Political and Diplomatic History of the Arab World 1900-1967

Political and Diplomatic History of the Arab World 1900-1967 A Chronological Study

Menahem Mansoor

The University of Wisconsin

Volume 3

1953-59

1972

NCR Microcard Editions

Library of Congress card no. 72-184866
ISBN 0-910 972-09-5

Published by NCR/Microcard Editions
901 26th Street, N.W., Washington, D.C. 20037

January, 1953

January 1

The British Government released 10 million pounds sterling from Egypt's blocked balances at the request of that Government and in accordance with the 1951 Anglo-Egyptian agreement.

The arrest of M. Caballero, Secretary General of the Algerian Communist Party, was announced. He was charged with attempts against the security of the State in connection with the distribution in Algeria of a pamphlet emphasizing the solidarity of the Algerian and Moroccan peoples.

Premier Nagib of Egypt stated in an interview with the newspaper al-Ahram that the three main problems occupying his attention were: British evacuation, the Sudan, and development of national resources. He spoke of the danger that foreign borrowing might lead to political interference, and declared that Egypt should make itself strong before accepting foreign aid.

January 2

A British Air Ministry employee was found stabbed to death in the Suez Canal Zone.

It was revealed in Egypt that formal charges of corruption and abuse of power involving six former Cabinet ministers and eight lesser politicians active under the old regime had been laid before Minister of State Fathi Radwan.

January 3

Eight hundred Egyptian officials were reported dismissed or resigned, in Premier Nagib's drive to purge the government of corruption.

General Nagib of Egypt announced that a Five Year Plan for the economic development of the country had been formulated. Hussein Fahmi, a former Finance Minister, would head a Permanent Council for the Development of National Production.

Premier Nagib of Egypt conferred with the West German Ambassador, Gunther Pawelke, on the Bonn-Israel reparations pact.

January, 1953

January 3

At the opening meeting of the Egyptian National Production Development Council, which was formed to bring about a planned increase in production, General Nagib promised that the Council would be given wide powers. It was composed mainly of experts in finance, industry, and agriculture.

At the Asian-Arab Conference, Fathi Radwan, Egyptian Minister of State, told the press that Colonel Gamal Nasser's statement of December 31, 1952, about guerrilla warfare against the British reflected the opinion of the nation.

Three Syrian political leaders — Akram Hourani, leader of the Arab Socialist Party, Michel Aflaq, leader of the Revival Party, and Revival Party Secretary Salah-ad-Din Bitar — sought political asylum in Lebanon. They bitterly attacked the regime of President Adib Shishakli in Syria.

January 4

Tunisian nationalist spokesmen revealed that they would call for a boycott of municipal elections to protest against the grant of voting rights to French colonists. They also protested the manner in which the municipal reform program was imposed on the country's ruler.

January 5

The Israel Ambassador to Washington, Abba Eban, discussed with US Secretary of State Dean Acheson Israel's anxiety over arms shipments to the Arab states.

It was announced in Damascus that the proposed economic talks between Syria and Lebanon were postponed indefinitely.

Press censorship of all outgoing and incoming messages was reintroduced by the Egyptian Government.

Egypt asked the Secretariat of the Arab League to convene a meeting of the Political Committee.

January, 1953

January 5

London and Cairo exchanged notes concerning the dam across the White Nile at Owen Falls, Uganda.

January 7

The US Government decided that it had no objection to a British plan to sell large quantities of jet aircraft to the Arab States.

The Israel Government presented a formal note to the United Kingdom protesting the sale of jet aircraft to Arab states.

A note was received by Britain from the Israel Government which repeated the arguments put forward by Moshe Sharett, Israel's Foreign Minister, December 28, 1952, against the supply of arms, especially jet aircraft, to Arab states, maintaining that it was inconsistent with the Three Power declaration of May, 1950.

Lebanese Premier Amir Khaled Chehab announced that, in accordance with international law, the three Syrian leaders who sought political asylum in Lebanon were considered political refugees by the Lebanese authorities.

Press attacks on the Shishakli regime in Syria were officially disowned by the Lebanese Government through its Premier, Amir Khaled Chehab.

The Syrian Government closed the frontier with Lebanon as a reprisal against attacks in the Lebanese press against Colonel Shishakli, the deputy Premier and Chief of Staff.

January 8

A food production conference was opened in Beirut, Lebanon, in connection with the inauguration of the Regional Center for Agricultural Guidance in the Middle East. Norris Dodd, Director General of the UN Food and Agriculture Organization (FAO), addressed the conference.

January, 1953

January 8

The Syrian frontier with Lebanon was reopened following a meeting on the border between Colonel Adib Shishakli, the Syrian Deputy Prime Minister, and Lebanon's Chief of Staff, General Fuad Chehab.

January 9

The Supreme Court of Aden ordered the disputed cargo of Iranian oil aboard the tanker Rose Marie turned over to the Anglo-Iranian Oil Company. The Court ruled that since no adequate compensation had been offered to the Company by the Iranian Government, the oil remained the Company's property.

The Egyptian Foreign Ministry announced that in an exchange of notes dated July 16, 1952, and January 5, 1953, the Egyptian and British Governments had approved the financial arrangements concerning the construction of a reservoir at Owen Falls, Uganda, to provide electric power for Uganda and to facilitate irrigation projects in the Upper Nile region.

January 10

An agreement between the Sudan and Egypt was concluded in Khartoum by Major Salah Salem representing the Egyptian Government and representatives of the Umma, National Unionist, Socialist Republican, and National parties of the Sudan. The text stated that the settlement had been reached after discussions during which the Sudanese parties had been informed of differences arising between the British and Egyptian Governments.

It was reported from Cairo that Anglo-Egyptian negotiations on problems of self government for the Sudan had entered the critical phase.

The four major Sudanese political parties agreed on a transitional constitution, to remain in effect during the three year period in preparation for self rule. They agreed to boycott any constitution which did not drastically curtail the powers of the British Governor General.

January, 1953

January 10

It was reported in Cairo that as a result of disturbances at Cairo University the previous week, 123 students involved were arrested and that all faculties except those of medicine and Arab studies were closed.

January 11

British Ambassador Sir Ralph Stevenson saw Egyptian Foreign Minister Mahmoud Fawzi and requested an early resumption of talks on the future of the Sudan with Premier Nagib, which were suspended December 22, 1952.

January 12

It was reported in London that the agreement of the four Sudanese parties would delay Sudanese self government.

The British Ambassador presented to the Egyptian Foreign Minister the British draft of an Anglo-Egyptian treaty on the Sudan, based on the Egyptian note of November 2, 1952.

A committee composed of 50 people from all professions, political views and religions to redraft the Egyptian Constitution, was announced.

At a meeting to commemorate the martyrs killed in the Suez fighting against the British, Egyptian Premier Nagib told several thousand students that Egypt's main aim was to clear all foreign troops from the Nile Valley.

The Lebanese Government signed an agreement with the US for technical assistance to agricultural schemes and a statistical survey.

January 14

The Political Committee of the Arab League met in Cairo. The principal item on its agenda was West Germany's reparations agreement with Israel.

January, 1953

January 17

David Rousset, president of the International Commission against Concentration Regimes, and three members of an investigating team arrived in Tunis to check into the issue of widespread arrests, deportation, and concentration camp methods going on in Tunisia under the French regime.

The first direct national parliamentary elections were held throughout Iraq. All parties had been abolished by Premier Mahmoud; all candidates ran as independents; almost half of them had already been declared elected, as their seats were uncontested. The dominance of the followers of Nuri-Said was apparent.

The Communications Committee of the Arab League met in Cairo and various resolutions were passed which would aim at establishing a Pan-Arab network of rail, road, air, and sea transport. Five subcommittees were appointed to study the technical aspects of the question.

January 18

Two persons were killed and six wounded by terrorists in Tunis.

January 19

Moroccan Sultan Sidi Muhammad Ben-Youssef asked France to resume negotiations on French reform programs for Morocco. The proposal was made in a letter to French President Vincent Auriol.

January 20

Egyptian Premier Nagib ordered the formation of a revolutionary tribunal to try persons endangering national security.

An Egyptian military court found Lieutenant Colonel Muhammad Husni al-Damanhuri, who had been appointed Governor of the Western Desert after the Army coup, guilty of attempting to incite rebellion among the armed forces on January 14, and his brother, Captain Hassan al-Damanhuri, guilty of failing to give information on the

January, 1953

January 15

Egyptian Premier Nagib declared that Egypt would never join a Western alliance for the defense of the Middle East so long as British troops were in the Suez Canal Zone.

The text was published in Cairo of a confidential letter dated December 29, 1952, addressed by Sir James Robertson, Civil Secretary to the Sudan Government, to officials in the Sudan.

Sir James Robertson, Civil Secretary of the Sudanese Government, accused the Egyptian Government of trying to damage Britain's reputation in the Sudan by spreading false rumors about the negotiations presently in process on the territory's future.

A bomb exploded in the Jewish quarter in Tunis, killing two children and wounding two others.

January 16

Fuad Galal, Minister of National Guidance, broadcasting over the Egyptian radio system in the name of Premier Nagib, said that a plot to overthrow the regime of the Premier had been discovered. As a result, the government abolished all political parties and confiscated their funds. A three year interregnum was established, during which Premier Nagib would rule unhampered and would prepare the country for democratic rule.

Twenty-five Egyptian Army officers were arrested on charges of conspiring to overthrow the Government.

January 17

The Egyptian Cabinet issued a decree extending the absolute powers of the Premier to July 23, 1953, formally abolishing all political parties and confiscating their funds. A nationwide roundup of Communists took place and six of their newspapers were closed.

Egyptian Foreign Minister Mahmoud Fawzi handed Egypt's reply to the British proposals on the Sudan to the British Ambassador.

The Egyptian Government requested the withdrawal of the British Information officer in Cairo.

January, 1953

January 20

plot. The former was condemned to death and the latter to five years imprisonment and dismissed from the Army.

The Aviation Subcommittee of the Arab League drew up a plan which would unify laws regulating civil aviation in the Arab countries. It also passed a resolution urging those Arab States which had not yet joined the International Civil Aviation Organization to do so.

A vote of confidence, 22-14, was given to the Government of Jordan.

A meeting took place at Mexera Homadi between General Augustin Guillaume, French Resident General in Morocco, and the High Commissioner in Spanish Morocco. A communique issued after the talks said the generals had agreed to maintain their collaboration on Moroccan questions and had decided to take commercial measures to aid fuller development.

January 23

A four day "Liberation Festival" was inaugurated in Egypt by a speech from General Nagib in which he announced the formation of a Liberation Front to replace the political parties dissolved on January 16.

The Israel Ambassador to London received an oral reply from British Foreign Secretary Anthony Eden to the Israel note of January 7 protesting against the supply of arms to Arab States. It was understood that the reply was on the lines of the Foreign Office statement of December 29, 1952.

January 24

Economic talks between Syrian and Lebanese representatives opened at Shtoura, Lebanon.

The Iraqi Regent, Abd-al-Ilah, opened Parliament and delivered the speech from the throne which laid emphasis on continuing the traditional policy of working for the independence of all Arab States and of supporting the Arab League.

January, 1953

January 24

The Iraqi Premier, Nur-ad-Din Mahmoud resigned as Prime Minister.

The Egyptian Council of Ministers announced a decree giving the Government the right to proclaim general mobilization in case of international tension, danger of war or the outbreak of war.

January 25

It was reported in Jerusalem that the situation on the border between Jordan and Israel was deteriorating.

January 26

Representatives of the Lebanese Government met with representatives of Syria at Shatura in an effort to negotiate an economic agreement to supplant the one that would expire February 4. Lebanese delegates submitted a draft agreement.

Colonel Mahmoud Riyad, Chief of Palestine Affairs in the Egyptian Government, told the press that Egypt had requested an immediate meeting of the Palestine Truce Committee because of an attack by Jewish soldiers on Egyptian territory in the Gaza-Rafah area on January 24.

The Aden Government ordered the deposition of Sheikh Shaher of the Subhaihi and the return of all rebel tribesmen from sanctuary in Yemen before January 29. Yemen was supplying the rebels with arms and ammunition to resist the combined Aden and Lahej force sent to restore order.

January 27

It was disclosed that on January 12 the Sultan of Morocco had sent a message to French President Vincent Auriol in which, it was understood, he had expressed his willingness to consider with favor some of the French reforms which he had formerly opposed.

January, 1953

January 28

Negotiations on the Sudan were resumed between Great Britain and Egypt. Egyptian Premier Nagib handed British Ambassador Sir Ralph Stevenson a draft agreement and an explanatory note on the Egyptian attitude on the situation in the negotiations.

A UN observer reported that an Israel force of over 150 men launched a premeditated, concentrated military attack upon the Jordanian village of Falma, near Tulkarm. The headman and ten others of the 70 inhabitants, including women and children, were killed.

Israel attacks led Jordan to make representations to the United Kingdom and the United States; it invoked its treaty of alliance with the former and demanded that the latter take action in accordance with the Tripartite Declaration of May, 1950.

The Joint UN Jordanian-Israel Truce Committee declared that an Israel attack upon the village of Rentee was a flagrant violation of the Truce, and warned the Israel authorities to stop their repeated aggressions upon Jordanian territory.

January 29

Jamil al-Midfai, a former President of the Iraqi Senate, formed the following cabinet with himself as Premier: Deputy Premier, Ali Jawdat al-Ayyoubi; Foreign Affairs, Tawfiq Suwaidi; and Defense, Nuri-Said.

It was reported both from Amman, Jordan, and Jerusalem that the border situation with Israel was very tense.

The British Government communicated with the Yemeni Government on the question of the rebel Subhaihi tribesmen.

In a speech to the American Club in Paris, General Augustin Guillaume, French Resident General in Morocco, declared that the main aims of the proposed French reforms were to give the Moroccans a bigger share in public life and progressively to democratize their institutions and decentralize the administration.

January, 1953

January 29

The Egyptian Government's note to Britain on the Sudan maintained that the proposed commission's function should be to complete Sudanization within three years (See February 12, 1953). The note accused Britain of trying to divide the south and the north and warned the British Government not to rely on the Sudan Government's version of events in the south.

The Sudanese Umma Party decided to support the Egyptian note on the Sudan political parties, but resolved to ask Egypt to include an article to the effect that neither Britain nor Egypt should indulge in propaganda during the self government period.

January 30

The Iraq Petroleum Company and its subsidiaries produced 18 million tons of oil in 1952, double the 1951 production.

January 31

The Jordanian Government invoked the Anglo-Jordanian Treaty of Alliance against Israel for alleged attacks on Jordanian villages.

February, 1953

February 1

Eleven officials and industrialists from West Germany, headed by the Under Secretary for Economic Affairs, Ludger Westrick, arrived in Cairo to discuss German trade relations with Egypt.

The General Secretary of the International Confederation of Free Trade Unions pointed out that the latest French concession, allowing Moroccan workers to form unions, stipulated that half of the membership of the national and regional governing bodies should be French and excluded agricultural workers who formed the greater part of the native labor force.

Selwyn Lloyd stated in reply to a question in Parliament that Her Majesty's Ambassador in Cairo had made representations to the Egyptian Government concerning the visit to the Sudan of the Egyptian Minister for National Guidance. He said the Government was unable to accept Major Salah Salem's description (reported in the press) of his visit as being "private and unofficial."

The Italian Defense Minister, Randolfo Pacciardi, with three officers of the Italian Army, Navy and Air Force, arrived in Cairo to establish contact with the regime of General Nagib.

February 2

Economic talks were resumed between Lebanon and Syria. Counter-proposals to the draft economic agreement presented to Syria were presented by Syrian representatives at Shatura.

The Iraqi Parliament met to hear a statement of policy from Premier Jamil al-Midfai. The two major issues outlined were strengthening of relations with other Arab countries, and local reform.

It was confirmed that Jordan had invoked the Anglo-Jordan Treaty of 1948 following Israel-Jordan border incidents.

February, 1953

February 2

The Egyptian Government concluded an agreement with the Government of East Germany on the exchange of $11,200,000 worth of goods. Under the agreement Egypt would send East Germany cotton, manganese ore and phosphates in exchange for fertilizers, agricultural machinery, printing presses and cardboard.

The Sudanese Socialist Republican Party endorsed the signature of the agreement of January 10 between Egypt and the Sudanese political parties.

The Sudanese Foreign Minister issued a statement that the British Minister of State, Selwyn Lloyd, had no right, either under the Anglo-Egyptian agreement on the Sudan or by common usage, to protest against Egyptian Minister of National Guidance Major Salah Salem's visit to the Sudan.

February 3

In Damascus four British jet fighters were reportedly delivered to the Syrian Air Force.

Foreign Minister Musa Mubarak of Lebanon resigned in protest when he was attacked by a number of Deputies for his supposed caution in the Syro-Lebanese economic talks. He later withdrew his resignation.

The Syrian Information Department issued a statement accusing Israel of carrying out an anti-Syrian campaign particularly by radio. The statement was especially critical of speeches made by two Druze members of the Israel Knesset.

Trade discussions opened in Cairo between representatives of the Arab States and a West German delegation headed by West German Under Secretary for Economic Affairs Ludger Westrick.

Sir James Robertson, the British Civil Secretary, reportedly met with the leaders of the Umma, Socialist Republican, and National parties of the Sudan and explained the British proposals to them. The National Unionists had declined to meet the Chief Secretary.

February, 1953

February 3

An agreement was signed by the Egyptian Government with the US Conorada Petroleum Corporation providing for a thirty year oil prospecting concession contract for an area of some 114,000 square miles in the western desert.

February 4

Selwyn Lloyd, British Minister of State, said in reply to a question in the House of Commons that the British Ambassador in Cairo had talked with the authorities and was told that guerrilla warfare would be renewed in the Canal Zone if British troops were not withdrawn. As a result, the Foreign Secretary had received the assurance of the Egyptian Foreign Minister that it was the Egyptian Government's intention to reach a settlement by negotiation.

Speaking at Tanta, Egyptian Minister of National Guidance Major Salah Salem declared that the Liberation Rally would ensure the evacuation of imperialist forces from the whole Nile Valley. He said that they would ask the imperialists to get out. . . . if they refused, they would resort to drastic action as already promised by General Nagib.

Foreign Minister of Israel Moshe Sharett told the Knesset that the Government was taking the necessary steps against the recent wave of incursions by Arab infiltrators.

Ludger Westrick, head of the West German Economic Mission, stated that he and his associates had not come to discuss his Government's restitution agreement with Israel, that his was an economic mission and he was not qualified to discuss political questions.

February 5

The American, British and French diplomatic representatives were invited to the Foreign Office to hear Israel Foreign Minister Moshe Sharett state the Israel Government's views on the border incidents involving Jordan.

February, 1953

February 5

The British Government announced that it had made urgent representations to Israel, at the same time expressing strong disapproval of Israel raids upon Jordan territory.

The Joint Israel-Jordan Mixed Armistice Commission accused both Jordan and Israel of violating their armistice agreement.

The British Ambassador in Tel Aviv called on the Foreign Office and asked that all possible steps be taken to restore tranquility and prevent incidents along the border with Jordan. A similar request was made in Amman of the Jordanian Government.

The British Government informed the Jordanian Government that Britain stood by its obligations under the 1948 Treaty to protect the Jordanian frontier and also by the Tripartite Declaration of 1950 in support of the status quo.

The Lebanese Government resumed economic discussions with representatives of Syria at Damascus. A Syrian proposal to establish a Joint Council with supra-national economic powers was accepted as a basis for discussion.

February 6

Lebanese Foreign Minister Musa Mubarak reportedly resigned again and Georges Hakim took over his duties temporarily.

An Egyptian military mission arrived on a good will visit to Saudi Arabia.

At a meeting between Egyptian and British delegates in Cairo, Sir Ralph Stevenson presented the British view on the agreement proposed by Egypt.

Egyptian Premier General Muhammad Nagib declared at a dinner given to the West German delegation that Egypt's warm reception to the delegation did not mean satisfaction with the West German offers. He added that Egypt would not fail to fulfill its decision to boycott West Germany economically as a result of the Bonn agreement for reparations to Israel. He said that the Arab States expected to receive something under the agreement.

February, 1953

February 7

Lebanese President Camille Chamoun arrived in Saudi Arabia on the first leg of a tour of Arab capitals.

Muhammad al-Sadr was elected President of the Iraqi Senate.

General Augustin Guillaume, French Resident General in Morocco, told the press that about 400 arrests had been made after the Moroccan riots December 7 and 8, 1952, and that of those arrested 380 had been detained.

February 8

The UN Truce Commission asked Israel to remove forcibly 130 persons occupying a building in Jerusalem in the no man's land between Israel and Jordan.

The Chief Jordanian Delegate to the Mixed Armistice Commission delivered a strong protest to the Assistant Chief of Staff of the UN Truce Observers against the February 7 occupation by Israel squatters of the Arab Teachers' College in the demilitarized zone against the south boundary of Jerusalem.

The Syrian Government demanded 49 percent of the savings made by Iraq Petroleum Company and Tapline through use of the pipelines instead of tankers.

An agricultural school in Libya was opened at al-Aweida under the auspices of the American technical assistance program.

February 9

The UN Assistant Chief of Staff informed the Jordanian Delegate that the Israel authorities had promised to remove the Israel squatters in the demilitarized zone within a few days.

Selwyn Lloyd, British Minister of State for Foreign Affairs, stated in reply to a question in the House of Commons that, after investigation of the attacks on the Jordanian villages of Falama and Rantis on

February, 1953

February 9

January 23 and January 28-29, the Mixed Armistice Commission had by majority vote held the Israel Government responsible. The Government had made representations to the Israel Government and had counselled moderation on the part of Jordan.

February 10

Egyptian Premier Muhammad Nagib issued a constitutional proclamation vesting in himself and a 13 member army council the power to rule Egypt for three years. A provisional Constitution was declared for the transitional period. Nagib further expressed his absolute faith in the need for establishing a complete constitutional and democratic system of government at the end of the transitional period.

Libya became a member of the International Telecommunications Union.

Egypt and Holland signed a trade agreement in Cairo.

February 11

It was announced in Syria that the police had arrested 60 members of the Syrian National Party for holding an unauthorized meeting in the town of Margayun and smuggling pamphlets and curculars about their party into Lebanon.

The West German Trade Mission to Egypt suspended talks with the Egyptian Government because of exaggerated Arab demands. The demands were reported to be a billion dollars in long term credits for Egypt and other Arab States, in reparation for the so-called damage caused the Arabs by the Bonn restitution agreement with Israel.

February 12

The Lebanese Government announced that it had allocated LL24 million to finance development schemes.

February, 1953

February 12

An agreement providing for the immediate introduction of self government in the Sudan and for the exercise of self determination by the Sudanese people was signed by the United Kingdom and Egypt. Under this agreement elections for a self governing legislature would be held immediately. The elections would be supervised by a commission of seven members: three Sudanese, one Egyptian, one Briton, one American, and one Indian. Within a period of three years the Sudan would be free to choose between complete independence and association with Egypt.

Anthony Eden, British Foreign Secretary, stated in the House of Commons that the Anglo-Egyptian Agreement of February 12 left the Sudanese with freedom to enter the British Commonwealth if they so desired.

The Egyptian Cabinet accepted from a French firm a bid of LE10,141,000 for the Aswan hydroelectric scheme.

It was announced that a Communist cell had been discovered in Basra, Iraq, in January, and that those arrested would be put on trial before a Military Tribunal on February 16.

The scheduled meeting of the economic conference between Lebanon and Syria was postponed to February 19.

February 13

It was announced that Georges Bidault, French Foreign Minister to Morocco, had sent a reply to the letter of January 19 from the Sultan of Morocco, Sidi Ben-Youssef, to the President. He expressed pleasure that the Sultan was ready to study the proposed French reforms and declared that the reforms were intended to develop democratic institutions progressively, while respecting Moroccan sovereignty and ensuring "the active cooperation of the French element." The reply had also emphasized French determination to negotiate with the Sultan and continue the modernization of the Moroccan economy and institutions to pursue progress in the social and intellectual spheres.

February, 1953

February 13

President Camille Chamoun of Lebanon returned from Riyadh after a six day official visit to Saudi Arabia. His projected tour of other Arab capitals was postponed.

February 14

The United States, through its Ambassador in Jordan, stated that it did not condone in any way Israel aggressions upon Jordan.

An East German trade delegation opened talks with Egyptian Government representatives in Cairo.

It was reported from Tripoli that Libya applied officially for membership in the Arab League.

Tawfiq Abu-al-Huda, Prime Minister of Jordan, arrived in Damascus en route for Lebanon and had talks with Syrian leaders.

The Governor General of Sudan, Sir Robert Howe, issued a statement in which he praised the wisdom and statesmanship of Egyptian Premier General Nagib in reversing the policy of previous Egyptian Governments.

February 15

The Lebanese Cabinet decided to remove all restrictions on women as to their political equality with men.

Tawfiq Abu-al-Huda, Prime Minister of Jordan, arrived in Beirut for a holiday and talks with Lebanese President Chamoun.

The West German trade delegation left Cairo without concluding any agreement with the Egyptian Government.

An agreement between Jordan and Syria on a hydroelectric and irrigation project on the Yarmuk River was signed. Its cost was estimated at $60 million.

February, 1953

February 16

It was announced that Libya would become the fifty-ninth member of the Civil Aviation Organization.

Egyptian Premier General Nagib declared in a broadcast to the Sudanese that any attempt to bring the Sudan into the British Commonwealth would invalidate the Anglo-Egyptian Treaty signed on February 12. He said that the agreement provided for two alternatives: union with Egypt or complete independence.

The Iranian Government protested to the Iraqi Government against a recent incursion and attacks on Sanjab tribesmen in the Kermanshah area.

February 17

The Lebanese Government signed an agreement with the US for technical assistance and hydroelectric power.

The Jordanian Government signed the Arab League agreement on nationality, reciprocal recognition of court sentences, extradition of criminals and powers of attorneys.

A branch of the US Information Service was opened in Amman, Jordan.

After debating the issue, the House of Commons rejected, 267-238, a condemnation of the British Government's policy of supplying jet planes to Arab States.

Diplomatic representatives of seven Arab League member states called on General Walter Bedell Smith, US Under Secretary of State. They claimed that giving help of any kind to Israel might endanger Middle East security.

British Foreign Secretary Anthony Eden reaffirmed that in the Government's view the phrase "complete independence" in the Anglo-Egyptian agreement of February 12 included the right of the Sudanese to choose any form of association with any other State on their achieving self determination. He affirmed that the Treaty could not prevent a choice of association with the British Commonwealth.

February, 1953

February 18

An economic and financial agreement was signed between Jordan and Syria. The agreement provided for the exchange of agricultural products and locally manufactured goods free of customs duty, and free transit between the two countries.

Egyptian Premier General Nagib declared in an address to army units that talks on evacuation of the Suez Canal would begin within a few days. He said there was perfect agreement on the principle, and discussion would be confined to points of detail and the period during which evacuation might be carried out.

A trade agreement between Egypt and East Germany was announced under which the two countries were expected to increase their trade to about LE4 million during the year.

February 19

An agreement was concluded between the Lebanese Government and the US for a preparatory survey of the Litani River irrigation and hydroelectric scheme.

February 20

A British Foreign Office statement was issued on additions to forces in Trucial Oman and Persian Gulf sheikhdoms, under protection of the British to maintain defense and suppress slave trade.

February 21

A law was enacted in Amman prohibiting non-Jordanians from owning immovable property, and forbidding non-Jordanians from renting property for more than a three year period.

The Egyptian Constitution Committee appointed by Premier Muhammad Nagib held its first meeting in Cairo, in the Chamber of Deputies. After a speech by the Premier, it elected as its chairman Ali Maher, the last Premier before Nagib took over.

February, 1953

February 22

The Egyptian Minister of Commerce announced amendments to the Mines and Quarries Law. The new law allowed foreign companies to exploit as well as prospect for mineral resources in Egypt.

A military spokesman stated that a Jordan force had crossed into Israel territory south of Hebron on February 19, and that in an ensuing clash with an Israel military unit one Israeli was killed.

February 23

A Point Four agreement between Egypt and the US, valid to June 30, 1954, was signed in Cairo by Foreign Minister Mahmoud Fawzi and US Ambassador Jefferson Caffery. It provided for $200,000 in assistance for the development of Egypt's industries and the exploitation of its mineral resources, especially oil.

Arab League headquarters issued a statement that on February 21 an Israel patrol had fired on Jordanian shepherds grazing their cattle in the Jordanian village of Sureef. Jordanian national guards had returned the fire and after half an hour exchange the Israel patrol had disappeared.

February 24

A joint meeting of the Egyptian Army Council of Revolution and the Egyptian Council of Ministers was held under the chairmanship of Premier Nagib.

India named Sukmar Sen as its representative on the seven member election commission which would arrange and supervise the Sudanese parliamentary elections.

February, 1953

February 25

Syrian and Lebanese representatives, meeting in Shatura, accepted an interim economic agreement which would run for six months from March 8, while negotiations for a permanent agreement continued.

An agreement regulating the legal status of Consolidated Refineries Limited and the Anglo-Iranian Oil Company was initiated in Tel Aviv.

Egypt and East Germany agreed on an exchange of goods to the amount of $11,200,000.

February 26

Arab League headquarters announced that a man, his twelve year old daughter and four boys had been killed by an Israel patrol while they were trying to lead back their flock of sheep and goats which had strayed three kilometers into Israel territory.

February 27

The chief Jordanian delegate to the Mixed Armistice Commission reported that two of four Jewish soldiers who had advanced from the Jewish side to the Jordanian village of Falamis had been killed by Jordanian defense guards.

An army spokesman reported that a Mixed Armistice Commission team had established that a border clash in the Hebron area on February 25 had taken place on the Israel side of the frontier.

March, 1953

March 1

The Egyptian police raided the secret headquarters of the Egyptian Communist Party at Shrubra, a Cairo suburb.

March 2

After a visit from Amir Faisal, Foreign Minister of Saudi Arabia, US President Eisenhower expressed his concern over some evidence that there had lately occurred a deterioration in the relations between the Arab nations and the United States. He declared that it would be his firm purpose to seek to restore the spirit of confidence and trust which had previously characterized those relations.

The Ministry of the Egyptian Interior announced that Communists and others arrested in Mansura, lower Egypt, during the weekend would be tried by a military court. It had been announced earlier that the arrests totalled 53.

March 3

Elections to the Tripolitanian Legislative Council were held. The Council was to be composed of 40 members, 30 elected and ten nominated.

March 4

The Governor General of Pakistan, Chardri Ghulan Muhammad, arrived in Riyadh for a five day official visit as the guest of King Ibn-Saud of Saudi Arabia.

John B. Blandford, Jr., Director of UNRWA, stated that the UN, in agreement with the Arab governments, had arranged for $100 million to be spent in the Middle East for the benefit of Arab refugees.

US Secretary of State John Foster Dulles cleared John Carter Vincent, Minister to Morocco, of disloyalty and security charges, but accepted his resignation and application for retirement.

March 5

The interim economic agreement between Lebanon and Syria reached on February 25 was signed. It was announced in Beirut that Lebanese President Camille Chamoun and the Syrian Deputy Premier, Colonel Adib Shishakli, had held a two and one half hour secret meeting, at the former's request, at the mountain resort of Bohmidan, to save the economic talks from collapsing.

March 6

The third conference of Middle East Medical Associations opened in Baghdad.

French authorities arrested Hedi Nouria, acting head of the Tunisian Neo-Destour Party, on charges of distributing anti-French propaganda.

Office spokesmen reported that the Saudi Arabian Charge d'Affaires had had discussions at the British Foreign Office on March 3 and 4 about the frontier dispute which had arisen between Saudi Arabia, the British protected Trucial Sheikhdoms, and the Sultanate of Muscat and Oman.

March 7

Two bombs exploded in the European section of Tunis.

A trade agreement between Libya and Egypt was signed in Cairo.

Egyptian Foreign Minister Mahmoud Fawzi and Fritz Kich, head of the East German delegation, signed a one year bilateral trade agreement.

A strike of railway and transportation workers began, bringing all transportation in the Sudan to a standstill.

March 8

The Egyptian Council of Ministers reportedly approved a $60 million program of the Permanent National Resources Development Board which would bring 37, 000 acres of land under irrigation and cultiva-

March 8

tion, improve the Nile Delta road network and distribute improved wheat and hybrid corn seed.

The Council of Ministers announced that it had approved a mining law which did away with a previous stipulation that oil and mineral leases could only be granted to Egyptian companies.

An Israel army spokesman said that during the week ending March 8, 15 marauders had been killed and 11 captured.

March 9

The Jordanian Government concluded discussions with financial representatives of the British Government. The British Government agreed that it would make 1,250,000 pounds sterling available to the Jordan Government for the fiscal year beginning April 1, 1953. It was also announced that Britain had offered to cooperate with Jordan in a five year plan of economic development.

Foreign Minister Mahmoud Fawzi of Egypt announced in Cairo that Egypt protested to Great Britain against oppressive measures by British authorities in the southern Sudan.

March 10

A law entitled "The Land Acquisition Law" was passed by the Government of Israel. It legalized the expropriation, without consent of the owners, of land belonging to the 180,000 Arabs living in Israel, if that land was needed for the purposes of development, settlement or security. Compensation paid would be based on the value of the land in 1950, with an additional three percent for each year thereafter, to be paid in Israel currency at the current rate of exchange. Under Israel law Arabs would not be allowed to acquire new land although several kubbutzin (collective farms) had rented out parcels of the newly acquired land to some of the Arabs who previously owned it.

The Lebanese Parliament ratified the economic agreement with Syria.

March 10

Prime Minister Muhammad Nagib of Egypt accused the British Government of breaches of the Anglo-Egyptian agreement on the Sudan, in particular of delaying the holding of elections by refusing to approve the Sudanese nominees to the Governor General's Commission. He also made allegations of maltreatment of the South Sudanese by British administrators.

Egyptian General Nagib made a statement on the Sudan in which he declared that Sudanese officials and others had complained that the British Administration was resorting to intimidation and some Sudanese had been imprisoned.

The British Government protested against Premier Nagib's accusations that Britain was violating the terms of the Anglo-Egyptian Sudan agreement. The accusations were described as unfounded.

Three agreements were signed with American Point Four administrators between Lebanon and the US.

An Israel army spokesman announced two further border incidents: the shooting of an Israeli by a member of the Arab Legion and the killing of an Israel policeman by infiltrators in the Kalkilya area.

A note was delivered from Iran to the Iraqi Embassy protesting against alleged activities by the British agents and spies along the Iraqi-Iranian border, and demanding that Iraq should cease allowing its territory to be used for a base for anti-Iranian activity by British agents.

Egypt signed a barter agreement with Russia, Bulgaria and Poland for an exchange of Egyptian cotton against 115,000 tons of wheat from the three countries.

March 11

Selwyn Lloyd, British Minister of State, told the House of Commons he had asked the Governor General of the Sudan for full information on all General Nagib's allegations about breaches of the Anglo-Egyptian

March 11

Agreement on the Sudan. He said he had little doubt that they would prove to be quite unfounded.

Prince Faisal, Foreign Minister of Saudi Arabia and leader of its delegation to the UN, made a statement to the press on the dispute with Britain concerning the Buraimi Oasis. He denied that the Saudi Arabian claim to the territory was in any way inspired by the discovery of oil, and complained that in spite of the standstill agreement, British officials were trying to extend their influence and British aircraft had repeatedly flown low over the area in an attempt to terrify the inhabitants into submission.

Visa requirements between Lebanon and Iraq were abolished.

Syria promulgated a decree law outlining the powers and responsibilities of the President of the Republic, and defining the future tasks of the Ministry of Defense and the armed forces.

Arab Legion headquarters reported that in a border incident on March 9, four Israel soldiers were believed to have been killed.

March 12

The Sudanese transportation workers ended their five day walkout.

British Ambassador Sir Ralph Stevenson called on Egyptian Foreign Minister Mahmoud Fawzi to complain against Egyptian Premier Nagib's statement accusing British officials of acts of coercion and intimidation.

March 13

The Afro-Asian bloc addressed two letters to the President of the UN General Assembly, Lester B. Pearson. One asked Pearson to intervene to stop the execution of 13 Tunisian leaders; the other accused French officials of arbitrary arrests of Moroccans and mistreatment of political prisoners.

March 13

In a letter to UN Secretary General Trygve Lie, the Syrian UN delegation criticized the report of Lieutenant General William E. Riley, Chief of Staff of the Truce Supervision Organization in Palestine, charging that it gave an inaccurate account of continuing Syrian-Israel disagreements.

A three man Egyptian delegation, headed by former Foreign Minister Muhammad Salah-ad-Din, was stopped from boarding a plane in Khartoum for Juba in the southern Sudan after the three failed to obtain the Sudan Government's permission to visit that area.

March 14

The US Government, in a note to the French Government, protested that the latter had violated the judgment of the International Court of Justice delivered August 27, 1952, and demanded that current legislation regulating trade between Morocco and the US be amended to comply with the above court decision.

The US formally joined Anglo-Egyptian negotiations on the withdrawal of British troops from the Suez Canal Zone.

March 15

Amir Boudhidu Kahia, local chieftain of Mahdia, was shot to death by assassins, in Tunisia.

It was announced that the Lebanese Government had voted to allocate LL2,500,000 to be spent over a period of four years for irrigation purposes.

Egyptian Premier Nagib declared emphatically that the US would take part in the Suez talks only to the extent of providing its good offices. He met separately with the American and British Ambassadors.

A treaty of friendship, commerce and navigation was signed by India and Muscat and Oman.

March 15

Egyptian Premier General Nagib reportedly sent a strong protest to the Governor General of the Sudan against his refusal to allow Salah-ad-Din, the former Wafd Foreign Minister, and a delegation of Egyptian lawyers to go to southern Sudan.

Syria signed a trade agreement with Lebanon providing for a tariff exemption on agricultural and a few industrial products and a 50 percent tariff reduction on other industrial products.

The text of a cable sent by the British Governor General, Sir Robert Howe, to General Nagib, Prime Minister of Egypt, was published. It said that the report of General Nagib's statement of March 10 suggested that he had been misled by irresponsible persons, and it declared that all members of the Sudan Government, whatever their nationality, were faithfully performing their normal duties.

The Iraqi Government denied the Iranian charges that Britain was conducting anti-Iranian activities from Iraqi territory. A statement said that the Iranian Government had been asked to prevent Tehran Radio from broadcasting mendacious reports which were harmful to friendly relations.

March 16

The Egyptian Army Council of Revolution and the Council of Ministers met jointly; they rejected US participation in the Suez talks beyond the extent of good offices.

March 17

The Saudi Arabian Embassy issued a further statement alleging breaches of the standstill agreement on the frontier dispute over the Oasis of Buraimi. It asserted that on March 9 armored cars twice passed by the area of Bani Kaab, a prohibited area, that weapons

March 17

had been taken by car from Sharga to Shurm for distribution among the Shuwaihiyyeen of Bani Kaab, and that later that day three armored cars had attacked Shurm.

March 18

US Ambassador to Egypt, Jefferson Caffery, declared that the US Government had no wish to take part in any discussions regarding the Suez question unless asked to do so by both Egypt and Great Britain.

Egyptian Foreign Minister Mahmoud Fawzi announced that John Foster Dulles, US Secretary of State, would visit Egypt in the course of a Middle East tour early in May.

Colonel Gamal Abdel Nasser, First Lieutenant of General Nagib, stated in a published article that Egypt wanted immediate, complete and unconditional evacuation of the Suez Canal Zone. He added that Egypt would not accord British military forces the right to return to the Canal Zone in the event of war, and that Egypt would not accord the Royal Air Force the use of airfields in the Canal Zone.

A Foreign Office spokesman in London declared that his Government and Saudi Arabia were deadlocked over the Buraimi incident.

March 19

The Egyptian Government signed an agreement with the US Government whereby the latter would aid in the reclamation of 20,000 feddans of marshland in the Nile Delta province of Buheria and 60,000 feddans of desert wasteland in Fayum province. The cost of the project was estimated at $25 million; the US would contribute $10 million.

March 20

The Lebanese Government took over the management of the French and Belgain owned Beirut Electricity Company because of the Company's failure to comply with government requirements.

March 20

Lebanon concluded an economic agreement with Yugoslavia.

Selwyn Lloyd, British Foreign Affairs Minister of State, left for the Sudan in connection with the implementation of the Anglo-Egyptian agreement of February 12.

March 21

A trade and payments agreement with the Netherlands was signed in Cairo.

The Sudan's self government status was signed by the British Governor General and came into force. Selwyn Lloyd, British Minister of State, and Major Salah Salem of Egypt were present at the signing.

It was announced at Vatican City that the Vatican and Syria had established diplomatic relations.

March 22

On the recommendation of the Foreign Affairs and Security Committee, the Israel Cabinet gave formal approval to the reparations agreement with West Germany.

Egyptian Premier Nagib, on a tour of upper Egypt, declared at Esna that if the British would not go of their own free will they would be forced to go. "We are ready for it," he said.

March 23

President Eisenhower told a delegation of the American Zionist Council that the US had only the friendliest feelings for Israel and the Arab States and intended to use its best offices to bring about peace in the Middle East.

The US and Lebanon concluded a mutal defense assistance agreement.

The French Ambassador to Lebanon, M. Balay, called on President Chamoun to inform him of the French Government's protest at the

March, 1953

March 23

seizure of the French and Belgian owned Beirut Electric Company. A note of protest had also been delivered by the Belgian Minister.

March 24

Lebanese President Camille Chamoun arrived in Baghdad for a six day official visit.

The American Independent Oil Company announced that it had struck oil in the neutral zone between Kuwait and Saudi Arabia. The territory was controlled jointly by the Sheikhdom of Kuwait and Saudi Arabia.

The first practical steps toward freeing one million pounds sterling of the estimated six million pounds in the blocked bank accounts of Arab refugees in Israel were taken when the Barclay's and Ottoman Banks began receiving applications from refugees seeking release of their accounts.

The Jordanian Government submitted a draft budget for 1953-1954 to the Chamber of Deputies. Expenditures would amount to JD14,670,618 and revenue was estimated at JD14,396,050.

The subcommittee of the Egyptian Constitution Committee reportedly decided to recommend that Egypt should have a republican form of government.

March 25

The British Embassy in Cairo formally announced the British Government's acceptance of the appointment of two Sudanese to the vacancies on the Governor General's commission. This cleared the way for the Governor General, in consultation with his commission, to appoint three Sudanese, which would complete the electoral commission.

D. M. H. Riches arrived in Khartoum as the first British Trade Commissioner to the Sudan.

March, 1953

March 25

At a press conference in Khartoum, Foreign Secretary Selwyn Lloyd reaffirmed British determination to carry out the Anglo-Egyptian Treaty in both the letter and the spirit, and urged that elections be held as quickly as possible. On the Sudan's future, he said that the British Government would desire a continuing friendship with the Sudan. If the Sudanese chose union with Egypt, arrangements would presumably depend on the Egyptian Government. If the Sudan chose independence, the British Government would welcome any relationship which could properly be entered into between two sovereign independent countries.

The British Ambassador had reportedly informed the Sudanese Government of British willingness to nominate Ibrahim Ahmad and Dardiri Osman as the Sudanese members of the Governor General's Commission.

March 26

A tense situation was created between Egypt and England when Minister of State Selwyn Lloyd mentioned in Khartoum the possibility that the Sudan, after it decided on its form of government, might join the Commonwealth.

March 27

It was announced in Ismailia that two Egyptians attacked and stabbed two British soldiers.

March 28

A communique issued after a meeting in Cairo between Egyptian Premier Nagib and British Minister of State Selwyn Lloyd stated that following a complete and frank discussion of the issues involved in the Sudan situation, both felt that a way had been found for improving matters in the implementation of the Anglo-Egyptian agreement on the Sudan.

It was reported from Tel Aviv that an armed Jordanian unit crossed the Israel frontier and was driven back after a six hour engagement in which two Israel soldiers were wounded.

March, 1953

March 28

The Egyptian Government for Sudan approved a decree setting up the Governor General's Commission.

The 18th ordinary session of the Arab League Council opened in Cairo. Egypt suggested that the Foreign Ministers of the various Arab countries attend the session to discuss the West German ratification of the Israel reparations agreement, British evacuation of the Suez Canal Zone, the forthcoming visit to the Middle East of the US Secretary of State, John Foster Dulles, and other important topics, but for various reasons the Foreign Ministers did not attend and the majority of the participants consisted of the regular Arab diplomatic representatives in Cairo.

The Council of the Arab League admitted Libya to full membership in the League.

March 29

The Political Committee of the Arab League began deliberations, under the chairmanship of Egyptian Foreign Minister Mahmoud Fawzi. A proposal by Lebanon that the League's meetings be held in public was approved in principle but detailed discussion was postponed for future consideration.

The Iraqi Government announced that it was abolishing, on a reciprocal basis, visa requirements for visitors from all Arab states and from India.

The Saudi Arabian Government issued a note to the British Government claiming that the latter had transgressed upon certain territories in the southwestern portion of Saudi Arabia and had violated the "standstill" agreement of October, 1952.

March, 1953

March 30

An agreement was signed between the Jordanian Government and UNRWA for the execution of the Yarmuk hydroelectric and irrigation scheme. The cost was estimated at $60 million.

The Tripolitanian Legislative Council met for the first time.

Fawzi Selo, Head of State, announced that the Syrian Government had decided to establish a central bank and to organize Syria's currency on a basis of financial independence. Colonel Adib Shishakli, deputy Premier and Chief of Staff, called it a "happy patriotic event no less important than the evacuation of foreign troops from our territories."

Colonel Muhammad Rashad Mehanna, member of the Egyptian Regency Council, was sentenced to 25 years imprisonment with hard labor for instigating a plot to overthrow the Government. Sentences ranging from 12 months to 15 years imprisonment were imposed upon 14 other military and civilian defendents who, it was alleged, had participated in the conspiracy.

The Arab League Committee discussed the attitude of the Arab countries toward the German-Israel reparations agreement.

March 31

The Lebanese Chamber of Deputies approved the statement of the Premier setting out the reasons for the Government's seizure of the Franco-Belgian Beirut Electricity Company. The Government rejected all protests against the seizure.

A decree promoted Syrian Colonel Selo to the rank of Major General, and Colonel Adib Shishakli to the rank of Brigadier.

April, 1953

April 1

The Egyptian Cabinet approved a law aimed at encouraging the investment of foreign capital in Egypt. It would allow for the transfer of foreign funds through any approved bank. Both currency and agriculture, mining, and industrial machinery would be considered as foreign capital. Under the law, profits might be transferred out of Egypt provided they did not in one year exceed ten percent of the registered value of the capital.

The Arab League Committee discussed the economic boycott of Israel.

The Saudi Arabian Government, through the Embassy in London, issued a statement explaining that the Buraimi Oasis was occupied in August 1952 by an official and forty men as Saudi Arabian territory. As it was claimed by the Sultan of Muscat and the Sheikh of Abu Dhabi, a standstill agreement was signed by Britain and Arabia on October 26 by which both sides were to maintain the status quo pending discussions. On nine occasions between November 11 and March 9 political officers, soldiers, or armored cars had visited the place, while restrictions were placed on trade or traffic with it from towns in the Trucial sheikhdoms.

April 2

In a note to the Saudi Arabian Government, the British Government requested that the Buraimi Oasis dispute be submitted to impartial arbitration.

The British Ambassador in Jedda handed the Government a note denouncing the Anglo-Saudi agreement of October 1952 on the Buraimi Oasis area.

The Egyptian Governor General's Commission on the Sudan had its first informal meeting.

British Minister of State for Foreign Affairs Selwyn Lloyd, in a statement in the UK Parliament on his visits to Cairo and Khartoum, assured the Sudanese that whatever difficulties might arise Her Majesty's Government would carry out its promise that Sudan should

April, 1953

April 2

have self government and the opportunity to determine its own future. He said that he had told the northern Sudanese how necessary it was to pay special attention to the problems of the south, and had urged those in the south to take a full part in the elections and the normal working of Parliament within a united Sudan. He further assured the people of Sudan that whatever direction they chose to take in the future Britain's feeling of friendship would continue toward them.

Selwyn Lloyd told the House of Commons that the Government had proposed to Saudi Arabia four months before that the Buraimi Oasis dispute should be settled by impartial arbitration. This had been rejected, but had been renewed nearly three months before. Her Majesty's Government had accordingly informed the Saudi Government that they reserved complete freedom of action in the matter and had renewed the offer of arbitration.

April 3

The Egyptian Governor General's commission on the Sudan approved the membership of the electoral commission.

The Foreign Ministers of Iraq, Syria and Lebanon reportedly declined to attend a special meeting of the Arab League Political Committee fixed for the next day. Reports were current that the Lebanese Government believed that Egypt wished to involve the other Arab States in a dispute with the Western Powers in order to obtain satisfaction of her demand for the evacuation of the Canal Zone.

April 4

A resolution was passed by the Council of the Arab League supporting Egypt's position in the Sudan controversy with the UK.

The Egyptian Minister of National Guidance Salah Salem said that the Anglo-Egyptian treaty was "not worth a dime." He said that the Egyptian Government would not negotiate on the evacuation of the Suez unless it knew beforehand that its demands would be accepted.

April, 1953

April 5

Sudan's Governor General, Sir Robert Howe, approved the three Sudanese members of the electoral commission: Abd-al-Salam Abd-al-Lahi, Under Secretary of the Ministry of Interior; Khalfallah Khaled, member Executive, National Unionist Party; and Gordon Bulli, representing the South.

The Iraqi Senate approved the establishment of a Higher Court comprised of eight members which would interpret the Constitution.

April 6

The Jordanian Government urged the Arab refugees to stop filing applications to partially recover blocked bank accounts in Israel because such applications would legally jeopardize their chances to recover the amounts deducted by the Israel Government on June 12, 1952, for a compulsory state loan.

The Syrian Government released statistics indicating that 96,499 Palestine refugees were in Syria.

April 7

The Sudanese Government announced the composition of the Electoral Commission, which would supervise elections, as follows: Sukumar Sen (India), chairman; J. C. Penney (Britain); Warwick Perkins (United States); Lieutenant Colonel Abd-al-Fattah Hassan (Egypt); and Abd-al-Salam Abd-al-Lahi, Khalfallah Khaled and Gordon Bulli (Sudan).

Jordan concluded an agreement with the US Government for technical assistance amounting to $1,915,000.

A meeting of the Egyptian Social Reform Union, held in Cairo, urged that the new Constitution stipulate social security as first among human rights. It also urged the Government to secure the necessary funds in order to implement the Social Insurance Law fully, and to prepare a comprehensive health insurance plan.

April, 1953

April 8

The Soviet Union had reportedly informed the Egyptian Government that the latter's participation in a Western organized Middle Eastern Defense Pact would be viewed unfavorably by the Soviet Government.

Egyptian Premier Nagib issued a statement saying that it was well known in Britain that unconditional and complete evacuation of the Canal Zone expressed the unanimous will of the Egyptian people and that absolute independence for Egypt was the primary objective of the army's movement.

The Political Committee of the Arab League Council announced that it had made the following recommendations on the Arab refugee question and relations with Israel: (1) the Arab Governments should spare no effort to defend the rights of the refugees and to secure the implementation of the UN resolutions on the subject; (2) they should undertake constructive projects (to be financed by the UN Relief and Works Agency) intended to provide work for the refugees resident in their territories and to raise their standards of living; (3) they should oppose the admission of Israel to the Eastern Mediterranean regional organization of the World Health Organization.

The envoys of the US, Britain and France were called to the Iraqi Foreign Ministry to hear the Government's views on the wave of Arab infiltrations.

April 9

Under a revised Graft Law issued in Egypt, new offenses were included, relating to acting against the interests of the nation by neglect or by infringement of law, and improper exploitation of influence to obtain or to allocate government, institutional or commercial positions. New penalties included deprivation of nationality or of the right to hold a directorship, public office, or to exercise a profession forming public opinion or education.

The Arab League's 20th session adjourned. Assistant Secretary General Ahmad Shukairy said that the resolutions adopted by the

April 9

Political Committee would be made public in due time. He also stated that the Anglo-Egyptian issue of the evacuation of the Suez Canal Zone had not been raised although all the Arab delegates expressed full support for Egypt.

Israel Foreign Minister Moshe Sharett was received by President Eisenhower, with whom he discussed matters concerning the situation in the Middle East.

April 10

A special Iraqi ministerial committee would reportedly investigate the large scale migration of Iraqi peasants to Kuwait.

Dag Hammarskjold began his term as Secretary General of the United Nations.

April 11

A conference of Arab journalists was convened in Cairo. A permanent Arab Press Union was agreed upon whose Executive Committee would meet within six months.

Colonel Gamal Abdel Nasser, in a statement to the press, said Egypt was willing to begin discussions at once with Britain for a just and practical solution to the Canal Zone question, but that it should be recognized in advance that Egypt would not discuss a "Middle East agreement," and that by a just solution he meant "evacuation of the Zone."

April 12

Colonel Gamal Abdel Nasser, Secretary General of the Liberation Rally and considered second in command after Egyptian Premier General Nagib, declared in Cairo that Egypt would expect the aid of British technicians in maintaining the Suez Zone base after the departure of British troops.

April 12

The Palestine Conciliation Commission urged Arab refugees to disregard the advice of Arab Governments against applying to Israel for the release of their blocked accounts in Israel banks.

A decree was issued appointing Colonel Adib Shishakli as Syrian Minister of Interior in addition to his post of Chief of Staff and Vice President of the Cabinet.

April 13

It was officially announced in Tel Aviv that seven Arabs were killed and a score captured in four clashes during the previous week between marauding Arab bands and Israel border units.

April 14

The Lebanese Government had reportedly issued a White Paper relative to its taking over the Beirut Electricity Company.

April 15

Sultan Sidi Muhammad Ben-Youssef sent a note to President Vincent Auriol of France, requesting that negotiations between his Government of Morocco and the French Government take place in Paris. The note deplored French repressive measures in Morocco, and the nomination and dismissal of Moroccan officials by the French Residency without his approval.

For discussions on outstanding questions with the Egyptian Government, which were expected to open shortly in Cairo, Her Majesty's Ambassador in Cairo and General Sir Brian Robertson had reportedly been appointed as the British representatives.

April 16

It was announced in Cairo that British and Egyptian representatives would begin discussions on the Suez Canal Zone question on April 27. They would deal with the technical problems involved in the evacuation of the British forces and the subsequent maintenance of the Canal Zone base.

April 16

The Ford Foundation announced that it had granted to 23 projects a total of $3,256,282 for basic research into the economic and social problems of the Near East, and for vocational training, village development and leadership training.

April 17

The twenty-third Middle East Medical Conference opened in Beirut.

The British Foreign Office stated that the Saudi Arabian Government had been informed that there was no foundation for reports that supplies were being prevented from reaching the eight villages of the Buraimi Oasis.

The Israel Foreign Ministry stated that a note requesting an opportunity for consultation on any aspect of the forthcoming Anglo-Egyptian negotiations likely to affect Israel interests had been sent to the United States as well as Britain because both parties to the negotiations were likely to consult with America.

April 18

A meeting of the Palestine Armistice Commission opened in Cairo, attended by delegates of Lebanon, Syria, Jordan and Egypt. General Nagib, Egyptian Premier, described Israel as a "cancer endangering all Arab States." He declared that existing Israel territory did not represent the limit of Israel ambitions. This view was endorsed by the Jordanian delegate who said that reports of the possibility of peace between the Arab States and Israel were baseless and ridiculous.

April 19

In a demarche to the US, British, French and Turkish Governments, the Israel Foreign Office drew attention to the "steadily deteriorating situation" in the Middle East that had led to an increasing number of border incidents and an attack on five Israel fishing boats.

April 19

A barter agreement with Greece was signed in Cairo. It provided for the exchange of Egyptian cotton for Greek olives, olive oil and tobacco.

The British Embassy issued a statement designed to counter misrepresentations in the Egyptian press concerning the Anglo-Saudi Arabian dispute over the Buraimi Oasis. It said that the British offer to submit the dispute to arbitration remained open and could be accepted by Saudi Arabia without loss of dignity if its conscience was clear.

April 21

After a heated debate on the interpretation submitted by an opposition Deputy on the legality of the decree issued by the Lebanese Government of Amir Khaled Chehab, Prime Minister, for administrative appointments and reorganization of the various governmental departments, the Deputies left the Lebanese Chamber.

President Camille Chamoun of Lebanon arrived in Cairo on an official visit.

A trade and friendship agreement between West Germany and the Kingdom of Yemen was concluded and signed.

April 22

A five hour battle broke out along the entire two mile border in Jerusalem.

Opposition members in the Lebanese Chamber of Deputies demanded the rejection of the State budget because it relied on foreign aid—British financial assistance and the American Point Four program.

April 23

A commercial agreement was concluded between Syria and Jordan.

April, 1953

April 23

An Israel Army spokesman reported that in the clash on the previous day, four men were killed and five injured on the Jordanian side of the armistice line, and four Israelis were injured.

Israel forces again opened fire on the Arab half of Jerusalem, until a truce was effected by Lieutenant General William E. Riley, Chief UN Truce Supervisor.

April 24

Lieutenant General William E. Riley submitted his resignation as Chief of Staff of the Truce Supervision Organization. The Secretary General accepted the resignation, effective as of May 15.

The Egyptian Foreign Office announced that the Jordan Government had appealed to Britain, France and the United States to end repeated Israel aggression.

Rural elections in Tunisia ended. The nationalists' boycott of the elections — by both the Neo-Destour Party and the Tunisian Trade Union Federation — was generally effective.

April 25

A public meeting of protest against the Land Acquisition Law, sponsored by the Society for the Defense of the Arab Minority Rights in Israel, was held in Haifa. The meeting was addressed by Israelis of all liberal, political and non-political groups such as the League for the Defense of Civil Rights, the Ichud and others.

April 27

Ahmad Hussein, former President of the Egyptian Socialist Party, imprisoned on charges of instigating and directing the anti-British riots of January 26, 1952, was granted an amnesty by a decision of the Egyptian Court.

Egypt and Iraq protested to the UN, accusing Israel of killing Arab civilians in Jerusalem.

April, 1953

April 27

It was reported from Cairo that a new traffic record for the Suez Canal was set in 1952 with 86,137,000 net registered tons of shipping passing through the Canal. This was 4,300,000 tons more than in the previous peak year, 1950.

The first meeting between Egypt and Great Britain on negotiations for the evacuation of the Suez Canal Zone was described in an official communique as "very cordial."

In a farewell message at the conclusion of his visit, President Camille Chamoun pledged Lebanon's full support of Egypt's demand for evacuation of the Suez Canal Zone.

April 28

Lebanese Prime Minister Khaled Chehab and his Cabinet resigned; President Camille Chamoun requested Saeb Salam to form a new Lebanese Government.

A new railway extension from Sennar to Singa was officially inaugurated in the Sudan.

Israel Prime Minister David Ben-Gurion stated before the Security and Foreign Affairs Committee of the Knesset that Israel would take the necessary measures to repel the planned infiltration of its territory by marauding Arab bands.

An Egyptian Government spokesman, speaking about the current talks with Britain, declared that Egypt was demanding that British troops withdraw unconditionally from the Suez Canal Zone. Once the evacuation was completed, he stated, admittance into Egyptian territory of any foreign troops would be freely decided by Egypt alone, and in conformity with Egypt's interests.

Lieutenant General William E. Riley, Chief UN Truce Supervisor, and his staff investigated the demilitarized zone of Mount Scopus on the complaint of the Jordan Government that Israelis were accumulating arms and ammunition there in defiance of the demilitarization agreement of November, 1948. No arms or ammunition were found in excess of those which were authorized in 1948.

April, 1953

April 29

The communique issued after the meeting between Egyptian and English negotiators stated that the two delegations agreed they should not make any further press statements until a fresh stage had been reached.

April 30

The French police announced the arrest of 11 Tunisians on charges of sabotage and terrorism.

May, 1953

May 1

Lebanese Prime Minister Saeb Salam reportedly had formed the following new Cabinet: Saeb Salam, Prime Minister, Interior and Defense; Georges Hakim, Foreign Affairs and Economy.

The British Ambassadors in Amman and Tel Aviv proposed that a special meeting of representatives of Israel and Jordan be convened to work out means of avoiding frontier incidents.

Abu-Bakr Naama was appointed Minister of Finance and Economics in Libya. He succeeded Mansour Qidar, who was appointed Minister to Great Britain.

Richard G. Casey, Australian Minister for External Affairs, made a statement in which he emphasized Australia's great interest in the negotiations proceeding in Cairo on the future of the Canal Zone and the importance which the Government attached to the building up of the Middle East Defense arrangements. He said the Government hoped the "statesmanship and soldierly sense of military reality" of General Nagib would enable a settlement to be reached which gave due recognition to the rights and needs of all whose security was involved.

May 2

King Hussein I was sworn in as King of Jordan on his eighteenth birthday.

King Faisal II assumed the throne of Iraq on his eighteenth birthday, bringing to an end the 14 year regency of Amir Abd-al-Ilah, his maternal uncle.

A note from French Foreign Minister Georges Bidault was conveyed to the Bey of Tunis, Sidi Muhammad al-Amin, in which the Bey was requested to put out a statement repudiating the nationalists and exhorting his subjects to vote in the forthcoming municipal elections.

The Deputy Mayor of Tunis, Chadly Kastally, considered pro-French, was shot to death on the eve of elections in which he was to have been a candidate for municipal councilor.

May 3

The Electoral Commission concluded a ten day visit to the Southern Sudan.

Several score Tunisians were arrested following the assassination of Deputy Mayor Kastally.

May 4

Prime Minister Muhammad Nagib of Egypt informed the Umma Party that he would not allow Egyptian politicians to make propaganda tours of the Sudan.

May 5

The Sudanese Electoral Commission announced that general elections, as simultaneous as possible, would begin in the second half of October.

The King of Jordan requested Fawzi al-Mulki, Ambassador to Great Britain, to form a government. Prime Minister al-Mulki announced the following new Cabinet: Fawzi al-Mulki, Prime Minister and Defense; Said al-Mufti, Deputy Prime Minister and Minister of State; Hussein al-Khalidi, Foreign Affairs and Acting Chief Justice.

In accordance with constitutional procedure, Prime Minister Tawfiq Abu-al-Huda and his Jordanian Cabinet tendered their resignation to King Hussein.

It was reported from Amman that Jordan again invoked the Anglo-Jordanian Treaty in connection with the clashes on the Israel-Jordan border. The Jordanian Foreign Minister also presented notes of protest against Israel to the Ambassadors of Great Britain, France and the US, guarantors of the frontiers under the 1950 Tripartite Declaration.

The Egyptian Constitution Committee, under the chairmanship of former Premier Ali Maher, approved a proposal that a republican system of government form the foundation of the constitution.

May 5

The Cabinet of Iraqi Prime Minister Jamil al-Midfai submitted its resignation, in accordance with constitutional practice. The King asked al-Midfai to continue in office and to enlarge the Cabinet.

May 6

A trade agreement was signed in Baghdad between Iraq and India.

The Foreign Ministry of Israel notified the diplomatic representatives of the powers directly concerned with the security of the Middle East of the situation on Israel's borders.

As of May 6, a total of 60 Tunisians had been arrested in connection with the assassination of Deputy Mayor Kastally.

Countrywide parliamentary elections in the Sudan were postponed until October because preparations could not be completed before the start of the rainy season in June.

After the sixth meeting of the Anglo-Egyptian negotiations a communique announced the adjournment of the talks. Colonel Gamal Abdel Nasser said the Egyptians refused to enter into any details without agreement on the basic issues. He thought it probable that the British representatives could not continue the discussions without consulting their Government.

May 7

Asked to form a Cabinet, Iraqi Prime Minister Jamil al-Midfai announced the following reconstituted Cabinet: Jamil al-Midfai, Prime Minister; Ali Jawdat al-Ayyoubi, Deputy Prime Minister; Tawfiq al-Suwaidi, Foreign Affairs.

A three day conference of Arab Foreign Ministers was opened in Cairo, at the end of which the Foreign Ministers reportedly agreed to support the Egyptian Government in its controversy with Great Britain. The conference recommended the immediate implementation of the Arab League Collective Security Pact, appealed to the West, particularly the UN, to effect a just settlement of the Palestine problem, and

May 7

reiterated its support of the nationalist aspirations of Tunisia, Algeria and Morocco.

May 8

It was reported from London that the British Government notified the Egyptian Government that the terms of reference the latter proposed for the negotiations on the future of the military base in the Suez Canal Zone were not acceptable to Britain.

Israel complained to the Israel-Jordan Mixed Armistice Commission of murders and abductions in the Jerusalem area.

May 9

US Secretary of State John Foster Dulles, accompanied by Mutual Security Director Harold E. Stassen, left for a tour of twelve Near Eastern and South Asian countries.

May 10

Egyptian Premier Muhammad Nagib indicated that he had abandoned hope of reaching a negotiated settlement with Britain in the dispute over the evacuation of the Canal Zone and that he washed his hands of the negotiations. He warned the Egyptians to prepare to gain their objectives in the impending big battle.

The Arab delegates in Cairo adopted a nine point declaration bearing on the general world situation, the Anglo-Egyptian problem, collective security, Palestine, Tunisia, and internal Arab League problems. They also passed a resolution calling on the UN to enforce the 1949 Palestine partition plan, the repatriation of Arab refugees, and the payment of compensation to those not returning.

May 11

Final returns of the Tunisian elections showed that 40 percent of the registered Tunisians in 25 towns voted in the series of municipal elections.

May 11

The Arab Cambers of Commerce ended their three day conference in Damascus. Among the resolutions adopted were the strengthening of the economic boycott of Israel, restriction of the rights of Jews to dispose of their property in Arab lands, and removal of barriers to investment of capital in any Arab country.

US Secretary of State John Foster Dulles and Mutual Security Director Harold E. Stassen arrived in Cairo. Dulles issued a statement indicating US support of the British view in the Suez Canal Zone issue: that the Canal Zone must remain on an efficient footing for future use by the forces of the free world. The Americans conferred with Premier Nagib and other high Egyptian officials.

In a statement on foreign policy in the House of Commons, Prime Minister Winston Churchill declared that the current British negotiations with Egypt were inaugurated at the direct request of the Egyptian Government, and that if the boastful threats of the Egyptians were converted into action against British troops in the Canal Zone, the latter would have no choice but to defend themselves. He told Premier Nagib that if Egypt had any proposals for the resumption of the negotiations, England would be willing to consider them.

Following talks with the Egyptian Foreign Minister and Premier Nagib, US Secretary of State John Foster Dulles issued a statement saying that the defense and well being of the Middle East were of great concern to the US. He said that the US favored a solution to the Suez Canal Zone problem consistent with full Egyptian sovereignty, with a phased withdrawal of troops to be arranged so that the Canal base could remain in good working order and be available for immediate use on behalf of the free world in the event of future hostilities.

Lieutenant General William E. Riley warned the Security Council of worsening Israel-Jordan relations and advised that there should be high level talks to ease the mounting tension.

A report to the UN Security Council by General Riley, the retiring Chief of Staff of the UN Truce Supervision Organization in Palestine, was published in Jerusalem.

May 12

Lebanese Premier Saeb Salam received a 37-31 vote of confidence for his administration.

Egyptian Premier Nagib issued a statement calling Britain an aggressor and not a defender of the free world.

As tension mounted Britain dispatched marine commandos to the Suez Canal area. The British Minister of State for Foreign Affairs told the Commons that there had been 30 attacks on British troops in the Suez Canal area since April 1.

May 13

The Egyptian Government charged that British forces in the Canal Zone had killed eight Egyptians and wounded 17 in 43 attacks of aggression since April 3.

US Secretary of State John Foster Dulles and Mutual Security Director Harold E. Stassen arrived in Tel Aviv where they conferred with Foreign Minister Moshe Sharett and other Israel leaders.

In reply to questions in Parliament, Defense Minister Nuri-Said stated that Iraq would not rush into a Middle East defense scheme, but would seek to ensure its national safety through cooperation with the Arab League Collective Security Pact.

May 14

The Egyptian Cabinet issued an order which would require special permission from the Supply Ministry to sell British military forces in the Suez Canal Zone food, alcoholic beverages, building materials and other goods.

French authorities arrested two brothers of Salah Ben-Youssef, former Tunisian cabinet minister, in connection with the Kastally murder.

After a round of conferences with Israel leaders, including Prime Minister David Ben-Gurion and President Yitzhak Ben-Zvi, US Secretary

May 14

of State Dulles and US Mutual Security Director Harold E. Stassen left for Amman, Jordan. They paid a courtesy visit to King Hussein and met with Government leaders.

May 15

Lieutenant General William E. Riley resigned as Chief of the UN Truce Supervision Organization.

Premier Fawzi al-Mulki of Jordan told US Secretary of State John Foster Dulles that there could be no talk of Middle East defense until the individual problems of the Arab States were solved. The Americans left for Syria.

US Secretary of State John Foster Dulles arrived in Damascus on an official visit.

A British Royal Marine commando brigade from Malta arrived in the Suez Canal Zone.

The Egyptian Embassy issued a list of 21 alleged "acts of assault" by British troops against the lives and property of Egyptian citizens in the Canal Zone between January and April. The list included six cases of alleged murder.

May 16

After a visit to Syrian Deputy Premier Shishakli and other Government leaders, US Secretary of State John Foster Dulles and Mutual Security Director Harold E. Stassen arrived in Beirut, Lebanon, where they called on President Chamoun. The parliamentary Foreign Affairs Committee advised Dulles that the US must remove from its mind any possibility of Arab peace with Israel.

Communists and students attempted to demonstrate against Dulles' visit to Lebanon but were dispersed by the police.

Lieutenant Colonel Gamal Abdel Nasser, second to General Nagib in the Egyptian Revolutionary Council, declared that negotiations for settlement of the dispute over the Canal Zone had broken down

May 16

because Britain had sought to impose terms that would have continued the British occupation under a new guise.

Egypt charged that British troops in the Canal Zone, pursuing a policy of provocation, kidnapped nine Egyptians, including four members of the armed forces.

May 17

An Israel Army spokesman reported that two Israel border patrolmen were killed by infiltrators in the Jerusalem border area. A complaint was filed with the Israel-Jordan Mixed Armistice Commission.

Egypt charged that British troops attacked the Abu-Hammad railway station in the Suez Canal Zone and kidnapped the station master and his assistants.

US Secretary of State John Foster Dulles arrived in Iraq and visited King Faisal II.

May 18

Before leaving for Saudi Arabia, US Secretary of State Dulles stated that the new American policies would be developed as a result of his fact finding tour of the Near and Middle Eastern countries.

Lieutenant Colonel Gamal Abdel Nasser was appointed Vice President of the Revolutionary Council. This placed him officially as second in command to Premier Nagib.

The Egyptian Government disclosed that three protest notes had been delivered to Britain concerning alleged attacks on Egyptians in the Canal Zone. They declared that 43 attacks had been made by British forces against Egyptians between April 3 and May 12, and that British troops had fired on the village of Kafr Abdu near the Suez on May 14. On May 17 British forces occupied Abu-Hammadi railway station and abducted the staff.

May 18

US Secretary of State John Foster Dulles conferred with officials of the Saudi Arabian Government and with representatives of the Arabian American Oil Company.

May 19

US Secretary of State John Foster Dulles reportedly had been given a note by the Iraqi Government which asked the US to implement the UN resolutions on Palestine, particularly those relating to the repatriation of Arab refugees and to the payment of compensation to the refugees, and also the 1948 resolution on the partition of Palestine.

May 20

The Syrian Cabinet approved the budget for the current year of SL205 million.

British civilians in Egypt were advised by the British Embassy to leave Egypt within the next few weeks unless they had compelling personal or official business.

The Lebanese Cabinet decided to establish a National Bank which would issue currency.

May 21

Jordan military authorities stated that national guard units repelled Israel attacks on four Arab villages along the Jordan-Israel armistice demarcation line during the past 24 hours.

The British Foreign Office in London announced that Robert Hankey, Minister to Hungary and an expert on the Middle East, was flying to Cairo to take over temporarily from Ambassador Stevenson, who was returning to England on sick leave.

May 22

Heads of the French diplomatic missions in the Arab States, Turkey, Iran and Ethiopia conferred in Beirut.

May 22

The Syrian Government reportedly protested in a note to Britain against Sir Winston Churchill's statement on the Middle East in his speech of May 11 in the House of Commons.

The President of the Iraqi Chamber of Deputies sent a message to the speaker of the British House of Commons for transmission to the members of Parliament and of the Government. It stated that the Iraqi Parliament unanimously condemned Sir Winston Churchill's statement on the Middle East for its biased support of Zionism and Israel, and disregard for Arab rights, and declared that the statement impaired British relations with Iraq and the Arab world and endangered peace and stability in the Middle East.

May 23

Sir Abd-al-Rahman al-Mahdi, religious Sudanese leader, en route to London for the coronation of Queen Elizabeth, conferred with Premier Nagib in Cairo.

May 24

A Syrian treaty of friendship with Iran was signed in Damascus.

Evacuation of British civilians began with the departure from Cairo of 16 women and 24 children.

The Jordanian House of Deputies approved a memorandum unanimously which protested Sir Winston Churchill's statement on Middle East policy in the House of Commons on May 11. The memorandum called for the support of Egyptian claims and for all possible measures to fight the British Government's policy of enmity to the Arabs.

The Jordanian Government issued a statement alleging that Israel attacks had been made against eleven Jordan villages on May 20 and 22 and that three villages in the Hebron district had been attacked on May 23. It accused the UN of supporting Israel aggression by refusing an investigation into these incidents.

May 24

The Jordanian Prime Minister, Fawzi al-Mulki, read a statement of policy which promised re-examination and revision of the Constitution to allow liberty of speech and the formation of political parties.

May 25

It was announced in Damascus that the new Constitution of Syria would be promulgated on June 19.

A six day conference of Arab Ministers of Finance and Economy opened in Beirut. The Trade Exchange Committee agreed to exempt agricultural produce from inter-Arab customs dues, and the Administrative Organization Committee agreed on a Lebanese proposal to establish a regional training center for financial and economic studies.

May 26

France and Iraq agreed to raise their respective diplomatic missions to embassies.

Jordanian Premier Fawzi al-Mulki received a 32-4 vote of confidence, with four Deputies abstaining, after the Chamber adopted the statement of policy of the new Government.

An Israel Army spokesman stated that Jordanian forces undertook coordinated and murderous action against three villages in the Shephela district near Lud; two persons were killed and six others, including three children, seriously injured. The incident was brought before the emergency session of the Israel-Jordan Mixed Armistice Commission.

A payments agreement was signed between Egypt and Greece which provided that the National Bank of Egypt should open a Collector Account in Egyptian pounds in the name of the Bank of Greece through which all payments between the two countries were to be effected. A trade agreement was also signed between the two countries in which they granted mutual most favored nation status.

May 26

A trade agreement with India, valid for one year, was initialed in Cairo. Egypt would receive jute and tea from India, in return for cotton, phosphates and manganese.

Muhammad Fuad Galal, Egyptian Minister of National Guidance, announced the names of four former Cabinet Ministers and seven others (among them the wife of former Premier Mustafa Nahhas Pasha) who were once powerful at the Court or in Parliament, to answer charges of irregular operations in the cotton market and other actions detrimental to national interests.

Egypt charged that British troops annihilated an entire Egyptian village in the Canal Zone by destroying its 300 houses.

May 28

General William E. Riley, Chief of the UN Truce Supervision Organization, agreed to remain at his post until the current situation was cleared up.

A pro-French city councilor, Muhammad Ben-Naceur of Zerkin, Tunisia, was murdered and his twelve year old daughter seriously wounded by anti-French Tunisians.

US Secretary of State John Foster Dulles and Mutual Security Director Harold E. Stassen arrived in Tripoli on an official visit to confer with Libyan leaders.

A payments agreement was signed between Egypt and Belgium.

May 29

A petition signed by 270 Moroccans, mostly Berbers, requesting that Sultan Sidi Muhammad Ben-Youssef be forced to abdicate, was submitted to the French Government. It was reported that the petition was instigated by the Pasha of Marrakech who was the Sultan's principal opponent.

May 29

The Foreign Ministry of France confirmed that 270 pashas and caids — two-thirds of the local governors of Morocco — had signed a petition for the deposition of the Sultan, Sidi Muhammad Ben-Youssef.

Israel proposed at a special meeting of the Mixed Armistice Commission that local commanders along the borders of Jordan and Israel resume meetings as a means of halting the long series of border incidents.

The American delegation of Secretary of State Dulles and Mutual Security Director Harold E. Stassen returned to Washington.

May 30

Lebanese President Chamoun dissolved Parliament and called for general elections in mid-July.

May 31

A conference of Arab Economic and Financial Ministers ended in Beirut after agreeing on recommendations designed primarily to establish a closer knit economy between Arab League States and to stimulate inter-Arab investment and trade exchanges.

The French Foreign Ministry issued a statement declaring that it did not intend at the present juncture to follow up politically the petition of pashas and caids, but it commented that the importance of Moroccan opinion from which it emanated should not be underestimated and that it could only reinforce the Government's will to give democratic expression to tendencies in Moroccan opinion.

June 1

A trade agreement was signed with Turkey at the Egyptian Ministry of Foreign Affairs. It provided for exchanges of goods on a barter system, for one year.

Adib Shishakli, Syrian Deputy Prime Minister and Chief of the Army Staff visited President Camille Chamoun of Lebanon.

US Secretary of State John Foster Dulles reported to the nation on his recent trip through the Middle East, underscoring increased US concern in the area and suggesting the likelihood of increased economic and military aid. He emphasized that the US should disregard the appearance of supporting colonialism.

June 2

In response to a plea for mercy submitted by his family, Premier Nagib commuted the death sentence of Lieutenant Colonel Muhammad Husni al-Damanhuri.

In reply to local chieftains' demand for his ouster, Sultan Sidi Muhammad Ben-Youssef of Morocco demanded that France, the protecting power, put an end to organized dissidence.

The Sudanese Electoral Commission decided that direct elections would be conducted in all but 24 constituencies, ten of which were in the north and 14 in the south. It was also decided that the number of direct elections constituencies should be raised to 68 and the number of indirect ones to 24.

An agreement on the Yarmuk irrigation scheme was concluded between Syria and Jordan. Syria would pay five percent of the cost of Point Four in Jordan.

It was announced at Amman that Jordan would exchange diplomatic representation with Yugoslavia.

Iraqi Prime Minister Jamil al-Midfai announced the immediate abolition of press censorship and the gradual reduction in the functions of

June 2

the Military Tribunals as a preliminary to the abolition of martial law, which was imposed in November, 1952. He also said a decree law governing the formation of political parties would be discussed by the Council of Ministers on June 6.

Moroccan Sultan Sidi Muhammad Ben-Youssef declared that the 270 local Moroccan chieftains, who on May 29 had asked for his ouster, were not qualified to speak out on government policy or on religious questions and that they could not act in the name of popular opinion since they did not derive their power from it. The Sultan was supported in this by the Moslem elders of Fez.

In a statement to the press Prime Minister Jamil al-Midfai expressed Iraq's full support for Egyptian National aspirations and a willingness to execute any decision taken by the Arab League Council to help Egypt. He declared that Iraq would never negotiate with Israel and had never considered joining the proposed Middle East defense command. Iraq was a member of the Arab League Collective Security Pact and its main duty was to defend Iraq territory and to fulfill its obligations to other member states.

June 3

Jordan conveyed to the Mixed Armistic Commission in Jerusalem its acceptance of the Israel proposal for a renewal of meetings between local commanders along the armistice lines. The first meeting was set for June 8.

The UN Mixed Armistice Commission found Israel and Jordan each guilty of recent armistice violations.

The Assistant Secretary General of the Arab League, Ahmad Shukairy, said that while US Secretary of State John Foster Dulles viewed the Arab issues from the angle of the dispute between East and West, the Arabs had to look at these issues from their viewpoint alone. The Beirut daily al-Hayat , commenting on Dulles' speech, asked for a "real change in American policy." An-Nasr of Damascus described the Dulles speech as "vague and contradictory."

June 3

The French Residency General in Tunisia released seven Tunisian trade union leaders from prison, including Professor Mahmoud Messadi, General Secretary of the UGTT (L'Union Generale Tunisienne du Travail), and Muhammad Krayem. Sixty-five other internees were to be released on June 21.

June 4

Israel officials announced that Israel was willing to negotiate the joint use of waters of the Jordan, Yarmuk and Litani Rivers with Jordan, Syria and Lebanon in advance of a general peace settlement.

A conference of senior elections officers and members of the Electoral Commission on the Sudan began.

The American Ambassador to Iraq informed the Iraqi Government that US Point Four aid to Iraq would be increased by 35 percent; the 1953 allotment was raised from $1,600,000 to $2,165,000.

An official of the Ministry of Foreign Affairs in Paris said that the difficulty between the local chieftains and the Sultan of Morocco was an internal matter of a mainly religious nature, and that France would not interfere so long as the country remained calm.

June 5

A statement issued on June 3 by four pashas from Morocco, including the Pasha of Sefrous and the Pasha of Fez, was made public. It severely criticized the petition of 270 pashas and caids for the deposition of the Sultan, and reaffirmed the Moroccan unity around the person of the Sovereign. It recognized at the same time the great French contribution to Moroccan progress and expressed the wish to safeguard legitimate French rights in Morocco.

The scene of the Anglo-Libyan discussions was shifted from Tripoli to London.

June 6

Lebanese Minister of Foreign Affairs and Economy Georges Hakim told representatives of Tapline (Trans-Arabian Pipeline Company) and the Iraqi Petroleum Company that the present Lebanese Government insisted upon modification of the agreements and demanded an increase of revenue.

June 8

Jordan and Israel signed a three month agreement in Jerusalem providing for regular meetings of local commanders along the armistice lines between the two countries to prevent border crossings and incidents.

An economic agreement was signed between Syria and Japan. It was to come into force 15 days after ratification. The agreement was valid for one year and was renewable.

June 9

Egyptian Minister of National Guidance Fuad Galal, at his weekly press conference, said there was no reason for optimism regarding resumption of talks with the United Kingdom regarding the Suez Canal, which were broken off May 6.

Foreign Minister Mahmoud Fawzi signed the Arab Nationality Agreement on behalf of the Egyptian Government.

Jordan's Council of Ministers approved the Yarmuk River Agreement in its final form, including the modifications recently introduced by Syria. Jordanian Foreign Minister Hussein al-Khaledi was authorized to sign it. King Hussein returned to Amman after a five day tour of the southern districts, where he was studying the economic potential of the area, accompanied by a number of American experts.

UN Secretary General Dag Hammarskjold announced that Major General Vagn Bennike, one time head of Denmark's Engineer Corps and a leader in the Danish resistance movement, had been appointed head of the UN Truce Supervision Organization in Palestine.

June, 1953

June 9

Iraq and Lebanon informed the Executive Board of UNESCO, meeting in Paris, that the Arab States would not attend the regional UNESCO conference because of Israel. The conference was therefore cancelled.

An Israel spokesman said that 12 hours after Israel and Jordan signed an agreement to combat infiltration along the armistice line, Arab marauders bombed two houses and killed a farmer in Tirat Yehuda.

A communique was issued after the final plenary session of the Commonwealth Prime Ministers' Conference. They had recognized the international importance of the Suez Canal and of the effective maintenance of the military installations in the Canal Zone. They agreed it was in the common interest that the outstanding issues in the Middle East should be settled on the basis of ensuring the peace and security of the Middle East countries, consistent with the sovereignty of each and promoting their social and economic development.

June 10

A series of decrees were issued in Lebanon to safeguard the freedom of the elections.

In a report to the Saudi Arabian Government, Aramco noted that during 1952 the Company produced 301,860,885 barrels of crude oil, compared with 277,962,605 barrels in 1951. The sale of refined products in Saudi Arabia rose from 635,000 to 1,002,000 barrels.

June 11

Israel Foreign Minister Moshe Sharett warned the Jordanian Government that if "nightly murders" by marauders who crossed the armistice lines continued, the situation could easily get out of hand, with disastrous results.

June 13

Lebanese President Camille Chamoun visited Deputy Premier Shishakli of Syria at Damascus.

June, 1953

June 14

A Turkish delegation arrived at Aleppo at the invitation of the Syrian Government to discuss transport questions between the two countries.

The Sheikhdom of Kuwait imposed stringent controls on exports and imports following reports received by the Kuwaiti authorities that attempts were being made to smuggle goods into Israel.

June 15

Middle East veterinarians began a six day conference at Nicosia, Cyprus.

The Egyptian Minister of Supply, Muhammad Sabri Mansour, the Minister of Public Works, Murad Fahmi, and the Minister of Communications, Hussein Abu-Zaid, resigned.

June 16

President Camille Chamoun of Lebanon arrived in Amman on a state visit at the invitation of King Hussein. He was accompanied by senior Lebanese officials and army officers, including the Lebanese Minister of Justice and Information and Colonel Khaled Chehab of the Lebanese Army.

The dissolved People's Front Party of Iraq, led by General Taha al-Hashimi, announced its support of the notes submitted by the National Democratic and Istiqlal Parties regarding the law governing the formation of political parties.

June 17

The Syrian Government and the Syrian Bank delegation resumed discussions regarding liquidation of the Syrian-Lebanese Banks Association preliminary to the establishment of a Syrian Central Bank.

June, 1953

June 17

Israel Foreign Minister Moshe Sharett assured the UN of Israel's readiness to cooperate with whomever was charged with the international supervision of the Holy Places in Jerusalem. He made clear, however, that such supervision could not possibly infringe upon Israel's sovereignty in New Jerusalem, or prejudice the status of Jerusalem as Israel's capital.

British Prime Minister Sir Winston Churchill stated in London that at the request of the British Government, the West German Government was investigating the recruiting of German technicians by the Egyptian Army.

The Sultan of Morocco issued a statement declaring the "effective collaboration of the French" and the "peaceful and brotherly cohabitation" of all inhabitants to be essential for Morocco's well being.

June 18

The Egyptian Military Council of Revolution announced that the Egyptian monarchy had been brought to an end and proclaimed a Republic with General Muhammad Nagib as President and Prime Minister. Some civilian ministers were dropped from the Cabinet and their positions taken by members of the Military Council. Gamal Abdel Nasser became Deputy Premier and Minister of the Interior, and Abd-al-Hakim Amer became Commander in Chief of the Armed Forces.

The Egyptian Council of the Revolution still characterized its rule as transitional, leading eventually to the restoration of the parliamentary government, and the election of the President by the people after the constitution making committee had finished its work and the regime had been stabilized. The period of transition would last three years.

Two Point Four agreements with Egypt signed in Cairo offered US technical assistance to Egypt on a broader range of technical problems, including rural and vocational training and in the field of public health.

June, 1953

June 18

In a communique the Sultan of Morocco said that an exchange of notes regarding the reform of administrative councils was proceeding with the French Resident General, but that complete accord could not be reached in an "atmosphere of terror and intrigue."

A statement issued by General John Glubb, Chief of Staff of the Arab Legion, referred to Israel Government and press allegations that bands of marauders from Jordan had been committing terrorist acts in Israel.

The Israel Government announced that it had sent a note to the head of the UN Truce Supervision Organization demanding an immediate reduction in the number of inhabitants of the Arab village of Issawiya, in the demilitarized zone on Mount Scopus, from the 1,000 recorded to be there to the 150 permitted under the armistice agreement of July 7, while nothing had been done to secure the reopening of the Hadasseh Hospital on Mount Scopus which had been specifically called for in the general armistice agreement.

Major General Vagn Bennike of the Danish Army arrived at Lydda Airport to replace Lieutenant General William C. Riley as Chief of Staff of the UN Truce Supervision Organization.

June 19

Representatives of Iraq and Saudi Arabia met in Riyadh to discuss the price of crude oil paid by Western concessionaire companies. A joint statement issued in Riyadh and Baghdad simultaneously said that the Iraqi-Saudi consultations also covered the questions of wireless and telephone communications between the two countries and travel to the Hejaz via a desert highway.

The Palestine Conciliation Commission announced that Jordan and Israel agreed to a new arrangement for the payment of the blocked bank accounts of Palestine Arab refugees.

President Muhammad Nagib of Egypt swore in the new Egyptian Cabinet.

June, 1953

June 20

Major General Vagn Bennike took over from General William E. Riley his duties as Chief UN Truce Observer in Palestine.

June 21

The US reportedly offered to conclude separate arms agreements with the Middle East states inasmuch as a unified defense organization was regarded as a future rather than an immediate possibility.

Leaders of the Lebanese opposition asked President Camille Chamoun for the appointment of a neutral Government to supervise the forthcoming parliamentary elections, but the President declined to dismiss Prime Minister Saeb Salam.

Brigadier Adib Shishakli announced the new Iranian draft Constitution.

A decree was issued inviting the Syrian people to take part in a plebiscite on the new Constitution and the election of the President of the Republic by secret ballot on July 10.

The Syrian political leaders, Akram Hourani, Michel Aflaq, and Salah-ad-Din Bitar, who were granted political asylum in Lebanon in early 1953 were ordered to leave that country within 24 hours.

Israel requested restoration of a "lawful situation in the Mount Scopus area" in accordance with the Israel-Jordan armistice agreement of April 3, 1949.

Tehran Radio gave the text of a note to Iraq which complained that the activities of an Anglo-Iraq military commission near the Iranian border on March 1 and excavations along the border by a British group were prejudicial to Iraq-Iranian friendship.

Muhammad Ali, Pakistan Prime Minister, and Jawaharlal Nehru, Indian Prime Minister, arrived in Cairo.

June, 1953

June 22

Air Commodore Hassan Mahmoud, Chief of Staff of the Egyptian Air Force, was relieved of his post and pensioned.

Premier Muhammad Ali and Foreign Minister Zafrullah Khan of Pakistan met with President Muhammad Nagib in Cairo and discussed with him the Suez Canal Zone issue.

French Resident General Augustin Guillaume, forbade Sheikh Abd-al-Rahman Ben-Musa to say the customary prayers for the Sultan over the Moroccan broadcasting system.

June 23

The Iraqi Chamber of Deputies approved the draft law submitted by the Development Board to establish a Ministry of Development which would carry on the Board's work of financing projects with revenues from oil. Nadim al-Pachachi, Chairman of the Board and Minister of State, would become Minister of Development.

The Iraqi Cabinet adopted the Ministry of Economy's suggestion that the Government enter into talks with the British Government to settle outstanding economic questions. A mission headed by Abd-al-Ilah Hafez, Governor of the General Bank, was to leave for London for this purpose towards the end of July.

An agreement was concluded between the Bahrain Government and a British firm for the building of a new port at Manama, the capital of Bahrain. The port was to be used to harbor commercial vessels carrying freight into the Persian Gulf.

The Anglo-Iranian Oil Company was offered exploration rights off Abu Dhabi and the Anglo-Iranian Oil Company and Compagnie Francaise des Petroles were granted joint rights off Dubai.

A three power conference was held in Cairo at which Anglo-Egyptian relations and the situation in the Sudan were discussed. Pakistani Prime Minister Muhammad Ali and Indian Prime Minister Nehru attended.

June, 1953

June 23

In his first speech as President, General Muhammad Nagib warned that Egypt "would not give an inch" on its rights.

Indian Prime Minister Nehru had private discussions with Egyptian President Muhammad Nagib, Foreign Minister Mahmoud Fawzi and other members of the Egyptian Government.

A delegation representing political personalities submitted to the Syrian Deputy Premier a letter signed by more than a hundred politicians criticizing the drafting of the Constitution by a committee of Government employees, and asserted that an elected constitutional assembly should have been entrusted with the task. Among the signers of the letter were former premiers and heads of political parties.

June 24

Lebanon's Premier Saeb Salam announced that the Government had abolished entry visas for the nationals of all Arab countries who wished to visit Lebanon.

A preliminary informal meeting was held in Libya with an Italian delegation led by Ambassador Bombieri, regarding disputed Italian property in Libya.

The Sudanese Financial Secretary, Sir A. L. Clark, reported that exports and re-exports fell from 64 million pounds sterling in 1951 to 43 million pounds sterling in 1952; in contrast, imports rose from 42 million in 1951 to 61 million pounds sterling in 1952.

Karim Thabet, press advisor to ex-King Farouk, was sentenced by the Graft Court and was deprived for ten years of the right to hold public office of any sort, to join a political party or a board of directors, or to practice any liberal profession.

June 25

A payments agreement was signed between Egypt and Libya.

June, 1953

June 25

Indian Prime Minister Nehru said in a press statement that he hoped there would be a peaceful settlement of the Suez issue, but Major Salah Salem, Egyptian Minister for National Guidance and Sudanese Affairs, said Egypt must "depend on herself," and did not feel there would be a speedy solution by way of mediation.

June 26

The British Government accorded de facto recognition to the new Egyptian Republic when it acknowledged the Egyptian note notifying it of the change of regime.

June 27

The Jordanian Council of Ministers at an extraordinary meeting decided to issue JD100,000 as loans to farmers and grain to the poor in the south who were suffering from a poor agricultural season.

The Jordanian Cabinet met in Jerusalem for the first time since the enforced partition of the Holy City into Arab and Jewish sections in 1948. The Cabinet decided to set up a central office in Jerusalem responsible to the Minister of State in Amman, to establish governmental offices in the Holy City, and to allocate JD50,000 for the creation of light industries.

King Hussein of Jordan arrived at Baghdad on a state visit to congratulate King Faisal on his coronation of May 2.

Sheikh Muhammad Hassan al-Bakhuri, Egyptian Minister of Waqfs, announced that 60,000 feddans of Waqf lands which the ex-King had usurped for himself had been returned to the Ministry.

The Egyptian Embassy received a note from Iraqi Foreign Minister Tawfiq al-Suwaidi stating that Iraq wished to see the Egyptian people exercise their full rights in deciding the kind of government they wanted.

June, 1953

June 28

Prime Minister Jamil al-Midfai of Iraq issued an order permitting Arab refugees living in Iraq to work on an equal footing with the nationals of the country. The order did not affect the Palestinian nationality of the refugees in any way.

Rashid Beidoun, Lebanese Minister of Health and Communications, resigned, creating a cabinet crisis.

June 29

Thirty-eight Moroccans were arrested following the discovery of an alleged secret nationalist organization in Rabat.

Maarouf al-Dawalibi, former speaker of the Syrian House and Premier prior to the Shishakli coup, who was arrested in January, 1953, in connection with an alleged plot to overthrow the Shishakli regime, was released.

The Government of Libya asked the International Bank for Reconstruction and Development for a $17 million loan to finance Libya's capital development plan.

At a meeting of Jordanian and Israel general staff officers, Jordan agreed to take measures to prevent the infiltration of Jordanians into Israel.

June 30

An agreement to provide work for Arab refugees was signed in Cairo between the Government of Egypt and the UN Relief and Works Agency for Palestine. The agreement called for economic and construction surveys to be made in the Gaza Strip and some parts of Sinai, with a view to providing work for refugees in these regions as a means of improving their living and social conditions. The UN Relief and Works Agency reported the number of Palestine refugees at 871,748.

After French Premier Joseph Laniel succeeded in forming a Government in France, the political committee of Neo-Destour in Tunis issued a markedly conciliatory statement calling for resumption of negotiations between Tunisia and France in a spirit of mutual understanding and respect.

July, 1953

July 1

Prince Azzedine Bey, heir presumptive to the crown of Tunisia, was assassinated.

The Egyptian Cabinet declared July 23, the anniversary of the military coup, and June 18, the day of the establishment of the Republic, national holidays.

The Anglo-Libyan talks in London entered the ministerial phase when Libyan Prime Minister Mahmoud Muntasir called on British Minister of State Selwyn Lloyd at the Foreign Office.

July 2

In an article in Syria's al-Liwa, Abu-al-Khair al-Miodani, head of the Ulema's Society, criticized the new Syrian draft Constitution from the Islamic point of view.

It was reported in Geneva that UN technical assistance to the Arab States increased more than 300 percent in 1953.

The Egyptian Government censorship on outgoing news dispatches, which had been in effect in one form or another since the beginning of the Palestine conflict in 1948 and with only brief interruptions since 1938, was lifted. The Government intended to invite some seventy foreign journalists to attend celebrations beginning July 23, marking the first anniversary of the military coup that put President Nagib in power.

July 3

Egyptian President Muhammad Nagib, in his first press interview since the lifting of the censorship on outgoing dispatches, said Egypt would continue to press for the withdrawal of British troops from the Suez Canal Zone but indicated there was no urgency about the matter and that the economy was the most pressing problem.

The Sultan of Morocco signed two decrees enacting new administrative and judicial reforms in Tangier. The first gave Spain and Italy as

July, 1953

July 3

much representation as they had after the Accord of 1928. The other permitted the inclusion of American, Moroccan, Dutch, Portuguese and Swedish judges to the already existing judges in the Mixed Tribunal.

The Bey of Tunis handed to the Tunisian Minister of the Interior, who was acting as Prime Minister in Salah-ad-Din Baccouche's absence, a note accusing the Prime Minister of undermining his authority and infringing his prerogatives.

July 4

A Ministry of Economy was established in Saudi Arabia to replace the Department of Economic Affairs. The new Ministry was placed under the direction of Abd-al-Sulaiman.

The Jordan Government announced that a law prohibiting trading with Israel had been issued at the request of the Control Office for the Economic Boycott of Israel.

The Sultan of Morocco gave General Guillaume, French Resident General in Morocco, a new protest to deliver to the French Government.

July 5

Muhammad Sadok Ben-Hussein, brother of the slain Tunisian prince, was named the new heir to the throne of Tunisia.

Abdallah Khalil, Secretary of the Sudanese Umma Party, and Abd-al-Fadel al-Mahdi, member of the Party's executive committee, left Cairo after a series of talks with President Nagib and other Egyptian leaders. Abdallah Khalil said the talks had resulted in "complete understanding" in outstanding matters between the Party and the Egyptian Government.

July 6

Sheikh Abdallah al-Salem al-Sabah, the Ruler of Kuwait, returned to Kuwait from Beirut. He had been undergoing medical treatment in France.

July, 1953

July 6

A decree by the Lebanese Government granted amnesty to Ahmad al-Barazi, who assassinated Major General Sami al-Hinnawi on October 30, 1950.

A trade and payments agreement was signed between Austria and Egypt in Cairo. Egyptian cotton and manganese were to be exchanged for Austrian industrial equipment, electrical appliances, trucks and prefabricated houses.

July 7

The Egyptian vessel Samir, captured in Israel territorial waters, was turned over to Egyptian authorities under the supervision of UN officials.

King Ibn-Saud donated LE25,000 to Arab refugees in Lebanon. His Majesty stipulated that, of this sum, LE4,000 be allocated toward the building of a refugee hospital at Tyre, Lebanon.

The Syrian and Jordanian Governments ratified at Damascus the Yarmuk Agreement for a major irrigation and hydroelectric scheme, estimated to cost 18 million pounds sterling, part of which would be borne by the United Nations Relief and Works Agency.

July 8

The Egyptian Government abandoned its threat of an economic boycott of West Germany when its representative in Bonn initialed a supplementary protocol to the 1951 trade and payments agreement of the two countries.

A trade agreement between India and Egypt providing for the most favored nation treatment was signed in Cairo.

July 9

Election meetings throughout Lebanon were banned after a bomb incident in which 13 persons were injured. Muhammad al-Garudi, a new

July 9

element in the political arena, had nominated himself in a Beirut constituency as a rival to Abdallah al-Yafi, former Prime Minister. Mrs. Emile Faress Ibrahim (Socialist) and Mrs. Alvira Lattof (Independent) were candidates for Beqa's and North Lebanon Governorates respectively.

Iraqi Director of Information Khalil Ibrahim announced at a press conference that the Government had sent a note of protest to Iranian authorities against the attacks by Iranian troops against some Iraqi villages.

July 10

Police in Lebanon arrested 120 persons, including 28 Communists and five members of the Lebanese Militia Party, for instigating the bomb incident on July 9. Pierre al-Jamil, Head of the Lebanese Militia Party, denied his party had any connection with the incident.

The Sudanese Umma Party decided at a meeting in Khartoum that a republican regime was the form of government to which the Sudan would look forward.

A plebiscite on the new Syrian Constitution and elections for the Presdent were held, with Shishakli unopposed. Brigadier Adib Shishakli was elected President of the Republic of Syria with 86.6 percent of the popular vote, and amalgamated the Prime Minister's office with that of the President.

The first meeting of the Union Generale des Etudiants Tunisiens in Paris was held. This conference requested all young Tunisians to unite and to join the national struggle in order to reconquer their sovereignty and to seize their independence.

July 11

The US agreed to increase Point Four aid to Libya from $1.6 million to $2.3 million.

July 11

Adib Shishakli assumed office as President of Syria.

A three day strike organized by the Executive Committee of the Electricity Workers in Sudan began at Khartoum because the Company refused to grant the request of the workers for a 60 percent wage increase.

General Sir Francis Festing, Commander of British forces in Egypt, protested to the Sub-Governor of Ismailia regarding the disappearance on July 9, of Leading Aircraftman A.V. Rigden. General Festing stated that if Rigden was not returned by 9:00 am on July 13, the General would take measures which would "cause serious disruption and inconvenience to the Egyptian community in the Ismailia area."

July 12

King Hussein of Jordan, the Jordanian Queen Mother and Jordan's Prime Minister arrived in Riyadh on a state visit.

Three persons were killed and three injured in clashes between demonstrators and police during parliamentary elections in the Beirut and Mount Lebanon districts of Lebanon.

Raif Abu-Lamaa, newly appointed Assistant Secretary General of the Arab League, contacted Arab envoys in Cairo to discuss the attitude of the Arab Governments toward the Israel decision to transfer its Foreign Ministry from Tel Aviv to Jerusalem.

Elections for the Lebanese Chamber of Deputies began with balloting in Beirut and Mount Lebanon Governorates.

July 13

Representatives of 15 Asian and African nations addressed a joint letter to the UN Secretary General, asking him to place the Moroccan question on the provisional agenda of the Eighth Session of the General Assembly.

July 13

British soldiers clamped down an iron ring of armored cars and machine guns around Ismailia to force the return of the missing British aircraftsman. All civilians entering and leaving Ismailia were searched. As a countermeasure, the Egyptian authorities stationed moving units of the Army around the government buildings.

Three leading Iraqi Communists, including Secretary General of the outlawed Communist Party, Baha-ad-Din Nuri, were sentenced to life imprisonment. Another party member was given five years at hard labor.

July 14

Nadim al-Pachachi was appointed Iraqi Minister of Development by Royal Decree.

An Israel spokesman said that seven Arabs were killed, two wounded, and 16 detained in clashes between Israel's security forces and armed infiltrators during the week ending July 9.

Major General Salah Salem, Egyptian Minister of National Guidance, said that many Egyptians were being killed, injured and robbed by British troops. Two people were killed in the Suez Canal Zone on July 13.

The British Government warned Egypt that it would take measures to protect British troops in the Canal Zone against attack.

The British Foreign Under Secretary stated in the House of Lords that the action taken by the GOC (General Officer Commanding) in Egypt was, in his judgment, necessary to safeguard the troops under his command.

King Hussein of Jordan and Amir Saudi, the Saudi Arabian Crown Prince, left Riyadh for al-Kharj region where they inspected agricultural farms and other projects in the area.

July 15

A decree was issued amalgamating the Syrian Prime Minister's office with that of the President.

Iraq, Syria, Lebanon and Egypt sent protests to the UN over the decision of the Israel Government to transfer its Foreign Ministry from Tel Aviv to Jerusalem. Notes were also sent to the Palestine Conciliation Commission and to the British, US and French Governments.

Egyptian Foreign Minister Mahmoud Fawzi said that Egypt demanded that Britain cancel the restrictive measures imposed in the Suez Canal Zone.

July 16

A decree was issued abolishing the old electoral law in Syria.

The Arab Transit Trade Committee, meeting at Bhamdoun, Lebanon, finalized a draft transit trade agreement among Syria, Lebanon, Jordan and Iraq. A further bilateral trade agreement was concluded between Syria and Lebanon.

British forces relaxed their security cordon around Ismailia.

Delegates of six Arab States called on Secretary General Dag Hammarskjold to present a complaint about Israel's transfer of its Foreign Office from Tel Aviv to Jerusalem.

July 17

Muhammad Ben-Mabrouk, pro-French official and Sheikh of the Beni-Kaddech tribe near Gabes, was shot and killed by an unidentified assailant in Tunisia.

July 18

Kamal Jumblat, leader of the Lebanese Socialist Progressive Party, was summoned by the Government to appear for questioning July 23 for having accused Prime Minister Salem and his Cabinet of interfering in the elections and for having alleged that a "foreign source" had

July 18

offered him one million Lebanese pounds if he agreed to drop his opposition to Middle East defense schemes.

July 19

The second part of the parliamentary elections was held in south Lebanon.

Syrian President Shishakli completed his Cabinet with Khalil Mardam Bey as Minister of Foreign Affairs.

July 20

The Syrian Minister of the Interior said elections would be held in the first week of October. He said that a new electoral law had been completed and was being studied by the Cabinet.

The American Ambassador to Egypt, Jefferson Caffery, met with Foreign Minister Mahmoud Fawzi in an effort to find a basis for resuming Anglo-Egyptian negotiations on the Canal Zone issue.

July 21

Syrian President Shishakli issued a general amnesty decree covering crimes against internal security between the time he seized power on November 26, 1951, and the date he was elected President.

The Egyptian Cabinet approved a state budget of LE197,500,000, to be in balance largely by a regime of austerity demanded of Government employees and general consumers.

July 22

The Jordanian Chamber of Deputies approved a general budget for the financial year 1953-54 of JD15,148,466. This included defense, which was covered by the British grant in aid of 8,250,000 pounds sterling.

July 22

At 11:00 pm a 101 gun salute inaugurated a four day celebration commemorating the first anniversary of the Egyptian Revolution. One of the highlights of the celebration was the distribution of land to poor farmers and former landless peasants, with 13,000 acres to be distributed.

July 24

An agreement was signed between Israel and Egypt providing for the return of ships forced to seek shelter in the territorial waters of the other in case of storm, mechanical breakdown, or circumstances endangering the ship's safety and the crew's lives.

Egyptian Premier Muhammad Nagib received a message of congratulation from President Eisenhower, who had spoken of the opportunity open to Egypt to strengthen peace and stability in the Middle East and thereby to contribute to the welfare of mankind.

Radio Mecca broadcast that special "Pilgrim Receipts" would be issued to pilgrims by the Saudi Monetary Agency against cash amounts from pilgrims. Redeemable at full value, the receipts would make it unnecessary for pilgrims to carry large amounts of gold coins, silver coins, or bank notes. Anyone in possession of the "Pilgrim Receipts" regardless of whether he had obtained them through business or any other means might exchange them for Saudi riyals or sovereigns at the rate of SR40 a sovereign without delay or formal procedures.

July 25

The Jordanian Government reportedly decided to abolish visas between Jordan and Iraq as from the beginning of August, except for "Communists, smugglers and other undesirables."

July 26

The Iraqi Minister of Agriculture, Abd-al-Rahman Jawdah, announced that 3,284 poor farmers had received parcels of state land under the

July 26

Government's plans for land redistribution estimated to total eventually nearly four million acres. He also said a special council was to be set up to organize the production of cotton and plans to increase mechanization.

Lebanese Foreign Minister Georges Hakim handed notes to the envoys of Turkey, India, Afghanistan, Pakistan and Greece expressing the wish that Lebanon and Arab countries develop closer economic relations with these countries.

July 27

The Jordanian Cabinet met for the first time in Jerusalem, as a move against Israel's transfer of its Foreign Ministry to that city.

July 28

Brigadier Shawkat Shukairy was appointed Chief of Staff to succeed Colonel Adib Shishakli of Syria.

A committee of sixty Arabs presented to the Knesset at Jerusalem a list of grievances of Israel's 175,000 Arabs, including the land expropriation law, the deprivation of freedom of movement of Arabs and difficulty of acquisition of Israel citizenship.

July 29

A 20 year treaty of friendship and alliance between Britain and Libya was signed in Benghazi. The treaty covered military, economic and financial relations between the two countries. Britain would be permitted to station armed forces in Libya on conditions agreeable to both Governments. Reassessment of the situation would take place at the end of each five year period.

A new Syrian Party Law reportedly was completed. The goal of the political parties must be the realization of the Arab National ideal.

A trade agreement was signed between Syria and Yugoslavia.

July 29

The Israel Foreign Ministry issued a reply to a criticism by US Secretary of State John Dulles, of the decision to transfer the Israel Foreign Ministry from Tel Aviv to Jerusalem. Mr. Dulles stated that the Israel Government was taking action "embarrassing" to the UN and "inopportune" in relation to the existing tension in the Middle East.

July 31

The Jordanian Government reportedly began recruiting labor for the Yarmuk irrigation and hydroelectric scheme. The number of workers to be employed was estimated to be 16,000, of whom 85 percent would be recruited from among the Palestine Arab refugees.

A joint Anglo-Egyptian communique was issued which stated that informal contacts concerning the Suez Canal problem had been made by Egyptian and British representatives and that the possibility of agreement would be further explored by this means before discussions were resumed.

August, 1953

August 1

A new 73 article Electorate Law was published in Syria. It provided that a general election would be held before December 11, 1953.

August 3

Because of a complication of serious illness, Fuad Sirag-ad-Din, last active leader of the dissolved Wafd Party, who had been arrested on suspicion of complicity in an alleged plot by officers against Egyptian Premier Nagib, was released from prison, where he had been since January, and permitted to return to his home.

An Egyptian spokesman made a statement at the end of a general meeting of the Cabinet and the Military Revolution Council. He said that unless the British submitted new proposals to a meeting of the two sides scheduled for the following day which were satisfactory to Egypt for a solution of the Suez Canal dispute, no more meetings would take place.

A debate was held in the UN Economic and Social Council during which the recently announced Anglo-Libyan treaty was strongly criticized by the Indian and Soviet delegates. The Council adopted by 15-3 (UUSR, Poland and India dissenting) a joint Egyptian-Turkish draft recommending UN financial and technical assistance to Libya.

Libya transmitted to the UN Economic and Social Council a detailed outline of a project included in a planned five year development program.

Hajj Thami al-Mezuari al-Glaoui, Pasha of Marrakech, in an interview at his palace said that a new petition signed by 365 Pashas was on its way to Paris, petitioning the removal of the Sultan. He said that he would not rest until Sultan Ben-Youssef was driven from the throne of Morocco.

August 4

Thami Al-Glaoui, accompanied by Sherif Abd-al-Hajj al-Kattani, leader of the Federated Confederation of Morocco, began a tour of the country.

August, 1953

August 4

According to an indictment issued by Lieutenant Colonel Anwar Saadat, Revolutionary Council member in Egypt, and Minister of State Fathi Radwan (who comprised the two man Draft Committee), the Government demanded that Fuad Sirag ad-Din, former Wafdist Interior and Finance Minister, pay LE22,000,000 damages for cotton market manipulations. No date was set for the trial.

The Sultan of Morocco signed the new statute for the International Zone. The new arrangements superseded those of the 1923 Convention which had lapsed under the Spanish occupations of 1940 and had been replaced by a provisional regime in 1945. They came into force immediately.

Diplomatic representatives of five Arab States, Jordan dissenting, called on Acting US Secretary of State Walter Bedell Smith to denounce Israel's transfer of its Government from Tel Aviv to Jerusalem. They accused the US of complicity in the transfer.

August 5

Two pro-French Arab leaders were assassinated in Tunis in a new outbreak of violence.

The Jordanian Government reportedly was preparing a detailed report on the possibilities of exploiting the mineral resources of the Dead Sea. The report, which was to be submitted to the Arab League, was the outcome of the Arab Finance Ministers' meeting which recommended the establishment of an Arab company financed by Arab Governments and individuals to exploit Dead Sea minerals.

An Israel Embassy spokesman in Washington charged that the Arab Governments had forcibly prevented peaceful internationalization of Jerusalem and accused them of unabashed cynicism when they said that Israel had upset the status quo of the Middle East by moving its capital to Jerusalem.

August, 1953

August 6

The Jordanian House of Deputies met for a short session in Jerusalem.

Egyptian and British negotiators met again informally to seek a basis for agreement on the Suez issue.

August 7

Muhammad Ennafaa, Secretary of the Tunisian Communist Party, stated that in spite of the hostility presented by the Western imperialist nations, the Communist Party was working toward the goal of a united front.

Abd-al-Rahman Azzam, first Secretary General of the Arab League, severely criticized Libya for signing the Treaty of July 29 with the United Kingdom without previous notification of its provisions to the Arab League.

Seventy year old Sayyed Omar Shennib, Chief of the Libyan Royal Ministry (Diwan), died of heart failure in Tripoli.

August 8

In the course of a speech to the Supreme Soviet, Premier Georgi Malenkov made the point that the restoration of diplomatic relations with Israel implied no weakening of Soviet relations with the Arab States with whom the Soviet Government would seek to strengthen friendly cooperation.

Major Salem, Egyptian Minister of National Guidance, left Cairo by air for Khartoum, despite the notification by British Ambassador to Egypt Robert Hankey to Egyptian Foreign Minister Mahmoud Fawzi that the visit was not in the spirit of the Anglo-Egyptian Agreement. Hankey also talked with the Foreign Minister regarding the necessity of preserving a friendly and neutral atmosphere in the Sudan.

Gunmen shot and seriously wounded Ahmad Belgarwi, prominent Tunisian politician and Sfax councillor who held pro-French views.

August, 1953

August 8

Tayeb Hussein, Pakistani Charge d'Affaires in Cairo and Chairman of the Sudan Governor General's Commission, called a meeting of the Commission in Khartoum.

August 9

At his first press conference since becoming Syrian President, Adib Shishakli said his primary concern regarding internal affairs was reform, and regarding foreign affairs, was the question of internationalization of Jerusalem.

An official Saudi Arabian Mission led by Amir Sultan, son of King Ibn-Saud, arrived in Damascus to congratulate President Shishakli on his election.

French Resident General in Tunisia, Jean de Hautecloque put new security measures into effect and warned that in case these measures proved to be insufficient, he had firmly decided to reinforce them as much as would be necessary.

The Jordanian Ministry of Reconstruction announced that it would build 326 houses for Arab refugees living in villages on the border of Israel. Each family was to be allocated about 18 acres of land and provided with seeds, cattle, agricultural machinery and money. The cost of the scheme would be met from $11 million which UNRWA had allocated for refugees in Jordan.

August 10

Fifty-one Communist Party workers were arrested in Egypt.

Major General Vagn Bennike, Chief of the Truce Supervision Organization, was called to New York by UN Secretary General Dag Hammarskjold for consultations. During the next three weeks he was to meet both Arab and Israel delegates.

Final and complete returns on the general elections from all parts of Lebanon were in. Premier Saeb Salam submitted his resignation to President Camille Chamoun.

August, 1953

August 11

Sheikh Taher al-Tabari of Nazareth, highest Moslem religious authority in Israel, pleaded for an exchange of population between Arab countries and Israel on a strictly voluntary individual basis.

The Egyptian Cabinet approved a LE1 million trade agreement with Russia providing for the exchange of Egyptian cotton for Soviet wheat and war machinery.

Iraq notified the Soviet Union that the transfer of the Soviet Israel legation to Jerusalem would be considered an unfriendly act in the Arab States.

The Moroccan Sultan sent an urgent note to the French President of the Republic in which he called on the French Government to stop subversive intrigues by people in authority.

August 12

Archbishop George Hakim, spiritual leader of the Greek Catholic Church in Israel, opposed Sheikh Taher's proposal made August 11. He stated that peasants who had remained on the land were in much better condition than during the days of the British mandate.

Iraqi King Faisal went to Amman for a four day visit to return the June visit of Jordanian King Hussein.

It was announced in Damascus that General Francisco Franco of Spain said his Government was ready to enter into negotiations with the Arab League States to conclude nonaggression, friendship and economic agreements.

French Premier Joseph Laniel ordered General Augustin Guillaume, the French Resident General to Morocco, to Rabat to cope with what the French Government described as a very serious situation.

Some 106,313 pilgrims arrived in the Hejaz, Saudi Arabia. By the end of the season, the Government expected to have approximately 120,000.

August, 1953

August 13

The Lebanese Cabinet of Saeb Salam resigned. The new Chamber of Deputies elected Abdel Usairan as Speaker and Ghassan Towani as Deputy Speaker.

General Guillaume, the French Resident General to Morocco, who had returned hurriedly from France the night before on the orders of the French Government, had an interview with the Moroccan Sultan during which the Sultan signed a number of decrees for internal reform.

August 14

Three hundred Moroccan caids, sheikhs and tribal chiefs assembled around al-Glaoui, Pasha of Marrakech, decided to depose Sultan Sidi Muhammad Ben-Youssef and to enthrone Moulay Muhammad Ben-Arafa, but at the request of France they held back their proclamation for 24 hours to allow time to discuss a plan to mediate between the two factions.

A seven man delegation of Asian and African members of the UN called on the Secretary General and accused France of instigating a plot to depose the Moroccan Sultan.

August 15

A joint statement signed by the Moroccan Sultan and the French Resident General revealed that the decrees signed by the Sultan concerned the reform of local government and the administration of justice, the creation of regional assemblies, and the delegation of the Sultan's executive powers to a small Cabinet, composed of the Grand Visier and two deputies and the Secretary General and two other representatives of the protecting Power.

August, 1953

August 15

Sidi Moulay Muhammad Ben-Arafa, uncle of the Sultan, was proclaimed supreme religious chief of Islam in Morocco by the al-Glaoui faction assembled at Marrakech. Two French and two Moroccans were killed in rioting following the naming of the new "Leader of the Faithful." Police arrested 35 demonstrators and blocked the gates of the town to break up the rioting.

August 16

Representatives of the six Arab member states of the UN decided not to ask that the Jerusalem issue be placed on the agenda of the forthcoming General Assembly.

The Sultan of Morocco, deposed as religious head by revolting Berbers, refused to accept the decision. Violence broke out in different parts of Morocco between supporters of the Sultan and the Berbers who proclaimed Moulay Muhammad Ben-Arafa supreme religious leader.

A payments agreement was signed between Egypt and Turkey.

August 17

Abdallah al-Yafi, who had been asked by Lebanese President Chamoun to form a government, named his Cabinet with himself holding the positions of Premier and Minister of Interior, Defense and Information. Alfred Naccache was named as Foreign Minister.

Egyptian President Muhammad Nagib left for Saudi Arabia on a pilgrimage to Mecca and important political conferences. Pakistan's Governor General, Ghulam Muhammad, who was also to be in Saudi Arabia, was expected to participate in the discussions.

August 18

Asian and African delegates to the UN circulated a memorandum once again accusing France of continuing repressive measures in Tunisia. They said these measures had seriously aggravated the already acute situation in that protectorate. The document was signed by fifteen nations.

August, 1953

August 18

Raif Abu Lamaa, Assistant Secretary General of the Arab League, told a press conference in Cairo that the member states of the League had each separately protested to Britain, France and the US on the developing situation in Morocco.

The Secretary General of the UN issued the following agenda for the Political Committee, which was to meet in Cairo on September 2: Nominations to the UN Security Council, Trusteeship Council, and Social and Economic Council; Tunisian, Moroccan and Algerian questions; Anglo-Libyan treaty; Palestine question, Arab refugee problem, and internationalization of Jerusalem.

Egyptian President Muhammad Nagib granted pardons to 130 Egyptians imprisoned for having taken part in the anti-Western riots of January 26, 1952.

Egypt and the Soviet Union signed a trade and payments agreement in Cairo.

Egyptian President Muhammad Nagib arrived to perform the pilgrimage to Mecca in Saudi Arabia.

The House of Representatives of Libya approved the treaty with Britain by a vote of 36-16.

French troops in Morocco surrounded the palace in Casablanca.

August 20

Moroccan Sultan Sidi Muhammad Ben-Youssef was banished to Corsica after armed Berber tribesmen had begun to converge on Rabat.

The French Government issued a statement announcing that according to information received from General Guillaume, French Resident General in Morocco, the General's mission of reconciliation had met with difficulties which could only be reduced by armed force.

A second communique issued by France later in the day, after the deposition of the Moroccan Sultan, said "in the face of the

August 20

impossibility of upholding the present Sultan without risking the outbreak of civil war" the traditional procedure was necessary to assure the succession to the throne.

August 21

Sidi Moulay Muhammad Ben-Arafa was solemnly proclaimed Sultan of Morocco at Rabat.

Fifteen Arab, Asian and African nations formally asked the UN Security Council to investigate, as a danger to international peace and security, France's ouster of the Moroccan Sultan.

Syrian President Adib Shishakli met the new Lebanese Prime Minister, Abdallah al-Yafi, at Falugha, Lebanon, to discuss restoration of economic unity between the two countries and the conclusion of a permanent agreement to replace the temporary one then in force.

August 22

The new Moroccan Sultan left Marrakech by special train for Rabat. At a ceremony at the great mosque of Tetuan in the Spanish Zone of Morocco, Abd-al-Khaleq Torres, leader of the Reformist (Nationalist) Party, made a speech denouncing the banishment of the former Sultan, and a crowd demonstrated against the new Sultan.

The US informed France of its deep concern over the developments which led to the removal of Moroccan Sultan Sidi Muhammad Ben-Youssef, and that it earnestly hoped for the restoration of order in the enflamed North African territory.

The Finance Ministers of the Arab League countries met in Beirut to resume their discussions on the question of closer economic cooperation between their countries.

An agreement was signed between the Egyptian Government and the Umma Party of the Sudan.

August 22

A conference of provincial committees of the Umma Party received a message from Sir Sayyed Abd-al-Rahman al-Mahdi declaring that he had agreed with Umma leaders that the Party of Sudan should advocate a democratic republican regime after the attainment of independence.

August 23

French authorities arrested more than 1,000 Arabs in an effort to wipe out the Istiqlal (Nationalist) movement of Morocco.

The UN Relief and Works Agency for Palestine Refugees decided to move some of its offices from Beirut to Jerusalem.

Government authorities in Egypt permitted Makram Obeid, leader of the dissolved Kotla Party, to hold a public meeting at the Cairo railway station square to commemorate the death anniversary of Saad Zaghlul, nationalist leader and founder of the Wafd.

Lieutenant Colonel Nasser, acting President in the absence of General Nagib, said the Government was studying new proposals made by the British in the informal Suez discussions.

Forty-five Tunisian political prisoners escaped from a French prison. By nightfall only four had been captured.

August 24

Iraqi Minister of Economy Diya Jaafar, leader of the financial delegation, said on his return from London that he had discussed with the oil companies operating in Iraq the means of carrying out the 50-50 principle, and that the Anglo-Iraqi financial committee was satisfied with the continual improvement of the sterling position.

August 25

A conference of the Arab Chiefs of Staff was formally opened at the Cairo Staff College by Colonel Nasser of Egypt. Libya was the only League state which had not ratified the Arab Collective Security Pact,

August 25

and was not represented. Abd-al-Khaleq Hassouna, Secretary General of the League, welcomed the delegates and said they had come to Cairo determined to accomplish complete mobilization of the Arab forces.

Saudi Arabian King Ibn-Saud appointed his son, Crown Prince Saud, Commander in Chief of the Armed Forces. The 48 year old Crown Prince had been Commander in Chief of the Armed Forces in the Nejd.

It was reported at the UN that the US decided to vote against putting the Moroccan case on the Security Council's agenda.

The Spanish High Commissioner said in a speech at Tetuan in Spanish Morocco that Spain could not be indifferent to the recent events in the French Zone and he deplored the French failure to consult Spain on questions concerning the Moroccan revolution.

August 26

President Chamoun of Lebanon discussed economic relations with Iraqi Finance Minister Ali al-Daftari.

The UN Security Council opened discussion on the question of putting the Moroccan issue on its agenda. France denounced the move, but Lebanon and Pakistan favored it.

The French Cabinet approved in principle a first series of governmental and administrative reforms for Morocco. It was agreed that the former Moroccan Sultan's signature of a decree on August 15 was valid and that the new Sultan would be expected to yield the legislative authority to the Grand Vizier. It also approved the creation of regional and local councils, the separation of the judicial and administrative powers and the creation of regional courts and election of the Council of Government by universal suffrage.

August 27

The US and Great Britain declared their opposition to putting the Moroccan question on the agenda of the UN Security Council.

August 28

American diplomatic missions in the Middle East began a two day conference in Cairo.

It was announced in Paris that the Bey of Tunis voluntarily signed a number of beylical decrees in his palace at Carthage. These decrees related to the appointment of local magistrates as part of the reform program that had been delayed because of nationalist opposition.

An official Jordanian statement announced that an Arab Legion patrol killed five Jewish soldiers at Beit Madkour, twelve and a half miles within the Jordan borders. The UN Mixed Armistice Commission had been informed.

August 29

The British Air Ministry in London issued a statement saying that Aircraftsman Anthony V. Rigden, who disappeared in Ismailia in Egypt on July 9, and whose disappearance resulted in four days of tension in Anglo-Egyptian relations, was in London and would be interrogated by the Royal Air Force.

August 30

Ahmad Shukairy, Assistant Secretary General of the Arab League, accused Israel of planning aggression to expand its territory.

The Moroccan Council of Ulemas of al-Azhar called for an economic and social boycott by Moslems against France and all supporters of French policy in Morocco.

September, 1953

September 1

The first Arab League Scientific Conference opened in Alexandria. Secretary General Abd-al-Khaleq Hassouna presided.

The third Middle East Regional Conference of the UN Food and Agriculture Organization opened in Cairo.

The sixth "informal" meeting between British and Egyptian negotiators in the Suez Canal base issue was held. Substantial agreement was reportedly reached on the following: (1) an Egyptian officer would be "commander" of the base; (2) a British deputy receiving orders from London would be "technical supervisor"; (3) about 4,000 British technicians would be retained until Egyptians could be trained to take over the skilled jobs; (4) the British garrison would be evacuated within 18 months after the signing of the agreement. Issues still to be settled included availability of the base for the return of British or Allied armies in the event, or threat, of war.

The new Sultan of Morocco, Sidi Moulay Muhammad Ben-Arafa, sealed an Imperial Decree delegating his executive powers to an Inner Council to be presided over by the Grand Vizier. The French Secretary General, Counsellor and Director of Interior were to sit on this council together with two assistant Viziers. This was the first French reform measure to be accepted.

September 2

The Palestine Conciliation Commission advised UN Secretary General Dag Hammarskjold that it could take no further action on the recent protests from Arab States on the transfer of Israel's Foreign Ministry to Jerusalem.

Israel began work on a canal for the diversion of waters from the Jordan River between Lake Huleh and the Sea of Galilee in connection with a projected hydroelectric power station. Syria protested the action to the Security Council.

Minister of Interior Husam-ad-Din Jumaa announced that Iraq had been in touch with Egypt and Syria regarding reciprocal abolition of visas. Jordan, Kuwait and Lebanon had already agreed.

September, 1953

September 2

Colombia stated its opposition to putting the Moroccan issue on the Security Council's agenda, while Chile expressed itself in favor.

Francis Mitterand, French Minister in charge of relations with the Council of Europe in Premier Laniel's Cabinet, resigned because of disagreement with the French Government's policy on North Africa.

The Political Committee of the Arab League began a four day meeting in Cairo.

Pierre Voizard, French Minister to Monaco since June 1950, was appointed Resident General to Tunisia, to replace Jean de Hautecloque. Voizard had been associated with Marshal Juin in Morocco in 1941 as Secretary General in the residency.

September 3

The Security Council of the UN rejected the Arab-Asian Bloc's request for an investigation of France's action in deposing the Moroccan Sultan, as "a danger to international peace."

The Lebanese Chamber of Deputies passed a vote of confidence in the Abdallah al-Yafi Government by a vote of 31-7 after hearing the Premier's statement outlining his foreign and domestic policies.

The seventh and last scheduled informal meeting between Egyptian and British representatives to discuss the Suez Canal issue took place.

The topic of the continuation of the function of the UN Tribunal in Libya was discussed in the UN.

Law No. 430 of 1953 regarding certain taxation measures to be taken for the support and development of the national economy of Egypt was signed.

An Egyptian law on the investment of foreign capital in economic development projects was passed.

September, 1953

September 3

President Eisenhower authorized a relief shipment of 10,000 tons of agricultural commodities to Jordan.

September 4

The conference of the Arab Chiefs of Staff closed with recommendations to the Arab Defense Council for the implementation of the Arab collective security pact.

Large forces of the army and police were stationed in the streets of Amman to prevent demonstrations in support of Morocco. Peaceful demonstrations took place after Friday prayers in Jerusalem, Nablus and Tulkarm.

Chief British negotiator, General Sir Brian Robertson, left Cairo for London.

The Supreme Defense Council of the Arab League, composed of the Foreign and Defense Ministers, began a five day meeting at Cairo.

A communique was issued after the meeting of the Supreme Defense Council in Cairo which said that the Council had reviewed the provisions of the Collective Security Pact and had decided to appoint a committee to formulate rules of procedure for the Council's work.

September 6

The Arab Liaison Officers for the Economic Boycott of Israel, meeting in Jerusalem, decided to warn banks which had branches in Israel to cease operations there. It also decided to recommend that the Arab countries facilitate the passage of Jordanian goods through Arab ports and that aircraft and ships which called at places in Israel not be allowed to call at Arab points. Specific warnings were directed to Barclay's Bank, the Ottoman Bank and Imperial Chemical Industries. The conference also recommended that Arab Governments reconsider facilities granted to Air France.

September, 1953

September 6

Egyptian authorities at Port Said intercepted the Greek freighter Parnon, carrying 500 tons of asphalt from Haifa to Elath.

September 7

The Political Committee of the Arab League transformed itself into the Arab League Council to approve resolutions adopted by the Political Committee and by the conference of the Ministers of Finance and Economy which had met in Beirut. Regarding political matters the Council resolved: to contribute one million Egyptian pounds to the maintenance of the Jordanian National Guard, and to continue political efforts on behalf of Morocco and Tunisia. The Council also approved two economic measures regarding favorable commercial exchanges between Arab countries, and transfer and investment of Arab capital within the Arab countries.

The Arab League Council decided to send Secretary General Hassouna to the United Nations as an observer.

A Saudi Arabian Ministry of Communications was established by Royal Decree, with Amir Talal Ibn-Abd-al-Aziz al-Saud, 16th surviving son of the King, as Minister. In addition to telegraph and telephone communications, the new ministry would have charge of roads, railroads and postal services.

A number of arrests were made in Cairo. The Director of the Military stated that "professional politicians and Communist elements" were conducting "an underground campaign to create unrest and to undermine the regime."

September 8

Kuwait's Director of Public Security Sheihk Abdallah Mubarak stated in Beirut that his country would join the Arab League as soon as it completed its internal development.

Jordan's Prime Minister, Fawzi al-Mulki, announced that Jordan had asked the Arab States for further aid of LE2 million for raising the living standards of Jordanians in "front line" villages and LE500,000 for reconstruction work in Jerusalem.

September, 1953

September 8

The Arab League Scientific Conference at Alexandria concluded its meeting with resolutions regarding the establishment of an Arab Scientific Federation, the teaching of Arab history in Arab countries and the translation of scientific works into Arabic.

Many arrests were made during Communist instigated demonstrations inside a Cairo textile factory.

The Israel Government instructed its delegation to the UN to lodge a complaint with the Security Council against the Egyptian seizure of 500 tons of asphalt destined for Israel from a vessel flying the Greek flag.

The pro-French sheikh of Bou Ficha of Tunisia, Abd-al-Rahman Mahmoud, was assassinated.

Jordanian King Hussein arrived in London for a sinus operation. He was accompanied by Queen Mother Zain, Crown Prince Muhammad, Prince Hassan, and Princess Basma.

September 9

The Umma (Independence) Party of Sudan sent a memorandum to President Nagib of Egypt saying that its leaders were convinced that the Egyptian Government had used propaganda and spent large sums of money to influence the views of the Sudanese people in favor of the National Unionist Party.

The Egyptian Ministry of Interior disclosed that a number of persons connected with a Communist sponsored organization known as the "Democratic Movement for National Liberation" had been arrested in Alexandria. Printing machines and leaflets attacking any Anglo-Egyptian agreement on the Canal Zone had been seized.

Saudi Arabian Minister of Health Amir Abdallah al-Faisal opened negotiations with the Bonn Government with the view of importing German medical equipment and supplies as well as equipment for broadcasting stations.

September, 1953

September 9

An Israel Foreign Ministry spokesman in Jerusalem charged the Government of Jordan with spreading false rumors about the massing of Israel troops in the Jerusalem area, which he said was for the purpose of getting aid from the other Arab countries. He declared that there was no truth in reports from Arab sources that Israel had been massing troops in Jerusalem for some time.

After the last of its meetings, the Defense Council of the Arab League issued a statement saying that the decisions it had taken were designed to unify the efforts and plans of the Arab States to reinforce and defend peace and security.

September 10

Lebanese Prime Minister Abdallah al-Yafi announced that he was opposed to the proposal to establish a senate, preferring to increase the number of deputies from 44 to 55 or more.

The Moroccan Sultan signed over his legislative powers to a Moroccan Council of Viziers and Directors composed of 14 Moroccans and 16 French directors of administrative departments. Legislation approved by this Council would go to the Sultan for his seal.

September 12

More than 2,500 refugees reportedly had left Jordan for Iraq because of feared concentration of Jewish forces.

An Egyptian prize court ordered the Greek freighter, the Parnon, to unload its cargo of asphalt and assembled motor vehicles. The captain declared that he would never allow anybody to take his cargo away.

Celal Tawfiq Karasapan, first Turkish Minister to Libya, arrived in Tripoli.

President Adib Shishakli of Syria decreed elections to be held October 9 to fill the 82 Parliamentary seats. The Government also announced it would soon define the manner in which the outlawed political parties might be revived to participate in the elections. The President stated that the Arab Liberation Movement would adhere to the rules laid down for political parties.

September, 1953

September 12

A new Parties and Organizations Law for Syria was issued as a legislative decree.

Hassan al-Hudaibi, Supreme Guide of the Moslem Brotherhood, in a speech at Mansura, declared that there was no misunderstanding between the Brotherhood and the current regime in Egypt.

September 13

Iraqi Premier Jamil al-Midfai announced the resignation of his Government. Fadel al-Jamali, former President of the Chamber of Deputies, was asked to form a government.

Saudi Arabia signed the two Arab States Trade and Payments Agreements.

Israel filed a sharp protest with the UN Security Council against the seizure of the Greek freighter Parnon by the Egyptian authorities.

Egypt ordered the release of the Greek freighter Parnon.

Lebanese Minister of Economy Rashid Karami discussed at Bhamdoun with Syrian Minister of Economy Awn Allah Jabri the establishment of a joint economic council to coordinate the economic policy of the two countries and the unification of their currencies.

President Adib Shishakli approved the re-establishment of political parties in Syria.

Hedi Chaker, a member of the policy committee of the Tunisian Nationalist movement, was murdered in Nabeul.

September 14

The Government of Egypt declared a state of emergency throughout Cairo.

Anthony Rigden, British airman who disappeared in the Suez Canal Zone in July and appeared seven weeks later in Paris, was released from custody by the Royal Air Force after a two week investigation.

September, 1953

September 14

The Jordanian Cabinet suspended the paper al-Hawadith for three months.

Fourteen Palestinian Arab families, absentees under Israel law, were evicted from the Umm al-Faraj cooperative farm in western Galilee and resettled two miles away on land abandoned during the Palestine war.

September 15

The British Air Ministry issued a statement on the case of Leading Aircraftman Rigden who had disappeared in the Canal Zone on July 9.

Major Salah Salem, Egyptian Minister of National Guidance and member of the Revolution Council, stated in Cairo that the Government had documentary evidence of an alliance between Egyptian traitors and foreign imperialists. A special court had been appointed to try the accused.

Egyptian President Muhammad Nagib, National Guidance Minister Salah Salem, and other government speakers addressed a crowd of 40-50,000 persons in Cairo. They gave notice that they were putting into operation a new tough policy designed primarily to smash a Communist-Wafdist inspired campaign to undermine the regime. They announced the formation of a Revolutionary Tribunal with Minister of War Abd-al-Latif al-Baghdadi as chairman and Colonel Anwar Saadat and Squadron Leader Hassan Ibrahim as members.

The 14 man high command of the Casablanca Istiqlal Party was arrested.

September 16

Muhammad Fadel al-Jamali was named to succeed Jamal al-Midfai as Premier of Iraq.

Israel was elected one of the seven vice presidents of the United Nations General Assembly.

September 16

The great majority of the dissolved political parties in Syria announced that they would not apply to the Government for permission to reorganize, in accordance with the provisions of the new Political Parties Law.

Premier Fawzi al-Mulki of Jordan called on the Arab nations to oppose the internationalization of Jerusalem.

The Syrian Government protested to the Governments of the US, Britain and France against Israel's drainage project in the Huleh swamp, charging violation of its frontier.

September 17

Iraqi Premier Fadel al-Jamali formed a Cabinet with Muhammad Ali Mahmoud as Deputy Premier and Abdallah Bakr as Minister of Foreign Affairs.

Syria became a party to the Inter-Arab Trade and Transit and Payments Agreements which were signed in Cairo and ratified by Egypt, Lebanon, Jordan, Saudi Arabia, Yemen and Syria. The Trade and Transit Agreement provided for the free exchange of agricultural products and a 25 percent reduction of customs duty on industrial products of a local origin.

Powers of the Egyptian Revolutionary Tribunal were laid down in a decree. Each accused would be allowed only one lawyer; the Tribunal could sit in public or in camera, as well as refuse to hear defense witnesses. Decisions were to be subject to approval by the Revolutionary Command Council.

September 18

A boycott of the elections in Syria was announced by the Shaab, Republican, and Baath (Arab Resurrectionist) Parties and a number of independents.

September 19

French authorities at Rabat said that all members of three units of the outlawed Istiqlal Party in Meknes had been arrested. They also said that one Moroccan was murdered and another wounded by nationalist terrorists the previous night.

Moroccan Sultan Sidi Moulay Muhammad Ben-Arafa signed a decree approving French proposals for municipal reforms.

General Sir Brian Robertson, British representative for talks with the Egyptian Government, returned from London to reopen negotiations on Suez.

France walked out of a meeting of the UN General Assembly because the delegates were debating the Moroccan and Tunisian issues.

At the first meeting of the new Iraqi Cabinet it was decided to abolish internal press censorship and to improve economic conditions. The Cabinet also discussed restoration of political parties and examined cases of political detainees.

September 20

A Libyan Royal Decree appointed Abu-Bakr Naama as Minister of Education and Ali al-Unaizi as Minister of Finance. Mahmoud al-Saqizli, former Minister of Education and also former Governor of Cyrenaica, was appointed Chief of the Royal Cabinet.

Lebanese President Camille Chamoun signed a decree for the allocation of an additional LL3 million for the purchase of arms and equipment by the Ministry of Defense.

Premier Abdallah al-Yafi of Lebanon said that he contacted the Tapline Company and the Iraq Petroleum Company and informed them of the Government's wish to amend the agreements with the companies to increase the annual royalties paid to Lebanon.

September 21

Numerous arrests were made in Egypt in the past two days, including former Wafdist Premier Nahhas and his wife, Hafez Afifi, former Chief

September 21

of the Royal Cabinet, former Saadist Prime Minister Ibrahim Abd-al-Hadi, Ibrahim Farag, Sulaiman Channan and Karem Thabet.

Two Egyptian fishing vessels captured in Israel waters were released by the Israel authorities.

Talks between Egyptian and British negotiators on the Suez Canal issue were resumed after the return from London of the chief British negotiator, General Sir Brian Robertson.

The Bey of Tunis, Sidi Muhammad al-Amin Pasha, asked for an end of terrorism before the arrival of the new French Resident General.

It was learned that the Syrian General Trade Unions Federation was discussing the formation of a Workers' and Peasants' Party.

Syria asked the UN Mixed Armistice Commission to halt Israel's drainage project in the Huleh swamp, charging that it would dry up 12,000 acres of Syrian land by diverting the waters of the Jordan River.

A Jordanian Government mission left for Iraq and Saudi Arabia to seek financial aid.

The Sultan of Morocco signed two new decrees which approved the new French reform program.

September 22

Jordan joined Syria in protesting the Israel canal project and added that Arab families living in Israel held territory had been expelled in contravention of the truce agreement. Lebanon filed a complaint with the Truce Commission over diversion of Jordan waters and demanded that work on the canal be halted.

The Israel Government termed baseless a Syrian protest to the Mixed Armistice Commission that the Huleh project was in violation of the Syrian-Israel Armistice Agreement, and that a part of the project designed to provide electric power for Israel would adversely affect Syrian farmlands.

September 22

An international exhibition, "The Conquest of the Desert," was opened in Jerusalem. The US and some other Western powers boycotted the exhibition because it was held in Jerusalem.

September 23

Following an investigation, Major General Vagn Bennike, Chief of Staff of the UN Mixed Armistice Commission, requested Israel to stop work on the Huleh canal until a settlement had been reached between Israel and Syria.

The Iraqi Cabinet abolished censorship of press cables going abroad.

The Saudi Arabian delegation to the UN protested strongly to the British Government about a series of "unjustifiable acts of aggression and the killing of innocent Saudi Arabian citizens" committed by the British officials and military authorities stationed around the Oasis of Buraimi on Saudi Arabian territory.

The Saudi Arabian Embassy at London made public two protests it had recently delivered to the British Foreign Office. One stated that on September 15 British soldiers had fired on inhabitants of Buraimi Oasis from 13 posts, killing several persons, and the second, that on September 19 British troops had forcibly confiscated caravans supplying Turki Ben-Ataishan and his men, opening fire without justification for ten minutes, killing and wounding caravan men.

The Tripolitanian Legislative Council in Libya had postponed the vote on amendments to the Tripolitanian Waliyat (Governorate) Organic Law until a later date.

September 24

A British Foreign Office spokesman, in his reply to the Saudi Arabian protests of September 23, 1953, stated that on September 15 a party of armed tribesmen attempted to enter the village of Hamsa, where Turki Ben-Ataishan, a Saudi Arabian official, had been detained since July, and were intercepted by a patrol of Trucial Oman levies who called on them to halt. The tribesmen had opened fire and the levies retaliated.

September 24

Israel rejected a request by the Chief UN Truce Supervisor, Major General Vagn Bennike, that work on the plan for diverting the Jordan River for a hydroelectric project be stopped as long as an agreement with Syria was not arranged. In his letter to General Bennike, Israel Foreign Minister Moshe Sharett declared that the request to halt the project was contrary to the United Nations Charter and the armistice agreement.

Ismail al-Azhari, President of the Sudanese National Unionist Party (NUP), left on a tour of al-Gezira district; another NUP mission left Khartoum to tour towns and villages in the North.

September 25

Radio reports from Damascus stated that Syria had cancelled all army leaves as a result of Israel's rejection of the request to stop the Jordan drainage work.

Most of the 349 candidates nominated to contest the 82 seats in the Syrian Parliament at the October 9 elections were members of the Arab Liberation Movement sponsored by President Adib Shishakli. Many Syrian political groups boycotted the elections and made no nominations.

Jordan sent notes to the US, Britain, France and Turkey saying it fully supported the Syrian view regarding the Israel canal project.

September 26

The United States asked Israel to stop work on the canal as requested by Chief UN Truce Supervisor General Bennike.

Ibrahim Abd-al-Hadi, a former Egyptian Premier and leader of the Saadists, pleaded not guilty before the Revolutionary Tribunal to the

September 26

charges in a six count indictment accusing him of treason, corruption, graft and complicity in murder.

September 27

Egyptian police raided the villa of former King Zog of Albania and seized a number of documents. The Government had removed Zog's diplomatic immunity in August 1953 and had withdrawn recognition of the Albanian legation.

King Idris al-Sanusi of Libya went to Lausanne for medical treatment. His brother, Prince Muhammad Reda al-Mahdi al-Sanusi, was to act as viceroy during the King's absence.

French Resident General in Tunisia Pierre Voizard paid his first official visit to the Bey. In an address he stated that no new task could be undertaken until public order was rigorously respected.

The provisional economic agreement between Lebanon and Syria was extended for another six months.

September 28

The Jordanian Government would reportedly prepare a special scheme for distribution of government lands to landless farmers, graduates of agricultural institutes and inhabitants of towns who wished to take up farming.

Lester de Witt Mallord was sworn in at Washington as new US Ambassador to Jordan to replace Ambassador Joseph C. Green.

The Egyptian Government announced that it had decided to confiscate the property of former King Farouk, previously placed in the hands of a sequestration commission.

The office of Colonel Gamal Abdel Nasser, Deputy Premier and Chief Egyptian negotiator in the Suez Canal issue, announced that an agreement between England and Egypt was "as good as signed."

September 28

A French military tribunal in Tunis condemned three Tunisians to death after finding them guilty of the assassination of Prince Azzedine Bey.

A Saudi Arabian report alleged that British authorities in al-Buraimi had warned that all persons trying to enter Hamsa would be killed.

Syrian Minister of Interior Ibish said candidates could conduct their campaigns with circulars and in the news, but government employees were forbidden to take part. He also prohibited the carrying of arms from October 3 to the end of the elections. Ten persons were injured in an armed clash in the Nabak area between supporters of opposing candidates.

Sudanese Under Secretary for Irrigation Abd-al-Rahman Abdun and the Sudanese Irrigation Adviser returned from Cairo after talks with representatives of the Egyptian Government. A statement issued at Khartoum by the Public Relations Office said that they had discussed the project to build a new high dam at Aswan.

Khairi al-Kaaki, publisher of *al-Sharq*, was sentenced *in absentia* to two months imprisonment and fined LL100 for publishing an article defaming the Egyptian Government in Lebanon.

Libyan Premier Mahmoud Bey Muntasir submitted his resignation to King Idris al-Sanusi.

September 29

Official quarters in London denied the Saudi Arabian statement of September 28. It was stated that the Saudi Arabian Government had been informed that visitors attempting to aid Turki Ben-Ataishan, a Saudi Arabian official, would be turned back, but that residents could come and go on legitimate business.

An Iraqi Royal Decree appointed Major General Rafiq Aref as Chief of Staff to replace General Nur-ad-Din Mahmoud, who had relinquished the post in November 1952.

Raymond Hare presented his credentials to Lebanese President Chamoun as US Ambassador to succeed Harold B. Minor.

September 29

The UN Relief and Works Agency for Palestine Refugees (UNRWA), in its Annual Report to the General Assembly, stated that the plight of the refugees had reached urgent proportions and gave the number of those still in need at 872,000.

The Egyptian Government accused Israel of occupying certain points in the demilitarized zone near al-Auja, Israel, and of erecting fortifications there. The spokesman said that the UN Truce Supervision Commission, Britain and the US had been notified.

September 30

A committee of legal and administrative experts appointed by the Iraqi Cabinet to inquire into the dissolution of political parties, which had been in effect since the imposition of martial law in November 1952, found that the abolition of martial law would automatically wipe out all measures arising from its imposition, including the ban on political parties.

The Jordan Regency Council confirmed a new press law to be effective October 1. New licenses for newspapers were to be applied for before the end of October.

The Arab envoys in Cairo met at the request of Egyptian Foreign Minister Mahmoud Fawzi to take up the al-Auja situation. Assistant Secretary General of the Arab League Shukairy declared that the other Arab States would support Egypt in any decision it might take.

A trade agreement between Iraq and Jordan was signed.

October, 1953

October 1

Ambassador Abba S. Eban, Israel's UN Delegate, denounced the Egyptian charges regarding al-Auja as completely untrue.

Former Egyptian Prime Minister Ibrahim Abd-al-Hadi was condemned by the Revolutionary Tribunal to death by hanging. In addition, the court ordered confiscation of all his property in excess of that inherited from his father. Another defendant, Ahmad Awzd, was convicted and sentenced to death on a charge of submitting reports to the intelligence services of some foreign powers on the activities of Egyptian commandos in the Suez Canal area in 1951 and 1952.

British Foreign Secretary Anthony Eden told a Conservative Party conference at Margate, England, that if an agreement was reached on the Suez question it would be one which the British Government was prepared to support and defend as in the best interests of the future peace of the world, Commonwealth, and Empire. Lord Salisbury, British Deputy Foreign Minister, addressed the same meeting in a similar vein.

Israel Foreign Minister Moshe Sharett announced that Israel agreed to temporarily suspend work on the hydroelectric project along the Jordan River.

October 2

Syrian Minister of the Interior Nouri Ebeiche went to Lebanon and sent his resignation to President Shishakli from there.

The Israel-Egyptian Mixed Armistice Commission rejected an Egyptian charge that Israel violated the Armistice Agreement by establishing a settlement in the demilitarized zone.

October 3

Egypt formally complained to the UN Security Council that Israel forces had built fortifications in the demilitarized area covered by the Egypt-Israel Armistice Agreement.

October, 1953

October 4

Israel complained to the UN Mixed Armistice Commission that Egypt was moving troops up to the al-Auja area and that Egyptian fighter aircraft had flown over the demilitarized zone.

The death sentence imposed on Abd-al-Hadi was commuted to life imprisonment in Egypt.

Colonel Zakariya Mohi-ad-Din, Egyptian Chief of Army Intelligence, was named Minister of the Interior to replace Colonel Gamal Abdel Nasser, who retained the post of Deputy Prime Minister.

A Jordanian economic delegation, headed by Deputy Premier Said al-Mufti and including three ministers of the Jordanian Cabinet, arrived in Saudi Arabia from Amman.

Sheikh Yusuf Yasin, Saudi Arabian Deputy Minister of Foreign Affairs, announced that the US had agreed to act as mediator between Saudi Arabia and Great Britain over the Buraimi dispute.

October 5

The International Monetary Fund announced that the initial par value of the Jordanian dinar would be at JD1= $2.80, and $1= JD0.357143.

Martial law was abolished in Iraq by Royal Decree. Kamel Chadirchi, leader of the Iraqi National Democratic Party, resumed publication of the daily al-Ahali.

Egyptian Deputy Prime Minister Abdel Nasser said the informal talks would be broken off if the British did not stop backtracking from previously agreed positions. He said the backtracking was aimed at placating US public opinion.

October 6

Ibrahim Farag, Egyptian Minister of Municipal and Rural Affairs in the Wafd Cabinet of Mustafa Nahhas, was sentenced to penal servitude for life on two counts of treason.

October, 1953

October 6

It was reported at Amman, Jordan, that the Iraqi Government had asked Jordan to restrict the migration of Arab refugees into Iraq.

October 7

Jordan notified General Bennike, Commander of the Mixed Armistice Commission, that it would boycott meetings of the Mixed Armistice Commission until work on the Israel canal project had been halted.

The US Congressional Technical Aid Committee arrived in Amman, Jordan.

The UN Political Committee began debate on the Moroccan question. Amjad Ali of Pakistan urged France to call a roundtable conference at which all political elements in Morocco, together with all French political parties, would be represented to discuss the future of Morocco. French Deputy Foreign Minister Maurice Schumann informed the committee by letter that France would not participate in the debate.

October 8

In the UN Political Committee, Hilmi Bahgat Badawi of Egypt attacked the deposition of Sultan Muhammad Ben-Youssef of Morocco and said that the so-called reforms would make the French settlers the real masters of the country. He called on France to grant Morocco its independence and protested against the absence of the French delegation.

Speaking before the UN Political Committee, Great Britain and Australia stated that French policy in the North African protectorate of Morocco was not the concern of the United Nations.

The Government of Sudan announced a five year development program with planned expenditures of 34 million pounds sterling for communications, 7,843,000 pounds sterling for productive schemes, 6,885,000 pounds sterling for social services development and 5,145,050 pounds sterling for public utilities.

October, 1953

October 9

Ambassador Abba Eban of Israel, in a letter to the Palestine Conciliation Commission, stated that the Government of Israel was engaged in preparatory work in implementation of its declared policy to offer compensation for abandoned lands in Israel.

The first elections since the Syrian Parliament was dissolved on December 2, 1951, were held throughout the country, with President Adib Shishakli's Liberation Movement assured of control of Parliament.

King Ibn-Saud of Saudi Arabia decreed the establishment of the first Saudi Cabinet, naming Crown Prince Saud as Prime Minister with extensive authority.

Jordanian Deputy Prime Minister Said al-Mufti and other members of the trade delegation which went to Saudi Arabia on October 4 returned to Amman. A joint communique was issued in Amman by the Saudi and Jordanian delegations saying that it was impossible to arrange an immediate loan.

Egyptian Deputy Prime Minister Nasser, responding to the speeches of British Prime Minister Eden and Deputy Foreign Minister Lord Salisbury, said that the period of British supremacy in Egypt had ended. He warned that if Britain could not come to recognize Egypt's complete rights, reactionary British elements should be prepared to face a popular organized struggle by millions of Egyptians who would rally as one man against Britain.

Two members of the US Congressional Technical Aid Committee arrived in Baghdad on a four day visit to study economic conditions.

Thirteen Asian and African countries presented a resolution at the UN calling on the General Assembly to recommend that Morocco become completely independent within five years.

October 10

After a three hour meeting of British and Egyptian negotiators, Egyptian Minister of Guidance Salem issued a statement for publication abroad, saying he firmly believed an agreement with Britain was impossible.

October, 1953

October 10

The International Confederation of Free Trade Unions urged the UN General Assembly to set up a good offices committee to try to work out a settlement of the disputes between France and the North African Nationalists.

The Jordanian trade delegation chief said that the delegation had concluded a commercial agreement with Iraq and that the door was open for further discussions with both Iraq and Saudi Arabia.

An official spokesman of the Saudi Arabian Government stated that his Government had proposed to Britain that a neutral international commission, including representatives of both parties to the dispute, be formed and dispatched to the oasis of Buraimi with a view to investigating recent incidents there.

The Arab Advisory Military Committee began a five day meeting at Cairo.

October 11

Crown Prince of Saudi Arabia Amir Saud appointed his brother, Amir Faisal Ibn-Abd-al-Aziz, as Deputy President of the Council of Ministers.

According to a British Embassy announcement, three armed Egyptians shot two British airmen near Ismailia, slightly wounding them.

Lebanese Prime Minister Abdallah al-Yafi told a press conference that the Government was determined to purge and reorganize the government machinery. He said that the Government would seek amendment of the oil contracts, and that he had submitted to Parliament a draft law for the reorganization of political parties.

The Libyan Cabinet decided to conclude a civil air agreement with Holland.

Israel officially informed the UN Truce Supervision Organization that it would temporarily suspend the work on the Jordan River hydroelectric project.

October, 1953

October 11

Yemen's Minister to Egypt, Ali al-Muayyed, deposited instruments of ratification of the Collective Security Pact at Cairo.

President Muhammad Nagib of Egypt said Britain could not defend the Canal Zone against a hostile Egypt. He also assailed political maneuvers on the part of the British designed to influence the November Sudanese elections.

Moscow Radio announced the appointment of Daniel S. Solod as Ambassador to Egypt to succeed Semen P. Kosyrev.

Syrian President Adib Shishakli's Arab Liberation Movement won 72 of the 82 Parliamentary seats. The National Socialist Party, a minor group, secured one seat, the Independents, nine.

October 12

Shafai Ahmad al-Sheikh, Secretary General of the Sudan Trade Unions Federation, reportedly had gone to Vienna to attend the Congress of the World Federation of Trade Unions which opened October 10. This was the first time Sudanese unions had been represented at an international congress held outside the Sudan.

A new Syrian press and publications law was issued in five sections: press, libraries, publishing houses, issuing of printed materials, and posters and bulletins. The holders of publishing licenses must have been Syrian citizens for at least five years. Papers must have three assistant editors and must subscribe to at least two world news agencies.

An imperial edict reforming the Council of Government was sealed by the Sultan of Morocco for promulgation on October 16. Under this decree, the Council would cease to be an adjunct of the French Residency and would become an integral part of the Moroccan Government.

British and Egyptian negotiations on the Suez issue were resumed.

October, 1953

October 13

Iraqi King Faisal left for the northern part of the country to attend the annual maneuvers of the Iraqi Army. He was accompanied by the Prime Minister and the Ministers of Defense, Finance and Economy.

The British Embassy in Cairo announced that 20 shots had been fired at Hamsa on a Trucial Oman levies post which returned the fire. Casualties were not known.

The US delegate to the UN General Assembly Political Committee expressed the hope that France and Morocco would move continually closer in achieving self government for Morocco. He strongly urged that nothing be done in the Assembly which might provoke disorder in Morocco.

October 14

Jordanian Minister of Finance Sukkar and Minister of Economy, Development, and Reconstruction al-Khatab began discussions in London with British representatives regarding financial aid for the Jordan five year plan, amendment of the 1951 financial agreement with Britain, and other matters.

Israel armed forces attacked the Jordan frontier village of Qibya, killing 53 persons and destroying all the houses and the school. Two other villages were shelled. An Israel Foreign Office spokesman stated that the raid had been organized by Israel villagers and that the army had not taken part.

During a Lebanese political rally in support of Morocco's independence, three sticks of dynamite were hurled at the speaker's platform when a speaker began criticizing the Lebanese Government. Three persons were arrested.

It was announced in Washington that Eric Johnston would go to the Middle East as President Eisenhower's personal envoy to undertake discussions regarding mutual development of the Jordan water resources on a regional basis.

October, 1953

October 14

The Sultan of Morocco signed a decree providing that the Council of Government should become entirely elective instead of a party nominated body, and that the French and Moroccan members should in the future sit together.

October 15

An Israel raid on the village of Qibya in Jordan led to passage by the UN Security Council of a resolution censuring Israel.

According to the Israel-Jordan Mixed Armistice Commission, 42 Jordanians were killed, 16 injured, and scores of buildings blown up by a unit of the Israel regular army that attacked three villages on October 14.

The Permanent Military Committee of the Arab League began six weeks of talks at Cairo Military College with Egypt's Chief of Staff Muhammad Ibrahim in the chair.

Lebanese Opposition leaders called a meeting to organize a strike in protest against the alleged Lebanese Government interference with their meeting of the previous day. Police tried to prevent Kamal Jumblat, leader of the Socialist Progressive Party, from attending the meeting. Several casualties were reported among a group of his followers in an encounter with the police at Bayt al-Nagadah.

Major General Vagn Bennike, UN Chief of Staff, Truce Supervision Organization, rejected the Israel offer of a temporary suspension of work on the Jordan River project. He insisted on his earlier request for a stoppage until an arrangement was made with Syria.

The Jordan Cabinet decided on a strict defensive policy for resisting Israel aggression. Protests were sent to the US, Britain and France.

October 16

The British Foreign Office issued a statement saying there was no possible justification for the Israel attack on Qibya.

October, 1953

October 16

Jordan complained to the UN Security Council of the Israel battalion attack on Qibya.

Syria asked the Security Council to place on its agenda for prompt decision Israel's Jordan River drainage project in the demilitarized zone. Syria claimed that the project was in violation of the provisions of the Syrian-Israel Armistice Agreement, for the effect of the work was to deprive the riparian inhabitants along the Jordan of the water they needed to irrigate their land. Syria pointed out that despite the request of the Chief of Staff of the Truce Supervision Organization that operations be halted, Israel was continuing with the project.

In a statement issued at the close of a conference of the Foreign Ministers of France, Great Britain and the US, it was stated that the Ministers viewed with grave concern the incidents which culminated in Israel's armed action in Qibya on October 14 and they would jointly request that an urgent meeting be called to consider the tension between Israel and the neighboring Arab States.

The Syrian UN delegate, in requesting the Security Council to take up the question of the Israel canal, charged that Israel had conducted military operations in the demilitarized zone and had carried out partial mobilization. He also said that diversion of the Jordan River infringed the right of inhabitants of the zone to exercise normal activities and that Israel authorities would prevent the Syrian reparian population from irrigating their lands with Jordan River waters.

Large crowds demonstrated in Amman, Jordan, demanding revenge for the victims of the Israel attack on Qibya village.

October 17

The Israel Army General Staff took precautionary measures along the armistice lines in response to reports that Jordan had moved Arab Legion units up to the border.

Jordan asked the Arab League to convene its Political Committee at Amman as soon as possible, and Jordan soldiers were ordered to shoot on sight any Israel troops crossing the border.

October, 1953

October 17

The Umma Party of Sudan complained in a note to the Sudanese Electoral Commission that Egypt was infringing the electoral freedom of the Sudanese people. The note also referred to evidence of non-Sudanese finance behind electioneering.

Lebanese President Camille Chamoun received a note from Kamal Jumblat and Abdallah Hajj, Deputy for Beirut, asking suspension of the current Constitution and the drafting of a new one. They also asked that the armed forces be responsible for maintenance of order and security in the country during the drafting period. The note also asked for the establishment of a National Bank.

It was reported from Amman that Jordan had called for military aid from the Arab States against Israel.

In separate but identical letters addressed to the President of the UN Security Council, to England, France and the US, Jordan requested the calling of an urgent meeting of the Council to consider the matter of tension between Israel and the neighboring Arab States. The letters also stated that it would be desirable to have a report in person from the Chief of Staff of the Truce Supervision Organization.

Sixteen thousand, about 90 percent of the total native workmen of the Arabian-American Oil Company, went on strike because of the Company's refusal to grant two demands of housing and an increase in cost of living allowances.

The UN representatives of the US, Britain, and France submitted identical letters to the UN Security Council proposing an immediate meeting on the Israel-Jordan border question and requesting that General Bennike be present.

October 18

In a statement issued at UN Headquarters, the Israel delegation declared that the Government of Israel would welcome a call by the Security Council to the parties concerned for full compliance with the Armistice Agreements and was ready to take all practical steps to insure this end.

October, 1953

October 18

Brigadier John Bagot Glubb, British commander of the Arab Legion, declared in Jerusalem, in the Jordanian section, that the Palestine War might resume. Acknowledging that Israel had been provoked by infiltration from the Jordan side, he said that the Israelis must deal with such infiltration within their country and not by military incursions across the border.

The US State Department issued a statement expressing sympathy for the families of those who lost their lives in Qibya, Jordan, and declared that those responsible should be brought to account and effective measures taken to prevent such incidents in the future.

The Revolutionary Tribunal sentenced Karim Thabet, ex-Egyptian King Farouk's Press Advisor, to life imprisonment at hard labor. Thabet was convicted of treason by contacting unnamed foreign quarters in 1953 and for corruption and abuse of office.

Armed Saudi Arabian troops were sent to Dhahran and martial law was declared there.

Former Syrian Head of State General Fawzi Selo left Damascus for Saudi Arabia to take up the post of counsellor to Crown Prince Amir Saud.

The Suez Canal Company announced a series of rate changes effective February 1, 1954, covering pilotage for non-transiting vessels, berthing and changes of berth and towage.

A London communique expressed grave concern over Israel armed action against Jordan and formalized the appeal to the UN Security Council. Washington was more critical of the "shocking attacks" and demanded that Israel take steps to prevent further incidents.

October 19

David Ben-Gurion, Prime Minister of Israel, categorically denied the allegation made by the Israel-Jordan Mixed Armistice Commission that the attack on Qibya was carried out by half a battalion of regular troops.

October, 1953

October 19

The UN Security Council met at the request of France, Britain and the US to deal with the border situation between Israel and Jordan. It decided to ask Major General Vagn Bennike, Chief of Staff of the UN Truce Supervision Organization, for a first hand account of the rising tension between Israel and its Arab neighbors. However, it failed to formulate the item for the agenda. General Bennike was summoned to New York to report on the situation.

A report prepared by Gordon Clapp of the Tennessee Valley Authority with backing of the US State Department for development of a land and water project for the Jordan Valley was presented to UNRWA.

The *ad hoc* Political Committee of the UN General Assembly rejected, 28-22, a resolution sponsored by the Afro-Asian Bloc calling for full independence of the French protectorate of Morocco within five years. By a vote of 31-18, it adopted a resolution by Bolivia and amended by India, calling for a reduction of tension in Morocco.

Governor General Chardri Ghulam Muhammad of Pakistan arrived in Baghdad to visit the Holy Places in Najaf, Kufa and Karbala in Iraq.

The Jordan Government addressed a memorandum to the President of the UN Security Council referring to the Israel attack on Qibya which it described as a criminal aggression which threatened an outbreak of hostilities and which called for immediate UN action, especially by the Western Powers as signatories of the 1950 declaration.

October 20

The Sudan Executive Council issued a law providing for sentences of up to 14 years imprisonment for direct or indirect advocacy of any subversive principle or theory, including Communism and fascism.

The National Unionist Party of Sudan, which favored eventual association of the Sudan with Egypt, complained to the Sudanese Electoral Commission that British Administrators were interfering with the electoral freedom of the Sudanese people, through their assistance to the Umma Party.

October 20

US Secretary of State John Foster Dulles indicated that the US was withholding further economic aid to Israel because of its refusal to stop work on the Jordan River project.

Israel formally asked the UN Security Council to take up charges of brutal assaults by Jordanian raiders on Israel civilians. It accused the Arabs of waging illicit economic warfare, maintaining their blockade of Israel and spreading war propaganda and threats against the territorial integrity and political independence of Israel.

The UN Security Council decided on a formula for the agenda which was a compromise between the three Western powers and Charles Malik of Lebanon. The agenda included the Palestine question, compliance with and enforcement of the General Armistice Agreements, with special reference to recent acts of violence and in particular to the incident at Qibya on October 14-15, and a report by the Chief of Staff of the Truce Supervision Organization, General Bennike.

Ahmad Hussein, Egyptian Ambassador to the US, said that the US decision to stop aid allocations to Israel would strengthen the faith of the Arab world in the United States.

It was reported in Amman that a Jordanian delegation composed of three senior officials of the Arab Legion were leaving for Cairo to seek payment for arms purchased and paid for by Jordan, held up in Egypt in transit and used by the Egyptian Army during the Palestine war.

According to a spokesman of the Arabian American Oil Company in Beirut, the strike in Saudi Arabia had ended.

October 21

President Eisenhower appointed George Wadsworth to succeed Raymond A. Hare as US Ambassador to Saudi Arabia and Minister to Yemen.

Demonstrations took place throughout Jordan during a three hour strike called by political leaders in protest against the Qibya attack. The French Embassy, the US Point Four offices and the British Council offices in Amman were stoned.

October 21

The six Arab members of the UN asked the Security Council to take up a general complaint of aggression by the armed forces of Israel committed against Jordanian villages.

At the request of Jordan, the Arab League Political Committee met in Amman to discuss the situation resulting from the Qibya raid.

General Vagn Bennike, Chief of Staff of the Truce Supervision Organization, arrived in New York.

The US State Department protested to the Jordan Government against the mob violence to the US Information Service office in Amman and also against an attack on a US Embassy car. The Jordan Government expressed its deep regrets.

Israel protested to the Mixed Armistice Commission that a train had been derailed on the night of October 20 by a land mine about three miles west of the armistice line, opposite the Jordanian town of Qalqilia.

A statement issued by the Israel Embassy in Washington rejected the US charge that Israel was acting in defiance either of the US or the UN.

A communique was issued after a meeting, the fifteenth in the series of informal discussions, between Egyptian and British negotiators on the future of the Suez Canal base, jointly agreed to by the British Embassy and the Egyptian Minister of National Guidance.

The Senate of Libya approved by a vote of 16-3 the 20 year treaty with Great Britain signed in July.

King Hussein of Jordan arrived in Amman from Rome.

Eric Johnston, Special Envoy of President Eisenhower, arrived in Beirut.

Debate on French rule in Tunisia was opened in the UN General Assembly's Political and Security Committee.

October 21

Akram Hourani, Michel Aflaq, and Salah-ad-Din Bitar returned from Rome. They were associated with the Arab Resurrectionists Party and the Arab Socialist Party, and had been living outside Syria since an attempted coup in December 1952.

October 22

An Israel note was handed to the First Secretary of the British Embassy in Tel Aviv in reply to a British note of protest of October 16 against the Israel attack on the Jordanian village of Qibya.

Eric Johnston, Special Envoy of US President Eisenhower, arrived at Amman, Jordan.

Eric Johnston conferred with the Premier of Jordan, Fawzi al-Mulki. It was reported in Baghdad that Premier Fadel al-Jamali told US Ambassador Burton Berry that Johnston would not be allowed into Iraq because he was a Vice President of the American Christian Palestine Committee.

The Saudi Arabian Government paid 85,000 pounds sterling to Jordan as its share toward developing the Jordanian National Guard.

The Israel Government asked for a meeting of the Mixed Armistice Commission to investigate reported Jordan troop concentrations in frontier areas where such concentrations were forbidden under the Armistice Agreement.

Sayyed Mansour Qidara presented letters of credence to Queen Elizabeth as Libya's first Minister to the Court of St. James.

Units of the American Sixth Fleet arrived in Lebanese waters for a five day visit.

Belief that the critical situation in the Middle East would not lead to a major conflict between Israel and the Arab States was expressed by Major General Vagn Bennike. The Chief of the United Nations Truce Supervision Organization in Palestine suggested changes in the

October 22

demilitarized zones. Israel charged that Jordan had concentrated large military forces inside Jerusalem.

October 23

The Arab League Political Committee adopted, according to Jordanian Premier Fawzi al-Mulki, several defensive, financial and political decisions in connection with the Israel-Jordan clashes. Included in the Amman meeting was the decision to quadruple aid to Jordan in September.

The Israel-Jordan Mixed Armistice Commission condemned armed Jordanians for mining the Israel train on October 20, and called on Jordan to take the most urgent and vigorous action to prevent the recurrence of such acts of violence.

Arab Legion Headquarters asserted that between October 18 and 20 eight Israel reconnaissance aircraft had flown over Jordan.

The Arab Chamber of Commerce, Industry and Agriculture, meeting at Beirut, asked the Arab Governments and the Secretariat General of the League to expedite formation of an Arab Economic Council in compliance with the charter of the Arab League.

Abdallah al-Yafi, Premier of Lebanon, said in Amman that the project of US Emissary Eric Johnston had been rejected by Lebanon, Syria and Jordan. He said it could not be accepted at any cost.

The US State Department announced that Eric Johnston, the US Emissary, had no plans to go to Iraq.

October 24

President Adib Shishakli of Syria opened the new Parliament for the first time since the beginning of the military dictatorship in December 1951. The President opened the Parliament with an inaugural address pledging Syrian support for Arab unity and opposition to Israel. Parliament elected Maamoun Kuzbari of the Liberation Movement as its presiding officer.

October 24

United Nations observers were requested by the Mixed Armistice Commission to investigate charges and countercharges by Israel and Jordan that troop deployments along the armistice lines were in excess of the limits permitted.

King Faisal II of Iraq gave 10,000 pounds sterling personally for aid to Jordan's frontier villages.

A $1,440,000 trade agreement was signed between Egypt and Rumania.

Five thousand volunteers enlisted in the Egyptian Home Guard. Companies and other employers were to pay the volunteers' salaries for 15 days of training or service. The Government would pay for any period exceeding 15 days.

October 25

Eric Johnston, Special Envoy of President Eisenhower, arrived in Cairo to enlist Egyptian support for the Jordan River irrigation development proposal. He and US Ambassador Jefferson Caffery conferred with Egypt's Foreign Minister, Mahmoud Fawzi. Johnston said that he also brought US proposals for development projects, mentioning the Sudd al-Ali Dam, proposed to create a large reservoir near the border of Sudan and irrigations projects for the Upper Nile.

Thirty-three prominent American religious, educational and civic leaders submitted to the President of the UN General Assembly, Vijaya Lakshmi Pandit, a memorandum on a six year program to resettle Arab refugees and develop the natural resources of the Middle East.

October 26

The Jordan Cabinet met to consider a report from a special three man ministerial committee appointed to investigate the failure of the Arab Legion to intervene during the Qibya attack.

Eric Johnston, the US Emissary, stated in Cairo that he saw a significant source of encouragement in the fact that the door had been kept open for discussion of the Jordan River development proposal.

October 26

French Resident General in Tunisia Voizard announced the lifting of the curfew and press censorship and the freeing of 22 of 80 nationalists interned in isolated camps.

The UN General Assembly's Political and Security Committee approved a resolution that all necessary steps be taken to lead to full sovereignty and independence for Tunisia, by a vote of 29-22-5.

Six Lebanese Jews suspected of being in contact with Israel and giving it information regarding military and economic activities in the Arab countries were arrested.

The Lebanese Ministry of Justice asked the Chamber of Deputies to withdraw parliamentary immunity from Deputy Abdallah Hajj for refusing to attend the Court for interrogation about strikes which took place in August.

The Libyan Cabinet completed discussion of the 1953-1954 budget estimated at LP6 million.

A 20 page report dealing with the Syrian complaint by Major General Bennike, Chief of Staff of the UN Palestine Truce Organization, was distributed at the UN.

Iraqi Prime Minister Fadel al-Jamali and Minister of Economy Abd-al-Rahman al-Jalili met Sir Herbert Todd, Chairman in Iraq of the Iraq Petroleum Company, and discussed the raising of prices of Iraqi oil to the level of world prices.

Anthony Eden, British Secretary of State for Foreign Affairs, stated in the House of Commons that the Saudi Arabian Government had agreed to submit to arbitration the question of defining the lines of demarcation in the Oasis of Buraimi. He added that talks in this connection were in progress between the British and Saudi Governments.

October 27

The UN Security Council began discussion of the Israel-Jordan border issue with a report by Major General Vagn Bennike, Chief of Staff of

October 27

the UN Palestine Truce Supervision Organization. He gave with his endorsement the findings of a subordinate, Commander E. H. Hutcheson of the US Navy, Acting Chairman of the Mixed Armistice Commission, that the raid on Qibya had been carried out by 250-300 well trained Israel soldiers. He stated that the raid might have been provoked by a Jordanian attack forty-eight hours earlier in which a mother and her two small children were murdered.

The UN Security Council took up Syria's complaint that Israel was diverting the waters of the Jordan in the demilitarized zone. Israel repeated to the Council the offer it made to General Bennike to suspend operations temporarily. This was to allow the discussions to proceed in an atmosphere more conducive ⁻ the Council's effort to solve the problem. After a lengthy discus n, the Council adopted a resolution expressing satisfaction with th uspension of operations by Israel, pending the urgent examination f the question without prejudice to either side.

The Government of Israel released a plan for harnessing the water resources of the country. It called for the siphoning of water from the Jordan River, from a Jordan tributary rising in Israel, from smaller rivers, springs, and so on. It was stated that Israel would prefer a regional water plan, but inasmuch as the Arab States refused to consider such a project, it could not be expected to halt its own development schemes.

Sayyed Sulaiman Touqan, Jordanian Senator and member of the former Regency Council, was appointed Counsellor to the King.

It was reported at Beirut that the strikers at the Dhahran Aramco plant had ignored a week old decree by the Saudi Arabian Prime Minister to return to work.

Eric Johnston, US Emissary, arrived in Tel Aviv to confer with Israel Government leaders regarding the TVA Unified Development Plan for the Jordan Valley.

The Secretariat General of the Arab League forwarded 100,000 pounds sterling to Jordan.

October 27

Lebanese Prime Minister Abdallah al-Yafi announced in the Chamber of Deputies that the Lebanese and Syrian Governments had agreed to present similar royalty demands to Tapline and the Iraq Petroleum Company.

Leslie J. Carver, Acting Director of the UN Relief and Works Agency for Palestine Refugees, in a joint report with UNRWA's Advisory Commission submitted to the ad hoc Political Committee, recommended that the UN extend its aid to the Arab refugee program until June 30, 1955.

The Egyptian Revolution Tribunal sentenced Ahmad Muhammad al-Nabib, former director of the Alexandria Moassat Hospital, to fifteen years imprisonment, and ordered the confiscation of his and his son's property and assets in excess of what they owned in September 1939. Nabib was convicted on charges of corruption, damaging the interests of the country through his close relationship with former King Farouk, and embezzelment of hospital funds.

October 28

President Eisenhower announced that in view of Israel's agreement to suspend work on the Jordan River project, as requested by the UN, US economic assistance would be resumed.

It was announced that Jews would be prohibited from leaving Lebanon without a permit from the Ministry of Foreign Affairs.

Jordanian Premier Fawzi al-Mulki said that the Government was strengthening its armed forces against another Israel attack.

Egyptian Minister of Guidance Salah Salem issued a statement saying that Egypt was anxious to discharge its international duties regarding the Suez Canal in accordance with all international conventions, but could not play this role satisfactorily until Egypt had acquired full sovereignty and rights.

Ambassador Abba Eban, Chief of Israel's UN delegation, told a press conference that the Qibya raid had been carried out by villagers who

October, 1953

October 28

had been supplied with technical materials like those used by the Israel Army, thus disputing General Bennike's report.

Abba Eban, chief of Israel's UN delegation, accused Israel's four Arab neighbors of carrying on a concerted campaign of not making peace with Israel and not letting Israel live in peace. This he said was decided on at a conference in Amman the previous November of the representatives on the Mixed Armistice Commissions of Egypt, Jordan, Syria and Lebanon.

Israel announced that it would discontinue temporarily work on the Huleh Canal, but that the suspension was without prejudice to Israel's rights, claims or position on the matter.

The Mixed Armistice Commission approved a report of UN observers that neither Israel nor Jordan had concentrated troops or equipment in the Jerusalem area in excess of limits imposed by the Armistice Agreement.

It was announced that Syrian authorities had handed over to Lebanese authorities Rashid Abu-Salman, the assassin of Riyad al-Solh, former Lebanese Prime Minister who was slain in Amman in 1951.

October 29

Abba Eban, chief UN delegate of Israel, stated that Israel's dependence on development of the Jordan contrasted with the situation of the Arab States which had such great rivers as the Nile, Tigris and Euphrates, and he charged in the Security Council that Syria's attempt to block Israel's diversion of waters from the Jordan River was part of its avowed political and economic warfare against Israel. The Syrian representative, Farid Zain-ad-Din, accused Israel of attempting to steal the water.

The representatives of France and Britain in the UN Security Council questioned General Bennike, Chief of Staff of the UN Palestine Truce Supervision Organization, on the organization of the work of the UN Truce Observers and on whether additional personnel should be provided. Sir

October, 1953

October 31

A conference, sponsored jointly by UNRWA and the UN Children's Emergency Fund, opened in Jerusalem to discuss plans for the education of refugee children. Delegates from Jordan, Syria, Lebanon, Egypt and Iraq attended.

Sidi Muhammad Ben-Youssef, deposed Sultan of Morocco, was recalled to France.

October, 1953

October 29

Gladwyn Jebb asked General Bennike to comment on the denial made by Israel Prime Minister Ben-Gurion that the Qibya raid had been carried out by members of the Israel Army. The General was also interrogated by the delegates of the US, Israel and Lebanon.

Eric Johnston, US Emissary to the Middle East, presented to Israel authorities the American sponsored international "little TVA" for the development of the Jordan River.

October 30

Eric Johnston, US Emissary, arrived in Beirut and conferred with Lebanese Foreign Minister Alfred Naccache. Authoritative sources said Minister Naccache told Johnston that Lebanon welcomed cooperation with the US but would not accept any compromise formula so long as Israel refused to implement UN decisions.

Eric Johnston, US Emissary, told US officials in Jerusalem that he believed skillful diplomacy could win Syrian and Jordanian approval for the US backed plan for developing a Jordan Valley irrigation and power system.

At the time of Eric Johnston's departure from Tel Aviv it was reported that the Israel Government did not believe that the TVA Jordan Valley plan would provide Israel with sufficient water for irrigation. It was felt that the Litani River should be included in the plan in order to supply sifficient water for the Negev area.

The US State Department announced that up to 10,000 tons of wheat would leave Philadelphia early in November for famine relief in Jordan.

The United States Assistant Secretary of State for Near Eastern Affairs spoke on the US position on French North Africa.

October 31

Eric Johnston, US Emissary, arrived in Damascus and conferred with Syrian President Shishakli. Informed sources said that Syria had little enthusiasm for the Jordan River plan despite promises of US financing.

November, 1953

November 1

A joint communique issued in London and Amman stated that Jordan would receive a grant of 2,350,000 pounds sterling, of which 1,600,000 pounds was to be an interest free loan and up to 750,000 pounds was to make up Jordan's budget deficit. Further aid might be given after needs were studied.

Opening the new session of Parliament, Jordanian King Hussein promised that laws would be enacted to give more freedom to individuals, and that the Government would continue to champion the policy of no compromise between Israel and the Arab States.

November 2

The Saudi Arabian Foreign Ministry reported to the Secretariat General of the Arab League that Saudi Arabia's losses from boycotting the air companies which passed through Israel had reached 10 million riyals.

Andrew G. Lynch, US Charge d'Affairs in Amman, said that the United States had no intention of withholding economic aid as a lever to win Arab acceptance of the unified TVA irrigation plan or any other proposals.

After meeting briefly with US Emissary Eric Johnston, Abd-al-Oseiran, Speaker of the Lebanese Parliament, said in Beirut that the Jordan Valley water development program backed by the US was unacceptable to Arab peoples and refugees.

The ad hoc UN Political Committee began discussion of the Arab refugee question with a statement by Leslie Carver, Acting Director of the UN Relief and Works Agency for Palestine Refugees.

Elections began in the 24 indirect constituencies in southern and eastern Sudan. Balloting in these and the 68 direct constituencies was expected to be completed by December 1. The five seats reserved to the Graduates' Constituency would be completed by December 7.

November 3

The compromise proposals on Moroccan independence adopted by the Political Committee October 19 failed to receive a two-thirds majority in the UN General Assembly, the vote being 32-22-5.

British Foreign Secretary Anthony Eden said in the House of Commons that Egypt was violating its agreement with Britain to keep hands off in the Sudanese elections.

November 4

US Delegate James P. Richards at the UN Political and Security Committee warned the Arab States and Israel that the US would not continue indefinitely to be the financial mainstay of the UN program for helping Arab refugees. His statement was linked with an endorsement of the soundness of the TVA Jordan Valley development plan Eric Johnston, US Emissary, was advocating. Richards presented a joint recommendation, co-sponsored by Britain, France and Turkey, asking that UNRWA be continued until June 30, 1955.

November 5

British Foreign Secretary Anthony Eden stated in the House of Commons that the British Government was not satisfied with the way the Egyptian Government was fulfilling the pledge, jointly made by Britain and Egypt in the February 12 agreement, that the Sudanese elections would be carried out in a free and neutral manner.

Mirghani Hamzah, spokesman for the Sudanese National Unionist Party, said his party wanted unity with Egypt in respect to defense, economic policy and foreign policy. He said that if elected his party would seek Sudanese admission to the Arab League and the United Nations.

In a statement denying British Foreign Secretary Eden's accusation that the elections in Sudan were not being carried out in a free and neutral manner, Egyptian Minister of State for Sudanese Affairs stated that Eden had announced the results of the Sudanese elections in advance. His statement was an admission of the defeat of British policy which wanted the Sudan to continue to be a British colony "to be milked dry."

November 5

Israel's Foreign Minister, Moshe Sharett, cabled General Bennike requesting UN intercession with Jordanian authorities who he charged were publicizing baseless allegations of Israel outrages, charges not backed up by official complaints to the Mixed Armistice Commission. The two specific charges to which Sharett referred were that Israelis blew up a water pipeline to Jerusalem's Old City on November 1, and that 60 Israelis raided the village of Budrus, near Qibya.

Talks looking toward economic unity between Syria and Lebanon began at the Lebanese border town of Shatura.

The UN conference on education for Arab refugees meeting at Jerusalem called on Egypt, Lebanon, Syria, Jordan and Iraq to assume their share of the educational burden for refugees within their borders.

Egyptian President Nagib said in a press statement that Egypt had sent Britain its final word on the Suez question and that Egypt did not consider that negotiation was the only means whereby its rights could be attained.

November 6

A communique was issued following talks between the Sultan of Morocco and the French Foreign Minister. The communique announced that His Majesty the Sultan of Morocco had confirmed his intention of constituting a Moroccan government to carry on affairs and to negotiate with France.

November 7

Lebanese Minister of Economy Rashid Karami denied reports that economic talks with Syria had broken down.

The Revolutionary Tribunal sentenced Colonel Abd-al-Ghaffar Uthman to 15 years imprisonment on charges of corruption and of conspiracy to supply the Egyptian Army with defective weapons during the Palestine War.

November 8

The Egyptian Revolution Command Council decided that the property and assets of all the members of the Muhammad Ali family, to which King Farouk belonged, be confiscated.

British authorities in Cairo said there was no truth in Egyptian press reports that British officers had been sent to the Sudan to carry on propaganda on behalf of or against any Sudanese party.

Libyan Finance Minister al-Unaizi told representatives of oil companies at a conference in Tripoli that his Government intended to create a Mining Department to deal with matters relating to the exploration and exploitation of minerals, including oil and gas. He said it had been decided to exempt from customs duties instruments and equipment used by oil companies for geological surveys.

November 9

It was announced in Jordan following a meeting with Kuwait authorities that Jordanians would be able to go to Kuwait after getting a visa from the British Embassy at Amman.

King Idris of Libya arrived in Tangier after a short visit to Spain. He was to leave the following day for Fez in French Morocco.

General Bennike, Chief of Staff of the UN Truce Supervision Organization, answered some 60 questions put to him by the members of the Security Council, Jordan and Israel. On the basis of these answers, France, Great Britain and the US declared that they held Israel responsible for the Qibya raid.

King Abd-al-Aziz Ibn-Saud of Saudi Arabia died at Taif. His son, Amir Saud, was proclaimed King. He in turn declared his brother, Amir Faisal, Saudi Arabia's Foreign Minister, Crown Prince.

November 10

Eric Johnston said in London that his mission to the Middle East had accomplished its purpose, which was to get Israel and the Arab nations to consider the Jordan River development project.

November 10

Syria's UN representative urged the Security Council to stop Israel's preparation to divert water from the upper Jordan River.

In London, Eric Johnston, President Eisenhower's personal representative, gave British Foreign Secretary Anthony Eden a report on his trip to the Middle East.

In a speech from the throne, King Saud guaranteed a welcome to further foreign investment in his Kingdom and promised a foreign policy of peaceful cooperation within the framework of the UN and the Arab League.

King Saud, accompanied by Heir Apparent Faisal and members of the royal family, left Taif, Saudi Arabia for Jedda, Saudi Arabia, where he was received at the airport by a party of notables including Amir Saif al-Islam Muhammad, son of the King of Yemen.

November 11

The UN General Assembly failed to win a two-thirds vote, 31-18, to adopt a resolution calling for more independence for Tunisia.

Arthur Lourie, Israel's Delegate in the UN Ad Hoc Political Committee, accused the Arab States of refusing, for political motivations, to help settle the Arab refugee problem, and even of hampering the welfare operations of the UN Relief Works Agency.

Jordanian Prime Minister Fawzi al-Mulki said Jordan would invoke the Anglo-Jordanian Treaty and request Britain to send more troops if Israel's forces made another attack like that of October 14 on Qibya.

November 12

The General Assembly's Special Political Committee approved by a 46-0 vote to continue UN assistance for Arab refugees and to spend $24,800,000 the following year for this purpose.

The UN General Assembly rejected all recommendations on Tunisia.

November, 1953

November 12

Israel's chief UN Delegate, Abba Eban, told the Security Council that a campaign of organized murder was being carried on across the central sector of the Israel-Jordan frontier, allowed, if not encouraged, by the Jordanian Government.

Charles Malik of Lebanon declared that an attempt was being made to drown the Qibya incident in a general debate, and that he would resist any attempt to deflect attention from the massacre.

The Iraqi Council of Ministers approved a decree to allocate ID100,000 for projects related to Arab cooperation, including delegations to carry out Arab propaganda in the US and opening propaganda offices.

November 13

Israel Ambassador Abba Eban called on UN Secretary General Dag Hammarskjold to discuss Israel's proposal for negotiations between Israel and Jordan which were to be held at UN headquarters.

British Foreign Secretary Anthony Eden charged in the House of Commons that the Egyptian Government was interfering in the parliamentary elections in the Sudan by buying votes for the party which favored union with Egypt.

November 14

Premier Fawzi al-Mulki of Jordan denied in Amman that Jordan had left the door open for further examination of the Jordan Valley irrigation and power project presented by Eric Johnston.

A Saudi Arabian Royal Decree was issued appointing Muhammad Surur al-Subban, former Adviser to the Ministry of Finance, as Minister of State on the Council of Ministers and Counselor to the King.

November 15

Speaking in the House of Commons, British Foreign Secretary Anthony Eden stated that the British Government deplored the events at Qibya and warned Israel that such outrages could only obstruct any chance of peace which Israel assured them it was anxious to obtain.

November, 1953

November 15

A joint meeting of the Arab League Secretariat and the Military Advisory Committee was held in Cairo to discuss implementation of the Collective Security Pact.

November 16

Ali Shukri Khamis, Director of the Egyptian Chamber of Commerce and member of an Egyptian economic mission, announced that the group would leave Cairo on November 29 for Beirut, Damascus, Amman, Baghdad, Kuwait, Mecca and Riyadh. It would later go to Libya.

The chief British military representative in the Anglo-Egyptian Suez discussions, General Sir Brian Robertson, was suddenly called back to London.

The Pakistani Chairman of the Sudan Governor General's Commission, an international committee of five which would carry on supervisory functions during the transitional period preceding self determination, arrived in Cairo but said that he would not go to the Sudan until the elections were completed.

Israel's UN representative, Abba Eban, urged the Security Council to expedite its decision on Israel's preparations for the Jordan River diversion project. He emphasized that this would in no way interfere with the US sponsored program for the development of the Jordan Valley. Eban said that Syria was attempting to exercise the right of veto over the development of the river. The Lebanese representative, Charles Malik, argued the question of jurisdiction over the demilitarized zone through which the Jordan River flowed. He insisted that Israel had no control over the area because of the circumstances of the Palestine War.

The Israel Government in Jerusalem formally called on the US, Great Britain and France to note its offer to meet with Jordan at UN headquarters in New York to "thrash out" all existing problems connected with the Jordan-Israel Armistice.

November, 1953

November 16

Jordan's UN delegate, Yusuf Haikal, rejected Israel Ambassador Eban's proposal of November 12 that Jordan and Israel delegates meet in New York to discuss means of preventing border incidents.

The Jordan-Israel Mixed Armistice Commission decided to extend for three months the Israel-Jordan meetings of army commanders to settle minor incidents and curb infiltration.

Anthony Nutting, Under Secretary in the British Foreign Office, stated in a written Parliamentary reply that the British Government had offered, subject to Parliamentary approval, to provide Jordan in 1954 to 1955 with funds totalling 2,350,000 pounds sterling, of which up to 750,000 pounds was to be devoted to meeting the expected deficit in Jordan's budget for 1954, and the remaining 1,600,000 pounds was to be an interest-free loan to be expended in 1954 to 1955 on certain specified projects in the plan when further information about them had been received.

November 17

Syrian suggestions for financial and economic unity with Lebanon as reported in the Beirut press included the creation of a body to deal with currency affairs, and to direct loan policy, financial and currency markets and banks. It also included creation of a body to deal with exchange questions and to guarantee stability of foreign currency prices.

Vice Admiral Jerald Wright, Supreme Commander of the American Naval Forces in the Mediterranean and East Atlantic, arrived in Beirut. He said his visit was purely a courtesy call and declined to comment on reports that the US intended to conclude a unilateral defense treaty with Lebanon.

Eric Johnston told President Eisenhower that the four Middle Eastern countries to which he presented the Jordan Valley development plan proposed by the US promised that they would give the project careful study. The White House announced that Johnston was expected to return to the Middle East, probably in February 1954.

November, 1953

November 17

Squadron leader Hassan Ibrahim, a member of the Egyptian Revolutionary Tribunal, announced that former King Farouk would be tried <u>in absentia</u>.

The Jordanian Government announced that it would adopt a liberalized import program enabling it to purchase $30,800,000 in goods and services abroad during the 1954 fiscal year.

November 18

The Jordanian Court of Appeals rejected an appeal by Barclay's Bank against a court order that the bank must meet demands on an Arab refugee's account with a branch at Jaffa, then in Israel.

Libyan Finance Minister al-Unaizi left for New York to attend the General Assembly debate on assistance to Libya recommended by the UN Economic and Social Council. Libya had asked the UN for LP6 million.

A three power (US, British, French) resolution censuring Israel was presented to the UN Security Council. It called on Jordan to strengthen measures to prevent crossing the demarcation line, proposed additional personnel for the Truce Supervision Organization, and asked General Bennike to report back to the Security Council within three months.

November 19

General Sir Charles Keightley, Commander in Chief of the British Middle East Land Forces, arrived in Benghazi on his first visit to Cyrenaica since taking over his new command.

The Israel delegation in the UN Security Council issued a statement condemning the three power (US, British, French) resolution of November 18 concerning the Qibya incident as "one sided and discriminatory."

November, 1953

November 20

Group Captain Hussein Dhu-al-Fiqar Sabri, Egyptian member of the Sudan Governor General's Commission, speaking on behalf of Egyptian National Guidance Minister Salah Salem, asked that elections in Kassala Province in the east and Equatoria in the south be suspended temporarily because of serious British interference, and that all British officials in those places, including the Governors, be removed.

Writing in the Cominform press, Khaled Bakdash, Secretary General of the Communist Party of Syria and Lebanon, stated that the failure of the US in trying to put together an aggressive military block of Arab and Near Eastern countries was due to the resistance offered by the Arab peoples.

In a press statement, Sudanese Prime Minister Sayyed Ismail al-Azhari emphasized that his Sudanese National Unionist Party did not recognize the Anglo-Egyptian Agreement of 1929 concerning the use of the waters of the Nile River which allocated only one twenty-third of the Nile waters to the Sudan. He intended to negotiate a new agreement, he said, whereby the Sudan would be allowed more water with which to develop its agriculture.

The Iraqi Istiqlal Party held a meeting at Baghdad attended by more than 1,000 persons. Mahdi Kubba, Leader of the Party, urged the Arab countries and their friends to form a third world bloc to strengthen world peace. He asked for the abrogation of the Anglo-Iraqi Treaty of 1930.

Colonel Gamal Abdel Nasser, Egyptian Deputy Premier, speaking in al-Minia al-Kamh, said that although there was talk in the American press of assistance to underdeveloped countries, none had been given to Egypt in the fourteen months since the revolution.

November 21

Egyptian President Muhammad Nagib, on the third day of his visit to Egyptian Nubia on the Sudan frontier, said he would visit the Sudan after the elections.

November, 1953

November 21

The Sudanese Electoral Commission turned down the Egyptian request of the previous day that elections in Kassala Province and Equatoria be temporarily suspended.

November 22

Israel Prime Minister David Ben-Gurion said in Jerusalem that the proposed resolution of censure would not weaken the Israel Government's resolve to protect the lives of its citizens. He blamed UN authorities for having "failed to bring to the notice of the Security Council the full tale of the tragedy of bloodshed" in Israel. He declared that the draft resolution discriminated between the blood of one people and that of another. He said that "while censuring Israel for the Qibya affair, the powers, by their silence, condoned in effect all murders committed by the armed forces hailing from the Kingdom of Jordan."

November 23

A 15 day conference under the auspices of the World Health Organization opened at Beirut.

Israel invoked Article XII of the Israel-Jordan Armistice Agreement which provided for the convocation by the UN of a conference of representatives of the two parties for the purpose of reviewing, revising or suspending any of the provisions of the agreement. Participation in such a conference was obligatory upon the parties.

November 24

It was announced that a draft law had been prepared for the establishment of a Syrian Council for National Wealth to prepare schemes for the development of agricultural, industrial and commercial resources.

King Idris returned to Libya.

November, 1953

November 24

The UN Security Council adopted a resolution condemning an Israel attack on Jordan as a violation of the July 15, 1948, Security Council ceasefire resolution.

It was announced that the Jordanian Cabinet had decided to establish a Supreme Council of Defense to be composed of the Ministers of Defense, Finance, Interior, and Foreign Affairs, the Chief of Staff of the Arab Legion, and two senior officers.

November 25

Lebanese Prime Minister Abdallah al-Yafi said arrangements for the Litani River hydroelectric scheme had been completed and that the Government had formed a company with a capital of LL100 million to implement the project. He also announced that an Industrial and Agricultural Loan Bank would be established with a capital of LL30 million.

November 27

The UN General Assembly adopted a resolution for continuing the UN Relief and Works Agency for Palestine Refugees. The UNRWA resolution was adopted 52-0. A budget of $248 million was authorized for the year ending June 30, 1954.

November 28

A number of Moslem Brotherhood dissidents, headed by Saleh Ashmawi, occupied the organization's headquarters at Cairo and announced the resignation of Hassan al-Hudaibi as Supreme Guide. Hudaibi had ousted four members of the executive council without explanation on November 23. The dissident faction also announced the formation of a four man provisional executive group to run the Brotherhood pending the election of a new council.

An Egyptian-Japanese agreement for the exchange of goods up to the value of $5 million was signed in Cairo.

November, 1953

November 29

Egyptian Government Radio reported that pro-Egyptian candidates had won a clear majority of seats in elections for the Anglo-Egyptian Sudan's first House of Representatives.

November 30

Because of Arab objections to working with Israel, the Food and Agriculture Organization of the UN, at a plenary session in Rome, voted to place Israel within the European region for purposes of administration.

British Foreign Secretary Anthony Eden said in the House of Commons that the British Government did not support the idea of an Israel-Jordan meeting at this time, but believed that it would be better to allow a little time to elapse in order to "bring the parties together in more reasonable conditions."

Egyptian President Muhammad Nagib declared in Cairo that the initiative in trying to reach an Anglo-Egyptian base had to come from Britain.

December, 1953

December 1

King Faisal II of Iraq delivered his speech from the throne and outlined the Government's policy.

Sudanese Prime Minister Sayyed Ismail al-Azhari reaffirmed that his Sudanese National Unionist Party did not recognize the Anglo-Egyptian Agreement of 1929 concerning the use of the waters of the Nile River.

It was announced in Baghdad that the Iraqi Cabinet approved a scheme for exploiting natural gas from the oil fields, at a cost of about $800 million.

December 2

In a note to the Iraqi Government, Saudi Arabia rejected the former's proposal for the abolition of visas between the two countries. The reason given was the special religious status of Saudi Arabia and the desire to safeguard the Holy Places.

Governor General Ghulam Muhammad of Pakistan arrived in Jedda, Saudi Arabia, on a special visit.

Egypt announced that foodstuffs would be placed on the list of contraband articles that would not be allowed to pass through the Suez Canal destined for Israel.

The Syrian Ministry of Economy warned foreign companies to comply by the end of December with the decree calling for the replacement of foreign directors with Syrians.

December 3

The World Islamic Conference began a seven day meeting at Jerusalem with representatives from 16 states.

Egyptian guns fired on a US vessel, the S. S. Albion, carrying wheat to the Jordanian port of Aqaba, in the erroneous belief that it was bound for the Israel port of Elath. After explanations the vessel was allowed to proceed.

December, 1953

December 4

Lebanese President Camille Chamoun accepted an invitation to visit Buenos Aires presented by the Argentine Minister. No date was set for the visit.

December 5

Five aircraft carrying the Jordanian Ministers of Interior and Communications, other Government officials, and representatives of the American Embassy and Point Four staff flew from Amman to Aqaba for the ceremonial acceptance of 9,600 tons of wheat donated by the US for the relief of drought sufferers.

Three Arab conferences opened in Cairo. A conference of the Ministers of Education was held at Arab League headquarters to discuss the coordination and unification of education courses and cultural cooperation among the Arab countries. The Ministers of Finance and Economy met at the Egyptian Foreign Office to deal with the financial and economic situation in the Arab States and with production problems. Crime prevention in the Middle East was considered at a conference held at the headquarters of the Geographical Society, under the auspices of the UN.

December 6

Basra Petroleum Company workers in Iraq went on strike for higher pay and better working conditions.

It was reported from Damascus that talks would be started to form a joint Saudi Arabian, Syrian and Jordanian committee to discuss the question of reopening the Hejaz Railway to Medina, Saudi Arabia.

December 7

An Egyptian trade mission arrived in Amman, Jordan, to study schemes which included the exploitation of phosphates, manganese and potash, marble quarrying and oil refining.

December, 1953

December 7

The British Embassy in Cairo received a note from the Egyptian Government replying to written and verbal protests against increasing lawlessness in the Canal Zone.

It was reported from Baghdad that most of the Iraqi newspapers were critical of the speech from the throne and of Premier Fadel al-Jamali for not referring to the Anglo-Iraqi Treaty.

Syrian President Adib Shishakli was elected President of the reorganized Arab Liberation Movement political party.

Instruments of ratification of the Anglo-Libyan Treaty of Alliance and Friendship and the military and financial agreements were exchanged at Benghazi, Libya.

December 8

Foreign Minister Crown Prince Faisal of Saudi Arabia said in Jedda that his Government would welcome a US offer of good offices in Saudi Arabia's dispute with Great Britain over the border oasis of Buraimi.

December 9

The World Islamic Conference at Jerusalem concluded its meetings after passing a resolution, among others, that the defense of Palestine was the concern of every Moslem and that the conclusion of peace or dealing in any way with Israel must be considered as high treason.

It was announced that the Jordanian Government had asked the Arab League Secretariat to bring to the notice of the Supreme Defense Council a proposal that the League should establish a munitions factory in Jordan.

Iraqi Minister of Social Affairs Hassan Abd-al-Rahman returned to Baghdad from Basra after intervening in the dispute among the oil workers of the Basra Petroleum Company. The Company had agreed to most of the workers' demands, including an increase in wages and a stricter application of the Iraqi labor law.

December, 1953

December 9

The British delegation to the Big Three conference at Bermuda asserted that Britain could make no further concessions regarding wearing of uniforms by British technicians who were to remain at the Suez base, and the conditions under which in time of a world crisis British troops could be sent back to the base.

Fuad Sirag-ad-Din, former secretary of the outlawed Egyptian Wafd Party, went on trial before the Revolutionary Military Tribunal on nine counts of abuse of power and of using the Wafd to uphold the regime of former King Farouk.

December 10

King Idris of Libya opened the third session of Parliament in Benghazi. The Speech from the Throne was read by Minister of Justice Mansour Fathi al-Kekhia in the absence of Prime Minister Mahmoud Bey Muntasir, who had gone to Tripoli because of ill health. The speech surveyed Libya's progress in the previous year and referred to the Government's policy to improve the friendly relations with the Arab States and other countries. It also said the Government planned to develop internal communications and improve social and health conditions.

The Syrian Chamber of Deputies approved a draft law allocating SL650,000 to aid Jordanian defense of its border with Israel.

Sheikh Omar Salim Dammani with 60 followers raided Marwahah and engaged Aden Protectorate levies in a two and one-half hour battle in protest against the construction of a 150 mile road from Lodar, in the Awdhali country, to Nisab in the Awlaqi State. He then took refuge in Yemen. The British Agent and the Awdhali Sultan protested to the Baidha Governor, who promised to warn the Sheikh that a recurrence would lead to his expulsion from Yemen.

The Lebanese Government forbade a meeting of the Arab and Oriental Peoples' Communist Conference organized by "Peace Partisans." The Criminal Court in Tripoli sentenced Ahmad Zaki al-Afyuni, owner of the Communist organ al-Sarkha, to one years imprisonment for publishing an article considered harmful to political relations between Lebanon and Syria.

December 10

Lebanese Colonel Aziz al-Ghazi and two other high ranking army officers were arrested. It was feared they were preparing a coup to seize power.

Sir Ralph Stevenson, British Ambassador, left London to resume his post in Cairo after a six month illness.

The Egyptian Government sent a note of protest to the British Embassy alleging that British armored cars had surrounded the town of al-Qurein five days earlier and had fired several rounds of shots at it.

December 11

Declaration was made of the final results of the elections to the House of Representatives in the Sudan, giving a majority to the National Unionist Party.

December 12

Egypt authorized conclusion of a detailed customs agreement with countries of the Arab League.

Egypt passed Law 621 on the organic status of the region under Egyptian military occupation in Palestine.

Sheikh Omar Dammani stated another raid in Aden, this time on a fortress occupied by the Protectorate Levies. Six soldiers were killed. RAF planes were flown to the fortress with reinforcements.

The first official meeting of the Sudanese Governor General's Commission was held under the presidency of Mian Zain-ad-Din of Pakistan. Among other things, the question of the appointment of Senators by the Governor General was considered.

The Sudan Government's Public Relations Department gave the following official election results: National Unionist Party, 50; Umma

December 12

Party, 22; Independence, 12; Southern Party, 7; Social Republicans, 3; South Political Organization, 2; Front against Colonialism, 1.

December 13

US Vice President Nixon was received in audience by King Idris of Libya.

The Arab Economic Council concluded its meeting after approving standing regulations setting up a headquarters in Cairo, but with provision for the regular conference of the Council to be held in any of the Arab capitals, once a year or more frequently if necessary. Subcommittees of the Council had studied schemes for the establishment of a bank to help in the development of Arab economy and exploitation of the Dead Sea mineral deposits.

December 14

A trade agreement with East Germany was initialled at the Lebanese Foreign Ministry.

US Vice President Richard M. Nixon returned to Washington from a good will trip to the Far, Middle and Near East.

December 15

Abd-al-Khaleq Hassouna, Secretary General of the Arab League, submitted his resignation.

Members of the Financial Committee of the World Islamic Conference left Jerusalem for Damascus to begin collection of contributions for a special fund to "save" the Holy Places in Palestine.

After conferring with Syrian President Adib Shishakli, Jordanian Prime Minister Fawzi al-Mulki cabled the Arab League Secretariat requesting a meeting of the Arab League Political Committee to discuss Israel's request at the UN of November 23 for direct talks on border tensions.

December 15

A rebel group of 36 Conservative members of the British House of Commons introduced a motion calling for the suspension of negotiations with Egypt on withdrawing British troops from the Suez Canal Zone base and for holding the base reduced in size.

The Lebanese Ministry of Justice informed Premier Abdallah al-Yafi that it was impossible to take any legal action against Tapline (Trans-Arabian Pipeline) and the Iraq Petroleum Company to oblige them to discuss the question of increasing annual royalties to Lebanon for their pipelines in Lebanese territory.

One striker was killed and several severely injured in clashes between the Basra Petroleum Company strikers and the police in Iraq. The Iraqi Cabinet announced the imposition of martial law in Basra.

December 16

France, the US and the United Kingdom submitted a compromise resolution to the UN Security Council which, inter alia, called upon the Chief of Staff of the Truce Supervision Organization to report back to the Security Council within 90 days after investigating the existing rights of Israel and Syria in the demilitarized zone.

Iraqi Minister of Interior al-Qazaz announced that the Cabinet had imposed martial law in Basra because of "Communist intrigues" to disturb the peace.

The Iraqi Cabinet suspended nine daily newspapers for one year.

The American Independent Oil Company announced that the first shipment of oil from the new field in the neutral zone between Kuwait and Saudi Arabia would be made on January 5 to Japanese refineries.

The US, Great Britain and France submitted a draft resolution in the UN Security Council on the Jordan River project dispute between Israel and Syria. The draft resolution placed full authority for the settlement of the dispute in the hands of Major General Vagn Bennike, Chief Truce Supervisor.

December 16

Egyptian authorities intercepted the Italian freighter, Franca Maria, carrying meat from Eritrea to Israel, as it passed Port Said, and confiscated its cargo.

December 17

The Arab Ministers of Education concluded their conference. They agreed on a plan to standardize education in the Arab countries at a period of six years for primary education and a period of six years for secondary education. They approved a cultural agreement for their countries together with proposals for the encouragement of the study of Arab archeology and the popularization of Arab classical literature.

British Prime Minister Sir Winston Churchill and Foreign Secretary Anthony Eden served notice on Egypt that Great Britain would not go back on the two essential conditions for its withdrawal from the Suez Canal Zone. Eden bluntly rejected the motion of the rebel Conservatives to suspend negotiations.

Drilling and production operations were resumed in Iraq by the Basra Petroleum Company. A Company spokesman said most of the strikers had returned to work.

The Istiqlal and National Democratic Parties protested against the Iraqi Government's proclamation of martial law in Basra in connection with the oil workers' strike.

The Public Security Department announced that forty-three Egyptians had been arrested for Communist activity.

The Egyptian Ministry of the Interior said that British troops had cordoned off several areas in the Canal Zone apparently in search for Egyptian commandos and had established a check point near Firdan Bridge over the Canal.

Farid Zain-ad-Din of Syria told the UN Security Council that the three power compromise resolution introduced on December 16 merely represented the Israel position. Israel representative Abba S. Eban said he wished the resolution had been more specific; he criticized various details, but he did not attack or reject it.

December, 1953

December 18

In protest against the imposition of martial law in Basra, the Popular Front Party decided to withdraw its two members from the cabinet—Hassan Abd-al-Rahman, Minister of Social Affairs, and Abd-al-Rahman Jalili, Minister of Economy.

Soviet delegate in the UN Security Council Andrei Vishinsky severely criticized the three power draft resolution on the Syro-Israel dispute over the Jordan River project. He supported the contention of Syria and Lebanon that the project must have Syria's consent. In urging the Council to postpone voting on the draft resolution, Vishinsky threatened to use his veto power on its key paragraphs.

Charles Malik of Lebanon opposed the UN tripartite resolution and submitted an alternative draft resolution according to which any resumption of the Israel canal project would be dependent on Syria's approval. The draft asked that General Bennike should try to bring about such an agreement. It also declared that Israel's unilateral action in contravention of the armistice agreement was likely to lead to a breach of the peace.

December 20

Final results of the Sudanese Senate elections and appointments were announced, with 31 seats for the National Unionist Party and seven for the Umma Party.

Israel and Jordan agreed to allow 3,000 Christians to cross from Israel into Jordan for their yearly pilgrimage to Bethlehem.

A 1,300,000 pounds sterling Government of Aden loan was advertised in London for financing development works, including a power station, a telephone exchange and major improvements to the water supply.

December 21

Five British Labor MP's issued a statement saying that they had decided to decline the Egyptian Government's invitation to visit Egypt with five Conservative MP's, owing to the latters' decision to withdraw their acceptances.

December, 1953

December 21

The Mixed Armistice Commission fixed the blame for the killing of two Israel soldiers on December 16 on "Jordanian irregulars." Blame for the death of an Arab Legion medical officer was fixed on "Israel irregulars."

Israel reminded the UN Secretary General that he was obliged to convene a conference between Israel and Jordan under the terms of the Armistice Agreement.

King Hussein conferred the Star of Jordan, First Class, on Charles Malik and Muhammad Zafrallah Khan, Lebanese and Pakistan delegates respectively in the UN Security Council, for their services to Jordan in its dispute with Israel. He also conferred the Order of Merit on Yusuf Haikal, Jordan's Ambassador to Washington.

Soviet delegate Andrei Y. Vishinsky demanded that the Security Council, instead of adopting the three power compromise resolution, call upon Israel and Syria to reach an agreement by direct negotiation.

United States UN Delegate Henry Cabot Lodge, Jr. submitted an additional paragraph for inclusion in the three power UN proposal which stated that "nothing in this resolution shall be deemed to supersede the Armistice Agreement or to change the legal statutes of the demilitarized zone thereunder."

After consultations with his commission the Sudanese Governor appointed ten National Unionists, four Umma, one Socialist Republican, three Southerners, and two independents as members of the Senate.

December 22

After futile attempts to amend the three power compromise resolution, the Security Council adjourned further discussions until December 29.

At a private luncheon at the Pakistan Embassy, the British Ambassador to Egypt, Sir Ralph Stevenson, and Egypt's Deputy Premier, Gamal Abdel Nasser, conferred on the Suez Canal Zone dispute.

December, 1953

December 22

The President of the Iraqi Lawyers' Syndicate sent a note to Prime Minister Fadel al-Jamali asking for the abolition of martial law, declaring that the Government's action was unconstitutional.

December 23

The Israel-Jordan Mixed Armistice Commission censured Israel for a raid on a Bedouin encampment four miles inside Jordanian territory on December 21 in which one refugee was seriously wounded, and said the attack had been carried out by Israel irregulars.

December 24

Amir Sultan was appointed Saudi Arabian Minister of Agriculture and Amir Fahd Minister of Education, by Royal Decrees establishing these Ministries.

Sheikh Abdallah Ibn-Salem al-Mubarak al-Sabah, Ruler of Kuwait, visited Riyadh to congratulate Saudi Arabian King Saud on his accession to the throne.

The Mixed Armistice Commission condemned Israel for a raid on Hebron on December 21 in which a woman and two men were killed. The blame was placed on Israel irregulars.

Major General Vagn Bennike left New York for Jerusalem. Israel asked General Bennike to adjudicate a dispute with Jordan over whether illegal crossing of the armistice lines by unarmed civilians was a breach of the Armistice Agreement.

The Turkish Foreign Office announced that it had protested to Egypt over confiscation of property of the Muhammad Ali family, the former Egyptian dynastic house which included a number of Turkish citizens. The Turks contended that the confiscation was a violation of both international justice and the 1937 Turkish-Egyptian Friendship Pact.

Sixteen persons were killed and 24 injured when a homemade bomb exploded in the central market at Casablanca.

December, 1953

December 26

At the request of Jordan, the Arab League Political Committee met in Beirut to consider the former's reply to the UN Secretary General following Israel's invoking of Article XII of the Jordan-Israel Armistice Agreement.

General Augustin Guillaume, French Resident General of Morocco, declared at the funeral of 16 terrorist victims that while the authors of the crime were as yet unknown, the responsibility was clearly established.

The Sultan of Morocco published a decree providing for the punishment of terrorist acts by the criminal section of the Sherikian High Court under conditions set forth by the Ulemas (Moslem theologists).

December 27

Colonel Abd-al-Fattah Hassan, Commander in Chief of Egyptian armed forces in the Sudan, was appointed Deputy Minister for Sudan affairs, to assist Major Salah Salem.

December 29

Soviet Delegate Vishinsky charged at the UN Security Council that the US was trying to use the Syrian-Israel dispute as a lever to gain control of the Middle East's economy. The Council adjourned discussion of the dispute until January.

A meeting of the Arab League Political Committee ended in Beirut.

US Secretary of State John Foster Dulles said in Washington that he hoped there would be meetings between Israel and Jordan, in good faith on both sides, to try to eliminate some of the points of friction between the two countries.

The permanent representatives of Egypt, Iraq, Lebanon, Saudi Arabia and Syria sent a letter to the President of the UN Security Council protesting against the murder, by an Israel armed group on December 18, of Mansour Mouawad, a Lebanese physician in the service of the Jordanian army.

December, 1953

December 30

It was officially announced in Rabat that 50 persons were killed and 117 wounded in the wave of terrorism which had swept French Morocco since the deposition of Sidi Muhammad Ben-Youssef as Sultan in August of 1953.

General Augustin Guillaume, French Resident General of Morocco, stated that he had pointed out to Ministers in Paris the responsibility of "certain foreign Powers" for the outbursts of terrorism in Morocco.

Egypt and Great Britain resumed informal negotiations on the control of the Suez Canal Zone after a ten week recess.

It was learned that the Ambassadors to Pakistan, India, Britain, the United States and the Soviet Union had been called to assist in an examination by the Egyptian Government of its foreign relations.

Sir Zafrullah Khan, Pakistan Prime Minister, arrived in Damascus on a four day official visit to Syria.

December 31

One hundred fifty leaders of western Jewry decided to broaden the Zionist movement. The resolution was supported by the US delegation to Israel.

Supplement to 1953

January

4 Tangier security police said that passports of seven Moroccan nationalists who went to New York to attend the UN General Assembly sessions the previous month had been canceled and they would not be readmitted to the International Zone of Morocco because their return might disturb public order.

5 British Foreign Secretary Anthony Eden, after rejecting a plebiscite in Saudi Arabia as not "appropriate," urged King Ibn-Saud to accept arbitration.

9 Saudi Arabian King Ibn-Saud stated that Israel to the Arab World was like a "cancer to the human body and the only remedy is to uproot it just like a cancer."

13 The USSR newspaper Pravda linked the Soviet "Doctor's Plot" in which a group of Soviet doctors, most of them Jewish, had been accused of plotting to kill a number of Soviet military leaders, with a "Zionist espionage organization."

16 A treaty of friendship was concluded between Pakistan and Lebanon.

17 Egyptian Premier Muhammad Nagib, at a press conference, confirmed the statement by Colonel Nasser made the same day, but denied that the arrested men's activities had been sufficiently serious to constitute a plot against the regime.

Dhufar signed an agreement with the Dhufar-Cities Service Petroleum Corporation.

Muscat and Oman signed an agreement with Philpryor Corporation, assigned to Cities Service Company.

20 British Foreign Under Secretary Lord Reading told the House of Lords that Britain's sale of arms to Arab States was justified by the 1950 Israel-Arab armistice pact.

21 Jordan asked Egypt to tighten the Arab nation's blockade of Israel.

Commenting on the agreement between Egypt and Sudan in the House of Commons, British Foreign Secretary Anthony Eden emphasized that the provisions in the draft Self Government Statute, giving the

Supplement to 1953

January

21 Governor General special powers to protect the interests of the Southern Provinces, should not be removed "without the voice of the Southern population being heard in the matter."

22 The Charter and Statement of Aims of the Egyptian Liberation Organization were issued.

25 The US and Saudi Arabia signed a technical cooperation agreement for aid to Saudi Arabia.

26 Egyptian Premier Muhammad Nagib pledged to Egyptians that he would liberate "the Nile Valley from all foreign soldiers."

28 British Ambassador to the US Sir Roger Makins, addressing the National Press Club, urged closer coordination of the US and British policies on the Middle East to avoid "a net loss to our combined position."

29 Moroccan Resident General Augustin Guillaume of French Morocco charged that Soviet and Arab League agents had provoked the Moroccan riots in December, 1952.

February

2 In reply to questions in the British House of Commons, Selwyn Lloyd, Minister of State, said that the UK had decided in November to release a limited number of jet aircraft from among those still outstanding on the Egyptian order, in view of the change of situation caused by General Nagib's accession to power.

8 On his return to Rome, Randolfo Pacciardi, Italian Defense Minister, said that his discussions with Egyptian Premier Muhammad Nagib had been "frank, friendly and useful," expressed the opinion that the Egyptian armed forces would constitute an important element in the defense of the Middle East, and announced that Egypt would send missions to Italy to "intensify the commercial, cultural, agricultural and industrial relations" between the two countries.

9 Spain's High Commissioner for Spanish Morocco, Lieutenant General Rafael Garcia Valino, announced that he had carried out an administrative reform program giving one million Moslems in the Spanish Protectorate a voice in the solution of local problems.

Supplement to 1953

February

12 The USSR recalled its legation to Israel and broke off diplomatic relations with the Israel Government.

13 Israel Ambassador to the US Abba Eban called on all free nations to give Israel increased moral and material support because, "of all Governments in the Near East, Israel had shown devotion to democratic causes."

14 Egyptian Premier General Nagib declared in a broadcast that the "good news" of the Anglo-Egyptian Agreement would "fill the heards of the Sudanese and their Egyptian brethren with joy," and added, "This agreement inaugurates a new era in the relations between Egyptians and their brethren the Sudanese—an era of close brotherhood, permanent love and solid confidence."

US Secretary of State Dulles sent a note of congratulation to UK Foreign Secretary Anthony Eden and Egyptian Foreign Minister Mahmoud Fawzi on the occasion of the accord reached on Sudan.

16 It was reported that Egypt had nominated Lieutenant Colonel Hussein Sabr Zulficar (one of the negotiators in the Anglo-Egyptian discussions) as Egyptian member of the Governor General's Commission in Sudan, and that the two Sudanese members would be Muhammad al-Hassan Diab, a leading member of the Nationalist Unionist Party, and Ibrahim Ahmad, Vice Principal of Gordon University College, Khartoum, and a former member of the Umma Party Executive.

Israel Prime Minister David Ben-Gurion issued a statement deploring the Soviet Union's decision to break diplomatic relations over the incident in which an explosion occurred in the yard of the Soviet Legation in Israel.

18 John Foster Dulles, the US Secretary of State, told a press conference in Washington that the US Administration was considering the formation of a Middle East defense organization—as first proposed by the US and its allies more than a year before—and that Israel would be welcome as a member.

21 The UK and Libya signed an agreement for the establishment of air services between and beyond their respective territories.

Supplement to 1953

February

26 The UN and Egypt signed an agreement concerning technical assistance for a demonstration center for the blind.

March

5 Winston Churchill, the British Prime Minister, warned that Britain had to be careful not to upset the balance between Israel and the Arab countries in the Middle East by supplying them with jet aircraft.

In reference to the August, 1952 incident at Buraimi, a British Foreign Office spokesman explained that six of the eight villages in the Buraimi Oasis were regarded by the British Government as belonging to the Ruler of Abu Dhabi, who was under British protection, and that the other two, Buraimi and Hamasa, were regarded as belonging to the Sultan of Muscat.

8 It was announced that the Egyptian Government had agreed to pay the equivalent of 96,000 pounds sterling at the official rate of exchange to British residents in Cairo who were injured during the riots of January 26, 1952, and to the relatives of those who had been killed.

9 A spokesman of the Saudi Arabian Foreign Ministry in Jedda announced that his Government intended to bring the dispute with Britain over the Persian Gulf Sheikhdoms before "international organizations" on the ground that its continuance could threaten international peace and security.

10 An agreement was signed between Egypt and the US providing for technical cooperation between the Egyptian Government as represented by the Permanent Council for the Development of National Production and the American Government as represented by the United States Operations Mission to Egypt.

Mahmoud Fawzi, the Foreign Minister of Egypt, stated in Cairo that his country was more eager than Britain to see the Sudan elections take place as soon as possible.

11 The Sudanese Government Agency in London stated that Egyptian Premier Muhammad Nagib's allegations of "maltreatment" of the Southern Sudanese were apparently based on exaggerated reports of a recent incident at Aweil.

Supplement to 1953

March

19 The President of the UN General Assembly issued notes on the question of Morocco and the Tunisian problem.

23 The US State Department announced its acceptance in participating on the Mixed Electoral Commission for Sudan.

The Egyptian Minister of National Guidance announced that Egypt had rejected an American offer to take part as a "third party" in the forthcoming Anglo-Egyptian negotiations on the evacuation of the Suez Canal Zone.

The US Ambassador in Cairo issued a statement pointing out that his Government "had no wish to take part in any discussions regarding the Suez question unless asked to do so by both Egypt and Great Britain."

25 An agreement was signed by Libya and the UK regarding certain financial matters connected with the transfer of power to the Libyan Federal and Provincial Governments.

27 Israel Foreign Minister Moshe Sharett stated that Israel was not prepared to respond to any peace proposals that did not contain guarantees of the full sovereignty of Israel and of no territorial concessions.

29 A trade agreement concluded between Syria and the Hashemite Kingdom of Jordan was ratified by the Syrian Council of Ministers and was to go into effect as soon as instruments of ratification were exchanged.

31 Egypt complained to the UN that an Israel armed boat forced the Egyptian ship Samir into Jaffa and interned its crew January 4.

April

2 WHO (World Health Organization) signed a basic agreement for the provision of technical advisory assistance to Tunisia.

5 In his capacity of Military Governor of Egypt, General Muhammad Nagib extended martial law for a further 12 months as of May 1.

Supplement to 1953

April

7 An agreement was signed for US aid to Iraq for the Miri Sirf (state owned lands) land development and resettlement project.

A basic agreement was signed between the United Nations and Yemen concerning technical assistance.

An agreement was signed between Syria and the Arab League facilitating trade exchanges and transit trade between the various countries.

9 The Secretariat of the Arab League was requested to arrange for the unification of the efforts of all organizations and parties interested in North African problems.

10 The Israel Government officially announced that it had decided to proceed to the gradual release of accounts held by Arab refugees in banks in Israel. To implement this decision, it was stated that a first installment of LE1 million was being made available and that the operation would begin on March 1.

In an address before the National Press Club in Washington, Israel Foreign Minister Moshe Sharett declared that "the conclusion of a negotiated peace settlement" between Israel and the Arab States was not "merely a matter of self interest but a world necessity," although he indicated that the losses resulting from the absence of peace in the Middle East were "far greater on the Arab side" than on that of Israel.

16 Abba Eban, Israel Representative to the UN, replying to Arab attacks on Israel in the UN Political Committee the day before, said that they had revealed "hysterial anti-Jewish vehemence."

27 Israel complained to the UN Mixed Armistice Commission against Jordan that the Arab Legion had moved reinforcements on April 26 to Augusta Victoria Hospital on Mt. Scopus (Jerusalem) a demilitarized zone open only to civilians, and thus in breach of armistice terms.

Syria and Turkey signed an agreement concerning the conditions of the operation of the telegraph and telephone services between the two countries.

Supplement to 1953

April

30 A basic agreement was signed by WHO and France for the provision of technical advisory assistance to Morocco.

May

5 US Secretary of State John Foster Dulles and Harold Stassen reported to the US Senate Foreign Relations Committee on US Middle East policy.

6 General Nagib, the Egyptian Premier, speaking at a ceremony to mark the fifth anniversary of the Palestine War, warned Britain that Egypt was now ready to "pay with the hot blood of her sons for her complete independence. We are approaching a great battle . . . . We have washed our hands of Algo-Egyptian negotiations and should be grateful to Britain for it."

9 The Arab League affirmed its concern for preservation of international peace. However, it concluded that the major Arab problems were the Egyptian and Palestine cases, the settlement of which would bring Arab solidarity.

12 UK Minister of State Selwyn Lloyd made a statement to the UK House of Commons on the Anglo-Egyptian negotiations, and disclosed that there had recently been a serious deterioration in the situation in the Suez Canal Zone, where a number of British soldiers and civilians had been attacked by armed Egyptians.

14 The UNTSO Chief of Staff transmitted a report on the results of an inspection made in the demilitarized zone of Mount Scopus April 28-30, following a number of requests from Jordanian authorities.

15 Referring to his visit to Israel, US Secretary of State Dulles commented that it had been a stimulating experience to call on Israel leaders and that he had been impressed with the good will expressed by the Israel people.

18 A term of five years for the Secretary General of the Arab League was provided by the Internal Regulations of the Secretariat General.

Supplement to 1953

May

18 Israel President Itzhak Ben-Zvi made public a letter from US President Eisenhower, delivered by Secretary of State Dulles, in which the President declared he was anxious that the tensions between Israel and the Arab States be overcome so that real peace might return to the Middle East.

19 Prime Minister Nagib of Egypt declared that the Anglo-Egyptian negotiations concerning the Suez Canal had been broken off because the United Kingdom had been unwilling to admit "the principle of total and unconditional evacuation of occupation troops from our territory." He called for Egyptian unity in the matter, denounced UK Prime Minister Churchill and the British Government, and declared that the Egyptian Government would not repeat past errors.

20 US Secretary of State Dulles and Mutual Security Director Harold Stassen, after a 10 day fact finding tour of seven Middle East nations, summarized their major impressions in press reports.

21 A petition accusing the Sultan of Morocco of pursuing a policy prejudicial both to the country's interests and to Moslem orthodoxy, and demanding his deposition, was submitted to Resident General Guillaume by 287 Moroccan notables, including 250 pashas and caids out of a total 346.

The US and Egypt signed an agreement for an agricultural, forestry and fisheries program.

25 Tunisian High Commissioner Jean de Hauteclocque announced that he proposed to ask the French Government to exercise clemency towards a number of political prisoners, and particularly the interned trade union leaders.

UN Armistice Comission Chief Lieutenant General William A. Riley said that an inspection of the Mt. Scopus area, requested by Jordan, failed to show Israel violation of the 1948 demilitarization pact.

Egyptian Premier General Muhammad Nagib, in a speech, said that the British could be "easily dislodged" at any chosen moment. He emphasized however, that Egypt must wait for that moment and appealed for "moral training, sacrifice, and patience against adversity in preparation for the struggle."

Supplement to 1953

May

26 US Secretary of State Dulles indicated he felt that any move to create a Middle East defense without Arab participation would permanently injure the West's relations with Mid-Eastern nations.

28 Syria and the International Civil Aviation Organization signed a basic agreement for technical assistance.

31 The Syrian Government announced that an underground movement aimed at overthrowing the Government had been crushed.

June

7 The Sultan of Morocco issued a declaration in which he reiterated his attitude towards a Franco-Moroccan agreement, in view of the inconclusive discussions which he had had with General Augustin Guillaume during February and March on the implementation of the French reform proposals.

9 The French-Maghreb Committee, a body supported by a number of leading figures in French public and intellectual life, was formed to collect and publish objective information on the North African situation, and to work for "the re-establishment of an honorable understanding, the termination of the present emergency measures, and the application in North Africa of "the principles of the Rights of Man inscribed in the French Constitution."

10 Heads of Lebanese Chambers of Commerce meeting in Beirut adopted a resolution urging the implementation of the proposed economic union between Lebanon and Syria. A plan to this effect had been submitted by the Syrian Government several months before, and preliminary talks between the two countries involved were due to take place shortly.

14 Colonel Gamal Abdel Nasser told a Liberation Front rally held in Cairo that the Government was distributing arms throughout Egypt "in preparation for the battle to throw British troops out of the Suez Canal Zone." Nasser, who was General Nagib's aide, said, "We are training the youth and distributing arms on a nation wide scale. We are enlarging the Army to include the entire population of 22 million. We have plenty of arms, but will choose our own time so as to ensure victory."

Supplement to 1953

June

17 The Egyptian Cabinet issued a decree bringing into force the Arab League's collective security and economic pact.

18 The Israel Embassy pointed out, in reply to Arab Legion Commander Sir John Bagot Glubb's accusations of June 18, that Israel losses from Arab attacks during the year totaled 26 dead, 71 wounded, and 2 abducted, and that the Armistice Commission had condemned Jordan for 5 episodes involving loss of life within the previous two weeks.

20 Egypt filed suit against Great Britain for $100,000 damages caused when British troops demolished the village of Salak Malak May 26.

A joint statement by the leaders and members of the Syrian political parties and independent personages was addressed in a letter to Syrian Chief of Staff Adib Shishakli concerning the situation in Syria. President Hashem al-Atassi also sent a letter to Shishakli in support of the statement of the politicians and party leaders.

21 To allay possible ill feeling in neighboring countries, Gamal Abdel Nasser, Egyptian Vice Premier and Minister of the Interior, declared that opposition to the "corrupt monarchical regime in Egypt" does not imply any hostility on Egypt's part toward monarchy in any other country. "Egypt regards the constitutional changes at home as her own domestic concern."

25 In his investiture speech as a member of the Academie Francaise, Moroccan Resident General Marshal Juin paid tribute to the Pasha of Marrakech as an "ardent defender of the cause of Franco-Moroccan friendship" and denounced the "criminal methods" of the Istiqlal.

27 The Acting Prime Minister of Libya sent a communication to the UN on the question of assistance to Libya.

Jordan's Arab League charged that Israel during March and April had driven 52 Arabs from Israel into Jordan, and that 15,000 such expulsions had occurred since December, 1949.

Saudi Arabia and the US exchanged notes constituting an agreement relating to mutual defense assistance.

Supplement to 1953

June

29 Saudi Arabia and the US signed an agreement on technical cooperation in the field of public health and disease control.

July

1 It was announced that, under an agreement recently concluded between the French Government and the Mutual Security Agency, a loan of 2.638 billion francs had been granted to France for the development of the Moroccan economy, of which 1.585 billion francs would be for electric power development, 653 million francs for the Moroccan railways, and 400 million francs for improvements to the port of Nemours.

2 The Political Committee of the Neo-Destour Party issued a statement denouncing the murder of Prince Izz-ad-Din Bey, heir presumptive to the Tunisian crown, as an "odious act" which was "obviously the action of a provacateur of Franco-Tunisian understanding," and condemned it "in the strongest possible terms."

3 Major Salah Salem, the Egyptian Minister for National Guidance said that there was no question of resuming negotiations unless Britain first agreed to the main principle of Egyptianization of the military base.

4 The National Congress issued a statement addressed to the Syrian people on the eve of a referendum on the Constitution appealing for popular support and public calm.

6 Israel Minister of Foreign Affairs Moshe Sharett sent a letter to USSR Foreign Minister Molotov regarding resumption of diplomatic relations between the two countries.

7 The Secretary General of the UN sent letters to Italy and Libya regarding the economic and financial status of Libya and its UN Tribunal.

10 The US Department of State was informed by the Israel Government of its intention to transfer the Israel Foreign Ministry to Jerusalem as of July 12.

13 Egyptian Major General Salah Salem, in a radio broadcast, appealed to Egyptians to remain calm as the Government would not let itself

July

13 be provoked by the British into a battle under unfavorable circumstances. If the Egyptians must fight, however, they would do so to the last man.

15 In the House of Commons British Minister of State Selwyn Lloyd defended the measures taken at Ismailia as "entirely reasonable," criticized Major Salah Salem's statements as "unnecessarily inflammatory" and stated that Anthony Rigden, a missing British airman, had last been seen "in the company of an Egyptian officer and a notorious character who is believed to work for the Egyptian Army Intelligence, and who is known to have taken part previously in similar actions, of an anti-British character."

USSR Foreign Minister Molotov replied favorably to Israel Minister of Foreign Affairs Moshe Sharret's July 6 letter regarding the resumption of diplomatic relations between the two countries.

19 Britain's chief negotiator in the suspended Suez Canal Zone talks, General Sir Brian Robertson, said that Britain would recognize full and unqualified Egyptian sovereignty over the area where Britain's Middle East defense base was located.

An Israel Foreign Ministry spokesman said in Jerusalem that Israel firmly opposed the shipment of arms to the Arabs as long as they refused to make peace with Israel. Under the existing conditions the arms could only threaten Israel's security and thus present a threat to peace in the Middle East, the spokesman said.

21 The French Foreign Ministry announced that the French Ambassador in Tel Aviv had been instructed to protest to the Israel Government against the transfer of the Israel Foreign Ministry to Jerusalem.

25 Egyptian President Muhammad Nagib told Egyptians, during a four day "liberation" celebration, that their safety depended on the evacuation of foreign oppressors from Sudan and the Suez Canal.

28 A trade agreement was signed by Lebanon and Yugoslavia.

At his press conference, US Secretary of State John Foster Dulles expressed his regret that the Israel Government had "seen fit to move its Foreign Office from Tel Aviv to Jerusalem.

July

30 On returning to Morocco from a prolonged visit to France, the Pasha of Marrakech announced at a press conference that the number of signatories to the petition of May 21 requesting the deposition of the Sultan had reached about 350.

Italian Minister of Foreign Affairs de Gasperi addressed a letter to the UN Secretary General concerning the UN Tribunal in Libya.

A commercial agreement was signed between Egypt and Yugoslavia.

August

7 The Arab League approved an agreement for facilitating trade exchange and transit trade between the Southern Region and the UAR, Jordan, Iraq, Saudi Arabia, Lebanon and Yemen.

13 Libyan Foreign Affairs Minister Mahmoud Muntasir sent the UN Secretary General a letter concerning the maintenance of the UN Tribunal in Libya.

17 Moroccan French Resident Augustin Guillaume issued a statement claiming that he had proof that the Moroccan disorders had been provoked by the Istiqlal, and appealing to Moroccans for calmness to to enable a settlement to be reached in an objective manner.

The Sultan of Morocco appealed to the people of Morocco to maintain order and avoid bloodshed. He attributed the disorders to "the emotion felt by our loyal subjects since a sacrilegious attack was made on the unbreakable laws of Islam" and expressed his sorrow that innocent Moroccans and Frenchmen had "fallen as victims to a series of attacks on the Moroccan throne.

18 The Pasha of Marrakech, in a statement, declared that if the French Government did not "respond immediately to the wishes of the Moroccan people" France would "no longer have any place in Morocco," and that he intended to "save Morocco at whatever cost, even if I have to deny a friendship which I have so much at heart."

Press censorship was imposed in Morocco.

August

23 In the Tangier international zone the new Sultan of Morocco was recognized by the official Sherifian representative in Tangier.

24 General Augustin Guillaume, French Resident General in Morocco said that France hoped to institute within three months a program of governmental reforms offered by the former Sultan 18 months before.

25 It was officially announced that 1,023 persons were under detention in Morocco on charges ranging from murder to carrying arms. Seventy-nine political leaders had been arrested, of whom 42 had subsequently been released.

26 French Delegate to the UN Henri Hoppenot told the UN Security Council that there was no threat to international peace in Morocco that would warrant UN intervention.

Egypt and the International Civil Aviation Organization signed an agreement regarding privileges, immunities and facilities in Egyptian territory.

28 Abdallah Yafi, Prime Minister of Lebanon, announced that his Cabinet had decided to limit imports as a first step of "drastic measures" to save the country's economy.

29 The Tunisian decrees of August 27 were denounced by the Neo-Destour delegation in France, which issued a statement saying that the Party regarded as null and void "any signature extracted from the Bey by blackmail or force."

31 Syria officially offered Jordan military aid if "new Zionist violations" of the Jordan armistice lines occurred.

September

4 The new Sultan of Morocco announced by proclamation that he had decided to abolish, as being contrary to the tenets of the Islamic religion, all ceremonies which might be interpreted as a manifestation of a cult for his person.

September

7 The UN decided to retain the UN Tribunal in Libya and continue to bear the expense of it.

It was officially stated by the French authorities that eight Tunisian officials known for their French sympathies had been murdered and four seriously wounded in recent weeks.

10 An Arab League spokesman stated that the member States would attempt to "obstruct the passage" in the Libyan Senate of the Anglo-Libyan treaty, and were prepared to take over all Britain's treaty obligations, including the annual grant of 4 million pounds sterling, if Libya rejected or amended that treaty.

13 An announcement was made of Lebanon's request for an increase in oil transit royalties on oil piped from Iraq.

28 US President Eisenhower, speaking at a press conference, expressed his satisfaction with Israel's decision, which was in conformity with the ruling given by the UN representative in Palestine (General Bennike), and announced that American economic aid to Israel would be resumed.

UN Representative Abba Eban made a statement to the UN General Assembly on Israel's policies and designs in the Middle East.

October

3 After having heard the statements of the delegates of Algeria and Tunisia regarding the cases of their two countries, the UN Political Committee declared its support for their national claims and recommended that the States of the Arab League should endeavor, according to the League Pact, to safeguard their future by all possible diplomatic means.

5 Speaking in Washington, Israel Ambassador to the UN Abba Eban made it clear that Israel was concerned over a recent American offer of military assistance to the Arab States for defense against the danger of Communist aggression. He said that Israelis had reason to fear the arms would be turned against them.

October

7 Gamal Abdel Nasser, the Egyptian Vice Premier, disclosed that Britain and Egypt had reached "an understanding to a certain extent" on the future of the Suez Canal Zone. He advised, however, against being "too optimistic."

8 Muhammad Allal al-Fassi, the leader of the Moroccan Istiqlal Party, told a French press correspondent that, as "all the peaceful means by which we have tried to recover our independence have failed," the nationalist movement needed arms in order to "answer with force."

The US, during debate of the UN General Assembly's Political Committee on independence for Morocco, opposed any specific UN action on Morocco for the time being and warned against action that would provoke disorder and confusion in the protectorate.

9 A basic agreement concerning technical assistance was signed by Lebanon and the UN.

13 UNRWA and Syria signed an agreement for the rehabilitation of 85,000 refugees in Syria at a cost of $30 million.

14 Egypt and UNRWA signed a project agreement for the development of the national production of the Republic of Egypt.

15 A meeting took place in Jerusalem between Moshe Sharett, Foreign Minister, and General Bennike, UN Chief of Staff. Israel was reported to have offered temporarily to suspend work on the Jordan diversion canal so as to enable the Chief of Staff to clear up any moot points regarding ownership of Arab lands and of water rights.

Egypt denounced the treaty of 1936 with the UK.

16 A manifesto issued by the Syrian opposition parties, after the election of October 9, denounced the "dictatorial" character of President Shishakli's regime, and announced that a "Free Syrian Government" had been established in Baghdad.

17 Figures issued by the Israel Government showed that 421 Israelis had been killed and wounded by raiders from Jordan since 1950, and that 128 cases of sabotage and of mining of roads and railroads had taken place during the same period, and that the Mixed Armistice Commission

October

17 had found Jordan guilty of 159 frontier violations and Israel of only 25, during the 12 months up to June, 1953.

18 An Israel Foreign Ministry spokesman denied after a Cabinet meeting that the attack on Qibya, Jordan had been made by regular troops, and attributed it to Israel villagers who had recently been issued arms for defensive purposes.

The Umma Party of Sudan sent notes to the Egyptian Government, the British Government and the UN, asserting that the National Unionists were receiving large scale financial support from Egypt.

19 The UK and Libya exchanged notes constituting an agreement concerning the Libyan Public Development and Stabilization Agency.

20 During UN Security Council debate on the Qibya incident, US Ambassador Lodge called for a complete UNTSO investigation of the incident.

General Bennike, UNTSO Chief of Staff, replied to the observations of Israel Foreign Minister Moshe Sharett and rejected every contention on the part of the Israel Government concerning the Huleh drainage project. He noted that he had studied the relevant issues and statements of competent UN organs since 1949 and thought his position concerning the project was consistent with them.

21 The US and Jordan signed an agreement on emergency wheat aid to Jordan.

The Jordanian Embassy in London issued a statement declaring that the attack on Qibya had been carried out by Israel armed forces, and accusing the Government of Israel of attempting to "divert public opinion from their brutality" by seeking to show that the attack was part of a series of border incidents. The Embassy stated in this connection that Arab penetrations across Israel's frontier were "nothing but isolated incidents by individuals who crossed the border to their homes or farms," and that the Jordanian Government had been constantly checking such infiltrations and had punished the individuals concerned.

24 Jordanian Minister to the US Yusuf Haikal stated that he had been instructed by his Government to reject the plan concerning development

October

24 of water resources in the Jordan River Valley. He had been told that the plan presupposed cooperation with Israel and was designed to benefit that country.

26 A special report of the Director and the Advisory Commission of UNRWA was issued.

27 US Ambassador Lodge declared in the UN Security Council that, since Israel representative Ambassador Eban had stated that there would be an immediate stoppage of drainage work in the Lake Huleh region of the Israel-Syrian demilitarized zone, and had given assurances "of future cooperation with the activities of the Security Council," further resolutions aiming at an immediate cessation of this work were "quite superfluous," and the thing to do was to proceed with substantive consideration of the problem.

28 An Order in the UK amended the 1937 and 1940 Orders respectively relating to the appointment of Deputies to the Adenese Governor and to his powers and appointment.

The UN First Committee submitted its report on Tunisia.

A report on the Qibya incident was presented to the Jordanian Cabinet by three of its members.

29 Egyptian Laws 518 and 519 approved agreements between Egypt and Arab League concerning trade facilities and commercial payments.

Egyptian Laws 513 and 517 approved agreements between Egypt and the US on agricultural programs and cooperation in the educational field.

31 A trade and payment agreement between Egypt and Japan was initialled.

November

2 Syrian Ambassador Farid Zain-ad-Din, in a television interview carried over the Dumont network from Washington DC said that ". . . the US public is misled, and it is misled by Zionist special groups, because when an individual becomes a Zionist, he acquires a double loyalty;

November

2 his allegiance is divided. If he is a strong Zionist, his allegiance will certainly go to Israel, even against his very country, be it the United States of Syria or any other country . . . "

President Muhammad Nagib of Egypt revealed that Suez Canal talks with the British had reached a "critical stage" and called for new proposals from Britain.

3 Arab League Secretary General Abd-al-Khaleq Hassouna, in a speech to the Overseas Writers, warned that the US might lose its strategic bases and economic resources in the Middle East if it continued a policy of friendship for Israel.

5 Lebanon said that the Arab refugee problem could be solved only by repatriation to Israel.

8 Twelve raids by Jordanian regulars and armed infiltrators since October 17 were reported by Israel.

9 US Secretary of State John Foster Dulles expressed regret at the death of Saudi Arabian King Ibn-Saud. President Eisenhower sent a note of sympathy to Saudi Arabia and good wishes to newly crowned King Saud.

11 Saudi Arabia said that the Arab refugee problem could be solved only by repatriation to Israel.

An Israel Government White Paper called for international planning of resettlement of 600,000 refugees in Arab States, proposed using a UN reintegration fund set up in 1951 as the financial frame for a $300 million program and offered Israel contributions to the fund.

14 An agreement between Egypt and Pakistan for cooperation between the two countries in the cultural, educational and scientific spheres was signed.

16 Egyptian Prime Minister Nagib sent a formal note to the British protesting against British interference in the Sudanese elections.

17 A joint communique was issued in London and Amman stating that Jordan would receive a grant of 2,350,000 pounds sterling of which 1,600,000 pounds sterling was to be an interest free loan and up to 750,000 pounds sterling was to make up Jordan's budget deficit.

Supplement to 1953

November

20 The Egyptian Government requested the Electoral Commission to suspend all electoral proceedings in the provinces of Equatoria and Kassala, to remove all British administrators, including the Governors, from the two provinces, and to fix dates for new elections in both areas.

28 British Minister in Cairo Creswell formally protested to the Egyptian Government against the increasing number of recent incidents in the Suez and Ismailia area.

A decree was issued in the UAR to the effect that all trade dealings with Britain should be boycotted.

29 The Jordanian Parliament approved an anti-Communism law providing for severe prison sentences or forced labor for Communists and even members of the World Peace Movement and its "sympathizers."

30 The Umma Party announced that it did not recognize the validity of the Sudanese elections and that it proposed to submit evidence of Egyptian interference to the Electoral Commission.

December

1 Eric Johnston, the Personal Representative of US President Eisenhower to the Middle East, delivered an address on Jordan River development.

2 The UK Foreign Office announced that Sir Ralph Stevenson, Britain's Ambassador to Cairo, would shortly leave for Egypt to resume his post, after a six month illness and convalescence in England.

7 Selwyn Lloyd, British Minister of State, delivered a statement in the House of Commons on British policy in Sudan following the recent elections.

11 Israel Foreign Minister Moshe Sharett stated at a press conference in Jerusalem that the conclusion of permanent peace depended entirely upon the Arab States since Israel was "always ready for it."

13 The Sudanese Electoral Commission delivered its report on recent elections.

Supplement to 1953

December

14 The Jordanian Legation to the US was raised to the rank of Embassy.

16 US Ambassador to the UN Henry Cabot Lodge, in remarks to the UN Security Council, indicated US views on the Israel-Syria problem.

17 Sukumar Sen, Chairman of the International Electoral Commission for Sudan, stated during his journey back to India that if there had been any interference in the elections by Britain or Egypt it had not been noticed by or proved by the Commission.

18 Israel protested to the UN against additional Egyptian blockages to Israel use of the Suez Canal.

A note from Yemen was handed to the British Representative to the UN. Yemen claimed that air and land forces of the British led Aden levies had "intimidated" the villages of Rabeiz and Druman on the borders of Yemen and the Protectorate.

23 A judicial convention was concluded between the Syrian Republic and the Hashemite Kingdom of Jordan.

24 Lebanon and Belgium signed an agreement for air services between and beyond their respective territories.

28 Egyptian Premier Muhammad Nagib in a statement to Egyptian journalists after receiving Ernest Bevin, said that the latter had assured him that the majority of the British people favored an agreement with Egypt, and that Bevin had also pointed out that there was some fear in Britain that Egypt might attack Israel after a British withdrawal from the Suez Canal.

31 The Air Navigation Agreement of April 24, 1950, between Egypt and Greece was promulgated.

The concession granted by Sudan to the Kassala Railway Company was terminated, and ownership was passed to the new Sudanese Company.

January, 1954

January 1

The Political Committee of the Arab League, meeting in Beirut, decided that Jordan should reject Israel's invoking of Article XII of the Armistice Agreement, but should indicate its readiness to discuss border issues in the UN Jordanian-Israel Mixed Armistice Commission.

In a reply to a Yemeni note, the British Government denied Yemeni allegations that Britain had, in violation of UK-Yemeni agreements, repeatedly committed acts of aggression against unarmed villages in the area.

The first elected Sudanese parliament was officially opened at Khartoum by Governor General Sir Robert Howe.

It was reported in Benghazi that the Libyan Federal Government refused a French offer of financial help in exchange for the establishment of French military bases in the Fezzan and air bases in Tripoli.

January 2

President Nagib of Egypt issued a new basic law for the Gaza Strip giving its permanent residents and Arab refugees increased self government under Egyptian military rule.

The Bank of England released at the request of the National Bank of Egypt, 5 million pounds sterling from Egypt's blocked sterling balances.

Jordan's Chamber of Deputies approved the Arab League Political Committee's decision to reject Israel's invoking Article XII of the Armistice Agreement.

January 3

The Governor General of Sudan refused to approve the election of Ibrahim al-Mufti as Speaker of the House of Representatives on the ground that he was partisan, but confirmed the election of Ahmad Yasin.

Egyptian Minister of National Guidance Major Salah Salem announced in Cairo the resignation of Education Minister Ismail al-Kabbani, and his replacement by Abbas Ammar, former Minister of Social Affairs, who was in turn replaced by Major Kamal-ad-Din Hussein of the Revolution Council.

January, 1954

January 3

Sir Zafrullah Khan, Pakistan Foreign Minister arrived on a visit to Jordan.

January 4

Jordan rejected Israel's proposal for high level talks on the application of the Israel-Jordanian Armistice Agreement, and informed the UN Secretary General that such talks should take place in the Mixed Armistice Commission.

It was reported at UN headquarters that the Government of Jordan rejected Israel's invoking of Article XII of the Jordanian-Israel Armistice Agreement, but that the UN Secretary General decided not to make the reply public because he considered that it was not a definitive rejection and that he intended to pursue the matter further with Jordan.

Arrangements had reportedly been concluded under which West Germany would make available to Israel the equivalent of 75 marks in blocked sterling for the purchase of oil from Britain.

Lieutenant General Aziz al-Masri, Egyptian Ambassador to the USSR, arrived in Cairo for consultations.

A special meeting in Cairo of the Egyptian Ambassadors to the USSR, the US and Great Britain, together with the Egyptian members of the UK-Egyptian negotiating team, discussed the foreign policy of the Nagib Government.

A US State Department spokesman indicated in Washington that the US Government was inclined to give military aid to Saudi Arabia and Iraq, which were considered potential targets of Soviet attack, but had no immediate plan to appropriate such aid to Israel, Lebanon and Syria, since these countries were not in danger of a sudden Soviet invasion.

January 5

Ismail al-Azhari, leader of the National Unionists, was elected first Prime Minister of Sudan.

January, 1954

January 5

Sudanese Prime Minister Ismail al-Azhari nominated District Judge Babikr Awadallah as Speaker of the House of Representatives. He was unanimously elected.

Turkish Ambassador Hulusi Fuat Tugay was ordered to leave Egypt after having denounced the Nagib regime following the confiscation of property belonging to his wife, a distant relative of ex-King Farouq. He left Egypt.

The Yemeni Government informed the Egyptian Government in a note that it had protested to Britain against acts of aggression and had notified all Arab States, asking members of the Arab League to include Yemeni charges on the agenda of the League Council meeting on January 9.

January 6

Turkish Foreign Minister Fuat Koprulu announced that the Turkish Government had delivered a note to the Egyptians protesting the recent expulsion of the Turkish Ambassador. His expulsion was called unprecedented in the history of the relations between civilized nations.

It was reported in Cairo that in an interview between US Ambassador to Egypt, Jefferson Caffery, and Ahmad Hussein, Egyptian Ambassador to the US, the Egyptian Government was notified that its current tactical flirtation with a policy of neutralism endangered its chances of obtaining American economic and diplomatic assistance.

January 7

The Governor of Aden, Sir Thomas Hickinbotham, announced to a meeting of Arab rulers the proposal to federate their states within the protectorate. He said he hoped there would be two separate federations, one in the western and one in the eastern area, with a High Commissioner at the head.

January, 1954

January 8

The Arab League Council opened its twentieth session in Cairo with an agenda of some 80 items.

Prime Minister Muhammad Fadel-Jamali of Iraq stated in Beirut, where he was interviewed on his way to the Arab League Council in Cairo, that Iraq and Lebanon had agreed on a common policy for the Council meeting.

Abd-al-Rahman al-Jalili, Iraqi Minister of Economics, and Hassan Abd-al-Rahman, Minister for Social Affairs, reportedly resigned as a protest against the continuance of martial law in the Basra area.

King Faisal of Iraq and Crown Prince Amir Abd-al-Ilah, who were due to arrive in Pakistan on January 17 had reportedly postponed their visit. No reason was given.

The Yemeni Legation issued a statement accusing the British Authorities in Aden of moving levies into disputed areas and terrorizing the inhabitants.

January 9

At the Arab League Council session in Cairo, Muhammad Fadel Jamali, Prime Minister of Iraq, proposed that the eight member states unify their Ministries of Foreign Affairs, War, Education, Finance and Economics.

Ismail al-Azhari, Prime Minister of Sudan, announced his Cabinet in which he assumed the Ministry of the Interior.

US Ambassador to Saudi Arabia George Wadsworth presented his credentials to King Saud at Dhahran.

King Saud of Saudi Arabia told a visiting press delegation from Jordan that the Arab nations should sacrifice up to ten million men if necessary to wipe out Israel. He also said the Arab nations would never hold direct talks with Israel because they did not recognize Israel as a nation.

Self government began in Sudan.

January, 1954

January 10

Iraqi Prime Minister Muhammad Fadel Jamali stated that his plan for federation with other Arab states would not be fully achieved at present, but that it could begin with the unification of at least two of the states. He said that he had not presented a detailed plan to the Arab League Council but had put forward the proposal in broad outline.

Colonel Nasser, Egyptian Vice Premier, announced Egyptian support for an Iraqi scheme for Arab unity in preparation for an Arab federation.

January 11

In an official communique, the Arab League Council gave its endorsement to Egypt's efforts against the West, but without definitely committing itself to formal neutralism.

The Supreme Defense Council (composed of the Arab League's Foreign and Defense Ministers) approved a plan to supply Jordan with arms for use against Israel aggression. It also approved a project for a joint defense fund to finance military operations. The Council announced its full support for Egypt in the UK-Egyptian dispute.

The Jordanian Government reached an agreement with Hassan al-Soliman, Managing Director of the Industrial Bank of Iraq, for the opening of a branch in Amman. The administrative unit of the branch would be composed of representatives of the two Governments, the Chamber of Commerce, factory owners and the bank itself.

January 12

Amir Salman Ibn-Hamad al-Khalifah, ruler of Bahrain, visited King Saud of Saudi Arabia in Dhahran.

Street fighting broke out in Egypt between student members of the Moslem Brotherhood and the Liberation Rally.

Jordan's Ministry of Justice drafted a law providing the death penalty for pro-Israel spies.

January, 1954

January 12

Four Cairo University students, supporters of the Nagib regime, were wounded as they clashed with members of the Moslem Brotherhood.

January 13

The Political Committee of the Arab League issued a statement thanking the Iraqi Premier for submitting his proposal for Arab federation and consigning it to study by the member states. This was considered a shelving of the plan.

The meeting of the UN Security Council to act on the three power draft resolution on the Jordan River dispute, scheduled for the period January 7-15, was postponed until January 21 at the request of the three Western powers.

A new Company Law was approved by the Egyptian Council of Ministers which replaced the 1947 law as amended.

Supreme Guide Hassan al-Hudaibi of the Moslem Brotherhood and 77 other leaders of the organization in Egypt were arrested and the organization dissolved on the ground that it had engaged in political activities. Similar action was taken against Brotherhood leaders in Alexandria and Port Said.

The Israel Government announced in Jerusalem that 136 Israelis were killed in 1953 in border incidents resulting from Arab infiltration.

January 14

A nationwide state of emergency was proclaimed in Cairo as police and troops arrested about 400 more leaders of the Moslem Brotherhood. The military regime in Egypt instructed newspapers and radio stations to avoid the subject of the arrest of Brotherhood leaders.

Israel was admitted to membership in the World Bank for Reconstruction and Development and the International Monetary Fund.

An Iraqi Army mission of four officers arrived in Tripoli to undertake the training of Libyan Army officers.

January, 1954

January 15

The military regime in Egypt accused the Moslem Brotherhood of plotting a coup and engaging in disloyal negotiations with the British Ambassador in Cairo.

A British Embassy spokesman, replying to allegations of the Egyptian Government, said that no meeting had taken place between Keppel Archibald Cameron Creswell and Hassan al-Ashmawi of the Moslem Brotherhood on 10 January, that Mr. Creswell had never heard of Hassan al-Ashmawi until he read the statement, and he had never met any members of the Moslem Brotherhood.

The Political Committee of the Arab League rejected the UN summons for direct talks with Israel.

Israel protested against the reported plans of the US to grant arms to Iraq and Saudi Arabia.

January 16

The Umma and Southern Parties of Sudan asked Great Britain and Egypt to keep their officials from visiting the country during its period of self determination. They threatened to place the matter before the UN.

An Egyptian economic mission arrived in Moscow to discuss trade exchanges.

It was reported in Washington that the US State and Defense Departments were considering requests for the grant of military aid to Iraq and Saudi Arabia.

January 17

The Tunisian Neo-Destour nationalist party asked the French to release its leader, Habib Bourguiba, since he was the only man capable of reaching a serious and honest compromise with France.

A British Foreign Office spokesman described as a "contemptible allegation without any foundation whatsoever" a statement by Major Salah Salem, Egyptian Minister of National Guidance, that the Egyptian Ambassador in

January, 1954

January 17

London had been approached by the British to ask the Minister to stop his anti-British campaign in exchange for medical treatment of his son.

January 18

The trade pact with Rumania, initialed in December, was ratified by Egypt.

A French cruiser, aircraft carrier, escort ship and flotilla of destroyers left Toulon, France for Mers-al-Kebir off the coast of Algeria near the Spanish zone of Morocco, ostensibly for maneuvers.

French Foreign Minister Georges Bidault called on the Spanish Ambassador in Paris to ask for explanation of reports that religious and tribal leaders of Morocco were going to meet in Tetuan to proclaim the Imperial Khalifah, Moulay al-Hassan al-Mahdi, as "Regent and guardian of the Sherifian throne" in the absence of the deposed Sultan Sidi Muhammad Ben-Youssef. Bidault warned the Spanish Ambassador that if the meeting in any way threatened the unity of the Moroccan empire, France would defend this unity by every means at its disposal.

January 19

The Turkish Foreign Ministry reportedly received a note from Egypt concerning the expulsion of the Turkish Ambassador. The note was said to be extremely conciliatory, although not a formal apology.

Iraqi Premier Muhammad Fadel Jamali stated in the Chamber of Deputies that the Iraqi Government would welcome a Jordanian offer of unity should Jordan decide upon it. He said that Jordan had two alternatives against Israel aggression: either cooperation with Britain, or union with Iraq, and that it was up to Jordan to choose one of these.

Yemen submitted a complaint to the Arab League Council meeting in Cairo stating pressure was being used to accomplish a Federation of Aden Protectorates among the nine border states claimed by both Yemen and Aden.

The Arab League Council announced its support for Yemen in its dispute with Great Britain over alleged aggression in the Aden Protectorate area,

January, 1954

January 19

and decided to send a mission to the Imam of Yemen to assure him of the League's support by all means in its power within the framework of the Arab League charter.

The Arab League Council approved the decision of the Political Committee that relations between the League states and the Asian nations should be improved by strengthening Arab diplomatic missions in Asia and by the development of economic and cultural relations. The Council also recommended the same policy with regard to Latin American countries.

The Arab League Council decided to establish a special fund to help the peoples of North Africa. Contributions were to be collected from the Arab states and other friendly governments.

January 20

France was reported to have asked the US to intercede with Spain to end a purported plan to reject the Sultan's authority in Spanish Morocco. The French authorities posted troops in all places in its zone where disorders might occur, particularly at the frontier of the Spanish Zone.

In Libya the Wali of Tripolitania announced that the Tripolitanian Legislative Council had been dissolved by Royal Decree and that a new council would meet within two months.

The Libyan Foreign Office denied reports that Libya had refused to grant military bases to France in the Fezzan. It said France had made no such request.

France, Britain and the US submitted a revision of their UN resolution presented on December 16, 1953, omitting all references to the goal of developing the natural resources of the Syria Israel demilitarized zone. This revision was done to avoid a possible Russian veto.

The Arab League Council approved a new scheme, obviating Israel cooperation, for the development of the River Jordan as an alternative to the US scheme suggested by Eric Johnston.

January, 1954

January 21

General Nagib announced that he had discussed with the British parliamentary delegation visiting Egypt the two outstanding issues in the Canal Zone negotiations. He had said that Egypt could not agree to the corps of British technicians in the zone wearing uniforms as that would imply that it had a military character. On the question of reactivization of the zone he said Egypt did not want to be tied to Turkey in case Turkey embarked on a war of aggression.

Following a meeting of 30,000 Moroccans and 1,500 of their leaders at Tetuan, a petition signed with 430 names was presented to the Spanish High Commissioner, General Rafael Garcia Valino. The petition was reported to protest the manner in which former Sultan Ben-Youssef was deposed, refused to recognize the authority of the new Sultan, asked for the temporary separation of the Spanish zone and proposed that the Khalifah be given full and independent sovereign prerogatives.

Moroccan Sultan Sidi Muhammad Ben-Moulay Arafa's Council of Ministers addressed a note of protest to Paris on the Tetuan meeting. The note said that the present agitation... probably resulted from the pressure of local Spanish Authorities, and asked the French Government to call the attention of the Spanish Government to this situation and to its present and future consequences.

General Valino, the High Commissioner of Spanish Morocco, stated in a reply to the notables that he would send their note of demands to General Franco. He declared that the two dangers in the world were Communism and colonialism. France, he felt, had acted against its obligations and Spain's advice and had ignored Spain's point of view. The French, according to General Valino, have said that Spain's attitude was dictated by the desire for material and territorial advantages in Morocco. General Valino denied this. He claimed that the petition had the support of all the inhabitants of Spanish Morocco.

January 22

General Valino endorsed and sent to Spain the January 21 petition of the Spanish Moroccan notables. He also announced an amnesty for all prisoners in Spanish Morocco serving sentences of less than two years to mark the occasion.

January, 1954

January 22

In a reply to the Spanish High Commissioner in Morocco, General Franco of Spain expressed his utmost satisfaction at the Tetuan demonstration and his feelings of unity with the Spanish Moroccan people.

In line with the Arab League's decision to tighten the blockade against Israel, Egypt placed new restrictions on ships passing through the Suez Canal en route to the Gulf of Aqaba.

The French Government protested to the Spanish Foreign Ministry against the action of Moroccan leaders in the Spanish Zone. The note asked Spain to cooperate to preserve unity throughout Morocco and to avert dangers that could arise from the position taken by the Arab leaders. French Resident General Augustin Guillaume in Rabat was asked to inform the Sultan of the French Government's action and to assure him that it would take all necessary steps to protect the unity and sovereignty of Morocco.

It was announced that the British and Egyptian Governments had exchanged notes of protest regarding recent Suez Canal Zone incidents.

The USSR vetoed a Western sponsored Security Council resolution on the Israel water power project which called upon the Chief of Staff of the Truce Supervision Organization to explore the possibilities of reconciling the Israel and Syrian interests involved in the dispute over the diversion of the Jordan waters.

UN Secretary General Dag Hammarskjold announced that he would be willing to take part in an Israel-Jordanian conference. He said that he was legally bound to call the conference since Israel invoked Article XII of the Jordanian-Israel General Armistice Agreement.

January 23

On the first anniversary of the proclamation of the formation of the Liberation Rally, President Nagib decried imperialist efforts to keep Egypt tied to an agricultural economy and announced that his regime would undertake great projects to stamp out poverty through industrialization.

January, 1954

January 23

Sir Ralph Stevenson, British Ambassador to Egypt, called on Foreign Minister Mahmoud Fawzi to discuss with him the growing number of serious attacks on British troops in the Suez Canal Zone area.

General Valino, Spanish High Commissioner in Morocco, informed the press that among the recommendations of an interministerial commission which had been studying the problems of the Spanish Protectorate was the creation of a free port zone at Ceuta as a counter influence to the free ports at Tangier and Gibraltar.

King Hussein of Jordan and King Saud of Saudi Arabia met near the Jordanian-Saudi Arabian border to discuss common problems.

January 24

Israel sought the intervention of the UN, US, Great Britain and other countries as well as the International Red Cross on behalf of the three Israelis arrested in Baghdad, Iraq, when a Tehran-bound plane from Cyprus made a forced landing.

At the request of the Israel Government, the Netherlands Government intervened in behalf of one of the three Israelis arrested in Baghdad when a Tehran-bound plane from Cyprus made a forced landing at the Iraqi capital.

Sultan Sidi Muhammad Ben-Moulay Ben-Arafa, in a proclamation addressed to all Moroccans, warned that disloyalty to him would mean expulsion from the Moslem community. The Sultan added that the Makhzen in the French Zone had gone on record as condemning the movement in the Spanish Zone.

The Arab League Political Committee called on its member nations to support Spanish General Franco in his disputes with France over Morocco and with Great Britain over Gibraltar.

Syria's delegate to the Cairo Conference of the Arab Regional Bureau for the Arab League Boycott of Israel stated that Arab states would be urged to conclude trade agreements with Turkey to minimize Israel's chances of trade with that country, and that the British firm of Imperial

January, 1954

January 24

Chemical Industries would be given until March to close its establishments in Israel.

It was reported from Jerusalem that the Israel Cabinet declared that because of the UN Security Council's failure to reach a decision on the Syrian-Israel dispute, Israel might resume work on the Huleh project. The reasoning given was that Israel had agreed to stop work pending a Council examination of the issues involved, that the Soviet's veto had ended that examination and the situation reverted to what it had been before the Council was brought into the picture.

Moshe Sharett formed a coalition government in Israel.

January 25

Ex-Sultan of Morocco Sidi Muhammad Ben-Youssef was flown from Corsica to Central Africa. It was reported that from there he would be taken to an island, probably in the Pacific, for exile.

January 26

US Minister to Libya Henry S. Villard handed over a gift of 2,200 tons of wheat from the US for relief of drought victims in Libya.

It was announced in Amman that a conference of Syrian, Jordanian and Saudi Arabian representatives successfully concluded talks on the reopening of the Hejaz railway to serve the three countries. The Damascus-Medina line was destroyed during World War I.

Premier Fawzi al-Mulki of Jordan was reported to have announced that the Arab countries would stop giving money to the Jordanian National Guard as of April 1954. Last year the Military Advisory Committee, the Supreme Defense Council and Council of the Arab League voted large sums to the Guard.

It was announced that the Arab League had invited General Franco of Spain to visit the Arab states. The invitation was accepted.

January, 1954

January 29

In a review of affairs in the colonial and dependent areas, the Cominform press stated that the people of Tunisia were struggling against colonial oppression and exploitation and for their national independence.

January 30

In Egypt the revolutionary tribunal sentenced Fuad Sarraq-ad-Din, former Wafd minister, to 15 years imprisonment on charges of abuse of office, corruption and working against the interests of Egypt.

January 31

President Muhammad Nagib of Egypt said that he considered a US defense pact with Pakistan would threaten to isolate the Arab nations and drive a wedge between them and the countries of Asia.

The Syrian Government announced that it had regained control over the dissident areas of the country.

It was reported from Cairo that American Ambassador Jefferson Caffery and British Charge d'Affaires Robert Hankey met with Egyptian Foreign Minister Mahmoud Fawzi and protested against the Egyptian embargo on Israel bound goods through the Suez Canal.

January, 1954

January 27

It was announced in Syria that ten political leaders were arrested. It was stated that they declined to reorganize on the Government sponsored plan for the Jordan River and were carrying on activities against the regime.

Israel called for Security Council hearings on Egypt's refusal to allow Israel bound ships to pass through the Suez Canal. It maintained that this was a violation of the Armistice Agreement and of the resolution of September 1951.

The Political Committee of the Arab League concluded its Beirut meeting with the completion of 12 items of business.

The Arab League Council issued a statement condemning the British move to organize a Federation of Aden Protectorates and urged the Sultans, Amirs and Sheikhs who had accepted the federation scheme in principle to refuse to believe imperialistic claims.

The Arab League Council approved the actions of The Political Committee and declared that its session would be continued on February 20.

January 28

President Adib Shishakli of Syria announced that martial law had been imposed in a number of areas. He said that the Syrian Army was engaged in maintaining the security of the country.

Britain made known its support of a pact between Turkey and Pakistan which may have also included Iraq.

The Mixed Armistice Commission condemned Jordan for the death of an Israel guard on January 27, and called on the Jordanian Government to prevent such occurrences.

January 29

The Israel delegation at the UN made public a memorandum which it submitted to the Security Council detailing alleged violations of the Council's 1951 resolution and of the Armistice Agreement between Israel and Egypt.

February, 1954

February 1

A joint Syrian, Lebanese, Egyptian and Jordanian mission visited Iraq to persuade Iraq not to join a pact with Turkey.

Forty-four persons were indicted on charges of plotting to establish a Communist regime in Egypt. The defendants were to be tried by the Supreme Military Court.

February 2

The Jordanian Cabinet approved a decision of the Jordanian Defense Council to instruct anti-aircraft batteries to open fire on any aircraft flying over Jordanian territory without permission.

A draft trade agreement with Jordan was approved by the Iraqi Chamber of Deputies.

The Deputy from Basra urged in the Chamber of Deputies that Iraq should be the dove of peace between the Syrian nationalist politicians and Syrian President Adib Shishakli. Replying to questions about secret Arab League decisions, Prime Minister Muhammad Fadel Jamali said Iraq was annually losing ID12 million as a result of preventing the flow of oil to Haifa, but that full cooperation among the Arab countries was indispensable. He also declared that Iraq aimed at the union of the Arab countries and would extend its hand to any Arab country which wished cooperation and union.

February 3

British Minister of State Selwyn Lloyd disclosed in the UK House of Commons that the supply of British war material to Egypt had been banned because of the latter's hostile attitude toward Britain.

The Conorada Company of America (a combination of the Ohio Company, the Continental Company and the Petroleum Corporation of America) signed an agreement with the Egyptian Government for exploration rights in Egypt's Western Desert.

February 3

The Riyadh agreement on the repair of the Hejaz Railroad was published in Amman. It provided that Jordan, Syria and Saudi Arabia should make available all possible assistance and exempt the railway administration from dues.

Egypt asked the UN Security Council to consider the al-Auja incident of September 28, 1953 in which Egypt charged that Israel had set up fortifications in the demilitarized zone.

General Bennike, Chief of Staff of the Palestine Truce Supervision Organization, called on Syrian President Adib Shishakli in Damascus to discuss the Syrian complaint before the UN Security Council regarding Israel's attempt to divert the Jordan waters.

February 4

After a long procedural wrangle, the UN Security Council decided to adopt an agenda combining Israel's charges of Egyptian armistice violation by the Suez Canal blockade and Egypt's claim that Israel violated Egypt's border in October of 1953.

In a speech in London Israel Ambassador Elath expressed apprehension regarding the stocks of arms and war materials which he said Egypt was accumulating.

February 5

Israel's UN Representative Abba S. Eban denounced before the UN Security Council the Egyptian blockade on ships bound for Israel as piracy. He called upon the Security Council to impose sanctions against Egypt unless the restrictions were immediately removed. Ahmad Ghalal-ad-Din Abd-al-Razzak, Egyptian UN Representative, said that Egypt was merely stopping shipments of food for the Israel Army.

Syrian authorities closed the frontier with Lebanon for 24 hours. It was understood in Beirut that this was in retaliation for the campaign conducted by a number of Lebanese newspapers against the present Syrian regime and the conference of Druze leaders held in Beirut.

February 5

The Syrian Government announced that the Iraqi Military Attache in Damascus was persona non grata and asked for his recall. He was accused of having carried out activities outside the framework of his official work and inconsistent with the present situation in Syria.

Following the closing of the Syrian-Lebanese border, Lebanese President Chamoun asked Abd-al-Aziz Ibn-Zaid, Saudi Arabian Ambassador to the Levant States, to mediate with President Adib Shishakli of Syria for its reopening.

As a reprisal for Syria's request for the withdrawal of the Iraqi Military Attache in Damascus, the Iraqi Government ordered the Syrian Military Attache to leave Iraq.

The Spanish reply to the French note of January 22 which was delivered at the French Embassy in Madrid stated that the protest to the Spanish Government against the action of Moroccan leaders in the Spanish Zone in the note constituted a political internal act and the public expression of the inhabitants' convictions.

The Lebanese Council of Ministers decided to buy the Franco-Belgian-Beirut Electricity Company for LL23, 500, 000. The Government had previously seized the Company's properties on the ground that it had failed to carry out its contract.

February 6

General Guillaume, French Resident General in Morocco, said in a speech at Marseilles that the reforms introduced after the accession of the Sultan had three aims: decentralization of power, the reorganization of justice and the closer association of Moroccans and the French in public affairs.

February 7

The Government of Israel announced that there was a relaxation of restrictions on the movement of Arabs in the Galilee area. The Ministry of Defense explained that the step had been taken because of improved security conditions in the area.

February 7

It was learned that the Government of Egypt received a note from Turkey refusing to accept the reasons given by Egypt for the expulsion on January 4 of Fuat Tugay, the Turkish Ambassador to Egypt.

February 8

Jordan reportedly informed the UN Secretary General that it would not agree to direct talks with Israel on the armistice question. UN Secretary General Hammarskjold declined to make the new reply public.

Egypt announced that merchant ships would not be blacklisted for calling at Israel ports if they did not touch Arab ports during the same voyage.

February 9

A Royal Decree was issued approving the agreement concluded between Jordan and the US Point Four Program for the year ending June 30, 1954.

General Francisco Franco of Spain, speaking to a delegation of Spanish Moroccan notables in Madrid, declared that the Spanish Zone of Morocco would continue under the sovereignty of the Khalifah appointed by the former Sultan and assisted by the Spanish High Commissioner.

A Lebanese court sentenced nine Arab refugees on charges of spying for Israel.

February 10

It was announced that the Egyptian National Production Council had reached an agreement with the West German firm of Demag, from Duisberg, for building an iron and steel works near Helwan, Egypt. The works would be run by an Egyptian company with a capital of LE10 million of which 51 percent would be Egyptian.

The Parliament of Syria unanimously condemned the plan for Arab federation submitted to the Arab League by the Iraqi Premier.
The Secretary General of the Foreign Ministry expressed

February 10

Syria's desire to restore economic unity with Lebanon and urged the Lebanese Government to oppose the partisans of separation.

Egyptian National Guidance Minister Salah Salem said that Egypt favored some sort of unity of the Arab states, but that Egypt had not offered any assistance to Syria in order to not interfere with the domestic affairs of any Arab nation.

It was reported in Washington that Saudi Arabia turned down an American offer to provide weapons for the expansion and modernization of Saudi Arabia's Armed Forces. King Saud was said to have notified the American Ambassador that he considered unacceptable the draft of a military aid agreement proposed by the US.

February 11

Iraqi Prime Minister Muhammad Fadel Jamali flew to Jordan with a private message from King Faisal to King Hussein and for conversations with Jordanian leaders concerning Iraqi-Jordanian relations.

The Spanish Government, in reply to a French inquiry, called the Arab meeting at Tetuan on January 21 an act of internal policy and a public expression of a state of mind of Spanish Moroccan inhabitants.

At a meeting of the French National Assembly's Foreign Affairs Committee, Under Secretary for Foreign Affairs Maurice Schumann called the Spanish reply to the French inquiry inadmissible.

February 12

Instruments of ratification of the trade agreement signed by Lebanon and Eastern Germany on December 14 were exchanged at the Foreign Ministry in Lebanon.

Addressing a crowd in Khartoum on the first anniversary of the UK-Egyptian Agreement on Sudan, Sudanese Prime Minister Ismail al-Azhari thanked Egypt for its part in fulfilling the agreement and warned Britain against occupying other people's lands against their wishes. He

February 12

declared that the freedom of Sudan would not be complete until foreign troops evacuated the Suez Canal Zone.

February 13

The Council of Ministers of France reaffirmed the Government's determination to safeguard the unity of the Sherifian empire and the sovereignty of the Sultan of French Morocco. The Council also emphasized the importance of the reforms envisaged in French Morocco and expressed the hope that they would be hastened as much as possible.

Emile Bustani, a prominent Lebanese deputy, arrived in Egypt as personal envoy of Lebanese President Chamoun to discuss the Syrian-Iraqi tension with Egyptian leaders.

Premier Jamali of Iraq flew to Beirut for conversations with Lebanese President Chamoun at the latter's request. It was reported that Jamali agreed that President Chamoun should use his good offices to remove friction between Iraq and Syria.

Iraqi Prime Minister Jamali stressed in conversations with Jordan's King and Prime Minister that the Iraqi plan for federation depended entirely on the will of Jordan and that Iraq was prepared to cooperate in economic, military or political spheres to the extent that Jordan desired.

February 14

Iraqi Prime Minister Jamali returned home after short visits to Jordan and Lebanon. It was stated that he had visited Beirut at the invitation of Lebanese President Chamoun who wished to discuss ways in which Lebanon could use its good offices to alleviate Syrian-Iraqi tension. The purpose of the Iraqi Prime Minister's visit to Amman was to reassure King Hussein that Iraq's federation proposals implied no threat to the Jordanian throne.

February 15

King Idris of Libya accepted the resignation of the Muntasir Cabinet of Libya. The task of forming a new government was entrusted to Sayyed Muhammad al-Saghisli, Acting Chief of the Royal Cabinet.

It was announced in Cairo that the Revolution Council ordered the Prosecutor General to release the former Saadist Premier, Ibrahim Abd-al-Hadi, because of the prisoner's health.

Abd-al-Hamid Ghaleb, member of the Egyptian delegation to the UN Security Council, said that Egypt had a right to search Israel bound ships passing through the Suez Canal and the Gulf of Aqaba. He declared that the Israel complaint against the restrictions lacked seriousness.

Abba Eban, speaking for Israel, asked the UN Security Council President to circulate the text of the Egyptian Decree of 1950, restricting the shipping to Israel of strategic supplies, and the amendments in 1953 extending it to comprise food stuffs.

Engineers from Egypt, Syria, Jordan and Lebanon, preparing a new Arab League plan for exploitation of the Jordan River waters, conferred in Amman and then left to inspect the terrain which would be affected by the scheme.

Prime Minister Muhammad Fadel Jamali of Iraq arrived in Amman to discuss the misunderstanding arising from his proposal for Jordanian-Iraqi union.

Lieutenant Colonel Gamal Hammad, Egyptian Military Attache to the Arab states, arrived in Baghdad to discuss the tension between Iraq and Syria. He carried a personal message from Egyptian President Nagib to Iraqi Premier Jamali.

February 16

A trade agreement between Yugoslavia and Jordan, providing that each party purchase commodities from the other to the amount of not less than ID100,000, was signed in Amman.

A special committee of the Arab League Economic Council met in Beirut to discuss a proposal by Lebanon and Syria that a joint Arab defense

February 16

fund be established from contributions taken from national budgets and oil royalties.

The Iraqi Council of Ministers decided to withdraw Iraqi nationality from 70 Jews who failed to return to the country from abroad within the prescribed time.

February 17

An Arab League mission left Cairo for Yemen to confer with King Ahmad about his complaint of British aggression in the area south of Yemen.

The Egyptian Government newspaper al-Gumhuriyah stated that Egypt favored simultaneous federation of the Arab states and was opposed to the formation of any blocs within the Arab League.

Iraqi Foreign Minister Abdallah Bakr presented to the Chamber of Deputies the Government's position on the federation plan sponsored by Iraqi Prime Minister Jamali in the Arab League Council. He denied that the Government had said the project would be carried out as soon as it was approved, but did assert that the Government would continue to advocate the idea as such until the Arabs were finally united.

Lebanese Prime Minister Abdallah Yafi submitted his resignation after winning an 18-16 vote of confidence in Parliament, a vote which he considered too slim a margin.

After a three hour meeting between the Lebanese President and the Cabinet, the Prime Minister announced that the President had refused to accept their resignation.

February 18

In Libya Sayyed al-Saghisli announced the members of his Cabinet in which he held the offices of Prime Minister and Acting Foreign Minister.

The first of 45 US stratojet bombers arrived at Sidi Slimane airfield near Rabat, Morocco.

February 19

UN Secretary General Dag Hammarskjold called on Israel and Jordan to meet in Jerusalem to try to solve the problems of keeping the truce between the two countries; he offered to act as chairman of the conference. This was in response to the invoking by Israel of Article XII of the Israel-Jordanian Armistice Agreement.

February 20

Group Captain Sabri issued a statement deploring the use of the radio to lash out at the Egyptian Government and attacking the Governor General's officials for the delay in setting up the Sudanization Committee. He exonerated the two Sudanese members of the Governor General's Commission from any blame.

King Faisal of Iraq signed an economic agreement with Jordan.

The Egyptian Government newspaper al-Gumhuriyah called the proposed Turkish-Pakistani Pact a conspiracy. It declared that the West would not succeed in luring any Middle Eastern Arab state into joining the open agreement between Turkey and Pakistan.

A Sudanization Committee was appointed in Sudan to affect nationalization of some industries there.

The leaders of both the left wing National Democratic Party and the right wing Nationalist Istiqlal (Independence) Party of Iraq submitted statements to the Prime Minister opposing Iraq's adherence to the Turkish-Pakistani Pact.

February 21

The US Government announced through its Point Four Program that it would offer Jordan $10 million from the fund for special economic aid for Middle Eastern countries.

February, 1954

February 22

Wing Commander Abd-al-Latif Baghdadi, Egyptian Minister of War and Marine, said in a press interview that it would not be in the interest of Egypt or any other Arab country to join a Turkish-Pakistani alliance or any other alliance before achieving full freedom and independence.

Wing Commander Abd-al-Latif Baghdadi, Egyptian Minister of War and Marine, stated in Cairo that Egypt would soon start a policy of non-cooperation with Britain which would paralyze operations in the Suez Canal Zone.

The subcommittee of the Arab League Economic Council ended a week long meeting in Beirut after recommending the establishment of an Arab Fund to finance the creation and maintenance of a unified Arab army. Money for the fund would be raised from oil royalties received by some Arab countries and from other sources.

Sultan Pasha al-Atrash and 35 of his followers fled from Syria and asked Jordan for political asylum. They were arrested and held for a decision on their status. Sultan Pasha was accused by Syrian President Adib Shishakli of plotting with opposition leaders to overthrow the Syrian regime.

February 23

Sultan Muhammad Shiqqi of Lower Yafai was interrogated at Baida by the Arab League mission investigating the Yemeni complaint for the Arab League Political Committee. Speaking for 11 regional leaders, he told the mission that there had been no attempt by the Adenese Government to influence their choice of joining the proposed federation.

Lebanese President Chamoun accepted the resignation of Abdallah Yafi's Government.

February 24

UN Secretary General Hammarskjold announced that Dr. Ralph Bunche would head a new committee to appraise both the TVA Jordan Valley Project and the Yarmuk Plan (devised by Jordan and Syria).

February, 1954

February 25

A rebellion of the Syrian Army forced President General Adib Shishakli to resign. He fled to the Saudi Arabian Embassi in Beirut. Insurgents controlled Aleppo and most of the southern part of the country. The Aleppo radio accused Adib Shishakli of suppressing education, falsifying the returns of last October's parliamentary elections and arresting students and lawyers.

The Arab League Technical Committee meeting in Beirut sent to Arab League member states its report on the TVA Jordan plan submitted to the Arab Governments by Eric Johnston. Among other objections to the plan, the report stated that it overlooked the possibility that Israel might be able to use wells for irrigating the northern Galilee area.

The Syrian Constitution of September 5, 1950 was readopted following the overthrow of the Shishakli regime.

Egyptian Minister of National Guidance Salah Salem announced that President Nagib had resigned the presidency three days before after being denied absolute autocratic authority by the Revolutionary Command Council. Colonel Gamal Abdel Nasser, Vice President and Vice Prime Minister, succeeded as Prime Minister and head of the Revolutionary Command Council. The presidency was to remain vacant until new elections could be held. General Nagib was kept under guard as a precaution against a popular demonstration. Colonel Nasser assured the Western powers that the new regime would not swing the country away from the West.

February 26

Major Salem, Egyptian Minister of National Guidance, said that the Revolutionary Command Council relieved General Nagib of his posts as President and Premier of Egypt because of a threat of assassination.

The Revolutionary Command Council named two new Vice Prime Ministers who were Abd-al-Galil al-Omari, former Finance Minister, and Wing Commander Gamal Salem, present Communications Minister.

The Sudanese Cabinet issued a statement regretting the events which led to General Nagib's resignation in Egypt but declaring that fraternal relations would continue.

February, 1954

February 24

UN Secretary General Hammarskjold stated that he planned to set a date for an Israel-Jordanian conference in Jerusalem unless the Jordanian Government came forward and agreed to a specific date.

The Jordanian Cabinet referred the third cable from the UN Secretary General to several Arab governments.

In reply to the UN Secretary General's proposal for an Israel-Jordanian conference, the Israel Government agreed to Jerusalem as the site for the conference and suggested that meetings be held alternately in the Israel and Jordanian parts of the city. It welcomed Hammarskjold's offer to preside, but expressed the hope that the parties themselves would overcome problems of procedure and agenda and then agree to assume direct responsibilities for the conference.

Iraqi Premier Muhammad Fadel al-Jamali stated that Iraq would buy arms from the West but would withhold any decision to side with the West in a war until the occasion arose. He said that Iraq was not invited to join the Western sponsored Turkish-Pakistani alliance but would consider such an invitation if received in the light of Iraq's interest. Replying to Egyptian press criticism of Iraq in connection with the alliance, the Premier said that like the other Arab states and everyone else, Iraq would sign any pact it liked when it saw fit to do so.

Anthony Head, British War Minister, stated in London that 16 British subjects were killed in Egypt in the past 13 months.

In a speech, Tunisian President Habib Bourguiba stated that France would not be able to retain its African world position if it did not refrain from violence toward a peaceful people who would not allow themselves "to be swallowed up by force nor by trickery." He stated that the Africans had proved themselves ready to deal freely with France in measures where their dignity was spared and their sovereignty respected.

Despite the demands of the Syrian Ministry of the Interior to hand Sultan Pasha al-Atrash and his followers over to the Syrian Government, Jordan granted them asylum on condition that they would not engage in political activities.

February, 1954

February 26

Abdallah Yafi formed a new Government of ten Ministers in Lebanon.

It was announced in Damascus that Maamoun Kuzbari, President of the Syrian Chamber of Deputies, assumed temporarily the President's office in accordance with the Constitution.

Army elements loyal to ousted Syrian President Adib Shishakli continued to control the capital city of Damascus. Maamoun Kuzbari, temporary President, pledged to uphold the constitution and promised elections for a new President within two months.

US President Eisenhower announced a decision to give US military assistance to Pakistan in order to strengthen the defensive capabilities of the Middle East.

February 27

At the end of a day long meeting among the representatives of the factions within the junta led by Major Khaled Mohi-ad-Din and Colonel Gamal Abdel Nasser, an announcement was made to the press by Major Muhammad Rabiah that General Nagib would come back to power as President of the Parliamentary Egyptian Republic. Street crowds shouted "Down with Salem!"

General Nagib, speaking from his home, told correspondents that the current dissension in Egypt had been "a tempest in a teapot." Colonel Nasser was quoted as saying that the events of the few previous days had been the "work of the devil" and that the Revolutionary Command Council would heal the breach and go on as before.

Damascus was placed under strict curfew after a day of demonstrations against the supporters of former Syrian President Adib Shishakli's regime. Sixteen persons were killed when demonstrators set fire to government buildings.

Ex-President Adib Shishakli of Syria left Beirut for Riyadh, Saudi Arabia.

Because of disagreement in the allocation of posts, the Yafi Cabinet in Lebanon resigned.

February, 1954

February 28

Lebanese President Camille Chamoun requested Abdallah Yafi to form a cabinet.

The Governor of Aden received an Arab mission headed by Muhammad Abd-al-Khaleq Hassouna, Secretary General of the Arab League, and replied to objections expressed by the delegation concerning federation in the Protectorate.

King Hussein of Jordan arrived in Iraq for a four day state visit.

Hashem Atassi was proclaimed Syrian President after an understanding was reached between the northern rebels and the pro-Shishakli army elements in Damascus. Maamoun Kuzbari, temporary President, announced his resignation over Radio Damascus.

Revolutionary Council spokesman Major Amin Chaker said immediately after General Nagib's speech that calling a constituent assembly and general elections were matters that concerned the ruling Egyptian Government and Revolution Council.

In a display of unity, General Nagib attended a Cabinet meeting and accompanied Egyptian Prime Minister Nasser on a visit to wounded demonstrators in a hospital.

Dissident members of the Egyptian Revolution Council restored General Nagib to power as President through a show of force, without actual violence. Colonel Abdel Nasser remained Premier.

General Nagib of Egypt was publicly reconciled with Colonel Abdel Nasser. Addressing a crowd before the presidential palace, Nagib announced a plan to establish immediately a provisional parliament composed of representatives of the professional, social and political communities.

March, 1954

March 1

The formal opening of the Sudanese Parliament was postponed for ten days when riots broke out between crowds welcoming Egyptian President Nagib and Umma Party followers. The Mahdist demonstrators were against the Government's policy of unity with Egypt.

Egyptian President Nagib and British Minister of State Selwyn Lloyd informally discussed the Suez Canal base issue when they met in Khartoum for the opening of the Sudanese Parliament.

King Hussein of Jordan visited with King Faisal during his stay in Iraq.

Hashem Atassi who took over the Syrian presidency from Maamoun Kuzbari, who had held it for two days, was enthusiastically greeted by crowds in Damascus on his arrival from Homs. A caretaker Cabinet pending elections (promised within two months) was sworn in.

The tacit renewal of a trade agreement of December 31, 1951, was signed between Iraq and Italy for a further period of one year.

Abdallah Yafi of Lebanon announced the formation of a new Government (the third attempt within six days) composed entirely of Independents.

March 2

President Nagib of Egypt said in a broadcast that the disorder in Sudan was in the interests only of Sudan's imperialist enemies who might use it as a pretext to remain in Sudan. He suggested that sedition in Sudan might be inspired by former British administrators to show Sudan as disunited.

In accordance with a Security Council resolution adopted on November 24, 1953, Major General Vagn Bennike, Chief of the Truce Supervision Organization, reported to the Security Council. He said that during the three month period tension between Israel and the Arab states had increased. During that time Israel had filed 294 complaints against Jordan while Jordan had filed 211 against Israel.

In Syria the Army returned to its barracks and the curfew was lifted.

March, 1954

March 2

His Highness Sidi Muhammad Lamine Pasha Bey invested a new Cabinet of eight Tunisians and five Frenchmen for Tunisia, with Muhammad Salah M'Zali as Prime Minister.

March 3

The Sudanese Government denied reports of a rift between pro-Egyptian Sudanese Premier Ismail al-Azhari and British Governor General Sir Robert Howe.

British Foreign Secretary Anthony Eden said in the UK House of Commons that a very large measure of responsibility for the riots in Khartoum must rest upon those who in the recent past sought to raise the emotional temperature in Sudan.

March 4

The Arabian American Oil Company reportedly discovered an oil pool at Uthmaniyah, Saudi Arabia, estimated to contain as much as all known US oil reserves (28 billion barrels).

The Neo-Destour Party in Tunisia commented on recent reforms by saying that the principle at the heart of the French-Tunisian dispute had not been settled and it regretted that the reforms did not protect the country against the evil consequences of co-sovereignty and the dangers of the integration of Tunisian national institutes in French ones. It pointed out that they did not effectively restore Tunisian sovereignty or secure the democratic conduct of public affairs.

Sidi Muhammad Lamine Pasha Bey approved a program of administrative reforms which gave Tunisians greater control over domestic affairs. Under this program the new Premier, Muhammad Salah M'Zali, assumed the full powers and responsibilities of that office, thus placing a Tunisian at the head of the country's affairs for the first time.

Following a conference with Egyptian President Nagib and Colonel Abdel Nasser, former Prime Minister Ali Maher announced that Egypt would elect a civilian constituent assembly within three months to take over from the military regime. This announcement was confirmed by Colonel

March, 1954

March 4

Abdel Nasser who said, however, that political parties would not be allowed to exist until after the adoption of a constitution.

The Egyptian Minister of Commerce announced an agreement between the Government and the Shell and Socony Vacuum Oil companies providing for a new price agreement to replace that of 1951 which was repudiated by the Wafd Government.

Syrian Premier Assali expressed approval of the announced military alliance between Turkey and Pakistan.

March 5

About 70 percent of the shops in the Arab quarter of Tunis closed in protest against the inadequacy of the new French reforms for Tunisia.

The Syrian Government dropped border restrictions with Lebanon.

Premier Yafi's new Government in Lebanon won a 23-8 vote of confidence in the Lebanese Chamber of Deputies.

Moroccan Sultan Sidi Muhammad Ben-Moulay Ben-Arafa was slightly wounded in an attempt on his life while he was praying at the mosque in Marrakech. Si Thami al-Glaoui, who was with the Sultan, shot the attacker.

March 6

Egyptian President Nagib said that the constituent assembly to be convened in July would have full legislative powers as well as the task of drafting a new permanent constitution.

Colonel Nasser, Egyptian Prime Minister, stated that if Britain wanted to resume talks on the Suez Canal his Government was ready.

March, 1954

March 6

King Hussein returned to Jordan after a five day visit to King Faisal of Iraq.

The Fourth Arab League Social Seminar opened in Baghdad, Iraq.

March 7

Colonel Nasser, Egyptian Prime Minister, became Military Governor in place of General Nagib with special powers under the martial law enforced on January 26, 1952.

Lebanese Prime Minister Yafi visited Damascus, Syria.

The Iraqi Premier submitted the resignation of his Cabinet to King Faisal. The King immediately asked Muhammad Fadel al-Jamali to form a new cabinet.

The Egyptian Revolutionary Tribunal found Zainab Abd-al-Wahed al-Wakil al-Nahhas, wife of the former Premier and Wafd leader Mustafa al-Nahhas, guilty of corruption and abuse of power. It ordered the confiscation of her property as well as that of her two brothers. Because of her poor health the court decided not to impose a prison sentence.

John Blandford, head of UNRWA, resigned. Leslie J. Carver became the acting Director.

March 8

President Nagib was reinstated as Egyptian Prime Minister and Head of the Revolutionary Command Council. All other Cabinet changes that followed the split in the Council on February 25 were annulled.

Muhammad Fadel al-Jamali of Iraq formed a 15 man Cabinet with himself as Prime Minister.

Israel Prime Minister Moshe Sharett told the Knesset that any grant of arms to Iraq by the US would be regarded by Israel as seriously detrimental to its security.

March, 1954

March 8

Saudi Arabia's first Cabinet meeting was held. King Saud read a policy statement which among other things spoke of unity of the Arabs within the sphere of the Arab League Charter and Collective Security Pact.

The Lebanese Minister of Defense announced that LL7 million had been allocated to increase the size of the Army and equip it with modern weapons and aircraft.

March 9

The Umma Party of Sudan issued a statement expressing readiness to cooperate with the Government if it abandoned its policy of taking sides with the Egyptian Government and pursued a Sudanese national policy.

Nuri-Said of Iraq, in a statement before leaving for Pakistan with King Faisal, urged consultations with neighboring countries including India and Pakistan with a view to ensuring collective strength.

Syrian Sultan Pasha al-Atrash, who had fled to Jordan for political refuge, returned to the Druze capital of al-Suwaida where he was greeted by the new Ministers of Interior, Finance and Agriculture.

March 10

The Syrian Parliament elected in 1949 was summoned by its Speaker, Nazim al-Kudsi, to meet on March 15. Thirteen members who had approved the Constitution of former President Adib al-Shishakli were not invited to attend.

The Lebanese Ministers of Interior, Economy and Health arrived in Damascus for economic discussions with the new President, Prime Minister and Minister of Economy of Syria.

UN Secretary General Hammarskjold warned the Government of Jordan that if it did not reply soon to his message convoking a conference with Israel, he would be obliged to set a date for the meeting.

A trade agreement providing for most favored nation treatment was signed between Russia and Egypt.

March, 1954

March 10

Nuri-Said, leader of the Iraqi Constitutional Party, called on the Arab states to establish a defense line, similar to the West's, with Pakistan, India and Turkey.

Saudi Arabia warned all international airlines that strong measures would be taken against any plane passing over Saudi Arabian territory to or from Israel.

Sir Robert Howe, Governor General of Sudan, opened Sudan's Parliament. In his speech he said that the advent of the era of self determination made the building up of an additional defense force imperative, and so the Army would be strengthened.

The French Foreign Affairs Committee of the National Assembly adopted a resolution urging bold measures to raise living standards in Morocco.

March 11

Tunisian Prime Minister Muhammad M'Zali announced that elections for the new assembly would be held in June, 1954.

The Executive Committee of the Union of French of Tunisia declared that the reforms had resulted in an extremely dangerous situation.

The French Ambassador in Cairo reportedly had been instructed to protest to the Egyptian Government against the unspeakable terms used by the "Voice of the Arabs" in a broadcast from Cairo announcing the attempt on the life of the Sultan of Morocco on March 5, 1954. The broadcast had described the Sultan in grossly insulting terms and had expressed the hope that the injuries to him would prove fatal.

By Royal Decree, the Iraqi Parliament was recessed for a month. No explanation was given.

A Labor motion deploring the British Government's handling of the UK-Egyptian negotiations was defeated in the House of Commons by 271-219.

Selwyn Lloyd, British Minister of State, said that all Sudanese of every political party recognized in private that many of the technical branches of the British administration would be needed long after self determination.

March, 1954

March 11

There would have to be conditions of law and order, publicly expressed confidence by Ministers in their officials and a degree of efficiency in general administration. The British Government would continue to try to work the agreement of 1953 and to prevent civil disturbance.

March 12

Iraqi King Faisal, accompanied by the Crown Prince, the Minister of Agriculture and Senator Nuri-Said, left for Karachi, Pakistan, on a state visit.

Mahmoud Azmi of Egypt defended before the UN Security Council the restrictions placed on Israel bound shipping through the Suez Canal on grounds that Egypt was exercising the right of visit, search and seizure, since it was still in a state of war with Israel. Israel Representative Abba Eban replied that Azmi was repeating the arguments used by Egypt in September 1951 in its unsuccessful attempt to prevent the Security Council from adopting its resolution calling on Egypt to end the restrictions on Israel bound shipping.

The Syrian Government ordered the confiscation of the property of former President Adib Shishakli and his brother Salah Shishakli, who was a senior official in the Customs Department.

Doria Shafik, leader of the "Daughters of the Nile" feminist movement, notified President Nagib of Egypt that she was undertaking a hunger strike until women were permitted representation in the constituent assembly.

March 13

The Lebanese Prime Minister announced that LL10 million had been allocated for enlarging and improving the port of Tripoli.

The Egyptian Government ordered indefinite closing of the country's main universities after 2,000 Cairo students demonstrated in defiance of emergency regulations for the ouster of Deputy Premier Abdel Nasser.

March, 1954

March 14

The Jordanian Government announced that it would open a legation in Pakistan.

The Egyptian Government proclaimed a general amnesty for all remaining political prisoners and internees. Among those already released, in addition to former Premier Ibrahim Abd-al-Hadi, were the former Wafd minister Ibrahim Faraq and former Secretary of the Wafd Party and minister Fuad Sirag-ad-Din. All Moslem Brotherhood internees except Hassan al-Hudaibi and Secretary Abd-al-Kader Auda were also to be released.

March 15

It was announced in Egypt that General Nagib would replace Colonel Abdel Nasser as Military Governor.

In Tunisia one person was killed and a score injured in a clash between French policemen and 700 demonstrators trying to storm Dar-al-Bey Palace, seat of the Government, protesting French refusal to grant full independence.

Two British soldiers were shot to death in a boat on the Suez Canal.

The Mixed Armistice Commission considered a complaint by Israel and a counter-charge by Syria concerning an incident on Lake Tiberias on March 11, 1954. According to the Israel account Syrian guns opened fire on Israel craft fishing in the eastern waters of the lake but no casualties were caused. The Syrians reported two casualties as the result of an Israel attack with 57 millimeter guns. The Commission censured Syria for its attack on fishing boats and Israel for answering with gunfire causing Syrian casualties.

Responding to a call by the Speaker of Parliament in Syria, Nazim al-Kudsi, the 1949 Syrian Chamber of Deputies met in Damascus to give legal effect to the decisions of the new Government. This Chamber, under the 1950 constitution, would remain in session until the election of a new parliament.

March, 1954

March 15

In a statement in the British House of Commons on the Sudanese disturbances of March 1, 1954, Selwyn Lloyd, UK Minister of State, said that in the past Sudan had been governed with very small security and police forces. Danger of deterioration in law and order might occur, he said, in both the north and south.

March 16

The Foreign Office of Britain stated that the Government had received indirect approaches from the Egyptian Government with a view to resuming the negotiations on the Canal Zone.

It was reported at UN headquarters that the Western powers agreed to back a resolution calling on Egypt to permit Israel bound ships to pass through the Suez Canal.

The Syrian Government decided to inform the signatories of the 1950 Tripartite declaration—Great Britain, France and the US—that it proposed to repel by force any further Israel attacks from Lake Tiberias. It was understood that Ministers had informed UN Truce Supervisory Organization Chief of Staff, General Bennike, of the need to strengthen the international observer machinery.

March 17

Tunisian nationalist demonstrators stoned street cars in Tunis, demanding the release of their interned leader, Habib Bourguiba.

Egyptian Foreign Minister Fawzi made a strong protest to Sir Ralph Stevenson, the British Ambassador, against the security measures reported to have been taken by the British military forces in the Suez Canal Zone following recent events. The British Ambassador replied that the reports of security measures had been grossly exaggerated and he made a counter protest about the recent disorders which had necessitated the measures.

Eleven Israelis were killed in a machine gun attack on a bus at Scorpion Pass, near Beersheba. Israel accused Jordan of the attack and called on the Mixed Armistice Commission to investigate.

March, 1954

March 17

Jordan rejected a third UN invitation for high level talks with Israel to discuss armistice problems.

March 18

It was reported in London that Colonel Nasser of Egypt, on February 25, 1954, had transmitted an offer through the US and Australia to Great Britain that Egypt would agree to the reopening of the Suez base to British forces in the event of a threat to or an attack on Turkey in return for Britain dropping its demand that the 4,000 technicians who would remain at the base wear British uniforms.

British military authorities denied exaggerated reports in the Egyptian press that inhabitants in the Suez Canal Zone had been terrorized.

Israel formally blamed the Jordanian Government for the massacre on Scorpion Pass.

Jordan denied that its citizens participated in the attack at Scorpion Pass and offered to join in the search for the perpetrators.

March 19

It was reported in Cairo that British Ambassador Sir Ralph Stevenson met with Egyptian President Muhammad Nagib and strongly protested the attacks on British soldiers in the Suez Canal Zone.

A conference of the Moslem Brotherhood organizations in the Arab countries opened in Damascus. Invitations had been sent to branches in Jordan, Iraq, Kuwait, Lebanon, Sudan, Yemen and Hejaz (in Saudi Arabia).

Israel called upon Jordan to take drastic measures to end the intolerable situation that brought on the attack on the Israel bus at Scorpion Pass on March 17, 1954, but accepted Jordan's offer to join in the search for the attackers.

March, 1954

March 19

New Zealand presented a resolution to the UN Security Council calling on Egypt to allow ships bound for Israel to pass through the Suez Canal. The resolution was supported by Great Britain, France and the US.

March 20

"The Voice of the Arabs" program of the Egyptian Broadcasting Service said that King Faisal's visit to Pakistan was an attempt to include Iraq in an imperialist alliance.

The USSR vetoed a UN Security Council resolution calling upon Egypt to comply with a 1951 Council resolution to end its blockade in the Suez Canal.

Representatives of Syria, Egypt, Iraq and Saudi Arabia presented UN Secretary General Dag Hammarskjold with official reports from their Governments concerning Israel troop movements along the borders with Syria, Jordan and Lebanon. They told him that if Israel attacked any of the Arab states, the other Arab nations would not remain idle.

The investigating staff of the Mixed Armistice Commission for the Scorpion Pass bus massacre lost the trail of the attackers while still in Israel territory.

King Saud of Saudi Arabia arrived in Cairo on a seven day visit, ostensibly to discuss with Egyptian leaders the Middle East situation, in view of Iraq's readiness to join the Turkish-Pakistani alliance and the possible resultant disturbances in the Arab League. He met with President Nagib, Colonel Gamal Abdel Nasser and other dignitaries. In a statement to the press he announced that Saudi Arabia had refused military aid from the US.

The explosion of five bombs in Cairo heightened the atmosphere of tension as King Saud was publicly welcomed. They were reportedly set off by opponents of the Nagib regime.

March, 1954

March 21

It was learned in Cairo that British Ambassador Stevenson had asked Egypt to withdraw from the Suez Canal Zone certain officers who allegedly did not cooperate in checking violent attacks on British forces and that Foreign Minister Fawzi had asked that Britain abolish check points at which Egyptian vehicles were stopped and searched.

The Egyptian Bar Association backed a recommendation for a return to civilian government made by 100 Egyptian lawyers.

It was announced that Mansour Fathi al-Kikhia had been appointed Libya's first Minister to the US and would leave shortly for Washington.

March 22

A joint communique issued simultaneously in Cairo and Moscow said that the Government of Egypt and the Government of the USSR had decided to strengthen and promote relations between the two countries and to raise their respective legations to the rank of embassies.

Egyptian Foreign Minister Mahmoud Fawzi told US Ambassador Jefferson Caffery that Egypt would resist by every means Iraq's joining the proposed Turkish-Pakistani Pact.

Iraqi Premier Muhammad Fadel al-Jamali summoned Hussein Sherif, the Egyptian Charge d'Affaires in Baghdad, to protest the virulent campaign against Iraq in the Egyptian press and the "Voice of the Arabs" broadcast.

British Foreign Secretary Anthony Eden announced in the UK House of Commons that resumption of the deadlocked Suez Canal talks was not possible so long as British soldiers were being murdered, wounded and kidnapped in the Canal Zone.

The British Ambassador delivered a note informing the Egyptian Government of the suspension of UK-Egyptian discussions and demanding the various measures specified by UK Foreign Secretary Eden in his statement.

The Iraq Petroleum Company announced the appointment of Muhammad Abd-al-Ghani al-Nagib, Director General of Oil Affairs in the Iraqi

March, 1954

March 22

Ministry of Economy, to the Board of the Iraq, Basra and Mosul Petroleum Companies. He was the second Iraqi director.

Previous decisions banning a number of foreign newspapers in Syria were revoked.

The Government of Aden reportedly protested to the Yemeni Government after a camel raid by Dham tribesmen of the Seiah Hadrami tribe in Quaiti State in the eastern Aden Protectorate. The raiders were intercepted on their return by guards of the Hadrami Bedouin Legion, two were killed, four captured.

It was reported in Jerusalem that the Israel authorities gave information to the Chairman of the Mixed Armistice Commission, Commander Elmo Hutchison of the US Navy, on the identity of some of the killers of the 11 Israelis on Scorpion Pass.

After a four hour session on the Scorpion Pass massacre, the Mixed Armistice Commission adjourned at the request of the Jordanian delegation.

March 23

Egyptian President Nagib declared that Egypt would not resume the UK-Egyptian discussions except on the basis of complete acceptance of all of Egypt's rights.

Egyptian President Nagib reaffirmed the decision to return quickly to constitutional government.

A military court sentenced seven Tunisians to hard labor for life for having sabotaged bridges during terrorist violence in 1952.

A delegation of seven Arab League nations served notice to US Secretary of State John Foster Dulles that the Arab League was prepared instantly to wage war against Israel should Israel take any expansionist or aggressive action.

The UN Security Council began hearings on the Israel-Egyptian dispute over Suez Canal passage rights.

March, 1954

March 23

The Israel Minister in Washington, Reuven Shiloah, told the US State Department of the grave view taken by Israel over the deteriorating security situation, the failure of the armistice machinery and the repudiation by Jordan of its obligations under the armistice.

US Secretary of State Dulles stated in Washington that the US had been supporting the UN Secretary General in his request that Jordan meet with Israel under Article XII of the Israel-Jordan Armistice Agreement to discuss armistice problems.

The Mixed Armistice Commission investigating the Scorpion Pass incident of March 17, 1954, refused to condemn Jordan for the attack. Israel announced that it would boycott the Commission, warning that it might be impossible to prevent retaliatory action.

In reaction to the statement made by British Foreign Secretary Eden in the House of Commons on March 22, 1954, President Nagib of Egypt said that Egypt did not want negotiations. He declared that Egypt did not want negotiations which would not give it full sovereignty and rights.

It was reported in Cairo that the Soviet Union informed Egypt and other Arab countries that it would consider the conclusion of any Western sponsored Middle East military pact an unfriendly and even hostile act directed against the USSR.

Sir Leslie Knox Munro, New Zealand representative in the UN Security Council, urged the Council to adopt the resolution calling on Egypt to lift its blockade on Israel bound shipping in the Suez Canal.

Egypt's representative in the UN rejected the resolution made by New Zealand. He said that the Security Council had no jurisdiction in the issue and insisted that Egypt was acting within its sovereign rights by imposing a ban on Israel bound traffic. He warned the members of the Council that Egypt would weigh their votes in the light of Egyptian sovereignty and that it would take an attitude toward those countries consequential to their votes.

March, 1954

March 24

UN Secretary Hammarskjold met with representatives of the US, Great Britain and France to discuss the mounting Arab-Israel tension.

Israel Prime Minister Moshe Sharett announced in the Knesset that the Israel Government asked the US, Great Britain and France to call an immediate session of the Security Council to discuss the massacre at Scorpion Pass.

It was reported from Amman that the Jordanian Government rejected a request of UN Secretary General Dag Hammarskjold to sit down with Israel at high level conferences on armistice disputes.

The temporary economic agreement between Syria and Lebanon was extended for a period of six months from March 7, 1954, pending the conclusion of a permanent agreement.

Colonel Nasser and Major Salah Salem failed to attend an Egyptian Government Cabinet meeting which had been preceded by a separate gathering of the civilian ministers.

March 25

US Secretary of State Dulles appealed to both Jordan and Israel for restraint and prudence and the avoidance of any statements or acts which might further disturb the general situation. He urged both parties to cooperate with the Mixed Armistice Commission.

The UN Secretary General said that he had given up efforts to arrange an Israel-Jordanian high level meeting to discuss armistice disputes.

Hussein Fakhri al-Khalidi, Jordanian Foreign Minister, said Jordan had rejected a conference with Israel because, although the UN Secretary General had said the agenda would be limited, Israel had already declared that the subjects would be unlimited. This meant that Jordan might be asked to take part in a peace conference in which it had repeatedly said it would not take part unless UN decisions regarding Palestine had been respected and executed by Israel.

The Revolutionary Command Council of Egypt (RCC) announced that it would transfer sovereignty to a constituent assembly on July 23, 1954,

March 25

that political parties could re-form immediately, and that the Council would not form itself into a political party.

Britain, France, US and Denmark supported the New Zealand resolution of March 19, 1954, and referred to the resolution passed by the Security Council in 1951 which explicitly rejected the claim that the parties to the Israel-Egyptian Armistice Agreement retained the status of active belligerents or any consequent right of visit, search and seizure for self defense.

A group of young Egyptian officers issued a statement threatening to kill President Nagib and other members of the Egyptian Revolutionary Council if officials of the Farouk regime were returned to power.

Orders were issued in Egypt for the release of political prisoners, including Hassan al-Hudaibi and Abd-al-Kader Auda of the Moslem Brotherhood, former Wafd Prime Minister Mustafa Nahhas and Colonel Rashad Mihanna, one of the Regents appointed after former King Farouk was dethroned.

A one day strike in Tunisia was called by the trade unions in protest against a recent Government wage awards which was stated to have been only partially effective.

March 26

Hundreds of political prisoners in Egypt were released, including former Wafd Premier Mustafa Nahhas, who was under house arrest and many other prominent political figures.

The Egyptian Charge d'Affaires in Baghdad handed Iraqi Premier al-Jamali the reply of the Egyptian Foreign Ministry to the Premier's protest against the "Voice of the Arabs" broadcasts critical of Iraq.

The Soviet Ambassador handed Prime Minister Fadel al-Jamali of Iraq a note warning Iraq that participation in any Western sponsored defense pact would be considered an unfriendly and hostile act.

March 26

An agreement was signed by Lebanon for the purchase of the Beirut Electricity Company from the Belgian-French owners. The price was reported to be LL25.5 million.

Israel's UN delegate, Ambassador Abba S. Eban, presented a formal note to US Secretary of State Dulles requesting the US, Great Britain and France to call an immediate session of the Security Council to discuss the Scorpion Pass incident.

The General Assembly of the Egyptian Bar demanded that the Council of the Revolution should dissolve itself immediately and that the officer members should return to their barracks with a vote of thanks from Egypt for their services.

Flood waters on the Tigris River were stated to have affected an area of a hundred square miles including crop bearing lands in Iraq.

March 27

Israel's Minister of Development declared before the International Planning Conference for Israel that US aid to the Arab states would be used to attack Israel and would hasten the resumption of war between the Arab states and Israel.

King Saud of Saudi Arabia arranged and attended a meeting between the Egyptian supporters of Nagib and those of Nasser.

Hassan al-Hudaibi, Supreme Guide of the Moslem Brotherhood, in a press interview, called for a jihad (holy war) as the only means of realizing Egypt's aspirations for control of the Suez Canal.

Students of the American University of Beirut demonstrated against Iraq's intention to join the Turkish-Pakistani Pact.

Three Tunisians were executed in Tunisia for the slaying of three French police agents on July 23, 1954.

Major Amin Chaker, aide to Colonel Abdel Nasser, charged that Egyptian President Nagib had become a tool of dishonest politicians of the old

March 27

regime, and followers of Nasser staged a sitdown strike against Nagib in their barracks.

Egyptian President Nagib collapsed at the airport when bidding farewell to King Saud and was confined to his home.

The Federation of Cairo Transport Workers began a hunger and sitdown strike on company premises, protesting restoration of political parties and calling for a boycott of elections.

A trade agreement was signed in Cairo between the USSR and Egypt providing for broader commercial ties.

March 28

Nine Jordanians were killed and 19 wounded in an attack on Nahhalin, eight miles southwest of Jerusalem, carried out by two companies of the Israel Army. The village mosque was sacked and six houses bombed before Arab Legion reinforcements arrived to drive the attackers back into Israel territory. Jordan lodged a complaint with the Mixed Armistice Commission.

The struggle in Egypt between General Nagib, who advocated a civilian government, and Colonel Abdel Nasser, who desired continued control by the Revolution Command Council, which had been going on for more than four days, brought forth the statement from Major Salah Salem, Minister of Sudanese National Guidance, spokesman for the Nasser faction, that the Revolution would continue.

The Cairo police officer's club passed a resolution of support for Colonel Abdel Nasser and his colleagues. Demonstrators stoned the offices of the Wafd newspaper, al-Misri, which was supporting General Nagib.

Youths of the Ismaili sect in Syria attacked school teachers and others at a village near Hama, protesting the Government decision that religious teaching would again be given in the schools.

Electricity company workers in Syria went on strike for higher pay and shorter hours.

March 29

Major Salah Salem announced that the Revolution Command Council of Egypt decided to revoke the concessions made to the Nagib faction on March 5 and 25, which were to hold elections in June for a constituent assembly that would approve the new constitution, to exercise interim parliamentary power, and to dissolve the Revolution Command Council on July 24, 1954.

Soviet delegate Vishinsky used his veto at the UN Security Council to defeat the majority sponsored New Zealand resolution supporting Israel's complaint against Egypt regarding passage of ships destined for Israel through the Suez Canal.

In protest against the threat of the Egyptian Revolutionary Command Council (RCC) to abdicate, a mob invaded the State Council and attacked the court president, Abd-al-Razeq al-Sanhuri, as a traitor to the ruling group. Major Salah Salem, Minister of National Guidance and Sudanese Affairs, came to the aid of Dr. al-Sanhuri and denied the allegations against him.

The Saudi Arabian Embassy issued a statement alleging that British soldiers had been shooting at civilians day and night without any due reason in the Buraimi Oasis and that on March 23, 1954, two men were killed as they walked along the street in Buraimi unarmed.

Students of the American University in Beirut, demonstrating in protest of the use of firearms against them on March 27, declared a strike. Twenty were arrested.

March 30

The Syrian Chamber of Deputies revoked 20 decrees of the former regime.

Thousands of Cairo University students demonstrated against the decision of the Revolution Command Council to continue its military rule.

Press censorship was reimposed in Egypt.

A clash between Deputy Kamal Jumblat and Premier Abdallah al-Yafi over the student demonstrations caused such disorder in the Lebanese Chamber of Deputies that the chairman was forced to adjourn the session.

March, 1954

March 30

Aleppo students in Syria boycotted classes out of sympathy for the student demonstrations in Lebanon.

At a meeting of the Mixed Armistice Commission unattended by Israel, the chairman and the Jordan delegation passed a resolution strongly condemning Israel for its aggression against Jordan at Nahhalin on March 28 and 29, and calling on the Israel authorities to take measures to prevent such aggression and to apprehend and punish those responsible.

A joint communique issued by the Egyptian and Turkish Governments said that both had agreed to consider closed the case of former Turkish Ambassador to Egypt Fuat Tugay and to continue the good relations between the two countries.

The Jordanian Chamber of Deputies approved the budget for the financial year 1954-1955. Great Britain's contribution to the budget was about 50 percent.

The Jordanian Prime Minister issued a statement alleging that Jews had fabricated the incident of the bus in Negev in order to regain world sympathy lost after the Qibya incident. The Jordanian Government would raise the case of Jewish aggression at Nahhalin in the Security Council.

The twentieth session of the Arab League closed with the approval of a budget of LE396, 000.

March 31

Several thousand Egyptian university students demonstrated against the re-entrenched military regime. Representatives of Communists, Socialists and the Moslem Brotherhood identified themselves by name and party and harangued the students demanding a return to parliamentary life.

France ordered Moroccan Resident General Guillaume to bring a speedy end to terrorism and to hasten implementation of reforms including provisions for regional and municipal assemblies.

Under the chairmanship of Sheikh Yusuf Yasin of Saudi Arabia, the twenty-first session of the Arab League Council opened in Cairo. The two major issues for consideration were regional defense and Israel.

April, 1954

April 1

Scott Murray, Managing Director of the Southern California Oil Corporation, stated in Cairo that his company drilled an oil well in the Eastern Desert and was definitely a commercial producer.

Charles Malik, Lebanon's delegate to the UN Security Council, submitted a demand on the part of Jordan that the Council take up the Israel attack on Nahhalin on March 28 as a flagrant breach of the armistice agreement between Israel and Jordan.

A conference of the Arab Chamber of Commerce, Industry and Agriculture opened at Baghdad with 12 states in attendance.

April 2

Iraq announced that it was ready to free three Israel citizens arrested in January when their plane made a forced landing in Baghdad, on condition that Israel agree to return the seven soldiers captured during the war in 1948.

Iran and Iraq were invited to join the alliance between Turkey and Pakistan for mutual defense and economic cooperation.

April 3

In their efforts to break up demonstrations against the military regime, police in Cairo arrested 50 students.

Egyptian military equipment for about 1, 000 men was handed over to the Sudanese Defense Force in accordance with a promise Egyptian President Nagib had made in January.

In a speech to the Zionist Federation of Britain, Eliahe Elath, Israel Ambassador, said that Israel anxiety at the tension with bordering Arab states was increased by the knowledge that Western Powers were still supplying arms to some of those states while it was obvious that such arms were more likely to be used against Israel than for the legitimate defense of the whole area against outside aggression.

March, 1954

US President Eisenhower called on the Arab states and Israel to restrain their extremists and to permit other nations to help them settle their disputes.

More than 100 students in Lebanon began a hunger strike aimed at forcing the resignation of the Cabinet for its repression of student demonstrations.

Lord Reading, Minister of State of the British Foreign Office, stated in reply to a question in the UK House of Lords that there were about 80 Germans employed by the Egyptian Ministry of War and Marine. Their main duty was to advise on training and establishment but a small number were concerned with arms manufacture and research.

April, 1954

April 3

Ten policemen and six students were injured when police clashed with students in Amman, Jordan who were demonstrating against the Turkish-Pakistani Pact, against Israel for the Nahhalin incident and against the arrest of students in Lebanon.

The Lebanese Government rescinded the order closing the American University of Beirut.

Security forces used tear gas to disperse student demonstrators in Egypt. Authorities at both Ibrahim University and Alexandria University announced that classes would be discontinued until April 8.

April 4

In Lebanon the students ended their five day hunger strike after their colleagues who were arrested for inciting demonstrations in protest against Iraq's proposed joining the Turkish-Pakistani Pact were released. Twenty-eight of the fasters were taken to a hospital.

The Israel-Egyptian Mixed Armistice Commission censured Israel for two raids into Egyptian territory on April 2, in which three Egyptian soldiers were killed and one wounded.

April 5

Major Salah Salem of Egypt stated that at a joint meeting of the ten members of the ruling Revolution Command Council and the civilian Cabinet members, measures were discussed to protect the Revolution from its opponents. It was understood that these were the press, university students and former political leaders.

A Middle East Afforestation Conference opened at Damascus under the chairmanship of the Syrian Minister of Agriculture.

King Saud of Saudi Arabia returned to Riyadh after a nine day visit to Kuwait.

April 5

Israel charged Jordan before the UN Security Council with repudiation of several provisions of the Jordanian-Israel Armistice Agreement and asked the Council for urgent consideration of these charges.

April 6

Major Khaled Mohi-ad-Din, a supporter of General Nagib in the Egyptian Revolution Common Council, left suddenly for Paris.

In a joint letter to Andrei Vishinsky, April's President of the UN Security Council, five member states of the Arab League supported the complaint of Lebanon against Israel, presented on behalf of Jordan.

Jordan demanded of Great Britain a full explanation of Britain's interpretation of the 1948 UK-Jordanian treaty of alliance and mutual defense, wishing to know under what circumstances Britain would come to the aid of Jordan in the event of hostilities with Israel.

Talks between the Iraqi Government and the Iraq Petroleum Company on outstanding questions began in Baghdad.

At the conclusion of the Arab League meeting in Cairo, the Arab League Political Committee resolved that their governments would stand as one bloc to resist any aggression directed against them. A proposal that food supplies to Israel be considered as contraband and the Arab League scheme for exploitation of Jordan Valley waters were referred to subcommittees. The Jordan Valley scheme was reported to provide water and power for the various countries as follows: Lebanon 35,000 dunums irrigated and 115,000 kilowatt hours of electricity, Syria 119,000 dunums and 30,000 kilowatt hours of electricity, Jordan 490,000 dunums and an unspecified amount of electricity.

April 7

The Jordanian Government announced that a Jewish force of about 100 men had crossed the border near Husan in the Bethlehem subdistrict. It fought with a Jordanian patrol and National Guards and after an hour's battle had withdrawn.

April 8

The UK Royal Air Force completed an eight day airlift during which it flew to Iraq 650,000 sandbags and 1,000 tents to help in the flood disaster.

US, French and British representatives to the Security Council requested a review of the entire Middle Eastern frontier situation. Charles Malik of Lebanon, on behalf of the Arab states, asked that the question of the attack on Nahhalin be considered separately.

The Libyan Government of Muhammad al-Saghisli resigned; King Idris al-Sanusi asked Mustafa Ben-Halim to form a new cabinet.

Radio Cairo broadcasted a statement by Egyptian Foreign Minister Mahmoud Fawzi that the Egyptian people and Government were in favor of banning atomic weapons. Fawzi stated that Egypt would continue its efforts towards that end in the UN.

April 9

King Saud of Saudi Arabia donated SR1.5 million for relief of flood victims in Iraq.

Pakistani Foreign Minister Zafrallah Khan called for a conference of Islamic states to consider the whole problem of Palestine so that a policy might be settled and remedies devised.

US Assistant Secretary of State Henry A. Byroade, delivering a policy address before the World Affairs Council at Dayton, Ohio, expressed the view that Israel should regard itself as solely a Middle Eastern nation and that the Arabs should accept it as such.

Bey Sidi Muhammad al-Amin of Tunisia asked the French Government to pardon all persons convicted of political crimes in Tunisia.

The Lebanese Minister of Public Health inaugurated the fourth Annual Middle East Medical Conference at Beirut.

A delegation of 75 persons representing many organizations went to Alexandria to invite former president Shukri Kuwatli to return to Syria

April 10

Muhammad Hassan al-Sulaimani, former valet of ex-King Farouk, and Ali Muhammad Hassanein, were sentenced to life imprisonment at hard labor for the murder of Army Lieutenant Abd-al-Kader Taha.

The Premier of Lebanon, Abdallah Yafi, announced in Beirut that Lebanon's Armed Forces would be increased to three times their present strength, from 5,000 to 15,000 men.

April 11

King Saud of Saudi Arabia arrived in Bahrain for a three day visit.

The Egyptian delegation to the Egypt-Israel Mixed Armistice Commission walked out after Colonel Hommel, the US Chairman, had refused them an adjournment of 24 hours to study the details of the Israel complaint. The Commission then accused Egypt of four violations of the Armistice Agreement which had occurred in the Negev on April 8 and 9, in their absence, and also called on Egypt to end aggressive acts along the Gaza Strip. The UN Chairman voted with the Israelis on three counts but abstained on the fourth. Egypt filed an appeal with General Bennike, saying its delegation should have been notified of the meeting 24 hours in advance and had not been.

The Syrian Prime Minister announced that an amnesty would be granted to all persons convicted in political cases under the al-Shishakli regime.

The Jordanian Cabinet voted to endorse an Arab boycott of the UN Security Council unless that body discussed the Nahhalin attack as a separate item.

April 12

The UN Security Council continued its debate on whether to take up the Lebanese complaint against Israel, or the entire issue of Arab-Israel relations as advocated by the Western Powers.

Charles Malik, speaking on behalf of the Arab states, told the UN Security Council that the Arabs would agree to general debate on the frontier situation provided it was understood that a resolution would

April 12

be passed later censuring the March 28 Israel attack on Nahhalin. Soviet UN delegate Vishinsky supported the Arab stand.

It was agreed that a new Assistant Secretary General for Economic Affairs of the Arab League be named, bringing the total of assistant secretaries general to five.

The Permanent Communications Committee of the Arab League approved seven recommendations of the Arab Aviation Committee, including the establishment of an Arab Civil Aviation Council.

A new Libyan Government under Mustafa Ben-Halim, Prime Minister and Minister of Communications, was sworn in.

April 13

The US State Department issued a statement regarding the Arab-Israel tension which said that all US efforts were directed to the ultimate goal of a peaceful adjustment of the relations between the Arab states and Israel.

The Sudanese Minister of Public Works announced that the Egyptian and Sudanese Governments had agreed in principle on the need to amend the Nile Waters Agreement of 1929. He said Sudan now needed a much larger share in the waters than it was given under that agreement.

In Aleppo, students demonstrated against the invitation extended to former President al-Kuwatli to return to Syria.

Syrian Minister of the Interior Buzo announced that elections would be held on June 15, on the basis of the 1949 electoral law.

Speaking at land distribution ceremonies at Faroukia, Colonel Abdel Nasser and Major Salem of Egypt criticized US policy regarding the Suez Canal issue and said that the US Point Four Program was a form of American colonial penetration in the Middle East.

April 14

In a letter to the UN Relief and Works Agency for Palestine Refugees (UNRWA), US Delegate Lodge stated that the US was willing to give the Agency $15 million for 1953-54 and $12 million for 1954-55. These amounts represented about 70 percent of those budgets respectively. Saudi Arabia and Yugoslavia announced contributions of $40,000 each.

Iraq's Foreign Minister reported that his Government officially welcomed the invitation by Zafrallah Khan for a meeting of all Islamic states to consider the Palestine question.

Elections were held in Tripolitania for 30 members of the Libyan Legislative Council.

Anticipating an attack by the Egyptian Revolution Command Council, the Press Syndicate issued a statement defending its members in the matter of receiving payments from secret funds.

King Saud of Saudi Arabia arrived in Karachi, Pakistan, on an official visit.

April 15

Major Salah Salem announced that the Egyptian Press Syndicate's ruling council had been dissolved. The law establishing the syndicate was to be revised to eliminate publishers from membership.

April 16

Nineteen American religious and civic leaders addressed a 173 page memorandum concerning the Middle East to US President Eisenhower. A copy was also presented to UN Secretary General Dag Hammarskjold.

Lebanon's President Camille Chamoun met with envoys of other Arab states in Beirut to discuss the possibility of Lebanon's withdrawal from the UN Security Council.

The Syrian Government ordered the family of Captain Salah Shishakli, brother of deposed President Adib Shishakli, to pay SL1.8 million.

April 16

as a fine for smuggling goods and drugs while he was director of the antismuggling office of the Customs Department.

Thirty-eight Egyptian ministers were deprived by the Government of political rights for ten years. Colonel Nasser explained that these ex-ministers were individually responsible for the actions of their parties' Cabinets and were therefore to blame for the corruption pervading Egyptian political life since February 6, 1942.

It was announced in Casablanca that the town was to be divided into ten arrondissements instead of six in the interests of better administration, and that armed Berber tribesmen had been temporarily enlisted and brought to Casablanca to reinforce the police and help preserve order in the Moroccan quarters.

April 17

General Guillaume, French Resident General of Morocco, said in a broadcast that the activities of a handful of agitators who for several months had been trying to impose their will on the country, had caused him, in agreement with the Sultan, to take exceptional measures with a view to re-establishing calm and confidence.

About 4,000 Moroccan Berber tribesmen, especially recruited as auxiliary policemen, took up posts in the Arab quarters of Casablanca to aid French efforts to stamp out terrorism.

The US Foreign Operations Administration requested the US Congress for a package of $130 million in aid for Israel, the Arab states and Iran. The State Department anticipating approval of the request authorized US envoys in Lebanon and Jordan to begin discussions on specific projects.

April 18

Major Salah Salem, Egyptian Minister of National Guidance, announced in Cairo that President Nagib had resigned as Premier and turned over the post to the Deputy Premier, Lieutenant Colonel Nasser. Nagib retained the post of President, Mahmoud Fawzi was selected Minister of Foreign Affairs.

April 18

Colonel Nasser of Egypt said that his Government would continue the domestic and foreign policies established by the Revolution in July 1952. According to the official announcement, the outgoing minister resigned for health reasons.

April 19

Egyptian Prime Minister Abdel Nasser presented land titles to 869 peasant families at Kaft-al-Dawar, near Alexandria.

King Hussein of Jordan sent an Easter radio appeal to Americans for help to relieve the plight of Arab refugees.

It was stated in Amman, Jordan, that Israelis had fired on Jordanian National Guards in two frontier areas.

April 20

Parliament approved a bill permitting any Arab residing in Lebanon to obtain Lebanese nationality.

A Lebanese sailing vessel and four sailors, seized by the Israel coastal patrol on April 19, 1954, were released at Jaffa.

Jordan's lower house of Parliament sent a resolution of thanks to Soviet UN Delegate Andrei Y. Vishinsky for his support of the Arab cause in the UN Security Council on April 12, 1954.

April 21

The US and Iraq exchanged notes at Baghdad, setting forth the conditions on which the US proposed to provide Iraq with military assistance.

Iraqi Premier Muhammad Fadel al-Jamali, presented the resignation of his Cabinet to the King. It was stated in Baghdad that the opposition's attack on the Premier's policy to join the Turkish-Pakistani Pact and his handling of the flood disaster caused his resignation.

April 21

The British member resigned from the Sudanization Commission after it had decided that it was within its powers to Sudanize the judiciary.

A three day conference of Spanish diplomats in the Middle East opened in Beirut.

April 22

Dr. Hussein Fakhri al-Khalidi, Jordanian Foreign Minister, referred at a press conference to treaty relations with Britain and said that after thorough study of the British Government's explanations the Jordanian Government understood that Britain would come to the aid of Jordan in any war against any country including Israel after Britain and Jordan had first eliminated the possibility of a peaceful settlement in discussions at which Britain was present.

The UN Security Council met for the third time to debate how to debate the Palestine situation and adjourned until April 29, 1954.

It was announced that a new agreement had been signed with the UN Technical Assistance Administration by which Jordan would receive $35 million annually.

Secretary General of the Arab League Muhammad Abd-al-Khaleq Hassouna left for Madrid for discussions with General Franco and other Spanish officials.

A Royal Decree was issued in Iraq announcing the resignation of Iraqi Foreign Minister Musa al-Shahbandar. It stated that he had been appointed Ambassador to the US.

April 23

French authorities in Paris announced that deposed Sultan Sidi Muhammad Ben-Youssef of Morocco would be permanently established in exile on the island of Madagascar. This action followed a written promise of the former Sultan not to engage in political affairs.

April, 1954

April 23

Jordanian Foreign Minister Hussein al-Khalidi said in Jerusalem that Eric A. Johnston, US President Eisenhower's special Ambassador to the Middle East, would be ill advised to come to Jordan.

After a visit by Abdallah Yafi, the Lebanese Prime Minister, for discussions with the Prime Minister and Foreign Minister of Syria, it was announced that Syrian and Lebanese frontier forces were operating under a joint command.

April 24

Israel Army headquarters at Tel Aviv reported that an Egyptian soldier was killed in the Negev in a clash with an Israel border patrol. The soldier was one of several covering Arabs who were illegally harvesting grain at Kisufim, an Israel communal farm.

The Egyptian Revolutionary Tribunal indicated Mahmoud Abu-al-Fath and Hussein Abu-al-Fath of al-Misri, former Wafd Party organ, and two other Cairo papers on charges that they committed acts against the interests of the nation and sought to corrupt the Government machinery. Hussein Abu-al-Fath was placed under house arrest; his brother was residing abroad. A third brother, Ahmad Abu-al-Fath, present publisher of al-Misri, was not indicted.

King Saud of Saudi Arabia left Pakistan for home. An official statement by Muhammad Ali, Prime Minister of Pakistan, indicated complete accord both on matters of immediate and common interest between Saudi Arabia and Pakistan and on all matters of general interest to Islam and Moslems.

April 25

Amir Abdallah al-Salem al-Sabah, Ruler of Kuwait, arrived in Amman, Jordan for a five day visit.

The International Islamic Organization Conference opened in Karachi, Pakistan, with Turkey participating. This conference was of an economic nature.

April, 1954

April 25

The US State Department confirmed that an agreement had been reached under which the US might supply military aid to Iraq. In the agreement it was understood that Iraq guaranteed to use the material only in self defense or to preserve its internal security.

April 26

Syrian Foreign Minister Faidi Atassi had further talks in Beirut with Lebanese Ministers.

Israel Army spokesmen in Tel Aviv reported that two Arab infiltrators from Syria were killed in a clash with Israelis near where the upper Jordan River flows into the Sea of Galilee.

Jordan accused Israel troops of firing across the armistice line on the village of Budrus.

Israel asked the chairman of the Egyptian-Israel Mixed Armistice Commission to convene an emergency meeting to discuss a heavy exchange of fire across the armistice line of the Gaza Strip.

Israel Ambassador Abba Eban called on the US State Department and protested against the US agreement to give arms to Iraq.

April 27

Egypt charged that Israel forces attacked Egyptian positions in the Gaza Strip area.

King Faisal of Iraq asked Senator Nuri-Said, leader of the Constitutional Union Party, to form a new Cabinet but he declined for reasons of health.

The Israel Foreign Affairs Ministry issued a statement criticizing the US grant of arms to Iraq.

UK Queen Elizabeth and the Duke of Edinburgh arrived in Aden for a one day visit in the course of their Commonwealth tour.

April, 1954

April 28

Major General Vagn Bennike voted with Jordan in the Jordan-Israel Mixed Armistice Commission condemning Israel for an all day siege of Budrus Village. Israel boycotted the Commission.

In Egypt, the ruling military junta held an all night session behind a heavy extraordinary guard of troops in battle dress manning anti-tank guns. No explanation was given.

The Egyptian Government arrested 12 Army officers and 40 civilians accused of plotting May Day disorders with Communists and other dissident elements.

The International Islamic Economic Organization, meeting at Karachi, approved a decision to open its membership to all Arab countries. It was formerly restricted to Moslem countries.

A new Iraqi Government under Senator Arshad al-Omari was announced. Muhammad Fadel al-Jamali, the retiring Prime Minister, was included as Foreign Minister and acting Minister of Education.

April 29

Israel Prime Minister Moshe Sharett declared in Jerusalem that the decision by the US to grant arms to Iraq could only have the effect of worsening Middle Eastern tension and placing a premium on opposition to peace. He also noted that an Israel request for US military aid had not been granted, although it was based on simple security needs and on considerations of regional responsibility.

The Mixed Armistice Commission condemned both Israel and Egypt for warlike acts across armistice demarcation lines.

April 30

An economic agreement was concluded with the Soviet Union and Lebanon by which each party could import goods from the other to the value of LL10 million.

April, 1954

April 30

Unofficial reports stated that between 32 and 50 officers of the Egyptian cavalry had been arrested. They were described as friends of Major Khaled Mohi-ad-Din.

Seven influential members of the Moroccan Istiqlal Party and two members of the Democratic Independence Party within Morocco were sent under protective custody to an unspecified part of Morocco.

The International Wheat and Barley Conference organized by the UN Food and Agriculture Organization concluded a meeting in Damascus.

May 1

Queen Elizabeth of Britain and the Duke of Edinburgh arrived by air at Tobruk, Libya, and were received by King Idris. They left later for Malta.

Egyptian Wing Commander Hassan Ibrahim left Tripoli after meetings with the President of Libya's Supreme Court and the Wali and Nazirs of Tripolitania which resulted in a reconciliation between the Tripolitania Administration and the court.

US Assistant Secretary of State Byroade, addressing the American Council for Judaism at Philadelphia, stated that the possibility of a formal peace treaty between Israel and the Arab States just did not exist, but the US could not abandon its policy in support of a peace settlement. He urged Israel to adopt a policy of restricted immigration.

May 2

It was reported that the Permanent Communications Committee of the Arab League had completed plans for an Arab Shipping Company with a capital of LE30 million.

Fawzi Mulki, Jordanian Prime Minister, and his Cabinet resigned. A Government spokesman said the resignation was the result of a memorandum from the British Government urging Jordan to accept the proposal of the Secretary General of the UN for a meeting with Israel representatives to discuss the situation on the Jordanian-Israel border, and to accept proposals made to the Security Council for discussing the disputes in general instead of confining them to Jordan's complaint about the Israel attack on Nahhalin. King Hussein asked Tawfiq Abu-al-Huda to form a new Government.

In a new drive against terrorists, police detained 300 persons in Casablanca, Morocco.

The Syrian Parliament voted punitive measures against supporters of former President Shishakli. The measures, aimed primarily at Cabinet officers and other high officials, provided for paying back all monies received in salaries and allowances while in power, and for the annulment of exceptional promotions and pensions.

May 3

Israel protested to the US against Assistant Secretary of State Byroade's speech on May 1.

For the fifth consecutive day the UN Security Council failed to come to a vote on whether to allow general debate on Israel-Jordanian border problems or confine the debate specifically to each nation's complaints.

A Pastures Conference organized by the Jordanian Government in cooperation with the US Point Four Administration opened in Amman.

The Iraqi Minister of Interior announced that elections would be held on June 9.

The Opposition Umma Party of Sudan protested to Governor General Sir Robert Howe over the replacement of Ibraham Ahmad on the Governor General's Commission. They also alleged that Egypt had interfered in the matter, which was a purely internal one and urged that Egypt and Great Britain try to find a settlement by which the Commission could act impartially, the two Sudanese members now both being members of the same party.

May 4

King Hussein of Jordan approved the Cabinet formed by Tawfiq Abu-al-Huda to replace that of Fawzi Mulki.

The Israel UN Representative asked whether Jordan, which was not a member of the UN, agreed to accept the obligations for a peaceful settlement provided in the UN Charter (Art. 35). He said that under the Charter non-members of the organization who submitted complaints must make a commitment to accept the peaceful settlement provisions of the Charter.

The Security Council voted to permit full debate on the entire situation along the Israel-Jordanian borders, in accordance with the Brazilian-Colombian resolution condemning Israel for the attack on Nahhalin on March 28 and calling on members of the UN to consider applying economic and diplomatic boycotts against Israel.

Mahmoud Abu-al-Fath, owner of al-Misri, was sentenced in absentia by the Egyptian Revolutionary Tribunal to ten years imprisonment and

May 4

ordered to forfeit LE358,438 (over $1 million) allegedly gained by illegal means. Hussein Abu-al-Fath, publisher of al-Misri, received a suspended sentence of 15 years imprisonment.

Major Salah Salem said in Cairo that some of the Egyptian Army officers arrested on April 28 confessed to a plot to overthrow the regime and set up Communist rule.

May 5

Governor General Howe left Sudan for London for discussions with the British Government.

Akram al-Hourani, leader of the fused Socialist and Arab Resurrectionist Parties in Syria, stated that he had turned down a cabinet post because the Government had not provided sufficient guarantees that forthcoming elections would be free.

Border restrictions between Syria and Lebanon were lifted.

The Secretary General of the Syrian Foreign Ministry had separate meetings with the diplomatic representatives of Britain, France, the US, Russia, Brazil and Turkey. It was understood that he expressed Syria's anxiety about continuing border tension and discontent at the ineffectiveness of the UN Truce Supervisory.

May 6

Syria's Prime Minister met with President Chamoun of Lebanon to discuss the defense of their countries in case of an attack by Israel.

The Lebanese Parliament voted to abolish preventive arrests of newspapermen.

Twenty more Egyptian Army officers were arrested in an alleged Communist plot to overthrow Egypt's military Government.

May 8

Lebanese President Camille Chamoun left for Brazil, Argentina and Uruguay. He was expected to sign treaties of friendship with these countries.

One Israeli and one Jordanian were killed in separate incidents on the Israel side of the Israel-Jordanian border.

A British soldier, Fusilier Edward McKinney, was sentenced to death by a British court martial for the murder of an Egyptian police officer. The court martial added a recommendation for mercy.

May 9

A Jordanian official charged that a band of 90 Israelis attacked Khirbet Ilin in the Hebron area and fired on an investigating UN team after two Israel soldiers had been killed. He also said that a Jordanian farmer had been killed in Jordan's northern sector.

A communique was issued by the Jordanian Royal Cabinet denying rumors that Jordan had been pressured from abroad on the direction of its foreign policy and that this had caused the resignation of the Mulki Cabinet.

May 10

Jordan filed a complaint with the Mixed Armistice Commission that a Israel force opened fire along a 12 mile sector of the armistice line and that in a seven hour exchange of shots, three armed Israelis and three Jordanian farmers were killed and three wounded near the village of Dair al-Ghusum.

Moshe Sharett, Prime Minister of Israel, said in the Knesset that Israel was ready at any time to negotiate a settlement with its neighbors, but it must be with Israel within its present boundaries and without the introduction of Arab refugees. He declared that Israel had always been ready to pay compensation to the Arabs for abandoned lands without making final peace an absolute condition for such payment.

May 10

Fire was set to a gunpowder factory near Gafsa and a train was fired on in the same area by bandits calling themselves the Tunisian Army of the Liberation.

May 11

The Mixed Armistice Commission (Israel not participating) condemned Israel for invading Jordanian territory at Khirbet Ilin in platoon strength, and for bringing UN Observers under fire.

It was disclosed that General Bennike, Chief of the UN Truce Supervision Organization, had written on April 30 to the Israel Prime Minister, urging him to instruct the Israel delegation to return to meetings of the Israel-Jordanian Mixed Armistice Commission.

US envoys from 13 Middle Eastern countries met in Istanbul under the chairmanship of US Assistant Secretary of State, Henry A. Byroade, to discuss regional problems.

A draft law regarding the Egyptian National Consultative Assembly was published. It provided for 240 members representing economic and social groups who could approve bills on the request of the Government and submit draft legislation, or "urge" the Government to amend or abrogate laws.

The Syrian Parliament adopted legislation aimed at punishing newspaper editors who collaborated with the deposed Shishakli Government.

May 12

The Security Council met to consider the Palestine question, but the issue raised at the last meeting by the Israel delegate not having been settled, the meeting was adjourned.

May 12

Combined floods of the rivers Tigris and Euphrates were stated to have wiped out ten villages around Nasiriyah in southern Iraq and to have made more than 15, 000 people homeless. All cattle and summer crops were destroyed.

Israel circulated its report of the May 9 Khirbet Ilin incident to the Security Council members. According to Israel, a 14 man police border patrol was attacked by Jordanian armed forces and two wounded Israelis were dragged into Jordan and murdered.

US Assistant Secretary of State Henry A. Byroade told the US envoys that the Soviet Union recently intensified its propaganda and political activity throughout the Middle East.

It was stated that the Chamber of Shipping made representations to the Ministry of Transport of Britain concerning an agreement under which Aristotle S. Onassis, a shipowner, had secured the right to transport all Saudi Arabian oil not shipped by tankers of the four US Companies associated in Aramco.

May 13

The Jerusalem Post called for the removal of Commander Hutchison from the Israel-Jordanian Mixed Armistice Commission as a prerequisite for consideration of Israel's return to the Commission, presumably for his vote condemning Israel for firing into an area where UN observers were investigating on May 11.

An agreement providing for US grant aid for economic development was signed in Amman.

Captain James Robinson of the US Navy was appointed a jurist on the Libyan Supreme Court.

May 14

US Assistant Secretary of State Byroade concluded a four day meeting with US Ambassadors of 13 Middle East countries at Istanbul to review, among other questions, the Israel-Arab dispute. The meetings favored

May 14

a joint US, British, French declaration that these countries would use force to prevent aggression by either Israel or the Arab countries, in reaffirmation of the Tripartite Declaration of May 25, 1950.

May 15

Khalafallah Khaled, Defense Minister of Sudan, received Abd-al-Fattah Hassan, Egyptian Deputy Minister for Sudanese Affairs, who was passing through Khartoum. In a statement to the press Khalafallah Khaled referred to activities in the Sudan Defense Force which he considered contrary to the country's interest as they were opposed to the duties and allegiance of army officers.

May 16

The Jordanian Government lodged two complaints with the Mixed Armistice Commission, one alleging an attack by Israel soldiers on shepherds in Jordanian territory and the other an attack by an Israel patrol near Jabaa village in the Hebron area.

Sir Zafrallah Khan, Foreign Minister of Pakistan, concluded a short visit to Egypt. The Egyptian Ambassador informed the press that Zafrallah Khan promised that Pakistan would spare no effort to defend the Holy Places in Palestine and to assist the Arab countries against any Israel aggression.

The Chiefs of Staff of the Arab League countries concluded a three day meeting during which they adopted recommendations which were not made public. The questions discussed were Israel and the standardization of training in military officer's schools.

May 17

The Israel Knesset approved by a vote of 60-4-12 a resolution expressing grave concern at the US decision to give arms to Iraq and at the trend expressed in recent speeches by US Assistant Secretary of State Byroade which were not in accord with the traditional friendship between America and the Jewish people returning to their homeland.

May 17

Five armed Egyptians held up two British civilians near Suez and fired at and slightly injured one of them.

King Faisal of Iraq signed a decree allocating ID3 million for flood victims. The Government also allocated LD3 million for a new oil refinery.

May 18

The Saudi Arabian Minister of Commerce, Muhammad Reza, who was passing through Cairo on his way to Hamburg for the launching of a 47, 000 ton oil tanker for the Saudi Arabian Maritime Company, informed Egyptian reporters that the company would be financed up to 75 percent by the Greek ship owner Onassis and the remaining 25 percent by his Government. He said that Saudi Arabia aimed at a tanker fleet of 500, 00 tons.

Moroccan Resident General Guillaume went to Paris for discussions with the French Government.

May 19

Dodds Parker, Under Secretary in the British Foreign Office, replying to a question in the UK House of Commons, said that in the period April 2 to May 13 there had been 52 attacks on British personnel in the Suez Canal Zone, as a result of which one British serviceman had been killed and four seriously injured.

The Egyptian Revolutionary Council Tribunal sentenced Abd-al-Khair Nagib, editor of the defunct extremist weekly al-Gumhur al-Misri, to fifteen years imprisonment and loss of civil rights for activity against the regime, aiding the Communists and blackmail.

It was reported from Cairo that an Arab plan for the utilization of the waters of the Jordan River had been worked out and would be presented to Eric Johnston, US President Eisenhower's personal ambassador, when he visited Cairo. The plan differed basically from that proposed by Johnston last October.

May 19

Following an outbreak of violence inspired by the Communist Partisans of Peace at a political meeting, the Governor of Baghdad announced that no electoral meeting could be held without his permission.

May 20

The Jordanian representative to the UN officially informed the Security Council that his Government no longer permitted him to represent it. This was a move to withdraw the charges against Israel and was obviously Jordan's answer to Israel's request that it obligate itself in advance to comply with the peaceful provisions of the UN Charter.

Jordan complained to the Mixed Armistice Commission of two alleged violations by Israel of the armistice lines.

Habib Bourguiba, leader of the Tunisian nationalist Neo-Destour Party, who had been under house arrest, was sent to France for residence on the island of Croix.

Francois Lacoste, a career diplomat, was named Resident General for Morocco by the French Government. The post had been refused by Marcel Edmond Naegelen on the grounds that the French Government was not unanimous in its support of his candidacy and that his own Socialist Party was opposed to his acceptance. General Guillaume was to retain his post as Inspector General of the French Forces in North Africa.

May 21

In a letter to the Security Council, Israel accused Jordan of having stirred up 37 border clashes in the 43 days between March 30 and May 11.

It was reported from Rabat that 37 terrorist attacks, resulting in the deaths of 14 Europeans and ten Moroccans, had taken place since April 10.

May 22

A concession for oil prospecting and exploitation in the Western Desert of Egypt was granted to the Egyptian Oil Exploration Company, owned by Cities Service Company of New York.

Colonel Nasser, Egyptian Prime Minister, was reported in a Cairo newspaper to have informed the Syrian Ambassador that he was not opposed to any fusion of Arab States which had the approval of the peoples concerned.

May 23

A five man American military mission headed by Brigadier General Henry Meyers left Iraq after completing a survey of the defenses needed within the framework of American military aid.

Five Nationalists were killed and one wounded and two French soldiers killed in a two day battle for a mountain peak in a lake near Bizerta, Tunisia.

May 24

The Jordanian Government lodged six protests with the Mixed Armistice Commission, alleging four attacks by Israelis, one case of setting fire to Arab grassland and flights by an Israel plane over Jordanian territory.

The Egyptian Revolutionary Command Council announced the establishment of a special five man tribunal to try the persons accused of planning May Day disturbances.

May 25

A statement which was issued by the Saudi Arabian Embassy in Cairo accused the British Government of having, on May 5, prevented food supplies from reaching the inhabitants of the village of Hammassia in the Buraimi Oasis. The statement also alleged that incidents had occurred, one on May 22, in which the British authorities opened fire on tribesmen, killing three, and one in which herds and flocks belonging to the people of Hammassia were stolen by British troops. The Govern-

May 25

ment challenged the British Government to agree to an international investigation.

The Jordanian Government protested to Major General Bennike, Chief of the UN Truce Supervisory Organization, that Israelis had opened fire on the Augusta Victoria hospital in the Arab sector of Jerusalem.

May 26

An official of the Egyptian Foreign Ministry stated that the British Government had made known its readiness to resume negotiations on the Suez Canal Zone.

The Foreign Office of the UK stated that Saudi Arabian allegations that the British Government was starving women and children in Buraimi were completely false.

Jordan filed a complaint with the Mixed Armistice Commission that four men had been killed at the village of Khirbet Jinba. UN observers followed the tracks of 30 or 40 men leading from and returning to Israel.

Five French settlers were murdered by Tunisian outlaws in attacks on two farms south of al-Kef, near the Algerian border. Pierre Voizard, French Resident of Tunisia, told the press in Paris he was convinced that the murders were the work of a small isolated group of irresponsible outlaws.

May 27

The Israel delegation to the Israel-Egyptian Mixed Armistice Commission submitted a resolution stating that three attacks had been made by armed Arab civilians on May 25 and called on the Egyptian authorities to insure the prevention of such acts. The resolution was approved, with the Egyptians abstaining.

May 29

French Resident General in Tunisia Pierre Voizard returned to Tunis after a weeks visit to Paris and announced that a large reinforcement of troops were being sent to the protectorate.

Tunisian Prime Minister M'Zali was shot at outside his palace but was unhurt.

Jordan's UN representative withdrew from UN Security Council discussions on Israel-Jordanian border tension.

May 30

Prime Minister Abdel Nasser of Egypt became head of the Liberation Rally's new High Council.

May 31

The Mixed Armistice Commission with Israel absent charged that two separate units of Israel soldiers fired across the Jordanian border at the village of Nazlat Isa, wounding five inhabitants and condemned Israel for violating the General Armistice Agreement.

The Egyptian Foreign Minister received the British Ambassador, who protested against the continuation of incidents in the Suez Zone.

An unannounced number of infantrymen crossed into Tunisia from Algeria and two squadrons of Mobile Guards were flown in from France.

French Resident General in Tunisia Voizard, in a radio address, said that 48 French combat groups would be stationed in the 48 principal regions colonized by the French. He also called for volunteers for the formation of territorial units to protect population centers.

According to a France Presse report, Egyptian General Nagib, President of Egypt, was expelled from the Supreme Council of the Liberation Movement, of which he was President. The office was then assumed by Gamal Abdel Nasser, formerly Secretary General of the Liberation Movement.

June 1

The Bey of Tunis, Sidi Muhammad al-Amin, and Habib Bourguiba, exiled leader of the Neo-Destour, both issued appeals for an end of violence and asked for French-Tunisian cooperation.

The Egyptian State Council decreed that every employer of more than 500 persons would in the future be completely responsible for the medical care of his workers.

The Egyptian-Israel Mixed Armistice Commission condemned Egypt for two separate incidents involving firing on Israel patrols in the Kissufim area near the border of the Gaza Strip and held Israel responsible for firing on Egyptian military posts.

The Jordanian-Israel Mixed Armistice Commission with Israel absent condemned Israel for shelling and machine gunning the Jordanian village of Nazlat Isa in the Tulkarm area.

Israel representatives in Washington handed Eric Johnston a Jordan Valley plan prepared by a US engineer, Joseph S. Cotton, as an alternative to his UN sponsored proposal.

June 3

The Saudi Arabian Embassy in London issued a statement proposing the setting up of a fact finding mission to look into the dispute over the Buraimi Oasis. A British Foreign Office spokesman declared that Britain thought the proposal inadequate.

Hassan al-Hudaibi, Supreme Guide of the Moslem Brotherhood, left Egypt for Saudi Arabia to discuss Moslem affairs with King Saud.

Details of the Israel Jordan River Development Project were made public. It covered the utilization of the Jordan River waters as well as those of the Litani River.

June 5

The world's largest tanker, named for King Saud, was launched in Hamburg. The 47,000 ton tanker, the first to fly a Saudi Arabian flag, was

June 5

to be followed by others under an agreement between Aristotle S. Onassis, the tanker magnate, and the Saudi Government.

President Camille Chamoun of Lebanon returned from a visit to Brazil, Argentine and Uruguay.

The Iraqi Ministry of Agriculture announced that 75,000 acres of cultivated land in southern Iraq were being distributed among small farmers.

June 6

The Syrian Finance Ministry announced that 60 percent of Syria's currency was covered by gold.

The Egyptian Revolutionary Tribunal charged Ahmad Ali Hassan al-Masri with leading an attempt to carry out a coup on April 27 in which Colonel Nasser was to have been arrested. Its intention was stated to have been to restore parliamentary government.

The Turkish press reported that the Egyptian Government had been "pestering" Turkish students in Cairo to write and talk against Turkey's secular regime. The students had allegedly refused to do so.

Major Salah Salem, Minister of National Guidance, left Egypt for Saudi Arabia to discuss with King Saud relations between the Arab states. His immediate aim was a unified policy to resist the entry of any Arab state into pacts with Western countries which might create divisions within the Arab world.

June 7

The Saudi Arabian Minister of Commerce stated that the oil transportation agreement with Aristotle S. Onassis did not give him a monopoly, but would give him fourth place in transporting Saudi Arabian oil.

The Egyptian Government denied responsibility for the fire at the British military depot in Port Said on May 29, and for the murder of two British soldiers at Ismailia. A reply was sent to the British note of May 31 about these incidents, an official spokesman stating that the Egyptian

June 7

police were cooperating with British military authorities to put an end to incidents in the Suez Canal Zone.

The US State Department announced that during talks with Arab and Israel leaders, Presidential Envoy Eric Johnston would discuss the Jordan River development schemes to define points of essential agreement and insofar as possible to narrow the differences on technical aspects.

June 8

Assistant Iranian Foreign Minister, Abd-al-Hussein Meftah, declared that the Saadabad Pact signed by Turkey, Iraq and Afghanistan in 1934 was null and void. He said Iran would participate in "a kind of Middle East defense pact."

The Iraqi National Front leaders complained to the Iraqi Prime Minister about interference with their candidates in the election campaign. The Minister of the Interior instructed the Governor of Baghdad and other officials to observe strict neutrality between the parties.

The Syrian Arab Socialist Resurrection Party opened an office in Aleppo. Religious leaders demonstrated against the party accusing it of being against religion.

June 9

Electors went to the polls to elect 135 Deputies to the lower house of Parliament in Iraq's first direct election.

Premier Ismail al-Azhari inaugurated the new 153 kilometer railway line which linked central Sudan with southeastern Sudan.

The US Foreign Operations Administration submitted to the Lebanese Government the outline of a project for the developing of the Litani River, at a cost of $97.8 million to be spent over a period of twenty-five years.

June 9

Pakistani Prime Minister Muhammad Ali arrived in Beirut and discussed Middle East defense problems with Lebanese Prime Minister Abdallah Yafi.

Egyptian Minister of National Guidance Major Salah Salem left Jedda, Saudi Arabia for Cairo. The two countries agreed to coordinate their armaments and to oppose Western efforts to bring Arab countries into regional defense pacts.

A French banking and trade mission staying in Cairo issued a statement jointly with the Egyptian Government saying that the foundation of financial and technical cooperation between the two parties had been established.

Israel was ready to negotiate any regional water development scheme for the Middle East, but would not forego its rights or interests or sovereignty over any portion of its territory, Israel Prime Minister Moshe Sharett declared in the Knesset while discussing the various proposed plans.

June 10

Complete returns from 94 of the 135 constituencies in Iraq revealed that the Conservative Party and independent candidates won 86 seats. The ultra-conservative Constitutional Union Party of Nuri-Said suffered a substantial reduction in strength, although it still held the largest single bloc of seats.

The Cabinet of Syrian Prime Minister Sabri Assali resigned. President Hashem Atassi began talks with leaders of political parties and independents regarding the formation of a new Government.

Yemen charged that Adenese troops under the command of British officers made two attacks on Yemeni territory from the neighboring Aden protectorate.

Saudi Arabia appealed to the International Red Cross and the World Health Organization to send vital food supplies to the blockaded village of Hamasa in the Buraimi Oasis.

June, 1954

June 11

On his return from Saudi Arabia, Egyptian Minister of National Guidance Major Salem stated that Egypt and Saudi Arabia agreed to pool their resources in war industries, armaments, defense and military training. He declared that the two countries decided to merge their armies and to reject independent Western plans for anti-Communist defense organizations in the Middle East.

The Egyptian-Israel Mixed Armistice Commission censured Egypt for mining an Israel command car traveling along the Gaza Strip and firing on the patrol in the car, and Israel for directing mortar fire against the Egyptian position.

June 12

Samir Rifai and a number of other persons applied to the Jordanian Government for a license to form a new political party to be called the Umma Party.

A trade and payments agreement was signed between West Germany and Lebanon under which previous restrictions on Lebanese produce entering West Germany were eased. The two countries also signed an agreement for economic cooperation.

After the arrival of King Saud of Saudi Arabia in Amman, Jordan, demonstrators shouted slogans against the US, British and Jordanian Governments.

The association of ex-servicemen of the wartime expeditionary force in Italy (a group of French settlers in Morocco) issued a broadsheet calling for the formation of a vigilance and action committee to oppose official French policy. The statement alleged that the Government was intending to liberate nationalist leaders and other measures even more criminal. Other French associations declared their support of the vigilance committee.

June 13

Iraq's Ambassador in Cairo complained that the Egyptian Government was spreading Arab hostility toward his country.

June, 1954

June 13

Testimony given by Arthur Z. Gardiner, Political and Economic Adviser in the US State Department's Bureau of Near Eastern Affairs, released by the House Committee on Foreign Affairs, indicated that the US Government hoped to make Iraq's army a stabilizing force in the Middle East.

Elections to the regional and municipal councils in Tunisia were postponed indefinitely because of unsettled conditions.

A group of Tunisian nationalist terrorists raided a village in the north and killed four Tunisians who were waiting to vote at French sponsored Consultative Economic Chamber elections.

Eric Johnston began a series of meetings with Arab experts in Cairo on proposals for the Jordan River Valley development. Arab delegates presented their plan, prepared in March, which would give Israel 20 percent of the Jordan River waters.

June 14

Major General Yigal Yadin, former Israel Army Chief of Staff, warned in New York against the dangerous assumption that Iraqi military power could be made a stabilizing force in the Middle East.

It was reported in Cairo that the Syrian Armed Command threatened that it would take over supervision of Syrian national elections unless politicians agreed on the formation of a coalition government.

Francois Lacoste arrived in Morocco to take up his duties as the new Resident General.

June 15

The US State Department announced the conclusion of an agreement with Jordan under which Jordan would receive US aid for economic development.

French paratroops were rushed from Dakar, Senegal, to Tunis to halt mass terrorism in Tunisia.

June, 1954

June 15

Henry R. Labouisse was appointed head of the UN Relief and Works Agency for Palestine Refugees in the Near East.

June 16

At the conclusion of talks between Arab experts and Eric Johnston, a joint communique was issued stating that the talks had served to define the bases of agreement on which, it was hoped, an acceptable plan would be formulated.

Tunisian Premier Salah M'Zali offered the resignation of his Cabinet to the Bey of Tunis and to the French Resident General.

Prime Minister Muhammad Ali of Pakistan arrived in Damascus for talks with Syrian officials.

The Legal Committee of the Arab League approved the scheme for a unified Arab passport.

June 17

The Tunisian Neo-Destour Party issued a statement saying that the situation in Tunisia had not been changed by the M'Zali Government's resignation.

King Saud of Saudi Arabia returned to Riyadh. It was announced that he had donated JD100, 000 to Arab refugees in Jordan.

King Saud of Saudi Arabia stated that his country would help pay for Jordan's national guard, the semi-military fighting force that guarded the border with Israel.

Following a meeting with the Yemeni Minister in Cairo, the Arab League issued a statement accusing Britain of threatening to use force against tribal chiefs in the disputed area between southern Yemen and the Aden Protectorates if they refused to obey the orders of the Adenese Government in implementing the British plan for a federation of Aden Protectorates.

June, 1954

June 18

Major Saleh Salem, Egyptian Minister of National Guidance, told a press conference that Egypt was waiting for a move from the UK regarding the Suez Canal Zone negotiations. If the UK accepted the Egyptian position on the outstanding issues the problem would be solved immediately.

The Saudi Arabian Embassy issued a statement accusing the British Government of warlike actions and aggressions in the Buraimi Oasis. It also claimed that the British were continuing to prevent food from reaching the inhabitants and said that a local Saudi Arabian doctor had appealed to the International Red Cross and the World Health Organization to intervene.

According to an Adenese Government announcement, a Yemeni force of from 100 to 150 men crossed the frontier of the Western Aden Protectorate from al-Suma and attacked the village of Marta in the Awdhali Sultanate. Protests were being lodged with the Yemeni Government.

June 19

Said Ghazzi formed a neutral caretaker Government in Syria of six ministers to supervise elections. It received a vote of confidence from the Chamber of Deputies of 67-9-1.

Three Israel soldiers were killed and one Jordanian woman wounded in a border incident near Wadi Foukim, in the Bethlehem sub-district. A letter from the Chairman of the Mixed Armistice Commission, asking the Israel Army authorities for permission to send observers to interview possible witnesses of the incident, was returned unopened in accordance with Israel practice since the withdrawal of the Israel delegation from the Commission on March 23.

The US Ambassador to Libya presented a check for $1 million to Libyan Premier Muhammad Ben-Halim in Tripoli in connection with economic development projects for Libya.

The French Government established a new Ministry of Tunisian and Moroccan Affairs with Christian Fouchet as its head.

June 20

Major General Muhammad Rafiq Aref, Iraqi Army Chief of Staff, and Brigadier General Abbas Ali Chaleb, Commander of the First Division, left for a three week tour of US military installations and training centers, at the invitation of the US Government.

The US and Great Britain, through their diplomatic representatives, proposed to Israel and Jordan a series of procedural measures designed to check violence along the border between the two countries.

Major General Marie-Antoine d'Hauteville, French Military Commander of Marrakesh, was seriously wounded by a Moroccan terrorist.

June 21

The Saudi Arabian Embassy in Amman announced that King Saud would contribute JD100,000 annually to charity societies and for refugees in Jordan.

Eric Johnston of the US conferred with Israel officials in Jerusalem on the Jordan River Development Scheme.

The Yemeni Ambassador in Cairo told a press conference that he had asked for an immediate meeting of the Arab League Political Committee to discuss an alleged British aggression against the inhabitants of Sanaa, the Yemeni capital. He spoke of a clash between British forces in which many were killed on both sides. He added that the Egyptian Government had promised Yemen all possible help in the dispute.

June 22

A Royal Decree dissolved Jordanian Parliament before it was to vote on a question of confidence for Premier Tawfiq Abu-al-Huda's Government.

Mustafa Nahhas, former Premier and leader of the Wafd Party in Egypt, and his wife were freed from house arrest.

Nine Egyptian Army officers were found guilty of mutinous conspiracy against the regime and were sentenced by the Revolutionary Tribunal to prison terms up to fifteen years.

June 22

Iraqi Foreign Minister Muhammad Fadel al-Jamali left for a tour of the US.

June 23

The Jordanian-Israel Mixed Armistice Commission, meeting without the Israel delegation, condemned Israel for the border incident of June 19 and for preventing UN observers from carrying out their functions on Israel territory under threat of being shot.

The British Ministry of Defense announced that its headquarters of the British Middle East Land and Air Forces would be moved from the Suez Canal Zone to the island of Cyprus.

The Yemeni Legation in Cairo issued a statement denying the British announcement that the clash between Yemeni and Aden Protectorate forces on June 18 had taken place within Aden's territory, and claiming that a force of Audhali tribesmen who owed allegiance to the British Government had attacked the town of al-Soumaa in Yemen with support from units of Aden levies and from four British military aircraft.

June 24

A US State Department representative told a congressional committee that the US had protested to Aristotle S. Onassis, the shipping magnate, against his large share of shipping of Saudi Arabian oil.

Pierre Voizard, the French Resident General of Tunisia, arrived in Paris to consult with the new Minister for Tunisian and Moroccan Affairs, Christian Fouchet.

An additional protocol to the payments agreement of May 28, 1953, between Egypt and Belgium was signed.

It was announced that closer cooperation between Turkey and Libya had been decided upon. This report set off rumors that Libya would be invited to join the Turkish-Pakistani Pact as a third member. Occasion for the announcement was a four day visit to Turkey by Libyan Prime Minister Mustafa Ben-Halim.

June 25

After a meeting in Cairo between Eric Johnston, US President Eisenhower's envoy, and the technical committee representing Jordan, Lebanon, Syria and Egypt it was announced that understanding had been reached on the main points of a prospective agreement for the development of the Jordan River to provide irrigation and power for the Arab countries concerned and Israel.

A spokesman of the French Residency in Tunisia, outlining emergency measures to curb terrorism, said that troops in seven specified areas where terrorists had been most active had been empowered to arrest civilians and search houses.

June 26

The Egyptian Finance Minister announced that the Government had concluded an agreement on prices with four foreign oil companies producing and marketing in Egypt. The agreement put an end to a long standing dispute and opened the way for expansion of the companies' activities.

Former Iraqi Prime Minister Tawfiq Suwaidi called for the formation of a new party, whose main object would be to combat Communism.

A trade agreement between Syria and Iran was signed in Damascus.

June 28

The Jordanian Cabinet rejected an application from the Socialist Arab Renaissance Party for a license to carry on political activities.

The US Foreign Operations Administration allotted $8 million to Jordanian development, reforestation and road construction projects.

Lebanese Prime Minister Yafi won an overwhelming confidence vote in an extraordinary session of Parliament.

Moshe Sharett, Prime Minister of Israel, told a press conference that Eric Johnston, the US envoy, had refused to consider the Israel plan for bringing the Litani River, in Lebanon into a regional water development program. He listed various Israel objections to Johnston's proposals,

June 28

and said that no regional scheme would be allowed to affect Israel's right to the Yarmuk waters already in use for irrigation and hydroelectric power schemes.

June 29

Egypt's Minister of National Guidance Salah Salem arrived in Lebanon for a five day visit. It was stated in Beirut that the main objective of the visit was to try to achieve unity between the Arab States.

Six Frenchmen were wounded, two seriously, by machine gun fire at Tebourba, west of Tunis. Their assailants escaped.

June 30

Dr. Emile Eyraud, managing director of the French newspaper La Vigie Marocaine, was assassinated by terrorists in Casablanca. He was an advocate of a strong anti-nationalist policy.

Widespread cases of crop burning continued to be reported in Morocco.

After sentencing the retired Colonel Ahmad Shawki to ten years imprisonment for inciting the Egyptian Armed Forces to revolt against the regime, Wing Commander Baghdadi announced the decision to close down the Egyptian Revolutionary Tribunal which was set up in September 1953.

The UN Information Officer issued a statement clarifying the status and duties of the UN observers under Security Council resolutions in the belief that they might not be fully understood by public opinion in Israel and by some Israel authorities.

It was stated that the Jordanian village of Awa in Hebron district had been fired on for some hours from Israel territory on June 29, causing damage to houses but no casualties. A truce observer and a Jordanian member of the Mixed Armistice Commission went to the scene and brought about a ceasefire.

June, 1954

June 30

Several persons were wounded in Jerusalem as gunfire and mortar shelling broke out between Arabs in the Old City and Jews in the New City.

The Arab League Council resumed its last ordinary session at Cairo.

The UN Relief and Works Agency reported the number of Palestine refugees at 887,058.

July, 1954

July 1

At a meeting of Israel and Jordan representatives, presided over by General Bennike, Chief of the Truce Supervision Staff, both sides agreed to order an unconditional and sincere ceasefire in Jerusalem. They also agreed that an investigation into the previous day's events in Jerusalem should be undertaken by UN observers with the cooperation of Israel and Jordan authorities.

Heavy firing was resumed in the southern part of Jerusalem while the meeting between Israel and Jordan representatives was in progress. Both Governments blamed the other side for having begun the attacks.

Notes of protest against alleged Israel attacks in Jerusalem were handed to the British, American and French Ambassadors by Jordan.

The American, British and French diplomatic envoys in Israel met in urgent session in Tel Aviv to consider joint action on the Jerusalem flareup, the most serious border clash in months.

It was announced that Syria had given up its territorial claim to the province of Hatay, to Turkey.

Saudi Arabia assured the US that the shipping arrangement with Onassis would not bar US tankers from Saudi Arabian oil.

French Resident General in Tunisia Pierre Voizard returned from Paris and issued an appeal for calm and concord. France gave its Defense Minister authority to call up reservists for an indefinite period following fresh outbreaks of terrorism in Tunisia.

Officials at Rabat announced that 4,000 French troops would arrive in Morocco beginning July 6.

July 2

French reservists living in Tunisia were called up.

Addressing more than 15,00 mourners at the funeral of Emile Eyraud, managing director of the French newspaper La Vigie Marocaine, French Resident General to Morocco Lacoste urged the people to avoid retaliating with blind violence.

July, 1954

July 2

The British Foreign Office stated that the British Ambassadors to Israel and Jordan had been instructed to urge those Governments to exercise restraint after the recent serious clashes on the border.

Israel Prime Minister Moshe Sharett telephoned the British Ambassador and said that Israel was ready to do anything to end the firing in Jerusalem; he urged the British Government to influence Jordan towards that purpose. A message was also sent to the American Charge d'Affaires.

Gunfire from the Old City of Jerusalem killed one soldier and wounded four other persons in the Israel sector; reports from the Arab side said that five were killed and 26 wounded.

July 3

It was announced in London that Great Britain and Libya would raise their diplomatic missions to embassies.

Envoys of the US, Britain and France in Jordan and Israel respectively called on the Foreign Ministries of the two countries to discuss steps to lessen the tension in Jerusalem.

On his arrival in New York from the Middle East, US Special Envoy Eric Johnston said that he believed there was a possibility of settling the dispute over the Jordan River project.

Francois Lacoste, the French Resident General in Morocco, flew to Paris to discuss with the Prime Minister and the Minister for Tunisian and Moroccan Affairs the measures required to deal with terrorism and the problem of reforms.

A detachment of Republican Guards from France arrived in Casablanca.

July 4

Four leaders of the Umma Party were found guilty by a Khartoum court of inciting the Khartoum riot of March 1.

July, 1954

July 4

Sheikh Hafez Wahba, Saudi Arabian Ambassador to London, arrived in Riyadh to brief King Saud on the latest developments in the negotiations over the Buraimi Oasis dispute.

King Hussein of Jordan appealed to other Arab States for material and moral support in his struggle against Israel.

July 5

Israel Defense Minister, Pinhas Lavon, declared in Jerusalem that the shooting outbreak in the capital represented a brutal attack organized by the Jordanian Government and carried out under orders of responsible officers of the Arab Legion.

Jordanian Minister Without Portfolio Isa Elbandak repudiated the charges of the Israel Defense Minister and said there was no doubt that Jewish authorities had planned the firing of the Holy City. He suggested the Israel plan was to see whether the three Western Powers would maintain their undertakings and if not to storm the western bank of Jordan and make its occupation the basis for a peace settlement.

Syria's Prime Minister Said al-Ghazi announced that he and Lebanese Prime Minister Abdallah Yafi had agreed on a program of military aid to Jordan.

Jordan's King Hussein sent messages to Arab monarchs and heads of state asking them to send aid for Jordan's National Guard against Israel aggression.

The Bey of Tunis accepted the resignation of the 19 year old Cabinet of Muhammad Salah M'Zali in the midst of a campaign of native violence against French authorities. Two thousand Moroccan troops were landed in Tunis to suppress terrorism. Government affairs were entrusted to permanent civil servants.

Three battalions of French troops landed at Tunis to strengthen the security forces. Seven rebels and three members of the security forces were killed in a clash at Jebel Orvata.

July 6

Eric Johnston reported to President Eisenhower on the results of his trip to the Middle East. He said Israel, Syria, Lebanon and Jordan had accepted the principle of international sharing of the waters of the Jordan.

The Association of Danish Steamship Companies joined international shipping organizations in protesting an agreement for the transport of Saudi oil between the Saudi Arabian Government and Aristotle S. Onassis.

An agreement was signed between Iraq and India by which the two countries would exchange cultural missions and establish cultural institutes in each other's country.

The Iraqi Government suspended the following newspapers for a year: al-Wadi, al-Hisab, al-Amal and Akhbar al-Yawm.

It was stated in Tunis that 58 rebels had been killed and eight captured in security operations since April 1954.

In a closing speech in the debate between Jordan and Israel, Pinhas Lavon, Defense Minister of Israel, said that while criticism of certain activities of the Truce Supervision Organization were warranted and had led to Israel's withdrawal from the Mixed Armistice Commission, general attacks on the Organization were to be deprecated.

An Egyptian Foreign Ministry official said that the Government would do everything in its power to help Jordan and had already given LE200, 000 for the strengthening of the Jordanian Guard, in accordance with the decision of the Arab League Council.

July 7

The Adenese Government claimed that Yemeni forces in al-Suma opened fire on a rationing party entering Marta in the Awdhali Sultanate, that later the same day about 15 Yemeni regulars shot at five Awdhali tribal guards near Marta, and that Government Guards had joined in an exchange of fire which followed.

The Iraqi Government decided to expand its oil refinery because of the increase in local consumption of petroleum in the last few years.

July 7

The principal witness in the investigation into the assassination attempt on General Marie-Antoine d'Hauteville, French Military Commander of Marrakech, was shot to death by an unknown terrorist in Morocco.

It was announced that Iraq had granted ID50, 000 to the Jordan Home Guard in response to King Hussein's appeal for funds to fight Israel aggression.

July 8

The British Foreign Office handed a note to the Yemeni Charge d'Affaires calling attention to the "very serious situation" on the Adenese-Yemeni frontier. It stated that the British Government had evidence that the Yemeni Government was fomenting rebellion in the Protectorate and that in spite of the agreements of 1934 and 1951, the Yemeni Government was giving color to the belief that it laid claim to the whole of the Western Aden Protectorate and had no intention of settling the frontier problem.

Neo-Destour leaders in Tunisia were reported to have denounced the French decision to form a provisional Government of senior officials of ministries. They had declared that it would only complicate an already grave situation.

July 9

The US Foreign Operations Administration submitted to the Lebanese Government a study outlining a possible development project for the Litani River. The scheme called for the irrigation of 69, 000 acres.

The British Ambassador informed the Egyptian Foreign Minister that the Bank of England had released 10 million pounds sterling from Egypt's blocked sterling balances in conformity with the Anglo-Egyptian sterling releases agreement.

July 10

The Aden Government reported two small raids on Mukeiras Airfield on the Yemeni border. The raiders, believed to be Yemeni tribesmen, were driven off after an exchange of fire.

Informal British-Egyptian talks on evacuation of the Suez Canal Zone were resumed.

Eighty persons were killed and 12 wounded by anti-French terrorists in Ferryville, Tunisia.

A temporary Tunisian Cabinet headed by Georges Dupoizat replaced that of Muhammad Salah M'Zali, which resigned in protest against outbreaks of nationalist terrorism.

The Egyptian newspaper Akhbar al-Yawm reported an agreement with the Yemeni Government for the dispatch of an Egyptian military mission to train the Yemeni Army in modern warfare.

It was announced that Jordan and Syria had agreed to open Legations in each other's capital for the first time.

The Yemeni Charge d'Affaires delivered to the British Foreign Office a note protesting against alleged flights by British Royal Air Force aircraft over the Yemen town of Beidha. It described the flights as open acts of provocation and said they were committed at a time when the Yemeni Government was endeavoring to comply with the British suggestion for a meeting of frontier officers.

The security services in Morocco made public the following figures on terrorism since August 20, 1953: 335 armed attacks; 118 explosions of bombs or grenades; six instances of railway sabotage; 390 cases of arson; 30 Europeans and 89 Moroccans wounded.

Lebanese Prime Minister Abdallah Yafi returned to Beirut after a visit to Cairo.

In a border clash in the Gaza Strip near Kissufim three Israelis were wounded, one of whom died later, and five Egyptians were reported to have been killed. Both sides lodged complaints with the Mixed Armistice Commission.

July 11

The Mixed Armistice Commission met to consider the UN observers' investigations into the shooting in Jerusalem from June 30 to July 2. General Vagn Bennike, Chief of the Truce Supervision Staff proposed the establishment of adequate supervision of frontier guards by officers and non-commissioned officers, a firm undertaking by both sides to refrain from retaliatory fire, orders forbidding sniping, prompt disciplinary action against violators of ceasefire orders and a sincere effort to reduce tension.

An Israel Army spokesman told the press after the Mixed Armistice Commission that General Bennike's five points should be addressed exclusively to Jordan: Israel could not accept them.

British and Egyptian negotiators reopened talks regarding the Suez Canal base which had been deadlocked since October 1953.

Egypt announced the removal of almost all restrictions on imports of goods from the sterling area.

In an interview published in Le Monde, Habib Bourguiba, the Tunisian Neo-Destour leader who was in exile on an island off Brittany, proposed terms for a Tunisian settlement. They included a return to the original 1881 Treaty of Bardo conferring on France the right to station troops in Tunisia and to undertake its diplomatic representation, the repeal by France of the 1884 decree under which decrees signed by the Bey were submitted to the French Resident General for approval and publication and a solemn reaffirmation by France of its intention to lead Tunisia to complete internal self government.

July 12

The Israel delegation presented to the UN Mixed Armistice Commission a resolution condemning Jordan, and the Jordan delegation followed with a resolution condemning Israel.

The Arab League Permanent Committee for Econimic and Financial Affairs, meeting at Cairo, decided to form a three man subcommittee to study a plan for establishing a joint institution to finance economic development schemes in the Arab countries.

July, 1954

July 12

The Sudanese House of Representatives gave a second reading to the Expatriate Officials' Compensation Bill which sanctioned the award of compensation to British officials whose posts were being Sudanized. The decision was unanimous except for one member who abstained.

The heads of the four chief Christian communities in Tunisia appealed for an end to terrorism and condemned absolutely the practice of reprisals.

July 13

The Yemeni Legation at London published a statement charging raids by Aden forces into Yemeni territory. It also said terrorizing flights by British aircraft over Beidha city and district were continuing.

The Aden Government reported two further small raids on Mukeiras Airfield on the Yemen border. The raiders, believed to be Yemeni tribesmen, had been driven off after an exchange of fire.

Shops remained closed in Casablanca and Rabat, Morocco, following an order by terrorists not to open on pain of reprisals. In Casablanca, food shops had been closed for five days.

July 14

The Saudi Arabian Embassy in Cairo issued a statement charging that Great Britain prevented food supplies from reaching the inhabitants of Hamassa village in the disputed Buraimi Oasis area.

July 15

Pierre Voizard, French Resident General in Tunisia, announced that the security forces had been instructed to enforce their regulations with the utmost strictness. He said he was determined to enforce law and order at whatever cost; every act of rebellion would be pitilessly repressed. He asked for the cooperation of the sound elements of the population.

July, 1954

July 15

The text was published in Paris of a letter to the Premier from a group of forty leading Frenchmen in Tunisia calling for the termination of "police methods" in favor of a policy of discussion.

British and Egyptian negotiators met for three hours and discussed a solution for the Suez question.

Meeting under the chairmanship of the Truce Organization's Chief of Staff General Bennike (Israel attending on a special basis), the Jordan-Israel Mixed Armistice Commission failed to fix the blame for the Jerusalem shooting as General Bennike refused to vote with either the Jordanians or the Israelis. Israel offered a six point program to avoid recurrences of the incident; the Jordanians refused to accept the proposals. General Bennike said he would report the situation to the UN Security Council.

US President Eisenhower sent a letter to Egyptian President Muhammad Nagib assuring him that simultaneously with the conclusion of a Suez agreement the US would enter into firm commitments with Egypt for economic assistance for strengthening the Egyptian armed forces.

The Yemeni Charge d'Affaires in London stated that no discussion of the dispute between Yemen and the United Kingdom could begin until the terrorizing flights of British aircraft over Yemen territory in the Beidha area had ceased.

July 16

It was announced that a general French reserve division would soon arrive in Tunisia to enforce law and order.

Israel was condemned by the Israel-Egyptian Mixed Armistice Commission for the Kissufim incident of July 10. At the same time Egypt was condemned for placing land mines that blew up an Israel vehicle and wounded five Israel soldiers on July 8.

It was reported in Washington that Saudi Arabia told the US it did not want any new technical aid funds because the amounts offered were too small.

July, 1954

July 17

Israel charged that the failure of the Israel-Jordan Mixed Armistice Commission to identify and censure those guilty of causing the armistice violation in Jerusalem on June 30-July 2 was liable to undermine the moral authority of the UN and serve as an encouragement to further aggressive violence.

King Saud of Saudi Arabia left for Sanaa, the capital of Yemen, on a three day state visit.

July 18

Syrian President Hashem al-Atassi issued a decree setting August 20, 1954 as the date for parliamentary elections within Syria.

Crown Prince Abd-al-Ilah of Iraq arrived in Beirut to discuss Arab affairs with Lebanese President Camille Chamoun.

Libyan Prime Minister Mustafa Ben-Halim arrived in Washington for discussions regarding conclusion of an air base agreement with the US.

Tunisian Neo-Destour leader Habib Bourguiba was transferred from the island of Croix, west of Brittany, to a chateau near Montargis, 65 miles south of Paris.

July 19

Yemen accused Britain of military and press maneuvers aimed at cutting off its territory.

In a note replying to the Yemeni note of July 10, the British Government categorically denied that Royal Air Force aircraft had flown over Beidha. The Foreign Office therefore rejected the Yemeni Legations' protest and regretted that the allegations should have been published.

British Minister of State for Colonial Affairs Henry Hopkinson stated that in the first half of July Yemeni regulars and irregulars had raided or fired on Western Aden Protectorate from Yemeni territory in at least four cases and that there had been 28 frontier incidents in areas of the Protectorate where Yemeni influence was known to be concentrated.

July, 1954

July 19

The Foreign Office of Britain confirmed that several representations had been made to the Spanish Government concerning the signing by Spanish manufacturers of contracts to supply arms to the Egyptian Government. A report put the value of the contracts at 1,250,000 pounds sterling.

Arthur Douglas Dodds-Parker, Under Secretary of the Foreign Office of Britain, stated in reply to a question in the Commons that in the Government's view the agreement between the Saudi Arabian Government and A. S. Onassis constituted flag discrimination by seeking to force buyers of oil to use tankers of one particular flag.

July 20

The Syrian Cabinet decreed that the number of seats for the new Chamber would be 117 for Moslems, 16 for Christians and six for Bedouin tribes.

Leaders of the Syrian Union of Labor Syndicates decided to call a general strike in Damascus for July 24 and in the other Governorates for July 26. The strike was postponed, however, to give the Government time to submit a special Labor Bill to Parliament.

The Syrian-Israel Mixed Armistice Commission censured Syria for firing on Israel patrol boats on Lake Tiberias; it also censured Israel for replying from shore batteries and patrol boats.

The Yemeni Legation at London issued a statement to clarify misconceptions over relations with Britain. After reviewing Yemen's point of view since 1941, the statement concluded with a denial of reports of internal dissensions in Yemen and of the allegation that the Imam hoped to enlist popular support by adopting an aggressive foreign policy.

The Supreme Economic Council of the Arab League met at Cairo. It referred the formation of an Arab Mercantile Company to a subcommittee for consideration, postponed consideration of a suggestion to exploit mineral depsits in the Dead Sea area to give Jordan time to study the question and approved the unification of Arab action to combat smuggling to Israel.

July, 1954

July 21

Iraqi Prime Minister Arshat Omari left for Turkey on a two week holiday.

Anthony Nutting, Under Secretary of the Foreign Office of Britain, said in answer to a parliamentary question that the British Ambassador in Cairo had been instructed to make an official protest regarding a series of Egyptian Government broadcasts in Swahili encouraging African, including Mau Mau, hostility to British colonial government.

July 22

The French authorities issued an order prohibiting all movement, except on main roads, within a wide area around Sbeitla and Kasserine, in western Tunisia, where anti-rebel operations were in progress. In an ambush near Sousse three Republican guards were wounded.

In a speech on the eve of the second anniversary of the Army revolution, Colonel Nasser, Egyptian Prime Minister, said that if Israel failed to comply at least with UN repeated decisions, the situation in the Near East was liable to explode. He called on the UN to do something in earnest for the execution of its decisions which Israel had "trodden over."

The conclusion of negotiations on a US-Libyan base rights agreement was announced in connection with a visit of Premier Mustafa Ben-Halim to Washington.

July 23

Egypt began a six day celebration of the second anniversary of the revolutionary regime.

The British Government announced that it was sending War Secretary Antony Head to Cairo for top level talks regarding the proposed British withdrawal from the Suez Canal base.

King Saud of Saudi Arabia donated JD150, 000 toward the development of Jordan's National Guard.

July, 1954

July 26

In his speech from the Throne at the opening of Parliament, King Faisal of Iraq said that lack of cooperation between the Chamber and the Government had led to the Cabinet's resignation.

In Iraq Abd-al-Wahhab Marjan, Deputy leader of the former Constitutional Union Party, was elected Speaker of the Chamber of Deputies, and Muhammad al-Sadr President of the Senate.

In Iraq the National Front, composed of the Istiqlal, the National Democratic Party and a number of Independents announced the formation of a parliamentary bloc pledged to the liberation of Palestine and the non-participation of Iraq in international blocs.

July 27

An accord, entitled "Heads of Agreement," was initialed by Egyptian Prime Minister Nasser and British War Secretary Anthony Head for the removal of the 83, 000 British troops from the Suez Canal Zone defenses but providing that the West might still use the base of aggression against an Arab State or Turkey. British sources estimated it would take a month to draft the details of a formal treaty.

Colonel Nasser, Egyptian Prime Minister, and Anthony Head, British Minister for War, announced in a communique that they had initialled the "Heads of Agreement" embodying the principles proposed for an agreement on the Suez Canal base. They expressed their conviction that, by removing sources of mistrust and friction, the agreement would lead to growing improvement in the two countries' relations and would contribute to the maintenance of peace and security.

Forty Tunisians were detained for questioning in connection with the murder of the Bey's chief guard.

July 28

The Syrian Chamber of Deputies approved an amendment to the Labor Code giving the Government the right to decide if a laborers' strike was legal and allowing it to grant salaries to laborers if the factory owners refused to open their factories.

July, 1954

July 23

The Iraqi Cabinet resigned during the absence of the Prime Minister, Nuri-Said being asked to form a new Government. He announced the dissolution of the Constitutional Union Party.

July 24

Colonel Rene de Benoit de Lapaillone, Chief of the Bey's Palace Guard, was shot and killed on the street in Tunis. Police ordered all Arab cafes in the city closed and roadblocks set up.

In a letter to Francois Lacoste, the French Resident General in Morocco, 124 leading Moroccans, mostly former politicians or members of the liberal professions, urged that the time had come to give practical substance to the principle of Moroccan sovereignty, and called for a frank and unequivocal discussion of the problem posed by the deposition of Sultan Sidi Muhammad Ben-Youssef.

July 25

The chairman of the Lebanese-Israel Mixed Armistice Commission called on Lebanon to keep elements suspected of border infiltration and attacks on Israel out of the frontier districts.

An Israel Foreign Ministry spokesman said about the possible grant of arms by the US to Egypt: "The US may be quite sincere about giving the Egyptians arms, so that they could defend the Suez Canal after Britain had left, but the Egyptians were equally sincere in wanting the arms so that they could attack Israel with a greater chance of success than they had the previous time."

The Syrian Chamber of Deputies was summoned to an emergency meeting to discuss a threat by trade union leaders to order a general strike in support of the Damascus textile workers, as well as to deal with the tension which had developed as a result of the election campaign.

July, 1954

July 28

British Foreign Secretary Anthony Eden announced that Britain and Saudi Arabia had agreed to arbitrate the Buraimi Oasis dispute. The arbitration tribunal would consist of five members, one nominated by Britain on behalf of the Sultan of Muscat and the ruler of Abu Dhabi, one by Saudi Arabia and three neutrals to be chosen by these two.

The Israel Prime Minister expressed concern over the change in the balance of power resulting from Anglo-Egyptian agreement on the Suez Canal evacuation which he claimed might be a spur to aggression if the settlement was not conditional on complete cessation of the blockade against Israel in the Suez Canal and if the US proposed to send arms to Egypt.

British Foreign Minister Eden outlined to the House the terms of the Suez Canal base agreement and reaffirmed the Government's intention of abiding by the Tripartite Declaration of May 2, 1950 relating to Arab-Israel relations. He said that both the US and French Governments were equally determined to uphold that declaration.

US President Eisenhower and Secretary of State John Foster Dulles both expressed great satisfaction at the conclusion of the Anglo-Egyptian Suez Canal base agreement.

July 29

A motion approving the "Heads of Agreement" initialled in Cairo on July 27 was approved in the British House of Commons by a vote of 257-26. The main body of Labor members abstained, and a number of Conservatives (the Suez Group) opposed the motion.

July 30

The Syrian-Israel Mixed Armistice Commission adopted two resolutions censuring both Syria and Israel for their participation in an incident on March 15, 1954.

The Shaab (Peoples') Party of Syria announced its decision to boycott the coming elections because of the belief that they would not be free.

July, 1954

July 30

Abd-al-Aziz Djellouli, a moderate member of the Tunisian Neo-Destour, returned to Tunis after conferences with French leaders in Paris.

It was announced that General Boyer de Latour du Moulin had been appointed French Resident General in Tunisia in succession to Pierre Voizard, and that the Cabinet had approved a new policy for Tunisia proposed by Premier Pierre Mendes-France which was designed to base Franco-Tunisian relations on a willingness to guarantee French interests and to respond to Tunisian aspirations by the realization of internal autonomy.

July 31

After French Premier Mendes-France arrived in Tunis, he told the Bey that France was ready to transfer the internal government of the country to Tunisia. France however, would continue in control of defense and foreign affairs.

Habib Bourguiba, the exiled Neo-Destour leader, described the French Government's proposals for Tunisia as a substantial and decisive stage along the road that led to the restoration of complete Tunisian sovereignty.

The first stage of a census in the cities and provinces of Libya was taken with the aid of a team from the UN Technical Assistance Administration.

August, 1954

August 1

Ali Maher, Chairman of the Constitution Drafting Committee of Egypt, presented the completed draft of the new constitution to Egyptian Premier Gamal Abdel Nasser.

The economic blockade of British troops in the Suez Canal Zone was lifted, permitting fresh food to go to troops through the Canal for the first time in two years.

The Federal Economics Ministry of the West German Government announced that the latter would underwrite the shipment of 65 million German marks worth of industrial equipment to Egypt.

Amir Mashaal, Saudi Arabian Defense Minister, concluded defense discussions with Egyptian Ministers.

The Israel Government replied to the 11 point note regarding border security presented to it by the Western Powers. The technical proposals were accepted; doubt, however, was expressed as to whether the measures suggested would check Arab infiltration into Israel territory. The proposals to extend the powers of the UN observers were rejected. The reply concluded by welcoming the initiative taken by the Western Powers to reduce the tension on the Arab-Israel borders, but stressed that the best way to put an end to such tension was through direct Arab-Israel negotiations.

The Anglo-Iranian Oil Company refinery, with a five million ton annual capacity, was commissioned.

Five persons were reported trampled to death in riots near Fez, and a Frenchman was reported shot to death in Casablanca, Morocco. The riots were touched off by rumors of the return of Sidi Muhammad Ben-Youssef, former Sultan.

August 2

It was reported in Cairo that the Government was studying the conditions under which the US would grant military and economic aid to Egypt.

A French educated moderate Nationalist, Tahar Ben-Ammar, was appointed by the Bey of Tunis as Prime Minister and instructed to pick his Cabinet. Habib Bourguiba appealed to Tunisians to cease all violence and called for a general ceasefire throughout the Protectorate.

August, 1954

August 3

US Secretary of State John Foster Dulles said that he hoped the Anglo-Egyptian negotiations on the Suez Canal Zone would dispose Egypt to comply with the 1951 Security Council resolution requesting an end to the anti-Israel blockade.

The Moslem Brotherhood proclaimed its opposition to all aspects of the Anglo-Egyptian agreement on the Suez Canal Zone and challenged the Egyptian Government to permit publication of the Brotherhood's arguments attacking the proposed agreement.

The "Voice of the Arabs" broadcast from Cairo urged Tunisians to continue their fight for independence. Bandits shot a French civil servant in Sousse and a Tunisian near Tatahouine.

In Morocco demonstrations for the return of the ex-Sultan led to riots in Petijean in which twelve people, including six Jews, were killed.

UN Secretary General Dag Hammarskjold announced the appointment of Major General E. L. M. Burns of Canada as Chief of Staff of the Truce Supervision Organization in Palestine, to succeed Major General Vagn Bennike of Denmark.

August 4

General Nuri-Said of Iraq, moderate leader of the former Constitutional Union Party, formed a Cabinet to succeed the caretaker Government of Arsha al-Omari. He would hold the positions of Prime Minister and Minister of Defense.

The King of Iraq dissolved Parliament. Nuri-Said announced the dissolution of the Constitutional Union party in preparation for the elections to be held in September. In a message to the King, Said outlined his foreign policy which was based on termination of the Anglo-Iraqi treaty and on establishing Iraq's cooperation with other nations in a manner compatible with the Charter of the UN.

French reinforcements continued to arrive in Tunisia; 700 Tunisians were searched and questioned in Sousse; a curfew was imposed from 8 pm to 5 am in Sfax.

August, 1954

August 4

Habib Bourguiba issued a statement in which he said that all trends of opinion, even minority ones, should be included in the new Tunisian Government.

August 5

Following the rejection of the Bey of his first list of Ministers, Tahar Ben-Ammar, Tunisian Prime Minister, submitted a second and more moderate list.

The text was published of a letter written on August 4 by Si Thami al-Glaoui, Pasha of Marrakech, to the French Resident General in Tunisia. In the letter al-Glaoui gave a warning of the danger threatening France in Morocco by reason of the "intrigues of agitators in favor of the ex-Sultan." He advised that firmness should be used and described himself as head of the movement which had favored the deposition in accordance with sacred Islamic precepts and had the unanimous support of the people.

August 6

A group of Yemenis, led by Hassan Aqel, attacked a trade truck, killing one person and wounding two others. The Aden Government authorized assistance to be given to the Maisari tribe so they could protect themselves against raiders and also assist the Protectorate levies and guards.

Colonel Nasser, Egyptian Prime Minister, left for Mecca to make a pilgrimage, to have political discussions with Saudi Arabian King Saud and to attend the Islamic congress.

The Syrian Government announced that the parliamentary elections scheduled for August 20 had been postponed to September 24. All nominations were cancelled.

August, 1954

August 7

In Tunisia, Prime Minister Tahar Ben-Ammar completed the formation of the new ten member cabinet which was to negotiate with the French. It was composed of four members of the Neo-Destour, one Socialist and five independents.

Secretary General of the Arab League, Muhammad Abd-al-Khaleq Hassouna cabled the UN Secretary General drawing his attention to the serious situation in Morocco and to the repressive measures taken by the French authorities in the Protectorate.

The Istiqlal Party of Morocco ordered its followers to carry out a general strike.

Former Syrian President Shukri al-Kuwatli returned to Damascus after nearly five years exile in Egypt.

Israel's Ambassador to the US, Abba Eban, conferred with Secretary of State John Foster Dulles on Israel's security in the light of the Anglo-Egyptian agreement on the Suez Canal Zone.

The Aden Government issued a statement saying that the Government of Yemen had agreed to the British proposal that British and Yemeni frontier officers consult with a view to restoring tranquility on the frontier, but that when on July 7 the British frontier officer approached his Yemeni counterpart, the Amir of Beidha, suggesting a meeting on or after July 14, he was told that the Yemeni frontier officer was ill at Taizz and that the meeting would have to be postponed. The statement continued that while these meetings were delayed, it became difficult not to doubt the sincerity of the professions of peace made by the Yemeni Government.

In Cairo, the Moslem Brotherhood accused the Neo-Destour Party of Tunisia of going back on an agreement for the liberation of the entire Maghreb by the appeal of Habib Bourguiba to the Tunisian people recommending the acceptance of the Mendes-France program.

August, 1954

August 8

It was announced in Cairo that US Ambassador Jefferson Caffery would retire from the Foreign Service in January 1955 and be replaced by Henry Byroade, Assistant Secretary of State for Near Eastern and African Affairs.

Muhammad Hassan al-Wassani, leader of the Moroccan Shura and Istiqlal Party, and Muhammad al-Makki al-Nasri, leader of the Moroccan Unity and Independence Party, living in self imposed exile in Egypt, wired Saudi Arabian King Saud urging the Islamic Conference in Mecca to adopt a resolution appealing to France to put an end to the present repressive measures in Morocco, to expedite the granting of independence to the Protectorate and to restore the ex-Sultan to his throne.

The Bey of Tunisia invested the following Cabinet of four Neo-Destourians, one Socialist, and five Independents, including the Prime Minister, Tahar Ben-Ammar. The Ministers of State were to be Muhammad Masmoudi, Mongi Slim and Abd-al-Aziz Djellouli. French directors were to remain in charge of Finance, Education, Public Works and Communications until the autonomy agreement had been concluded by the Cabinet with the French Government.

August 9

About 1,000 persons were confined by French and North African soldiers as a result of rioting in the principal cities of Morocco.

The Nationalists of Morocco issued a general strike order to Moroccan workers.

August 10

Thousands of Berber tribesmen armed with knives and rifles forestalled nationalist outbreaks in Morocco which were planned to prevent observance of the religious feast of Aid al-Kabir in protest against the removal of the former Sultan.

In the first stage of the withdrawal of Britain's garrison from the Suez area, a detachment of 300 British troops sailed for England.

August, 1954

August 10

General Bennike, Chief of the UNTSO, reported to the UN Security Council that it was impossible to place responsibility on either Jordan or Israel for the violence in Jerusalem between June 30 and July 2, 1954.

It was reported from San Sebastian, Spain, where the Spanish Cabinet was meeting, that the Spanish Government was framing a statement on Moroccan policy which would censure France and reaffirm Spain's refusal to recognize France's unilateral ouster of Sultan Sidi Muhammad Ben-Youssef in August 1953.

By a vote of 398-126, French Premier Mendes-France obtained postponement of a full dress debate on the situation in Morocco and Tunisia. He told the Assembly that his present objective was to restore peace in Morocco and that the Government would ignore claims for the return of the former Sultan. He defended his program for Tunisia and concluded with a strong appeal to the Moroccans to refrain from violence.

The Tunisian Neo-Destour Executive issued a statement which expressed satisfaction with the French decision to grant Tunisian autonomy and to review Franco-Tunisian relations. The statement called for a democratic regime which would guarantee French interests so long as these did not infringe upon Tunisian sovereignty or the rights of Tunisian citizens. But it added that the negotiations had no chance of success so long as repressive methods such as exile, deportation and imprisonment continued.

August 11

The Feast of Aid al-Kabir, normally one of prayer and rejoicing, was commemorated as a day of mourning by Moroccans in obedience to an Istiqlal order.

The Ambassador of Israel to the US, Abba Eban, was called home for discussions of US policy in the Middle East and its effect on Israel.

August, 1954

August 12

Muhammad Ali, Prime Minister of Pakistan, said that during his recent pilgrimage to Mecca he had discussed with Egyptian Prime Minister Colonel Nasser problems of a much wider range than mutual defense.

August 13

Ahmad Zabarah, Yemeni Charge d'Affaires in Washington, protested at the National Press Club in Washington against Britain's proposed federal plan for the Aden Protectorate.

August 14

Lieutenant General Rafail Garcia Valino, High Commissioner in Spanish Morocco, addressed a gathering of Moorish chiefs at Tetuan on the final day of the Aid al-Kabir festival. He said that Spain was pushing its policy of giving Moroccans an increasing share in the administration of the Spanish Zone and criticized French policy in the neighboring zone.

The French Foreign Ministry announced that Tunisian Prime Minister Tahar Ben-Ammar and Minister of State Muhammad Masmoudi would visit Paris August 17 and 18 as official guests of the French Government to settle details of the forthcoming formal negotiations for Tunisian autonomy.

The Saudi Arabian Government announced that it would reject all future US Point Four aid and that the present mission would be terminated immediately.

August 15

French troops marched into Fez, ancient capital of Morocco, where they occupied the Arab quarters and arrested nationalist leaders.

A Syrian submarine chaser seized a 50 ton Israel fishing boat in the Mediterranean and took it to Latakia harbor. An Israel Foreign Ministry spokesman called the seizure an act of piracy in contravention of international law and usage.

August, 1954

August 15

US Secretary of State John Foster Dulles sent congratulatory messages to Egyptian Premier Nasser and Foreign Minister Mahmoud Fawzi on the conclusion of the accord with Britain; he sent a similar message to British Foreign Secretary Anthony Eden.

Major Salah Salem, Egyptian Minister of National Guidance and Sudanese Affairs, accompanied by Muhammad Riyad, Director of the Foreign Ministry's Department of Arab Affairs, flew to Iraq for conferences with King Faisal and other important Iraqi political leaders. The primary objective of the mission was reported to be the eradication of the distrust and friction which had accumulated in relations between Egypt and Iraq in the past decade.

The Iraqi Minister of the Interior announced that general elections would be held in Iraq on September 12, 1954.

August 16

The Netherlands Ship Owners Association asked its Government to intervene in the transport agreement between the Saudi Arabian Government and Aristotle S. Onassis. This was the seventh national group to protest the agreement as a monopoly and a serious limitation on the transport of Saudi Arabian oil and oil products by other ship owners.

Amir Faisal, Crown Prince and Foreign Minister was named Premier of Saudi Arabia by Royal Decree.

Eight Sudanese were promoted to the post of Provincial Governor to replace British officials.

August 17

In the first big withdrawal of British forces from the Suez Canal Zone under the Anglo-Egyptian agreement of July 27, 2,000 British troops sailed from Port Said.

An official announcement in Jerusalem stated that since the establishment of the Israel State, 4,800 Arabs had been permitted to settle in

August, 1954

August 17

Israel: 1,750 came from Jordan; 2,270 from Lebanon; 150 from Syria and 620 from Egypt.

It was announced in Iraq that the Umma Party had been dissolved and that its members would stand for election as independents.

Following talks in Iraq between Nuri-Said, Iraqi Prime Minister and Major Saleh Salem, Egyptian Minister of National Guidance, it was announced that full agreement had been reached on all matters discussed including a decision to surmount all obstacles hindering full cooperation between the Arab States.

Jordanian Premier Tawfiq Abu-al-Huda suspended five weekly newspapers for attacking the newly formed government.

The Jordan-Israel Mixed Armistice Commission, with Israel absent, condemned Israel for violation of the Armistice Agreement on August 3, 1954.

The US Defense Department announced that six Egyptian Army officers were in the US for six weeks of intensive study of Army quartermaster and ordinance activities.

August 18

Saleh Jabr, leader of the Iraqi Umma Party that was dissolved on the previous day, returned from Beirut.

Forty Ulemas (Moslem theologians) who had recently signed a letter in favor of the ex-Sultan were removed by the Sultan's guards from the Mosque of Moulay Idris in Fez (a place of sacred sanctuary) and taken with about thirty other Moslems who were in the sanctuary in Rabat to await the Sultan's decision.

Major Salah Salem of Egypt completed several days discussions with King Faisal of Iraq and Iraqi Government officials. A joint declaration stated that one of the results of the talks would be the reinforcement of the Arab Collective Security Pact.

August, 1954

August 18

The Institute of International Education of New York reported that 1,664 students from Arab League countries and 857 from Israel were enrolled in American colleges and universities. Egypt was not included as the Egyptian Embassy refused to give out the number of Egyptians studying in the US.

Syria released the captured 50 ton Israel fishing boat captured in the Mediterranean on August 15, along with its crew and master.

French and Tunisian leaders in Paris agreed to a conference in Tunis in September to establish Tunisia's internal autonomy.

August 19

Major Salah Salem, Egyptian Minister of National Guidance, said in Baghdad that Egypt was not opposed to closer union between any of the Arab States so long as that union had the support of the countries concerned.

King Faisal of Iraq reportedly had accepted an invitation to visit President Nagib of Egypt the first week of November.

Egyptian Prime Minister Nasser told a press conference that leaders of Egypt, Pakistan and Saudi Arabia, who had met in Mecca, had decided on a missionary campaign in Africa to compete with Christian missions there.

The new UN Chief of Staff of the UN Truce Supervision Organization in Palestine, Major General E. L. M. Burns, arrived in Jerusalem.

The Jordan Press Office said that 150 Israel troops had penetrated Jordan territory in the Hebron area that evening and after a clash with Jordan forces had retired leaving three Israeli dead.

Arab League Secretary General Abd-al-Khaleq Hassouna left Cairo for a tour of Jordan, Syria and Lebanon.

Tunisian Prime Minister Tahar Ben-Ammar and Minister of State Muhammad Masmoudi left Paris for Montargis to confer with Neo-Destour leader Habib Bourguiba.

August, 1954

August 19

Moshe Sharett, Israel Prime Minister, said that he was not satisfied with certain verbal assurances given to Abba Eban, Israel Ambassador to the US, by US Secretary of State Dulles, in connection with American policy in the Middle East. Israel was convinced that arms sent by Western countries to the Arab States would be used against Israel.

In Morocco one of the Caliphs of the Pasha of Casablanca and another official were slain in Casablanca and two of the Caliph's guards and two passing motorists were injured.

August 20

A bipartisan group of US Senators and Representatives, headed by Senator Leverett Saltonstall (Republican, Massachusetts) of the Senate Armed Services Committee, conferred with Secretary of State Dulles and registered concern over three points of critical importance to the stabilization of relations between Israel and other countries of the Middle East: the bearing of the preliminary Anglo-Egyptian Suez agreement on Egypt's blockade of Israel shipping; the effect on Israel's security of the military agreements between the US and the Arab nations; and American military assistance to Israel.

On the first anniversary of the deposition of the former Sultan of Morocco, Ahmad Balafrej, Secretary General of the outlawed nationalist Istiqlal Party, speaking at Geneva, Switzerland, declared that the first condition for peace in Morocco was the transfer of the deposed Sultan from exile in Madagascar to France where he could negotiate with the French Government.

A general strike was called by nationalists and Communists in Morocco.

August 21

In Iraq, the National Democratic Party and the Istiqlal Party dissolved their National Front. The former decided to boycott the coming elections; the latter to contest them.

Colonel Nasser, Prime Minister of Egypt, declared at a public meeting that no joint defense or alliance was implied by the Suez Canal Zone

August 21

agreement with Britain. Egypt had no objection to receiving military aid from the US or Britain, provided that it was unconditional, he said.

August 22

Amir Turki Ibn-Utaishan, the Saudi Arabian official who had been in Hamasa (Buraimi Oasis) for two years, and the Trucial Oman levies and Abu Dhabi irregulars occupying parts of the disputed territory were ordered to withdraw in accordance with the arbitration agreement with Britain.

After hearing a report from Israel Ambassador Abba Eban of his talks with US Secretary of State John Foster Dulles, Israel Prime Minister Moshe Sharett stated that Israel would continue to oppose the US policy of arming the Arab States, and would not be satisfied with mere verbal guarantees of its security, then in even greater danger as a result of the Anglo-Egyptian agreement on Suez that had brought about a change in the Middle East balance of power.

August 23

King Hussein of Jordan arrived in Istanbul for a four day official visit to Turkey.

French Resident General of Morocco, Francois Lacoste, flew to Paris for discussions with the French Minister of Tunisian and Moroccan Affairs.

Egypt demanded that the UN Truce Supervision Organization reopen the case in which Israel was accused of maintaining a fortified stronghold disguised as an agricultural settlement at al-Auja, from which Israel made a military attack into the demilitarized zone on September 27, 1953. The demand was based on evidence given by an Israel deserter.

August 24

It was reported in Washington that the US Government refused to underwrite a $100 million Litani River development project for Lebanon although the plans had been prepared by a Point Four mission.

August 24

The Jordanian Moslem Brotherhood's newspaper al-Kifah al-Islamiah was suspended for six months to protect public interests.

The Jordanian Government forbade the entry of Sheikh Hassan al-Hodaibi, former supreme leader of the Egyptian Moslem Brethren, and Allal al-Fasi, Moroccan Independence Party leader.

August 25

The Umma Party of Iraq announced that it decided to boycott the elections; according to its leader, Saleh Jabr, it was not satisfied that the Government would be neutral during the electoral campaign.

August 26

The French Minister of Tunisian and Moroccan Affairs told the French National Assembly that the Government had prepared a vast program of action to lead Morocco to sovereignty and democracy.

The bishops of Christian communities within Lebanon met to discuss sectarian demands and counter demands touched off by a booklet by George Shaker, which contained statements considered offensive to the Prophet and which caused violent Moslem demonstrations in Beirut. The National Organization (a Moslem group) had demanded that the Government either abolish sectarianism or make a correct census of the population.

Sir Reader Bullard, a British diplomat, was named Britain's representative on the arbitration tribunal on the Buraimi Oasis.

August 27

The French national assembly voted 451-122 to support the reform policies for granting more self rule to Morocco and Tunisia of French Premier Mendes-France.

Speaking at the end of a two day debate on North African policy, French Premier Mendes-France told the French Assembly that the Government,

August 27

through its Resident General in Morocco, would begin a frank and loyal discussion with representatives of all forms of Moroccan opinion, who would be asked to form a council to discuss basic reforms.

Lebanese Premier Abdallah Yafi left for Baghdad for talks with Iraqi political leaders on the strengthening of Arab unity.

August 28

A Royal Ordinance required the dissolution of all political parties in Iraq.

August 29

Following a call on Colonel Nasser by the Saudi Arabian Ambassador, Major Saleh Salem, Egyptian Minister of National Guidance, revealed that a high Arab personality (understood to be King Saud) had protested against the statement by Major Salem during his recent visit to Iraq that Egypt did not object to unions between Iraq, Syria and Jordan provided that they were founded on the will of the peoples concerned.

August 30

The Iraq Government suspended 18 political newspapers and magazines, bringing the total of newspapers suspended during the month of August to 31.

In a debate in the Knesset, Israel Prime Minister Moshe Sharrett strongly attacked British policy and the Anglo-Egyptian agreement which he interpreted as an abandonment of Israel and described as an unprecedented act of territorial ostracism. Sharrett also attacked the US for granting economic and military aid to Iraq and Egypt, declaring that it would increase the military inequality already existing between Israel and Egypt.

The Jordanian Press and Publicity Bureau stated that an Israel contingent had crossed the demarcation line that morning in the Hebron district and had fired on two villages with mortars and automatic weapons. Men of the Arab Legion and National Guards had returned the fire, and after an

August 30

exchange lasting three hours, the Israelis had withdrawn. One Jordanian was killed and three wounded; the Israelis reportedly suffered heavy casualties.

The British Government announced its decision to lift the embargo, imposed in October 1951, on the export of arms to Egypt. The statement made clear that the export of arms to Egypt, other Arab countries, or Israel would have to conform with the Tripartite Declaration of May 1950 which stated that these countries had given assurances to the three Western Powers that any arms purchased by them would not be used for aggression.

September 1

It was officially announced that some Cabinet changes had been made in Egypt with the aim of bringing in the only two members of the Revolution Command Council not holding ministerial office. This followed the resignation of the Finance Minister and the Minister of Education.

General Boyer de Latour du Moulin, the French Resident General in Tunisia, promised sympathetic consideration to political prisoners and a pardon to all those who laid down their arms, but said he would remain implacable towards murderers. He gave an assurance that the new agreements to be negotiated would fully guarantee French settlers rights and the rights of France in respect of defense, foreign affairs and the maintenance of order.

In a statement during the debate in the Knesset on foreign policy, Israel Prime Minister Moshe Sharrett declared that Israel was ready to meet any movement towards peace with Egypt.

According to an Aden Government announcement, 15 Yemeni soldiers crossed into the Awdhali Sultanate in the Western Aden Protectorate and attacked farmers, but were dispersed by local guards.

The Sudanese Government accused the Appeals Court of involving itself in political controversy, departing from constitutional principles, usurping the functions of Parliament, trying to adjudicate on Government responsibilities, and abuse of the Government.

An officer and four parachute troops, all French, were killed in a clash with rebels in Tunisia on the Jebel Orbata, east of Gafsa. Rebel casualties were believed to be serious. In another clash with about seventy rebels, a few miles to the east, two members of a Franco-Tunisian unit were wounded.

The Egyptian Supreme Military tribunal sentenced two women and 19 men to prison for terms ranging from one year to life on charges of conspiring to overthrow the Government.

In Iraq three Royal Decrees were issued in an effort to tighten the reins on Communist activities.

September 2

Major General E. L. M. Burns of Canada took over as Chief of Staff of the UN Truce Supervision Organization in Palestine.

Egypt's Revolutionary Command Council issued a policy statement emphasizing Egyptian support of the West although public opinion was not ready to accept a formal treaty arrangement. The statement also declared the only major threat to the area would be an invasion by the Soviet Union.

Egypt's Minister of National Guidance, Major Salah Salem, arrived in Amman for a five day visit.

King Hussein of Jordan informed the British and US Ambassadors that Jordan would have to reconsider its attitude to the armistice agreement unless Israel ended its repeated aggressions on the armistice line. He said Jordan had always been careful to observe the armistice terms.

The Jordan Press Office announced that Jordan had lodged two complaints with the Mixed Armistice Commission charging Israel with violations in the Ramallah area. It stated that in the two encounters two Arab Legion soldiers had been killed, five wounded and three were missing.

Christian Fouchet, French Minister of Moroccan and Tunisian Affairs, announced that legal status had been restored to the Tunisian Neo-Destour Party. Some political prisoners were freed and the state of siege was partially lifted.

The Damascus International Fair opened with 26 nations taking part.

The Shaab Party of Syria decided to lift its boycott and participate in the elections set for September 24.

The Iraqi Government ordered the dissolution of the National Democratic Party led by Kamel Chadirchi and the suspension of its organ Sawt al-Ahali because of its criticism of the decrees of September 1, 1954.

September 3

Lebanese Prime Minister Abdallah Yafi returned from a five day visit to Iraq. The Prime Minister was reported to have said that his talks in

September 3

Baghdad did not touch on the question of union between Iraq and Syria, or between Iraq and Jordan.

The UN Mixed Armistice Commission condemned Israel in strong terms for an incident at the Jordan village of Beir Liqya in which, according to its report, a force of Israel troops, estimated at battalion strength had crossed the demarcation line and opened fire on the village killing two members of the Arab Legion, wounding one and abducting three.

Former Chief of Staff of the Truce Supervision Organization, Major General Vagn Bennike, left Jerusalem for New York to report to UN Secretary General Dag Hammarskjold.

It was learned that in the clash in southern Tunisia on September 1, there were four more French killed than first reported, making nine in all.

September 4

It was announced that Sir Thomas Hickinbotham, Governor of Aden, had accepted an invitation from the Imam of Yemen to visit Taizz to discuss the Aden-Yemen dispute.

General Boyer de Latour du Moulin, French Resident General in Tunisia, published a decree abrogating the sixteen year old order outlawing the Neo-Destour Party.

Negotiations on Tunisian self government opened with a ceremony at the Bey's palace at Carthage.

Yusuf Haikal, Jordanian Ambassador to London, called at the Foreign Office of Great Britain. In a statement afterwards he said he visited in relation to new Israel military aggression against Jordan which had been carried out by a larger force than usual.

Four political parties in Syria and the League of Labor Trade Unions announced that they had agreed to merge in a general national union under the leadership of former President Shukri al-Kuwatli.

September 5

In a blistering attack on Hassan al-Hodaibi, Supreme Guide of the Moslem Brotherhood, as well as on the Brotherhood as a whole, Premier Nasser defended the Suez Canal agreement with Great Britain.

A Communique issued in connection with the visit of Egyptian Minister Salah Salem stated that Egypt and Jordan had reached agreement on foreign policy and methods for military cooperation among the Arab countries.

As a move to lessen the tension along the border, Israel returned five prisoners to Jordan.

Lebanese Director of Public Security Fares Chehab returned to Lebanon from a visit to Baghdad, where he reached an agreement with Iraqi authorities on unified measures to combat Communist activities in the two countries.

King Saud of Saudi Arabia donated 20,000 pounds sterling to Palestinian refugees in the Gaza sector for the purchase of winter clothing.

September 6

A thirty year concession for the exploitation of the Ras Matarma oil fields in the Sinai Peninsula by the Anglo-Egyptian Oil Fields Company and Socony Vacuum Oil Company was signed in Cairo.

The Jordanian Government lodged four new complaints against Israel with the Mixed Armistice Commission. Two of them concerned alleged flights by Israel aircraft over Jordan areas of Jerusalem and the other two alleged firing and stone throwing at Arab Legion units in the Old City of Jerusalem.

The Political Committee of the Arab League met in Cairo; all the member states were represented by their diplomatic agents in Egypt except Lebanon, represented by its Foreign Minister Alfred Naccache, and Iraq by ex-Premier Fadel al-Jamali.

September 8

Lebanese President Camille Chamoun accepted the resignation of Prime Minister Abdallah Yafi's Cabinet.

An Israel Army spokesman accused the Egyptian authorities in the Gaza Strip of responsibility for acts of sabotage along the border and warned them that if they continued they would be responsible for any entanglements caused.

An Egyptian military mission headed by Brigadier Fathi Rizk Ahmad left Cairo for Saudi Arabia to inspect the Saudi army and military factories and to undertake the task of coordinating military plans of the Saudi and Egyptian armies.

In Algeria the town of Orleansville was devastated by an earthquake in which over 1,000 people were estimated to have lost their lives.

In Iraq, one hundred and eleven candidates were declared elected since there was no opposition to their nominations. Only 24 seats were to be contested by 43 candidates on September 12.

September 9

The Arab League Political Committee decided to ask Saudi Arabia, Jordan and Yemen to become members of the International Labor Office; to ask that the member states instruct their delegates to the forthcoming UN General Assembly to use their good offices with Great Britain and Greece for an amicable settlement of the Cyprus dispute; to support Indonesia in its dispute with the Netherlands over Western New Guinea; and to support the Moroccan nationalists.

A twenty year agreement was signed between the US and Libya, by which the US would have the right to use a number of air bases in Libya in return for $40 million in economic aid.

It was announced in Egypt that Major Salah Salem, Minister for National Guidance and Sudanese Affairs, had been granted a leave of unspecified duration and that Colonel Hussein al-Shafei would undertake his duties.

September 10

After a long meeting between Major Salah Salem and Premier Nasser, it was announced that the former's leave had been cancelled and that he was returning to his duties.

Saudi Arabian Minister of Education Amir Fahd Ibn-Abd-al-Aziz disclosed that 270 schools had been established in the Kingdom during the previous six months.

September 12

It was announced that a complaint had been lodged with the Mixed Armistice Commission concerning an alleged attack by an Israel patrol in the Ramallah sub-district of Jordan which had led to a clash in which one Israeli was killed and one wounded. Official communiques reported two further border incidents for which responsibility was attributed to Israel but in which no casualties were reported.

September 13

The Egyptian-Israel Mixed Armistice Commission condemned Egypt for the killing of an Israel tractor driver by two armed infiltrators from the Gaza Strip, and for the blowing up of a water pipeline near the Nir Am settlement by a well trained and organized group of four from the Egyptian controlled territory.

The Jordan-Israel Mixed Armistice Commission condemned Israel in the strongest terms for a brutal attack on Jordanian citizens.

In Aden the town of Marta was attacked by raiders from across the Yemen border.

French Resident General in Tunisia Pierre Boyer de Latour du Moulin reported from Paris that bands of semi-political outlaws known as Fellaghas were continuing to make attacks on French residents in the Protectorate

September 13

despite repeated admonitions that violence must cease as a preliminary to conclusions of the new agreement.

French Resident General Boyer de Latour in Tunisia issued an order that the rights to requisition for lodging and quartering of troops would be exercised in all the territory of the Regency of Tunisia.

Talks regarding the implementation of the internal autonomy within Tunisia, promised by French Premier Mendes-France on July 31, began between representatives of the French and Tunisian Governments. Mongi Slim and Muhammad Masmoudi were the principal Tunisian representatives.

An Egyptian Government Order decreed that Friday sermons in all mosques throughout Egypt should be written by authority of the Ministry of Waqfs in a concise manner and that disputed religious, social and political questions would be avoided.

Sudanese Prime Minister Ismail al-Azhari sent a letter to tribal chiefs in southern Sudan explaining the Government's intentions regarding the South in hopes of warding off the formation of a Southern Bloc led by the Southern Freedom Party, which had announced a meeting for opposition elements to be held in Juba October 17.

September 15

The Saudi Arabian Ministry of Foreign Affairs announced that India and Saudi Arabia would exchange diplomatic representatives at the Ministerial level.

Nuri-Said, Iraqi Prime Minister, arrived in Egypt en route to London having discussions on the way with Camille Chamoun and Abdallah Yafi, the Lebanese President and Prime Minister designate.

September 16

Colonel Saadat, member of the Egyptian Revolutionary Council and temporary Secretary General of the Islamic Congress, announced a draft charter for the Congress which described its aims as to spread Islamic culture;

September 16

to prepare Moslem peoples to adhere to Islamic teachings and to raise social and educational standards; to coordinate the economic policies of Moslem nations with the best financial and administrative systems; to cooperate with the Arab League and Moslem organizations; and to cooperate with any international organizations with similar principles, such as the Arab-Asian group and the educational, social and economic bodies of the UN.

A joint communique issued by the Iraqi and Egyptian Premiers after long discussions between them said that they reached an agreed viewpoint on steps to be taken in the interests of the Arabs.

At the opening of the new Iraqi Chamber of Deputies, King Faisal's Speech from the Throne outlined the Government's program, laying particular stress on internal development.

Egyptian Chief of Staff Major General Muhammad Ibrahim and four other high army officials arrived in Washington to begin a three week tour of US army installations.

Three Iraqi members of the Moslem Brotherhood arrived in Ankara to solicit funds and to establish a branch of the Society for the Liberation of Palestine from the Jews.

September 17

Nuri-Said, Iraqi Prime Minister, told the press that since 1949 Arab foreign policy as laid down by the Arab League had been based on cooperation with the West once agreement had been reached on the Palestine and Suez issues. They had rejected cooperation with the Communist countries because they could not have it without becoming Communists and obeying the Kremlin.

In Lebanon a new Cabinet was sworn in with Sami al-Solh as Prime Minister and Minister of General Planning.

Two raids, on September 14 and 15 from across the Yemen frontier into Aden in the neighborhood of Mukeiras, were reported.

September, 1954

September 17

It was reported from Cairo that the conference between Iraqi Prime Minister Nuri-Said and Gamal Abdel Nasser left a divergence of views on the immediate military needs of the Middle East. The Iraqi Premier urged quick action in the acceptance of arms aid from the West, while the Egyptian Premier claimed that his country could not accept a US military mission to supervise the distribution and use of arms aid. Nuri-Said maintained that it would be impossible to depend on the Arab Collective Security Pact without arms aid from the West.

The heads of the Arab diplomatic mission in London called at the Foreign Office and handed Selwyn Lloyd, Minister of State, an aide memoire on the Arab-Israel situation. It touched on the issue of the Arab refugees, the danger of Communism which the Arabs were fighting with the arms they secured from the West and the dangerous border incidents between Jordan and Israel.

Prime Minister Adnan Menderes of Turkey declared that relations with the Arab and Islamic countries were getting better from day to day and that Turkey would create a defense system with them.

Secretary General of the Tunisian Communist Party, Muhammad Ennafaa, reviewed the achievements and shortcomings of the Communist Party.

September 18

Iraqi King Faisal and Prime Minister Nuri-Said arrived in London, where it was believed discussions regarding the Anglo-Iraqi Treaty would be undertaken, although the visit was described as unofficial.

The Israel Embassy in London issued a memorandum in reply to the Arab statement delivered at the Foreign Office September 17. It said that Israel had announced its readiness to negotiate a peace settlement but that the Arab States had refused and threatened a second round of war against Israel. It was only natural therefore that the Israel Government should hold the view that arms deliveries to Middle Eastern States should be dependent on a complete cessation of hostil activities.

Three alleged members of the Moslem Brotherhood ordered out of Turkey by the Turkish Government left the country.

September, 1954

September 19

Syrian Premier Said al-Ghazzi, accompanied by his Army Chief of Staff, arrived in Cairo for a day long conference with Premier Gamal Abdel Nasser. The intensified anti-Egyptian Government activities of the Moslem Brotherhood, centered in Damascus, were described in Cairo as the primary object of the visit.

The temporary trade agreement between Syria and Lebanon was extended for another three months.

September 20

French Resident General in Morocco Francois Lacoste outlined in a radio broadcast the first steps the French administration planned to take towards political, economic and social reforms in the protectorate. He announced the establishment of a Council for Studying Reforms, which would be open for the expression of all tendencies of opinion and which would examine the reorganization of central power in the country.

The French news agency reported that 14 killings had taken place in Casablanca between September 13 and 19. Three of the victims were French and the rest Moroccans. The new outbreak of terrorism was blamed partly on retaliation for the murder of a Moroccan lawyer and partly on the Nationalist boycott of the French owned cigarette monopoly.

September 21

It was reported in Baghdad that oil revenues for the year were expected to be about ID70 million as a result of the recent agreement between the Government and the Iraq Petroleum Company.

In his reply to the Arab aide memoire of September 17, British Minster of State Selwyn Lloyd stated that the British Government, while desirous of adding to the defense strength of the Middle East, an area where the free world's defenses were not strong enough, it believed that economic development and reform were strong weapons for resisting Communist infiltration and subversion.

September, 1954

September 22

A new Societies' Law was promulgated in Iraq dissolving all existing political parties. New application for the formation of political parties had to be made.

September 23

Israel charged that UN observers violated its sovereignty by patrolling the border without its authorization.

In Israel the extreme right wing Herut Party and the left wing United Workers' Party (Mapam) both rejected the British statement of policy and the offer of good offices to arrange Israel-Arab talks.

The Egyptian Revolution Command Council issued an order stripping five prominent Moslem Brotherhood leaders of their Egyptian nationality. Among them were Abd-al-Hakim Abdin, Secretary General, and Muhammad Ramadan, Controller General of the Moslem Brotherhood.

September 24

Syria held its first general election since 1948. Independents won 53 seats; Peoples Party, 34; Nationalists, 25; others, 30.

Egypt's ruling junta was openly challenged by the Moslem Brotherhood, which refused to depose its anti-regime leader. Hassan al-Hudaibi, who had been acting head of the Moslem Brotherhood, was elected Supreme Guide for life.

September 25

In a broadcast in Arabic, an Israel Foreign Ministry spokesman told Israel's Arab neighbors that: Israel was resolved to initiate a practical scheme for paying compensation to the refugees; a practical plan could be found for interregional communications across the Negev; Israel was ready to grant Jordan facilities in Haifa harbor and transit rights for goods through Israel territory.

September, 1954

September 25

The Israel Army ordered its forces not to permit UN observers to patrol the Jerusalem border unless accompanied by Israel officers.

The White House announced that the US legation in Libya had been elevated to the status of an embassy, and that John L. Tappen had been nominated Ambassador.

Syrian Premier Said al-Ghazzi presented the Order of Merit to General Vagn Bennike, former UN Chief of Staff of the Truce Supervision Organization.

As part of a program to purge the three universities of political dissidence, the Egyptian Revolutionary Command Council dismissed 40 professors. Among those discharged were the deans of Cairo University's Faculties of Law, Medicine and Commerce, and the head of the English section of the Faculty of Arts and seven of his colleagues.

September 26

A letter dated September 23 from the Israel Government was published inviting the Chief of Staff of the UN Truce Supervisory Organization to study conditions on the border and offering to furnish all pertinent information.

Sheikh Mustafa al-Sibai, Controller General of the Moslem Brotherhood in Syria, strongly condemned the Egyptian Government for depriving five members of the Brotherhood of their nationality.

September 27

An agreement between Israel and the Palestine Conciliation Commission provided for the release to Arab refugees of all funds they had on deposit in the banks of Israel; the total amounted to about $8.5 million.

Curfew was reimposed on the district of Kef after a new outbreak of anti-French terrorism within Tunisia.

September 28

The French Resident General to Tunisia, still in Paris, again appealed to the Fellaghas to lay down their arms and stated he believed they were partly beyond the control of Tunisian nationalists and acted under the orders of fanatical or totalitarian inspiration from foreign countries.

The Lebanese Chamber of Deputies voted confidence in Premier Sami al-Solh's new Cabinet.

It was officially announced in Baghdad that an Iraqi mission would visit Tehran to exchange information with the Iranian Government on oil agreements and prices.

The Arab Bureaus for the Boycott of Israel completed a week's conference at Damascus. Resolutions taken were to be submitted to the Arab League Council.

Egypt charged that an Israel merchant ship fired on and wounded inhabitants of the Red Sea coast of Egypt, south of Suez. The vessel, the Bat Galim, was taken into custody by Egyptian authorities.

An Israel spokesman in Tel Aviv denied the Egyptian accusations that the Israel ship fired on Egyptian territory. He stated that the Bat Galim was entirely unarmed, fired at no one, and that the ship was seized only after it had entered the Canal.

Anthony Nutting, British Parliamentary Under Secretary for Foreign Affairs, arrived in Cairo to take part in the final stages of the Anglo-Egyptian agreement on the Suez Canal base.

The Secretary of the Arab League, Abd-al-Khaleq Hassouna, told the press in Cairo that he saw no reason for Iraq's joining the Turkish-Pakistan alliance, because the Arab League States held the key to Middle Eastern defense.

The Libyan Parliament began debate on the US air bases agreement.

The President of the UN Security Council received a letter from the permanent delegate of Israel stating that the seizure of the Bat Galim would have to be viewed against the background of the mounting number

September 28

of "murderous Egyptian attacks" against Israel territory in recent weeks. Israel demanded the release forthwith of the vessel and its crew.

September 29

The Israel Government informed the Western Powers that the Egyptian story of the Bat Galim having fired on Egyptians was absolutely without foundation. The vessel was on a normal trade run and had a perfect right to pass through the Suez Canal.

In an attempt to neutralize the effectiveness of the Communists in Egypt, the Egyptian Government tried Communists accused of printing and distributing propaganda pamphlets, forming cells and plotting to overthrow the Government.

September 30

Major Salah Salem, Egyptian Minister of National Guidance and Sudanese Affairs, flew unexpectedly to Khartoum for urgent conferences with Sudanese political leaders. From there he was scheduled to fly to Saudi Arabia for meetings with King Saud.

Lebanese Prime Minister Sami al-Solh announced his proposal to appoint 22 new deputies instead of holding new elections.

October 1

Security authorities arrested seven Communists in Kafr Kala for taking part in a demonstration to celebrate the return to Syria of Khaled Bakdash, leader of the Syrian Communist Party, during the Syrian elections.

October 2

In Tunisia some 65 terrorists were killed or wounded in a clash with security forces near Sidi Bou Zid.

The Umma Party Executive cabled Governor General Sir Robert Howe, Prime Minister al-Azhari, Egypt's Major Salah Salem and the Egyptian Government protesting Major Salem's visit as an infringement of the neutrality supposed to prevail during the three year transitional period before Sudan became fully independent.

October 3

It was reported in Baghdad that the Iraqi Government agreed to a proposal to unify the oil policies of Iraq, Iran and Saudi Arabia.

The Israel-Egyptian Mixed Armistice Commission called on Egypt to halt, finally and immediately, attacks on Israel's borders by Arab infiltrators from Egyptian held territory.

The southern members of the Sudanese National Unionist Party announced that they were in complete accord with the party's policies.

October 4

The US Point IV administration allocated $4, 071, 782 to Jordan for the fiscal year 1954/55.

The Syrian UN delegate asserted before the General Assembly that Israel should be expelled from the UN. He proposed that a new Palestine Commission composed of the five permanent members of the Security Council and with wide powers be set up in Jerusalem to put into effect the previous UN resolutions on Palestine.

October 4

Israel asked the Security Council to take up the complaint charging Egypt with interference with Israel bound shipping in the Suez Canal, as evidenced by the seizure of the Bat Galim.

Major General Burns reactivated the Higher Appeals Committee of the Israel-Egyptian Mixed Armistice Commission, which had not functioned for more than three years.

An Israel Foreign Ministry spokesman, in a statement, intimated that reprisals against Jordan would be taken if frontier incidents continued at their current frequency and intensity. The Israel Government announced that it was appealing to the International Red Cross to investigate the conditions under which the crew of the Bat Galim were being held in Egypt.

Major Salem, Egyptian Minister for Sudanese Affairs, said in Khartoum that Egypt was prepared to give the various Sudanese political parties equal consideration and to cooperate with them all to serve Sudan, Egypt and Arab interests.

October 5

A Cairo court dismissed an appeal by the master of the Bat Galim against its detention at Suez and authorized it continuation for another month to allow completion of the investigation into the alleged shooting.

A state of emergency was declared in Cyrenaica following the assassination of Libyan Chief of the Royal Estates Ibraham al-Shalhi. Al-Shalhi was assassinated on the steps of the Federal Government House in Benghazi by Sharif Mohi-ad-Din Sanussi, nephew of the Libyan Queen.

The Egyptian Minister of the Interior announced that the security forces had broken up an Israel ring conducting espionage and subversive activities in Egypt.

October, 1954

October 6

Abba Eban, Israel delegate to the UN, called upon the Arab States to join Israel in concluding nonaggression pacts to bring peace to the Middle East.

The Syrian election returns revealed that independents won 53 seats; Shaab (Peoples) Party, 34; National Party, 25; Baath Socialist Party, 15; National Socialists, 3; Social Cooperative, 2; Communists, 1; tribes, 9.

October 7

An Egyptian spokesman for the Ministry of Interior confirmed that 109 high ranking police officers had been dismissed within the previous ten days.

The arrest in Cairo was announced of seven more persons accused of espionage on behalf of Israel.

October 8

Hassan al-Hudaibi, Supreme Guide of the Moslem Brotherhood in Egypt, was arrested. The police reported that his arrest followed the circulation of signed leaflets inciting the people against the Egyptian Government.

The term of the Saudi Arabian Consultative Council was extended for one year from August 30, 1954.

October 9

Israel agreed to the appointment of Lieutenant Colonel Charles F. Brewster of the US Army as new Chairman of the Israel-Jordan Mixed Armistice Commission. He succeeded Commander Elmo H. Hutchison to whom the Israelis had been opposed since his abstention from voting on a censure of Jordan for the Scorpion Pass incident in March 1954.

October, 1954

October 10

Arab League Secretary General Muhammad Abd-al-Khaleq Hassouna told a convention of the Syrian and Lebanese-American Federations in Washington that the Arabs were planning a propaganda campaign in the US aimed at winning American support for the Arab League against Israel.

The Algerian Revolutionary Council for Unity and Action decided to launch the revolt against the French on November 1.

Nasib al-Bakri arrived at Amman, Jordan, as Syria's first envoy to Jordan since the severance of diplomatic relations in 1949.

October 13

Henry R. Labouisse, head of the UN Relief and Works Agency, reported to the UN General Assembly on the situation of the Arab refugees. The report stated that the Agency was caring for 887,000 refugees, 8,000 more than in the previous year.

October 14

The Egyptian Government granted two new contracts for oil prospecting in the Eastern Desert, one for thirty years to a West German firm for oil production in twenty-nine areas to the northeast of Sinai, the other to the Egyptian National Petroleum Company.

After hearing statements on the seizure of the Israel freighter Bat Galim from the Egyptian and Israel representatives, the UN Security Council adjourned until the Egyptian-Israel Mixed Armistice Commission had completed an on the spot investigation of the incident.

Syrian Premier Said al-Ghazzi submitted the resignation of his Cabinet to President Hashem al-Atassi.

The Libyan House of Representatives approved 39-2 the air bases agreement with the US.

October, 1954

October 15

It was reported from London that over 100 Jews had been arrested in Egypt in addition to 13 Jews arrested earlier and accused of being spies for Israel.

Members of the Moslem Brotherhood demonstrated in the streets of Damascus protesting the Egyptian Government's recent actions against the organization.

The Egyptian Government closed the Egyptian news agency (MENA) allegedly for misquoting Government officials.

By a vote of 30-5, the Lebanese Chamber of Deputies granted the Solh Government exceptional powers for three months.

Israel returned to the Mixed Armistice Commission and submitted 356 complaints of alleged armistice violations which had accumulated in the seven month period during which it was boycotting the commission.

The Israel and Jordanian military commanders in the Jerusalem area met to sign an agreement for direct contact to enable them to take immediate action in the event of any incident on the demarcation line. A last moment hitch prevented the signature, the Israel delegates said that they had no authority to sign the agreement if witnessed by General Burns and the Jordanian representatives refused to sign if they did not.

October 16

Jordanians went to the polls to elect a new Chamber of Deputies. At least nine persons were killed in disturbances, principally at Amman, and the library of the US Information Agency was set on fire. King Hussein ordered the appointment of a commission to investigate the cause of the disturbances. Election results were as follows: Independents, 37; Umma (Nation) Party, one; Liberation Party (outlawed), one; National Democratic (Communist unregistered), one; total, 40.

The Sudanese Syndicate of Primary School Teachers submitted resignations of 700 teachers to the Ministry of Education, giving three months notice, since their demands for better wages and working conditions had not been met.

October, 1954

October 16

Turkey sought to persuade the Iraqi Premier to abandon his proposals for a broad Middle East Defense Organization in favor of direct links with Turkey and Pakistan.

October 17

Syrian President al-Atassi asked Khaled al-Azm, leader of an independent bloc, to form a new Cabinet.

The US closed its foreign aid mission in Saudi Arabia after that country demanded that the aid program be halted.

The Libyan Senate approved the US-Libyan air bases agreement by a vote of 15-4.

Post election demonstrations occurred in various parts of Jordan. The number of persons dead in the previous day of riots was reported as having reached 18.

Libyan King Idris ordered the arrest of seven young members of his family. They were ordered deported to Houn in the southern Libyan Desert.

October 18

In reply to a question about Sudan, Major Salem, Egyptian Minister for Sudanese Affairs, said that Egypt would not intervene to define the form of union. That would be left to the National Unionist Leaders. If the Sudanese wanted complete independence and complete separation from Egypt, Egypt would respect their decision and remain a loyal friend. If they chose some form of union, Egypt would be ready to cooperate in putting that choice into effect after its endorsement by the Sudanese Constituent Assembly. He also stated that the Sudanese should choose their own rulers.

Nuri-Said, Iraqi Premier, whose visit to Turkey had attracted great publicity, gave a press interview. He declared that there was no need

October, 1954

October 18

to talk about the sincerity of the friendship between Turkey and Iraq because it was self evident.

Egyptian Minister of National Guidance Major Salem told the press that all differences in connection with the agreement with the British had been overcome and he and all his colleagues believed in the agreement which they thought would give Egypt great advantages. He claimed that the evacuation of British troops would remove a major obstacle to full cooperation between Arab countries.

October 19

A 13 article main agreement accompanied by two annexes, 17 exchanges of notes and an agreed minute elaborating the articles of the main agreement was signed between Great Britain and Egypt in final settlement of the Suez Canal negotiations. Principal points provided for the withdrawal of all British troops by June 18, 1956, termination of the 1936 UK-Egyptian Treaty, a seven year period during which British or other Allied troops might re-enter the Suez Canal Zone in case of attack upon the Arab states or Turkey, the 1888 Constantinople Convention guaranteeing freedom of navigation to be upheld. The agreement was to be in force seven years from the date of signature.

Britain and France ended their long dispute over the Suez Canal by signing an agreement returning control of the area to Cairo.

At the end of a visit of Nuri-Said, Iraqi Prime Minister, a statement was issued which said that Iraq and Turkey were agreed on the necessity of organizing immediately a Middle East security front comprising all nations sincerely attached to UN principles and determined to withstand aggression. It also said that the Turkish Prime Minister gave assurances that Turkey would never follow a policy opposed to the legitimate interests of Arab countries.

Iraqi Prime Minister Nuri-Said returned from a trip abroad, his last stop having been Turkey.

An Adenese Government statement said that armed Awadhi tribesmen from Yemen had again raided Aden Protectorate territory on October 18, killing

October, 1954

October 20

A Royal Decree in Libya establishing the line of succession to the throne restricted the royal family to king, queen and their descendants.

October 21

After a meeting of the Moslem Brotherhood's full General Assembly in Egypt, Deputy Supreme Guide Khamis Hamada announced that the October 20 decisions of the anti-al-Hudaibi faction were invalid.

Egypt objected to the examination of the Bat Galim incident by the Egyptian-Israel Mixed Armistice Commission at an emergency meeting.

Jordan's Prime Minister Tawfiq Abu-al-Huda tendered the resignation of his Cabinet. The King asked him to form a new Government.

October 22

French Premier Mendes-France conferred in Paris with Christian Fouchet, Minister of Moroccan and Tunisian Affairs, and Francois Lacoste, Resident General of Morocco.

Tawfiq Shamandi, Yemeni delegate at the UN, protested against information being given by Great Britain to the UN Trusteeship Council on conditions in Aden and the surrounding territory on the grounds that Yemen did not recognize British jurisdiction in that area. Specifically, he objected to placing the so-called Aden and the West and East Protectorates in the category of non-self-governing territories, asserting that they formed an integral part of Yemen.

The agreement between the UK and Egypt on the Suez Canal base, with annexes and exchanges of notes, was published by the UK Government as a White Paper.

October 23

Khaled al-Azm reported to the Syrian President that he was unable to form a Cabinet. The Shaab and National Parties refused to cooperate.

October, 1954

October 19

one person and injuring three. It added that on October 15, Yemenis from the Assomaa tribe had crossed into Awdhali Sultanate in the western Aden Protectorate but had been driven off by Marta tribesmen.

October 20

The Yemen delegation at the UN protested against the designation of the Aden Crown Colony as British territory, and asserted that it was rightfully Yemeni territory.

The Yemeni Legation in London reported that UK Royal Air Force planes had recently carried out raids in the southern region of Yemen, terrorizing the inhabitants, and that Aden levies had attacked tribes who had restricted themselves to defensive action.

Colonel Nasser of Egypt, speaking of the impact of the agreement with Britain on Egypt's foreign policy, said that Egypt had no aggressive designs against Israel. Any such designs would be incompatible with plans for internal reconstruction.

Major General Abd-al-Hakim Amer, Egyptian War Minister and Commander in Chief of the Army, said the Army would have to be increased but the expansion would be no more than was necessary to take over responsibility for the security of the Suez Canal Zone base and would in any case be limited by financial considerations.

About 70 members of the Moslem Brotherhood's General Assembly in Egypt and other members met and declared that Supreme Guide Hassan al-Hudaibi was "on leave." The group also named a new eight man provisional committee.

US President Eisenhower in discussing US efforts to achieve a just peace in the Middle East emphasized that the US would make sure that any arms provided to strengthen the security of the entire Middle East would not be used to create local imbalances which could be used for intimidation of or aggression against any neighboring nations.

Egypt began a two day holiday in celebration of the signing of the UK-Egyptian Suez Canal Zone Agreement.

October, 1954

October 24

At the close of the Arab League conference of economic experts which began on October 16 Chairman Nadim Dimishkiya, of Lebanon, stated that it was decided to recommend a reduction in customs duties, ranging up to 50 percent, on some industrial products. The conference also approved the amendment of the inter-Arab Trade and Payments Agreement which aimed at facilitating the transfer of capital from one Arab country to another. (Iraq and Yemen had not ratified this agreement.)

A new Cabinet composed of nine Deputies and three Senators was announced in Jordan. Tawfiq Abu-al-Huda became the Prime Minister and Walid Salah became Minister of Foreign and Social Affairs.

October 25

The Syrian President asked Fares al-Khouri to form a Cabinet.

Sixteen national Jewish organizations in the US protested to US Secretary of State John Foster Dulles against the arming of Arab states as long as they refused to make peace with Israel. They urged that Israel be invited to participate in planning the defense of the Middle East.

Rashid Ali al-Gailani, the Iraqi anti-Allied rebel during World War II, arrived in Cairo and was received by Egyptian Premier Nasser.

October 26

While Premier Nasser of Egypt was addressing a crowd on Republic Avenue in Alexandria, he was shot at eight times but escaped unharmed. The would-be assassin, Mahmoud Abd-al-Latif, a Cairo tinsmith, was seized and identified by the authorities as a member of the Moslem Brotherhood.

The Israel delegation asked the UN Security Council for an urgent meeting to consider the question of Egypt's blockade of the Suez Canal against Israel bound shipping.

The UN Truce Supervision Organization in Jerusalem reported to the Security Council that Egypt prevented the Mixed Armistice Commission

October, 1954

October 26

from considering the seizure of the Israel freighter, Bat Galim, in the Gulf of Suez.

October 27

Ahmad Mukhtar Baban, Minister of State of Iraq, was appointed Deputy Prime Minister by Royal Decree.

French Resident General Lacoste stated in Rabat, Morocco, that he would continue his efforts to negotiate with local leaders on a reform program.

It was stated that during a visit of the Governor of Aden to Yemen, frontier disputes and troubles had been the chief questions discussed with the Yemeni Government.

Mass arrests of Moslem Brotherhood members and leaders in Egypt brought to 400 the number arrested in the 24 hours after the attempted assassination of Egyptian Premier Nasser.

October 28

The Egyptian-Israel Mixed Armistice Commission condemned Egypt for the blowing up of the main water pipeline in the northern Negev, and Israel for the crossing of the demarcation line by armed Israelis and the wounding of an Arab.

October 29

The new Syrian coalition Cabinet was formed, headed by Fares al-Khouri as Premier and Faidi al-Atassi as Foreign Minister. The Cabinet was composed of five Shaab Party members, three of the National Party, two independents, and one representing the tribes.

Three Egyptian members of the Moslem Brotherhood who had taken political asylum in Syria were placed under surveillance by Syrian authorities.

November, 1954

November 1

The Algerian Army of the National Liberation began guerrilla operations against the French. Rebels were led by the revolutionary Committee for Unity and Action which became the National Liberation Front (NLF). Three hundred Mobile Guards arrived in Algeria from Marseilles as well as 600 Republican security troops. French Premier Mendes-France announced that three battalions of parachutists would also be sent.

The Jordanian Government asked Britain, France and the US to stop Israel from diverting the waters of the Jordan River. Jordanian Foreign Minister Walid Salah asked the three Ambassadors to intervene under the terms of the 1950 Tripartite Declaration which guaranteed the status quo in the Palestine situation.

In Syria, Fares al-Khouri presented his Government to the Chamber of Deputies.

Moulay Merbah, Secretary General of the extremist Algerian Nationalist Party, the Movement for the Triumph of Democratic Liberties, was arrested.

In his Speech From the Throne at the opening of Parliament, King Hussein of Jordan called for the establishment of a fighting air force. He pledged no peace and no negotiations with Israel.

The Egyptian Revolutionary Command Council issued an order setting up a three man Special Tribunal to consider acts of treason or action against the national security, whether committed at home or abroad, and acts directed against the military regime or against the principles on which the revolution was based. The tribunal, whose powers were retroactive, was headed by the Deputy Premier, Wing Commander Gamal Salem; its other two members, Anwar Saadat and Colonel Hussein al-Shaffei, were also in the Cabinet.

November 2

The Jordanian Ambassador in Washington protested to the US State Department regarding presentation of credentials by the new US Ambassador to Israel in Jerusalem rather than in Tel Aviv. He stated that even the trip to Jerusalem by the Ambassador for this purpose would have serious

October, 1954

October 29

Tunisian Resident General Boyer de Latour du Moulin conferred in Paris with the French Premier and the Minister of Tunisian and Moroccan Affairs and then with the Neo-Destour ministers regarding direct talks with Fellaghas leaders and the proclamation of a truce, which the Neo-Destour leaders desired.

The Arab League Council passed a resolution in Cairo congratulating Egypt on the signing of the UK-Egyptian agreement on the Suez Canal Zone.

The Egyptian Ambassador in Ankara issued a statement on Turkish-Egyptian relations. He declared that there was no matter outstanding which would make it impossible for the two countries to reach agreement.

October 30

Prime Minister Abdel Nasser of Egypt told a rally of workers that his bloodless army movement would turn into a bloody revolution if necessary, to stamp out Moslem Brotherhood terrorism.

The Arab League Council opened the first meeting of its twenty-second session in Cairo with Sheikh Ibraham al-Fadl of Saudi Arabia as chairman.

Egyptian Minister of National Guidance Major Salah Salem announced the arrest of Hassan al-Hudaibi, accused of plotting to overthrow the Egyptian Government with scores of assassinations. President Nagib was excepted from the list. Major Salem said the terrorist group within the Moslem Brotherhood was headed by al-Hudaibi, retired army colonels Abd-al-Moneim and Abd-al-Rauf, retired police Major Salah Shadi, and Yusuf Talaat.

November, 1954

November 2

implications throughout the Middle East. US Secretary of State John Foster Dulles replied that presentation of credentials in Jerusalem did not mean that the US had reversed its refusal to recognize Jerusalem as the capital of Israel.

Eliahu Elath, Israel Ambassador, addressing the UK-Israel Association, said that the Israel Government was willing to discuss an amicable, just and honorable settlement with the Arab States at any time, anywhere and without prior conditions on either side.

Two French armored columns in Algeria succeeded in partially clearing the Arris region of rebels, who continued to occupy mountain heights in the vicinity.

Radio Cairo urged the formation of a united liberation command to coordinate operations in Tunisia, Morocco and Algeria in the Maghreb struggle against French imperialism.

November 3

US Secretary of State Dulles told the Ambassadors of the Arab League States who called on him to protest the US decision that the new US Ambassador to Israel present his credentials in Jerusalem, that the Ambassador would do so, but that this implied no change in the US attitude regarding the status of Jerusalem.

The Israel Foreign Ministry announced in Jerusalem the acceptance of Arab proposals for the release of the blocked bank accounts and safe deposits belonging to refugees of the Palestine war. The proposals were submitted to Israel by the Executive Committee of the General Refugee Congress of Palestine.

The UN Security Council began debate on the Israel complaint against Egypt's blocking of Israel bound shipping in the Suez Canal. During his speech to the Council, the Chief of the Egyptian Delegation, Mahmoud Azmi, collapsed and died less than two hours later. With his collapse, the Council adjourned without setting a date for the next meeting. Omar Loutfi, an official of the Ministry of Foreign Affairs, became the acting head of the delegation.

November, 1954

November 3

Premier Nasser of Egypt announced that 447 members of the Moslem Brotherhood had been arrested since the attempt on his life, in addition to 200 members previously taken into custody. Nasser declared that the assassination plan was submitted to the Moslem Brotherhood Supreme Guide who had approved it.

A new Government was formed in Syria under the Premiership of Fares al-Khouri, an Independent. He announced, however, that he would resign if by March 21 he had failed to form a parliamentary bloc comprising a working majority in the Syrian Chamber of Deputies. After prolonged discussion the Chamber of Deputies voted confidence in the new Khouri Cabinet.

An outbreak of terrorism in Algeria led to the dissolution of the Algerian Nationalist Movement for the Triumph of Democratic Liberties.

November 4

The Ambassadors in London of the eight Arab League States called at the British Foreign Office and protested against the reported intention of the new British Ambassador to Israel to present his letters of credence to the Israel President in Jerusalem, on the ground that this implied British recognition of Jerusalem as the capital of Israel. They were told by Anthony Nutting, UK Minister of State, that the new Ambassador would present his letters of credence in Jerusalem on November 10, but that this would be done purely on the grounds of international courtesy and had no political implications. A statement issued after the meeting said the decision had been taken in consultation with the US and French Governments.

The Jordanian Minister responsible for Arab refugee affairs announced that no persons had been authorized to negotiate with Israel regarding blocked bank accounts and that unauthorized negotiators would be guilty of treason for making contact with the enemy. Jordan insisted that any

negotiations regarding refugees be carried on with the sponsorship and participation of the UN.

Two French columns attacked some 1,000 rebels in the heights above Foum Toub in the Aures area of Algeria.

Ferhat Abbas, leader of the Union of the Algerian Manifesto (a nationalist group), issued an appeal for calm within Algeria.

November 5

Francois Mitterand, French Minister of the Interior, stated that security troops in Algeria would be increased by four more companies.

The French Cabinet declared the Movement for the Triumph of Democratic Liberties dissolved. Raids were made on the party's headquarters both in France and in Algeria.

November 6

An agreement was signed with the US whereby the US would grant Egypt $40 million for modernization of its economy. Current plans called for construction of a new dam at Aswan and road and railroad improvement. The new dam was expected to bring under cultivation an additional two million acres and ultimately to provide ten billion kilowatt hours of cheap electric power for industry.

Alfred Naccache, Lebanese Foreign Minister, handed to the Papal Nuncio for transmission to the Pope an appeal to the Pope to use the Vatican's good offices with the Western Powers to prevent a step which implied recognition of Jerusalem as capital of Israel.

November 7

Jordanian Premier Tawfiq Abu-al-Huda told the Chamber of Deputies that the international situation, the new UK-Egyptian agreement and the projected new treaty between Britain and Iraq gave Jordan the right to seek a revision of its treaty with Britain.

It was announced that Turkish Prime Minister Menderes would visit Egypt in December and the Egyptian Prime Minister would visit Turkey during January. A pact of mutual friendship would be signed by the two countries to be later followed by another pact of a military nature which might include other Arab states. A Turkish-Egyptian friendship pact would probably be signed during Nasser's visit.

The French Government protested against the arrest of French citizens among the 13 Jews arrested in Cairo and Alexandria on charges of spying for Israel.

The Iraqi Government decided to close its Legation in Moscow for reasons of economy.

Muhammad Khalil al-Gumati, Tripolitanian Minister of Justice, was appointed President of the Libyan Supreme Federal Court by Royal Decree.

November 8

Sudanese Prime Minister Ismail al-Azhari and several other Sudanese officials arrived in London for a ten day visit.

The British Government reported a rejection by Saudi Arabia of a British protest against a proposed grant of an oil shipping monopoly to Greek ship owner Aristotle Onassis.

The British Foreign Office confirmed that the Jordanian Government had made informal approaches about a revision in certain respects of the UK-Jordanian Treaty of 1948.

Algerian rebels retreated before advancing French armored forces. At the same time the French Government dissolved the Movement for the Triumph of Democratic Liberties, described as an extremist group headed by an Algerian exile, Messali Hadj.

November 9

Egypt became the second signatory (after Jordan) to the Arab Nationality Agreement approved by the Arab League Council on April 5, 1954.

It was reported from Amman that British Ambassador Charles Duke called on the Premier of Jordan and told him that although the 1948 UK-Jordanian Treaty of Alliance contained no provision for modification for 15 years, and the present approach was perhaps a little premature, the British Government would consider Jordan's views should the Jordanian Government care to formulate them.

The Lebanese Government banned public religious demonstrations throughout the country.

November 10

In a letter to the UN Secretary General representatives of six Arab nations asked that measures be taken to stop Israel from changing the status of Jerusalem. They charged the UK and the US with flagrant violation of UN decisions to internationalize Jerusalem by sending their Ambassadors to that city to present their credentials.

The French Government sealed off the border between Tunisia and Algeria to prevent infiltration of Tunisian terrorists into Algeria.

The Jordanian Chamber of Deputies voted 35-3 confidence in the Abu-al-Huda Government.

November 11

On the recommendation of General Burns, the UN Security Council decided that Egypt's seizure of the *Bat Galim* should take priority over other matters on the agenda of the Israel-Egyptian Mixed Armistice Commission.

It was announced that the Governor of Istanbul, Turkey, would visit Egypt on November 21 as a guest of the Egyptian Government.

November 12

Major Salah Salem, Egyptian Minister of National Guidance and Sudanese Affairs, flew to Saudi Arabia to discuss questions of military cooperation with King Saud.

November, 1954

November 12

The French National Assembly voted in favor of Premier Mendes-France's proposal to postpone indefinitely a full dress debate on the Algerian situation.

The French Government defined its policy in Algeria as one of firm sanctions but no reprisals.

Speaking in the French National Assembly in a debate on Algeria, Premier Mendes-France said, in reference to the activities of Cairo Radio in spite of French protests, that France desired to maintain its traditional friendship with the Arab world and it would maintain with Egypt a correct and friendly attitude, but the Egyptian Government should accept its responsibilities. If it persisted in its present course the French Government would not hesitate to take the necessary measures, but he hoped that negotiations would permit a satisfactory solution.

November 13

Nabil Ibrahim Sanusi, Libyan Ambassador in Cairo and member of the Libyan Royal Family, was recalled. He refused to return and asked for political asylum in Egypt.

An Egyptian Government spokesman announced that the Government had recalled its Ambassador in Syria, Major General Ali Nagib (a brother of President Nagib) because Syria had done nothing to curb the activities of the Moslem Brotherhood.

The Arab League Secretariat issued a statement calling on the French Government to revise its attitude toward the nationalist movement in North Africa and offer the North African peoples independence and sovereignty.

Ismail al-Azhari, Prime Minister of Sudan, told the press that Sudan would soon join the Arab League.

The Governor and Mayor of Ankara, Turkey, Kemal Aygin, visited Egyptian Premier Gamal Abdel Nasser in Cairo.

November, 1954

November 15

At the opening of a foreign affairs debate in the Knesset, Israel Prime Minister Moshe Sharett sharply criticized the US policy of granting arms to Egypt and declared that it was difficult to imagine a more blatant contradiction in terms than the granting of arms to the ruling junta in Egypt in order to strengthen regional stability and the defense of democracy.

Witnesses at the trial of the Moslem Brotherhood asserted that the plan to overthrow the Government of Egypt was worked out on the basis of agreement between the Brotherhood's secret organization and President Nagib and pro-Nagib elements in the Egyptian Army.

November 16

In Iraq, a new press and publications law went into effect whereby about 300 newspapers, including many already suspended, were closed. New permits for publication would have to be applied for. Party newspapers could henceforth be suspended by order of the Cabinet rather than by a Court Order.

Henry R. Labouisse, Director of The United Nations Relief Works Agency (UNRWA), spoke before the Special Political Committee of the General Assembly and criticized the Arab countries and Israel for not fully co-operating with UNRWA in solving the problems of the Arab refugees.

The executive of the Umma, one of the two licensed parties in Jordan, issued a statement dissolving the party. It declared that the political situation in the country did not favor the existence of political parties.

November 17

The Revolutionary Command Council of Egypt (RCC) invested the Cabinet with the powers of President of the Republic. The Cabinet in turn empowered Premier Nasser to exercise the presidential powers on its behalf. Nasser assumed the offices of Head of the State of Egypt and President of the Revolution Council.

A trade and payments agreement between Egypt and Ceylon was signed in Cairo.

November, 1954

November 13

The Cairo daily al-Gumhuriyah carried an interview with Prime Minister Mustafa Ben-Halim of Libya which stated that Libya would not join the Turkish-Pakistani Pact or any other military bloc.

November 14

The Revolutionary Command Council (RCC) dismissed Egyptian President Muhammad Nagib from his official duties and placed him under house arrest. Prime Minister Abdel Nasser assumed the presidential duties, although the office itself was declared vacant for the time being.

French sources in Tunis reported that 20 Tunisian nationalists and one French soldier had been killed in clashes near Djebel Garbou in the previous two weeks.

November 15

The concession of the Jordanian Petroleum Company was terminated. The agreement provided for a final payment by the company to Jordan of 400, 000 pounds sterling.

Tunisian Nationalist leader Habib Bourguiba, living under guard about 25 miles from Paris, stated in an interview that the French were obstructing the talks with Tunisians regarding autonomy and were thus forcing the Tunisians to fight for their independence.

The National Council of the Tunisian Neo-Destour Party, meeting in Tunis, refused to take a stand against the Fellaghas and demanded that the French call off their military operations against them.

The Egyptian Council of the Revolutionary Command issued a statement in which it was alleged that General Nagib had become envious of Colonel Nasser who had defeated his attempts to gain power, and that Nagib had joined the camp of the Communists and the Moslem Brotherhood who were trying to create anarchy and undo the revolution and who had used General Nagib as a tool.

November, 1954

November 17

UN Truce Chief Major General E. L. M. Burns proposed a series of measures to curb incidents along the Israel-Egyptian frontier, including patrolling of sensitive sections of the line by a joint team composed of Israelis, Egyptians and UN representatives.

The Egyptian Government published names of 133 wanted members of the Moslem Brotherhood, and arrested some of them, including Supreme Guide Hassan al-Hudaibi and Yusuf Talaat, chief of the terrorist section.

Tahar Ben-Ammar, Tunisian Prime Minister, saw Edgar Faure, French acting Prime Minister, and Christian Fouchet, French Minister for Tunisian and Moroccan Affairs. A joint statement issued afterwards said that the French ministers had expressed surprise at the resolutions of the Neo-Destour Council.

November 18

The Suez Canal Company's London agency announced that a scheme to widen and deepen the Suez Canal had been approved by the Company's International Advisory Works Commission.

King Faisal of Iraq, accompanied by the Crown Prince, the Deputy Prime Minister, the Foreign Minister, the President of the Royal Cabinet, and a number of court officials, left for visits to Jordan and Lebanon.

Shops were closed in the Arab quarters of most of the large cities of Morocco in a three day demonstration of support for the exiled Sultan, Sidi Muhammad Ben-Youssef.

The French Government announced that an agreement in principle had been reached with representatives of the Tunisian Government on how to deal with terrorist bands in Tunisia.

The Government of Iraq issued an ordinance banning public meetings in the streets and laying down certain conditions for the holding of demonstrations.

November, 1954

November 18

A three man court martial in Syria began the trial in absentia of Brigadier Adib al-Shishakli, former President who was charged with the murder of Naji al-Bahri, an army officer.

November 19

Addressing the UN Special Political Committee of the General Assembly, which was discussing the Arab refugee question, the US representative asked for tangible evidence that the Arab states would cooperate in public works projects designed to make Arab refugees self supporting.

The Israel-Egyptian Mixed Armistice Commission accepted an Israel resolution declaring that the terms of the armistice agreement had not been violated by the Bat Galim's attempt to reach Suez and that the ship's crew had not fired on any craft at the Suez Canal mouth. The UN chairman had earlier abstained from voting on an Egyptian contrary resolution which was therefore rejected.

A four man delegation from the Sudanese National Unionist Party arrived in Cairo. It conveyed to the Government the anxiety of the majority party in Sudan about future Sudanese-Egyptian relations should any harm befall Egyptian General Nagib, who was a popular personal symbol for party supporters and of unity and harmony between Egypt and Sudan.

The French Cabinet approved the agreement of November 18, by which the Tunisian Government would share responsibility for public order with the French in areas where the Fellaghas bands were operating. Varying time limits in different areas would be allowed for the Fellaghas to respond to an appeal to lay down their arms.

November 20

The Egyptian Foreign Minister announced that the Egyptian Government ratified the UK-Egyptian agreement on the Suez Canal Zone.

Egyptian Minister of National Guidance Major Salah Salem announced that the Egyptian Revolutionary Command Council had offered the office

November, 1954

November 22

The French and Tunisian Governments issued a joint statement in Paris and Tunis containing a solemn appeal to the Fellaghas to hand over their arms, a guarantee that they would not be troubled or persecuted and a promise of measures to help their adaptation to a normal family life.

Supreme Guide of the Egyptian Moslem Brotherhood Hassan al-Hudaibi went on trial on charges of plotting to overthrow the Revolutionary Command Council.

November 23

A resolution calling on the Arab Governments to cooperate with the UN in carrying out projects to make the Palestine refugees then living in their countries self supporting, and to place the United Nations Relief Works Agency (UNRWA) on a long term basis, was introduced by the US, UK, France and Turkey in the Special Political Committee of the Assembly.

November 25

Egyptian authorities sold the cargo of the Bat Galim at public auction.

The special committee of the Egyptian-Israel Mixed Armistice Commission upheld the Commission's resolution on Egypt's complaint in the Bat Galim case.

It was announced in Tunis that military operations against the Fellaghas would cease for three to six days to allow the terrorists to heed the appeal of November 22.

November 26

French Interior Minister Francois Mitterand arrived in Algeria to inspect the Constantine Department. He announced that the situation was not critical.

November, 1954

November 20

of President to Ahmad Loutfi, an 84 year old scholar and former Foreign Minister.

Egypt appealed the decision of the Israel-Egyptian Mixed Armistice Commission on the Bat Galim.

November 21

An announcement issued simultaneously by the Egyptian Government and the Sudanese National Unionist Party delegation stated that the question of ex-President Nagib's participation in the movement of Moslem Brotherhood Leaders accused of planning to overthrow the regime was finally considered closed. The frequent mention of his name during recent trials had caused much suspicion. The statement stated flatly that Nagib would not be brought to trial.

Fares al-Khouri, Syrian Prime Minister, arrived in Beirut for talks with Iraqi King Faisal. They were the first to take place between Syrian and Iraqi leaders since diplomatic relations were broken off during the regime of Brigadier al-Shishakli.

The Syrian Government approved a proposal to pardon all political crimes committed by individuals against the unconstitutional regime which existed between November 29, 1951, and March 1, 1954.

King Faisal of Iraq arrived in Beirut on a four day visit, his first to Lebanon since his accession to the throne.

November 22

It was announced that on January 1, 1955 and in January of subsequent years the British Government would relase the 10 million pounds sterling due Egypt under the Sterling Release Agreement of 1951. The release date was previously left to the UK Government's discretion, which caused Egypt some hardships and uncertainties.

Ahmad Loutfi announced that he had declined the offer of the office of President of the Egyptian Government.

November, 1954

November 26

Israel reaffirmed its willingness to the UN to consider compensation for Arab lands abandoned in Israel by refugees and to enter into negotiations through the UN on the question of compensation.

November 27

The session of the Arab League Council was opened; only the heads of the Arab diplomatic missions in Cairo attended.

Egypt's Interior Minister Lieutenant Colonel Zakariah Mohi-ad-Din stated that about 1,000 of the 200,000 members of the Moslem Brotherhood were under arrest.

November 29

Annual financial talks between Jordan and the UK opened in London. Among the members of the Jordanian delegation were Anistas Hanania, Minister of Finance, Khalusi al-Khairi, Minister of Economics, and Dr. Yusuf Haikal, Jordanian Ambassador to Great Britain.

Twenty-two Tunisian representatives accompanied by 22 French officers left Tunis to make contact with Fellaghas groups and to offer them safe conduct to their homes.

November 30

The Arab Agricultural Credit Conference held in Beirut under the auspices of the FAO and the Ford Foundation concluded its work after meeting for fifteen days. It recommended to the Arab Governments that they subsidize bank loans for farmers and that the Arab Governments establish technical centers to help farmers improve their crops and find markets for their produce.

The UN Special Political Committee voted 40-0 to extend UN assistance to Arab refugees for another five years.

November, 1954

November 30

Israel Prime Minister Moshe Sharett told the diplomatic representatives of the US, the Soviet Union, Great Britain and France that Israel could not be expected to acquiesce indefinitely to the denial of free passage to Israel ships through the Suez Canal.

Following a request by Israel that the Security Council should resume consideration of the Bat Galim incident, Moshe Sharett, Israel Prime Minister, held discussions with the representatives in Israel of the permanent members of the Security Council (Britain, France, US and the USSR).

December, 1954

December 1

Fares al-Khouri, Syrian Prime Minister, told a press correspondent that there would be no settlement of the Palestine question until the UN or the Western Powers, or the Arabs themselves, had brought the Jews to a state of reasonableness by force.

Sudanese Prime Minister Ismail al-Azhari conferred with Egyptian Prime Minister Gamal Abdel Nasser.

John Tappen, US Ambassador to Libya, officially handed over 3,000 tons of wheat, a gift from the US to victims of famine areas.

Lasar Chraibi, one of the two most prominent chiefs of the Fellaghas bands in Tunisia, agreed to the truce accord under which the rebel forces would lay down their arms and end their struggle against the regime. Twenty-two rebels surrendered near Mateur in northern Tunisia.

An Egyptian newspaper printed an article by Premier Gamal Abdel Nasser concerning Turkish-Egyptian relations. The headline quotation in Afer read: "If Turkey is secure we Egyptians are likewise secure. Turkey and Egypt are members of the same family. Today the two countries are brothers as they were in the past."

The Lebanese press and radio reported that Iraqi King Faisal, opening the Iraqi Parliament, announced Iraq's intention to denounce the UK-Iraq treaty of 1930 which would expire in January 1956. King Faisal declared that Iraq wished its relations with Britain to be founded on the principles of the UN Charter.

December 2

It was learned that Dr. Ridken, special envoy of West German President Theodore Heuss, had returned from a special mission to King Saud of Saudi Arabia with an agreement to establish diplomatic relations. He had also persuaded the Saudi Arabian Government to allow four West German businessmen to leave Saudi Arabia. They had been prevented from doing so after incurring the disapproval of the authorities.

December, 1954

December 4

Following a meeting of Arab League Foreign Ministers, Musa Shahbandar, Iraqi Foreign Minister, told the press that Iraq would conclude a new agreement with Britain, to replace the 1930 agreement which would expire in 1956 under which British troops would be allowed to re-enter Iraq in the event of an attack on Iran.

On completion of his fact finding tour, Sir Evelyn Shuckburgh, Assistant British Undersecretary for Foreign Affairs in charge of Middle Eastern Affairs, presided over a conference in Beirut of British diplomatic envoys in the area.

Syrian Premier Fares al-Khouri stated in Parliament that his Government was holding to its decision not to join any Western defense pact or program for the Middle East.

Seven Moslem Brotherhood leaders were condemned to death for complicity in the attempted assassination of Egyptian Prime Minister Nasser on October 26. The sentence for Supreme Guide Hassan al-Hudaibi was later commuted to life at hard labor.

The UN General Assembly extended the mandate of UNRWA (UN Relief and Works Agency) to June 30, 1960.

December 5

More than 15,000 Syrian students in Damascus left their schools to take part in a protest demonstration against the sentencing of the Moslem Brotherhood members in Egypt.

The President of the Islamic Conference, Sheikh Anjad Zahawil, and representatives of other religious and political organizations in Baghdad cabled Premier Nasser to halt the death sentences of the Moslem Brotherhood leaders.

The Foreign Ministers of six Arab states (Yemen not included) met in Cairo to work out a common policy on international issues. This was reported to be preliminary to a meeting of the premiers of the same states. This meeting took place outside the framework of the Arab League.

December, 1954

December 6

Egypt announced that it intended to release the ten man crew and the cargo of the Israel freighter Bat Galim. Israel stated that while it welcomed the intended release of the seamen and the cargo, it did not regard the case as closed. The only solution which Israel could accept was the unconditional release of the ship together with its crew and cargo so that it could complete the journey which Israel said Egypt had not the slightest right to interrupt in the first place.

Instruments of ratification of the UK-Egyptian agreement on the evacuation of the Suez Canal were exchanged in Cairo.

A joint French-Tunisian statement reported that 1,404 Tunisian rebels had surrendered to French authorities.

The Egyptian UN representative notified the Security Council that the Egyptian judicial authorities had set aside, because of insufficient evidence, the charges against the Bat Galim, and the men and the cargo would be released.

December 7

The UN Security Council reopened debate that was suspended in November on Israel's charges that Egypt was restricting passage through the Suez Canal of ships trading with Israel.

The six condemned Moslem Brotherhood members were hanged in Cairo despite numerous protests from many Moslem countries.

December 8

One thousand secondary school students paraded before the Egyptian Embassy in Amman protesting Egypt's hanging of six Moslem Brotherhood members convicted of plotting to overthrow the Egyptian Government.

December 9

At the opening of a debate on North Africa in the French National Assembly, Rene Mayer attacked the policies of French Premier Mendes-France

December 9

and reaffirmed France's intention to remain in Morocco as well as in its other North African territories.

Twelve Asian and Arab countries submitted a resolution to the UN recommending that an atmosphere be created that was conducive to peaceful settlement of the Morocco question and that negotiations take place between France and the true representatives of the Moroccan people.

Syria proposed in the UN General Assembly's Political Committee to call an international conference to consider the unification of Morocco as a sovereign independent state.

In the Speech from the Throne at the opening of the fourth session of Parliament, Mustafa Ben-Halim, Libyan Prime Minister, said that relations with Britain were good and based on complete respect for the terms of the UK-Libyan Treaty. He expressed satisfaction with modifications in the Libyan-American agreement which ensured more US help for development.

The Arab League Political Committee concluded its meeting in Cairo and presented its resolutions to the Arab League Council.

In the Speech from the Throne read by Libyan Prime Minister Mustafa Ben-Halim, the King reiterated Libya's demand for the withdrawal of the French garrison from Fezzan.

December 10

In the continuing debate on North Africa in the French National Assembly, Premier Mendes-France stated that those who opposed his Tunisian policy had forgotten that home rule had been the declared policy of previous Governments. The security situation in Tunisia had improved, he said, and a very large number of troops had been sent to Tunisia, Algeria and Morocco. Attention was called to the decline of terrorism in Morocco and he said that political and social reforms were being prepared for that country. Mendes-France further put his Government on record as opposing independence for Tunisia or the other French territories in French North Africa.

December 10

Christian Fouchet, French Minister for Moroccan and Tunisian Affairs, speaking in an Assembly debate on the Government's North African policy, explained that under the home rule agreement France would retain responsibility for defense and foreign relations. The Tunisians could not be excluded from all responsibility over the police, though for many years the higher posts would remain in French hands. The rights of French citizens would be protected by special agreements.

A general strike was proclaimed in Amman in mourning for the Moslem Brotherhood members executed in Egypt.

A joint French-Tunisian statement announced that 2,514 Fellaghas had responded to the appeal offering an amnesty to those laying down their arms. The French Resident General and the Tunisian Government had agreed on the necessary steps to deprive the remainder of the possibility of doing further harm.

Francois Mitterand, French Minister of the Interior, revealed that 20,000 French troops had been sent to Algeria since the troubles began there on November 1, and further reinforcements would be sent. He said that the French Government could not accept the separation of Algeria from the mainland.

General Burns, Chief of Staff of the UN Truce Supervision Organization, in a letter to the senior Jordanian delegate to the Mixed Armistice Commission, agreed that the use of mortar fire by Israel forces during an incident on December 3 was not justified and said he would request the Israel military authorities to instruct border guards not to use mortar fire as a retaliatory measure or to cover the withdrawal of elements.

December 11

The Arab League Council began consideration of the proposals of its Political Committee which included exploitation of oil and prevention of it being smuggled into Israel, the strengthening of the Collective Security Pact, Israel's diversion of Jordan waters and the question of North Africa.

The Arab League Council adopted the recommendations of the Political Committee including the participation of the Arab countries in the

December 11

Djakarta Conference called by Indonesia, that the Egyptian scholar Taha Hussein be appointed Chairman of the League's permanent Cultural Committee, that Jordan's home guard be strengthened, that Syria would lodge a complaint with the UN Security Council on behalf of Jordan against Israel's diversion of Jordan River water.

The French Assembly approved the Government's North African policy by a vote of 294-265-60.

The Syrian Chamber of Deputies passed a law pardoning all political crimes committed before March 1, 1954, during the regime of Brigadier General Adib Shishakli.

Sharif Mohi-ad-Din Sanusi, nephew of the Jordanian Queen, was sentenced to death for the premeditated murder in October of Ibrahim Shalhi, Chief of the Royal Estates.

The Egyptian Supreme Military Tribunal began trial of 13 persons accused of spying for Israel. Two were to be tried in absentia, having escaped the country before the arrests took place.

December 12

It was announced in Libya that diplomatic representation with Turkey had been raised to Embassy status.

The Economic Council of the Arab League convened in Cairo.

The Egyptian Special Tribunal sentenced five more members of the Moslem Brotherhood to death by hanging on charges of plotting to assassinate Premier Nasser.

December 13

The Saudi Arabian Minister of Finance and National Economy announced that if no agreement was reached between the Government and Aramco (Arabian-American Oil Company) regarding modification of the Onassis tanker agreement by January 15, 1955, the dispute would be referred to an arbitration commission.

December 13

Despite US opposition, the Afro-Asian bloc succeeded in having a resolution passed in the UN Political Committee 39-15 to keep the Moroccan item on the agenda, but to postpone further consideration of the issue for the time being. Those opposing included Britain, US, Belgium, Australia, Denmark, Netherlands, New Zealand, Norway, Sweden and South Africa.

The Egyptian-Israel Mixed Armistice Commission censured Egypt for six truce violations and Israel for one.

The Egyptian Revolutionary Command Council commuted to life imprisonment the death sentences imposed on December 12 on five members of the Moslem Brotherhood.

Speaking in the Knesset in the name of the Israel Government, Prime Minister Moshe Sharett protested the use of medieval methods of torture to force confessions of guilt from the 13 Egyptian Jews standing trial in Cairo on charges of espionage and terrorism on behalf of Israel.

December 14

Syria sent a letter of protest to the UN Security Council against Israel's interception and seizure of a Syrian civilian airliner on December 12.

US envoys in the Middle Eastern countries met in Damascus to discuss problems of the area, especially defense.

December 16

A conference of Arab Foreign Ministers, supplementary to the Arab League Political Committee and Council meetings, ended with tentative agreements for the evolution of a foreign policy toward the Western Powers, including such matters as Iraq's intention to seek cancellation of the UK-Iraqi Treaty.

An agreement was signed between Turkey and Lebanon extending for an additional two years the provisions of the Lausanne Treaty of 1924,

December 16

by which persons of Lebanese origin living in Turkey were able to claim Lebanese nationality if they wished.

The UN Political Committee passed a resolution 54-0-3 expressing confidence that the current Tunisian negotiations would produce a satisfactory solution and deferring for the time being discussion of the issue.

December 17

The General Assembly of the UN adopted a resolution expressing confidence in the satisfactory outcome of negotiations on the Tunisian question.

December 18

At the conclusion of the discussions, the US Embassy in Damascus issued a statement outlining the five points of US policy in the Middle East which included complete and strict impartiality toward the Arab states and Israel, friendship with all the Middle Eastern countries, support of those countries in their efforts to maintain strong and stable governments, adherence to the 1950 Tripartite Declaration guaranteeing the territorial integrity of Israel and the Arab countries and support for the UN Truce Supervision Organization.

The Egyptian police arrested eighteen members of the dissolved Moslem Brotherhood on charges of having taken a secret oath to carry on the organization's message.

Ismail al-Azhari, Sudanese Prime Minister, issued a statement drawing public attention to a serious situation. He said that one of his Ministers had asked for the removal of certain of his colleagues from the Cabinet, stating that otherwise he and other Ministers would cooperate with the opposition Umma Party and cause the Cabinet to fall.

Iraqi Foreign Minister Musa Shahbandar stated in Cairo that the Iraqi Government would seek to renegotiate its treaty of alliance with the UK on a basis similar to the UK-Egyptian agreement covering the evacuation of the Suez Canal Zone.

December 19

King Hussein of Jordan, accompanied by Prime Minister Tawfiq Abu-al-Huda and Anwar Nusaibah, Minister of Defense, arrived in London for talks with the British Government on revision of the UK-Jordan Treaty of 1948.

In Libya, changes in several ministerial posts occurred. Mustafa Ben-Halim became Prime Minister and Abd-al-Salam al-Busairi became Minister of Foreign Affairs.

Ahmad Ramzi, Egyptian Ambassador in Ankara, declared that Turkish Premier Adnan Menderes had helped turn a new page in history by following a policy based on good sense and the practical course of events. He referred to Menderes' statements regarding a reconciliation with Egypt.

Major Salah Salem, Egyptian Minister of National Guidance and Sudanese Affairs, declared that three Sudanese Cabinet members planned to kidnap Egyptian President Muhammad Nagib before his dismissal and take him to Sudan to place him in the presidency there.

The first shipment of US military aid arrived in Basra, Iraq.

December 20

Egyptian Prime Minister Nasser announced that his Government would restore democratic constitutional life by January 1956.

A gift from Turkey of 12 mortars and six field guns, together with ammunition, was handed over to Libya in a ceremony at Palace Square.

Mirghani Hamzah, Sudanese Education Minister, Khalafalla Khaled, Defense Minister, and Ahmad Jali, State Minister, issued a statement in reply to Prime Minister al-Azhari. They denied that they had threatened to cooperate with the Umma Party to overthrow the Government.

Israel requested the Security Council to resume consideration of Israel's complaint against Egyptian restrictions on the passage of Israel ships through the Suez Canal.

December 21

The People's Tribunal of Egypt sentenced sixty members of the Moslem Brotherhood to prison sentences for conspiracy to overthrow the regime by force.

It was learned that the Egyptian Government was sending a protest to members of the UN Security Council against the sentence in Tel Aviv of four young Palestinians accused by Israel of spying for Egypt. The Egyptian Government maintained that the charges were trumped up as reprisals for the trial of Zionists in Cairo.

Israel Ambassador to the UN Abba Eban, in a letter to the President of the Security Council, stated that the Bat Galim had not been released by Egypt with its crew and cargo nor permitted to proceed on its journey. He asked for an early meeting of the Security Council to consider the matter further.

Talks between Jordanian Premier Tawfiq Abu-al-Huda and Anthony Nutting, British Minister of State, on revision of the 1948 UK-Jordanian Treaty of Alliance, began at the Foreign Office in London.

Ismail al-Azhari, Sudanese Prime Minister, asked Major Salem, Egyptian Minister of National Guidance, to stop making capital out of Sudanese ministerial crises and to use his influence with the Egyptian press to stop the campaign against the three rebel ministers in the Sudanese Cabinet.

December 22

It was announced simultaneously in London and Amman that as a result of financial discussions between Jordan and the UK, Jordan would receive 2,500,000 pounds sterling in economic aid from Britain during 1955. Of this, 1,750,000 pounds sterling would be an interest free loan to be spent on certain projects of Jordan's Five Year Plan.

The Egyptian Minister in Ankara, Sadek Salem, announced that Egypt was not then prepared to join either the Turkish-Pakistani Pact or a Middle East Defense Pact.

December 23

The Egyptian Government, in a letter to the UN Security Council, stated that the crew of the Israel freighter Bat Galim would be released on January 1, 1955.

Five members of the Moslem Brotherhood were sentenced to life terms for terrorist activities against the Egyptian Government, 35 others were given sentences of from ten to 15 years, and 45 others received ten year suspended sentences.

Three Sudanese Cabinet members were dismissed as a result of dissension in the Cabinet.

A statement issued after the end of the talks between Jordan and Britain on revision of the UK-Jordanian Treaty said they were exploratory and the matter would be considered further.

December 25

In the reshuffled Sudanese Cabinet, Ismail al-Azhari became Prime Minister, Minister of the Interior and Minister of Defense.

A Saudi Arabian Royal Decree approved the budget for the Hijrah year 1374 (beginning August 3, 1954). Revenue was estimated at SR1,043,010,500 and expenditures at SR1,355,000,000, leaving a deficit of SR311,989,500.

December 26

The Jordanian Cabinet approved the terms under which the country would receive $5 million in economic aid from the US. The money would be used in a Jordanian five year development plan which called for a dam on the Yarmuk River, irrigation projects, roads and factories.

December 27

In a special statement on policy, Turkish Premier Menderes told the Arab states that they must collaborate closely with the rest of the free world if a viable defense system was to be created in the Middle East.

December, 1954

December 27

This was taken as a flat rejection of Egypt's attempt to persuade Turkey to join a regional alliance based on the Arab League and the 1950 Arab Collective Security Pact.

A military tribunal in Lebanon sentenced three members of a Zionist terrorist ring to death, two of them in absentia and 27 others, seven in absentia, to prison terms ranging from two to 20 years.

December 28

Major Salah Salem, Egypt's Minister of National Guidance, told visiting Syrian journalists that Egyptian defense policy was based on the Collective Security Pact of the Arab League and excluded any alliances with Powers outside it. Egypt had refused an offer by the US of tens of millions of dollars worth of arms if it would sign a military aid agreement. He said that the Arab League Security Pact should be made a reality and he called for unification of armaments, training, planning and command. He said that Egypt would not make peace with Israel even if Israel agreed to execute the UN resolutions on partition and refugees because Israel was a danger to Egypt as well as to the rest of the Arab world.

The Syrian-Israel Mixed Armistice Commission refused to censure Israel for the seizure of the Syrian plane on December 12.

A People's Tribunal in Egypt sentenced to death five officers and men of the Egyptian armed forces for their part in a Moslem Brotherhood conspiracy to overthrow the Government. Twenty-four others received sentences of imprisonment ranging from five years to life.

It was announced at Beirut that the Medrico Oil Company would resume operations in Lebanon now that an agreement had been reached with the Government on a price for products from the company's refinery in Sidon.

A ministerial delegation led by Libyan Prime Minister Mustafa Ben-Halim flew to Paris on the French Government's invitation to negotiate on the question of the French bases in Fezzan.

December, 1954

December 29

A Middle Eastern Parliamentary Group was formed to establish and maintain relations among Iraq, Iran, Afghanistan and Pakistan with the object of broadening cultural relations.

The Sudanese Cabinet approved all recommendations of the Sudanization Committee regarding the Railways and Posts and Telegraphs Administrations. The Minister of Communications was charged with putting them into effect.

French troops and police arrested 200 suspected Arab terrorists in a two day mopping up operation in the mountains of the northwestern part of Algeria.

It was announced that the tribunal to consider the Buraimi dispute between the UK and Saudi Arabia would consist of Charles de Visscher of Belgium as chairman, and one representative each of Britain, Saudi Arabia, Cuba and Pakistan.

December 30

A military tribunal in Egypt passed sentences of imprisonment on 36 Egyptians and ordered the dissolution of the Communist inspired Democratic Movement for National Liberation to which they belonged.

A military tribunal in Cairo sentenced 64 Moslem Brotherhood leaders to prison terms ranging from ten years to life and 52 others were given ten year suspended sentences.

The temporary economic agreement between Lebanon and Syria was extended for three months from January 1, 1955.

December 31

It was announced in London and Cairo that the resignation of Sudanese Governor General Sir Robert Howe had been accepted and that he would be succeeded by Sir Alexander Knox-Helm early in 1955.

Supplement to 1954

January

1 At a press conference given at the Indian Embassy in Cairo, Ernest Bevin said that he was hopeful of an Anglo-Egyptian agreement, and that the main difficulty consisted in presenting an agreement which was "sufficiently attractive psychologically" to both countries.

Sudanese Governor General Sir Robert Howe paid tribute in his inaugural speech to the sense of responsibility among the electorate, shown both by the size of the poll in most constituencies and by their orderly behavior during the elections, despite the fact that the procedure of democratic elections had been unfamiliar to them.

5 At an Arab League Council meeting Egypt accused Iraq of planning a revival of the Pact of Saadabad. The members of the Saadabad Pact were Turkey, Iraq, Iran and Afghanistan.

6 The Palestine Conciliation Commission delivered its thirteenth progress report to the UN Secretary General. It stated that the Commission had had "no real opportunity of exercising its general function of conciliation" during the past year.

7 The Yemen Federation Scheme of three councils was established: 1) a council of chiefs; 2) a legislative council; and 3) an executive council—all under direct British control.

10 It was proclaimed at a meeting of the Arab heads of state that Arab foreign policy would be free of all foreign influence.

11 The US and Libya exchanged notes constituting an agreement relating to emergency wheat aid to Libya.

The Sudanese Cabinet decided that Parliament should adjourn for six weeks to enable the Ministers to become acquainted with their departments, and the Prime Minister to announce his program. It was also agreed to invite Sir Winston Churchill of the UK, Egyptian President Nagib, and representatives of the US, India, Palestine and the Arab States to attend the reopening of Parliament.

In an interview published in the Cairo Weekly Akhbar al-Yawm, Sudanese Prime Minister Ismail al-Azhari said that his Government would "use its influence to realize unity with Egypt, by which he meant a system whereby each country would have equal rights and obligations.

Supplement to 1954

January

14 At the end of its sessions the Arab Mutual Defense Council issued a communique in which it confirmed that the armed forces of the Arab nations were uniting and co-ordinating their efforts to assure the safety of the Arab nation.

15 The Egyptian Council of the Revolution Command dissolved the Moslem Brotherhood and charged it with violence and propagandizing.

16 Muhammad Fadel al-Jamali told the Iraqi Parliament that Iraq had not approached the US for military aid and that reports of such a proposal were "pure fabrication."

17 A spokesman of the Egyptian Council of the Revolution said that Ahmad Hassan, Supreme Guide of the Moslem Brotherhood, and his close associates would be brought to trial before the Revolutionary Tribunal on charges of conspiracy to overthrow the regime.

18 The Bey of Tunis requested Muhammad M'Zali to form a new Government.

19 The Iraqi Premier stated that Jordan could not remain independent much longer, for if it did not unite with Iraq of its own free will it would be attacked by Israel.

20 An agreement was signed by Saudi Arabia and Aristotle Onassis, Greek shipping magnate, for the organization of a tanker company to transport oil.

The Moroccan Sultan's Cabinet decided to send a note to Paris protesting against the attacks which had been made on the Sultan's spiritual and temporal sovereignty by the press and radio in the Spanish zone.

21 The Arab League Council approved a resolution for cooperation between the States of the Arab League and the States of the Asian-African Bloc.

22 The UN Ad Hoc Political Committee approved a resolution, drafted jointly by Great Britain, the US, France and Turkey, after consultations with the Arab States, for a three year relief plan for Palestine Arab refugees.

January

23 French Resident General for Morocco General Augustin Guillaume alleged in a press statement that the Tetuan demonstration had been organized by the Spanish High Commissioner's Office, that Spanish officers had lived among the tribes for weeks past to prepare it, and that the Spanish authorities had deliberately "paralysed" local movements of support for the new Sultan.

A resolution congratulating Libya on its attainment of independence, and recommending that country for UN membership, was passed without a dissentient vote, the Soviet group abstaining, by the UN Ad Hoc Committee.

25 The Egyptian Government announced that new controls would be imposed on all ships passing through the Suez Canal en route to the Gulf of Aqaba, with the object of preventing cargoes from reaching Eilat, the Israel port in the Gulf.

29 President Shishakli proclaimed himself Military Governor of Syria, appointed Deputy Military Governors (responsible only to himself) for the Jebel Druze area and for the cities of Damascus, Aleppo, Homs and Hama, and forbade assemblies of more than five persons.

30 An agreement was signed by representatives of the Yugoslavian and Jordanian Governments which provided that Yugoslavia accept payments in Jordanian goods for the services rendered by Yugoslav firms in Jordan, and that Jordan undertake to make the prices of its exports competitive, particularly prices of phosphate.

An agreement was concluded between the UK and Syria for scheduled civil air services between and beyond their respective territories.

February

4 The Egyptian Government newspaper al-Gumhuriyah said that Egypt would apply a new policy if Britain failed to respect its demands for the evacuation of the Suez Canal Zone.

5 An agreement was concluded between Syria and the United Kingdom for the establishment of wireless telegraph service between Syria and the United Kingdom.

February

9 A press report stated that the Jordanian Cabinet had approved a trade agreement with Yugoslavia.

The Syrian Parliament endorsed the action taken by General Adib Shishakli against political leaders detained on charges of illegal political activity.

10 Major Salah Salem, the Egyptian Minister of National Guidance, said in Cairo that Russia had offered to contribute to Egypt's major construction projects and would probably carry out some of them "if all details are agreed." "But we shall not be satellites of either Eastern or Western powers," he told reporters.

24 In accordance with the provisions of the UN Security Council's resolution of November 24, 1953, Major General Vagn Bennike, Chief of Staff of the UN Truce Supervision Organization in Palestine, reported to the Council on developments during the preceding three months.

27 Tunisian constitutional reforms were approved by the French Cabinet after discussion with Pierre Voizard, the Resident General in Tunisia.

The Egyptian Council of the Revolution received a letter from General Nagib stating that he had resigned voluntarily to enable the Council to achieve its aims, including "the expulsion of the usurping enemy still occupying part of our land"; recognizing that the Council had accepted his resignation from entirely disinterested motives; and appealing to all Egyptian patriots, both inside and outside the Army, to unite behind the Council of the Revolution.

28 A joint statement issued by the Egyptian Cabinet and the Council of the Revolution attributed the incidents which had occurred in Cairo to "vicious elements and opportunists" who had taken advantage of the national rejoicing at President Nagib's restoration to achieve their aims.

March

2 In a statement Syrian President Atassi announced that the Constitution drawn up by the Constituent Assembly in 1950 had been restored; that preparations would be made for the holding of general elections; and that a referendum would be held authorizing the future Parliament to draw up a new Constitution.

March

2 The Umma Party denied that its supporters had been responsible for the Sudanese riots, alleged that the Police had attacked them without provocation, and accused the Government of having brought a "reign of terror" to the Capital.

3 An official Egyptian spokesman announced that 119 persons, including 46 members of the Moslem Brotherhood, 21 Socialists and several Wafdist and Communists, had been arrested in connection with demonstrations and would be tried by special courts on charges of creating a "state of anarchy."

Lebanon and Switzerland signed an air transport agreement.

5 The Arab Socialist and Baath Parties fused into one party, the ASRP (Arab Socialist Renaissance Party).

The main Tunisian Trade Union,. the UGTT, declared in response to the proposed legal and administrative changes in the country, that they legalized the inequitous and anti-national idea of co-sovereignty.

6 Faidi al-Atassi, the Syrian Foreign Minister, said that the new Government would conduct general elections as soon as possible to strengthen the country's position internationally and domestically.

Colonel Nasser announced that all Egyptian political detainees would be released after a rapid examination of their cases; that all sentences imposed by the Revolutionary Tribunal would be revised; and that the Tribunal itself would be abolished when the trial of Madame Nahhas had concluded.

7 In an interview Colonel Nasser declared that General Nagib was purely the President of the Republic of Egypt and had no vote in the Revolutionary Council.

Press censorship was lifted in Egypt except for matters relating to defense.

Tunisian President General Pierre Voizard maintained that the interests of France and the French community had been completely safeguarded, described the Tunisian reform decrees as "the fruit of patient and sincere research by the Bey and myself," and said that he and the Bey

March

had sought to find "the balancing point where the just aspirations of some can be harmonized with respect for the legitimate interests of others."

8 A proclamation was issued naming Colonel Gamal Abdel Nasser as Vice President of the Council of Ministers in Egypt.

9 In a statement Pierre Voizard, Tunisian Resident General, pointed out that, in the event of a difference of opinion between the Tunisian Assembly and the French Representative Delegation, the Executive would "take the decision which, in the light of their previous discussions, appeared to be most in conformity with public interests."

Lieutenant Colonel Gamal Abdel Nasser declared that he had relinquished the Premiership in favor of Nagib "in order to demonstrate the unity of the Egyptian people."

Saudi Arabian King Saud opened the first meeting of Saudi Arabia's first Cabinet, recently appointed by himself. In a Speech from the Throne the King stated that he would follow in the footsteps of his father, Ibn-Saud.

11 The most important of the Tunisian political parties, the Neo-Destour, proclaimed its opposition to the proposed legal and administrative reforms of the Government.

Major Salah Salem, the Egyptian Minister of National Guidance, stated that members of the Council of the Revolution proposed to form a "Republican Socialist Party" to contest the forthcoming general elections, with a program of social reforms, economic development and "expulsion of imperialists."

The Iraqi Senate and Chamber of Deputies in a joint session approved a Regency Council to rule during the absence of King Faisal who was scheduled to leave for Pakistan on a ten day visit.

12 A letter was sent from the Representative of Egypt to the Secretary General of the UN.

Egyptian President Nagib appealed to students in a broadcast to refrain from "actions which might stir up feelings and widen the range of

March

disputes," and to follow the example of the Council of the Revolution whose members had "forgotten their quarrels in the interests of national unity."

13 Sir Robert Howe, Governor General of Sudan, and Ismail al-Azhari, the Sudanese Prime Minister, in a joint statement denied that there was a "serious crisis" between them.

16 The Egyptian Minister of the Interior, Lieutenant Colonel Mohi-ad-Din stated that 100 of the 450 members of the Moslem Brotherhood arrested after the dissolution of that organization had been released, but denied reports that a general amnesty had been granted to its members.

17 Lebanese Foreign Minister Alfred Naccache said that Israel had withdrawn most of its troops from the Syrian and Lebanese borders.

The Egyptian Government extended martial law in the Sinai Peninsula and the Red Sea Province.

The Egyptian Customs demanded the sum of LE30 million from the British forces as customs duty on goods which these forces had forcefully removed from the customs area.

18 Jordan and Syria announced that precautionary measures had been taken in view of Israel Army maneuvers alleged to be taking place near its frontier.

Egyptian President Nagib declared that he was "not eager" to reopen discussions with the UK, and that, although he would accept better terms if they were offered, he was "not prepared to make an overture."

Majid Arslan, the Lebanese Minister for National Defense, announced in Beirut that about 3,000 Palestine Arab refugees camped near the Lebanese-Israel border would be removed elsewhere with the aim of avoiding frontier incidents with Israel.

19 Maarouf al-Dawalibi, the Syrian Defense Minister, said that Syria was preparing to teach Israel a lesson as a result of the Lake Kinnereth incidents. Syria would no longer be content with UN protests, but would "repulse future attacks by fire and iron."

March

20 Doria Shafiq agreed to call off her hunger strike protesting the fact that women were not permitted representation in the Egyptian Constituent Assembly after General Nagib had assured her that the petition would be considered by the commission charged with the formation of the Constituent Assembly.

23 An agreement was concluded between the USSR and Egypt concerning transformation of diplomatic missions into Embassies.

Egyptian President Muhammad Nagib announced that he did not intend standing as a candidate for the Presidency of Egypt at the elections due to be held in June. "I leave that for the will of the people," he told reporters.

24 The demand for a coalition Government in Egypt, drawn from the Wafd, the Moslem Brotherhood and the Socialist and Communist parties, was put forward in the Wafdist organ <u>al-Misri</u> by Colonel Seddeq, who had been expelled from the Council of the Revolution a year earlier for his alleged Communist leanings.

25 Colonel Nasser denied that there were any divisions within the Egyptian Council of the Revolution.

UN Secretary General Hammarskjold said that he had given up efforts to arrange high level Israel-Jordan peace talks because Jordan insisted that the Armistice Commission was the only appropriate channel for negotiations.

Abba Eban, the Israel Representative at the UN, described Jordan's refusal as "the most serious breach of the armistice agreement since it was signed," adding that Israel would determine her future course of action in the light of this development.

In a note to the US Government Israel expressed "grave concern" at the negotiations for a military aid agreement in progress between the United States and Iraq, accusing Iraq of being a prime instigator of the Arab countries' attack on Israel, and quoting recent statements by Iraqi Ministers to show that hostility toward Israel remained the basis of Iraq's policy.

March

27 The "Free Officers" demanded that the Egyptian Council of the Revolution should remain in power until the aims of the revolution had been achieved, and that any of its members who did not support the principles of the revolution should be expelled.

In Egypt the civilian members of the Cabinet who had resigned the previous day withdrew their resignations.

Egyptian President Nagib denied that he had wanted a plebiscite on whether or not he should remain in office, instead of a general election.

29 Major General Abd-al-Hakim Amer proclaimed a state of seige in Egypt after a large mob attacked the offices of the Council of State and other departments.

Egypt promulgated the cultural agreement between Spain and Egypt, signed at Cairo April 26, 1952.

A letter was sent from the UN representative of Israel addressed to the President of theSecurity Council. It concerned three incidents on the Israel-Jordan border.

30 Egypt promulgated the agreement between Egypt and the UN Bureau for Refugee Affairs, signed at Cairo February 10, 1954.

Moshe Sharett, Israel Prime Minister, claimed that the Israel attack on March 29 of the Jordanian village of Nahhalin was a local reaction, perhaps in retaliation for the killing of a watchman at a nearby Israel village on March 26.

April

1 The Israel Government submitted a resolution to the UN Secretary General alleging that General Bennike's report of February 24, 1954, had shown bias in Jordan's favor by ommitting reference to incidents for which Jordan had been responsible, and that he had minimized Israel's attempts to reduce tension on the border.

April

3 According to Resolution 753 of the Arab League the Secretary General was directed to maintain contact with the Yemeni Government on the issue of British "aggression" in southern Yemen with the objective of deciding upon appropriate assistance to render Yemen in order to maintain the country's security.

The Arab League passed a resolution to send a protest addressed to the UN against French terrorism in Tunisia and Morocco.

Abdallah Yafi, the Lebanese Premier, told reporters that his Government would not sign any military or political treaty with any other Government, because such a treaty would strike at its sovereignty.

4 The Arab League Council approved a resolution to place LE15,000 at the disposal of the Secretariat General for aid to victims of French policy in North Africa.

5 According to Resolution 759 of the Arab League the Secretary General was requested to make a survey of member states to determine their positions on a proposed joint Arab League-UNRWA program for the education of Arab refugees.

Representatives of all the nationalist parties in French North Africa signed an agreement at the Arab League's headquarters in Cairo setting up a "Liberation Committee" (<u>Comite de Liberation du Maghreb Arabe</u>), with its seat in the Egyptian capital. The agreement, officially known as the "Pact of the Liberation Committee of the Arab Maghreb," laid down (a) that the Committee would fight for the complete independence of Morocco, Algeria and Tunisia, and for their adherence to the Arab League; (b) that it would reject union with France; and (c) that all the nationalist parties concerned would have a joint delegation in each of the three countries.

6 The Arab League Council had adopted a resolution asking the nine Aden Protectorate territories to refuse to commit themselves to any plan which was contradictory to the national spirit and which might separate them from their Arab colleagues, especially in Yemen, and offering to cooperate with Yemen in assisting the rulers of the territories to strengthen their positions and preserve their integrity.

April

6 Egyptian Minister of National Guidance Salah Salem announced that the Egyptian Press would be purged and "corrupt elements" would be removed in a series of sweeping measures to "protect the revolution."

7 Saudi Arabia and Aristotle S. Onassis, Greek shipping magnate, exchanged letters relating to an agreement signed on January 20.

Israel Ambassador to the UN Abba Eban said that the Israel-Jordanian truce machinery had suffered a complete breakdown and that recent Soviet vetoes of Security Council resolutions criticizing Arab States indicated that the Council could take only actions congenial to Arab opinion.

8 During a discussion of the Israel-Jordanian border situation in the UN Security Council, US Ambassador Lodge made it clear that the United States was "seriously concerned" when any Government, and especially a UN member, presumed to take the law into its own hands "in a policy of reprisal and retaliation," as it had made "perfectly clear" in connection with the Qibya incident. Noting the attack on the village of Nahhalin, he indicated that the situation along the Israel-Jordan demarcation lines had not improved, despite resolutions of the Security Council, and declared that separate incidents must be considered as interrelated.

Israel Ambassador to the UN Abba Eban sent a letter to the President of the UN Security Council in which he presented a list of ten border incidents on the Israel-Jordan frontier from March 21 to March 28.

11 King Hussein of Jordan declared that the Arab homeland had been partitioned and a strong race created in its midst, but the Arabs would never accept this destiny.

14 Lebanon told Jordan that it had earmarked LL250,000 for the Jordan National Guard.

It was announced in Cairo after a joint session of the Cabinet and the Revolution Council that all members of the former Wafdist, Saadist and Liberal Constitutional parties in Egypt during the past twelve years would be deprived of their political rights for ten years.

April

15 Representatives of the Tunisian political parties, the trade unions and the Chambers of Commerce and Agriculture, meeting under the chairmanship of Tahar Ben-Ammar, unanimously adopted a memorandum which condemned the reform decrees of March 4 on the grounds that they neither restored Tunisian sovereignty nor democratized Tunisian institutions.

18 It was announced that Major General al-Banna (President Nagib's aide de camp,) Major General Hamdi (Chief of the Army Establishment) and Colonel Seddeq (a former member of the Council of the Revolution who had published an appeal on March 24 for the formation of a broadly based coalition Government) had been placed on the retired list.

19 Figures published by the Suez Canal Company showed that traffic passing through the Canal in 1953 reached the new records of 92,905,000 net tons of shipping and 90,299,000 tons of merchandise, compared with 86,136,000 net tons of shipping and 83,448,000 tons of merchandise in 1952.

20 UN Secretary General Dag Hammarskjold announced that Israel had complied with the Iraqi terms for releasing three Israel citizens imprisoned in Baghdad when their plane was forced down.

The General Union of Tunisian Workers (UGTT), the leading trade organization, condemned the reform decrees of March 4 and recommended a boycott of the elections envisaged therein.

22 The Israel Foreign Ministry issued a statement describing the alleged US-Iraqi agreement as "prejudicial to the prospects of peace in the Middle East" and as "bound to endanger Israel's security."

23 The Jordanian Foreign Minister, in response to a proposal by Eric Johnston that Israel and Jordan work on joint development of the Jordan and Yarmuk River Valleys, said that the Arab countries found this proposal utterly unacceptable.

A trade agreement was concluded between Egypt and Portugal.

26 The Israel Representative to the UN sent a letter to the President of the Security Council refuting complaints by Jordan concerning frontier incidents.

April

27 Jordanian King Hussein declared that Jordan did not have enough financial resources to defend its borders with Israel, and that it was the duty of all Arab Governments to share the cost.

The UN Security Council delayed for a third time a decision on procedure in considering cross complaints of Israel and Jordanian armistice violations.

29 The Iraqi Parliament was dissolved by Royal Decree following the swearing in of a Caretaker Government under the Premiership of a former Independent, Arshal Omari.

US President Eisenhower said that any US military aid to Middle Eastern countries was designed only to safeguard the area against Communism and not to assist local quarrels.

30 A "common market" for the cereal crops produced in metropolitan France and Tunisia during the four year period August 11, 1954-July 31, 1958, was set up by a decree promulgated in Paris.

May

1 A communique was issued on the signing of a trade and currency agreement between the USSR and Lebanon.

3 The Permanent Representative of Syria to the UN sent a letter to the President of the Security Council concerning an Israel-Syria border incident in the Shamalneh sector.

Saudi Arabia had not asked the United States for military aid, the Saudi Arabian Legation stated in Baghdad.

King Saud of Saudi Arabia had called a conference of Moslem countries to consider providing military aid to Arab forces in the "Palestine" area, the Saudi Arabian Minister announced in Karachi.

4 Charles Malik of Lebanon introduced a resolution in the UN Security Council condemning Israel for a March 28 attack on Nahhalin and calling for a UN economic and diplomatic boycott of Israel.

May

4 Tawfiq Abu-al-Huda, the new Jordanian Premier, said in Amman that his Government would not discuss peace with Israel and would maintain its former attitude in the Security Council. Addressing a press conference, he added that the "Palestine case" would remain the major consideration of his Cabinet.

5 The Egyptian Council of the Revolution decided to ban the further publication of al-Misri, to pay the employees of that paper their full salaries until they had found new employment and to place the Societe Orientale de Publicite under the custodianship of a Government trustee pending payment of the fine imposed on Mahmoud Abu-al-Fath.

Israel Prime Minister Moshe Sharett charged that "the great powers" were vying with each other for Arab friendship by injuring Israel.

6 The Syrian Government decided to try the former dictator General Shishakli in absentia, on charges of staging a coup and violating the Constitution. This was announced in the Chamber of Deputies by Izzat Sakkal, the Syrian Minister of Justice.

10 The Syrian Representative to the UN sent a letter to the President of the Security Council concerning its protest to the UNTSO Chief regarding the adjournment of a meeting of MAC.

12 Selwyn Lloyd, UK Minister of State for Foreign Affairs, said in London that in view of the shift of power in Egypt it would be just as well to see how things settled down before the Government embarked on negotiations with Egypt.

A treaty of friendship, commerce and navigation was concluded between Brazil and the Lebanese Republic and signed by the Presidents of the two countries. The treaty was a confirmation of the most favored nation treatment accorded the nationals, goods and ships of either country by the other.

13 Directors of the Suez Canal Company approved a $9,714,285 program for widening and deepening the 104 mile long waterway, it was announced in New York.

17 The Israel Representative to the UN sent a letter to the President of the UN Security Council concerning the legality of a Lebanese complaint and Jordanian participation in the Security Council.

May

23 Major Salah Salem, Egyptian Minister of National Guidance, commenting on London reports that new overtures would be made to resume Anglo-Egyptian Canal Zone talks, said that Egypt had "heard of such reports before."

Jordan's high court ruled that banks with branches in both Jordan and Israel were liable for Arab accounts blocked in Israel.

26 Switzerland and Syria signed an agreement concerning regular civil air services.

An emergency shipment of six tons of garden seed would be sent to Iraq by air on May 27, it was announced by the FOA.

29 Gamal Abdel Nasser, the Egyptian Premier, told 500 Arab students in Cairo that "Crusades will never end until the Arab World is freed from the fetters of imperialism."

31 Egypt approved a cooperation agreement between the Egyptian Ministry of Commerce and Industry and the United States Operations Mission to Egypt.

Sir Ralph Stevenson, British Ambassador to Egypt, lodged a strong protest with Egyptian Foreign Minister Mahmoud Fawzi after further violence in the Suez area.

Selwyn Lloyd, UK Minister of State for Foreign Affairs, stated that the allegations that British troops were starving women and children in the Buraimi Oasis were without foundation, though he explained that "restraints" had been put on the movement of Saudi Arabian tribesmen in order to limit their "illegal activities."

June

8 Tawfiq Abu-al-Huda, the Prime Minister of Jordan, told an extraordinary session of the Lower House of Parliament that Jordan's policy towards Israel remained unchanged.

14 A Decree Law was published authorizing the Egyptian Government (in virtue of Law No. 131 of 1954) together with the Permanent Production Council, the Industrial Bank, Bank Misr, Societe Misr pour

June

14 la Filature et le Tissage, Societe Misr d'Assurances and the German Demag Company to establish a new company: The Egyptian Iron and Steel Company.

16 Anthony Nutting, Under Secretary at the British Foreign Office, stated that 47 British servicemen had been killed in the Suez Canal Zone between October 16, 1951, and June 1, 1954; that seven more were missing, presumed killed; and that there had been 3,297 thefts of British official property, of which 1,767 were of Army telecommunications cable, and ten cases of deliberate sabotage by arson.

The British War Office categorically denied reports that the partial evacuation of the Suez Canal Zone would start within a fortnight. It said that there was absolutely no truth in reports that British troops would be moved to Libya and Cyprus shortly. Discussing the recent conflicting reports regarding the imminent evacuation of the Suez Canal Zone by the British forces, Zeev Laquer commented in the Jerusalem Post.

17 An address was made by the French Premier candidate, Pierre Mendes-France, in the National Assembly containing a statement on French policy in Morocco.

The agreement on a common Arab nationality was unanimously approved by Egypt.

18 Eric Johnston, President Eisenhower's Special Representative to the Middle East, said on his arrival in Jerusalem that "no decisions were reached and none were sought" during the six day talks he had just concluded in Cairo with representatives of Lebanon, Syria, Jordan and Egypt on the Jordan River project. He asserted that progress was being made.

The US and Lebanon exchanged notes constituting an agreement relating to special economic assistance.

19 The UNTSO Chief of Staff reported on the Nahhalin incident, fixing guilt on the Israel residents, and also on the Scorpion Pass incident.

A unified customs tariff for the three provinces of Libya came into force and duties were chiefly on an ad valorem basis.

June

24 A US State Department spokesman stated that the US had protested to the Saudi Arabian Government against the agreement between Saudi Arabia and Aristotle Onassis, which it considered might eventually give Onassis "a virtual monopoly" in the transportation of Saudi Arabian oil. The spokesman added that the State Department had received notes expressing "strong concern" at the agreement from Norway, Denmark, Sweden, Finland, Western Germany, the Netherlands, Italy and Spain, and that Onassis had approached "three other countries" with a view to concluding similar agreements with them.

25 The US Department of State announced approval of a gift of 6,000 tons of wheat for delivery to Libya. The first shipment of 2,000 tons was to be loaded on June 25 and to arrive in Tripoli within a few weeks. The action was taken in response to a Libyan appeal to the United States for grain to alleviate shortages resulting from continued droughts.

According to a report of the Mixed Armistice Commission, an attack on a Jordanian village made March 29 had been perpetrated by a large group of militarily trained Israelis.

26 Brigadier Mahmoud Riyad, Egyptian Director of Arab Affairs, accused Israel of attempting to amplify Jordan River water to increase irrigation of its land and make room for more immigrants.

30 A special agreement concerning technical assistance was signed between Iraq and the UN, ILO (International Labor Office), FAO (Food and Agricultural Organization), UNESCO, ICA (International Cooperative Alliance) and WHO (World Health Organization).

July

1 The US sent messages to the Government of Israel and the Government of Jordan on Jerusalem violence on June 30.

Both Israel and Jordan sent letters to the President of the UN Security Council concerning the June 30 Jerusalem incidents.

An agreement concerning the conditions of the operation of the telegraph and telephone services between Turkey and Syria and the measures to

July

1 be taken to improve and expand the telecommunication systems of the two countries was signed.

Egyptian Minister of National Guidance Major Salah Salem declared that the liberation of the entire Arab world since it would not be wise to make another adventure in Palestine while the British Army controlled its rear lines of communication.

2 The Israel Representative to the UN sent a second letter to the Security Council President protesting further fighting in Jerusalem.

5 Lebanon sent a letter to the UN Security Council concerning the June 30 incidents in Jerusalem.

8 A trade agreement was reportedly signed by Syria and Yugoslavia.

Egypt approved an agreement signed on May 6 by the Egyptian Government and UNFAO (UN Food and Agricultural Organization) for extending technical cooperation to certain Near East countries through the establishment of an Arab Training Center.

12 It was announced that a large number of goods from the sterling area, whose importation had lately been prohibited, would again be permitted entry into Egypt, including motor cars, textiles, electrical goods and confectionery.

19 The Syrian Representative to the UN sent a letter to the UN Security Council President concerning Israel's resumption of work on the Jordan River project in the demilitarized zone.

The US State Department said it had inquired in Madrid about Spanish exports of arms to Egypt and other countries and expressed concern that such exports might violate terms of the US-Spanish military aid pact.

22 The Arab Tourism Conference issued a resolution annulling visas between Arab nations.

It was announced by the British Foreign Office that Spain had agreed to ban the export of arms to Egypt after representations by the UK Ambassador in Madrid, Sir John Balfour.

July

27 Israel protested to the UN Security Council concerning acts of aggression by Jordan against Israel.

28 Fourteen Middle Eastern and Asian countries sent a letter to the UN Secretary General requesting the inclusion of the Tunisian question on the agenda.

29 Richard Gardiner Casey, Australian Minister of External Affairs, said of the Egyptian-British Suez agreement: "This agreement . . . should not be regarded as a victory for one side or the other but rather as a compromise based on statesmanship and mutual good will."

British Prime Minister Churchill explained in the UK House of Commons that the "appalling" development of nuclear weapons had made the Suez base obsolete.

British State Secretary for War Antony Head told the House of Commons that his Government had agreed to the Suez evacuation because: 1) nuclear arms development virtually eliminated the threat of a major Soviet attack in the Middle East, 2) Turkey's entry into NATO and its military ties with Pakistan created a new Mideast defense line and 3) Britain could not afford to keep 80,000 troops in Suez militarily.

30 An arbitration agreement was concluded between Saudi Arabia and the UK concerning the dispute over the Buraimi Oasis. It was also agreed that all forces should be withdrawn from Buraimi except a 15 man police detachment to be maintained by each party in the Oasis.

August

2 Senator Colonna (who represented the French population of Tunisia in the Council of the Republic), in an interview with Le Monde, made a bitter attack on the French Prime Minister, whom he accused of having proposed "the dissolution of the Franco-Tunisian community." In particular, he criticized the decision "to reduce the French inhabitants to a position of foreigners in the country which they have contributed to building up," and deprecated the value of the proposed conventions on the ground that there was no guarantee that they would not be unilaterally abrogated.

August

3 Christian Fouchet, French Minister of Tunisian and Moroccan Affairs, explained in a press statement that the new Tunisian Government would still have four French members, heading, as hitherto, the departments of Finance, Public Works, Education and Posts, and that the transfer of these departments from French to Tunisian hands would not take place until the Franco-Tunisian conventions had been concluded.

Egyptian Prime Minister Colonel Gamal Abdel Nasser stated that Egypt needed peace in order to solve its internal problems, and suggested that the US act as a mediator between Israel and the Arab countries.

UK Foreign Secretary Anthony Eden sent a letter to US Secretary of State John Foster Dulles concerning the agreement reached on July 28 between the UK and Egypt.

Egyptian Foreign Minister Mahmoud Fawzi issued a statement to the UK concerning the settlement of the Suez controversy.

4 Christian Fouchet, French Representative to Tunisia, stated in the Foreign Affairs Commission of the Council of the Republic that there would be seven conventions dealing respectively with cultural, defense, diplomatic and judicial matters, Franco-Tunisian cooperation in the implementation of the economic modernization plan, administrative and technical cooperation in the Civil Service (including protection for French Civil Servants, of whom there were about 10,000 in Tunisia), and a customs union.

A manifesto issued by the moderate nationalist Democratic Independence Party of Morocco demanded the restoration of the ex-Sultan and the formation of a provisional Government which would negotiate a new treaty between Morocco and France.

5 The USSR and Lebanon established diplomatic relations.

6 General Vagn Bennike, the UN Truce Supervisor in Jerusalem, commenting on the armed border clashes that had occurred between Israel and Jordan between June 30 and July 2, said that it was impossible to fix the blame for beginning the firing and offered a plan to avoid new outbursts.

August

19 In an interview, Egyptian Prime Minister Colonel Nasser said that defense pacts between the Arab world and the Western powers would have to wait until the Arabs had overcome their residual suspicions of Western intentions.

21 A communique was issued following Major Salah Salem's visit to Iraq. This communique was later clarified by Radio Cairo when it reported that Major Salem remonstrated with Iraqi Prime Minister Nuri-Said about making alliances outside of the Arab League, but did not get much change out of the latter.

24 Iraq and Pakistan exchanged notes consituting an agreement relating to air services.

31 Egyptian Commander in Chief Major General Abd-al-Hakim Amer said he accepted the conditions of the British arms embargo lifting "without reluctance" because Egypt had no intentions of attacking Israel or any other country.

In a press interview, Egyptian Prime Minister Gamal Abdel Nasser told the correspondent of the American publication US News and World Report that the Arab nations could not possibly join the big Western nations in any defense pact of the Middle East because the Arab people believed that such an organization would only be a form of masked imperialism.

September

2 The UNTSO Chief of Staff, Major General E. L. M. Burns, complained of lack of cooperation, particularly on the part of Israel in connection with an incident in the Beir Liqya area. He declared that the holding of military maneuvers in Israel near the demarcation line increased anxiety on the other side.

4 Christian Fouchet, French Minister for Tunisian and Moroccan Affairs, after observing that France could not abandon the responsibilities for the defense of Tunisia imposed upon it by "ineluctable strategic necessities," pointed out that the seven main conventions would have to be negotiated.

September

4 The US State Department informed Israel Minister in Washington Shiloah that the US viewed the attack on Beir Liqya with "great concern." Although the US Government recognized that infiltration from Jordan constituted a serious problem, Israel's apparent policy of armed retaliation—which had been condemned in the past—had increased rather than diminished tension along the armistice line.

7 The UNTSO Chief of Staff reported to the UN Secretary General concerning the incident of September 1-2 in the Beir Liqya area of Jordan, on the basis of an investigation of the incidents between Israel and Jordan by the Mixed Armistice Commission.

In his first report submitted to the UN Security Council, General Burns gave warning that recent incidents on the Jordanian border could develop into hostilities which might spread "like bushfire."

8 Israel, in response to a State Department admonition, justified its policy of organized retaliation in Beir Liqya on the grounds that after such attacks as those of Qibya or Nahhalin, infiltration was substantially reduced.

13 A joint manifesto denouncing the Egyptian Government was issued by the Supreme Guides of the Moslem Brotherhoods of Syria, Jordan and Iraq.

14 A report was submitted by the Chief of Staff of the UN Truce Supervision Organization to the UN Secretary General concerning the incident in the Beir Liqya area.

16 The French President reportedly recognized the right of Algerians to self determination.

17 An order was issued permitting Habib Bourguiba to move freely throughout France, except in the Paris area, although not to leave the country.

The Israel Embassy replied to the joint statement made that same day by eight Arab envoys stating that urgent measures must be taken "to deter Israel from any further aggression" to avoid an outburst in the Middle East. The reply said that if arms were supplied to the Arab States then Israel must insist on receiving arms in the same measure so that the balance of power would be preserved and not be impaired

September

17 to "the advantage of those who continued to threaten Israel's annihilation."

20 Egyptian President Colonel Nasser stated that he had warned Syrian Prime Minister Said al-Ghazzi that the Moslem Brotherhood was using Syria as a base for propaganda, and accused it of forming secret cells in the Egyptian Army and Police for the purpose of committing terrorist acts.

23 An official Israel reply to UN Truce Supervisor in Palestine General E. L. M. Burns' report described it as incomplete in fact, since it was based solely on Jordanian evidence. The Israel Government therefore suggested that General Burns should undertake a general survey of border conditions and should try to obtain Jordan's consent to a definite demarcation line.

Saudi Arabia protested against an alleged UK attack on September 15-16 in which several people were said to have been killed.

Tawfiq Abu-al-Huda, the Jordanian Premier, in a statement in Amman, vigorously denied all recent reports and rumors regarding a possible Arab peace settlement with Israel, according to the Arab News Agency.

28 After returning to Paris from Orleansville, Algeria, the scene of a violent earthquake, French Minister of the Interior Francois Mitterand announced that the French Government had approved a sum of two billion francs to be spent on the reconstruction of the devastated town and the surrounding area.

29 The Egyptian Representative to the UN informed the President of the UN Security Council that the Israel ship Bat Galim had approached the harbor of Suez at 6 am (GMT) on September 28. Without any provocation, it was charged, the Bat Galim had opened fire, using small arms, on Egyptian fishing boats within Egyptian territorial waters. The authorities had taken the preliminary measures of arresting the crew of the ship and of ordering an immediate inquiry to determine responsibility for the incident.

October

19 US Secretary of State Dulles pronounced the Anglo-Egyptian settlement of the Suez problem "an event of far reaching importance and an occasion for renewed congratulations to both countries."

20 Sir Anthony Head, UK Secretary of War, announced the recommendations for the future operation of the Suez Canal Base by civilian contractors made by a group of engineers from the Federation of British Industries.

The British Foreign Office published a communication made to the Israel Ambassador in London Eliahu Elath in which British assurances were given to Israel concerning the effect of the Anglo-Egyptian Agreement on that country's security.

21 Libya ratified an agreement with the US relating to military bases in Libya.

25 Anthony Nutting, British Minister of State, in a statement to the UK House of Commons on the Anglo-Egyptian Agreement, said that the most important point was that Britain now had for the first time a legal right to maintain a base in Egypt.

26 In a note sent by the UK to Saudi Arabia, the UK proclaimed a new line of boundary between Saudi Arabia and the Trucial Sheikhdoms. The new line of boundary followed, in general, the Riyadh Line of 1935. The UK warned Saudi Arabia of violations of the new line.

27 In a message to Egyptian President Colonel Nasser, Hamadah, the Acting Head of the Moslem Brotherhood, condemned the attempt on Nasser's life October 26 (which had been done by a member of his organization).

An announcement was made of a joint request by Lebanon and Syria to Iraq for increase in oil transit royalties.

28 Sheikh Mustafa al-Sibai, Supreme Guide of the Moslem Brotherhood of Syria, issued a statement declaring that the organization was opposed to political assassination, but adding that "suppression of liberties can only provoke such explosions."

October

3 Saudi Arabia signed an increased prices agreement with the Arabian American Oil Company.

7 An Egyptian complaint was sent to the Egypt-Israel Mixed Armistice Commission on the Bat Galim incident.

A convention for facilitating trade exchange and the regulation of transit trade between the States of the Arab League was signed.

10 Major General Muhammad Ibrahim, Chief of Staff of the Egyptian Army, announced that he had invited the US Army to send a military mission to Egypt.

12 The Governor General of Algeria, speaking in the Algerian Assembly, stated that the reconstruction of Orleansville, scene of recent earthquakes, would take the form of a "pilot project" involving a number of improvements—e. g. in rural housing—of a type which it was ultimately hoped to extend throughout the whole of Algeria.

13 Egyptian Minister of National Guidance Major Salah Salem announced in a broadcast that concessions had been made to the Southern Sudanese, raising rates of pay to those of Northerners in the same grades.

14 A statement by the Chief Egyptian Delegate to the UN Mahmoud Azmi was made, alleging that since March, Egypt had refrained from "any interference with vessels conveying goods to Israel or coming from Israel ports and passing through the Suez Canal."

19 Following the signing of the Anglo-Egyptian agreement on the Suez Canal Base, a statement was issued. Egyptian President Colonel Nasser, Joint Parliamentary Under Secretary at the British Foreign Office Anthony Nutting and Sir Ralph Stevenson, British Ambassador to Egypt, said that both delegations had "labored intensively to achieve a comprehensive agreement which constitutes a constructive measure in the cause of peace," and that both Governments were sincerely desirous of "promoting a new spirit of friendship and understanding between our peoples."

The Israel Foreign Ministry issued a statement on the Anglo-Egyptian Agreement, expressing concern over the Agreement and its effect on the balance of power in the Mideast.

October

29 Egypt sent a letter to the President of the UN Security Council concerning the Bat Galim incident.

30 The US and Egypt exchanged notes constituting an agreement concerning relief supplies and equipment, its duty free entry into Egypt and exemption from internal taxation.

November

1 Fares al-Khouri, new Syrian Premier, said that Syria would continue to support "the struggle of Palestine Arabs."

3 The US and Libya exchanged notes constituting an agreement on emergency wheat aid to Libya.

5 The Special Report of the Director of the Advisory Commission of the United Nations Relief and Works Agency (UNRWA) for Palestine refugees in the Near East was issued.

It was officially announced in Algeria that 175 nationalists had been arrested, ten terrorists killed and large quantities of munitions seized in police operations.

9 British Prime Minister Sir Winston Churchill gave a speech at the Lord Mayor of London's annual banquet held at Guildhall in which he commented on the settlement of the Egypt situation.

11 A trade protocol regulating exchanges of goods between Lebanon and Czechoslovakia was signed by a Lebanese delegation in Prague.

A report was submitted to the UN Security Council by the Chief of Staff of the United Nations Truce Supervision Organization in Palestine General Burns, concerning the situation between Egypt and Israel in the area of the Gaza Strip.

13 The Israel Foreign Ministry announced the release of the blocked bank accounts and safe deposits of the Arab refugees.

The Libyan Government informed the French authorities that it did not propose to renew a provisional agreement, concluded in December, 195

November

13 and due to expire on December 31, 1954, under which France had been permitted to maintain 400 troops and an air base in Fezzan.

14 The Syrian Government announced that a ban had been imposed on all activities which might harm relations with other Arab States and that refugees had been warned to abstain from political activities on pain of expulsion.

15 Jordanian Ambassador to the UN Abd-al-Moneim Rifai sent a letter to the Chairman of the UN Ad Hoc Political Committee concerning relief for Jordanian refugees.

Mubarak Zarrouq, Sudanese Minister of Communications, gave a warning that any further action against General Nagib of Egypt would "weaken the unity of the Nile Valley."

16 The Moslem Brotherhood in Syria accused the Egyptian authorities of resorting to torture and persecution to force members of the Brotherhood to confess in the trials before the Cairo Military Tribunal.

17 The Council of Ulema (Moslem theologians) of al-Azhar University, Cairo, which was regarded as the supreme religious authority by orthodox Moslems, issued a fatwa (religious edict) condemning the Moslem Brotherhood as heretical, and warning Moslems not to be misled by its practices and aims.

The Egyptian Council of the Revolution issued a statement deploring the fact that some Arab Governments "still wink at the Moslem Brotherhood's activities."

In a statement over Cairo Radio, Gamal Abdel Nasser, the Egyptian Premier, said that the Suez Canal would belong to Egypt after the current concession ended in 1968.

19 French Premier Mendes-France told the National Press Club that North Africans were being provoked to violence by systematic propaganda emanating from Budapest and Cairo, which was being bolstered by a supply of arms and infiltration of agitators.

20 A joint communique was issued by US Secretary of State Dulles and French Premier Mendes-France after their talks of November 17-20,

November

20 wherein Dulles promised serious consideration of external influences that compromised the security of the North African region.

22 At a press conference, General Boyer de la Tour du Moulin, the French Resident General and Commander in Chief in Tunisia, announced that joint teams of French officers and Tunisian Government representatives would visit the areas where the fellaghas were active to inform them of the offer contained in the declaration.

Habib Bourguiba, in an interview published by the Tunis Petit Matin, suggested that those fellaghas who surrendered should be incorporated in a Tunisian Army, "as the maquis was in the French Army," although care should be taken to exclude "undesirable sham patriots."

23 After discussions between French Premier Mendes-France and Charles Malik, the Lebanese Ambassador in Washington and spokesman of the 15 nation Asian-Arab Bloc in the UN, Charles Malik declared that Mendes-France had made it clear that all he wanted was an opportunity to put his plans into effect, and that it was his personal view "that the French Premier should be given this opportunity and be helped in every possible way to carry out his good intentions."

25 Gamal Abdel Nasser said that he would spare no effort so suppress the Moslem Brotherhood, which he accused of trying to overthrow his regime by force and assassination.

26 Lebanon and UNRWA exchanged notes constituting an overall agreement.

27 It was officially announced that civilian, military and police casualties in anti-fellagha operations in Tunisia during the six months May 1-November 1 were 42 civilians and 34 police and soldiers killed and 31 civilians and 89 soldiers and police wounded. In the same period, 38 people had been killed by individual fellagha acts of terrorism in the towns. The fellaghas had lost 147 killed and 51 captured during the six months.

29 A report was made by the Chief of the UN Truce Supervision Organization to the UN Secretary General concerning the Bat Galim incident.

Sir Anthony Eden, the British Foreign Secretary, signed the instrument of ratification of the Anglo-Egyptian Treaty, under which about 70,000

November

29 British troops would be withdrawn from the Suez Canal Zone, a Foreign Office spokesman said in London.

30 A Franco-Tunisian amnesty offer to fellagha rebels was conveyed by Tunisian Government emissaries. The guerrillas were promised immunity from prosecution if they turned in their firearms by December 9.

The Jordanian Parliament passed a law forbidding the carrying and possessing of firearms in a belt ten kilometers wide along the armistice lines, except by special permission.

December

1 The transfer of the General Headquarters, British Middle East Command, from the Suez Canal Zone to Cyprus officially came into effect, on which date it began operating under the joint command of General Sir Charles Keightley, Commander in Chief, Middle East Land Forces, and Air Chief Marshal Sir Claude Pelly, Commander in Chief, Middle East Air Forces.

Reports from Tripoli said that the Libyan Government had notified France that all French troops stationed in Fezzan, Libya's third province, must be withdrawn by December 31, or would then be considered "illegal."

2 An Algerian offical spokesman stated that the security forces had regained control of three quarters of the Aures Massif, that traffic between Batna, Foum-Toub and Arris and between Biskra and M'Choumeche was once again possible without interference or danger and that the systematic mopping up operations by the security forces under General Gilles were not confined to the southeastern part of the mountains, through which the seasonal migration towards the northern fringes of the Sahara took place.

4 In Pakistan, representatives of the Moslem League and other political and religious organizations signed a message to the Egyptian Government giving a warning that the Moslems of the world would approach the United Nations unless the "atrocities" perpetrated against the Moslem Brotherhood were ended.

The Arab League Trade and Payments Agreements were ratified by Iraq.

December

4 Egypt announced preparation to release the Bat Galim crew members captured in a test of Suez denials to Israel. Israel had protested in the UN.

5 The Egyptian Council of the Revolution officially confirmed its earlier order dissolving the Moslem Brotherhood.

6 Musa Shahbandar, the Iraqi Foreign Minister, stated that his country was urging the other Arab States to allow Iran to become a member of their defense agreement. He said that it was essential for the Arab collective security pact to be extended to include Iran.

8 A UN General Assembly Resolution provided for the extension of assistance to the Arab refugees for another five years, approved the allocation of $25.1 million for relief and $36.2 for rehabilitation, and provided also for the extension of some help to the economic refugees.

9 A five year trade and friendship agreement between Yemen and West Germany came into force.

12 The leaders of the Moslem Brotherhood in Damascus elected Sheikh Mustafa al-Sibai, head of the organization in Syria, as Supreme Guide, in succession to Sheikh Ahmad Hassan al-Hudaibi.

13 Egypt and Pakistan signed an agreement for the establishment of scheduled air services between and beyond their respective territories.

Iraqi Foreign Minister Musa al-Shahbandar said in Cairo that in any revised treaty Britain would be given the right to return to the Habbaniya Air Base if Iran were attacked after the expiration of the Anglo-Iraqi Treaty in 1957. Iraq would also reserve the right to call in British troops to help defend her frontiers against attack.

14 In an interview with a correspondent of the Paris Le Monde, Libyan Prime Minister Mustafa Ben-Halim denied that his policy was in any way hostile to France and stated that his Government had demanded the withdrawal of French troops from Fezzan because "we are proud of our independence and wish to feel ourselves free."

Supplement to 1954

December

15 US envoys in the Middle Eastern countries meeting in Damascus issued a statement of US policy in that area. They announced "strict impartiality" and "friendship" with all Arab States and Israel, adherence to the May 25, 1950, Tripartite Declaration and support for UNTSO.

Nuri-Said Pasha informed the Iraqi Parliament that it was his Government's intention to terminate the Anglo-Iraqi Treaty before its expiration in October, 1957.

17 French Prime Minister Mendes-France proposed that he negotiate directly with Libyan Prime Minister Mustafa Ben-Halim concerning the temporary military agreement of 1954.

19 The presence of Israel in the midst of the Arab World was one of the main obstacles hindering close Egyptian and other Arab cooperation with the West, Major Salah Salem, Egyptian Minister of National Guidance declared to a visiting Turkish press mission in Cairo.

20 Mirghani Hamzah, Khalafallah Khaled and Jali, all members of the Sudanese Cabinet, in a statement denied that they had threatened the Sudanese Government and accused the Prime Minister of having had secret meetings with Egyptian Major Salah Salem during his visit to the country, of favoring certain Ministers and giving them access to Government secrets and of ignoring others who did not accept "Egyptian domination."

Israel sent a letter to the UN Security Council protesting Syria's complaint of December 4.

21 Iraqi Prime Minister Nuri-Said announced that agreement had been reached with the oil companies operating in Iraq to increase Iraq's royalties for 1954 in accordance with the increased royalties of neighboring countries.

In Beirut, Musa Shahbandar, Iraqi Foreign Minister, told a press conference that the Arab League Council had decided to cooperate with the West on Middle East defense provided certain conditions were fulfilled.

Supplement to 1954

December

21 The Iraqi Government notified Britain of its decision not to renew or extend the Anglo-Iraqi Pact. Making this announcement in Baghdad, Nuri-Said, the Premier, added, however, that although Iraq would not enter into such a pact with Britain, it would take into consideration the security problems of Arab countries and the Arab League Collective Security Pact.

22 The Jordanian Minister of Economy announced that Jordan would receive further US financial aid amounting to $7 million which would be spent on the Yarmuk River hydroelectric and irrigation projects, industrial loans and road construction.

23 Libyan Prime Minister Mustafa Ben-Halim agreed to negotiate directly with French Prime Minister Mendes-France provided that the negotiations would begin before December 31, the date set for the termination of the temporary military agreement.

24 Colonel Gamal Abdel Nasser, the Egyptian Premier, said that his country was looking forward to closer Anglo-Egyptian cooperation, especially in the economic field.

27 Egypt would refuse to conclude peace with Israel even if the latter were to implement all UN resolutions regarding its frontiers, Major Salah Salem, Egyptian Minister of National Guidance, declared, according to the Jordanian paper al-Difea.

28 The Jordanian Parliament approved a commercial agreement between Jordan and Yugoslavia exchanging goods and strengthening economic relations between the two countries.

30 It was announced in London that Britain would release a further 15 million pounds sterling of Egypt's blocked sterling balances on January 1, 1955.

January, 1955

January 1

British authorities turned over to Egypt control of an 87 mile oil pipeline between Suez and Cairo, under the terms of the agreement for British evacuation of the Suez Canal Zone.

The captain and crew of the Israel ship Bat Galim were released from Egypt and put across the border into Israel.

Jordanian Premier Tawfiq Abu-al-Huda returned to Amman after unsuccessful talks in London on revision of the 1948 Treaty of Alliance.

Addressing the Iraqi Chamber of Deputies, Premier Nuri-Said stated that he officially impressed upon the British Government that Iraq did not wish to have its treaty of alliance with Great Britain either revised or renewed. He said that in any future arrangement, Iraq must take into consideration the safety of neighboring nations such as Iran and Turkey. Nuri-Said also told members of Parliament that there was an alliance against the Arabs between the Zionists and the Communists.

January 2

Israel Prime Minister and Foreign Minister Moshe Sharett spoke during a major Knesset debate on foreign policy. He denounced the Soviet Union as the factor principally responsible for the new Palestine crisis.

It was announced in Amman that the British-Jerusalem Electric Company would turn over to Jordan its installations serving the Old City of Jerusalem.

Under the terms of the compensation ordinance, 71 British technicians in Khartoum resigned, and 15 were given notice by the Sudan Government.

January 3

Salah Ben-Youssef, Secretary General of the Tunisian Neo-Destour Party, stated at Geneva, Switzerland, that five months of negotiations over the form of autonomy to be given Tunisia had shown that the Government of Mendes-France was determined to perpetuate the colonial regime in Tunisia.

January, 1955

January 3

The Iraqi Foreign Ministry informed the Soviet Charge d'Affaires in Baghdad that Iraq was closing its legation in Moscow.

January 4

Negotiations between France and Tunisia regarding autonomy were resumed at Paris.

During the debate in the UN Security Council on the Bat Galim case, Great Britain, France and the US supported Israel's demand that its ships be allowed to pass through the Suez Canal without Egyptian interference. These same powers also praised Egypt for its conciliatory attitude. Egyptian Foreign Minister Mahmoud Fawzi said in Cairo that his Government's decision to release the vessel would not affect its position on its right to refuse Canal passage to Israel shipping.

Twelve British judges of the Sudan judiciary gave notice of their resignation and requested their release in February or March. All five British specialists of the Health Ministry and five British nurses also gave notice.

At discussions held between Qadi Muhammad al-Shami and the British Agent in the western Aden Protectorate, in the presence of the Sultan of Lahej, the Qadi reportedly stated that he had removed Muhammad al-Shahir and other dissidents from the frontier and had warned the Qubati tribesmen living along the Yemen border against causing disturbances.

January 5

In a letter to the UN Security Council, Saudi Arabia protested that ruthless military operations by France against Algerian nationalists were a threat to peace. A copy of the letter was sent to all the member states of the UN.

January, 1955

January 6

Turkish Premier Adnan Menderes, accompanied by the Ministers of Foreign Affairs and Communications and nine members of the Turkish National Assembly, arrived in Baghdad for discussions with Iraqi Government leaders.

Mirghany Hamzah, who was ousted from his post as Sudanese Minister of Education, Irrigation and Agriculture, together with the two other ousted Ministers, organized a new political party, the Republican Independence Party.

The Secretariat of the new Sudanese Republican Independence Party, under the leadership of the three ministers dismissed from the Cabinet on December 23, issued a statement of its aims and principles. Among the aims were the establishment of an independent Sudanese Republic and cooperation with Egypt on economic, cultural and other questions in a way compatible with the sovereignty of both countries.

The Libyan Prime Minister, returning from Paris, announced that an agreement had been reached regarding the future of the French garrison in the Fezzan. Details of the agreement were to be discussed in Tripoli.

The Israel-Egyptian Mixed Armistice Commission (MAC) discussed measures which might lessen the tension and decrease the number of incidents on the frontier in the vicinity of Gaza.

A 22 man Syrian parliamentary committee was appointed to work out a new oil policy for the country.

Representatives of the regional, civil and military authorities in Morocco met and decided on future measures for the maintenance of law and order.

USSR Ambassador D. S. Solod called Egypt Foreign Minister Mahmoud Fawzi to express the sympathy of the USSR Government in connection with the disastrous floods in that country caused by heavy rains. He informed the Minister that the USSR Red Cross and Red Crescent Society had decided to donate 60,000 rubles to the Egyptian Red Crescent Society for use to relieve distress in the flood areas.

January, 1955

January 7

Deputy Prime Minister Fatin Rustu Zorlu of Turkey left for Baghdad by special plane to join Premier Menderes.

January 8

The International Bank for Reconstruction and Development announced that the Government of Iraq had cancelled the unused balance of $6.5 million of the $12.8 million 15 year loan made by the Bank in 1950.

An International Bank mission, which had been studying the Litani River project to provide water and electric power for southern Lebanon, left for Washington.

Moscow Radio announced the USSR's decision to recall its diplomatic mission from Iraq in view of Iraq's unfriendly attitude.

January 9

British Minister of State for Colonial Affairs Henry Hopkinson arrived in Western Aden Protectorate for talks with Arab tribal chiefs. He was received by the Awdhali Sultan.

Further resignations of British officials in Sudan brought the total to 600.

A Turkish Foreign Office statement denied that Turkish Deputy Prime Minister Zorlu's trip to Baghdad had anything to do with his conversations with the American, British and Israel Ambassadors. It was made known that Menderes had been invited to Damascus by the Syrian Government.

January 10

Hassan Marai, Egyptian Minister of Commerce, announced discovery of a potentially rich oil field near Wadi Firan on the Red Sea coast of the Sinai Peninsula.

January, 1955

January 12

The Soviet Legation in Iraq was closed down.

In a Knesset debate, Israel Prime Minister Moshe Sharett announced that an exploratory trade mission would leave for Communist China to look into the possibilities of a trade agreement.

It was announced in Baghdad that agreement in principle had been reached between the Iraqi Government and the oil companies for a new price fixing formula for oil produced in Iraq. This would increase the Government's oil revenue by one-fifth.

At the end of their discussions, a joint communique was issued by the Turkish and Iraqi leaders announcing that their two countries proposed to enter into a military alliance and to extend a pressing invitation to other Middle Eastern countries to join them.

An official statement was issued stating that the Sudanization Committee had decided that of the 1,036 posts held by British expatriates, 598 affected the free and neutral atmosphere requisite for self determination. Ten of the posts were considered redundant, and the remaining 427 were non-influential.

January 13

A majority of the UN Security Council agreed that Israel should be allowed to use the Suez Canal. Sir Leslie Knox Munro of New Zealand, President of the Security Council, declared that most of the eleven members clearly upheld a three year old resolution in which Egypt was called on to desist from restricting the passage through the Canal of any vessels from Israel.

The French Minister for Moroccan and Tunisian Affairs, Christian Fouchet, received Resident General Francis Lacoste as he arrived in Paris after failure of discussions among representative elements of the Moroccan population for a reform program. Nationalists remained adamant over the question of the return of the former Sultan.

Police clashed with student demonstrators in Damascus who were attempting to stage a protest parade against the visit of Adnan Menderes, the Turkish Prime Minister.

January, 1955

January 13

It was reported from Baghdad that the Iraqi Government would renew its bid for larger allocations of US military equipment in the light of the decision to conclude a military alliance with Turkey.

Fares Khouri, Syrian Prime Minister, was quoted as saying that he hoped the Government would be able to discuss a number of outstanding questions with Turkish Prime Minister Adnan Menderes. Syria was anxious to build up friendly relations with Turkey, he stated.

A Turkish Foreign Office spokesman welcomed the announcement of a prospective Turko-Iraqi defense agreement as most promising.

The Iraqi Ambassador called on the Foreign Minister of Egypt. A spokesman of the Egyptian Foreign Ministry said afterwards that the Turko-Iraq Pact arranged in Baghdad was contrary in spirit to the Arab League collective security pact.

January 14

The UN Security Council issued a report submitted by General E. L. M. Burns, Chief of Staff of the Palestine Truce Supervision Organization. In it General Burns traced the history of the dispute, expressed the view that a lasting settlement would be possible only by negotiated revision of the terms of the Armistice Agreement, and suggested as a provisional arrangement the division of the demilitarized zone into areas within which either Israel or Syria would have administrative responsibility.

Before leaving for Syria, Turkish Prime Minister Adnan Menderes issued a statement saying that the decision of Iraq and Turkey to cooperate was not intended to be exclusive but was meant to achieve the cooperation of the other Middle Eastern States.

Turkish Prime Minister Adnan Menderes, en route to Beirut from Baghdad, stopped in Damascus for a short talk with Prime Minister Fares al-Khouri. Following the meeting it was announced that Turkey and Syria had agreed to form a committee to study the question of property held by Turks in Syria and by Syrians in Turkey.

January, 1955

January 14

The Turkish Premier Adnan Menderes met with Lebanese Premier Sami al-Solh. He showed him a copy of the Turko-Iraqi draft agreement and invited Lebanon to adhere to it.

Prime Minister Tahar Ben-Ammar from Tunisia held a Cabinet meeting to discuss ways of ending the impasse in the talks with French leaders regarding Tunisian autonomy.

Henry Hopkinson, British Minister of State for Colonial Affairs, said in Aden that the British Government was determined to carry out fully its obligations under the treaties with the Protectorate States.

January 15

Henry Hopkinson, British Minister of State for Colonial Affairs, said that Britain planned to give Aden self government when its people proved their worth.

Addressing a delegation from Gharbiya Province, Egyptian Premier Gamal Abdel Nasser said that when he stated that the transition period would be over in 1956, it did not mean that the Revolution would be ended by then. He added that when the British would evacuate the Canal Zone, it would not mean that the Revolution would withdraw after them.

In demonstrations in Aleppo protesting the visit to Syria of the Turkish Premier, 35 persons were seriously injured, among them ten policemen.

Turkey's Prime Minister Adnan Menderes invited Lebanon to join the Turko-Iraq Defense Pact. The Jordanian Prime Minister flew to Beirut to talk with the Turkish and Lebanese Governments about the pact. Egypt delivered notes to the Arab Governments opposing the pact.

Alfred Naccache, Lebanese Foreign Minister, said that Adnan Menderes had invited Lebanon to join the proposed Turko-Iraq Pact and had expressed Turkey's readiness to conclude favorable economic agreements with Lebanon and other Arab States.

January, 1955

January 15

The Tunisian press reported that Egypt's displeasure with the Turko-Iraqi draft agreement was based on two reasons: (1) fears that Egypt's role of leadership among the Arab countries would be challenged, and (2) a preference by Egypt's leaders, after all their recent internal troubles, to avoid raising another controversial issue at this time.

January 16

The ninth session of the Arab League Cultural Committee was opened at Jedda by Amir Fahd, Saudi Arabian Minister of Education. Taha Hussein, Director of the League Cultural Department, presided. The teaching of Arabic in both Eastern and Western countries was one of the principal topics on the agenda.

Egypt called an emergency conference of Arab Prime Ministers to discuss Iraq's decision to conclude an alliance with Turkey. Egypt subsequently announced that it would secede from the Arab League Security Pact when the Turko-Iraq Pact was formalized and would work for a new military alliance of Arab States opposed to foreign alliances. Saudi Arabia endorsed the Egyptian stand.

Students tried to storm the main government building in Damascus, demanding release of the Aleppo students who had been detained by police on January 15.

It was officially announced that Lebanese President Camille Chamoun had accepted an invitation to visit Turkey, the date to be set later.

The Turkish press reported that Lebanon would join the Turko-Iraqi Pact. The Syrian Foreign Minister announced that he would resign if Syria did not approve cooperation with Turkey.

January 17

Eric Johnston, President Eisenhower's special envoy to the Middle East, left for Israel and the Arab countries in a renewed effort to settle the Jordan River controversy.

January, 1955

January 17

Mahmoud Fawzi, Foreign Minister of Egypt, saw the British Ambassador and the US Charge d'Affaires and explained to them the Egyptian attitude towards the proposed Turko-Iraq Pact.

Egypt opened a campaign to prevent the Arab countries from cooperating with Turkey.

January 18

An official communique issued in Baghdad stated that the Iraqi Government's decision to sign a pact with Turkey was based on the fact that Iraq occupied a special geographical position and that it already had three treaties with Turkey, signed in 1926, 1937 and 1946.

Southern opposition members of Sudan's Parliament met at Juba to discuss partitioning of the Sudan into North and South, and also the establishment of a Federal Government which would include North and South Sudan and Egypt.

Israel lodged a complaint with the UN commission in Jerusalem that two Israel farmers had been killed by Jordanians in the Jerusalem corridor.

The Algerian Assembly convened in extraordinary session. Speaker Raymond Laquiere read a letter from French Interior Minister Francois Mitterrand promising that his reform plan would be submitted to the Assembly in time for consideration during its present session.

General Boyer de Latour, French Resident General of Tunisia, declared at the funeral of five French soldiers who had been captured and presumably murdered by fellaghas, that France would remain in Tunisia even though its "will for agreement" was not believed and "its generous offers" rejected.

The Israel Foreign Ministry, in a letter to General Burns, stated that the latter's suggestion to partition the demilitarized zone between Israel and Syria was unacceptable.

January, 1955

January 18

Turkey and Lebanon concluded four days of talks on the issue of Middle East defense pacts.

President Eisenhower nominated Donald A. Heath to be US Ambassador to Lebanon, to succeed Raymond A. Hare.

In three engagements in and around the Aures Mountain region in Algeria, French casualties were eight killed and three wounded. The rebels lost eight killed and three captured. Fifty-eight arrests were made in the Department of Constantine.

The Arab liberation movement formed by the ousted Syrian Premier, Brigadier Adib Shishakli, resumed its activities.

Henry Hopkinson told newsmen that it was the earnest desire of the British Government and the Aden Government to maintain the friendliest relations with Yemen and that they attached great importance to a strict observance of all agreements with that Government.

January 19

It was announced by the Iraqi Embassy in Cairo that because of illness Premier Nuri-Said would not attend the conference of the Arab League states on January 22. Arab diplomats in Cairo assumed that the decision was motivated by "diplomatic illness."

The Soviet radio and publications violently attacked the Turko-Iraq Pact as a threat to peace.

Clark Gregory, US Director of Point Four administration in Jordan, said in Amman that Jordan would need five to ten years to become self supporting.

January 20

It was reported in Cairo that the major oil companies began a boycott against the oil tanker fleet of Aristotle S. Onassis in the hope of forcing modification of his allegedly monopolistic contract with the Saudi Arabian Government.

January, 1955

January 20

The Saudi Arabian Government announced that talks for the reopening of the Hejaz railway which began in Riyadh on January 16 had been concluded. The resolution passed would be submitted to the Governments of Saudi Arabia, Jordan and Syria in the form of a draft agreement for their approval.

The anticipated visit of Turkish Prime Minister Menderes to Egypt was reportedly not acceptable to the Egyptian Government.

January 21

Egyptian newspapers attacked the Iraqi Prime Minister, and reported that it was thought that Iraq would withdraw from the Arab League. Iraq was criticized for not having consulted the Arab League before announcing its intention to sign a pact with Turkey. A news item from Karachi reported that Pakistan might enter a pact with Iraq similar to the Turko-Iraq Pact.

A statement was issued by Turkish Prime Minister Adnan Menderes in which he pointed out that he regretted the attitude of the Egyptians toward a Turko-Iraq Pact, because Turkey attached great importance to relations with Egypt. He added that he was ready to meet with Egyptian leaders at anytime, anywhere.

A number of new Ministers took office in the Caliphate Government of Spanish Morocco. For the first time the National Reformist Party was represented through its leader Abd-al-Khaleq Torres, Minister of Social Action.

January 22

Arab Premiers and Foreign Ministers met in Cairo with Egypt, Saudi Arabia, Jordan, Syria and Lebanon present. Egypt declared that the proposed Turko-Iraq Pact would undermine the foundations of the Arab League and contravene the Arab Collective Security Pact, and warned that it could commit all the Arab States to go to war if Turkey were attacked.

January, 1955

January 23

Iraq and Lebanon refused to censure the Turko-Iraq Pact in the Arab League meeting in Cairo. Iraq did not attend, although it was expected to do so later in the week. Yemen and Saudi Arabia supported the Egyptian proposal to censure the Pact, although no one from Yemen was actually attending. The meeting broke up in discord.

The Syrian Government directed the Foreign, Finance and Economic Ministries to seek larger royalties from the foreign petroleum companies operating in the country.

Negotiations on home rule for Tunisia were resumed in Paris by French and Tunisian delegations headed respectively by the two Prime Ministers.

January 24

It was announced at Paris that French and Tunisian delegates meeting there had reached agreement on 18 of 20 points on Tunisian home rule, in a nine hour session.

Iraq's Deputy Prime Minister Ahmad Mukhtar Baban flew to Beirut to discuss with Lebanon's President Camille Chamoun Egypt's strong reaction to the proposed Turko-Iraq Pact.

It was reported from Cairo that Egyptian efforts to build a solid Arab opposition to the projected defense pact between Iraq and Turkey were not successful.

The Israel-Egyptian Mixed Armistice Commission condemned Egypt for an attack by Egyptian forces on an Israel patrol post near the demilitarized zone in the Gaza area.

January 25

Israel called on the WHO (World Health Organization) to change the current arrangements under which Israel was prevented from participating fully in and obtaining the benefits of WHO activities in the Middle East because of the anti-Israel political campaign of the Arab countries.

January 25

Israel Prime Minister Moshe Sharett conferred with the Turkish Ambassador in Jerusalem on the implications for his country from the projected Turko-Iraq Pact.

Iraq's acting Foreign Minister Burhan-ad-Din Bashayan and Fadel al-Jamali joined Iraqi Deputy Prime Minister Ahmad Mukhtar Baban in Beirut for further discussions with Lebanese President Chamoun.

Lebanese President Camille Chamoun met with the Egyptian Ambassador in Beirut.

January 26

Egypt proposed to the Arab League a twelve point resolution as a reaction against the proposed Turkish-Iraqi Pact. Saudi Arabia, Yemen and Syria were said to support the resolution, but the position of the other Arab states was not clear.

A three man Iraqi delegation, led by former Prime Minister Fadel al-Jamali, arrived in Cairo to attend the emergency session of Arab League Prime Ministers. Yemeni Prime Minister Amir Saif al-Islam Hassan also arrived, while Libyan Ambassador Khalil Kallal was permitted to attend on behalf of his Government.

Prime Minister Moshe Sharett from Israel told the Knesset that the proposed defense pact between Turkey and Iraq would alter the political and military strength in the Middle East to Israel's detriment.

Eric Johnston arrived in Tel Aviv to resume negotiations regarding joint development by Israel and the Arab States of the Jordan River Valley. He was also to visit the Arab capitals.

Jacques Soustelle was appointed French Governor General of Algeria by Premier Mendes-France.

January 27

The Supreme Egyptian Military Tribunal made public its sentences against ten of the 13 Jews being tried for espionage: two were

January 27

sentenced to death, and the rest to various sentences of hard labor.

An Egyptian Government spokesman told the press that the "secret of Nuri-Said's illness" was opposition in his own country to the proposed Pact with Turkey. He warned Arabs not to be deceived by the idea that the Pact was to protect them against aggression from Israel as well as from outside the Middle East.

The Iraqi delegates held a private meeting with the Egyptian Prime Minister, Foreign Minister, and Minister of National Guidance.

Eric Johnston met with Israel Prime Minister Sharett to discuss the plan for regional development of the Jordan Valley.

January 28

Libyan Prime Minister Mustafa Ben-Halim arrived in Cairo to participate in the emergency meeting of Arab League Prime Ministers.

At a meeting of the Arab League, the group named a committee to draft a compromise acceptable to Iraq and Egypt in their dispute over Iraq's close relations with Turkey. Iraq charged that Egypt had been conferring secretly with Soviet diplomats.

The Egyptian Ambassador in Turkey denied having contacted Russian representatives in Ankara, a charge made by a number of Turkish newspapers.

January 29

At the twelfth meeting of the Arab League emergency conference, a five man committee was appointed to draft a communique on results of the deliberations. The chief Iraqi delegate, Fadel al-Jamali, proposed that the communique should include a clause recognizing Iraq's right, as a sovereign power, to conclude military pacts outside the scope of the Arab Collective Security Pact. The Egyptian delegation rejected the Iraqi proposal and the meeting adjourned without action.

January 30

The Egyptian delegation failed to secure the assent of the Syrian, Lebanese and Iraqi delegations to a resolution which: (1) reaffirmed a resolution of an earlier conference which based the defense of the Middle East on the Arab Collective Security Pact, subject to reservations by Iraq (which, as interpreted in Baghdad, covered a treaty such as the proposed Turko-Iraq Pact), and (2) committed all Arab countries to abstain from adhering to the Turko-Iraq Pact.

After Premier Gamal Abdel Nasser threatened that Egypt would withdraw from the Arab Collective Security Pact should Iraq sign a treaty with Turkey, it was decided to send a mission to Baghdad to discuss the situation with Iraqi Premier Nuri-Said.

An appeal by the Egyptian delegates for at least a postponement of the Turko-Iraq Pact was received unsympathetically by Fadel al-Jamali, leader of the Iraqi delegation.

The Turkish Embassy in Baghdad was dynamited. The Turkish press blamed the Zionists and Communists.

Protest meetings against the death sentences imposed by the Supreme Egyptian Military Tribunal on two Jews tried for espionage were held in all parts of Israel. Protests were also made in London, Paris, New York and Washington.

January 31

The Arab League delegation stopped in Beirut on its way to Iraq and had talks with the President. A Foreign Ministry spokesman said the Lebanese, Syrian and Jordanian members of the mission were seeking to mediate between Iraq and Egypt. He said the Lebanese Prime Minister would urge Iraqi Premier Nuri-Said to delay signing the Turko-Iraq Pact.

The Arab League mission arrived in Baghdad and conferred with Iraqi Premier Nuri-Said.

Lebanese Deputy to the President Emile Bustani arrived in Baghdad with a special message from President Chamoun to King Faisal. He told newsmen that in his view the Turko-Iraq Pact was a blow to Israel.

January 31

Speaking in the Knesset, Israel Prime Minister Moshe Sharett accused the Egyptian Government of spilling Jewish blood in an attempt to strengthen its position against rivals within Egypt and opponents in the Arab countries. French Foreign Minister Edgar Faure told the Egyptian Ambassador in Paris, officially, that France was upset by the executions. The State Department in Washington stated that everything that could be done was done on behalf of the two men.

President Tito of Yugoslavia arrived in Aden for a short visit.

February 1

The entire country of Israel went into an unofficial state of mourning for the two Jews hanged in Cairo.

It was reported from Washington that Israel was seeking military ties with the US, Great Britain and France. It was pressing for formal security guarantees that would make it part of the Western defense system and for renewed promises that the balance of power in the Middle East would not be upset.

Premier Fares Khouri of Syria stated in Damascus that the weakness of the Arab Collective Security Pact was responsible for Iraq's move.

President Camille Chamoun inaugurated Lebanon's second oil refinery, located at Sidon and named the Mediterranean Refinery.

February 2

The terms of the proposed Turko-Iraq Pact were published in Beirut and subsequently confirmed in Baghdad. The terms provided in general for an exchange of information on internal security, with exchange also of technical information methods, and for the right of transit of arms to Turkey via Iraq without customs, and vice versa. The Pact was to be open for adherence by any Arab state or other friendly state having interests in the region. It was to have a validity of five years and to be terminable only at a year's notice.

Abdel Nasser, Egyptian Prime Minister, confirmed that Egypt would secede from the Arab League Collective Security Pact if Iraq concluded the proposed defense agreement with Turkey. He added that Egypt would then propose that all Arab States opposed to the Turko-Iraq Pact should enter into a pact with Egypt not to accept any offers of alliance from powers outside the Arab League and to stand together in mutual defense against Israel.

A statement issued at the end of the talks between Iraqi representatives and the Arab League delegation announced a proposal by President Camille Chamoun of Lebanon, in a message to Iraqi King Faisal, that the Prime Minister, Nuri-Said, and the Egyptian Prime Minister, Colonel Gamal Abdel Nasser, should meet in Lebanon and attempt to solve their differences.

February 2

Iraq reportedly rejected an alternative proposal made by Lebanese President Camille Chamoun that Iraq should delay signature of its pact with Turkey.

The debate on French North Africa opened in the French Assembly with strong attacks on the French Government's policy from General Aumeran and Qilici, right wing deputies for Algiers and Oran, respectively, and from Bardoux (Peasants) and Dronne (Gaullist). General Aumerman asserted that it was the arrival of Premier Pierre Mendes-France to power and his encouragement of the Neo-Destour in Tunisia which had set off the terrorist movement in Algeria, and he declared that internal autonomy in Tunisia was incompatible with the preservation of French influence.

Bardoux accused the Libyan Government of supplying arms to Tunisian fellaghas and of operating training camps for them. He said Libya was virtually a British protectorate and spoke of foreign intrigues for the expulsion of France from North Africa. Dronne accused both Britain and America of passive complicity in Libya's support for the fellaghas.

February 3

After their mission to Baghdad reported that its efforts had failed, the Arab League Premiers met again in Cairo but recessed without achieving any result.

On the second day of the French Assembly debate on North Africa, Mayer, the Radical former Premier, announced that he would vote against the Government, and he made it plain that this was not only because of North Africa but also because of general policy. He accused the Government of contradictions, particularly in the appointment of Soustelle as Governor General of Algeria, and of failing to protect the loyal Moslem population in Algeria.

Discussing Tunisia, French Premier Mendes-France reminded deputies that the Assembly had three times approved the principle of negotiations for internal autonomy, and he pointed out that any agreement reached would not enter into force until ratified by the Assembly. It was essential in his view that the Neo-Destour Party

February 3

should be involved in the negotiations so that they would not be able afterwards to reject the agreement. There were only two choices, Mendes-France declared, a policy of entente and reform, or one of repression with all its consequences. He had chosen the first and would defend it to the limit of his abilities.

February 4

It was revealed in Cairo that at the Arab League Premiers' meeting Lebanon proposed that another conference be held in Beirut in about ten days, to try again to reconcile Egyptian and Iraqi views on the question of the Turko-Iraq Pact.

A spokesman of the French Mouvement Republicain Populaire said that his party would vote against the Government, in spite of its agreement on North Africa, because of its disapproval with its record on the German problem.

February 5

French Premier Mendes-France was defeated in a vote of confidence ostensibly on his North African policy.

Marshal Tito visited Egyptian Premier Gamal Abdel Nasser in Cairo.

February 6

Egypt's attempt to organize a unified opposition by the Arab States to the proposed Iraqi treaty with Turkey ended in failure. The Arab League Premiers' meeting ended after sixteen days of conferences and diplomatic maneuverings with no results and not even an approved communique.

Iraqi Prime Minister Nuri-Said sent a reply to Colonel Nasser, Prime Minister of Egypt, saying that he would have been pleased to meet him had not the Egyptian condition been unacceptable.

Iraqi Premier Nuri-Said told the Chamber of Deputies that in spite of Egyptian opposition, Iraq would consummate the proposed defense treaty with Turkey. He received a unanimous vote of confidence.

February 6

The Coalition Cabinet of Syrian Premier Fares al-Khouri collapsed as the National Party withdrew from it.

February 7

A note was presented by Iraq to the Egyptian Ambassador protesting against the use of diplomatic channels for the introduction into Iraq of publications inciting Iraqis against the Turko-Iraq Pact and seeking to create disturbances and foment hatred for the Government.

Egyptian Minister of National Guidance Salah Salem told a delegation of Lebanese journalists visiting Cairo that Egypt would secede from the Collective Security Pact the day Iraq signed the proposed pact with Turkey and would seek to conclude a new military alliance with like-minded Arab States opposed to foreign alliances.

A communique issued in Cairo stated that Eric Johnston had reached an understanding with Jordan, Syria and Lebanon on the general principles of a plan for exploiting the waters of the Jordan River for the mutual benefit of the Arab States and Israel.

February 8

Turkish Premier Adnan Menderes, in a public statement, thanked Syria and Lebanon for the deep understanding and good will shown by them during the recent Cairo Conference. He insisted that one of the main principles of Turkish foreign policy was to maintain friendly relations with all the Arab States, and that the road Turkey and Iraq had taken was admired by all the Arab States.

Amir Faisal, Prime Minister of Saudi Arabia, said after a visit to Colonel Gamal Abdel Nasser that if Egypt seceded from the Arab League Security Pact, Saudi Arabia would also secede. His Government was in full agreement with Egypt on all questions of Arab foreign policy.

The British Ambassador in Amman handed Premier Tawfiq Abu-al-Huda a note in reply to the Jordanian Government's request for

February, 1955

February 8

negotiations for the revision of the Anglo-Jordanian treaty of alliance. The note maintained that the question of revising the treaty might be considered only in the light of a comprehensive defense system for the Middle East.

Tunisia's Resident General Pierre Georges Boyer de Latour flew to Paris to seek emergency relief for Tunisia to avert a threat of famine caused by drought.

February 10

Premier Tawfiq Abu-al-Huda announced that Great Britain had agreed to grant 350,000 pounds sterling annually for a period of five years for the Jordanian Home Guard which served as a reserve of the Arab Legion.

Speaking at a press conference, Jordanian Prime Minister Tawfiq Abu-al-Huda announced that he had received a note from Britain embodying its viewpoint on the various points raised during the December talks in London.

Syrian President Hashem Atassi asked Fares al-Khouri to form another Cabinet, but the latter admitted defeat within 24 hours. Sabri al-Assali, Secretary General of the Syrian National Party, was then assigned the task.

February 11

King Saud of Saudi Arabia declared that separatist Arab tendencies to conclude defense pacts with outside countries had brought the Arab League to the verge of collapse.

February 12

Addressing the Arab peoples from Mecca, Saudi Arabian King Saud stated his determination to oppose military alliances between the Arabs and foreign powers.

February, 1955

February 15

The Syrian High Court cancelled the membership of four deputies on charges of having contravened regulations during the October elections, bringing to 17 the number dismissed since the formation of the new Chamber.

Israel sent a reminder to the UN Security Council that Egypt still held the Israel freighter, Bat Galim, and requested that Egypt be asked whether it would arrange for the release of the ship and cargo and for the ship's passage through the Suez Canal.

French Governor General of Algeria, Jacques Soustelle, arrived in Algiers to take up his duties.

February 16

It was reported from Damascus, where Eric Johnston was holding negotiations with Arab leaders, that Israel, Jordan, Syria and Lebanon had agreed to the use of Lake Tiberias as the main water storage reservoir in the proposed Jordan Valley development plan. The chief remaining item of disagreement was the share of the water each state would get.

Indian Prime Minister Jawaharlal Nehru left Cairo after two days of talks with Egyptian officials. Before his departure a joint communique was issued declaring identity of views of the two Governments regarding international issues.

Fadel al-Jamali, representative of the Iraqi Prime Minister, had talks in Beirut with Lebanese President Camille Chamoun. He said Iraq would terminate the treaty with Britain when the pact with Turkey was signed. Referring to the talks he had just had in Damascus, he expressed the view that a majority of the peoples in Syria and Iraq favored a union of the two countries.

British Foreign Secretary Anthony Eden told the House of Commons that Britain would grant a special subsidy of 350,000 pounds sterling for the Jordan National Guard, and that subject to parliamentary approval further support up to a maximum of 250,000 pounds sterling would be given for the following four years. This was to be in addition to the annual subsidy for the Arab League.

February, 1955

February 12

The second anniversary of the conclusion of the Anglo-Egyptian Sudanese Agreement was celebrated with prayers at the mosques and churches, public parades and celebrations.

February 13

Sabri al-Assali announced the formation of a new Cabinet in Syria, composed of three political parties and two Independents. Sabri al-Assali was the acting Interior Prime Minister, Kakhr al-Kayali, Minister of National Economy, and Khaled Azm, Prime Minister for Foreign Affairs and acting Defense Minister.

February 14

In his speech opening the third session of Parliament, the Governor General of Sudan, Sir Robert Howe, expressed the Government's concern that a substantial part of the cotton crop had not yet been sold and that foreign exchange reserves had consequently dropped appreciably.

King Hussein flew to Baghdad for a private visit. It was believed that he would attempt to ease tension between Egypt and Iraq.

Yemen's Foreign Minister Qadi Muhammad Omari told newsmen in Cairo that his country was prepared to follow the example of Egypt and Saudi Arabia and withdraw from the Collective Security Pact if Iraq signed the proposed pact with Turkey.

Fadel Jamali, who was visiting the Levant States as personal representative of the Iraqi Prime Minister, Nuri-Said, had talks with the new Prime Minister and Foreign Minister of Syria.

February 15

Tribal representatives, the Islamic Socialist Bloc, and a number of Independents, totalling about 30 in all, formed a "United Constitutional Front" in the Syrian Chamber.

February, 1955

February 16

Following bread riots at Tunis, Beja and Sfax, French officials gave a warning that the situation might become catastrophic if emergency relief measures were not taken promptly. The situation was due to the winter drought.

February 17

The British Embassy issued a statement giving details of the progress made in implementing the Anglo-Egyptian Agreement. It showed that the withdrawal of British forces from the Canal Zone was ahead of the prescribed timetable.

February 20

Sir Anthony Eden, British Foreign Secretary, who was on his way to the Manila Pact conference at Bangkok, stopped over in Cairo for talks with Colonel Nasser, Egyptian Prime Minister. A joint statement after their talks said they had reviewed the world situation and the task of promoting peace, and had noted with satisfaction the progress of Anglo-Egyptian relations since the signing of the Suez Canal base agreement.

In Syria, eight thousand secondary school students walked out of their classes, and 500 demonstrated in protest against the projected Turko-Iraq Pact.

Egyptian Minister of National Guidance Salah Salem flew to Beirut with Prime Minister Gamal Abdel Nasser's reply to an invitation by President Camille Chamoun that Nasser meet Prime Minister Nuri-Said of Iraq in Beirut to iron out Egyptian-Iraqi difficulties. Nasser replied that he would welcome a meeting with any Arab leader to discuss unification of the Arabs.

Eric A. Johnston, special US envoy to the Middle East, opened negotiations at Jerusalem on the US sponsored plan to develop Jordan and Yarmuk River resources to benefit jointly the states of Israel, Jordan, Lebanon and Syria.

February 21

King Hussein of Jordan arrived in Cairo for a six day visit.

Sabri al-Assali, Syrian Prime Minister designate, announced that Syria would not conclude any alliance with a non-Arab state.

February 22

Syria's new Prime Minister, Sabri al-Assali, announced that Syria would not join the Turko-Iraq Pact.

Egypt complained to the Joint Egyptian-Israel Mixed Armistice Commission that an Israel Army unit had kept up mortar fire for a half hour on an Egyptian Army position near Rafah, causing serious injuries to four Egyptian soldiers.

February 23

The Egyptian and US Governments agreed to use $23,337,000 of the $40,000,000 American Economic Development Assistance Fund for four major projects: highway improvement; piping for a new potable water supply system; improvement of the port of Alexandria; and equipment for the Ministry of Public Works machine shops.

Premier Adnan Menderes of Turkey arrived in Baghdad for the signing of the Turko-Iraq Pact.

February 24

The Turko-Iraq Pact was signed in Baghdad. It had a validity of five years, and was renewable for further five year periods.

The Turkish National Assembly's Affairs Committee approved the Turko-Iraq Pact, after a speech by Adnan Menderes, Turkish Prime Minister.

Following the signature in Baghdad of the Turko-Iraq Pact, a Government spokesman said that Egypt would invite the signatories of the Arab Security Pact, except Iraq, to meet to revise the agreement. Egypt would ask for the expulsion of Iraq from the pact.

February 24

Syrian Parliament voted confidence, 66-53, in the new Government's statement that the time was not ripe for Syria to join the Turko-Iraq Pact.

February 26

The Iraqi Government disclosed that the defense alliance with Turkey carried a pledge by both states to take measures guaranteeing enforcement of the UN resolutions on the Palestine question.

The Turkish Parliament ratified the Turko-Iraq Pact by a vote of 449-0. The Iraqi Parliament ratified it by a vote of 116-4. It was announced that Turkey had invited the US, Great Britain and Iran to join the Pact. A joint communique from Baghdad concerning the Pact included statements in regard to the UN decisions on Palestine, thereby identifying Turkey more closely with the Arab position.

In the debate on the Turko-Iraq Pact in the Iraqi Chamber of Deputies Nuri-Said said it was hoped that Britain and the US would adhere to the treaty and that Pakistan and Iran would also be welcomed. He stated that Iraq would terminate the Anglo-Iraqi Treaty of 1930 when other countries intimated their wish to join the pact. He listed three principles on which Iraq would cooperate with the other signatories.

Egypt's Minister of National Guidance, Salah Salem, arrived in Damascus for a five day visit.

Major Salem, Egyptian Minister for National Guidance, said in Damascus that with Iraq's signature of the alliance with Turkey the Arab Collective Security Pact no longer existed.

February 27

The Israel Government, in an official statement on the Turko-Iraq Pact, referred to the hostile intent towards Israel in the exchange of letters between Iraqi Prime Minister Nuri-Said and Turkish Premier

February 27

Adnan Menderes. Israel said that the Turko-Iraq Pact was liable to encourage Arab belligerent tendencies, foment aggressive ambitions and undermine the peace and stability of the area.

King Faisal of Iraq gave the royal assent to the Turko-Iraq Pact.

Two persons were killed and eight persons injured in Deir al-Zor, a town near the Iraqi border, when supporters of the Baath Socialist Party who were demonstrating against the Turko-Iraq Pact clashed with supporters of the Syrian Popular Party. Troops were called out to end the clash.

The Jordanian Government accepted a suggestion made by Colonel Brewster, chairman of the Mixed Armistice Commission, that the local commanders' agreement should be implemented and put into force as of March 1.

Henry A. Byroade arrived in Cairo to take up his duties as US Ambassador to Egypt.

February 28

Israel armed forces of about half battalion strength crossed the armistice lines at Gaza and destroyed the Gaza Garrison Headquarters of the Egyptian Army. Thirty-eight Egyptians were killed and 31 wounded. Israel casualties were unknown.

Lieutenant Colonel Nachman Karni of the Israel Army accused the Egyptian Army of operating an extensive intelligence network in southern Israel. He said that 24 Egyptian agents were apprehended during 1954, ten others had been killed and five escaped.

The Iraqi Chamber of Deputies approved the five year program of the Development Council. The cost was estimated at ID303 million.

It was reported from Damascus that after several days of secret talks between Egypt's Minister of Guidance Salah Salem and Syrian leaders, the two countries had decided to sign an agreement for the setting up of a new Arab alliance, excluding Iraq.

February 28

Edgar Faure, new French Premier, called for resumption of negotiations with the Tunisian Government on proposed internal autonomy for the protectorate.

The French Government decided to send wheat and other foodstuffs immediately to Tunisia to relieve the shortage caused by drought.

March, 1955

March 1

Egypt protested to the UN Security Council against an act of aggression by Israel that led to the death of 38 persons at Gaza.

The Israel delegation at the UN declared that the military clash of February 28 must be viewed against the background of mounting Egyptian military pressure against Israel, synchronized with a vicious propaganda campaign which had in recent weeks reached a peak of hysteria.

The UN Truce Supervision Organization said that Israel Army units had penetrated Egyptian territory as far as the Gaza railway station and had carried out an attack with mortar fire, grenades and automatic weapons on the Egyptians, killing 37 and wounding 30.

Israel lodged a complaint with the MAC (Mixed Armistice Commission) that on the night of February 28 a routine Israel patrol was ambushed by an Egyptian force, and in the running fight which ensued a number of Israel soldiers were wounded.

The Egyptian Foreign Minister received the Ambassadors of the five permanent members states of the UN Security Council and the Turkish Ambassador and informed them of the grave view taken by the Egyptian Government of the incident near Gaza and of the decision to make a strong protest to the UN and to request an urgent meeting of the Security Council.

Lieutenant Colonel Salah Gohar, Director of Palestine Affairs for the Egyptian Army, said in Cairo that Israel forces attacked Gaza on February 28, killing 37 Egyptians and wounding 39.

An Israel Army announcement said that an Egyptian unit opened fire from Israel territory against an approaching Israel unit which returned the fire and pursued the Egyptians some distance into their territory.

The British Foreign Office deplored the extremely grave incident in the Gaza area.

Students besieged and stoned the headquarters of the UN Truce Supervision Organization in Gaza. They burned a UN jeep and pulled down the UN flag.

March, 1955

March 1

Sherif Moulay Idris, founder of the Moroccan Democratic Party of Free Men, in opposition to the Istiqlal Party, was assassinated in Casablanca.

March 2

After five days of secret talks with Egypt's Minister of National Guidance, Major Salah Salem, an agreement was signed with Syria defining the principles of a proposed alliance to replace the Arab League Collective Security Pact. Other Arab States were asked to study the plan.

A trade agreement was signed between Egypt and Indonesia. The agreement was valid for one year and provided for reciprocal most favored nation treatment to be given to both parties.

The acting Foreign Minister of Iraq telephoned to the Iraqi Ambassador in Cairo asking him to assure the Egyptian Foreign Minister of Iraq's fullest support in connection with the Israel attack in the Gaza region.

Rioting by Arab refugees occurred in Gaza and other towns in the border region. Many of the refugees attacked and looted UN relief stores, shouting that they wanted arms, not food, and demanded to be allowed to go home. Five men were reported wounded when police fired cautionary shots.

Israel Prime Minister Moshe Sharett warned in the Knesset that if Egypt proclaimed that it was maintaining a state of war against Israel, it must face the consequences, including armed clashes.

Moshe Sharett, Israel Prime Minister, said that the Turko-Iraq Pact was the result of US and British policy and that these two countries were therefore inevitably responsible for the effect of their activities upon the position of each state within the region.

March 3

The Foreign Minister of Iraq instructed the Iraqi Ambassador in Cairo to make a formal protest against allegations by Egyptian Ministers that the Israel attack at Gaza had been incited by the Iraq Government.

March, 1955

March 3

As a result of the Egyptian-Israel border incident on March 1, a spokesman for the Turkish Government announced that Turkey shared the grief of Egypt in its losses.

After Egyptian Minister of National Guidance Salah Salem visited Amman to invite Jordan to join a pact with Egypt, Jordanian Foreign Minister Walid Salah asked for time to study the proposal in the light of the situation in Jordan and the attitude of the other Arab countries.

It was announced in Tel Aviv that eight Israelis were killed and 13 wounded in the Gaza clash of March 1.

Israel requested the UN Security Council to consider violations of the Armistice Agreement by the Egyptian Government. The request listed six accusations of continuous violation by Egypt which endangered international peace.

Egyptian Premier Gamal Abdel Nasser warned Israel that Egypt would not depend on the UN but would meet force with force. He said he had heard Israel threaten Egypt on March 2 and that if Israel "wanted a battle" Egypt would "give them a harsh lesson." Nasser said that Egypt did not count on the Security Council because "that body has helped the Israelis to attain their objectives."

March 4

British Foreign Secretary Sir Anthony Eden arrived in Iraq on his way back to Britain from the SEATO (Southeast Asia Treaty Organization) conference and had talks with Nuri-Said, Prime Minister of Iraq. A joint statement said that the two statesmen had reviewed the world situation and that Sir Anthony Eden had congratulated the Iraqi Government on the conclusion of the Turko-Iraq Pact which he hoped would prove an important step in fortifying the security of the Middle East and ensuring peace.

Britain and Iraq signed in Baghdad a new agreement for defense cooperation to replace the Treaty of Alliance of 1930.

March, 1955

March 4

The UN Security Council placed on its agenda the Egyptian and Israel complaints regarding the Gaza incident of February 28. It then adjourned to await the report of Major General E. L. M. Burns and the decision of the Egyptian-Israel MAC (Mixed Armistice Commission) after investigation of the incident.

Egyptian and Israel troops exchanged fire for about ten minutes on the Gaza frontier. No casualties were reported on the Egyptian side.

Turkey presented three aircraft to the new Jordanian Air Force.

March 5

Khaled Azm, Syrian Minister of Foreign Affairs, and Major Salah Salem, Egyptian Minister of National Guidance, arrived in Riyadh for talks with Saudi Arabian King Saud and Crown Prince Faisal on the new Egyptian sponsored accord.

Turkish Premier Adnan Menderes said that in the Syrian-Egyptian Agreement both parties had agreed to enter into no commitments with nations other than Arab states and to refuse all cooperation with Turkey and Iraq. He declared that if Syria and Egypt continued their present policy and activity, it would be impossible not to feel anxiety at the future relations between Syria and Turkey, who had a sincere desire to be friendly.

UK Foreign Secretary Sir Anthony Eden praised the Turko-Iraq Defense Pact as a step toward strengthened Middle East security, at a stopover in Baghdad on his return from the Bangkok Conference.

In view of new Arab demonstrations against UN representatives in Gaza, the wives and children of the Truce Observers were evacuated from Gaza through Israel territory to Arab Jerusalem.

The Imam of Yemen instructed his Minister at Cairo to bring to the attention of the Arab League an attack in southern Yemen in which a number of persons were killed by a British force from Aden. He also alleged that a Yemeni Army barracks had been destroyed.

March, 1955

March 5

President Celal Bayar of Turkey arrived in Baghdad for a five day visit.

US Special Envoy Eric A. Johnston gave President Eisenhower an encouraging report on his efforts to work out an agreement between Israel and the Arab States on the Jordan River development project.

Addressing Jewish national organizations in Washington, Nahum Goldmann, Chairman of the Jewish Agency for Palestine, declared that the State Department was excluding Israel from Middle East defense. The methods being used implied a de facto withdrawal of recognition from Israel and denial of its existence.

A 60 man Egyptian military mission arrived in Beirut for a six day visit as guests of the Lebanese Government.

Donald A. Heath arrived in Beirut to take up his duties as US Ambassador to Lebanon.

March 6

Egypt, Syria and Saudi Arabia announced they proposed to place their armed forces under unified command, ready to act collectively against any state which might attack them. They would form a permanent joint command with a centralized headquarters to control the training, arming, organizing and employment of the armed forces which pact members would place at its disposal.

Turkey assured Syria that it would not support Iraq in the realization of the Greater Syria plan which would embrace Syria, Lebanon and Jordan in a union with Iraq.

Members of the Syrian Socialist-Resurrectionist Party clashed with landowners near al-Maarrah in the Aleppo Governorate. Thirty persons were injured, some seriously.

The Egyptian-Israel Mixed Armistice Commission voted that there had been a prearranged and planned attack in the Gaza area ordered by the Israel authorities. The charge by the Israel representative on the Commission that Egypt started the fight was not accepted. The Israel delegate said that the Commission's decision would be appealed.

March, 1955

March 6

It was announced at Damascus that Syria had complained to the Syrian-Israel MAC (Mixed Armistice Commission) that 200 Israelis had entered a demilitarized zone and fired at a Syrian outpost.

The conference of US Jewish national organizations adopted a five point program for the attainment of peace, development and defense in the Middle East that would faithfully serve the highest interests of the security and welfare of the peoples of the US and the free world.

John D. Jernegan, Deputy US Assistant Secretary of State, asserted that Israel could not be included in any defense pact with the Arab States until tensions were resolved.

March 7

Egypt's Minister of National Guidance, Major Salah Salem, left Beirut for Cairo after talks with Lebanese leaders regarding the Turko-Iraq Pact of February 24 and the proposed Egyptian-Syrian-Saudi Arabian alliance. Before leaving he stated that Lebanese leaders had emphasized their "neutrality."

British Minister of State Anthony Nutting rebuked Israel for its part in the Gaza incident.

March 10

The Saudi Arabian Ambassador to Jordan announced that Saudi Arabia and Jordan had agreed to form a joint committee to supervise the demarcation of their common boundaries in July of 1955.

The Jordan-Israel MAC (Mixed Armistice Commission) charged Israel with the murder of five Arab Bedouins.

Turkey sent a note to Damascus protesting against Syria's participation with Egypt and Saudi Arabia in an alliance which was directed against the Turko-Iraq Pact.

March, 1955

March 11

General E. L. M. Burns, Chief of Staff of the UN Truce Supervision Organization, ruled against any altering of the factual findings in the condemnation of Israel for the Gaza incident by the MAC (Mixed Armistice Commission). However, the MAC changed some of the wording in the resolution to make it less severe.

Turkey and Iraq agreed to admit Great Britain to their alliance without waiting for other Middle Eastern states to accede to it.

The Shah of Iran and Queen Soraya arrived in Iraq for a 24 hour visit on their way back to Iran.

March 12

Iraq's Foreign Minister Fadel Jamali arrived in Beirut for talks with Lebanese President Camille Chamoun and Syrian Foreign Minister Khaled Azm preliminary to the visit of a Syrian delegation to Baghdad.

March 13

The Turkish Government sent a second note to the Syrian Government concerning the contemplated Egyptian-Syrian Pact. It said that the origin of the agreement was the desire of Egypt to isolate Iraq and to destroy the effects of the Turko-Iraq Pact. The Turkish Government drew the attention of the Syrian Government to the dangers of persistence in this hostile attitude towards Turkey and to the adverse effect such an attitude was bound to have on Turkey's relations with Syria.

March 14

Jordan's Foreign Minister Walid Salah stated that his country was opposed to the Turko-Iraq Pact but had not yet determined its attitude to the proposed Egyptian-Syrian-Saudi Arabian alliance.

A Syrian delegation headed by Foreign Minister Khaled Azm arrived in Baghdad to attempt to mediate the hostile feelings between Iraq and Egypt over the Turko-Iraq Pact. They met with an Iraqi delegation led by Iraqi Deputy Prime Minister Ahmad Mukhtar Baban.

March, 1955

March 15

French and Tunisian negotiators resumed talks regarding Tunisian autonomy that were interrupted by the fall of the Mendes-France Government on February 5. Although it was admitted in principle that the points previously agreed upon would not be open to question, French Minister for Moroccan and Tunisian Affairs Pierre July asked for modifications in the preamble of the proposed convention establishing the principle of a "federal" link between the two countries. Points still unsettled were control of the southern zone and the length of time before the police force would become wholly Tunisian.

On his arrival in New York to report personally to the Security Council on the Gaza incident, Major General E. L. M. Burns, Chief of Staff of the UN Truce Supervision Organization, stated that he did not expect full scale fighting to break out between Israel and its Arab neighbors. Since the Gaza incident, he said, both sides had seemed willing to show restraint and to forego provocations that would lead to more bloodshed.

March 16

A report of the Secretariat of the UN Economic Commission for Europe, released in Geneva, stated that the price of Middle East oil in Europe could be substantially lowered; it blamed the US oil policy for the present high, commercially unjustified, world price level. As an example of oil profits, the report estimated that the Arabian-American Oil Company in Saudi Arabia made a profit of about $1.40 on each barrel of crude selling for $1.75.

The Arab Postal Conference met in Cairo to consider, among other things, the admission of Libya and Yemen to the Arab Postal Union.

March 17

The UN Security Council resumed consideration of the Gaza incident of February 28. Major General Burns, Chief of Staff of the UNTSO, reviewed the March 6 decisions of the Egyptian-Israel MAC, submitting a complete list of the complaints lodged by both sides during the preceding four months. He referred to his report to the Security

March, 1955

March 17

Council on November 11, 1954, in which he had recommended that the two parties set up joint patrols and barbed wire obstacles along certain portions of the demarcation line and negotiate a Local Commanders' Agreement. Burns said that he felt that if such an agreement were honestly carried out, infiltration could be reduced to an "occasional nuisance."

The Egyptian UN delegate, Omar Loutfi, insisted that the UN Security Council do more than pass a resolution on the Gaza incident; he demanded that sanctions be invoked against Israel.

March 18

Israel reported to the Egyptian-Israel MAC (Mixed Armistice Commission) that infiltrators had crossed the border and were harvesting inside Israel. An Israel patrol approaching them was fired on from across the border by Egyptians. The Israelis replied and in the ensuing exchange of fire two of the infiltrators were killed.

Egypt complained to the Egyptian-Israel MAC (Mixed Armistice Commission) that Israel soldiers had killed two Arab children who had crossed the demarcation line four miles south of Gaza.

An agreement was signed with the US Point Four administration by which Lebanon would receive $25,400 for health projects.

March 19

At the close of five days of talks with Syrian leaders, the Iraqi Government issued a communique stating that Iraq was still adhering closely to the Arab League and the Arab Collective Security Pact.

Israel complained to the Jordan-Israel MAC that an Israel farmer was shot at and his companion wounded in an ambush in Jezreel, a village on Mount Gilboa near the Jordanian border.

March, 1955

March 19

French authorities at Tunis banned al-Irada, official organ of the old Destour Party, for "inciting to racial hatred" by publishing a violently anti-Jewish article.

March 20

The conference of the Premiers of Egypt, Syria and Saudi Arabia, scheduled for this date, was indefinitely postponed.

Syria assured Turkey that its alliance with Egypt and Saudi Arabia was not directed against Turkish interests, in a memorandum sent to Ankara in respect to Syria's relations with the Arab States.

The Turkish Government refused to accept a Syrian memorandum on the relations of Arab countries following the signing of the Turko-Iraq Pact. Adnan Menderes, Turkish Prime Minister, in handing the memorandum back to the Syrian Ambassador, said that Syrian-Turkish relations had entered a serious phase. The information in the memorandum about Turkish-Syrian relations and the aim of the alternative defense pact proposed by Syria and Egypt could not be accepted as the truth, he added.

Egypt's Minister of National Guidance, Salah Salem told pressmen that Egypt might join Western defense plans if Israel would cede the Negev to Egypt, thus creating a land link between Egypt and its Arab neighbors.

The Egyptian RDD (Revolutionary Command Council) appointed Ahmad Khairat Said as Deputy Foreign Minister, a new post in the Government.

Despite a ban on trade union activities, members of the Union Generale des Syndicats Confederes du Maroc met in Casablanca and organized a new labor group to be known as the Union des Travailleurs Marocains. The meeting was the outcome of efforts of the International Confederation of Free Trade Unions to get a labor movement started in Morocco.

March, 1955

March 21

An Israel Foreign Ministry spokesman labeled as "war propaganda" the statement by Egyptian Minister of National Guidance Salah Salem that he would make a deal with the West in return for the Negev. The spokesman declared that no part of Israel territory was at the disposal of anyone to serve as a quid pro quo for political or military arrangements of any kind, nor for any other purpose.

The French Resident General to Morocco flew to Paris for further talks with the Minister for Moroccan and Tunisian Affairs, Pierre July.

Israel protested to the UN truce authorities about two new attacks in the Gaza area, alleging that a band of ten Egyptians had penetrated Israel territory near Nahal Oz, and that an Egyptian patrol had fired near Kissufim.

Lebanese President Camille Chamoun left for a two week visit to Italy and Turkey.

The French Cabinet approved a bill granting the Government wide powers to deal with terrorism in Algeria. The bill, still to be approved by Parliament, provided for a six month state of emergency.

March 23

Syria's Foreign Minister summoned all the foreign envoys stationed in Damascus and gave them details of the notes exchanged between the Syrian and Turkish Governments.

Speaking before the UN Security Council, Israel's Delegate to the UN, Ambassador Abba Eban, asked Egypt to renounce useless hostility and join Israel in a code for peace in the Middle East. Eban insisted that through cooperation, Egypt and Israel could become the keystone to Middle East peace.

March 24

The Lebanese Government reportedly approached the Turkish Government with a view to having the latter reconsider its attitude toward Syria.

March, 1955

March 24

The Sudanese Chamber of Deputies rejected a motion by the Umma Party suggesting that self determination be put into immediate effect by the evacuation of all foreign troops.

It was reported at UN headquarters that representatives of the US, Great Britain and France conferred with UN Secretary General Dag Hammarskjold and General E. L. M. Burns, Chief of Staff of the UNTSO, on the Gaza situation.

A new oil agreement was signed in Baghdad by Nadim al-Pachachi. Iraqi Economics Minister, and the representative of the Iraq Petroleum Company and associated companies. The agreement amended Iraq border prices for Iraq oil and readjusted the discount allowed to Iraq Petroleum and its associated companies.

An Israel Army statement said that armed Egyptians threw bombs at a wedding party at Patish, in the Negev, killing one woman and wounding 18 persons.

March 25

Israel complained to the UN Security Council regarding the incident at Patish on March 24, charging that the Egyptians' "premeditated assault" was one more instance of Egypt's policy of ceaseless harassment of Israel villages. It said 13 incursions and attacks from Egypt had occurred since March 3.

An agreement was signed with France by which France would extend LL45 million credit to Lebanon to buy French goods. The credit was to be returned within five years. France would supply Lebanon with capital goods and would import citrus fruits and tobacco; France would also encourage investment of French capital in Lebanon.

March 26

Over 1,500 students in Syria left their classrooms to demonstrate against the Turko-Iraq Pact.

March, 1955

March 26

The Turkish Government charged that Syrian planes had violated the air frontier.

The Prime Minister of Yemen informed Egypt's Minister of National Guidance Salah Salem that Yemen would joint the projected pact between Egypt, Syria and Saudi Arabia.

An International Bank mission arrived at Amman for talks regarding Jordan's economy.

Israel's Prime Minister, Moshe Sharett, invited the British and American Ambassadors to Israel for the purpose of bringing to their attention the situation along the border of the Egyptian held Gaza Strip. He referred to the proposal thrown out by the Egyptian Minister that Israel cede the Negev to the Arabs; he told the Ambassadors that their Governments had a degree of responsibility for the Egyptian statement as it concerned the regional defense plans that they were advocating.

March 27

The Arab League Council opened its 23rd ordinary session at Cairo. An agenda of 29 items was approved, including Yemen's request for discussion of its dispute with Britain.

Syrian Foreign Minister Khaled Azm assured the Turkish Government that no Syrian planes violated the Turkish air territory.

Syria delivered a note to Turkey alleging that two Turkish aircraft had violated the Syrian frontier.

The Egypt-Israel MAC (Mixed Armistice Commission) found Egypt responsible for a "brutal and murderous act of aggression" in the attack on the wedding party in the village of Patish.

March 28

Israel Prime Minister Moshe Sharett talked with the Ambassadors of Soviet Russia and France about the situation along the Gaza border.

March, 1955

March 28

The British, French and American delegates in the UN Security Council submitted a draft resolution condemning Israel for the February 28 attack on Egyptian forces in the Gaza area. In a second draft resolution, the three powers called on both parties to cooperate in carrying out the practical measures to reduce border tension proposed by the UNTSO Chief.

Israel Ambassador to the UN, Abba Eban submitted proposals for amending the first joint draft resolution by France, the UK and the US noting that infiltration from Egyptian controlled territory had been one of the main causes of the present tension.

Mumtaz Faik Fenik wrote in a page one editorial in the Ankara daily, Zafer, that the anti-Turkish Syrian Government was a tool of Communist Agents.

King Faisal of Iraq arrived at Amman for a four day visit with the royal family.

March 29

The Arab League's Political Committee approved the Secretariat's report on the harsh treatment of Arabs living in Israel. The report recommended that the question be raised at the UN.

The UN Security Council adopted the three power resolution censuring Israel for its February 28 attack on Egyptian forces in the Gaza area.

The Syrian Parliament passed a resolution stating that all parties and organizations, irrespective of political trend, unanimously supported the government's opinion that the country should take a united stand against the foreign pressure being exerted on Syria.

Sir Alexander Knox-Helm arrived at Khartoum to take up his duties as Governor General of Sudan.

March 30

Turkey announced that it was closing its customs border with Syria.

March, 1955

March 30

British Foreign Minister Sir Anthony Eden announced in the House of Commons that Britain had decided to join the Turko-Iraq Defense Pact. This was simultaneously announced by Iraqi Premier Nuri-Said in Baghdad. A White Paper was issued by Britain giving the text of the proposed agreement with Iraq. It provided for the maintenance and development of peace and friendship between the two countries, for cooperation for their security and defense in accordance with the Turko-Iraq Pact, and for the termination of the Anglo-Iraqi treaty of June 30, 1930, on the entry into force of the agreement.

The UN Security Council adopted a resolution calling on both Israel and Egypt to cooperate in reducing tension along their borders.

Jordan and Israel were blamed in turn by the Israel-Jordan MAC (Mixed Armistice Commission) for a shooting incident near the Jordanian village of Zeita, on the border north of Tulkarm.

A clash between Israel and Egyptian soldiers in the Gaza Strip was reported in Jerusalem.

March 31

The Egypt-Israel MAC (Mixed Armistice Commission) took note of the aggravation caused by repeated acts of "aggression" by Egypt against Israel.

The Arab League Council concluded its session at Cairo.

A trade agreement was signed between Egypt and Poland. It provided that the two countries would grant each other most favored nation status in respect of customs duties and other import taxes.

April, 1955

April 1

The National Assembly of France approved a bill creating a new legal concept intermediate between the rule of law and a state of siege, called a "state of urgency," by a vote of 379-219. The bill was made applicable to Algeria forthwith for a period of six months. It gave the Governor General increased powers for maintaining order.

French authorities in Tunis arrested 22 members of a secret committee for the liberation of Tunisia.

President Camille Chamoun of Lebanon arrived in Ankara. This was interpreted in some Arab quarters as a move which would ultimately lead to Lebanese accession to the Turko-Iraq Pact.

Eleven Syrian Deputies, headed by Speaker Nazem al-Kudsi, left for Yugoslavia for a four week visit at the invitation of the Yugoslav Government.

April 2

Turkey and Lebanon signed a commercial agreement.

The son of King Ahmad of Yemen, Saif-al-Islam Muhammad al-Badr, fled to Hajja.

Saif al-Islam Abdallah, brother of Imam Ahmad of Yemen, supported by part of the Army, asked the Imam to abdicate in his favor. Ahmad signed the abdication papers and handed them over to a delegation of religious leaders.

The last of the British troops in the Suez Canal Zone left the area and the remaining British installations were taken over by the Egyptians.

April 3

Abdallah, brother of the Imam of Yemen, ordered the withdrawal of Ahmad's bodyguard from Elurdhi Fortress in Taizz where the ex-King was staying. He ordered the Prime Minister, Amir Saif-al-Islam al-Hassan, Ahmad's older brother, who was in Cairo, not to return to Yemen.

April 3

Egyptian Premier Gamal Abdel Nasser stated in Cairo that the US and England obtained the tenuous allegiance of Iraq at the price of re-awakening Arab fears of foreign domination and arresting what had been a trend toward closer political, economic and military links between the Arab States and the North Atlantic Powers.

Israel complained to the MAC that two soldiers were killed and 19 wounded in a clash with Egyptian troops at Nahal Oz when an Israel patrol car was blown up by a land mine and an Egyptian patrol opened fire. Egypt complained that Israelis opened fire on one of its frontier posts.

It was reported in London that the US Government notified Great Britain that it preferred to wait for Middle Eastern affairs to settle down before it joined the new Turko-Iraqi-British Defense Pact (Baghdad Pact).

Negotiations in Cairo on the Egyptian sponsored new Arab League Collective Security Pact were suspended when the Syrian delegation, headed by Foreign Minister Khaled Azm, left for consultations in Damascus.

April 4

On April 1 the Turkish and Iraqi Governments issued identical invitations to Pakistan to join the Baghdad Pact.

Saif-al-Islam Muhammad al-Badr, Yemen's Crown Prince, at the head of some 8,000 armed men, attacked Taizz. He called Secretary General Hassouna of the Arab League from Hajja, which was held by the Loyalists, to tell him that it should be obvious to Hassouna that the sedition was harmful to the Yemen, the Arabs and Islam.

Israel asked the UN Security Council for an urgent meeting to consider new charges against Egypt; it accused Egypt of "repeated attacks" from across the border on Israel civilians and soldiers. It enumerated three specific charges.

Israel Prime Minister Moshe Sharett informed the American Ambassador, Edward B. Lawson, that Israel's policy was to continue the

April 4

motorized patrols along the Gaza Strip. He drew attention to the incident of the previous day as the best example of the Egyptian practice of blowing up Israel patrol cars and shooting Israel soldiers after their cars were wrecked.

After being seriously pressed by the opposition in connection with Britain's accession to the Baghdad Pact, UK Foreign Secretary Sir Anthony Eden said in the House of Commons that Britain would, if requested, guarantee a settlement that might be worked out between Israel and the Arab States. Such a settlement would have to include agreement on the refugee problem, Arab-Israel frontiers and utilization of the Jordan River waters, he added.

The new defense treaty with Great Britain providing for termination of the 1930 Anglo-Iraqi treaty and British adherence to the new Turko-Iraq Defense Pact was signed in Baghdad.

Representatives of Britain, Egypt and the UN signed an agreement for technical assistance to the Sudan.

April 5

The UK concluded an agreement with Iraq under which British bases in Iraq would be taken over by Iraq under the Baghdad Pact.

The eldest son of Imam Saif-al-Islam Ahmad reportedly attacked the rebel forces in Yemen which were besieging a fortress at Taizz where the former Imam had taken refuge, and had restored his father to the throne. Prince Abdallah was reportedly fleeing toward Saudi Arabia, and other disloyal soldiers were seeking refuge in the British Aden Protectorate.

Egypt addressed a letter to the Security Council giving its version of the Nahal Oz incident of April 3. It stated that about 80 Israel soldiers opened fire with 120 millimeter mortars, killing two Egyptian soldiers and wounding four.

Israel Prime Minister Moshe Sharett said during a visit to Nahal Oz in the Negev that it should be clear to all concerned, and in particular to Israel's adversaries in the area, that it was determined to

April 5

do everything within its rights of self defense "to assure quiet, security, work and peaceful development in this vital area of our State."

April 6

A Treaty of Friendship was signed between Egypt and India.

After months of preliminary discussions, negotiations were begun between Egypt and the Sudan for revision of the 1929 Nile waters agreement.

An agreement of economic cooperation and trade was signed between Argentina and Lebanon in Buenos Aires. The agreement was in general terms and embodied various arrangements for strengthening the economic, commercial and cultural relations between the two countries.

The UN Security Council convened to hear Israel's charges against Egypt. The Israel representative, Ambassador Abba Eban, charged that Egypt had embarked on a relentless siege of border violence that threatened the six year old Palestine armistice. He further complained that in the period March 24 to April 3 sixteen border incidents had occurred and Egypt's campaign of hostilities seemed to have increased since the Security Council first met in March to deal with the situation. During March the Mixed Armistice Commission had adopted six resolutions condemning four "serious" violations of the agreement. A purposeful military design was emerging in the Egyptian assaults. Omar Loutfi, the Egyptian representative, said that Israel's new complaint was mere propaganda.

The Egyptian-Israel Mixed Armistice Commission condemned Egypt for shooting across the border on March 30.

At the suggestion of the British UN Delegate, Sir Pierson Dixon, further debate was postponed until the findings of the Mixed Armistice Commission were received.

Al-Badr cabled the Egyptian Premier, Gamal Abdel Nasser, that he received news from his father at Taizz that the revolt in Yemen had been crushed.

April 6

A communique issued in Ankara at the conclusion of the conference between the Lebanese President and Turkish leaders said that both governments agreed that peace and stability in the Middle East were vital factors for world peace. This stability, it stated, required friendship among Lebanon, the Arab States and Turkey, as well as practical cooperation among the countries responsible for the welfare of the region. The communique further contended that there existed no clash of interests among Lebanon, the Arab countries and Turkey to prevent cooperation among them.

The Egyptian semi-official organ al-Gumhuriyah noted that the text of the Turkish-Lebanese communique was strikingly similar to the joint communique issued after Iraqi Premier Nuri-Said's visit to Ankara the previous year, which resulted a few months later in the conclusion of the Baghdad Pact.

The Anglo-Iraqi agreement of April 4 came into effect.

The French Ministry of Interior declared a state of emergency in four parts of Algeria, one along the Tunisian-Algerian border and three in the interior of the country.

April 7

The Egyptian-Israel MAC (Mixed Armistice Commission) blamed Israel for a shooting affray on March 31.

The Yemeni legation at Cairo announced that Prince Abdallah had been arrested by Yemeni authorities while attempting to escape into Saudi Arabia.

Talks with Sudanese delegates for revision of the 1929 Nile waters agreement with Egypt were suspended indefinitely when the two sides were unable to agree on a basis for discussion.

Egypt charged that a second attempt to reach agreement with the Sudanese on the Nile waters broke down because Sudanese delegates insisted on injecting political implications into the discussions; the talks were suspended.

April, 1955

April 8

Khadr Hamad, Sudanese Minister of Irrigation, said that the Government would consider referring its dispute with Egypt on the Nile waters to international arbitration.

April 9

The executive committee of the Sudanese NUP (National Unionist Party) adopted a resolution advocating full independence for the country.

The Israel-Egyptian MAC (Mixed Armistice Commission) condemned both Egypt and Israel for the incident of April 3.

April 10

Egypt's Minister of Social Affairs returned to Cairo from Yemen with the report that six leaders of the abortive coup against Imam Saif-al-Islam Ahmad had been condemned and beheaded. Two of the Imam's brothers, Prince Abdallah and Amir Saif-al-Islam Abbas, were expected to be tried. A third brother, Prime Minister Amir Saif-al-Islam Hassan, who was in Cairo, was ordered to remain abroad. The Imam's oldest son, Amir Saif-al-Islam Muhammad al-Badr, was named Crown Prince.

President Camille Chamoun and the Prime Minister of Lebanon left Turkey after a nine day visit in which they toured the Izmir and Istanbul areas as well as conducting discussions in Ankara. Chamoun said that in order to find the road to progress, the East should turn to Turkey, not the West.

April 11

In a letter to the UN Security Council, Israel's representative, Abba Eban, complained of five new frontier attacks by Egypt and asked that the Council resume debate with the utmost urgency.

The French and Tunisian Premiers, Edgar Faure and Tahar Ben-Ammar, resumed negotiations in Paris on national autonomy for Tunisia.

April, 1955

April 16

The Foreign Ministry of the USSR charged in Moscow that the Western Powers were trying to turn the Middle East into a battleground and to reduce the people of the region to colonial enslavement. It warned that the Soviet Union could not remain indifferent to the Western sponsored military alliances in the region, and threatened to appeal to the UN if such pacts continued to be made.

Egypt addressed a letter to General E. L. M. Burns, Chief of Staff of the UNTSO, agreeing to the setting up of joint patrols along the demarcation line as proposed by Burns. Egypt was also prepared to consider ways and means of erecting a barbed wire fence along certain portions of the line.

April 17

Israel complained the MAC (Mixed Armistice Commission) that marauders had blown up a house in the Jerusalem corridor five miles inside the Israel border. Five persons were injured.

On the basis of a survey completed a year before, the International Bank recommended to the Syrian Government a five year development program to cost $350 million. It endorsed two irrigation projects already begun and four smaller projects as well as improvement of agricultural products and services, industrial development, and expansion of transport facilities and public utilities.

Ghaleb Shishakli, former member of Syrian Parliament and cousin of ousted President Adib Shishakli, was killed during a political clash.

The Soviet Union denounced the Baghdad Pact as a method to achieve colonial enslavement of countries of the Middle East.

April 18

Israel and Jordan agreed on an arrangement to prevent infiltration in the area around Jerusalem. Guards would not be allowed to fire without authorization by a commissioned officer unless in danger of attack by superior numbers.

April, 1955

April 13

The USSR Foreign Ministry issued a statement protesting against the creation of military groups in the Middle East, and threatening to raise the question before the United Nations. The statement referred to the Turkey-Pakistan and the Turko-Iraq Pacts and accused the Western Powers of "pressure and threats" towards countries in the area.

April 14

The Secretary General of the UN circulated a report from General E. L. M. Burns, Chief of Staff of the UNTSO, which stated that from March 1 to April 13 Israel had submitted 35 complaints to the MAC (Mixed Armistice Commission) and Egypt, 49. Egypt had been condemned in seven cases and Israel in four. General Burns believed that the majority of these incidents were the result of tension owing to the Gaza incident of February 28.

In Yemen two of the Imam's brothers, Abdallah and Abbas, were hanged at Taizz.

April 15

The Baghdad Pact took effect with a ceremonial signing in Ankara.

Major General E. L. M. Burns, Chief of Staff of the UN Truce Supervision Organization, reported to the Security Council that both Israel and Egypt were ready to work out an agreement whereby local commanders would cooperate to check infiltration. Both sides also pledged to keep only disciplined regular troops in the froniter vicinity.

April 16

An official statement over Radio Mecca announced the deportation from Saudi Arabia of the well known author and orientalist, H. St. John Philby. It said that Philby had been deported because he had "of late pursued a course of action both inappropriate and tactless."

April, 1955

April 18

Thami Glaoui, Pasha of Marrakech, rejected the suggestion that a third man be found to occupy the throne of Morocco. He stated that the dynastic issue was settled once and for all with the accession of the present Sultan, Sidi Muhammad Ben-Moulay Ben-Arafa.

Delegates of eight Arab countries at Bandung, Indonesia, reached agreement on Middle Eastern problems, but on other issues were seriously divided between the neutralist and pro-Western camps. In deference to the desire of the sponsoring powers to avoid controversy, they agreed not to use pressure on the other twenty-one nations to endorse the Arab position on Palestine or to condemn Israel.

April 19

The UN Security Council resumed consideration of the Israel complaint against Egypt but concluded that there was no need for new action by the Council at the time, as the matter was already covered by the resolutions of March 29 and 30.

The UN Security Council, through its President, appealed to Egypt and Israel to continue forward with a program to avoid future war clashes. It took no action against Egypt as requested by Israel.

King Hussein of Jordan married Princess Dina Abd-al-Hamid al-Awn, a distant cousin, at Amman. Queen Dina had been a lecturer in English literature at Cairo University.

In a memorandum submitted to the Afro-Asian Conference in Bandung, Indonesia, the Jordan delegation declared that efforts to establish peace and stability in the Middle East were "a sheer waste of time and money" so long as the Israel border and refugee problems remained unsettled.

April 20

The Onassis tanker dispute between Aramco and the Saudi Arabian Government was reportedly to be submitted to international arbitration in Geneva on June 15.

April 20

Israel complained to the MAC (Mixed Armistice Commission) that infiltrators from the Egyptian controlled Gaza Strip penetrated into the Negev but were dispersed by a patrol which opened fire on them.

Chou En-lai, Premier and Foreign Minister of Communist China, announced that he was prepared to support a resolution expressing Arab demands for territorial revisions in Palestine and recognition of Arab refugees. This was seen as a bid by Communist China for the good will of the Arab States.

April 21

The Political Committee of the Afro-Asian Conference at Bandung, Indonesia, passed a resolution supporting the Arab position on Palestine.

The Israel-Jordanian MAC (Mixed Armistice Commission) blamed Jordan for dynamiting an Israel house on April 17.

April 22

An agreement was reached between the Premiers of France and Tunisia on principles for local self government for Tunisia.

Prime Minister Tahar Ben-Ammar returned to Tunisia.

Habib Bourguiba, the exiled Neo-Destour leader of Tunisia, called in to the French-Tunisian negotiations by French Premier Edgar Faure, expressed whole hearted approval of the agreements. He stated that they set the seal on Franco-Tunisian friendship and should open a period of long hoped for reconciliation.

French Premier Faure announced that all restrictions were removed from the movements of Habib Bourguiba and that he was free to return to Tunisia if he wished.

A Syrian Army sergeant, member of the National Socialist Party, assassinated Colonel Adnan Malki, who supported the proposed

April 22

Egyptian-Syrian-Saudi Arabian alignment and opposed the Iraq Greater Syria Plan. Malki was slated to become Syrian Army Chief of Staff.

French Governor General of Algeria Jacques Soustelle decreed censorship of the press in accordance with the state of emergency proclaimed April 6.

In reply to General Burns' January suggestion that the demilitarized areas on the Israel-Syrian frontier be partitioned, Syria replied that it might be considered under certain circumstances. Syria suggested that a map be prepared by UN truce officials, that preliminary negotiations be conducted by the Syrian-Israel MAC (Mixed Armistice Commission), and that the section of the armistice agreement concerning the demilitarized pockets be revised.

Israel reportedly accepted three of the four proposals made by General E. L. M. Burns, Chief of Staff of the UN Truce Supervision Organization, for reducing incidents along the Gaza Strip border. The three were: (1) consultation by area commanders of both sides, (2) the erection of physical barriers along the border, and (3) the stationing of regular forces only as guards in the frontier area. Israel had rejected the proposal to set up joint Israel-Egyptian patrols.

Israel sent a message to the Afro-Asian Conference at Bandung, Indonesia, deploring the resolution adopted by the Political Committee. Prime Minister Moshe Sharett of Israel expressed astonishment and profound regret that the Afro-Asian Conference from which, despite its principles of universal representation and full international equality, Israel was expressly excluded, had deemed it fair and expedient, in Israel's absence, to discuss and resolve upon issues which vitally affected Israel's future and its relations with neighboring states.

April 23

About 800 members of the Syrian National Socialist Party were arrested in the wake of Malki's assassination.

April 23

Saudi Arabia issued Royal Decrees (1) abolishing elementary and secondary education in foreign schools for all Saudi Arabian students and imposing restrictions on those wishing to enroll in foreign universities, and (2) prohibiting the movement of currency from the Kingdom except for trade and import purposes and providing for the return to Saudi Arabia of funds invested abroad for use in local development projects.

The signing of the Protocol of Agreement as a prelude to home rule in Tunisia precipitated mixed reactions. The Tunisian nationalists were jubilant, and the European residents attacked the accord as endangering their position.

A group of French settlers met in Tunis and issued a statement declaring that they would fight against the application of the new Franco-Tunisian agreement which they proclaimed to be invalid because it sacrificed the interests of Tunisia and France and could end only in the rapid and total ruin of the Franco-Tunisian community.

V. M. Molotov, USSR Minister of Foreign Affairs, received the Syrian Minister to the USSR, Farid Hani, who conveyed appreciation for the USSR statement of April 16, 1955, on the Mideast.

April 25

A communique issued by the Afro-Asian Conference in Bandung stated that in view of the existing tension in the Middle East caused by the situation in Palestine, and of the danger of that tension to world peace, the Conference declared its support of the "rights of the Arab people of Palestine" and called for implementation of the UN resolutions on Palestine and of the peaceful settlement of the Palestine question. A further statement was issued, stating that in view of the unsettled situation in North Africa and of the persisting denial to the peoples of North Africa of their right to self determination and independence it urged the French Government to bring about a peaceful settlement of the issue without delay.

French authorities announced the arrest of 179 Moroccans charged with plotting a revolution against French rule.

April 25

Imam Ahmad of Yemen decided to open the private safe which had belonged to his father, reputed to contain 100 million pounds sterling, and to use it in development projects for the benefit of the people.

April 26

France reported that a military command would be created in Algeria from May 1 covering all the emergency areas in the Department of Constantine.

April 27

A trade agreement between Egypt and the Soviet Union was signed in Cairo. Russia would supply kerosene to the value of LE2 million and would buy 14,000 bales of cotton valued at LE300,000. An agreement was also signed with Rumania under the terms of which the latter would purchase about LE1 million worth of cotton yarn.

Mustafa Ben-Halim of Libya, who earlier submitted his Cabinet's resignation and had been asked by King Idris to form a new Government, announced his new Ministry in which he himself was Foreign Minister as well as Premier.

David Ben-Gurion, Defense Minister of Israel, spoke at Ramat Gan, and referred to British Foreign Secretary Sir Anthony Eden's recent statement in the House of Commons; a revision of frontiers was put as a condition for an Arab-Israel settlement.

April 28

US Ambassador Lester Mallory gave visas to 22 Arab refugees at Amman for entry into the United States. They were the first of 2,000 such refugees being allowed to immigrate.

April, 1955

April 29

The Mixed Armistice Commission censured Israel for a flagrant violation of the Armistice Agreement in the Gaza Strip on April 18, 1955.

Fatin Rustu Zorlu of Turkey, on his return from the Bandung Conference, declared that during the meetings a group consisting of Turkey, Iraq, Pakistan, Lebanon, Iran and Libya had worked very closely. He declared the conference was "a success from the point of view of those Asian-African countries who represented the collective security system."

April 30

The Finance Minister of Iraq and the British Ambassador signed an agreement in Baghdad settling outstanding debts between the two countries resulting from the use of each other's services and facilities during the war.

May, 1955

May 2

On his return from the Bandung Conference, Premier Gamal Abdel Nasser told a welcoming crowd that he had declared in the name of the Egyptian people at the Bandung Conference that their internal policy was to establish social justice and to eliminate feudalism and imperialism and its supporters, and that their foreign policy was a fully independent policy.

Major Salah Salem returned from Damascus after receiving Syria's signature to an Egyptian plan for a new alliance which had the backing of Saudi Arabia. The text of the agreement was not to be published until other Arab States had a chance to study it.

The British turned over the air bases at Habbaniyah and Sheiba to the Iraqi Army.

Representatives of Israel and Egypt, under the chairmanship of Major General E. L. M. Burns, Chief of Staff of the UN Truce Supervision Organization, met to consider United Nations proposals for reducing tension in the Gaza area. General Burns proposed that contact between the commanders on each side be established. The meeting concluded with no result except that the representatives would meet again.

May 3

General Boyer de Latour, French Resident General in Tunisia, ordered the arrest and deportation of General Rime-Bruneau, president of the right wing Prescence Francaise movement, who had denounced and had threatened members of the Movement for Free Franco-Tunisian Cooperation.

The Tunisian Resident General flew to Paris for consultations with French Premier Faure on measures to counter the opposition to the announced agreement on autonomy. Before leaving, he appealed for order by radio and cited attacks on three Frenchmen who favored home rule.

The State Department announced that 45 Palestine Arab refugees were granted visas for permanent residence in the US. These were the first of 2,000 Arab refugees whose admission under the Refugee Relief Act of 1953 had been authorized.

May, 1955

May 5

An official statement issued in Baghdad said that Radio Free Iraq, which had been attacking Iraqi leaders, was operating in Egypt. This was considered an act of open hostility and the Government intended to protest to Egypt.

May 6

An agreement was signed with Pakistan by which Lebanon would supply Pakistan with cotton yarn valued at $600,000.

May 7

The Syrian Government dissolved the National Socialist Party and confiscated its assets when an investigation of the assassination of Colonel Adnan Malki, deputy Chief of Staff, revealed the party was behind the crime.

May 8

The cabinet of Nuri-Said was reshuffled by Royal Decree in Iraq. Foreign Minister Musa Shahbandar became Ambassador to Washington; Minister of State Burhan-ad-Din Bashayan became Foreign Minister.

May 10

Representatives of Jordan and Israel signed an agreement to treat any captured soldiers or police as prisoners of war in accordance with Geneva Convention provisions.

The Iraq Petroleum Company announced that construction of a 24 inch pipeline ending at Tripoli on the Lebanese coast would begin soon.

May 15

The Egyptian Minister of State for Sudanese Affairs issued a statement saying that the Sudan was invited to the Bandung Conference as a result of Egyptian insistence, with Indian support.

May, 1955

May 16

Tunisian delegates returned to Paris to complete the convention establishing Tunisian internal autonomy.

The Egypt-Israel Mixed Armistice Commission censured both Israel and Egypt for a shooting exchange on April 19, Egypt for firing at an Israel position and command car from across the Gaza border, and Israel for returning the fire.

May 18

The French Ministers of Defense and the Interior announced in a joint statement the decision to extend the emergency regulations in Algeria to the whole of the department of Constantine and to the regions of Biskra and al-Oued, in the Southern Territories.

Sudanese Premier Ismail al-Azhari said in Cairo that the Sudanese people would decide the future of their country and that public opinion favored complete independence. The National Union Party, of which he was the leader, favored the establishment of an independent sovereign Sudanese republic which would cooperate with Egypt on a basis of complete equality.

May 19

Substantial reinforcements of French troops and police were reportedly to be sent immediately to Algeria and Algerian troops on operational service in Algeria were to be relieved by French units from Germany. The measures would bring the total of armed forces in Algeria up to about 100,000.

Premier Nasser told Egyptians that a National Parliament would be established in January 1956 as originally planned by the military junta. It would exercise a rule based on the working classes; there would be no political parties, feudalism, capitalism or any foreign power. Nasser did not mention elections and he did not indicate how the parliament was to be established.

The Egyptian Revolutionary Command Council issued a decree ruling that members of boards of directors of companies over 60 years of age be dismissed. The declared purpose of the decree was to

May, 1955

May 19

destroy the present monopoly of the financial and industrial fields and afford opportunity for young manhood to direct and supervise the investment field.

May 20

Major Salem, Egyptian Minister of National Guidance, announced in Cairo that Egypt and the Sudan had reached agreement on the distribution of the Nile waters on a satisfactory and fair basis.

Jacques Soustelle, French Governor General in Algeria, made a statement to the press in which he declared that France would never renounce its peaceful mission among the population which was loyal, but would show "pitiless severity" to rebels and to all who gave them aid or comfort in any form.

May 23

King Idris of Libya arrived at Alexandria for a month's visit in Egypt.

May 25

President Camille Chamoun of Lebanon inaugurated the Near and Middle East Economic Conference at Beirut. India, Iran, Turkey, Greece, Pakistan, Afghanistan, Ethiopia and seven Arab League member states were represented. Saudi Arabia, which had received an invitation, was not represented.

May 26

French Premier Edgar Faure announced that he was sending to Algeria an Army division then under the command of the North Atlantic Treaty Organization. He said that France's obligation to NATO would not be permitted to interfere with the re-establishment of order in Algeria by military force.

May, 1955

May 29

France withdrew one of its NATO divisions from Germany for use in Algeria.

Premier U Nu of Burma arrived in Israel for a seven day state visit. He cancelled a three day call in Cairo when Egyptian authorities asked him to abandon his Israel visit if he wanted to visit Egypt.

May 30

Habib Bourguiba left Paris on his return journey to Tunisia after two years exile in France. He was expected to arrive in Tunis on June 1.

A new government was formed in Jordan by Premier Said Mufti, who also took the position of Minister of Foreign Affairs.

May, 1955

May 27

A British Foreign Office spokesman reported that 12 Arabs were believed killed in Oman in a clash between tribesmen and forces of the Sultan of Muscat. He denied that the clash had been between British troops and Saudi Arabian settlers in an area bordering the Buraimi Oasis.

May 28

The Cabinet of Tawfiq Abu-al-Huda of Jordan resigned.

The Near and Middle East Economic Conference adopted a proposal to set up a regional organization in Beirut to organize economic relations among the fifteen member states.

Israel and Egyptian forces exchanged heavy mortar fire for 24 minutes in the Egyptian held Gaza Strip. Both sides accused the other of firing first.

Iraqi King Faisal flew to Amman for a four day visit with the Jordanian royal family.

The Egyptian Minister of Commerce announced that an oil well, producing 3,000 barrels a day, had been brought in by the National Petroleum Company at Balaeem No. 2 in Wadi Firhan, in the Sinai Peninsula.

May 29

Sheikh Yusuf Yasin, Deputy Foreign Minister of Saudi Arabia, issued a statement in Mecca denying Lebanese and Iraqi press reports that there were disturbances in Saudi Arabia and that three persons were condemned to death for plotting against King Saud.

The Egyptian Government announced that it would send an economic mission to Communist China early in June.

King Hussein of Jordan accepted the resignation of Prime Minister Tawfiq Abu-al-Huda and asked former Prime Minister Said Mufti to form a cabinet.

June, 1955

June 1

Additional members of the Syrian National Socialist Party were reportedly arrested in connection with the assassination of Colonel Adnan Malki on April 22.

Nationalist leader Habib Bourguiba returned triumphantly to Tunisia from exile. He warned France that force could not solve the crisis in North Africa.

Egypt and France initialed a Trade and Payments Agreement whereby French industry would contribute to some of Egypt's development projects and France would buy much of its cotton requirements from Egypt.

At Mostorod, ten miles east of Cairo, Premier Nasser laid the cornerstone of a $10 million government oil refinery which would have a 2.3 million ton annual capacity.

It was announced in Khartoum that the US had contributed $120,000 of technical aid to the Sudan.

June 2

General E. L. M. Burns, Chief of Staff of the UNTSO, ended two days of talks with Prime Minister Nasser regarding the continuing clashes in the Gaza area. Prime Minister Nasser rejected General Burns' bid for top level talks with Israel.

Secretary General Dag Hammarskjold said that in spite of intensive UN efforts to ease the Egypt-Israel border tension, the prospects were not bright. He declared that the results so far did not entitle him to say that he felt very happy about the situation. He saw little chance that the two countries could then be persuaded to sit down together.

June 3

As terrorist attacks continued, the French Government announced that 9,000 veterans were being recalled for duty with the army in Algeria.

June, 1955

June 3

An agreement was signed between France and Tunisia granting internal autonomy to Tunisia, while at the same time protecting French interests and preserving the close links with France. Under this agreement the Resident General would be replaced by a High Commissioner, acting as Foreign Minister, with control over all defense and police matters — together with Bizerta and the Southern Frontier Zone.

A ten day meeting of the Near and Middle East Economic Conference ended in Beirut. The Conference recommended to the 15 member states that a permanent Regional Economic Organization be established in Beirut. It was also recommended that the next session of the conference be held in November 1956.

The US agreed to lease 13.2 pounds of enriched uranium to Israel for development of peaceful uses of atomic energy.

June 4

King Hussein of Jordan and his bride, Queen Dina, left for state visits in Spain and Britain.

June 5

Prime Minister Nehru of India, en route to Moscow, talked for an hour at the Cairo airport with Prime Minister Abdel Nasser and other Egyptian leaders.

Prime Minister U Nu of Burma, completing a nine day visit to Israel, said that he would be happy to mediate the Arab-Israel differences if invited by both sides.

King Idris of Libya took a second wife in ceremonies in Cairo.

The UN Secretary General sent a new appeal to Israel and Egypt to refrain from committing any acts that would increase tension in the Middle East.

Premier Nasser proposed the creation of a demilitarized zone around the Gaza Strip.

June, 1955

June 6

A military mission of senior Iraqi officers left for consultations in Turkey.

The Egyptian Government rejected the UN proposal for a conference of Egyptian and Israel officials to ease the tension along the Gaza Strip.

The Israel Government received a letter from UN Secretary General Dag Hammarskjold containing the Egyptian proposal for a demilitarized zone, In reply to this, Israel Prime Minister Moshe Sharett declared that restoration of quiet along the border depended on the Egyptian troops desisting from firing "in a systematic and entirely unprovoked manner" against Israel patrols moving within their own area, and on the cessation of "mine laying outrages" from Egyptian controlled territory.

June 7

The Egyptian-Israel Mixed Armistice Commission, meeting in Jerusalem, adopted an Egyptian resolution censuring Israel for the death of two Egyptian soldiers on May 11.

The British Foreign Office accused Egypt of interfering with the freedom of the Sudanese people to choose their own future status.

King Saud of Saudi Arabia offered Egypt full military and financial support in the event of an Israel attack on the Egyptian held Gaza Strip.

The Israel Foreign Ministry issued a statement attacking Egypt for its "bombastic declarations" and "sabre rattling" and reminded it of what happened when the Egyptian Army marched against Israel in 1948.

Henry Cabot Lodge, the US delegate to the UN, warned both Egypt and Israel that unless their attacks in the Gaza vicinity ended, the UN Security Council would have to reconsider the situation there.

June, 1955

June 8

French Governor General in Algeria Jacques Soustelle reportedly proposed the following major changes in Algerian policy to the Faure Government of France: further troop reinforcements, the beginning of a public works program, lower prices on foodstuffs, increased decentralization of the government.

Egyptian and British representatives met in Cairo to discuss the formation of an international commission to oversee the process of self determination in the Sudan, as required under the terms of the Anglo-Egyptian Agreement of 1953.

June 9

A Parliamentary inspection committee arrived back in Paris from Algeria and issued a report which called for "profound economic and social reforms" which would be intended to put an end to the "shocking inequality between man and man, the destitution and the unemployment created by the massive and continuous increase in the population and the achievement of a real economic equilibrium.

Egypt was reported as willing to send a high level army officer for talks with a similar representative from Israel provided that a representative of the UN be included in the talks.

It was announced in Damascus that agreement had been reached on six major points in the proposed tripartite pact between Egypt, Syria and Saudi Arabia. The agreement would provide for a common foreign policy, a joint economic planning council, an Arab bank and the establishment of a combined army with headquarters in Damascus.

Premier Khaled Azm of Syria told Parliament that the US had asked Syria to join the Baghdad Pact. He declared that Syria opposed the Pact because it divided the Arab States and that Syria would continue to back an Arab defense pact.

Syria assured the Lebanese Government that it would take effective measures to stop the press campaign against President Camille Chamoun of Lebanon.

June, 1955

June 11

The French Minister of Defense announced that a division of France's NATO committed troops was being sent to Algeria.

June 12

East Germany concluded a payments agreement with the Sudan and a clearing account in Egyptian pounds was opened with an Egyptian bank in Khartoum in the name of the Deutsche Notebank of Berlin.

A rather formidable list of new customs regulations went into effect in Iraq.

Israel insisted that the proposed talks with Egypt be undertaken by high diplomatic officials, while Egypt said that they should be limited to military matters and carried on by the local military commanders.

June 13

The Egyptian-Israel MAC (Mixed Armistice Commission) found Egypt guilty of a flagrant violation of the Armistice Agreement, firing mortar shells at an Israel truck in the al-Auja area, about 60 miles southeast of Gaza, on May 18. It also found that Egyptian troops opened fire on the UN team investigating the incident on the spot.

Radio Free Iraq announced in Cairo that it would cease transmitting.

The Casablanca branch of the French Socialist Party issued a statement pointing out that, though Moroccan terrorists were sometimes arrested and condemned, not one of the counter terrorists' murderers had ever been disturbed, though the police certainly had the means of identifying them.

June 15

Celal Bayar, President of Turkey, left for a state visit to Lebanon.

The French Cabinet gave its qualified approval to Governor General Jacques Soustelle's reform plans. It clearly rejected the idea of

June, 1955

June 15

Algerian autonomy. Instead, it stated that Algeria would be integrated more fully into the French nation, although there would be increased Arab participation in a decentralized Algerian Government.

The UN Truce Supervision Organization issued a communique in Jerusalem on the seizure of an Egyptian military jeep by Israel in the demilitarized zone of al-Auja. General Burns asked Israel to return the jeep.

The Egyptian-Israel Mixed Armistice Commission censured Israel for a raid on the Egyptian post at Deir-al-Balah on May 18 as a flagrant violation of the armistice.

Two British officers in a Government convoy were killed in Aden by Rabizi tribesmen in the north of the Protectorate.

June 16

Sir Ralph Richardson, British Ambassador in Cairo since 1950, retired. He was to be succeeded by Sir Humphrey Trevelyan.

Turkish Prime Minister Adnan Menderes, who was expected to go to Lebanon for an official visit, sent his apologies. He was unable to go because of the press of state business.

June 17

Countering Egypt's proposal for a demilitarized zone, Israel suggested that a mined security zone be established along the Gaza Strip with joint patrols to watch the 100 meter wide area.

June 18

Imam Ahmad of Yemen dismissed Amir Saif al-Islam al-Hassan as Prime Minister and assumed the full powers of that position himself.

The first wireless telephone service between Saudi Arabia and Egypt and between Saudi Arabia and Syria was opened.

June, 1955

June 18

The Egyptian Government rejected an Israel proposal for a meeting of ambassadors or chiefs of staff to discuss measures to reduce tension in the Gaza area.

A new opposition bloc in the Syrian Chamber of Deputies was created. Known as the Constitutional Front, it was composed of the Islamic and tribal groups in the Chamber.

Eight persons were killed in Algeria in incidents involving guerrillas.

June 19

The Egyptian-Israel Mixed Armistice Commission censured Israel for a violation of the armistice in a border incident on May 20 in which an Arab farmer was wounded.

June 20

Gilbert Grandval, chief of the French diplomatic mission to the Saar, was appointed Resident General of French Morocco, succeeding Francis Lacoste.

A second meeting was held in Cairo to discuss the international commission on Sudanese self determination.

The third phase of the British evacuation of the Suez began. It was expected that by October 75 percent of the British troops would have been withdrawn.

The Jordan-Israel Mixed Armistice Commission censured Jordan for a clash near Qalqilia on June 17 in which a Jordanian corporal was killed.

June 21

Premier Edgar Faure of France told the French National Assembly that the Government resolved to carry out a new policy in Morocco. This would involve a gradual transfer of authority from French to Moroccan hands, and the concomitant development of modern Moroccan political institutions.

June, 1955

June 21

The Egyptian-Israel Mixed Armistice Commission censured Israel for attacking an Egyptian post at Deir-al-Balah on May 21.

Tribal forces in the Mukalla area attacked and cut off 500 soldiers of the Aden Government after the Government ordered the substitution of its trucks for camel transport between Mukalla and Wadi Hadramaut.

King Saud of Saudi Arabia decided to contribute LS2 million toward financing a technical study needed before repair work on the Hejaz Railway could begin.

June 22

Egypt accepted General Burns' invitation to participate in talks on reducing tension in the Gaza area, but rejected his suggestion that the meeting be held in the no man's land in Jerusalem. For consideration at the meeting were the proposals made by General Burns, counterproposals by Israel and proposals by Egypt.

The Egyptian-Israel Mixed Armistice Commission condemned Egypt for an attack on May 23 on Israel settlers near the Gaza area.

The Jordan-Israel Mixed Armistice Commission censured Jordan for a grenade attack on an Israel border settlement.

An exchange of shots continued for nearly two hours between Israel and Jordanian troops. It marked the fifth consecutive day of clashes on the front after several months of relative quiet.

French authorities seized three Moroccan nationalist outlaw groups and held eight policemen on charges of illegal counter terrorist activities.

President Bayar of Turkey left for Ankara after a six day visit and the signing of a trade agreement with Lebanon.

Israel and Jordanian troops fought for nearly two hours on the banks of the Jordan River near Naharayim, south of the Sea of Galilee. Firing from Jordanian territory on an Israel border patrol brought return fire from the patrol.

June, 1955

June 22

King Faisal left for a summer of official and unofficial visits in Lebanon, Turkey, England and Western Europe.

June 23

Iraqi Prime Minister Nuri-Said arrived in Turkey for an official visit.

Egypt declared that Israel's proposal for a mined security zone was "propaganda" as the suggestions were practically identical to proposals made by General Burns in November which Egypt had accepted and Israel turned down.

June 24

More than 200 suspected Arab terrorists were rounded up by French security forces in eastern Algeria.

June 25

A conference of ranking Syrian Government officials was held to discuss the economic crisis which had resulted from heavy drought damage to crops.

Three hundred members of secret anti-French organizations were arrested in the Constantine Department in Algeria.

Israel and Egypt agreed to meet under UN supervision to discuss means of quieting the Gaza strife, including General Burns' original proposals of joint patrols, barbed wire fences on the border, the use of regular troops only, and contact and cooperation among the commanders to maintain peace.

June 26

King Faisal II of Iraq arrived in Istanbul for an extended visit to Turkey.

June, 1955

June 27

Lebanon seized an Israel ship, the Bracha Fold, which had been forced within Lebanon's territorial waters by high seas.

King Faisal II of Iraq arrived in Ankara, Turkey, amid much fanfare.

The Rabat Chamber of Commerce published a resolution sent to Faure, French Prime Minister, asking him to stop the issuing of official statements which gave the impression that Moroccan disorders were caused by counter terrorists.

The Saudi Arabian Director of Oil Affairs discussed a "united oil policy" with the Iraqi Minister of Economy.

The Egyptian-Israel Mixed Armistice Commission censured both Egypt and Israel for acts of aggression in an exchange of fire along the Gaza Strip on May 28.

June 28

A joint Syrian, Saudi Arabian and Jordanian committee on proposed repairs to the Hejaz Railway completed its meetings in Amman. The committee agreed to set up an office in Damascus.

Israel and Egyptian representatives met under the chairmanship of General E. L. M. Burns, Chief of Staff of the UNTSO, to discuss border tension. The main consideration was the agenda of the meeting.

The USSR Supreme Soviet and the Syrian Parliament exchanged messages on the proposed visit of a Syrian parliamentary delegation to the USSR.

Egypt's budget for 1955-1956 was approved. It totalled LE315,259,572, the largest in the country's history.

The surrounded British troops in Aden were rescued with the aid of British jets.

The Iraqi police raided the two main centers of the Arab Renaissance Socialist Party and arrested about 100 of its members, including the party's secretary.

June, 1955

June 29

The Egyptian Minister of Waqfs returned from an official visit to the Far East, including Communist China.

Foreign Minister Alfred Naccache of Lebanon announced his resignation from the Government.

June 30

The trial opened for 30 leaders of the Syrian National Socialist Party who were charged in the death of Colonel Adnan Malki. The Syrian Government claimed that the accused leaders had been negotiating with the US in order to take over the Syrian Government and then join the Baghdad Pact.

Pakistan agreed to join the Baghdad Pact formed in February 1955 between Turkey, Iraq and Britain.

A third Anglo-Egyptian meeting was held in Cairo to prepare for the international commission on Sudanese self determination.

The UN Relief and Works Agency reported the number of Palestine refugees at 905,986.

The first census in the history of Sudan began.

June, 1955

June 28

A conference to discuss the future relations between northern and southern provinces in the Sudan opened at Juba, but was immediately adjourned because a number of delegates had not yet arrived.

General E. L. M. Burns, Chief of Staff of the UNTSO, chaired the first meeting of the Egyptian-Israel talks on Gaza.

Terrorist bombs blew out the front of the US Information Center in Tunis.

Fourteen Algerian rebels were killed in a clash with Foreign Legion troops.

June 29

A meeting between Israel and Egyptian representatives on the Gaza conflict continued for six hours, then adjourned until July 6. There was agreement to place the proposals of General E. L. M. Burns, Chief of Staff of the UNTSO, on the agenda, as well as Egyptian proposals for a wide demilitarized zone. Egypt objected to including Israel's suggestion that Egypt cancel its "order" to fire on all Israel patrols.

Resignation of the Government of Israel was succeeded by a caretaker government to carry on till the general election.

A report of the French Parliamentary mission to Algeria was issued.

The Syrian prosecutor submitted a list of 300 members of the National Socialist Party whom he charged with plotting the overthrow of the Government. He demanded the death sentence for a number of them, for others life imprisonment, and for the rest, heavy prison terms. The majority of those for whom the death sentence was asked were out of the country.

Conversations took place in Ankara among Iraq, Turkey and Pakistan. Pakistan Minister of National Defense General Ayub Hanin was then in Ankara, as was Prime Minister Nuri-Said of Iraq.

July, 1955

July 1

Jacques Soustelle, Governor General of Algeria, reported to Paris that the drive against terrorists had met with success and that the Algerian outlook had improved.

Nearly 1,000 British troops were flown into Aden from Suez to assist the local government levies and British air force.

July 2

Algerian terrorists burned French plantations and clashed with police and troops.

As scattered Arab terrorism and French counteractions continued, in Morocco Marshal Alphonse Juin, former Resident General of Morocco, sharply criticized French residents of Morocco who ignored the government's policy of conciliation.

July 3

Britain invited Jordanian financial representatives to visit London for discussions on the Arab Legion budget and the question of Britain's contribution to a proposed oil refinery.

The French Socialist Party announced that it favored a new Algerian electoral law which would give equal rights to both Arabs and French.

Three thousand persons suspected of aiding the terrorists were rounded up by French authorities in western Algeria.

Egyptian shore batteries fired at the British ship Anshun which was passing through the mouth of the Gulf of Aqaba bound for Aqaba.

One European and two Moroccans were killed and five Moroccans wounded in Casablanca.

Muhammad Nur-ad-Din, recently dismissed Sudanese Minister of Public Works, attacked Prime Minister Ismail al-Azhari for his dictatorial methods and for deviating from the National Union Party's mandate for union with Egypt.

July 4

The Iraqi Government announced that it had agreed to enter into negotiations with Indonesia for a treaty of friendship similar to that existing between Iraq and Pakistan.

The Egypt-Israel Mixed Armistice Commission condemned Egypt and Israel for clashes on May 30: Egypt for opening up with automatic and mortar fire from an outpost east of Deir al-Balah, in the Gaza Strip, on the Israel settlements of Nir Am En Ha Shelosha and Kissufim, killing two Israelis and wounding seven others; Israel for firing heavy artillery at the Egyptian outpost, killing one Egyptian soldier and wounding two others and one civilian.

A Syrian military prosecutor announced in Damascus that the Government would ask France to surrender former President Adib Shishakli to answer a charge of fatally beating a Syrian soldier.

New terrorist attacks took place in Philippeville and Robertville, Algeria.

July 5

The British Foreign Office instructed its diplomatic representative in Cairo to protest the shelling of the Anshun by Egyptian shore batteries.

July 6

The Gaza talks reopened and agreement was soon reached on an agenda which included suggestions presented by General E. L. M. Burns, Chief of Staff of the UNTSO, and the question of the right of both Israel and Egypt to make additional proposals. Talks continued on the first two of General Burns' points: joint patrols and cooperation among field commanders.

A note was received by Egypt from the British Government protesting against the shelling of the British ship Anshun by Egyptian shore batteries on July 3.

The British Embassy revealed that an incident similar to the shelling of the Anshun had occurred on April 10, and had also led to a note of

protest. On that occasion the British ship Argobec, carrying grain from Aden to Aqaba, had been fired on but later allowed to proceed, as it had not been damaged.

Anthony Nutting, British Minister of State for Foreign Affairs, declared in the House of Commons that the Government did not recognize the legality of the Egyptian blockade of the Suez Canal or of any other waters leading to Israel ports.

The French Council of Ministers issued a statement saying that Gilbert Grandval, the new French Resident General in Morocco, would be granted wide liberty of action but that his general task was to restore order. He was to act within the framework of the Protectorate Treaty of 1912, giving that treaty its normal application through the progressive abandonment of direct administration by French officials and the grant of increased Government responsibility to Moroccans, and also to seek to reconcile the various tendencies of opinion.

July 7

Another day of Gaza conferences between Egypt and Israel was marked by some progress. Disagreements were chiefly on the degree of detailed cooperation between front line commanders for both sides.

Lebanese Premier Sami al-Solh denied that his Cabinet resigned.

July 8

Lebanese Premier Sami al-Solh's Cabinet reportedly resigned because of difficulties with Foreign Minister Alfred Naccache over diplomatic appointments. Solh had asked Naccache to resign. Naccache's refusal reportedly forced the Premier to resign.

July 9

The agreement on Tunisian self rule was approved by the French Chamber of Deputies by a vote of 540-43.

July 9

A new oil law was promulgated in Libya stating that all oil concessions must be on a 50-50 profit sharing basis, and that within ten years of signing a concession 75 percent of the staff of such companies must be Libyan nationals.

An international court awarded Libya eight of the 25 pieces of property which had been in dispute with Italy since the declaration of Libyan independence.

Prime Minister Sami al-Solh of Lebanon announced the reformation of his Cabinet following a dispute with Foreign Minister Alfred Naccache. The new Cabinet was as follows: Sami al-Solh as Prime Minister and Minister of Planning, Hamid Franjiah as Minister of Foreign Affairs.

The press reported that Iraq would soon pay Turkey 100 million lira on the Mosul oil account.

July 10

Israel's Prime Minister, Moshe Sharett, warned Egypt that if any attempt were made to close the port of Elath by force, Israel would not hesitate to use force to break the blockade, since free passage was their right. They would, he said, use all peaceful measures against the Egyptians' blockade, but would use force against aggression.

The Aden Government accused Yemen of supplying cash, grain, arms and ammunition to the rebellious tribes.

July 11

The Egypt-Israel MAC (Mixed Armistice Commission) found that an Israel observation post was shelled from Egyptian controlled territory on May 30.

Prime Minister Nehru of India spent 24 hours in Cairo on his return trip to Delhi. Prime Minister Nasser and he announced their general agreement on the international matters they discussed.

A Syrian parliamentary delegation headed by Rafik Bashur, Vice Chairman of the Chamber of Deputies, arrived in Moscow at the invitation of the USSR Supreme Soviet.

July 12

Yemen denied the British claims and stated that the real reason for the recent difficulties was that the tribes had been "robbed of their livelihood by decree."

The Egyptian-Israel MAC blamed both Egypt and Israel for an exchange of fire on June 5 in the neighborhood of the MAC's meeting place.

Premier Jawaharlal Nehru of India and Premier Gamal Abdel Nasser of Egypt issued a joint communique in New Delhi and Cairo denouncing military alliances as hindrances to peace.

July 13

Salah Ben-Youssef, Secretary General of the Tunisian Neo-Destour Party, denounced the Franco-Tunisian Conventions as dangerous and compromising irremediably the future of the Tunisian nation.

The new French Resident General in Morocco, Gilbert Grandval, ordered the release of 31 Moroccan political prisoners. He indicated that others would be pardoned later if public tranquility was preserved.

July 14

Lebanese Premier Sami al-Solh won a vote of confidence in Parliament for his new Government, 22-11-2.

A bomb explosion in Casablanca killed six persons and injured 35; all were reported to be Europeans.

July, 1955

July 15

The arrival of new Resident General Gilbert Grandval in French Morocco was marked by rioting in which 15 persons were killed and many were injured.

A military tribunal in Syria sentenced deposed President Adib Shishakli in absentia to 20 years imprisonment for beating to death Sergeant Naji Bahri.

In Morocco,French and Arab mobs grew in strength throughout the day. A curfew was established throughout Casablanca.

July 16

Riots continued in Morocco after the arrival of the French Resident General with deaths totaling 27. There was much local French opposition to the moderate policies of the new Resident General, Gilbert Grandval.

A declaration of state of siege at Casablanca followed a series of outrages.

French mobile gendarmes and Foreign Legionnaires opened fire on rioting Moroccans in Casablanca, killing five and wounding 19.

The Sudanese Government agreed that the International Commission to supervise Sudanese self determination should be composed of representatives of neutral states, which had neither connections with the Sudan nor interests in the outcome of self determination, and that neither Britain, Egypt, nor the Sudan should sit on the Commission.

July 17

Moslem Terrorism and European counter terrorism caused arson and murder throughout Casablanca, Morocco.

Native Moroccans wrecked shops in the native Jewish quarter of Casablanca. Eight persons were killed and 20 injured.

July, 1955

July 17

Militant mobs continued to gather in the Arab section of Casablanca. Deaths totaled about 60.

C.W.W. Greenidge, secretary of the British Anti-Slavery Society, charged in London that there were between 100,000 and 125,000 slaves in Saudi Arabia, and 750,000-1,000,000 in the whole of the Arabian Peninsula.

July 18

Lebanon and the US signed an "atoms for peace" agreement.

The British Embassy protested the "violent" attacks in the Egyptian press on Britain's role in the Buraimi Oasis dispute.

President Sukarno of Indonesia paid a one day visit to Baghdad.

Robert Hugh Turton, Under Secretary for the British Foreign Office, replying to a Parliamentary question, said that the Egyptian Acting Minister for Foreign Affairs, in an oral reply to the British note of protest at the shelling of the Anshun by Egyptian shore batteries, had said that none of the shots fired was aimed at the ship, but he recognized that there might have been some confusion regarding signals exchanged between ship and shore.

Several French police officials in Morocco were dismissed by the Resident General for not taking action against French counter-terrorist groups.

July 19

A barter agreement was signed with Czechoslovakia, by which Egypt would exchange cotton and phosphates for Czechoslovakian light and heavy industrial products.

President Sukarno of Indonesia arrived in Egypt for a six day state visit.

July, 1955

July 19

It was announced in Jerusalem that $6 million in frozen Arab accounts in Israel were paid out to Arab refugees, and that valuables and documents in safe deposit boxes were returned to their owners through the medium of the UN and a British bank, acting as agents for the Israel Government.

July 20

Fifteen Asian and African nations requested that the North African situation be included on the agenda of the General Assembly session in September. They also asked that Secretary General Hammarskjold use his personal position to help solve French-Arab differences.

King Saud of Saudi Arabia made a statement to foreign journalists in which he appealed to the West to restore to Arabs in Palestine their rights, to liberate North Africa as well as southern and eastern Arabia, and to respect Arab independence and not to obstruct their unity.

July 21

Representatives of Israel and Jordan exchanged drafts of a proposed commanders' agreement. This would put arrangements into effect along the Israel-Jordan frontier similar to those in the Jerusalem area, where opposing commanders met from time to time and communicated by telephone to prevent incidents.

French Resident General in Morocco Gilbert Grandval traveled to Marrakech to talk with Thami Glaoui about replacing the present Sultan. His arrival was met with new nationalist demonstrations.

A strong Egyptian protest was lodged with the Joint Armistice Commission following reports that a number of Israel aircraft had flown over Gaza.

July 22

Prime Minister Gamal Abdel Nasser inaugurated the festivities marking the third anniversary of the Egyptian revolution. In a three

July, 1955

July 22

and one-half hour speech he reviewed the accomplishments of his regime and again promised that "parliament will be inaugurated in January."

Sudanese Prime Minister Ismail al-Azhari and seven Cabinet ministers arrived in Cairo to attend the celebration of the third anniversary of the Egyptian revolution.

It was estimated that 10,000 Moroccans lost their homes during the past week as a result of arson.

A curfew was imposed on the Arab quarter of Rabat, Morocco, after two French corporals were murdered there.

UN Secretary General Dag Hammarskjold announced that Major General E. L. M. Burns had signed a contract to serve as UN Truce Supervisor for another year.

July 23

The British Charge d'Affaires in Jedda was instructed to deliver a very strong protest to the Saudi Arabian Government against their refusal to allow Britain to send relief to the village of Hamasa in the Buraimi Oasis.

It was announced in Jerusalem that Israel and Jordanian troops fought a four hour battle in the border area south of Lake Tiberias. Jordanian soldiers shot at an Israel patrol on Israel territory; the Israelis returned the fire and withdrew safely.

Seven Algerians were killed in scattered assassinations and in a clash between troops and a rebel band.

July 24

Israel Defense Minister David Ben-Gurion offered to confer with Egyptian Premier Gamal Abdel Nasser or any other Egyptian statesman in an effort to pacify the Middle East.

July, 1955

July 24

The Jordan Government asked the US to delay the proposed visit to the Middle East of Eric Johnston, President Eisenhower's special envoy, who was working on a plan for the development of the Jordan River.

July 25

London announced that two destroyers would be sold to Egypt, the aim being to balance the two sold to Israel earlier.

French Resident General Gilbert Grandval's arrival in Meknes, Morocco, was the occasion for riots there.

The Syrian Army along the northern border announced the shooting of a Turkish soldier during a brief clash between Turkish and Syrian patrols.

Egypt offered its official regrets at the shelling of the Anshun in the Gulf of Aqaba.

July 26

Ex-King Farouk made a statement in Paris in which he denounced the Egyptian Government in the strongest terms by saying that it had plunged the country into an unprecedented reign of terror and almost inextricable economic difficulties. He said all his efforts were directed to ending the suffering of the Egyptian people.

The Egyptian Government of Premier Gamal Abdel Nasser imprisoned 100 Communists, including Communist leader Professor Omar Tantawi.

French Resident General Gilbert Grandval, in Morocco, cancelled a visit to Fez.

July, 1955

July 27

Robert Hugh Turton, Under Secretary for the British Foreign Office, told Parliament in a written reply that the Egyptian reply to the British protest against the attack on the Anshun was received on July 14. The note repudiated all liability. Turton said the note was most unsatisfactory.

The Egypt-Israel Mixed Armistice Commission found Egypt guilty of violating the armistice on July 19 when Egyptian infiltrators blew up a water pipeline near the Israel settlement of Kissufim.

July 28

It was reported in Paris that fierce fighting in eastern Algeria cost the lives of 24 French soldiers.

A thousand workmen in Nzara, southern Sudan, rioted until brought under control by police fire. The rioting followed the conviction of an official who was known to favor unity with Egypt.

July 29

Sudanese Premier Ismail al-Azhari stated that relations between Sudanese and Egyptian leaders had nearly reached a breaking point. The major issues between the two were the division of the Nile waters, and the repudiation by the al-Azhari Government of its previous support of unity with Egypt.

Al-Ahram, Cairo daily newspaper, reported that the Secretary General had sent all member governments of the Arab League proposals for amendments to the Pact, which included: (1) a consultative assembly composed of parliamentary representatives from the several member states, and (2) a binding majority vote in the League Council.

Fourteen Asian and African nations requested that the UN Security Council and General Assembly act in connection with the situation in French North Africa.

July, 1955

July 30

Crown Prince Amir Muhammad Rida al-Mahdi Sanusi of Libya died at the age of 65.

French troops trapped a band of the Moslem insurgent Army of God in eastern Algeria.

August, 1955

August 1

Arabs living in Paris rioted in sympathy with the Arabs of Morocco.

Announcement was made in Khartoum of the completion of Sudanization of government services.

August 2

The Egyptian-Israel discussions to ease tension along the border came to a halt when Egypt refused to accept Israel's proposal for the erection of a physical barrier along the border.

Sudanese Prime Minister al-Azhari completed several meetings with leaders of the opposition Umma Party regarding the work of the forthcoming Parliamentary session.

Eight southern Sudanese tribal leaders announced from their Cairo headquarters that they would work for an independent status for the southern region, with only a general federation link with the north. They also attacked Prime Minister al-Azhari for the "oppressive measures" he had used in the south. The leaders appealed to Egypt for help in achieving their aims.

August 3

Iraqi Prime Minister Nuri-Said returned to Baghdad from Turkey, where he had been since June.

August 4

Egyptian and Israel negotiations on the Gaza dispute were stalemated on the degree to which UN officers would be used in the proposed contacts between field commanders on either side. Israel favored direct contact between the two sides, while Egypt insisted on using representatives of the UN as intermediaries.

The Sudanization Committee notified the Government that Sudanese had replaced foreigners in all responsible administrative jobs.

August, 1955

August 4

The British Foreign Office issued a statement saying that after a fire at Hamasa in the Buraimi zone the Government had sent 4,000 pounds sterling worth of supplies to the stricken people.

Israel and Jordan agreed to extend their new truce arrangements throughout the length of their common border. Direct telephone communication between local commanders would be used to reduce the threat at points of contact.

An Egyptian mission arrived in Syria to discuss economic aid for Syria.

Thami Glaoui, Berber leader in Morocco, refused to accept a French plan whereby Sultan Sidi Muhammad Ben-Moulay Arafa would abdicate, at least temporarily, for a regency council. This statement was made in a letter to the French Premier.

August 5

France's Premier Edgar Faure managed to keep a free hand in dealing with Morocco by rejecting attempts to halt concessions to nationalism there. He withstood severe attacks from right wing deputies before the National Assembly recessed for the summer.

August 6

It was announced that Tripoli would be the terminus for a new Iraq Petroleum Company pipeline to supply the oil refinery there with an additional nine million tons annually.

In a note to all Arab League members, the Secretariat proposed that an Arab League General Assembly be established to serve in an advisory capacity to the League Council. The Assembly delegates would be members of the parliaments and other institutions in the member states.

August, 1955

August 7

Details of the report of the Sudanization committee were made public. Of the 1,222 posts studied, 734 had been Sudanized by July 31. Of the remaining 488 posts, 281 were abolished, and the remainder, occupied by both British and Egyptian officials, were not considered of the type that could sway the Sudanese vote in the forthcoming election.

The Prime Minister of Sudan, acting as leader of the National Union Party, dismissed Muhammad Nur-ad-Din as Vice President of the party and Said al-Tayib Muhammad Khair as Assistant Secretary. Nur-ad-Din said that the action was illegal and he would not recognize it.

August 8

A barter agreement was signed between Egypt, Russia and Rumania.

The Chief Israel Truce Negotiator warned that Egypt's policy might be leading toward ominous confirmation that direct contact between the two countries was possible only in war or border incidents.

Nine persons were killed and eight wounded in a battle between French infantrymen and Algerian rebels.

August 9

After a deadlock developed, the Egyptian-Israel negotiations on armistice security measures were adjourned for ten days to permit representatives of both countries to consult with their governments.

Prime Minister Gamal Abdel Nasser of Egypt accepted an invitation to visit Moscow in the spring of 1956.

Disagreement continued in the Egyptian-British discussions on an international commission to oversee the self determination process. Egypt insisted that Britain, Egypt and the Sudan should be represented on the commission, though with a majority of neutral members, while the British representatives thought that only neutral members should be selected.

August, 1955

August 10

The Iraqi Ministers of Interior and Economy left for Ankara, Turkey, for discussions on combatting subversive movements and the extension of trade.

Moroccan Resident General Gilbert Grandval arrived in Paris for talks on French policy toward the Moroccan nationalists.

An Egyptian trade delegation arrived in Peking.

The Egyptian Government announced a barter agreement with Russia and Rumania under which Egypt would provide Russia with 60,000 tons of rice and Rumania with LE1.8 million worth of cotton yarn in exchange for Russian oil and Rumanian paraffin.

Prime Minister Mustafa Ben-Halim of Libya signed with the French Ambassador a pact by which the small French garrison would evacuate the province of Fezzan by November 30, 1956. Four protocols attached to the treaty arranged for the evacuation, made arrangements for the movements of nomads across the desert, established cultural missions from each of the two countries, and regulated the transfer of money from the sterling area to the franc area and vice-versa.

August 11

After negotiations with Communist Chinese officials in Cairo, it was announced that China had agreed to buy about LE8 million worth of Egyptian cotton.

Israel protested to the UN Security Council that Egypt was interfering with the passage of Israel bound shipping through the Suez Canal. It reported that on July 8 Egyptian authorities had removed a civilian automobile from a vessel bound for the port of Haifa and held the ship for two days.

The Arab League Secretary General announced that the League Political Committee would meet on September 3.

August, 1955

August 12

A split in the French Cabinet between conservative and more liberal groups was avoided by a compromise policy ("the Grandval plan") which was arranged in discussions with the French Resident General in Morocco. Gilbert Grandval requested that the Sultan form a new government representing all shades of Moroccan opinion. If he failed in this task, a regency council would be formed. As soon as the council was formed, negotiations with France would begin for major reforms in Morocco.

August 13

Great Britain sent another note to Egypt over the shelling of the British freighter Anshun. The Egyptian reply to the first note was described as most unsatisfactory.

A rump session of the Sudanese National Union Party meeting at the home of Muhammad Nur-ad-Din expelled Prime Minister Ismail al-Azhari and some of his colleagues from the party. The Prime Minister said that the action was not legal and would be ignored.

Sayyed al-Mirghani, leader of the Khatmia sect in Sudan, issued a statement calling on the Sudanese people and political leaders to agree to determine the future status of the country by a plebiscite instead of by the election of a Constituent Assembly.

The Syrian Chamber of Deputies approved a budget for the coming year of SL260,500,000, including 40 percent for defense and internal security.

French Premier Edgar Faure gave himself a month for settlement of the Moroccan crisis under a new plan adopted by the Cabinet.

It was announced that King Hussein of Jordan would visit King Saud of Saudi Arabia during September.

Sudanese Prime Minister Ismail Azhari announced that he and his ministers had visited Cairo July 23-28, 1955, to tell the Egyptian Government two things: one, that their two countries must be friends and attacks by one against the other must cease; two, that the Sudanese people had an ever increasing desire to cling to their independence.

August 14

An Egyptian note was delivered at the British Embassy proposing that the question of the composition of the international commission to supervise the process of Sudanese self determination should be referred to the Sudanese Parliament for decision. The note gave an account of the negotiations between the British and Egyptian delegations in Cairo on the question.

The Egypt-Israel Mixed Armistice Commission condemned Egypt for the blowing up of the main water pipe to the Kissufim settlement on June 25.

The outlawed Istiqlal (Independence) Party of Morocco said that it would probably not participate in any coalition government which the French attempted to form.

French Resident General Gilbert Grandval brought to Sultan Sidi Muhammad Ben-Moulay Arafa in Rabat letters from French Premier Edgar Faure and President Rene Coty, offering him a proposal that he form a broad based government for Morocco which would exercise powers then held by the Sultan and France.

August 15

Israel Army Headquarters in Tel Aviv reported that armed Egyptians penetrated the Negev on August 14 to a depth of eight miles and were driven back across the armistice line.

August 16

The text of a note from the British Government to the Governor General of the Sudan was published in London. It informed the Governor General that the Government, in order not to hold up the process of self determination, had accepted the Egyptian proposal that the composition of the international supervisory commission should be left to the Sudanese Parliament to decide, but it pointed out that British views on the neutral nature of the Commission had not changed.

As its special session opened, the Sudanese Parliament unanimously approved a resolution calling for the evacuation of British and

August 16

Egyptian troops within 90 days. The next step, according to the British-Egyptian Agreement of 1953, would be the election of a constituent assembly, which would decide the country's future. Prime Minister al-Azhari said that he hoped elections could be called by early December.

August 17

In a letter to President Coty of France, Sultan Sidi Muhammad Ben-Moulay Arafa accepted the French proposal that he form a new government but turned down two key aspects of this plan: that the government be formed within a few days and that all segments of Moroccan politics be represented. The Sultan was understood to have said that he would not include anyone in the government who was hostile to himself, i. e., any of the nationalist groups.

Former President of Syria, Shukri Kuwaitli, who fled the country during the Zaim coup in 1949, was the strongest candidate for the presidency.

A mutiny broke out in two companies of the Equatoria Corps at Torit in the southern Sudan. Reports stated that the revolt was partly a protest against the use of northern Sudanese officers who were replacing the British under the process of Sudanization of all officers' positions, partly the result of orders transferring the troops to the north, and partly the result of widespread propaganda from Egypt. A state of emergency was declared throughout the area.

August 18

Former President Shukri al-Kuwaitli, National Party leader, was elected Syria's ninth president by the Chamber of Deputies. He defeated Foreign Minister Khaled Azm by a vote of 91-41. Azm resigned as Foreign Minister and Acting Defense Minister and announced that he would become leader of the opposition.

The Egyptian negotiator in the Gaza border talks stated that the discussions were deadlocked. Egypt objected to the proposals that there be direct communications between the military commanders, that Israel and Egyptian officers meet without the presence of UN

August 18

officers, and that the proposed arrangement be signed by the two countries without the UN being a party to it.

Despite objections of the right wing members of his Cabinet, French Premier Faure said that he could not agree to the formation of a Moroccan Government composed of only friends of the Sultan. However, the Premier did grant a few more days for the Sultan to consider the French proposal. He expected the crisis to be solved by September 12, when talks would begin on far reaching reforms.

The Sudanese Government issued a statement saying that an unofficial plebiscite had been exercised on August 16 by the people who had unanimously expressed their preference for independence. It asked Egypt and Britain to meet the Sudanese wish by declaring the independence of the Sudan, provided the Sudanese Parliament agreed to the course. It held that the matter had become so obvious that it needed no plebiscite.

August 19

Eric Johnston left for Amman, Jordan, to attempt a settlement of the division of the waters of the Jordan River and its tributaries.

The French Government decided to enter into direct consultations with the leaders of Moroccan public opinion, including Istiqlalists.

Thirteen persons were killed during riots in Khenifra, Morocco.

Marshal Voroshilov, President of the USSR, sent a message of congratulations on the beginning of the Moslem Near Year to Colonel Nasser, Egyptian Prime Minister.

August 20

Nearly 200 Arabs and French troops were killed as a result of terrorist outbreaks marking the second anniversary of the deposition of the exiled Sultan of Morocco, Sidi Muhammad Ben-Youssef. It was coordinated with the operations of the NLF in Algeria.

Edgar Faure, Premier of France, in a statement on the disorders in North Africa, said that the Government would not permit terrorist bands to attack the destiny of French Algeria.

King Faisal II of Iraq left Turkey after a prolonged visit.

It was reported from Paris that about 300 North Africans and Frenchmen were killed in widespread clashes in Morocco and Algeria.

Berber tribesmen in Morocco sacked the European section of the town of Oued Zem, killing 50 Europeans and leaving the section in a shambles.

About 200 persons were killed during terrorist outbreaks in the Constantine Department of Algeria.

Major Salah Salem, Egyptian Minister of Sudanese Affairs, denied reports that Egypt was inciting southern Sudanese against the north Sudan. He suggested that both Britain and Egypt send troops into the southern Sudan to aid in quieting rebellious conditions there. In the meantime, government troops advanced into the south and retook one village from the mutineers.

August 21

Widespread violence in Algeria and Morocco resulted in over 700 deaths. French Premier Edgar Faure and four cabinet members went to Aix-les-Bains to confer with Moroccan leaders in an effort to restore peace.

August 22

French Premier Edgar Faure and a committee of cabinet ministers opened at Aix-les-Bains a conference which was to eventually

August, 1955

August 22

include conversations with all segments of the Moroccan population. These talks, the second major step in the Grandval Plan, were begun because of the Sultan's delay in forming a coalition government. It was hoped that they would assist in the formation of a government and serve as a preliminary sounding board for the development of reform plans. In the first day of the conference, the French talked with Thami al-Glaoui, Grand Vizier al-Mukru, and other conservative Moroccan leaders.

It was reported in Washington that the US Government was prodding France to move more swiftly in search of political solutions in North Africa.

General Raymond Duval, Commander of French troops in Morocco, was killed in a plane crash.

A Chinese-Egyptian trade agreement and protocol on mutual deliveries for the 1955-56 fiscal year was signed in Peking.

Israel troops crossed the armistice line after Egyptians attacked a three car convoy making a routine patrol of the demarcation line, and stormed and captured an Egyptian outpost in the Gaza Strip. After a ceasefire was arranged by UN observers, the Israelis left the post.

The Sudanese Parliament recommended that the international commission to oversee the process of self determination be made up of representatives from Czechoslovakia, Yugoslavia, Sweden, Norway, India, Pakistan and Switzerland.

Egypt proposed that Britain join with it in sending troops to put down a revolt in southern Sudan. The offer was expected to be refused.

A Sudanese communique said that the Prime Minister had called on the mutineers at Torit to surrender and had promised them a fair and detailed inquiry into their grievances.

French troops leveled nine villages in the vicinity of Constantine, Algeria, which were thought to have been the center of the local terrorist organizations. The death toll approached 1,000.

August, 1955

August 24

The mutiny of troops in southern Sudan was reported to be assuming the proportions of a popular uprising against Egyptian and British control.

French Resident General Gilbert Grandval was booed in Morocco by some 2,000 Frenchmen at the funeral of General Raymond Duval, former Commander of French troops in Morocco.

August 25

Special US Ambassador Eric Johnston opened talks with the Jordanian Government on the question of developing the waters of the Jordan River.

Talks between France and Morocco continued at Aix-les-Bains, with an assortment of city and tribal leaders present. The French delegation talked with leaders of the outlawed Istiqlal Party. Unconfirmed reports indicated that French Resident General in Morocco, Gilbert Grandval, would soon resign, although the essence of his plan would be followed in working out future arrangements for Morocco.

General surrender and peace proceedings continued between French troops and Moroccan tribes.

The US expressed concern to France about the use of American military equipment against North Africans.

France notified NATO that another contingent of troops would soon be sent to North Africa, leaving only two of the five NATO committed divisions on the continent. The first contingent of six battalions would be sent to Algeria.

Salah Ben-Youssef, Secretary of the Neo-Destour Party, said in Cairo that he opposed the agreement for Tunisian autonomy signed by other members of his party with France.

The Egyptian Government took over operation of the Sugar Company of Egypt because of back taxes owed by the managing director, Ahmad Abboud.

August, 1955

August 22

Sudanese Governor General Sir Alexander Knox-Helm flew back to Khartoum from his vacation in Scotland.

August 23

Egypt and Britain agreed to withdraw all their troops from the Sudan within three months.

The mutinous troops at Torit agreed to surrender if British or Egyptian troops replaced the Sudanese forces in the nearby city of Juba. Prime Minister al-Azhari said that he would accept only unconditional surrender.

French troops were active in rounding up arms from surrendering Berber tribesmen in central Morocco.

With over 1,000 persons killed in North African rioting, French Premier Edgar Faure summoned French reservists to the colors.

The French delegation at Aix-les-Bains talked with representatives of the Moroccan Democratic Party of Independence. The conservative parties represented in the Faure Government criticized any such contacts with the nationalists and stated their opposition to the Grandval Plan.

Iraq, Lebanon, Burma, Egypt, Liberia, Iran and India asked UN Secretary General Hammarskjold to assist in halting the bloodshed in French North Africa.

Major General E. L. M. Burns, Chief of Staff of the UNTSO, said in Cairo that Egypt had accepted his proposal that the Gaza frontier be manned only with regular troops.

August 24

Egypt formally broke off the Gaza talks because it felt that Israel was aiming at the removal of international supervision and the possibility of direct talks between Egypt and Israel.

August, 1955

August 25

Sir Alexander Knox-Helm, Governor General of the Sudan, ordered the Sudanese mutineers to surrender without resistance within 24 hours.

Egyptian President Nasser received US Ambassador Henry A. Byroade and informed him that he condemned the use of the North Atlantic Treaty Organization armed forces to suppress the national liberation movement in North Africa.

Israel's Prime Minister Moshe Sharett discussed with the American and British Ambassadors the situation created by Egypt's withdrawal from the discussions to ease tension along the Gaza frontier.

August 26

The International Bank announced a loan of $10 million for additional electric power development in Algeria.

US Secretary of State John Foster Dulles proposed a new plan for settling the long standing Arab-Israel conflict: (1) The fixing of borders between the Arab nations and Israel; if requested, the United States would assist in this process. (2) An international guarantee of the new borders, a guarantee in which the United States would participate. (3) An international loan to Israel to help that country pay compensation to the displaced Arab refugees. The United States would make a substantial contribution to this loan.

Indications from Aix-les-Bains showed that a general agreement on the Moroccan problem was nearing, although a number of points remained unresolved. Uppermost among these was whether French Resident General Grandval or Sultan Sidi Muhammad Ben-Moulay Arafa should leave his position first, the prestige of each and his followers being involved in the decision.

French authorities in Rabat announced that in putting down the uprising in the Oued Zem area of Morocco their troops had killed 700 natives.

The French Socialist Party issued a request that French Resident General Gilbert Grandval be left at his post.

August, 1955

August 26

The International Bank for Reconstruction and Development granted Lebanon a loan of $27 million for the development of the Litani River.

Egyptian patrols ambushed and killed several Israelis during the night.

August 27

The British Government stated that it would join in any international guarantee that might be developed for the Arab-Israel borders.

In the Middle East, all of the countries involved announced that they were studying the Dulles proposals for Middle East peace presented on August 26.

The southern rebels in the Sudan agreed to a complete surrender, with Governor General Sir Alexander Knox-Helm promising to investigate their grievances.

In Morocco, Sultan Sidi Muhammad Ben-Moulay Arafa continued to be reluctant to abdicate, while the Istiqlal Party said that it would not join any government until he was out of office.

Sidi Muhammad al-Amin, the Bey of Tunis, ratified and sealed the conventions granting internal autonomy to Tunisia.

August 28

Prime Minister Designate David Ben-Gurion of Israel said that he was opposed to any revision of Israel's borders as fixed by the Armistice of 1949.

August 29

Egyptian and Israel jet fighters met over the Gaza frontier. Israel declared that four Egyptian planes penetrated into Israel air space. Two Egyptian planes were shot down on Israel territory.

August, 1955

August 29

The full French Cabinet debated the plans developed at Aix-les-Bains. General agreement was understood to have been reached on all key points. Gilbert Grandval would be replaced as Resident General by Lieutenant General Pierre Georges Boyer de Latour, present Resident General in Tunisia; Sultan Sidi Muhammad Ben-Moulay Arafa would be allowed to leave under honorable circumstances, and a regency council formed. The former Sultan, Sidi Muhammad Ben-Youssef was to be moved from his place of exile on the island of Madagascar to France during October, and preparations would be completed for the formation of a national Moroccan Government.

The Sudanese Parliament approved a resolution asking Egypt and Britain to allow the Sudan to organize a direct national plebiscite which would provide the means for Sudanese self determination.

The US urged Egypt and Israel to refrain from further hostilities along the Gaza Strip frontier and to resume the talks which had been broken off by Egypt.

Religious leaders throughout Iraq asked that all relations with France be broken as a protest against the French administration of its North African colonies.

August 30

US Secretary of State John Foster Dulles said that he had learned that the Soviet Union had offered arms to Egypt.

Britain and Egypt agreed on a means of settlement of Britain's wartime debt to Egypt. The total remaining debt of 135 million pounds sterling (about 265 million pounds sterling had already been paid under the agreement of 1951) would be returned to Egypt in annual payments ending in 1963.

A decree was published in Algeria extending the state of emergency to the whole of Algeria.

As raids and counter raids continued at Gaza, the Egyptian Government announced acceptance of a ceasefire proposal put forth by General E. L. M. Burns, UN Truce Supervisor. Israel asked that Egypt accept responsibility for the terrorist activity of the past two days.

August, 1955

August 30

The first contingents of an additional regiment of French troops arrived in Casablanca, Morocco.

The Israel Foreign Office notified the UN Security Council of the situation in a report which stated that in incidents of August 29 and 30 five Israel civilians had been killed, four civilians and one officer wounded and a radio station destroyed.

The Israel Embassy in London issued a statement attributing full responsibility to Egypt for the breaking off of talks and for the situation in the Gaza area. It said that since the rupture of the talks there had been 13 attacks on Israel villages, 12 attacks on Israel patrols, and seven cases of Egyptian aircraft flying over Israel territory.

August 31

The Israel Foreign Ministry issued a statement which said that since warnings conveyed to Egypt of its violations of the armistice agreement had proven futile and since the scope and range of its aggressive acts had become threatening, Israel had no choice but to resort to self defense.

Israel said that it would not accept a ceasefire until the Egyptians assumed full responsibility for the terrorism in the Gaza region.

The UN Truce Commission announced the acceptance by Egypt of ceasefire proposals in the Gaza border area.

The revision of the Anglo-Egyptian sterling releases agreement of 1951 was concluded in an exchange of notes.

The Israel Army attacked an Egyptian military camp in Khan Yunis which served as a base of operations for the Egyptian terrorist squads that killed 15 Israelis inside Israel territory.

An official Sudanese statement said that a few mutineers surrendered at Torit and that most of them had fled to neighboring villages. Eleven northerners had been found killed at Torit.

August, 1955

August 31

Ambassador Eric Johnston of the US arrived in Cairo after five days in Amman. The Egyptian Government announced that after Johnston's departure representatives of the Arab States would meet in Cairo to discuss his proposals.

Major Salem of Egypt reportedly resigned from his ministerial positions, although there was no word on his place as a member of the Revolutionary Command Council. Prime Minister Nasser would assume the duties of Minister for Sudanese Affairs; the new Minister for National Guidance would be Lieutenant Colonel Abd-al-Kader Hatim, the present Director General for Information.

Lieutenant General Pierre Georges Boyer de Latour du Moulin of France arrived in Rabat to take up the post of Resident General in Morocco after Gilbert Grandval secretly resigned.

France and Tunisia exchanged ratifications on Tunisian autonomy agreements.

Imam Ahmad of Yemen formed a Cabinet with himself as Prime Minister, as well as a six man advisory council of religious leaders, elders and chieftains. The Cabinet was as follows: Imam Ahmad as Prime Minister, Crown Prince Amir Saif al-Islam Muhammad al-Badr as Deputy Prime Minister, Minister of Foreign Affairs, and Minister of Defense.

Le Monde published a letter sent by Gilbert Grandval to the President of France on August 17 explaining why he wished to resign. The Prime Minister's office protested against the publication of the letter and it was announced that an inquiry would be made into how it came to be published.

Cairo Radio formally announced formation of the Egyptian fedayeen.

September, 1955

September 1

Prime Minister Moshe Sharett of Israel stated that there would be no further attacks against Egypt provided that all forms of Egyptian attacks ceased. The Egyptian Government said that it was considering the Israel ceasefire request.

Two Egyptian jet fighters were lost in action near Gaza, Israel claiming that the planes had been shot down.

Britain reportedly consulted with the US and France about the inflamed situation in the Gaza Strip. The British informed both sides that they supported United Nations Truce Supervisor General Burns' proposals and warned them of the dangers of a policy of retaliation.

The Israel Knesset passed a resolution at a special session to discuss the situation of North African Jewry, declaring immigration to be the only way of ensuring the safety of the Jews in Morocco, and requiring the Government to present a program for the financing and intensified immigration and absorption.

A joint Egyptian-Lebanese statement issued after five day talks with the Lebanese Foreign Minister, Hamid Faranjiah, recorded agreement on the need to strengthen the Arab League and on measures for increasing trade and economic and cultural relations.

A communique was issued summarizing the three opening statements of the chief delegates at the London Tripartite Conference on the Eastern Mediterranean and Cyprus.

The new French Resident General in Morocco, Lieutenant General Pierre Georges Boyer de Latour du Moulin, had an audience with Sultan Sidi Muhammad Ben-Moulay Arafa. He attempted to persuade the Sultan to withdraw in order to pave the way for the appointment of a three man regency council to introduce the necessary reforms.

Eric Johnston, President Eisenhower's special envoy, met with Egyptian Premier Gamal Abdel Nasser and discussed with him the US sponsored plan for the regional development of the Jordan River Valley waters.

September, 1955

September 1

An agreement was signed between the Syrian Government and the Banque de Syrie et du Liban terminating the 1938 convention as of the end of July 1956 and settling all outstanding claims between the two parties.

In Sudan, fifty-seven men and two officers who took part in the mutiny at Torit returned to Khartoum and surrendered to Defense Force troops.

The US State Department said that it had instructed its diplomats to seize every opportunity to impress Egypt and Israel with the gravity of the situation resulting from the fighting in the Gaza Strip.

An Iraqi Royal Decree nationalized the Baghdad Light and Power Company, and stated that compensation of two million dinars would be paid the company. The decree ended a 50 year concession which was due to expire in 1978.

September 2

France announced it would send nine more battalions of troops to Algeria and at the same time revealed that new reform measures were being drawn up to reduce tension. In Morocco, prospects for a political settlement took a turn for the worse when the new Resident General took no action toward removing the Sultan, regarded by the nationalists as a usurper.

After an initial audience with Moroccan Sultan Sidi Muhammad Ben-Moulay Arafa, the new French Resident General, Pierre Georges Boyer de Latour, visited the interior of the country where he removed from office a number of French and Moroccan officials.

Egypt and Israel agreed to an unofficial ceasefire, after ten days of fighting in the Gaza Strip.

Iraq offered full military and other aid to Egypt in the event of an Israel attack on the Gaza Strip.

September, 1955

September 2

Egypt and Lebanon signed an agreement to consult together and exchange information on matters relating to foreign policy, defense and public security.

Egypt announced that its forces captured 18 Israelis. It was learned in Cairo that 11 were taken during the past few days by infiltrators working inside Israel. The other seven were understood to have been captured on September 1; all were brought into Egypt across the Gaza Strip.

September 3

There was a heavy exchange of mortar fire along the Gaza border. General E. L. M. Burns, UN Truce Supervisor, immediately requested that both sides accede to his ceasefire request. Israel announced its acceptance of this request.

UN Truce Supervisor General Burns cabled UN Secretary General Hammarskjold and requested that the UN Security Council take action to prevent further Israel-Egyptian hostilities.

A payments agreement was signed between Egypt and Saudi Arabia providing that the National Bank of Egypt would open an account in Egyptian pounds in the name of the Saudi Arabian Monetary Fund representing the Saudi Arabian Government, in which all current accounts would be recorded.

The Arab League's Political Committee met in Cairo. Discussion centered on the agenda for the UN General Assembly, nominations for vacant UN posts, the Palestine question and the French position in North Africa. The members agreed to support Greece in the Cyprus dispute.

September 4

UN Truce Headquarters announced that both Egypt and Israel had given unconditional agreement to an urgent appeal for enforcement of a general ceasefire in the Gaza area.

September, 1955

September 4

Jordan announced that if Israel broke the armistice with Egypt, then Jordan would consider its truce with Israel ended.

Egyptian Deputy Premier Gamal Salem confirmed in Karachi that the Soviet Union made an arms offer to his country.

After the French Resident General of Morocco's visit to the Sultan, it was reported in Rabat that a plan to settle the Moroccan problem had emerged. The plan called for Sultan Sidi Muhammad Ben-Moulay Arafa to abdicate and the Regency Council to ask a prominent Moroccan to form a government representing all the elements of Moroccan opinion.

Iraq and Turkey signed an agreement for full cooperation and exchange of information in combatting subversive and Communist activities. Iraq already had similar agreements with Jordan, Syria, Egypt and Iran.

September 5

It was reported from Cairo that the ceasefire in the Gaza Strip was broken during the night by an exchange of shots near Tabet al-Assra; four Israelis were killed.

Cairo reported that the Egyptian Government had received an explanation that the break of the Gaza ceasefire had resulted from an Israel patrol's mistake.

Special Envoy Eric Johnston arrived in Beirut to discuss the American backed plan for regional water development with Lebanese officials.

More than 300 arrests were made in France as the Government attempted to end agitation among Algerians living there. The French Government also criticized the activities of "foreign inspires" and specifically protested to the Syrian Government because of provocative broadcasts from Damascus. It was further announced that similar representations had been made to the Arab League on September 2.

September, 1955

September 5

An Algerian nationalist band cut off the water supply for the city of Philippeville.

The special French Government envoy, General Georges Catroux, met with the exiled Sultan, Sidi Muhammad Ben-Youssef, in Madagascar and consulted with him on France's plans for Morocco.

It was officially announced in Cairo that Premier Gamal Abdel Nasser accepted an invitation to visit Hungary.

Major Salah Salem, whose resignation from the Egyptian Cabinet was announced the previous week, called on Premier Nasser.

King Hussein of Jordan flew his private plane to Saudi Arabia to confer with King Saud.

Following a call on Sultan Moulay Ben-Arafa of Morocco by the French Resident General, a statement was issued at the palace saying that the Sultan had affirmed his conviction of the divine character of his mission and his determination not to lay it down except with his life.

September 6

Egypt and Russia signed a barter agreement by which Egypt would exchange 60,000 tons of the current rice crop for 500,000 tons of crude oil from Russia.

The Government of Syria was dissolved.

Of those arrested on September 5 in France, about 200 Algerians were flown to Algiers to stand trial for extortion to help finance nationalist activities.

Governmental authority in Philippeville and Constantine, Algeria, was transferred from civilian to military hands, although martial law was not declared.

Twelve members of the 44 man Holy Synod of the Coptic Orthodox Church asked the Egyptian Government to remove Patriarch Anba Yusab II from office.

September, 1955

September 7

In Cairo, Allal al-Fassi, exiled leader of the Istiqlal Party, condemned the French plan for Moroccan reform and insisted on the immediate return of Sidi Muhammad Ben-Youssef to the throne. Al-Fassi thus openly broke with those Istiqlal leaders who had been negotiating with the French Cabinet for the past month.

French authorities in Morocco announced the formation of temporary protection units composed of armed civilians to reinforce army and police forces.

Lebanese Foreign Minister Hamid Franjiah and Minister of Finance Pierre Edde resigned from the Cabinet. The disagreement was thought to result from the Foreign Minister's negotiations with Egypt, at which he had agreed to cooperate with Egypt in certain matters of common interest.

The United Nations published a report of General E. L. M. Burns, Chief of Staff of the Palestine Truce Supervisory Organization, on the recent incidents in the Gaza area.

Algerian rebel terrorists killed a mother and her two daughters near Philippeville, starting a new wave of rage and fear.

September 8

Iraqi Prime Minister Nuri-Said left for a two week visit in Turkey. During his absence Muhammad Ali Mahmoud, Minister of Communications and Works, acted as Prime Minister.

Five Moroccans were killed in police counter fire against native terrorists in Casablanca.

King Hussein of Jordan returned to Amman after a three day visit with King Saud of Saudi Arabia.

Iraqi Premier Nuri-Said arrived in Istanbul and was met by Turkish Prime Minister Adnan Menderes.

The United Nations Truce Council unanimously condemned Israel for the Gaza Strip raid of February 28.

September, 1955

September 6

In an attempt to win Arab agreement to the American plan for hydroelectric development of the Jordan, United States Special Envoy Eric Johnston announced new concessions which regarded the storing of water in the Yarmuk Basin and in Lake Tiberias.

It was reported in Washington that Israel indicated qualified support for Secretary of State John Foster Dulles' proposals for the solution of the Israel-Arab conflict, and that it requested further details as to the guarantee of the borders between itself and its Arab neighbors.

The Egyptian-Israel Mixed Armistice Commission condemned both Israel and Egypt for violations of the armistice on August 22, leading to nearly two weeks of violence and about 70 deaths in the Gaza area.

Shukri al-Kuwatli was sworn in as Syria's new president. The Cabinet of Sabri al-Assali tendered its resignation. President al-Kuwatli asked Nazem al-Kudsi, leader of the Shab Party, to form a new Government, but the request was turned down for reasons of health. The President next asked Said al-Ghazzi, an independent deputy, to form a Cabinet.

Egypt told the UN Security Council that Israel had launched a large scale attack on Khan Yunis (Gaza region) causing the death of 36 Egyptian soldiers and Arab refugees. The Egyptian complaint said the attack occurred August 22.

September 7

The French delegation to discuss reform plans with ex-Sultan Sidi Muhammad Ben-Youssef on Madagascar gave an optimistic report on the chances of agreement with the former Sultan. The delegation was seeking approval of French plans for a regency council to replace Sultan Sidi Muhammad Ben-Moulay Arafa.

The Executive Committee of the Istiqlal Party of Morocco at the conclusion of a meeting in Rome announced that negotiations between Moroccans and French would be impossible unless proper legal conditions in Morocco were first restored.

September, 1955

September 8

It was reported that former Moroccan Sultan Sidi Muhammad Ben-Youssef had accepted the French reform proposals. With the completion of talks between the ex-Sultan and the French officials, the Government permitted a nationalist delegation to fly to Madagascar.

The UN Security Council unanimously approved a British-French-US resolution calling on Israel and Egypt to cooperate with UN Truce Supervisor General Burns in fixing tighter border controls.

September 10

Before leaving Madagascar, General Georges Catroux of France pledged his Government to the creation of Morocco as a free sovereign state permanently tied to France by an act of independence.

Abd-al-Krim, exiled Moroccan nationalist leader, denounced from Cairo the plan for a regency council and demanded complete French evacuation of Morocco.

The Israel-Jordanian Mixed Armistice Commission censured Jordan for a series of sabotage incidents on September 6, but the UN member of the Commission complimented Jordan for its earnest efforts to halt such actions.

French Resident General in Morocco, General Boyer de Latour du Moulin, proposed to the Sultan's Government that it give native Moroccans the right to form labor unions.

September 11

A state of alert was proclaimed in Constantine, Algeria, following attacks on French military personnel.

The arbitration board of five members appointed to settle conflicting claims to the Buraimi Oasis opened its hearings in Geneva. A British document on the Buraimi dispute was submitted to the International Arbitration Tribunal.

Egypt officially announced that all ships sailing into the Gulf of Aqaba had to have prior permission from the Egyptian authorities;

September, 1955

September 11

such permission had to be obtained at least 72 hours before the ship entered Egyptian territorial waters. An Israel spokesman challenged Egypt's right to control traffic through the Gulf of Aqaba. He declared that by international law a strait was deemed to be a high sea if it led to a gulf or sea serving territories of more than one country, and therefore Egypt had no right to legislate over the Strait of Tiran.

General Catroux and Yrissou returned from Madagascar bringing a letter from the ex-Sultan of Morocco, Sidi Muhammad Ben-Youssef, which expressed approval for the Government's proposals for the creation of a Council of the Throne and the formation of a representative Moroccan Government.

A decree was announced granting Moroccans the same right to form trade unions as Europeans.

September 12

The French Cabinet gave final approval to Premier Edgar Faure's plan to remove the Sultan of Morocco under honorable conditions, form a regency council, and negotiate with a representative Moroccan Government for internal reforms.

Georges Bidault, the Foreign Minister in the former French Premier Joseph Laniels' Government responsible for the deposition of Sidi Muhammad Ben-Youssef in 1953, issued a statement saying that the French Government's proposals for Morocco could not and would not be accepted.

The Egyptian-Israel Mixed Armistice Commission censured Egypt for a cattle rustling raid across the border during which an Israel Bedouin shepherd was killed. It also called on Egypt to return 100 sheep that were stolen from the Bedouin.

Great Britain challenged Egypt's right to control the movement of ships in the Gulf of Aqaba. The Foreign Office maintained that the Gulf was an international waterway open to ships of all nations.

The French Cabinet approved a series of reforms for Algeria aimed at improving conditions of farmers in backward areas.

September, 1955

September 13

A group of ten right wing Moroccan deputies sent a letter to the French Premier in which they referred to a declaration in process of being drafted by the Government, setting out the Government's proposals for the future framework of Franco-Moroccan relations. They said this definition would dominate future Franco-Moroccan relations and was obviously a precondition of any measure of application whatever. The deputies stated that they had learned "with astonishment" that the Government proposed putting its proposals at least partially into effect before Parliament had been consulted. They therefore wished to make clear that they would not consent to be confronted with a fait accompli.

September 14

General Burns of the Mixed Armistice Commission began talks in Cairo where the Egyptian Government said it was considering the UN proposal for a neutral zone and barrier along the Gaza border.

Eric Johnston, Special Envoy from the US on Jordan Valley Development, arrived in Cairo and went into immediate session with Egyptian officials.

Israel Prime Minister Moshe Sharett said in an interview that the proposals for a peaceful settlement of the Palestine problem made by US Secretary of State Dulles on August 26 were constructive, but they raised several important questions. Chief among these was the need for assurance that the Arabs would use the proposed reimbursement money for the refugees as intended.

The Bey of Tunis named Tahar Ben-Ammar as Premier.

It was reported from Paris that last minute differences within the French Cabinet delayed the implementation of the proposed plan for Morocco.

Lebanon allowed Israel police to cross the border in their search for the group of raiders of September 13.

In Rabat, Morocco, some 500 French colons protested the projected French policy in a demonstration before the Residency.

September, 1955

September 12

The French Government outlawed the Algerian Communist Party because of its support of recent nationalist activities. Police raided Party offices throughout Algeria.

September 13

French President Rene Coty diplomatically proposed in a personal letter to Sultan Sidi Muhammad Ben-Moulay Arafa of Morocco that he retire to Tangier.

Salah Ben-Youssef, Secretary General of the Neo-Destour Party of Tunisia, returned from exile.

Lebanese Prime Minister Sami al-Solh resigned after four members of his Cabinet had resigned during a heated parliamentary attack on the Prime Minister. President Camille Chamoun asked Rashid Karami, Minister of Economy in the outgoing government, to form a new cabinet.

The new Syrian Cabinet was formed by Said al-Ghazzi to replace that of Sabri al-Assali. The Cabinet included representatives of the Shab Party, the Constitutional Bloc, the Democratic Bloc and several independents.

The Government of Tunisia was dissolved.

Roger Seydoux of France was named Resident General of Tunisia, succeeding General Boyer de Latour, the new Resident General of Morocco.

Israel formally warned Egypt of its determination to run the blockade of the Gulf of Aqaba. The Foreign Ministry declared that Israel would protect the exercise of the rights of free passage through the international channel at whatever time and by whatever method it saw fit.

Alma, a village in Galilee three miles south of the Lebanese border, was attacked. According to a report of the Israel Army, delayed action explosives were placed on window sills of a number of buildings.

September, 1955

September 14

The Egyptian Cabinet approved the establishment of trade offices in Communist China.

September 15

Delay in beginning the French plan for Morocco continued as the Cabinet and Moroccan nationalists were unable to reach an agreement on the proposed regency council.

September 16

Sir Reader Bullard, British member of the Buraimi Arbitration Board, resigned on the ground that the Saudi Arabian member, Yusuf Yasin, had "hopelessly compromised the position of the tribunal" by acting as a member of the Saudi Government rather than "as an impartial arbitrator."

The Saudi Arabian official reply to the resignation of Sir Reader Bullard, British member of the Buraimi Arbitration Board, was a statement deploring that the decision of the tribunal should have been paralyzed by it, and expressing a firm determination to press for the appointment by the British of a new member of the tribunal.

September 17

The Bey of Tunis approved the formation of a new Cabinet under Tahar Ben-Ammar, an independent. The new Cabinet, which included five Neo-Destour Party leaders and one Jewish member, did not include a Minister of Defense or Foreign Affairs, as France would continue to handle these functions.

Scattered incidents of violence occurred in various towns in Morocco.

Governor General Jacques Soustelle proposed that in the September 27 meeting of the Algerian Assembly new measures should be passed to substitute elected local councils for direct French administration in rural communities.

September, 1955

September 17

French Resident General Boyer de Latour, of Morocco, journeyed to Paris to participate in talks on the makeup of the regency council.

The Syrian Government announced the formation of a three minister committee to negotiate with foreign oil companies for revision of the oil agreements.

The official inquiry into the August mutiny in the southern Sudan opened.

September 19

The Lebanese Government promised the Lebanon-Israel Mixed Armistice Commission (MAC) that it would not permit further acts of sabotage to be planned or launched by infiltrators from Lebanese territory. It accepted full responsibility for the September 13 attack on the settlement Alma where two homes and a barn were bombed.

A new Cabinet was formed in Lebanon with Rashid Karami as Prime Minister and Minister of the Interior, Fuad Ghusn as Deputy Prime Minister, and Amir Majid Arslan as Minister of Defense.

September 20

It was reported from Paris that Premier Edgar Faure finally succeeded in obtaining the endorsement of all his cabinet members for the proposed plan for Morocco of a three member Council of Guardians.

Egyptian troops withdrew 500 meters from the Gaza border and began erecting barbed wire fences along stretches of the new line. The Egyptian Government stated that this served as Egypt's answer to General Burns' request for a neutral zone between Egypt and Israel, and that it was now up to Israel to demonstrate equal good will.

September 21

Saudi Arabia's King Saud expressed regrets that Sir Reader Bullard had resigned from the arbitration board, thus making completion of its work impossible. He hoped that a new appointment would be made soon.

September, 1955

September 21

Moroccan Resident General Latour returned to Rabat with full authority from the French Cabinet to settle the stalemated negotiations for a regency council.

Iraqi Premier Nuri-Said left Turkey for Baghdad.

Twenty persons were killed in a bomb attack in Rabat, Morocco.

The Egyptian Government ordered the suspension of Coptic Patriarch Anba Yusab II and called a meeting of the Holy Synod to select a three man committee to assume his functions.

The French Cabinet unanimously approved the declaration drawn up by a committee of Ministers on the future pattern of Franco-Moroccan relations.

Israel troops entered the demilitarized zone of al-Auja in the southern Negev. The Foreign Ministry stated that the troops would remain until Egypt had withdrawn two military groups alleged to be in the zone in violation of the armistice agreement. Chief of Staff of the UNTSO General Burns strongly protested the action to the Israel Government.

It was reported in Jerusalem that when Israel's Ambassador to Moscow, Yosef Avidar, called at the Soviet Foreign Ministry on September 12 to inquire about statements by Syrian and Egyptian officials concerning the USSR's readiness to sell arms to their countries, the Soviet Foreign Ministry replied that it was authorized to say that the statements were devoid of any foundation and were nothing but fantasies.

September 22

Israel apologized for having seized the UN headquarters building in al-Auja but refused to withdraw from the demilitarized zone until Egypt had given up its two nearby outposts.

The UN General Assembly's Steering Committee defeated the motion of 15 Asian and African nations that the Algerian situation be included on the Assembly's agenda.

September, 1955

September 22

Oil was struck in Israel at Helez at a depth of 4,906 feet. The quality of the oil was about the same as that of Iraq and Kuwait.

Three Moroccans were killed and four persons wounded during demonstrations in several cities in Morocco.

September 23

The Pakistani Government acceded to the Baghdad Pact between Turkey and Iraq, to which Britain had also adhered.

The Jordanian Government decided to nationalize the British Telegraphs and Wireless Company and entered into negotiations to buy the firm's equipment.

The French Ministry of Defense recalled Pierre Montel, pro-colon chairman of the National Assembly's defense committee, who had been in Morocco inspecting defense arrangements.

September 24

Arab infiltrators killed three passengers on a bus eight miles south of the Lebanese border, according to an Israel announcement.

The new Syrian Cabinet of Said al-Ghazzi was given parliamentary approval by a vote of 88-33. The opposition was made up of the Socialist Renaissance Party, the National Party and a number of independents.

The Egyptian Government reportedly abolished, as of January 1, 1956, the entire system of Sharia and non-Moslem religious courts.

September 25

Prime Minister Designate Ben-Gurion declared that Israel would open the Gulf of Aqaba to its use within a year even if force were needed.

September, 1955

September 25

It was reported in Washington that the State Department sent a message to Cairo that the US was willing to sell weapons to Egypt on credit. This was considered a move to dissuade Egypt from buying arms from the Soviet Union.

The Libyan Government announced that it had agreed to establish diplomatic relations with the USSR.

French Premier Faure stated in a radio speech that France intended to keep Algeria as an integral part of France.

French troops and planes began a major offensive against Algerian terrorists on the edge of the Sahara, southeast of the Aures Mountains.

September 26

Moslem representatives in the French National Assembly and in the Algerian Assembly announced plans to oppose French Premier Faure's program for further integration between France and Algeria.

New violence broke out in various towns in Morocco in protest against the delay in the implementation of the French plan.

In a note to France, Spain stated that it should have equal rights with France in arranging any major change in the status of Morocco.

A US State Department spokesman told the press that the Government had "agreed in principle" to sell quantities of arms to Egypt, but that no definite arrangements had yet been made. Whatever might go to Egypt in the future would be in small quantities to avoid encouraging aggression against Israel.

US Secretary of State John Foster Dulles discussed with UK Foreign Secretary Harold Macmillan the question of supplying arms to Egypt, in the light of the US decision to sell arms to Egypt and the confirmation that specific items were being considered.

Turkish President Celal Bayar asked Iran to join the Baghdad Pact.

September, 1955

September 26

King Hussein of Jordan arrived in Istanbul, Turkey.

Moroccan stores in Marrakech and Fez closed in response to a strike called by nationalist organizations.

September 27

The Alexandria Cotton Futures Market, closed for three years, resumed operation in Egypt.

UN Truce Headquarters in Jerusalem announced that both Israel and Egypt agreed to withdraw their forces from the al-Auja zone, but Israel's conditions necessitated postponement.

The Foreign Ministers of Great Britain, France and the US expressed grave concern about the arms pacts between Egypt, the Soviet Union and Czechoslovakia, and warned that a race to supply arms to the Middle East would inevitably increase tensions in the area.

The Czechoslovakian Government issued a statement which referred to an intensive campaign of pressure on Egypt to cancel its agreement with Czechoslovakia and said that the Government rejected all interference in normal relations between sovereign States and would strictly carry out the agreement.

Egypt announced an agreement with Czechoslovakia for the exchange of cotton in return for arms.

Algerian Governor General Jacques Soustelle cancelled the scheduled meeting of the Algerian Assembly after the Moslem members announced a boycott of the Assembly.

September 28

Prime Minister Moshe Sharett of Israel summoned US Ambassador Edward B. Lawson and requested clarification about reports that the US was ready to sell arms to Egypt.

The official Israel view about the report of Egypt's purchase of arms from Czechoslovakia was stated in Jerusalem to be that Israel must

September, 1955

September 28

object to the supply of arms to Arab countries from whatever source as long as those countries refused to make peace with Israel, and even asserted, as Egypt did, that a state of war still existed between them and Israel.

US Assistant Secretary of State George V. Allen flew to Cairo to discuss the Czechoslovakian-Egyptian arms agreement with Premier Nasser. The British Government officially protested to Egypt about the arms agreement.

Mahmoud Fawzi, the Egyptian Foreign Minister, issued a statement in New York saying that the question of arms for Egypt had a direct bearing on his country's security, sovereignty, and honor, and his Government would not accept "tutorship" by anyone.

September 29

As a measure to prevent border incidents, the Lebanese Army ordered everyone without a Lebanese passport to move at least six miles from the Israel border.

In a letter to the UN Security Council, the Israel delegation stressed that the Strait of Tiran, the entrance to the Gulf of Aqaba, was an international waterway and that Egypt's blockage was illegal.

By a vote of 28-27-5, the UN General Assembly voted to overrule its Steering Committee and add the Algerian problem to the agenda. French Foreign Minister Pinay stated that his Government would consider as null and void any recommendation which the Assembly might make in this connection.

September 30

Reports stated that Moroccan Sultan Sidi Muhammad Ben-Moulay Arafa had finally agreed to abdicate, but only under several conditions, the most important of which was that he be succeeded by a member of his family rather than a regency council.

September, 1955

September 30

Britain and Egypt announced an agreement to remove all of their troops from the Sudan by November 12.

The Saudi Arabian Ministry of Finance solicited bids for a Riyadh-Medina-Jedda railway.

October, 1955

October 1

The French Government issued its declaration of intentions for Morocco in which it was stated that Morocco should be given greater responsibility, although at the same time recognizing the permanence of the link between France and Morocco.

Sultan Sidi Muhammad Ben-Arafa left Rabat for the International Zone of Tangier "without in any way renouncing our rights" to the throne. He left the "affairs of the crown" in the hands of his distant cousin, Moulay Abdallah Ben-Moulay Abd-al-Hafid.

Moroccan nationalist leaders indicated that they would not participate in any government under Sultan Ben-Moulay Ben-Arafa's cousin, Moulay Abdallah Ben-Moulay Abd-al-Hafid.

The French Government, bitter because the UN General Assembly approved debate on the Algerian issue, ordered the withdrawal of its Assembly delegation. The boycott did not extend to the Security Council or to the sub-commission on disarmament.

The Council of the Arab League met in Cairo and sent congratulations to Egyptian Premier Gamal Abdel Nasser on his arms deal with Czechoslovakia. It also discussed general political matters, Oman's membership application, the condition of Palestinians in Cyprus, the establishment of a League aviation council and other matters.

George V. Allen, US Assistant Secretary of State for Near Eastern, South Asian and African Affairs, discussed the Egyptian arms situation with Egyptian Premier Gamal Abdel Nasser in Cairo for two hours. Premier Nasser also conferred with the British, French and Soviet Ambassadors.

Commenting on the Egyptian-Czechoslovakian arms agreement, the Soviet Government said that it held the view that every state had the legitimate right to provide for its own defense and to purchase arms for its defense needs from other states at usual commercial terms.

Prime Minister Nehru of India announced in Parliament that Egypt had been asked to look after Indian interests in Portugal. He spoke of increased Egyptian-Indian cooperation and commended Egypt for its policy of nonalignment with "Big Power Blocs."

October 2

The Moroccan Government issued a statement defining the principles of French policy in Morocco.

Moroccan Nationalist attacks and demonstrations broke out in a number of cities, especially strong and organized in the north near the border of Spanish Morocco. French troops were immediately sent into action near Fez.

French Minister of the Interior Maurice Bourges-Maunoury told the French National Assembly that a series of reform measures would have to be passed immediately as a first step toward meeting nationalist demands in Algeria, and that the rest would have to come within 30 days. He indicated that the whole conception of French administration of the area would have to be revised.

Israel Ambassador Abba Eban said in Washington that if the balance of power in the Middle East was being disturbed, then the United States should sell arms, but not to Egypt, to Israel. Egypt, he stated, had only one objective internationally, that being to harass, besiege and if possible destroy a neighboring state. To give arms to Egypt was to condone this, he added.

Egyptian Premier Nasser said in Cairo that he intercepted British and French documents which proved that the West had sold arms to Israel despite a British report that Israel was probably more aggressive than Egypt. He charged the West with deceit when it declared that a supply of arms to Egypt would disturb the balance of power in the Middle East, while at the same time it continued to sell arms to Israel.

The USSR news agency Tass published a statement on the attitude of the USSR Government to the increasing pressure exerted on certain Mideast countries, e.g., Egypt, to compel them to buy arms for their defense only from Western countries and on the latters' conditions.

Under the supervision of UN observers, Israel and Egypt withdrew their military forces from the al-Auja demilitarized zone.

October 3

French representatives in the Moroccan Council of Government sent a telegram to the President of the Republic saying that the French Resident General, Boyer de Latour, had assured them there would be no Council of the Throne but merely a delegation of the seal to a single person approved by Moulay Ben-Arafa. The telegram complained that the creation of a Council of the Throne was again being imposed by the French Government, and it asked the President to intervene to ensure that the Resident General's promises would be kept.

The French Government ordered Resident General Boyer de Latour in Morocco to follow its instructions in arranging for a regency council to replace the Sultan. The Government also provided him with five more battalions to fight the recent uprising in northern Morocco.

Attacks against French posts in Morocco by tribes from the Atlas Mountains, the most serious such incidents in recent days, were brought under control by French troops.

A proclamation was signed by Allal al-Fassi, exiled President of the Istiqlal Party, announcing the unification under a single command of armed resistance movements in Algeria and Morocco which would, in the future, be known as the "Army for the Liberation of North Africa from the Foreign Invader." It said the new force had its headquarters inside North Africa and went into action for the first time on October 1.

The Premiers of Syria, Lebanon and Jordan met in Damascus to discuss recent developments in the Arab world, among which were the amendments to the Johnston plan for the development of the Jordan River, the Dulles proposal for settling the Middle East question, and the Egyptian agreement with Czechoslovakia for the purchase of arms.

Nikita Khrushchev, First Secretary of the Communist Party, in an interview published in Pravda, said that Russia's attitude to the North African question was one of sympathy and moral support for the strivings of people for national liberation. The question could be solved if the legitimate rights and interests of the people of the French Union were taken into account. Russia did not intend to interfere with French internal affairs and the Soviet Government believed a correct decision could be found.

October 4

US Secretary of State Dulles told Russia's Foreign Minister, Vyacheslav Molotov, that delivery of arms from the Soviet Bloc to Egypt would not help relax tensions between the US and the Soviet Union.

The Israel Charge d'Affaires in Prague told the Czechoslovakian Government that Israel would regard deliveries of arms to Egypt as an unfriendly act.

Israel warned that if the Arab States rejected the Johnston Jordan River Development Plan it would regard itself free to resume work on its national water scheme such as the hydroelectric project north of the Sea of Galilee.

Sir Alexander Knox-Helm, Governor General of the Sudan, issued a decree dissolving the Sudanization Committee.

October 5

It was reported in Washington that the US, Great Britain and France were devoting all their diplomatic efforts to blocking the Soviet arms deal with Egypt.

Egyptian Premier Gamal Abdel Nasser said that he informed Washington in June that Egypt would buy arms from the Soviet Union if the US would not supply them.

George Allen, US Assistant Secretary of State, transmitted an offer of American arms to the Lebanese Government under the conditions that they would not be used for aggressive purposes and that an American mission would be sent to train the Lebanese in their use. Rashid Karami, Prime Minister, welcomed the offer provided it was accompanied by the minimum of conditions.

October 5

French Resident General General Boyer de Latour issued a statement saying that to avoid erroneous interpretations he wished to define publicly the aim of his policy which was that of the French Government. The return of the ex-Sultan Muhammad Ben-Youssef being exluded, his policy was to form a Moroccan Government representing the different tendencies of opinion, to build with this Government a new Morocco, to find an acceptable solution to the problem of the throne, and to take into account the realities of the country which must not be plunged into civil war.

The French Government demanded that Spain take action to stop guerrillas in Spanish Morocco from entering the French Zone.

October 6

French Premier Edgar Faure dismissed four members of his Cabinet because they disagreed with his policy of conciliation toward the Moroccan nationalists.

The Syrian Parliament approved a declaration supporting Egypt's arms deal with Czechoslovakia.

It was announced that the Egyptian Government had signed a preliminary agreement with a British firm to act as consulting engineers for the Aswan High Dam project.

A trade agreement with a Polish trade mission was initialed in Damascus. It provided for an exchange of Polish heavy industrial machinery for Syrian cotton, wool, yarn and olive oil.

October 7

It was reported from Beirut that Lebanese Premier Rashid Karami conferred with the Czechoslovakian Minister on the possibility of exchanging Lebanese citrus products for arms.

Foreign Minister Amir Faisal of Saudi Arabia confirmed reports that the Soviet Union had offered his country arms.

October, 1955

October 7

According to a statement by the British Foreign Ministry, the Spanish High Commissioner in Tetuan had assured the French Resident General in Rabat that any armed forces penetrating the Spanish Zone would be disarmed and interned and there would be an increased watch to prevent clandestine crossings of the frontier.

French Premier Edgar Faure sent General Pierre Billotte, newly appointed French Defense Minister, to Morocco in an effort to speed the application of the projected reforms.

The Moroccan Istiqlal Party proposed that it act as intermediary between French troops and guerrilla bands in the Rif Mountains if it were given "a political basis to work from."

Saudi Arabia described as "fantastic" British charges that it offered bribes totaling $100 million to gain control over the oil rich Buraimi Oasis.

Of the 480 French reservists who were called for active duty in North Africa, 200 refused to leave the barracks in Rouen, France, and were supported by local Communists.

October 8

British Prime Minister Sir Anthony Eden warned the Soviet Union that it was increasing the danger of war in the Middle East by permitting Czechoslovakia to supply arms to Egypt.

French Premier Faure pleaded with the National Assembly to accept his program of conciliation in Morocco. His personal representative to Morocco, Francois de Panafleu, resigned because of despair over the outlook for a Moroccan settlement.

Lieutenant General Rafail Garcia Valino, High Commissioner for Spanish Morocco, said that he had strengthened patrols along the French Moroccan border in order to prevent aid from being given to rebel forces in the French Zone.

From Cairo Muhammad al-Fassi pledged a Maghreb Liberation Army of Moroccan and Algerian freedom fighters under the command of

October, 1955

October 10

Israel charged that Egypt was maintaining military posts on the Sinai Peninsula which were larger than those permitted under the 1949 Armistice Agreement.

French colonists in the major towns in Morocco staged a 24 hour strike against French Premier Faure's reform policy for Morocco.

Daniel A. Solod, Soviet Ambassador to Egypt, made public the decision of his Government to offer technical assistance to underdeveloped Arab and Asian countries.

October 11

The Israel Ambassador in Washington, Abba Eban, told US Assistant Secretary of State George V. Allen that his Government held that the US, Britain and France were committed under the joint 1950 Declaration to maintain the balance of power between Israel and Arab States. This meant the US would have to supply arms to Israel to equal the arms shipment from Czechoslovakia to Egypt.

Egyptian Deputy Foreign Minister Ahmad Khairat Said informed US representative Eric Johnston in Cairo that the Arab League's Political Committee decided to defer a final decision on the US sponsored Jordan Valley Development Plan. It was reported in Cairo that the Arabs had produced a modified version of the original American Plan. The new plan, which would exclude Israel, would cost about $200 million.

Iran announced that it would join the Baghdad Pact, a defense alliance between Iraq, Turkey, Britain and Pakistan.

The Lebanese Cabinet empowered Premier Rashid Karami to enter into negotiations with the Syrian Government for the reorganization of economic relations between the two countries and for the harmonization of their attitudes toward the oil companies whose pipelines crossed their territories.

October, 1955

October 8

Ben-Bella. This force, he claimed, would place Muhammad V on his rightful throne in Morocco.

One hundred fifty experts on agriculture, representing thirteen Middle Eastern countries, opened a three day conference at Salah Eddin in Iraq.

The British Foreign Office issued a statement saying that the "official French document (referred to by Egyptian Prime Minister Colonel Nasser on October 2 to support his charges of British sales of arms to Israel) was in fact an unofficial newsletter published in Paris on May 20. The statement added that "nearly all the figures quoted were inaccurate and were grossly exaggerated."

October 9

Salim Lahoud, Lebanese Foreign Minister, in a statement in Cairo on the Johnston plan for the use of the Jordan waters, said that Lebanon was not prepared to accept any scheme which even by implication meant recognition of Israel as a state.

It was reported from Cairo that Moslem extremists began a campaign to defeat the American plan for integrated development of the Jordan River for the benefit of both the Arab States and Israel.

The Foreign Ministers of the Arab League countries met in Cairo.

French Premier Edgar Faure by a vote of 477-140 won approval in the National Assembly of his reform plan for Morocco. This plan included the abdication of Sultan Sidi Muhammad Ben-Moulay Ben-Arafa, the formation of a three man regency council, and the establishment of a representative government to negotiate with France on detailed reforms.

The exiled Grand Mufti of Jerusalem, Hajj Amin al-Husseini, announced his complete opposition to the Jordan River development plans being put forth by US Ambassador Eric Johnston.

October, 1955

October 12

The announcement of Iran's decision to adhere to the Baghdad Pact brought a Soviet protest that such action contradicted the friendly relations of Iran and the Soviet Union. Iran replied that the Pact membership was only a means for legitimate defense.

In a formal statement, the US State Department welcomed the Iranian decision to adhere to the Baghdad Pact and declared that this decision was in no way hostile or threatening or directed against any other nation. The statement analyzed the objective of the alliance and the pertinent provisions of the 1921 Soviet-Irano Treaty and found no contradictions or clashes.

The US State Department said that it had indications that the Soviet Bloc might be willing to supply arms to Israel as well as to the Arab States. An Israel Embassy spokesman said that no Communist state had made any formal approach to Israel, but that if one were made, he was convinced his country would turn it down. He said that Israel was definitely opposed to the basic intention of such offers, which were to promote an arms race.

An extraordinary meeting of the Israel Knesset opened at the request of the opposition parties to discuss Israel's defense position in view of the Communist sale of arms to Egypt.

US Representative Eric Johnston flew from Cairo to Jerusalem after failing to dissuade Arab leaders from deferring action on the Jordan River Development Plan.

Salah Ben-Youssef was removed from his post and expelled from the Tunisian Neo-Destour Party for opposition to the Franco-Tunisian agreement of June 2, 1955, and for party splitting activities.

The French Cabinet proposed several immediate reforms for Algeria and promised a complete review in the near future of the 1947 statute bringing Algeria into the French Union. The immediate reforms would include a greater degree of local autonomy, redistribution to small owners of land then being insufficiently used, separation of Moslem religious activities from state control, and increased school instruction in Arabic.

October, 1955

October 13

French Premier Edgar Faure opened a major parliamentary debate on Algeria. In discussing his program for Algeria, he listed the immediate reforms which had been announced on October 12, emphasized the need to steer a middle course between assimilation and separation for Algeria, and promised free, democratic elections to provide a basis for future reforms. He then asked Parliament to approve a four point, middle of the road reform plan for Algeria. He said its passage would justify France's refusal to accept United Nations interference there.

Jordan announced, with the approval of Egypt, that new regulations would require four days prior notice for ships entering the port of Aqaba.

Fifteen Democratic Congressmen from the US called on the administration to ship jet planes and tanks to Israel to balance the arms Egypt was getting from Czechoslovakia. They also urged the US to embark immediately on establishing a security pact with Israel guaranteeing the integrity of its borders and those of its Arab neighbors.

Wing Commander Hassan Ibrahim, Egyptian Minister of Production, said in Cairo that the Soviet Union made an offer directly to Premier Gamal Abdel Nasser to help finance the projected Aswan High Dam.

The Egyptian Commerce Ministry announced that it concluded a deal to import $5,600,000 worth of iron from Communist China.

The Foreign Ministers of Jordan, Syria, Lebanon and Egypt met as a subcommittee of the full Foreign Ministers committee. They announced that they had studied the Jordan River development proposal of US Special Envoy Eric Johnston and had decided that the plans required further work and for this purpose had returned them to a committee of technicians.

Following talks between Israel Ministers and US Special Envoy Eric Johnston, a statement was issued saying that Johnston had informed the Israel representatives that the differences between the Arab States and Israel on the technical aspects of the Jordan waters project were so small as to be, in his view, insignificant, and he was confident that they could be resolved.

October, 1955

October 14

The Prime Ministers and Foreign Ministers of the Arab League countries, meeting in Cairo as the political committee, decided to support self determination rights for Algeria and to continue support for Tunisia until it achieved "its national aspirations." It issued a statement which condemned France's "repressive" policy in Algeria and said that NATO help was threatening peace in the area.

The French National Assembly failed to approve Premier Edgar Faure's Algerian policy; he was forced to present the issue for a vote of confidence.

The New China News Agency announced the ratification of a trade agreement with Egypt, signed on August 22, under which the trade would be balanced and payments made in transferrable sterling if no other currency were suitable.

It was reported from Washington that the US and Great Britain cautioned Israel, in connection with the Aqaba Straits, against any thought of preventive war against Egypt. They also urged Israel to refrain from proceeding with its plans for the Jordan River waters, even though the Arab States rejected the Johnston Joint Arab-Israel Development Plan.

The Israel Embassy in Washington issued a statement saying that accounts appearing in certain newspapers describing alleged representations by the US to Israel bore no resemblance to conversations in Washington between Israel representatives and the Department of State. Some of the subjects, Israel's Jordan River project and the question of the Aqaba Straits, did not even figure in the State Department conversations.

October 15

The Moroccan Istiqlal Party council issued a statement alleging that their good faith had been abused in regard to the composition of the council and that the proclamation represented the Council as holding the throne on behalf of Sidi Muhammad Ben-Moulay Ben-Arafa whom the Moroccan people had never recognized as having any right to it.

The Grand Vizier of Morocco, Hajj Muhammad al-Mokri, declared the throne to be vacant and announced that the Council of the Throne

October, 1955

October 15

would act in the place of the Sultan. The French Government announced the following four members of the Council: the Grand Vizier; Si Bekkai Ould M'Barek, former Pasha of Sefrou; Si Tahar Ouassou, a Berber chieftain; and Hajj Muhammad Sbihi, Pasha of Sale.

The Director of UNRWA issued a special report on claimants for relief not on UNRWA rolls, particularly children and needy inhabitants along the demarcation lines.

The Spanish Government sent a note to the French Government which stated that unless French accusations of Spanish responsibility for the disturbances in Morocco ceased, Spain would lay the matter before the UN and would also offer the UN facilities for investigating the allegations.

The Arab League Council of Foreign Ministers announced the adoption of several resolutions during its Cairo meeting. An Arab League flag was approved and arrangements were completed for the establishment of information offices in Latin America and the Far East. Various resolutions relating to Palestinian refugees and a unified passport for all Arab States were postponed until the next session of the Council.

October 16

General Boyer de Latour, French Resident General in Morocco, issued a statement saying that it was "notorious" that the dissident tribes had been afforded aid and comfort from the Spanish Zone. The French authorities in Morocco had great difficulty in establishing contact with the Spanish authorities.

The French Residency General in Morocco charged that French troops had been fired upon from the Spanish Zone of Morocco.

October, 1955

October 16

The press published statements made by Colonel Nasser, Egyptian Prime Minister, to an American journalist, in which he had said that the US was under the domination of strong Zionist organizations and was therefore being led to support Israel against the Arabs.

October 17

Following a meeting in Cairo between the Russian Ambassador to Egypt and Qadi Muhammad al-Emary, Acting Foreign Minister of Yemen, it was announced that Russia and Yemen had agreed to exchange diplomatic representatives. They had also agreed to renew the Russo-Yemen Treaty of Friendship of 1927 which was allowed to lapse in 1954, and to strengthen trade and economic relations.

The Truce Supervision Organization in Jerusalem asked UN Secretary General Dag Hammarskjold to take diplomatic action with the Egyptian delegation in connection with an attack on UN personnel. This referred to an attack on UN observers from across the border in the al-Auja area.

Syrian guns opened fire on an Israel police launch in the Sea of Galilee.

The Moroccan Council of the Throne was installed in Rabat. A proclamation declared that its first task would be to form a Moroccan Government representative of all the tendencies of Moroccan opinion. The task of the Government would be to manage public affairs and to seek, with the French Government, a new definition of the permanent links that united the two countries. The proclamation added that the Council recognized that the French population in Morocco, which by its works and activities had brought much to the country, would have to be protected and have its rights and legitimate interests guaranteed.

French Foreign Minister Pinay handed a note the Spanish Ambassador rejecting the Spanish note which had denied the French allegations of Spanish aid to Moroccan rebels.

The Arab League refused to reply to a British note in which it was claimed that Oman, which had applied for League membership, was

October, 1955

October 17

not independent and thus not a potential member. The note had stated that Oman was under the jurisdiction of the Sultanate of Muscat.

October 18

The Faure Government of France won a 308-254 vote of confidence in the National Assembly on its moderate reforms for Algeria. With the Government staking its existence on this vote, the Deputies decided not to initiate a government crisis on the eve of the Geneva Conference.

French Premier Edgar Faure stated that four immediate steps were envisioned for Algeria: the complete application of the Algerian Statute of 1947, the application of the Soustelle program of agrarian and administrative reform, the application of the Maspetiol Plan involving an investment program of 150 million francs, and the establishment of the necessary machinery to guarantee free elections.

Henry R. Labouisse, Director of UN Relief and Works Agency for Palestine Refugees, in his annual report to the General Assembly, implied that many of the refugees would give up their idea of returning if they recognized that their old homes were gone and that conditions had changed drastically since 1948.

Moshe Sharett, Prime Minister and Foreign Minister of Israel, opened a debate on foreign affairs in the Knesset. He claimed that the arms agreement between Egypt and Czechoslovakia implied a political and military bond between Egypt and the entire Soviet Bloc, and said it had created a situation liable to bring about a revolutionary and ominous change in Israel's security. Israel wanted a security pact with the US and considered that it was entitled to it. Sharett pointed out that neither Russia nor Egypt had even pretended that the arms were not to be used against Israel, and he asked what relation such Russian policy bore to its avowed intention of lessening tension. He also strongly criticized the Western Powers for supplying arms to "Israel's enemies."

The Egyptian Government announced that it sent out invitations to the seven countries selected by the Sudanese Parliament to sit on

October, 1955

October 21

The Moroccan Istiqlal Executive Committee issued a statement announcing that it would not support the Council of the Throne which it claimed to be inconsistent with the agreements reached at the Aix-les-Bains conference. It also complained that the exiled Sultan had not yet been transferred to France where he could better appreciate the situation. The Committee was critical of the French Government statement of policy, saying that it was inadequate because it was based on the 1912 protectorate treaty which was incompatible with the exercise of Moroccan sovereignty and the realization of Moroccan independence "in the framework of relationships of interdependence freely negotiated."

Syrian Prime Minister Said al-Ghazzi flew to Egypt, presumably to discuss the newly signed Egyptian-Syrian defense pact.

October 22

The Syrian Government said that its military pact with Egypt was the most bold official step ever taken toward achieving Arab unity on a practical, legal and correct basis.

Four Soviet ships loaded with arms for Egypt arrived in Alexandria. A fifth, an Egyptian freighter, had arrived previously.

Israel Prime Minister Moshe Sharett left for Geneva to warn the Big Four Foreign Ministers of the "danger which looms over Israel" as a result of the Czechoslovak-Egyptian arms deal.

The British Foreign Office issued a statement saying that it could not welcome the Egyptian-Syrian defense agreement since it was conceived in hostility to the Baghdad Pact to which Britain had adhered.

British Ambassador to Egypt, Sir Humphrey Trevelyan, called on the Egyptian Minister of the Interior to protest against the Egyptian invitations to the International Commission on Sudan. He urged that Egypt should take into account a proposal made by the Sudanese Prime Minister Ismail al-Azhari, in a statement on October 18, that

October, 1955

October 18

the international commission which would supervise the self determination of the Sudan. Terms of reference for the commission were attached to the invitations. It then informed the British Embassy in Cairo of the invitations and asked the British Government to send out similar invitations.

October 19

Premier Moshe Sharett of Israel accused the Soviet Union of creating the danger of a Middle East war but rejected the idea of a preventive war against Egypt.

The Iranian Senate ratified, 38-4, the bill authorizing the Government to join the Baghdad Pact.

Egyptian Premier Nasser accepted an invitation to visit Poland.

Saudi Arabian Foreign Minister Amir Faisal said in Cairo that the Soviet Ambassador to Iran informed King Saud that the Soviet Union wished to exchange diplomatic missions.

The Egyptian Government informed the British Embassy that it had sent invitations to the seven Powers to be represented on the international commission to supervise the process of self determination in the Sudan. It had also sent terms of reference for the commission.

October 20

Syria and Egypt signed a military agreement providing for a unified command for their armies. Under its terms, a joint defense council would be formed composed of the Prime Ministers and Ministers of Defense and Foreign Affairs of the member countries. Each country would regard an attack on the other as an attack on both.

The first shipment of Czechoslovakian arms to Egypt arrived at Alexandria on board a Soviet vessel.

It was reported in Washington that the US was ready to contribute substantially to the financing of the Aswan High Dam in Egypt.

October, 1955

October 22

the procedure of a plebiscite for self determination should be abandoned in favor of a vote in the existing Parliament.

Two experts from the International Bank arrived in Cairo to continue discussions regarding a loan for the construction of the High Dam at Aswan.

In Morocco, Si Bekkai published a telegram from ex-Sultan Ben-Youssef approving the Council of the Throne as constituted and urging the political parties to accept it.

Moroccan Premier Designate Ben-Slimane accepted the regency council's invitation to form a government. He said that his major aim would be to work out a new relationship between France and Morocco so that Morocco could exercise its full sovereignty while still guaranteeing the legitimate interests of France.

The Democratic Independent Party of Morocco announced its approval of the new regency council. The Presence Francaise joined the Istiqlal Party in saying that the council was illegal, although giving different reasons for the illegality.

French troops continued heavy action against nationalists on the Algerian-Tunisian border.

It was reported in Washington that the State Department had received assurances that Israel would delay its plan to divert waters from the Jordan River at least until the end of the rainy season.

October 23

Israel sent a letter to the UN Security Council accusing Syria of repeated attacks against Israel citizens and property.

The Soviet Union categorically denied that any member of the Soviet Bloc intended to deliver arms to Israel.

British Foreign Secretary Harold Macmillan said in London that when the four Foreign Ministers met in Geneva the question of the Soviet

October, 1955

October 23

diplomatic offensive in the Middle East would be raised with Vyacheslav Molotov by the three Western ministers.

Pakistan formally joined the Baghdad Pact.

The Iranian Majlis approved the bill providing for the adherence of Iran to the Baghdad Pact.

October 24

A resolution in the Knesset expressed anxiety over the arming of Egypt and Iraq and called on the "powers" to aid Israel with arms. It was approved by an 84-5 vote, all parties backing the motion except the Communists.

A letter was received from the Saudi Arabian delegation to the UN drawing the attention of the UN to the Buraimi Oasis dispute, and reserving the right to call a meeting of the Security Council to discuss it.

October 25

In Morocco the powerful Pasha of Marrakech, Thami Glaoui, joined nationalist factions demanding the return of former Sultan Muhammad Ben-Youssef, then in exile.

It was reported in Washington that Egypt's arms deal with the Communist Bloc totaled about $80 million, with the price of the weapons one-tenth to one-fifth of what Western countries would have charged. Egypt supposedly contracted to buy 200 Soviet MIG jet fighters, 100 Russian tanks, a half dozen submarines and a sizeable number of artillery pieces. The Egyptians were charged $50,000 for a MIG fighter and $1,500,000 for a submarine, prices which were reported to be an unprecedented low.

The Egyptian Public Services Council authorized the purchase from China of 60,000 tons of steel worth LE2.5 million, in return for Egyptian cotton and rice.

October, 1955

October 26

In a statement to the UN on the Buraimi Oasis dispute with the UK, the Saudi Arabian Delegate to the UN stated that he deplored the "arbitrary" resort to force against the Saudi Arabian oasis, recalling the Saudi Arabian proposal for a plebiscite in the area, and accusing Britain of deliberately sabotaging the efforts of the arbitration tribunal in order to force the issue to an armed conflict.

Saudi Arabian troops were forced out of the Buraimi Oasis and other areas to the west by British led Arab levies from the Trucial Coast. In announcing the action, British Prime Minister Anthony Eden said that a fair boundary would be the "1952 line," but that Britain was willing to uphold a line which was more "favorable to Saudi Arabia."

The Buraimi Oasis was occupied by the Sultan of Muscat and the Ruler of Abu Dhabi, who expelled the Saudi Arabian police detachment located there.

Lincoln White, press officer in the State Department in Washington, said that the US received "further information" on Communist approaches to Israel in the matter of supplying arms. This was denied by the Israel Embassy.

Israel Prime Minister Moshe Sharett flew to Paris for conferences with US Secretary of State Dulles and British Foreign Secretary Macmillan on the possibility of arms aid for Israel.

UN Truce Supervisor of the Mixed Armistice Commission, General Burns arrived in New York to report to UN Secretary General Hammarskjold.

The French Government's position in Morocco worsened as Moroccan religious leaders joined the nationalists in urging the return of former Sultan Muhammad Ben-Youssef.

October 27

Egyptian Prime Minister Gamal Abdel Nasser and Crown Prince Amir Faisal, Prime Minister of Saudi Arabia, signed a five year defensive alliance in Cairo.

October, 1955

October 27

Premier Nasser said that Egypt's mutual defense pact with Saudi Arabia was a powerful factor for the liberation of the Arab nation and its advance on the road to full independence free from foreign domination and foreign guardianship.

On his arrival in Geneva, Israel's Prime Minister Moshe Sharett said that he hoped his country would not be driven to a preventive war against the Arab States.

Saudi Arabian Amir Faisal described the occupation of the Buraimi Oasis by British officered forces as a "ghastly armed aggression." He declared that his Government would take all possible measures to safeguard the interests of Saudi Arabia and its nationals in Buraimi.

The British Foreign Office disclosed that 25 Saudi Arabian troops were taken prisoner during the Buraimi occupation.

The Iraqi Finance Minister announced an agreement with Britain under which Iraq would be allowed to buy five million pounds sterling worth of gold from Britain, and dates from Iraq would be imported duty free into the UK in return for the lifting of certain duties by Iraq. Britain also agreed to provide, when necessary, $2 million to cover Iraq's obligation to the International Monetary Fund, and to an increase in the Iraqi-dollar working balance.

By a vote of 53-0, the Political and Security Committee of the UN favored a resolution endorsing progress made toward the establishment of an international Atoms for Peace Agency. Six Arab States abstained but the Soviet Bloc supported the measure despite defeat of its proposed amendments.

October 28

Demonstrations demanding the return of former Moroccan Sultan Ben-Youssef took place in several cities in Morocco. Three persons were killed and 19 wounded in Oujda.

The Syrian Government sent a letter to the UN Security Council saying that "aggressive acts" by Israel against Syria had increased

October, 1955

October 28

during October. Six acts of aggression were listed as constituting conclusive proof of Israel's warlike intentions.

A frontier clash between Turkish and Syrian soldiers was reported. Syria later charged that the shooting began at Kitaca, where a Turkish patrol allegedly penetrated more than 300 yards into Syria.

An Egyptian communique in Cairo declared that the Egyptian attack at al-Auja was directed against regular Israel Army troops, not police.

October 29

Egypt informed Britain of its approval of the principle of a plebiscite in the Sudan to choose between full independence and a link with Egypt. This indicated that Egypt had given up hope of influencing the self determination choice and was prepared to accept the complete independence of the Sudan.

The Saudi Arabian Government protested to Britain against the reoccupation of the disputed Buraimi Oasis.

British Foreign Secretary Macmillan warned Soviet Foreign Minister Molotov at Geneva that the flow of arms from Communist centers to Egypt threatened the peace of the Middle East.

The Egyptian Government signed a contract with a British firm of consulting engineers for the construction of a High Dam at Aswan.

The Israel Foreign Ministry charged that the Egyptian Command apparently decided to extend the front. It warned that if Egyptian troops continued to occupy Israel territory in the al-Auja zone responsibility for continuation of the present tense situation would rest entirely with Egypt.

Major General E. L. M. Burns, Head of the UN Truce Supervision Organization, addressed identical notes to Egypt and Israel. He called to the attention of both parties the grave moral responsibility that would be borne by the party which took offensive action of any kind, which in this situation would result in the gravest consequences.

October, 1955

October 29

He was authorized by the UN Secretary General to state that he had seen the letter and that the demarche was made also on his behalf.

Egypt raided the Israel settlement at Nir Am, northwest of al-Auja near the Gaza Strip.

October 30

Saudi Arabia called for an emergency meeting of the Arab League Political Committee to discuss the occupation of Buraimi on October 26, 1955.

In a letter to the UN Security Council, Britain charged that Saudi Arabia invaded the border area of the Buraimi Oasis and that the inhabitants of the area were subjected to bribery and intimidation.

Edwin W. Pauley, a US oil developer, signed a 55 year agreement with the Government of Jordan under which Pauley would be granted eight months to explore the country and then select an area one-third the size of the entire country for intensive oil explorations. In the event that oil should be discovered, profits would be divided on a 50-50 basis.

Sultan Muhammad Ben-Arafa abdicated the Moroccan throne. The French Government acknowledged for the first time that former Sultan Muhammad Ben-Youssef, exiled since 1953, would return to the throne.

US Secretary of State Dulles conferred in Geneva with Soviet Foreign Minister Molotov and Israel's Prime Minister, Moshe Sharett. He protested to the former the arms shipment from Czechoslovakia to Egypt which might have led to new warfare between the Arab countries and Israel, and he told the latter that the US would consider sending a certain amount of arms to Israel.

The Israel Government announced that it had been informed by the UN Truce Supervisory Organization that its requests to Egypt to withdraw its troops from the position they occupied in the al-Auja zone had met with no response. Egyptian troops were still entrenched in Israel territory, holding a line in depth throughout the southern part of the zone.

October, 1955

October 30

Egypt informed the Sudan and Britain that it approved of the Sudanese suggestion of August 29, 1955, to hold a national plebiscite as the means of self determination.

October 31

Israel Prime Minister Moshe Sharett conferred with the Soviet Foreign Minister in Geneva, and appealed to him not to ignite a war in the Middle East by arming the Arabs.

It was reported from Geneva that Israel was informed by a Soviet satellite Government that in the event of war Egypt would not honor its treaty obligation to readmit Britain to the Suez Canal base.

An Egyptian Government spokesman in Cairo characterized as "malicious nonsense" a report that Egypt promised the Soviet Union that it would not honor its treaty obligation to re-admit Britain to the Suez Canal Zone in the event of war.

The British Minister of State for Foreign Affairs stated that Britain, wishing to guarantee a settlement in the area rather than guarantee the existing unsettled state of affairs, did not consider it the right moment to give a guarantee of Israel's borders.

Said al-Ghazzi, Prime Minister of Syria, arrived in Jordan and held discussions with the Jordanian Prime Minister and the Cabinet. A joint statement issued afterwards said that the policy of both Governments was based on the consideration that the armistice demarcation line was one Arab defensive line and that any aggression on any part of that line would be considered aggression of all of its parts.

UN Truce Supervisor General Burns said in New York that he thought some action was required by Britain, France and the US to deal with the current situation in Palestine.

A five year treaty of friendship between Russia and Yemen was signed at the Soviet Embassy in Cairo by the Soviet Ambassador and Abd-al-Rahman Abu-Taleb, Yemen Minister. The treaty provided, inter alia, for measures to promote trade and for the exchange of diplomatic representatives when necessary.

October, 1955

October 31

Former Moroccan Sultan Ben-Youssef landed in France after two years of exile at Madagascar and prepared to confer with French Foreign Minister Pinay about his return to the Moroccan throne.

November, 1955

November 1

Israel Prime Minister Moshe Sharett said on leaving Geneva that his trip to Europe to discuss the Middle East situation with the Big Four Foreign Ministers was definitely worthwhile. He declared that he left with the feeling that the views of the Israel Government and the gravity of the situation which faced the State had been fully and authoritatively presented in fairly lengthy conversations with the distinguished representatives of the major powers. On the question of security, Sharett declared that the future government would observe meticulously the Arab-Israel armistice agreements and would insist on similar observance by neighboring nations. He said that it would "take effective measures for protection of frontier settlements and danger areas and relief of tension along the borders."

US Secretary of State John Foster Dulles promised sympathetic consideration of an Israel arms list to be submitted to the State Department. He added that consideration would be limited to defensive weapons.

Israel protested to the UN Security Council against Egypt's invasion and continued occupation of the demilitarized al-Auja area.

Radio Mecca announced that the Saudi Arabian Government reserved all its rights in Buraimi and that it would not recognize any concessions which were granted or might be granted to any person, company or government unless such concessions were granted by itself. The Government further warned that it would not be responsible for loss of life or property suffered by unrecognized concessionaires.

The Syrian Cabinet approved a program that provided for free medical care, medicine and hospitalization for low income groups. Anyone with an income of less than $70 a month would be eligible.

November 2

A new Government of Israel was formed by David Ben-Gurion.

Israel Prime Minister Ben-Gurion, in a speech presenting his Cabinet to the Knesset, offered to meet with Arab leaders in an attempt to avert the threat of war. Egypt refused the invitation.

November, 1955

November 2

The Jordan Government summoned the ambassadors of Britain, France and the US and asked them to call on their governments to put an end to unilateral diversion of the waters of the Jordan River by Israel. A spokesman for the Israel Government cautioned the Western powers against supplying arms to Arab countries.

Turkey's President Celal Bayar arrived in Jordan on an official state visit.

Lord Reading, British Minister of State for Foreign Affairs, in a reply in the House of Lords to a question on the situation in southern Sudan, said the Government believed strongly that the future interests of the Sudan could only be served if the Sudan Government's authority was maintained and strengthened.

The acting Secretary General of the Arab League said no Arab leader with any pride would agree to meet with or talk to the Israel Prime Minister. He added that Israel must first carry out the UN resolutions on Palestine.

The Moroccan Istiqlal Party announced that it would not participate in any government formed by Fatmi Ben-Slimane.

The members of the Throne Council of Morocco offered their resignations to the former Sultan in a move to bring him back to the throne.

November 3

The Israel Army announced that it attacked and occupied a position established by Egypt inside the al-Auja demilitarized zone. An Israel Foreign Ministry spokesman said that the action was aimed at expulsion of Egyptian forces from Israel territory.

An Egyptian Army spokesman said that 70 Egyptians were killed or were missing in the al-Auja clash, and that 200 Israelis were killed.

Egyptian Premier Gamal Abdel Nasser said that Israel's attack on the Egyptians the previous day determined his answer to Prime Minister Ben-Gurion's invitation to discuss means of reaching a mutual settlement.

November, 1955

November 3

UN Secretary General Dag Hammarskjold made new proposals to Egypt and Israel aimed at restoring order in the al-Auja area. These proposals had the support of the US, Great Britain and France. The Secretary General also expressed grave concern to the Israel representative over the Israel Army's military action in the al-Auja area.

Egypt admitted that it had inevitably advanced some check posts into the al-Auja demilitarized zone several days before, but denied that this was sufficient reason for the Israel attack on al-Sabha, as claimed by the Israelis.

Britain protested the Israel military action at al-Sabha.

Iran's membership in the Baghdad Pact became official.

The Syrian Government announced that two clashes with Turkish soldiers occurred on the Syro-Turkish frontier.

November 4

Italy and Lebanon signed a trade agreement under which barter trade would take place up to a limit of LL8 million. The agreement also provided for Italian investment in and economic aid to Lebanon.

The British Government informed the Governor General of the Sudan that it accepted the proposal made by the Sudanese Parliament for a plebiscite and was issuing invitations to the Governments chosen to participate in the international commission to supervise the plebiscite.

A letter was received at the UN from the Syrian delegation saying that Syria would be obliged to exercise its legitimate right of self defense against any future Israel aggression.

November 5

Lebanese sources reported that Syrian troops had shot down an Israel plane. Egyptian-Israel exchange of fire continued both at the Gaza Strip and near al-Auja.

November, 1955

November 5

The Ambassadors of Egypt and Israel were called separately to the US State Department and informed by George V. Allen, Assistant Secretary of State, of the Government's deep concern at the rising tension between their two countries. A statement issued afterward said the US deplored the use of force for the settlement of disputes and strongly supported the UN proposals, especially those of General Burns, UNTSO Chief.

The French Cabinet officially recognized Muhammad Ben-Youssef's right to return to the Moroccan throne. The Cabinet also reaffirmed its earlier decision to make Morocco a modern, free and sovereign state within a framework of interdependence.

Britain announced that it was supplying Jordan with ten jet fighters as well as personnel to train Jordanian pilots.

The Arab League's Oil Committee opened a four day meeting in Cairo to discuss means of coordinating the oil policies of the member states, promoting the Arab oil industry and combatting the smuggling of Arab oil into Israel.

The Syrian Chamber of Deputies unanimously ratified the mutual defense pact with Egypt signed on October 20, 1955. Said al-Ghazzi, Syrian Prime Minister, said that the two armies had been established under joint command and would be able to repel any aggression by Israel.

November 6

Sidi Muhammad Ben-Youssef was reinstated as Sultan of Morocco.

Moroccan Sultan Ben-Youssef and French Foreign Minister Pinay issued a joint declaration that Morocco was to become a democratic state under a constitutional monarchy. The Sultan said that his new Government and France would conduct negotiations destined to make Morocco an independent state, united to France by permanent ties of an interdependence liberally defined and agreed to.

Israel claimed that Egypt was maintaining troops in prohibited numbers on the Egyptian side of the al-Auja zone. Under the armistice

November, 1955

November 6

agreement, Egypt was permitted to maintain only check posts in that area.

November 7

The US State Department declared that the US would agree to sell Israel a significant quantity of arms.

Britain agreed to the holding of a Sudanese national plebiscite.

British Foreign Secretary Macmillan, in a statement in Parliament, said that the situation in the Buraimi Oasis had been completely quiet and normal since the reoccupation of October 29, 1955.

November 8

Moroccan Sultan Ben-Youssef granted royal pardon to his once powerful opponent, Thami Glaoui, Pasha of Marrakech.

Speaking at the ceremony of exchanging the signed texts of the Syro-Egyptian Mutual Defense Pact, Egyptian Premier Gamal Abdel Nasser accused the US of pursuing a policy of promise and postponement toward the Arab world. This, he said, obliged him to obtain arms from the Soviet Bloc.

The newly created Egyptian-Syrian Defense Council selected Major General Abd-al-Hakim Amer, Commander of the Egyptian Army, as the first joint Commander of the armies of the two nations.

Fastin Rustu Zorlu, Turkish Foreign Minister, saw Lebanese President Camille Chamoun, the Prime Minister and the Foreign Minister and invited Lebanon to join the Baghdad Pact. He was told by the Prime Minister, Rashid Karami, that Lebanon was not anxious to join any pact which split the Arab States and that Lebanon's main interest was to unify the Arabs against the danger from Israel.

Turkey's President Celal Bayar returned from Jordan.

November 8

An Israel Foreign Ministry spokesman said in Jerusalem that Israel supported Secretary General Hammarskjold's proposals for a cease-fire in the al-Auja area in so far as they aimed at bringing about full compliance of the parties with the provisions of the general armistice agreement signed by both Egypt and Israel.

The Sudanese Government requested that Britain and Egypt allow the simultaneous holding of elections for a constituent assembly and the national self determination plebiscite.

November 9

The French Government named Andre Dubois, Paris Prefect of Police, as French Resident General in Morocco.

The head of the East German Foreign Trade Department announced in Cairo a new agreement with Egypt extending the barter agreement of 1953. He added that East Germany had offered Egypt economic and technical assistance in building the High Dam at Aswan.

Speaking at the Mansion House dinner in London, British Prime Minister Sir Anthony Eden made a long statement about Israel-Arab tension in the Middle East. He offered his own services and those of the British Government in settling the dispute.

The Egyptian Ambassador in Washington, Ahmad Hussein, warned the US against selling arms to Israel.

The UK received a further note from Saudi Arabia on the occupation by Trucial Oman levies of the Buraimi Oasis.

The Sudanese Council of Ministers despatched notes to the Egyptian and British Governments regarding the necessity of taking the opinion of the Sudanese Government into account before a final agreement about the terms of reference of the International Commission to supervise Sudanese self determination.

A statement by President Eisenhower on the situation in the Middle East said that the US, while willing to consider needs for legitimate self defense, did not intend to contribute to an "arms competition"

November 9

because it did not think such a race was in the true interest of any of the participants. The US would, however, continue to play its full part and would firmly support the UN which had already done so much to minimize violence in the Middle East.

November 10

The Sudanese Prime Minister, Ismail al-Azhari, resigned after his Government had been defeated by 49-45 on the second reading of the budget. The four Parliamentary undersecretaries who resigned the day before voted against the Government.

It was reported in London that Britain and Egypt reached an agreement on the safe passage of British ships entering the Gulf of Aqaba on the Red Sea.

Egypt was reported to have bought 30 Vampire jet fighter planes from an Italian concern.

A trade agreement was signed between Syria and Italy.

US diplomatic representatives in the Middle East warned the governments of the countries of the area that the US would be strongly opposed to the side that started a war, and conversely, would be very favorably disposed to the side that convinced the US that it desired to maintain peace.

The Israel Embassy issued a statement recalling that, on the withdrawal of the mandatory power from Palestine, the Arab countries had attacked Israel in order to prevent the enforcement of UN resolutions in 1947.

November 11

The Italian Government banned licenses for the export to Egypt of British Vampire jet fighters made in Italy under license.

France announced its intention to resume the sale of arms, including jet fighters, to Egypt. The sale had been suspended two months

November 11

before because of anti-French broadcasts from Cairo to French North Africa.

A Syrian economic delegation signed a trade agreement with Saudi Arabia.

A Libyan Royal Decree dissolved Parliament and fixed January 8, 1956, as the date for new elections.

November 12

Sheikh Yusuf Yasin, Saudi Arabian Deputy Foreign Minister, stated in Cairo that his Government proposed to Great Britain that the question of the Buraimi Oasis be referred back to international arbitration, and that in the meantime the Oasis be put under the supervision of an international body such as the UN.

UN Truce Supervisor General Burns arrived in Cairo to discuss the November 3, 1955, peace proposals of UN Secretary General Hammarskjold with Egyptian officials. Although the details of the plan were not made public, it was announced that Egypt objected to the proposals because they included the assumption that the al-Auja demilitarized zone belonged to Israel. Egypt contended that al-Auja must remain neutral and demilitarized until its ownership could be determined.

Egyptian Minister of Finance Abd-al-Moneim al-Kaissouni, arrived in Washington for discussions with the International Bank for Reconstruction and Development on the financing of the LE200 million Aswan High Dam project.

Prime Minister Nasser of Egypt said that British Prime Minister Eden's speech of November 9, 1955, marked the first time that a major Western leader had taken a constructive attitude toward the Palestine controversy.

Lebanon and East Germany signed a trade and payments agreement under which Lebanon would export agricultural products and import manufactured goods.

November 12

Acting from Paris, Sultan Ben-Youssef of Morocco dismissed the cabinet ministers who served during his exile.

The withdrawal of Anglo-Egyptian troops from the Sudan was completed.

November 13

Yaacov Herzog, Director of the American division of the Israel Foreign Ministry, reiterated that his country was still offering the Arab States routes across its territory, free port facilities at Haifa, and compensation for land abandoned by refugees when they fled in 1948.

It was reported from Jerusalem that official and public opinion in Israel was indignant at British Prime Minister Sir Anthony Eden's suggestion that Israel negotiate peace with the Arab States on the basis of the surrender of some of its territory. Eden was accused of embarking on a straight appeasement policy.

Said al-Ghazzi, Syrian Prime Minister, said that Syria would not conclude a bilateral pact with Iraq because in its view the Arab Collective Security Pact was sufficient to secure Iraq support for any Arab State subjected to Israel aggression. He said that he could not fix a date for his proposed visit to Iraq.

The Saudi Arabian Embassy in Cairo charged that British led Arabs looted and wrecked two villages in the disputed Buraimi Oasis.

November 14

US Secretary of State Dulles told the Foreign Ministers Conference in Geneva that continued supply of weapons to Egypt and other Middle East states threatened the foundations of any peace between the Communist and non-Communist worlds.

It was learned in Cairo that Marshal Voroshilov, President of the USSR, in a message to King Saud on the anniversary of his accession (November 9), had reviewed the Russian offer of arms to Saudi Arabia and had offered "material and moral help" on the Buraimi dispute.

November 14

Henry R. Labouisse, Director of the UN Relief and Works Agency for Palestine Refugees, told the special Political Committee that unrest in the Middle East would continue as long as thousands of Palestinian Arabs clamored in vain to go back to their lands in Israel.

Israel offered to exchange 90 Egyptian and Syrian prisoners for eight Israel soldiers held by the Arab States.

Abd-al-Rahman Abu-Taleb, Yemeni Minister to Cairo, said that his Government would welcome any offer of Soviet arms.

Abd-al-Jabbar al-Tikerli was appointed Iraqi Minister of Justice and Muhammad Ali Mahmoud was transferred from the Justice Ministry to that for Development and Reconstruction.

November 15

In a letter to Rabbi Abba Hillel Silver, to be read at a mass meeting at Madison Square Garden in New York, President Eisenhower reaffirmed his administration's willingness to enter into formal treaties with Israel and its neighbors to guarantee peace in the Middle East. The President declared that the US was willing to consider requests for arms needed for legitimate self defense, adding that it did not intend to contribute to an arms competition in the Near East.

Israel Prime Minister David Ben-Gurion told the Knesset that UK Prime Minister Anthony Eden's offer that Britain mediate the Israel-Arab border dispute was unacceptable.

Jordan and Israel agreed that their border would be opened during the Christmas season to permit Christians within Israel to visit Bethlehem.

The Political Committee of the Arab League adopted a resolution on the Buraimi dispute. It announced that Britain's action was a unilateral violation of the arbitration agreement, and supported wholeheartedly the attitude of the Saudi Arabian Kingdom. It further decided that the case would be settled amicably by means of returning to arbitration on the basis of the withdrawal of the occupying forces from Buraimi and the restoration of the situation to what it

November 15

was during the arbitration. A neutral international commission would be formed to watch over the situation in the areas under dispute.

A reply from Saudi Arabian King Saud to Marshal Voroshilov's message was handed to the Soviet Ambassador in Cairo. It was understood to have welcomed the idea of assistance.

Ismail al-Azhari was rechosen Prime Minister of Sudan by the Parliament after a switch in votes gave him majority support, 48-46-1. The Cabinet would be the same that had resigned on November 10, 1955, except for the Minister of Animal Resources.

The Egyptian National Production Council approved the building of a LE3.6 million shipyard in Alexandria for building and repairing ships, as well as a LE2.5 million drydock.

November 16

Egyptian Ambassador to Washington Ahmad Hussein told the State Department that his country had received the proposal from UK Foreign Secretary Anthony Eden enthusiastically. He called it an objective approach to constitute the basis for negotiating a peaceful settlement. Israel Ambassador Abba Eban explained to the State Department that his country could not accept the proposal since Eden was suggesting in advance of his mediation to let the Arabs "take a big bite out of Israel."

Egypt warned the US that if the latter agreed to Israel's request for arms, Egypt would be compelled to buy more arms from other sources.

Israel formally asked the US to sell it arms under the most lenient conditions of credit and price. The list submitted by Israel Ambassador Abba Eban specified the weapons his country was seeking.

Speaking in the Special Political Committee, the US Delegate to the UN, James J. Wadsworth, urged the Arab States not to let their political quarrels with Israel block plans to help the Palestine Arab refugees. He insisted that a start be made on those programs that would mean a better life for the refugees and would benefit the

November 16

whole Arab world. He mentioned specifically plans for the development of Egypt's Sinai region and the Jordan River Valley.

The Israel Government officially indicated acceptance in principle of the UN proposal for pacifying the al-Auja demilitarized zone.

Syria signed a trade and payments agreement with the Soviet Union in Damascus, running for a year and automatically renewable with payments to be made either in sterling or dollars. Syria was to export agricultural products for Soviet industrial goods.

Moroccan Sultan Sidi Muhammad Ben-Youssef arrived in Rabat, ending over two years of exile.

Moroccan Sultan Sidi Muhammad Ben-Youssef, in reply to an address by Andre Dubois, the French Resident General, said that his desire was to be the constitutional monarch of a modern democratic and independent state. He asked Dubois to assuage the anxieties of the French settlers in Morocco and to assure them of his desire to see them live in fruitful cooperation with his subjects in a new but ever hospitable Morocco.

November 17

The national convention of the Neo-Destour Party in Tunisia voted to exclude from Party membership Salah Ben-Youssef, leader of the extreme nationalist wing.

Britain and the US announced plans to present Libya with equipment for the development of an armored car squadron.

Jordan was promised full support for its admission to the UN simultaneously with 17 other nations.

Al-Akhbar, Cairo newspaper, reported that the Iraqis took the initiative in proposing to the Arab League that a joint Arab Army be formed, to be maintained by the Arab League, with the mission of defending the borders of Palestine.

November 18

Moroccan Sultan Sidi Muhammad Ben-Youssef, in a major speech in Rabat, declared the end of the 43 year old French protectorate over Morocco. He said that his first aim would be to form a responsible and representative government. He emphasized the need for a continuing close association with France, both for purposes of external defense and internal improvements.

In a statement on Prime Minister Eden's offer to mediate between Israel and the Arab States, the US State Department declared that while the US and Great Britain saw eye to eye on the imperative necessity of the methods that should be employed, the US did not necessarily support Sir Anthony Eden's specific proposals. This apparently referred to the proposed territorial compromise in the plan.

The Tunisian Neo-Destour Party unanimously elected Habib Bourguiba as its President for the next two years, 1956 and 1957.

The Neo-Destour Convention in Tunisia recommended an economic development program for Tunisia which included the expansion of producer cooperatives, heavy investments in power development, the nationalization of large farm areas belonging to religious foundations if they were not used to their fullest extent, and a revision of the major 99 year industrial concessions made within the past three years.

Tunisian Salah Ben-Youssef, former Secretary General of the Neo-Destour Party, spoke to a rally in Tunis, criticizing the Neo-Destour's friendly relations with France and emphasizing that Tunisia was an indivisible part of the Arab world.

Israel rejected repatriation of Arab refugees living outside its territories and charged that the Arab States were keeping the refugee problem alive solely for political objectives. It emphasized before the Special Political Committee of the UN that the only solution to the problem was the willingness of the Arab countries to accept the refugees as new citizens.

November 19

King Hussein of Jordan arrived in Beirut for a six day visit.

November 19

In connection with the first meeting of the Baghdad Pact Council in Baghdad, the US formally announced the establishment of military and political liaison with the five nation Pact organization. The American Ambassador to Iraq, Waldemar Gallman, was designated head of the liaison group, and he would maintain contact with the Pact body after the initial sessions. Admiral John H. Cassady, Commander in Chief of the US naval forces in the eastern Atlantic and Mediterranean, and Brigadier General Forrest Caraway were to attend the initial meetings as military observers.

The al-Azhari Cabinet in Sudan refused to consider reforming itself on a non-partisan basis as had been suggested by the opposition.

A series of shooting and mob actions occurred throughout Morocco. In a village near Meknes, four persons were killed and 26 wounded including six French police, in a clash between a demonstrating crowd and the police.

Egyptian Deputy Premier Gamal Salem discussed with Soviet Ambassador to Egypt Daniel Solod the financial problems connected with the building of the Aswan High Dam.

An official communique stated that Syria and the USSR had decided to raise their diplomatic representation to embassy level in order to consolidate their relations.

November 20

The Saudi Arabian Government issued a communique denying reports of rebellious movements in the country, and that there were differences between Saudi Arabia and Egypt. The communique also denied reports that Saudi Arabia had accepted an offer of Soviet arms and that King Saud had suggested to USSR President Marshal Voroshilov that representatives of their two countries should meet in Cairo to discuss an arms deal.

Jordanian Deputy Prime Minister Hazza al-Majali announced that Jordan would remain outside the Middle East Treaty Organization at least temporarily.

November 20

Fourteen persons were killed and 60 wounded in Morocco in what appeared to be a breakdown of law and order as a result of the confused situation in the inter-regime period.

November 21

Talks between the International Bank and an Egyptian delegation on financing the High Dam at Aswan opened in Washington.

Jordan announced that it would remain neutral in relation to the Baghdad Pact, the Syrian-Egyptian Defense Pact and the Egyptian-Saudi Arabian Defense Pact.

Death sentences were confirmed for 80 civilians involved in the August uprising in the southern Sudan.

The Sudanese Government informed Egypt that it would welcome the resumption of talks on the division of the Nile waters and also sent a series of proposals which were "fair to both sides."

A French army officer and a civilian were killed in the Rif area near Fez in Morocco. Resident General Andre Dubois issued instructions that French military and civilian authorities should suppress by force all manifestations of violence.

The first meeting of the representatives of the Baghdad Pact opened in Baghdad with the Prime Ministers of Iraq, Iran, Pakistan and Turkey and the UK Foreign Secretary Harold Macmillan present. The US established military and political liaison with the conference.

November 22

The two day organizational meeting of the newly named Council of the Baghdad Pact ended with the announcement that permanent military and economic committees and a secretariat would be formed in Baghdad. In addition, the Council would continue to function, with the ambassadors of each country to Iraq serving as members. The next meeting of the Council at the Foreign Ministers' level would

November 22

occur in Tehran in April 1956. The US would continue its informal association with the committees working in Baghdad.

The Moroccan Sultan appealed to the people to prevent further disorder.

The Yemen Development Corporation in Washington signed a 30 year agreement with Yemen for exclusive exploration and development rights for oil and minerals. The agreement covered a 40,000 square mile area; all net profits were to be divided on a 50-50 basis. Should petroleum in commercial quantities and minerals not be found in six years, the agreement would be void.

Egyptian Premier Gamal Abdel Nasser accepted an invitation to visit Bulgaria.

Egyptian officials in Washington said that they were seeking a formal commitment from the International Bank to help finance the High Dam at Aswan.

Israel informed General Burns, UN Chief Truce Supervisor, that it had accepted Secretary General Hammarkjold's proposals for the settling of differences in the al-Auja zone.

November 23

The UK rejected proposals for arbitration of the Buraimi Oasis dispute.

New violence in different parts of Algeria resulted in 20 deaths.

British Foreign Secretary Macmillan, en route from Baghdad, stopped briefly in Beirut to urge the Government to consider an economic tie with the Baghdad Pact powers even though it could not consider complete affiliation with the organization.

French Resident General of Morocco Andre Dubois asked that the authorities in Spanish Morocco cooperate with the French in ending the recent incidents.

November 24

British Prime Minister Sir Anthony Eden, under pressure in the House of Commons on the territorial compromise he asked of Israel in his November 9, 1955, proposal, suggested that the end of Egypt's blockade of Israel and the return of Arab refugees to Israel were types of concessions that might lead to a settlement of the Israel-Egyptian dispute.

Great Britain dismissed as unrealistic a Saudi Arabian proposal that the dispute on the Buraimi Oasis be referred back to arbitration.

The Egyptian Cabinet approved amendments to the penal code specifying penalties against anyone guilty of publishing false news and unable to prove that it was done unintentionally.

Egypt ended its press and radio attack on French activities in North Africa in exchange for France's resumption of shipments of previously ordered arms.

November 25

Ahmad Balafrej, leader of the moderate wing of the Istiqlal Party in Morocco, announced his party's views toward future government organization. The Istiqlal's program would recognize the need for continued French control of Moroccan foreign and defense affairs in the immediate future. It would demand that the Istiqlal have at least twice as many cabinet posts as any other party, and that these included the Ministries of Interior and Justice. The Istiqlal Party demanded the annulment of the 1912 Treaty of Fez which established the protectorate, and that the Sultan be deprived of legislative power under a democratic constitutional monarchy.

The UN General Assembly unanimously adopted a resolution stating that it had decided not to consider further the item entitled "The Question of Algeria." This enabled France to return to the Assembly.

Italy and Libya agreed to establish a mixed arbitration commission to exercise jurisdiction over questions arising between the two governments. This commission would replace a UN tribunal which had exercised the same function for the past five years. Italy and Libya would each appoint a member to the commission and a third member would be appointed by the Secretary General of the UN.

November, 1955

November 26

Egyptian War Minister and Commander in Chief of the Armed Forces, General Abd-al-Hakim Amer, who was also Chief of the Joint Command of Syrian and Egyptian Forces under the Syro-Egyptian Mutual Defense Pact, arrived in Damascus for talks with Syrian Government and Army leaders.

The French Government announced that by the end of December, 16 additional infantry battalions and three armored squadrons would be sent to reinforce the troops already stationed in Algeria. It was also stated that 16 companies of Algerians would be formed, beginning in January, 1956.

Lebanese Foreign Minister Salim Lahoud said in Beirut that British Foreign Secretary Harold Macmillan had invited Lebanon to join the Baghdad Pact's economic committee, not the Pact itself.

The Soviet Union warned Iran that its frontiers were endangered by Iran's membership in the Baghdad Pact. It asserted that Iran violated its treaty obligations to the USSR and contradicted good neighborly relations between the two countries, and that it would have to answer for possible consequences.

November 27

Syria and East Germany signed a trade and payments agreement, valid for one year and with an automatic renewal clause.

Berber guerrillas in the Rif area of Morocco ambushed a military convoy, killing 15 French soldiers and wounding ten.

In a drive against Algerian nationalist rebels, French police and troops killed 30 in scattered clashes in the Constantine Department.

Syria announced a final payments agreement with the Iraq Petroleum Company in connection with its pipeline across Syria. IPC agreed to pay SL80 million for use during the past three years and SL65 million annually in the future. The Government also announced that negotiations for new royalty arrangements with Tapline would begin soon.

November, 1955

November 27

King Saud of Saudi Arabia arrived in India for a 17 day visit.

November 28

By a vote of 49-0-5, the UN Political Committee adopted a resolution expressing confidence that impending negotiations between France and its Moroccan protectorate would reach a satisfactory solution and hence postponed discussion of the question.

The US, Great Britain and Turkey introduced a resolution in the Special Political Committee of the UN calling on all governments to continue supporting the UNRWA. By implication, the resolution called on the Arab States to cooperate with the UN on land development plans aimed at getting the refugees out of relief camps and resettled.

A report emanating from Cairo said that authoritative Egyptian and British sources believed that a negotiated settlement of the Arab-Israel dispute was becoming a tangible possibility for the first time since 1948.

Colonel Nasser, Egyptian Prime Minister, commented to the press on Sir Anthony Eden's proposals on the Palestine issue. He said that his reference to the UN resolutions of 1947 indicated that the Palestine Arabs' rights had not been abandoned by the Big Powers and that the time had come for a revival of those resolutions. Colonel Nasser emphasized that the Palestine problem concerned all the Arab States and that no Arab State was entitled to deal with it alone.

The first meeting of the Ministerial Council of the new Baghdad Pact was held in Baghdad under the chairmanship of the Iraq Foreign Minister. The others present were the ambassadors to Iraq of the other four member countries. The US ambassador attended as an observer.

November 29

The French delegation returned to the UN General Assembly after the latter dropped the question of Algeria from its agenda for the current session.

November, 1955

November 29

James J. Wadsworth, US delegate on the UN Special Political Committee, advised the Arab States to cooperate on long delayed efforts to develop agricultural land for the benefit of Palestine Arab refugees; he warned that nations would not pay indefinitely for refugee relief work when the refugees could be made self supporting by large land development projects.

The Arab States attacked the three power resolution on the refugee problem. They insisted that the only solution was to return the refugees to Israel.

It was reported from Jerusalem that Israel regarded hints in Cairo about possible negotiations for an Arab-Israel settlement as a smokescreen to cover up preparations for aggression.

It was reported from Cairo that Egypt and Syria completed arrangements for establishing a joint military command against Israel, and that the Egyptian Air Force dispatched a squadron of jet fighter planes to Syrian airfields for joint air exercises.

The US informed Israel and the Arab Governments that it saw real prospects for bringing peace between them.

Great Britain and Egypt agreed to amendments and additions to the Anglo-Egyptian agreement on the Sudan legalizing the plebiscite requested by the Sudanese Parliament to determine the future status of the country and the setting up of the international commission to supervise self determination.

The Libyan American Oil Company, a subsidiary of the Texas Gulf Producing Company, was granted an oil concession in Libya. If oil was discovered, the agreement would require a payment to the Government of 12.5 percent royalty on all oil and gas up to 15,000 barrels a day. Above that point net profits would be shared on a 50-50 basis.

November 30

The UN Special Political Committee adopted, 38-0, the three power resolution on Arab refugees.

November, 1955

November 30

Lebanese Minister of Finance Jamil Chehab resigned in protest against the Government's acceptance of a $27 million loan from the International Bank for the Litani River development scheme.

The Egyptian military mission to Syria, under General Amer, arrived in Amman, Jordan, for a four day visit.

M'Barek Bekkai was designated Moroccan Prime Minister.

Syria and Communist China signed a trade and payments agreement providing for the exchange of commercial representatives and the encouragement of trade.

In a reply to parliamentary questions, Harold Macmillan, British Foreign Secretary, said that no formal agreement with the Egyptian Government about shipping proceeding to the Gulf of Aqaba had been signed. Ships to Aqaba from the north continued to notify the customs authorities at Port Said and Suez. Ships from the south notified the British Embassy in Cairo who informed the Egyptian authorities. The Government maintained its legal position regarding the freedom of shipping in international waters, but adopted a de facto arrangement.

Saudi Arabia protested to the UN Security Council that its air space had been violated repeatedly by British military aircraft.

December, 1955

December 3

Britain and Egypt signed a formal agreement in Cairo which would permit the Sudan the right of self determination by means of a national plebiscite, with elections to a constituent assembly to take place at the same time. A seven nation commission was to oversee the process of self determination.

In reply to the Sudanese Council of Ministers note of November 9, 1955, the Governor General of the Sudan considered that the talks concerning the terms of reference of the International Commission to supervise Sudanese self determination had reached an advanced stage and that it was therefore impractical to afford the Sudan the chance of participating in the talks, without delaying the setting up of the International Commission.

Sudanese leaders Ali al-Mirghani of the Khatmia sect and Abd-al-Rahman al-Mahdi of the Ansar sect met for the first time since 1946 and expressed their hope that all parties would unite to form a national Government for Sudan during the months of self determination.

The plenary session of the UN Tenth General Assembly unanimously endorsed the reports and recommendations on the Moroccan question, as well as other major resolutions. It also adopted a resolution supporting the continuation of the work of UNRWA.

December 5

The Syrian Chamber of Deputies, by a vote of 56-19-17, approved the new royalty arrangements completed on November 27, 1955, with the Iraq Petroleum Company (IPC) in connection with their pipeline across Syria.

The UN Economic Committee unanimously passed a resolution inviting Governments to provide financial assistance to Libya through the UN and requesting all concerned to give favorable consideration to Libyan requests for technical assistance.

A skirmish between French and nationalist forces in a village near the Algerian-Tunisian border resulted in at least 17 nationalist deaths.

December, 1955

December 6

General Sir Gerald Templer, Chief of Britain's General Staff, arrived in Amman, Jordan, to hold talks with King Hussein and high Government officials.

A major resolution was adopted in the UN General Assembly terminating the UN Tribunal for Libya.

Sudanese Prime Minister Ismail al-Azhari announced that the National Union Party would be willing to join a coalition government during the self determination period if several conditions were agreed to, the most important being that the present Parliament be used as the vehicle for self determination rather than a national plebiscite, and that the Parliament also be given the powers of a constituent assembly.

December 7

Morocco's Prime Minister M'barek Bekkai's newly announced Cabinet was sworn in by Sultan Muhammad Ben-Youssef. In so doing, the Sultan for the first time formally relinquished many of his absolute powers, although stating that the Cabinet would remain responsible to him until a national assembly had been elected. The Cabinet members were M'barek Bekkai (independent) as Prime Minister and Muhammad Zechare (independent) as Deputy Prime Minister.

December 9

The Communist Party of Lebanon published an appeal for peace and against "the US-UK imperialists" who were intensifying their pressure on the Arab countries in order to draw them into the Baghdad Pact.

December 10

French Premier Mendes-France put his Government on record as opposing independence for Tunisia or the other territories of French North Africa.

December, 1955

December 10

It was reported that Lebanon had ratified an agreement with West Germany dealing with German industrial property.

The French Cabinet announced that Algeria would not participate in the national elections scheduled for January 2, 1956. Algeria would have elected thirty deputies to the National Assembly, but because of "the exceptional situation" in Algeria and the probable boycott of both candidates and voters there, the elections were postponed to a later date.

December 11

An Iraq-Jordan joint statement announced an agreement providing that Iraq should pay its share of 625,000 pounds sterling for financing the Jordan potash project as soon as the requisite company had been formed and its shares offered for sale. Iraq also undertook to lend ID1 million for the financing of Jordan's super-phosphate project. The agreement also provided for joint consultations on securing the necessary funds for financing other Jordan projects, the establishment in Jordan of branches of the industrial and agricultural Iraq banks, and an Iraq contribution of ID100,000 for Jordanian national guards.

The Sudanese Cabinet announced that it had protested to Britain and Egypt that it was not consulted when the two countries agreed on the procedure for Sudanese self determination. It had also stated that it wanted representation on the plebiscite commission, and it said that public opinion rejected the terms of reference of the international plebiscite commission.

Heavy loss of life resulted from an Israel raid on Syrian territory near Lake Tiberias. Truce Supervisor Burns held Israel responsible.

December 12

UN Truce Observers found that at least 56 Syrians had been killed in the Israel raid of December 11. Israel sources said that all Syrian installations near the northeast corner of Lake Tiberias had been destroyed.

December, 1955

December 12

Opening a debate on the Middle East in the Commons, Harold Macmillan, British Foreign Secretary, said that it was not surprising in view of the resistance to Communism in the West and a temporary lull in the Far East that the struggle for power had developed in the Middle East.

The British Foreign Office announced that Sir Alexander Knox-Helm, Governor General of the Sudan, wished to resign for personal reasons. The Egyptian Government had been informed that it was not intended to nominate another British candidate, and that consultations were taking place with the Egyptian Government on the steps to be taken.

King Saud of Saudi Arabia declared in Bombay that if he failed to have a peaceful settlement of the Buraimi Oasis dispute it would be his duty to defend the rights of his kingdom in every possible way. He claimed that the Oasis had been an integral part of his kingdom for over 250 years, and said that he wished to try all diplomatic channels to settle the dispute although it was difficult to restrain the enthusiasm of his people to reoccupy the Oasis. In a reference to the Baghdad Pact, he said that Iraq had done great harm to Arab unity by joining it.

December 13

Syria requested that the UN Security Council meet to consider charges of armed aggression by Israel.

The Syrian military tribunal trying the accused persons in the death of Colonel al-Malki on April 22, 1955, announced that eight persons were given death sentences, one given life imprisonment and 17 given shorter prison terms.

Yugoslavia and the Sudan signed a trade agreement under which Yugoslavia would buy 300,000 pounds sterling worth of Sudanese cotton in the next year and the Sudan would be free to buy the goods of its choice from Yugoslavia.

M'Barek Bekkai, Moroccan Prime Minister, outlining the Government's future policy, said that it would have to democratize the

December, 1955

December 13

country's institutions, reorganize the functions of the Moslem chiefs, reform the legal system, restore trade union freedom, and develop industry, agriculture, housing and education. He described Morocco as a country which geographically and economically belonged to the West and at the same time belonged to the great Moslem Bloc. He said that his ambition was to make Morocco the great meeting place of two civilizations. Speaking of relations with France, he said the Government's first task was to negotiate a new agreement, but the Fez Treaty of 1912 would have to be abrogated. Morocco, he said, needed French economic, technical and military aid.

December 14

Iraq offered military assistance to Syria at any time to defend Syrian territory against Israel aggression.

Libya's application for UN membership was approved by a vote in the General Assembly.

Jordan became a member of the UN.

The Prime Minister of Jordan, Said al-Mufti resigned after four members of his Cabinet quit in protest over British suggestions that Jordan join the Baghdad Pact.

Awni Khalidi of Iraq was appointed Secretary General of the Baghdad Pact.

December 15

Israel notified UN authorities that it was prepared to exchange all Syrian prisoners it held for Israelis held as prisoners in Syria.

Egyptian Prime Minister Nasser cabled UN Secretary General Hammarskjold that any further Israel attacks such as that on Syria on December 11, 1955, would be met by the united action of Egypt and Syria under their new Mutual Defense Pact.

December, 1955

December 15

Generalissimo Franco of Spain declared that Spain would not permit the establishment of a Western democratic system of government in the Spanish Zone of Morocco.

The Government of the Sultan of Muscat announced that the Sultan's forces had that day occupied without opposition the Oasis of Nazwa which it described as the focus of a conspiracy. The statement added the Sheikh Ghaleb Ibn-Ali, the Imam of Oman, who had put forward pretensions to independence had left Nazwa on December 14, 1955.

December 16

A new Government of Jordan was formed by Hazza al-Majali who was also Foreign Minister and Economic Minister.

Widespread rioting occurred in Jordan in protest against proposed Jordanian membership in the Baghdad Pact.

The UN Security Council opened its debate on the Israel raid against Syria. The Syrian representative called for the expulsion of Israel from the UN and the imposition of economic sanctions against Israel. The ten members of the Council present, including Britain, France, the US and the Soviet Union, criticized the Israel attack against Syria.

The US and UK offered to contribute $56 million and $14 million, respectively, to help Egypt finance building of the Aswan High Dam.

December 17

The accused defendants in the trial for the assassination of Colonel Adnan al-Malki in Syria appealed the tribunal's decision of December 13, 1955, to the higher court.

An eight hour daily curfew was imposed on Meknes, Morocco, because of the renewed outbreak of violence there.

December, 1955

December 17

The French announced that at least ten persons had been killed during the preceding 24 hours by Algerian terrorists in Algeria. It was also stated that French troops had attacked a nationalist arms convoy crossing the border from Tunisia. Seven of the nationalists in the convoy were killed.

December 18

The Soviet Ambassador to Egypt declared that his Government was still prepared to assist in financing the Aswan Dam. US officials indicated that it was implicit in the US-British offer that Soviet aid would be excluded.

Nuri-Said formed the new Government of Iraq.

Ambassador Awni Khalidi, Iraq's representative to the UN, announced that he had been selected by members of the Baghdad Pact Council as Secretary General for the Pact.

Demonstrations against the new Jordanian Government and the Baghdad Pact broke out in Amman, Jericho and Hebron. In the latter town, the UNRWA (UN Relief Works Agency) headquarters was attacked.

Jordan's Prime Minister Hazza al-Majali issued a statement outlining the course of recent events in Jordan.

Jordan's Minister of the Interior announced that defense regulations would be enforced within Jordan. He said that his policy was that no Arab State might alone decide questions affecting the grand Arab nations or the Palestine question.

December 19

In Egypt three French Catholic priests were arrested but immediately released on bail after they had protested the Government's plans to abolish all religious courts, as announced on September 27, 1955.

December, 1955

December 19

The Sudanese House of Representatives unanimously adopted a resolution declaring Sudan's independence and requesting Egypt and Britain to recognize the declaration. Parliament also agreed to elect a five man commission to assume the duties of the Governor General.

Lieutenant General Garcia Valino, High Commissioner for Spanish Morocco, said that he would make every effort to prepare Morocco for self rule and would give increased responsibilities to those Moroccans participating in the Government of Spanish Morocco.

As demonstrations continued in Jordan's major towns, Prime Minister al-Majali resigned and suggested to King Hussein that Parliament be dissolved and new elections held. Six members of the Cabinet resigned earlier in protest against the Prime Minister's plans to dissolve Parliament. King Hussein issued a decree dissolving Parliament and calling for a general election within four months.

Details of Israel's peace proposals for Palestine were announced in Washington. It was later confirmed that they also had the approval of the Israel Government. The main points were: (1) Israel would agree to mutual adjustments of the 1949 armistice line but would not consider negotiating on the basis of the 1947 line; (2) Israel would consider granting the Arab States land and air transit rights for the free flow of trade between Lebanon and Egypt and across the Negev between Egypt and Jordan; such concessions would, however, have to be reciprocated by similar transit concessions on the part of the Arabs; (3) Jordan would be offered free port rights in Haifa and the necessary transit rights to reach the port by land; (4) Israel would be ready to raise funds to compensate Arab refugees and would accept the US offer of a loan for resettlement and rehabilitation; the refugees would, however, have to be resettled in Arab States and not in Israel; (5) Israel would accept the Jordan River development plan proposed by US Special Envoy to Egypt Eric Johnston under which more than half of the water would go to the Arabs.

December 20

Demonstrations against the US, the UK and Turkey occurred in Damascus. Crowds shouted for the return of the Hatay to Syria.

December 20

Crowds in Jerusalem attacked the US, French and Turkish consulates. At the request of King Hussein, Ibrahim Hashem, President of the Senate, formed a caretaker Government to rule until the new elections.

Syria signed a trade agreement with Saudi Arabia. The Saudi Arabian Government extended an interest free loan of $15 million to Syria and postponed the repayment period of the 1950 loan of $6 million.

The new Prime Minister of Jordan was Ibrahim Hashem. The new Deputy Prime Minister and Minister of Foreign Affairs was Samir al-Rifai.

December 21

Britain announced that, in exchange for some 2,750,000 pounds sterling worth of equipment left behind on the airfields recently evacuated by Britain, Iraq would purchase 2 million pounds sterling of military equipment from Britain during the next two years.

Lord John Hope, British Under Secretary of the Foreign Office, in a statement in the House of Lords, said it seemed likely that the disturbances in Jordan were deliberately incited by misrepresentation of the Jordan Government's policy from outside Jordan, especially in connection with the Baghdad Pact. He gave details of four attacks on British personnel and property in one of which a British sergeant was injured.

French authorities announced that attacks on nationalists scattered throughout Algeria had resulted in the deaths of 89 rebels.

The report of General Burns, Chief of the Palestine Truce Organization, was published.

December 22

The Jordanian Government announced that 41 persons had been killed and 150 injured during the demonstrations of the past week.

December 22

Israel expressed willingness to consider UNTSO Chief General Burns' request for a gentlemen's agreement to abide by the armistice terms, although it objected to the Truce Supervisor's proposal that the use of Israel patrol boats on Lake Tiberias be limited.

The Sudanese Senate approved unanimously the lower House declaration of Sudan's independence.

The forces of the Sultan of Muscat and Oman took Rustak, the last stronghold of the Imam of Oman.

December 23

Thirty-five Algerian guerrillas in the Djurdjura Mountains were killed in a raid by French troops.

The Lebanese Chamber of Deputies approved the $27 million loan granted Lebanon on August 26, 1955, for the development of the Litani River.

December 25

Leaders of the recent demonstrations within Jordan met in Amman to form an organization, the National Committee, to prepare for the forthcoming elections. The committee's aims were declared to be opposition to the Baghdad Pact and termination of British influence.

December 26

Mendes-France, French Prime Minister, speaking at Lyon, said that in Algeria there should be a reciprocal agreement between the populations living there. He promised to hold free and honest elections in Algeria within six months, if he and his allies were returned. The Moslem and European electoral colleges would need to be put on a footing of equality. He proposed that the next Prime Minister should take over the Algerian question and establish himself in Algeria for as long as was necessary to overcome opposition of all sorts.

December 26

Egypt and Saudi Arabia announced, in Cairo, the first steps in the implementation of their mutual defense pact of October 27, 1955. Major General Abd-al-Hakim Amer, Commander of the Egyptian Army and the recently selected joint commander under the Syrian-Egyptian Mutual Defense Pact, was chosen as the first Joint Commander. A war council was established consisting of the Chiefs of Staff of both countries.

December 27

It was announced that British and Yemeni officers who had met at Awabel to investigate frontier disorders had agreed: (1) that the Yemeni authorities would cause all the dissident Shuibis, including the ex-Shuibi sheikh, to be removed from the frontier; (2) that both Governments would withdraw all soldiers from the frontier; (3) that each Government would appoint one observer but not from the Shuibi or Mureibi tribes; (4) that both sides would stop fighting forthwith; (5) that a committee of four, consisting of two members appointed by each Government, should investigate compensation claims, and that compensation would be paid for the damage caused to Mureibi property within the Yemen by accidental bombing.

The Sudanese Governor General, Sir Alexander Knox-Helm, reportedly would not return to Sudan from his Christmas leave, and a five member Council of State would assume sovereign power on January 1, 1956.

December 28

The US suggested that Britain and Saudi Arabia resume direct negotiations, whether bilaterally or through an arbitration commission, in order to reach an agreement on the Buraimi dispute.

President Tito of Yugoslavia arrived in Cairo for a state visit.

It was announced in Brussels that Belgium had shipped surplus tanks and other war equipment bought from Britain to Egypt.

December 28

A group of members of the dissolved Jordanian Parliament issued a protest stating that the dissolution was illegal because the Prime Minister at that time, Hazza al-Majali, had recommended the dissolution on his own without consulting with the Minister of Interior, as required by the constitution.

A communique by UN Truce Supervisor General Burns stated that violations of the armistice by both Israel and Egypt had occurred. It added that Egypt had not yet formulated its final position on Hammarskjold's proposals.

December 29

After conversations with Egyptian officials, UN Truce Supervisor General Burns talked with Israel leaders about new peace guarantees in the al-Auja demilitarized zone. Israel announced that talks had broken down because of Egyptian objections to the UN proposals.

The Bey of Tunis issued a decree establishing a National Constituent Assembly to meet in April, 1956, to draw up a constitution.

A meeting of the Mapai Party of Israel endorsed the "line of action" taken by Prime Minister Ben-Gurion in his handling of Israel's affairs. Of particular concern in the vote was the generally accepted fact that the Prime Minister had been solely responsible for the raid on Syria on December 11, 1955.

A US State Department spokesman, commenting on reports that Saudi Arabia was banning trade with American firms owned by Jews, accused Arab League nations of boycotting foreign firms doing business with Israel and said that certain nations had regulations which prohibited the granting of visas to people of the Jewish faith. He expressed the disapproval of the US of the actions mentioned.

The USSR press announced that the USSR Red Cross and Red Crescent Society had allocated 50,000 rubles to help flood victims in Tripoli, Lebanon.

December, 1955

December 30

Britain announced that its economic aid to Jordan would be increased by 3,350,000 pounds sterling. The additional money would be used for development work on the port of Aqaba. Plans announced also included construction of a highway from Amman to Aqaba. Britain's military subsidy to Jordan, amounting to 7,500,000 pounds sterling, would be continued unchanged during the following year.

UN Truce Supervisor General Burns reported to the UN Security Council that Syria, prior to the Israel raid of December 11, 1955, had fired on an Israel patrol boat in Lake Tiberias.

December 31

Egypt announced that it recognized Sudanese independence as of January 1, 1956.

Supplement to 1955

January

1 The Arabs must miss no opportunity to arm themselves against the "great danger of Zionist expansion," Nuri-Said, the Iraqi Premier, told his Parliament during the budget debate.

3 It was announced in Benghazi that the Libyan Government would set up embassies in Paris and Rome.

5 Francois Mitterrand, French Minister of the Interior, submitted to Pierre Mendes-France's Cabinet a series of proposals for economic, administrative and educational reforms in Algeria.

6 The Iraq Petroleum Company concluded a transit fee agreement with the Government of Lebanon.

Following Israel and Syrian complaints, and discussions in both Damascus and Jerusalem, the UNTSO Chief of Staff reported to the Secretary General concerning the situation in the demilitarized zone.

8 The UN announced that Yemen had established a Permanent Mission to the UN, with Kamel Abd-al-Rahim to have the rank of Ambassador.

15 Adnan Menderes, Turkish Prime Minister, explained in a press statement that the Lebanese Government had expressed the desire to see a sound Middle Eastern defense organization established, but was unwilling to take independent action without the approval of the Arab League.

16 Iranian Foreign Minister Entezam, commenting on the Turko-Iraqi Pact, said that Iran had no intention of entering into any defense alliance at that time.

18 Saudi Arabian King Saud told the Arab League powers that he condemned the Turko-Iraqi Pact.

20 An Israel Foreign Ministry spokesman denounced the Turko-Iraqi Pact as containing references clearly directed against Israel.

Egypt turned down Iraq's request for a postponement of the Arab Prime Ministers' Conference called for January 22 to discuss the Turko-Iraqi Pact. The Iraqi Ambassador in Cairo told the Egyptian Foreign

Supplement to 1955

January

20 Minister that General Nuri-Said, Iraqi Prime Minister, would not attend the Conference because his doctors had forbidden him to travel.

23 An offer by Turkish Prime Minister Adnan Menderes to meet Egyptian Premier Colonel Nasser in Cairo, Ankara or any other place which he might select was rejected by the Egyptian Government.

27 Pakistani Prime Minister Muhammad Ali declared in a press interview in New York that he would welcome a tripartite alliance between Pakistan, Iraq and Turkey.

Iraqi Foreign Minister Fadel al-Jamali told the Egyptian Press that it was "necessary for the free nations to cooperate in accordance with the principles of the UN Charter." He added that "neutralism is impossible in existing circumstances" and that "we have an interest in profiting from the economic and military advantages of the West for our own defense."

28 Iraq refused to join other Arab League members in a statement that the League rejected all outside alliances, and maintained that its nearness to the USSR required that Iraq seek protection immediately.

30 Fadel al-Jamali, the Iraqi Delegate to the Arab Premiers' Conference, declared that he was insisting on an alliance that included Turkey, Pakistan, Iran, Britain and the United States. He extended an invitation to all Arab Governments to join the Turko-Iraqi Pact. Jamali said his country was a sovereign state and could not abide by others' decisions.

February

1 The US and UK issued a statement on the Turko-Iraqi Pact of January 12.

2 Ali Yawar Jung, the Indian Ambassador to Cairo, conferred for one hour with Gamal Abdel Nasser, the Egyptian Premier, concerning the Turko-Iraqi Pact.

6 Fadel al-Jamali, Iraqi Representative to the UN, addressed the Iraqi Chamber of Deputies about the Turko-Iraqi Pact.

Supplement to 1955

February

8 Vyacheslav Molatov, speaking to the Supreme Soviet, said that in the Soviet State the Arab States had and would continue to have a "reliable bulwark in the cause of defense of their sovereignty and national independence."

Lebanese Prime Minister Sami al-Solh told Parliament that Lebanon had made no promise to join the proposed Turko-Iraqi Pact.

Syrian Foreign Minister Faidi al-Atassi issued a communique on Syrian policy at the Arab League Conference.

9 Fares al-Khouri, Syrian Prime Minister, issued a statement on the Arab League Conference.

Jordanian Prime Minister Tawfiq Abu-al-Huda said at a press conference that two amendments to the treaty proposed by Jordan remained outstanding—namely, that Jordan should be supplied with fighter aircraft, and that payments of the Arab Legion subsidy of 7.5 million pounds sterling a year should be made directly to the King of Jordan instead of into the Legion's account in London.

10 The Deputy Foreign Minister of Iraq said that Iraq would guarantee the defense of Lebanon, Jordan and Syria if these three countries joined hands with Iraq in its proposed military alliance with Turkey.

11 The Turkish Grand Assembly unanimously approved a proposal for the presentation of three Turkish military aircraft to the Jordanian Government, as a gesture of friendship to that country.

12 At anniversary celebrations of the conclusion of the Anglo-Egyptian-Sudanese Agreement, Sudanese Prime Minister Ismail al-Azhari praised the cooperation of the UK and its Governor General in the implementing of Sudanization.

14 New Syrian Premier Sabri al-Assali said in his first statement to the press that Syria's Arab policy would be based on the Arab League Charter and the Arab Collective Security Pact. His Government's foreign policy was based on Syria's interests in particular and Arab interests in general. He considered Arab problems as a single unit.

Supplement to 1955

February

15 Iraqi Representative to the UN Fadel al-Jamali charged that Egyptian Premier Nasser had broken a promise, made 13 months previously, to help Iraq create a Middle Eastern Security organization after the Anglo-Egyptian Suez dispute was settled.

The Lebanese Foreign Ministry, in a communique, denied reports that Lebanon had offered military bases to the United States on its territory.

17 Syria denied reports that it had agreed to use of the Sea of Galilee as a main reservoir for the Jordan Valley.

20 Egypt and Yugoslavia signed an agreement concerning regular air transport services.

22 Emile Bustani, a member of the Lebanese Parliament's Foreign Affairs Committee, said that Egypt had agreed to reconsider its opposition (pressed via the Arab League) to the Turko-Iraqi Pact, and announced Egyptian Premier Nasser's acceptance of a Lebanese invitation to meet with Iraqi Premier Nuri-Said in Beirut to negotiate on compromise defense proposals, drawn up by Lebanon.

23 Addressing the Algerian Assembly, French Governor General Jacques Soustelle announced that the French Government would make a contribution to the Algerian budget for the first time in order to cover certain expenses in the field of education and justice and would also contribute 40 billion francs to the investment budget.

26 The Prime Minister of Yemen, Prince Saif al-Islam Hassan, said that the Turko-Iraqi Pact did not violate the Charter of the Arab League. Iraq had declared its good intention in signing the Pact. Its action was not regarded as a withdrawal from the Arab League.

March

2 Iraq and the US signed an agreement relating to a technical cooperation program of community welfare.

3 In an official communication to the Foreign Office in London and the State Department in Washington, Israel expressed its concern at the

Supplement to 1955

March

11 UK Foreign Minister Sir Anthony Eden in a BBC radio broadcast declared that the decision to evacuate the Suez Canal Zone had enormously improved Anglo-Egyptian relations.

The Lebanese Foreign Minister announced that his country would not attend the conference of Arab Prime Ministers called by Egypt in Cairo for March 20. He declared that Lebanon would not take part in any conference which was not attended by representatives of all Arab countries.

15 John Foster Dulles, US Secretary of State, told his press conference that the Gaza incident caused a setback to American plans to extend the security considerations desired by Israel.

16 Najib al-Rawi, Iraqi Ambassador to Cairo, said after meeting with Gamal Abdel Nasser, the Egyptian Premier, that relations between the two countries were "much improved." Arab sources saw in this statement an indication that Egyptian hostility regarding the Turko-Iraqi Pact was beginning to be tempered.

17 Soviet Delegate to the UN Arkady Sobolev urged the Security Council not to overlook Israel's statements regarding tension in the area. He said the facts of the Gaza incident showed that responsibility must be borne by Israel, and that the incident was a violation of the Armistice Agreement.

21 Egyptian Prime Minister Gamal Abdel Nasser told an Indian press delegation that his country's independent foreign policy was the result of an inner conviction, and not of expediency.

23 The UN Technical Assistance Administration announced it had opened an Institute of Public Administration in Cairo in cooperation with Egypt to help Arab countries train personnel.

Egypt and Iraq signed an agreement for the establishment of scheduled air services between and beyond their respective territories.

25 The Iraqi Government issued a communique to the effect that although not asked to mediate, Iraq felt it its duty to see that no misunderstanding should ever exist between any Arab country and Turkey.

Supplement to 1955

March

3 Turko-Iraqi Treaty and asked the British and US Governments to issue statements expressing their reservations regarding the "anti-Israel aspects" of the Treaty.

The UN Conciliation Commission for Palestine submitted its fourteenth progress report (for the period from December 31, 1953, to December 31, 1954).

5 Turkish Premier Adnan Menderes charged that Egypt had exerted pressure on Syria for an agreement on an exclusive Arab defense pact with no links to the Western powers. He warned that Turkey would not condone a policy equivalent to forcibly depriving a country of its freedom of action.

7 Egypt and the UN exchanged notes effecting an agreement relating to an informational media guarantee program.

8 The Yemeni Government announced its support for the new Arab treaty proposals.

It was stated in Beirut that the Lebanese Government had suggested that the proposed Arab treaty be amended to include Iraq and that Major Salah Salem, Egyptian Minister of National Guidance, had agreed to this provided Iraq gave definite assurances that it would not conclude a separate peace with Israel.

9 In a protest note handed to the Libyan Embassy, Egypt protested against the nomination of an Iraqi national as Head of Libya's armed forces and also against the dispatch of an Iraqi military mission to Libya.

10 Foreign Minister of Syria Khaled al-Azm announced that Egypt, Saudi Arabia and Syria were placing part of their armed forces under a Unified Arab Command. Negotiations were going on with Jordan and Lebanon with a view to persuading those countries to join the new Arab alliance.

In a statement Syrian Foreign Minister Khaled al-Azm announced that Syria did not want to see Iraq excluded from the Arab community, and that he wished to explain the proposed new Arab pact and its benefits.

Supplement to 1955

March

25 A trade payments agreement was signed by Egypt and Indonesia under which both countries agreed that trade between them in 1955 would amount to LE150,000.

28 Yemeni Minister to Egypt Abd-al-Rahman Abu-Taleb said that his country had challenged Britain to agree to the setting up of an international committee to inquire into an alleged attack by British troops from Aden on March 26.

The UNTSO Chief of Staff sent a report to the UN Secretary General transmitting complaints by Syria on his report on the observations of the general armistice agreement between Israel and Syria.

In a speech at the Officers' Club in Cairo, Egyptian Premier Colonel Nasser declared that it would require a miracle to obtain any arms from the United States.

29 In a statement before the UN Security Council, US Ambassador Lodge, who recalled the attempts of the UN and of the US to deal with the disturbed Palestine situation and the hope of the US "that patience, understanding, and a real desire to put an end to hostility were beginning to prevail," condemned Israel for the "terrible event" at Gaza.

31 Indian Premier Jawaharlal Nehru said the military alliance currently being forged in the Middle East changed the situation for the worse. As a result of the Turko-Iraqi Military Pact, the Middle East had been split into hostile camps.

April

4 Iraqi Premier Nuri-Said sent a letter and memorandum to the British Ambassador concerning the Baghdad Pact.

Egyptian Premier Colonel Gamal Abdel Nasser stated that London and Washington had obtained the tenuous alliance of Iraq at the price of reawakening Arab fears of Western domination. He called the Baghdad Pact a victory for NATO.

7 The Ruler of Yemen announced that order had been restored and that he had pardoned "all misguided soldiers" who had taken part in the

April

7 uprising. In recognition of Amir al-Badr's services, and in order to end the rivalry within the royal family over the succession, the Ruler officially proclaimed Badr heir to the throne.

Mustafa Ben-Halim, the Libyan Premier, told Parliament that the Libyan Government "found no reason" to join the Turko-Iraqi Pact. The Pact meant military cooperation between two neighbors who were very near to the Communist danger, he said.

10 Major General E. L. M. Burns, Chief of Staff of the UN Truce Supervision Organization, warned both Israel and Egypt that the Gaza Strip incidents had resulted in a deteriorating situation which could and should be ended.

At a press conference Egyptian Minister of National Guidance Major Salah Salem said that Egypt was opposed to joining military alliances sponsored by the West, which were contrary to its best interests, and was pursuing a policy of neutrality between world blocs.

12 Egyptian Prime Minister Colonel Nasser and his colleagues proceeded to Delhi, where the Egyptian Prime Minister held further talks with Indian Prime Minister Nehru.

13 Lebanese Premier Sami al-Solh said that Lebanon would play a leading role in the political moves for "striking a balance" between the two rival regional pacts in the Middle East—the Turko-Iraqi Pact and the Tripartite Arab Alliances.

17 Musa Shahbandar, the Iraqi Foreign Minister, rejected the Soviet allegation made on April 16 that the Arab States were under constant pressure to form military blocs against their will in the Middle East area. Radio Ramallah quoted Shahbandar as saying that Iraq had concluded the military alliance with Turkey purely because of security reasons.

18 The Egyptian UN Representative informed the President of the UN Security Council that Egyptian military authorities would shortly begin to construct barbed wire fences within Egyptian controlled territory along certain essential positions on the Demarcation Line.

April

19 The Soviet Government declared that the establishment of a new power bloc and military bases in the Far and Middle East had "a direct bearing on the security of the USSR."

US Assistant Secretary of State David McKay, temporary US Representative to the UN, addressed the UN Security Council endorsing the proposals of UNTSO for reducing tension in the Gaza Strip.

21 Egyptian Minister of National Guidance and Sudanese Affairs Major Salah Salem said that closer relations with Communist China might grow out of trade talks.

The Israel Foreign Ministry described the UN Security Council's decision not to act on Israel's complaints, as a "manifest and disconcerting instance of partiality," likely to encourage further acts of hostility against Israel. The statement added, "The Powers which determined the outcome of the Security Council debate have assumed a heavy responsibility for its baneful results."

British Ambassador in Paris Sir Gladwyn Jebb stated that North Africa was "absolutely necessary" to France which was itself an essential link in the Western alliance.

25 Attorney General of the Syrian Army Muhammad al-Rifai told the Government at an emergency meeting that investigation had revealed that the Social National Party had ordered the assassination of Colonel Adnan Malki.

26 Syrian Prime Minister Sabri al-Assali stated in the Syrian Chamber that Colonel Malki's assassination had been part of a plan to stage a coup d'etat with the aid of "a foreign power," and that 75 civilians and 30 army officers and other ranks had been detained for interrogation.

May

4 Egyptian Minister of Finance Abd-al-Moneim Kaissouni announced that the National Bank of Egypt had agreed to advance up to 100 million pounds sterling free to help finance development schemes including a new giant dam on the Nile at Aswan.

May

9 After discussions with Egyptian officials in Cairo, UNTSO Chief General Burns announced that Egypt had accepted, with reservations, his four main proposals. These proposals included an Egypt-Israel border patrol and a barbed wire border barrier.

10 Syria warned Lebanon that it would close their frontier unless energetic steps were taken to seek out George Abd-al-Masah, leader of the Syrian National Party, who was known to have found asylum in Lebanon.

11 Saudi Arabia sent a memorandum to Lebanon urging authorities to abandon their policy of "neutrality regarding the Arab Defense Pact.

12 The USSR and Egypt signed a protocol concerning extension of validity of trade lists.

Egypt and Belgium signed a payments agreement.

14 Alfred Naccache, the Lebanese Foreign Minister, reported that relations between Lebanon and Saudi Arabia, which had demanded abandonment of the Lebanese policy of "neutrality," would be "normalized" soon.

17 Syria replied to an Iraqi note protesting against the proposed new Arab alliance between Egypt, Syria and Saudi Arabia. In the reply Syria rejected the allegation that the proposed alliance was a hostile act aimed at Iraq and said its policy was based on national aspirations and Arab interests in general.

18 Israel broke off Mixed Armistice Commission talks on Gaza truce difficulties.

19 The economic and financial clauses of the Convention between France and Tunisia, completed during May, were published.

Syria and the Menhall Prospecting and Exploitation Company signed a concession for exploration rights for the following four years in a 6,000 square mile concession area in northern Syria.

The Israel Army announced that it had staged a retaliatory attack for the detonation of a land mine in a road near the Gaza Strip May 17 in which two Israel soldiers were killed and three wounded.

April

19 Secretary General Dag Hammarskjold of the UN said that the world organization was leaving nothing untried to prevent a resurgence of tension along the Gaza Strip.

23 The Union of South Africa came out in support of France in the Algerian situation.

A communique was broadcast by Cairo Radio concerning an Egyptian-Israel clash in a demilitarized zone over the Egyptian border.

30 Libya and the US exchanged notes constituting an agreement relating to economic assistance.

31 Egypt and China initialled an agreement on cultural cooperation between their two countries.

June

1 Iraq sent a note to Syria warning against joining the projected Saudi Arabian-Egyptian-Syrian defense pact, it was reported in Damascus.

2 The new Jordanian Government would strengthen the country's Air Force "to repulse any further aggression on the armistice lines," the new Premier, Said Mufti, told his first press conference in Amman.

6 The Arab League officially welcomed the Franco-Tunisian Agreement.

7 A law was passed Egyptianizing joint stock companies and subjecting their capital to the national system in the public interest.

Israel Prime Minister Moshe Sharett told UNTSO Chief Burns during discussions on the Gaza situation that full responsibility for the current situation in the Gaza area rested with the Egyptian authorities. He said that Israel supported the UNTSO Chief's call for a high level meeting between both sides.

9 The British Government sent appeals to Colonel Nasser, Egyptian Premier, by Henry Bryoade, US Ambassador in Cairo, to refrain from any acts that would increase tension.

Supplement to 1955

June

11 The Iraqi Cabinet approved a Five Year Plan for development of the nation's resources.

13 Cairo Radio reported that Egypt had rejected the Israel proposal of direct talks between the two countries to discuss the situation along the troubled border area.

14 British Foreign Secretary Harold Macmillan appealed to the Egyptian and Israel Ambassadors in London to refrain from any acts that would increase tension.

15 A conference of some Lebanese parties and politicians issued a statement denouncing the Turko-Iraqi Pact and alliances with Turkey and asking the Lebanese Government to refrain from signing the Turko-Iraqi Pact. The statement ended, "Lebanese public opinion is determined to stand in the face of any policy which is likely to tamper with the Constitution, national sovereignty, Lebanese interests or common Arab aims."

18 US Attorney General Herbert Brownell, Jr., delivered an address on American-Israel friendship before the Zionist Organization of America.

19 The Petroleum Law of Libya was published.

21 The US and Syria signed an air transport services agreement.

Sudanese Minister of Irrigation Hammad stated that negotiations with Egypt on the Division of the waters of the Nile between the two countries were "in a state of complete deadlock" and that the Government was considering asking the World Bank to appoint mediators.

27 Czechoslovakia offered economic aid and credit to Egypt for the construction of a shoe factory and rubber processing plant.

30 A trade and payments agreement was concluded between Egypt and France.

Supplement to 1955

July

21 An agreement and memorandum of understanding in the area of technical cooperation was concluded by Libya and the US.

23 Egypt was "preparing to speak the language of force" with Israel, Major General Abd-al-Hakim Amer, War Minister and Commander in Chief, said in Cairo when armed forces paraded on the occasion of the third anniversary of the Egyptian Revolution.

25 Iraq and the US exchanged notes to effect an agreement concerning the disposition of surplus equipment and materials.

26 The Lebanese Parliament unanimously rejected the US proposed project for development of the River Jordan Valley, because it provided for an Israel share of Lebanese water.

An air agreement between Iraq and India was concluded in Baghdad.

28 An agreement was concluded between the US and Libya for technical cooperation and a public health program.

29 A joint statement was issued by the USSR and Syria at the conclusion of a visit to the USSR by a Syrian parliamentary delegation.

August

1 Egypt and Czechoslovakia signed a payments agreement.

6 A communique said that during the State visit of Indonesian President Sukarno to Saudi Arabia, he and King Saud exchanged views on preserving and strengthening the existing friendly relations between the two countries. There had also been an exchange of views on Islamic matters.

10 US Secretary of State Dulles issued a statement in praise of the Franco-Tunisian Convention.

13 Libya and WHO (World Health Organization) signed a basic agreement for the provision of technical advisory assistance to Libya.

Supplement to 1955

July

1 Egypt and the UK signed an agreement for the release of blocked sterling.

3 Egypt and Syria signed an agreement concerning scheduled air transport services between and beyond their respective territories.

6 Gamal Abdel Nasser, the Egyptian Premier, reiterated in al-Faiyoum, south of Cairo, that Egypt could not negotiate with Israel.

8 David Ben-Gurion, Israel Minister of Defense and former Prime Minister of Israel, speaking at Beersheba, said that the port of Eilat would be completed and passage to the Indian Ocean assured, and that this would be done "if necessary with the help of the Israel Navy, Air Force and Army."

9 Changes in the command structure of the Middle East Air Force, necessitated by the redeployment of RAF forces in the Middle East in accordance with Britain's agreement with Iraq, were announced.

Syrian Minister for Foreign Affairs Khaled al-Azm gave a foreign policy speech to the Syrian Chamber. He referred to the Turko-Iraqi Pact and what accompanied it and said that the immediate contacts Syria had with Arab and foreign states convinced Syria that it did not stand alone in the battle for freedom.

13 British Foreign Secretary Harold Macmillan said that the British note of July 6 made it clear that the UK Government did not recognize Egypt's claim to obstruct the right of innocent passage through an international channel, even though such a passage lay within Egyptian territorial waters.

15 A joint communique issued by delegates of Israel and Egypt in discussions over Israel-Arab border incidents expressed hope for a final draft of a security arrangement for the Gaza area within a week.

17 In Cairo, Ahmad Khairat, Acting Foreign Minister, reitereated "Egypt's right to halt ships entering the Gulf of Aqaba because it is in a state of war with Israel."

18 Libya and the US exchanged notes constituting an agreement relating to emergency wheat aid.

Supplement to 1955

August

13 Major Salah Salem, Egyptian Minister of National Guidance and Sudanese Affairs, said that Egypt wanted the USSR to serve on the five nation neutral commission which was to supervise the Sudanese plebiscite on independence.

16 Sudanese Prime Minister Ismail al-Azhari remarked in the Sudanese Parliament that the longer a foreign rule persisted in an "unfortunate" land, the harder was the task of those nationals who took over.

18 A letter from the Higher Arab Committee for Palestine was presented to the Heads of Arab Governments, Foreign Ministers, the Secretariat General of the Arab League, and to leaders of political parties and parliamentary blocs, concerning Eric Johnston's scheme for the Jordan River Valley.

24 Burhan-ad-Din Bashayan, the Iraqi Foreign Minister, called on all civilized nations to cooperate in using every possible means to end the "French massacre" in Morocco.

26 The Lebanese Government announced that it had decided to break off the American Point Four aid.

UN Secretary General Hammarskjold said that US Secretary of State Dulles' plan for settling the Arab-Israel conflict might be the beginning of a general stabilization of Middle East conditions.

27 Egyptian Premier Colonel Nasser informed the United States Ambassador in Cairo that every Moslem country regarded the French use of NATO forces in North Africa as implicating the whole Atlantic Alliance and as an act of aggression against Arabs everywhere.

28 The Prime Minister of Pakistan declared that Pakistan sympathies rested "entirely with the people of Morocco and Algeria."

Sir John Kotelawala, Prime Minister of Ceylon, declared that US Secretary of State Dulles' plan for an Arab-Israel settlement would "provide a useful starting point" for a "further sincere and determined effort" to settle outstanding Arab-Israel differences. Ceylon, he said, was ready to assist "in the search for a peaceful solution."

Supplement to 1955

August

29 The Pasha of Marrakech and al-Kittani published a statement asserting that the removal of the Sultan of Morocco would violate "the rule of Islam" and the Protectorate Treaty.

31 The Egyptian Foreign Ministry announced that representatives of the Arab States would meet in Cairo August 26 to discuss the US plan proposed by Secretary of State Dulles to promote peace and progress in the Middle East, after special US Ambassador Eric Johnston, then in Cairo, completed his Middle East tour.

An Egyptian spokesman announced that an Egyptian "commando" party had dynamited the mast of a radio station nine miles inside Israel territory after it had broadcast warnings to Egypt of the consequences of attacks on Israel nationals.

September

1 The Prime Minister of Libya addressed a letter to the UN Secretary General on the question of Libya.

A protest of the violation of Israel air space was made by Israel to the UN Truce Supervision Organization.

An Israel Foreign Ministry statement was issued stating that Egypt's offer of a ceasefire in the Gaza Strip was deceitful, since Egyptian military bands were still roaming the country.

2 An additional grant of emergency wheat aid was issued to Libya by the US.

4 Egyptian Deputy Premier Gamal Salem confirmed that the USSR had offered arms to Egypt.

5 The Government of Israel apologized for an incident on the previous night in which an Israel patrol had crossed the border and had subsequently withdrawn after a clash with Egyptian troops in which two Israel soldiers were killed.

Supplement to 1955

September

19 The question of assistance to Libya was discussed in the report of the UN Secretary General.

21 On the advice of the Acting French Commander in Chief in Tunisia, in his capacity as Tunisian Minister of Defense, the Bey of Tunis issued a decree ending the state of seige in Tunisia, which had been in force since 1939.

The Egyptian Cabinet ratified a barter agreement with China whereby China would become one of the foremost consumers of Egyptian cotton.

26 UNTSO Chief General Burns sent messages to the Egyptian and Israel Governments calling upon them to withdraw their forces from the al-Auja demilitarized area simultaneously and immediately, under UN supervision.

The new Syrian Prime Minister, Said al-Ghazi, announced in the Syrian Chamber of Deputies that Syria rejected any plans or attempts for the conclusion of peace with Israel, including the proposals of US Secretary of State Dulles.

27 The UN Secretary General reported on the question of the continuation of the United Nations Tribunal in Libya.

A letter was sent from the Permanent Representative of Israel to the President of the UN Security Council concerning recent Egyptian regulations regarding passage of shipping through the Straits of Tiran into the Gulf of Aqaba.

Israel Ambassador to the UN Abba Eban indicated that his Government might seek US arms to balance any weapons Egypt got from Russia.

Speaking in the UN General Assembly, Yemeni Representative Prince Saif-al-Islam Hassan said that his country would take its dispute with Britain over the borders of the Aden Protectorate to the United Nations if a settlement was not reached through diplomatic channels.

29 Israel's Prime Minister protested to the Soviet Charge d'Affaires against the Soviet and Czechoslovakian agreements to sell arms to Egypt. He expressed Israel's grave concern at the agreements and requested the

Supplement to 1955

September

5 The Chief of Staff of the United Nations Truce Supervision Organization in Palestine, General Burns, reported to the Security Council on the recent incidents between Israel and Egypt in the area of the Gaza Strip.

6 Lieutenant Colonel Anwar Saadat, Egyptian Minister of State and a member of the Revolution Command Council, said that Egypt would buy arms from anyone it wished.

7 A letter was sent from the Permanent Representative of Israel addressed to the President of the UN Security Council concerning additional incidents in the Gaza Strip area.

US, Britain and France called for a September 8 meeting of the UN Security Council to consider border reforms to prevent further Israel-Egyptian fighting in the Gaza area.

Addressing Parliament, Syrian President Kuwatli said it was the duty of every Arab Government to lend support to Egypt in its current struggle against Israel.

8 The Israel Foreign Ministry stated that Israel supported UNTSO Chief General Burn's suggestion for the erection of a physical barrier between the forces of the two sides in the Gaza area.

9 Israel Prime Minister and Foreign Minister Moshe Sharett issued a statement to the press in Jerusalem on security in the Middle East.

11 A decision was made by the Israel Government setting Israel's territorial waters limit at six nautical miles, presumably of 1,852 meters, in the Gulf of Aqaba.

17 In a statement, the French Foreign Ministry said that the Government had suspended contracts for supplying arms to Egypt following "anti-French broadcasts by Cairo Radio."

18 In a speech to the Israel Knesset, Israel Prime Minister Moshe Sharett declared that the supply of arms to Egypt by Czechoslovakia had cast a "deep shadow over the entire scene of Israel's foreign and defense affairs" and was "liable to bring about a revolutionary and ominous change in Israel's security situation."

Supplement to 1955

September

29 Charge d'Affaires to obtain clarification from his Government of its Middle East policy.

It was announced that Egypt and Czechoslovakia had decided to raise their diplomatic missions to Embassy status.

30 The 14 Asian-Arab nations that sponsored the Algerian resolution in the UN argued that the Algerian problem was a matter for UN debate and not an internal affair of France, because France maintained its position in Algeria by force.

In regard to the Palestine situation, UK Prime Minister Harold Macmillan said, "It is clearly the duty of the United Nations to moderate and allay the animosities between Israel and her Arab neighbors."

US Ambassador to the UN John Cabot Lodge said that an Algerian debate in the UN would involve fundamental changes in the French Constitution and that in such a course lay grave dangers to the future of the UN.

October

1 By an exchange of letters the volume of trade between Lebanon and the Soviet Union for the period September 12, 1955 to September 11, 1956 was fixed at LL10,000,000.

3 Syrian Delegate Ahmad Shukairy, speaking in the UN General Assembly, said that Syria accepted no intervention from any side in the exercise of its right to build up its defense and that to be unarmed invited aggression.

Czechoslovakia declared that it would carry out its agreement to supply arms to Egypt in spite of pressure brought to bear on Egypt by the Western powers to cancel.

6 A technical cooperation agreement was concluded between the US and Libya.

Supplement to 1955

October

7 The Israel Foreign Ministry issued a statement claiming that the Government of Israel was in possession of information proving that the Egyptian authorities had decided, after the ceasefire arrangements of September 4, to continue raiding operations against Israel by gangs of saboteurs (fedayeen) from the Gaza Strip, and also to organize similar guerrilla attacks from territory of other Arab States.

In an interview with the correspondent of The New York Times, Premier Colonel Nasser said that Egypt had informed the US in July of its intention to buy arms from Eastern Europe if the Western countries continued to persist in their refusal to supply arms to Egypt. Since the US did not give any attention to the matter he said that his country would now get jet aircraft from the Soviet Union.

8 In a speech at a conference of Foreign Ministers of several Arab League nations, Egyptian Prime Minister Nasser gave details of his negotiations with the West for purchase of arms and the circumstances under which the arms deal with Czechoslovakia had been concluded.

9 The International Bank for Reconstruction and Development approved Syria's request for a $25 million loan to be used to finance a number of development projects.

10 A cultural agreement between Egypt and Indonesia was signed.

A regulation was issued by the Queen of England regulating income tax in Kuwait.

11 Jordan declared its acceptance of the obligation contained in the UN Charter.

It was announced by Cairo Radio that the Soviet Union had offered economic aid to Egypt and in particular had undertaken to assist in financing the Aswan Dam project.

13 It was announced in New York that the United Jewish Appeal had raised over $10 million to resettle the Moroccan Jews in Israel, and that a mission was leaving for that country to survey "priority Jewish immigation, settlement, welfare and rehabilitation needs."

Supplement to 1955

October

15 The Liberation Committee of the Arab Maghreb meeting in Cairo expelled Habib Bourguiba, President of the Neo-Destour, and the member of the party's political bureau, and announced that it recognized Salah Ben-Youssef as the only legitimate representative of the Neo-Destour.

16 Said Ala-ad-Din, Jordan Minister for Economic Affairs, said that Jordan, Egypt, Saudi Arabia, Iraq and Lebanon had agreed to take part in a project to exploit potash deposits in the Dead Sea.

The Syrian Government had issued a sharp warning to Lebanon that relations between the two countries would rapidly deteriorate if it did not take steps to arrest the man accused of the murder of Adnan Malki, the Syrian Deputy Chief of Staff.

17 The Spanish Foreign Ministry replied to a French protest stating that it could not be proved that the Spanish troops had fired on French troops in Morocco.

Egypt requested France to reconsider its decision to cancel the dispatch of French tanks and jet planes ordered by Egypt.

Egyptian Ambassador to the US Ahmad Hussein told US Secretary of State Dulles that Egypt would rather have the US and the International Bank finance the Aswan Dam project than the USSR.

18 Egyptian Ambassador to the US Ahmad Hussein told reporters that he had personally assured US Secretary of State John Foster Dulles that his country's decision to buy arms from Czechoslovakia would not affect American-Egyptian relations.

US Secretary of State Dulles commented on the Egypt-Czechoslovakia arms deal in a news conference. He indicated that the US would adhere to the 1950 Tripartite Declaration in the Mideast, but that the US had not yet decided to send arms to Israel.

19 The Sudanese Cabinet approved the opening of liaison offices in Khartoum for Russia and Czechoslovakia.

20 Syria and Denmark signed an agreement concerning regular civil air services.

Supplement to 1955

October

21 Lebanon and Denmark signed an air transport agreement.

22 The United Nations Truce Supervision Organization submitted its reports on Israel attacks.

An Israel force killed three Syrian soldiers, wounded six and took at least five prisoners in what the UNTSO termed a "well planned operation."

24 The British delegation sent a letter to the UN setting out the British version of the Buraimi Oasis dispute. After describing events leading up to the occupation of the Oasis, it said that the action was taken to protect the legitimate interests of the Ruler of Abu-Dhabi and the Sultan of Muscat, after the Saudi Arabian Government had shown itself no more willing to reach an equitable solution by arbitration than it was previously by negotiation.

Egypt and Hungary agreed to raise their respective diplomatic representatives from Charge d'Affaires to Ministers Plenipotentiary.

25 An Egyptian-Saudi Arabian mutual defense pact was signed.

Libyan Ambassador to the United States Sadiq Muntasir wrote to the UN Secretary General with regard to discontinuance of the UN Tribunal.

26 Jordan applied for membership in the United Nations.

30 The Iraq Foreign Minister summoned the Lebanese Ambassador and the Syrian Charge d'Affaires and told them that Iraq "after full consideration of the bilateral military pacts between Egypt and Syria would welcome negotiating similar pacts with Syria and Lebanon.

November

1 Jordanian Prime Minister Said al-Mufti announced, when reading the Speech from the Throne on behalf of King Hussein, that Jordan intended to reinforce its armed forces with heavy modern weapons and to build up an effective air force. He declared that the Government's policy with regard to Palestine was based on the principles of the Arab League, that Jordan regarded itself as the Arabs' "front line

Supplement to 1955

November

1 against the Zionist danger" and that a solution to the Palestine problem should be found within the framework of a complete understanding between the Arab countries.

Burhan-ad-Din Bashayan, the Iraqi Foreign Minister, declared that if a pact were concluded with Syria, it would not affect his country's obligations under the Baghdad Pact with Britain, Turkey and Pakistan.

It was reported that Syria and Jordan had agreed in principle to set up a joint command over the Syrian Armed Forces and the Jordan National Guard on the Israel border.

2 David Ben-Gurion, Israel Premier, openly criticized Great Britain for selling arms to Egypt while refusing to supply Israel, and the United States for arming Iraq.

Syrian Premier Said al-Ghazi told US, British and French representatives that, because of repeated Israel aggression, Syria no longer felt bound by its international agreements.

3 The Egyptian Representative to the UN addressed a letter to the President of the UN Security Council regarding the situation in the al-Auja area.

4 The Secretary General of the Arab League said that no responsible leader in any Arab country would negotiate with Israel Premier Ben-Gurion or even meet him.

A UK Foreign Office communique said that Anthony Nutting, UK Minister of State at the Foreign Office, and General Burns, UNTSO Chief, had "a most useful talk about ways of restoring tranquility on the Israel-Egypt border."

8 The Saudi Arabian Government granted Syria a loan of $10 million to enable Syria to meet its current economic difficulties and its commitments under the defense pact with Egypt.

9 Israel Prime Minister David Ben-Gurion repeated the desire of the Israel Government for peace and cooperation with Egypt when he received UNTSO Chief Major General E. L. M. Burns.

Supplement to 1955

November

10 The Saudi Arabian Ambassador sent a message to the American Assistant Secretary of State on behalf of the Arab countries stating that any pact signed by the US with Israel or any guarantee given to Israel would be considered by all the Arab States as an act of hostility directed against them.

11 The Opposition agreed to form a coalition Government in Sudan under the leadership of Mirghani Hamzah, who had formed the Independent Republican Party after his dismissal from the Government in December, 1954.

Israel Foreign Minister Moshe Sharett, replying to British Prime Minister Sir Anthony Eden's speech of November 9, said that there was no justification whatsoever for calling for compromise between Israel and the Arab States on the issue of territorial waters.

12 Egyptian President Nasser said in an interview that if the Western countries supplied Israel with arms, the Arab States "would enter a real arms race." He added that the Arabs could get more arms from the Soviet Union if Israel got arms from the West.

13 In a letter to The New York Times, Fadel al-Jamali, Chairman of the Iraqi Delegation to the Tenth Session of the UN General Assembly, denied that the Egyptian arms deals with the Soviet Bloc were primarily due to the Baghdad Pact.

A group of armed Jordanians tried to blow up a house at Rosh Haayin, frontier village of Sde-Hemed, causing some damage but no casualties. An inquiry was instituted by the Israel-Jordanian Mixed Armistice Commission.

14 Moroccan Sultan Sidi Muhammad Ben-Youssef issued a message to the Moroccan people in which he spoke of a "free and independent" Morocco where tolerance and harmony would prevail and all inhabitants would feel safer in their persons, their interests and their freedom. He appealed for the preservation of law and order on the occasion of his return.

The Saudi Arabian Minister to Egypt denied that the Soviet Union had offered to sell arms to his country.

Supplement to 1955

November

21 not launch an offensive war no matter what the provocation and that peace in the Middle East should be based on the maintenance of the status quo.

22 Moroccan Sultan Sidi Muhammad Ben-Youssef told a New York Herald Tribune reporter that US bases in Morocco were in defense of peace, and the Moroccan Government was not opposed to them.

The Israel UN Representative brought to the notice of the President of the UN Security Council the "grave threat created by acts of aggression" against Israel by Egypt.

23 The French National Assembly passed a bill granting a complete amnesty for all political prisoners in Tunisia between January 1, 1952, and August 3, 1955.

The French Cabinet approved the proposed Franco-Tunisian customs union.

US Ambassador to Iraq Waldemar Gallman said in a press statement that in the current circumstances the US Government did not intend to join the Baghdad Pact organization, although its eventual adherence was not excluded. At the moment, however, the US Government considered that it could make a more efficacious contribution by staying outside the Pact.

25 The French Foreign Office denied that licenses had been granted for export of Mystere jet fighters to Israel but said slower Ouragan jets had been shipped to that country.

Egyptian Deputy Foreign Minister Ahmad Khairat, in a press conference in New York, intimated that Egypt would be prepared to negotiate with Israel on the outstanding issues through a third party.

26 British Foreign Secretary Harold Macmillan, in Beirut on his return from the inaugural meeting of the Baghdad Pact, told Lebanese leaders that Jordan would join the Pact. King Hussein was on a state visit to Lebanon at that time.

Israel Premier David Ben-Gurion told the Jerusalem correspondent of The New York Times in an interview that he thought Britain wanted the

Supplement to 1955

November

15 British Prime Minister Anthony Eden asked for a compromise of the Israel-Egyptian dispute.

16 Prime Minister of Libya Mustafa Ben-Halim announced that the British and US Governments, in response to a request by the Libyan Government, had decided to supply the Libyan Army with full equipment for one battalion, including armored cars. He added that there were no conditions of any kind and that the arms supplies were "a new proof of the strong ties which bind Libya with Britain and America."

The Political Committee of the Arab League ended a six day special session. Announcement was made of a decision to have the Arab States work collectively and individually to "destroy the attempts by Israel, world Zionism and its collaborators to obtain arms." On the question of Buraimi it was decided to recommend withdrawal of occupying forces, formation of an arbitration commission and jurisdiction by an international body in the interim.

UK Foreign Minister Anthony Nutting reaffirmed the 1950 Tripartite Agreement by which Britain, together with the US and France, guaranteed existing frontiers between Israel and neighboring Arab States.

17 Salim Lahoud, the Lebanese Foreign Minister, admitted in Beirut that Lebanon had recently signed an arms agreement with the US with no conditions attached.

19 An official spokesman disclosed that Egypt had proposed to the UN Secretary General that the entire al-Auja demilitarized zone should be marked instead of only the western side, as Dag Hammarskjold had suggested.

Israel Foreign Minister Moshe Sharett declared in New York that Israel's attitude to UK Prime Minister Sir Anthony Eden's offer to mediate between Israel and the Arab States would be no different if the US were the author of the idea. He said he was not aware that the US had approached Israel to accept the British initiative.

21 Israel Foreign Minister Moshe Sharett, in a major foreign policy speech, told the National Press Club that the US was under a moral obligation to counterbalance Communist arms sales to Egypt, that Israel would

Supplement to 1955

November

26 Negev to be given to Jordan in order to provide a large, secure base for the British Middle East forces.

29 At his news conference, US Secretary of State Dulles indicated that despite so called Soviet offers in the Middle East and Southeast Asia and the probability that the situations in those areas would be focal points for a time, the United States had a distinct initiative.

The British Foreign Office claimed that Britain was promoting a compromise peace settlement between the Arab nations and Israel.

December

3 Iraq and the US exchanged notes constituting an understanding relating to the disposition of equipment and material pursuant to the mutual defense assistance program.

6 Syria and Iraq signed an oil transit agreement.

A Soviet offer to provide Syria with an oil refinery was reported.

In a communication to the President of the UN Security Council, the British UN Representative denied that it was British policy to allow British aircraft to fly over any part of Saudi Arabian territory without prior permission. He apologized for infringement of Saudi Arabian airspace.

Israel Foreign Minister Moshe Sharett told US Secretary of State Dulles that Israel was willing to discuss minor border adjustments but was opposed to territorial concessions.

8 A letter was sent from the Representative of Israel to the President of the UN Security Council concerning incidents along the Gaza Strip.

10 Israel appealed to the West to move swiftly to reduce the "perils of disparity" in the armed strength of itself and its Arab neighbors caused by Egypt's import of Soviet Bloc weapons. Abba Eban, Israel Ambassador to the US, told the UN General Assembly's Political Committee that he saw in the "Middle Eastern arms crisis nothing but a reflection in miniature of all the perils which arise from a lack of political

December

10 agreement combined with a lack of concern over the equilibrium of armaments."

12 The Sultan of Lahej asserted that he wished to be totally independent, "freed from both the English and the Yemenis."

The Secretary General of the Lebanese Foreign Ministry said that Lebanon was not thinking of joining the Baghdad Pact. He added that his country intended to negotiate trade agreements with Egypt, Syria and Jordan.

A joint statement issued in New Delhi said that there had been a "friendly and informal" exchange of views between Saudi Arabian King Saud and Indian President Nehru on matters of mutual interest, including recent developments in the international situation.

An Israel Government statement issued said that the aim of the December attack had been to silence Syrian batteries which had shelled Israel fishing boats and their police escorts on December 10.

14 The US and Egypt signed a surplus commodities agreement.

General Sir Gerald Templer, British Imperial General Staff Chief, during a week long series of talks with Jordan, presented British conditions for Jordan's joining the Baghdad Pact: continuation of economic aid and Britain's annual subsidy of 11 million pounds sterling to Jordan's Arab Legion.

The Sudanese National Unionist Party proposed that a commission of three, consisting of a Government supporter, an Opposition nominee and a Southern representative, should be appointed to fulfill the functions of Head of State.

15 US Secretary of State Dulles, Britain's Foreign Secretary Harold Macmillan and French Foreign Minister Antoine Pinay reached an agreement to coordinate Western policies to meet Soviet penetration in the Middle East.

The UNTSO Chief of Staff made his report for improving the situation in the Lake Tiberias area.

December

15 Sudanese Prime Minister Ismail al-Azhari stated that his Government had completed its first two tasks, the Sudanization of the Administration and the evacuation of foreign troops, and that it only remained for Parliament to proclaim the country's complete independence.

16 In a statement before the UN Security Council, US Ambassador Lodge, in commenting on the Israel action against Syria on December 11-12, declared that the United States opposed "such acts of military violence" although it realized that there might be provocations for such action for which there was no excuse.

17 UK Foreign Secretary Harold Macmillan stated that the Soviet Union could deal a serious blow to the economy and standards of living of the West if it could get control or cause turmoil in the Middle East.

18 A trade agreement was signed by Syria and Pakistan.

19 A Sudanese Government spokesman announced that the state of emergency imposed after the mutiny in August had been lifted in the provinces of Upper Nile and Bahr-al-Ghazal.

In a British Foreign Office statement, Britain welcomed the declaration by the Sudanese Parliament regarding the independence of Sudan and said that it was consulting the Egyptian Government "about the formal steps necessary to put the resolution into effect."

Saudi Arabian Representative Abd-al-Rahman Azzam protested against the happenings in Oman before the UN.

20 The British Foreign Office announced that the UK intended to give financial aid to Jordan during the fiscal year 1956-57 totalling 12.5 million pounds sterling.

21 An Israel White Paper listed 55 Israel and Zionist statements of good will toward the Arab nations since 1947 against which, it said, the Arabs had maintained a posture of defiance.

22 Israel Ambassador to the UN Abba Eban introduced into the UN Security Council a series of alleged Syrian documents which he said showed that Syrian gunners had been instructed to fire upon Israel vessels in Lake Tiberias.

December

22 The US, UK and France jointly presented a resolution to the UN Security Council to condemn Israel's "flagrant attack" on Syria. The USSR also presented a resolution to censure Israel.

Details of a new Anglo-Jordanian financial agreement were announced in London following discussions between a Jordanian delegation, led by the Ministers of Finance and Economics, and British Treasury officials.

The US and Libya exchanged notes constituting an agreement relating to duty free entry and exemption from internal taxation of relief supplies and equipment.

Syrian Representative to the UN Ahmad Shukairy presented a resolution to the UN Security Council calling for the expulsion of Israel from the UN and the imposition of economic sanctions against Israel for its attack on Syria on December 11.

25 The Jordanian Government announced that the recent talks in London with the British Government on financial matters had been a "success." Britain had agreed to pay over three million pounds sterling to finance various development projects in the country.

26 Egypt, Saudi Arabia and Syria formally announced their readiness to provide Jordan with a grant of eight million pounds sterling if it agreed to reject a yearly British grant of the same amount.

27 Israel Prime Minister David Ben-Gurion offered to meet with the Egyptian Representative "to do everything possible to restore peace" during a meeting that would be held in accordance with the armistice terms.

29 Nikita S. Khrushchev, in an address to the Supreme Soviet, said that Israel had been "threatening her neighbors and pursuing a policy hostile to them . . . from the beginning of her existence."

Tunisia and France signed a protocol of customs union.

31 The UK extended its approval of independence for Sudan.

January, 1956

January 1

The Sudan was proclaimed an independent and democratic republic.

Both former codomini Great Britain and Egypt, officially recognized the independence of the Sudan.

A provisional constitution was brought into operation in Sudan comprising 11 chapters and 121 articles, and largely repeating the Ordinance on Autonomy of 1952.

January 2

Under the terms of the revised Anglo-Egyptian Sterling Agreement of August 29, 1955, Great Britain released the 1956 installment of Egypt's blocked sterling balances.

In answer to a Labor attack in Commons, the British Government reaffirmed that it intended to do all in its power to prevent an arms race in the Middle East, whatever the source of supply.

In a general debate in the Knesset on the security situation, Israel Prime Minister David Ben-Gurion rejected the idea that Israel might start or provoke war as a solution to its security anxieties.

India and the US recognized Sudan as an independent state.

January 3

In a letter to the Security Council, Israel assured the United Nations that it was willing to negotiate with Syria on means of settling border conflicts.

The British Government rejected strong Labor demands for Parliamentary debate on the export of surplus war material to Belgium, which had been reaching Egypt.

Iraqi Prime Minister Nuri-Said's new Cabinet was given a vote of confidence by the Chamber of Deputies, 91-10.

The Soviet Union recognized the independence of Sudan.

In his capacity as Iraq's Defense Minister, Premier Nuri-Said took delivery of 12 Centurion tanks at al-Rashid military camp.

January, 1956

January 3

It was reported in Damascus that under pressure from the Parliamentary Financial Committee and from university students, the Syrian Government recalled its delegation which was negotiating for a loan from the International Bank for Reconstruction and Development.

January 4

A group of 61 leading Algerian officials presented a three point demand to the French National Assembly. The group asked that France recognize Algerian nationality, that the Assembly arrange for direct talks on the country's future with Algerian representatives, and that all political prisoners be released immediately. They threatened to resign their offices in a body if their requests were not met.

The Jordan High Council declared the Royal Decree which dismissed Parliament on December 19 was unconstitutional and illegal. The Cabinet cancelled plans for the new elections scheduled for April.

A one year trade agreement was signed between Lebanon and Poland. Poland was to buy citrus fruit, apples, olive oil and tobacco, in exchange for chemicals, textiles, agricultural machinery and dyes.

The Texas Company and Standard Oil of California announced that their California subsidiaries, Texaco Overseas Petroleum Company and California Asiatic Oil Company, were granted concessions in Cyrenaica and Tripolitania covering about 14.2 million acres.

French Premier Designate Guy Mollet outlined a plan for settling the Algerian problem. It included the institution of a single electoral college; Moslems and non-Moslems on an equal basis; elected representatives with whom France would consult about a new status for Algeria.

January 5

The Western Big Three agreed that Israel should be censured in strong and unequivocal terms for the December 11 raid, but opposed the extreme demands of Syria that Israel be expelled from the UN and that sanctions be imposed.

Syria demanded that Iraq recall its military attache to Damascus, Colonel Salah Mahdi, on grounds that he was engaging in activities against the Syrian Government.

January, 1956

January 5

President Tito of Yugoslavia and Prime Minister Nasser of Egypt issued a joint declaration in which they agreed to remain outside of any major power bloc.

January 6

France refused to permit Spanish participation in the forthcoming negotiations with the Moroccan Government on the future status of French Morocco.

The first Soviet Ambassador to Libya, M. Generalov, arrived in Tripoli.

January 7

President Tito of Yugoslavia denounced the Baghdad Pact, asserting that it did not serve the interests of the people of the Middle East and that it disunited them.

The steamship al-Kahira arrived in Alexandria with a consignment of 114 British tanks from Antwerp, Belgium.

A general election was held in Libya.

Jordanian Premier Ibrahim Hashem resigned.

Demonstrating mobs in Jerusalem, Jordan, stoned the US Consulate; in Amman similar groups burned the US Technical Aid Center.

January 8

An Israel attack on Syria in the Lake Tiberias region caused over 50 Syrian deaths. The Security Council condemned Israel action.

US Secretary of State John Foster Dulles summoned the Jordanian Charge d'Affaires, Taysir A. Touqan, and personally delivered to him a protest against the inadequate police protection of American lives and property during the previous day's violence. The American Ambassador in Amman was instructed to deliver a similar protest.

January, 1956

January 9

Standard Oil of New Jersey announced that the Libyan Government granted its affiliate, Esso Standard Inc. (Libya), seven concessions covering 18.8 million acres. Four concessions were in the province of Tripolitania, two in Cyrenaica and one in Fezzan.

A new Jordanian cabinet, pledged against participation in the Baghdad Pact, was formed and headed by Samir al-Rifai. Stern measures were instituted to quell the present rioting, believed by many to be led by political opponents of the Government.

A British Foreign Office spokesman denied that Britain put pressure on Jordan to join the Baghdad Pact. He said that General Sir Gerald Templer, whose visit to Jordan touched off a riotous political crisis, had not been sent there by Britain but had been invited by the Jordanian Government.

In the bloodiest day in 15 months of disorders, 64 persons were killed in clashes with nationalist rebels in Algeria.

Experts representing the five members of the Baghdad Pact concluded four days of meetings in Baghdad on coordinating Middle East economic resources.

Syria's demand that Israel be condemned for an "outrageous attack" was supported by the Soviet Union. The USSR, in a resolution submitted to the UN, indicated that it might favor sanctions and other extreme measures against Israel if Israel indulged in further raids.

January 10

The British Government ordered about 1,600 paratroopers to be flown to Cyprus "in view of the disturbed position" in the Middle East. It was believed in London that the move was intended to bolster the regime of King Hussein in Jordan.

January 10

The newly named Jordanian Premier, Samir al-Rifai, charged that broadcasts from Egypt and Saudi Arabia helped instigate the violence sweeping through Jordan.

Marshal Tito of Yugoslavia stated in Belgrade that Egypt wanted peace and was not threatening anyone.

January 11

The US, France and the UK asked the Security Council to condemn the Israel attack of December 11, 1955 on Syrian forces. A jointly sponsored resolution assailed the raid as a flagrant violation of the UN Charter and the Syrian-Israel Armistice. The resolution did not call for penalties, thereby differing from the Soviet resolution of January 9.

US Secretary of State Dulles made a strong plea to the US to support the President's long term foreign aid program to counter Soviet penetration of the Middle East and South Asia. He said that defeat in this contest could be as disastrous as defeat in an armaments race.

The coastal area of the Kabylia Mountains in Algeria was put under military rule prior to a major effort of the French Army to eliminate the rebels in that area.

Jordanian Foreign Minister Hussein Fakhri al-Khalidi denied that Egypt, Syria and Saudi Arabia officially offered to extend financial aid to Jordan.

The UK announced a revision of its plans for withdrawing troops from the Suez Canal Zone. Evacuation had been proceeding ahead of schedule as arranged in the Anglo-Egyptian Treaty of 1954, but because of the crisis in Jordan the UK decided to use the entire period allowed for evacuation.

Egypt recalled its Military Attache in Baghdad at the request of the Iraq Government, implicating the Attache in a plot against the regime of Premier Nuri-Said.

January 11

Syria's Prime Minister handed a memorandum to the Charge d'Affaires of Jordan, in the presence of the Egyptian and Saudi Arabian Ambassadors, proposing financial aid to Jordan in the name of Syria, Egypt and Saudi Arabia.

January 12

Evelyn Shuckburg, Assistant Under Secretary in the British Foreign Office and Senior Expert on the Middle East, arrived in Washington, in preparation for the forthcoming meeting of President Eisenhower and Prime Minister Eden, to explore with US officials the possibilities for a common Middle East policy.

Jordanian Premier Samir al-Rifai summoned the Egyptian Ambassador and the Saudi Arabian Charge d'Affaires to complain that hostile radio broadcasts from Egypt and Saudi Arabia were aggravating the situation in Jordan.

The Security Council resumed discussion on the Israel attack on Syria. While the Western Big Three and the Soviet Union called for the condemnation of Israel, they differed in two respects: the Soviet Union made no reference to acts of provocation by Syria, the Western Powers did; and while the Soviet Union asked that sanctions be applied, the Western Powers did not mention sanctions.

An agreement was signed providing for air transportation on a regular basis between Egypt and Saudi Arabia.

The British ship Memphis arrived in Alexandria but was not permitted to take on supplies and its crew was forbidden ashore. It had previously been blacklisted by Egyptian authorities for dealing with Israel.

About 50 persons were killed in a series of clashes between French and nationalist forces in Algeria.

Salah Ben-Youssef, the former Secretary General of the Neo-Destour Party in Tunisia, declared "open war" against his former party and its leader Habib Bourguiba. Ben-Youssef had requested a new Neo-

January 12

Destour congress but the Political Bureau denied the request on grounds that it would create public disorder and that it came from an illegal party.

January 13

UN Secretary General Dag Hammarskjold said that he would be available for talks with Arab and Israel leaders during his forthcoming visit to the Middle East.

USSR Ambassador Extraordinary and Plenipotentiary to Libya, N. I. Generalov, presented his credentials to Amir Muhammad Idris al-Sanusi at Tobruk.

Debate on the Israel censure motion continued in the Security Council. All 11 members agreed that some form of censure should be approved.

Syria and Lebanon completed negotiation on a bilateral defense pact. As agreed, the pact called for joint retaliations in the event of outside attack on either of the signatories.

January 14

The UK complained to Yugoslavia against Marshal Tito's public intervention in the dispute over the Baghdad Pact.

Jordanian Premier Samir al-Rifai in a statement to the press, apparently aimed at the Egyptian and Saudi Arabian efforts, said that Jordan would never allow anyone to interfere in its affairs.

Jordan lifted the curfew imposed in Amman, Jordan-held Jerusalem and other towns as the situation returned to normal. Censorship on outgoing cablegrams was also lifted.

A trade and payments agreement between Syria and Rumania was signed in Damascus.

January 15

UN Secretary General Hammarskjold left New York for talks in the Middle East with Arab and Israel leaders.

The French reported that 71 nationalists and three French soldiers had been killed during the previous 24 hours in Algeria.

Saudi Arabia gave Syria $3 million to complete the terms of a $10 million loan previously offered to Syria.

January 16

Premier Gamal Abdel Nasser presented a new constitution to Egypt.

Israel indicated opposition to the suggestion of voluntary payment for damages to Syria.

January 17

Syria asked the US to cut off economic aid to Israel and said that it would regard continued aid in the face of the recent attack as unfriendly.

Differences between Syria and Lebanon caused indefinite postponement of the initialing of the proposed military defense pact.

January 18

The Government of Prime Minister al-Azhari of Sudan was defeated in Parliament on a budget question by a vote of 46-44. The Prime Minister refused to resign but called for a vote of confidence in his Government.

Egypt and Israel agreed to resume meetings of their Mixed Armistice Commission to hear some 130 complaints which had accumulated since meetings were discontinued in September, 1955.

January, 1956

January 19

The al-Azhari Government of Sudan won a 49-46 vote of confidence.

A UK White Paper was published on the export of British war surplus material and shipments of reconditioned British tanks from Belgium to Egypt (Cmd. 9676).

Syria joined Egypt in an arms deal with the USSR.

The Council of the Arab League approved Sudan's application for membership in the League. Sudan was elected as the ninth member of the Arab League in a meeting of the League Council in Cairo.

The Israel raid on Syrian military posts was unanimously condemned by the UN Security Council.

January 20

Saudi Arabia recognized Sudan.

A high official in the Arab League indicated that Saudi Arabia would take its dispute with Britain over the Buraimi Oasis to the Security Council.

January 21

The Military Council of the Baghdad Pact powers met for the first time in Baghdad.

UN Secretary General Dag Hammarskjold arrived in Cairo for a two day visit.

The Jordanian Government closed three schools in Amman because of a student demonstration on January 19 demanding the release of persons arrested during recent riots.

The Spanish Government announced that under no circumstances would it recognize any authority of the Nationalist Government of French Morocco over the affairs of Spanish Morocco.

January, 1956

January 22

Libyan Premier Ben-Halim formally opened the Libyan University at Benghazi.

French authorities reported that after a week's intensive drive in Algeria, 580 rebels had been killed.

In his first Speech from the Throne, read by Prime Minister Ben-Halim at the first Parliament session, Libyan King Idris stressed that Libya would remain neutral and not join any pact.

January 23

Italy and Libya signed an agreement regulating problems involved in the transfer of Italian sovereignty to the new Kingdom of Libya.

After meeting with Egyptian Premier Nasser and Foreign Minister Fawzi, UN Secretary General Hammarskjold said in Cairo that he felt continued optimism about finding a solution for the Arab-Israel conflict. He left for Tel Aviv.

The Iraqi Government announced that it had broken off talks with the Iraq Petroleum Company about the revision of the existing royalties agreement for the transit of oil by pipeline across Lebanese territory.

The Saudi Arabian Embassy in Washington said that it received a cable from King Saud advising the Embassy to deny that Saudi Arabia had anything to do with the recent disturbances in Jordan.

It was reported in Cairo that Jordan agreed to a meeting with the Foreign Ministers of Egypt, Syria and Saudi Arabia to discuss possible economic aid to Jordan.

Press censorship was imposed in Jordan.

Thami al-Glaoui, Pasha of Marrakech, Morocco, died after an illness of several months.

January, 1956

January 24

Jordan and Israel accepted UN truce proposals to ease Middle East tension.

The UN Truce Supervision Organization published the Secretary General's proposals, accepted by Israel and Egypt, for relieving tension in the Middle East.

UN Secretary General Hammarskjold met with Israel Prime Minister David Ben-Gurion and Foreign Minister Moshe Sharett.

Iraq announced its decision to refer to arbitration its dispute with the Iraq Petroleum Company on oil royalties for the year 1953.

About 80 Algerian nationalist rebels seized the village of Izhil Bouamas in the Kabylia Mountains near Michelet. After setting fire to the rural school, the rebels withdrew to the hills.

Arab League Secretary General Muhammad Abd-al-Khaleq Hassouna informed the West German Ambassador to Egypt of the League's desire that West Germany reconsider the German-Israel reparations agreement, now that it had become independent.

UN Secretary General Dag Hammarskjold announced that Egypt had accepted three proposals to ease tension in the vicinity of the demilitarized zone at al-Auja.

January 25

UN Secretary General Hammarskjold arrived in Amman. After conferring with government leaders he flew to Beirut.

King Ahmad of Yemen sent a special plane to transport four Soviet economics experts from Egypt to Yemen to hold talks with the Yemen Government.

US Secretary of State John Foster Dulles told Israel Ambassador Eban that the US was not prepared at this juncture to meet Israel's request for arms. He assured him, however, that the US would consider the matter further.

January, 1956

January 25

Egypt protested to Iraq after a messenger at the Egyptian Embassy had been arrested and charged with plotting to assassinate high Iraqi officials.

January 26

A voluminous British dossier on alleged Saudi Arabian moves against Western interests in the Middle East was shown to US Government officials in Washington. This material allegedly confirmed British charges that the Saudi Arabian Government was spending large sums, derived from Arabian American Oil Company revenues, to promote its influence with Egypt and to combat American and British political aims in the Middle East.

Jordanian Premier al-Rifai in Parliament pledged his Government to reject all alliances.

The Economic Council of the Arab League concluded a three day session. It was decided to institute an Arab Financial Establishment for Economic Development, with capital of LE20 million, to which member states would subscribe in proportion to their share in the League's budget. The Council also decided to establish a petroleum office in the Arab League Secretariat to coordinate the policies of the Arab oil producing countries.

Syria accepted an invitation to discuss with General Burns, Chief of Staff of the UN Truce Supervision Organization, means of reducing tension along the Israel border.

The US announced relinquishment of its extraterritorial rights in Morocco.

Allal al-Fassi, leader of the Moroccan Istiqlal Party, arrived at Baghdad to discuss the Moroccan question with Arab leaders.

The trial of the Egyptian Embassy messenger opened, along with that of two Israelis also charged with smuggling bombs into Iraq to assassinate certain officials.

January, 1956

January 27

A new short wave radio station in Jordan broadcasted a report that during the recent disturbances Saudi Arabia was massing troops along Jordan's frontier.

It was reported in Paris that the French Government sent notes to the US and Great Britain urging them not to extend the Baghdad Pact.

Egyptian Premier Nasser gave a speech violently attacking Iraq and the Baghdad Pact.

January 28

Bulgaria and Egypt signed a trade agreement, exchanging Bulgarian tobacco for Egyptian cotton.

Yemen officially protested a concession granted by the British Government for oil explorations on Kamaran Island in the Red Sea.

Eugene R. Black, President of the IBRD (International Bank for Reconstruction and Development), began discussions with Egyptian Prime Minister Nasser on the proposed International Bank loan for the construction of the Aswan High Dam.

The new Tunisian Government acted against the ultra-nationalists, led by Salah Ben-Youssef, by arresting about 40 of his associates.

All the Egyptian envoys to Middle Eastern countries met in Cairo to discuss inter-Arab tensions.

Egyptian Premier Nasser asked that a meeting of the Arab League Council be called to discuss the dispute over the arrest of a messenger of the Egyptian Embassy in Baghdad.

Former US President Harry S. Truman, Mrs. Franklin D. Roosevelt, and Walter P. Reuther, Vice President of the AFL-CIO (American Federation of Labor-Congress of Industrial Organizations), issued a joint plea that the US supply Israel with defensive arms.

UN Secretary General Hammarskjold arrived in Baghdad after concluding talks in Syria.

January, 1956

January 30

Sudanese Premier Ismail al-Azhari bowed to demands of the Opposition to form an all party government.

The Iraqi Council of Ministers approved the treaty of friendship with Indonesia.

The Egyptian Foreign Ministry said it was calling an Arab League Council meeting to discuss not only the case of the arrested messenger but also the deteriorating relations between Iraq and Egypt, which threatened the unity of the Arab world.

Abba Eban, Israel Ambassador to Washington, appealed to US President Eisenhower and UK Prime Minister Eden to make it possible for Israel to buy arms.

January 31

The Sudanese Government formally submitted an application for membership in the UN.

The Jordanian House of Representatives approved the appointment of al-Rifai as the new Premier of Jordan.

Foreign Minister Lahoud stated that the Iraq Government offered to mediate between the Lebanese Government and the Iraq Petroleum Company in their dispute over oil royalties.

The Saudi Arabian Foreign Ministry issued a statement calling for the re-establishment of friendly relations with Britain, but saying that the Government would not permit any Saudi Arabian territory to be unjustly taken.

US President Eisenhower and UK Prime Minister Eden discussed the possibility of stationing UN armed forces on the Arab-Israel frontiers. Amid reports that neither Egypt nor Israel favored the idea, it was indicated that the UK and the US also disagreed.

January, 1956

January 28

It was reported in Washington that the US was seeking to use its good offices in the dispute between Britain and Saudi Arabia over the Buraimi Oasis.

January 29

A new radio station in Amman, set up to rival the Egyptian "Voice of the Arabs" station, began broadcasting. Its first transmission was a violent attack on Israel.

Three Sudanese ministers resigned from the government because the Premier failed to accept a list of ministers proposed for an all party government.

The Jordanian Government of Samir al-Rifai won a 35-3 vote of confidence in Parliament.

The Spanish Government announced that additional authority would be gradually assigned to Moroccans in the Spanish Zone, although final approval of any reorganization must be given by General Franco.

Proposals by French Premier Designate Guy Mollet to modify the French administration in Algeria in order to give a greater role to the Algerians encountered wide opposition as French residents in the area demonstrated against any appeasement.

King Faisal of Iraq received Moroccan leader, Allal al-Fassi, and expressed his sympathy with the cause of the Arab Maghreb.

An Iraqi spokesman in Baghdad said that his Government opposed a meeting of the Arab League Council on the ground that such a body was not a high tribunal for hearing a criminal case.

Syria signed a trade agreement with Egypt providing for free exchange of agricultural products, 25 percent reduction in tariffs on some industrial products and 50 percent reduction in some others. This agreement also provided for settling payments through an account in Egyptian pounds.

February, 1956

February 1

UK Prime Minister Anthony Eden and US President Eisenhower issued the Declaration of Washington DC reaffirming their joint policy in the Middle East.

The first consignment of British arms and equipment was turned over to the Libyan Army in a ceremony at Tripoli.

February 2

The head of the Jordanian delegation to the meeting of the Arab League Economic Council said in Amman that Egyptian Premier Nasser told him that the Egyptian Government would contribute LE125, 000 to Jordanian economic plans.

Ismail al-Azhari of Sudan formed a coalition government consisting of eight members of his National Union Party and eight members of opposition parties.

In Algiers, an estimated 100, 000 Frenchmen demonstrated against the announced policies of French Premier Mollet and against appointed Minister Resident Catroux.

New figures published in an official US Government document gave proved oil reserves in the Middle East as 230 billion barrels, as compared with 97. 5 billion barrels previously reported by the Department of the Interior.

February 3

Israel's Foreign Minister Sharett said in Tel Aviv that posting UN military forces along the Israel-Egyptian frontier would be likely to increase Middle East problems rather than to solve them.

February 4

More than 4, 000 Algerian Europeans paraded in the rain to protest the nomination of General Georges Catroux as Minister Resident in Algeria.

February, 1956

February 4

Egypt lodged an official protest with the UN Armistice Commission over an Israel attack on an Egyptian outpost south of Gaza.

The Soviet Union protested for the third time against Iran's accession to the Baghdad Pact.

The Bey of Tunis ordered nationalization of Tunisia's two privately owned railroads.

February 5

Press censorship in Jordan was officially lifted.

February 6

Talks began in Cairo between Egyptian and Hungarian envoys toward replacing the present Hugarian-Egyptian short term agreement with a long term trade and payments agreement. Talks also began with Bulgarian and Communist Chinese trade delegations.

Canadian Prime Minister St. Laurent announced that his Government had lifted its three week embargo on arms to the Middle East and that future orders would be handled on their merits.

Syrian laborers demonstrated in Aleppo against a decree which prevented members of labor syndicates from belonging to a political party or organization.

The Security Council unanimously approved the admission of Sudan as the seventy-seventh member of the UN.

On his arrival in Algiers, French Premier Mollet was met by a wildly hostile demonstration of Frenchmen protesting his proposed negotiations with Algerian national leaders. The Premier announced that he accepted the resignation of General Catroux as Resident Minister in Algiers.

A Soviet delegation arrived in Yemen.

February, 1956

February 6

A Lebanese security squad arrested three Israel agents in Bint Jubail, near the Israel-Lebanese border. They were tried and convicted of spying for Israel.

Tunisian nationalist rebel, Salah Ben-Youssef, escaped into Libya where he was granted political asylum.

The Polish engineering delegation scheduled to rebuild the Hejaz Railway arrived in Amman.

Iraq received 12 Centurion tanks under the military assistance agreement between itself and the US.

Jordan's Premier Samir al-Rifai said in Baghdad that Iraq accepted an invitation from King Hussein to attend a conference in Amman of Arab chiefs of state and premiers.

The Trans-Arabian Pipeline Company accepted in principle Syria's demand for increased royalties on the passage of oil by pipeline through Syrian territory.

Replying to a request by 127 members of the US Congress that Israel be allowed to purchase arms, US Secretary of State Dulles said that he felt that Israel's security could be better assured by means other than an arms race.

February 7

The French Foreign Ministry declared in Paris that France was ready to negotiate on Tunisian independence. Habib Bourguiba, Tunisian political leader and President of the Neo-Destour Party, stated that agreement was reached for Tunisia to have its own army and diplomatic representation.

Moderate nationalists of Algeria expressed the view that the French Government had stripped them of political authority, leaving the NLF (National Liberation Front) as the only representative for Algerian Moslems.

February, 1956

February 7

Four experts from India engaged for services with the Post and Telegraph Administration arrived in Khartoum, Sudan.

A delegation of lawyers demanded the resignation of Sudan's Prime Minister al-Azhari.

French Premier Mollet promised French settlers in Algeria that his Government would never abandon Algeria.

February 8

Ten Libyan cadets arrived in Baghdad to receive training at Iraqi military schools.

Crowds in Casablanca welcomed Moroccan Sultan Ben-Youssef's first public appearance outside Rabat since his return from exile November 16.

The weekly magazine Akher Saah published pictures of the arms Egypt had received from Czechoslovakia.

US President Eisenhower said that everything he could constitutionally do to prevent an outbreak of hostilities in the Middle East would be done. Under Secretary of State Robert D. Murphy conferred with the British and French Ambassadors to implement Eisenhower's policy.

Egyptian Finance Minister Kaissouni said that his Government accepted in principle the terms of a loan from the International Bank for Reconstruction and Development to finance part of the Aswan High Dam project.

Law Number 32 was issued in Egypt requiring Egyptians to obtain permission before taking employment with foreign organizations in Egypt. Egyptians already working for such organizations would have to obtain the permission of the Ministry of the Interior within three months.

February, 1956

February 9

Muhammad Ali Isa, an employee of the Egyptian Embassy in Baghdad, was sentenced to four years imprisonment for heading a conspiracy against the Iraqi Government and conspiring to blow up the embassies of the Baghdad Pact powers.

Premier Mollet named Economics Minister Lacoste, Resident Minister in Algeria. He told the Algerian Europeans again that France would not abandon Algeria, and at the same time told the Algerian Moslems that the "gigantic" injustices from which they had suffered would be redressed.

Elections were held in Bahrain for a six member committee to supervise health affairs. The elections were the first in the history of the Persian Gulf.

Robert Lacoste arrived in Algiers and assumed his new post of Minister Resident in Algeria.

One of the British Army's three overseas supply reserve depots at Al-Kirsh was handed over to the Egyptian Army.

The Soviet Union announced an atomic aid program to Egypt.

The Iraqi Minister of the Interior ordered the withdrawal of residents' visas from 20 Palestinian Arabs after information was obtained that the Palestinians were cooperating with subversive elements. They were asked to leave the country immediately.

February 10

Jordanian Premier al-Rifai, accompanied by the Chief of the Royal Cabinet, arrived in Cairo, the third stop on his tour of Arab capitals on his avowed mission to settle Arab antagonism, particularly between Egypt and Iraq. He conferred with Egyptian Premier Nasser and Foreign Minister Fawzi.

February, 1956

February 11

French Premier Mollet returned to Paris after a week visit in Algeria with no evident solution to the 15 month old rebellion.

While Jordanian Premier al-Rifai was visiting Egypt, 200 Jordanian students gathered at the Jordanian Embassy in Cairo to protest against the Baghdad Pact.

Limited home rule was restored to Morocco in a protocol signed by Premier Bekkai and Resident General Andre DuBois, in accordance with an agreement of November 6.

The Belgian Association of Merchants, Exporters and Importers called on the Belgian Government to take action against Arab business firms and to aid Arab economic warfare against Israel by demanding that Benelux businessmen reveal any Jewish connections.

Terrorism reappeared in Tunisia following the flight of Rebel leader Ben-Youssef to Tripoli. Plastic explosives were used against the Neo-Destour offices in Tunis. Tahar Lassoued, outlaw chieftain, issued a manifesto announcing the creation of a Tunisian National Liberation Army. The announcement coincided with ten bombings and attacks on French soldiers in Tunis.

February 12

It was reported in Cairo that the Jordanian Government dropped its plan with Syria to build a $40 million dam on the Yarmuk River.

Sheikh Larbi Tebessi, presiding alim of Algeria, told reporters that the ulama would not discuss the Algerian problem with French Resident Minister Lacoste until the French Government promised Algeria independence.

The Algerian Assembly convened in Algiers for the first time since November. After a brief formal session, it adjourned until February 21.

The Soviet Union officially announced that it would consider the sending of British and US troops to the Middle East a threat to peace and an object of legitimate concern. This implied that the USSR would

February, 1956

February 16

It was reported in Washington that Egypt no longer insisted that it select the contracts for the Aswan High Dam without advertising for competitive bids.

The US Department of State announced that 18 tanks were being shipped to Saudi Arabia. Israel denounced the shipment.

Premier Mollet announced to the French National Assembly his Government's determination to maintain its link with Algeria by rendering economic, social and political justice to its population.

February 17

The Algerian policy, defined February 16 by French Premier Mollet, was received coolly in Algiers. The nationalists expressed bitterness over the denial of nationhood. Europeans expressed hostility to the proposal for a common electoral roll composed of the eight million Moslems and one million Europeans, who had previously been on separate rolls.

The Egyptian Ambassador to Washington stated that he was reassured that the US cotton selling policies would seek to avoid upsetting the world market.

The White House announced the suspension of all arms shipments from the US to the Middle East. This step was taken following a protest by members of Congress and by the Israel Ambassador on the scheduled shipment of tanks to Saudi Arabia.

Both nationalists and Algerian Europeans demonstrated against Premier Mollet's single electoral roll proposal.

February, 1956

February 12

ask the Security Council to deal with any US-British troop movements to the Middle East.

Moroccan Sultan Muhammad Ben-Youssef arrived in Paris as head of a delegation whose purpose it was to negotiate with France on freer relations between the two countries.

It was reported in Cairo that Premier Nasser was urging Jordan to join Egypt in a bilateral defense pact; this was interpreted as an effort to keep Jordan from joining the Baghdad Pact. The Egyptian Premier was reported also to have rejected the Jordanian proposal for a meeting of Arab chiefs of state to discuss action on Arab unity.

February 14

Israel Premier David Ben-Gurion disclosed that Israel would hold up work on the Jordan Valley Project, pending another attempt by the US to obtain Arab political agreement on joint development of the plan.

Egypt told the US that any sharp reduction in the amount of long staple cotton the US permitted to be imported might result in the end of US-Egypt trade relations.

It was reported in Washington that the three Western powers would resume consultations on joint measures to prevent war in the Middle East. This was interpreted as a refusal by the Big Three to be sidetracked by the Soviet protest.

British Prime Minister Eden said in reaction to the Soviet statement about the Middle East that the 1950 tripartite declaration against aggression was in full harmony with the United Nations Charter.

February 15

Syrian President Kuwatli sent a special message to the Chamber of Deputies urging all parties to unite against external danger.

February, 1956

February 18

The Saudi Arabian Ambassador to Washington protested the suspension of the shipment of American tanks to Saudi Arabia.

Lieutenant General Richard A. Hull, Commander of British troops in Egypt, moved his headquarters from Moscar to Port Said, inaugurating the fourth and final stage of British withdrawal from Suez.

The US Department of State announced the lifting of the embargo on the shipment of arms to the Middle East. This meant that 18 tanks would go to Saudi Arabia as scheduled.

February 19

A violent clash occurred in Kosti between Sudanese farmers and police. The farmers were demonstrating in support of their demands for higher crop prices. Police jailed 281 of the demonstrators, including women, overnight in a small windowless room; 192 persons died of suffocation during the night.

US Senator Walter F. George (Democrat, Georgia) declared that the Senate Foreign Relations Committee would undertake an inquiry into the Administration's entire foreign policy.

After a flight of nine MIG jets over Cairo, Premier Nasser claimed that if war came to the Middle East, Egypt would be ready for it.

The Cairo newspaper al-Ahram published a report that Syria had joined Egypt in concluding an arms pact with Russia.

February 20

It was reported in Amman that King Saud of Saudi Arabia had accepted an invitation to attend a conference of Arab chiefs of state to consider the question of Arab unity.

The UN Mixed Armistice Commission censured Egypt for an Arab-Israel ceasefire violation on August 26, 1955.

February, 1956

February 20

Israel patrolmen captured a member of the Jordanian National Guard inside Israel territory.

February 21

Two proposals made by Syria, which would have modified the provisions of the Syrian-Israel armistice agreement, were rejected by Israel. The proposals were to permit Syrian farmers to cross the ten meter strip of Israel territory along the northeast coast of the Sea of Galilee, and to forbid Israel patrol boats from approaching within 800 feet of that shore.

Seven members of the outlawed Syrian Nationalist Party were arrested in Damascus on a charge of conspiring to assassinate three Syrian officers and a member of Parliament.

Three exchanges of gunfire between Israel fishermen and Syrian riflemen broke the 10 week truce on Lake Tiberias.

February 22

Premier M'Barek Bekkai said, at the start of formal negotiations between France and Morocco, that Morocco would undertake discussion on interdependence as a sovereign state and on an equal footing. The Premier outlined the Moroccan position demanding abrogation of the 1912 protectorate treaty, control over their military, diplomatic and security affairs and complete territorial unity.

A Soviet economic development mission on a tour of the Middle East arrived in Beirut. The Soviet Minister, Sergei P. Kiktev, called on President Chamoun and offered the services of Soviet technicians in increasing Lebanon's trade with the Soviet Union.

US Secretary of State Dulles said he knew nothing about the tanks to Saudi Arabia controversy but would investigate the matter.

February, 1956

February 23

The International Bank for Reconstruction and Development announced that it had granted a $27 million loan to Lebanon in August, 1955.

Sudanese student rioting broke out in Khartoum over the death of the tenant farmers in the Kosti prison.

Hajj Messali, Algerian nationalist leader, said that French recognition of Algerian independence was a prerequisite for re-establishing peace.

February 24

A UN Headquarters communique stated that Syria had informed the Joint Armistice Commission that villagers were responsible for the three shooting incidents of February 21-23.

US Secretary of State Dulles told the Senate Foreign Relations Committee that the decision regarding the controversial tanks was that of Under Secretary of State Hoover. Mr. Dulles told the group that the Free World was stronger than it had been a year before and that Russia had had to revise and replace a bankrupt strategy. He asserted that the Soviet Union had made very little progress in the Middle East. The tanks were to go to Saudi Arabia.

An Algerian guerrilla leader said in Cairo that his forces would accept arms from the Soviet Bloc or "even from the devil himself" to carry on their fight for liberation from French rule.

February 26

It was reported in Amman that King Hussein had invited all the Arab states to participate in a conference to plan a united Arab front against Israel.

Tunisian Premier Ben-Ammar, with other Tunisian leaders, arrived in Paris to begin talks with French leaders on Tunisian independence.

February, 1956

February 26

The Saudi Arabian Defense Minister, while touring Egyptian military installations, told a group of Palestinian refugees that their "day of salvation is at hand."

A Syrian delegation left Damascus for Turkey to conclude a trade and payments agreement.

Egyptian Minister of Commerce and Industry Nusair said that the Government had signed an agreement for the importation of 375,000 tons of wheat from the US. He stated that 30,000 tons had already been received.

Mobs of Algerian Moslems and French settlers engaged in street battles with French policemen in Oran and Constantine.

Nine men were tried in a Baghdad court on a charge of forming, without prior permission, a political party called al-Tahrir (Liberation).

Iraq formally offered military aid to Lebanon and Syria in the event of Israel's diversion of the Jordan River.

February 27

UN Secretary General Hammarskjold, after visiting with leading Arab and Israel statesmen, said that he saw no basis for panicky reactions to the situation in the Near East. He said that there was no need for action by either the Security Council or the General Assembly.

Teachers at private schools in Lebanon resumed their work after being on strike for ten days, demanding equal treatment with teachers in government schools.

Sudanese government officials and school teachers demonstrated in Khartoum in protest against the Kosti affair.

A Japanese trade fair opened in Cairo.

February, 1956

February 28

Robert Lacoste, French Minister Resident in Algeria, was reported to have asked for 200,000 additional soldiers to guard the four African Departments against rebels.

French Premier Mollet broadcast an offer to Algerian rebels to choose between a ceasefire, followed by elections and discussions of Algeria's future status, or all out war. He announced decisions taken at a cabinet meeting February 27 to offer justice and equality to Moslems and protection of rights to Europeans living in Algeria.

Tunisian Premier Tahar Ben-Ammar demanded, at the start of negotiations with France for Tunisian independence, that the protectorate treaty be discarded.

Israel asked the US for a definite answer as to whether it would be allowed to buy arms in the US.

Agriculture Secretary Benson announced that the US Government would put all federally owned surplus cotton on the world market beginning August 1. Reports of the plan sent cotton futures tumbling by $3 a bale on the Cotton Exchange. Egypt officially protested the action.

February 29

Cairo held its first full scale civil defense exercise.

The Sudanese Court in Kosti sentenced a government deputy and prominent member of the Anti-Imperialist Front Party, the Secretary of the Party, and the President of the Workers' Syndicates Union to six months imprisonment for taking part in a protest demonstration in Kosti.

Jordan officially informed Syria of its decision to suspend the work of the Joint Syrian-Jordanian Yarmuk Committee until further notice.

The French Government reorganized its High Military Command and requested special powers to deal with the Algerian revolt.

March, 1956

March 1

The Secretary General of the Moroccan Istiqlal Party said that between a week and ten days would be needed before a ceasefire order, sent to nationalists fighting the French in the Rif and northeastern Morocco, reached all of them and stopped hostilities.

The Budget Committee of the Syrian Chamber of Deputies approved the Syrian civil defense budget of SL18, 500, 000.

A trade agreement was reached between Jordan and Yugoslavia, replacing the 1954 agreement.

Jordanian King Hussein issued a Royal Decree relieving Lieutenant General Glubb of his command of the Arab Legion. The decree also terminated the services of three other high ranking British officers of the Legion. It named Brigadier General Radi Innab as the new Commander of the Legion. Demonstrators milled in the streets of Amman celebrating the dismissals made by King Hussein.

British Foreign Secretary Lloyd opened talks with Premier Nasser in Cairo in an effort to bolster British prestige in the Middle East.

Egypt signed a contract with Communist China to import 5, 000 tons of cottonseed oil.

The Standard Oil Company of New Jersey had proposed to the Syrian Government the construction of an oil refinery at company expense to provide petroleum products for the local market.

The 1951 trade agreement between Iraq and Italy was extended for a further year.

In London the British Government expressed deep shock over the dismissal of General Glubb. The sudden action of Jordan's King Hussein was conceded to be a fresh blow to British prestige in the Middle East.

French Premier Mollet asked the National Assembly for unlimited powers to carry out reforms and pacification in Algeria.

March, 1956

March 2

Cairo viewed Jordan's dismissal of General Glubb as a far reaching victory for Premier Nasser and as a blow to the prestige of Britain and the West.

The independence of Morocco was recognized in a joint declaration by France and Morocco. A protocol to govern relations during further negotiations was also signed.

Israel Ambassador Eban called upon US Secretary Dulles, as the latter was about to leave for Karachi, to review the problem on arms shipments to Israel. No definite answer was given to him concerning his request to purchase arms.

March 3

From Beirut it was reported that the dismissal of General Glubb cheered anti-Western forces throughout the Middle East.

The Jordanian Government announced that it would honor the 1948 treaty of friendship with Britain which granted Britain bases in Jordan.

The Syrian Chamber of Deputies approved bills setting up model villages and an Arab civil aviation council, and ratified an air agreement with Denmark.

An economic agreement was signed between Turkey's Foreign Ministry and a Syrian delegation.

Saudi Arabia received two fighter planes from Egypt.

The Egyptian Cabinet approved the new electoral law. It gave women optional voting rights and made voting compulsory for men.

March 4

Iraq's King Faisal pardoned the Egyptian Embassy messenger, Muhammad Ali Isa, who was sentenced in February to four years imprisonment for subversive activities.

March, 1956

March 4

An Egyptian trade delegation arrived in Prague to visit Czechoslovakian industries.

An Arab postal conference in which representatives from all the Arab countries except Yemen and Sudan participated, opened in Baghdad.

The chief of the Soviet engineering mission on a visit to Syria told newsmen in Damascus that the mission wished to offer Syria an oil refinery.

In Amman, Jordanian Premier Samir al-Rifai was reported to have commented on General Glubb's dismissal that he thought this would help Jordan's friendship with Britain and the Western world. Glubb's going removed the stigma under which Jordan "has so long labored in the eyes of our fellow Arabs, of not being our own masters."

March 5

Jordanian Premier al-Rifai said that the termination of General Glubb's service was to be regarded as a purely internal affair. He declared that Jordan's treaty relationship with Britain should be based on common interest, not on individuals.

After three meetings with Indian Prime Minister Nehru and other leaders, British Foreign Secretary Selwyn Lloyd said that there was not much point to India's argument that the Baghdad Pact tended to split Arab unity.

Britain recalled 15 top officers from the Arab Legion as a result of the Glubb dismissal which Prime Minister Eden had called a violation of the spirit of British-Jordanian accords.

Moroccan Sultan Ben-Youssef received a tumultuous welcome in Rabat upon his return from France after having secured Morocco's independence.

March, 1956

March 6

British Ambassador to France, Sir Gladwyn Jebb, praised French policy in North Africa in a report to Associated Regional Newspapers in Paris.

Egyptian Premier Nasser, Syrian President Kuwatli and King Saud of Saudi Arabia opened a conference in Cairo to discuss the future of Jordan and a unified Arab front.

Syria complained to the Mixed Armistice Commission of Israel's violation of Syrian air space on March 5.

The first issue of the Communist French language newspaper Syria was published in Damascus.

French Premier Mollet summoned the Egyptian Ambassador in Paris to discuss aid allegedly given by Egypt to Algerian rebels.

Israel Prime Minister David Ben-Gurion told the Knesset that his Government would not start a war. He declared that although he was less hopeful, he still thought that war could be prevented. But if war broke out, moral responsibility would fall on the United States and the Soviet Union, which had supplied arms to Egypt.

March 7

Sultan Ben-Youssef broadcast criticism of Spanish troops for their brutality in breaking up demonstrating Moroccans on March 4 and 5.

The first American shipment of aid to Palestinian refugees was unloaded in Beirut.

In a letter to the Security Council, Israel accused Syria of two flagrant acts of aggression on March 4 and 5.

British Prime Minister Eden warned Egypt that it could not combine professions of friendship with incitements to hostility and maintain cordial relations with the West. In the light of the Glubb dismissal, the annual British subsidy to Jordan might be reviewed.

US President Eisenhower called on the United Nations for urgent and early action to pacify the Middle East.

March, 1956

March 8

Lieutenant General Rafael Garcia Vallino, High Commissioner of Spanish Morocco, was called to Madrid for a meeting with Generalissimo Franco.

The US State Department emphasized that the lead in seeking Middle Eastern peace should be taken by the UN.

A Turkish parliamentary mission arrived in Iraq.

The new Chief of Staff of the Arab Legion, Major General Radi Innab, denied reports of disagreement among Arab officers of the Legion.

Yemen and the Soviet Union signed a trade agreement.

The six members recently appointed to the new Bahrain Education Council to complement the elected members were asked to resign by the Higher Executive Committee of the Government because of non-cooperation.

Robert Lacoste, French Minister Resident in Algeria, told the French National Assembly that a major military, economic and social effort was necessary to check the tide of rebellion in the protectorate.

Meeting in Cairo, King Saud of Saudi Arabia, Premier Nasser of Egypt and President al-Kuwatli of Syria sent King Hussein a note outlining the decisions they had taken regarding Jordan. Syrian Premier Said al-Ghazzi flew to Amman with a special message for King Hussein from the three conferees.

An official communique issued by the three Arab leaders meeting in Cairo stated that they had reviewed the Baghdad Pact and the pressure brought to bear on Arab states as a result of the Pact. They had also analyzed the "weakening effect the Pact had on the Arab world and its disuniting influence."

March 9

Egypt concluded a trade transaction with North Vietnam.

March, 1956

March 9

A French mob wrecked the buildings of the US Consulate General and the US Information Service Library in Tunis.

Prime Minister Eden declared that his policy toward the Middle East would be one of watchful waiting.

In support of the revolt in their homeland, 10,000 Algerians marched toward the National Assembly in Paris.

King Hussein rejected an offer from three Arab leaders to replace Britain in subsidizing Jordan's defense forces, on the condition that Jordan drop the present subsidy.

March 10

In Paris, officials declared that workers in the March 9 Algerian strike were under orders from a clandestine nationalist organization.

Moulay Hassan Ben-al-Mahdi, the Sultan's chief representative in Spanish Morocco, said that his country would resist any action endangering its unity and independence.

The French Government condemned the wrecking of the US buildings in Tunis and conveyed a formal apology to the American Ambassador in Paris, offering to pay the full cost of repairs.

March 11

Israel modified its position on compensation. Israel stated that when Arab Governments agreed to reverse the present trend of tightening their economic blockade against Israel, Israel would be ready to make known its detailed plans for compensation.

A consignment of 7,500 tons of Russian wheat arrived in Alexandria.

Israel asked the UN to check the massing of troops by Egypt on its frontier, and asked for an urgent meeting of the Israel-Jordan Mixed Armistice Commission.

March, 1956

March 11

Muhammad Kabir, acting head of the Algerian rebel chieftains, urgently appealed for arms to the heads of Egypt, Saudi Arabia and Syria as they met in Cairo.

A general strike occurred in Bahrain in support of the campaign to oust the British adviser.

The Lebanese Government announced its support of a conference, proposed by Jordan, of the heads of all Arab states. The proposals ran counter to the Cairo negotiations between the leaders of the "big three" Arab states.

March 12

The leaders of Egypt, Saudi Arabia and Syria concluded their conference by approving all inclusive plans for a united defense against Israel and for the counteraction of Western efforts to strengthen the Baghdad Pact.

The Sudanese Government and the Soviet Union agreed to exchange ambassadorial representatives.

A three year trade and payments agreement was signed by Egypt and Bulgaria.

March 13

King Hussein said that Jordan had no aggressive intentions toward Israel and that he planned no change in his foreign policy.

The French National Assembly voted 455-76 to grant Premier Mollet's Government extraordinary powers to pursue its policies in Algeria.

March, 1956

March 14

The turning over of Moscar, Egypt, a former British Army garrison on the outskirts of Ismailia, to the Egyptian Army, was completed.

French Foreign Minister, Christian Pineau, opened talks in Cairo with Premier Nasser about Egyptian support of nationalist rebels in North Africa. France accused Egypt of supplying arms to the rebels.

Moroccan Nationalist leaders announced that their resistance fighters had been instructed to suspend hostilities against the French.

Baghdad announced that Iraq had made a substantial loan towards a superphosphate project in Jordan.

British Foreign Secretary Lloyd stopped in Tripoli for a brief talk with Libyan Premier Ben-Halim before flying to Rome.

An unexpected and unannounced meeting between King Hussein of Jordan and King Faisal of Iraq took place near the border of the two countries. An official statement was issued after the meeting.

The Egyptian Cabinet announced it would float a new production loan of LE25 million divided into a five year loan of LE5 million at two and one-half percent and a 15 year loan of LE20 million at three and one-half percent.

March 15

Lebanese Premier Rashid Karami submitted his Cabinet's resignation to President Chamoun after four Ministers resigned in protest against the Premier's policies.

The Sudanese Government completed an agreement with the Soviet delegation visiting Sudan to establish a Soviet Embassy in Khartoum.

The Saudi Arabian Government gave Jordan JD100,000 as a first installment of promised assistance to the Jordanian National Guard.

March, 1956

March 15

Deputy Minister of Foreign Affairs, Sheikh Yusuf Yasin said that Saudi Arabia was negotiating with Britain for a peaceful settlement of the Buraimi Oasis dispute.

Tunisia's first national election campaign began when the Neo-Destour Party issued its National Front platform.

The Jordanian Cabinet dissolved the municipal Council of Ramalah. and replaced it with a new council presided over by the District Officer.

A UN commission condemned both Jordan and Israel for a battle in the village of Bartaa on March 12.

The British Secretary of State for War arrived in Suez to inspect the final stage of withdrawal of British forces.

British Prime Minister Sir Anthony Eden hinted in the House of Commons that the Big Three Western allies had drawn up new military and political plans aimed at guarding present Middle East frontiers against sudden attack.

March 16

Lebanon's President Chamoun appointed Abdallah al-Yafi as Premier and asked him to form a new Government.

Three earth tremors, said to be the most serious in a quarter of a century, hit Beirut and nearby areas.

Algiers was placed under curfew in the wake of terrorist raids on the night of March 15.

Syria lodged two complaints with the Turkish-Syrian Joint Border Commission.

Nearly $1 million (300, 000 dinars) was collected during the week in voluntary contributions for funds for the National Guard Militia of Jordan, a force organized to supplement the Arab Legion in the event of war.

March, 1956

March 17

The USSR and Sudanese Governments reportedly decided to set up embassies.

A Soviet cultural delegation arrived in Damascus to present a Stalin peace award to Syrian religious leader Sheikh Muhammad al-Ashmar.

In Bahrain, agreement between the strikers and the authorities resulted in a general return to work after five days of stoppages and violence.

UK Secretary for War Anthony Head told a press conference in Cairo that the last British soldier would be out of the Suez Canal Zone before June 18, the final date for evacuation.

The French Cabinet announced plans to transfer troops from West Africa and two divisions from West Germany to Algeria.

In a sudden move after two weeks of negotiations, French Foreign Minister Christian Pineau announced French recognition of Tunisian independence. It was expected that responsibility for foreign affairs, defense and security would be turned over to Tunisia.

A member of the Istiqlal Executive Committee announced that a satisfactory solution of the Rif question in Morocco had been reached.

March 18

The leader of the Istiqlal Party said that the Moroccan Government would respect foreign interests in the Tangier International Zone, but insisted that foreign rule must end.

Premier Ben-Gurion forecast an attack on Israel by the Arab states within the next few months. He said that this would be almost certain unless Israel could obtain sufficient arms in the immediate future.

Egypt announced that it had made a grant in aid for the Jordanian National Guard.

March, 1956

March 19

Arab Legion troops attacked an Israel force near Beersheba.

Syrian students demonstrated against French violence in Algeria.

A Bulgarian trade delegation arrived in Damascus.

In Baghdad, Iraqi Premier Nuri-Said reported that Iraq would help any Arab state attacked by Israel.

A meeting of the Algerian Assembly, attended only by members of the Sixty-One, a group of moderate Algerian politicians, produced a manifesto calling for immediate abolition of the Assembly and of all other local elected bodies. Twelve out of 58 Moslem delegates to the Algerian Assembly defied Algerian rebels by taking their seats.

New decrees were issued limiting trade by Algerians living in France.

March 20

Dillon, American Ambassador to France, gave a speech on US views of France's North African problems.

Israel Prime Minister David Ben-Gurion said in Tel Aviv that Israel did not propose to start work on the Jordan Valley if there was a chance that the US regional water project would be accepted by the Arabs.

The US Defense Department announced that a battalion of 1, 800 marines was to join the Sixth Fleet in the Mediterranean. Washington officials said this was designed as a show of force.

Tunisian leader Bourguiba told his people that they could not be truly happy until their sister nation, Algeria, regained its sovereignty.

The protocol in which France recognized Tunisian independence was signed.

The US called for an urgent and early meeting of the Security Council to review the current causes of tension in the Middle East. Although

March, 1956

March 20

the letter was signed only by the US, the move was understood to have been the result of intensive discussions among the three signatories of the 1950 tripartite declaration.

Lebanese Premier Yafi formed a new Cabinet after three days of political maneuvering following the resignation of the previous Cabinet on March 15.

Egypt signed an agreement with Afghanistan providing for cultural exchanges between the two countries.

The US submitted a draft resolution to the Security Council calling upon the Secretary General to go to the Middle East to prepare a survey of the various aspects of enforcement of, and compliance with, the four general armistice agreements between Israel and its Arab neighbors. He would also determine the extent of compliance with the Security Council resolutions passed during the previous year.

March 21

A trade delegation from Communist China completed a three day visit to the Aswan High Dam site. The Hungarian Minister of Communications, a guest of the Egyptian Government, was also scheduled to visit the site.

French Foreign Minister Pineau invited US Secretary of State Dulles and British Foreign Secretary Lloyd to discuss Middle East policy in Paris during the NATO Council meeting early in May.

President Eisenhower called on the Arabs and Israelis to accept a form of mediation to resolve their dispute.

It was reported that Britain had completed a plan for effective military action within 24 hours of the outbreak of an Arab-Israel war. Action would be taken under the 1950 tripartite declaration.

At the Aden oil refinery, 5, 000 workers went on strike for higher wages, recognition of public holidays, union work hours and controlled rent.

March, 1956

March 21

The Sudanese Government decided that the official name of its country would be the "Republic of the Sudan."

Libya assured Egypt that it would not permit the US and Britain to use military bases for an attack on the Arab states in the event of war with Israel.

March 22

USSR Minister to Lebanon, S. P. Kiktev, conveyed to President Camille Chamoun the condolences of the USSR Government and people in connection with the recent earthquake in Lebanon. The USSR Red Cross and Red Crescent Society contributed 100,000 rubles to the Lebanese relief fund.

The first conference of Arab labor unions opened in Damascus.

The Syrian Minister of Public Works said that 28 offers to build an oil refinery in Syria had been received from abroad.

At UN headquarters the USSR gave assurances that it would support in general the draft resolution submitted by the US.

The President of the Security Council announced that the Council would meet on March 26 to consider the American draft resolution of March 20.

Transport workers who had joined the strike of oil refinery workers returned to work in Aden Colony.

Israel's Ambassador to the US met with the Assistant Secretary of State for Near Eastern and African Affairs to discuss the question of Israel's purchasing defensive arms.

Sultan Ben-Youssef assumed responsibility for the enforcement of law and order in Morocco by taking the title of Supreme Commander of the Royal Armed Forces. Prince Moulay Hassan was designated Chief of the General Staff and Minister of State Guedira was named Head of the Ministry of National Defense.

March, 1956

March 24

The Sudanese Government earmarked LE19,000 as compensation to the families of the farmers who died at Kosti.

The Sheikh of Kuwait authorized the Iraq Petroleum Company to survey a route for a pipeline across Kuwait.

The UNRWA (UN Relief and Works Agency) in Palestine issued a statement requesting UN Headquarters to review the question of continuing its work in Syria, after Syrian Minister of Health, Dr. Badri Abbad, had charged that the agency was deliberately exterminating Arab refugees.

Moroccan Sultan Ben-Youssef told US Ambassador to France Dillon that he supported the Algerian drive for independence.

An Egyptian official said that his Government was sending men to the Soviet Union, Poland and Czechoslovakia for extensive training in the use of recently purchased Communist weapons.

Syrian police threw a heavy guard around the French, British and US embassies as thousands of students milled through the streets shouting protests against French policy in North Africa.

An agreement was reported between Jordan and Syria uniting the frontiers of the two countries.

French Premier Mollet advocated the early establishment of an embargo on arms shipments to the Middle East.

After long talks in Amman between British and Jordanian delegations, a joint communique was issued stating that all British officers in the Arab Legion, except for a number engaged in technical and training work, were to return home.

Syria and Lebanon asked Sir Pierson to postpone the scheduled March 26 meeting of the Security Council. Although they were not members of the Council but only parties concerned, they wanted more time to consider the US draft resolution of March 20.

March, 1956

March 22

Violent demonstrations broke out in Tunis, inspired by adherents of exiled political leader Salah Ben-Youssef, Bourguiba's opponent.

French Resident Minister Lacoste announced a ban on importation or sale in Algeria of firearms, gunpower, explosives and weapons parts, including empty cartridges.

March 23

The French Cabinet voted a series of economic decrees in Algeria at the request of Resident Minister Lacoste.

A minor official of the Neo-Destour Party was kidnapped and killed in Tamarza by a secret terrorist organization, the Black Sword, which supported exiled political leader Salah Ben-Youssef.

Intensive conferences were held between Syrian Premier Ghazi and Lebanese Premier Yafi to work out unified Arab plans for dealing with the Arab-Israel dispute over the Jordan River. The leaders discussed what action to take if Israel decided to go ahead with its own plan for using the river, plans for backing Syria if it brought the dispute before the UN and the Arab position on the modified Jordan plan proposed by the West for the mutual benefit of Arabs and Israelis.

Tunisia's Habib Bourguiba assailed the speech by US Ambassador Dillon in Paris which supported France's position toward Algeria.

Violence erupted in the wake of the continuing Little Aden refinery strike. The Government announced a new daily wage schedule.

The British Government made known its intention to spend more than $25 million to support Jordan's Armed Forces and economy in the fiscal year 1956-57.

A British Foreign Office spokesman stated that Russians were training large numbers of Egyptian military men in the use of the newly acquired armaments from Czechoslovakia. He asserted that 200 army and navy commissioned and noncommissioned officers were undergoing secret training by Russian instructors at a Soviet base near the harbor of Gdynia, Poland.

March, 1956

March 25

On behalf of the Lebanese Parliament, its speaker Adel Usairan accepted an invitation from the Chairman of the USSR and the Soviet Nationalities, A. P. Volkov and V. T. Lacis, for a Lebanese Parliamentary delegation to visit the USSR.

Moderate candidates of the National Front won a resounding victory in Tunisia's first national election for a constituent assembly.

The British Foreign Office challenged a statement by Premier Nasser of Egypt that he was not opposed to British interests in the Middle East. Officials declared that anti-British propaganda by Egypt contradicted this statement.

Iraq Petroleum Company workers in Homs and other parts of Syria went on strike.

The Lebanese Government announced in Beirut that it would seek to have discussion of the US UN resolution postponed for a month. It also requested that Egypt, Jordan and Lebanon take part in the debate.

March 26

All Sudanese Government workers began a three day strike to protest the Government's refusal to negotiate with the Sudan Workers Federation.

An unknown terrorist killed the Secretary General of the Neo-Destour Federation at Gafsa, who had just been elected to the constituent assembly in Tunisia.

The British Foreign Secretary told the House of Commons that Britain, the US and France had yet to evolve a joint plan for preventing war between the Arab states and Israel under the tripartite declaration. He said that the British Government intended to honor that declaration.

Premier Ben-Halim officially opened the National Bank of Libya.

Libyan Premier Ben-Halim formed a new cabinet.

March, 1956

March 26

The UN Security Council denied Syria and Lebanon's request to postpone consideration of the US resolution, but invited the four Arab states—Egypt, Lebanon, Syria and Jordan—and Israel to participate in the debate as interested parties.

March 27

Seven decrees providing for economic and social reforms in Algeria were published in Paris.

The head of the Soviet technical mission visiting the Arab states said in Cairo that the Soviet Union had agreements to build grain elevators, oil reservoirs and a cement factory in Syria. He also stated that the USSR was ready to give technical aid to Egypt and help carry out development schemes in return for Egyptian cotton.

Libyan King Idris approved the new Cabinet.

March 28

The 18 tanks ordered from the US and shipped on February 18 to Saudi Arabia arrived in Damman.

A squadron of Egyptian jet aircraft arrived in Jedda and was delivered to Saudi Arabia under the terms of the bilateral alliance with Egypt.

A special Egyptian committee recommended wide propaganda for the adoption of trousers in place of all other forms of dress.

Egypt and Syria asked for assurance that the UN Secretary General would limit his proposed mission to the Middle East to the obtaining of compliance with Israel-Arab armistice agreements. They opposed any plan which would empower Mr. Hammarskjold to suggest a solution to the broader problems. The US delegate Henry Cabot Lodge, Jr.

assured the Arab delegates that Mr. Hammarskjold would act within the framework of the armistice agreements.

The Jordanian Government freed 115 persons arrested during the anti-Baghdad Pact riots in December 1955 and January 1956.

March 29

Israel asked UN authorities to investigate three Egyptian attacks on its border.

The Lebanese Chamber of Deputies voted confidence in the new Yafi Government.

Israel and Syria exchanged prisoners. Four Israel soldiers and one civilian were exchanged for 35 Syrian soldiers and six civilians in the culmination of the UN's efforts to persuade the Syrians to agree to a prisoner exchange.

March 30

Libya's Parliament supported the rejection made by Premier Ben-Halim on March 29 of Soviet offers of economic and technical aid.

French Foreign Minister Pineau summoned the ambassadors of Syria and Lebanon and protested against an Arab League resolution offering full support to Algerians in rebellion against French rule. Pineau cancelled his visit to Syria and Lebanon which was scheduled to begin April 5.

France denied shipment of 12 jet planes to Israel.

An 8 pm to 6 am curfew was imposed on the city of Tlemcen, in western Algeria, in retaliation for the continued harassment of French forces.

It was reported in Washington that the US told the other Western powers that while it was not ready to supply arms to Israel, it would raise no objection if Britain joined France in doing so.

Thirty chiefs of the Moroccan Army of Liberation from the Rif swore fealty to Sultan Ben-Youssef in a ceremony at Rabat.

March 31

Abd-al-Karim Ben-Abdallah, Moroccan Secretary of the Communist Party, was assassinated in Casablanca.

The leader of the Nationalist Chinese trade delegation visiting Jordan said that Nationalist China was ready to buy Jordanian phosphate.

The last major British military units left Port Said, Egypt.

Easter services were held in Jerusalem (Jordanian sector). Fewer pilgrims than usual attended because of the threat of war.

Claude Bourdet, editor of the weekly newspaper France-Observateur, was arrested on charges of demoralizing the French Army because his editorials attacked the Government's policy toward Algeria.

The Iraqi Chamber of Deputies ratified a bill establishing Iraq's first university, to be known as Baghdad University.

US Consul General Clark visited Algiers to underscore the new US policy of firmly backing France's attempts to stay in North Africa through liberal reforms.

Algerian nationalists appealed to the US for help and charged that France was conducting a colonial war of reconquest.

Syrians freed by Israel as war prisoners told reporters that they had been tortured in an attempt to wrest military secrets from them.

The annual report of the Suez Canal Company showed that 14,666 vessels used the waterway during 1955, an increase of 11 percent over 1954.

Farid Mustafa, Director of the Finance Ministry in Egypt, urged that the US reconsider its cotton policy as a significant gesture of friendship for Egypt. He indicated that if the recent decisions on American supplies were carried out, Egypt would be forced to turn to other countries for relief.

Iraqi Premier Said reported in London that Egyptian Premier Nasser once considered joining the Baghdad Pact but did not join only because it would interfere with his dreams of personal glory.

A conference of the rulers of the Aden Protectorate States was held to discuss proposals for the federation of the states of the Western Protectorate.

An automatically renewable trade agreement was signed between Lebanon and China and would go into effect ten days after each notified the other of its ratification.

April, 1956

April 1

Egyptian Minister of Commerce Nusair opened a Chinese Communist trade fair in Cairo.

Egyptian military authorities in the Gaza area announced measures to stop Arab infiltrations from the Gaza Strip into Israel.

Iraqi Minister of Public Works Bustani stated in Baghdad that Premier Said promised to mediate in the dispute between the Lebanese Government and the Iraq Petroleum Company over oil transit royalties paid to Lebanon.

A Moroccan nationalist leader declared that nationalist rebels would not move against French troops in Moroccan territory, including the territory bordering on Algeria.

Egyptian Premier Nasser declared that he was still holding a Soviet offer to help finance the construction of the proposed High Dam at Aswan.

The National Bank of Libya was opened for business. The Libyan Currency Commission began to transfer its assets and responsibilities to the new bank.

April 2

King Faisal II of Iraq dedicated a dam on the Tigris River at Samara.

Premier Azhari stated that since joining the Arab League, Sudan considered itself at war with Israel.

One thousand French troops landed in Algiers. The authorities reported that the death toll since Good Friday morning was 341. Algerians demonstrated at Metz, Thionville and Maubeuge, France.

The Jordanian Cabinet approved the formation of a new political party, the Arab Constitutional Party.

Rulers of 14 British protectorates in the Aden area, meeting under the British Governor of the Protectorates, organized a committee to study

the formation of a federation. The committee was also empowered to draw up a constitution for any union agreed upon.

April 3

Hungary offered to participate in the Egyptian High Dam project by supplying machinery and building roads.

The Iraqi Minister of Interior said that Communist penetration of Iraq seemed to be directed from Syria.

Changes were announced in Jordan's Cabinet Ministry posts.

Syria and the USSR ratified trade and payments agreements.

The Lebanese Chamber of Deputies passed a resolution recommending that the Arab League approve an economic, political and cultural boycott of France if it continued aggressive policies in Algeria.

The USSR charged in the UN Security Council that certain Western nations were planning armed intervention in the Middle East.

US Secretary of State Dulles said that in an emergency US forces might be sent into action in the Middle East without Congressional authority. He added that he was unaware of any emergency that would require such an action.

Yemen's Foreign Minister said in Cairo that consultations were under way with other Arab states to foil a British sponsored plan to federate the tribes in the Aden area.

The Spanish Government issued a communique declaring the end of Spain's protectorate over part of Morocco. Moroccan independence and unity were thus recognized.

April 4

The Saudi Arabian Defense Minister announced that Saudi Arabia was buying several squadrons of jet planes from Egypt and that the first squadron had arrived a month before.

About 5,000 Tripoli high school students in Libya clashed with police in a protest against French actions in Algeria and the sale of French jets to Israel.

Representatives of the Baghdad Pact met in Tehran to discuss Communist subversion in the area covered by the Pact.

The Israel Government requested an emergency meeting of the Israel-Egypt Mixed Armistice Commission.

Sultan Muhammad V arrived in Madrid to confer with Generalissimo Franco about ending Spanish rule in Morocco.

Israel Foreign Minister Moshe Sharett discussed Israel's security position vis-a-vis the Arab countries with US Ambassador Lawson at Tel Aviv, and expressed dismay over President Eisenhower's continued refusal to send arms to Israel.

The UN Security Council voted unanimously to send Secretary General Hammarskjold to the Middle East to negotiate with Israel and its four Arab neighbors concerning compliance with the armistice agreements. The Security Council rejected all the amendments proposed by the USSR.

April 5

Israel armed forces shelled Gaza, Deir-al-Balah, Khan Yunis and Kisan for five hours. UAR troops launched retalitory artillery attacks on Israel frontier communities, causing fires in some. Armed clashes lasting until 6:30 pm occurred along the entire demarcation line.

The Chairman of the Egyptian-Israel Mixed Armistice Commission negotiated a ceasefire after an extraordinary ten hour battle along a ten mile front of the strife torn Gaza Strip armistice line. Israel frontier villages and military positions were attacked throughout the day with 120

millimeter mortars and machine guns from Egyptian fortified positions. The Israelis returned the fire.

The Egyptian delegate to the UN filed a complaint with the President of the Security Council. Israel's Foreign Minister demanded that the Truce Supervision Organization take firm action to stop the attacks on the Gaza Strip.

Saudi Arabian King Saud officially inaugurated the extension of the Holy Mosque in Mecca.

Iraq protested to France against France's policy in Algeria.

The Arab League Council met in Cairo for the second time.

At a meeting between Israel Foreign Minister Moshe Sharett and General Burns, the former said that the responsibility for the Gaza violence fell squarely upon the Egyptians who refused to issue the ceasefire order as demanded by the UN.

It was reported in London that King Saud was reviving the Ikhwan (Moslem Brotherhood) as a precaution against growing revolutionary sentiment. Revolutionary activity was reported to be especially strong among Saudi Arabian army officers, in the tiny middle class growing up under the impact of oil production and in the illegal labor movement in the oil areas.

Secretary General Hammarskjold announced that he was going to Rome where he would confer with the Chief of Staff of the Truce Supervision Organization, General E. L. M. Burns. From Rome he would go to Beirut on April 10, and from there to Cairo on the 11th. He said at a news conference that he did not expect his mission to the Middle East to accomplish miracles.

The French Minister in Algeria, Lacoste, won approval of his project for sending 100,000 additional French troops to Algeria.

King Faisal dedicated a flood control barrage on the Euphrates River.

Franco told Moroccan leaders that Spain was determined to respect Morocco's independence and territorial unity.

April, 1956

April 6

Israel artillery shelled the Gaza Strip for three hours.

The conference of the Syrian, Lebanese, Jordanian and Kuwait committees of "Every Citizen is Sentry" was ended in Damascus. It adopted resolutions that the Arab boycott of Israel should be tightened.

Five thousand employees of the Iraq Petroleum Company in Syria ended their 11 day strike for higher wages.

UN Secretary Hammarskjold left for the Middle East to try to arrange a peaceful settlement in the Arab-Israel dispute.

As a result of the tense situation, the UNTSO Chief of Staff postponed his meeting in Rome with Secretary General Hammarskjold.

A Kuwait oil tanker company was formed under the auspices of the Sheikh of Kuwait with a nominal capital of 3, 700, 000 pounds sterling.

King Idris called for US President Eisenhower's active intervention in North Africa in a note to US Ambassador Tappin.

Two thousand Adenese dock workers went on strike for a pay increase.

It was reported in Paris that US Secretary of State Dulles, UK Foreign Secretary Lloyd and French Foreign Minister Pineau would meet in Paris on May 4 in an all out effort to coordinate Western policy in the Middle East in an attempt to avert a possible large scale war in that region.

Although the US still refused to join the Baghdad Pact, it was sending a US observer delegation to the Pact meeting in Tehran April 16-20.

Israel Foreign Minister Sharett talked with the US Ambassador in Tel Aviv about US policy toward Israel.

April 7

Eight persons were killed and 30 wounded in a Syrian tribal clash near the Iraqi border.

April, 1956

April 7

Secretary General Hammarskjold arrived in Rome and immediately went into conference with his advisers, General Burns' advisers and the head of the UN Relief and Works Agency.

Spanish and Moroccan leaders signed in Madrid a joint declaration and protocol recognizing in principle Moroccan independence and unity. Only the need for free collaboration between Spain and Morocco was recognized, whereas the French-Moroccan agreement described a need for interdependence.

The Tunisian Government took over control of the local police from the French, following four days of negotiations.

Khatabi Abd-al-Krim, leader of the Rif warriors, appeared before the Arab League Political Committee to demand an Arab boycott of France and support of North African nationalist aims. He urged boycott in all fields—economic, political and cultural.

Iraq's Minister of Development Diar Jaafar announced a 30 percent expansion in public works projects financed by oil revenues.

The British Government officially announced that all UK Air Force units had been moved out of Habbaniya and Shaiba, Iraq, in accordance with the agreement of April 4, 1955.

The Libyan Government revealed that the US would increase its economic and military aid to Libya. Libya had recently rejected a Russian offer of assistance.

A trade agreement was signed between Sudan and Yugoslavia which would be valid for a one year period.

A commercial and payments agreement was signed between Syria and China which would enter into force on ratification and be valid for a one year period.

April, 1956

April 8

The Council of the Arab League met in Cairo and discussed the situation in the Middle East and the mission of UN Secretary General Hammarskjold.

Iran announced that it intended to press its claim to Bahrain Island by amicable and direct negotiation with Britain.

Moroccan workers at US air bases in Morocco scheduled a wage strike for April 9.

Saudi Arabia's King Saud expressed his support of Egypt in its conflict with Israel over the Gaza sector.

UN Secretary General Hammarskjold cut short his visit to Rome and prepared to leave for the Middle East earlier than intended, due to mounting tension there.

The UNTSO (UN Truce and Supervision Organization) Chief of Staff met with Israel Prime Minister Sharett and discussed the penetration into Israel of terrorist bands.

Habib Bourguiba was elected president of Tunisia's National Assembly.

Izvestia, the official newspaper of the Soviet Government, charged that the US fomented recent armed clashes on the Israel-Egypt border as a pretext for armed intervention in the Middle East.

April 9

In a statement issued by US Presidential Press Secretary Hagerty, the US pledged itself to oppose Middle East aggression within constitutional means and to assist the victims of aggression.

An Israel military court sentenced to death an Arab commando caught inside Israel.

It was reported in Damascus that orders had been issued to mass Syrian army forces all along the Syrian-Israel frontier.

April, 1956

April 9

The US Ambassador to Cairo, Henry A. Byroade, discussed the daily raids and counter raids of the violent Israel-Egypt border situation with Premier Nasser.

The Egyptian Minister of State blamed the Western Big Three for the recent increase in tension in the Middle East.

Five thousand teachers in Jordanian Government schools went on strike for higher wages.

King Hussein of Jordan arrived in Damascus for a three day state visit and political discussions with Syrian President Kuwatli.

Israel sent a letter to the UN Secretary General charging that Egypt had committed a warlike act of the gravest kind in sending armed sabotage and murder gangs deep into Israel territory to terrorize civilians.

President Eisenhower issued a three point statement of US Middle East policy.

April 10

Yemen's Imam Ahmad initialed a pact aligning Yemen with "The Arab Alliance" of Egypt, Saudi Arabia and Syria. He stated that he considered it a necessary link in Arab unity.

Habib Bourguiba agreed to become Premier of Tunisia at the invitation of the Bey.

The Israel Foreign Ministry issued a statement declaring that Egypt's failure to comply with the UN ceasefire terms within 48 hours left Israel no choice but to reserve to itself freedom of action. A UN spokesman said that the period was the most dangerous since the armistice.

Washington officials expressed to the Israel Government the gratitude of the US Government for the restraint shown by the Israel armed forces during the Egyptian raids of the last few days.

April, 1956

April 10

It was reported in Washington that the US Government was using all its influence to persuade Egypt to join Israel in a ceasefire. The US President and the Secretary of State were warned by the Israel Government that it must put a time limit on its tolerance of raids by Egyptian suicide squads across the Israel border.

Israel sent two letters to the Security Council; each charged that the assaults by Egyptian murder gangs were carried out on orders from Cairo officials.

Hammarskjold began talks in Cairo. It was made known that Israel and Egypt had promised Hammarskjold to refrain from warlike acts.

The Economic Council of the Baghdad Pact held its first session and announced that Britain offered 250, 000 pounds sterling ($700, 000) for technical assistance over a five year period in addition to funds already reserved for an automatic energy training center.

April 11

A joint communique was issued in Damascus on the talks between President Kuwatli and King Hussein, reaffirming Syria's and Jordan's resolve not to participate in foreign military pacts. A Jordanian-Syrian communique issued in Amman stated that the two countries agreed to coordinate their defense plans. They also agreed to steer clear of any foreign pacts.

Tunisian Premier Ben-Ammar resigned. The Bey named Habib Bourguiba Premier.

A Cairo radio broadcast said that Arab commando raids had accomplished their mission of revenge for the Israel bombardments of Gaza the week before; the 300 fedayeen sent across the Gaza frontier had completed fifty suicide attacks against Israel.

Israel sent a third letter to the Security Council complaining of new Egyptian acts of hostility.

US Ambassador to Israel Lawson praised Israel for its restraint and composure in the face of Arab suicide squad terrorism.

April, 1956

April 12

The Israel Foreign Ministry reported four Israeli dead and 16 injured by guerrillas and charged Egypt with a vicious and calculated renewal of aggression.

French Finance Minister Ramadier announced that the Administration was asked to make an across the board budget reduction to help pay for Algerian military operations and new social benefits.

April 13

Berber tribes in Ifni rose in protest against the Spanish ban on Moroccan independence celebrations.

Winston Churchill said in a speech that Britain's honor required it to assist Israel if the latter were attacked by Egypt. He predicted that Britain and the US would halt any aggression.

The Tunisian Constituent Assembly adopted a new Constitution.

French Premier Mollet offered to negotiate a ceasefire with Algerian rebels, but refused to consider discussions with rebel leaders on Algeria's future status. It was the first indication that the French considered negotiating with leaders of the National Liberation Front as representatives of the Algerian people. However, the discussions offered pertained to purely local matters in connection with a ceasefire.

Hammarskjold asked Israel for assurance that it would order its troops to abstain from warlike actions on the Egyptian border.

The Tunisian Assembly adopted the basic law of vesting sovereignty in the people and ignoring the titular ruler Muhammad al-Amin, Bey of Tunis.

April 14

In a letter to Secretary General Hammarskjold, Israel Foreign Minister Sharett pressed the question of Egypt's closing of the Suez Canal to Israel ships and the blockage of the Gulf of Aqaba. The Secretary

April, 1956

April 11

UN Secretary General Hammarskjold met with Egyptian Premier Nasser. It was believed that Hammarskjold would return to Cairo after visiting other Middle East capitals.

April 12

France decreed the dissolution of the Algerian Assembly.

The 15 day session of the Council of the Arab League and the League's Political and other permanent specialized committees ended in Cairo. The Council adopted a resolution recognizing the independence of Tunisia and Morocco and offering them assistance in their independent national development. The Political Committee condemned French actions in Algeria and voiced support for its liberation struggle.

Syrian Minister of Defense Barmada received a delegation of Kuwaiti youth who presented a check for $145, 000 toward Kuwait's contribution to the equipment of the Syrian Army.

The strike of workers at US military bases in Morocco ended with the understanding that negotiations would begin at once to establish a new wage scale.

The French Government called up the reservists to reinforce the active forces in Algeria.

The UN Secretary General sent to the Security Council correspondence between himself and high government officials of Egypt and Israel in which both countries promised to refrain from warlike acts along their border. Each nation reserved to itself the right of self defense should further incidents occur.

Israel Prime Minister Ben-Gurion forwarded a communication to the UN Secretary General, pointing out that Egypt continued its open violation of a pledge given to Mr. Hammarskjold only a few days before to refrain from further hostilities and to observe the provisions of the armistice agreement. The Israel UN Mission published the communication.

April, 1956

April 14

General informed Israel that under the Council mandate he could not at that time discuss the closing of the Suez Canal to Israel shipping.

The Syrian Government refused to conclude a loan with the IBRD (International Bank for Reconstruction and Development) because of a condition that IBRD loans be used through contractors and technical advisors only from countries who were members of the IBRD.

The Bey of Tunis approved a new cabinet.

Abu-Suweir, the last British controlled Suez base, was vacated by Britain.

A trade and payments agreement was signed between Lebanon and Rumania. The agreement also provided for commercial representation and contained a most favored nation clause.

Secretary General Hammarskjold left Cairo for Beirut. He indicated that he was satisfied with his talks with Nasser and his advisors. On the way to Beirut he toured the Gaza area and held an informal conference with Israel officials at Lydda.

It was reported in Washington that Israel took delivery of eight Mystere IV jet fighter planes from France; four more were expected soon. Washington approved the diversion of the 12 Mysteres from NATO to Israel.

April 15

A statement attributed to Algerian rebels and published in the Tunis newspaper L'Action said that an Algerian ceasefire was contingent on French recognition of Algeria's independence.

Israel Prime Minister Ben-Gurion gave an Independence Day broadcast outlining future prospects for Israel's security.

It was announced in Damascus that Syria and Burma agreed to exchange diplomatic representatives.

Egypt signed a cultural treaty with Communist China.

April, 1956

April 15

The chiefs of the Baghdad Pact delegations met in Tehran to draft the agenda for the opening session of the Ministerial Council.

In Washington, US officials declared that the US was planning special economic assistance for the Baghdad Pact nations.

Sudanese Premier Azhari disclosed that a Czechoslovakian military mission had offered to sell arms to Sudan, and that the Soviet Union had offered economic and technical aid. He declared that Sudan stood with Egypt on the question of Israel.

Three members of the Sudanese opposition Umma Party were released from jail. They were serving sentences of 5-14 years for disorders committed during the opening of Parliament in March, 1954.

The Bey of Tunis swore in the Bourguiba Government.

April 16

Representatives of 16 Asian and African nations sent a joint letter to the UN Security Council calling attention to the deteriorating situation in Algeria and declaring the developments were likely to endanger peace and security in the area.

An exchange of fire occurred between Syrian army units and a Turkish patrol.

Negotiations between Britain and Jordan on the future status of the Arab Legion's British officers ended with the agreement that Britain would continue to lend officers for training and technical duties until Jordanian officers were available to replace them.

In a new exchange of letters between Israel and the UN Secretary General, the former insisted that the pledge Egypt made the previous week to live up to a strategic clause in the armistice agreement had to be interpreted as a readiness by Cairo to lift the Suez Canal blockage against Israel shipping. Hammarskjold told Israel that he was not authorized to discuss the closing of the Suez Canal to Israel shipping.

April, 1956

April 16

The Baghdad Pact Council held its second annual meeting in Tehran, Iran, attended by US observers.

The USSR offered to support a UN settlement of the Arab-Israel dispute.

Communist China and Egypt concluded a new trade agreement.

Lebanese leaders promised UN Secretary General Hammarskjold that they would accept all proposals to reduce tension in the Middle East, providing such proposals would not prejudice a just Palestine settlement, violate any Arab sovereignty and be within the scope of Arab-Israel armistice agreements.

The US told the Baghdad Pact members that it would discuss economic cooperation through the Pact organization, but implied that it would not join the Pact because of the objections raised by Egypt, Saudi Arabia and Syria.

April 17

Syria celebrated its tenth anniversary of the withdrawal of foreign troops in 1946.

The Greek Government granted permission to an undisclosed number of French and Czechoslovakian fighter aircraft with Egyptian markings to fly over Greece and refuel, if necessary, while en route to Egypt.

The Ministerial Council of the Baghdad Pact approved a proposal to take collective action against subversion in the territories of the member states, and to pool their police resources and information on subversive groups.

The British War Office announced that Britain would continue to lend officers to Jordan's Arab Legion until Arab officers were able to replace them.

Tunisian Premier Bourguiba told the National Constituent Assembly that his Government was pledged to oppose poverty and unemployment. He noted that Article 1 of the new Constitution, approved on April 13, vested Tunisian sovereignty in the people.

April, 1956

April 17

Syrian workers in the Homs Electric Company went on strike.

Israel Prime Minister Ben-Gurion and Foreign Minister Sharett conferred with the UN Secretary General.

Two French residents of Morocco were arrested in the garden of the French High Commissioner in Rabat and charged with attempting to murder radical leader Mendes-France.

The Soviet Foreign Ministry issued a statement in Moscow clarifying the Soviet stand on the Arab-Israel dispute. It called upon the Arab states and Israel to settle their conflict on a basis acceptable to both sides.

April 18

The US joined the Economic Committee of the Baghdad Pact.

A ceasefire agreement arranged by the UN Secretary General between Egypt and Israel came into force at 6:00 pm.

Sudan decided to accept an Egyptian offer of military equipment, including tanks and armored cars.

The Tunisian Government assumed full responsibility for internal security. An amnesty was announced for all persons convicted of crimes committed before March 20.

British Foreign Secretary Lloyd said that although the Soviet Foreign Ministry statement on the Middle East included evident misstatements and inconsistencies, Britain welcomed the Soviet's emphasis on the need to preserve peace and to reach an Arab-Israel settlement.

In reaction to the statement by the Soviet Foreign Ministry in which was implied a willingness to cooperate with the UN in its efforts for peace in the Middle East, the White House commented that if the statement demonstrated a real desire and determination on the part of the Soviet Union to back the United Nations effort, the US President welcomed this support.

April, 1956

April 19

The head of the US observer unit to the Baghdad Pact meeting stated that his Government agreed to establish a military liaison office, headed by a general or an admiral, at the permanent headquarters of the Baghdad Pact organization; to join as a full member of the Committee to Fight Subversion and the Economic Committee; and to pay a share of the cost of the permanent secretariat.

A four day session of the Baghdad Pact Permanent Council ended in Tehran.

Lebanon's Premier Yafi called the Soviet statement supporting UN efforts to obtain peace in the Middle East a victory for American diplomacy.

French citizens demonstrated in southern France to try to prevent young reservists from leaving for service in Algeria.

Imam Ahmad of Yemen arrived in Jedda for talks with King Saud.

Nineteen Czechoslovakian motor torpedo boats arrived in Alexandria for the Egyptian Navy.

The Tunisian Cabinet announced the formation of a High Court of Justice to try political offenses and acts detrimental to national interests.

Israel and Egypt issued ceasefire orders to all their armed forces; the orders included the cessation of terrorist activities in Israel by Egyptian commandos. Secretary General Hammarskjold announced simultaneously in Jerusalem and Cairo that Egypt and Israel agreed to an unconditional ceasefire on their borders. Both Governments barred trespassing as well as shooting across the demarcation lines; the orders applied to regular and military like troops as well as to nonregular forces. Israel agreed to greater freedom of movement for UN truce observers and to the creation, on an experimental basis, of fixed observer posts along the Gaza Strip.

Hammarskjold announced that Egypt and Israel had agreed to carry out a ceasefire as of 6:00 pm, April 18.

April, 1956

April 20

The Israel Prime Minister told the Secretary General that Israel felt free to resume work on the Jordan River irrigation project at any time. Syria, Egypt and Jordan threatened war if Israel were to start digging the diversionary canal in the demilitarized zone along the Syrian frontier.

Egyptian Premier Nasser flew unexpectedly to Jedda to join in talks with King Saud and the Imam of Yemen.

April 21

A commercial and payments agreement was signed between Syria and Egypt which would be valid for a one year period and would go into effect 15 days after the exchange of the instruments of ratification. Most favored nation treatment was included.

A commercial and payments agreement was signed between Syria and Rumania and would go into effect 15 days after the exchange of the instruments of ratification. The agreement would be valid for one year and most favored nation treatment was mutually accorded.

A Modus Vivendi was concluded between Lebanon and Turkey which dealt with the mutual accord of most favored nation treatment. It would enter into force seven days after the Lebanese ratification documents were deposited with Turkish authorities.

A commercial agreement was concluded between Lebanon and Turkey which aimed at encouraging trade and would be valid for one year.

An Atoms for Peace exhibition set up by the American Embassy opened in Damascus under supervision of the Syrian Ministry of Education.

Egypt, Saudi Arabia and Yemen signed a military agreement setting up a unified command under an Egyptian leader for five years.

April, 1956

April 22

Sudanese Foreign Under Secretary Yasmin left for Addis Ababa to discuss settlement of Sudanese property in Gambala, an important coffee trading center under Ethiopian control.

The pilot of a US military transport plane forced down by Egyptian jet fighters denied that the plane had been flying over a prohibited military area. The plane was carrying members of the US military mission to Iran on a tourist flight to Cairo.

Reacting to US President Eisenhower's April 9 statement of policy on the Middle East, Israel Prime Minister Ben-Gurion said that Israel did not consider the UN Charter alone a substantial guarantee of Israel's security, or any deterrent to the aggressors who planned war against Israel. He declared Israel had two needs: a firm Arab renunciation of intent to wipe Israel from the map, and a supply of arms to Israel that would render any such intent unfeasible.

April 23

Egyptian War Minister Amer was named Head of the Joint Command of the Armies of Egypt, Saudi Arabia and Yemen. This made him the Supreme Commander of the three armies, as well as the Army of Syria.

Exiled leaders of the Algerian rebellion said in Cairo that four of the more moderate Algerian leaders joined the National Liberation Front.

Secretary General Hammarskjold arrived in Damascus and conferred with Syrian Premier Ghazzi in an effort to obtain an unconditional ceasefire on the Israel border.

Italy's Foreign Minister Martino stated that his country would participate in any international agreement affecting the Mediterranean and the Middle East.

The British Government protested to Yemen against a raid by Yemeni tribesmen in the Aden Protectorate. Aden's British Governor Hickenbotham withdrew his ultimatum to Yemen to withdraw its troops from

April, 1956

April 23

the Western Protectorate, because Yemen had proposed a meeting at Beihan to settle the problem.

April 24

Syria announced readiness to respect a ceasefire on the Israel border provided Israel observed the decision of the UN Security Council.

Three Israel surveyors and the driver of their car were ambushed and killed near the Jordanian frontier. Israel Foreign Minister Sharett sent an urgent message to Hammarskjold in which he said that the incident bore signs of resumption of raids by Arab commandos.

It was reported in Cairo that Egypt made a gift to the Sudan of $1, 500, 000 worth of arms.

Fakhri al-Khalidi resigned as Jordanian Foreign Minister.

April 25

The Umma Party in Sudan issued a statement of its new policy.

Abbas, leader of the Algerian moderates, announced that he had joined the rebel Algerian Liberation Front to fight the French.

All but 1, 000 of the striking dock workers in Aden returned to work and agreed to refer their dispute to arbitration.

An Egyptian five year, $8 million program for the Productivity and Vocational Training Center was described by Dr. Sidqi, Director of the Center. He said that the program would set up vocational training centers in the major industrial cities to train skilled workers, graduating 30, 000 foremen within four years to meet the needs of local factories.

The British Parliament rejected the demands of Opposition members that financial aid for the Aswan High Dam project be withheld until Egypt dropped its anti-British policy entirely.

April, 1956

April 25

Secretary General Hammarskjold arrived in Amman and conferred with Jordanian Premier Rifai on a ceasefire.

The French Government announced a reorganization of top officials in the Algerian civil administration, and accelerated military measures to deal with the rebellion.

The International Cooperation Administration asked the US Congress for an $884, 318, 000 aid appropriation, twice that of 1955, for the Middle East. Most of the increase was for military aid to members of the Baghdad Pact.

April 26

A British delegation arrived in Jedda for talks on Saudi Arabian-British differences.

King Muhammad V named Ahmad Balafrej, Secretary General of the Istiqlal Party, as Foreign Minister, giving the Istiqlal a majority of one in the Moroccan Cabinet.

Egypt accepted all the principles and most of the specific items in Hammarskjold's plan for ending Arab-Israel tensions. The only ostensible deadlock was the question of how far troops were to withdraw from the demarcation line.

An Anglo-Soviet joint communique was issued in London at the conclusion of the visit of Soviet leaders Bulganin and Khrushchev on the situation in the Middle East.

UN Secretary General Hammarskjold obtained a ceasefire agreement from Jordan.

The Israel-Jordanian Mixed Armistice Commission condemned Jordan for the murder of four Israel civilians in the Negev on April 23, and declared that it viewed with grave concern the increase in incidents along the Israel-Jordan demarcation line in recent weeks.

April, 1956

April 26

The Soviet Union agreed to be restrained in supplying arms to Egypt and promised to support UN efforts toward a settlement of the Arab-Israel dispute.

April 27

French Resident Minister in Algeria Lacoste declared that the French Government would not negotiate with the nationalist rebels.

Before leaving England, Khrushchev stated that the USSR was willing to cooperate in an arms embargo in the Middle East, with certain reservations.

The UN Secretary General conferred in Beirut with Lebanese officials on eliminating border tension with Israel.

April 28

A Jordanian military mission arrived in Cairo to discuss military cooperation with Egypt.

Poland delivered four minesweepers to the Egyptian Navy in Alexandria.

The UN Secretary General and UNTSO Chief of Staff returned to Cairo to work out detailed provisions to guarantee the ceasefire more fully.

Eight members of the Syrian National Socialist Party were sentenced to death by a military court on a charge of conspiracy to assassinate Deputy Army Chief of Staff, Malki.

A general strike took place throughout Syria in protest against French policy in Algeria. In Damascus 30,000 demonstrators urged a French boycott.

In Alexandria, Egypt, dock workers who went on strike for higher pay on April 27 returned to work after receiving an increase.

Egyptian Foreign Minister Fawzi signed the Arab Broadcasts Agreement.

April, 1956

April 29

Saudi Arabia ordered the British Desert Locust Control Mission to leave the country by May 1.

A ceasefire agreement arranged by the UN Secretary General between Israel and Jordan came into force.

West German banks offered to lend Syria $72 million to buy West German products at world prices.

Three Sudanese workers left for Peking to represent the Federation of Sudanese Trade Unions in May Day celebrations.

Israel Foreign Minister Sharett sent an urgent message about renewed Egyptian attacks of aggression to UN Secretary General Hammarskjold in Cairo.

The President of the Aden Association sent a note to Governor Hickenbotham demanding self government.

April 30

The Jordanian Government decided to carry out the Dead Sea potash scheme by itself, since none of the other Arab states accepted the invitation to cooperate.

Secretary General Hammarskjold arrived in Jerusalem on the last stop of his Middle East mission, amidst a tense situation created by the latest incidents near the Gaza Strip. Israel's Foreign Minister Sharett asked him what explanation Premier Nasser had offered for Egyptian violation of the new ceasefire agreement.

All nine Moroccan members of the Tangier International Legislative Assembly walked out on a procedural question after a Moroccan delegate introduced a surprise motion tending to limit the Assembly's legislative powers. The question was then ruled out of order, based on the view that the Assembly had no power to amend the Tangier Statute.

Moroccan Foreign Minister Balafrej on a visit to Tangier said that the non-Moroccan delegates to the Assembly had indicated full agreement to the principle of unifying Tangier with Morocco.

April, 1956

April 30

UN Secretary General Hammarskjold opened the final truce talks with Israel Premier Ben-Gurion.

Iraq and Indonesia signed a treaty of friendship.

May, 1956

May 1

It was revealed that an Israel agricultural settlement had been strategically established about one-half mile east of the demilitarized zone on the Beersheba-al-Auja Road.

Frachon, the Communist Chief of the General Confederation of Labor in France, called for united labor opposition to French military tactics in Algeria.

Premier Bourguiba announced that Tunisia would not open negotiations with France on interdependence unless France recognized Tunisia's full independence and negotiated with it as an equal.

The Lebanese ministerial committee in charge of negotiations with the Iraq Petroleum Company refused to resume negotiations for higher royalties on the basis of assessing royalties according to the length of pipe across Lebanese territory. The head of the committee said that the kilometric-ton basis was unjustifiable and detrimental to Lebanese interests.

In Jerusalem the UN Secretary General ran into unexpected trouble in his attempt to obtain an unconditional ceasefire agreement from Syria. The Syrian leaders insisted on a guarantee that Israel would not attempt to divert the waters of the Jordan River for irrigation purposes; Israel refused to give this guarantee. Jordan and Lebanon were reported to be stalling on ceasefire agreements, insisting on the same guarantee from Israel as Syria demanded.

Secretary General Hammarskjold announced in Jerusalem an agreement between Israel and Egypt on measures aimed to reduce frontier strife near the Gaza Strip.

A decree issued in Amman ordered imports from Poland, Czechoslovakia, East and West Germany, Holland, Belgium and France to be licensed only on condition that delivery be made through the port of Aqaba. This would seriously affect Beirut, which hitherto had handled the bulk of Jordan's import trade.

May 1

Angered at the occupation of the Buraimi Oasis by British led forces, the Saudi Arabian Government requested the UN Food and Agriculture Organization to liquidate the British Locust Control Mission in Jedda by May 19, 1956. UN officials expressed concern that the action could lead to reduced food crops in the Middle East and in northeast and central Africa.

May 2

King Faisal opened Baghdad's television station, the first in the Middle East.

Israel released a KLM (Royal Dutch Airlines) plane intercepted on May 1 and allowed it to proceed to Cairo. The plane used for aerial mapping was flying under charter to the Egyptian Government.

Full agreement was announced by Sudan and Ethiopia on the settlement of Sudanese property in Gambala.

Sudan's Foreign Minister Zarrouq said that until the currency question was settled between Egypt and Sudan, he would not agree to talks on the division of the Nile waters between the two.

A ceasefire agreement between Syria and Israel was arranged by the UN Secretary General.

An agreement was reached between Egypt and the Suez Canal Company whereby the Company would invest $60 million of its reserves in Egyptian development projects.

May 3

Britain withdrew its Locust Control Mission from Jedda, Saudi Arabia, and the UNFAO was asked to raise new non-British teams to carry on its work.

Some 260 Lebanese assistant judges went on strike for higher wages. Premier Yafi said in the Chamber of Deputies that the Government

May 3

would not submit to pressure and that it would ensure operation of the courts in spite of the strike.

In Jerusalem, Hammarskjold cautioned Israel against the resumption of the Jordan River project as incompatible with the 1953 Security Council resolution against the project. Israel took strong exception to the warning.

The UN Secretary General left Israel for Cairo en route back to the US, reportedly satisfied with the results of his mission. He submitted a progress report to the Security Council.

The London Daily Telegraph reported that Czechoslovakia and Syria had concluded an arms agreement providing for shipment to Syria of 100 tanks, 100 armored cars and 25 MIGs.

Eighteen more supporters of al-Glaoui were killed in riots in Morocco.

May 4

The Jordanian Government decided to stop the printing of propaganda leaflets by Arab and other diplomatic missions in Jordan.

The April 30 edition of The New York Times was removed from newsstands in Lebanon by the police. No reason was given for the removal.

May 5

Riots in Marrakech caused 46 deaths. The Moroccan Minister of the Interior resigned. The Sultan announced over the government radio that an investigation would be undertaken to find those responsible for the massacre of Opposition leader Glaoui's followers.

The USSR offered Lebanon the free services of engineers to rebuild villages destroyed by an earthquake on March 16.

Jordanian Defense Minister Falah Madadhah said that Jordan had not yet issued its ceasefire order. He stated that it was waiting for a

May 5

firm pledge from Israel to Syria not to proceed with diversion of the Jordan River.

Moroccan Foreign Minister Balafrej left for Paris for consultations on Morocco's future relations with other countries.

Yemeni Deputy Foreign Minister Imari announced in Cairo after a meeting with Czechoslovakian Ambassador Karpisek that Yemen would conclude a treaty of friendship with Czechoslovakia.

May 6

Egypt and Jordan issued a joint communique announcing agreement on plans to unify and coordinate their armies.

Secretary General Hammarskjold returned to New York and was acclaimed by a welcoming group of UN diplomats on the success of his mission.

The Soviet Army newspaper Red Star charged that certain persons in Israel encouraged by the US were trying to provoke war in the Middle East.

The strike of Lebanon's assistant judges ended.

May 7

Arab newspapers reported the discovery of a conspiracy to overthrow the Government of Jordan. The conspirators were supporters of the Baghdad Pact.

Tunisia rejected a French compromise plan on the issue of the former's right to establish diplomatic relations abroad.

The World Zionist Congress in Israel adopted a closing series of resolutions condemning the right wing faction in Israel for favoring war with the Arab states, and denouncing the Arab economic boycott of Israel as a violation of UN principles.

May 7

Tapline (Trans-Arabian Pipeline Company), a subsidiary of the Arabian American Oil Company, offered to share its profits equally with the four Middle Eastern countries through which its pipeline passed. However, since Tapline was not a profit making organization, it offered to change into a commercial firm.

US Secretary of State Dulles said in Washington that there was increased hope of preventing the Israel-Arab conflict from erupting into a global conflict because the Soviet Union seemed increasingly aware of the dangerous consequences of reckless action.

May 8

Israel blamed the Chairman of the Mixed Armistice Commission for refusing to find Jordan guilty of a breach in the ceasefire.

Business was paralyzed in Beirut because of a sympathy strike against French policy in North Africa. There was no violence.

Irving Brown, Chief European Representative of the US AFL-CIO, was banned from Algeria by the French Government for anti-French activity.

UN Truce Supervisor, Chief of Staff Burns, conferred in Gaza with Gohar, Egyptian expert on the Palestine armistice, on the implementation of the Egypt-Israel ceasefire agreement.

Israel Foreign Minister Sharett sent a cable to Secretary General Hammarskjold expressing grave concern at recent incidents along Israel's frontiers with Egypt and Jordan.

A trade agreement with Hungary was signed in Damascus, Syria.

May 9

UN Secretary General Hammarskjold reported to the UN Security Council that he had received from Israel, Egypt, Syria, Lebanon and Jordan written assurances that ceasefire provided for in 1949 armistice agreements would be observed.

May, 1956

May 9

Sudanese Minister of Communications Tawfiq ended a visit to Cairo with the statement that relations between Egypt and Sudan were entering a new phase of mutual cooperation. He said that the progress of talks between Sudanese delegations and Egypt on the question of currency and the Nile waters heralded favorable settlements in both cases.

Secretary Dulles explained publicly for the first time the reason for the refusal of the US to supply arms to Israel.

French Minister Lacoste said that his reason for banning Irving Brown of the AFL-CIO from Algeria was that Brown had encouraged the labor forces in Algeria seeking separation; this action was in line with the aims of Algerian rebels to oust the French from North Africa through foreign intervention and pressure.

May 10

The eastern third of Algeria was put under martial law as a result of the continuing French-Algerian conflict.

Syrian Minister of Justice Munir al-Ajlani resigned.

UN Secretary General Hammarskjold submitted his final report on the Middle East situation to the Security Council.

May 11

Hundreds of demonstrators demanding independence for Aden mobbed the car of British Parliamentary Under Secretary for the Colonies Lloyd during his visit to the colony.

French police impounded the Communist newspaper L'Humanite for circulation of an article by its Algerian correspondent describing alleged eyewitness reports of French reprisals against Moslems.

UN Secretary General Hammarskjold rebuked Israel for an incorrect version of the Nirim incident of May 7, which claimed that the Egyptians had staged the incident.

May, 1956

May 11

UN Secretary General Hammarskjold said that he had no plans to return to the Middle East, though he was willing, if asked, to continue his services as a negotiator. He said he would not himself make any recommendations about possible next steps on the very long road to a Palestine solution.

May 12

The Lebanese Government made attempts to convince Saudi Arabia, Jordan and Syria that the royalties for oil pipelines crossing their territories be equally divided without regard to the distance covered.

Twelve more jet planes to complement the previous month's shipment were released for delivery to Israel from France with the tacit approval of the US. The US did not press its priority claim to these planes in its military aid program to NATO.

King Hussein of Jordan arrived suddenly and unexpectedly in Beirut.

The British Government granted 26,000 pounds sterling to relieve famine among Bedouin tribes in the north of Eastern Aden Protectorate.

Egyptian Premier Nasser paid a surprise visit to the Egyptian held Gaza Strip. He declared that his Government considered the Strip a part of Egypt.

May 13

In Algeria, downtown Constantine was placed under military guard after a new outbreak of violence.

The new Royal Moroccan Army of 15,000 troops swore allegiance to Sultan Ben-Youssef and his Government.

The Israel Foreign Ministry acknowledged that the Israel Government wrongly accused Egyptians of violating the frontier on May 7 at Nirim near the Gaza Strip. A spokesman said that Israelis and not Egyptians crossed the demarcation line in that incident.

May, 1956

May 14

In an address to army officers in Cairo, Premier Nasser declared that the Egyptian Army would continue to be the strongest army in the area and would continue to enjoy superiority whether the West liked it or not and whether Israel liked it or not. If the West would give more arms to Israel, Egypt would get more arms also.

French forces cordoned off the Jewish quarter of Constantine, Algeria.

A delegation of six citizens of Aden explained their demands for self government within the British Commonwealth to British Foreign Secretary Lloyd in Aden. In addition to the requests made April 29 to the Governor, they asked for the formation of a militia and for stiffer immigration laws.

Two senior officers of the Jordanian Army faced trial and seven were under house arrest on a charge of plotting an armed coup to seize control of the Arab Legion and overall power in Jordan.

May 15

Moroccan guerrillas released six French Senegalese soldiers captured May 7 and presented them to Moroccan Sultan Muhammad V.

Israel rejected a suggestion by UN Truce Chief Burns that the Mixed Armistice Commission resume meetings in the al-Auja (Nitsana) demilitarized zone, now occupied by Israel forces. It claimed that occupation of al-Auja was necessary for its security, but agreed to hold meetings at a third neutral site to discuss arrangements for implementation of the Palestine ceasefire.

In Algiers, 2,000 European university students asked French Minister Lacoste to waive their national service postponement so that they could be mobilized for service in Algeria.

King Hussein returned to Amman, Jordan, after conferring with Lebanese leaders.

May, 1956

May 16

British officials announced that six modern airfields built by Britain in the Suez Canal Zone were now in Egyptian hands.

Studies resumed in most Catholic schools in Lebanon at the request of the Maronite Patriarch of Lebanon, after the Government had promised aid for private primary education.

An East German trade mission arrived in Cairo.

The US Defense Department confirmed that a consignment of ammunition and other military material was being prepared for shipment to Saudi Arabia. The value of the cargo was about $1 million. Senator Lehman (Democrat, New York) demanded the fullest possible inquiry into this shocking action on the part of the US Government. A State Department spokesman said that no major weapons were in the shipment.

The Egyptian Government announced that it had recognized Communist China.

The Jordanian Ministry of Development and Reconstruction invited the UN Relief and Works Agency for Palestine Refugees to share in the Dead Sea potash scheme. The Ministry suggested an Agency contribution of about $5 million, approximately one-third of the total investment cost.

May 17

Communist China's Foreign Minister issued a statement in Peking expressing gratification over Egypt's recognition of the Peking Government.

The Nationalist Chinese Government broke diplomatic relations with Egypt and recalled its Ambassador to Egypt.

Sir Charles Belgrave, advisor to the Ruler of Bahrain, announced that press censorship would end in Bahrain on May 21 for the three Arabic biweekly newspapers in the sheikhdom.

May 17

The Foreign Ministers of Egypt, Syria, Jordan and Lebanon met in Damascus to discuss the report of the UN Secretary General on his mission to the Middle East.

The Egyptian Cabinet approved a law providing compulsory primary education for all children from the age of six.

May 18

Iraq's King Faisal arrived in Madrid for a state visit at the invitation of Generalissimo Franco.

Adenese Government spokesmen said that two Yemeni leaders had received the equivalent of $1,400,000 and 5,000 rifles and ammunition from King Saud of Saudi Arabia.

The Foreign Ministers of Egypt, Syria, Jordan and Lebanon agreed to adopt a common policy of action if Israel resumed work on the diversion of the Jordan River for irrigation and power generation.

May 19

A joint communique signed by Soviet leaders and French Ministers Mollet and Pineau reflected Soviet doubt on France's ability to find a solution in Algeria.

An Egyptian reporter completed a five day tour of Israel under the guise of a Brazilian journalist. He reported to Premier Nasser that Israel Premier Ben-Gurion, Foreign Minister Sharett and Labor Minister Myerson had separately expressed willingness to meet Nasser "anywhere, anytime" to discuss Arab-Israel frictions.

Turkey sent an official note to Syria protesting that the latter's plans for irrigation and drainage in the al-Ghab area would harm Turkey's agricultural border lands.

Morocco and France signed a diplomatic agreement permitting Morocco to extend diplomatic recognition to a number of countries.

May 19

The Israel-Jordanian MAC condemned Jordan for violating the General Armistice Agreement on May 15, when two Israelis were wounded in an ambush near Megiddo. Noting that a series of acts had been committed against Israel highway traffic since the beginning of the year, the Commission called on Jordan to take immediately the strictest measures to ensure forthwith the cessation of violation of the general armistice agreements.

Addressing a graduating class of naval cadets in Alexandria, Premier Nasser said that Egypt was free to buy arms from any place it liked and in any quantity it liked. He vowed to resist with all force any foreign effort to limit the quantity of arms Egypt received. He alleged that the Western Big Three had agreed at the Paris meeting of the NATO Foreign Ministers to send sufficient arms to Israel to keep that country militarily superior to the Arabs.

The Political Committee of the Arab League, meeting in Damascus, announced that it would bring the Algerian question before the UN Security Council as a case concerning a threat to peace.

In a statement to the Legislative Council of Aden, the British Government declared that there was no possibility in the foreseeable future of any change in the status of the colony of Aden.

May 20

King Hussein of Jordan dismissed Premier Rifai and asked Said al-Mufti to form a new government.

In Aden, 130 armed tribesmen, coming in trucks from the direction of Saudi Arabia, were forced to surrender to local security forces by British jets, as Arabs demonstrated against the British Parliamentary Under Secretary for the Colonies.

Cairo Radio announced that Egypt and Poland had concluded an agreement for Polish arms to be supplied to Egyptian military forces.

Five Algerian rebel political leaders, including Abbas, left Tripoli for Europe in a search for more foreign support.

May 20

A Rumanian economic mission arrived in Cairo to negotiate a long term trade and payments agreement.

Azzouz, the leader of the small Tunisian National Party, was killed in an exchange of fire with guards outside Bourguiba's house in a suburb of Tunis.

May 21

Israel reluctantly agreed to truce talks with Egypt at the al-Auja site.

The British reported that the tribesmen seized in Aden on May 20 were from Najran, Saudi Arabia. It was announced that the report of demonstrations against Lord Lloyd was unfounded.

Lebanese statesman Malik said that the Western powers must adopt a sound policy toward the Arab countries or see them ally with the USSR.

Jordanian Premier Mufti formed a new government and announced that he would request a revision of the defense treaty between Jordan and Britain.

Israel Premier Ben-Gurion confirmed the statement made by an Egyptian reporter that he was ready to meet Premier Nasser "any time, any place." He added, however, that no more Egyptian journalists would be invited to visit Israel unless Israel journalists were permitted to visit Cairo.

It was announced in Beirut that Lebanon and Jordan agreed to coordinate their defense plans and unite their forces in case of war. A Jordanian military mission left Lebanon and returned to Jordan after talks leading to this agreement. The agreement was described as not involving either country in commitments to the other except in case of an emergency.

The Israel Foreign Ministry informed General Burns that it was willing to permit the Israel-Egyptian MAC to meet in al-Auja to approve the

May 21

Secretary General's plan to strengthen enforcement of the ceasefire along the Gaza Strip.

The Syrian Minister of State resigned because there was no harmony between the members of the Cabinet. He resigned after the resignation of Minister of Justice Haroun al-Ajlani.

A 72 member cultural mission from Communist China arrived in Damascus for a ten day visit.

Syrian Premier Ghazi said in Damascus that the Government was considering recognizing Communist China.

May 22

A shipment of US military equipment arrived in Tripoli for the Libyan Army. It was the first of three shipments promised to Libya as part of a joint British-American arms grant totalling $1 million.

Premier Nehru of India declared in the Indian Parliament that he supported the Algerian nationalist demands, but at the same time he praised the French. He called for an Algerian ceasefire based on five suggestions.

In reaction to Egypt's recognition of Communist China, US Secretary of State Dulles stated that it was an action that the US regretted. He also said that the US would probably not help Egypt on the Aswan High Dam if the USSR had a share in the project.

It was reported in Beirut that, in Arab opinion, the change of Government in Jordan was a definite loss of Western power in the Middle East.

May 23

Iran complained about the unfriendly attitude of the Egyptian press in reporting an alleged coup d'etat in Iran.

A Bulgarian mission led by the Deputy Minister of Foreign Trade arrived in Damascus to negotiate a trade and payments agreement with Syria.

The Iraq Chamber of Deputies approved a five year development scheme to cost ID500 million.

Three hundred French reservists called to duty in Algeria demonstrated to show their protests and tried to stop a troop train.

Libyan Premier Ben-Halim said that the principal issues which could cause friction between Libya, Britain and the US were the attitudes of the two Western countries toward Israel and Algeria.

The Israel Foreign Ministry expressed its readiness to discuss measures to improve truce supervision along the Gaza Strip, and dropped its insistence that such measures be first adopted by the Egyptian-Israel MAC. Furthermore, Israel agreed to set up six observation posts along its side of the truce line to correspond with six Egyptian posts already agreed upon.

Iran told India in a memorandum that the Baghdad Pact powers had a right to discuss anything about the Kashmir question which might violate international peace. The memorandum was sent in reply to an Indian protest of April 27 against a statement made by the Baghdad Pact countries in their April meeting in Tehran urging early settlement of the dispute.

The Soviet Ambassador to Egypt presented Premier Nasser with an Ilyushin-14 aircraft as a token of Soviet-Egyptian friendship.

Mendes-France resigned from the French Cabinet in disagreement over government measures to counter the rebellion in Algeria. He said that the Government's failure to accompany its massive military effort with political action designed to restore Moslem confidence in French intentions would result in the loss of Algeria.

May 24

The Egyptian Government officially announced that Premier Nasser had accepted an invitation to visit Communist China. It was reported that the Egyptian Government had decided to invite the Communist Chinese Premier, Chou En-lai, to visit Egypt in July for the celebration of the third anniversary of the revolution.

Czechoslovakian Premier Siroky revealed that Czechoslovakia and Syria were negotiating a trade agreement and that Syria was interested in arms.

Major General Radi Innab resigned as Chief of Staff of the Jordan Arab Legion; King Hussein named Ali Abu-Nuwar, Chief of Military Operations, to succeed him. Hussein said that Jordan wanted to retain its close ties with Britain and dismissed any suggestion that Jordan would abrogate the defense treaty.

UN Truce Chief Burns announced that Israel had refused to sanction meetings of the Mixed Armistice Commission at al-Auja on grounds that the demilitarized area was Israel territory. He also censured Jordan for an attack on Israel Forces on Mount Scopus.

May 25

Major General Ali Abu-Nuwar announced plans for enlarging Jordan's Army.

Lebanon began trade talks with Nationalist China.

The French Army began to close off the Algerian-Moroccan frontier with a barbed wire fence. When completed, the fence would be a 100 mile barrier from Port Saya south to al-Aricha on the edge of the Sahara.

King Faisal of Iraq arrived in Rabat, Morocco, for a two day official visit.

French policemen arrested 100 Algerians in an effort to destroy the nationalist underground in Algiers and Oran. French Resident Minister Lacoste put press correspondents in Algeria on military censorship.

May 25

Algerian nationalist representatives addressed a meeting of Asian and African delegates to the UN and charged France with greatly increased repressive measures against Algerian rebels. The UN delegates decided to ask the Security Council to take up the Algerian question.

May 26

Premier Nasser conferred with the British Ambassador to Egypt for the first time since March 16 in an apparent effort to restore good relations.

Jordanian Defense Minister Ajlouni announced plans to merge the Arab Legion with the National Guard to create an expanded Jordan Army.

Libya and Egypt signed new trade and payments agreements.

The British tanker Verenia was blacklisted in Alexandria after a report that it had taken oil to Israel.

May 27

Sultan al-Qaiti of Shihr and Mukalla and Premier of the Eastern Aden Protectorate died in Aden at the age of 78.

Between 20 and 30 persons were arrested in Kuwait for alleged Communist activities in a series of raids. A large quantity of Communist literature was found.

An Egyptian health delegation arrived in East Berlin to tour hospitals and medical installations in East Germany.

Iraq's King Faisal flew to Paris after an official visit to Sultan Muhammad V of Morocco.

Former Premier Rifai accused King Hussein of leading Jordan to the solution of problems by force when moderation was needed.

May 28

Egypt said that the Arab states would accept any resolution adopted by the UN Security Council regarding the Palestine ceasefire so long as it did not contradict the terms of the Arab-Israel Armistice Agreement.

The 18 sentences imposed on officials of the Syrian Popular Party for the assassination of Colonel Malki were reversed.

French Defense Minister Bourges-Manoury said that the ambitions of the Egyptian dictator were without limit. According to his own writings, he planned to bring under his grasp not only the Middle East and North Africa but a very large part of Africa south of the Sahara as well. Bourges-Manoury said that the French Army in Algeria was fighting to halt Nasser's expansionist plans.

Several thousand Communist led workers rioted in St. Nazaire in France against the government recall of reservists for service in Algeria.

French and Moroccan officials signed a treaty designed to bring the foreign policies of their Governments into harmony. Morocco agreed to be bound by the international treaties which France had made in its name.

Leaflets were distributed in several parts of the Aden Protectorate calling on the people to revolt against their rulers.

May 29

The UN Security Council discussed UN Secretary General Hammarskjold's report on his tour of the Middle East.

French Minister Lacoste said that the problem of Algeria was an internal one and would never be resolved in an international setting.

A Rumanian economic delegation arrived in Cairo to discuss economic relations and negotiate the exchange of Egyptian cotton for oil.

British UN Delegate Sir Pierson Dixon asked the UN Security Council for approval of a resolution urging that UN Secretary General Hammarskjold "continue his good offices" toward an enforcement of Arab-Israel armistice agreements.

May, 1956

May 29

Syrian President Kuwatli arrived in Amman on a state visit.

The Syrian Government banned the export of wheat to France or Algeria. This action followed reports that Syrian merchants had sold 9,000 tons of wheat to the two countries for the use of French forces fighting Arab nationalist rebels.

A majority of the Security Council delegates indicated their approval of the British draft resolution. To meet Arab objections, the British Delegate revised some expressions in the resolution, but the Arabs asked for more precision and greater clarity and maintained that the Secretary General must be strictly bound by the framework of the armistice agreements.

Tribesmen coming from Qaiti State into the Eastern Aden Protectorate equipped with arms from Saudi Arabia were strafed by RAF (Royal Air Force) planes and retreated to the northeast.

May 30

The Iraq Chamber of Deputies passed a new income tax bill.

The Sudanese Foreign Minister Zarrouq said that his country would take no action on recognition of Communist China until Sudan's application for UN membership was approved.

Tunisian Premier Bourguiba declared that diplomatic prerogatives had not been accorded to Tunisia by France and declared his country solidly in support of Algerian independence.

The irregular Moroccan Army of Liberation, which carried on guerrilla warfare with the French prior to independence, issued a communique accusing French troops still in Morocco of provocations and demanded their immobilization.

June, 1956

June 1

In a new political program published in Davar, the official Israel trade newspaper, Premier Ben-Gurion said that Israel would refrain from war even if provoked.

Former French Premier Reynaud called on Premier Mollet to define France's peace aims in Algeria as a prerequisite to ending the rebellion. He said that he and most of his fellow Independents supported the Government's efforts to pacify the country by blanketing it with troops, but asked for a clear statement that military measures now in effect would suffice.

Premier Gamal Abdel Nasser promised to end military rule in Egypt and to turn the country into a cooperative society. He announced in a major policy speech that the Revolution Command Council would be dissolved on June 23, when Egypt's new constitution was to be voted on.

In an effort to solve the problem of integrating the Tangier Zone with Morocco while protecting financial investments made during the period of international control, the Tangier Committee of Control agreed with the Moroccan Foreign Minister that the local Government of Tangier should be allowed to operate as before.

Radio Cairo's Voice of the Arabs program broadcast practical instructions in propaganda to all Arabs outside the Arab World.

Arab states representatives in the UN refused to support a modified British resolution toward a settlement in Israel. They objected to the phrase a mutually acceptable solution as perpetuating the existence of Israel, *de jure* as well as *de facto*.

June 2

A spokesman for the British Foreign Office declared in London that the British Ambassador in Jedda was holding discussions with the Saudi Arabian Government to draw up an agenda in preparation for scheduled talks in which the two countries would attempt to solve the outstanding problems between them.

May, 1956

May 31

The French National Assembly opened debate on Premier Mollet's North African policy. He was attacked by both moderate and conservative groups and extreme radicals.

In UN Security Council debate, Syrian delegate Shukairy charged that history had proved that Palestine was nothing but southern Syria. Israel Delegate Eban replied that Shukairy's statement betrayed Syrian designs on Israel.

President of the Sudanese Sovereignty Council, Salah, was replaced by al-Maghrabi.

After a visit to Amman by Syrian President Kuwatli, Jordan and Syria announced in a joint communique several agreements, including a military pact.

Arab representatives to the UN violently attacked the British draft resolution. Their two major objections were the failure to state the exact authority to be granted the Secretary General, and the endorsement of a peaceful settlement on a mutually acceptable basis.

Israel UN Delegate Eban gave approval to the draft resolution. He renewed Prime Minister Ben-Gurion's offer to negotiate with any of the Arab states and declared that since history had decreed that the Israelis and Arabs must live together for all time, they should settle their differences and join in promoting regional and international peace.

The USSR Delegate to the UN supported two of the Arab demands: that the Secretary General's future activities be confined to compliance with the armistices, and that references to freedom of movement for UN observers in all areas be deleted.

Premier al-Yafi's Government in Lebanon won a vote of confidence. The Government had asked for the vote after a motion by the opposition National Bloc censuring the government controlled electricity company had been approved by the Lebanese Chamber of Deputies.

Tunisia joined the World Health Organization.

June, 1956

June 2

Premier Mollet offered Algeria wider self rule when peace was restored. He said that increased autonomy would include voting by Moslems and Europeans in a single college, instead of separately as in the past. He asked the National Assembly for a vote of confidence on the Government's policies at home and abroad.

The Syrian Cabinet of Premier Ghazi submitted its resignation. The President asked former Premier Haffar to form a new government.

Eleven men in Aden were sentenced and fined 625 pounds sterling for organizing an illegal procession on May 11 on the arrival of British Foreign Secretary Lloyd.

A trade agreement was signed between Syria and Turkey.

The Iraqi Director of Propaganda and Guidance said that his country had decided to open information offices in several Arab capitals and in London and Washington.

A *Modus Vivendi* was signed between Syria and Turkey which granted most favored nation treatment to the two countries.

Students occupied the Syrian Ministry of National Economy and asked that the exportation of cereals to France and Algeria be prohibited.

June 3

A Saudi Arabian Government spokesman denied that his country would recognize Communist China or establish diplomatic relations with Soviet Russia.

In preparation for the June 23 balloting, eight members of the Egyptian Cabinet toured the Nile Delta provinces to explain Premier Nasser's concept of a cooperative state to voters.

It was reported in Washington that 33 delegations from the Communist countries had visited Egypt in 1955 and 30 delegations arrived there in the first three months of 1956. Egypt and India reportedly were the main targets of the Soviet Bloc's rapidly expanding program of cultural, scientific and trade exchanges with the non-Communist world.

June 4

A new Arab newspaper, al-Shaab (The People), was started in Cairo by Major Salem, former Minister of National Guidance in Premier Nasser's Revolutionary Command Council; he had been ousted from his post in August, 1955.

In response to Arab demands, Britain agreed to withdraw the mutually acceptable solution clause from its UN proposal for an Arab-Israel peace.

Salah Ben-Youssef, Tunisian rebel leader, was named Commander of the Tunisian Liberation Army, which opposed Premier Bourguiba's Government.

The Jordanian Cabinet reversed its decision of April 30 that Jordan alone should finance the Dead Sea potash scheme and approved the formation of a company with Arab capital. The initial capital was fixed at JD1 million.

The Security Council adopted unanimously a British resolution aimed at consolidating the gains of Secretary General Dag Hammarskjold's Middle East peace mission. The final draft called on the Secretary General to continue his good offices with Arabs and Israelis and to cooperate with them in securing full compliance with the Palestine armistice and in adopting measures to reduce border incidents.

Finance Minister Hamad said that Syria had decided in principle to recognize Communist China.

The Egyptian Representative on the Suez Canal Company's Board declared that Egypt would not extend the Company's 99 year concession on its expiration in 1968.

Finance Minister Paul Ramadier said that the first installment on the cost of keeping Algeria French was $285 million and he set the total cost of military measures in North Africa in the current budget at 215 billion francs ($613 million). He said that the Government was considering tax increases and rises in the cost of state monopoly tobacco to produce this additional revenue.

June 5

The UN Truce Supervision Organization announced completion of 12 new observation posts on the Gaza Strip frontier, six on each side.

All copies of The New York Times for June 2 were seized by Lebanese authorities from the newsstands. The newspaper had carried an editorial severely critical of Arab policy in Palestine.

The Lebanese Cabinet resigned over the purchase of the port of Beirut from a company that operated on a concession and over disagreement on how to spend the 100 million pounds sterling reserved for earthquake emergencies.

Lebanon became the twenty-third country to ratify the UN Convention on the Political Rights of Women.

French Premier Mollet won a vote of confidence in the National Assembly for his Algerian policy by a vote of 271-59-271.

French Foreign Minister Pineau politely rejected Indian Prime Minister Nehru's offer for settlement of the Algerian issues, because it involved recognition of the Algerian national entity.

June 6

After accepting the resignation of Prime Minister Abdallah al-Yafi, Lebanese President Chamoun asked him to choose a new cabinet.

Resigning Syrian Premier Ghazi was asked to form a new cabinet.

France agreed to let Morocco proceed with its establishment of diplomatic relations with any country, although the Franco-Moroccan agreement allowing it to do this had not been ratified by the French Parliament.

The first diplomat accredited to Morocco was Spanish Ambassador Alcover, formerly Spanish Consul General in Rabat.

The Adenese Government denied that a British patrol had been killed by tribesmen in a clash south of Yemen.

June 6

Israel complained formally to the Mixed Armistice Commission that Jordan had established a detachment of troops on its territory. The Jordanians had withdrawn when challenged, the complaint added.

June 7

A riot of 2,000 workers in Le Havre, France, delayed the departure for Algeria of 15 reservists for more than an hour.

The Cabinet of Libya ratified the trade agreement with Egypt.

UN Secretary General Hammarskjold said that there could be no lasting settlement in Palestine unless it was mutually acceptable to Israel and the Arab countries.

Wholesale merchants in Khartoum, Sudan, began a four day strike in protest against profit fixing on certain goods.

Israel notified the Security Council that Egypt had detained a Greek ship bound for the port of Elath, Israel.

The Syrian Head of the Security Department said that he had asked the US Information Service in Damascus to appoint an employee to censor all books, newspapers and magazines that it received.

June 8

Lebanese Premier al-Yafi formed a new government, retaining all former members of the Cabinet except al-Bustani and George Hakim, former Minister of Economy. The two new officers in the Cabinet were Alfred Naqqash, Minister of Justice, and Fuad Ghusn, Minister of National Education. The new Government won a vote of confidence in the chamber by 30-5-2. Al-Bustani remained Director of the Reconstruction Department.

June 8

Moroccan Foreign Minister Balafrej said that the US should negotiate directly and immediately with Morocco on the future of US air bases there.

The President of Standard Oil of New Jersey in the US declared that he was concerned over the political situation in the Middle East but did not believe that it would greatly affect oil operations in the Arab countries.

The USSR announced that Foreign Minister Shepilov would go to Cairo on June 18 to participate in Egyptian Evacuation Day ceremonies, celebrating the departure of the British from the Suez Canal Zone.

The Yemen Legation in London formally protested to Britain the alleged bombing on June 3 of a Yemeni customs port by RAF (Royal Air Force) planes. The British Foreign Office said that the Government had no information on the matter. It added that the British Charge d'Affaires in Taizz, the present capital of Imam Ahmad, had been instructed to protest an incursion into the Beihan area of Aden Protectorate by a large number of Yemeni tribesmen.

According to reports, Israel Premier Ben-Gurion decided not to force the resignation of Foreign Minister Sharett.

June 9

Dockers at Port Said refused to unload the ship Yangtse, in transit from China to Rumania.

A strike of Luke Thomas Company employees began in Aden.

The Casablanca police ordered the dissolution of Cadima, a society engaged in assisting Jews to emigrate from Morocco to Israel.

The Sudanese Cabinet approved the recommendations of the ministerial committee set up to draft a permanent constitution for Sudan.

Prime Minister Ben-Gurion said that the danger of Israel becoming embroiled in a war would prevail that summer with greater intensity

June, 1956

June 9

than before because of the acquisition by the Arab countries of arms.

June 10

Lebanon announced the roundup of a huge spy ring in Beirut and said that it was preparing to try more than 20 persons for spying for Israel.

The Egyptian Government and the Suez Canal Company reached an agreement under which the Company would transfer over 20 million pounds sterling to Egypt over the next eight years.

Moroccan Foreign Minister Balafrej arrived in Spain for talks on the procedure of incorporation of Spanish Morocco into the rest of the country.

The Crown Prince of Yemen said in Cairo that the purpose of his impending visit to the USSR was an attempt at establishing trade between Yemen and the Soviet Union.

Deputy Foreign Minister of Yemen, al-Amari, said in Cairo that Aden would gain independence sooner or later despite British opposition.

The Jordan and Iraq treaty of friendship was renewed for five years.

French Premier Mollet won support from the Socialist Party's National Council after he made a standing truce offer to Algerian rebels. Reversing his former position that a ceasefire was akin to surrender, Premier Mollet stated a willingness to make contact with Algerian rebels to discuss a ceasefire.

Former Syrian Premier Haffar abandoned his efforts to form a new cabinet. The President asked former Premier Assali to form a new cabinet.

June 11

Bulganin of the USSR sent messages to Tunisian Premier Bourguiba and Moroccan Premier Si Bekkai announcing the recognition of the

June, 1956

June 11

The US established an Embassy in Rabat, Morocco, and named former Consul General Porter to the position of Counsellor and Charge d'Affaires pending the arrival of an Ambassador.

June 12

The UN Trusteeship Council received a complaint from Somaliland that Egyptian propagandists were exerting undue pressures on the Somalis to join the Arab League upon attaining independence in 1960. The complaints stated that Egyptian educators sent to Somaliland were causing Somali students to fear that they would be divorced from Islam unless they cemented their ties with Egypt.

June 13

A communique issued after the conclusion in Madrid of the Spanish Moroccan talks said the two sides agreed to start preparations for the transfer of the powers hitherto exercised by the Spanish to the Moroccan authorities.

The last British troops left the Suez Canal Zone after 74 years of occupation.

Britain rejected Yemen's claim to the Aden Protectorate.

The Social Democratic Party refused to discuss peace in Algeria with nationalist Ferhat Abbas because he did not stress indissoluble ties with France.

A trade and payments agreement was signed between Lebanon and Bulgaria.

After a deputy suggested that Turkey might export Lebanese goods to Israel, the Lebanese Parliament refused to ratify a Lebanese Turkish trade agreement made previously.

The Union of Civil Servants in Tangier, affiliated with the Moroccan Trade Union Federation, went on strike for 48 hours to demand immediate integration of Tangier into Morocco.

June, 1956

June 11

two countries as sovereign independent states by the USSR, and its readiness to establish diplomatic relations with them.

Sudan was admitted to the ILO (International Labor Organization). The four day strike of Khartoum merchants ended.

Cairo announced that new naval units had arrived at Alexandria to reinforce the Egyptian Navy. The units were presumed to be two destroyers of Skoryi class sold to Egypt by the Soviet Government.

The Crown Prince of Yemen left for Moscow in a Soviet plane. His arrival in the USSR was described by Pravda as proof of the growing ties and cooperation between the Soviet Union and the Arab States.

The Iraq Development Board announced a six year housing program.

An Israel military court sentenced two Egyptian commandos to 20 years imprisonment on charges of armed infiltration and recording lists of military traffic in the Negev.

The Iraqi Government banned Ahmad Ben-Bella, leader of the Algerian Liberation Army, from entering Iraq.

Tunisia was admitted to membership in the ILO.

The Egyptian Interior Ministry issued an order restricting travel abroad for Egyptians except on business or for medical treatment. The measure was designed to save currency.

Syria prohibited grain exports to France in protest against the latter's Algerian policy.

Libya asked all foreign missions, including the US Information Agency, to stop the general distribution of all printed materials from their countries and to ban public movies, meetings and lectures. This action was taken to protect Libya from a large increase in Egyptian and Soviet propaganda activities.

Morocco was admitted to membership in the ILO.

June, 1956

June 14

The Yemeni Representative to the UN accused Britain of repeated aggressive acts over Yemeni territory, in violation of the 1934 Anglo-Yemen treaty and the UN Charter.

Morocco lifted a ban on collective Jewish emigration to Israel.

Pennsylvania Governor George Leader, visiting Israel at the invitation of the Government, was refused permission by Jordan to visit the holy places of Arab controlled Jerusalem.

French Resident Minister Lacoste said that rebel military strength in Algeria had been broken. He forecasted a peaceful settlement with the nationalists.

Official statistics published in Cairo listed Czechoslovakia as the largest buyer of Egyptian cotton from September 1, 1955 to May 25, 1956. India was second and France third; Britain was at the bottom of the list.

June 15

The impending visit of Foreign Minister Pineau of France sparked a warning from a spokesman for the Arab governments against US support of France's position in Algeria—specifically against the use of US equipment from NATO to crush Algerian nationalists.

France and Tunisia signed an agreement confirming Tunisia's independence in foreign affairs. France in turn received no assurance of Tunisian cooperation.

Premier Habib Bourguiba threatened to renew the fight against France unless French Armed Forces were evacuated from Tunisian soil.

June, 1956

June 15

A Syrian Government of National Union was formed by Sabri al-Assali of the National Party.

The former French High Commissioner presented his credentials as French Ambassador to Morocco in Sudan.

Two members of the French Cabinet told a group at Tindouf, Algeria, in the Sahara, that reinforcements airlifted to the area had eliminated the danger of further attack by rebels. A previous attack on the small French post of Cum-al-Hachar, 100 miles north of Tindouf, on June 1, was the first in the Sahara regions of Algeria and Morocco.

June 16

The British Consul in Tunisia was named first Charge d'Affaires to independent Tunisia.

In a conference in Karachi, Pakistan, Iran and Iraq agreed to form a joint shipping company. The company was to be mutually financed and would provide coastal service between Pakistan and Persian Gulf ports.

Soviet Foreign Minister Shepilov arrived in Cairo and called for closer Soviet-Arab ties and an end of the Western control of the Middle East. It was reported that he offered Russian help to Egypt on the Aswan Dam project.

June 17

The trial of 13 persons accused of murder in the "black hole" incident at Kosti in February, 1956, began.

Premier Mollet said in Narbonne that the Algerian situation had been completely righted by France's resolve to make political and social reforms and by the courage of its soldiers.

Libyan Premier Ben-Halim arrived in London for talks with Britain on the British subsidy to Libya, caused by the basing of the 10th Armored Division there.

June, 1956

June 19

Workers of the Arabian American Oil Company at Dhahran, Saudi Arabia, struck over the arrangements for the transportation of workers to and from their jobs.

The President of the World Bank arrived in Cairo with an offer to finance the Aswan Dam.

The Jordanian committee organizing an Arab Workers' Union decided at its Amman meeting to open a branch in Beirut, work to establish a Yemen labor union movement and create a special syndicate in Arab countries.

Two Algerian rebels were executed, bringing to a close the period of leniency during the Algerian crisis.

Israel Premier Ben-Gurion outlined a forceful new policy for Israel, but warned against preventive war. He said that the change in the Foreign Ministry from Moshe Sharett to Golda Myerson had been arranged to achieve greater coordination between the Defense and Foreign Ministries. The new policy included no evacuation of the demilitarized Sinai border zone so long as Egypt maintained its aggressive policy, reprisal tactics against future Arab cross border raiders, refusal to accept any unenforceable settlement of Arab-Israel relations, and increased colonization of underdeveloped parts of the country.

It was reported that the Soviet Union had increased its offer of a loan to Egypt of $1.12 billion at two percent for the construction of the Aswan High Dam. Soviet Foreign Minister Shepilov, in Cairo, offered economic and technical aid for other industrial developments as well.

Premier Nasser proclaimed the end of martial law in Egypt which had been in effect since the overthrow of King Farouk four years before. He also ended press censorship and announced that all political prisoners had been freed. In a two hour speech, he called for a free Algeria and for good relations with Britain.

Salah Ben-Youssef, exiled Tunisian nationalist leader, left Italy by plane for Cairo at the suggestion of the Italian police. After being permitted to enter Italy for medical treatment on the condition that he

June, 1956

June 17

Egypt announced the freeing of nearly 600 political prisoners, mostly Communists or members of the outlawed Moslem Brotherhood. The pardon was believed to be a feature of Liberation Day.

June 18

Independence and Republic Day was celebrated in Egypt.

The Director of the International Bank for Reconstruction and Development arrived in Riyadh on a special Saudi Arabian plane.

Moshe Sharett, Foreign Minister of Israel since 1949, resigned and was replaced by Minister of Labor, Golda Myerson.

Thirteen Asian and African members of the UN formally requested a Security Council meeting to consider the grave situation in Algeria.

A national holiday in Syria was called to celebrate the evacuation of foreign troops from Egypt.

Egyptian Premier Nasser formally proclaimed the end of British control over Suez.

The Algerian rebel flag, green and white with a red star and crescent, was flown in Tangier for the first time at a mass meeting organized by the Moroccan Istiqlal Party.

French prospectors struck oil in the Sahara Desert area of Southern Algeria, according to a Paris report by the French State Oil Organization.

June 19

The US and Saudi Arabia agreed to extend the Dhahran Airbase Agreement to July 18, 1956, pending the outcome of present negotiations between the two countries. The agreement expired on June 18, 1956.

June, 1956

June 19

refrain from political activity, he had issued a violently anti-French statement on June 18.

Oil exploration in Libya got underway with the transfer of 11 members of the geological staff of the Ohio Oil Company to the Oasis Oil Company of Libya, under terms of the former's one-third interest in the latter.

French Secretary of State for Tunisian and Moroccan Affairs Savary told the Advisory Council for the Republic that the French-US statute on Moroccan air bases could not be modified without French consent.

A new electoral law for the Iraqi Chamber of Deputies was enacted.

The Istiqlal Party leader, in a speech at Tangier, demanded the incorporation into Morocco of southwest Algeria, Mauritanian area of French West Africa and Spanish Rio de Oro.

June 20

A Royal Order was issued strictly prohibiting the exit from Saudi Arabia of Saudi Arabian currency, whether Saudi Arabian gold pounds or silver riyals.

The Lebanese Minister of State and Chairman of the Ministerial Oil Committee arrived in Riyadh for talks with the Saudi Government on the Tapline offer to share the oil royalties between Saudi Arabia, Syria, Jordan and Lebanon.

The Yemeni legation in Washington accused Britain of repeated border violations along the Adenese-Yemeni border, and of trying to impose a federal union on the nine Yemen cantons adjacent to the Aden Protectorate.

The Israel Navy was reinforced by two British destroyers of the Zambesi class, purchased in 1955.

The third day of celebrations marking the end of British occupation of Suez was highlighted by a military parade in Cairo that prominently displayed Egypt's newly purchased weapons.

June, 1956

June 20

The Iraq Petroleum Company gave Syria's Premier a check for SL2, 500, 000 in part payment for outstanding claims of SL8, 500, 000.

Israel asked the UN to censure Jordan and Syria for armistice violations inherent in the hostile pronouncements by their leaders before the Security Council and other public forums.

The head of the IBRD held another conversation with Egyptian Premier Nasser about the IBRD proposed loan to help finance the Aswan High Dam.

The French Cabinet approved the breakdown of Algeria's four departments into 12 new and smaller ones to solve the problem of under-administration.

The first consignment of Egyptian arms for the Sudanese Army arrived at Port Sudan.

June 21

The Algerian National Liberation Front published a handbill warning that 100 French civilians would be killed for every patriot executed by French authorities.

The USSR extended a loan to finance the construction of the Aswan High Dam project in Egypt.

The discovery of oil in a wildcat well on the Persian Gulf coast of Saudi Arabia was announced by the Arabian American Oil Company. The well was located approximately 80 miles northwest of Dhahran.

Egypt, Jordan, Syria, Iraq, Lebanon, Saudi Arabia and the Arab Bank signed an agreement to set up an Arab potash company with a capital of JD1 million. Jordan was to contribute JD500, 000, the other countries proportional amounts.

Jordan's Premier said that the new Government would never conclude a peace agreement with Israel. He told Parliament that he would

June, 1956

June 21

seek the return of Palestine Arab refugees to their former homes and that military pacts with Syria and Egypt were intended to encircle Israel.

June 22

A joint Egyptian-USSR communique was issued on the conclusion in Cairo of talks between the USSR Foreign Minister Shepilov, and Egyptian Prime Minister Nasser. A wide exchange of opinions took place on relations between the two countries as well as on international problems of mutual interest.

The Pan-Islamic Conference opened its meeting in Damascus with delegates from all Islamic countries from Indonesia to Morocco. The issues of Palestine and Algeria were discussed.

USSR Foreign Minister Shepilov arrived in Damascus on the invitation of the Syrian Government.

The Bey of Tunis reduced his civil list, which supported members of his family and retainers under the French Protectorate, by a decree reducing his royal allowance from 420 million francs to 181 million francs.

The Soviet Foreign Minister, on a visit to Damascus, received a popular demonstration on his arrival from Cairo.

June 23

Advertisements appeared in Los Angles (US) newspapers seeking to recruit aviation technicians for the Algerian Liberation Army with salaries up to $1, 500 monthly.

Egyptian voters went to the polls for the first time in seven years, nationally, to elect a new president and to approve or reject the new constitution. Premier Nasser was the only candidate for president.

June, 1956

June 23

Lebanon announced receipt of a grant in aid of $3, 670, 000 from the US on the eve of USSR Foreign Minister Shepilov's visit. Of the amount, $3 million was earmarked for construction of a highway from Beirut to Damascus, Syria, and $470, 000 for the expansion and modernization of Beirut's International Airport.

A communique from Moscow said that the USSR agreed to give Yemen economic assistance and favorable trade conditions. Both countries agreed to friendly cooperation and an exchange of diplomatic representatives.

Syrian Premier Assali conferred with Soviet Foreign Minister Shepilov, but was unable to get public backing from him for Arab attitudes against Israel.

June 24

Premier Bourguiba paraded his Tunisian Army before French and allied officials and proclaimed Tunisia's solidarity with Algerian rebels.

Moroccan Acting Secretary General of the Istiqlal Party Ben-Barka returned from a trip to Tangier with al-Fassi, leader of the Party, and outlined Moroccan claims to Mauritania in French West Africa and the Colomb-Bechar-Tindouf regions of the Sahara. The two leaders also claimed the coastal enclave of the Spanish Sahara, and they disputed Algerian claims to Colomb, Bechar and Tindouf.

Premier Nasser won the presidential election with over 99 percent of the votes of Egypt's more than five million voters. Nearly all registered voters indicated approval of the new constitution along with their preference for him as president.

Yemen and the Soviet Union agreed to exchange diplomatic representatives at the conclusion of the visit to Moscow by Crown Prince Badr.

June 25

Yemeni Crown Prince al-Badr and his party left for East Germany after a two week visit to the USSR.

June, 1956

June 25

The Egyptian Cabinet resigned in accordance with the results of the election. Final tabulation of the ballot showed that 5, 508, 291 persons out of Egypt's total population of 23 million voted, including 150, 000 women.

USSR Foreign Minister D. T. Shepilov arrived on an official visit to Beirut after a three day visit in Damascus where he held talks with Syrian leaders.

A police officer and nine soldiers were sentenced to two years imprisonment by the Sudanese Supreme Court at Kosti for their part in the Kosti incident. Three others were acquitted.

It was announced that provisory credits totalling over 21 billion francs had been established by Morocco for government expenses for June and July.

June 26

A joint USSR-Syrian communique was issued on the talks that Shepilov held while in Damascus. It stressed that the development of relations between the USSR and Syria would make for closer friendship and would be an effective contribution to international peace and security.

The Saudi Arabian Government issued a decree against strikes, with severe penalties including banishment for violators. The decree barred work stoppage under agreement by three or more persons, demonstrations and lockouts and the use of violence or coercion to cause work stoppages.

Lebanese leaders attempted unsuccessfully to have visiting Soviet Foreign Minister Shepilov declare himself definitely in favor of the Arab countries in the Palestine question.

A new Sudanese political party, the Democratic People's Party, was formed. Its membership consisted of 21 deputies and 14 senators, formerly members of Premier Azhari's National Unionist Party. Its program called for continued independence, a constitution assembly to be

June, 1956

June 26

formed to draft a permanent constitution, a rise in the standard of living and—in foreign policy—peace, neutralism and support for the resolutions of the Bandung Conference.

Tunisian Premier Bourguiba declared that he would not sign an alliance with France while the Algerian war continued.

France increased by one-third the ceiling on the number of US Air Force troops permitted in Morocco. The increase was authorized as France relinquished its protectorate over Morocco, and after three years of French refusal to accept US demands for more men in the US air bases there.

The UN Security Council refused to debate the Algerian issue by a vote of 7-2-2.

Libya concluded an agreement with Great Britain covering financial, military and educational matters.

Jordan's King Hussein dismissed Parliament at the request of Premier Mufti.

June 27

Syria warned Turkey that the increase in border clashes between the two countries would be detrimental to good neighborly relations. It formally demanded the release of 38 Syrians held as hostages after a clash on June 23.

Egypt and Lebanon signed a trade agreement calling for a free exchange of goods, at the rate of eight and one-half Lebanese pounds per Egyptian pound.

The first step toward carrying out major economic reforms in Algeria was taken. The French Cabinet authorized the expropriation of large agricultural lands for distribution to landless Moslems.

June, 1956

June 30

Jordan's King Hussein accepted the resignation of Premier Mufti and his cabinet to allow for the organization of a caretaker government to hold elections for a new parliament.

Yemen and East Germany signed a trade and payments agreement.

At a Socialist Party rally, French Premier Mollet said that President Nasser was suffering from delusions of grandeur and megalomania.

June, 1956

June 28

Israel's tougher line was displayed in meetings of the Israel-Jordanian Mixed Armistice Commission. Israel delegates refused to accept the normal MAC practice of determining whether action of either country was a breach of the armistice. Instead, they insisted that the commission should make a clear distinction between aggressors and defenders.

At the conclusion of a trial that began June 9, Egypt sentenced 40 members of the Egyptian Communist Party to prison terms from two to seven years; 29 others were acquitted. The names of those sentenced were not given.

June 29

A bill to be passed by the Lebanese Parliament at the special request of Lebanese President Chamoun would abolish retroactively the tax exemption granted in Lebanon to certain foreign business interests. It was aimed primarily at the Iraq Petroleum Company but would affect other foreign investments, such as the American owned Tapline, the concessionary company operating the port of Beirut, the tobacco monopoly and the Damascus Railroad. Unless returned by the President to Parliament for reconsideration, the bill would become law at the end of July.

Discussions began in Lebanon on technical work for a US financed highway from Beirut to the Syrian border. The highway would be a 40 mile, four lane road, but only the 18 mile stretch from Beirut to Sofar figured in the discussion.

June 30

The UN Relief and Works Agency reported the number of Palestine refugees at 922,279.

President Nasser replaced three of his former Revolution Command Council colleagues and increased his cabinet to 18 members by adding two new ministries to control industry and agrarian reform.

July, 1956

July 1

The Syrian Government recognized and agreed to exchange diplomatic representatives with Communist China.

A caretaker government in Jordan was formed by Senate President Hashem.

Former Jordanian Premier Abu-al-Huda hanged himself at his home in Amman. He had been premier several times, the last in May, 1955.

A trade and payments agreement was signed between Egypt and West Germany.

The French Socialist Party issued a resolution supporting Premier Mollet's moderate Algerian policy.

Nasser obtained credits and technicians from the USSR for the Aswan Dam.

In a report submitted to the 48th annual stockholders meeting in Paris, the Suez Canal Company said that canal traffic in 1956 was the greatest in the history of the waterway.

July 2

Commander Terrill was relieved of his post as Chairman of the Israel-Jordanian Mixed Armistice Commission after Israel criticized his support of a Jordanian resolution censuring Israel for its part in a border clash on June 24. Commander Terrill was succeeded by French Colonel Costaguay.

The Lebanese Government seized all the Iraq Petroleum Company's installations on Lebanese territory.

British Foreign Secretary Lloyd said in Parliament that Israel still held the balance of power over the Arabs in armaments.

French officials, after meeting with Moroccan leaders, agreed to suspend further movements of French troops. This resolution followed a

July 2

protest from Sultan Muhammad V against French troops reinforcing Agadir, in southern Morocco, after the kidnapping of a French officer.

Five thousand men of the Moroccan Army of Liberation joined the Sultan's Royal Moroccan Army.

July 3

Israel reported increasing difficulty in buying arms from Western countries. France and Canada halted shipments of jet planes to Israel because of the US delay in authorizing comparable weapons for Israel.

Syrian Premier Assali announced his country's recognition of Red China.

Lebanese Premier Yafi said in Cairo that the USSR had offered Lebanon arms and economic aid.

Libyan Premier Ben-Halim stated that Britain had undertaken to train and equip an Arab legion in Libya.

July 4

President Nasser's new civilian cabinet announced a record breaking budget.

Israel's Prime Minister Ben-Gurion categorically denied British Foreign Secretary Lloyd's assertion that the Middle East arms balance favored Israel despite the arms delivered to Egypt by the Communist Bloc. He declared that the Egyptian Air Force was the strongest in the area.

Lebanon pledged the Arab states the support of its constabulary units in the event of an Arab-Israel War.

Algerians went on strike both in France and in Algiers on the 126th anniversary of the French conquest of Algeria.

July 4

Jordan charged that Israel was massing troops near the armistice line. Israel refuted this charge.

The Syrian Chamber of Deputies voted to abolish passports between Syria and the Arab countries on condition of reciprocity.

The Tunisian Government rejected French protests about Arabic language broadcasts on Tunis Radio attacking French policy in Algeria. Tunisia protested the French halting and searching of Libya's Ambassador to Tunis.

The Moroccan Government announced that troops led by Prince Hassan would proceed to the Agadir Tissint region of Southern Morocco to take over outposts occupied by French forces.

French troops were parachuted into Foum-al-Hassane near Agadir, contradicting the Moroccan announcement of July 2 that troop movements would be suspended.

Premier Nuri-Said of Iraq arrived in Morocco for an official visit.

Sudanese Premier Azhari, in office since January 1954, resigned following a 60-31 vote of no confidence in the House of Representatives.

July 5

Arab troops massed at Israel's border in response to an unconfirmed report that Israel was preparing to attack. Major General Burns of UNTSO reported that there was no evidence of Israel mobilization.

In Prague, the Yemeni Crown Prince signed two friendship and trade agreements with Premier Sikory of Czechoslovakia.

UN Secretary General Hammarskjold said that he was more optimistic than at any previous time about the chances for an ultimate settlement in the Middle East.

The Sudanese House of Representatives elected Abdallah Khalil, Secretary General of the Umma Party, Premier of Sudan. His sole opponent was former Premier Ismail al-Azhari.

July 5

Syria's Parliament unanimously approved plans for a committee to negotiate with Egypt for a federal union of the two countries.

July 6

Iran, Iraq and Pakistan signed the agreement made in Karachi on June 16, providing for the establishment of a joint shipping company with 15 million pounds sterling capital to handle regional traffic.

Israel Ambassador Abba Eban called on the UN to follow up his Government's complaint that Egypt had held up the Greek vessel, Panagia, in the Suez Canal and confiscated its cargo of cement destined for Israel.

The US State Department said that the US was still waiting to help Egypt build the Aswan Dam, although the funds earmarked for the project had been allocated for other purposes. The Department was reported to be taking a second look at its offer, made in December, because of Egyptian Government policies.

July 7

Jordanian Army Chief of Staff Ali-Abu-Nuwar warned Britain in a note to the British Ambassador in Amman that it must aid Jordan's defense in case of an Israel attack, or face abrogation of the mutual defense treaty between the two countries. He also pledged UN Truce Chief Burns that he would withdraw his troops from the Jerusalem sector if he received first hand assurances from UNTSO that there was no excess of Israel troops on the other side of the line.

A new Sudanese coalition cabinet was formed by Premier Khalil.

The Soviet Union came out unequivocally in support of Algerian independence and condemned French Premier Mollet's policy in editorials in Pravda.

The Syrian Chamber of Deputies approved a draft law considering Palestinians living in Syria as Syrian in regard to appointment, work

July 7

and military services. However, they would keep their original Palestinian citizenship.

Minister of State Salam said that Lebanon had accepted a US offer of mediation in a royalties dispute with the Iraq Petroleum Company.

The Fezzan Legislative Council of Libya was dissolved by Royal Decree for noncooperation with the administration.

July 8

Sultan Muhammad V named the first Governor of Morocco's new Province of Tangier. It was the first step implementing the provisional agreement reached the previous week between the Tangier International Zone Control Committee and the Moroccan Government.

An Egyptian trade mission headed by Minister of Commerce Nusair arrived in London for talks on British-Egyptian commerce.

It was reported in Cairo that Egyptian exports to the Soviet Bloc increased to 27 percent of all exports, totalling $383 million in 1955, compared with 14 percent the previous year. Egypt's imports from the Soviet Bloc rose from $26,320,000 to $35 million.

July 9

The head of UNTSO sought to arrange a special inspection of the Israel-Jordan frontier within a few days as a means of allaying fears on each side of a military buildup by the other.

Three persons were killed and 15 injured in demonstrations in the Tawahi, Aden, area over the detention of three men.

The French Government approved US shipments of wheat to Tunisia.

July, 1956

July 10

A group of Moslem pilgrims left Moscow by plane for the Hejaz on a pilgrimage. Among the Soviet pilgrims were the Imam of the Grand Mosque of Moscow and other Moslems from the Asian Republics of the USSR.

The Israel Ambassador to the US complained to Secretary of State Dulles that Egypt was increasing its blockage of Israel shipping in the Suez Canal.

Israel's Foreign Minister Myerson called UN Truce Chief Burns to a conference to complain about continued Jordanian violations of the ceasefire agreement.

UN Secretary General Hammarskjold announced a change in plans to include a trip to Israel and Egypt July 19-22, as a follow-up to his previous truce mission.

July 11

Five persons—two Syrians and three Turks—were killed in an outbreak of violence along the Syrian-Turkish frontier.

Egypt's President Nasser arrived in Yugoslavia for a visit with Marshal Tito and India's Prime Minister Nehru.

The Commander of the Syrian Police and seven members of the dissolved Nationalist Party were arrested for distributing propaganda leaflets.

Major General Burns said that in his opinion Israel Premier Ben-Gurion had threatened armed retaliation against Jordan. He made this statement when informed that Israel Ambassador Eban had denied the Ben-Gurion statement.

Jordan lodged six complaints with the Mixed Armistice Commission over Israel planes flying over its territory.

July, 1956

July 12

The World Jewish Congress protested Arab efforts to boycott Jewish concerns in Europe and the US.

A USSR-Egyptian agreement on cooperation in the peaceful uses of atomic energy was signed in Cairo.

Yemen accused Britain of sending a force of 200 armed troops and vehicles to the border at Noman near Beihan.

July 13

Morocco applied for membership in the UN.

President Nasser held his first official talk with President Tito of Yugoslavia and decided on a list of questions to be submitted to Indian Prime Minister Nehru as an agenda for their discussions.

Tunisian representatives broke off talks on French-Tunisian cooperation because of the unfriendly attitude of the French Council of the Republic and the unyielding speech of French Foreign Minister Pineau before the National Assembly on July 12. The Council of the Republic, advisory Upper House of the French Assembly, voted 164-132 to cancel 16 million francs in economic aid to Tunisia for 1956, on the grounds that France was getting meager cooperation from Tunisia since the latter became independent March 20.

July 14

Premier Bourguiba threatened to renew fighting with the French unless French troops were withdrawn from Tunisia. The statement followed one by French Foreign Minister Pineau that French forces intended to remain in Tunisia and Morocco to seal off help for Algerian rebels.

French and Moroccan spokesmen expressed confidence that they had reached a basis of day to day cooperation between their armed forces. Their agreement was called a gentlemen's agreement rather than a formal military accord.

July, 1956

July 14

Britain protested to Yemen an attack by tribesmen on villages in the Western Protectorate.

A trade and payments agreement was concluded between Egypt and Lebanon which would go into effect 15 days after the exchange of instruments of ratification. Most favored nation treatment was included.

An announcement from the office of the French Resident Minister said that civil servants who had participated in a July 5 general strike ordered by the National Liberation Front would be treated leniently. The announcement also said that certain categories of persons detained in internment camps would be freed.

The Presidents of Egypt and Yugoslavia concluded private talks in preparation for the three power meeting with Indian Prime Minister Nehru.

July 15

It was reported from Beirut that the Arab countries were divided over Syria's proposed union with Egypt. Many Arab diplomats were said to discount the proposal as propaganda and impossible of fulfillment. Premier Yafi of Lebanon said that he welcomed the idea and hoped for other steps toward Arab unity. Saudi Arabia was reportedly opposed.

President Nasser was greeted with a parade by Yugoslavian Moslems in Sarajevo, Yugoslavia.

The Jordanian-Israel MAC censured Jordan for an incident in which two Israelis were killed. It declared that the incident appeared to be of a pattern of attacks from Jordanian controlled territory against Israel and it issued a strong call to the Jordanians to heed continuous exhortation of the Commission to terminate such repeated incursions into Israel. The Jordanian delegate, apparently feeling that the Commission was going further than usual in its condemnation, walked out of the meeting.

July, 1956

July 15

Two Egyptian colonels, who were victims of recent bomb plots, were named by Israel's intelligence chief on October 7, 1955 as organizers of guerrilla raids into Israel. One colonel, Mustafa Hafez, was killed in Gaza on July 11 by a letter bomb.

The Mayor of Oran said that Eastern Morocco belonged to Algeria and should be annexed.

President Eisenhower asked for Senate confirmation of four new ambassadorial appointments to strengthen the US position in the Middle East, especially in Cairo and Athens.

July 16

Cairo press reported that the Egyptian Government declined the US proposal to participate in the Atoms for Peace program on the grounds that this proposal involved definite conditions.

Egypt and Rumania signed a three year trade agreement in Cairo. The exchange of goods during the first year was to be limited to LE4.5 million ($12,915,000).

The formal report issued by the US Senate Appropriations Committee ordered the administration to spend no mutual security money on the Aswan Dam in Egypt.

The abolition of passports between Syria and Jordan was put into effect.

Iraq's King Faisal arrived in London for a three day state visit.

Jordan lodged two complaints with the MAC.

It was reported in Damascus that Syrian authorities closed the Syrian borders.

July 17

It was reported in Washington that Egyptian Ambassador Hussein returned from Cairo with orders from President Nasser to reach a final

July 17

agreement as soon as possible with the US and Great Britain on aid in building the Aswan High Dam on the basis of the US-British offers of December 16.

Prime Minister Nehru of India arrived in Paris. He participated in talks with French leaders which resulted in significant but undisclosed terms on the French side for a truce in Algeria.

The Tunisian delegation to Paris returned to Tunisia.

The Soviet Union signed an agreement to increase its deliveries of oil to Israel, despite Russian friendship with Arab countries.

A military tribunal in Beirut, Lebanon, sentenced 16 persons to prison terms of up to eight years for spying for Israel. Seven others were acquitted.

Jordan returned to meetings of the Mixed Armistice Commission, ending a two day walkout.

Israel protested to the UN Security Council that Jordan had stepped up border attacks aimed at Israel's main arteries of communication.

July 18

Tunisia applied for membership in the United Nations.

French troops in the Tunisian frontier town of Moulares discovered a group of armed Algerian rebels in uniform and killed two. Tunisian Vice Premier Ladgham protested to French Ambassador Seydoux against a violation of Tunisian sovereignty.

President Nasser of Egypt, Prime Minister Nehru of India and Yugoslavian President Tito met at Brioni Island, in the Adriatic Sea, for talks on the world situation and the role of their countries as mediators in the cold war. Joining the Yugoslavian and Egyptian leaders, Nehru made it clear that he did not attach extraordinary importance to the conference.

July 19

The US withdrew its offer of a grant to help Egypt build the Aswan Dam. The withdrawal was explained in a statement saying that Egypt had failed to reach agreement with the Sudan and other riparians on a division of Nile waters, and that Egypt's ability to devote adequate resources to the project had become more uncertain than at the time the offer was made.

UN Secretary General Hammarskjold conferred in secret with Israel Prime Minister Ben-Gurion for five hours.

July 20

India, Yugoslavia and Egypt appealed in a joint communique for a ceasefire in Algeria and a settlement that would protect the interests of the million French inhabitants.

Britain cancelled its offer of $14 million as an initial step in the building of the Aswan Dam, in line with the previous American withdrawal of aid offers.

Egyptian officials were angered and surprised by the US and British withdrawal of their offers of economic assistance for the development of the Aswan Dam.

It was reported in London that Arab sources hostile to Egypt were delighted with the withdrawals of US and UK aid for development of the Aswan Dam. They interpreted them as a final abandonment of the belief in President Nasser as a positive force for stability and progress in the Middle East.

Secretary General Hammarskjold ended talks with Israel Prime Minister Ben-Gurion. A joint communique issued indicated that the talks had

July 20

been fruitful toward keeping peace in the Middle East. Hammarskjold announced that he would fly to Amman, Jordan.

The Security Council unanimously approved Morocco's application for membership in the UN.

July 21

The semiofficial Egyptian Government newspaper, al-Gumhuriyah, declared that the reasons given by the US and Britain for withdrawing their aid offers were invalid. It warned that America should be well advised to draw a good lesson from its refusal to arm Egypt's forces. This refusal had not hindered Egypt from obtaining arms elsewhere. Likewise, Egypt would set up its great project, "to the consternation of America and the grief of Britain."

Soviet Foreign Minister Shepilov said in Moscow that the USSR was not considering aid to Egypt in the construction of the Aswan Dam, but that it would be ready to consider sympathetically Egypt's request for aid in developing its industries. Referring to the Dam, Shepilov said that this problem was not put here in such an acute form as the US thought it was. He had the impression after his visit that there were now more vitally important problems for the Egyptian economy, particularly problems in industrialization, although he did not minimize the importance of the Aswan Dam, Shepilov said.

After meeting with Jordanian leaders, UN Secretary General Hammarskjold arrived in Cairo and met with Egyptian leaders, including President Nasser.

UN Secretary General Hammarskjold held talks in Amman with Jordanian leaders. The Egyptian Military Attache in Amman, Jordan, died of injuries suffered in a bomb explosion at his Embassy.

India's Prime Minister Nehru arrived in Lebanon for a day visit.

July 22

The statement of the Soviet Foreign Minister that the Soviet Union was not considering any offers of help in the construction of the Aswan Dam was taken as evidence that Egypt was using inflated reports on Soviet aid offers as a bluff to obtain Western assistance, and also that the USSR was a party to the Egyptian game. Shepilov's statement was the first that any Soviet spokesman had made denying or even qualifying reports by the Egyptians that they had received highly attractive offers of help from the Soviet Union for the project.

July 23

In reply to US criticism of the economic soundness of the Aswan project, the Egyptian Finance Ministry reported that only ten days before the US and Britain withdrew their offers of aid it had received assurances from the IBRD that the project was economically sound.

The Syrian-Turkish border was reopened and the ban on travel was lifted. It was reported in Damascus that Turkey promised to release the Syrians taken in the border clash of June 23.

The IBRD said that its offer to Egypt of $200 million in a loan for the construction of the Aswan Dam had automatically expired with the withdrawal of the US and British funds.

UN Secretary General Hammarskjold said in Cairo that the Arab-Israel ceasefire was "in good working order." He left Cairo for Switzerland.

Israel Premier Ben-Gurion demanded an accounting from UN Secretary General Hammarskjold on the attitude of Jordan toward implementing the ceasefire agreement.

July 24

United States Ambassador to Greece, Cavendish Cannon, was confirmed as Ambassador to Morocco.

US President Eisenhower sent the following appointments to the Senate for confirmation: Ambassador to Egypt, Byroade, as Ambassador to the

July 24

Union of South Africa; Assistant Secretary of State Allen (Near Eastern, South Asian and African Affairs) to replace Cannon as Ambassador to Greece; Deputy Assistant Secretary of State Rountree, to replace Allen as Assistant Secretary.

French Minister of Finance Ramadier told the Finance Committee of the National Assembly that he would accept a bond issue as a means of financing military expenditures in Algeria; however, it would have to be accompanied by provisions guaranteeing adequate return to the Government, including the right to levy a ten percent increase.

Two UN military observers and a Jordanian officer, investigating a clash between Israel and Jordan, were wounded severely on Mount Scopus when a mine accidentally went off. General Burns warned against any attempt by either party to seize Mount Scopus.

President Nasser accused the US of lying about Egypt's economy when it withdrew its offer to help build the Aswan Dam. Soviet Ambassador to Egypt Kislev stated, after Nasser's speech, that the USSR stood ready to finance the Aswan Dam if Egypt asked for help. He said that he was merely repeating the statement made previously by Soviet Foreign Minister Shepilov in Moscow, which had been exaggerated by Western newsmen. Later in the day the Soviet Embassy's press attache in Cairo denied that Ambassador Kislev made his statement.

Egypt reached an agreement with the Japanese shipbuilding company, Harima, for construction of a 300 ton dredge to deepen the port of Alexandria.

In the national elections in Egypt, 98 percent of the votes were cast for Premier Nasser. The proposed new constitution received 96 percent of the votes.

Thirty-five Syrians released by Turkish authorities complained of ill treatment.

July 25

Jordanian villagers attacked a UN observer team near Jerusalem and seriously wounded Swedish Colonel Thalin. The attack came after an Israel-Jordanian exchange of fire which reportedly wounded ten Jordanians.

Former Colonel Roussan of the Arab Legion, who was sentenced to jail in May for having plotted to seize power in Jordan, was appointed Jordanian Minister and Charge d'Affaires in Washington. His sentence was commuted by Royal Decree, but his army service was ended.

French Premier Mollet agreed to a public loan to finance the Algerian campaign. He and his cabinet advisors worked out a compromise proposal to raise the necessary 300 billion francs by first launching a 150 billion franc public loan. The Government would have the right, if the loan were not fully subscribed by mid-autumn, to impose new taxes to make up the difference.

Israel demanded an emergency meeting of the Jordanian-Israel Mixed Armistice Commission to hear charges that Jordanian forces killed two Israelis and wounded a third in a four hour border clash.

The Security Council met to decide whether to place the Algerian question on its agenda.

The US Senate Foreign Relations Committee adopted a resolution requesting the Government to include antidiscrimination principles in all negotiations with foreign governments. The move was aimed at Saudi Arabia's discrimination against American Jews.

July 26

Foreign Minister Mahgoub of Sudan told newsmen that Sudan would reject foreign offers to finance its development if they carried any conditions restricting the country's independence and sovereignty.

President Nasser's Government nationalized the Suez Canal and announced that all profits from the Canal would be used to build the Aswan Dam. Nasser said in a speech that a decision of the Cabinet and Council of Ministers had dissolved all bodies controlling the Canal. He also said that all stockholders would be reimbursed at

July 26

the prevailing Cairo stock market price and Paris Bourse. Navigation through the Canal was placed under the jurisdiction of a special board attached to the Ministry of Commerce.

UN Secretary General Hammarskjold sent a new appeal to Israel and the Arab countries to enforce the ceasefire agreement.

Israel notified the Security Council that it would stop presenting resolutions of censure to the Mixed Armistice Commission concerning Arab attacks. It said that the resolutions had had little effect on securing implementation of even adverse verdicts of the Commission against Jordan.

President Eisenhower named G. Lewis Jones, a career diplomat, as the first US Ambassador to Tunisia.

The USSR denied that its policy toward the Arab states had changed and declared that Soviet-Arab friendship was based on a community of interest. It accused the US of showing antipathy towards the Arabs.

It was reported in Washington that Saudi Arabia demanded a $50 million yearly rental for the American air base at Dhahran. The US informed Saudi Arabia it would not pay rent for its Dhahran air base inasmuch as the base was maintained for the mutual benefit of the host country and the US.

The Security Council unanimously approved Tunisia's application for UN membership.

July 27

The Egyptian Government proclaimed martial law on the operations of the nationalized Suez Canal. Egyptian troops and policemen stood guard throughout the Canal Zone.

After an emergency meeting, the French Cabinet indicated that France would favor military occupation of the Suez Canal Zone if Britain joined it. The French Government sent a strong protest to Egypt

July 27

against the nationalization of the Canal and denounced President Nasser as a dictator who had broken his word.

The US Department of State issued a statement apprehensive of the nationalization of the Canal.

Britain protested sharply to Egypt against nationalization of the Canal, calling the action a serious threat to navigation. Prime Minister Eden told the House of Commons that the British Government had in mind a number of retaliatory measures. He later summoned the military service chiefs to an emergency Cabinet meeting.

The American and French diplomatic representatives in London met in an emergency session with British Foreign Secretary Selwyn Lloyd.

July 28

President Nasser warned the Western powers that any interference with his seizure of the Canal would obstruct navigation. He declared that Egypt would meet force with force and would fight to the last drop of blood to protect its independence, freedom and rights.

The British Treasury blocked all Egyptian accounts in the UK.

The spokesmen of the different Syrian parties stated their support of Egypt in the nationalization of the Suez Canal Company.

President Nasser was hailed in Egypt and the Arab world by anti-Western groups.

Reports from Russia indicated that USSR Foreign Minister Shepilov's offer of aid to Egypt was misleading; the USSR had no intention of financing the Aswan Dam.

July 28

A mine killed a UN truce observer near the Gaza Strip.

The French National Assembly voted 273-163 to approve Premier Mollet's plan to finance the Algerian campaign. The plan would authorize the Government to raise 150 billion francs in order to finance half the cost of maintaining 400, 000 troops in Algeria for the present year.

British Foreign Secretary Lloyd, French Foreign Minister Pineau and US Under Secretary of State Murphy met in London to discuss the Suez Canal crisis and to work out measures to be taken.

US Under Secretary of State, Herbert Hoover, Jr., called in the Egyptian Ambassador and protested vigorously the tone and contents of President Nasser's statement with respect to the US in his speech in Alexandria on July 26.

A law was adopted in Lebanon imposing taxes, retroactively to January 1, 1952, on certain foreign concerns in that country. It was primarily aimed at the oil companies whose pipelines ran through Lebanon.

A commercial agreement was signed between Syria and Hungary which would go into effect 15 days after ratification. Most favored nation treatment was mutually accorded and the agreement was valid for one year.

July 29

Britain agreed to loan 12 British technicians to the Jordanian Army.

Egypt banned all exports to Britain and its colonies unless payment was made through a third state with acceptable currency. Four ships preparing to sail to Britain with goods from Alexandria were ordered unloaded. All shipments of goods to be paid for in sterling were suspended.

July 29

After a five hour meeting of the Big Three diplomats in London, a statement was issued declaring that the Canal must be preserved as an international waterway open to the ships of all nations.

Secretary of State Dulles declared in Washington that nationalization of the Suez Canal by Egypt was a grevious blow to international confidence.

France blocked all Egyptian assets in retaliation for the seizure of the Suez Canal.

Britain and France urged the US to join them in devising a policy to put the Suez Canal under international jurisdiction. Under their plan, Egypt would be guaranteed a special position in the administration of the canal and a substantial share in operating revenues. The principle of free passage to all ships in peace or war would be reaffirmed under a consortium better adapted to modern conditions than the 1888 Convention.

Varying reactions from other countries were reported on Egypt's seizure of the Suez Canal. Spain expressed approval. Turkey accused Egypt of a unilateral act of violence. Israel condemned the action. Jordan defended Egypt's right to nationalize. The Sudan did not officially comment, although a statement by Premier Khalil expressed wishes for Egypt's success.

The Soviet Union announced its support of Egypt's nationalization of the Suez Canal. It stressed that it regarded President Nasser's action as not only correct but legal.

July 30

The Egyptian Government announced that during the past week tolls could continue to be payed to the Suez Canal Company in London, Paris or Cairo. Beginning the next week, however, vessels using the canal would have to make payments directly to Egypt.

Egypt rescinded the order halting all exports payable in sterling in an attempt to avoid economic warfare in which Egyptian losses could

be heavy. It was reported that Britain had assured Egypt that the freezing of Egyptian assets did not apply to goods imported from Egypt. The four ships held in Alexandria were permitted to reload. At the same time, Egypt imposed strict monetary controls on foreign bank accounts.

Dr. Bahgat Badawi, new Egyptian head of the Suez Canal Company, said that he would assume his duties within a few weeks.

British Prime Minister Sir Anthony Eden announced in the House of Commons a ban on exports of war materials to Egypt. He declared that Britain would never accept any arrangement which would leave the Suez Canal under unfettered control of any single power. He rejected President Nasser's plan to use canal tolls for the projected Aswan High Dam, and warned Egypt against keeping British Suez Canal Company employees on their jobs under duress.

The Israel-Jordanian Mixed Armistice Commission found Jordan guilty of aggression in the incident in which Jordanian infiltrators threw a hand grenade into an Israel children's home July 23.

The US Government position on Egypt was outlined in Washington as follows: President Nasser had the sovereign right to nationalize the Suez Canal Company which handled the technical operation of moving ships through the canal, but the canal itself was a free waterway by international treaty and Egypt had no right to block the flow of traffic through it.

The Jordan Defense Ministry said that the Arab states would ask the UN to replace Burns as head of the UN Truce Supervisory Mission in Palestine. It accused the General of bias in favor of Israel.

The Jordanian Cabinet released and deported the head of the Jordan Communist Party.

A Syrian was killed and three injured in two Turkish mine explosions on the Turkish-Syrian border.

The Upper House of the French Parliament approved a bill passed by the National Assembly on July 28 to raise money for the Algerian campaign.

July 31

US Secretary of State Dulles flew to London to talk with British and French officials who sought US assistance for their plan for international supervision of the Suez.

President Nasser said that nationalization of the Suez would in no way affect Egypt's international obligations, that Egypt would honor the 1888 Convention and the Anglo-Egyptian agreement of 1954 regarding freedom of navigation through the canal. His political aide said that checks for canal fees must be made payable to the order of the Suez Canal Authority, but that banks in London and Paris had refused to accept checks made out in this manner. He denied reports that foreign employees of the company were being forced to work under threat of imprisonment.

Immediately after US Secretary of State Dulles' departure for London, the US Treasury Department froze temporarily all the assets in that country of the Egyptian Government and the Suez Canal Company.

The British Admiralty announced that certain naval moves had been ordered to meet the possibility of serious trouble in the Eastern Mediterranean. Warships in Britain's three chief home ports received orders to prepare for an immediate state of readiness.

Khrushchev appealed to the Western powers to be moderate in their reaction to the nationalization of the Suez Canal. While endorsing Egypt's action, Khrushchev stressed Russia's interest in keeping the canal free to international shipping.

Italy reproved Egypt for nationalization of the Suez Canal, but made it clear that it had no intention of taking action in the matter.

The Suez Canal Company notified all shipping companies throughout the world that it was no longer responsible for the safe operation of ships in the canal.

Syrian officials denied reports that Syria would nationalize oil properties.

August 1

The Spanish Zone of Morocco was officially transferred to the Moroccan authorities.

It was reported from Paris that the French were disappointed with the decision to call an international conference, since it entailed no immediate action by the Western powers. The French public was prepared by its Government for some severe moves in relation to Suez.

Canadian Minister of External Affairs, Pearson, said in the House of Commons that Canada favored international control of the Suez Canal, preferably under the aegis of the UN.

Radio Moscow said that Egypt had never sought Soviet aid to build the Aswan High Dam, but that any request for such aid no doubt would be considered sympathetically.

Sheikh Khalifah of Bahrain rejected demands for the dismissal of his British adviser, Sir Charles Belgrave. He said that Belgrave was a loyal servant and obeyed orders.

An underground radio station broadcasting in Arabic called upon Egypt to overthrow President Nasser before he brought the country to destruction.

Egyptian Minister of Commerce Nusair called the first meeting of the Egyptian Suez Canal Authority.

President Nasser declared that he had the backing of all Arabs in the nationalization of the canal.

Sudanese demonstrated in Khartoum in support of Egypt's nationalization of the Suez Canal.

Opposition members of the West Pakistan Assembly in Lahore walked out after defeat on a motion of approval for the nationalization by Egypt of the Suez Canal.

An Arab youth congress meeting in Cairo, under the sponsorship of President Nasser, called for the nationalization of all oil resources and foreign companies in the Arab world. It also recommended that all Arab governments extend material aid to Algerian nationalists.

August 1

The Jordanian-Israel Mixed Armistice Commission censured both countries for shooting across the border on July 25.

Premier Nehru of India said in Bombay that Egypt's nationalization of the canal was a sign of the weakening of European domination of Asia and the Middle East.

Egypt said that it would await formal notice before commenting on the London conference plan.

It was reported in Washington that Egypt urged the US to use its influence to prevent nervous actions in the Suez crisis from building up into war.

It was stated in Washington that US President Eisenhower instructed Secretary of State Dulles to oppose the use of force, even as a last resort, as long as Egypt continued to keep the canal open and ships moving normally.

The US, British and French Foreign Ministers decided to call a conference of the principal nations using the Suez Canal to establish some form of permanent international control over the waterway. Both Egypt and the USSR were to be invited.

US President Eisenhower made a statement stressing the gravity of the Suez Canal situation.

Prince Faisal of Saudi Arabia stated that the resolutions adopted at the Brioni Conference agreed with the interests of all the people of the world, and that the decision of the British and US Governments to withdraw from assisting the financing of Egypt's Aswan High Dam project was not in the interest of these two Western countries.

The Syrian State Bank was inaugurated and the Currency and Credit Administration transferred to the Syrian Government.

Syrian and Jordanian officials began conferences on an economic and customs union announced as a project in June.

August 2

UK and French nationals left Egypt.

The British Foreign Office warned British subjects in Egypt to leave unless their duties required them to remain.

The US international Cooperation Administration Chief stated in Washington that the US planned to continue economic aid to Egypt, barring orders to the contrary from Secretary of State Dulles.

The US, the UK and France invited 24 nations to a conference in London on August 16 to set up an international control over the Suez Canal consistent with legitimate Egyptian interests.

Soviet newspapers and magazines, banned until this date, were placed on sale at newsstands throughout Egypt.

Jordan's Arab Legion Chief of Staff Ali Abu-Nuwar arrived in Beirut for a "vacation."

Syrian President Kuwatli presented his resignation to the Cabinet because he refused to sign the death warrants of three Syrian National Socialists implicated in the 1955 assassination of Chief of Staff Malki.

Canadian Secretary of State for External Affairs Pearson said that the decision to send a shipment of 24 F-86 jet planes to Israel would be postponed until he could determine the relationship of Egypt's seizure of the Suez Canal to the situation in Palestine.

The French National Assembly adopted a resolution 422-150 condemning Egypt's President Nasser and urging Premier Mollet to take the most energetic measures to counter the seizure of the Suez Canal.

Gaitskell, leader of the UK Labor opposition, supported UK Prime Minister Eden in a policy of firmness toward Egypt in the Suez crisis.

Newspapers in Communist China continued to approve of nationalization of the Suez Canal.

UN Secretary General Hammarskjold said a will to peace still existed in the Middle East despite recent Israel-Egyptian border incidents.

August 2

British Prime Minister Eden announced in the House of Commons that Queen Elizabeth would empower the Government to call up all Britain's organized reserve forces, more than 500,000 men. At the same time, the Royal Navy and Air Force ordered sea and air units to the Middle East.

The Mixed Armistice Commission condemned Israel for the flight of a military plane over Jordanian territory on July 25. The Israel delegates voted against the resolution on grounds that there was no proof that the plane was a military one.

August 3

On returning from London, US Secretary of State Dulles, in a radio address, expressed confidence that the forthcoming international conference would be able to draw up a workable plan for administration of the Suez Canal.

The British Government obtained emergency powers to requisition merchant shipping and call up military reserves for its last-resort plan to restore international control of the Suez Canal.

French Premier Mollet and Foreign Minister Pineau told the National Assembly that the French Government was ready to take military action, if necessary, to restore international control of the Suez Canal.

The Soviet newspaper Pravda condemned the UK for reassigning naval forces in the Mediterranean nearer the Suez Canal.

A political adviser to President Nasser said in Cairo that the Big Three Western powers took no notice of Egypt's right in their declaration on the Suez nationalization.

Egypt accused the Western Big Three of having invited it to the conference on the Suez Canal under threat of armed force and planned economic pressure.

Chief of UNTSO Burns conferred with Egyptian leaders in the Gaza Strip on ways of easing tension.

August 3

The Trans-Arabian Pipeline Company accused the Lebanese Government in a formal note of repudiating the principle of sanctity of contract by its new retroactive tax law. The Company said that it would not continue negotiations with Lebanon on a 50-50 share of profits between Syria, Jordan, Saudi Arabia and that country.

August 4

The UK halted all normal releases of army troops and officers from active duty as a part of a military buildup for possible reoccupation of the Suez Canal area.

France announced that it would stop publishing casualty figures in Algeria because the publication of lists of rebels killed there would shock French public opinion and also aid the Nationalists.

Syrian President Kuwatli withdrew his resignation on conditions that no more executions be carried out for complicity in the Malki assassination.

South Africa restricted sterling payments to Egypt.

The Jordanian Government suspended the newspaper, al-Urdun, indefinitely on the ground that it was affecting Jordan's relations with Iraq by attacking Iraqi policy toward other Arab states.

Acceptances to the August 16 London conference on the Suez were received from Greece, Ceylon, Australia, Italy, Norway, Pakistan and Portugal. India requested more information before deciding.

August 5

The Arab League set a meeting for August 7 to vote formal support for Egypt's nationalization of the Suez. Lebanon and Jordan were the first members to announce their attendance.

Lebanon declared its support of Egypt.

August 5

Syria and Jordan announced an agreement on economic unity which would give citizens of both countries equal rights to work, residence and freedom of movement. The two countries planned to form a unified customs area.

The British aircraft carrier Theseus, the first of three carriers ordered to the Mediterranean, sailed from Portsmouth.

Egypt called up a limited number of its enlisted reserves. It was also reported that the Cabinet had drafted a quick general mobilization in the event of war over the Suez. No Egyptian answer was given to the West's invitation to attend a London conference on international control of navigation.

The Soviet Government made it clear that Moscow would not support the West's proposal for an international conference on the Suez unless Egyptian sovereignty was guaranteed.

Great Britain cancelled the export license of the Egyptian cargo ship, Star of Luxor, scheduled to sail for Lebanon with a cargo of arms.

An Iraq Government communique said that Iraq stood beside Egypt and that nationalization was the undoubted right of any nation.

August 6

President Nasser conferred with Soviet and Indian envoys.

An Israel military court condemned an Egyptian member of a suicide squad to death. The prisoner had been caught on April 5.

Communist demonstrators paraded outside the British High Commission and the French Embassy in New Delhi in support of the Egyptian nationalization of the Suez Canal.

The Mixed Armistice Commission produced a Jordanian charge against Israel of violating the armistice agreement August 2.

August 6

The Syrian Government prepared a draft plan for a federal union between Syria and Egypt, to be presented to Egypt within ten days.

Egypt announced that it would devote a large part of the revenues from the Suez Canal to deepening and widening the canal to permit the passage of the new super tankers being built for the oil companies.

The Suez Canal Company instructed its non-Egyptian employees to choose before August 15 between their contract with the company and cooperation with Egyptian authorities. The departure date was to be communicated later.

Jordan charged that Israel had assembled the equivalent of a division of troops plus artillery in the Jerusalem area. Syria complained to the Security Council that Israel was violating armistice terms in the demilitarized zone by maintaining regular uniformed troops and digging fortifications.

Egypt accepted an invitation to join the Colombo powers in talks on the Suez Canal crisis at a conference to be held in Djakarta, Indonesia, as an alternative to the London conference.

Britain clamped new restrictions on military information as the aircraft carrier Ocean sailed from Plymouth for the Middle East. Reinforcement of the Middle East was designated Operation Magic.

India, West Germany, Japan and Ethiopia accepted invitations to attend the London conference on the Suez Canal crisis.

It was announced in Cairo that wives and children of British civilian contractors who operated military supply bases along the Suez Canal were being evacuated on orders from London.

August 7

The Egyptian Embassy in London issued a statement declaring that it was a matter of vital interest to Egypt that navigation not only be

August 7

maintained but intensified and increased in the Suez Canal.

Two Algerian moderates stated that Egypt's seizure of the Suez Canal had encouraged Algerian rebels to the point where they might be able to prolong their fight against the French.

Secretary of State Dulles said in Washington that if the London conference failed to restore international control of the Suez Canal, economic pressure might be brought to bear upon Egypt.

August 8

France expelled three Egyptians and a Lebanese, all former Arabic language announcers on the French National Radio System. The expulsion coincided with increased French-Egyptian tension over the Suez Canal but was based on an earlier dispute, when the four had refused to broadcast a dispatch deemed harmful to Egypt.

India decided to attend the London conference on Suez, but made it plain that it backed Egypt's right to nationalize the canal and resented British and French mobilization.

The Hejaz Railway announced in Damascus that the bid to prepare studies for the restoration of the railway between Damascus and Medina was granted to an American company, the International Resources Engineering and Exploration Group.

UK Prime Minister Eden told the British people in a radio and television address that Egypt's President Nasser was solely responsible for the dispute over Suez. He said that Britain's quarrel was not with Egypt but with Nasser and called free use of the canal a matter of life and death for Britain and Europe.

The Arab economics experts' conference in Cairo approved Article 1 of the project proposed by the Secretariat General of the Arab League, calling for complete economic unity among the Arab states.

US President Eisenhower expressed confidence that the Suez Canal crisis would be settled around the conference table.

August, 1956

August 8

Israel accused Syria of increased military preparation on the border and of deliberately spreading false reports to increase tension.

Egypt indicated that it would reject an invitation to the London conference.

August 9

The airlift of British wives and children from the Suez Canal Zone began.

At Wau, in Sudan, trial began for former Minister of Mechanical Transport, Paysama. He was charged with subversion in advocating a federal form of government for Southern Sudan.

The USSR accepted, with reservations and dissents, the British invitation to the London conference.

President Nasser announced the formation of a new National Liberation Army incorporating the National Guard and youth organization volunteers under a single command. Minister of Education Hussein was named Commander of this Army. Training began immediately.

The Tapline Company agreed to resume talks with the Lebanese Government over increasing Lebanon's profits to 50 percent on oil passing through that country.

The Egyptian Cotton Committee in Alexandria announced a stoppage on sale of its cotton stocks effective August 8 to aid farmers in selling their current crop.

The Egyptian Embassy in London said that UK Prime Minister Eden's attack on President Nasser in a speech was incompatible with international courtesy and responsible relations between governments.

August, 1956

August 10

President Nasser postponed indefinitely his trip to the USSR.

In Cairo, a group called the Strike Group for the Liberation of the Moslem People organized a rally calling for a general strike throughout Islam on August 16, the day of the London conference.

Two British employees of the Shell Oil Company refinery at Port Suez were arrested and expelled by Egyptian authorities. No reason was given for the action.

The Egyptian destroyer Ibrahim, which had been refitting in Malta for three months, staged its first sea trials.

The Egyptian Government announced that small arms production had been put on a 24 hour a day basis.

The British Board of Trade imposed a virtual embargo on trade with Egypt by advising exporters that no payments woud be permitted from Egyptian sterling accounts for goods shipped after July 27.

Syria announced that it would exchange diplomatic relations with Communist China at the embassy level.

The Arab Workers Federation met in Cairo and issued a number of resolutions of support for Egypt's action on Suez.

Tunisian Premier Bourguiba announced several new decrees relating to marriage and divorce as forthcoming in Tunisia's new social revolution.

The UK, France and the US circulated written proposals for solving the Suez problem to the nations preparing for the London conference.

The UK rejected the Soviet suggestion to ask 22 other nations to the conference in addition to the 24 already invited, and to hold it later in the month.

President Nasser declared in Cairo that his great objective was to arouse Arab nationalism.

August, 1956

August 10

Yugoslavian President Tito expressed surprise that Yugoslavia had not been invited to the London conference. Hungary also stated that it should have been invited as heir to the Austrian-Hungarian Empire, a signatory to the 1888 convention.

Greece refused to attend the London conference.

The former Sudanese Minister of Mechanical Transport Paysama was sentenced to 18 months imprisonment.

The Indonesian Parliament approved by unanimous voice vote a resolution supporting Egypt's nationalization of the Suez Canal.

August 11

Acting Premier Qallal said that Libya would not permit any foreign power to launch an attack on Egypt from its territory, and that it had already supported Egypt's nationalization of the Suez.

August 12

Iraq's King Faisal left the UK for France at the end of a vacation following his state visit of July.

The Arab League Political Committee expressed support for Egypt's nationalization of the Suez and called on the West to stop threatening Egypt.

President Nasser rejected the British invitation to attend the London conference and proposed instead a conference to be attended by all the countries whose ships used the canal, and to conclude an agreement reaffirming and guaranteeing freedom of navigation through the canal. Nasser also stated that the IBRD (International Bank for Reconstruction and Development) had offered Egypt a $1 billion loan to improve the Suez Canal or build a new one.

An IBRD official in Washington said that the IBRD had never offered Egypt a loan to enlarge the Suez Canal.

August, 1956

August 12

Britain announced a major airlift to the Middle East, moving about 5,000 men and equipment during the forthcoming week.

A fund started by Sultan Muhammad V of Morocco to provide relief in stricken areas and to stimulate Morocco's economy was announced as totalling one billion francs after 45 days.

After meeting with Congressional leaders, US President Eisenhower and Secretary of State Dulles expressed hope for a peaceful solution of the Suez dispute but warned that there was still danger of war in the Middle East.

A nationwide draft of civilians including women was announced in Damascus, Syria.

August 13

The Council of the Arab League said that it would consider any attack on Egypt as an attack on the League, and would give Egypt full military support. The League also supported Nasser's suggestion for an Egyptian sponsored conference of the 45 nations that used the canal, following the London conference.

The Labor Opposition in the UK broke with the Eden Government over the use of force in internationalizing the Suez Canal, demanding assurance that the Government's military policy was merely a precaution against possible aggression.

Israel Opposition Leader Beigin called on the Israel Government to abandon its passive policy on the Suez Canal issue and denounced Egyptian President Nasser as Israel's biggest enemy since Hitler.

Syria warned the UK and the US that in the event of Western aggression against Egypt over the Suez dispute, it might not be able to prevent sabotage of oil pipelines.

Iraqi lawyers meeting in Baghdad called the Western threat of force against Egypt over the nationalization of Suez a clear violation of international law and the UN Charter and an interference in Egypt's domestic affairs.

August, 1956

August 13

The US said that it was in full accord with Britain and France on means of solving the Suez Canal dispute by the London conference.

August 14

The US formed a Middle East Emergency Committee to ensure an adequate supply of oil for the UK and Western Europe in the event of an interruption in supplies. The committee was composed of 13 representatives from US oil companies.

The French Cabinet approved a plan for full international control of the Suez Canal to be backed by military force, if necessary.

Sir Belgrave, the Bahraini Sheikh's adviser for thirty years, announced his retirement, saying that it might ease the present political tension in Bahrain. He added that it was not a second Glubb affair.

US Secretary of State Dulles left the US for the London conference.

The UK restricted the export of all aircraft and aircraft spare parts to Egypt, closing a loophole in Britain's previous restrictions on aircraft exports to that country.

The Bey of Tunis, Amin, signed the law abolishing polygamy in Tunisia and placing in effect—as of January 1, 1957—other decrees described by Premier Bourguiba on August 10.

The office of the Governor of Casablanca lifted the ban on passports imposed 17 days before on Moroccan Jews.

The US announced the appointment of Raymond Arthur Hare as Ambassador to Egypt, succeeding Byroade.

The Syrian Arab Committee organized a mass meeting in Damascus for the support of Egypt.

Egyptian authorities ordered five minutes of mourning on August 16, at the moment the 22 nation conference on the Suez Canal was to open London.

August 14

British Foreign Secretary Lloyd declared in London that Egypt's nationalization of the Suez Canal Company was a greater threat to Britain than the Berlin blockade or the Korean War.

Israel charged that Egypt had detained ten ships carrying cargoes to Israel.

August 15

The Suez Canal Company denied charges by Nasser that it had attempted to perpetuate its concession beyond the 1968 expiration date.

The US Democratic Party Convention in Chicago adopted a Middle East plank in its platform.

The West German delegation to the London conference left Bonn with instructions to endorse a compromise solution on the Suez crisis acceptable to Egypt.

Indian Prime Minister Nehru warned that use of force in the Suez crisis would start a world war.

President Nasser's chief political aide and Cabinet head Ali Sabri flew to London as an observer of the London conference.

The Governments of Syria, Lebanon, Iraq and Jordan sanctioned strikes and set mass rallies in support of Egypt's nationalization of the Suez Canal.

Cairo police began checking on the 1,700 Americans in Egypt as to name, address, date of birth and other personal information.

A British liner, the S. S. Largs Bay, was ordered to go around the Cape of Good Hope instead of through the Suez Canal en route to Australia.

A 57 member Egyptian cultural mission arrived in Amman, Jordan.

Saudi Arabian Deputy Foreign Minister Yasin met with President Nasser. After the meeting, Yasin said he had no news of reports that Saudi

August 15

Arabia's King Saud had threatened to cut off Western oil supplies in his Kingdom if the UK and France used force against Egypt.

August 16

Lebanese Premier Yafi said that the Government had begun to collect taxes from oil and other companies pursuant to the law of July 28, 1956, levying taxes back to 1952 on all companies hitherto exempted by special agreement.

The Iraqi Foreign Ministry said that Egyptian Foreign Minister Fawzi had officially asked Iraq to mediate in the Suez Canal dispute but that the question had not been fully settled.

The London conference opened with 22 nations participating. US Secretary of State Dulles presented what was in effect a US-British-French plan for operating the Suez Canal under an international board associated with the UN and having Egyptian representation.

The Egyptian Government protested that the UK was trying to use the London conference to impose international domination or, rather, mixed imperialism on an indivisible Egypt.

A 24 hour countrywide strike was proclaimed by the Egyptian Government in protest against the London conference. The only activity not affected was the daily convoy passage of ships through the Suez Canal. Similar strikes were held in Syria, Jordan, Libya and Lebanon.

The Suez Canal Company said in Paris that there was a definite shortage of pilots in the canal accounted for by Egypt's refusal to accord entry visas to foreign candidates for pilots' posts during 1955 and 1956.

The Egyptian Embassy in London said that the number of convoys southbound through the Suez Canal was being reduced from two to one a day because a number of foreign pilots had not returned from vacations in Europe.

August 17

At the London conference, Soviet Foreign Minister Shepilov rejected the creation of an international authority to operate the Suez Canal.

Acting Under Secretary of Foreign Affairs Mumayiz said that Iraq had not taken steps to mediate in the Suez dispute and could not do so while the London conference continued.

UN Secretary General Hammarskjold appealed for an end to acts of violence on the Israel-Arab borders for the second time in two days.

French Foreign Minister Pineau said at the London conference that the Suez Canal Company should be kept in existence as an investment company and that the proposed international board for running the canal should be nonprofit.

Egyptian newspapers reported the organization of an Arab underground from the Atlantic to the Persian Gulf ready to strike against the imperialist West.

Indonesia's President Sukarno defended Egypt's right to nationalize the Suez Canal and urged all newly independent states to warn the West not to interfere with Egypt's action.

Two Soviet ships carrying Czechoslovakian arms to Egypt arrived in Alexandria.

King Hussein of Jordan visited Damascus, Syria, for talks of a political and military character in which he was joined by Jordan Chief of Staff Abu-Nuwar.

August 18

In Sudan, supporters of the National Unionist Party staged demonstrations in various towns in protest against the Government decision to circulate banknotes bearing the signature of Former Premier Azhari.

August 18

Iraq Minister of Finance Kannah said that the idea of an oil pipeline to Turkey, to bypass possible troubled areas in the Levant, was impractical because of the time involved to construct such a line.

Jordan charged an invasion of its territory by four Israel soldiers in a jeep and lodged a complaint with the Mixed Armistice Commission.

Egypt emphatically denied reports from Baghdad that it had sought the help of Iraq in mediating the Suez issue.

Egyptian Cabinet Head, Ali Sabri, said in London that Egypt would be willing to agree that violation of free navigation of the Suez Canal would be an act of aggression under the UN Charter.

British Foreign Secretary Selwyn Lloyd told the London conference that the US, France and the UK had abandoned their intention of seeking approval of a detailed plan for operation of the canal and would ask instead for a declaration of principles.

President Nasser reaffirmed his earlier declaration that he would not accept internationalization of the Suez Canal.

The American Association for the United Nations urged that the future of the Suez Canal be decided within the UN.

August 19

One of the planks in the US Republican National Convention platform contained a pledge to support the independence of Israel against armed aggression.

Suez Day, a day of solidarity with Egypt and condemnation of the Western powers' policy towards it, was marked in India under the auspices of the All India Peace Council.

The Syrian press reported that seven persons were killed and 257 injured in pro-Egyptian demonstrations in the British Protectorate of Kuwait. The British Foreign Office denied this and declared that it had no knowledge of anti-British demonstrations in Kuwait.

August 19

Turkey and Syria signed an agreement permitting farmers from either country to enter the territory of the other to gather their crops and setting controls over lands cultivated for narcotics. Agreements were also reached about extradition and smuggling control.

The Istiqlal Party of Morocco criticized Moroccan Premier M'barek Bekkai's Government for losing sight of nationalist goals. Foreign Minister Balafrej, also Secretary General of the Istiqlal Party, said at a party conclave in Rabat that the Government should undertake a rapid conclusion of economic and financial accords and define the status of French interests in Morocco.

Egypt announced that a group of Egyptian scientists would go to Moscow on August 21 to prepare for the establishment of a nuclear laboratory in Egypt by the Soviet Government.

Pravda accused the West of attempting to take over the Suez Canal under the aegis of an international authority.

US Secretary of State Dulles circulated among the delegates to the London conference a declaration of principles which called for operation of the Suez Canal by an international board on which Egypt would be represented.

In Egypt, the Gulf Oil Corporation called for firm and reliable international control of Suez.

Commander of the Egyptian Youth Legion Shuhaib said that he had received several applications from members of youth organizations in Communist countries to join Egypt's new Liberation Army if war broke out over the Suez Canal issue.

Tunisian Secretary of State for Youth and Sport, Rebai, returned from a visit to Cairo with an invitation for Premier Bourguiba to visit Egypt.

Libyan Premier Ben-Halim announced that the UK had sent a written confirmation to Libya that it would not use its Libyan bases for an attack on Egypt.

Israel announced that manufacture of certain items in its military production had doubled, and in some cases tripled, in the last 12 months.

August 19

Syrian Defense Minister Raslan said that Syria, Egypt and Saudi Arabia had agreed to extend permanent financial aid to Jordan's National Guard to equip it against the Israel threat.

A rebel statement listed four conditions for a ceasefire in Algeria. They were: 1) recognition of an indivisible Algerian nation, with its natural Sahara extensions; 2) unconditional recognition of Algerian independence; 3) release of all Algerians interred, imprisoned or exiled for "political" activities; 4) recognition by France of a provisional Algerian government qualified to negotiate a treaty between France and Algeria.

Jordanian authorities suspended efforts to deport Armenian Archbishop Diran Nersoyan accused of having direct contact with the Soviet Armenian Republic.

August 20

Both Syrian and Turkish regular army forces withdrew from the common border and were replaced by security and police units.

A conference of 500 tribal leaders from the Egyptian deserts was held in Cairo. The conferees decided to set up 20 battalions of tribal warriors under the National Liberation Army. Each tribe would equip, arm and supply its own battalion.

In the name of his own Government and that of the UK and France, US Secretary of State Dulles formally submitted the proposed declaration of principles to the London conference.

Deposits of iron ore estimated at 29 million tons were discovered in the Western Desert in Egypt.

At the London conference, India declared that it was impossible to impose international control over the Suez Canal and submitted a set of principles of its own.

The Israel-Jordanian Mixed Armistice Commission urged Jordan to stop Arab raids into Israel territory.

The NLF elected a 54 member National Council of the Algerian Revolution, stating it was the only body empowered to take any decision on the future of Algeria.

August 20

The Syrian Minister of Education and the Soviet Deputy Minister of Culture signed a cultural agreement.

The Lebanese Government was reported to have prepared a draft of legal measures to seize foreign oil pipelines in the event that the deadlock over retroactive tax payments was not broken.

In Morocco, the Istiqlal Party's National Council asked the Executive Committee of the Party to withdraw its ministers from the coalition government and undertake consultations with Sultan Muhammad V for a new government.

The Democratic Party of Morocco asked the Sultan to permit free elections for a representative assembly.

August 21

Egypt agreed to negotiate on Suez, provided French and British forces sent to reinforce the Middle East were withdrawn beforehand. At the London conference, the revised plan offered by the US for control of the canal won a vote of confidence by 18-4. The plan was favored over an Indian one which would create an international board merely for consultation.

The Suez Canal Company confirmed in Paris that its pilots on leave had been advised to delay their return to duty.

Egyptian Finance Minister al-Kaissouni said that his ministry had taken all necessary measures to continue Egypt's cotton trade abroad.

Yemen recognized Communist China.

The Iraq Petroleum Company further complicated the dispute over the new Lebanese retroactive tax law by declaring a net loss for 1955 of 600, 000 pounds sterling.

Pakistani Prime Minister Ali ordered the release of all persons arrested in Karachi for defying a ban on processions and assemblies in the city. The arrests had begun on August 16 while Karachi workers were on strike in support of Egypt's nationalization of the Suez Canal.

August 22

Nabih Yunis, Under Secretary of the Egyptian Ministry of Finance, threatened to give priority in the Suez Canal to all ships over those of Britain and France if British and French Canal pilots left their jobs.

A French agency report from Casablanca said that 5,500 Moroccan Jews would be allowed to leave Morocco soon.

India's Prime Minister Nehru told Indian leaders that the Suez crisis had eased. He said that India had taken part in the London conference to help reach a settlement, although he had doubts about its representativeness.

The USSR and India blocked a proposal of the London conference to ask Egypt to negotiate with the other nations for international control of the Suez Canal. New Zealand suggested that a committee selected from those supporting the proposal approach the Egyptian Government with the US statement.

August 23

The London conference ended with 18 of the nations agreeing to ask Egypt to discuss international operation of the Suez. A committee of representatives of five nations—Australia, Ethiopia, Iran, Sweden and the US—was formed to make plans for approaching Egypt. Only the USSR, India, Indonesia and Ceylon opposed the decision of the conference.

To help Egypt evade the UK's freeze on Egyptian sterling accounts, China deposited 20 million Swiss francs in Egyptian accounts in Swiss banks. India and Egypt agreed to continue to exchange goods without payment for the present.

Soviet Communist Party leader Khrushchev said that if war broke out over the Suez crisis, the Arabs would not stand alone. There would be volunteers.

The US International Cooperation Administration said that it would not send additional technicians to Egypt or begin new aid projects in that country until the Suez crisis was over.

August 23

A skeleton headquarters for a French Mediterranean force was announced as having been set up in Algiers under the command of Major General Beaufre, Commander of the 2d Mechanized Infantry Division stationed in Eastern Algeria.

The US State Department announced that an informal agreement was reached with Saudi Arabia extending indefinitely the right of the US to use the Dhahran Air Base.

Some 5,500 Moroccan Jews, held since the suppression of the Kadima Society, left for Israel.

The Ministry of Finance and National Economy in Saudi Arabia announced that it would send a number of Saudi Arabians on scholarship to the International Statistics Center in Beirut, Lebanon, to train for a period of six and one-half months beginning October 25, 1956.

August 24

Representatives of the five nations selected to present the London Conference Plan for international control of the Suez Canal met for the first time.

The Egyptian Embassy in Bonn said that applications were being received from West German pilots on the Kiel Canal to work on the Suez Canal.

Egypt declared Adabiyah, 15 kilometers south of the Suez Canal entrance, a free port, in answer to a request by Indonesia for a free zone for its goods imported into Egypt.

A six months payments agreement was signed between the Sudanese and Saudi Arabian Governments in Khartoum.

The Egyptian destroyer, al-Qahar, left England for Egypt without ammunition for its guns, due to the British embargo on arms shipments to Egypt.

August 25

US Secretary of State Dulles expressed the hope that Egypt would accept the London conference suggestions for international operation of the Suez Canal.

British Labor Party leader Gaitskell urged his Government to appeal to Suez Canal pilots to remain on their jobs.

The Saudi Arabian Government paid the Jordanian Ministry of Economy JD125,000 as its share in financing the Jordan-Arab Potash Company for extracting salts from the Dead Sea.

Seven Bulgarian geologists arrived in Damascus, Syria.

"Algeria Week," during which money was collected to help the Algerian nationalist movement, began in Syria.

An agreement was announced between Egypt and East Germany for Egypt to import 90,000 tons of fertilizer in exchange for Egyptian cotton.

Jordanian Under Secretary of Economy Farhan called for a revision of the US aid program to give all administrative and executive responsibilities to Jordanian ministries, leaving the US officials with technical and supervisory functions over particular projects.

Talhouni, chief of King Hussein's household, flew to Beirut, reportedly carrying a personal message for King Idris I of Libya.

The British Foreign Office placed the full record of the eight day Suez conference in the hands of the Egyptian Embassy for transmission to Cairo.

It was reported in Cairo that Egypt was considering the possibility of seeking action by the UN Security Council against British and French troop movements in the Eastern Mediterranean.

August 26

The Suez Canal Company issued a statement that it could not assure the safety of its staff in Egypt.

August 26

A mass student demonstration was held in Khartoum in support of Egypt's decision to nationalize the Suez Canal Company.

Egypt began stamping all outgoing mail with the cancellation slogan: "Free navigation of the Suez Canal guaranteed."

The Syrian Minister of Economy left for Egypt to conclude the sale of 100,000 tons of wheat to Egypt.

Statistics published by the Egyptian Customs Administration revealed that 26 percent of Egypt's exports had gone to Soviet Bloc countries in 1955, as compared to 14 percent in 1954.

Red Star, the Soviet Union's most authoritative military voice, warned the UK and France against the use of force in the Suez Canal crisis.

Mahdi, leader of the Ansar religious sect in Iraq, arrived in Cairo for medical treatment and talks with President Nasser.

A section of the members of the Syrian Cooperative Socialist Party united with the Nationalist Party, and a new committee was chosen for the Damascus branch of the Nationalist Party.

Israel Premier Ben-Gurion said that peace would not be established in the Middle East unless Israel was assured complete freedom of navigation in the Red Sea Strait and through the Suez Canal.

August 27

It was reported in Damascus that Syria, Lebanon, Jordan and Saudi Arabia accepted in principle the offer of the Trans-Arabian Pipeline Company to share its profits equally with the four states.

Saudi Arabia agreed to loan Egypt $100 million to bolster its hard currency.

The Egyptian Government expelled correspondents of the Daily Mail, Evening Standard and Toronto Star.

August 27

King Saud held talks in Jedda with the West German Minister to Saudi Arabia, Von Richthofen, and a number of heads of big West German companies.

Marshal Pierre Juin, spokesman for the ultraconservative French colonials, said in a speech that Algeria should be given a large measure of internal autonomy.

Jordan's Chief of Staff Abu-Nuwar said that war between the UK and Egypt would lead to an inevitable alliance between the Arab world and the USSR.

August 28

President Nasser agreed to meet with a five nation delegation, appointed by the London conferees, charged with presenting the US proposal for international operation of the Suez Canal.

US Secretary of State Dulles said that President Nasser made a contribution toward a solution of the Suez problem by agreeing to receive the five nation committee. He declared also that the USSR was attempting to obstruct a peaceful solution to the Suez crisis.

Egypt received a loan of $100 million from Saudi Arabia because of assets frozen in England and France.

Egypt admitted it was seeking qualified American pilots to work in the Suez Canal.

A Chinese Communist mission arrived in Jordan for talks.

August 29

Prime Minister Nehru announced that he would visit Saudi Arabia on September 24.

The UN Mixed Armistice Commission censured Israel for a violation of the truce agreement in a skirmish with Jordanian troops August 26.

August 29

France agreed to turn over to Tunisia French built and operated radio installations in Tunis.

France received Britain's permission to station troops on Cyprus, due to tension over the Suez Canal and the need to protect French nationals and their interests in the Eastern Mediterranean.

Egyptian authorities in Cairo reported that they uncovered a British plot to overthrow the Government of President Nasser. Two British diplomats were asked to leave the country.

Egypt and Syria signed a trade agreement for Egypt's purchase of 100,000 tons of wheat at 20,000 tons a month.

US President Eisenhower appealed for world support of the London conference proposal for a peaceful solution of the Suez crisis.

August 30

The Permanent Council of NATO was called to a meeting set for September 5 to discuss the Suez Canal dispute.

In retaliation for Egypt's action on the previous day, the UK ordered two Egyptian diplomats to leave London within 72 hours.

A Czechoslovakian economic mission to Syria, headed by Deputy Minister of Industry Yavorik, arrived in Damascus.

President Nasser called in US Ambassador Byroade to protest against President Eisenhower's statement of August 29 that the Suez Canal had been internationalized by the 1888 Convention. Nasser said that the canal was an integral part of Egypt.

August 31

Egypt charged that 13 of its soldiers were killed in three simultaneous Israel raids across the armistice demarcation lines, and filed a com-

August 31

plaint with the Mixed Armistice Commission. Egypt also reported an Israel violation of Egyptian air space in Gaza.

The British Government rejected an Opposition demand for a special session of Parliament within 15 days to discuss the Suez situation.

Egypt commissioned the Israel freighter, *Bat Galim*, the only vessel ever to attempt to pass through the Suez Canal flying the Israel flag, into its navy. The *Bat Galim* was seized in 1954.

Abba Eban, Israel's UN representative, warned member states that Egypt might discriminate against their shipping in the Suez Canal, as it had done before.

President Eisenhower said that the US was not challenging Egypt's ownership of the Suez Canal, but merely pointing out the right of other nations under the 1888 Convention to use it in perpetuity.

French Premier Mollet said he would go to Algiers the following week in a major effort to settle Algeria's political future.

Moroccan Premier M'Barek Bekkai defied Istiqlal Party demands that its ministers resign from the coalition government. He said that the program of the Sultan's Government necessitated the mobilization of all the country's efforts.

September 1

President Kuwatli inaugurated Syria's third annual trade fair in Damascus. Eight of the 30 participating countries were members of the Communist Bloc; their exhibits were chiefly of heavy industry products. The US, represented officially at the fair for the first time, had a display featuring consumer export goods. France was not represented.

According to a report in the *Akhbar-al-Yawm*, the Egyptian Government intended to start a lawsuit against the former Suez Canal Company, accusing it of illegally spending funds that no longer belonged to it.

The Tunisian Government took over Tunis Radio under an agreement signed in Paris on August 29.

An advance guard of 150 French soldiers arrived in Famagusta as part of the UK-French buildup in Cyprus due to the Suez crisis.

A commercial agreement was signed between Syria and Bulgaria which was valid for a one year period. It provided for most favored nation treatment.

The final preparatory meeting of the Committee of Five, set up by the London conference on the Suez Canal, was held in London. Proposals for internationalization of the waterway, to be presented to President Nasser on behalf of the 18 nations, were formulated. The committee was composed of representatives of the US, Sweden, Iran and Ethiopia and was headed by Australian Prime Minister Menzies.

September 2

The British Government advised wives and children of personnel stationed in Jordan to begin leaving the country.

The five member committee from the London conference arrived in Cairo. President Nasser stated that he would accept any solution to the Suez Canal question that would not affect Egyptian sovereignty. He said that international control would infringe upon Egypt's sovereignty.

September, 1956

September 2

French Foreign Minister Pineau stated again that France would use force, if necessary, against Egypt in the Suez Canal dispute. He also castigated the USSR for endangering world peace by its pressure on Egypt's President Nasser to reject all Western offers of mediation over the dispute.

Syria and Egypt reached an economic agreement for industrial cooperation and for the formation of joint companies with joint capital.

Jordan received ID125, 000 from Iraq as the latter's share in the proposed Arab Potash Company.

September 3

Israel's Prime Minister, Ben-Gurion said that many countries which previously were ready to acquiesce in closing the Suez to Israel shipping had now realized that their own interests, too, were directly at stake.

The Suez Canal Company in Paris requested its non-Egyptian staff to continue their work against their will beyond September 1 in consideration of the mission given to Australian Premier Menzies by the London Conference.

Leaders of the Trades Union Congress at its 84th conference at Brighton, England, approved a resolution opposing force to settle the Suez dispute.

Australian Prime Minister Menzies presented the 18 national proposals for internationalization of the Suez Canal to Egyptian President Nasser.

One hundred French civilians arrived in Paris from Egypt, saying that they had left Egypt upon the recommendation of French consular authorities.

French reports stated that more than 3, 063 civilians had been killed by Algerian rebels since the revolt against French control began November 1, 1954. Of these, 2, 700 were Algerian Moslems and 363 were French.

September, 1956

September 3

Syrian President Kuwatli accused the West of trying to instigate a third world war to block Arab liberation. He said that any aggression against Egypt would be aggression against Syria.

In Syria, two men convicted of complicity in the 1955 assassination of Colonel Malki were executed.

September 4

An agreement whereby the USSR would sell Egypt 200, 000 tons of wheat for LE6 million and would use the proceeds to purchase Egyptian goods, including cotton and rice, was signed in Cairo.

The first group of British Embassy staff families—14 women and children—left Amman for England, following the advice of the British Government.

The Saudi Arabian Embassy in Cairo said that King Saud had asked Egypt, Iraq, Syria and Lebanon to send military representatives to Riyadh for an urgent meeting on the Arab-Israel crisis.

King Hussein of Jordan invited President Chamoun of Lebanon and President Kuwatli of Syria to confer with him on current Arab problems.

Egypt said that it had received almost 200 offers from pilots wishing to work for the Egyptian Suez Canal Authority.

It was reported from Washington that Egyptian purchases of heavy arms from Communist countries exceeded $250 million, and could reach $300 million, under pressure from President Nasser for accelerated deliveries.

A Soviet parliamentary delegation arrived in Syria.

September 5

Syrian Defense Minister Raslan told newsmen that Syria, Egypt, Lebanon and Jordan had instructed their UN delegates to file notes

September, 1956

September 5

about Arab uneasiness over the supposedly pro-Israel attitude of UNTSO Chief Burns.

The Netherlands protested orally to Egypt about the latter's refusal to release two Dutch dredgers that had completed their work in the Suez Canal.

The Suez Canal Company said that it was unable to retire some of its bonds or pay interest on others because of a freeze on its funds in Egypt.

At the close of the fourth secret meeting between Egyptian President Nasser and the five nation committee, President Nasser said that each side had finished presenting its views.

The NATO Council, meeting in Paris to discuss the Suez situation, received a report on the military precautions taken by France and the UK and gave full backing to the 18 nation plan for international control of the Suez. Foreign Minister Spaak of Belgium said that the West must not yield to any intimidation by Egypt.

A member of the Syrian Socialist National Party said that leftist pressure had forced President Kuwatli to accept Soviet arms on condition that Communist and socialist officers be assigned to key military positions in the army.

The UK was reportedly disturbed by indications that the US was softening its Suez policy.

A clash between Sudanese army troops and mutineers at Torit, Equatoria Province, resulted in a number of casualties on both sides.

President Eisenhower said that the US was committed to a peaceful solution of the Suez problem, and one that would insure to all nations the free use of the Suez Canal for the shipping of the world.

Israel sent a letter to the UN Security Council charging Egypt with pretending to guarantee free shipping on the Suez Canal while resorting to a brazen blockade of Israel bound vessels.

September, 1956

September 6

At the invitation of King Saud of Saudi Arabia, military representatives of Egypt, Iraq, Syria and Lebanon met at Riyadh to discuss joint measures to strengthen Jordan against Israel.

Sudan and Ethiopia signed an air transport agreement.

Tunisian Ambassador to the US Slim presented his credentials to President Eisenhower. He declared that Tunisia wanted to be a buffer state between the Arab and European worlds.

The French troopship, Athos II, carrying 2, 500 French paratroopers, docked at Limassol, Cyprus. Three French cargo ships arrived in Cyprus, bringing to seven the number of French vessels arriving with military supplies during the past week.

Police in Casablanca, Morocco, arrested four members of the Presence Française accused of inciting anti-nationalist Berber tribesmen to revolt against the Government.

France protested against the expulsion of two French nationals implicated in a plot against the security of the Tunisian State. Tunisia replied with a protest against the French abduction of four Tunisians in the Ain-Draham frontier region.

French Resident Minister Lacoste told French Army and civil officials that he had all the military means necessary to effect peace in Algeria. He said that 200, 000 additional French troops had arrived in the past three months.

Prime Minister Eden summoned the British Parliament to an emergency meeting to discuss Suez.

Baghdad ulema sent a telegram to Pakistan Prime Minister Ali denouncing Pakistan's attitude on the Suez Canal problem during meetings of the London conference.

Jordan sent a delegation to the meeting of the Arab Chambers of Commerce in Damascus, Syria. The meeting was called to determine measures to be taken by the Chambers of Commerce in the event of British or French aggression against Egypt.

September 6

It was reported from Sweden that four days after President Nasser nationalized the Suez Canal Company, an Egyptian export company offered 100,000 tons of Russian light fuel oil for sale at 25 percent above the world market average. This was interpreted as a gamble on Western fears that the canal might be closed.

September 7

The military conference at Riyadh, Saudi Arabia, opened. Discussions dealt with the question of providing Jordan's National Guard with a fixed annual budget and the necessary equipment to fight in the event of Israel aggression.

French Premier Mollet arrived in Algiers and held discussions with Resident Minister Lacoste and the Commander of French Forces Lorillot.

Australia's Prime Minister Menzies called an end to his committee's mission to Cairo and said that Egypt's attitude left no room for an accord.

French officials said that President Nasser had shown no sign of making the slightest concession to the West in talks with the Menzies committee.

US Secretary of State John Foster Dulles met twice with British and French diplomats because of the failure of the Menzies talks in Cairo.

Egyptian authorities agreed to release the Greek freighter Panagia on condition that it return to Haifa. The ship had been held in Port Said since May 25, when it was prevented from entering the Suez Canal on its way to the port of Elath, Israel, on the Gulf of Aqaba. Cairo authorities maintained that the question of blockading Israel shipping did not apply to the Panagia since the freighter was stopped outside the canal and did not enter it.

September 8

Former Rif leader Abd-al-Krim sent a telegram from Cairo to Moroccan Minister of State Lyoussi supporting the latter's campaign in the Middle Atlas area of Morocco for national unity under the Sultan.

It was reported from Paris that France had completed all military preparations to retaliate in the event of President Nasser's flat rejection of the Western proposal to internationalize the Suez Canal, or of his attempt to obstruct free passage of ships through it.

The Menzies committee announced an extra meeting with Nasser in an effort to break the deadlock over the internationalization of the Suez Canal.

Premier Mollet and Foreign Minister Christian Pineau of France accepted an invitation to discuss the stalemate in the Cairo negotiations with UK Prime Minister Eden and Foreign Secretary Lloyd in London.

Egypt began advertising in Canada for pilots to work at the Suez Canal.

Yemen accepted an offer from Czechoslovakia to send student missions to Czechoslovakian universities to take courses in engineering and medicine free of charge for a six year period.

Officials from Communist China arrived in Beirut to supervise execution of the trade agreement signed between Lebanon and China August 20.

A state of emergency was proclaimed in the area of Mosul, Iraq, due to a strike of butchers against increased duties on meat. The Government said that the strike had been instigated by subversive elements engaged in smuggling sheep into Israel.

September 9

Syria and Albania signed a one year trade pact to exchange Syrian agricultural products for Albanian coal and asphalt.

The Sudanese Government issued an order prohibiting all processions, meetings and demonstrations in Khartoum, Omdu[illegible] Khartoum West and the suburbs.

September 9

The Suez Canal talks between the Menzies committee and Egyptian President Nasser ended in deadlock. Nasser declared that any attempt to impose international control over canal operations would plunge the area into turmoil.

French Premier Mollet said that his Government favored international operation of Suez by force, if necessary.

US Secretary of State Dulles said that he was not surprised at Nasser's rejection of the plan for international control of Suez.

September 10

The Arab Refugees' Conference ended in Jerusalem with recommendations that the only solution to the refugee problem was repatriation.

UN Headquarters reported that the bodies of six Israel soldiers, killed in a clash with a Jordanian patrol in the Hebron foothills, were found in Jordanian territory. An Israel Army spokesman said that the bodies had been dragged into Jordan across the armistice line.

The Greek freighter, Panagia, which had been prohibited from passing through the Suez Canal with a cargo of cement for Israel, returned from Port Said to Haifa after three and one-half months of detention in Egypt.

The Royal Rotterdam Lloyd Line ordered its flagship Willem Ruys to make a 4,000 mile detour to avoid the Suez Canal.

A Jordanian military delegation returned from talks in Saudi Arabia.

Syria announced an imposition of restrictions on the passage of American and British military planes over its territory. Forty-eight hours notice to the Ministry of Public Works was required.

September 10

The Egyptian Government circulated a note on the Suez issue deploring the show of strength against Egypt and stressing that a settlement could be achieved without detriment to its sovereignty and dignity through peaceful negotiations.

Australian Prime Minister Menzies declared in London that Egypt would have nothing to do with international control of the Suez Canal.

Egypt proposed a special negotiating body to work out agreements covering the rights of all states concerned in navigation through the Suez Canal.

In reply to President Nasser's proposal for another international conference on the Suez issue, the British Foreign Office commented that the Egyptian statement did not appear to suggest any basis for negotiation.

British and French officials met to coordinate their policies on the second phase of the canal dispute with Egypt.

British Governor General Harding of Cyprus said that the island would be an absolutely crucial base of operations for any military move against the Suez Canal to protect British interests.

The French Ambassador to the US Herve Alphand said that French troops were sent to Cyprus as a precautionary measure.

The West German Foreign Ministry criticized the Egyptian Government for attempting to lure West German pilots to the Suez Canal.

US Secretary of State Dulles expressed disappointment with Egypt's rejection of the London conference proposals.

Iraq sent an official protest to France over French troop concentrations in the Mediterranean.

The Tunisian Government announced a capital outlay budget of 19 billion francs for the next 12 months. All but 500 million francs of the amount was to be financed by French loans. The budget was 48 percent more than the previous one.

September, 1956

September 11

An Israel Army spokesman said that two guards were killed and one was missing after an attack by Jordanian infiltrators on the village of Hatseva near the Dead Sea.

Iranian Foreign Minister Ardalan returned from conferences on the Suez Canal issue with President Nasser. He said that Iran would never agree to the use of force to settle the issue.

Egypt announced that the ambassadors of all Arab, African and Asian states in Cairo had expressed their support of President Nasser's proposal for new talks on Suez.

Egypt lodged a complaint with UNTSO that Israel raiders had killed five Egyptians and injured one in a clash inside Egyptian territory, at El-Quseima. The attack came 24 hours after the blowing up of the Israel railway line north of Beersheba.

The instruments of ratification for the commercial exchanges and economic agreements which had been signed by Lebanon and Italy on November 4, 1955, were deposited in Rome and the agreements therefore entered into force.

The UK and France agreed to promote a mutual economic campaign against Egypt to force it to accept international control of Suez. The first move was for the Suez Company to order its pilots to leave their jobs.

President Eisenhower ruled out any possibility of US participation in an Anglo-French military action against Egypt under the existing circumstances.

The International Confederation of Free Trade Unions said that it would protest strongly the Saudi Arabian anti-strike law recently promulgated by Royal Decree.

The Moroccan Government issued an order expelling more than 50 French settlers who were members of the French colon organization "L'union pour la Presence Francaise," previously implicated in a plot to incite Berbers to attack Moroccan Arabs.

September, 1956

September 12

The US State Department confirmed Prime Minister Eden's statement that the US would participate in a canal users' association.

In a letter to the UN Security Council, the UK and France declared Egypt's refusal to negotiate on the basis of the 18 nation plan for internationalization of the Suez Canal an aggravation of the situation.

French Premier Mollet warned President Nasser that if he rejected the canal users' association plan he would be violating the 1888 Convention, and that every nation would be free to seek its rights through the UN or by any other means.

The USSR newspaper Soviet Russia hailed Egypt's rejection of the 18 nation proposal for international control of Suez as another blow against colonialism.

Egypt said that the proposal for a users' association to operate the Suez Canal was a step toward war and announced its intention to abide by the terms of the 1888 Convention. It refused to give up its legitimate rights or sovereignty.

The Egyptian Government announced that the Suez Canal pilots who resigned were free to leave Egypt and that their departure would be facilitated through exit visas.

The Egyptian delegate to the UN said that Egypt had a legal right to nationalize the canal. He repeated the Egyptian proposal for another international conference.

The conference in Riyadh decided to allocate JD3,600,000 for the Jordanian National Guard, to be contributed by Saudi Arabia, Egypt, Iraq, Syria and Lebanon.

September 13

Egypt declared that it could run the Suez Canal without foreign help.

Israel hailed the Western plan for an association of Suez Canal users.

September, 1956

September 11

UN Chief of Staff Burns called on both the Arab states and Israel to halt border conflicts.

France ended military government of the Ouzou mountain area east of Algiers.

Syria charged Turkey with massing troops on its border as part of a Western plan to besiege Syria and Egypt.

The chairman of the new Egyptian Suez Canal Authority warned that any employee leaving without notice or permission was committing sabotage.

The British Prime Minister and his Foreign Secretary and the French Premier and his Foreign Minister issued a statement at the conclusion of their talks in London that the refusal of President Nasser to negotiate on internationalization of the Suez Canal created a very grave situation.

Referring to the British-French communique, President Nasser's political aide said that the two Western countries had a plan to stop navigation in the canal in order to create incidents which would give them an excuse to rob Egypt of its legal rights in the Suez after they had failed to prove that Egypt had violated any international agreement.

President Eisenhower declared that the US could approve the use of force by Britain and France only after all peaceful means were exhausted, or if Egypt committed some kind of aggression against peaceful use of the Suez.

The Suez Canal Company authorized its non-Egyptian employees to leave their posts on September 14 or 15, and instructed them to ask for diplomatic help in leaving the country.

September 12

British Prime Minister Eden told an emergency session of Parliament that the UK, France and the US had agreed to create a Suez Canal operating authority.

September, 1956

September 13

UN Secretary General Hammarskjold called on the Arab states and Israel to honor their pledges under the Palestine Armistice Agreement.

The Egyptian Ambassador to the US, Hussein, delivered an oral message to US Secretary of State Dulles warning that the scheme which Sir Anthony Eden wanted to impose on Egypt was an open and flagrant aggression of Egyptian sovereignty, and its implementation would mean war.

Indian Prime Minister Nehru appealed to the UK, France and the US to reconsider their decision to establish the Canal Users Association.

Indian Prime Minister Nehru warned the West that it was running a grave risk of war with its users' association plan. He said that Egypt's proposal for a second conference opened the way to negotiations, whereas the Western plan would close the door to further negotiations.

UK Prime Minister Eden announced that his Government would take the Suez Canal dispute to the Security Council rather than use force, but that the UK could not give an absolute pledge not to use force in an emergency.

UK Prime Minister Eden told the House of Commons that an Egyptian attack on Israel would result if President Nasser succeeded in nationalizing the Suez.

Omar Loutfi, Egypt's permanent representative to the UN, addressed letters to Secretary General Hammarskjold and all member states stressing that his country would hold the UK and France responsible for any impediment to navigation in the Suez Canal.

The official representative of the ruler of Kuwait said that the oil sheikhdoms of the Persian Gulf would be forced by Arab public opinion to stop the flow of oil from their countries to the West in case of war with Egypt.

Soviet Premier Bulganin urged France to negotiate and use moderation in the Suez crisis. Yugoslavian President Tito accused the UK and France of obsolete saber rattling tactics against Egypt.

September 13

US Secretary of State Dulles said that the users' association plan was not yet sufficiently understood by the Egyptian Government, and that the US would detour its shipping around Africa rather than fight its way through the canal. He said that a detailed plan was worked out to supply oil to Western Europe from the US and Venezuela, to counteract temporary oil shortages should the Suez Canal be replaced by the Cape route.

The National Liberation Front ordered a general boycott of all Algerian public schools, to begin during the present year. The boycott was intended to stigmatize the French war of extermination, and to complete the break in relations with French authorities.

Morocco notified France that henceforth visas would be required for entry by French citizens.

September 14

The Jordanian Government authorized the resumption of the daily newspaper al-Urdun.

In its reply to the note on the Suez issue circulated by the Egyptian Government, the USSR Government said it was ready to take part in the international conference on the revision of the 1888 Convention.

UN Secretary General Hammarskjold sent almost identical notes to Israel and Jordan warning that they must be held fully accountable for continued border fighting.

King Hussein of Jordan visited Baghdad, Iraq.

Resident French Minister Lacoste said that his Government would announce its plan for political settlement in Algeria within a month.

Sudan expressed full support for Egypt in the Suez crisis and opposed the formation of a Suez Canal users' association.

Moroccan Finance Minister Benjelloun announced that France agreed to give his country about 24 billion francs ($68 million) to help balance its budget.

September 14

The British Foreign Office announced that invitations were sent out on behalf of the Western Big Three to 15 nations to join in an organizational conference to form a Suez Canal users' association.

Egypt took over full operation of the Suez Canal with almost entirely Egyptian personnel after about 400 foreign employees, including pilots, left their jobs. The Egyptian Canal Authority issued a statement that to completely preserve normal navigation in the canal the pilots would have to double their working hours.

September 15

Egypt announced that 41 ships were moving through the canal, 28 northbound and 13 southbound.

The agenda for the forthcoming Suez Canal users' association conference was drawn up.

President Nasser said that Egypt would fight to the bitter end if the West attempted to force the proposed users' association on it.

Saudi Arabian Minister of State Sulaiman said that King Saud supported Egypt and President Nasser wholeheartedly.

The first Soviet pilots for the Suez Canal were reported to have arrived in Egypt. In the first official Soviet statement on the crisis, the USSR accused the UK and France of planning to seize the canal by an act of aggression and announced its intention of attending the conference proposed by Egypt.

The Egyptian Ambassador to Jordan Saif-ad-Din said that Jordan could depend upon Egyptian military support.

Iraq denounced recent Israel aggression against Jordan and pledged military aid under its 1947 treaty of alliance with Jordan.

Lebanon and Bulgaria signed a trade pact.

September 15

A general strike began in Tunisia in protest against a French plane attack on a village which killed a child and wounded five persons.

September 16

A USSR statement on the necessity of a peaceful settlement of the Suez issue was published.

It was reported in Cairo that Ismail, an Egyptian, was appointed Chief of Staff of the Unified Syrian-Egyptian Command set up under the defense pact signed in October, 1955.

In Washington, the US Department of Commerce reported that Egypt's sales of cotton behind the Iron Curtain increased its export earnings 35.6 percent above the first half of 1955. Egypt arranged to trade cotton for arms after the US refused to furnish it with weapons.

Fifteen Soviet pilots began training to handle Suez Canal shipping.

US Sécretary of State Dulles was reported prepared to grant half a billion dollars in credits to Western European countries to help them meet the expense of rerouting their oil shipments.

President Nasser declared that Egypt would not allow the Western proposed canal users' association to function through the Suez Canal.

The Communist led World Federation of Trade Unions cabled the Egyptian Trade Union Congress in support of the Egyptian appeal for labor solidarity against Anglo-French threats to stop the Suez Canal from functioning.

An Iraqi military delegation arrived in Amman to discuss military cooperation between Jordan and Iraq. This discussion was an outgrowth of the previous meeting of Jordanian King Hussein and King Faisal of Iraq.

September 17

Omar Loutfi, Egypt's permanent representative to the UN, conveyed to the Security Council his Government's note on the situation arising after the nationalization of the Suez Canal Company. The note stressed that France's actions and those of the UK constituted a serious threat to world peace and security and grossly violated the UN Charter.

The Suez Canal Company denied charges that it had bribed French and British pilots not to work for Egypt.

The Arab League Political Committee endorsed Egypt's nationalization of Suez.

Egypt told the UN Security Council that France and the UK aimed to take possession of the Suez Canal.

The Saudi Arabian Government denounced the formation of an international Suez Canal users' association.

Egypt told the UN that the proposed users' association was a violation of the UN Charter and the 1888 Convention.

The British Foreign Office said that all the nations invited to the users' association conference in London had accepted. Five nations of the 15 invited indicated opposition to the users' association plan. The objectors were Pakistan, Sweden, Norway, Denmark and Iran.

Iraq's Premier Nuri-Said told his Cabinet that he had warned the UK and France against setting up a Suez Canal users' association, and that Iraq would not accept any solution imposed on Egypt by the Western powers.

Two left wing candidates for the Jordanian Parliament were arrested on grounds that their activities were harmful to the present situation.

The Jordanian Government told UNESCO that neither Jews nor Communists were welcome to Jordan on educational missions.

Syria returned an American and a Briton captured by a Syrian patrol in Israel and taken across the border.

September, 1956

September 17

The Jordanian-Israel Mixed Armistice Commission condemned Jordan for the attack on September 10 in which the bodies of six Israel soldiers had been carried across the border into Jordan.

Egypt charged that an Israel patrol had attacked an Egyptian defense position in the Sinai Desert.

The first shipment of arms to Jordan under the terms of the Riyadh conference began.

September 18

Egypt's Suez Canal Administration Chief declared that the pilot crisis was over.

Egypt decreed a ban on the activities of Christian missions and congregations, and declared a policy of trade boycott of the West in retaliation for severe economic sanctions placed on it.

A conference of Arab national and political organizations opened in the Syrian Chamber of Deputies to formulate practical measures to consolidate the Arab struggle against imperialism.

Australian Prime Minister Menzies said that to permit Egypt to repudiate the convention on international use of the Suez Canal would lead to an "open season for military dictators."

The British Government advised all British nationals to leave Jordan if there was no pressing reason for their staying.

All doctors and nurses in hospitals were forbidden to leave Jordan, and leaves of all government doctors were curtailed.

The US Commission on UNESCO approved a resolution condemning discriminatory practices by foreign governments against American citizens of Jewish faith. The action, aimed at the practice of certain Middle Eastern states of barring entry to persons of the Jewish faith, followed Jordan's announcement that Jews were not welcome on UNESCO missions to that country.

September, 1956

September 19

The Jordanian-Israel MAC condemned Israel for hostile and warlike acts in the September 11 raid on a Jordanian police post.

The US International Cooperation Administration announced a forthcoming shipment of 45,000 tons of wheat to Tunisia as a gift to help prevent a threatened shortage.

Jordanian Foreign Minister Abd-al-Hadi revealed that his country planned to protest to the Security Council that Israel was concentrating troops near its border.

Israel said that in the past six months Jordanian attacks resulted in the death of 29 and the wounding of 35 Israelis.

The first consignment of Egyptian arms and ammunition for the Jordanian National Guard arrived in Amman.

Soviet Premier Nikolai A. Bulganin declared that the USSR was willing to meet immediately with the leaders of Egypt, India, the UK, France and the US to seek a solution of the Suez dispute.

Forty persons, including two French doctors and several other Europeans, were arrested in Algiers in connection with the discovery of a secret Communist cell in Western Algeria. The group known as the Freedom Fighters was described as planning to aid the National Liberation Front.

Three Syrians were killed in an armed clash with Turkish border guards in the Ein-al-Arab area.

President Nasser convened a special session of the Cabinet to report on Suez developments. In Cairo the Association of Ulemas of Al-Azhar University called for a political, economic and cultural boycott of Western imperialist countries.

Speaking at the opening session of the 18 nation emergency conference in London, US Secretary of State Dulles outlined a six point plan for a canal users' association.

September, 1956

September 19

Five nations—Holland, Italy, Sweden, Norway and Denmark—announced their opposition to an economic boycott of Egypt because it would affect them adversely.

September 20

King Faisal of Iraq met with King Saud of Saudi Arabia at Dammam, Saudi Arabia.

September 21

US Air Force Secretary Quarles conferred with Moroccan leaders on US air bases in Morocco.

The Soviet press attacked Israel for siding with the West in the Suez dispute and declared that Israel leaders ought to profit by the crisis.

Egyptian President Nasser revealed plans to meet King Saud of Saudi Arabia and President Kuwatli of Syria in Saudi Arabia to discuss the Suez crisis.

The conference in London ended. A draft plan for a Suez Canal Users' Association was announced.

British Foreign Secretary Lloyd issued formal invitations to the 18 governments represented at the second Suez conference to send delegates to a meeting in London on October 1 to establish the Suez Canal Users' Association.

US Secretary of State Dulles declared on his return from London that the door to a peaceful and fair solution was kept widely opened if only the Government of Egypt would choose that way.

Canada agreed to sell Egypt 250,000 tons of wheat worth $20 million.

Canadian Prime Minister St. Laurent announced his Government's approval of the sale of 24 Sabre jet fighter planes to Israel. The US said that it had no objection.

September, 1956

September 22

King Saud of Saudi Arabia ended meetings begun earlier in the week with King Faisal of Iraq to consolidate fraternal relations between the two royal families.

President Nasser flew to Saudi Arabia for meetings with King Saud and Syrian President Kuwatli.

The Ministry of Agriculture announced a plan to grow green tea in Morocco. The experiments would be undertaken with the help of the Food and Agriculture Organization of the UN, which Morocco had recently joined.

France decided to join the Suez Canal Users' Association (SCUA) with reservations and reserve freedom of action to seek full international control over the waterway.

Israel Finance Minister Eshkol warned that the Suez crisis had aggravated the possibility of an attack against Israel.

September 23

King Saud met with President Nasser of Egypt and President Kuwatli of Syria at Riyadh for talks on the general world situation.

Convoys in the Suez Canal fell three hours late as a reduced pilot staff worked around the clock.

French Premier Mollet expressed anxiety and bitterness over Western disunity on the Suez Canal crisis.

US Secretary of State Dulles warned that the danger of war would recur if Egypt continued to reject a solution in accordance with the principles of justice and international law.

The UK and France requested the President of the Security Council to call a meeting for September 26 to discuss the Suez Canal dispute.

Prime Minister Nehru of India criticized President Nasser for [illegible] method of nationalizing the Suez Canal.

September, 1956

September 23

The French War Veterans Coordinating Committee in Algiers voted to reject proposals for a federal relationship between France and Algeria to solve the Algerian crisis.

A trade and payments agreement was signed between Libya and Egypt.

Delegates to an Israel Archaeological Society Congress in Jerusalem were fired on from Jordan. Three Israelis were killed and 15 wounded.

September 24

Israel rejected Jordan's explanation that a soldier who had gone berserk was responsible for the machine gunning of the archaeological party.

Communist China announced recognition of Yemen and establishment of diplomatic relations on the ministerial level.

President Nasser returned to Cairo with pledges of full support from Syria and Saudi Arabia in the Suez dispute. A joint communique issued by chiefs of the three Arab states demanded that the West negotiate with Egypt on control of the canal.

Egypt filed a counterprotest with the UN Security Council on the Suez Canal dispute and called for an urgent meeting.

It was reported in Baghdad that as of this date Iraq had received 20 consignments of heavy and light military equipment from the US and the UK.

The Algerian moderate leader Fares shifted from support of Algerian integration with France to support of the National Liberation Front.

September 25

Dr. Anwar of the Saudi Arabian Ministry of Finance said that King Saud was anxious to prevent the Suez crisis from becoming a wedge for Communist penetration into the Middle East. He said the King was also concerned about what would happen, in the event of a shutdown, to

nations whose economies were dependent on the canal for exports of oil and imports of food.

The Jordanian-Israel MAC censured Israel for the attack on the Gharandel police post on September 13.

Fifteen Arab, Asian and African states asked the UN General Assembly to consider the Algerian question in its forthcoming session.

The US Treasury Department disclosed that it was investigating whether regulations barring payment of Suez tolls to Egypt would apply to US owners of vessels flying foreign flags. The effect would be to reduce by one-half the present 35-45 percent of tolls now received by Egypt.

The US formally notified Egypt's Suez Canal Authority that Soviet pilots would not be taken aboard US warships passing through the canal.

A NATO Council, meeting in Paris, was informed by British representatives of the results of the London conference on the Suez Canal.

Mr. Menzies of Australia defended setting up the Suez Canal Users' Association.

"The Voice of the Arabs" radio station in Cairo declared that so long as the Arabs were united, they would become the masters in Palestine, secure victory in Algeria, obtain full liberation in Bahrain, Qatar, Kuwait and Oman, and reaffirm their indisputable rights to the Buraimi Oasis region in Alexandretta and the Suez Canal.

September 26

Israel Foreign Minister Meir told UNTSO Chief Burns that Israel would maintain its pledged ceasefire on the basis of reciprocity.

The UN Security Council voted to include in its agenda the complaint lodged by the UK and France against the Egyptian Government's unilateral action regarding the Suez issue, and Egypt's complaint against the actions against Egypt by some powers, particularly France and the

UK, which constituted a danger of international peace and security and were serious violations of the UN Charter.

Egypt issued a stamp commemorating the July 26 nationalizing of the Suez Canal.

The UK-French talks opened in Paris and were devoted to working out a common stand on the Suez issue.

France and the UK conferred about a possible reversion to a tough policy on Egypt. US Secretary of State Dulles said that Egypt would eventually have to accept a reasonable settlement of the Suez dispute because economic consequences would automatically follow nationalization.

The French Cabinet postponed definition of a new status for Algeria due to the Suez dispute.

The Foreign Minister of Jordan visited Baghdad to seek additional military support.

Five US pilots arrived in Ismailia to work for the Egyptian Suez Canal Authority.

September 27

Minister of State Salam announced that the Government of Lebanon rejected a proposal from the Iraq Petroleum Company for arbitration on the tax dispute.

Iraq said that it would ask Canada to stop delivery of jet planes to Israel.

The International Monetary Fund verified a loan of $15 million made to Egypt the previous week to help it meet payments for wheat and other essential imports. The amount represented the approximate gold and dollar contribution made by Egypt to the fund.

Seven nations—Turkey, Italy, Holland, Australia, Denmark, West Germany and Pakistan—accepted invitations to the third Suez parley called by the West.

The Iraq Development Ministry announced an agreement with Hilton Hotels International to build a Hilton Hotel in Baghdad.

The Arab literary conference at Bloudan, Syria, ended with an appeal to writers all over the world to support Arab national causes, including the Suez, Palestine and Algeria.

US President Eisenhower said in a press conference that Egypt's blockading of the Suez Canal to Israel shipping was against the principles of the 1888 Convention. He expressed hope for the success of the Canal Users' Association.

At the end of long discussions, British Prime Minister Eden, Foreign Secretary Lloyd, French Premier Mollet and Foreign Minister Pineau announced that they planned to continue cooperation during the Suez crisis.

A joint statement issued by India's Prime Minister Nehru and King Saud of Saudi Arabia said that political and economic pressure on Egypt would only retard peaceful settlement of the canal dispute.

UNTSO requested an emergency meeting of the Israel-Jordanian MAC to investigate the latest flareup along the border.

September 28

UN Secretary General Hammarskjold told the Security Council that unless Israel and Arab states showed a will to peace and acted to halt violence, the ceasefire would become a dead letter.

September, 1956

September 28

Moroccan officials refused to comment on reports that the USSR had protested that it had not been invited to the October 8 Tangier conference.

War risk rates on shipments through the Suez Canal were reduced 50 percent.

The Societe Nationale de Recherche de Petrole en Algerie announced that oil was struck in the Algerian Sahara, 62 miles from Ouargla.

Minister of State Salam said that Lebanon welcomed the proposed laying by Iraq of pipelines across Lebanese territory to the sea. He emphatically approved diversion of the Kirkuk-Haifa pipeline from Mafrak, Jordan, to Dison, Lebanon.

September 29

Iraq and Kuwait agreed to unify their oil policies.

Egyptian airport traffic control officials threatened to boycott planes of any country taking part in any aggression against Egypt over the Suez Canal.

Sultan Muhammad V of Morocco urged the establishment of firm relations between the French and Algerians that would give satisfaction to the aspirations of the Algerian people for liberty, and at the same time respect the superior interest of France and guarantee the interests of the French who had chosen to live in Algeria.

The Egyptian Government signed an agreement with the USSR for an additional 200,000 tons of wheat, to be paid for in Egyptian currency.

Ten American pilots were reported to be training for the Egyptian Suez Canal Authority.

September, 1956

September 30

The British Foreign Office said that all 18 nations invited to the October 1 Users' Association Conference had accepted. Japan, Pakistan and Ethiopia would attend without a commitment to join the association. Iran would agree to join on condition that it would not force its way through the Canal.

Lebanon asked that a conference of Syria, Jordan, Egypt and Lebanon meet to coordinate defense measures.

French Premier Guy Mollet declared that the unshakeable French-British solidarity, the certainty that the responsible men of the US were profoundly in agreement with the UK and France on the objectives to be reached made the UK and France confident of their success.

October, 1956

October 1

Israel delegates to the Mixed Armistice Commission walked out of a meeting after the commission chairman had supported Jordan's version of the Ramat Rahel incident of September 23.

Arab children boycotted public primary schools in Algiers in response to a previous request of the National Liberation Front. Elsewhere in Algeria Arab attendance was normal.

Syrian Premier Assali said that his Government would not accept an Iraq Petroleum Company decision to transfer pipelines from Lebanon to Syria to evade the Lebanese retroactive tax law on foreign companies.

A Saudi Arabian spokesman denied reports that a Saudi Arabian delegation representing Saudi Arabian labor unions was among the Arab labor delegations recently visiting Peking.

The Egyptian Canal Authority said that 1,192 ships passed through the Suez Canal in September, as compared with 1,197 for September, 1955.

British Labor leader Gaitskell charged that the British Government had not given a clear assurance that it would not resort to force in the Suez Canal without UN authorization.

A Suez Canal Users' Association was formally inaugurated with a membership of 15 nations. Of the Middle Eastern nations, Pakistan and Ethiopia sent observers to the inauguration but did not join. Iran and Turkey became members.

October 2

Preparation of a new decree which would introduce trial by jury into Moroccan criminal courts for the first time in modern history was announced.

A spokesman of the Indonesian Foreign Ministry announced that Indonesia was opposed to the establishment of the so called Association of Canal Users and held that the Suez issue could not be solved without Egypt's participation.

October, 1956

October 2

The Iraqi Parliament approved a five year industrialization plan to cost about ID454 million ($1,270,000,000).

According to a report from Mexico City, the newspaper Al-Popular published a statement by the Confederation of Latin-American Workers appealing to all the trade unions in that part of the world to solidarize with Egypt on the Suez Canal nationalization issue and condemn the UK and France and the US for interfering in Egypt's internal affairs.

King Zaher Shah of Afghanistan received a message from President Nasser of Egypt thanking him for his country's continuous support during the Suez Canal crisis.

US Secretary of State Dulles said that there were differences of a fundamental nature between the US and its European allies on the Suez Canal question, arising from the independent position of the US on the issue of colonialism.

Jordanian Foreign Minister Abd-al-Hadi left Baghdad after five days of talks on Iraqi military support for Jordan, including the stationing of Iraqi troops in Jordan.

Italy and Libya signed a treaty settling certain mutual problems resulting from Libya's independence.

Fifteen Asian-African nations accused France in the UN of genocide in Algeria.

October 3

Israel announced its intention to boycott further meetings of the Israel-Jordanian Mixed Armistice Commission because of the failure of the commission to distinguish between attacker and attacked.

The French Cabinet approved the transfer from two private companies of 200,000 acres in Algeria to landless, rural, mostly Moslem families. Long term loans and the establishment of planting, harvesting and marketing cooperatives were to be created to assist development of these lands.

October, 1956

October 3

Resident Minister Lacoste reported to the French Cabinet that the pacification campaign in Algeria was making progress despite an apparent intensification of rebel activity.

The Yemeni Minister in Cairo met with the Secretary General of the Arab League to discuss British aggression in Southern Yemen.

Talks between Iraq and Jordan on Iraqi military aid to Jordan were reported to have broken down.

The French and British were described as bitter over US Secretary of State Dulles' linking of the Suez question with colonialism.

Chairman Badawi of the Egyptian Suez Canal Authority arrived in New York for talks with the US oil and shipping executives. He said that his major objective was to seek a larger volume of traffic from the US.

October 4

Egypt cut off local currency issuances to British shipping agents. Under new regulations, all foreign currency transfers in Egypt were required to be approved by exchange control authorities.

Moroccan Foreign Minister Balafrej returned from Paris and said that lack of cohesion in the Moroccan Government was a major obstacle to the signing of a permanent convention regulating Morocco's relations with France.

The Suez Canal Users' Association agreed to set its operating budget at $140, 000 for the first three months, with each member contributing equally.

The head of the Egyptian Suez Canal Authority said that Egypt would not consider any arrangement with a consortium organized to improve the Suez Canal if the arrangement removed the toll collecting function from Egyptian authorities.

Preliminary work began on the construction of the Wadi Hanifah Dam near Riyadh, Saudi Arabia.

October, 1956

October 5

Opposition deputies in the Lebanese Parliament attacked the Government's inept policy of retroactive taxation of foreign companies, claiming that it was losing revenue for Lebanon.

The Iraq Petroleum Company said that its decision to build the new pipeline to the Syrian port of Banias, instead of to the Lebanese port of Tripoli, because of the dispute with the Lebanese Government over taxes, was final and that work had begun on the new link in Syria. The announcement followed a statement by Premier al-Yafi that Lebanon was still ready to negotiate with the IPC for a new pipeline through its territory.

October 6

The Syrian Chamber of Deputies began its new session.

Syrian President Kuwatli said that union between his country and Egypt would become an actuality in the near future.

Jordan announced that it would withdraw permits allowing foreign consuls to pass from Jerusalem through the Mandelbaum Gate to Israel occupied Jerusalem for a week, after which consuls entering the Israel portion of the city would have to apply for entry permits. The step was taken to prevent consuls from carrying unauthorized material into Israel.

Urging a just and peaceful settlement of the Suez question, US Secretary of State Dulles said that the Egyptian Government had seized the Suez Canal to promote the so called grandeur of Egypt by being able to exert economic pressures upon other countries.

Twelve more foreign mariners, including four Russians, passed their final examinations as pilots on the Suez Canal, making a total of 36 accredited to the Canal Authority.

The Iraq Development Board agreed to lend the Ministry of the Interior ID2 million a year for four years to improve rural administration. The loans were without interest and could be paid back over a period of 20 years.

October, 1956

October 4

The UN Conciliation Commission for Palestine reported that, in view of the unchanged attitudes of the parties and their failure to avail themselves of the Commission's services, the Commission had had no opportunity of exercising its general function of conciliation with any prospect of success.

An explosion in an office building in Hamburg, Germany, revealed a large scale arms export business to the Middle East and North Africa.

Qureshi, a Pakistani financial adviser to the Saudi Arabian Government, said that the Suez crisis had not led to any pressure in Saudi Arabia to make American oil companies pay higher royalties and that there was no drive to nationalize the oil properties.

The Jordanian-Israel Mixed Armistice Commission, with Israel absent, censured Israel for planned and unprovoked aggression in the retaliatory raid on Husan on September 25.

October 5

The UN Security Council opened deliberations on the Suez issue.

The Canal Users' Association organizational conference ended without clearly defining the body's functions and purposes. Britain, France, the US, Italy, Iran and Norway were named to the seven member executive group. The seventh seat was left temporarily vacant.

The UK and France submitted a joint resolution to the UN Security Council, asking for endorsement of the principle of international operation of the Suez Canal and recommending that Egypt cooperate by negotiation on the basis of the 18 nation proposals.

US Secretary of State Dulles said that his Government would support the Anglo-French proposal for UN endorsement of a plan for international operation of the Suez Canal.

India's Chief Foreign Affairs Advisor Menon met with President Nasser to discuss the Suez crisis.

Egyptian Foreign Minister Fawzi said that Egypt was in favor of direct negotiations on the Suez question and would press for establishment by the Security Council of a negotiating committee to take up the question.

October, 1956

October 6

The Iraq Petroleum Company dismissed 120 Lebanese employees in its dispute with the Lebanese Government over the law imposing retroactive taxes on foreign oil pipelines.

Iraq and Saudi Arabia raised their diplomatic missions to embassy level.

October 7

Britain urged that the US stop its ships from paying tolls to the Egyptian controlled Suez Authority.

The US and Moroccan Foreign Ministries announced that the US had renounced its extraterritorial treaty rights in Morocco. American residents, like all residents, would be subject to Moroccan justice.

October 8

Iraqi Premier Nuri-Said appealed for a settlement of the Palestine problem through the persuasion of Israel to negotiate with the Arab states on the basis of the 1947 UN partition proposal.

The Sultan of Morocco insisted on noninterference by foreign powers in Tangier's rule by Morocco, stating that he would consult with foreign powers on the best way to safeguard their economic interests in Tangier.

Israel withdrew from the Israel-Jordanian Mixed Armistice Commission.

Egypt and the USSR rejected international operation of the Suez Canal in the UN but said there was room for negotiation on an undefined amount of international participation.

In answer to Egypt's statement before the UN Security Council that it had kept the Suez Canal open to international shipping, Israel charged that Egypt had barred the canal to 103 vessels from at least 14 countries.

October 8

The list included 45 British ships blocked as of February, 1956, 8 ships (US) under Panamanian registry, and smaller lists from other countries including Sweden, Greece and Morocco.

October 9

The Jordanian Ministry of National Economy said that the potash project was not making satisfactory progress; the Arab states were delaying payments for their shares of the capital and appointment of their representatives to the Board of Directors. The deadline for payments was August 7.

The UK renewed an offer, made 11 months before, to formulate a compromise settlement of the Arab-Israel dispute based on the 1947 partition plan and Israel's position at the time of the 1949 armistice.

Replying to Egypt's declaration favoring direct negotiations on the Suez question, US Secretary of State Dulles told the Security Council that there should be a system to insure that the Suez Canal could not be used by any country as an instrument of its distinctly national policy.

The Palestine Conciliation Commission reported that Israel had released 80 percent of the blocked bank accounts belonging to Arab refugees.

Following the Security Council meeting, the Foreign Ministers of Britain, France and Egypt met privately with UN Secretary General Hammarskjold to try to work out a compromise solution to the canal question.

In the UN Security Council, France formally charged Egypt with gun running for the Algerian rebels.

Moroccan Sultan Muhammad V told the Tangier International Control Board that Morocco had just established full and complete sovereignty over all its territory, including Tangier. He said that henceforth he would consider the Board's role to be advisory only.

Jordan lodged complaints with the Jordanian-Israel Mixed Armistice Commission that an Israel plane violated airspace over Jordanian held

October 9

Jerusalem, and that Israel forces opened fire from a Jerusalem border post.

October 10

Tunisian Premier Bourguiba said that he had urged the French to proclaim independence for Algeria as the only basis of negotiation with rebel leaders.

Jordan expelled Archbishop Nersoyan, the second ranking prelate of the Armenian Church in Palestine, for allegedly engaging in politics.

Two Iraqi transport planes carrying arms arrived in Amman, Jordan. The Iraqi Embassy described them as the second consignment sent to Jordan under the 1947 treaty of alliance.

The first consignment of Egyptian arms for Sudan was brought to Khartoum.

Jordanian Foreign Minister Abd-al-Hadi arrived in Cairo to discuss strengthening Jordan's armed forces.

Leader Butler of the British House of Commons said that the Conservative Party was a bit critical of US policy in the Suez dispute.

It was reported from Washington that the US and the UK would approve the stationing of Iraqi troops in Jordan.

October 11

US President Eisenhower said that it was an error to contend that US policy in the Suez crisis had not been clear and firm. He denied any fundamental rift with Britain and France, and declared that a final solution must guarantee that the canal would not be operated for the political purposes of any one single country.

UN Truce Headquarters in Jerusalem confirmed an Israel report that a Jordanian police post at Qalqilya was captured and demolished during the night.

October 11

The West German Minister told the Syrian Foreign Minister that West Germany would sever diplomatic relations with any country that recognized East Germany. The statement referred to a request for the opening of an East German consulate in Damascus.

Most of the 2,500 employees of the Iraq Petroleum Company went on strike after 200 had received dismissal notices at the Tripoli refinery. The company said that the dismissed employees were not needed since the Lebanese Government's attitude prevented planned expansion of the IPC.

October 12

The Governor of the National Bank of Libya returned to Tripoli from the last meeting of the Libyan Currency Commission in London. He said that the National Bank of Libya had taken over all responsibilities and powers of the Commission.

Algerian Nationalist leader Messali called on France to consult with Algerian nationalists on Algeria's future.

After four days of secret meetings with UN Secretary General Hammarskjold, the Foreign Ministers of the UK, France and Egypt agreed on six general principles to govern operation of the Suez Canal. The talks were suspended, however, when no agreement was reached on the means of putting the principles into operation.

US President Eisenhower said that the progress made in the settlement of the Suez dispute at the UN was most gratifying, and that it looked as if a very great crisis was over.

President Eisenhower authorized the Office of Defense Mobilization to make a survey of US tanker needs and, if necessary, to construct more tankers to bypass the Suez Canal.

After an emergency meeting of the Jordanian Cabinet October 11, King Hussein reviewed a request for military aid from Iraq, Syria and Egypt.

October 12

The UK warned Israel orally that it was prepared to fulfill its obligations to Jordan under the 1948 treaty of alliance and mutual defense.

October 13

The UN Security Council refused to hear Israel and Arab views on the Suez Canal issue.

The UN Security Council concluded its deliberations on the Suez issue after unanimously adopting the first part of the UK-French draft resolution (to which the Egyptian representative agreed) and rejecting the second part (to which the Egyptian representative objected). The USSR and Yugoslavia voted against the resolution.

The UK and France urged the Security Council to approve international operation of the Suez Canal.

British Prime Minister Eden declared that force was the last resort and it could not be excluded in the Suez dispute. He said that what was at stake in this dispute was whether the sanctity of contracts was to be respected or not.

Israel submitted a memorandum to the Security Council demanding equal rights with other countries in any plan for revising or reinforcing the 1888 Suez Canal Convention.

Bonn announced that West Germany had recalled its Charge d'Affaires from Syria on the latter's agreement to the opening there of an East German consulate.

A financial pact was signed between Saudi Arabia and Egypt. Under its terms Saudi Arabia would receive $15 million to be used for buying Egyptian goods or for investment in Egypt. The agreement would permit Egyptian investors in Saudi Arabia to transfer profits up to a 15 percent limit of the Egyptian capital invested there.

October, 1956

October 14

The Israel Government expressed alarm and amazement at British military intervention and recalled its ambassadors from Washington, London, Paris and Moscow for consultations on Arab moves to bolster Jordan's defenses.

King Saud received Makkawi, the first Sudanese Minister to Saudi Arabia.

Arab League Secretary General Hassouna said that the six principle resolution adopted by the UN Security Council could be the first acceptable basis for a peaceful solution of the Suez Canal crisis.

The UK asked the US to help start operation of the Suez Canal Users' Association without the completion of organizational details.

October 15

Shareholders of the Suez Canal Company at a general meeting in Paris approved the action taken by the Company since the Egyptian Nationalization Decree.

Jordan requested the Security Council to deal with the situation arising from Israel raids September 25 and October 10-11.

Israel Ambassador Eban conferred with US Secretary of State Dulles on Israel's alarm at the prospect that Iraqi troops might move into Jordan.

Soviet Deputy Premier Mikoyan said that all states, including Israel, should have equally free use of the Suez Canal.

France and Morocco agreed to draw up a new military agreement setting November 12 for negotiations to give French troops a new status.

Egypt's Foreign Minister Fawzi denounced the UK's suggestion of using force as a last resort over Suez. He said that this contradicted the third principle of the Anglo-Franco-Egyptian resolution that the Suez Canal should be insulated from politics.

October, 1956

October 15

Israel Premier Ben-Gurion told the Knesset that Israel reserved freedom of action if Iraqi troops marched into Jordan. He denounced the appeal by Iraqi Premier Nuri-Said for an end to the Palestine dispute on the basis of the 1947 partition proposals as a disguised attack on the integrity of Israel's borders. He appealed for US arms.

October 16

Jordanian Chief of Staff Abu-Nuwar said that British jet aircraft and Iraqi troops were available immediately if Jordan needed them against any Israel aggression. He said that all points of disagreement on the terms of Jordanian-Iraqi cooperation had been settled in talks with an Iraqi military delegation, which were concluded October 15.

Syria announced the shipment of the first installment of heavy weapons into Jordan, and alerted troops under the Syrian-Jordanian Defense pacts in case of an attack by Israel.

US Secretary of State Dulles said that the US stood by its pledge to oppose aggression in the Middle East and to assist victims of aggression.

Sudan returned Gambela, a frontier trading station on the Ethiopian border, to Ethiopia.

October 17

Israel Premier Ben-Gurion called Egypt's President Nasser Israel's "number one peril" in a speech to the Knesset. The Knesset voted down resolutions to commit Israel to military action in the event of Iraqi troops entering Jordan. The Israel Premier received a 76-13 vote of confidence.

President Nasser said that the USSR was willing to give Egypt long term loans to build the Aswan High Dam, but that a decision on the loans would be deferred until he visited Moscow.

October, 1956

October 17

Israel submitted a counter complaint to the Security Council accusing Jordan of persistent violations of the 1949 Palestine Armistice Agreement.

The UK announced that its newest jet fighters would reinforce the RAF squadron stationed in Jordan.

A committee of the Council of Europe proposed a new international body to run the Suez Canal in accordance with the 1888 Convention. Voting rights would be decided on the basis of shipping tonnage using the Suez Canal and the extent of dependence of a nation's economy on canal traffic.

France's Ambassador to the US said that the Suez dispute could be settled only by international operation, unless Egypt devised a more efficient system. He said that an efficient system must apply the six principles, be accompanied by a system of operation or sanctions in case of violation, and guarantee the rights of all powers concerned.

The French National Assembly began a new debate on Algeria's future, but without new proposals.

Tunisia announced that it would take control of its Algerian border away from French troops to prevent Algerian-French fighting from spreading to Tunisia. French units would be replaced by Tunisian Army and National Guard units.

October 18

French officials at Oran claimed to have proof that the Egyptian Government was supporting the Algerian rebels. They announced seizure of a ship carrying arms, which they said were loaded at Alexandria under the supervision of an Egyptian naval officer.

The Arab League reaffirmed unanimous support of Egypt in the Suez dispute.

A leading British civil engineer said that if the Aswan Dam were built, it would become a dwindling asset because of silt.

October, 1956

October 18

Libya told the UN Security Council that any French-British action against Egypt over nationalization of Suez would cause trouble in the Middle East.

Yemeni tribesmen clashed with a British convoy en route from Salah to Aden.

In response to an appeal by Lebanese President Chamoun, the striking Iraq Petroleum Company employees in Tripoli returned to work.

In a letter to the Security Council, Secretary General Hammarskjold warned that Israel was jeopardizing the Palestine armistice by dealing with border incidents without UN supervision.

The eight nation conference on integration of Tangier opened in Fedala attended by representatives of Belgium, the UK, France, Italy, Holland, Portugal, Spain and the US. Sultan Muhammad V, in the opening address, emphasized that the only purpose of the conference was to discuss ways of safeguarding foreign as well as Moroccan economic interests in the exclusively Moroccan city. The Moroccan Foreign Ministry announced that the Tangier conference had unanimously accepted the report of its committee on concessions and communications in the Tangier Zone.

The Council of the Suez Canal Users' Association held its first meeting in London.

October 19

A conference of Arab chambers of commerce opened in Tripoli, Lebanon. Its agenda included a discussion of the principle of nationalization.

Six persons were killed on the Sudanese-Ugandan border in another clash of mutineers against the Government authority and the Sudanese Defense Force.

Israel Foreign Minister Meir told American Jewish communal leaders that the entry of Iraqi troops into Jordan would be a new and grave threat to Israel security.

October, 1956

October 19

At a Security Council meeting on the Palestine question, Jordan called upon the Council to impose diplomatic and economic sanctions against Israel.

Soviet Foreign Minister Shepilov denied that his country was considering financing the Aswan Dam in Egypt.

Bartels, Danish Consul General in New York, was named Administrator of the Suez Canal Users' Association.

France seized an Egyptian ship off the coast of Algiers which was allegedly loaded with arms for Algerian rebels. France demanded an explanation from Egypt.

The nine power conference on the abolition of international rule over Tangier agreed on the status of Tangier's civil servants and the compensation to be paid to those who would lose their jobs because of the integration of Tangier with Morocco. The US accepted the principle of Moroccan monopoly of communications in Tangier in a new formula which stipulated that existing installations, including the Voice of America relay station, could continue operations pending regularization of their statutes.

October 20

Referring to the shipment of arms seized by the French, which allegedly came from Egypt, the Egyptian Embassy said that the international situation of Egypt did not permit it to deprive itself of modern weapons.

The Tangier Conference adjourned after reaching general agreement on a formula for liquidating the zone's international status. No agreement was reached concerning the economic status of Tangier.

Four new British jets arrived in Amman, Jordan.

Authorities in Jordan warned the public that voting in the elections for Parliament October 21 and thereafter would have to be peaceful. Voters were forbidden to carry arms and were told not to demonstrate or gather in groups after voting, but to return to work.

October, 1956

October 21

Five major leaders of the Algerian revolt conferred with Sultan Muhammad V in Morocco.

The Iraq Petroleum Company said that it had dropped its plan to build a pipeline to Tripoli, Lebanon, because of the Lebanese Government's refusal to arbitrate the tax dispute. It stated that work had already begun on a new link to Banias, Syria, instead.

October 22

The French seized five top Algerian rebel leaders en route to Tunis after their conference with the Sultan of Morocco in Rabat October 21. The five leaders were on their way to a conference with French and Moroccan officials on the Algerian situation.

Anti-French riots began in Tunisia.

The protocol for the second year of the Chinese-Egyptian long term trade agreement and a new payments agreement was signed in Cairo.

Results of the election of 35 out of 40 members of the Jordanian Parliament indicated that the majority would be anti-Western. The pro-Egyptian National Socialist Party emerged with the largest bloc of seats and at least three Communists were elected.

October 23

The October 22 arrest of five Algerian rebel leaders by the French resulted in widespread rioting in Morocco.

A proclamation by the Neo-Destour Party of Tunisia condemned the French arrest of the five Algerian leaders as a violation of international law.

Military leaders from Egypt and Syria arrived in Amman for talks with Jordanian military leaders.

Lebanon instructed its UN delegation to work for the inclusion of Algeria on the General Assembly agenda opening November 12.

October, 1956

October 23

The UK and France agreed to reject vague Egyptian advances toward a reopening of the Suez negotiations as having no real foundation.

October 24

In a letter to Mr. Mahmoud Fawzi, Egyptian Minister of Foreign Affairs, UN Secretary General Hammarskjold presented a broad outline for general operation of the Suez Canal. He emphasized the Constantinople Convention and the principle of organized cooperation between Egyptian authorities and users of the canal.

French Premier Mollet won a 330-140 vote of confidence in the National Assembly on his Algerian policy. All 140 opposing votes came from the Communist Bloc.

Muhammad Khider, one of the five arrested Algerian rebel leaders, reportedly told the French police that the income of the committee directing the over all rebel strategy came largely from Arab League grants.

Jordanian Chief of Staff Abu-Nuwar said that Jordan had accepted the principle of over all Egyptian command in case of war. He added that this applied only to strategic command.

It was reported from Washington that the US Government had set aside funds in the 1957 foreign aid program in anticipation of Moroccan and Tunisian requests for aid to supplant French support.

Deputy Director of the Suez Canal Authority, Yunis, said that 233 foreign pilots were working in the Suez Canal, about 180 of them fully qualified and the rest in training.

Diplomatic relations between Saudi Arabia and Japan were established.

India released a revised plan for operation of the Suez Canal in an attempt to reopen negotiations between Egypt and the Western powers.

October, 1956

October 25

Jordan, Egypt and Syria signed a military agreement putting Egypt's Minister of War Amer in charge of their armed forces in the event of war.

Ten British tanks and a quantity of arms, part of a consignment of military equipment purchased by the Government of Iraq, arrived in Basra, Iraq.

Israel assured the UN Security Council that it would never start a war, but that it would not sit back and suffer the consequences of a unilateral Arab belligerency.

More rioting swept Morocco and Tunisia. At least nine Europeans were killed in Meknes, adding to the previous toll of 31. The French Ambassadors to both countries resigned.

Jordanian King Hussein announced that the National Socialists had gained 11 seats in the recent elections, thus becoming the largest party in the 40 member House of Representatives.

The Council of the Suez Canal Users' Association held its second meeting in London.

Five Egyptian Vampire jet fighters were presented to the Royal Jordanian Air Force.

October 26

A rumor that Jordan's King Hussein had been assassinated proved to be false.

France appealed to the Security Council to take up its charges that Egypt had been supplying military aid to Algerian rebels.

Moroccan Premier Bekkai's Government resigned. The Sultan immediately called on Bekkai to form a new cabinet.

October 27

Israel partially mobilized its army reserves.

Millionaire tanker fleet owner, Onassis, presented the Egyptian Government with a formal application to lay a 120 mile pipeline along the Suez Canal from Port Tawfiq to Port Said. The line would be capable of handling 150, 000 barrels of oil a day. According to Onassis, the cost per ton of moving oil through the pipeline would be about one-half the present Canal tolls for tankers.

The US said that it was continuing its $40 million aid program for Egypt despite the Suez dispute.

It was reported from Washington that foreign aid shipments to Egypt, halted briefly because of the Suez crisis, had been resumed.

Al-Azhari, President of Sudan's National Unionist Party and former Premier, and Umma Party President al-Mahdi condemned French policy in Algeria.

Moroccan Premier Bekkai formed a new government. The Istiqlal Party took the portfolios of Foreign Affairs, Interior and National Economy. Total Istiqlal ministries were eight out of fourteen, the remaining six being given to independent or nonparty ministers. The opposition Democratic Independence Party was eliminated from the Cabinet.

Jordan's King Hussein called on Nabulsi of the National Socialist Party to form a government.

Tunisian civilians and irregular forces clashed with French troops in five places in Tunisia because of the French arrest of five Algerian rebel leaders.

October 28

Jordan's Government announced that a number of reserve battalions had been mobilized and stationed along the borders of neighboring Arab states as a precautionary measure and to safeguard the security of Israel's borders and border settlements.

October 28

The UK denied having planned exploratory talks with Egypt and France over the Suez crisis after the opening of the UN General Assembly.

The five captured Algerian rebel leaders were transferred to Paris for trial by a military tribunal.

Saudi Arabia's King Saud sent telegrams to the Sultan of Morocco and the Bey of Tunis expressing concern over the arrest by France of the five Algerian nationalist leaders on their way to Tunisia.

Demonstrators in Jordanian held Jerusalem burned the French Consulate in protest against the arrest of five Algerian nationalist leaders.

A 24 hour general strike in Egypt, protesting the French arrest of the five Algerian leaders, halted all normal business.

King Saud contributed SR1 million for the families of Algerian war victims. Committees were formed throughout Saudi Arabia to collect contributions for Algeria.

Israel mobilized army reserves on its borders. US President Eisenhower warned Israel Premier Ben-Gurion against taking any forceful initiative in the Middle East.

Soviet arms equipment sent to Egypt during the last 14 months under the Egyptian-Czechoslovakian arms deal had reportedly helped to create the strongest Egyptian Army in modern times.

October 29

Jordanian Premier Nabulsi formed a new Cabinet.

British ships sailed from Malta.

US nationals were instructed to leave Egypt, Syria, Jordan and Israel, unless compelled to remain.

British subjects were advised to leave Egypt and Jordan.

October 29

An Israel force invaded the Sinai Peninsula, allegedly to eliminate fedayeen bases, and speared to within 20 miles of Suez before halting.

Ben-Youssef proposed a sacred union with Tunisian President Bourguiba calling for a settlement of differences and a reuniting of the Neo-Destour Party.

Egypt's high command said that no clash had taken place between Egyptian and Israel forces.

The US asked for an emergency meeting of the Security Council to deal with the new threat of war in the Middle East caused by Israel's advance into the Sinai Peninsula.

International control of Tangier ended with the signing of the formal act of the Tangier Conference. Under the act, the nine foreign powers attending the conference renounced all rights and left the Moroccan Sultan to determine what special privileges, if any, would be enjoyed by foreign citizens.

In the Security Council, France charged that Egypt was shipping contraband to the Algerians.

The French Government formally charged the five Algerian rebels with treason, an offense punishable by death. Algerians being French citizens were subject to charges of treason.

October 30

Israel forces were reported within 20 miles of Suez on a 70 mile front. The capture of Quseima was announced.

The Iraqi Government officially announced that its forces were ready to help Egypt to repulse Israel's aggression.

The Security Council resolution calling upon Israel to refrain from the use of force in Suez was vetoed by France and the UK.

Aerial warfare commenced between Israel and Egypt.

October 30

Jordan appealed to the Security Council to immediately stop Israel's invasion of Egypt.

Cairo's International Airport was closed to commercial flights until further notice.

The West German Government asked its missions in Cairo, Damascus and Amman to evacuate German citizens from dangerous Middle Eastern areas.

British Prime Minister Eden announced in the House of Commons that the British and French had issued a joint ultimatum to Egypt and Israel to halt fighting and withdraw to positions ten miles from the Suez Canal within 12 hours. If the ultimatum was rejected, British and French troops would intervene and move into key positions at Port Said, Ismailia and Suez.

Premier Mollet informed the French National Assembly of the British-French ultimatum.

Egyptian President Nasser said that the British-French ultimatum could not in any way be accepted. He ordered general mobilization.

Cairo reported that British and French planes bombed targets and large cities in Egypt in an attempt to force Egypt to evacuate its troops from the Suez.

The US protested to the UK and France against their ultimatum to Egypt, and said that it was prepared to stop economic aid to Israel until that state withdrew its troops from Egyptian soil.

As a result of the Israel attack on Egypt, King Saud ordered general mobilization in Saudi Arabia and called on all Arab heads of state to prepare their armies to oppose Israel's attack.

King Saud of Saudi Arabia sent a telegram to US President Eisenhower thanking him for the announcement that the US would stand by the country subjected to aggression in the Israel-Egyptian fighting.

October 30

Amid rising tension in Jordan over the Israel attack on Egypt, the French community in Amman moved to Beirut and British RAF (Royal Air Force) personnel were moved to Mafraq. Jordan assured Egypt of support.

The UK and France vetoed two separate US and Soviet resolutions in the UN calling for an immediate ceasefire between Israel and Egypt. The reason given was that the UN could not act quickly enough to deal with the conflagration.

Canada decided to delay shipment of 24 jet fighters to Israel until the UN decided whether or not Israel was guilty of aggression against Egypt.

Tunisia declared that France's act of bad faith in the kidnapping of the five Algerian rebel leaders was proof that France was not prepared to seek a settlement in Algeria.

Syrian President Kuwatli left for a ten day visit to the USSR. He was accompanied by Defense Minister Abd-al-Hasib Raslan, Foreign Minister Salah Bitar, Agriculture Minister Rashad Jabri and financial and military experts.

An Egyptian communique stated that British aircraft had bombed Cairo, Alexandria, Port Said and Ismailia. British Foreign Secretary Selwyn Lloyd declared that the air operations were being strictly limited to military targets, with the objective of achieving Egyptian compliance with the British-French demand that Egypt withdraw from the Suez Canal with the minimum loss of life and the minimum destruction.

October 31

After shelling Haifa for several hours, the Egyptian warship Ibrahim Awal was captured by Israel forces in Haifa Bay and brought into port.

The US sent aid to Israel.

The Security Council adopted a Yugoslavian resolution calling for an emergency session of the General Assembly as provided for in the "Uniting for Peace" resolution of November 3, 1950.

October 31

France and the UK attacked the Suez Canal area, ignoring UN efforts to avert warfare.

The USSR Government's statement on armed aggression against Egypt by Israel was published.

Syria's President Kuwatli arrived in Moscow on an official visit at the invitation of the Presidium of the USSR Supreme Soviet and K. Y. Voroshilov.

Indonesian Premier Ali Sastroamidjojo cabled the Premiers of India, Ceylon, Burma and Pakistan on the aggression against Egypt. A Foreign Ministry spokesman branded the UK-French-Israel attack as open aggression.

An Israel communique said that Egyptian forces in the Sinai Desert had been virtually engulfed and that mobile Israel armored forces had penetrated the ten mile neutralized zone near the Suez Canal.

Israel agreed to the British-French ultimatum, provided that Egypt responded affirmatively.

The British House of Commons, by a majority of 52, endorsed the UK Government's intervention in the Suez, if necessary. Foreign Secretary Lloyd asserted that because the Security Council was blocked by the Soviet veto, the UK and France had to protect peace and property in the Suez. He denied that collusion existed between the UK, France and Israel before the Israel attack.

The French National Assembly approved by a vote of 368-182 the ultimatum to Egypt and Israel that was expected to lead to French-British occupation of Suez within a few hours.

India's Prime Minister Nehru denounced Israel, France and the UK for aggression against Egypt and expressed appreciation of US efforts to keep the war from spreading. The USSR also branded the three countries as aggressors.

October 31

The Sudanese Cabinet held an emergency meeting to debate Anglo-French aggression against Egypt. Premier Khalil said that the ultimatum addressed to Egypt was a violation of international law.

Lebanon's President Chamoun invited all Arab heads of state to an urgent meeting to discuss Israel's attack on Egypt. Lebanon and Jordan declared states of emergency.

Iraq proclaimed martial law.

Jordan proclaimed a state of emergency, imposed press censorship and declared general mobilization.

General Sir Charles Keightley was appointed Commander in Chief of Allied Forces for intervention in Egypt.

President Nasser ordered general mobilization in Egypt.

President Eisenhower said that the US would not become involved in the Middle East hostilities, but that disapproval of actions taken in the Middle East did not lessen US friendship with the countries involved.

Replying to US President Eisenhower's message, Israel Prime Minister Ben-Gurion said that Israel was indebted to the American President for his constant efforts to ease the tension in the Middle East, but that President Nasser had created a unified command of Jordan and Egypt for the purpose of destroying Israel and that the Israel Government felt morally obliged to defend its people.

The UN Security Council, by a vote of 7-2 called an emergency meeting of the General Assembly to debate actions undertaken against Egypt.

British and French troops on Cyprus were ready to move into Egypt immediately if the order for such action was given.

The US suspended plans to supply the UK and France with oil in the event that their supplies from the Middle East were cut off.

October 31

Canada announced suspension of all shipments of arms to Israel. The West German Government debated halting all deliveries to Israel under the 1952 restitution agreement.

A special envoy from France to Morocco, with the mission of trying to heal the breach between the two countries, left Morocco without having seen Sultan Muhammad V.

November, 1956

November 1

The USSR Committee of Asian Solidarity, meeting in Moscow, issued a statement condemning the criminal action of the UK, France and Israel against Egypt.

Indian Prime Minister Nehru sent a telegram to the UN Secretary General condemning the Anglo-French invasion of Egypt.

Soviet Premier Nikolai Bulganin sent US President Eisenhower a letter on the Middle East crisis.

Jordan broke off diplomatic relations with France. Premier Nabulsi told the UK that Jordan would not allow British forces to use its bases for attacks on Egypt or any other Arab state.

Iraq ordered full mobilization, following the declaration of martial law, in readiness for any Israel attack on Jordan.

Censorship went into effect in Beirut, Lebanon.

The Anglo-French Joint Command announced that more than 50 Egyptian airplanes were believed to have been destroyed on the ground and 40 others seriously damaged in two days of bombing raids on Egyptian airports.

The British Admiralty announced that a British cruiser had sunk an Egyptian frigate in the Gulf of Suez at the southern entrance to the Suez Canal.

November, 1956

November 2

The UN General Assembly adopted a resolution for a ceasefire in Egypt by a vote of 64-5. The Asian-African Bloc then appealed to Secretary General Hammarskjold to deal with the situation.

British Prime Minister Eden told the House of Commons that the UK and France both rejected the General Assembly's call for a ceasefire.

French Foreign Minister Pineau hurried to London to consult with UK Prime Minister Eden on a way to complete the occupation of the Suez Canal before a UN ceasefire could go into effect.

Israel's Ambassador to the UK Elath said that Israel would not withdraw its forces from Egypt until it was guaranteed freedom from further Egyptian attacks.

Syria informed the US State Department that it had placed its armed forces under Egyptian command, according to the terms of the Syrian-Egyptian defense pact.

A detachment of British troops arrived in Bahrain.

A protest demonstration against the Anglo-French intervention in Egypt resulted in some damage to British establishments in Bahrain.

All public meetings, demonstrations and strikes were banned in Kuwait. The order cancelled a mass meeting called for November 3 to seek removal of all British subjects from Kuwait.

In Yemen, Imam Ahmad issued a proclamation calling for volunteers to join Egyptian forces opposing the British-French invasion. A recruiting center opened in Sanaa.

President Nasser announced that Egyptian forces in the Sinai Desert had completed their withdrawal safely.

The US State Department revealed that minor military shipments to Israel had been stopped.

A four hour general strike was staged in Tunisia to show national support of Algerian independence. Tunisia gave full moral support to Egypt and

November, 1956

November 1

Britain was divided on the intervention in Egypt; Laborites and students bitterly attacked it. Ceylon, Indonesia and India condemned the UK, while Australia called the move necessary. UK Prime Minister Eden said that the UK and France would welcome eventual assumption of control of the Suez Canal area by the UN, but only after Israel and Egyptian forces had been separated and the situation in the area was stabilized. The House of Commons voted 324-255 in support of Eden's policy.

President Nasser of Egypt promised his people that he would fight with Egypt for its freedom to the last drop of his blood.

The US proposed a ceasefire in Egypt and the withdrawal of Israel forces behind the Egypt-Israel armistice line. This proposal was made at the opening of an emergency UN General Assembly session.

An Israel Foreign Ministry statement declared that Israel took the opportunity to assure other Arab countries with which it shared borders that it wished now, as in the past, to live with them in peace and quiet. If attacked by another Arab state, Israel would strike back, but would not be the first to attack.

Israel forces captured the town of Rafah in the Gaza Strip.

November 2

President Nasser announced the seizure of all property at the British bases on the Suez Canal.

Gaza fell to Israel. The Israel Government announced that its military operations were practically completed.

Syria broke diplomatic relations with the UK and France.

Egypt's Major General Muhammad Fuad Al-Dajawi, Eighth Division Commander, surrendered control of Gaza in talks arranged by a UN truce observer, US Lieutenant Colonel Robert Bayard.

November, 1956

November 2

denounced the British-French intervention. Resolutions pledged Tunisian support of any UN measures taken to stop the action.

November 3

The US offered the UN a two part plan for peace in the Middle East. It called for the establishment of two committees—one to seek a final settlement of the Palestine dispute, the other to obtain immediate reopening of the Suez Canal.

Strict censorship went into effect in Amman.

Canada proposed the immediate creation of a UN force to obtain and supervise a ceasefire in Egypt.

The UK and France rejected the UN call for a ceasefire and offered the General Assembly a counterproposal designed to bring their independent military action under UN authority.

The Israel Mission to the UN issued a statement declaring that Israel's decision to move into the Sinai Peninsula and the Gaza Strip was that of the Israel Government alone.

It was reported in Beirut that pipelines carrying more than a half million barrels of oil daily from Iraq to the Mediterranean coast had stopped operating and that the Iraq Petroleum Company's three pumping stations in Syria had been blown up.

The Egyptian Government sequestered the Anglo-Egyptian Oilfields Ltd.

A communique from British-French headquarters in Cyprus reported the virtual destruction of the Egyptian Air Force as a fighting unit. The report also said that the emphasis of the allied air attacks had been switched from the airfields of the Egyptian Air Force to the Egyptian Army.

The Iraqi and Jordanian Governments confirmed that Iraqi and Syrian troops had entered Jordan November 1-2.

November, 1956

November 3

The British Minister of State in the Foreign Office resigned because of disagreement with the Government's intervention in Egypt. Prime Minister Eden announced that Britain would guarantee the withdrawal of Israel forces after the Anglo-French occupation of Suez.

Syrian President Kuwatli left Moscow for home.

China protested to the UK and France against the aggression in Egypt.

Heeding the General Assembly call to ceasefire in the Gaza Strip and the Sinai Desert territory, France and the UK announced that they would stop military action.

An Egyptian communique stated that Egyptian forces repelled a British-French invasion of the southern entrance to the Suez Canal.

The USSR pledged assistance to Syria to reinforce the latter's independence. The pledge was made during a reception in Moscow honoring President Kuwatli prior to his return to his own country.

November 4

The US introduced two resolutions to the UN General Assembly embodying long range solutions of Suez and Palestine problems. Neither resolution was adopted.

Israel Army Headquarters announced that all operations in the Sinai Peninsula had stopped. The job was complete and done. The four day battle for Sinai gave Israel control of the passage to the Gulf of Aqaba after an Israel unit had occupied Sharm-el-Sheikh at the entrance to the Gulf, thus breaking the Egyptian blockade of the port of Elath.

An Emergency UNRWA team flew into the Gaza Strip to look after the 215,000 officially certified Arab refugees there. Israel occupation of the strip added 100,000 refugees, previously living on Egyptian relief, to Israel's population responsibility.

November, 1956

November 4

The Government of Sudan declared a state of emergency following the Israel attack on Egypt.

Following a Canadian recommendation, UN Secretary General Dag Hammarskjold urged that the UN set up a command force to supervise a ceasefire in the Middle East.

Soviet notes to the UK and France accused the two countries of being aggressors and violators of international agreements, and protested their closing of ports of the Mediterranean and Red Seas to commercial shipping.

President Kuwatli, returning to Syria from Moscow, declared that his country had plenty of arms. However, Syria denied being the center of a Soviet arms buildup. Kuwatli described his talks with Soviet leaders as more than successful.

The US Government tried to allay fears of increased Soviet military development in Syria.

A Syrian source announced that 20,000 members of Syria's regular forces were already mobilized in Jordan.

A top Algerian rebel commander, Ajoul, surrendered to French authorities and urged his followers to rally to France. He called the Algerian conflict profitless.

The UN General Assembly adopted a Canadian resolution requesting the UN Secretary General to produce within 48 hours a plan for an emergency international UN force to secure and supervise hostilities in the Middle East. The vote was 57-0-19. Abstentions included the UK, France, Israel and Egypt. Egypt later accepted the resolution and stated readiness to cease military operations by 8:00 pm.

November, 1956

November 5

A joint Syrian-USSR communique on the talks held by the leaders of the two countries was published.

Thousands of Moscow workers held protest demonstrations in front of the UK, French and Israel Embassies. Demonstrations of solidarity and friendship were held in front of the Egyptian Embassy.

The UN General Assembly passed a resolution, 57-0-19, establishing an international emergency police force command to end hostilities in Egypt. UNTSO Chief of Staff Burns was named Chief of Staff of the new command. The resolution stipulated that participants in the command could not come from the permanent Security Council members.

Israel informed UN Secretary General Hammarskjold that it had unconditionally accepted the UN ceasefire and that Israel-Egyptian fighting had halted.

The UN rejected a Soviet suggestion that a US-Soviet force be sent to Egypt to stop the fighting.

Egypt reported acceptance of the ceasefire and the international police force voted by the General Assembly.

British and French paratroops landed in Port Said, Egypt. Surrender terms were accepted by the local Egyptian commander, but later rejected by Cairo.

The British and French Governments replied to the UN welcoming the idea of an international police force.

Soviet notes were sent to the British and French Prime Ministers calling for immediate cessation of Anglo-French aggression in Egypt and alluding to the possible use of rocket weapons against the UK and France.

The UK and France announced that all bombings would stop forthwith throughout Egypt and that air action would be limited to supporting necessary operations in the Suez Canal Zone.

November, 1956

November 5

The US warned the Soviet Union that it would oppose any effort by the USSR to intervene by force in the Middle East, and termed unthinkable Premier Bulganin's proposal that the US join the Soviet Union in a bipartite employment of military forces to stop the fighting in Egypt.

The USSR announced that it was recalling its ambassador to Israel and told Israel to duly evaluate this warning.

The Afghanistan Cabinet, in an extraordinary session, reaffirmed the Government declaration of November 1 calling the attention of the UN to the Anglo-French-Israel attack on Egypt as a violation of the UN Charter.

The Lebanese Government rushed reinforcements to the Tripoli area after an oil pipeline there was cut.

Tapline, the oil pipeline running from Saudi Arabia to Sidon, Lebanon, remained in operation.

Leaders of the Baghdad Pact countries, except for the UK, met in Tehran to discuss the Middle East crisis.

November 6

Anglo-French amphibious assault forces landed at Port Said and Port Faud.

Israel announced the end of the Sinai campaign and claimed that Sinai, up to a ten mile buffer zone before Suez, was Israel's.

The USSR Ambassador A. N. Abramov left Israel in accordance with the decision of the USSR Government.

A British Foreign Office spokesman said that the UK wanted Israel to withdraw its troops at once.

The UK and France agreed to a ceasefire in Egypt.

British-French ground troops landed on Egyptian soil and advanced south toward Ismailia.

November, 1956

November 6

British Prime Minister Eden told the House of Commons that the UK and France had agreed to put the ceasefire into effect immediately and to halt the advance of troops, as called for in the November 2 General Assembly resolution.

Israel Prime Minister Ben-Gurion said that his country was ready at all times to make peace with Egypt and that if Nasser wished peace, let him send his authorized representatives to meet Israel representatives and there would be peace.

The total number of volunteers from Yemen for Egypt reached 21,179.

Egypt broke diplomatic relations with Australia.

Saudi Arabia broke diplomatic relations with the UK and France. Orders were issued to those concerned forbidding oil to be shipped or supplied to British or French ships or to ships that carried Saudi Arabian oil to these two countries.

The National Union Committee in Bahrain was dissolved, and four of its members were detained.

Nineteen Asian and African nations submitted a joint draft resolution to the UN calling for immediate withdrawal of British, French and Israel forces from Egypt.

The USSR warned the UK, France and Israel of its preparation to use force to restore peace in the Middle East.

The Security Council refused to hear a Soviet suggestion that a military force, including American and Soviet troops, go to Egypt.

Moscow Radio broadcasted an appeal from the Egyptian Government for aid and volunteers in its fight against the UK and France. An Egyptian Embassy spokesman said that a number of Soviet reserve officers had applied to the Embassy and were accepted.

UN Secretary General Hammarskjold presented his plan for the UN command to police the Egyptian battle area from the Suez Canal to the Egyptian-Israel armistice line.

November, 1956

November 7

It was reported from Baghdad that oil was discovered in the central part of the country near the Habbaniya Air Base. The territory was under concession to the Mosul Petroleum Company, a subsidiary of the Iraq Petroleum Company.

Morocco and Tunisia became members of UNESCO.

November 8

UN Secretary General Hammarskjold appointed the first salvage firms to clear the Suez Canal.

USMC (US Marine Corps) Leary was named Acting Chief of Staff of the UNTSO, filling the vacancy created by the appointment of Major General Burns as Chief of the new UN Command in the Middle East.

Burns arrived in Cairo and reported that Egypt had agreed to permit a team of ten UN observers to supervise the ceasefire in the Suez Canal area.

The Chinese Communist Government issued a statement supporting Egypt.

Israel agreed to withdraw its troops from Egyptian territory in response to a UN resolution but did not mention specific territory such as the Gaza Strip or two islands in the Gulf of Aqaba.

Israel Prime Minister Ben-Gurion replied to USSR Premier Bulganin's message of November 5 and to US President Eisenhower's note of November 7.

A motion of nonconfidence in the Ben-Gurion Government, moved by the Herut Party in criticism of the policy to withdraw Israel troops from Sinai and to accept an international police force, was defeated 66-13.

Israel claimed that Arab fedayeen from Jordan had crossed the border and attacked an installation near Shaar Hagai.

November, 1956

November 6

The Grand Mufti of Jordan, Sheikh Qalqili, urged a holy war against Britain, France and Israel.

November 7

By a vote of 64-0-12, the General Assembly adopted a seven power resolution designed to speed completion of the proposed UN force to supervise the ceasefire in Egypt.

The UN General Assembly, by a vote of 65-1-10, called for a British-French-Israel withdrawal from Egypt.

US President Eisenhower sent a cablegram to Prime Minister Ben-Gurion of Israel urging him to comply with the UN resolution of November 4 calling for the withdrawal of troops from Egypt.

Israel Prime Minister Ben-Gurion rejected the General Assembly resolution calling for the withdrawal of troops.

British Prime Minister Eden said that until the UK and France were convinced that a UN police force would be effective, there was no question whatever of the withdrawal of the UK or its allies from Egypt.

The UN General Assembly adopted a resolution setting up an Advisory Committee under the chairmanship of Secretary General Hammarskjold to develop those aspects of the planning and operation of the UNEF not already dealt with by the Assembly.

British and French troops ceased fire in Egypt and stopped their advance on the Suez Canal zone. They were reported 30 miles south of Port Said.

Peking Radio announced that 280,000 Chinese had volunteered for military service in Egypt. The USSR also was reported receiving volunteer requests.

The Jordanian Government sent a note to the USSR thanking it for its positive stand on Arab problems.

November, 1956

November 8

President Nasser sent a message of congratulations to Soviet President Voroshilov on the thirty-ninth anniversary of the Bolshevik Revolution.

France reported the presence of jet planes in Syria.

Baghdad Pact members Turkey, Pakistan, Iraq and Iran condemned Israel aggression and called on Israel, British and French forces to withdraw from Egypt.

The British War Office announced that British Army personnel attached to the Jordanian Army would temporarily discontinue their technical and advisory duties in Jordan.

France barred all Egyptians from leaving the country.

Indonesia announced that it would participate in the UN emergency police force for the Middle East.

Fighting in the Suez Canal area ceased. British-French forces were fixed at the ceasefire line at El-Cap, about 20 miles south of Port Said.

The Tunisian Government banned publications of La Presse de Tunisie, the country's leading French newspaper, for an indefinite period.

Shops in Kuwait began refusing to serve British and French customers. Schools were closed. Contributions totaling $1,400,000 were made to the Aid of Egypt Fund.

November 9

Advance units of the UN police force, composed of Danes and Norwegians, started for Egypt.

Egypt agreed provisionally to the formation of a UN police force for the Suez Canal.

President Nasser said that the Egyptian Air Force was intact and that the Army was prepared to continue fighting if the British, French and Israel forces were not withdrawn quickly.

November, 1956

November 9

The UK said that its ground forces would be redeployed in the Eastern Mediterranean after withdrawal from Egypt.

Iraq cut diplomatic ties with France and announced a boycott of any meeting of the Baghdad Pact nations attended by the UK.

Israel announced that raiders from Syria and Jordan had crossed into its territory for the second successive night.

King Saud of Saudi Arabia issued his order to transfer SR2 million to the Egyptian Red Crescent Society to be spent on the victims of the Anglo-French-Israel aggression against Egypt.

Saudi Arabia paid the second installment of money to the Jordanian National Guard, in accordance with the decisions of the Arab Military Conference in Riyadh.

November 10

The first contingent of UN police troops bound for Egypt arrived at Naples from Denmark.

The UN voted to place the Middle East crisis before the regular annual session beginning November 12 as a matter of priority.

The USSR announced that unless British, French and Israel troops were withdrawn from Egypt, it would permit volunteers to join the Egyptian forces.

Jordanian Premier Nabulsi banned the import of all French goods into his country.

Israel Foreign Minister Meir said that the Gaza Strip was an integral part of Israel and that as far as the Strip was concerned, Israel had no intention of withdrawing to the 1949 armistice lines.

King Faisal of Iraq flew to Beirut to attend a meeting of Arab rulers to discuss the Middle East crisis.

November, 1956

November 11

The Egyptian Government issued military orders which classed the British and French as enemy nationals, provided for the confiscation of their assets and prohibited transactions with British and French citizens.

King Saud left Riyadh to attend the meeting of Arab heads of states which was scheduled to begin in Beirut November 12.

An official statement issued by the Sudanese Information Service indicated that the Sudanese Ministry of Finance and Economics issued the necessary instructions to the banks to remove the credit restrictions which had previously been imposed on importers.

The British Government issued a special report that the USSR was in a position to form military units in the Middle East very quickly because of the large quantities of Soviet Bloc arms in Egypt and the presence of a large number of Communist technicians. The report said that in a little over a year President Nasser had received 150 million pounds sterling ($420 million) worth of war materiel from the Communist Bloc, and that 1,000 Soviet Bloc technicians had been sent to Egypt. Syria's Army of 25,000 had received weapons valued at 20 million pounds sterling ($56 million) from the same sources.

November 12

UN Secretary General Hammarskjold announced that Egypt agreed to accept UN troops on its soil.

Egyptian Ambassador to the USSR al-Koni said that more than 50,000 Soviet citizens had volunteered to serve with Egyptian forces.

November, 1956

November 12

An order signed by the Egyptian Third Infantry Division Commander, dated February 15, 1956, captured by Israel, was made public. The order called for a stepped up training program to prepare Egyptian troops for annihilation of Israel in as little time as possible.

French Premier Mollet said that he did not intend to impose an Algerian solution by force and that he was ready to negotiate with the rebels for a ceasefire. He outlined three principles governing French policy in Algeria: equality of rights, political predominance of neither Europeans nor Moslems, and final decisions resting with France.

Egypt accepted the stationing of the UNEF in its territory.

The Iraq Petroleum Company's pipeline southwest of Irbid, northern Jordan, was blown up.

French Premier Mollet said in Paris that the British-French military intervention in Egypt revealed a Soviet intrusion in the Middle East.

The UK announced that it would keep the Suez Canal open after it had been cleared for the benefit of all nations.

The British House of Commons rejected by 321-259 votes a motion of censure of the Government's Suez policy.

King Saud of Saudi Arabia urged US President Eisenhower to take positive action in the Middle East to avert a world war.

Iraq warned the Arab states to avoid any action in the Middle East that might lead to a third world war and particularly stressed the danger of inviting Russian technicians and advisors.

Sudan, Morocco and Tunisia were unanimously elected to membership in the UN.

Sultan Muhammad V inaugurated the first Moroccan Parliament, the National Consultative Assembly. He said that his purpose was to establish a representative system within the framework of a constitutional monarchy, guaranteeing liberty, equality and justice for all individuals and groups. He also said that royal nomination of all 76 members of

November, 1956

November 12

the Assembly must be replaced by popular election. The Assembly elected Ben-Barka of the Istiqlal Executive Committee as its President.

November 13

The Iraqi Government issued a memorandum stating that it was fully convinced that the uprooting of Israel was the only practicable method to secure peace and order in the Middle East.

Israel Foreign Minister Meir called for a round table conference between Israel and the Arab states to establish a lasting peace in the Middle East.

The nine member states of the Arab League met in Beirut. The delegates included King Saud of Saudi Arabia, King Hussein of Jordan, King Faisal of Iraq, President Chamoun of Lebanon, President Kuwatli of Syria and representatives of Egypt, Libya, Sudan and Yemen.

Ten UN observers arrived in Port Said.

The USSR charged the US with military preparations in support of the aggressors in Egypt. The US warned that it would oppose any Soviet intervention in the Middle East.

British, French and Israel leaders asked for clarification of the UN mission before withdrawing troops from Egypt.

The departure of the first contingent of troops for the UN police force in Egypt was postponed.

The local press in Saudi Arabia announced that no payment for cash against documents would be made if the documents were dated later than November 13, 1956. Letters of credit opened before that date would not be affected but subsequent letters of credit were to be opened only with the permission of the Saudi Arabian Ministry of Finance. Essential foodstuffs were exempted from the restriction.

In Tunisia, a government decree amended the penal code to extend jurisdiction of courts to infractions committed in Tunisia. France protested that the decree was a violation of the French-Tunisian agreement of

November 13

June 3, 1955, which put French nationals under the jurisdiction of French courts.

November 14

Official Cairo sources denied that Egypt had asked the USSR for volunteers.

UN Secretary General Hammarskjold left for Egypt to work out plans for the projected UN police force.

President Eisenhower declared that the US would oppose, through the UN, any Soviet military intervention in the Middle East.

Viscount Lord Hailsham of the British Admiralty declared that the UN should call upon the UK to clear the Suez Canal, regardless of the view of President Nasser.

It was reported from New York that the Arabian American Oil Company had complied with Saudi Arabia's demand that no petroleum be shipped to France and the UK.

In Israel, the Knesset voted 66-13 against a motion censuring the Government for its offer to withdraw troops from Sinai. The motion was introduced by the Herut Party.

The Prime Ministers of India, Indonesia, Ceylon and Burma denounced British-French aggression in Egypt.

Employees of the Arabian American Oil Company collected more than SR178,000 for the Egyptian Red Crescent Society. The Company agreed to pay an amount equal to that collected by the employees.

November 15

Nine members of the Arab League threatened to end diplomatic relations with the UK and France unless the two countries immediately withdrew troops from the Suez Canal.

November 15

The representatives of the nine Arab states issued a communique expressing their satisfaction with the measures taken by the General Assembly of the UN regarding British-French-Israel action in Egypt.

Soviet Premier Bulganin sent notes to the UK, France and Israel demanding that their troops be withdrawn without delay from Egyptian territory, and that Egypt be compensated for the destruction caused by their aggression.

Ninety-five Danish and Norwegian riflemen, advance units of the UN police force, arrived at Abu-Suweir, the Egyptian air base near Ismailia.

The British Foreign Office said it had received information that units of the Syrian Army had carried out demolitions of the Iraq Petroleum Company pipeline in Syria. The UK declared that it held the Syrian Government directly responsible for these acts of sabotage and for causing the flow of oil to cease, and it called on Syria to repair the line and insure its continued operation.

Canada suggested that the UN General Assembly take up the question of a permanent settlement of the Suez Canal and Palestine disputes.

November 16

Indian Prime Minister Nehru told the House of the People that all foreign forces ought to be withdrawn from Egypt.

Peres, Director General of the Israel Defense Ministry, listed three conditions for Israel's withdrawal from Sinai and the Gaza Strip: the Strip was not to be used as a fedayeen base, Sinai was not to be remilitarized as an invasion springboard and Israel shippings were to have free access to the Port of Elath.

UN Secretary General Hammarskjold arrived in Cairo to oversee deployment of the UN police force. US, British and French officials agreed that the force should be stationed along the Suez Canal and the Israel-Egypt border.

November 16

The Afghan Embassy in New Delhi announced that Afghanistan had offered troops for the UN police force in the Middle East. It also said that thousands of Afghans were volunteering to fight in Egypt.

Israel turned the municipal administration of Gaza over to Gaza's most recently elected mayor.

US Acting Secretary of State Herbert Hoover, Jr. told the UN General Assembly that the UN would be obliged to take action if Soviet volunteers were sent to the Middle East, and that the US would fully support such action.

The Arab League concluded discussions in Beirut with resolutions to act independently of the UN Security Council in taking any necessary measures against France, the UK and Israel. They agreed that in case of further fighting in Egypt they would apply Article 2 of the 1952 Arab Collective Security Pact.

In a published report, the Israel Government revealed that from January to October 1956, 74 persons had been killed and 209 injured in 93 cases of sabotage and 590 armed clashes with Arabs.

Lebanese President Chamoun accepted the resignation of Premier al-Yafi and his Government.

November 17

The Egyptian Government announced that all British and French citizens in Egypt would be placed in forced residence for their own personal safety.

A trade agreement was signed between Lebanon and Bulgaria under which the two Governments undertook to develop commercial relations. Most favored nation treatment was mutually accorded.

The Syrian Army moved tanks into the outskirts of Damascus, but did not enter the city.

November 18

The Egyptian Government handed UN Secretary General Dag Hammarskjold a note on the refusal of the UK, France and Israel to abide by the UN resolutions of November 2 and 7, 1956, calling for a cease-fire and withdrawal of foreign forces, and demanded their full implementation.

Egypt asked the UN to assist in clearing the Suez Canal of obstructions. The UN police force was increased to 500 with the landing of 150 Scandinavian soldiers.

A Baghdad Pact meeting, excluding the UK, was held in Baghdad.

US Secretary of State Dulles declared that it would be a great mistake to believe that stability and tranquility could be permanently established in the Middle East merely by emergency measures to stop the fighting. It would be necessary, he said, to attack the basic problems of the area.

Israel rejected a Soviet demand that it pay war damages to Egypt. Israel Premier Ben-Gurion said that the invasion was fully justified by Egypt's acts of aggression and its repeated violations of the UN Charter since 1948.

The French reported that the arrest of Omar, political and military rebel chief in Oran Department, had broken the rebel chain of command in Western Algeria.

Moroccan Sultan Muhammad V called on foreign residents to stop fleeing his country. He promised to protect them from mob attack.

The USSR Government made a statement on the disarmament and reduction of international tension in the Middle East and referred specifically to the UK-French-Israel invasion of Egypt as imperialist aggression.

A statement issued by the Jordanian Communist Party was published by the local press for the first time since the banning of Communism.

November, 1956

November 19

According to a France Presse report, Jordan decided to establish relations with the USSR and the Peoples' Republic of China.

UN Secretary General Hammarskjold told a General Assembly advisory committee that he agreed with Egypt that the UN emergency force should leave the Suez Canal Zone after the withdrawal of British and French forces.

The UN began investigating the first truce break, reported when Egyptians fired on Allied positions near al-Cap. Egypt accused France and the UK of brutality against civilians in Port Said.

Canada decided not to send combat troops to Egypt but to provide ferry planes and administrative help.

President Nasser said that there were no volunteers in Egypt and added that Egypt did not ask for Soviet volunteers or troops from any other country.

Israel Army Headquarters reported 171 Israel soldiers killed in the Sinai Peninsula campaign.

Syria complained to the UN that British, French and Israel planes had repeatedly violated Syrian airspace.

A British shipment of armaments was unloaded at Basra, Iraq. This was the second delivery of the year under a contract providing for acquisition by Iraq of almost 3 million pounds sterling ($8, 400, 000) worth of British war materiel.

November 20

The Egyptian Government notified the Swiss legation in Cairo that British and French citizens under house arrest would be permitted freedom of movement and would be given exit visas on request.

Egypt demanded that the UN set up a committee to investigate the barbarous aggression of the UK, France and Israel on Egypt. Egypt charged the three nations with conspiring to attack it.

November, 1956

November 20

Egyptian Foreign Minister Fawzi stated that the continued presence of foreign troops on Egyptian soil precluded every possibility of clearing the Suez Canal of sunken ships.

The Lebanese Army took control of Beirut in the wake of several days of anti-Western demonstrations and bombings, reportedly in protest against Lebanon's refusal to break off diplomatic relations with the UK and France.

Jordan's Parliament unanimously recommended abrogation of the alliance with the UK, recognition of the USSR and Communist China and substitution of Arab aid for the $33, 600, 000 annual British subsidy.

Thirty-five Iraqi Government officials were suspended by the Government Purge Committee.

Acting US Secretary of State Hoover explained that the UN wanted to work through the Organization for European Economic Cooperation to help Europe's emergency oil needs.

UN Secretary General Dag Hammarskjold asked the UK, France and Israel to explain why they had not withdrawn their forces from Egypt.

November 21

Twenty-two Asian and African delegations in the UN sent a communication to the UN Secretary General Hammarskjold, expressing concern for the fate and welfare of the Gaza area population, which included 200, 000 Arab refugees from Palestine, and requesting him to use all the machinery at his disposal to secure immediate withdrawal of Israel troops from the area.

The first UN Emergency Force company arrived at Port Said. A crowd of about 20, 000 Egyptians greeted the arrival of the first UN police force contingent in Port Said with a noisy demonstration.

November, 1956

November 21

UN Secretary General Hammarskjold submitted reports to the General Assembly on his talks with President Nasser concerning regulation of the UN emergency force and clearance of the Suez Canal.

President Nasser said that the Egyptians would never surrender their political and ideological freedom. He also said that Egypt's basic objective was the radical improvement of the economic and social conditions of the Egyptian people, but that this objective could not be advanced until certain highly inflammable problems were solved.

Members of the Baghdad Pact, except for the UK, continued meetings in Baghdad begun November 18. President Mirza of Pakistan left for Saudi Arabia to try to persuade King Saud to join the talks.

France informed the UN that it would withdraw its forces as soon as the Emergency Force could take over control of the Suez. Foreign Minister Pineau said that one-third of the French naval personnel in Egypt had been withdrawn. The UK announced that one of its battalions had left Egypt as a gesture of good faith. Israel stated that its forces had withdrawn along the entire Egyptian front.

Syrian Foreign Minister Bitar reported to UN Secretary General Hammarskjold that Israel, together with the UK and France, was massing troops on the Syrian and Jordanian frontiers. He asked for an immediate examination by the General Assembly.

Israel admitted the presence of French planes and pilots in the recent Sinai campaign.

Iraq's Government declared the entire Kirkuk oil area a military zone, and barred outsiders from entering the Basra oilfields in measures to guard oil installations.

November 22

The British conditions for withdrawal from Egypt were stated in the UK House of Commons.

November, 1956

November 22

The French Assembly voted in favor of ratifying the French-Libyan treaty with the stipulation that ratification should not be deposited until the Algerian-Libyan frontier had been delimited.

Authoritative sources in Cairo reported that the Egyptian Government had begun large scale deportation of all enemy nationals by ordering Zionists, British and French nationals to leave the country.

Brazil approved a law to authorize sending one battalion of troops to the Suez Canal for the UN force.

Rural Affairs Minister al-Latif of Egypt was put in charge of clearing the Suez Canal.

UN Secretary General Hammarskjold asked the General Assembly for $10 million to cover the initial cost of the UN Emergency Force in Egypt.

Major General Burns landed in Cairo to assume command of the UN Emergency Force.

USSR Minister of Foreign Affairs D. T. Shepilov delivered a speech at the plenary session of the UN General Assembly in which he branded the Egyptian-Israel war as an imperialist conspiracy and said that the UN should bar the road to forces of aggression and reaction.

Egypt rejected the UK-French condition that the British and French withdraw from the Port Said area only after the UN police force became effective, and said that Egyptian forces would resume fighting and accept foreign volunteers if the Anglo-French-Israel troops did not leave quickly.

Security authorities in Lebanon linked Egypt's Assistant Military Attache to the bombings and disorders in Beirut, which were considered part of a terrorist campaign to oust the new Government.

US representatives at the UNESCO conference in New Delhi, India, opposed the Arab states' restrictions on travel of persons of Jewish faith engaged in nonpolitical activities.

November, 1956

November 23

French Resident Minister in Algeria, Robert Lacoste, won unanimous confidence of the French Cabinet for his policy of ending the nationalist rebellion mainly by force.

The Moslem members of the Baghdad Pact declared that they would take all necessary measures against subversion in the Middle East and pledged to work in harmony with the UN Charter.

The Syrian Army said that it discovered a plot, allegedly instigated by the Iraqi Government, to "stab Syria and its army in the back."

The Egyptian Government was reported to have begun deporting Jews on charges of collaboration.

In a communication to the General Assembly, UN truce observers reported that they had found no evidence on the Israel side of the Syrian and Jordanian frontiers to support Arab charges that Israel troops were massing along the borders with French and British help.

Soviet Foreign Minister Shepilov demanded the immediate withdrawal of the UK, France and Israel from Egypt. He gave complete endorsement to Egyptian demands that the UN Emergency Force be withdrawn from the Suez Canal Zone after the British-French withdrawal and that it leave Egypt entirely when told to do so by the Egyptian Government. The Asian-African Bloc in the UN supported Shepilov.

November 24

Syrian military authorities claimed the seizure from Iraq of British made arms intended for use against the Syrian Government.

Iraq protested to Syria against Syrian allegations that large quantities of arms seized in Damascus had been sent to Syria by Iraq.

Twenty-one Egyptian students arrived in Moscow to study nuclear physics.

The Eleventh General Assembly of the UN adopted a resolution approving an agreement with Egypt on the stationing of UNEF troops in Egypt. The vote was 65-0-9.

November, 1956

November 24

The UN General Assembly authorized the Secretary General to proceed with negotiations for clearance of the Suez Canal. Mr. Hammarskjold appointed a three member team to direct clearance operations.

The UN, by a vote of 63-5, called on the UK, France and Israel to withdraw from Egypt.

The Saudi Arabian customs tariff was extensively revised with the duties on some goods increased to offset the reduction or exemption from duty of staple foodstuffs and cheaper grades of textiles.

The Egyptian Government confirmed that it was deporting Zionists and British and French citizens.

Israel Ambassador Eban reported to the General Assembly that two Israel infantry brigades had been withdrawn from Egyptian territory into Israel.

The first battalion of troops under the Anglo-French command withdrew from Port Said.

The Moroccan Development Board reported completion of the irrigation of 123,000 acres of government owned land. This was the first part of a project designed to irrigate 741,000 acres to be distributed among smallholders.

November 25

Nearly 20,000 French and British nationals prepared to leave Egypt after having been given a choice between expulsion and internment.

Egyptian Foreign Minister Fawzi said that what Egyptians did with the Suez Canal was Egypt's own business.

The Atlas Construction Company, a US concern working on American air bases in Morocco under a French contract, said that it would cease

November, 1956

November 25

operations December 31. Its contract had not been renewed by the Moroccan Government.

The Egyptian Ministry of Education announced that the administrative and faculty staffs of 45 British and French secondary schools were being replaced by Egyptians.

Major General Burns conferred with British and French commanders in Port Said on the military and logistic aspects of further UN force movement into the Suez Canal area.

The USSR accused Iraq of sponsoring an armed attempt to overthrow the Syrian Government. Moscow claimed that the Syrian High Command had seized a large consignment of Iraqi arms intended for the coup.

November 26

Britain charged that Egypt's expulsion of British and French nationals was a violation of the 1949 Geneva Convention protecting noncombatants. Egypt denied the charge and stated that the nationals had been placed in protective custody because of the people's anger, but were subsequently free to leave.

Iraqi Ambassador Shahbandar asked the US to speed arms deliveries to his country.

The Iraqi Government warned Syria in a note that it would use every possible means to defend itself against attacks by the Syrian Government.

In Lebanon several new loads of arms were discovered by security forces in a roundup of subversive elements.

Ethiopia asked Egypt to recall its Military Attache in Addis Ababa for alleged activities contrary to Ethiopian state security.

November, 1956

November 26

Libyan Premier Ben-Halim told Parliament at its opening session that his Government was attempting to review its obligations under the British-Libyan treaty in the light of new developments. He said that Libya would support any Arab state in the struggle to protect independence.

The General Assembly, by a vote of 52-9, approved a resolution appropriating an initial $10 million for the expenses of the UN emergency police force.

The Israel Army turned over the municipal administration of Gaza to its Mayor Shawa.

November 27

The World Jewish Congress said that Egypt's Rabbi Nahum had resigned in protest against treatment of Jews there.

The Israel delegation to the UN requested the President of the General Assembly to ask Egypt to desist from its inhuman policy of mass deportation of Jews and the closing of Jewish hospitals in Cairo and Alexandria.

Egyptian Foreign Minister Fawzi informed the UN that his Government would ask for sanctions against the UK, France and Israel if they did not give a satisfactory answer as to the date they would complete withdrawal of their troops from Egypt. Egypt added that it was engaged in a full scale buildup of defenses in Cairo and the Suez Canal Zone because of suspicion of British and French intentions.

US President Eisenhower said that the Suez crisis had not weakened NATO or British-French-US relations.

About one-third of the Conservative Party in the British House of Commons assailed the US and the UN for their attitude toward the UK in the Suez crisis.

Al-Solh was named Premier of Lebanon. He formed a new cabinet.

November 27

Settlement was announced of a labor dispute which had delayed the unloading of ammunition for US forces in Morocco.

Major General Burns announced that the UNEF in Port Said would be increased to the size of a battalion and that it would be stationed in Port Said and Port Fuad. The arrival of 160 Indian troops increased the unit to 1,415 men.

November 28

British Foreign Secretary Lloyd said that the difference between Britain and the US on Middle East policy remained unchanged.

Norway charged that Egypt had refused to permit two stranded Norwegian ships to leave the Canal. Egyptian authorities had described the ships as too big to pass an emergency channel opened by the British and French the previous week.

UK Foreign Secretary Selwyn Lloyd said in the House of Commons that the buildup of the UNEF in Egypt must have an important relationship to a phased withdrawal of allied troops.

The Soviet Union suggested that the Israel invaders of Egypt should be tried as war criminals.

The American Jewish Committee charged in Paris that Jews in Egypt were being imprisoned, threatened with expulsion or internment, and faced with loss of citizenship.

Israel Premier Ben-Gurion charged Egypt with imposing a reign of terror on Egyptian Jews. The Knesset adopted a resolution demanding action by the UN to halt the persecution.

UN Secretary General Hammarskjold said that within a fortnight the UNEF would have 4,100 men in Egypt.

Premier Nabulsi told Parliament that Jordan would abrogate the 20 year treaty of alliance with the UK as soon as Egypt, Saudi Arabia and Syria implemented their offer to replace the annual 12 million pounds sterling subsidy.

November 28

The US informed Syria of its concern over reports of substantial Soviet arms shipments.

November 29

A Yugoslavian force of 721 men for the UNEF reached Port Said, Egypt.

A report of the apparent seizure of Anglo-Egyptian Oilfields Ltd., by Egypt, substantiated a November 3 publication in the Journal d'Egypte of a military proclamation providing for sequestration of the company.

The lower house of the Jordanian Parliament backed Premier Nabulsi's plan to terminate the Anglo-Jordanian treaty.

Foreign Minister Menderes of Turkey and Secretary General Burgi arrived in London to discuss their country's concern over the growing Soviet influence in Syria.

Syrian Foreign Minister Bitar denied that his country had bought Soviet arms since the start of hostilities in Egypt in October. He said that Syria had been made the target of a vicious propaganda campaign as preparation for subversion.

Major General Ragheb, Military Commander of the Baghdad Martial Area, warned that strikers and instigators of disorder in Iraq would be severely punished.

A spokesman for the Iranian oil consortium said that the effect of the closing of the Suez Canal had not been felt. He expected that shipments would fall off as much as 25 percent in the next month, but that the drop would be temporary.

The US announced that it would view with the utmost gravity any hostile move against the Middle East members of the Baghdad Pact.

The French Assembly ratified a treaty of friendship with Libya which provided for withdrawal of 450 French troops from that country by November 30, some border adjustments along the Algerian Frontier in Libya's favor and some strategic concessions to France, such as the right to use military airports.

November 29

Premier Bourguiba deposited Tunisia's ratification of the UN genocide convention at the UN.

November 30

Danish troops of the UNEF took over British frontline positions in al-Cap to form a buffer between UK-French and Egyptian forces.

Egypt said that British-French intervention in Egypt had forstalled a unified move by the Arab states to aid Egypt against the Israel invasion.

According to an authoritative source, the UK planned to speed the removal of its troops from the Suez because of assurances of US support of clearances of the Canal and of an international agreement guaranteeing free passage through the Canal. Removal of French troops was expected to follow shortly.

The French Foreign Ministry said that French citizens in Egypt were being treated in violation of the principles of international law. The Ministry claimed that 65 French nationals were being held in prison.

Diplomatic sources in Baghdad reported the arrest by Iraqi Government authorities of five opposition leaders for signing a plea to permit the free functioning of political parties. All schools and colleges were closed indefinitely because of student rioting.

Premier Habib Bourguiba said that Tunisia intended to retain a neutral foreign policy toward the Arab nations.

The US made effective its emergency oil plan to supply European nations with 500,000 more barrels of oil a day, following the British announcement of hastened removal of its forces from the Middle East.

US President Eisenhower reactivated the work of the Middle East Emergency Committee.

The first tanker to reach Britain via the Cape of Good Hope since the Suez Canal had been blocked arrived in the Mersey River.

December 1

King Faisal of Iraq suspended Parliament and decreed martial law for a month at the request of Premier Nuri-Said. All political activity was frozen.

It was reported that Britain's base at New Mafraq, Jordan, was under virtual siege.

A Danish infantry company and a detachment of Canadian engineers of the UNEF moved into the area along the Suez Canal separating the British and French forces from the Egyptian positions.

The Syrian Government complained to the UN that the UK, France, Israel, Turkey and others were preparing to attack it, and were manufacturing false and tendentious news.

December 2

The Israel Army announced that all Israel forces remaining in the Sinai Peninsula had been withdrawn to positions more than 30 miles east of the Suez Canal. The total strength of soldiers withdrawn was three brigades (about 11,000 men).

British occupation authorities in Port Said gave an ultimatum to shopkeepers ordering them to open for business. Ninety percent of Egyptian shops had been closed for almost a month in protest against the invasion.

Egyptian Foreign Minister Fawzi stated in the UN that the UNEF assembling in his country must leave the Suez Canal Zone the minute the British and French forces pulled out from that area. After the withdrawal from the Canal Zone was completed, the force could stay for a while near the demarcation line between Israel and Egypt.

It was reported in Beirut that the Syrian Army, which controlled the press and radio, was barring all information from the West. The Army's strong man was Colonel Sarraj, Chief of Intelligence, who was USSR oriented and an admirer of President Nasser.

December 2

Turkey's Foreign Minister Menderes declared in London that the Turkish and British Governments had reached complete understanding on all questions touched upon in talks concerning the Syrian question.

After conferring with US President Eisenhower, US Secretary of State Dulles stated that he and the President had agreed that the prospects for peace in the Middle East were reasonably good, and that the outlook had improved considerably in the past month.

It was reported in Cairo that the Iraqi Government sent a strong warning to Syria to cease its propaganda attacks.

The Colombian Ambassador to the US urged that a UN buffer force be established between Iraq and Syria to prevent hostilities.

French forces began evacuating the Fezzan region of Libya, following French parliamentary ratification of the treaty signed in July between Libya and France.

December 3

UN Secretary General Hammarskjold ordered the UNEF to be ready to take over British and French forces in the Port Said area by the middle of the month.

The US urged speed in clearing Suez, suggesting that clearance operations begin immediately on the British-French promise to withdraw from Egypt.

British Foreign Secretary Lloyd announced that the UK and France would withdraw troops from Egypt without further delay.

The Commander of the British and French forces in Egypt declared that he could carry out a complete withdrawal within two or three weeks.

December 3

The British Admiralty suggested a three stage program for clearing Suez.

Through an arrangement made by the International Red Cross, two chartered Italian planes flew 27 wounded Egyptian prisoners of war from Tel Aviv to Cairo.

Egyptian Minister of the Interior Mohi-ad-Din said that 288 Jews were being held in Egypt for reasons of security.

Israel Foreign Minister Meir reported to the UN Secretary General that Egypt ordered 21, 000 Jews, out of a total of 50, 000 in the country, to leave within seven to thirty days; imprisoned approximately 1, 900 (holding 900 as hostages in undisclosed concentration quarters); and seized or froze assets amounting to well over $100 million.

Israel Prime Minister David Ben-Gurion declared that his country would withdraw from most of the Sinai Peninsula, provided that there were guarantees that the territory would not again become an Egyptian base.

Israel Premier David Ben-Gurion said that Israel would rebuild and enlarge its air force, in view of the Soviet planes which were allegedly pouring into Syria.

It was reported in Damascus that the US informed Syria that it would tolerate no further aggression in the Middle East.

It was reported in Damascus that the Iraqi Army was ordered to quell serious demonstrations in Mosul and that several members of the Iraqi Parliament had petitioned the King to dismiss Premier Nuri-Said and to withdraw from the Baghdad Pact.

Moroccan Minister of National Economy Bouabid announced a series of severe measures to reduce Government spending in view of the country's precarious economic situation.

The Saudi Arabian Government rescinded its prohibition of representation of animate objects on imported merchandise.

December 4

The Egyptian shadow administration in Port Said imposed a total boycott on UK-French forces.

British Foreign Secretary Lloyd said that the UN failure to keep peace in the Middle East had led to UK-French intervention in Egypt. He declared that the operation had halted a general war there and exposed Soviet infiltration.

India's Prime Minister Nehru denounced the British suggestion that a Suez settlement be on the basis of the 18 nation proposal adopted in London in August. He said that no settlement could take place until the foreign troops were withdrawn.

British Chancellor of the Exchequer Macmillan told the House of Commons that Britain's financial reserves had been reduced by $279 million during November as a result of the Suez crisis. He outlined a series of emergency measures to check the flight from sterling and avert the threat of a further devaluation of the pound.

A Yugoslavian motorized contingent of the UNEF moved into positions in the Sinai Peninsula previously held by Israel troops at a point 30 miles from their furthest penetration.

On his arrival in Haifa from Italy with 29 Jews expelled from Egypt, the Head of the Immigration Department of the Jewish Agency said that 30, 000 Jews in Egypt had been outlawed and lost all protection of law. The properties of many had been confiscated.

In Baghdad, Iraqi Foreign Minister Bashayan urged that Egypt and the US join the Baghdad Pact.

France approved loans of 48 billion francs; 32 billion to Morocco and 16 billion to Tunisia. The vote was 315-252. A special provision of the loans was that part or all of the money would be spent to aid French colonists. The grant was accompanied by a warning that the two countries adopt a friendlier attitude and cooperate more with France.

December 4

The UNESCO conference in New Delhi ended with resolutions to promote better understanding between East and West and to carry out scientific research on arid lands.

December 5

The French Cabinet adopted decrees authorizing the dissolution of 333 Algerian municipal councils controlled by Europeans and authorizing the creating of new ones. European leaders in Algeria called the decrees unjust and unconstitutional.

A tour of Syria by American and other correspondents at the invitation of Foreign Minister Bitar showed no evidence of Soviet arms.

Jamali, Head of the Iraqi delegation to the UN, stated in New York that his country's tense relations with Syria could be explained in one word: oil. He said that if the Syrian situation threatened this oil, Iraq's vital interest, something would have to be done.

Israel disputed Egypt's President Nasser by declaring that the former's forces had encountered two Egyptian battalions at Sharm-el-Sheikh in South Sinai during the Israel invasion.

Jordan informed the UK of its desire to terminate their alliance.

The UK-French Command began the first phase of withdrawal of troops from Egypt.

Syria and Jordan ratified an economic agreement providing for customs and monetary union.

Four members of the Baghdad Pact—Pakistan, Iraq, Turkey and Iran—asked the US to make a stronger and more explicit pledge to come to their assistance in the event of attack.

December 6

Soviet Foreign Secretary Shepilov said that Soviet Bloc arms had been sent to Syria, but that this small amount of arms could not threaten peace.

December 6

Iraq told Israel that the Arab world was united in support of Egypt in the Palestine crisis.

The British House of Commons endorsed the Eden Government's policy of of intervention in Egypt, after two days of debate, by a vote of 327-260.

More than 1,500 Europeans in Port Said prepared to leave Egypt.

Addressing the General Assembly, Iraqi delegate Jamali said that the UN had these alternatives: The first was that of restoring Arab rights to their own homes in Palestine and removing the Israel danger from the Middle East. The second was letting the situation drift and deteriorate in such a manner as to endanger the peace of the whole world. He said it would not be the Arabs who would be the cause of such a catastrophe.

Major General Burns, Commander of the UNEF, conferred with Israel Chief of Staff Dayan regarding the further advance of UNEF troops into Sinai and an Israel withdrawal.

December 7

President Kuwatli declared that Syria was the second major target after Egypt in an UK-Franco-Israel plan to destroy Arab nationalism and partition the Middle East into spheres of influence.

A two hour general strike was called in Jordan to protest Iraqi Premier Nuri-Said's policy toward Syria and his detention of opposition leaders.

The US Navy announced that it would send a goodwill fleet to the Middle East later in the month.

About 3,000 Egyptians paraded in Port Said mourning for residents killed in the fighting.

The Australian Ambassador to the US urged that the UNEF remain in the Suez Canal Zone until a general Middle East settlement had been reached. This settlement would provide for clearing the Canal of obstructions to navigation, for firm assurances that the Canal would

December 7

remain open to ships of all nations and for ending the present state of hostilities between Egypt and Israel.

December 8

Moroccan Foreign Minister Balafrej said that the US would give financial aid to Morocco.

Iraq announced the removal of its troops from Jordan, sent on November 3. Meanwhile a number of Jordanian organizations sent telegrams to King Faisal demanding the removal of Premier Nuri-Said and Iraq's withdrawal from the Baghdad Pact.

In a protocol to the trade and payments agreement of 1954 between Lebanon and the USSR, the value of trade exchanged between the two countries would be increased.

The British seized large quantities of arms smuggled into the Port Said area and arrested six Egyptians.

Lieutenant General R. A. Wheeler, named as aid to UN Secretary General Hammarskjold in charge of the Suez clearance project, arrived in Cairo.

The USSR withdrew its threat to send volunteers to the Middle East to fight along with the Arabs. It said that the UK-French-Israel pledge to withdraw from Egypt had made the promise unnecessary.

December 9

Tunisian Premier Bourguiba returned to Tunis from a visit to the US. He praised France for having agreed to evacuate the Suez Canal Zone.

Port Said was declared out of bounds for British and French troops as the UNEF moved in. The Egyptian boycott of allied forces ended.

December 9

Egypt's Interior Minister Zakaria Mohi-ad-Din said that 1,452 out of a total of 18,000 British and French citizens had been expelled from the country.

Syrian authorities forced an Iraqi airlines passenger plane, en route to Beirut, to land at the Damascus Airport.

It was reported in Baghdad that Syrian sabotage of the oil pipelines was costing Iraq $700,000 a day in loss of revenue. This was about one-fourth of its income for normal budget expenditures, and three-quarters of the income for the six year development plan.

December 10

Israel authorities reopened 23 elementary schools in the Gaza area. Postal and telegraph communications were restored.

The British commander in Port Said protested to the UN against an Egyptian ambush of a British patrol. There were no casualties in the attack.

Intelligence Chief Sarraj of the Syrian Army said that his country had bought arms from the Communist Bloc because the West imposed impossible conditions.

December 11

The US State Department informed Egypt of its concern over reports of mistreatment of Jews there.

The US issued a master plan for providing emergency oil for Europe.

Israel informed the UN that it would withdraw further from the Sinai Peninsula and turn the area over to UN forces.

Foreign Minister Golda Meir said that while Israel would withdraw from Egypt, the Gaza Strip was a special problem.

December 11

The Lebanese Government protested to the Syrian Government against the crossing of a Syrian military contingent into Lebanese territory, and the arrest and brief detention of a detachment of Lebanese *gendarmes*.

Iraq said that its troops had been withdrawn from Jordan because the Jordanian Government had demanded that they be put under Egyptian command.

Mahmoud, Director General at the Ministry of Development, said that Iraq's development program had not been affected by loss of oil revenue. He said also that the program had unspent balances and cash reserves sufficient for more than a year if the emergency continued that long.

The Egyptian underground in Port Said informed Allied military authorities that a British lieutenant kidnapped that day had been killed.

In Kuwait, a series of bomb explosions set one oil well on fire and damaged another; sabotage was attempted on two other wells, but only slight damage was caused. The oilfield was barred to unauthorized persons and strict security measures were enforced.

The mayors of 83 Algerian cities and towns agreed to resign on the day the French Cabinet's new decree, dissolving 333 municipal councils, went into effect.

Jordan announced a ban on the traditional Christmas diplomatic pilgrimage to Christian holy places in Jordanian held Jerusalem.

December 12

Israel officially acknowledged the killing of 48 Israel Arabs by Israel border police acting without orders in the village of Kafr Qasim on the Jordanian border on October 29. It was said that those responsible would stand trial and that compensation would be paid to the families of the victims.

France and the UK protested to the UN against Egyptian mistreatment of their citizens in Egypt.

December, 1956

December 12

As a New Year's goodwill gesture, French Resident Minister in Algeria, Robert Lacoste, instructed the prefects in Algiers, Oran and Constantine to arrange for the release of some 600 political prisoners.

Prime Minister Nehru of India said in New Delhi that the US should take the bull by the horns and deal with Russia on a Middle East settlement.

West German oil technicians began intensive exploration in northwestern Syria, along the Iraqi-Turkish borders, under a concession granted by the Syrian Government.

December 13

Sudanese Premier Khalil met with President Nasser after arriving in Egypt December 12 on a state visit. The two leaders conferred on ways to develop closer cooperation between their countries.

Egyptian Foreign Minister Fawzi said in Washington that his Government had interned 1,573 Britons, Frenchmen and Jews for valid reasons of public security.

Israel submitted a letter to the President of the UN General Assembly on the mistreatment of Jews in Egypt.

France asked the UN to take up Egypt's treatment of French citizens in Egypt. The French said that 740 French citizens had been arrested since the November 7 ceasefire, and the 8,000 French residents of Egypt had been told to leave the country by December 18.

The UK said that it would not allow salvage ships of the Royal Navy to be used for clearing the Suez Canal unless their crews were also employed.

December, 1956

December 14

The US called on Syria to restore pumping through the Iraq Oil Company pipeline to prevent cold and hunger not only in Europe, but also in Asia and South America.

A Yugoslavian contingent of the UNEF reported that it had been halted by Israel forces while on its way to the Gaza Strip.

Eleven Arab states accused Israel before the UN of inhuman treatment of the Arabs living in Israel, the Gaza Strip and the Sinai Peninsula.

The 11 Arab states in the UN charged that Israel had applied a scorched earth policy to Sinai before evacuating the Peninsula. They also protested the October 29 shooting of 48 Arab residents in Israel.

The NATO Council urged the USSR to withdraw its troops from Hungary. In a communique issued at the close of a four day meeting, the Council called for rapid clearance of the Suez Canal, an Israel-Arab settlement and stronger Atlantic Pact defenses.

The French Assembly approved by 316-162 a bill to create a single administration for the economic development of the Sahara region.

December 15

Iraqi Minister to Syria al-Rawi left for Damascus to discuss the repairing of the oil pumping stations which had been blown up by the Syrian Army.

Syria stated that it would not permit any oil to cross its territory until the Middle East situation had returned to the status which existed before the British, French and Israel invasions of Egypt.

UN troops opened fire on Egyptian guerrillas in Port Said to break up an attack on a French jeep. UN Chief Burns protested to Egypt against the attack.

December, 1956

December 16

Jordanian Premier Sulaiman Nabulsi urged an Arab federation of Jordan with one or more Arab states, as a solution to his country's problems. Commenting on a recent purge of Jordanian officials, Premier Nabulsi said only four persons had been affected and that those dismissed were not sincere nationalists; they were corrupt persons, and not up to standards of efficiency.

Iraqi Premier Nuri-Said defended his Government's policy of consistently demanding the eradication of Israel. He said that 13 months before Egypt's President Nasser had tried to initiate a final peace settlement with Israel and blamed Egypt for weakening Arab unity.

British forces turned over all but a narrow waterfront perimeter of Port Said to UN forces.

Serious fighting broke out in Port Said between the British and Egyptians.

Egyptian Foreign Minister Fawzi said that his Government would not permit British and French salvage crews to help clear the Suez Canal, but would allow those countries to contribute equipment.

Israel declared that its forces had captured sufficient gasoline on Sinai to supply the needs of its entire Army for several months.

December 17

The UK and France protested strongly against UN Secretary General Hammarskjold's barring of British crews from the British salvage ships he was planning to use in clearing the Suez Canal.

Britain said that if the safety of British crews and salvage equipment were not guaranteed by the UN, the salvage fleet would leave Egypt along with the withdrawing troops.

A one day shutdown of the press, private businesses and public enterprises, in protest against Iraqi policy, took place in Syria. In Cairo, streetcars and buses were stopped for two hours.

December, 1956

December 17

A general strike took place throughout Jordan in protest against the policies of Iraq Premier Nuri-Said and the arrest of Jamil, President of the Iraqi Bar.

Gasoline rationing went into effect in the UK. Motorists received coupons for about 200 miles of motor travel a month: this amounted to about a 30 percent cut.

Lebanon informed the Syrian Government that it would be unable to provide Syria with further supplies of refined oil products after January 10, when the present stock of crude oil at the Tripoli refinery would be exhausted.

December 18

Israel Premier Ben-Gurion said that his country would not allow Egypt to return to the Gaza Strip. He advocated demilitarization of the Sinai Peninsula and the Strait of Tiran, which leads into the Gulf of Aqaba and gives access to the port of Elath.

A crowd of 2,000 Egyptians demonstrated without violence in Port Said against the arrival of Egyptian police reinforcements.

Iraqi Foreign Minister Bashayan said that his Parliament had offered more than once to send forces to help repel Israel aggression.

Syrian Foreign Minister Bitar called upon the Arabs to save Iraq from the chains of servitude with which the Baghdad Pact was tying it.

Syria rejected US and Italian requests for emergency repairs on the pipelines carrying oil from Iraq across Syrian territory to the Mediterranean.

December 19

UN Secretary General Hammarskjold gave the UK and France the UN program for clearing the Suez Canal. He said that the crews of six British salvage vessels should be neutrals (that is, not citizens of

December 19

Britain, France, Israel or Egypt), and he agreed to allow the UK to place three officers on each vessel as observers.

Seven Swedish officers of the UNEF became temporary administrators of Port Said, taking over from the British the supervision of civil affairs through the last stages of the evacuation and pending Egyptian resumption of control.

Saudi Arabian crude oil production in November, 1956 averaged 719,754 barrels a day as compared with 1,041,098 barrels in November 1955.

The Iraqi Government announced that two oil pipeline pumping stations and an area of three kilometers around them had been placed under curfew.

The UN General Assembly elected Iraq to a two year term on the Security Council.

December 20

The UK agreed to place its salvage vessels under the UN flag and protection in clearing the Suez Canal.

A UN General Assembly committee approved by a vote of 57-8 a compromise plan for raising the first $10 million of the cost of the UNEF in Egypt. Under the plan the cost would be prorated among the 80 UN members on the same basis as the regular budget.

An Egyptian Government sponsored newspaper said that the kidnapped British officer had died of suffocation while being hidden from British searching parties.

The French National Assembly upheld Premier Mollet's Egyptian policy by a vote of 325-210 after three days of dispirited debate.

Hayim Nahum, Chief Rabbi of Egypt, said that no foreign government, especially Israel, was authorized to speak on behalf of the Egyptian

December 20

Jews. He denounced UK-French-Israel aggression against Egypt.

The Iraq Petroleum Company announced that total oil production in Iraq in November was 728,868 tons, as compared with 3,105,470 tons in October, and that Iraq had been losing about $4.8 million weekly since the pipeline flow had been halted November 2.

The Moroccan Government asked France to accept the jurisdiction of the new World Court at The Hague to settle their dispute over the arrest of five Algerian rebel leaders October 22.

December 21

Secretary General Hammarskjold told the UN that Israel had promised to withdraw its troops from Sinai by January.

US Export-Import Bank lent $20 million to the UK for purchases in the US, including oil, because the blocking of the Suez Canal had cut off more than half the UK oil supplies.

The US agreed to lend the UK $500 million to help finance British purchases of American oil, coal and other raw materials.

December 22

Sultan Muhammad V approved a prospective federation of North African labor unions that would unite Moroccan and Tunisian workers with the Nationalist Workers Union of Algeria.

Schools rebpened throughout Egypt, except for 50 British and French schools scheduled to reopen later under Egyptian control and with Egyptian teachers.

The evacuation of British and French forces from Egypt was completed. Port Said and Port Fuad were taken over by the UNEF.

West Germany's Foreign Minister said that he was urging his Government to stop paying reparations to Israel and to pay them to Egypt instead.

December 22

Syrian Premier Assali submitted the resignation of his Cabinet to President Kuwatli.

In Syria, a military judge ordered the court-martial of 47 prominent Syrian political figures on charges of plotting to set up a pro-Iraqi Government. Twenty-nine of those charged were under arrest; 18 fled to Lebanon. The court-martial order accused Lebanon of housing conspirators.

December 23

The second phase of UNEF operations in Egypt began. Indian troops began moving east to follow up the Israel evacuation of Sinai.

Egypt banned participation by British crews in clearance of the Suez Canal. The Egyptian Army entered Port Said.

The US delegate to the UN, James J. Wadsworth, told the UN General Assembly that the US had received information that an indeterminate number of persons, including British and French nationals and persons of Jewish origin in Egypt, had been subjected to pressure and intimidation and, in some instances, had been ordered deported.

Iraqi Premier Nuri-Said said that Iraq, and not Egypt and its satellites, would decide what was good for Iraq. He called Egyptian President Nasser a dictator.

Moroccan Foreign Minister Balafrej said that his country was ready to negotiate a military base agreement with the US.

Five members of the outlawed Committee of National Unity were sentenced to long prison terms on charges of plotting to kill Sheikh al-Khalifah, the Ruler of Bahrain.

French officials denounced Tunisian aid to Algerian rebels.

India's Prime Minister Nehru asserted that conditions in Algeria were worse than in Hungary.

December 24

The Head of the Israel Foreign Ministry accused Egypt of continuing a policy of armed conflict in defiance of the November 2 UN resolution.

UN Secretary General Hammarskjold announced that in order to speed the clearance work on the Suez Canal, he was sending to Egypt his chief assistant, Cordier, and the UN Deputy Under Secretary Katzin in charge of secretariat planning for clearing the Canal.

Egypt submitted a draft resolution to the UN General Assembly calling on Secretary General Hammarskjold to make arrangements to assess the damage caused by the military operations on Egyptian territory, and requesting him to report to the Assembly on the required assessment as a basis for the payment by Israel, France and the UK of adequate compensation to Egypt.

Iraq called on the US to become a full member of the Baghdad Pact to help secure peace and security in the Middle East.

The Saudi Arabian Ambassador to Egypt gave the Egyptian Government a check for LE3,645 for the welfare of Israel aggression victims.

December 25

Israel accused Egypt of defying the UN call for an end to commando raids.

Premier Bourguiba called on Egypt to cancel measures taken against Jews living in that country and holding Tunisian passports.

Israel Premier Ben-Gurion refused to debate a possible withdrawal of Israel forces from the Gaza Strip on the grounds that it was not in the public interest.

A motion to debate the issue concerning the Gaza Strip, introduced in the Knesset by Menahem Beigin, leader of the Herut Party, was defeated by a vote of 52-18.

Egypt said that no work would begin on clearing the Suez Canal until the last Israel forces left Egyptian soil, including the Gaza Strip.

December 26

Israel asked the US to use its good offices to stop Egyptian directed raids into its territory.

Egypt announced that clearance of the Suez Canal had begun at Ismailia and Suez.

Syria told the Iraq Petroleum Company that it would not permit the repairing of damaged pipelines until Israel forces withdrew from Sinai and the Gaza Strip.

Moulay Merbah, the Algerian nationalist leader who had flown to Switzerland from France to escape arrest, left for New York to appeal to the UN. He was Secretary General of the nationalist movement.

Syria accused the UK, France and Turkey of instigating a plot to overthrow its Government. Syria said that Iraq had financed and conducted the plot. The accusation was made at a preliminary hearing, in court, of Syrians involved in the plot.

A treaty was signed between Libya and France which set the limit of the southeast Tunisia border.

December 27

Israel delivered notes in London, Washington and Paris reporting renewal of Egyptian fedayeen activity on Israel territory, mainly from Jordanian bases.

A number of Jordanians working in Iraq were deported by the Iraqi Government.

President Nasser sent warm greetings to the USSR and expressed hope that the friendship between the two countries would grow in strength. His message was broadcast over Radio Moscow.

The UK announced an agreement with Libya to review their current mutual defense treaty.

Morocco protested to France against new French legislation for developing the Sahara regions.

December 27

Merbah, the Algerian nationalist leader, arrived in New York and said that he hoped that the US would adopt a more liberal policy toward Algeria's desire for independence.

December 28

The Yemeni Charge d'Affaires in London protested to the British Government against an alleged British raid on Qataba. The Foreign Office denied this accusation.

December 29

Anti-Moslem riots occurred in the European part of Algeria.

After prolonged negotiations between UN and Egyptian authorities, salvage crews started clearing the southern end of the Suez Canal.

US President Eisenhower announced that his administration would ask Congress for authority to use political, economic and, if necessary, military force to oppose Soviet aggression in the Middle East.

More than 400 Canadian soldiers sailed for Egypt as part of Canada's contribution to the UNEF.

December 30

Egypt consented to the start of full scale salvage operations on the Suez Canal.

The Yemeni Government protested to the UK Government against attacks on Yemeni towns and villages.

Egypt began disarming civilians in Port Said.

Lieutenant General Wheeler estimated that by May the Suez Canal would be open for the largest type vessels adapted to its depth. By

December 30

early March ships of 25 foot draft would be able to go through the waterway; this would suffice for oil tankers and other craft of about 10,000 tons.

Jordanian Premier Nabulsi rejected any suggestion that he might call on the USSR for aid if financial assistance from the Arab states was not forthcoming.

Moroccan Sultan Muhammad V granted an audience to a French official for the first time since October 22. Negotiations were resumed on a joint convention to formalize the distinctions already in practice regarding a personal status law for Europeans.

An Iraq Petroleum Company survey team started an 800 mile tour of sabotaged oil installations in Syria.

December 31

Egypt appealed to the US to release Egyptian dollar assets, worth $50 million, frozen in US banks following the Suez Canal nationalization act.

Israel Premier Ben-Gurion credited French cooperation with having prevented the annihilation of his country by Egypt.

The UN assured Egypt's President Nasser that it would exert utmost pressure on Israel to speed up withdrawal from territory occupied in their attack on Egypt.

US Secretary of State Dulles conferred with UN Secretary General Hammarskjold on the latest developments in the Middle East and the impending statement of policy which President Eisenhower was to make to Congress.

The Syrian Ambassador to the US said that the US plan to protect the Middle East was caused by Israel and the Zionists rather than by Soviet penetration, and that Syria's policy was one of noncommitment. He noted that Syria's relations with the US were regulated by the UN

December 31

Charter and that Syria was uninterested in any action outside that framework.

Syrian Premier Sabri al-Assali formed a new Cabinet.

January, 1957

January 1

The UN salvage fleet began work on major obstacles in the Suez Canal.

The Foreign Ministry of Yemen charged that two British planes had bombed dwellings near Harib in southeastern Yemen on December 31.

An Egyptian Interior Ministry circular to public prosecutors' offices declared that Egyptians would lose their nationality if they were found to be "Zionists."

A decree by President Nasser abrogated, as of October 31, 1956, the 1954 treaty granting Great Britain the right to use bases in the Suez Canal Zone in the event of an attack on any Arab state or on Turkey.

The Saudi Arabian American Oil Company announced a decision to cut its expenditures for development projects during 1957 by $10 million.

Sudanese Foreign Minister Muhammad Ahmad Mahgoub told a press conference that his country observed complete neutrality and was hostile to all military pacts.

January 2

French authorities executed two Moslems for associating with terrorists in Algeria.

French forces reportedly killed 18,000 Algerian rebels during 1956 and lost 2,435 of their own men.

Prime Minister Assali of Syria ordered the IPC (Iraq Petroleum Company) to dispose of any of its crude oil — an estimated 180,000 tons — stored in its installations in Syria without a special permit from the military governor.

After considerable maneuvering, Prime Minister Assali of Syria formed a new cabinet.

Abdallah Rimawi, Jordanian Minister of State for Foreign Affairs, said that Jordan would pursue a policy of neutrality between

January, 1957

January 3

The World Federation of Trade Unions published the memorandum it had addressed to the UN General Assembly, expressing its hope that the UN would use its authority to put an end to bloodshed in Algeria.

January 4

Major General Burns, commander of UNEF (United Nations Emergency Force), talked with Israel Chief of Staff Moshe Dayan on the progress of the Israel withdrawal from Sinai.

Egyptian President Nasser lifted press censorship, which had been imposed two months previously, and censorship on other outgoing cables.

In his annual report to the General Assembly, Labouisse, Director of the UN Relief and Works Agency, declared that Egypt, Jordan, Syria, and to a lesser degree Lebanon, had put so many obstacles in the way of the refugee relief effort that the Agency might have to suspend or terminate its activities unless those governments gave full and open cooperation.

Passage was opened to medium shipping at least halfway down the Suez Canal as the east span of the Firdan Bridge was lifted by German salvage vessels.

January 5

Egypt reaffirmed its decision not to negotiate directly with Britain and France on Suez but rather to seek a settlement through the UN.

In a request to Congress, now known as the Eisenhower Doctrine, President Eisenhower asked for authorization to use US armed forces in the Middle East against "overt armed aggression" from any nation controlled by international Communism.

Lebanese Foreign Minister Malik said that the Arab governments had agreed to oppose the raising of the Palestine issue at the current session of the UN General Assembly.

January, 1957

January 2

East and West. He added that Jordan would not accept economic aid given with political objectives.

Cairo Radio announced that Britain's Suez base was liquidated and no longer existed. Britain denied, however, that its 1954 pact with Egypt was void, despite the announcement by President Nasser that the treaty had been unilaterally abrogated as of October 31, 1956.

The Libyan Chamber of Deputies rejected a motion for abrogating the Anglo-Libyan Treaty.

January 3

It was announced in Rabat that France and Morocco concluded an agreement granting Morocco 17 million francs ($4,857,000) in credits. The credits were part of the 1956 French aid appropriations.

The US told Israel not to expect American support for its efforts to draw international advantages from the attack on Egypt, and advised Israel to comply with the UN resolution of November 2, 1956 requiring an Israel withdrawal behind the 1949 armistice lines.

Yemen requested UN Secretary Dag Hammarskjold to intervene in its dispute with Great Britain over attacks from Aden.

The US announced that it would lend the UN up to $5 million to help meet the initial cost of clearing the Suez Canal.

Yemeni troops armed with modern weapons made in Czechoslovakia gained ground in border attacks into Aden.

General Fuad Chehab resigned as Minister of Defense and resumed his position as Army Commander in Chief of Lebanon.

The Arab League Secretariat issued a statement condemning Britain's actions in Yemen.

January, 1957

January 5

Syrian President Shukri Kuwatli left by plane on an official visit to Pakistan and India.

January 6

Premier Habib Bourguiba of Tunisia and Libyan Premier Mustafa Ben-Halim signed a treaty of friendship. A joint declaration annexed to the treaty called for recognition of Algeria's right to independence. Premier Bourguiba explained the treaty as part of his own concept of a greater "Arab Occident" and said that Algerian independence was a prerequisite to the formation of such a confederation.

British jet planes attacked Yemeni troops and rebel Aden tribesmen in western Aden.

Israel newspapers criticized the Eisenhower Doctrine for the Middle East as threatening new competition between the US and the Soviet Union.

The Basra Petroleum Company announced that it had achieved its export goal of eight million tons of crude oil from southern Iraq in 1956.

US officials said that the area covered by President Eisenhower's special aid program for the Middle East might be extended to include Morocco, Tunisia and Afghanistan.

January 7

Great Britain formally condemned Egypt's intention of closing the Suez Canal to British and French shipping until Israel forces withdrew from the Gaza Strip.

The Colonial Office in London announced that RAF fighters were in action to protect the Aden Protectorate against incursions from Yemen.

January 7

Iraq received 28 more Centurion tanks from Britain.

Israel military forces completed withdrawal to the east of al-Arish, Egypt.

January 8

Libyan Premier Ben-Halim told Parliament that the new treaty with Tunisia was the first step toward forming a unified Arab nation from the Persian Gulf to the Atlantic.

A military court in Damascus opened the trial of 47 Syrians, including former President Adib Shishakli, on charges of attempting to overthrow the government and replace it with a pro-Western administration. Eighteen of the accused, including Shishakli, were being tried in absentia.

Moroccan Minister of National Economy Bouabid stated that Morocco had asked the US for economic aid amounting to $37,143,000 during the current fiscal year. This assistance would be used to undertake public works and economic development largely to reduce the unemployment figure of 200,000. However, the US State Department said that reports of a specific Moroccan request for aid were premature.

Britain formally rejected a Yemeni charge that the RAF (Royal Air Force) had bombed Yemeni targets on December 31, 1956.

Britain protested against the action of the Yemeni Government in failing to restrain its subjects from entering the Aden Protectorate.

The Egyptian Government announced that it could not resume the Suez talks with Britain and France and that it would discuss the matter only within the framework of the UN.

January 9

The British Foreign Office reported that jet fighters were again in action in Aden to repel invaders from Yemen.

The French Government published a document reiterating the French contention that the UN was incompetent to deal with the Algerian problems and warning the UN not to interfere in Algeria.

The Asian-African nations in the UN demanded Israel's withdrawal behind the armistice lines.

Yemen announced it would receive arms from Czechoslovakia. The Yemeni Charge d'Affaires in Bonn said Russian volunteers would be requested if it became necessary against the British.

The US State Department expressed official concern to Egypt over reports that Egyptian Jews had been deported or otherwise mistreated, and urged President Nasser to adopt moderate policies towards Egypt's Jews.

Diplomatic sources reported that the Soviet Union delivered about a dozen MIG-17 jet fighters to Syria in the past three days.

Egyptian newspapers criticized the Eisenhower Doctrine as "one legged" and "one eyed."

January 10

Jordan charged in the UN that Israel was concentrating troops near its frontier.

In a statement on President Eisenhower's Middle East policy speech, the Syrian Government declared that it rejected the theory of a "power vacuum" in the Middle East. It asserted that there was no Communist threat in Syria and that maintenance of peace and security in the Middle East was solely the responsibility of the peoples of that area.

January 10

Abd-al-Rahman al-Baidani, Yemen's Minister to West Germany, asserted that unless British aggression against Yemen stopped, his country would if necessary call on Russian volunteers.

The US proposed that the Suez Canal Users' Association undertake a study of how the flow of international trade could best be restored after the reopening of the Canal. The proposal was made at a meeting of the Association.

Following talks with Soviet Ambassador to Egypt, Kiselev, the Yemeni Ambassador challenged Britain to allow neutral observers into the Aden-Yemen highlands where tension was very high.

UNEF (United Nations Emergency Force) Chief Burns said that Israel would vacate a captured Egyptian base in northern Sinai but would not withdraw from Sharm el-Sheikh.

Ambassador Dillon, speaking to the American Club in Paris, said that the US had no intention of replacing France in North Africa.

January 11

Egypt accused Israel of murdering more than 8,000 Arab youths in the Gaza Strip.

UN Secretary General Dag Hammarskjold submitted a report to the General Assembly on arrangements for clearing the Suez Canal. The arrangements included an agreement with President Nasser that the undertaking would be regarded as a United Nations enterprise and its personnel would be under obligation to discharge their functions and regulate their conduct solely in the interests of the United Nations.

In a speech at Tozeur, Tunisian Premier Bourguiba gave unqualified approval to the Eisenhower Doctrine for the Middle East. He said the plan, if adopted, would wipe out the "last vestiges of colonialists."

January 11

French Foreign Minister Christian Pineau told US Secretary of State John Foster Dulles that France would not recognize UN intervention in Algeria; it considered the issue a private, French matter.

British officials charged that Yemen had begun a full scale military campaign against the sheikhdoms in eastern Aden.

Yemen called a meeting of the joint command of the Egyptian-Saudi Arabian-Yemeni armies to discuss the British military action on its border.

Algerian nationalist leaders in Morocco said that Premier Mollet's program of ceasefire in Algeria followed within three months by election of representatives from Algeria who would negotiate, offered no new way to settle the conflict. The leaders also said that Mollet's statement did not mention Algerian independence and that a ceasefire would leave Algeria under the control of the French Army, which would supervise elections.

January 12

Lebanon's Foreign Minister Charles Malik said in a speech in Paris that Communists had penetrated certain Arab states deeply enough to make a bid for power.

Former Conservative M.P. (Member of Parliament) Cyril Banks said after interviews with President Nasser that Nasser would welcome a new Prime Minister because the change would enable Britain and Egypt to reopen negotiations on a variety of subjects.

In a once secret testimony made public, Secretary of State Dulles voiced the definite belief that the Middle East would be lost to the Communists without prompt economic aid and military backing. He said that if it was lost, it would be the

January, 1957

January 12

greatest victory that the Soviet Communists could ever have gained because if they got this area they in effect "would have gotten Western Europe without a war." He added that if volunteers were used in any organized way, that it would be regarded as an open, overt aggression.

Britain denied that major military operations were taking place on the Aden-Yemen border.

The Soviet Union warned that the Eisenhower Doctrine measures planned for the Middle East, aiming at the possible use of US armed forces in that area, could lead to dangerous consequences. The Soviet Union would regard this as a flagrant interference in Arab affairs and a contradiction of the principles of the UN, full responsibility for which would rest with the United States Government.

The Foreign Minister of Lebanon, Charles Malik, said that he had had long and fruitful talks with President Nasser, and that he was in a position to affirm that no settlement of the Suez affairs was possible until Israel withdrew behind the armistice line.

Ahmad Ali Zabarah, Yemen's Charge d'Affaires in Washington, appealed to the US to intervene against British aggression in Yemen. He confirmed reports that Yemen had recently purchased arms from Czechoslovakia.

January 13

Soviet party leader Khrushchev said that the Eisenhower Doctrine was doomed to failure against the "granite rock" of the Soviet Union.

January, 1957

January 14

Canadian External Affairs Minister Pearson welcomed the Eisenhower Doctrine as evidence of the increased US interest in the Middle East.

Great Britain offered to hold talks with Yemen on ending the Aden border dispute.

Israel forces began blowing up Egyptian military installations in al-Arish, before abandoning the town to UNEF (United Nations Emergency Force) troops. The destruction was in defiance of warnings by UN Secretary Hammarskjold.

Henry Labouisse, head of UNRWA (UN Relief and Works Agency), said that Israel had restored law and order to the Gaza Strip.

January 15

Israel forces evacuated al-Arish. Yugoslav troops of the UNEF entered al-Arish and found that all military installations except the airstrip had been blown up by Israel troops before their withdrawal.

President Nasser initiated a program of Egyptianization under which only Egyptian citizens born in Egypt could be shareholders in Egyptian companies located in Egypt. All British and French banks and insurance companies had been "Egyptianized"; other foreign banks and insurance companies had to conform within five years. Minister of Finance Qaysuni announced the formation of an Economic Organization to control the assets of all these companies.

The US agreed in principle to an interim accord on Suez covering maintenance, toll collections, and ship movement priorities, as a working arrangement until a permanent settlement could be negotiated.

January, 1957

January 13

UN observers reported that they had found no basis for Jordan's complaint that Israel was massing troops along the armistice line in the Tul Karm sector.

British Labor Party Leader Bevan said that the Eisenhower Doctrine was calculated to plunge the world into total war.

Subhi Omari, a former Member of Parliament on trial for allegedly plotting armed revolt in Syria, told the military court that the British had been aware of the plot and had encouraged it.

Tass published a statement on the Eisenhower Doctrine, pointing out that it ran counter to the purposes and principles of the UN Charter and constituted a serious menace to the peace and security of the Middle East.

January 14

Former French Premier Mendes-France joined Premier Mollet in opposing UN action in Algeria. He blamed the French press for not presenting the Algerian issue fairly and intelligently.

Lebanese Foreign Minister Charles Malik declared in London that Soviet penetration into the Middle East had been increasing and that, in some countries, it affected government policy.

President Nasser issued a decree establishing, under his own chairmanship, a Supreme Council on National Planning whose functions would include laying down the state's economic and agricultural objectives and deciding on phased plans of economic development.

The Egyptian Ambassador to Washington, Ahmad Hussein, appealed to the US for the release of more than $40 million worth of Egyptian assets frozen after nationalization of the Suez Canal Company.

January, 1957

January 15

Prime Minister David Ben-Gurion of Israel announced the minimum conditions for Israel's withdrawal from Sharm el-Sheikh and the Gaza Strip: a treaty safeguarding freedom of navigation through the Gulf of Aqaba, to be signed by Israel, Jordan, Saudi Arabia and Egypt, or the stationing of UNEF troops at Sharm el-Sheikh until final settlement was reached between Israel and Egypt; and retention by Israel of control under a civilian police force of Gaza's internal security and a suitable arrangement with the UN for Israel to continue supervision of public services in, and economic development of, the Gaza Strip. Ambassador Eban presented Israel's proposals to UN Secretary General Hammarskjold and informed him that Israel would not withdraw from the two areas without assurances against their renewed use by Egypt for hostile actions.

Israel Ambassador Abba Eban informed Secretary General Hammarskjold that Israel would withdraw its forces from the Sinai Desert by January 22, and that it was willing to discuss the remaining questions of the Sharm el-Sheikh area, the Gulf of Aqaba, the Straits of Tiran, and the arrangements envisioned for Gaza.

The US issued a statement declaring that the American Government had urged and would continue to urge the greatest restraint by Britain and Yemen in the current border warfare.

The Bey of Tunis signed a decree introducing military conscription in Tunisia.

January 16

Explaining the Government's "Egyptianization" move, Minister of Finance Abd-al-Moneim al-Kaissouni of Egypt declared that British and French banks and insurance companies "had been at war against us instead of helping us to realize our economic policy and to raise the standard of living of our people."

January 16

Australia announced it would lend the UN $1 million toward clearing the Suez Canal. The offer brought the total raised for this operation to $12 million, out of the $15 million necessary.

Prince Saif-al-Islam al-Hassan, Yemeni representative to the UN, lodged a complaint with Carlos Romulo, President of the Security Council, against the British aggression against his country.

January 17

President Nasser of Egypt made his first public comment on the Eisenhower Doctrine. He said certain parts were vague. He said he was neither pro-East nor pro-West.

The US asked Mr. Hammarskjold to arrange for deployment of the UNEF along the Egyptian-Israel armistice line and at the entrance to the Gulf of Aqaba to replace withdrawing Israel forces in order to assure the maintenance of the ceasefire and to safeguard the Armistice Agreement.

It was revealed in Amman that Jordan was asking the US for $30 million annually in foreign aid, without any American control over the choice of projects or their administration. Total American aid to Jordan since February, 1951, had been about $34 million, with the usual restrictions the US placed on technical assistance program aid.

Israel officials suggested than an association of nations using the Gulf of Aqaba be formed as a means of ensuring Israel's freedom of passage through the Straits of Tiran.

Britain and the protectorate rulers of Aden agreed to talks with Yemen about border hostilities. The British Foreign Office announced that the talks would begin January 18 at Sanaa in Aden.

January 17

The Syrian President, Shukri al-Kuwatli, arrived in Delhi on a state visit.

January 18

The Soviet Union and Communist China condemned the Eisenhower Doctrine for the Middle East and promised the necessary support for nations in the area to oppose aggression and interference in their affairs. The two nations also demanded that Britain, France, and Israel pay Egypt reparations for damages inflicted during their attack on it.

Britain called for internationalization under the UN of controversial areas in the Middle East as a shield against possible war. Minister of State Allan Noble told the General Assembly that the Gaza Strip and the Gulf of Aqaba should be held under UN control pending a settlement of the dispute.

The Yemeni Legation in Cairo said it had received the names of 10,000 Egyptians who had volunteered to help Yemen against the British. It said 6,000 youths, mostly fedayeen, and some officers had registered at the legation.

January 19

Egypt, Saudi Arabia and Syria signed a joint ten year solidarity pact with Jordan to give that country $36 million annually to replace the British subsidy. Egypt contributed $14 million, Saudi Arabia, $14 million, and Syria, $7 million.

The offices in the Arab countries that organized the boycotting of Israel opened their eleventh conference in Beirut, Lebanon.

A statement issued after a conference in Cairo by King Saud of Saudi Arabia, Premier Sabri al-Assali of Syria, and President Nasser of Egypt asserted: "All agreed on rejection of the

January 19

'vacuum' theory and decided that Arab nationalism was the sole basis on which Arab policy could be formulated."

Yemen accused Britain of invading its territory and besieging a town 25 miles inside the country with tanks and planes. The British Foreign Office denied the charge as completely imaginary.

The Lebanese Government rejected a request from the fuel distribution companies for an increase in prices of all fuels based on oil.

Jordan received 250,000 pounds sterling from Britain as a first installment of 900,000 pounds sterling allocated for building a 187 mile road from Amman to Aqaba.

The UN adopted by 74-2 an Asian-African resolution calling for Israel withdrawal from Egypt.

The Premiers of Iran, Iraq, Pakistan and Turkey met in Baghdad and agreed to support the American Middle East program.

A Soviet exhibition, with more than 10,000 industrial and agricultural items, opened in Cairo.

January 20

Yemen announced that it would not cancel its 1934 and 1950 treaties with Britain.

A French Government survey reported that blockage of the Suez Canal and destruction of Middle East oil pipelines were costing France an average of $20 million a month.

January 21

A British communique said that about 250 dissident tribesmen from Yemen invaded upper Yafi Protectorate and withdrew after seizing six Yafi tribal leaders.

Great Britain announced that it had requested immediate negotiations with Jordan on the future of the Anglo-Jordanian treaty of friendship.

Britain handed a strong note of protest to Yemen's Charge d'Affaires in London, against their aggressions in the Aden Protectorate.

The exchange of 5,850 Egyptian prisoners of war for four Israelis, arranged by the International Red Cross, began.

In a communique issued after their meeting in Ankara, the four Moslem Baghdad Pact nations announced their support for the Eisenhower Doctrine for the Middle East.

At the conclusion of two days of talks in New Delhi, Prime Minister Nehru of India and President Shukri al-Kuwatli of Syria issued a joint statement opposing a military approach to the solution of Middle Eastern problems. They declared that intervention by the big powers in the form of military pacts and alliances was detrimental to peace and stability in the Middle East.

January 22

French officials in the Algerian Government charged that Algerian rebels were receiving arms and other assistance on an increasing scale from Morocco and Tunisia. The charges claimed instances of Algerian and Moroccan raids into Algerian territory from Moroccan bases.

Yemen announced its willingness to enter ceasefire talks with Britain over the ending of the border dispute in Northern Aden.

January, 1957

January 22

Jordanian Premier Nabulsi said that negotiations would begin with Britain in February toward ending the 1948 Anglo-Jordanian treaty of alliance.

The Lower House of Jordan's Parliament approved the plan to replace the annual British subsidy to Jordan with equivalent aid from Egypt, Syria and Saudi Arabia.

The Lebanese Chamber of Deputies approved an amended trade agreement between Lebanon and East Germany negotiated in 1955. East Germany agreed to buy 5,000 tons of Lebanese citrus fruit every year for three years in return for East German manufactured goods.

Egypt threatened to stop clearance work on the Suez Canal if Israel did not comply with the UN resolution ordering withdrawal of its forces.

Israel forces pulled back into the Gaza Strip from Sinai, thus evacuating all Egyptian territory except Sharm el-Sheikh at the entrance of the Gulf of Aqaba.

January 23

The arrival of 857 Egyptian Jews in Greece brought to over 10,000 the number expelled from Egypt since November.

Egypt announced that all imports from the US would be canceled unless the exporters accepted payment in Egyptian pounds.

Sharif Hussein Ibn-Ahmad Amr Muhsin, ruler of the Beihan tribal state, appealed to Britain for more reinforcements against Yemen. He said that his state was in danger of being overrun, and that propaganda broadcasts had caused about 350 of his tribesmen to go over to Yemen after being promised free arms, ammunition and food.

January, 1957

January 25

Egyptian newspapers reported that Egypt had agreed to exchange LE12,000,000 worth of cotton for Soviet steel and agricultural equipment.

Syrian Premier Sabri al-Assali declared that the Arab countries were determined to take whatever measures were needed to drive Israel out of Gaza and Sinai.

French Premier Guy Mollet declared that in Algeria, as well as in the rest of Africa, France intended to insure the total liberation of the peoples it had in charge.

January 26

The Jordan Senate unanimously approved the January 19 Cairo agreement.

Israel Ambassador Abba Eban asked the US for support in obtaining special UN guarantees of protection before Israel withdrew its troops from the Gaza Strip and the Gulf of Aqaba area.

January 27

An Israel Foreign Ministry statement criticized UN Secretary General Hammarskjold's report as "negative and unconstructive" and declared that it did no more than seek to restore the regime which had already ended in disaster. Furthermore, it said, there was no indication that the Secretary General had taken the situation into proper account or that he had even inquired from Egypt whether Egypt was prepared to abandon the state of war with Israel and make peace.

The only Israel soldier captured during the Sinai campaign was returned to Israel with three other Israelis captured in 1955. The Egyptian prisoners were already returned to Egypt.

January, 1957

January 23

Israel informed Hammarskjold that it would not withdraw from the Gaza Strip or the Gulf of Aqaba without binding guarantees that these would not be used by Egypt for hostile acts against Israel.

French military sources estimated that about 2,000 weapons a month were involved in the arms traffic from Tunisia and Morocco.

January 24

Two Arab village councils, those of Rafah and Deir-al-Balah, adopted resolutions welcoming Israel's declaration not to withdraw from Gaza.

It was reported in Jerusalem that Yaochim al-Antoni, head of the Coptic Christian community, was arrested for spying for Egypt.

January 25

Hammarskjold rejected Israel demands for special guarantees in exchange for an Israel withdrawal from the Gaza Strip and the Gulf of Aqaba. He said that the 1949 armistice agreement provided for Egyptian administration of the Strip. He added that the UNEF would establish itself in the Gulf of Aqaba area following Israel withdrawal in the same way as in other parts of Sinai.

Israel said that it would be inconceivable for the UN to vote economic sanctions against Israel if the problems of the Gaza Strip and Gulf of Aqaba were not solved immediately. Israel spokesmen said that such an act would apply a double standard of morality.

January, 1957

January 27

Sudan signed the contract for the main excavation of the Managil extension to the Gezira cotton scheme with the West German firm of Julius Berger Tiefbau AG and Philipp Holzmann AG (two separate firms working together). Under the terms of the contract, worth about five million pounds sterling, about 83 miles of canals would be constructed and work would be completed by July, 1959.

The first Sudanese coins were put into circulation. Minted in Pakistan, they were designed to replace, eventually, both British and Egyptian coinage as legal tender.

Israel voted to begin commercial and agricultural development of the Gaza Strip, and indicated that it would not withdraw from the area without guarantees against renewed aggression.

January 28

UN representatives at Gaza protested to Israel against the internment and expulsion of 18 Egyptians employed by UNRWA (United Nations Relief Works Agency), and charged Israel with removal of equipment and livestock from a training school for Palestine Arab refugees.

British Home Secretary and Lord Privy Seal R.A. Butler expressed support of President Eisenhower's Middle East proposals and declared that the purpose of this policy, far from provoking war, was to prevent it.

Lebanese Foreign Minister Charles Malik declared that President Eisenhower's program was a countermove to Communism in the Middle East. He said he had no doubt that if things were left at the rate at which the situation was deteriorating, before long the area would have been pretty nearly lost to Communism.

Israel Ambassador Eban asked the UN General Assembly to adopt a resolution enabling the withdrawal of forces to become

January 28

a link in a chain of constructive developments. He declared that Israel aspired to a new system of relations between itself and Egypt.

The principal contract between the UN and the salvage contractors clearing the Suez Canal was signed. The signers were Secretary General Hammarskjold and representatives of L. Smit & Co., Netherlands, and Bendt-Goth-Bendtzen of Copenhagen.

The US told the General Assembly that it was essential that UNEF be stationed at the Gulf of Aqaba between Israel and Egyptian forces.

Israel Premier Ben-Gurion said that the Sinai Peninsula should be controlled by UN forces until Egypt was prepared to sign a peace treaty or a nonaggression pact with Israel.

Algerian Moslems began a country-wide general strike scheduled to last a week. About 50 percent of the Algerian workers in France obeyed the strike, which was called by the National Liberation Front.

The Yemeni Government warned that no peace could be arranged until Yemen's claims to the Western and Eastern Aden Protectorates were recognized.

Great Britain protested strongly a Yemeni raid on the Aden airfield at Dhala on January 26 and demanded that the attacks cease forthwith.

January 29

The Soviet Union demanded unconditional withdrawal of Israel forces from the Gaza Strip and the Gulf of Aqaba.

January 29

The Commander of the British forces warned that if Yemenis penetrated deeper into Aden or staged larger raids, they would have to face aerial strafing and bombardment.

January 30

King Saud of Saudi Arabia conferred with the President and other US leaders in Washington. Agreement on increased US aid and a five year extension of the Dhahran Base Agreement (to April 1, 1962) was formalized.

The Iraq Petroleum Company announced it had paid Syria 4,890,000 pounds sterling for transit of oil through the country up to November, 1956.

The Arab League Secretariat said that Hungary, Czechoslovakia and Bulgaria had halted trade with Israel.

Imam Ahmad declared that the British refused to yield Aden to Yemen because they had hoped to find a lot of oil there. Concerning the border controversy, the Imam asserted: "There is no border between Yemen and Aden."

By a vote of 355-61, the US House of Representatives approved a resolution in support of President Eisenhower's plan.

Edward Greenwood, a Washington businessman, said at a Cairo press conference that the Egyptian Government had approved a 30 year investment plan submitted by him as chairman of the Middle East Settlement Committee comprising US financial groups.

January 31

The US and two other "imperialists" — Britain and France —

January 31

were accused by a prosecution lawyer in the Damascus trial of unifying reactionary elements in Syria with the intent of stirring up civil war, which would be followed by invasion and military occupation of Egypt. It was the first mention of the US in the course of the trial.

President Nasser signed laws providing for "Egyptianization" of all foreign banks and insurance companies, including two US concerns.

It was reported in Washington that King Saud told President Eisenhower that his country urgently needed $250 million worth of armaments to equip 12 brigades and to build a small jet air force.

February 1

The US proposed that Israel withdraw from the Gaza Strip and the Sharm el-Sheikh area immediately. The US also put before the UN a resolution asking that the UNEF be stationed on the Egyptian-Israel armistice line following the withdrawal.

UN and Israel troops fired on one another near the Israel frontier.

British RAF jet fighter planes strafed two Aden villages which were seized by Yemen. Governor Sir William Luce declared that Great Britain was determined to continue to honor treaty obligations to protect the Aden sheikhdoms, and that Yemen had no legal claim to the Protectorate.

The Iraq Petroleum Company announced that it was discharging some 800 of its British and Arab employees, or about one-third of its labor force. The Company discharged all except 450 of its 3,700 employees in Syria.

US Secretary of State John Foster Dulles declared that the talks between President Eisenhower and King Saud of Saudi Arabia went extremely well and that a good many misunderstandings about US policy in the Middle East had been cleared up.

February 2

Egypt told the UN it would not agree to an expanded role for UNEF following Israel's withdrawal from its territory. Egyptian delegate Fawzi said that Egypt's consent to the entry, stationing and deployment of the UN force was an indispensable prerequisite.

King Hussein warned Jordan against Communist infiltration, and urged Premier Nabulsi to take steps to destroy destructive propaganda.

February 2

A resolution calling upon Israel to withdraw behind the Egyptian-Israel armistice demarcation line without further delay was adopted by the UN General Assembly, 74-2 with two abstentions. A second resolution proposing the stationing of UNEF forces on the demarcation line was passed by a vote of 56-0 with 22 abstentions.

February 3

Israel refused to withdraw its troops from Gaza or Sharm el-Sheikh, despite a UN resolution, without guarantees from the UN.

A British delegation arrived in Amman, Jordan, to commence talks on the cancellation of the 1948 mutual defense treaty; they were then to decide on the terms of canceling this agreement and on future relations between the two countries.

King Saud of Saudi Arabia said that the Arab world would find the Eisenhower Middle East plan acceptable if the points Saud had raised could be clarified to the Arab world as they had been to him.

The Moroccan Government was advised by the United States that American economic aid to Morocco for the fiscal year ending June 30, 1957, would probably not exceed $20 million.

February 4

Premier Nabulsi said that Jordan wished to remain a friend to Britain despite the termination of their treaty.

French Foreign Minister Christian Pineau told the Political Committee of the UN General Assembly that France would never accept UN competence on the question of Algeria. He warned that if Algeria became a foreign land it would be

February 4

pledged to fanaticism and by its very poverty, would be open to Communism.

France told the UN it was preparing a long range plan to create a Franco-African community based on cultural, economic and strategic interests, and inviting Tunisia and Morocco to become members in free association.

British Foreign Secretary Lloyd said that Britain might submit its dispute with Yemen over Aden to the UN.

Crown Prince Abd-al-Ilah of Iraq paid an informal visit to the US.

The UN and Egypt signed an agreement on the status of the UNEF in Egypt.

February 5

US Secretary of State Dulles declared that the US would apply economic sanctions against Israel if the UN required such measures.

In talks between UN Secretary General Dag Hammarskjold and Israel leaders, Israel asked Hammarskjold for assurances that Egypt would not blockade Israel shipping.

The Red Cross announced completion of the repatriation of 5,500 Egyptian prisoners taken by Israel forces during their invasion of Egypt.

February 6

Security police began confiscating all Communist publications and Russian newspapers in Jordan. The Government banned the showing of Soviet movies in any public theater.

February 6

King Saud of Saudia Arabia endorsed the Eisenhower Doctrine in general terms at a Washington news conference.

Jordan proposed that Britain evacuate its Mafraq and Aqaba bases by March 31.

Egypt urged Hammarskjold to initiate a General Assembly debate on economic sanctions for Israel.

Britain and France asked Hammarskjold to negotiate an interim settlement of Suez Canal shipping, a definitive settlement of this problem being unlikely before the Canal would be partly reopened the following month.

President Eisenhower's statement — "We are committed to the support of the United Nations" — was considered an indication that the US would support UN imposed economic sanctions against Israel.

Turkey's Premier Menderes said that aid under the Eisenhower Doctrine should go first to governments endeavoring for peace rather than those endangering it. He named Syria and Egypt in the latter class.

The Algerian Oil Research and Exploration Company announced a program of oil exploration and expansion in Algeria.

The US told the UN to avoid taking any action that would hamper a peaceful settlement of the Algerian revolt. US policy was described by Ambassador Lodge as having two goals: an end to violence in Algeria, and a climate of opinion permitting the Algerians to work out a solution with the French which would satisfy their aspirations.

France and Morocco signed an agreement on administrative and technical cooperation to come into effect February 15.

February 7

The Soviet Union announced the cutting off of oil supplies to Israel because of its aggressive action against Egypt.

Egypt and Jordan agreed to allow each other's fishermen to fish in either country's waters in the Gulf of Aqaba.

Cuba warned the UN that any resolution insisting on a French arranged ceasefire and UN supervised elections in Algeria would violate the UN Charter. Cuba said that such a resolution would set a dangerous precedent, particularly in Latin America.

The US State Department declared that it was concerned over reports that Soviet arms were continuing to move into Egypt.

February 8

King Saud and President Eisenhower issued a communique following talks between the two leaders during King Saud's ten day visit to Washington. Agreement was reached on the renewal of the US five year lease on the Dhahran Air Base in exchange for American arms deliveries.

Britain and France demanded that Egypt cease oppressing their nationals in Egypt.

Ambassador Abd-al-Moneim Rifai of Jordan, spokesman for the Arab-Asian Bloc in the UN, stated that that group would seek sanctions against Israel unless it withdrew unconditionally from the Aqaba and Gaza areas.

Fadel al-Jamali, Iraqi representative at the UN, declared that French recognition of Algeria's independence was a prerequisite to achievement of the Pineau plan for settling the Algerian problem.

February, 1957

February 8

Israel said that it intended to retain its civilian administration in Gaza, and would not withdraw from the Gaza Strip and Sharm el-Sheikh without further specific guarantees from the UN.

February 9

Soviet Marshal Georgi K. Zhukov declared that President Eisenhower's program for the Middle East was a policy that would lead to war, not peace. He saw it as a new edition of an old colonialist policy.

The Egyptian Eastern Petroleum Company was established by the signature of articles of association in Cairo to carry out prospecting as well as to operate Government oil refinery at Suez and market its products.

February 10

The Sultan of Morocco arrived in Madrid by air on a private visit.

King Saud of Saudi Arabia arrived in Madrid where he was welcomed by General Franco and met with the Sultan of Morocco.

An Egyptian decree was issued stipulating that the Arabic language be obligatory for all business transactions.

February 11

Secretary of State Dulles told Ambassador Eban that in exchange for Israel's withdrawal from Aqaba and the Gaza Strip, the US would support the principle of free navigation in the Gulf of Aqaba, the stationing of UNEF troops in Gaza and the increase of UN observers in the area.

February, 1957

February 11

Secretary General Hammarskjold reassured Britain that Egypt would permit the passage of British ships through the Suez Canal.

Secretary General Hammarskjold was frustrated in his attempts to get the Israelis out of the Gaza Strip. He suggested that the General Assembly, as a matter of priority, tell him what to do next.

A Soviet proposal was issued for a joint four power declaration on the Middle East, based on six principles outlined in Mr. Shepilov's speech to the Supreme Soviet, and presented in the form of Notes to the United States, United Kingdom, and French Ambassadors in Moscow.

Spain and Morocco signed diplomatic and judicial conventions in Madrid.

An Aden newspaper reported that the Soviet Union had offered to build modern harbors for Yemen on a 15 year repayment basis.

February 12

The US offered a plan by Secretary Dulles by which Israel forces would be withdrawn from the Gulf of Aqaba and the Gaza Strip, and the US would use all its influence to establish the Straits of Tiran as an international waterway with free passage to all nations and to replace Israel troops with UNEF soldiers in the Gaza Strip and place the Strip under a de facto UN trusteeship.

The French Government introduced a bill in the National Assembly declaring the Universal Company of the Suez Canal a purely French company not subject to the laws of any foreign state. The bill was designed to eliminate any possible Egyptian claim to the company's assets under French law, and to permit the company to amend its statutes and engage in new

February, 1957

February 12

lines of activity without submitting its projects to the Egyptian Government.

The Soviet Union published a six point plan for peace in the Middle East. Of the six points the only new proposal was an end to arms shipments by all countries to the Middle East.

Soviet Foreign Minister Dimitri Shepilov suggested that the Big Four pledge economic aid to the Arab countries in the Middle East.

Spanish Foreign Ministry announced that Spain had agreed to represent Moroccan interests in Argentina, Bolivia, Brazil, Chile, Colombia, Cuba, Dominica, Ecuador, El Salvador, Guatemala, Haiti, Honduras, Nicaragua, Panama, Paraguay, Peru, the Philippines, Uruguay and Venezuela. The French protested that this was incompatible with the Franco-Moroccan diplomatic convention lodged in Rabat.

February 13

It was announced in London that Britain and Jordan had agreed to terminate their 1948 treaty of friendship no later than April 1, 1957.

February 15

Israel rejected the US proposal for the former's withdrawal from the Gulf of Aqaba and the Gaza Strip. Instead, Israel offered to withdraw only under certain conditions.

The US Department of State announced with regret that Israel did not seem responsive to the United States position on Israel troop withdrawal.

February, 1957

February 15

Resolution 1012 of the UN General Assembly (Session XI) — expressing hope for a peaceful, democratic and just solution in Algeria — was passed. France did not vote.

Ethiopian Emperor Haile Selassie, in a statement that was issued in Addis Ababa, accused Egypt of fomenting unrest among the Moslem population of Ethiopia.

February 16

US Secretary of State Dulles said that it was up to Israel to make the next move toward breaking the deadlock over its withdrawal from the Gaza Strip and the Gulf of Aqaba.

The Government of the United Kingdom submitted a memorandum to the United Nations Security Council on evidence that Communist countries and Egypt had supplied arms and military assistance to Yemen.

February 17

Iraqi Minister of Economy Nadim al-Pachachi said that Iraq was planning to lay a pipeline linking its northern and southern oilfields and carrying oil to the Kuwait port of Ahmadi. He added that Iraq would not agree to the transfer from the Arab countries of any of its present pipelines.

President Eisenhower announced publicly that Israel would receive no further concessions as a price for its withdrawal from the Gulf of Aqaba and the Gaza Strip.

Israel declared that any one of three alternatives would be sufficient to guarantee the removal of Israel troops from Egyptian territory: (1) a guarantee from any major world power that an Egyptian blockade of Aqaba would not be tolerated, (2) the stationing of a UNEF force at Sharm el-Sheikh to insure

February, 1957

February 17

freedom of passage, or (3) an agreement among the nations bordering the gulf (including Egypt) which would permit the free passage of the ships of all nations.

King Saud of Saudi Arabia visited the Sultan of Morocco at Rabat (February 17-21), and a communique was issued.

February 18

The US promised another financial contribution to the UN aid program for Palestine refugees, but suggested that the agency prepare to discontinue operation, scheduled to end in 1960.

February 19

The US, Great Britain, France and Norway submitted a plan to the UN for interim operation of the Suez Canal by which the canal was to be operated by Egypt, but tolls were to be collected by an outside agency.

February 20

President Eisenhower declared in a radio and television address that in the interests of peace the UN had no choice but to exert pressure upon Israel to comply with the withdrawal resolutions.

February 21

The US Government asked eight leading non-Zionist Jews to help influence Israel to withdraw its troops from the Gaza Strip and the Gulf of Aqaba.

February, 1957

February 21

Premier Ben-Gurion rejected President Eisenhower's plea for immediate withdrawal of Israel troops. However he said that Israel would make a further effort to break the deadlock.

King Saud of Saudi Arabia met the Bey of Tunis and Premier Bourguiba in Tunis.

Israel agreed to pull out its last troops if the UN Emergency Force stationed peacekeeping troops on the Aqaba Gulf and in the Gaza Strip. The UN Emergency Force troops were so stationed.

February 22

In a report to the General Assembly, Secretary General Dag Hammarskjold stated with confidence that it was the desire of the Government of Egypt that the takeover of Gaza from the military and civilian control of Israel would be orderly and safe, as it had been elsewhere.

The French Foreign Ministry issued a statement declaring that France could not support President Eisenhower's position on the withdrawal of Israel troops from Egyptian territory.

The Arab-Asian Bloc urged the UN to vote economic sanctions against Israel, in view of its continued defiance of seven resolutions calling for withdrawal from Egypt.

Britain demanded that Yemeni troops be immediately withdrawn from the Aden Protectorate.

King Saud visited Tripoli for two days of talks with King Idris.

February 23

The UN Political Committee approved economic aid for Arab refugees to help them become self sufficient.

February, 1957

February 23

Syria and Bulgaria ratified a trade agreement reached on June 2, 1956.

France lodged a protest in Rabat against the incursions of Moroccan irregulars into Mauritania and Algeria.

February 24

Following talks between King Saud of Saudi Arabia and King Idris, the Libyan Government issued a communique saying that the two kings had called for unconditional withdrawal of Israel troops from the Gaza Strip and the Gulf of Aqaba area, and that they were in accord in their appreciation of President Eisenhower's understanding of Arab problems.

February 25

The Israel Knesset gave Prime Minister Ben-Gurion a 72-29 vote of confidence on his insistence that guaranteed security and freedom of shipping for Israel must precede the final withdrawal of its troops from the Gaza and Gulf of Aqaba areas.

British Prime Minister Harold Macmillan told the House of Commons that Israel should withdraw from the Gaza Strip.

The US offered financial aid to the Sudan. Sudanese Premier Khalil said that there were no political or economic strings attached to the offer.

Heads of State of Egypt, Jordan, Saudi Arabia and Syria met for two days in Cairo to continue discussion of the Middle East situation and to hear a report from King Saud on his visit to the United States.

February, 1957

February 26

The UNEF began aerial observation of the Israel-Egyptian demarcation line as an experiment.

Numerous politically prominent Syrians were sentenced at the conclusion of a sensational treason trial.

February 27

President Nasser of Egypt, King Saud of Saudi Arabia, President Shukri al-Kuwatli of Syria, and King Hussein of Jordan issued a communique at the end of their conference in Cairo. They demanded immediate, unconditional withdrawal of Israel forces from Gaza and Aqaba; support for Egypt's unilateral control of the Suez Canal, and its claim for compensation from Great Britain and France; the denunciation of British aggression against Yemen; and support for the Arabs of Algeria in their fight against France.

It was reported from Washington that as a basis for withdrawal of its troops from Gaza and Aqaba, Israel accepted in principle US assurances on Israel security, through the UN, from Egyptian raids from Gaza, and support of the principle of free navigation in the Gulf of Aqaba.

February 28

The UN voted to continue aid to 925,000 Palestinian Arab refugees and asked its members for help.

Egyptian Foreign Minister Mahmoud Fawzi denounced US efforts to secure Israel's withdrawal from Gaza and Aqaba.

Israel Ambassador Abba Evan informed the US of Israel's decision to withdraw its troops from the Gaza Strip and the Gulf of Aqaba area.

February, 1957

February 28

A communique issued at the end of three days of talks in Washington between President Eisenhower and French Premier Mollet stated their common conviction that solutions to problems of the Middle East area could be achieved by peaceful means, in conformity with the principles of justice and international law. It also reaffirmed their adherence to the six principles regarding free use of the Suez Canal, as adopted by the UN Security Council the previous October.

US Vice President Nixon began visits to Morocco, Ghana, Liberia, Uganda, Ethiopia, the Sudan, Libya and Tunisia.

March, 1957

March 1

Israel agreed to withdraw its troops from the Gaza Strip and the Gulf of Aqaba area. Israel Foreign Minister Golda Meir said that the withdrawal decision was based on the assumptions that free navigation in the Gulf of Aqaba would continue, and that the Gaza Strip would be administered by the UNEF until a peaceful settlement or a definite agreement on the future of this territory was reached.

The Tunisian Embassy in Cairo announced that as of April 1 the Tunisian Government would end the services of all the 10,000 French officials in its employment.

Secretary of State John Foster Dulles assured the representatives of nine Arab states that Israel obtained no promises or concessions whatsoever from the US in return for the withdrawal of its troops, and that stories about a secret understanding between the US and Israel were "Communist propaganda."

Israel's Foreign Minister, Golda Meir, told the UN General Assembly that any interference with Israel shipping in the Gulf of Aqaba or the Straits of Tiran would be regarded as an act of war.

UNEF forces were maintained in Sharm el-Sheikh which was then demilitarized.

March 2

Following an emergency meeting of the Knesset, Israel held its withdrawal promise in abeyance pending clarification of the US position on the future control of Gaza.

Premier Bourguiba rejected the position of neutrality taken by representatives of Egypt, Syria, Jordan and Saudi Arabia in their parley in Cairo. He declared that the Communist doctrine would not work if applied in Tunisia.

March, 1957

March 2

President Eisenhower sent a letter to Prime Minister David Ben-Gurion assuring him that Israel would have no cause to regret its decision and urged that the withdrawal go forward with the utmost speed.

The US Senate gave the Eisenhower Doctrine a vote of confidence by rejecting a motion to strip the program of its military and economic features.

The United Kingdom and Morocco announced an agreement to negotiate a new treaty of commerce and navigation.

March 4

Prime Minister Ben-Gurion ordered the Israel Army to withdraw from the Gaza Strip and the Gulf of Aqaba area.

The Soviet Union and India attacked the assumptions under which Israel had agreed to withdraw from the Gaza Strip and Gulf of Aqaba on the ground that these would lead to indefinite UNEF occupation.

In a statement handed to Raymond A. Hare, American Ambassador to Egypt, the nine Arab League Member States protested any plans to enforce freedom of Israel navigation in the Gulf of Aqaba and to impose UN administration in the Gaza Strip.

March 5

A Presidential Decree ended the general mobilization ordered in Egypt on October 29, 1956.

March, 1957

March 5

UN Secretary General Hammarskjold informed the UN that UNEF would take over provisional administration of Gaza within 48 hours.

Secretary of State Dulles declared that there had been a tendency on the part of Egypt to drag its feet in clearing the Suez Canal.

Prime Minister David Ben-Gurion told the Knesset that Israel was evacuating the Gaza Strip on the assumption that the UN administration would remain there until a peace settlement was concluded, and that freedom of action was reserved if there was a return to the conditions of deterioration which existed previously.

March 6

The UNEF took over the administration of the Gaza Strip.

Prime Minister Ben-Gurion won an 84-25 vote of confidence on his Government's decision to withdraw Israel forces from Sinai and Aqaba.

Premier Sulaiman Nabulsi of Jordan asserted that any attempt by the US to enforce freedom of navigation for Israel shipping in the Gulf of Aqaba would be considered an attitude of enmity by the Arab world.

An Egyptian state of emergency, proclaimed at the outbreak of Suez intervention, was lifted, together with a blackout and other restrictions then imposed.

March 7

The Egyptian Cotton Administration denied reports that Czechoslovakia had bought Egyptian cotton and resold it to West Germany for ten percent less than the market price.

March, 1957

March 7

The Jordan-Israel Mixed Armistice Commission (with Israel absent) censured Israel for an infringement of Jordan's air space on March 4.

The Iraq Petroleum Company said that Syria had offered on January 4 to restore all IPC (Iraq Petroleum Company) activities except repair of the pumping stations.

The Egyptian Suez Canal Authority said that all ships which paid tolls to Egypt would be allowed transit through the Canal.

The US House of Representatives adopted by 350-60 the Senate version of the Eisenhower Doctrine.

Israel troops blew up Egyptian military works at the mouth of the Gulf of Aqaba in preparation for withdrawal.

March 8

UN Secretary General Dag Hammarskjold informed the General Assembly that Israel forces had been completely withdrawn behind the 1949 armistice line and that UN units had moved into both Gaza and Aqaba.

The Egyptian Government opened the Suez Canal to vessels under 500 tons on payment of tolls to Egyptian authorities.

Iraq Petroleum Company's repair teams entered Syria and the following day began the repair of oil pumping stations that were blown up by the Syrian army on November 2, 1956.

March 9

Egypt rejected the UN plan for interim operation of the Suez Canal and insisted that all tolls be paid to the Egyptian Canal Authority.

March, 1957

March 9

French and Tunisian representatives signed a convention according Tunisia judicial autonomy in conformity with its independent status previously recognized by France.

Iraq Petroleum Company agreed to make Iraq an interest free advance on future royalties of 25 million pounds sterling.

US President Eisenhower signed a revised joint congressional resolution authorizing the military and economic aid provisions of his Middle East Doctrine.

March 10

Egypt and Czechoslovakia completed an expanded trade agreement, establishing a total exchange of goods between the two countries at LE50 million before 1958.

Diplomatic relations were restored between France and Tunisia. They had been broken off on October 22, 1956.

According to the New Times, a Soviet weekly magazine, there were mass meetings in Gaza, Rafah, and Khan Yunis demanding the return of Egyptian administration and protesting against the plans for internationalizing the Gaza area.

March 11

Egypt appointed General Hassan Abd-al-Latif civil governor to take over administration of the Gaza Strip.

Washington was described as shocked and surprised by Egypt's appointment of a governor for Gaza.

March, 1957

March 11

The US rejected a Soviet proposal for a four power declaration on the Middle East offered in February to the UN. The declaration would have barred military alliances, foreign bases, and arms shipments to the area.

Pumping of crude petroleum from Iraq to the Mediterranean was resumed through a newly repaired pipeline damaged by sabotage in November, 1956.

Egypt accused UNEF of exceeding its authority in the Gaza Strip and announced its intention of taking over administration of the area at once.

March 12

The US State Department appealed to all parties concerned to continue to cooperate with the UN and its agencies in efforts to maintain peace and tranquility in the Middle East.

Egypt told UN representative Bunche that it would not send an army of administrators into Gaza.

The US asked Egypt to cooperate in keeping peace in the Middle East.

Saudi Arabia lifted the ban on oil shipments to Britain and France.

Ambassador James P. Richards, special presidential representative under the US Middle East resolution, began visits to Lebanon, Libya, Turkey, Iran, Pakistan, Afghanistan, Iraq, Saudi Arabia, Yemen, the Sudan, Greece, Israel, Tunisia and Morocco.

March 13

Israel Premier Ben-Gurion declared that Israel still had the right to act if the Egyptians returned to Gaza.

March, 1957

March 13

The 1948 British-Jordanian treaty of friendship came to an end following an exchange of notes between the two governments.

March 14

Egypt took over the civil administration of the Gaza Strip from the UNEF.

The US contributed $8,042,000 to UNRWA.

Gaza's Governor, Major General Abd-al-Latif, arrived in Gaza to set up an Egyptian Administration.

British Foreign Secretary Lloyd told the House of Commons that UNEF should administer the Gaza Strip until a permanent settlement could be negotiated.

The Soviet Union agreed to deliver 500,000 tons of oil to Egypt in exchange for Egyptian goods under an agreement signed in Cairo.

March 15

Libyan Premier Ben-Halim strongly endorsed the Eisenhower Doctrine in his country.

The US announced resumption of economic aid discussions following Israel's withdrawal behind armistice lines.

An official Egyptian source announced that President Nasser would not allow Israel to use the Suez Canal.

Cairo Radio reported a Saudi Arabian statement which described the Gulf of Aqaba as absolute Arab territory.

March, 1957

March 16

Following two days of talks between US Ambassador Richards and Lebanese leaders, a joint statement was issued in Beirut announcing agreement in principle that the US would provide the Government of Lebanon certain equipment needed to strengthen the Lebanese armed forces. This was in addition to a recent grant of military equipment for the same purpose.

A Soviet Government delegation, headed by A. F. Gorkin, Supreme Soviet Deputy and President of the Soviet Supreme Court, left Moscow for Tunisia.

Egyptian army reconnaissance units moved into al-Arish, forty miles from the southern end of the Gaza Strip.

March 17

It was announced in Damascus that the Syrian Government approved a contract with the Technoexport concern of Czechoslovakia to build an oil refinery.

UN officials confirmed that UNEF troops had yielded Sinai-Gaza border checkpoints to Egyptian troops.

March 18

In a joint American-Israel communique, Israel Foreign Minister Golda Meir expressed deep concern at the return of Egypt to Gaza, the re-establishment of its control therein and the reduction of the responsibilities of the UN in the Gaza area, in contradistinction to the assumptions and expectations expressed in the UN. Secretary of State Dulles said the US stood firmly by the hopes and expectations it had expressed with regard to the situation which should prevail in the area with respect to the exercise of the UN in Gaza, the free and innocent passage of the Straits of Tiran by the ships of all nations and the settlement of the Suez Canal problem.

March, 1957

March 18

Radio Cairo reported that Gaza's Governor, Major General Abd-al-Latif, announced that UNEF would evacuate its headquarters and all occupied buildings in Gaza within 48 hours. Egyptian military vehicles entered Gaza. The vanguard of 150 Canadian troops scheduled to reinforce the Canadian UNEF force arrived in Cairo. Israel seized two armed Arab infiltrators from the Gaza Strip.

An Israel freighter sailed through the Gulf of Aqaba to the Red Sea without incident.

An Egyptian memorandum was sent to foreign missions in Cairo stating that, on reopening, Suez Canal dues should be paid in advance to the Egyptian Canal Authority or its authorized agents.

March 19

Following a state visit to Saudi Arabia, Iran's Shah Muhammad Riza and King Saud issued a joint communique stating that all international problems should be solved through peaceful means in accordance with the UN Charter.

Israel asked the United States to live up to its moral commitments in regard to UN control of Gaza.

The UN Secretary General left for Cairo to confer with Egyptian President Nasser on arrangements for the UNEF in Gaza.

March 20

The International Red Cross announced that 993 Jewish refugees had sailed from Alexandria.

March, 1957

March 20

The Egyptian Government's memorandum on the reopening of the Suez Canal was published in Cairo.

March 21

A joint US-Libyan communique said that Libya would receive further economic aid under the Eisenhower Doctrine.

UN Secretary Hammarskjold visited Cairo for discussions with President Nasser. He also visited the Suez Canal area.

March 22

The US offered to join the Military Committee of the Baghdad Pact, but said it would not become a full member of the Pact.

A communique issued at the conclusion of Ambassador Richards' mission to Turkey revealed that an offer of American financial aid was made for several regional projects of the Baghdad Pact.

March 23

Moscow Radio criticized the US decision to join the Military Committee of the Baghdad Pact as "dangerous to the existence of Arab countries."

March 24

A joint communique issued at the end of a conference in Bermuda between President Eisenhower and British Prime Minister Harold Macmillan expressed agreement on the following points dealing with the Middle East: (1) willingness of the United States to participate actively in the work of the

March, 1957

March 24

Military Committee of the Baghdad Pact; (2) need for the speedy implementation of recent resolutions of the UN General Assembly dealing with the Gaza Strip and the Gúlf of Aqaba; (3) importance of compliance both in letter and in spirit with the Security Council resolution of October 12 concerning the Suez Canal and on support for the efforts of the Secretary General to bring about a settlement in accordance with its provisions.

Israel submitted a written request to Secretary General Hammarskjold before his departure for Cairo that he ask President Nasser whether Egypt still considered itself at war with Israel.

Menahem Beigin, leader of the Opposition in the Israel Parliament, announced a nation-wide campaign to dissolve the Knesset and hold new national elections. He accused Premier Ben-Gurion and his Cabinet of breaking their pledge of office by voting to withdraw from Gaza.

The Middle East press criticized the new US link with the Baghdad Pact as indicative of an American intent to pursue Britain's traditional Arab policy.

Iraq announced the end of the boycott of the United Kingdom in the Baghdad Pact organization.

March 25

Iraq and the Sudan issued a joint communique stating that the two countries had reached complete agreement on political, economic and cultural relations.

A cultural agreement between Egypt, Syria and Jordan was reached, unifying the curricula in schools and colleges.

March, 1957

March 25

The Egyptian Government took over all the branches in Egypt of the British owned Barclay's Bank as part of its program to Egyptianize all foreign banks and insurance companies.

Tunisia's Premier Bourguiba arrived in Rabat for a state visit.

March 26

Tunisia and the US signed a pact giving Tunisia $5,500,000 in economic aid.

Secretary of State Dulles declared that under the 1949 armistice agreement, Egypt had no authority to exercise belligerent rights against Israel. He also questioned whether Egypt had the right arbitrarily to expel UNEF forces from Gaza and Aqaba until there was assurance of tranquility which would indicate that the initial mission was wholly accomplished.

Premier Nabulsi of Jordan said that the US had revealed its true policy toward the Arabs by joining the Baghdad Pact Military Committee.

Lebanon and Saudi Arabia said they had agreed that the Gulf of Aqaba and Straits of Tiran were purely Arab territorial waters. Saudi Arabia began moving troops into Aqaba under an agreement with Jordan. The troops were to be replacements for British troops evacuating Aqaba following termination of the Anglo-Jordanian treaty.

The US announced that a project was under way to build an international pipeline for oil running from Iraq through Turkey to the Mediterranean.

March 27

President Nasser reportedly had accepted a gentleman's agreement to do nothing to disturb the peace in the Gaza Strip and Gulf of Aqaba.

March, 1957

March 29

Israel was amenable to the UN proposal to erect a mined fence along the Gaza border. However, Israel stipulated that UN troops and not Egyptians must patrol the barrier on the Gaza side.

President Nasser declared that he would continue to bar Israel shipping from the Suez Canal until the problem of the Arab refugees was settled.

A nine ship convoy began the first passage through the Suez Canal since the previous November.

Premier Mollet received a vote of confidence from the French National Assembly on his Algerian policy by a vote of 221-188, with 111 abstentions.

A Tass statement that Israel's French supported aggression against Egypt might have serious consequences for world peace was published in Moscow.

March 30

Under an interim arrangement concluded between Egypt and the UN, UN troops began forming a Palestine Arab police force for joint patrolling of the Gaza Strip.

President Nasser accused the US of trying to starve the Egyptian people by refusing to sell wheat to his country, in contrast to the 600,000 tons supplied the previous year by the Soviet Union.

March, 1957

March 27

Egypt, Saudi Arabia and Jordan agreed that Saudi Army units would encamp in the port of Aqaba, Jordan, following withdrawal of British units.

Speaking to the National Assembly, French Premier Mollet said that France would back Israel's right to answer with force any Egyptian attack in the Gulf of Aqaba or launched from the Gaza Strip.

A French company was formed to exploit mineral resources of the Sahara.

March 28

President Nasser submitted a memorandum containing his proposals for operation of the Suez Canal to the US and six other countries. The Egyptian Suez Canal Authority would have full control over the canal. Egypt would respect the 1888 Constantinople Convention; disputes arising between parties would be settled in accordance with the UN Charter or referred to the World Court; tolls would be levied in accordance with the 1936 agreement, and be payable to the Authority in advance to any bank authorized by it; a Suez Capital Land Development Fund would be established for developmental needs of the canal, and 25 percent of all gross receipts paid into this fund; and the Authority would pay the Government of Egypt five percent of all gross receipts as royalty.

The Soviet Union warned France and Israel of heavy retaliation for any attack on Egypt.

March , 1957

March 30

Tunisian Premier Habib Bourguiba concluded his five day visit to Morocco by signing a treaty of friendship and alliance with that country.

March 31

The Israel Foreign Ministry expressed its willingness to negotiate with Egypt concerning the Arab refugees.

Iraqi King Faisal opened the Baghdad Pact nuclear center near Baghdad, thus bringing to an end Iraq's boycott of Britain since the invasion of Egypt. Britain supplied most of the technical equipment for the center.

A US note was presented in Cairo containing suggestions whereby Egyptian proposals for operating the Suez Canal could be brought into line with six principles enunciated by the UN Security Council, October 13, 1956.

Saudi Arabia, in a memorandum, claimed islands of Tiran and Sanafir at the mouth of the Gulf of Aqaba as Saudi territory and the Straits of Tiran as Saudi territorial waters.

The Arab League Council concluded its session. The Council protested against the actions of certain Western powers as encouraging Israel's aggressiveness and creating a threat to peace and security in the Middle East.

April 1

UN Secretary General Dag Hammarskjold declared in a statement that UNEF would assist the Egyptian administration of the Gaza Strip in preventing infiltration into Israel.

The US State Department lifted restrictions imposed October 31, 1956 on travel to Egypt, Israel, Jordan and Syria.

Britain's Prime Minister Macmillan said the US and his country would reject any proposal for a Suez settlement that did not conform fully with the six principles approved by the Security Council.

British insurance underwriters announced that war risk premiums for British and French ships using the Suez Canal would be double the additional rate payable by ships of other nations for each passage.

Khaled Azm, Syrian Defense Minister ad interim, categorically refuted Western allegations that the Soviet Union was interfering in his country's domestic affairs.

April 2

Britain began evacuating its base at Maan, in south Jordan.

Arabs in Gaza celebrated the raising of the Egyptian flag over the Government building.

Maurice Faure, French Secretary of State for Foreign Affairs, told the Council of the Republic that French interests and influence in Morocco and Tunisia would not be replaced by US dollars and technicians.

Secretary of State Dulles said that Egypt's future hinged on its answer to US proposals for operation of the Suez Canal.

April 2

Morocco and the US signed an agreement under which Morocco would receive $20 million in economic aid.

April 3

Six US Senators called on President Eisenhower to lead in establishing a bypass to the Suez Canal for the long term protection of Western interests.

In a letter to Secretary General Dag Hammarskjold, the Algerian National Liberation Front accused France of conducting a "systematic war of extermination" against the Algerian people.

French shipowners said they would continue to boycott the Suez Canal until further notice.

Israel announced it might erect a barbed wire fence along its border with the Gaza Strip to keep out Arab infiltrators.

Jordanian Premier Sulaiman Nabulsi's Government announced its intention to establish diplomatic relations with the Soviet Union at ambassadorial level.

April 4

Secretary General Hammarskjold declared that he had relayed to Egypt Israel's inquiry as to whether the former still considered itself in a state of belligerency with Israel. He asserted that while the absence of a peace settlement was "highly regrettable," it did not violate the UN Charter, and added that the state of no peace in the technical and legal sense was something with which we regrettably had to live.

Premier Sami al-Solh of Lebanon asked Parliament for formal approval of his cabinet's decision to work with the US for mutual defense against Communism.

April 4

Premier Sulaiman Nabulsi of Jordan said that if offered Soviet aid, his country would accept.

The Canadian Ambassador to Egypt, Mr. E. H. Norman, committed suicide following allegation by the US Senate Internal Security Subcommittee of "Communist associations."

April 5

France announced plans to set up a permanent commission to safeguard human rights in Algeria, in answer to charges of excessive French brutality in the suppression of the revolt there.

In a joint communique with Egypt the Sudan agreed to follow Egyptian policy of "positive neutrality."

April 6

A US oil tanker, the Kern Hills, sailed along the Gulf of Aqaba and arrived at Elath, Israel, in a test of the principle of innocent passage in the Gulf.

Lebanon signed a trade agreement with Nationalist China to improve mutual trade. Payment for goods, either exported or imported, would be made in US dollars or any other currency agreed on by the importers and exporters in accordance with regulations.

Premier Nabulsi of Jordan asserted that his country would maintain a "positive neutralism" in its dealings with the Soviet Union and the US.

The Netherlands Government advised its ships not to use the Suez Canal until further notice.

April 6

The Soviet Ambassador to Israel returned to Tel Aviv.

April 7

Israel granted greater rights to Druze and Arabs serving in Israel defense forces; they would now be eligible for full membership in the Federation of Jewish Labor and exempt from restrictions on border area travels.

Britain announced it would reinforce its troops in Aden within a week with the sending of a squadron of hussars with scout cars from Malaya.

Egypt charged that an Israel patrol had violated the Gaza demarcation line April 1. Egypt asked the Mixed Armistice Commission to investigate.

The Libyan Government ordered the closing of the Egyptian Club in Tripoli. No official explanation was given. Most of the club's members were described as civil servants seconded to the Libyan Government.

Egypt and the UK signed an agreement concerning the Sudanese currency exchange.

April 8

The US agreed to provide $12,500,000 to the Baghdad Pact nations for regional road, rail, and telecommunications projects.

The US State Department announced that the Saudi Arabian Government extended for five years the agreement permitting the US Air Force to use the Dhahran Air Base.

April, 1957

April 8

Israel accepted a proposal by UNEF commander General Burns that it build a barbed wire fence and a mined strip between its territory and the Gaza Strip.

Egypt complained to the Mixed Armistice Commission that Israel patrols had kidnapped two Arabs in the Gaza Strip.

In a letter to the Security Council, Israel's Ambassador Abba Eban stated that the "continuation of marauding and infiltration" from the Gaza Strip into Israel was a matter which "my Government could not avoid viewing with extreme concern."

The Egyptian frigate Abukir, last wreck blocking normal Suez Canal traffic, was raised.

A communique issued at the end of two days of talks between Special Ambassador James A. Richards and Iraqi Premier Nuri-Said affirmed that the US would assist in developing Iraq's telecommunications and railway network and would provide additional military assistance.

The Sudanese pound came into circulation.

An Egyptian decree authorized the sale or liquidation of sequestrated British and French banks and insurance companies; the sale and transfer of contracts was completed and signed on April 17.

April 9

Two tankers of about 20,000 tons each passed through the Suez Canal.

An Israel patrol fought a running battle with five Jordanian infiltrators in Israel territory at Beit Guvrin.

April, 1957

April 9

An order issued by the Finance Ministry permitted Egyptian shipping companies to deal with their British, French and Australian counterparts.

April 10

Jordanian Premier Sulaiman al-Nabulsi's Government resigned at the request of King Hussein.

The Asian-African Bloc in the UN charged that the General Assembly's resolution on Algeria was being frustrated and negated.

The Jerusalem Electricity Company, a British concession since the Palestine Mandate, became the property of the Jordan Government under an agreement signed to that effect.

Kamal Ramzi Istino, the Egyptian Minister of Supply, reported that Egypt was receiving two-thirds of its imports from the Soviet Union; formerly, nearly 100 percent of Egypt's imports came from the West.

The Suez Canal was declared open to all but the largest vessels following clearance operations by a UN salvage team.

It was reported in Washington that official connection between the Egyptian Government and the fedayeen guerrillas who had been raiding Israel had been established through documentary evidence.

Two UNEF Indian soldiers were killed in a land mine blast in the Gaza Strip.

The French National Assembly passed a bill decreeing that the Suez Canal Company remained subject to French law despite Egyptian unilateral action in nationalizing it.

April, 1957

April 11

The Saudi Arabian Government declared that any attempt at giving the Gulf of Aqaba international character would constitute "encroachment on the sovereignty of Saudi Arabia and a threat to its territorial security."

Great Britain announced willingness to permit Egypt to transfer 15 million pounds sterling ($42 million) of its blocked sterling balance to the Sudan.

The US State Department announced that in a joint statement issued by King Saud and Ambassador Richards following their conference in Riyadh, the former had reaffirmed his promise to oppose Communism and any other threat to Middle East peace.

Saudi Arabia announced that it would not let Israel shipping pass through the Gulf of Aqaba.

April 12

The US reaffirmed its support of the principle of innocent passage in the Gulf of Aqaba, and declared it would do so unless there were a ruling to the contrary by the World Court.

Israel asked the UN to ascertain if Egypt still considered itself at war with it.

The Intergovernmental Committee for European Migration voted to finance the transportation to Israel of 12,500 Jewish refugees from Egypt.

April 13

A Syrian armored regiment entered the northern part of the country of Jordan to reinforce the 3,000 man Syrian brigade already there.

April, 1957

April 13

The Egyptian Government reimposed censorship on outgoing radio broadcasts.

The Egyptian Embassy in Washington, in a formal statement, asserted that the principle of freedom of navigation in the Suez Canal was fully applied and respected by the Egyptian operating authority.

Foreign Minister Golda Meir of Israel declared that Israel would view with concern any change in the status quo in Jordan.

Abd-al-Halim al-Nimr, Arab nationalist and Deputy Premier and Defense and Interior Minister in the Nabulsi Government, became the new Premier of Jordan.

Jordanian anti-American demonstrations against the Eisenhower Doctrine took place in Amman and continued in towns west of the Jordan for three days.

April 14

Clashes between army units loyal to King Hussein of Jordan and pro-Egyptian army units followed a military coup by the King. He forced pro-Egyptians out of the army and the government.

Major General Ali Abu-Nuwar of Jordan, Army Chief of Staff, left for Syria. King Hussein appointed Major General Ali Hayari as Acting Chief of Staff. Nabulsi and other former cabinet members were placed under house arrest.

Premier Guy Mollet revealed that France had sent 700,000 soldiers to Algeria to combat the rebellion.

The Cabinet of Premier al-Nimr of Jordan was dissolved before it could take office, due to non-participation of a majority of members. King Hussein asked Senate President Said al-Mufti

April, 1957

April 14

as Premier designate to form a caretaker Cabinet.

US Special Representative James Richards arrived in Yemen.

April 15

Italy declared that Egypt had broken the 1952 Italian-Egyptian agreement on Suez Canal fees by requiring an Italian ship passing through the canal to pay tolls in cash rather than Italian goods and services.

A new Jordan coalition government was formed under Hussein Fakhri al-Khalidi.

The Asian-African Bloc complained to the UN that "violent and mass repression" was being used to crush the Algerian nationalists.

April 16

The Lebanese Ambassador protested to the US against the passage of the US tanker Kern Hills through Arab territorial waters. The Kern Hills was chartered by the Israel Government to carry oil from Elath to Aqaba.

Egypt complained to the Security Council against Israel's "continued acts of provocation and aggression against the inhabitants of the Gaza Strip."

The Iranian Foreign Ministry declared that the Government of Iran had instructed the National Iranian Oil Company to avoid all transactions with Israel.

Syria and Iraq protested to the US against the Kern Hills' voyage.

April, 1957

April 17

A decree blacklisted 13 foreign firms for trading with Israel despite warnings from the Arab League. The blacklisted firms included Swiss, American, Cypriote, French and seven British companies.

Iraq reinforced troops along the Jordanian frontier to help King Hussein if necessary.

April 18

A one year trade pact was signed between Morocco and the Soviet Union.

Seven banks and 17 insurance companies were "Egyptianized" after contracts had been signed for their sale to Egyptian companies.

A trade agreement was signed between Egypt and Rumania.

Israel forces engaged Syrians and Jordanians in separate gun battles. No casualties were reported.

Major General Burns, commander of UNEF, lodged five complaints with Israel authorities concerning violations and incidents in the Gaza Strip since the start of UNEF activity there.

A group of 174 French scientists and professors wrote to French President Coty denouncing torture in Algeria.

The US denied any commitment to use force in helping to defend Jordan.

A Japanese petroleum company signed a provisional agreement with King Saud for oil exploration rights in Saudi waters in the Persian Gulf.

April, 1957

April 16

The newspaper al-Jihad reported that King Saud placed at King Hussein's disposal all the Saudi troops which had been in Jordan since the Anglo-French-Israel action in Egypt the past November.

A mission from Syria to Saudi Arabia returned after securing an agreement that Saudi Arabia would release SL21 million in blocked funds.

April 17

King Hussein in a broadcast issued a warning to those who might wish to partition Jordan.

President Eisenhower affirmed American willingness to assist Jordan if it should become the victim of aggression.

Five Hunter Mark VI jet fighters presented to Iraq by Britain arrived at Habbaniya Air Base in Iraq.

Warren Pierson, president of the International Chamber of Commerce, outlined a program to be called Eurofrics, for a proposed union of six Mediterranean countries. Italy, France, Spain, Morocco, Tunisia and Algeria would constitute the union, essentially one of joint economic development.

An agreement to increase trade between Lebanon and Saudi Arabia was signed in Riyadh.

The Arab League advised its members that Yemen needed extensive military, political, and economic aid to "resist British aggression."

April, 1957

April 18

Exiled Major General Ali Abu-Nuwar's resignation was accepted by King Hussein of Jordan. Major General Hayari became army head by Royal Decree.

The Asian Legal Consultative Committee held its first session in New Delhi, and representatives of Burma, Ceylon, India, Indonesia, Iraq, Japan and Syria attended.

April 19

Jordan's new Chief of Staff, Ali Hayari, was reportedly taking steps to "Bedouinize" the army.

The US warned Israel against any possible action taken against Jordan.

A general French amnesty offer to rebels, which stated that if they surrendered and had only served as combatants they would not be punished, was recognized only by scattered individuals.

French Minister of Interior Jules opened a new campaign to end terrorism among North Africans living in France.

The first British ship, West Breeze, to pay tolls to the Egyptian Suez Canal Authority entered the waterway.

Lebanese Minister of Public Works Muhammad Sabra said that a provisional agreement had been reached with the French concessionary Beirut Port Company enabling Lebanese to own most of the company's stock shares and a majority of seats on the board of directors, and for the transfer of the head office from Paris to Beirut.

The Soviet Government's notes on peace and security in the Middle East were transmitted to France, the United Kingdom and the US.

April 20

Syrians opened fire on an Israel patrol east of Lake Huleh, according to a report by Israel spokesmen.

Jordanian General Hayari resigned while on a military mission to Syria. He asked for political asylum in that country and accused the Palace of preparing a plot in cooperation with "foreign non-Arab military attaches in Amman" against Jordan's independence and liberty.

The State Department announced that US economic aid to Israel was being resumed.

Britain completed evacuation of its armored base at Maan, Jordan.

Major General Hafez Majali replaced Major General Hayari as Chief of Staff in Jordan.

Moscow Radio reported that Jordan's Foreign Minister Nabulsi had appealed to the Soviet Union for aid in opposing Israel imperialist aggression.

Six US transports with 1, 800 marines on board anchored off Beirut; fifty ships of the US Sixth Fleet carried out air defense maneuvers in the open sea.

April 21

Foreign Minister Nabulsi charged meddling by some diplomatic envoys in Jordan's affairs.

Israel charged that General Burns, Commander of the UNEF, had shelved the idea of a mined fence between its border and the Gaza Strip and claimed that the UNEF was coming increasingly under the control of Egypt's President Nasser.

April 21

Arab raiders ambushed an Israel patrol between Tel Aviv and Haifa. There were no casualties.

Security police in Riyadh uncovered a terrorist plot to kill King Saud and made numerous arrests in a series of raids.

The Soviet Union asked the US, Britain and France to join in renouncing the use of force to settle the problems in the Middle East.

The Jordan Government stated that diplomatic relations would be established with the Soviet Union and that it would receive Mr. Richards, President Eisenhower's special assistant.

April 22

Premier Khalidi of Jordan branded as "without foundation" accusations by Syria and Egypt of American meddling in Jordan's political affairs.

An exchange of diplomatic correspondence between Soviet Premier Nikolai A. Bulganin and former British Prime Minister Sir Anthony Eden prior to the Anglo-French invasion of Suez was published in London and Moscow. Britain disclosed that the diplomatic correspondence with the Soviet Union from the fall of 1956 had pleaded with the Soviets to recognize the legitimate interests of nations using the Suez Canal and help the West reach a settlement with Nasser.

The Soviet Union disclosed that it had warned Britain and France before their attack on Suez that "little wars can turn into big ones."

Premier Khalidi of Jordan cautioned neighboring Arab countries against excessive statements about the political situation in Jordan.

April 22

The Jordanian Finance Ministry said that Saudi Arabia had given five million pounds sterling in aid to Jordan.

The Sudanese Prime Minister, Sayed Abdulla Khalil, arrived in Addis Ababa for a six day visit.

April 23

Following talks with the mission led by Ambassador Richards to explain the Eisenhower Doctrine to the Middle East, the Sudan Government revealed that it had told the mission that the Doctrine might lead to a cold war in the area, with Russian retaliation.

Secretary of State Dulles said that American shipping companies still had instructions to pay the Egyptian Canal Authority only under protest.

The Soviet newspaper Izvestia published the letters on the Suez Canal issue exchanged by the Governments of the Soviet Union, the United Kingdom and France on the eve of the British-French-Israel expedition against Egypt.

April 24

Egypt published a declaration stating its conditions for management and operation of the Suez Canal.

Premier al-Khalidi's cabinet resigned amid popular disturbances in Jordan.

It was reported from Baghdad that the Ministry of Education was no longer hiring Egyptian school teachers.

President Eisenhower declared that the US regarded the independence and integrity of Jordan as vital.

April 24

King Hussein charged that Jordan's troubles were due to international Communism.

The first US ship to transit the Suez Canal since its reopening, the S. S. President Jackson, reached Port Said.

Pravda accused the Baghdad Pact countries and Israel of preparing direct intervention in the affairs of Jordan.

April 25

Great Britain declared that Jordan's independence and integrity were essential elements to Middle East peace.

The US dispatched its Sixth Fleet to the eastern Mediterranean as a "precautionary" move against the threat to Jordan of "international Communism."

The King of Jordan appointed Ibrahim Hashem as Premier.

President Shukri at-Kuwatli of Syria flew to Cairo to confer with President Nasser.

The British Government advised its shipowners to avoid using the Suez Canal.

Dag Hammarskjold suggested that the International Court of Justice might rule on the question of Israel's right to use the Suez Canal.

The US Navy announced that the Atlantic Fleet Amphibious Force ships carrying a battalion of Marines would sail in a few days for the Mediterranean.

April, 1957

April 25

The Soviet Union accused the US of endangering peace in the Middle East by dispatching the Sixth Fleet to the eastern Mediterranean.

The Suez Canal Company decision to make a technical study of the Channel tunnel project was announced.

King Hussein of Jordan accused Egyptian press and radio of spreading untrue propaganda about him; martial law was proclaimed in Jordan, political parties were dissolved, frontiers sealed, air services to Cairo, Damascus, and Beirut were suspended, military courts created and a National Military Governor appointed.

April 26

A special Syro-Egyptian mission headed by President Kuwatli and Wing Commander Ali Sabri, President Nasser's chief political adviser, flew to Saudi Arabia to discuss the Jordanian situation with King Saud.

King Hussein received a cablegram from King Saud congratulating him on his maintenance of military security and order in his country.

The US Department of State disclosed that it had advised the Middle Eastern governments, particularly Egypt, Syria and Israel against any moves which might precipitate trouble in Jordan.

Henry Cabot Lodge, chief US delegate to the UN, told the Security Council that the Egyptian declaration in its present form did not fully meet the six requirements of the Security Council.

On the recommendation of the US, the Security Council took no action on Egypt's declaration on the Suez Canal.

April, 1957

April 26

Soviet broadcasts accused Israel of mobilizing along the Jordan border.

April 27

President Kuwatli of Syria returned to Cairo to report to President Nasser on his talks with King Saud of Saudi Arabia.

King Hussein of Jordan refused to approve a decree promulgated by the former Nabulsi Cabinet calling for establishment of diplomatic relations with the Soviet Union.

Egypt denied any intent or desire to threaten the independence of Jordan.

Premier Khalil announced full agreement between the Sudan and Ethiopia on closer political and economic cooperation, following talks with Emperor Haile Selassie.

The Egyptian owned Middle East News Agency in Jordan closed and all journalists except one were expelled from Jordan.

April 28

King Hussein flew from Jordan to Riyadh to confer with King Saud.

April 29

An offer to Jordan of $10 million in aid from the US was accepted by King Hussein.

Diplomatic representatives of Iraq, Jordan, Lebanon, Saudi Arabia and Syria called on Foreign Minister Ali Ardalan in

April, 1957

April 29

Tehran to thank him for his Government's assurance that Iran would not sell oil to Israel.

The Soviet Union warned that the US must bear responsibility for grave consequences that could develop out of the Jordan crisis.

King Hussein of Jordan and King Saud of Saudi Arabia stated that the crisis in Jordan was an internal affair.

April 30

US State Department Press Officer Lincoln White said that the Soviet Union was responsible for the recent crisis in Jordan.

King Hussein said he had no intention of binding Jordan to any treaty commitment under the Eisenhower Doctrine, and that there was no special reason for his having accepted US aid at this particular time.

Yemen complained to the UN that British forces had attacked a group of villages near Harib and another group in the Sharaf region near al-Baida.

Reliable sources in London reported that Britain would accept Egypt's provisions on the use of the Suez Canal by British ships.

Libya signed an agreement with the Export-Import Bank and the International Cooperation Administration for a $2,500,000 loan.

The Israel Foreign Ministry announced that Prime Minister David Ben-Gurion had invited UN Secretary General Dag Hammarskjold to Jerusalem for talks.

A UNEF vacation center was established in the Lebanese mountains near Beirut. Major General Burns, UNEF Commander, said that every member would get a weeks leave.

April, 1957

April 30

The Secretary General of the International Civil Aviation Organization, an autonomous UN body, said that the plane carrying five Algerian rebel leaders which had been forced down in Algiers on October 22, 1956, had been a French aircraft.

King Hussein declared that the crisis in Jordan had ended. He rejected Soviet allegations that the US was interfering in his country's affairs.

May, 1957

May 1

Britain reiterated its conviction that Israel ships should use the Suez Canal.

The Jordanian Government banned trade unions and employees' associations, effective May 2.

Mobil Oil Canada Limited reported finding natural gas in quantity in its first well in Fezzan, Libya.

May 2

James Richards, Special Assistant to Middle Eastern Affairs, arrived in Israel to discuss the Eisenhower Doctrine program.

It was announced in Washington that President Eisenhower ordered Ambassador Richards to return to the US without visiting Egypt, Syria and Jordan.

May 3

Syria and Czechoslovakia signed a trade agreement in Prague renewing Czechoslovakia's promise to build up Syria's economy.

Sir Winston Churchill criticized the UN for failure to help Britain in its Suez intervention, and defended his country's action.

The US Sixth Fleet left the eastern Mediterranean.

May 4

The US sent eight jet planes to Saudi Arabia.

Ambassador Richards of the US arrived in Tunisia.

May, 1957

May 5

Tunisian women voted for the first time in nationwide municipal elections.

King Hussein of Jordan declared that his battle waged against Leftist elements in his country had succeeded.

May 6

Major General Hafez Majali's appointment as Jordanian Chief of Staff was approved by King Hussein.

The Arab League blacklisted the US tanker Kern Hills for having carried oil to Israel.

US Secretary of State John Foster Dulles left Paris after a conference with Premier of France Guy Mollet and Foreign Minister Christian Pineau about the Suez Canal situation.

James P. Richards, US Special Envoy to explain the Eisenhower Doctrine to the Middle East, arrived in Morocco.

A Czechoslovakian-Egyptian agreement on scientific and technical cooperation was signed in Cairo.

May 7

General Raymond Wheeler, who supervised the UN Suez Canal clearance job, said that Egypt was capable of improving the Canal.

Syria protested to Turkey that military concentrations on the Turko-Syrian frontier were harming relations between the two countries.

The Lebanese Government announced the end of martial law and of press censorship.

May, 1957

May 7

Former Premier Nabulsi of Jordan was officially placed under house arrest.

May 8

The Lebanese Government banned importation of all Egyptian newspapers and magazines during elections.

The Neo-Destour party of Tunisian Premier Habib Bourguiba received 90 percent of the vote in the municipal elections throughout Tunisia.

Saudi Arabia sent a protest to the UN Secretary General against recent Israel naval and air activity.

May 9

Negotiations began in Rabat over continued US use of four air bases in Morocco.

The Suez Canal Users Association noted that the Egyptian plan for the Suez did not meet its demands for equitable settlement; each member state was left free to decide whether or not it would use the Canal.

Secretary General Hammarskjold, accompanied by UN Undersecretary Ralph J. Bunche, arrived in Jerusalem and conferred with Prime Minister Ben-Gurion and Foreign Minister Golda Meir.

May 10

Tunisian Premier Bourguiba sharply criticized US aid policies as applied by the Richards mission to the Middle East. He said that the US supported imperialism in North Africa by

May, 1957

May 10

continuing to regard Tunisia as a French sphere of influence.

United Nations Secretary General Dag Hammarskjold ended discussions with Israel Premier David Ben-Gurion and Foreign Minister Golda Meir. No major decisions were reached.

US Ambassador J.P. Richards revealed that he had committed about $120 million to the 15 Middle Eastern countries he visited. Nearly half the money was allocated for "guns, tanks and things of that kind," and the remainder for economic aid projects.

May 11

A reconciliation between Saudi Arabia and Iraq was effected as King Saud paid an official visit to Baghdad.

The spy trial of four Britons, 11 Egyptians, and a Yugoslav began in Cairo.

Six hundred Jews left Egypt for Israel.

Syria announced full payment from Saudi Arabia of its SL21 million in blocked funds.

Tunisia's Prime Minister Bourguiba arrived in Libya for a state visit.

The Libyan Government said that US economic and technical aid during the year ending June 30 would total more than $23 million, including that promised by the Richards mission.

The curfew was lifted in Jerusalem.

Jordan published details of an alleged plot by Egypt, Syria and the Soviet Union to overthrow the four Arab kings and the Lebanese republic.

May, 1957

May 12

Premier Ben-Halim of Libya told Parliament in a joint session that Libya would give all the aid in its power to Algerians fighting against French rule.

May 13

Colonel Noel Massignac, Chief of Staff to the French Commander in Chief, stated that the three year old rebellion in Algeria had cost about 12,000 lives, 8,000 of them Moslems.

Israel's Foreign Ministry revealed that Israel planned to send a ship through the Suez Canal; if Egypt tried to stop the ship, Israel would regard the action as "an act of war."

The Egyptian Government demanded the death penalty for one Briton on trial for spying, James Swinburn, and life sentences for three others.

Syria asked the UN Security Council to hear its charge that Israel's construction of a bridge in the Lake Huleh area was a violation of the 1949 Palestine Armistice.

Despite opposition from Conservative members of Parliament, Britain lifted its ban on use of the Suez Canal.

Morocco and Tunisia signed a trade agreement in Tunis agreeing to exchange scientific and technical missions and to expand their trade relations.

The US said that it would not block any attempt by Israel to send a ship through the Suez Canal.

May 14

Jon Kimche, editor of the Jewish Observer, was expelled from Lebanon.

May, 1957

May 14

Yemen protested that British forces were being concentrated on Kamaran Island, in the Red Sea, off Yemen, but administered from Aden.

Egypt named a delegation to open talks with Britain concerning the renewal of diplomatic and economic relations.

King Hussein of Jordan asked King Saud of Saudi Arabia and King Faisal of Iraq for additional loans or grants totalling $21 million.

In a communique issued in Amman, King Hussein expressed his regrets at being unable to meet with King Faisal of Iraq and King Saud of Saudi Arabia in Baghdad, "due to present circumstances."

May 15

President Kuwatli of Syria gave an Algerian National Liberation Front mission SL2,250,000 raised during "Algerian Week" in October, 1956.

Eight persons were killed and five wounded in a clash in Kuwait between government security forces and supporters of the Malik family, a distant branch of the ruling family.

The French Cabinet appealed to the UN Security Council to ask Egypt to agree to the six principles the Council had adopted for the Suez Canal. France refused to agree to Egypt's terms.

May 16

The US and Britain pledged financial aid to the Baghdad Pact

May, 1957

May 16

countries at meetings of the Economic Committee in Karachi. The US pledged $12,570,000 of Eisenhower Doctrine funds. Britain pledged two million pounds sterling. Pakistan also contributed RS200,000 for technical assistance projects.

Israel announced deferral of its intent to send a test ship through the Suez Canal.

The House of Commons defeated a Labor party vote of censure on the British Government's Suez policy by 308-259.

Syrian Foreign Minister Salah al-Bitar said Syria was determined to pay its share of the Arab subsidy to Jordan.

May 17

Egypt declared it would invoke its right of self defense against any Israel attempt to send a ship through Suez.

Following his state visit to Libya, Premier Bourguiba announced that cultural, health and communications agreements had been made between Tunisia and Libya. Teachers and students would be exchanged under the cultural agreement. Opening of a new radio link was also announced. The Premier also announced that Tunisia and Libya would seek to arrange talks between Algerian rebels and France on the French offer of free Algerian elections with neutral observers.

King Hussein of Jordan approved death sentences by hanging for four persons accused as traitors who had dealt with Israel.

May 18

The Russians, Poles and Czechs were reported bitter about Egypt's insistence that Suez tolls must be paid in dollars or Swiss francs.

May, 1957

May 18

Iraq and Saudi Arabia issued a joint statement following talks between King Faisal and King Saud. The statement condemned Communism, Western imperialism and Zionism and promised a new era in relations between the two countries and among all Arab states.

A Czech trade official was arrested as he prepared to leave Morocco; he was held on charges of paying a Moroccan official for documents.

President Nasser published a decree naming July 3 as the date for the general election for the proposed National Assembly.

Egypt and Afghanistan announced closer cooperation, both economic and cultural, in a statement issued at the end of a state visit to Egypt by Afghan Prime Minister Daud.

May 19

The Soviet Union branded Jordanian reports, issued May 11, of a Communist plot to overthrow four Middle Eastern monarchs, a complete fabrication.

The Soviet shipping agent in Port Said announced that the Soviet Union had set up a special Swiss franc account to pay tolls so that for some time to come no dispute would arise between Russia and Egypt over toll payments.

May 20

Arab League Secretary General Abd-al-Khaleq Hassouna proposed that Israel accept the 1947 UN partition plan as a basis for peace talks.

President Nasser proclaimed a new espionage law providing possible death penalties for treason and similar offenses.

May, 1957

May 20

The UN Security Council met at the request of the French delegation on May 15 to resume discussion of the Suez Canal question. No decision was reached.

Saudi Arabia informed Egypt that it considered the Gulf of Aqaba "Arab territorial waters" and that it supported any attempt to prevent Israel shipping from passing through.

The Yemeni Government protested to the UN against aggression by British troops on the Yemen frontier.

May 21

Sudanese Foreign Minister Mahgoub said in Parliament that the Sudan would not enter into any military pacts, nor into a defensive alliance with any other Arab nation. He called the Bandung conference a clear failure. He said that the Sudan's policy of positive neutralism meant not taking sides in world conflicts, but that it did not prohibit the acceptance of aid from any quarter. He declared that while no Arab country had rejected the Eisenhower Doctrine, the Sudan had decided after careful study not to give an opinion on it as of yet.

France cut off all aid to Tunisia, due to the Tunisian attitude of support for Algerian rebels. The Franco-Tunisian aid convention signed a month earlier had provided for French payment of 12 billion francs in several installments to Tunisia.

Saudi Arabia paid Jordan JD1,500,000 as the balance of the first installment of Saudi aid due under the Arab solidarity agreement replacing Britain's subsidy.

The Egyptian Government took over the Marconi Radio Telegraph Cable Organization in Egypt. It had been mainly British owned.

May, 1957

May 23

An American airplane belonging to Aramco (Arabian American Oil Company) was ordered to land at Damascus while en route from Saudi Arabia to Turkey, on grounds that it was infringing upon Syrian air space.

Syrian Airways began regular service to Sanaa, Yemen.

Agreement was reported on the draft of a franchise whereby the Moroccan Government would permit RCA to operate its radio relay station in Tangier for 20 years, subject to ratification by the RCA board of directors and the Moroccan Ministries of Economic Affairs, Finance and Labor.

The Baghdad Pact nations began secret discussions on Communist subversion in the Middle East and ways to combat it. The US participated in the discussions.

Syria asked the UN to order Israel to remove a bridge from a demilitarized zone in the Lake Huleh area. Syria charged that the bridge had a capacity of 45 tons and could be used to transport war equipment. Israel said the capacity of the bridge was only 12 tons and that its purpose was to transport earth-moving and dredging machinery to a land reclamation project.

May 24

Britain and Egypt began talks in Rome on financial problems resulting from the British-French intervention in Suez.

Eleven Arab governments, the nine members of the Arab League plus Morocco and Tunisia, asked the US to discontinue aid to France on the ground that this assistance was being used for suppression of freedom in Algeria.

May, 1957

May 21

The Karachi conference for joint economic planning among Baghdad Pact nations ended; plans were approved for a network of highways, railroads and telecommunications to link Pakistan, Iran, Iraq and Turkey.

A declaration issued in Jerusalem stated that the Government of Israel welcomed the support of the United States for the preservation of the independence of Middle Eastern states and for the development of economic strength dedicated to the maintenance of their independence.

The UN Security Council adjourned after a two day meeting, without taking any action on the French demand that it challenge Egyptian terms for the operation of the Suez Canal.

May 22

Four US naval vessels sailed through the Suez Canal.

May 23

Premier Bourguiba of Tunisia renounced the 1955 economic convention with France following French refusal to commence aid payments to Tunisia under this convention because of Tunisian support of Algerian nationalists.

Jordan asked Syria to withdraw its troops, which numbered about 5,000.

Premier Khalil of the Sudan said that he had protested to Egypt's ambassador in Khartoum and to President Nasser about reports that Egypt was financing newspapers and Communists in the Sudan.

A group of Sudan Army officers reported that an Egyptian embassy official had attempted to influence them to send all Sudanese officers to Egypt for training instead of to England.

May, 1957

May 24

The Jordanian Government decided to lift the midnight to dawn curfew in Amman, which had been imposed April 27.

The Syrian Government announced in Damascus that it was withdrawing its troops from Jordan at the request of King Hussein.

King Idris of Libya accepted the resignation of Premier Mustafa Ben-Halim and asked Abd-al-Majid Kobar, Deputy Premier and Foreign Minister, to form a new government.

May 25

The Egyptian Government authorized the resumption of operations by British airlines in Egypt, then cancelled the authorization.

The Soviet Union accused the US in an official statement of sending special agents into Jordan and engaging in imperialist intrigue in the Middle East by sending the Sixth Fleet there. The statement said the Soviet Union was a true friend of the Arab people.

May 26

Jordan announced that Syrian troops had completed their withdrawal from the Mafraq region in Jordan's north border area.

In Libya, ex-Deputy Premier Kobar formed a new cabinet with himself as Premier.

A Tass statement on the Jordan events was published in the Soviet press.

Ali Chekkal, President of the defunct Algerian Assembly, was assassinated in Paris.

May, 1957

May 27

Iraq lifted martial law imposed November 1, 1956, because of the Suez crisis.

Paris police rounded up 1,000 Algerians for suspected complicity in the killing of Ali Chekkal.

Special Ambassador Richards returned from his tour to the Middle East. He said that the Eisenhower Doctrine had already been notably successful. He said the US still held a large reservoir of good will there.

Saudi Arabia complained to the Security Council that an Israel plane and destroyer had violated its territory in the Gulf of Aqaba.

May 28

President Nasser appointed himself leader of the new National Union, Egypt's only political party.

The British Petroleum Company Ltd. raised the price of crude oil at Persian Gulf ports 13 cents a barrel, about a seven percent increase. It also raised prices for petroleum products in cargo lots at the Abadan refinery, where it received 40 percent of the output. The increase was designed to bring Persian Gulf prices into line with those of the US, Latin America and Mediterranean ports.

May 29

The Arab League Economic Council reached agreement on the building of an Arab tanker fleet and refineries in Arab countries to block the export of crude oil.

Egypt blacklisted the Norwegian tanker Noeck Eagle for unloading oil consignments at Haifa in November, 1956 and February, 1957.

May, 1957

May 31

Six Tunisians were killed and 17 wounded in a three and a half hour battle between French and Tunisian forces in the Ain Draham area near the Algerian border. French casualties were put at three wounded.

The British air base at Mafraq was transferred to Jordanian sovereignty.

Saudi Arabia announced approval of the established Nationalist Chinese Embassy at Jedda.

Awni Khalidi, Secretary General of the Baghdad Pact, said that the organization had "graduated from youth to manhood" during the Suez crisis. He said the main factor keeping the four Moslem members together was the keen awareness of Communist subversion and the threat of international Communism.

The Tunisian Cabinet amended customs regulations to permit reciprocal tariff agreements with countries other than France. It also formed a permanent committee to regulate imports and exports, and established a fund to guarantee foreign investments in Tunisia and permit the withdrawal of profits in foreign currencies.

May, 1957

May 29

King Hussein of Jordan charged that certain ministers in the ousted Nabulsi Cabinet had accepted bribes from Soviet agents in Syria. He said that the bribes were as large as ID100,000. He did not identify the ministers.

May 30

Government security forces of Lebanon killed five and wounded several persons in election clashes. Most of the casualties were inflicted when police attempted to break up mass meetings of Opposition members. Former Premier and Opposition leader Saeb Salam was among those arrested.

The Anglo-Egyptian talks begun May 24 were suspended.

The US Embassy in Tripoli gave $3,066 to the Government of Tripolitania for relief of victims of the January flood which had occurred at the Meginine River. The money was collected from members of the American community in Libya.

Saudi Arabia reportedly proposed to the Arab League Economic Council, meeting in Cairo, that an all Arab company be formed to build a network of oil pipelines from Middle East oilfields to Arab ports.

May 31

A joint French-Moroccan cultural convention was published in Rabat. It was to retain schools and programs for French children. France was to provide the Moroccan Department of Education with qualified assistants, help establish Moroccan universities, and make an annual financial contribution to Morocco's cultural program.

Egypt signed a trade pact with North Vietnam.

June, 1957

June 1

The Egyptian Government said that the latest figures showed 974 Egyptians killed in the Anglo-French attack on Port Said.

Britain released six million pounds sterling in frozen Egyptian accounts to cover Egyptian contracts made prior to the beginning of the Suez crisis in July, 1956. Egypt agreed to pay up the pensions of Britons who formerly worked for the Egyptian Government.

French President Coty called for world condemnation of the Algerian rebellion.

Following clashes between 350 French soldiers and 100 Tunisians, Premier Habib Bourguiba asked France to open negotiations immediately for the withdrawal of French Army troops. He declared that the movement of French forces was prohibited without government authorization.

Lebanese Premier Sami al-Solh said that the rioting of the previous week and the calling of a general strike was an attempt to overthrow President Camille Chamoun of Lebanon, whose term ended in 1958.

Jordan banned all Egyptian newspapers and magazines.

June 2

Jordan reportedly asked Egypt to fulfill its part of the agreement whereby Egypt, Syria and Saudi Arabia would replace the annual subsidy for Jordan formerly given by Britain. Saudi Arabia was the only country that had paid.

June, 1957

June 2

The Moroccan press accused Spain of colonialism in its enclave of Ifni.

It was reported in Damascus that more than 80 Syrians, most of them workers, had been expelled from Lebanon following election rioting the previous week.

June 3

The US became a member of the Baghdad Pact's Military Committee. Britain took part in the four day meeting of Pact members at Karachi; this was the first time Britain had participated since the British-French attack on Egypt in November. The US had made $12,570,000 available for four Baghdad Pact projects under the Eisenhower Doctrine.

It was reported in Cairo that trade between Egypt and the Soviet Union during the first four months of 1957 had increased tenfold compared with the corresponding period of 1956.

In Lebanon, the Opposition National Front Bloc called off a general strike, accepting the addition of two neutral ministers to the Cabinet and assurances from Army Chief of Staff Fuad Chehab that elections would be fair.

The Israel Knesset approved, 59-5 with 39 abstentions, Prime Minister Ben-Gurion's endorsement of the Eisenhower Doctrine.

At the opening session of the Baghdad Pact Ministerial Council, Britain offered 500 thousand pounds sterling a year in cash and in kind to build military defenses in the Baghdad Pact countries.

June, 1957

June 3

Moroccan Minister of Economic Affairs Bouabid told the Consultative Assembly that he had drawn up an emergency program permitting the start of certain development projects on credit. He said he had already allocated 22 billion francs in provision credits backed only by promises of foreign aid, and was counting on French and US aid to balance the 30 billion franc deficit in the 1957 budget.

June 4

The Arab League Economic Council formulated plans for group blacklisting of foreign concerns selling vehicles, goods and services to Israel. It also set up a unified boycott system to control imports and exports between Arab states and others so as to prevent Arab goods from reaching Israel.

Economic experts from Saudi Arabia, Jordan, Syria and Yemen signed an agreement setting up an Arab financial organization with a capital of $56 million for Arab economic development.

The Norwegian tanker Vestvard was refused permission to pass through the Suez Canal en route from Tel Aviv to the Persian Gulf.

Tunisia charged France in the UN with having caused "serious incidents" on the border between Algeria and Tunisia.

The Spanish-Moroccan commercial treaty of 1861 was abrogated by joint declaration; pending the conclusion of a new customs agreement, Morocco was to grant Spanish imports special treatment.

June 5

The ban on the Norwegian tanker Vestvard was lifted.

June, 1957

June 5

In a letter to the UN Security Council, Saudi Arabia charged that Israel destroyers had bombarded coastal positions near Taba.

The Cairo newspaper al-Shaab said Egypt would make its first payment to Jordan under the Arab subsidy agreement on July 1.

Morocco's new customs tariff went into effect. It was described as elastic and designed to protect local industry and attract new capital investment without seriously affecting living costs.

Two ships carrying milk, cheese and corn meal from the US for Moroccan needy, arrived in Rabat. These shipments of US surplus foodstuffs were organized by the National Catholic Welfare Conference.

The "Egyptianization" of six British and French pharmaceutical companies that had been sequestered by Egypt in 1956 was announced.

June 6

The Baghdad Pact Ministers' Council ended its four day meeting in Karachi with an agreement to establish a joint military planning staff in Baghdad with US participation.

Lebanon closed its frontier with Syria in anticipation of the June 9 elections. All Palestinian refugees were confined to their camps.

Saleh Jaber, senator and leading opponent of Premier Nuri-Said of Iraq on domestic issues, died of a heart attack on the Senate floor.

UN Secretary General Dag Hammarskjold said that fundamental changes for the better had taken place in the Middle East situation.

June, 1957

June 7

King Faisal of Iraq commissioned architect Frank Lloyd Wright to design a $45 million cultural center for Iraq.

President Kuwatli of Syria flew to Cairo for medical checkups and talks with President Nasser.

Prime Minister David Ben-Gurion of Israel warned the Arab countries that force would be answered with force if they attempted to stop Israel shipping from using the Gulf.

Scattered skirmishes took place between Tunisian and French forces in southeastern Tunisia. Seven French soldiers were reported killed and four injured near Gabes. Tunisian casualties were at least four killed and ten wounded.

June 8

Premier Nuri-Said of Iraq unexpectedly resigned.

King Saud of Saudi Arabia began a state visit to Jordan.

Lebanon received 40 jeeps equipped with anti-tank rifles from the US. It was the first material sent to any Middle Eastern country under the Eisenhower Doctrine.

Lebanon took stringent precautions against further election rioting. All arms permits were suspended. Alcohol sales were banned for 48 hours, as were political meetings.

Italy and Egypt initialled a new payments agreement.

June 9

The Jordanian Government ordered the expulsion of Colonel Ahmad Fuad Hilal, Egyptian military attache in Amman, on

June, 1957

June 9

charges of incitement to assassination. Also ordered to be expelled was Brigadier Muhammad Abd-al-Aziz, Egyptian consul general in Jerusalem.

The election of one-third of the single chamber Lebanese Parliament supported the pro-Western incumbent government of Premier Solh in Lebanon.

Egypt said it was prepared to accept free sterling in transit tolls for French shipping. This action cleared the way for French resumption of use of the Suez Canal.

June 10

Iraq signed two agreements under which the US would pay a total of $12, 500, 000 to the Moslem members of the Baghdad Pact for telecommunications and highway projects.

The Israel freighter Atlit arrived at the port of Elath.

Egypt ordered the expulsion of Jordanian Ambassador Abd-al-Moneim Rifai as a retaliatory measure for the expulsion of Colonel Hilal from Jordan.

The US State Department said that it was continuing promising discussions with Yemen for a possible US aid program there.

In a letter to the UN Security Council, Israel Ambassador Abba Eban categorically denied contentions by Saudi Arabia that Israel naval units and aircraft had violated Saudi territorial rights. Eban asserted that Israel vessels in the Gulf of Aqaba were under strict orders not to attack vessels or coastal positions under any circumstances and that the incidents alleged had never taken place.

An Egyptian court sentenced Amin Mahmoud, an Egyptian schoolmaster, to death for spying for Britain, but postponed

June, 1957

June 12

Moslem pilgrims traveling to Mecca to avoid the Gulf because of the unsafe situation as a "result of aggressions by Israel in the gulf waters."

A military court in Cairo sentenced 65 persons to prison terms and fined them LE5, 982, 158 on charges of smuggling Egyptian currency abroad during the invasion.

The Arab League central office blacklisted the tanker Memory, which flew the Liberian flag, for carrying strategic cargoes to Israel, and the Danish tanker Ulla Danielsen, which was under charter to the Zim Israel Navigation Company.

A Greek tanker about to enter the Suez Canal with a load of crude oil from Kuwait was damaged by a mine explosion.

The United States, the United Kingdom, and the French Governments delivered replies to the second series of Soviet notes on the Middle East, reiterating the substance of their rejections of March 11.

Burma and Israel signed an agreement for economic cooperation.

The French Government issued an authorization for French ships to use the Suez Canal.

June 13

The Jordanian Government announced the arrest of 19 persons in the Hebron district for their relations with the Egyptian Military Attache and Consul General.

King Hussein of Jordan and King Saud of Saudi Arabia, in a communique issued at the close of their talks, reaffirmed their support of military collaboration among Egypt, Syria, Jordan and Saudi Arabia in accordance with the agreements concluded among them.

June, 1957

June 10

verdicts on four Britons also on trial on the same charge. The death sentenced remained subject to approval by the Mufti of Egypt.

Egypt charged that its military attache in Amman and consul-general in Jerusalem had been falsely accused by Jordan.

The state of Yemen rejected US economic aid and the Eisenhower Doctrine.

June 11

Oil was struck in a third well at the Hassi-Messoud field in the Sahara in Algeria.

France and Morocco signed a judiciary convention establishing a modern system of justice for Morocco.

The Sultan of Morocco paid an official visit to Marrakech.

European teenage gangs rioted in Algiers, destroying Moslem shops and homes. The official casualty toll was five Moslems dead and 17 wounded. Eight Europeans were wounded and one killed. About 200 rioters were arrested.

The Soviet Ambassador in Beirut handed a note to the Lebanese Foreign Minister categorically denying Soviet interference in Lebanon's internal affairs.

Egypt signed conventions on Arab economic unity and the establishment of.an Arab financial center. The conventions envisioned economic cooperation by members of the Arab League.

June 12

King Hussein of Jordan and King Saud of Saudi Arabia ordered

June, 1957

June 13

Queen Elizabeth II conferred knighthood on General Charles F. Keightley, Commander of the Suez expeditionary force, and two of his aides.

France ended its boycott of the Suez Canal. The new government of Premier Bourges-Manoury accepted Egypt's terms for toll payments, to be made in British pounds transferable into dollars.

Egypt closed the Suez Canal for minesweeping to gard against repetition of the explosion that damaged a Greek tanker June 12.

The Quai D'Orsay revealed that the French Government had decided to allow French ships to use the Suez Canal, now that the Egyptian government had agreed to accept payment in sterling.

June 15

Syrian Minister of State Khaled al-Azm accused King Saud and King Hussein of cooperating with US policy for Israel's benefit, and of imperialism.

Syria attacked the joint communique of King Saud and King Hussein of June 13; Syria refused payment to Jordan of the first annual contribution of LE2. 5 million promised on January 19.

A major battle between French forces and Algerian insurgents took place at Tebessa, Algeria, near the Tunisian border.

June 16

The freighter Picardie became the first French ship to use the Suez Canal in seven months. It paid transit tolls amounting to LE1650 to Egypt's Suez Canal Authority.

June 16

The second phase of Lebanon's election ended with the Government represented by 38 deputies and the National Union Front by four.

The Libyan Government issued a protest against articles published in the Cairo newspaper al-Ahram accusing former Premier Ben-Halim and his Government of helping Britain attack Suez. The statement said that Libya had supported nationalization of the Canal, denounced the Anglo-French intervention, refused British troops the use of Libyan bases, and forbade British ships carrying military equipment to call at Libyan ports during the campaign.

Jordan announced it would close its embassy in Cairo.

June 17

King Faisal of Iraq asked Ali Jawdat to form a new government.

President Nasser released an approved list of candidates for the parliamentary elections in Egypt.

More than 350 rebels were reported slain in heavy weekend fighting near the Tunisian-Algerian border. French losses were put at 24 dead and 40 wounded.

In Lebanon, the two neutral ministers appointed to the Cabinet to supervise the elections resigned. They refused to tolerate the general atmosphere of the Lebanese election.

It was reported in Amman that Egypt was closing its embassy in Jordan in retaliation for the latter's intention to close its embassy in Cairo.

June 18

The Jordanian Cabinet suspended Parliament for three months. No reason was given for this action.

It was reported in Cairo that three submarines purchased from the Soviet Union had arrived.

A new transit record since the reopening of the Suez Canal was set when 51 ships passed through the waterway.

June 19

Israel warned Egypt against using submarines to blockade the Gulf of Aqaba.

Saudi Arabia told the UN that Israel planes and torpedo boats had violated air space and territorial waters June 12 and 13.

The Saudi Arabian Embassy in Cairo announced that the US tanker Kern Hills was blacklisted by royal decree of King Saud.

In Tunis, Tunisia and Yugoslavia signed a one year trade agreement under which Tunisian phosphates, salts and olive oil would be exchanged for Yugoslav meat, tobacco, lumber and machinery.

The new government of Ali Jawdat of Iraq was announced by Royal Decree.

June 20

Three Soviet warships passed through the Turkish straits to the eastern Mediterranean.

Tunisian Premier Bourguiba urged the creation of a French-North African community in which Algeria would have independent status like Morocco and Tunisia. He suggested in an

June 20

interview that General Charles De Gaulle might persuade France to adopt this policy.

Egyptian police arrested Charles A. Muse, an American archaeologist, and accused him of trying to smuggle antiquities out of Egypt.

June 21

The Algerian National Movement protested to Secretary General Hammarskjold over French treatment of Algerian prisoners, particularly the detention of 117 Algerians at Lille, as "criminal offenders" when they should be "political prisoners."

The Egyptian Canal Authority informed shippers the Suez Canal would be closed for 11 hours during the weekend. No reason was given for the closing.

June 22

James C. Swinburn, former business manager of the British operated Arab News Agency, was sentenced to five years at hard labor on charges of heading an alleged spy ring. Another Briton was sentenced to ten years imprisonment; two others were freed for lack of evidence.

The Libyan Council of Ministers ordered a gradual transfer of the seat of the Federal Government to Baida, in Cyrenaica, where new residences and office space were being completed.

Syrian Foreign Minister Salah Bitar declared that his country would maintain neutrality in order not to hamper its foreign policy. He added that Syria was ready to accept any foreign

June 22

economic aid, apart from the Eisenhower Doctrine, to consolidate its independence and speed up development.

King Faisal, King Hussein, and Cabinet ministers from Iraq and Jordan held talks on Iraqi economic aid to Jordan.

June 23

Following proper notification, two Soviet destroyers and a tanker passed through the Suez Canal. These were the first Soviet warships to do so since World War I.

The US circulated a statement among all shipping companies and masters of US registered ships reaffirming the right of free and innocent passage in the Gulf of Aqaba.

British Overseas Airways resumed flights across Syria after a 230 day interruption.

June 24

Twenty-nine French soldiers were killed in the ambush of two columns by Algerian rebels.

A two day conference of Moslem religious leaders from Syria, Tunisia, Morocco and Algeria, held at Damascus, proclaimed the National Liberation Front as the legitimate government of Algeria.

King Faisal and King Hussein issued a communique at the end of their talks declaring that they had decided that no Arab country should intervene in any other Arab country's internal affairs, and reaffirming their desire to fulfill their commitments and obligations under the treaty of alliance concluded between Iraq and Jordan in 1947.

June 24

A Presidential Decree placed all banking operations under the central control of the National Bank of Egypt.

Premier Solh's Government had won 42 of 66 seats at stake in Parliament at the end of the three-quarter mark in the election in Lebanon.

Lebanon accused the Soviet Union of interference in its private affairs because the Soviet Union had criticized its acceptance of the Eisenhower Doctrine.

June 25

The first British ship to do business with Egypt since the invasion, the Athelbeach, arrived at Alexandria.

Shareholders of the Universal Suez Canal Company voted to keep the concern in business despite a 50 percent cut in profits for 1956 following Egypt's nationalization. The company reported that in 1956 it had netted 5, 154, 903, 045 francs.

Minister of Economy Nadim al-Pachachi said that the Iraq Petroleum Company had agreed to pay Iraq seven million pounds sterling as settlement of its 1953 oil account.

The Iraqi Senate unanimously ratified economic and civil aviation agreements with Saudi Arabia.

Former Premier Fadel al-Jamali of Iraq said he would apply in a few weeks for permission to form a new political party on nationalist, progressive and democratic bases.

It was reported in Damascus that the Saudi Arabian Ambassador to Syria was recalled in protest against criticism of King Saud by Syrian Defense Minister Khaled al-Azm.

June 26

French Interior Minister Jules issued decrees outlawing the two principal Algerian nationalist organizations operating in France. At the same time, Defense Minister Morice announced that the Algerian border with Tunisia would be brought under tighter control with the withdrawal of French troops from Tunisia.

Security forces arrested seven teachers for taking part in the recent attempt to overthrow the Jordanian Government. Also arrested was George Terjuman, a prominent Communist leader.

The Lebanese Cabinet approved a bill authorizing the detention before judicial inquiry of any journalist whose writing was considered to offend the Government.

A Lebanese diplomat, Jamil Makkawi, accepted the key position, carrying the deciding vote, on the mixed commission set up by Franco-Moroccan agreement to inquire into the arrest of five Algerian rebel leaders October 22, 1956, while flying in a Moroccan chartered plane to Tunis.

Yugoslavia and Egypt signed a long term trade and payments agreement envisioning an annual exchange of goods worth $28 million.

The Ministry of Finance of Egypt said that it had decided to invite a British financial mission to Cairo to discuss questions regarding sequestered British property compensation and the unfreezing of Egyptian sterling balances in Britain.

The Egyptian Government agreed to permit British airliners to resume service to Egypt.

Premier Ali Jawdat said he would continue Iraq's past policy of cooperation with the West.

June 27

A new oil refinery with a capacity of 200, 000 tons opened at Alexandria, Egypt.

President Nasser was named patron of a nationwide fund raising campaign for victims of war in Algeria.

France admitted that at least 10, 000 Moslems had been moved from their homes in the Philippeville area to other parts of Algeria. Four areas near Philippeville were declared forbidden military zones.

Finance Minister Mahasan of Syria resigned to become Ambassador to Morocco.

The State Department reaffirmed the US position supporting free and innocent passage in the Gulf of Aqaba and through the Strait of Tiran.

June 28

The State Department rejected a request by 11 Arab nations that the US suspend military aid to France on the ground that the aid was being used to suppress Algerian nationalism.

Akram Hourani, one of the Government's most influential supporters, said that Saudi Arabia's deputy Foreign Minister, Yusuf Yasin, was working to overthrow the Syrian Government and replace it with a regime that would come to terms with American imperialism.

The royal family of Jordan announced that King Hussein had obtained a Moslem divorce from Queen Dina.

June 29

It was announced in Amman that the US Government would

June 29

promptly supply the Jordanian Army with $10, 000, 000 worth of military equipment. Jordan requested this military aid grant in order to maintain the level of efficiency of the Jordanian Army.

Egypt officially supported the plan of Greek shipowner Aristotle Onassis to build an oil pipeline along the Suez Canal. An official statement said that an Egyptian stock company would be established to build the pipeline. Not more than 49 percent of foreign capital would be allowed.

The commissioner of the Arab offices for the boycott of Israel said he hoped that the Sudan would open such an office shortly. He said that Libya had adopted a boycott law in accordance with a resolution from the Arab League.

June 30

The Lebanese elections ended with Premier Solh's Government winning 46 of the 66 seats and the opposition 16; four seats remained undecided.

State Department officials disclosed that the US had granted Jordan $10 million in economic aid, in addition to the $10 million grant announced on June 29.

July, 1957

July 1

Crown Prince Faisal of Saudi Arabia arrived in New York to undergo medical treatment.

President Nasser stated in an interview that his personal relations with King Saud were good and that there was no doubt that his views were pro-Arab.

July 2

US Senator John Kennedy called on the Administration to stop supporting France's Algerian policy and start working for Algerian independence. He introduced a resolution in the Senate following his speech, urging that the good offices of the Premier of Tunisia and the Sultan of Morocco or NATO be used to obtain such a settlement. He said that he favored Algerian interdependence with France and its North African neighbors.

Saudi Arabia filed its seventh complaint with the UN against Israel for violations of its territory by Israel armed forces.

The Directorate General of Broadcasting, Press and Publications announced that publications offices would be opened in Jedda, Mecca, Medina, Riyadh, Damman, Arar and Qaryah, Saudi Arabia.

Ahmad Shukairi, representative for Syria at a number of assembly sessions and in the Security Council of the UN, was appointed head of the Saudi Arabian delegation to the next General Assembly session with the rank of Minister of State.

Secretary Dulles said he would like to see a revival of the Eric Johnston plan to develop regions in both Israel and Jordan by irrigation from the Jordan River.

Czechoslovakia announced a new trade agreement with Egypt

July, 1957

July 2

under which the latter would purchase four complete factories to produce ceramics, cement, shoes and bicycles.

A trade and payments agreement was signed between Tunisia and Egypt.

July 3

The Standard Vacuum Oil Company opened a $1, 100, 000 ship bunkering terminal at Aden.

France's Defense Minister suggested that US Senator Kennedy was encouraging Algerian rebels to prolong their revolt against French rule.

More than five million Egyptians voted in the first post revolution elections for representatives to Parliament. Sixteen persons were reported killed as rival tribesmen began pushing one another to vote in the village of Qina, 250 miles south of Cairo.

Abd-al-Rahman Azzam, special adviser to the Saudi Arabian King, met with US Secretary Dulles for an hour and a half. He later stated that Saudi Arabia shared Egypt's leadership of the Arab world and that King Saud favored Arab federation.

The first Ambassador to Saudi Arabia from Iraq, Sheikh Ibrahim al-Suwail, presented his credentials to King Saud.

US Senator Humphrey proposed the formation of a UN good offices commission to explore means of solving the problem of the 900, 000 Arab refugees.

July 4

Delegates of the American Jewish Committee received

July, 1957

July 4

assurances in Morocco and Tunisia that the individual emigration of Jews to Israel would be maintained.

All remaining British soldiers and airmen left Aqaba, ten weeks before the final date fixed in an agreement ending the British-Jordanian treaty of 1948.

The Egyptian Government announced that it would charge an American archaeologist, Charles A. Muses, with the theft and smuggling of antiquities from a newly discovered pyramid.

A terrorist bomb exploded in the American Consulate in Algiers.

A visiting Syrian journalist published an interview with the Saudi Minister of Defense and Aviation, Amir Fahd. He stated that the Saudi base in Aqaba would be under the joint command of the Arab armies.

Egyptian Defense Minister Major General Abd-al-Hakim Amer flew unexpectedly to Jedda to confer with King Saud of Saudi Arabia.

July 5

Algerian laborers went on strike in various places throughout France, marking the anniversary of the revolt in Algeria against French control.

Two squadrons of jets arrived in Jedda from Egypt, a partial fulfillment of the 1956 agreement between Saudi Arabia and Egypt. The remainder were to be delivered in August.

French Minister for Algeria, Robert Lacoste, outlined plans for sealing the Tunisian frontier against the flow of arms to Algerian nationalists. He said the National Liberation Front was receiving 1, 000 rifles and submachine guns monthly from Tunisia.

July, 1957

July 5

Voting returns in Egypt showed that run off elections would have to be held for about two-thirds of the membership of the National Assembly. The Ministry of the Interior announced that returns from 189 constituencies showed only 68 Deputies chosen by clear majorities. In 121 other constituencies, no single candidate won a majority.

July 6

Moscow Radio said that Egypt's first atomic electric station had been set up in Cairo with Soviet help.

France was to receive $34 million worth of Egyptian cotton under a barter agreement concluded between the Egyptian National Bank and a Swiss bank.

The British War Office announced that the Royal Navy and troopships would soon resume use of the Suez Canal.

Jordanian Foreign Minister Samir al-Rifai condemned Egyptian and Syrian propaganda directed at Jordan and said the two nations did not realize the danger to the general welfare of all the Arab countries.

July 7

King Hussein of Jordan, in a nationwide broadcast, warned against a growing danger of atheism and called for greater Arab unity.

General Amer of Egypt left Saudi Arabia for Cairo after four days of discussions in which he and King Saud achieved a "complete identity of views" on joint military support of the blockade against Israel.

Israel Prime Minister David Ben-Gurion announced the relaxation of inter-village travel restrictions for Arabs in the Galilee

July 7

area. He also declared that government aid for water, road and education programs in Arab villages would be increased.

Egyptian sources said that Arab states would declare that Israel had no legal right to the Aqaba Gulf port of Elath and should not be permitted to send ships through the gulf. Arguments stated that the gulf had for centuries belonged to Arabs and Israel's seizure did not constitute legality; also that the gulf lay entirely within Arab territory.

The first French vessel to reach Elath arrived in port.

Spain and Morocco signed four agreements dealing in principle with the withdrawal of Spanish pesetas from the Moroccan Northern Zone, trade and payments, Spanish technical and administrative assistance to Morocco and the cultural convention.

July 8

Defense Minister Sulaiman Touqan said that Jordan was grateful for US economic aid, especially since there were no conditions attached to it. He also hoped that the US would be able to give more.

Egypt announced the acceptance of the French offer to buy Egyptian cotton to the value of LE12 million.

July 9

Sultan Muhammad V designated his eldest son, Moulay Hassan, Crown Prince and heir apparent to the throne of Morocco.

Syrian and Israel forces waged a ten hour battle in the Lake Huleh area. One Israel civilian was reported killed and seven

July 9

policemen wounded; Syrian casualties were unspecified. The fighting stopped after the fourth UN call for a ceasefire. Secretary General Hammarskjold issued a special appeal to the two governments to take steps to prevent further shooting.

July 10

Saudi Arabia wrote to the President of the UN Security Council charging that Israel ships had passed through Saudi Arabia's territorial waters on June 26 and 27.

Asian and African union leaders, attending the International unions congress in Tunisia, placed full blame on France for the conflict in Algeria and urged the world's unions to demonstrate in every way possible their desire to bring peace and freedom to the Algerian people.

The Embassy in Washington issued a denial that any representative of Jordan had engaged in negotiations in Rome with Israel representatives on the Arab refugee problem.

Pakistan gave Saudi Arabia seven million Saudi coins minted in Lahore, in accordance with an agreement.

Indian Prime Minister Nehru visited Cairo for talks with President Nasser (July 10-12).

July 11

French security forces arrested Abd-al-Majid Chaker, Tunisian political leader, as he stepped off the plane in Paris. He was carrying messages from Permier Bourguiba to Ambassador Muhammad Masmoudi. The French gave no reason for the arrest.

July 12

Tokyo announced the formation of the Japanese Oil Export Company. Delegates would go to Saudi Arabia to sign an agreement with the government. Japan would give the government cash guarantees equivalent to two billion yen.

France charged Abd-al-Majid Chaker with endangering the security of the state in attempting to pass a message to Ahmad Ben-Bella, Algerian nationalist leader imprisoned in France.

The British Foreign Office denied reports from Cairo that Indian Prime Minister Nehru was acting officially on behalf of the British Government in the Indian Prime Minister's efforts to mend relations between Britain and Cairo.

Mr. Nehru visited Khartoum for talks with the Sudanese Prime Minister.

July 13

A trade agreement between Tunisia and the Soviet Union was signed providing for an exchange to the value of 650 million francs.

July 14

Moulay Merbah, Secretary General of the Algerian National Movement, charged that Secretary Dulles' "hands-off" policy on Algeria was benefiting France in the Algerian independence fight.

Nationalists destroyed a municipal power station and caused an explosion that killed eight people in Laghouat, 200 miles south of Algiers.

Premier Ali Jawdat ordered suspension of the six month old jamming of broadcasts of the Voice of the Arabs, the Cairo

July 14

Radio and Damascus Radio. He also announced the revision of a previous decision not to participate in a coming consumer goods fair sponsored by Egypt.

Cairo Radio announced that Egypt had started sending jets to Saudi Arabia in accordance with a 1956 agreement between the two countries.

Dr. Ibrahim Fahmi al-Minnawi, chosen to head the 350 member Egyptian Parliament, died of a heart attack.

The Egyptian Interior Ministry announced that two persons were killed and fifteen injured in clashes during the run-off elections. Additional elections to the Egyptian National Assembly were held in those districts of Egypt where no candidate obtained the necessary number of votes on July 3, 1957.

July 15

In Egypt Madame Rawia Attia, a captain in a women's commando unit, and Madame Amina Shukri, Alexandria social welfare leader, defeated their male opponents and became the first women ever elected to any Arab Parliament.

The Egyptian Government decided to throw open to international bidding a contract for the construction of an oil pipeline paralleling the Suez Canal. The Ministry of Finance said a proposal by Aristotle Onassis to provide financial backing for the project had been rejected.

In Algeria, two Moslem women accused of cafe bombings were sentenced by a French military tribunal to die on the guillotine. They were the first women to be tried by the military court since the start of the Algerian revolt.

July, 1957

July 15

The US Embassy in Beirut announced that Lebanon would receive $10 million in economic aid and $4, 700, 000 in military aid during the fiscal year 1958 under the Eisenhower Doctrine. The announcement coincided with the arrival of the second shipment of military equipment. This was the first report on actual aid to be furnished under the Eisenhower Doctrine.

July 16

A three nation arbitration commission met to examine Morocco's claim that an airplane with five Algerian rebel leaders had been illegally seized by the French in October of 1956.

A number of Fighters for Liberation, an underground group of the banned Algerian Communist party, were recently arrested, the Algerian police announced.

The Egyptian Suez Canal Authority named Colonel Muhammad Yunis chairman of the board, to succeed the late Dr. Hilmi Badawi. Colonel Yunis was to continue as managing director of the Authority as well.

Secretary of State Dulles told a news conference that perhaps the US should take a lesser role than in the past in the search for solutions to Arab-Israel conflict.

The JordanianGovernment set aside JD13, 500, 000, more than half its 1957-58 budget, for the army.

The brother of President Nasser, Shawki Abd-al-Nasser, won a seat in the new National Assembly. He had been a school teacher in Alexandria.

King Saud of Saudi Arabia sent 20, 000 pounds sterling to assist refugees of the Iranian earthquake.

July, 1957

July 16

Israel agreed to the establishment of UN lookout posts on its side of the Israel-Syrian border. Staffed by UN observers, the posts were set up on a 30 day trial basis.

Cairo authorities disclosed that a dozen Army and Air Force officers and at least three leaders of the outlawed Wafd Party were being held on suspicion of conspiring to overthrow the regime and install a civilian government under Muhammad Salah-ad-Din, former Foreign Minister in the Wafd Government.

July 18

In Jedda, the newspaper al-Qahira reported that the joint Saudi-Egyptian command headed by Major General Abd-al-Hakim Amer, Egyptian Minister of War, began fortifying the entrance to the Gulf of Aqaba "to defend the waterway against Israel aggression."

It was disclosed in Washington that President Eisenhower, in a personal letter to King Saud, sought to clarify the US position on freedom of navigation in the Gulf of Aqaba. He stressed American support of the principles of innocent passage and the three mile limit of territorial waters.

Twenty-one Asian and African nations joined in a request that the agenda for the next General Assembly meeting include an item on the situation in Algeria.

The Egyptian Government wrote into law its promise not to discriminate against any Suez Canal users, but barred Israel shipping.

July 19

British led forces of Sultan Said Ibn-Taimour were reported battling a tribal revolt centered in Nizwa, capital of Oman.

July, 1957

July 19

Maurice Bourges-Maunoury, newly appointed French Premier, won special powers from the National Assembly to deal with Algerian rebel terrorism in France.

In Egypt, a Supreme Military Court was appointed to try 14 persons accused of plotting to assassinate President Nasser. It was to be headed by Major General Muhammad Fuad al-Digwi, who had supervised the last military court in 1954 when leaders of the Moslem Brotherhood were sentenced to hang for plotting against the President.

The Imam of Oman revolted against the Sultan of Oman, who requested British aid.

July 20

The French Government discussed the outlines of a ten year plan of economic development designed to reduce the poverty in Algeria.

The tribal revolt in Oman was reportedly led by Ghaleb Ibn-Ali, exiled Imam.

An official British spokesman said that Britain had agreed to help the Sultan of Oman and Muscat against tribesmen fighting for the Imam of Oman.

July 21

Trade talks began between the Ministers of Commerce of Saudi Arabia and Egypt.

The former Saudi Ambassador to Britain, Sheikh Hafez Wahbah, stated that Saudi Arabia had broken off relations with Britain because of violations of the countries' agreement over Buraimi

July, 1957

July 21

and Britain's alliance with France and Israel in attacking Egypt.

The British Government announced that certain local troop movements, on a small scale and of a precautionary character, were ordered for British forces in the Persian Gulf area in response to a request from the Sultan for help in putting down the revolt in Oman.

July 22

In Tunisia a meeting of the Constituent Assembly was called for July 25 by the National Committee of the Neo-Destour political party.

Twelve Frenchmen, including a Roman Catholic priest, were charged with treason after being accused of sheltering Moslems who were being hunted by French paratroopers during the arrests in Algiers in February and March of 1957.

President Nasser opened Egypt's first post-revolution Parliament.

Egyptian Foreign Minister Mahmoud Fawzi told UN Secretary General Dag Hammarskjold that Egypt would accept "on condition of reciprocity" the compulsory jurisdiction of the International Court of Justice on all legal disputes arising out of the 1888 Convention or the Egyptian declaration of April 24, 1957.

Egyptian authorities granted permission to a Danish vessel under charter to Israel, the Birgitte Toft, to go through the Suez Canal on its way to Haifa; they arrested an Israel member of the crew, Raphael Eylon. Israel protested to the UN Security Council against the arrest.

July, 1957

July 22

Israel filed a complaint with the UN charging that Syria had violated the armistice agreement by making "aggressive threats."

Syria lifted the state of martial law except in areas bordering on Israel, and the free entry of foreign newspapers was again permitted, but press messages abroad remained subject to censorship.

July 23

In Egypt, Soviet built military equipment was paraded in celebration of the fifth anniversary of the Egyptian revolution.

Britain gave Arab rebels 24 hours to clear out of points they had seized in Muscat and Oman or else face an aerial "show of strength."

Sir Bernard Burrows, British Political Resident for the Persian Gulf, declared that the rebels of Oman were using automatic weapons which had never been seen before in the area. It was "sufficiently clear someone on the outside was helping, but there was no concrete evidence who."

In Britain, Mr. Lloyd told Parliament that RAF jet planes were authorized to go into action if the rebels of Oman did not evacuate the Nizwa area within 48 hours.

King Saud arrived in Ethiopia on an unofficial visit with Emperor Haile Selassie.

July 24

The Egyptian Government distributed 20,578 acres of land to peasants under the agrarian reform program.

July, 1957

July 24

Syrian Defense Minister Khaled al-Azm headed a delegation to Moscow and secured broad promises of economic aid.

Following the expiration of a 48 hour ultimatum, British jet fighters attacked the rebel held fort of Izki, Oman, 20 miles east of Nizwa, causing severe damage.

July 25

Sir Bernard Burrows, British Political Resident in Bahrain, flew to Muscat to talk with the Sultan.

The fort at Nizwa was attacked by the RAF in 12 sorties. The flight commander said the planes flew in at 700 feet and fired on the roof of the fort with rockets and 20 mm. cannon. He said that the pilots did not notice any return fire.

The National Constituent Assembly proclaimed Tunisia a Republic, deposed the Bey, Sidi Muhammad al-Amin Pasha, and unanimously elected Premier Habib Bourguiba as President.

Syrian-Soviet talks were held in Moscow.

July 26

A British spokesman in Bahrain stressed that the British were not engaged in combat with the Imam's forces; rather, the strategy was to impress them so strongly with the modern weapons that could be used against them that they would give up the idea of resisting.

Air attacks were suspended at the fort of Izki after the red flag of the Sultan of Oman had replaced the white flag of the Imam.

President Bourguiba accepted the resignation of the Tunisian Cabinet.

July, 1957

July 26

The British Foreign Office criticized Cairo Radio for broadcasting a series of increasingly wild statements on Oman.

In a speech marking the first anniversary of the nationalization of the Suez Canal, President Nasser accused the US of trying to isolate Egypt from the rest of the Arab states and of trying to destroy Arab nationalism.

The Suez Canal Company and representatives of interested British, French and American groups signed an agreement setting up a Channel Tunnel Study Group.

July 27

The military trial of alleged pro-Egyptian plotters opened in Amman, Jordan.

The RAF dropped leaflets over Oman asking for support of the Sultan.

A spokesman in Bahrain said that the Sultan's flag now appeared at three places held by the Iman's forces: Izki, Araqi and Ainain.

President Nasser watched recently acquired Soviet built submarines take part in navy maneuvers.

The Finnish Government announced its decision to withdraw Finnish troops from UNEF in Egypt at the end of 1957.

A spokesman of the Syrian Foreign Ministry announced that his Government resolutely condemned British interference in Oman's domestic affairs.

July 28

Imam Ghaleb Ibn-Ali, leader of the rebellion in Oman, sent

July, 1957

July 28

word through one of his agents in Dammam that he would welcome aid from other Arab states.

The Egyptian State Prosecutor announced the indictment of the two former Cabinet members and 12 other persons charged with plotting to overthrow the government.

Sir Bernard Burrows said that the trouble in Muscat and Oman seemed to have been fostered from outside the country, and was very much exaggerated in reports to the outside world.

July 29

A spokesman for the Sultan of Oman said that loyal forces were closing in on the last small area held by followers of the Imam. He attributed the revolt and a similar one in 1955 to Saudi Arabian influence.

Tunisian President Bourguiba reorganized his government; the new cabinet included 12 Secretaries of State and three Under Secretaries. The term "secretary," which replaced "minister," was an indication that the new government was modeled on the US rather than the French system.

The Egyptian delegate to the UN, according to Egyptian sources, was instructed to deliver a memorandum to Secretary General Hammarskjold, in compliance with a UN request for information on the seizing of an Israel seaman aboard a Danish freighter in the Suez Canal.

After a three day lull in operations in Oman, British jet fighters attacked a rebel held fort at Birkat al-Moz, five miles west of Izki. British sources reported the movement of a small detachment of British troops from Sharja to Buraimi.

July, 1957

July 30

Egypt blacklisted the Birgitte Toft, the Danish vessel under charter to Israel.

Cairo Radio accused US military officials in Jordan of having engineered the conspiracy behind the trial of 22 Jordanians in Amman on a charge of having plotted to kill King Hussein.

Charles A. Muses, American writer and amateur archaeologist, went on trial in an Egyptian court. He denied the multiple charges of theft and smuggling.

July 31

In Egypt, suitcases full of old marble, pieces of pottery and segments of gold leaf were produced as evidence in the trial of Mr. Muses.

In Oman the RAF received orders to stop all vehicular traffic in the area still believed to be in the control of Imam forces.

August, 1957

August 1

President Bourguiba, in his first post-republic interview, emphasized that Tunisia was part of the free Western world and would remain so.

In Oman, RAF jet planes attacked rebel held forts at Bahlah and Nizwa.

The Egyptian State Prosecutor asked that Mr. Muses be sentenced to five years imprisonment on a charge of attempted smuggling and that he be fined $156, 291 on a charge of dealing illegally in currency while in Egypt.

The Imam of Oman, Ghaleb Ibn-Ali, appealed for intervention by the African and Asian states to stop aggression against the Omanians, according to his Cairo representative, Muhammad al-Harithi.

Two newspaper publishers of Lebanon were sentenced to 15 days imprisonment for articles deemed insulting to President Chamoun.

General Ma Pu-Fang was appointed Nationalist Chinese Ambassador to Saudi Arabia.

Cities Service Company announced that one of its subsidiaries had discovered a new oil well in the province of Dhufar in the Sultanate of Muscat and Oman. Preliminary tests indicated a producing capacity of 2, 000 barrels a day at a depth of 3, 200 feet.

Spokesmen for the Imam in Cairo reported the capture of Tareq Ibn-Taimour, brother of the Sultan, near the town of Ibri. The British Foreign Office denied the report.

August 2

RAF fighter planes attacked a movement of Yemeni forces into Aden.

August, 1957

August 2

Egypt placed a ban for an indefinite period upon newsmen entering the Gaza Strip.

Tunisian President Bourguiba warned that if the Algerian guerrilla war continued for another year, the nationalists would seek Communist support.

The British stepped up the tempo of their air war against the forces of the Imam of Oman. For the first time, they omitted the customary 48-hour warning before an air attack against rebel camps.

August 3

British ground troops advanced inside the Sultanate of Muscat and Oman in support of the Sultan.

The Syrian Government declared that it had rejected an ultimatum from Jordan threatening to break off diplomatic relations and to use military force unless Syrian newspapers halted a campaign against Jordan. Jordan denied that an ultimatum had been intended.

The Imamate of Oman appealed to the Bandung countries to take measures in putting an end to the British aggression against Oman.

August 4

President Chamoun of Lebanon called for a full Arab summit conference on the highest level to stop "bickering" among Arab nations.

Egypt blacklisted the Israel chartered Italian freighter Monte Pellegrino after it had passed through the Suez Canal.

August, 1957

August 4

The Cairo newspaper al-Akhbar declared that Egypt would go to Syria's aid if that country was attacked by Jordan.

A British spokesman said that white flags of the Imam were seen in Sharqiya Province. RAF planes dropped leaflets asking tribesmen to support the Sultan of Oman.

Pakistan Prime Minister Suhrawardi and King Hussein pledged common resistance to any aggression or subversive activities in the Middle East. Mr. Suhrawardi left Jordan for Lebanon.

August 5

It was reported in Cairo that the Soviet Union agreed to allow Syria to defer payment for arms bought from the Communist Bloc in the previous two years.

All funds and property of the Bey of Tunisia and his immediate family were confiscated. This was remuneration for the total of funds given to the Bey of Tunisia since 1943 beyond the amount provided in the annual civil list.

Syrian Foreign Minister Salah al-Bitar declared that the US was behind what he termed Jordan's "warlike ultimatum" of August 3.

A statement issued by Jordan's Foreign Minister Rifai, and Syria's Charge d'Affaires in Amman, Ahmad Rahbi, said that the misunderstanding between their countries had been cleared up.

The Cairo representative of the rebel chief, Imam Ibn-Ali, delivered notes to the embassies of the US and the Soviet Union, asking that the two countries try to halt British military intervention and bring about a ceasefire in Oman.

August, 1957

August 5

RAF jet fighters made six strafing attacks on rebel supplies in Oman.

A committee of the National Liberation Front said that Algerian nationalism was not turning toward the Communist world, but that nationalists would accept aid from any source to hasten their liberation.

In his first formal report to Congress on his Doctrine, President Eisenhower revealed that $174,200,000 in military and economic aid had been distributed in the Middle East since adoption of the Doctrine on March 9. He declared that the Doctrine had played a major role to build strength against the threat of international Communism.

State Minister and Minister of Syrian National Defense, Khaled Azm, head of the Syrian Government Delegation visiting the Soviet Union, held a reception.

August 6

The British Government announced that it had agreed to grant Jordan an interest free loan of 1,130,000 pounds sterling ($3,164,000) for economic development.

The Minister of Agriculture from Saudi Arabia was invited to pay an official visit to the Soviet Union. This was the first Soviet invitation to the Saudi Government.

A joint Syro-Soviet communique issued in Moscow announced agreement on Russian economic and technical aid to Syria. The Soviet side stated that this economic and technical co-operation would be carried out without any political or any other conditions.

The Egyptian National Assembly unanimously adopted a resolution condemning French and British aggression in Algeria and Oman.

August, 1957

August 6

Secretary of State Dulles revealed that the US had received an appeal from the Imam of Oman for assistance in halting British attacks in Oman.

August 7

RAF planes attacked a Yemeni force in the Beihan area of Aden.

In Oman, British forces were reported to have moved into the village of Izz, 12 miles from Nizwa.

The Saudi Arabian Government signed a contract with a Belgian company to build an electric railway linking Jedda to Mecca and Arafat. The project would take five years to complete and was estimated to cost LE4 million.

A delegation headed by Syrian Defense Minister Khaled al-Azm arrived in Prague from Moscow on the invitation of the Czechoslovakian Government.

UN Secretary General Hammarskjold circulated a report that Israel opposition had prevented the establishment of a full-time observation post along the Israel-Syrian border. The acting chief of the UN Truce Supervision Organization said that Israel felt the proposal was not in conformity with the general armistice agreement and also that it was not needed, since the area was visited twice daily by UN military observers.

The International Chamber of Shipping protested against a proposal to pay for clearance of the Suez Canal by levying a surcharge on shipping through the Canal, adding that such a plan was being considered by the UN.

An Israel chartered Norwegian cargo vessel bound for Haifa from Capetown with a cargo of fishmeal, jute and tanning chemicals was allowed to go through the Suez Canal.

August, 1957

August 8

In Oman, British ground forces and native troops captured two rebel outposts near Nizwa.

British sources reported the arrival in Yemen of six shiploads of Soviet arms, including tanks, anti-aircraft, and ground attack aircraft.

Secretary General Dag Hammarskjold declared that the Arab economic boycott of Israel was a deadweight on UN efforts for a settlement in the Middle East.

The Middle East News Agency carried a statement from the Imam saying that free Omanis were still holding fast against the Muscat forces backed by planes and forces of the British imperialists. He said that they would not stop fighting until they obtained full rights to freedom, independence and sovereignty in spite of the "brutality and savagery of the aggressor who had not hesitated to slaughter pregnant women, old men and children."

British led forces of the Sultan ran into heavy rifle fire on the outskirts of Farq. About 40 of the Imam's men resisted until they were fired on by rockets from jet planes. The Omani escaped to the hills with no known casualties.

President Bourguiba of Tunisia appealed to Egypt and other Arab states for arms for Tunisian forces.

August 9

Unexpected resistance by the forces of the Imam of Oman forced a mixed British and Muscat force to withdraw slightly before attacking Farq, where the major rebel forces were located.

August, 1957

August 10

An Aden Government spokesman said that all was quiet along the border between Yemen and the Western Aden Protectorate.

It was reported in Algiers that in the 33 months of the nationalist uprising about 35,000 insurgents had been killed and 20,000 captured. French security force losses were 3,900 killed, 9,000 wounded and 700 missing. Civilian casualties were 6,000 Moslems killed, 3,700 wounded and 2,300 missing; 945 Europeans killed, 2,700 wounded and 140 missing.

A Saudi National Reform Front statement published in a Damascus newspaper said that a Saudi-Syrian amnesty would mean little unless Syria and Egypt explained to King Saud the need for reforms.

In Oman, British bombers made repeated strikes with small fragmentation bombs as opposing forces dug into a hillside near Farq.

The Sultan of Oman gave two reasons for the bitter resistance against him. One was support from outside and the other was that the rebels knew that "if they were captured it would be their end."

A communique on the visit of the Syrian Government delegation to Czechoslovakia was published in Prague.

August 11

Sultan Muhammad V abandoned his traditional title for that of King, since his Sherifian Empire had become the Kingdom of Morocco.

British and Muscat troops broke the resistance at Farq and seized Nizwa without a fight. Representatives of Nizwa met the political representative of the Sultan to announce their recognition of the Sultan's sovereignty.

August 12

Algerian nationalists in New York appealed to UN Secretary General Dag Hammarskjold to intervene with the French Government, on behalf of two Moslem girls under sentence of death in Algiers.

The French Military Command in Algeria announced that French forces had put 800 rebels out of action in more than 200 military engagements within six days. French losses were not disclosed.

In Egypt, a special Supreme Military Tribunal opened the trial of 13 Egyptians, including two former Cabinet ministers, accused of plotting to assassinate President Nasser so as to establish a new regime.

The British Foreign Office said that the action of the Imam against the Sultan invalidated a treaty signed in 1920 granting limited autonomy to tribes in the interior of Oman.

The white flag of the Imam disappeared from all but the village of Jabrin, 20 miles west of Nizwa.

Yemen's legation in London charged that on August 5 the RAF bombed the post at Shukair for eight hours.

Nationalist China announced the establishment of diplomatic relations with Jordan on an ambassadorial level.

The Arab League agreed to ask for a meeting of the UN Security Council to act on the question of British efforts to put down the revolt in Oman. The decision was reached after the League received approval from Iraq and Libya.

August 13

A communique issued in Aden reported the unloading, at the Yemeni port of Salief, of the seventh shipload of arms from the

August 13

Soviet Union. The shipment was accompanied by some 50 technicians, advisers and pilots.

President Bourguiba warned Algerian nationalists against launching attacks from Tunisia on the French in Algeria. He said he did not want the Algerians to give France cause to say Tunisia was incapable of assuming the responsibilities of an independent and sovereign state. He also said that such a state could not permit attacks from its own soil on a neighboring country.

Syria expelled three American Embassy officials after accusing the US of having plotted to overthrow President Kuwatli's regime. The three officials were Lieutenant Colonel Robert Malloy, military attache, Howard Stone, second secretary for political affairs, and Francis Jetton, vice consul.

Mr. Muses, the American archaeologist, was convicted of attempting to smuggle antiquities out of Egypt and of violating currency exchange laws. He was fined $51,840 and given a 13 month suspended sentence. His attorney said that he would appeal. A defendent repudiated his alleged confession that he had plotted to overthrow President Nasser's regime, charging that he had been tortured until he signed.

British armored cars in Oman led the advance into Tanuf. Twenty miles away the Sultan's troops seized Bahlah.

August 14

In Lebanon, Premier Sami al-Solh and his Cabinet resigned.

Nationalist China announced the signing in Baghdad of a ten year cultural pact with Iraq. It was the first such agreement made between the Formosa Government and an Arab country.

August 14

The US expelled Syrian Ambassador Farid Zain-ad-Din and a member of his staff, and lodged a strong protest with Damascus against the "government-inspired slanderous campaign" which had been carried on against the US by the Syrian press and by the official Syrian radio, and against the allegations regarding US involvement in a plot against the Syrian Government.

Arkansas Democrat Senator William Fulbright accused US Secretary of State Dulles of acting against expert economic and diplomatic advice in withdrawing the US offer to help build the Aswan Dam. The results were Nasser's seizure of the Suez Canal Operating Company, the British, French and Israel invasion of Egypt, the deterioration of the North Atlantic Treaty Alliance, deeper Soviet penetration of the Middle East, and intensification of the difficulty in settling the Arab-Israel conflict.

Rafi Eylon, the Israel seaman seized aboard a Danish freighter in the Suez Canal July 22, was released from an Egyptian jail.

In Oman, Sultan Said Ibn-Taimur declared that the tribal insurrection had ended.

Defense Minister Khaled al-Azm of Syria returned to Damascus from Moscow where he had obtained assurances of economic and technical aid for his country.

In Egypt, a second defendant in the conspiracy trial told the military tribunal that he had been beaten and starved until he had signed a confession.

August 15

Cairo Radio reported that Egypt had shipped a second consignment of fighter planes to Saudi Arabia under the terms of their 1956 military agreement.

August 15

Eleven Arab nations requested an urgent meeting of the UN Security Council to discuss British armed aggression in Oman.

Colonel Ibrahim Husseini, Syrian Military Attache in Rome who was accused of participating in an American conspiracy against the Syrian Government, was recalled to Damascus but was reported as having refused, promising to comply with the order later, when sentiments cooled and facts were known.

In Oman, British Venom jets destroyed a rebel held fort at Sait.

Premier Sabri-al-Assali announced the resignation of General Tawfiq Nizam-ad-Din, Chief of Staff of the Syrian Army.

The Tunisian Government announced its intention of issuing its own national currency by the end of 1957.

The newly elected Lebanese Parliament opened. About two-thirds of the single chamber legislature were supporters of the Premier.

August 16

British forces began withdrawing from the Sultanate of Oman.

A spokesman in Bahrain said that statements had been taken from captured Omani youths who said that supporters of the Imam's brother, Taleb Ibn-Ali, were trained at Dammam, in Saudi Arabia.

British forces and the Oman troops moved their camp from Farq to Izki as the first step to final withdrawal.

Colonel Husseini declared that Syria was headed "in giant steps" toward a Communist dominated military dictatorship. He denied that he had been involved in any plot and expressed doubt that any such conspiracy had ever existed.

August, 1957

August 16

The Moroccan Government announced that the sovereign of the country was King Muhammad V, and that the Sherifian Empire was officially the Kingdom of Morocco.

August 17

By decree of President Shukri Kuwatli of Syria, General Afif Bizri, a well known leftist, was appointed Chief of Staff; Brigadier Amin Nafouri was named as his Deputy.

Arab League Secretary General Hassouna met with Jordan Foreign Minister Rafai.

A Turkish tanker ran aground in the Suez Canal, damaging the ship's rudder and holding up canal traffic for ten hours.

Greek Premier Constantin Karamanlis arrived in Cairo for talks with President Nasser.

Jordan would refuse to contribute to the expenses of the UN Emergency Force because it did not agree with stationing forces on the Aqaba Gulf. Instead, the Government would make a grant of $70,000 to the UN funds for the upkeep of the Palestinian refugees.

August 18

French Foreign Minister Christian Pineau declared that although France never would accept orders from the UN concerning Algeria, there was no question of France's leaving the UN.

Reportedly, thirteen army officers either resigned or were ousted from Syria and a number of them fled to Beirut.

August, 1957

August 18

Sir Bernard Burrows, British Political Resident for the Persian Gulf, flew to Muscat to confer with the Sultan.

British troops began arriving at Azeiba airfield to board planes for Bahrain or Aden.

Lebanese Premier Solh formed a new cabinet; Charles Malik remained as Foreign Minister.

August 19

Spanish forces killed seven Moroccans in the enclave of Ifni in 48 hours of sporadic clashes.

Syrian Foreign Minister Salah al-Bitar declared that his country had been the target of destructive activities aimed at making it accept the Eisenhower Doctrine. He also said that it was already known that the main object of the "conspiracy" to overthrow the Syrian and Egyptian regimes was to set up governments that would change from liberal foreign policies and join the imperialistic line.

Authorities permitted the Norwegian freighter Hubro, loaded with potash from Israel, to transit the Suez Canal.

Jordan announced that it would lodge a complaint with the UN Security Council alleging that Israel had attacked the demilitarized zone of Jerusalem July 21.

Premier Karamanlis of Greece and President Nasser concluded their talks.

The Foreign Minister of Muscat and Oman said that the Sultan did not recognize the right of the UN to discuss the conflict with the Imam.

August, 1957

August 19

The Yemen Minister in Cairo said that continued British aggressive acts against Yemen could turn the current war into a major war.

Beirut Radio officially announced the formation of a new Lebanese Government by Sami al-Solh.

August 20

The Soviet Union supported an 11 Arab nation demand that the Security Council investigate British efforts to put down a tribal revolt in Oman.

The British Foreign Office denied Soviet charges concerning Britain's role in the Oman conflict.

By a vote of 5-4 with one abstention and one "not participating," the UN Security Council rejected a request by the Soviet Union and 11 Arab nations to consider British aggression in the Sultanate.

Three leaders of the Oman revolt were reported fleeing toward the coast with Muscat forces in pursuit. British aircraft flew over the area dropping leaflets signed by the Sultan, warning that any who helped the men would be punished.

A Saudi Embassy was established in Addis Ababa. Omar al-Saqqaf, Director of the Political Department of the Ministry of Foreign Affairs, was appointed Ambassador.

British troops completed their withdrawal from Oman.

Major General Afif Bizri charged that he was marked for assassination in a plot that the US allegedly was directing against Syria. At the same time, Syria told the UN that the US had conspired to overthrow the Damascus Government but that Syria had refrained from asking for UN action.

August, 1957

August 21

US President Eisenhower declared that the ultimate aim of the Soviet Union was to control Syria, but that the situation did not at that time justify any kind of action at all under the Mideast Doctrine.

Syria announced officially the arrest of ten army officers accused of conspiring with the US.

The Soviet Union sent a note to Sudanese Premier Khalil offering the purchase of crops to help the Sudan "liberate itself from imperialist influence."

The Lebanese Government asked the Chamber of Deputies for emergency powers to arrest anyone considered a threat to the country's security.

King Faisal of Iraq discussed developments in Syria with Turkish officials in Istanbul.

A Tass statement on Oman was published. It said that UN members should immediately stop colonialists' intervention in that country and put an end to their interference in the domestic affairs of the Arab nations.

August 22

The Ambassador to the US signed an agreement with the World Bank, calling for a Saudi Arabian subscription of $10 million.

Saudi Arabia strongly protested the presence of British forces in Buraimi, considering this a violation of the Arbitration Agreement with Britain in 1954 and of international law.

Syrian Defense Minister Khaled al-Azm asserted that the Soviet Union and Czechoslovakia had no designs on the Middle East other than seeing the Arab nations entirely independent and free from any influence either from the West or from the Soviet Union itself.

August, 1957

August 22

Jordan asked the US for support of its action in the UN Security Council to halt Israel construction work on Mount Mukabbir in Jerusalem.

The Syrian Defense Minister and the Secretary General of the Foreign Office charged that the Eisenhower Administration was putting the brand of Communism on Syria as a "propaganda weapon" to push US ambitions in the Middle East.

King Hussein of Jordan arrived in Istanbul to confer with Premier Menderes of Turkey and King Faisal of Iraq on the Syrian situation.

Loy W. Henderson, US Deputy Under Secretary of State, left for the Middle East on what the State Department termed a fact finding mission.

August 23

Israel protested to the UN Security Council in the strongest terms against the detention of the Norwegian freighter Mars.

The British Foreign Office said that British and native troops supporting the Sultan of Oman had killed about 30 followers of the Imam during the fighting. No Sultan supporters were reported killed.

Syrian officials reported that no final agreement had been reached on the proposed expansion of Soviet aid to Syria and Soviet-Syrian trade.

Reports said that the French Government's proposals for a new Algerian statute had aroused suspicion among the European population and disappointment among Moslems.

President Kuwatli declared that Syria would never turn Communist, but said that the West, particularly the US, should not interfere with his country.

August, 1957

August 23

The Lebanese Internal Security forces held urgent meetings to cope with a wave of sabotage.

August 24

Loy Henderson, US Deputy Under Secretary of State, conferred in Istanbul with Premier Menderes both before and after the latter's meetings with King Faisal and King Hussein of Iraq and Jordan.

Russia charged that the US was preparing the ground for American intervention in Syria.

A Syrian official said that Moscow had expressed readiness to provide all experts and technicians necessary to carry out the country's long range development projects.

Syrian Minister of Public Works Fakher Kayali reported on his return from the Soviet Union that good response and excellent understanding of problems was reached. He added that the Soviet Union told of its willingness to support Syria and did not require anything from Syria.

August 25

President Kuwatli of Syria returned to Damascus after what he termed very successful talks with President Nasser. Both felt that the present situation was solid and they were determined to stand against all kinds of pressure.

August 26

British planes attacked the village of Sharaijia in central Oman where Imam Ibn-Ali and two other rebel leaders were reported to have taken refuge.

August, 1957

August 26

The British Foreign Office rejected a protest by the Yemen delegation against alleged British attacks on August 19 and 23, and declared that their troops and aircraft had strict instructions not to cross the frontier.

In Cairo, the special envoy of the Imam of Oman said that Oman would not conclude a peace treaty or enter into negotiations as long as one single Briton was in Oman.

Saudi Arabia became the 62nd member of the International Bank for Reconstruction and Development and of the International Monetary Fund.

King Hussein of Jordan left Turkey for a visit to Spain.

August 27

Secretary of State Dulles told a news conference that Syria's neighbors were alarmed by the large quantities of Soviet weapons in Syrian hands.

Three Syrian planning officials flew to Moscow to negotiate a proposed Soviet economic and technical assistance loan.

August 28

The British Foreign Office announced that RAF bombers had launched an attack against Yemeni troops in the Djebel-Dahat-Shukair Massif area of Aden.

US Deputy Under Secretary of State, Mr. Henderson, arrived in Beirut and conferred with the Lebanese Premier, President and Foreign Minister on recent events concerning Syria.

The Algerian National Movement rejected the French Government's incomplete plan to reorganize Algeria into virtually

August, 1957

August 28

autonomous regions, calling it a step backward from the 1947 Algerian Statute.

The Syrian Foreign Ministry announced that Soviet leaders Khrushchev and Bulganin would visit Syria.

Hassan Jabbara, Chairman of the Syrian Council of Economic Development, and his advisors arrived in Moscow to discuss certain aspects of Syrian-Soviet economic cooperation.

August 29

The Lebanese Premier declared that Lebanon was determined to continue its cooperation with the US and that it was resolved to remain on the side of the free world. He stressed that no development could take place in Syria without having direct repercussions in Lebanon as well.

Abd-al-Latif Benjelloun, Governor of Tangier, announced that King Muhammad V had signed the Charter of Tangier, replacing the international statute abolished when Morocco's independence was recognized.

A trade agreement was signed between Morocco and Switzerland.

August 30

Eighteen Egyptians were indicted on charges of being members of an underground Egyptian Communist Party.

French military and security officers asserted that their troops and police had smashed the National Liberation Front's command for the Algiers region and forced what remained of it to function from neighboring Tunisia.

August, 1957

August 30

The Saudi Arabian Broadcasting Office in New York reported that Shukairy would head the Saudi Arabian delegation in the next UN General Assembly session.

Britain rejected a new protest from Yemen that the Royal Air Force was continuing aggression against that country. Britain maintained that its attack had been made against Yemeni forces inside Aden.

A spokesman announced that the US was cutting down its embassy staff in Damascus as a result of the crisis in American-Syrian relations.

The Moroccan government issued a Royal Charter confirming the status of Tangier as a free money zone. It guaranteed that no change in that status would be enacted without six months advance notice.

August 31

King Saud received the Japanese oil company delegates who arrived in Saudi Arabia to discuss oil trade.

US Under Secretary of State Henderson completed his Middle East mission in Lebanon and was expected to return immediately to Washington.

September, 1957

September 1

Israel expressed its concern over the US airlift of arms to Jordan.

Opening the fourth annual Damascus trade fair, Minister of National Economy Khalil al-Kallas declared that economic freedom should be limited in Syria because all advanced European countries had abandoned it; he praised the Soviet Union as the great power that backed his country's cause.

French troops crossed into Tunisia from Algeria in pursuit of Algerian nationalist guerrillas.

September 2

Prague Radio announced the conclusion of a trade agreement between Czechoslovakia and Egypt; Czechoslovakian machinery and industrial products were to be exchanged for Egyptian cotton.

A diplomatic source said the Soviet Union had agreed to provide Syrian airlines with new TU-104 jet airliners.

September 3

Rebel attacks continued in western Oran and in Constantine in the face of French optimism about the success of pacification in Algeria.

Israel was condemned by a vote of the UN chairman and the Jordan delegate to the Israel-Jordanian Mixed Armistice Commission for two border incidents. No Israel delegate attended the meeting.

Lieutenant General Raymond Wheeler, who directed the clearing of the Suez Canal of wrecked ships, was sent back to the Suez Canal by the UN to confer with the Egyptian Canal Authority on his work in clearing the waterway.

September, 1957

September 3

The UN Security Council held an emergency meeting. The Council reportedly had proof that Syria was connected with the wave of subversive activities in Lebanon.

Syrian and Egyptian delegates signed an agreement in Damascus to form a joint committee to suggest, within three months, measures for the final economic unification of the two countries.

It was revealed in Beirut that during the past 49 hours security officers had seized 15 Czechoslovakian submachine guns coming from Syria.

The Soviet Notes to the US, Britain and France, third series, urged the renunciation of force in the Middle East.

September 4

The French Government announced that it would call Parliament into special session toward the end of the month to debate a bill to reorganize Algeria's administration.

Loy Henderson declared, on his return to the US from his fact-finding mission, that the situation in Syria was extremely serious.

US General Wheeler said that the Egyptian management of the nationalized Suez Canal was excellent.

US State Department officials said that the US was considering the possibilitv of providing economic aid to Yemen and the Sudan.

Jordan requested an urgent Security Council meeting to press a charge that Israel digging operations near Jerusalem constituted an attempt to grab territory that was a no man's land of about 600 acres between the Jordanian and Israel lines.

September, 1957

September 4

The Soviet press published a communique on the talks held in Moscow between a Syrian delegation, headed by Hassan Jabbar, Chairman of the Syrian Council of Economic Development, and the Soviet State Committee on Economic Relations with Foreign Countries.

September 5

A military court in Old Jerusalem sentenced 30 persons to prison terms ranging from one to two years for anti-government demonstrations in Jordan during the political crisis in the spring.

The French Foreign Office disclosed that France had delivered tanks to Lebanon.

It was announced in Washington that the US would fly arms to Jordan from depots in Europe. The State Department revealed that special shipments of arms would be made to Lebanon from US supplies in Europe. Commitments already made to Turkey and Iraq would be accelerated.

Abd-al-Khaleq Hassouna was elected to a second five year term as Secretary General of the Arab League.

The Sudan became the 63rd member of the International Bank for Reconstruction and Development and of the International Monetary Fund.

September 6

The US State Department confirmed dispatch of arms to Jordan and other Middle East countries at their request, following Russian arms shipments to Syria.

September, 1957

September 7

U S Secretary of State John Foster Dulles said of Mr. Henderson's report on his mission that the Undersecretary found in the Near East deep concern at the apparently growing Soviet Communist domination of Syria and the large buildup which could not be justified by any purely defensive needs. There was particular concern over border incidents and intensive propaganda and "subversive activities directed toward the overthrow of the newly constituted governments of Syria's Arab neighbors." Mr. Dulles announced President Eisenhower's reaffirmation of his pledge to help the nations of the Middle East resist international Communism through the Eisenhower Doctrine.

President Eisenhower pledged to use whatever powers necessary to protect pro-Western Arab governments from overthrow by the pro-Soviet government of Syria.

Syria condemned the arms shipments to Lebanon, Turkey, Iraq and Jordan, saying that it would not tolerate any action against its security.

The Syrian economic mission returned from Moscow.

East Germany and Egypt signed a protocol fixing the volume of trade between the two countries at more than $25 million, an East German news agency announced. It was also agreed that Egypt would establish a trade mission in East Berlin.

King Saud of Saudi Arabia arrived unexpectedly in Beirut, on his way to Germany to confer with Lebanese President Camille Chamoun.

Syrian Premier al-Assali summoned his Cabinet into emergency session, reportedly to discuss US aggressive intentions against Syria.

According to the Lebanese newspaper al-Siyasah, King Hussein of Jordan, visiting Madrid, asked the US for military aid

September, 1957

September 7

in the form of air, land, and naval forces on the plea that his country was being threatened by international Communism.

September 8

US Lieutenant General Wheeler, who directed the clearing of the Suez Canal, left Cairo to report to UN Secretary General Hammarskjold.

An international conference on nuclear physics opened in Israel.

September 9

The Syrian Government accused the US of sending warships and possibly planes close to Syrian territory in an open challenge to that country.

President Nasser declared in a press statement that Egypt would continue to give unlimited and unconditional support to Syria, and attacked US Middle East policy.

Tunisian President Habib Bourguiba declared a state of emergency along the Tunisian-Algerian frontier because of border clashes involving French troops and Algerians.

The first shipment of arms under the US accelerated airlift program arrived in Amman, Jordan.

The Soviet Union warned that it could not be indifferent to any US moves against the Syrian regime.

September 10

Secretary of State Dulles tempered earlier official US expressions of alarm over Syria by saying he did not think that developments would require direct armed intervention under the terms of the Eisenhower Doctrine.

September, 1957

September 10

The Jordanian Foreign Minister, Samir al-Rifai, denied that US arms were intended for use against Syria.

The Syrian Cabinet met in an urgent session.

Soviet Foreign Minister Andrei A. Gromyko accused Turkey of massing troops on the Turkish-Syrian border, and asserted that a threat of armed intervention in the internal affairs of Syria was being created.

Ghana and Israel signed an agreement to establish the Black Star Shipping Line.

Soviet Premier Bulganin, in a personal letter to Turkish Premier Menderes, accused Turkey of deploying its army in preparation for an attack on Syria planned by the US.

September 11

The Turkish Foreign Ministry denied charges that Turkey was concentrating troops along the Syrian border.

Syrian criticism of the West was abandoned as officials protested that they did not wish to worsen the present poor relations with the US.

The Norwegian freighter Mars, carrying Israel cargo and bound for Burma, was permitted through the Suez Canal after being held up 24 hours by Egyptian authorities.

Syria sent notes to Iraq, Jordan and Lebanon asking whether they had expressed anxiety to the US over the buildup of arms in Syria.

President Bourguiba said that Tunisia must purchase arms, if not from the US, then from the Communist powers, in order to protect its borders from French aggression.

September, 1957

September 11

Major General Afif Bizri, Army Chief of Staff in Syria, and Lieutenant Colonel Abd-al-Hamid Sarraj, chief of intelligence, flew unexpectedly to Cairo to confer with President Nasser and War Minister Major General Abd-al-Hakim Amer.

Soviet Ambassador M. S. Ryzhov transmitted to Turkish Premier Menderes, N.A. Bulganin's message on the Middle East situation.

September 12

Major General Bizri said that his talks with President Nasser and Egyptian military officials were very amiable and that the armies of the two countries were one, with one command and one plan.

King Hussein returned to Amman from a three week vacation in Turkey and Spain.

Syrian General Bizri paid a duty call on the commander of the joint Egyptian-Syrian armed forces in Cairo.

The Assistant Chief of Staff of Syria said that the Americans had incited Turkey to concentrate a huge army on the Syrian border, ridiculing the explanation that the troops were only on maneuvers.

Following a meeting with the US Ambassador, the Tunisian President assured his countrymen in a radio address that Tunisia would get arms.

King Saud told Washington leaders to modify their stand toward Syria because current developments there had been exaggerated.

Israel Ambassador Abba Eban asked US Secretary Dulles to enlarge upon US policy towards aggression in the Middle East. Dulles offered no further clarification except to point out

September, 1957

September 12

President Eisenhower's Doctrine of the Middle East, and the President's affirmation of that policy the past week.

The US State Department denied that King Saud had intervened in Syrian-American relations.

September 14

Suez Canal Authority Director, Muhammad Yunis, announced that the canal would be deepened by January of 1958 to accommodate ships of up to 35 foot draft.

The Jordanian Government Radio said that the rifles sent by Egypt to Jordan the previous year were unserviceable.

A US Embassy spokesman said that an American Air Force plane took off for Nicosia after being delayed an extra day by Egyptian authorities. The authorities expressed suspicion that the plane's crew had photographed an Egyptian military airport. The pilot said he had mistaken the airport for Cairo International airport.

Syrian Foreign Minister Bitar asserted that Turkey had sent assurances that its army was not poised to attack Syria, and that troop movements inside Turkey were routine maneuvers carried out every year at this time.

The Commission to Safeguard Individual Rights and Liberties, which was set up by France to guard the Algerians against French brutality in the suppression of the revolt there, submitted its report to the French Government.

September, 1957

September 15

The Arab Confederation of Labor said that Arab workers would hit back hard if the US moved against Syria.

Announcement was made of the engagement of King Faisal II of Iraq and 16 year old Princess Fadilah, distant cousin of former King Farouk of Egypt.

Major General Bizri, Army Chief of Staff for Syria, renewed charges that the US was threatening to attack Syria.

September 16

Yemen charged that British planes bombed Shukair and that ground forces had attacked four other posts the previous week.

King Hussein of Jordan signed the UN Convention prohibiting the white slave trade.

Representatives of Baghdad Pact nations and the US met in London and planned a customs union stretching from the Black Sea to India.

A committee representing European war veterans and student organizations in Algeria threatened a general strike in protest against the proposed reorganization law.

Syrian Foreign Minister Salah al-Bitar charged that the campaign of the Western powers to change Syria's present democratic regime was a threat of aggression and a violation of the UN Charter.

The Jordanian Government announced that it had prohibited distribution of a number of Arabic language books because of their Communist propaganda content.

September, 1957

September 16

An Egyptian offer of arms as a gift to Tunisia was announced.

The Mongolian Government recognized the sovereignty of Sudan and Tunisia.

The Middle East News Agency published a statement by the International Federation of Arab Unions, condemning the US imperialist plot against the freedom and independence of Syria.

A delegation of the Society for Promoting Cultural Exchange between Syria and the Soviet Union, headed by its Vice President Nur-ad-Din Hatum, and including Muhammad Nuri Rifai, well known Syrian lawyer and public figure, Sheikh Muhammad Murshid Abdi, a judge from Damascus, and Professor Muhammad Anwar Naaman of Syrian University, arrived in Moscow.

September 17

The Undersecretary of the Sudanese Ministry of Finance left for Washington to attend a World Bank meeting. The Sudan had become a full member of the Bank the previous week.

The Jordan Government charged that the "devils of communism" in Syria had drawn up a plan and were preparing to attack sister states.

September 18

A Soviet economic and technical mission arrived in Damascus to discuss questions arising out of the Syro-Soviet economic cooperation agreement.

Poland and Outer Mongolia pledged to support the fight for independence waged by countries of the Middle East against "colonialist powers."

September, 1957

September 18

Moscow Radio reported that two Soviet warships, the cruiser Zhdanov and the destroyer Svobodny, were en route to Syria for a friendly call at the invitation of the Damascus Government.

It was reported in Washington that Tunisia formally requested American weapons to defend itself against what it called border attacks by French units operating from Algeria.

Yemeni King Ahmad announced that British planes had resumed raids on southern Yemen.

The Cairo representative of the Imam of Oman stated that British air raids on Omani territory were continuing.

September 19

In a note handed to the Syrian Charge d'Affaires, Amman accused Syria of activities intended to create disorder and an atmosphere of confusion in Jordan. It reminded Syria that that country had broken its promise to give financial aid to Jordan under the Arab Solidarity Agreement, thus failing in its obligations under the international agreement made among Arabs.

The British Government announced that Yemeni forces had withdrawn from the much disputed Djebel-Dhat-Shukair area in western Aden which they had occupied for several months.

Secretary of State Dulles said that Turkey faced a growing military danger from the major buildup of Soviet arms in Syria.

A spokesman of the Algerian National Liberation Front, Muhammad Yazid, suggested a round table conference be held by France, Morocco, Tunisia and Algerian nationalists in order to settle the Algerian question. France said that it would not oppose a debate in the UN General Assembly, although it considered Algeria an integral part of France.

September 19

In Oman, a representative of the Imam said that he would protest to the UN against British aggression.

In answer to Syrian charges that the US was interfering in Jordanian affairs, Jordan accused Syria of meddling in its domestic business.

US Secretary of State John Foster Dulles told the UN General Assembly that the Soviet Communist effort had made progress in Syria, where political power "had increasing been taken over by those who depended upon Moscow." He declared that one consequence of this was that Turkey now faced growing military danger from the major buildup of Soviet arms in Syria on its southern border, "a buildup concerted with Soviet military power on Turkey's northern border."

September 20

Soviet Foreign Minister Gromyko accused the West of turning the Middle East into a hotbed of international conflict and called upon the UN General Assembly to defend the independence of these countries.

A conference of French Government and political leaders adjourned without agreement over the controversial issue of whether or not the Algeria bill should leave a way open for Algeria's secession from France.

Ireland called on France in the UN to allow free elections in Algeria supervised by UN observers, so that Algeria could determine its own political future.

Police ordered the arrest of a Baghdad lawyer who led 130 Iraqis to the International Youth Festival in Moscow. Sixteen other members of the group were also arrested.

September 20

King Hussein of Jordan declared that the present regime in Syria, if left to achieve its subversive aims, would endanger the national existence of Syria and endanger the whole Arab world.

September 21

Two Soviet warships, the first ships of the Soviet fleet ever to visit Syria, arrived at the port of Latakia.

The Jordanian Government announced the seizure of large amounts of Czechoslovakian manufactured arms near the Syrian-Jordanian border.

A group led by the Vice President of the Syrian Parliament arrived in Budapest on a visit to Hungary.

Damascus Radio announced an immediate curfew on highway traffic linking Syria's main cities because of general movements and maneuvers to be carried out by the Syrian Army.

Soviet Foreign Minister Gromyko renewed charges against the West, presenting two requests to debate the issue in the UN General Assembly.

The French Government announced intentions of selling shares of its oil companies to the public.

King Saud reportedly pledged to Egypt and Syria that his kingdom would give full support to Syria against any aggression.

The Deputy Chief of Protocol for King Saud was barred from the main buildings upon his arrival at the Capetown Airport because of South Africa's segregation laws.

French Premier Bourges-Manoury, meeting with Algerian political leaders, worked out a modification in the text of the proposal on Algeria. All political leaders except the Communists

September 21

and the Poujadists agreed. The bill now proposed that Algeria be divided into semi-autonomous regions, roughly along ethnic lines, so that heavily outnumbered Europeans could rule their own local affairs in areas where they were concentrated. It also proposed a central executive and assembly, allowing for an over-all Algerian federation and a freer relationship with France. The independence demanded by the nationalists was implicitly barred.

The Political Affairs Committee of the Western European Union Assembly endorsed French policy in Algeria and urged its support by the UN.

The Tunisian Government ordered suspension of the Italian language weekly newspaper L'Italo Tunisino and expulsion of its director, Vito D'Alessandro, for publishing articles which it felt could harm Italian-Tunisian relations.

The Jordanian Government approved a proposal to establish a branch of the Riyadh-Saudi Bank in Jordan.

September 22

Three hundred Jordanians called on King Hussein to assure him of their support of the Government in the wake of criticism leveled by Egypt and Syria.

Major General Bizri said that he and the Syrian Government were willing to talk directly with anyone from the US on American-Syrian relations.

Syrian jet fighters intercepted two Lebanese airplanes taking members of a Brazilian Parliamentary delegation to Beirut from Jordan. One airplane was forced to land in Damascus, but the other reached Lebanon.

September 22

President Camille Chamoun opened work on the Litani River power and irrigation project to double Lebanese electric power.

Back from an inspection trip to the Syrian-Turkish border, the Governor of Aleppo, Syria, reported to President Kuwatli that Turkey was concentrating its forces near the frontier.

September 23

After meeting in Washington with President Eisenhower, Crown Prince Faisal of Saudi Arabia declared that Syria posed no threat to its Arab neighbors.

The Jordanian Minister of Development and Agriculture told newsmen that Jordan was preparing to ask the US for an extra $10 million in economic aid during the current year.

Syrian authorities released the Lebanese airplane intercepted the previous day, explaining that the company that had chartered the plane for the Brazilian officials had failed to inform Syria of the plane's flight over Syrian territory.

Tunisia's new Ambassador to Egypt announced his government's acceptance of an offer of arms from President Nasser.

Representatives of the Baghdad Pact nations and the US discussed secret intelligence reports about Communist penetration in the Middle East.

September 24

The Egyptian Coast Guard seized an Israel fishing vessel near al-Arish, alleging that it was inside Egypt's territorial waters; the six man crew was arrested.

September 24

Saadi Yazid, Chief of the National Liberation Front, and Zorah Drif, a woman revolutionary, both condemned to death *in absentia* by a French military tribunal, were captured by French paratroopers in Algeria.

Italy offered to sell arms and ammunition to Tunisia.

The Tunisian Embassy in Washington denied that the acceptance of arms offered by Egypt foreshadowed any change in Tunisia's relations with the US.

The US, Great Britain and France refused to meet with the Soviet Union to iron out their Middle Eastern rivalries. In a note, the Soviet Union accused the US Government of illegal interference in Syrian affairs and of provoking trouble throughout the Middle East.

Premier Ali Jawdat of Iraq arrived in Beirut to confer with Lebanese leaders.

British Foreign Secretary Selwyn Lloyd told the General Assembly that Great Britain viewed the Syrian situation with grave concern. He declared that Soviet arms shipments to Arab countries could have been to pre-stock forward bases for the Soviet Union itself.

Israel announced that the second part of an oil pipeline from Elath on the Gulf of Aqaba to Ashdod on the Mediterranean had been completed.

Argentina and Israel signed a cultural cooperation agreement.

September 25

The Lebanese Government indicted 400 persons, including former Premiers Abdallah al-Yafi, Saeb Salam and Hussein Uwaini, on charges of attempting an armed coup and inciting to riot during the election campaign the previous May.

September 25

King Saud of Saudi Arabia arrived in Damascus to confer with Syrian leaders.

The US announced that it would not supply Tunisia with arms directly, but would instead act as broker with friendly European countries to help equip the country with its needs.

The Secretary General of the Arab League, Hassouna, advised the Western powers to cease interfering in the Middle East and North Africa.

The French Government avoided attempts to delay the debate on the Algerian reform plan.

In Jordan, a Jordanian was sentenced to death by a military court for spying for Israel. A life sentence was imposed on another, and a third accused was sentenced to hard labor for a term of five to fifteen years.

Generals Abu Nuwar and Hayari, former Foreign Minister Abdallah Rimawi and two other officers in Jordan were sentenced in absentia to 15 years imprisonment. Twelve other officers were sentenced, four in absentia, to ten year terms, and five were acquitted for lack of evidence concerning their part in the April riots.

A Jordanian Royal Decree ordered Parliament to convene October 1. The Parliament of Jordan was suspended three months previously by King Hussein.

The Egyptian National Assembly unanimously adopted a proposal to appeal to the UN General Assembly to take all necessary steps at its current session to ban the manufacture and use of atomic and hydrogen weapons.

September 26

In Jordan, the ban imposed on Egyptian publications the previous April was lifted from some 20 weekly and monthly social and technical periodicals.

September 26

The Bahrain Government announced that beginning January 1, 1958 goods passing in transit through Manama, the capital city, would no longer be subjected to customs duty.

Director General Henry Labouisse, of the UN Relief and Works Agency, discussed the status of Palestine refugees in Jordan with King Hussein and his ministers.

US Secretary of State Dulles said he would be glad to extend the same courtesy of seeing the Syrian Foreign Minister as he had to other foreign ministers in the US for the opening of the General Assembly.

Iraq's Premier visited Damascus to confer with Syrian leaders and King Saud of Saudi Arabia.

Libya, Morocco, Tunisia and Malaya were elected to membership in the World Bank and the International Monetary Fund.

President Bourguiba of Tunisia announced that Western arms shipments would reach Tunisia during October and said he hoped that France would not waste time and effort in opposing the deliveries.

President Habib Bourguiba of Tunisia said that he had received a letter from the State Department expressing the will of the US to help Tunisia resolve the arms problem and find sufficient equipment for its army. He announced acceptance of the US offer.

US diplomatic officials agreed that the position of their government in the Middle East had deteriorated because of recent US moves in that area, especially in relation to Syria.

September 27

The Baghdad Pact nations and the US agreed to expand their

September 27

program of defense against Communist subversion in the Middle East.

The US conceded that tactical clashes with friendly Arab nations had damaged its propaganda position in the Middle East.

The Middle East News Agency said that 120 Jordanian Army officers had threatened to resign unless the officers convicted of plotting to overthrow King Hussein were released. The protesting group criticized Hussein's regime for allowing US interference in Jordan's affairs, the agency report said.

King Saud left Syria to return to Saudi Arabia. He promised to help defend Syria in the event of any aggression from any source.

In a policy speech in the General Assembly, Turkey's chief delegate, Saifallah Esin, accused the Soviet Union of seeking to spoil Syrian-Turkish relations by rumoring that Turkish troops were poised for attack on Syria's frontier.

September 28

Israel was reported to be looking forward to the use of nuclear power for irrigation, industry and the development of mineral resources.

Following his visit to Damascus, Iraqi Premier Jawdat assured Syria that aggression against its or any other Arab country would be considered aggression against Iraq.

Egyptian newspapers published President Nasser's interview with US correspondents in which he said that his country was prepared to render every assistance to Syria in its struggle against imperialism.

September 29

Tourists wishing to visit Jordan via Israel would not be allowed to use the same route on the return journey, a Jordanian official announcement said.

Syrian soldiers seized two UN border observers and an Israel army liaison officer near the frontier and took them to Damascus. They were released later in the day.

Ten Syrians, including former President Adib Shishakli and Colonel Hussein, were ordered court martialed on charges of plotting with the US.

September 30

It was reported in Washington that President Eisenhower had sent word to King Saud that the US would not condone aggression in the Middle East by Turkey or any other country, but that he still considered the situation in Syria to be serious.

Mr. Labouisse left Beirut for New York to present a new plea to the UN General Assembly for funds to keep nearly one million Arab refugees from starvation.

In Lebanon it was revealed that Czechoslovakian arms bearing the stamp of the Syrian Army had been seized.

A Council of National Defense was set up in Egypt under the chairmanship of President Nasser.

The Omani Imam's representative asked the UN Secretary General to send a neutral observer group to Oman to investigate Britain's aggression against that country.

The Damascus Fourth International Fair with twenty-seven countries including the Soviet Union participating, closed.

October 1

The Algerian National Liberation Front declared, in a memorandum submitted to the UN General Assembly's Political Committee, that it was prepared to consider any formula of free cooperation between France and North Africa, such cooperation taking into account the legitimate interests of France.

A 40 mile road across the Rif Mountains, linking Fez with the Mediterranean port of Alhucemas, Morocco, and built by 10,537 young volunteers, was completed.

Tunisia protested to France that a French plane had flown over Tunisian territory and fired on a Tunisian military post and a customs station, wounding three Tunisians.

Three Algerian nationalist leaders touring Latin America were accused of being Communist agitators and expelled by the Guatemalan Government.

King Hussein of Jordan expressed his gratitude to Saudi Arabia as the only country which had made its payments under the Arab Solidarity Agreement.

Saudi Arabia and Thailand agreed to establish diplomatic relations.

King Saud of Saudi Arabia sent a memorandum to the Shah of Iran concerning measures to prevent oil reaching Israel and efforts to stop Israel from free navigation of the Gulf of Aqaba.

The Soviet cruiser Zhdanov and the destroyer Svobodny left Latakia after a ten day visit to Syria.

Iraq's National Economy Minister arrived in Damascus to negotiate a trade and payment agreement with Syria.

The new Assiut University in Upper Egypt was opened.

The Jordanian Parliament opened for the first time since the April crisis.

October 1

The Sudanese Prime Minister, Sayyed Abdallah Khalil, arrived in Cairo by air from Europe to meet President Nasser.

The charges against the participants in the recently exposed anti-Government plot in Syria were published. Investigations showed that the leading role in its organization was played by US Embassy officials.

October 2

The Saudi Arabian delegate to the UN, Ahmad Shukairy, denounced US Secretary of State Dulles' suggestion that the UN discuss the Syrian situation. Shukairy said that the UN had no right to interfere with Soviet arms shipments to Syria.

All French nationals living in Sakiet and in Kef, the principal town of the area, were expelled by Tunisian authorities.

Tunisia protested that two French aircraft bombed and machine-gunned the Tunisian border village of Sakiet Sidi-Youssef and that a mortar attack was launched on the village from Algeria.

The French National Defense Ministry issued a communique to the effect that French planes flying over Algeria near the Tunisian border had been fired upon on 13 occasions with automatic weapons from Tunisian territory. The communique asserted that the French planes had used the right of retaliation on October 1 when they returned Tunisian fire.

An Aden Government guard was killed and two others were wounded near the Yemeni border when they came under fire from the village of al-Hussein.

October 3

The head of the French delegation to the UN reiterated the French stand that the question of Algeria was not the business

October 3

of the UN and implied that there were parties at the UN interested in taking advantage of France's present political crisis.

The Sudanese Prime Minister, Khalil, said in Cairo that his government was studying a Russian proposal for an economic and trade agreement.

Hamid Khoja, the Syrian Minister of Agriculture, announced that the Soviet Union had guaranteed the purchase of Syria's entire surplus agricultural produce. Half would be paid for in cash, half in agricultural and other machinery.

Egyptian Foreign Minister Mahmoud Fawzi told the UN General Assembly that Egypt "would not tolerate that even a fingertip of Syria be ruffled, by any aggressor," and said that if aggression was attempted, Egypt would immediately rise to a man and stand four square with its Syrian sister state.

Saleh Akel, the Syrian Minister for Information, announced in Damascus that the Syrian Government had decided to cancel the licenses of 40 newspapers and weeklies because they failed to comply with press regulations.

President Eisenhower said that he had received a message of warm friendship from King Saud and did not know what particular thing had inspired the speech of Saudi Arabia's Shukairy in the UN. As to the Syrian situation, he felt that it seemed to be solidifying to some extent. Eisenhower also felt that the original alarm of countries like Lebanon, Jordan, and Iraq and, to some extent, Saudi Arabia, seemed to have been quieted by what they had learned. Just exactly what grounds they had for that, he said he didn't know.

Tunisian President Bourguiba announced the recall of Muhammad Masmoudi, Ambassador to France, following frontier incidents in which French aircraft and Tunisian batteries were involved.

October, 1957

October 3

Senior officials of the Saudi Ministry of Agriculture left for Moscow to study agricultural progress in the Soviet Union.

France asked Tunisia to delay the expulsion of 12 French nationals from Kef.

The leader of the French delegation to the UN, Guillaume Georges-Picot, declared that the Algerian question was not a legitimate concern of that organization.

October 4

The Syrian Foreign Minister, Salah al-Bitar, told a meeting of UN correspondents that Syria lacked sufficient arms for its own defense.

Tunisia charged that two French aircraft machine gunned a coal caravan inside Tunisian territory, killing three muleteers and nine mules.

The US pledged $21 million and Great Britain almost $3 million toward UN aid for Palestine refugees.

October 5

President Bourguiba of Tunisia canceled an order recalling the Tunisian Ambassador from Paris "in view of the friendly disposition" and conciliatory intentions shown by the French leaders.

In his reply to the Soviet note of September 11 protesting Turkey's massing of troops on the Syrian border, Premier Menderes categorically denied that Turkey had aggressive intentions toward Syria.

October, 1957

October 6

It was announced in Algiers that work was begun on a 93 mile oil pipeline from Hassi Messaoud in the Sahara to Touggourt.

It was reported in Damascus that Syria had accepted a Russian offer to build a naval base north of the Mediterranean port of Latakia.

October 7

In an interview with James Reston of The New York Times, Nikita S. Khrushchev charged US Secretary of State Dulles with inciting Turkey to wage war against Syria.

Syrian authorities canceled the visa of a US Foreign Service courier without explanation.

Gunfire was exchanged by Turkish gendarmes and Syrian border guards for 45 minutes between Nizip and Jerablus in a disagreement involving a search of Turkish railroad workers in a "free zone" area at the point where the Istanbul-Baghdad railroad crossed the border.

The Tunisian Secretary of State for Coordination and National Defense, Bahi Ladgham, told the UN that French military commanders in North Africa were seeking a pretext to invade his country.

Syrian Foreign Minister Salah al-Bitar, speaking before the UN General Assembly, accused the US of seeking to establish political domination over Syria by means of economic, financial, political and military pressure.

October 8

An Egyptian delegation left for Rome to resume talks with British representatives regarding the restoration of their trade relations.

October, 1957

October 5

French authorities announced that a Foreign Legion platoon had clashed on October 3 with a group of rebels who had crossed into the Sahara region from Libya. Libyan authorities contended that a French unit had crossed into Libya and attacked a military post there.

A French communique acknowledged that two French planes which had been over Tunisian territory during a storm on October 4 had returned the fire of a mule caravan.

Egypt's clandestine Communist Party accused the Government of persecuting Communists to please the US.

The Secretary General of the Saudi National Commercial Bank arrived in Hamburg for economic talks.

The Sudanese Premier and the Minister of the Interior, Ali Abd-al-Rahman, held a two hour conference with President Nasser in Cairo about the Nile water talks and general Arab questions.

France and Morocco signed a convention on the execution of judicial decisions and extradition orders, and also a cultural convention relating primarily to former French schools in Morocco.

Soviet Foreign Minister A.A. Gromyko and US Secretary of State John Foster Dulles met in Washington to discuss the Middle East question, disarmament, the situation in Europe and Soviet-US contacts.

October 6

A second consignment of US military aid for Jordan, including tanks and other heavy equipment, was unloaded from a US ship.

October, 1957

October 8

Israel protested to the UN Security Council and demanded the immediate release of a fishing trawler and its crew, which had been seized by Egypt.

Lebanon's Foreign Minister, Charles Malik, told the UN General Assembly that his country unreservedly ranged itself on the side of the free world, but that it would instantly come to the support of Syria if it was attacked.

Soviet Communist Party Secretary Nikita S. Khrushchev warned Turkish leaders that they had not been very sensible. They had concentrated so many Turkish forces against Syria that they had left their frontiers with Russia almost bare.

The Tunisian Government charged that the French Army had shelled Tunisian territory in the al-Hammam border area.

The Syrian Foreign Minister complained to the UN Secretary General that Turkey's massing of troops along the Turkish-Syrian border was a threat to the peace of Syria.

The Tunisian delegation to the UN announced that it would present the Algerian nationalist viewpoint during the debate on Algeria scheduled for the following month. Bahi Ladgham of Tunisia said that his country had concluded a thorough investigation of the political situation in Algeria, that the National Liberation Front was in control of Algerian nationalist activity and that the Algerian Nationalist Movement no longer represented active elements within Algeria.

The Syrian Government, in a note to Turkey, alleged that Turkish troops were concentrated on the Syrian frontier, Turkish planes had flown over Syrian territory, and Turkish guards had fired on and wounded Syrian civilians.

The Soviet Committee of Asian Solidarity published a statement resolutely protesting against British-US interference in the internal affairs of Middle Eastern nations.

October 9

Khrushchev charged that US Secretary of State Dulles sent Loy W. Henderson to the Middle East to incite certain Arab states against Syria, and that the US was pushing Turkey into war with Syria. Khrushchev said that he would do everything to prevent war between Turkey and Syria.

President Nasser ordered all branches of the Government and the press to represent Egypt as a strictly neutral country and to make every effort to bring about a more equitable balance between Eastern and Western trade.

A Turkish Foreign Ministry spokesman rejected mounting charges that Turkey was threatening peace in the Middle East.

The Egyptian Minister of Finance said that officials of the International Bank for Reconstruction and Development had expressed willingness to help finance a huge project for widening the Suez Canal to permit two way traffic.

October 10

King Saud arrived in Beirut for a five day visit.

An arms cache seized near Latakia was described by the Syrian press as being part of an American plot to overthrow the current regime.

Secretary of State Dulles announced that the US would honor its obligations under the North Atlantic Treaty and the Eisenhower Doctrine to come to the defense of Turkey in case of an attack.

The State Department declared that Khrushchev's charges were completely unfounded. It warned the Soviet Union to be under no illusions about US determination to support Turkey and fulfill its treaty obligations.

October 10

The Syrian Government claimed that Turkish border patrols raided three Syrian villages during the previous week, and that Turkey was continuing to mass troops on the Turkish-Syrian border.

It was reported in Beirut that the Parliamentary Foreign Affairs Committee formally asked the Government to clarify the joint Lebanese-US communique of March 16 confirming Lebanon's acceptance of the Eisenhower Doctrine.

The Egyptian Ministry of Education announced that the Government had prohibited all Egyptians from working in Iraq, in retaliation for that country's cancellation of a request for 240 Egyptian school teachers.

It was reported in Aden that Soviet technicians had started to build a military airport near Sanaa.

Abd-al-Rahman Abu-Taleb, Yemen's Ambassador to Egypt, announced that Yemen and the Soviet Union had agreed to raise their missions to embassy level.

October 11

Britain's First Lord of the Admiralty expressed confidence that his country would support US assurances of defending Turkey in the event of aggression.

The UN Secretariat said that Secretary General Hammarskjold had been holding private talks with Egyptian and Suez Canal company officials for several months.

Egypt told the UN Security Council that it had seized the Israel trawler Doron the previous month because the boat had violated Egyptian territorial waters.

October 11

French reports announced the capture, in Algeria, of 108 nationalist guerrillas in three days of fighting, and the killing of 80 more. The increase in surrenders was viewed hopefully as a sign of nationalist fatigue by the French authorities.

The managing director of the Egyptian Suez Canal Authority said in Zurich that Egypt had asked the UN Secretary General to mediate the settlement of Suez Canal stockholders' claims.

In Jordan, the security police arrested an undisclosed number of persons and seized a quantity of arms at refugee camps.

King Saud of Saudi Arabia and President Chamoun of Lebanon were reported to have agreed that a conference of all Arab leaders on the Turkish-Syrian crisis should be called.

Acting Foreign Minister of Lebanon, Jamil Makkawi, said that Lebanon would consider any aggression against Syria as an aggression against itself.

October 12

The Secretary General of the UN, Mr. Hammarskjold, announced in a 47 page report that the UN Emergency Force in Egypt was $12,800,000 in arrears and suggested that the General Assembly vote $20,000,000 more to carry the force on for ten months into 1958 and $6,000,000 above that if the Assembly decided to reimburse participating nations for the special overseas pay they were giving their troops.

The French Army announced that 30,000 land mines had been planted in the barbed wire and in a strip of no man's land along the Moroccan frontier.

It was announced in Amman that Jordan had received the second installment of Saudi economic aid amounting to $1,500,000.

October 12

It was announced in Amman that repairs would start in six months on a 523 mile stretch of the Hejaz Railroad that had been derelict since World War I.

Mr. Khrushchev sent identical letters to the Labour and Socialist Parties of the United Kingdom, France, western Germany, Italy, Belgium, the Netherlands, Denmark and Norway, referring to a Turkish and US conspiracy against Syria, and urged them to do everything necessary to prevent aggression and preserve peace in the Middle East.

King Ahmad of Yemen appointed Abd-al-Rahman Abu-Taleb, the Yemeni Minister to Egypt, his first Ambassador to the Soviet Union.

October 13

Sharif Gaschout, the Libyan Charge d'Affaires in Cairo, announced that Egypt was giving Libya six armored cars and 100-200 Egyptian made rifles.

The joint command of Egyptian and Syrian armed forces announced from its headquarters in Cairo that Egyptian armed forces had sent "basic elements" to Syria since September 11 to reinforce its forces and strengthen its defensive capabilities. Egyptian naval units carrying troops arrived in the port of Latakia, Syria.

US Representative Frances P. Bolton, who was on a fact finding mission in Jordan, met the Minister of Development and Reconstruction, who told her that America was responsible for the odd situation in the Middle East.

King Hussein had a five hour meeting with Iraq's King Faisal at an oil pumping station on the Iraqi-Jordanian border. They were reported to have discussed the $20,000,000 deficit in the Jordanian army budget due to the failure of Egypt and Syria to pay subsidies pledged under the Arab Solidarity Agreement.

October 13

A supplementary trade agreement was signed in Cairo between Hungary and Egypt.

King Saud announced in Beirut that Saudi contributions to Palestine refugees would be increased from $40,000 to $100,000.

The Saudi Arabian Ministry of Defense and Aviation announced the opening of the first Saudi Naval Academy in Dammam.

King Saud was reported to be laying the groundwork for a conference of all Arab Chiefs of State during his visit in Beirut.

October 14

Authoritative sources in London said that the Egyptian troops sent to Syria amounted to less than one battalion.

A military court in Amman sentenced Khaled Himshawi to 18 years hard labor for Communist activity in Jordan.

Israel accused the Arab nations of carrying out an economic war against Israel by boycotting goods produced in Israel and blacklisting ships going to and from Israel.

Security police arrested seven leading Communists, including two women, in Hilla, south of Baghdad.

Turkey denied Soviet charges that the US had sent troops to build up Turkey's defenses.

Egyptian troops which landed October 13 at Latakia were being massed on Turkey's border.

The Peking Radio reported that Communist China reached a trade agreement for 1958 with Morocco under which the latter would send phosphate, superphosphate, fertilizer, frozen

October 14

mutton, cotton, wheat, sardines and olive oil, in exchange for Chinese tea, cotton cloth, machinery and silk.

The Foreign Affairs Committee of the Lebanese Parliament approved a trade agreement with Saudi Arabia.

An Egyptian gift of armored cars, light arms, and ammunition arrived in Libya. The Libyan Foreign Minister announced that this gift was a symbol of Arab solidarity.

October 15

In a letter to Secretary General Dag Hammarskjold, Turkey denied the charges made by Syria on October 8. Turkey accused Syria of launching a series of propaganda actions in order to support the allegations and statements previously made by the Soviet Government on behalf of Syria.

October 16

Secretary of State Dulles reiterated at a news conference that a Soviet attack on Turkey would bring American retaliation against the territory of the Soviet Union.

Italian Foreign Minister Guiseppe Pella told the Chamber of Deputies that Italy did not offer Tunisia the arms it had requested the previous month.

Moroccan Foreign Minister Ahmad Balafrej announced that the Spanish Government had agreed to turn over a vast expanse of its southern Moroccan territory to the Kingdom of Morocco.

The US delegation declared that it welcomed UN General Assembly consideration of the situation in the Middle East.

October 16

In a letter to Sir Leslie Munro, President of the UN General Assembly, Soviet Foreign Minister Andrei A. Gromyko charged that there was reliable information that the Turkish General Staff, together with American advisers, had elaborated detailed plans for an attack on Syria, after the elections in Turkey on October 27. He accused the US of prodding Turkey to commit aggression against Syria.

King Hussein of Jordan declared full support for Syria in the event of an attack; he said that any such attack would be considered an attack on all Arab states.

King Saud conferred in Beirut with Lebanese President Chamoun on the landing of Egyptian troops in Syria.

The Yemeni representative to the UN said that British attacks against Yemen from the Protectorate of Aden had increased in violence and frequency since the first of the year of 1957.

Damascus Radio declared that the Soviet Union would come to Syria's aid if Syria was attacked by Turkey.

In a letter to the UN Secretary General, the Syrian Foreign Minister urged that a commission be set up by the General Assembly to make an impartial and international investigation of the situation on the Syrian-Turkish border.

The Syrian Government declared a state of emergency in Syria.

The USSR Communist Party's messages to the British and Norwegian Labor Parties were published, drawing their attention to the extremely serious situation in the Middle East, notably in the region of Syria.

October 17

In Algeria a company of Shaamba Camel Cavalry mutinied, killed eight French soldiers and fled into the desert.

October 17

President Bourguiba announced the formation of a company with American and Tunisian capital to prospect for minerals.

Ali Gholi Ardalan, Iranian Foreign Minister, said that Iran threatened to break off diplomatic relations with Syria if the latter continued its propaganda attacks against his country.

King Saud met for the second day with President Chamoun of Lebanon; he also conferred by telephone with President Kuwatli of Syria.

The weekly newspaper of the Moslem Brotherhood, in Jordan, was suspended for an indefinite period.

It was reported in Damascus that the Syrian Army was placed in a state of alert and that arms had been distributed to the Popular Resistance Movement, a civil defense organization.

Syrian acting Foreign Minister Khalil al-Kallas said that he had received a note from Turkey denying any military threat to Syria and expressing concern over developments in Syria.

Israel Premier Ben-Gurion called on the West to supply Israel with defensive air power and anti-submarine weapons to match the Soviet arms shipments to Egypt and Syria.

Five members of the Jordanian Chamber of Deputies resigned; four were members of the Nationalist Socialist Party and one of the pro-Communist National Front.

Despite the Government ban, demonstrations and meetings were held in France to protest the war in Algeria.

The Soviet press published the message of the Communist Party of the USSR to the French Socialist Party, drawing its attention to the situation in the Middle East, notably in the region of Syria. Similar messages were sent to the Italian, West German, Danish, Belgian and Dutch Socialist Parties on October 12.

October 18

Representatives of two French oil companies that were exploiting the Hassi Messaoud field announced that they would begin pumping 600 metric tons of crude petroleum to the rail head at Toggourt, Algeria, in January, 1958.

King Faisal of Iraq flew to Tehran for a ten day visit.

The Soviet Union declared that it had learned of a "top secret plan" for combined Turkish-US aggression against Syria, and reiterated that it would "take all necessary measures" to aid Syria if that country was attacked.

An Israel newspaper said that the Royal Dutch-Shell Group in Israel had sold their marketing holdings to the French oil company Petrofrance and a British chain store magnate.

Premier Ben-Gurion said that Israel faced more danger from underdevelopment of its southern desert than from the military forces of the Arab states.

Reportedly, Lebanon gave up hope of general Arab talks, owing to the opposition of Egypt's President Nasser.

Egyptian warships visiting the Syrian port of Latakia were ordered to remain there.

The UN General Assembly's Steering Committee recommended UN debate of the Syrian situation.

The General Assembly agreed, by a vote of 66-0, with one abstention, to debate Syria's complaint about alleged threats to its security.

October 18

It was reported in Beirut that ten of Jordan's 40 Parliamentary Deputies were under arrest for not submitting a written vote of confidence in the cabinet of Premier Ibrahim Hashem.

October 19

Egypt signed cultural cooperation agreements with the Soviet Union, Czechoslovakia and Bulgaria.

The Kremlin invited the US and Great Britain to call for talks among the three powers to discuss the Syrian-Turkish crisis.

King Saud and President Chamoun issued a joint communique pledging themselves to the united Arab front; they warned that an attack on Syria would be considered aggression against all the Arab states.

The trial of 18 alleged Communists opened in Cairo.

A Turkish Government spokesman accused the Soviet Union of "nonsensical lies" in charging that the US had plans for a joint attack on Syria by Turkey, Iraq and Jordan; he said the claim was beneath the dignity of a formal Government denial.

President Bourguiba opened Tunisia's fifth international fair in Tunis.

The Moroccan Minister of the Interior said that passport requests from 2,000 Moroccan Jews waiting at Marseilles for permission to re-enter Morocco would receive sympathetic attention.

The Tass statement on the situation in the Middle East and US intrigues against Syria was published.

October 20

The Iraqi Government expressed confidence that Turkey had no aggressive intentions against Syria.

A Jordanian military court sentenced two Arabs to prison for spying for Israel.

The Saudi Arabian Radio announced that in order to promote confidence and peace and foster the bonds of fraternity between Syria and Turkey, King Saud had offered to mediate. The two countries had accepted this mediation and official delegations would arrive in Dammam within two days. However, the Syrian Foreign Ministry denied that Syria had accepted any mediation offer.

Former Foreign Minister Muhammad Salah-ad-Din, former Defense Minister Abd-al-Fattah Hassan, and eight other defendants indicted in July were convicted on charges of conspiring to assassinate President Nasser and overthrowing his regime. Nasser approved the verdicts.

A UN subcommittee left for Aqaba to investigate a Jordanian complaint that an Israel jet fighter had attacked a Jordan Airways Liner on October 19.

Sudan and Saudi Arabia signed a payments agreement in Khartoum.

October 21

The Arabian American Oil Company announced the discovery of

October 21

oil about 150 miles southwest of Dhahran; it was estimated that the well would produce 3,000 barrels per day.

Vice Admiral Charles R. Brown, commander of the US Sixth Fleet, said that 6,200 Marines and a flotilla of warships scheduled to return to the US three weeks before had stayed on with the Fleet during the Turkish-Syrian crisis.

Israel Prime Minister Ben-Gurion told the Knesset that a fundamental transformation had taken place in the Middle East situation: he said that the forces contending in the area were not so much the forces of the area itself but the world blocs of the East and the West, headed by the US and the Soviet Union.

Turkey announced acceptance of King Saud's mediation offer. Syrian diplomats issued a statement at the UN that Syria did not reject the offer of King Saud, but that reports of a mediation move were "not in conformity with the facts."

An official Iraqi communique denied Soviet charges that Iraq was plotting with Jordan, the US and Turkey to attack Syria. It accused Russia of raising suspicion and mistrust between the Arab nations in order to "achieve a chaotic atmosphere for the attainment of the objectives of international communism."

It was reported in Washington that the US welcomed King Saud's offer to mediate.

October 22

Acting Foreign Minister Jamil Makkawi confirmed that Lebanon had asked for revision of the US-Lebanese communique on the Eisenhower Doctrine issued March 16. He asserted that his Government sought clarification, not a change in policy.

By a vote of 37-10 with 34 abstentions, the UN General Assembly suspended its debate on the Syrian-Turkish dispute pending

October 22

the outcome of King Saud's mediation efforts. An amendment sponsored by the Soviet and Arab Blocs, calling for the debate to be resumed automatically in three days, was adopted.

The British Embassy in Jerusalem said that four of five British warships scheduled to pay a courtesy call to Israel during the week, would not make the trip because of the international situation.

October 23

A Turkish delegation arrived in Dhahran, Saudi Arabia, to discuss King Saud's offer of mediation.

The American oil company Conorada obtained a five year prospecting concession on 10,000 square miles of the Sahara Desert in southern Tunisia.

An Air Force spokesman in Washington said that the Soviet charge that US jet bombers had been sent to Turkey was false.

Damascus formally rejected King Saud's offer, with the explanation that the crisis was not something which could be subject to mediation and that the Syrian Government did not understand the King's message as a mediation offer, but merely as an expression of his noble sentiments toward Syria and Arabism and his preparedness to spare no effort to avoid the threat of a catastrophe. The statement said that the crisis could be resolved only by the withdrawal of Turkish troops from the Syrian border and an end of Turkish interference in Syria's internal affairs.

Major General Afif Bizri, Syrian Army Chief of Staff, accused the US Sixth Fleet of sending planes deep over Syrian territory.

A shooting fray occurred on the Turkish-Syrian border involving Turkish tobacco smugglers.

October 23

Syrian sources at the UN said that their Government would press for immediate appointment of a commission to inquire into Syria's charges against Turkey.

Delegates from 21 Asian and African countries meeting in Cairo expressed their support of Syria in its crisis with Turkey.

Morocco's new Supreme Court was inaugurated.

Former Premier Guy Mollet, named to head a new French Government, was reported ready to establish contact with Algerian nationalist leaders to obtain a ceasefire. Mollet told the radicals and other political groups that he would resubmit to Parliament the Algerian Reform Bill which had caused the fall of Premier Bourges-Maunoury on September 30.

Egyptian authorities announced that two Gaza Strip Arabs convicted of spying for Israel were hanged in Tanta Prison near Cairo. Three others had been hanged on October 21.

Arab states, with the exception of Egypt, urged Syria to accept Saud's mediation offer.

The Lebanese press reported that the US Sixth Fleet was concentrating in the Turkish port of Izmir. Turkish troops were massing on the Syrian border, and US warships were cruising 25 miles off the Syrian coast.

October 24

The Arab News Agency stated that the Syrian President, Kuwatli, had requested that King Saud withdraw his mediation offer so that the UN could resume discussion of the border crisis.

Diplomatic sources in Moscow reported that the Syrian and Egyptian Ambassadors to Moscow had been called home.

October 24

The Sudanese Charge d' Affaires in Czechoslovakia presented his credentials.

The nine executive chiefs of the Algerian National Liberation Front, meeting in Tunis, issued a communique announcing that a new nationalist military offensive had been opened October 20 to mark the third anniversary of the rebellion. The French military command in Algiers said that there had been no unusual rebel activity since that date.

The People's Movement, a Moroccan political organization formed early in the month of October, was banned by the Interior Ministry on the ground that it was illegally constituted.

An Israel Army Intelligence Corps Lieutenant was sentenced to death in Amman, Jordan, for spying for Israel.

The Israel Ambassador to Canada predicted that peace would not come to the Middle East until the Arab world was convinced that Israel was an "immutable factor;" he warned the West not to join the race with the Soviet Union to supply arms to the Arab League countries.

October 25

A joint Turco-Saudi communique issued at Jedda at the close of a long conversation between King Saud and the Turkish Minister of State, Fatin Rustu Zorlu, reiterated King Saud's hope that the doubts and anxieties which had arisen between the two parties would be dispelled through the assistance and cooperation of the Turkish and Syrian Governments to the benevolent efforts which he would make. The note stated that Turkey had in no way an aggressive policy against any of its neighbors, including Syria, and expressed that country's intention to remain in close cooperation with King Saud.

October 25

The UN resumed debate on the Syrian complaint. Ambassador Henry Cabot Lodge denied Soviet charges that the US was prodding Turkey into war with Syria and accused the Soviet Union of creating an artificial war scare.

At the conclusion of talks in Washington, President Eisenhower and British Prime Minister Harold Macmillan issued a declaration of common purpose, expressing full agreement that: Soviet threats directed against Turkey gave solemn significance to the obligation, under Article Five of the North Atlantic Treaty, to consider an armed attack against any member of the Alliance as an attack against all.

It was reported in Cairo that Major General Abd-al-Hakim Amer, Egyptian Minister of War and joint commander of Egyptian and Syrian forces, went to Damascus to investigate flights by unidentified planes over the Syrian capital. Syria charged that the planes were from the US Sixth Fleet.

The first air raid alert of the Syria-Turkey crisis was sounded in Damascus.

It was unofficially stated in Cairo that Egyptian financial talks with Britain would not be resumed unless Britain agreed to release 27,800,000 pounds sterling from Egypt's sterling assets in London. Both delegations to Rome had been recalled.

October 26

US Vice Admiral Brown stated categorically that no aircraft of the Sixth Fleet had been over Syria or even near Syria.

Ahmad Bekhat, 27 year old Secretary General of the French Federation of the Union of Algerian Workers, was assassinated in Paris.

The Syrian Government announced that King Saud had responded to its appeal and withdrew his offer to mediate the border crisis.

October 26

A trade agreement was signed in Cairo between East Germany and Egypt.

A trade agreement was signed in Berne between Tunisia and Switzerland.

October 27

The Israel Government reported that 200 Arabs, the majority of whom had been admitted under the Government's family repatriation plan, were settled during the past year.

Jordan declared the entire Syrian border region a restricted and closed area in the interests of public security.

Kadim Jaafar, leader of the 110 member Iraqi delegation to the Moscow Youth Festival, was arrested on his arrival home on charges of spreading Communist propaganda by his attendance at the festival.

The Syrian Government announced that 30 fully armed Turkish soldiers crossed the border on October 25 and withdrew only on the arrival of Syrian security forces.

The Syrian Government signed an economic cooperation agreement with the Soviet Union.

It was announced in Amman that the US Secretary of Agriculture, Ezra Taft Benson, would visit Jordan for three days starting November 3.

The US paid Jordan $3,000,000 of the $20,000,000 in economic aid promised in June of 1957, according to an announcement from the Jordanian Foreign Ministry and the US Embassy.

An official statement in Damascus said that the Turks continued their provocation on the Syrian border.

October 28

The Syrian Foreign Ministry disclosed the text of the economic agreement with the Soviet Union. An annex to the agreement listed 19 projects on which the Soviets would aid Syria in planning and construction.

It was reported from Tunis that an arrangement by which Britain and the US could join in providing arms to Tunisia was under consideration.

The US Embassy in Damascus sent a formal note of protest to the Syrian Government over the disappearance of a Syrian employee of the US consulate in Aleppo.

The Syrian Foreign Ministry expressed belief that Turkey might attack Syria during exercises of US, British and Turkish forces scheduled to begin on October 31.

The Turkish delegate to the UN, Selim Sarper, declared that the Russians and the Syrians had brought unfounded and inconceivable charges against Turkey and the US in an attempt to dissolve NATO and the Baghdad Pact.

King Saud reaffirmed his offer to mediate despite Syria's formal announcement that he had withdrawn the offer.

It was announced in Paris that the Sinclair Oil Company would direct oil exploration operations in the Sahara Desert for a group of French and American investment companies.

Lebanese President Camille Chamoun arrived in Madrid for talks with Generalissimo Francisco Franco.

In a communique issued at the end of the Iraqi ruler's ten day visit to Tehran, King Faisal and Shah Muhammad Riza Pahlevi emphasized the necessity of strengthening the Baghdad Pact which was an effective element in creating good understanding and security for peace in this region.

October 28

The Bureau of the World Peace Council decided to send a message to the UN General Assembly on the situation in the region of Syria.

The Israel Parliament re-elected President Itzhak Ben-Zvi for another five year term.

October 29

On the anniversary of the beginning of the British-French and Israel attacks on Egypt, President Nasser said that Egypt felt no rancor against those who had attacked them.

The newspaper Le Monde estimated that the Algerian war had cost almost 41,000 European and Moslem lives and the equivalent of $1,764,280,000 in the past three years.

Premier Ben Gurion and Foreign Minister Golda Meir were slightly wounded when a young Israeli threw a hand grenade into the Knesset building. Two other cabinet members were seriously wounded.

October 30

At the conclusion of their five day meeting in Tunis, the leaders of the Committee of Coordination and Execution of the National Liberation Front issued a communique calling on the UN to take a firm position and halt as quickly as possible the three year old war in Algeria. The nationalists offered to negotiate peace with France only after recognition of Algerian independence had been granted by France. The communique also called for an early conference with Tunisia and Morocco to work out the hastening of Algerian independence.

It was reported from Tunis that Algerian nationalist leaders there were optimistic about their fighting chances and claimed a force of 100,000 combatants. The French officially estimated nationalist strength at a total force of 65,000. Colonel

October 30

Lakhdar Ben-Tobbal, nationalist commander of north Constantine, attending the meeting in Tunis, asserted confidently that his men in the mountains could go on fighting indefinitely.

Moderates among the Algerian leaders said unofficially that the reaffirmation of the position demanding the recognition by France of Algerian independence prior to negotiations was a tactical move to give the Liberation Front's representatives in the UN a stronger bargaining position from which to arrive at a compromise resolution.

An International Cooperation Administration survey mission arrived in Khartoum to discuss the possibilities of American assistance to the Sudan.

Israel policemen clashed with Communist demonstrators in the Arab town of Nazereth in Galilee.

The Governor of Rabat was suspended for opposing the Government ban on the political organization, the People's Movement.

The Western powers proposed that the UN General Assembly endorse efforts by Secretary General Dag Hammarskjold, at his discretion, to settle the Turkish-Syrian dispute.

Syria introduced a resolution in the UN General Assembly calling for the creation of a fact finding commission for the purpose of investigating the situation on the spot in both Turkey and Syria.

Syrian and Turkish officials met at the southeast Turkish frontier town of Assibin to discuss cattle rustling and kidnappings across the border.

A contract for the Egyptian-Italian-Syrian wheat deal was signed in Cairo.

An Egyptian ship, the Sinai, was launched at the Polish port of Szezecin. It was the second of six ships being built by Poland for Egypt.

October, 1957

October 31

Tunisian President Habib Bourguiba chided the Algerian National Liberation Front. He said that their position could neither increase the number of partisans of the Algerian cause nor favor the search for a solution that would achieve Algerian independence. His disappointment was caused, he said, by the declaration issued by the Algerian leaders on October 30 reaffirming that they would not negotiate peace until France recognized Algerian independence. He further stated that the new Tunisian Ambassador to Morocco would immediately approach the Moroccan Government to seek agreement on a conference to work out the hastening of Algerian independence.

King Faisal of Iraq opened the $9,408,000 lubricating oil refinery south of Baghdad built by the American-British Foster Wheeler Company.

An Egyptian military court sentenced 13 members of the outlawed Communist party to prison terms for anti-state activities.

The Council of the Arab League unanimously approved a resolution renewing pledges that any attack against Syria would be considered an attack against all Arab nations.

A French court martial in Constantine passed death sentences on eight Algerian insurgents taken prisoner in battle. Similar sentences were passed on patriots in Algiers and Oran.

Israel completed its drainage of the Huleh swamps.

November, 1957

November 1

President Kuwatli launched "Fortification Week" in Damascus, a week devoted to digging around the Syrian capital defensive fortresses that would "break every criminal hand" and would repel any raider or aggressor.

The UN General Assembly concluded debate on the Syrian-Turkey border crisis. No action was taken.

Marshal Rodion Y. Malinovsky, the newly appointed Soviet Defense Minister, welcomed Major General Abd-al-Hakim Amer, Egyptian War Minister, at the Moscow Airport on his arrival for a two week visit in the Soviet Union as the Marshal's guest.

The chairman of the Syrian National Economic Development Council said that the total cost of the 19 projects to be undertaken with the Soviet Union would be at least $570,000,000.

Thirteen oil companies prospecting in Libya were expected to spend $43,000,000 in 1958, company spokesmen in Tripoli said.

The UN General Assembly concluded discussion of the Syrian complaint after adopting the proposal of Ali Sastroamidjojo of Indonesia to ask Syria and Turkey to settle their differences on the basis of the Bandung Conference peace principles. With both sides agreeing, no decision was taken. The question of the threat to Syria's security and world peace remained on the General Assembly's agenda.

November 2

The al-Ferdan Bridge over the Suez Canal, damaged during an attack the previous year, was restored to service.

November, 1957

November 2

President Nasser issued a decree calling for the final organization of the National Union to realize the objectives of the revolution.

The US filed three protests with the Syrian Government over the arrest and detention of an American Marine and two Syrian employees of the American Embassy. These arrests brought to ten the number of incidents involving US Embassy personnel since August 13, when Syria charged the US with plotting to overthrow its Government.

The French press reported that 30 young miners, recently recalled from military service in North Africa on account of manpower shortages in the coal industry, were arrested and imprisoned by the military authorities in Lille, France. These men took part in the strike called by miners in defense of their rights on October 7, and in the stop-the-war-in-Algeria demonstrations on October 17.

A Soviet scientific-technical exhibition on the peaceful uses of atomic energy opened in Cairo.

November 3

The Arab League's Political Affairs Committee decided that member states should not contribute toward the expenses of the UN Emergency Force in the Gaza-Sinai region.

The Spanish Foreign Ministry announced that Lebanon's President Camille Chamoun and Generalissimo Francisco Franco had reached complete agreement on Middle Eastern problems in talks held during the former's state visit to Madrid October 28-31.

The Soviet Communist Party newspaper Pravda charged continuing suspect military activity of the countries belonging to the aggressive North Atlantic Alliance near the Syrian frontiers.

November, 1957

November 3

Farid Zain-ad-Din, Syria's representative to the UN, asserted that war could still come at any time on the Syrian-Turkish frontier.

US Secretary of Agriculture Ezra Taft Benson had an audience with King Hussein following talks in Amman with senior Jordanian agriculture and economy officials.

An Israel seaman was seized by the Egyptians from a Dutch freighter.

November 4

Syria charged that eight unidentified aircraft had violated Syrian air space.

The Arabic press in Damascus hailed the launching of the second Soviet satellite.

The Soviet Union abruptly resumed "propaganda attacks" against Turkey with a charge that the latter was starting to move hundred of tanks toward the Syrian border.

A Jordanian Government spokesman denied Egyptian allegations of Jordanian-Israel Government contacts.

President Nasser abruptly dismissed the head of his huge desert reclamation project "Liberation Province."

The head of the UN aid program for Arab refugees said at the UN that a curtailment of international assistance could have dangerous political repercussions in the Middle East. Mr. Labouisse emphasized in his report the urgency of getting additional financial contributions for the agency in the amount of $40,700,000.

November 4

Robert Lacoste, French Minister for Algeria, declared in a telegram to the New York Times that the figure given by the Algerian nationalist leaders, meeting in Tunis, of 700 French soldiers killed since the start of the nationalist offensive on October 20, was extravagant and erroneous. Lacoste asserted that French losses in the week following October 20 amounted to 38 killed and that 457 nationalists were killed. The nationalists had stated that their losses had been negligible. All French and nationalist reports of military figures were at wide variance.

The US Secretary of Agriculture conferred with Premier Ben-Gurion in Hadassah Hospital in Israel.

The Jordanian Government accused Egyptian leaders of treason to the Arab cause, saying that it had evidence of secret Egyptian-Israel contacts.

The Syrian Government announced that anti-aircraft guns had fired at six unidentified planes over Latakia; it listed five other incidents which, it said, had occurred on the Turkish border in the four days prior to November 4.

Dr. Aziz Sidqi, Egyptian Minister of Industry, announced a new oil strike in a field about 75 miles south of Suez.

New Times reported that a Turkish unit had crossed the Syrian border in the area between Abu-Sun and Gibda. This was followed by an exchange of fire lasting half an hour.

November 5

Egyptian financial circles in Cairo stated that Egypt would pay compensation to British and French nationals whose property had been appropriated, if the present negotiations between Egypt and Britain proved successful.

November 5

UN Secretary General Hammarskjold proposed that the General Assembly authorize a voluntary surcharge of three percent on Suez Canal tolls to repay more than $8, 000, 000 spent by the UN in clearing the canal.

Great Britain announced that Crown Prince Saif-al-Islam Muhammad al-Badr had accepted an invitation to visit London to discuss British-Yemeni border disputes.

The Syrian Minister of National Economy and Acting Foreign Minister, Khalil Kallas, said that unless Turkey withdrew its troops from the Syrian border, Syria would ask the UN General Assembly to reconsider its complaint.

US Secretary of State Dulles asserted that although Soviet charges of Turkish aggression against Syria had collapsed, this did not necessarily mean that the situation in the Middle East was free of danger and that the independence of these Arab states was secure. Dulles said that it was in danger.

Anglo-Egyptian talks on claims resulting from the British-French attack on Suez were resumed in Rome.

November 6

The World Bank announced that its President, Eugene R. Black, had accepted an Egyptian invitation to visit Cairo to advise Egypt on possible compensation of stockholders of the old Suez Canal Company.

The Syrian Parliament unanimously approved the economic and technical assistance agreement with the Soviet Union.

The Syrian armed forces had been ordered to fire on aircraft or military patrols violating Syrian territory, a Foreign Ministry spokesman said.

November 6

In Lebanon, an attempt by terrorists to dynamite the Parliament Building and Government House was thwarted; Abd-al-Aziz Shehab, Director of the Lebanese Ministry of the Interior, stated that the attempt was part of a wave of terror instigated by Communists and the outlawed Syrian Nationalist Party.

Egypt demanded that the UN Emergency Force pay rent to Gaza residents for property that it was occupying in the Gaza Strip along the Israel border.

It was reported at the UN that the US had agreed to make a special contribution of more than $5 million to prevent UNEF from withdrawing from the Gaza area due to lack of funds.

Jordan demanded an urgent meeting of the UN Security Council to hear a complaint against Israel's afforestation operations in no man's land near Jerusalem.

King Saud attended the opening of King Saud University in Riyadh.

Moroccan authorities denied an emigration freeze on Moroccan Jews, stating that 5000 Jews had left Morocco with regular passports from July through September 1957.

Arab oil representatives meeting in Baghdad from November 2 to 6 adopted a plan to unify policy of Arab countries toward oil companies operating in their territories. The plan was to be submitted to the Arab Economic Council.

November 7

The Lebanese Government confiscated all copies of the November 5 issue of The Manchester Guardian, owing to a dispatch commenting critically on the inefficiency of city administration in Lebanon.

November 7

President Camille Chamoun of Lebanon arrived in Athens for a four day official visit.

Saudi Arabia complained to the UN General Assembly and the Security Council that an Israel plane had violated its air space on October 28.

At the request of UN military observers, Israel work crews were withdrawn from the area along the Syrian border where an Israel policeman had been killed. An Israel Foreign Ministry spokesman said that the work in the demilitarized zone — deepening a drainage ditch — would be continued at safer points.

Egypt and Ghana agreed to exchange diplomatic missions.

Syrian Foreign Minister Salah al-Bitar told reporters at the UN that he was trying to improve Syria's relations with the US.

William M. Rountree, US Assistant Secretary of State for Middle Eastern Affairs, held lengthy discussions with the Syrian Foreign Minister in New York.

Well informed sources in Beirut said that many Western reports on Soviet arms deliveries to Syria were exaggerated to "the point of fantasy."

The Nationalist Chinese Foreign Minister and other leading officials arrived in Riyadh, Saudi Arabia.

New Times reported that a patrol from Turkey opened fire on the Syrian village of Jkara, forcing a unit of Syrian people's militia to retaliate.

November 8

Cairo Radio reportedly had begun to broadcast propaganda

November, 1957

November 8

aimed at stirring Jordanians and Palestine refugees to rise against King Hussein of Jordan and to restore a pro-Nasser government in place of his regime.

Turkey gave Libya $5, 500, 000 worth of arms, including Turkish made heavy and light field weapons.

Jordanians demonstrated for the second consecutive day in support of King Hussein against Egyptian propaganda attacks.

The Chief of Staff of the northern district of Syria, Colonel Tawfiq Chatila, charged that a great number of American officers and men had been serving with an estimated 50, 000-60, 000 Turkish troops on the Turkish-Syrian border. The US Departments of Defense and State issued a prompt denial, declaring that US personnel were at the border merely to act as advisers.

Syrian authorities released a Syrian employee of the US consulate in Aleppo.

Secretary of State Dulles reportedly had written to Premier Ben-Gurion of Israel, urging him to allow UN officials to help solve a recent series of border incidents with Jordan. In answer to Mr. Dulles' letter, Mr. Ben-Gurion gave no assurance that Israel would return to the Mixed Armistice Commission.

President Bourguiba of Tunisia sent a messenger to King Muhammad V of Morocco with a message believed to contain a proposal for a North African conference to pave the way to peace in Algeria.

November 9

A Jordanian Government spokesman said that the Jordanian Development Board planned to ask eight UN financial experts

November, 1957

November 9

In a letter to the UN Security Council, Israel declared that there was not a vestige of truth in the allegation that an Israel aircraft had violated Saudi air space on October 28.

November 10

A $40 million five year plan to improve rural conditions was announced in Iraq.

Eugene R. Black was reported to have told Egypt that the World Bank would consider helping finance the Aswan High Dam project if Cairo settled its dispute with the Suez Canal Company.

The Syrian Government reported three air violations over Syria's northern border by two Turkish and three unidentified planes.

In reply to an offer by Iraqi religious leaders to mediate between Jordan and Egypt in the vilification campaign by the Egyptian radio and press, King Hussein criticized Egyptian rulers "who had sold themselves to communism and exploited Arab nationalism to divert Egyptian public opinion away from the deteriorating situation at home."

On his arrival in London, the Crown Prince of Yemen declared his hope that his visit could start for Anglo-Yemen relations a new era of constructive understanding and positive progress on the basis of mutual respect and appreciation of the legitimate rights and interests of both parties.

Egyptian newspapers labeled King Hussein a traitor for alleged secret negotiations with Israel over the Palestine issue.

Foreign Minister Samir al-Rifai of Jordan received the Egyptian Charge d' Affaires to discuss the mounting radio and press war between the two countries.

November, 1957

November 9

to draw up a five year plan aimed at making Jordan economically independent.

Jordanian King Hussein broadcast his thanks to the people for showing their loyalty to him and their resentment over "lies fabricated recently by the hired trumpets of propaganda in Egypt against Jordan with the intention of stirring mutiny."

Major General Hafez Majali, Jordanian Chief of Staff, said that it had been proved that automatic weapons and explosives had recently been smuggled into Jordan from some Arab states.

Following several politically motivated bombings and murders, an official source in Beirut said that about 500 Syrians, Jordanians and Palestinian refugees, believed to be endangering the country's security, had been deported.

The Syrian Foreign Minister returned to Damascus, having presented his Government's charges against Turkey at the UN.

The Syrian Government charged that Turks and Syrians had fought a 30 minute gun battle on the northeastern border on November 8.

World Bank President Eugene R. Black proposed in Cairo that Egypt confer with officials of the former Suez Canal Company within a month to negotiate a settlement of compensation and other problems. He had a three hour talk with the Minister of Finance, Abd-al-Moneim Kaissouni.

The Moroccan Foreign Minister, Ahmad Balafrej, declared that Morocco supported the Algerian cause and favored diplomatic attempts to find a solution to the conflict. He also said that Moroccan foreign policy dictated an independent position between East and West and that, while Morocco favored the idea of an Arab League, it could not join until the Arab countries had settled their disputes.

November, 1957

November 10

A Jordanian Government spokesman said at the UN that his country was pressing for an early debate in the Security Council of its complaint against Israel soil digging operations in a neutral zone near Jerusalem.

Moscow Radio accused Jordanian King Hussein of being a tool of the West and an enemy of the Arab states.

November 11

Talks between the Yemeni Crown Prince and British Foreign Secretary Selwyn Lloyd began "in an exceedingly cordial atmosphere."

World Bank President Black concluded two days of talks with President Nasser.

The semi-official Egyptian newspaper al-Gumhuriyah charged King Hussein with treachery for allegedly holding "secret negotiations with Israel for the liquidation of the Palestine issue."

Eugene R. Black said in Geneva that the World Bank had offered to act as mediator in any future negotiations on the compensation of stockholders of the Suez Canal Company. He denied reports that he had discussed a World Bank loan to Egypt for financing the Aswan High Dam.

King Hussein told the first Arab refugee conference held in Amman that Jordan would never give way on the Palestine issue. The conference adopted a resolution denouncing "the unjust campaign of lies and intrigues launched against Hussein by the trumpets of Egyptian propaganda."

Thousands of Palestinian refugees, demonstrating in Damascus, called for the death of King Hussein of Jordan for alleged dealings with Israel.

November 11

An agreement to develop Saudi Arabian oil fields was reached between the Saudi Arabian Government and the Japanese Federation of Economic Organization, a non-government body.

Government officials in Ankara said that they had received no reports about an alleged incident on the Syrian border in which a Turkish soldier was arrested on Syrian territory.

Arab nations meeting in Cairo agreed to establish propaganda measures to offset anti-Arab, Zionist statements.

The Egyptian Government announced that the head of the Egyptian delegation to the Franco-Egyptian economic talks would proceed to Geneva.

Iraq and Morocco signed an amity agreement.

Major Turkish troop movements, one of them involving a unit with over 300 vehicles, were reported from Syria's northern frontier. The Syrian Cabinet held an emergency meeting to discuss the situation on the border.

November 12

An unofficial source in Tunisia reported that the French arms offer to Tunisia precluded Tunisia's acceptance of arms from any other source.

The President of the British Board of Trade stated in the House of Commons that Great Britain shipped 62,000,000 pounds sterling worth of arms to the Middle East between 1946 and 1957.

Mustafa Khalifah, Speaker of the Jordanian Parliament, telegraphed the leaders of the other Arab states to ask them to assist Jordan and put an end to the Egyptian propaganda campaign against King Hussein, which was "poisoning the Arab atmosphere."

November 12

The US accused the Soviet Union of joining Egypt and Syria in a campaign to dethrone King Hussein on fabricated charges that he was secretly dealing with Israel.

The anniversary of the accession of King Saud was celebrated. In his address, King Saud stated that Saudi Arabia would not rest until the Arabs of Palestine had regained their homeland.

A Moroccan Royal Decree established an office for Saharan and Frontier Affairs in the Moroccan Ministry of the Interior.

The Iranian Government announced that the Shah had been instructed that a Bill be put before Parliament declaring Bahrain the 14th Iranian province; the United Kingdom declared Bahrain an independent Arab state under British protection.

Three Algerian patriots were executed in Algeria by the French.

The Jordanian Government decided to join the Baghdad Pact's Economic Committee and the Anti-Subversion Committee, and in principle accepted the Eisenhower-Dulles Doctrine.

The French National Assembly passed by 344-211 a bill on the renewal of the Government's emergency powers in Algerian and metropolitan France.

November 13

The French Cabinet met in emergency session to discuss reported notes from the US and Great Britain, expressing the desire of those two countries to proceed forthwith to supply arms to Tunisia.

A French unit pursuing a group of Algerian rebels clashed with a Tunisian patrol near the Sakiet-Sidi Youssef frontier post; an unspecified number of Tunisian soldiers were killed.

November 13

The Lebanese Government expelled Michael Adams, Middle East correspondent of The Manchester Guardian.

Casualty figures for the three year Algerian rebellion were listed as: 4,200 French military killed, 9,200 wounded and 750 missing; 44,000 rebels killed and 25,000 captured; 1,100 European civilians dead, 3,000 wounded, 180 missing; 7,000 Moslem civilians killed by rebels and 2,700 missing.

Lebanese Foreign Minister Charles Malik denied a report that he had informed his government that the US was about to scrap the Eisenhower Doctrine.

King Hussein belittled the Arab Solidarity Pact as "not worth the paper it was written on." Under the agreement of April 1957, Saudi Arabia, Egypt and Syria promised to replace the $30 million subsidy Jordan had received annually from Great Britain; only Saudi Arabia had paid its share. He accused Egypt and Syria of a conspiracy against Jordan through press propaganda.

The Egyptian Government signed a trade and payments agreement with Syria designed to develop trade relations between the two countries preparatory to comprehensive economic union.

November 14

King Hussein of Jordan celebrated his twenty-second birthday.

King Saud of Saudi Arabia and King Faisal of Iraq called upon Egypt and Syria to hald their propaganda attacks against King Hussein. The Saudi monarch said that he regretted the current campaign and promised to work to the utmost to eliminate it. The ruler of Iraq declared that he fully shared his opinion in deploring radio attacks conducted by an Arab state against others. He said that these campaigns would benefit only the enemies of Arabs and Moslems.

November 14

Sheikh Muhammad al-Hamad al-Shubaili was appointed Saudi Ambassador to Pakistan.

The US and Britain announced that they would proceed with shipments of small arms to Tunisia on the grounds that Tunisia had freely chosen to identify itself with the West and therefore the West should reciprocate by giving Tunisia the opportunity to provide for its internal security and self defense.

The French were reported to be deeply resentful of the US-British action.

World Bank President Black reported to UN Secretary General Hammarskjold on his talks with Nasser concerning a settlement of the Universal Suez Canal Company's compensation claims against Egypt.

General Burns, Commander of the UN Emergency Force, said that he believed that an international force must remain between Egypt and Israel for the foreseeable future.

Syria accused Turkish troops of having opened fire on Syrian Army engineers removing Turkish mines planted inside Syrian territory on November 13.

Turkey issued an official denial of charges made on November 6 that Turkish planes and ground troops had violated Syrian territory.

King Hussein's birthday was marked throughout Jordan by strikes and mass demonstrations protesting against the Government's policy.

November 15

President Bourguiba of Tunisia expressed satisfaction over the arms deliveries from Britain and the US. He said that his country was duty bound to encourage America in its present orientation which could help toward a solution of the Algerian problem.

November, 1957

November 15

France registered an official protest with the British Foreign Office against British arms shipments to Tunisia. The Foreign Office replied that the action they had taken was designed to protect the interests of the West as a whole.

A report from Paris stated that the appeal by the Communist led General Confederation of Workers for demonstrations and strikes against the war in Algeria went apparently unobserved throughout France.

French oil officials in Algiers indicated that further petroleum deposits might be found before the end of the year in the Algerian oil field of Hassi Messaoud, besides the three wells already equipped for production. The officials said initial findings at three or four other wells also appeared quite promising.

Premier Felix Gaillard said in the National Assembly that France had sought guarantees that the arms France was willing to give Tunisia would not be given in turn to the Algerian rebels, in order to protect the lives of Frenchmen fighting in Algeria. He said President Bourguiba had refused to give these guarantees when approached by the French Ambassador on November 13 because he had already received assurances of British and American arms. Premier Gaillard further stated that unless "a clear and unequivocal solution" were forthcoming, the NATO conference in December would be seriously affected.

Syrian Foreign Minister Bitar said that the US was moving toward a change in its anti-Syrian policy.

Great Britain declared Bahrain an independent Arab state under British protection.

The French Council of the Republic passed by a majority vote a bill granting the Gaillard Government emergency powers in Algeria.

November, 1957

November 15

The US and British arms consignments to Tunisia of November 14, 1957, provoked the French delegations to leave the NATO conference.

More than 200 Egyptian scientists signed an appeal urging cessation of nuclear weapon tests.

November 16

Syria denounced the Iranian move to proclaim sovereignty over the British protected island of Bahrain.

Robert Lacoste, French Minister for Algeria, sharply criticized the delivery of US and British arms to Tunisia.

Reliable sources reported that West Germany sympathized with France in the dispute of US-British arms to Tunisia.

At a reception in Moscow in honor of Egypt's War Minister, the Soviet Defense Minister, Marshal Rodion Y. Malinovsky, told Major General Abd-al-Hakim Amer that Egypt had friends who were ready to give aid when needed.

The Middle East News Agency reported that Egypt had received from the Soviet Union all the necessary parts for an atomic reactor to be assembled under the supervision of Soviet experts.

James P. Richards, US Ambassador at Large to the Middle East, said that it was France's last minute shift in policy which had caused the present rift; he said that Secretary of State Dulles had thought until the last minute that France would not require the conditions objected to by Tunisia in its arms offer.

An authoritative source in Paris said that the French government would seek three promises from the US and Britain in the dispute over arms sent to Tunisia: the two powers' limitation

November, 1957

November 16

of their arms shipments to amounts that the existing Tunisian forces could use; the prevention of the arms being diverted to other uses; and no further shipments without prior consultation with France.

A trade agreement was signed between Tunisia and Denmark.

November 17

An authoritative member of the Moroccan Administration said that French excitability over the Tunisian arms question appeared to be an attempt to pressure the US into supporting the French position on Algeria in the UN.

President Nasser was reported to have called an abrupt halt to Egypt's violent propaganda campaign against King Hussein of Jordan.

The Acting Defense Minister of Syria, Khaled al-Azm, became Finance Minister as well.

November 18

Tunisian Ambassador to the US Habib Bourguiba, Jr., declared that the Soviet Union had offered arms to Tunisia and that the offer had been rejected.

The head of the UN aid program for Palestine refugees made another appeal at the UN for contributions to the aid program.

The Arab Cultural and Antiquities Conference opened in Baghdad.

Premier Ben-Gurion rejected suggestions that Israel loosen its ties with the West as a means of improving its relations with the Soviet Union.

November, 1957

November 18

King Saud expressed to Jordan his regret over the dispute among the Arab states in answer to a request that he use his good offices to end the Egyptian propaganda campaign against Jordan. He expressed his readiness to mediate the dispute.

The Syrian Parliament, in a joint session with 40 visiting members of the Egyptian Parliament, unanimously approved the proposal to expedite the federal union of Egypt and Syria.

Syrian and Egyptian armed forces held armed maneuvers.

November 19

Mr. Dulles disclosed that Tunisia had asked the US for arms in September and had been assured that it would receive arms from the West by the end of October. He said that, in view of the fall of the French Government, the Tunisians had agreed to postpone the date until November 12. Mr. Dulles said that it had looked as if the French would make the delivery, but a last minute refusal by France had left the US responsible for the fulfillment of a firm and definite commitment.

Secretary of State Dulles and French Foreign Minister Christian Pineau agreed in Washington to seek means by which Western arms could be delivered to Tunisia without reaching the Algerian nationalists.

Saudi-Egyptian negotiations were reportedly under way to renew the agreement for Saudi export of oil to Egypt which expired in August.

Informed sources in Jerusalem said that about 1,200 Jews from various Moroccan villages were stranded in Tangier without passports to emigrate to Israel.

The Soviet Union announced in Moscow that it had agreed to give Egypt economic assistance and also that agreement had been reached on military matters.

November, 1957

November 19

Soviet Premier Nikolai A. Bulganin told General Amer that in response to Amer's and President Nasser's request, the Soviet Union had agreed to help Egypt in building up its national economy. A communique on the Soviet-Egyptian talks issued earlier noted that both countries were satisfied with results of the discussions on questions of political and economic collaboration, as well as on military questions.

A friendship treaty between Jordan and Nationalist China was signed in Amman.

Rigid controls were announced over all Palestinian refugees living in Lebanon in order to halt subversive activity. The entry of refugees into Lebanon was prohibited.

The US announced an increase of $1,500,000 in rehabilitation and relief aid for Arab refugees.

Turkey started a general withdrawal of troops from the southern section of the country adjoining the Syrian border.

November 20

The Saudi Arabian chief delegate to the UN said that the Western powers must adopt a new policy on the Palestine dispute if they wanted to regain the good will of the Arabs.

Syria's Minister of National Economy announced that he would head a delegation to Cairo the following week, to negotiate economic union with Egypt.

Negotiations between Britain and Yemen ended without a formal communique.

Tunisian President Bourguiba flew to Rabat for a conference with Muhammad V of Morocco to try to find a solution to ending the war in Algeria.

November, 1957

November 20

It was announced in Cairo that the Soviet Union had offered to lend Egypt 700 million rubles at two and one-half percent interest, to implement Egypt's industrialization program. The first installment was to be repaid at the end of five years, and payments were to continue for 12 years thereafter.

State Department officials confirmed that the US had released about one-fourth of the $40 million in Egyptian assets frozen since the nationalization of the Suez Canal. They also reported that the US had recently paid $600,000 into a joint fund for rural development in Egypt under the terms of a previous agreement.

General Amer returned to Cairo from Russia and conferred with President Nasser.

Ahmad Shukairy delivered a speech to the Special Political Committee of the UN General Assembly regarding the Arab refugee problem. He called for a ban on Zionist propaganda and the return of Jewish immigrants in Israel to their homelands.

Saudi Arabia sent representatives to the Arab Cultural Conference in Baghdad.

The new Syrian Ambassador to Saudi Arabia, Dr. Zaki al-Jabi, presented his credentials to King Saud.

Former Iraqi Premier Nuri-Said left Baghdad for a tour of the Middle East, Western Europe, and North America to discuss a solution of the Palestine refugee problem and Baghdad Pact support.

November 21

King Muhammad V of Morocco and President Habib Bourguiba of Tunisia addressed an urgent appeal to the French to begin negotiations for ending the war in Algeria.

November, 1957

November 21

The Jordanian Deputy Prime Minister and Foreign Minister was received by King Saud.

It was reported in Madrid that Moroccan nationalists had clashed with a Spanish garrison in the enclave of Ifni.

Tunisia recalled its Ambassador to Syria before his credentials had been presented. This action was taken because President Kuwatli of Syria had received Salah Ben- Youssef, a Tunisian leader condemned to death for anti-government activity.

Moroccan Minister of Economy, Abd-al-Rahim Bouabid, reported that he had agreed to postpone a decision to re-evaluate the Moroccan franc at the request of French officials.

Fathi Radwan, Egyptian Minister of National Guidance, left for the Soviet Union in response to an invitation. He expressed the hope that his visit, concerned with culture and thought, would support the results of the Commander in Chief, General Amer, in the fields covered by his discussions and talks.

November 22

Egyptian authorities refused a Jordanian airliner permission to land at Cairo Airport. An airport spokesman said that the airliner had been turned away because it had exceeded the number of weekly flights stipulated in the Egyptian-Jordanian air agreement.

The UN General Assembly adopted a 21 nation resolution authorizing the expenditure of up to $3.5 million to the end of 1957 and up to $25 million in 1958 for the UNEF in the Middle East. Communist delegations said that the expense should be borne by the countries which invaded Egypt.

November, 1957

November 22

Jordan complained to the UN Security Council about Israel's planting of olive trees in a neutral area near Jerusalem. Israel replied that this complaint was part of an anti-Israel campaign being carried out by Jordan to show Egypt that Jordan harbored no friendly feeling toward Israel.

French Foreign Minister Christian Pineau announced in the UN that France could not accept the offer of Morocco and Tunisia to use their "good offices" to settle the Algerian question because these countries were not neutrals, and also because the offer had excluded some of the nationalists presently fighting in Algeria.

Seventeen members of the Syrian Parliament were stopped at the frontier and refused permission to enter Lebanon.

The French Army reported that it had virtually wiped out the Algerian rebels sabotaging petroleum developments in the Sahara: 42 rebels were killed and ten were taken prisoners.

Moroccan Foreign Minister Ahmad Balafrej indicated that Morocco was considering a temporary solution of the question of US air bases in Morocco.

Morocco agreed to postpone a re-evaluation of the franc, by which 100 Moroccan francs would be worth 110-115 French francs. Moroccan officials confirmed that the French Government had promised to hand over 5,000,000,000 francs to counteract the 20 percent devaluation of the French franc.

The UN Security Council met to discuss Jordan's complaint against Israel's illegal activity in the Jabal Mukabbir demilitarized zone.

November, 1957

November 23

A report that the US would give unlimited additional financial aid to Lebanon under the Eisenhower Doctrine circulated in Beirut, but was denied by the local ICA (International Cooperation Administration) director.

A spokesman for an Algerian nationalist organization , a rival of the Algerian National Liberation Front, accused King Muhammad and President Bourguiba of injecting new seeds of dissension among the Algerians. He said this approach made for civil war in Algeria.

Two Communists were arrested and charged with having joined the outlawed Egyptian Communist Party.

A Jordanian airliner, turned back on November 22, landed without incident in Cairo.

The Technical Education Conference of Arab countries was opened in Cairo.

Announcement was made in Rabat of a trade agreement with Communist China calling for the exchange of goods to the value of 5, 880, 000, 000 francs.

King Hussein approved the formation of a military court to try all persons held in concentration camps.

November 24

King Muhammad V left Rabat on a trip to the US. He announced that a solution of the question of maintenance of US air bases in Morocco would be the subject of talks with President Eisenhower.

Moroccan sources revealed that the tribe of Ait Ba Amrane had revolted against Spanish authorities in Ifni, a Spanish enclave surrounded completely by Moroccan territory.

November, 1957

November 24

Jordan asked the UN Secretary General to remove Colonel Byron Leary from his post of Acting Chief Truce Supervisor in Palestine because of his alleged bias in favor of Israel. The UN Secretary General, however, appealed to Jordan to continue cooperation with Colonel Leary and expressed his personal confidence in him.

The Saudi Arabian Ministry of Finance announced a new Saudi gold sovereign to be issued in December.

A military court sentenced ten Jordanians to prison terms on charges of membership in the Communist Party and plotting against the Government.

November 25

A spokesman for the UN Secretary General announced that Mr. Hammarskjold would leave for Amman to discuss Jordan's charge that Colonel Leary, the acting head of the Palestine Truce Supervision Organization, was biased in favor of Israel.

Colonel Leary was summoned to an emergency conference with Israel Government leaders to discuss the rising tension along Israel's borders and the delay in the departure of the Mount Scopus convoy.

Britain renewed a pledge to contribute $2, 900, 000 for aid to Palestine refugees during six months of 1958.

Premier Sami al-Solh confirmed reports from Damascus that Lebanon had barred Palestine refugees, residing in Syria, from entering the country.

The State Security Council of Lebanon decided to reinforce the guards on the Lebanese-Syrian border.

November, 1957

November 25

Soviet Premier Bulganin sent another note to the Turkish Government charging that Turkey had become an arsenal, and warning against continued participation in plans to attack Syria.

Saudi troops stationed in Jordan received orders to be ready for an emergency. King Saud sent a letter to King Hussein stating that Saudi Arabia was ready to assist Jordan.

Moroccan King Muhammad V arrived in Washington.

Egyptian officials disclosed that a shipload of Egyptian arms had been delivered to Tunisia.

It was announced in Cairo that Czechoslovakia had agreed to give Egypt industrial credits worth about LE20 million.

President Nasser announced that he was sending his Foreign Minister, Mahmoud Fawzi, on a mission to the US.

A ten man Egyptian trade mission began talks with the Liberian Government in Monrovia.

The Baghdad Pact countries — Great Britain, Iraq, Turkey, Iran and Pakistan — and the US started naval and air maneuvers in the northern part of the Arabian Sea. The exercises were to continue until December 10.

November 26

France told the UN that it was willing to admit 10, 000 observers from countries that had free elections, for the proposed Algerian elections.

French authorities imposed a travel ban throughout the oil areas of the Sahara, claiming that they were acting in order to insure the security of oil exploitations and prevent information leaks to rebels active in the area.

November, 1957

November 26

After two days of discussions on North Africa, British Prime Minister Harold Macmillan and French Premier Felix Gaillard issued a communique placing responsibility for a solution of the Algerian question with France.

Syrian Foreign Minister Salah al-Bitar said that Syria would ask the UN General Assembly to take up its complaint anew against Turkey if Turkish troop concentrations were not reduced by the next month.

The US turned over $15 million worth of arms to Libya for that nation's self defense, under the terms of a pact signed June 20, 1957.

Foreign Minister Charles Malik told Parliament that, regarding US aid, the assistance destined for Lebanon was in principle unlimited. He said that the American Government was entirely disposed to contribute to the realization of all new economic projects proposed by the Lebanese Government.

The Egyptian Ministry of Supply signed an agreement with the Soviet Union for the importation of 100, 000 tons of Russian wheat.

Reports from Rabat stated that Spain had launched a counterattack against Moroccan nationalists in Ifni and that a state of siege had been declared.

Saudi Arabia protested to the UN Security Council against violation of Saudi air space over the Gulf of Aqaba by Israel military planes November 14.

King Muhammad V, visiting Washington, conferred for two hours with Secretary of State Dulles.

The Tunisian Government published a law made on November 19 under which Tunisians who had willingly given either direct or indirect help to the French Protectorate authorities before July 31, 1954, would be held guilty of "national indignity."

November 26

The Israel-Jordan Mixed Armistice Commission, in an emergency meeting, declared Israel's capture of a so-called infiltrator from Jordan five days earlier a hostile act.

The Soviet press published an interview granted by N. S. Khrushchev to Muhammad Hassanein Haikal, Editor in Chief of the Egyptian al-Ahram, on November 18, 1957.

November 27

A Cabinet decision on the offer of Morocco and Tunisia to mediate in negotiations on Algeria concluded that France would consider the good offices of these countries in stopping the shooting in Algeria, but would not tolerate outside interference in political affairs.

France urged the UN not to interfere with the reforms the French planned to put into effect in Algeria. French Foreign Minister Christian Pineau added that France would take the initiative of inviting governments of democratic countries to observe the proposed elections in Algeria. He asserted that the freedom of action of Morocco and Tunisia was jeopardized by the large entrenchments of the National Liberation Front in those countries. He accused Egypt and Syria of inciting and supplying arms to the Algerian nationalists.

A Tunisian communique said that French troops had penetrated about 220 yards into Tunisia and had kidnapped four Tunisians and an Algerian; the four Tunisians were released three hours later, according to the communique.

In a joint statement issued at the White House, King Muhammad V and Secretary of State Dulles declared a desire to work out a provisional solution of the problem of US bases in Morocco. The Secretary of State, according to the statement, assured the King of US readiness to assist Morocco's efforts to stabilize and expand its economy.

November 27

Nationalist sources in Rabat said that the Spanish military post of Tiliouine fell to Ifni rebels and that 50 Spanish soldiers had been killed and 65 wounded. Spain reported four killed and 34 wounded, and estimated Moroccan casualties at 100.

Spain sent military reinforcements to its bases in the Canary Islands and Spanish West Africa, following the recent Moroccan rebellion at Ifni. All was reported to be quiet at Ifni.

Moroccan Crown Prince Moulay Hassan ordered his armed forces to fire on all foreign planes flying over Morocco's southern border territory. The Prince, who was regent while King Muhammad V was in the US, declared that foreign planes had bombed Moroccan territory and that the disorder in Ifni had spread into southern Morocco.

President Eisenhower appointed Donald R. Heath as US Ambassador to Saudi Arabia.

The British Foreign Secretary, reporting on talks with the Crown Prince of Yemen, said that it was made clear that Britain could not agree to any claim to foreign sovereignty over Aden.

The Lebanon Government of Premier Sami al-Solh won a 40-10 vote of confidence after a two day debate on its pro-Western policy.

The Suez Canal Authority announced that ships of 33.5 foot draught could pass through the canal after December 16.

November 28

Moroccan officials at Tiznit accused Spain of bombing Moroccan territory near Ifni for the third consecutive day. The Spanish Foreign Ministry declared that the charges that

November 28

Spanish forces, either by land or in the air, had carried out any aggression against Moroccan territory, were false.

Moroccan Crown Prince Moulay Hassan charged that Spanish forces had made forays into Moroccan territory from Ifni, and ordered his Army to shoot back.

President Habib Bourguiba of Tunisia said that the Algerian National Liberation Front was ready to start negotiations with France without requiring from its previous recognition of Algerian independence.

President Bourguiba called for a fresh shipment of arms from France. He said neither the US-British arms deliveries nor those expected from Egypt would be enough for his country's self defense.

Prime Minister Harold Macmillan disclosed to Parliament a British pledge to send no further arms to Tunisia without first consulting France.

The Libyan Ministry of Defense reported that Libya was expecting a valuable consignment of arms from Arab states.

A press dispatch from Cairo quoted the Egyptian Finance Minister as having said that US aid to Egypt had been resumed on the pre-Suez scale.

The Jordanian Minister of Economy received a note from the Saudi Legation in Amman requesting that a Jordanian delegation come to Riyadh to discuss Saudi-Jordanian economic relations and fishing rights in the Gulf of Aqaba.

Jordan announced an agreement with George Zimiri, an Arab financier living in Guatemala, to drill for oil in a 13,000 square mile area.

King Hussein of Jordan approved the formation of a military court to try all persons in concentration camps so that those

November 28

who proved they had not taken part in the April conspiracy could be released.

The US officially handed over the second consignment of American arms to arrive in Libya under a military pact.

Ahmad al-Shukairy submitted a memorandum to the Chairman of the UN Security Council replying to Israel's criticism of King Saud's Accession Day speech.

The Foreign Office reported from London that, two months before, France had refused a Yemeni request for arms on the grounds that these arms might be used against British forces in the Aden Protectorate.

November 29

US State Department officials denied reports from Cairo that the US had resumed economic aid to Egypt on the same scale as before the Suez Canal nationalization.

It was reported in Rabat that the fighting between Moroccan nationalist and Spanish colonial forces had spready 265 miles south of Ifni to the Spanish Sahara, which was claimed by Moroccan Irredentists.

The newspaper al-Alam reported that at least 180 persons in Ifni had been killed by Spanish bombers.

Spanish parachute troops sent into the Ifni area drove the Moroccans back across the border, Spanish military sources announced.

French Foreign Minister Pineau met at the UN with the heads of the Tunisian and Moroccan delegations to discuss steps toward a solution of the Algerian dispute.

November, 1957

November 29

A Saudi Arabian spokesman stated that the Turkish Government had decided to withdraw an important part of its defense forces from its southern frontiers.

The police placed a heavy guard around the US Embassy and the Turkish Legation in Damascus as a crowd demonstrated against the Palestine Partition, calling for the return to Syria of the Alexandretta District from Turkey.

UN Secretary General Hammarskjold left for the Middle East to discuss Jordan's complaint that Colonel Leary had been unwilling to investigate Israel activity on Mount Scopus where Jordan alleged Israel was building military fortifications.

The statement of President Bourguiba of Tunisia on November 28, that the Liberation Front no longer insisted on French recognition of Algerian independence before negotiating, confused rebel headquarters in Tunisia. Liberation Front sources announced that President Bourguiba could have made a slip of the tongue.

A trade agreement was signed between Morocco and Denmark.

November 30

The French National Assembly approved two reform bills for Algeria, one granting limited home rule, and the other instituting a system of proportional representation between the European and Moslem communities. The Algerian National Liberation Front rejected the reform bills on the grounds that the Algerian people had always demonstrated their will to determine their own destiny.

French authorities reported six French soldiers and 41 rebels killed on November 29 in a clash 20 miles south of Algiers.

December, 1957

December 1

Military sources in Madrid indicated that Spanish forces were in command of the situation in Ifni.

Mr. Hammarskjold arrived in Amman. After a two hour meeting, a joint communique was issued to the effect that discussions had been started on the problems relating to the strengthening of UN Truce Supervisory Organization authority, particularly in the Mount Scopus area.

Secretary of State Dulles said that he would be happy to talk with Foreign Minister Mahmoud Fawzi of Egypt.

December 2

The Spanish Government confirmed that fighting with Moroccan irregulars had spread from Ifni to Spanish West Africa. The Spanish announcement said that an armed band, believed to be part of the Moroccan Liberation Army, had attacked an armed convoy en route from the coast to Aiun in Spanish West Africa.

A number of British Parliament members said that President Nasser had offered to arbitrate the financial aspects of the Suez dispute with Britain.

Egypt announced its support of Jordan in the Mount Scopus issue.

In a joint communique issued at the conclusion of talks with the UN Secretary General, the Jordanian Government affirmed its desire to maintain the fullest cooperation with the UN Truce Supervision Organization.

The Saudi Arabian, Lebanese and Iraqi envoys announced their opposition to the French reform program for Algeria at the UN.

November, 1957

November 30

The Government of Jordan announced that it had received an official communique from the US informing Jordan that it had decided to grant $10,000,000 for economic projects in Jordan under the economic development program which was presently being prepared by the Development Board. The funds would come from the Point Four Program.

A Jordanian Army delegation arrived in London. Unofficial reports said the delegation was planning to sound out the British Government on a renewal of military and economic assistance.

Syria charged at the UN that the NATO was being used to make a so-called free world "safe for oppression" by assisting France in its Algerian policy.

Rebels in Ifni reported that they were under attack by planes, warships and 6,000 Spanish troops, and that villages in Rio de Oro, 200 miles south on the Atlantic, had been bombed.

French Premier Bourges-Maunoury submitted his resignation after the National Assembly rejected his government's plan on Algeria in a vote of 279-253.

December, 1957

December 2

Israel protested to UNESCO against the projected supply of radar equipment in Egyptian secondary schools, which the Chairman of the UNESCO Executive Board had announced.

December 3

The US representative to the UN, Henry Cabot Lodge, endorsed the French Foreign Minister's appeal of the previous week against interference with the reforms that France had planned for Algeria. He also gave high praise to the offer of Tunisia and Morocco to mediate in the Algerian conflict.

King Muhammad V appealed for a peaceful settlement of the Ifni dispute. Crown Prince Moulay Hassan, speaking on behalf of his father, described as "fantastic" the Spanish charge that Moroccan irregulars had attacked Ifni from outside the enclave.

Spanish Iberia Airlines reopened civil air traffic to Ifni for the first time since the fighting began.

Spanish Army communiques said that the communications point of Telata de Esbuia had been liberated and that a lighthouse at Cape Bojador in the Spanish Sahara had been attacked by armed bands.

Mr. Hammarskjold arrived in Israel and conferred with Premier Ben-Gurion in a three hour meeting which failed to yield a solution of Israel's border dispute with Jordan.

King Faisal of Iraq arrived in Riyadh on a six day state visit to Saudi Arabia.

December 4

Representatives of two Israel oil corporations appeared in a Moscow court to seek $2,396,440 in damages from Soyuzneft-

December 4

export for unfulfilled contracts. The Soviet oil export corporation had stopped deliveries and cancelled contracts after Israel's attack on Egypt.

The US and French representatives conferred at the UN in an attempt to work out a compromise resolution on the Algerian question.

A US representative told the UN that Israel and the Arab states must assume the primary responsibility for the fate of Arab refugees from Palestine.

The UN Secretary General engineered a settlement of the Mount Scopus issue. Israel was reported to have agreed to discuss the possibility of an inspection of Mount Scopus.

Instruments of ratification for cultural, economic and trade agreements drawn up between Iraq and Saudi Arabia were exchanged.

Al-Alam reported that nationalist guerrillas in Ifni had pushed Spanish troops back 12 miles toward the sea, and that the Spanish had bombed a Moroccan village in retaliation.

The Spanish Foreign Ministry reported that a relief column had brought the whole southern region of Ifni back under Spanish control after ten days fighting with the Moroccan "Army of Liberation."

December 5

President Nasser, in his first public address in several months, reiterated his determination to keep Egypt free from all foreign influences.

The Egyptian Manager of the Suez Canal, Mahmoud Yunis, said in Washington that Egypt was running the Canal more

December 5

efficiently than did the old Suez Company. He conferred with Eugene R. Black on a loan for improvement and widening of the Canal.

The Spanish Embassy in Rabat declared that Spain was willing to renew negotiations on Ifni in the fraternal spirit characteristic of Hispano-Moroccan relations.

Moroccan Crown Prince Moulay Hassan announced that Syria, Jordan, Saudi Arabia, Lebanon and Tunisia had offered to mediate in the Ifni dispute.

The Moroccan newspaper al-Alam said that only the capital of Ifni remained in Spanish hands.

Spanish forces, reported to number 12,000 men, advanced through the central and southern areas of Ifni in an attempt to sweep Moroccan troops back into Morocco, according to a Spanish Army communique.

President Bourguiba announced the evacuation of French troops from six posts in southern Tunisia.

Dag Hammarskjold and Lebanese Foreign Minister Malik met for a talk in Beirut at the end of the UN Secretary General's Middle East visit.

It was announced in New York that a personal representative of the UN Secretary General would be assigned to discuss a broader settlement of the Mount Scopus issue.

December 6

It was reported in Rabat that nationalist guerrillas had captured the Spanish military post at Tilouine in Ifni.

December 6

The Spanish Embassy in Rabat said that Madrid was willing to renew negotiations on Ifni. The Embassy further announced that Spain had offered to submit the Ifni question to an International Court in the event the negotiations between the two countries did not produce agreement.

Italy proposed that the US and Western Europe join in a program of economic development for the Middle East based on a Marshall Plan formula.

A resolution containing an urgent appeal for funds for Palestine refugees was approved 49-0 by the Special Political Committee of the UN General Assembly.

The UN General Assembly's Administrative and Budgetary Committee recommended that expenditures for the UN Emergency Force be held to less than $10 million for the first half of 1958.

The Political Committee of the General Assembly was unable to adopt either an Asian-African resolution calling for negotiations between France and the Algerian nationalists, or a Western move designed to meet the French viewpoint. The results of the committee debate were therefore to be forwarded to the General Assembly without recommendation.

Syrians reportedly invaded a Lebanon police post, removing arms and ammunition. The Lebanese Internal Security Council was called to discuss the situation.

December 7

King Faisal and King Saud issued a joint communique whereby they pledged themselves to support Arab unity.

The Moroccan Government protested against violation of its territorial waters as a Spanish flotilla of six, and possibly

December 7

eight, warships arrived off the Moroccan port of Agadir. Moroccan sources that that there were 17 Spanish warships in Moroccan coastal waters including naval units reported off the Moroccan town of Mirlaft just north of Ifni.

The Saudi Arabian Government and Aramco agreed to arbitrate their five year old dispute on the allocation of more than $100 million in royalties.

A trade agreement was signed in Rabat between Morocco and Hungary

December 8

The Crown Prince of Yemen arrived in Bucharest at the invitation of the Rumanian Government.

The Lebanese Army was reported to have taken over the border zone of the northeast, where raiders from Syria had attacked a post the night before.

Former Iraqi Premier Nuri-Said arrived in Washington on a visit.

A Spanish communique confirmed that Spanish troops had withdrawn from the army posts of Tiugsa, Zoco del Tenin and Tiliouin. The communique reflected a new strategy to draw back to the enclave's capital of Sidi Ifni and strike out from there with reinforcements from Spain.

The US Ambassador to Morocco informed the Moroccan Acting Foreign Minister that the US hoped that restraint would be exercised by both countries in the Ifni dispute.

Reports from Agadir said that the Spanish fleet was moving south in the direction of Ifni, and that Moroccan Army troops had taken up positions in the port and had installed 105 mm. cannons.

Foreign Minister of Iran Ali Gholi Ardalan reasserted Iranian claims to Bahrain.

December, 1957

December 8

Saudi Arabia and Japan signed an agreement on the formation of the Japan Petroleum Trading Company, Limited, for off-shore prospecting of oil in the Saudi Arabian half of the neutral land zone shared with Kuwait.

December 9

French officials reported a toll of 270 nationalists killed and 70 taken prisoner over the weekend. This figure included 103 nationalists killed in fighting near the Tunisian border December 7. French losses were given at five men killed and four wounded.

The Egyptian Foreign Minister and Secretary of State Dulles conferred in Washington.

Syria announced that it would no longer cooperate with Colonel Christian Moe of Norway, the chairman of the Israel-Syrian Mixed Armistice Commission.

A Syrian economic delegation left for Moscow to work out the details of the Syrian-Soviet economic agreement.

The Tunisian Ambassador to Yugoslavia presented his credentials.

At a dinner in New York in his honor, King Muhammad expressed regret that Spain had disregarded Morocco's friendly relations with Spain and had abandoned the method of peaceful solution and amicable negotiation in the dispute over Ifni. King Muhammad stressed that the best method for seeking a solution was through free and harmonious negotiation.

Reports from Madrid said that Spanish armed forces were building a defensive perimeter five miles in depth around Sidi Ifni on the personal order of Generalissimo Francisco Franco, in order to lure the attackers deeper into Spanish territory.

December, 1957

December 11

The military trial of ten Syrians accused of conspiring with the US to overthrow the regime, opened in Damascus.

An economic agreement was formally signed in Moscow by the Syrian and Soviet Deputy Premiers.

The UN announced that Colonel Christian Moe of Norway would be succeeded by Colonel J. G. Bertran of Canada as Chairman of the Israel-Syrian Mixed Armistice Commission.

The Jordanian Minister of Justice, Construction and Development, Walid Salah, resigned.

France was expected to consider again the possibilities of Tunisian and Moroccan mediation in the Algerian issue.

The National Liberation Front noted with satisfaction the UN resolution on Algeria, interpreting it as a call for negotiations on the basis outlined by King Muhammad V and President Bourguiba. Foreign Minister Pineau termed the resolution acceptable, and said that France must be left alone to work out a settlement of the rebellion.

French authorities reported at least 218 rebels killed in the northeast in two engagements taking place December 10.

The Ankara meeting of the Moslem members of the Baghdad Military Pact — Turkey, Iran, Pakistan and Iraq — agreed in principle to the Pact's proposed merger with NATO.

December 12

Al-Alam reported that tension was mounting in the Spanish possessions of Ceuta and Melilla in northern Morocco.

December, 1957

December 9

King Muhammad V was joined in New York by his four daughters.

Crown Prince Moulay Hassan read a message to the Moroccan people from King Muhammad V congratulating them on their wisdom and restraint in the Ifni dispute.

Al-Alam reported that Spanish warships had bombarded a small village in Moroccan territory.

December 10

The UN General Assembly adopted a compromise resolution on the Algerian situation calling for pourparlers, or talks. The French accepted the resolution as a testimony of confidence in the French position.

A Tunisian delegation left for Bonn to negotiate a trade agreement with West Germany.

Egypt decided to release the South African freighter which had been held since November 23 on suspicion that it belonged to Israel.

Jordanian Foreign Ministry sources said that Jordan had expelled two Syrian political attaches and the secretary of the Syrian Embassy for reasons not disclosed.

Iraqi Premier Ali al-Ayyoubi al-Jawdat resigned.

The Syrian Government delegation, headed by Deputy Premier Khaled Azm, concurrently Minister of State, Defense, and Finance, arrived in Moscow.

Trade agreements between the Korean Peoples' Democratic Republic and Egypt were signed in Phyongyang.

December, 1957

December 12

Al-Alam identified four posts in Spanish West Africa reported captured by Moroccan irregulars as Tantan, Mesid, Smara and Guelta Zemmur.

It was announced in a joint communique that the British-Egyptian financial talks in Rome had been adjourned temporarily to permit the two delegations to report to their respective governments.

Reports from Ifni said that operations were virtually over in the hinterland and that Spanish forces withdrew to Sidi Ifni, the capital.

President Bourguiba confirmed the arrival of a shipment of Egyptian arms for the Tunisian Army.

The UN General Assembly adopted a resolution appealing to member States to meet the critical need for funds for Palestine refugees.

The Australian delegate to the UN announced that his nation would increase its contributions to the Arab refugee fund from $112,000 to $200,000.

Moslem leaders of the Baghdad Pact, meeting in Ankara, issued a statement on the Middle East situation in advance of a NATO meeting.

The Sudanese Prime Minister arrived in Lagos for an eight day visit to Nigeria.

December 13

The Paris newspaper Le Monde published a long delayed and hotly disputed report on savagery and brutality in the Algerian war, prepared by 12 Frenchmen who constituted the official Commission for the Safeguard of Rights and Individual Liberties. Robert Lacoste, Minister for Algeria, issued a statement from

December 13

Algiers regretting the publication of the report before the Government had completed its comments on rebel atrocities which were to accompany the criticisms of French actions.

The US Army was completing a mapping survey of Libya vital to the conduct of missile warfare from North African bases.

King Muhammad V of Morocco left New York for Rabat.

December 14

The UN General Assembly passed, 54-0, with 19 abstentions, a resolution calling for an eight percent voluntary surcharge on Suez Canal tolls to cover the cost of clearing the waterway.

French-Egyptian talks in Geneva on compensation claims resulting from the Suez crisis were adjourned without agreement.

Israel Foreign Secretary Golda Meir said that any attempt by the North Atlantic Treaty Organization conference to ease Middle Eastern tension by rolling Israel borders back to comply with the 1947 partition agreement would create greater tension in the area.

Mr. Abd-al-Wahhab Marjan formed an Iraqi Government after Premier Ali Jawdat had resigned.

December 15

The Jordanian Government announced that it had granted political asylum to Air Vice Marshal Abd-al-Raouf of Egypt, who was under sentence of death.

Finance Minister Levi Eshkol disclosed that in the past ten years Israel had spent $700 million on defense and security,

December 15

and had invested between $1. 5 and $1. 75 billion on development projects. Local investments for the same period amounted to IL3. 8 billion.

King Muhammad V praised US statesmen for the good intentions and comprehension they had shown toward the problems facing Morocco and Algeria. He said the ties of friendship which united Morocco and the US had been strengthened, and the cooperation broadened, by his trip to the US.

The US State Department confirmed that President Eisenhower had sent a special letter to President Camille Chamoun of Lebanon assuring all the Arab states that no decisions affecting their interests would be taken at the NATO conference without their being consulted.

Egypt and the Sudan opened talks on regulating the flow of the Nile River for the projected irrigation and hydroelectric dam at Aswan.

Defense Minister Abd-al-Wahhab Marjan of Iraq was sworn in as Premier following the resignation of Ali Jawdat.

Reportedly, Spain ordered its Foreign Legion to reinforce its post at Villa Bens in Spanish West Africa.

In a statement published by Le Monde, Lacoste said that disciplinary action had been taken against persons guilty of ill-treating prisoners or other acts of violence in Algeria on 495 occasions — in 363 cases by order of military courts.

December 16

A leading Tunisian newspaper accused France of giving planes to Spain for use in the Ifni fighting.

A Government spokesman announced that Jordanian security

December 16

forces had seized a large cache of arms and had arrested two Communists in a raid at Nablus.

Saudi Arabia's oil administrator said that his country would not seek revision of an American oil concession on the basis of a more advantageous deal made with a Japanese group. He also said that the concession to the Japanese for offshore rights off the Neutral Zone between Kuwait and Saudi Arabia was valid, even if Kuwait did not enter into an agreement with the Japanese.

Dr. Francisco Urrutia, Colombian diplomat, was appointed to mediate the Mount Scopus dispute between Jordan and Israel.

US Ambassador Lester D. Mallory would leave his post in Jordan, it was announced by the US Embassy in Amman.

France and Sudan announced a trade agreement under which France would buy substantial quantities of Sudanese cotton.

The Shah of Iran arrived in Beirut for a five day State visit to Lebanon.

Rumanian-Yemeni talks in Bucharest ended in the establishment of diplomatic relations between the two countries and in the signing of a friendship treaty and trade agreement.

December 17

Major General Burns, Commander of the UNEF, was promoted to the rank of Lieutenant General by the Canadian Defense Department.

Premier Abd-al-Wahhab Marjan of Iraq said that his Government would follow Arab national policy and would work within the Baghdad Pact.

December 17

Musallem Bisaiso of Jordan, former editor of the Middle East News Agency, was sentenced to 15 years imprisonment at hard labor for membership in the Communist Party.

December 18

Mustafa Khalifah, President of the Jordanian Chamber of Deputies, received a cable from King Saud, in reply to his message regarding the Egyptian radio campaign against Jordan, expressing regret for the existing dispute between certain Arab states which had led to vituperation and abuse, a matter which benefitted no one but the enemies of both countries. He said that both countries were duty bound to work toward removing differences and whatever else tended to harm Arab solidarity and Arab unity.

December 19

The Jordanian Government signed a friendship treaty with Nationalist China.

A tentative agreement was reached under which France would present the compensation claims against Egypt by the old Suez Canal Company.

A meeting of the UN Security Council on the Israel-Jordanian dispute over an Israel tree planting program near Jerusalem was postponed for at least two weeks.

The British Council Building in Beirut was bombed.

December 20

President Bourguiba of Tunisia conferred in Rabat, Morocco, with King Muhammad V on means to end the three year old Algerian rebellion.

December, 1957

December 20

Secretary of State Dulles conferred with Generalissimo Franco on the attack on Ifni and the state of military alert in Spain's other areas in Morocco and West Africa.

The Syrian National Peace Committee appealed to public opinion in Arab countries to protest against flights by US atomic and hydrogen bomb planes over their territories.

December 21

Dr. Charles Malik made a vigorous defense of Lebanon's policy of cooperation with the US which had been denounced by the Opposition.

New York Senator Jacob K. Javits urged a new Middle Eastern policy that would make the US North Atlantic allies a party to US commitments to Israel.

The Spanish Government publicly stressed the potential importance to NATO of the Canary Islands and Spanish bases on the northwest African coast. The Spanish Minister of War told a full session of the Spanish Parliament that left wing elements of Morocco's Istiqlal Party had organized the Moroccan Liberation Army with the aim of subverting King Muhammad V's power and driving all Europeans from North Africa and the Sahara.

The Egyptian Canal Authority announced that 69 ships had passed through the Suez Canal, the largest number for a single day since the canal opened.

December 22

The New China News Agency announced that Egypt and Communist China had signed a trade agreement for the exchange of $72,000,000 worth of goods in 1958.

December, 1957

December 23

The US contributed an additional $12,000,000 to the cost of maintaining the UNEF in the Middle East.

Robert McClintock was named American Ambassador to Lebanon to replace Donald R. Heath; the appointment was subject to Senate confirmation.

Twenty members of a Moroccan armed band were killed in the Spanish Sahara territory on December 15, according to a Spanish Army Ministry communique which further stated that no important activity had taken place on the Western coast of Africa since December 12.

In Warsaw, Poland and Yemen agreed to exchange diplomatic representatives and also signed an agreement on economic and technical cooperation.

West Germany and Tunisia concluded a 15 month trade agreement.

The Crown Prince of Yemen arrived in Belgrade on a six day official visit to Yugoslavia.

President Camille Chamoun of Lebanon and Shah Riza Muhammad Pahlevi of Iran ended week long discussions.

UN Secretary General Dag Hammarskjold arrived in Cairo. According to an official release, he was to discuss issues pending between Egypt and the UN.

December 24

Eleven Jordanian supporters of the outlawed Communist and Socialist Baath Parties were sentenced to prison terms for participation in the April coup against King Hussein.

December, 1957

December 22

A Jordanian economic delegation left for Saudi Arabia to negotiate a trade and economic agreement.

The Government of Iraq prohibited all banks from investing more than 30 percent of their capital and deposits outside of Iraq.

It was reported in Tunis that the passage of a 16 inch oil pipeline from eastern Algeria through Tunisian territory to the port of La Skirra had been approved in principle by the Tunisian Government.

A Moroccan source said that the General Tire and Rubber Company of Ohio would build a subsidiary plant in Casablanca.

A Syrian note of protest to Turkey was announced which asked for Turkish cooperation in excluding the Middle East from the Cold War.

December 23

President Nasser paid a visit to Port Said to celebrate the first anniversary of the departure of British and French troops and was nearly mobbed by welcoming citizens.

The Algerian National Liberation Front reported that nationalist guerrillas had intensified their military action in the Wilaya command of Oran near the Moroccan border. The report further asserted that 47 French were killed and many were wounded in the Sebdou engagement December 18. The nationalists put their losses in this engagement at eight dead and three wounded, in contradiction to the French figures given for the battle. The nationalist communique said that 25 Frenchmen and two nationalists had been killed in two ambush attacks against the French forces in Oran December 20.

The UN Secretary General left for a Christmas visit to the UNEF and Arab refugee camps in the Gaza Strip.

December, 1957

December 24

Jordanian Premier Ibrahim Hashem won a vote of confidence in the Lower House of Parliament on the 1957-58 budget.

President Eisenhower nominated Charles W. Yost as US Ambassador to Syria.

The French police sized the Christmas Eve issue of the Communist newspaper L'Humanite because of articles on soldiers imprisoned for refusing to fight in Algeria.

The French Military Court of Oran imposed a death sentence on Abd-al-Kader Moqaddem, convicted as the instigator of a nationalist bombing December 17.

Prince Muhammad Abd-al-Moneim, a second cousin of former King Farouk, was arrested in Cairo.

Premier Ben-Gurion said that Israel was seeking weapons from West Germany to cope with Arab threats against ships carrying Israel bound refugees.

December 25

Secretary General Hammarskjold conferred with Dr. Mahmoud Fawzi, Egyptian Foreign Minister, in Cairo.

Iraq recalled its permanent representative to the UN for voting against Turkey in the recent Cyprus debate. The Government deplored the action of its representative because he had violated clear instructions.

The Government of Lebanon reportedly sent a note to Cairo suggesting talks to settle any outstanding differences between Lebanon and Egypt.

December, 1957

December 26

President Bourguiba said that French military forces in Tunisia must be evacuated before March 20, according to a report from the French News Agency.

Dag Hammarskjold conferred with President Nasser.

The International Red Cross Committee said in Geneva that the Algerian nationalists had broken their promises to permit Red Cross visits to French prisoners in nationalist hands.

Over 400 delegates from 39 Asian and African countries attended the opening of a people's conference in Cairo.

December 27

Egyptian authorities opened an inquiry into an alleged plot to overthrow President Nasser and restore the Egyptian monarchy.

Lebanese Deputies reportedly complained of what they called miserly US economic and technical aid to Lebanon.

Generalissimo Francisco Franco's Moorish Guard of Honor was disbanded because of anti-Moroccan sentiment.

The Soviet Union told the Asian-African nations meeting in Cairo that it would provide, to the best of its capabilities, money in the form of loans or aid, to assist those nations.

December 28

In a speech praising Saudi Arabia addressed to Saudi troops in the Jordan River Valley, King Hussein criticized Egypt and Syria for not supporting Jordan.

Yugoslavia and Yemen established diplomatic relations and signed a friendship treaty and scientific and technical cooperation pacts.

December, 1957

December 28

Bourguiba declared that all French troops must be removed from Tunisia by March 20, 1958.

December 29

Dr. Francisco Urrutia, representative of the UN Secretary General to negotiate the Mount Scopus issue, arrived in Jerusalem.

East Germany had offered aid to Syria, similar to that of Russia and Czechoslovakia, it was officially stated in Damascus.

Mr. Norman Thomas, the US socialist leader, who had recently met President Nasser and other Arab leaders, urged that the US should make a frank attempt to negotiate with Russia on what he called Russia's surprisingly decent proposals for a Middle Eastern settlement.

The US Secretary of State, John Foster Dulles, would attend the meeting of the ministerial council of the Baghdad Pact opening in Ankara January 27, it was announced. The State Department said there was no plan for the US to join the Pact at present, although it was a member of its economic, counter-subversion, and military committees. Mr. Dulles was to visit Tehran before Ankara.

A three day congress of the Tunisian Communist Party opened in Tunis; delegations from the French, Italian, Moroccan and Albanian Communist Parties attended.

Egyptian President Nasser reportedly was concerned because of the strong pro-Communist line taken by the Asian-African delegates. He had ordered the Egyptian press to play down the conference.

The Egyptian Finance Ministry Under Secretary announced that Egypt and France had reached a new trade agreement.

December, 1957

December 30

The Colonial Office in London said that Yemen had distributed between 2,000 and 3,000 rifles to tribesman of the British Aden Protectorate within the past six weeks, and that 200 protectorate tribesmen had been detained as hostages to insure that the rifles would not be used to cause disturbances in the Protectorate.

A large group of Yemeni tribesmen and regular soldiers had attacked government guards of Ghania, in the Aden Protectorate, on Christmas Day, according to an official comminique.

Egypt announced that it would not pay its share of the promised Arab subsidy to Jordan.

The Crown Prince of Yemen arrived in Moscow on an official visit.

West Germany assured Syria, in reply to an inquiry, that it could not supply arms to Israel, it was officially stated in Damascus. The Jordanian Defense Minister, Sayyed Akef al-Fayez, said that if West Germany did so, it would endanger its reputation in the Arab countries.

The Supreme Soviet invited a delegation from the Egyptian National Assembly to visit Russia in 1958.

Generalissimo Franco declared that Spain was fighting in the vanguard of the West's struggle against Communist penetration of Africa through its holding operation in Ifni.

A palace spokesman announced that Princess Lalla Aisha of Morocco had written a personal letter to President Coty of France, asking him to spare the life of a young Algerian woman condemned to death by a French military court in Algiers for terrorist activity.

December, 1957

December 31

An Esso Standard Oil prospecting team had struck oil in Western Libya, the Libyan Petroleum Commission announced. The oil deposits were found in the Atshan area near the Algerian border. This was the first of 13 oil companies prospecting in Libya to find oil.

Britain and Egypt had agreed to appoint a neutral accountant to assess the "Egyptianized" British property, it was stated in Cairo.

Foreign Minister Samir al-Rifai said that Jordan would need an average of $50,000,000 a year in US aid for the next five to ten years to help finance its economy and armed forces. The Foreign Minister also said that martial law would be lifted when there was a halt in Syrian and Egyptian intrigues to incite revolt.

Israel's Prime Minister, Mr. Ben-Gurion, resigned.

A trade agreement was signed between Iraq and Italy.

January, 1958

January 1

The Afro-Asian Conference closed with the unanimous passage of a resolution establishing a permanent body, to be known as the Afro-Asian Peoples' Solidarity Organization, with headquarters in Cairo. The Soviet Union and Communist China were to be represented on the ten member Secretariat.

An Israel seaman seized from a Dutch freighter, November 3, and held by Egyptian authorities since then, was released.

A comminique from Aden said that British forces in the Protectorate repulsed a Yemeni attack on Sanaa, a village close to the frontier.

Crown Prince Faisal of Saudi Arabia arrived in Alexandria, Egypt, for a state visit.

The director of the Egyptian Information Bureau said that Egypt agreed to help Jordan under the Arab Solidarity Pact in order to strengthen Arab unity and save Jordan from "imperialism and foreign occupation forces."

The outgoing Israel Prime Minister, David Ben-Gurion, accepted a mandate from the President to form a new Government provided that all parties in the proposed coalition agreed to the principle of collective responsibility.

The Moroccan Government abandoned the Spanish peseta as an official medium of exchange in Tangier. The Moroccan franc was now always to be used in both public and official transactions.

January 2

Egyptian Commerce Ministry Undersecretary Mustafa Khalifah said in Hong Kong that Egypt would supply Communist China with cotton, cotton yarn, textiles and rice under a LE103 million trade agreement, in exchange for soybeans, meat, oils, iron, timber, tobacco, tea, trucks and machinery.

January, 1958

January 2

UN Secretary General Hammarskjold said that although there were issues still to be settled concerning the Suez Canal, he did not regard the Suez Canal problem as a matter of concern.

The Turkish Foreign Ministry denied press reports issued in Arab countries that West German arms had been sent to Israel through Turkey.

An Egyptian-Chinese Friendship Society was inaugurated in Cairo.

Faisal, Crown Prince and Premier of Saudi Arabia, said that efforts were made by certain American circles to prevent conclusion of the Saudi-Japanese offshore oil agreement.

January 3

Soviet Premier Bulganin told newsmen that the return of Marshal Konstantin Rokossovsky from his Transcausasian command in Syria was proof that the Syro-Turkish crisis was easing.

By unanimous vote, Yusuf al-Sibai of Egypt was elected President of the Afro-Asian Peoples' Solidarity Organization for a two year term.

The first installment of a gift of weapons from Iraq (anti-tank guns) arrived in Benghazi, Libya.

A $6.7 million trade agreement between Morocco and Egypt provided for the exchange of Moroccan ores and agricultural products for Egyptian sugar and cotton.

The US State Department reported that the Soviet Union allocated nearly $1.9 billion to ten underdeveloped countries in 1956-1958. Recipient Middle East countries were: Egypt, $380 million, Syria, $280 million, and Yemen, $10 million.

The Tunisian Secretary of State for Foreign Affairs, Sadok Moqaddem, protested to the French Ambassador against the violation of the Tunisian border by French troops on January 2.

January, 1958

January 3

The US Army announced that the Chief of Staff, General Maxwell D. Taylor, would visit Libya, Iraq, Iran and Saudi Arabia during a tour later in the month.

January 4

President Nasser said that nine clandestine British and French radio stations in the Middle East were beaming "programs of vilification" at Egypt with the aim of overthrowing him.

A Russian jet airliner arrived in Cairo to pick up the Egyptian Minister of Industry and a large delegation who were to go to Moscow on January 6 to settle details of a loan.

A trade agreement was signed between Morocco and Norway.

Enrico Mattei, President of the Italian National Hydrocarbons Authority, said that US oil companies blocked concession negotiations between his firm and Libya in 1957.

A Syrian delegation led by the chairman of the Economic Development Board arrived in Prague for economic talks with the Czechoslovak Government.

January 5

Ali Amini, Iranian Ambassador in Washington, said that the Baghdad Pact members sincerely hoped the US would become a full member in the near future and give more adequate and consistent economic assistance to the underdeveloped Arab States.

Farid Zain-ad-Din, whom the US ceased to recognize as Syrian Ambassador in Washington, said that current US efforts were probably aimed at establishing missile bases in the Middle East.

Dr. Francisco Urrutia, personal representative of UN Secretary General Hammarskjold to mediate in the Mount Scopus conflict, conferred with King Hussein and Premier Samir al-Rifai of Jordan about the Arab-Israel dispute.

January, 1958

January 6

Israel Prime Minister Ben-Gurion ended a three week crisis by forming a new coalition of the five parties which he led before the split.

Jordan and Saudi Arabia concluded an economic agreement.

The Permanent Secretariat of the Afro-Asian Peoples' Solidarity Council, set up by the Cairo Conference, was inaugurated in Cairo.

A 47 man economic mission headed by Aziz Sidqi, Egyptian Minister of Industry, arrived in Moscow for talks on the LE62.5 million worth of economic aid which Russia had promised Egypt for industrialization projects.

January 7

It was reported in Cairo that the Soviet Union contributed 5,000 pounds sterling toward a maintenance fund for the Afro-Asian Solidarity Secretariat.

Israel was reported to have told Western Ambassadors at the UN that the work of the special mission sent to settle the Mount Scopus dispute in Palestine would be jeopardized if the Security Council debated the question.

The new Israel Cabinet with David Ben-Gurion as Prime Minister and Minister of Defense won a 76-33 vote of confidence in the Knesset.

Syria announced that it had sent notes to all Arab nations warning them of serious developments in relations between Israel and West Germany.

Lord Salisbury, who had resigned from the British Government the previous year over the handling of the Cyprus problem, said that Turkey, if its interests were not considered in any settlement, might lapse into neutralism and thus remove the main barrier to Russian infiltration throughout the Middle East.

January, 1958

January 7

It was reported that the US was considering lowering the interest rate on loans to underdeveloped areas including the Middle East.

January 8

Morocco protested to France against attacks on Moroccans living in the Paris region.

January 9

Russia was planning to give economic aid to Yemen similar to that for Egypt and Syria, it was reported in Cairo. A US mission which had visited Yemen in the fall recommended modest economic aid to develop roads and agriculture.

A Saudi-Jordanian joint statement granting free entry of agricultural and animal products and reciprocal entry and work opportunities for citizens was issued.

Tunisian President Bourguiba said that he would appeal to members of NATO if France did not withdraw most of its troops from Tunisia soon.

President Bourguiba said that Tunisia would remain "firmly and with conviction" in the western camp.

Abd-al-Aziz Chehab, Director General of the Interior Ministry, said that the Lebanese Government, in an effort to end terrorism in the country, was considering the establishment of concentration camps for suspect foreigners. He confirmed that the measure was aimed at Palestinian refugees.

The Russian armed forces newspaper, Red Star, said that the US was pursuing a policy of turning Turkey into a NATO military bridgehead which created a danger to peace in the Middle East.

January, 1958

January 11

A major clash between a large group of Algerian insurgents and a French army unit was reported near the Algerian-Tunisian border.

Abba Eban, Israel Ambassador to the US, said that Israel would consolidate its economic framework and secure its position as a democratic state in the Middle East despite international tensions.

January 12

President Nasser received a 41 page letter from Soviet Premier Bulganin. Official sources said that it proposed a high level conference that would include heads of neutral governments.

President Nasser welcomed President Sukarno of Indonesia to Egypt.

The French Ambassador to Tunis, Georges Gorse, formally protested against the asylum that he said the Tunisian Government had given to Algerian rebels accused of the January 11 attack.

General Afif al-Bizri, Syrian Commander in Chief, and other senior officers arrived in Cairo for talks with officers of the Egyptian armed forces.

Communist China promised to send technicians and other skilled workers to Yemen under a 10 year agreement between the two countries, who also signed a five year trade agreement.

Communist China affirmed its support of Yemen's claim to territories under British protection. The announcement marked the end of formal talks between Premier Chou En-lai and Crown Prince Saif-al-Islam Muhammad al-Badr.

The government owned bourse in Cairo reported that the Russian mission which had gone to Yemen was offering economic aid worth about LE20 million.

January 13

The British Prime Minister, Harold Macmillan, said at a Karachi press conference that it was wrong to believe that the Baghdad Pact caused tension among the Arab countries.

January, 1958

January 10

US Secretary of State Dulles said that he decided to attend the Baghdad Pact meeting as a concrete demonstration of continued American interest both in the drive against Communist imperialism in the area and in solving economic problems. He added that the US had no intention of joining the Pact.

The Cairo press criticized President Eisenhower for not accepting Soviet Premier Bulganin's newest summit meeting proposal.

Marshal Bulganin, Russian Premier, in a letter to the British Prime Minister, suggested a nine point agenda for a summit conference, including steps to reduce Middle East tension.

The Algerian National Liberation Front sent a note to all foreign missions in Tunis and to the International Monetary Fund, requesting that no financial aid be given to France while it continued its war of aggression in Algeria.

January 11

French authorities in Algeria charged Tunisia with helping Algerian rebels.

US General Maxwell Taylor arrived in Baghdad to confer with Iraqi army leaders.

E. D. Kiselev, Russian Ambassador to Egypt, flew to Yemen from Cairo with 11 Russian economists and industrialists. Extension of Soviet aid to Egypt was expected to be discussed.

The first crude oil from the Hassi Messaoud field in the Sahara arrived at the Mediterranean port of Philippeville, Algeria.

It was reported from Rabat, Morocco, that Spanish warships had shelled Moroccan territory bordering the Spanish enclave of Ifni.

Lebanon and Afghanistan signed an air convention.

January, 1958

January 13

Iraqi Prime Minister Nuri-Said arrived in Turkey for the Baghdad Pact meeting.

General Moshe Dayan, Israel Chief of Staff, said in London that the military situation in Israel was satisfactory.

An interministerial Cabinet committee in Israel recommended the expenditure of IL10 million over the next three to four years for the rehabilitation of some 20,000 Arab refugees who had returned to Israel.

Israel's Ambassador to the US, Abba Eban, conferred with UN Secretary General Dag Hammarskjold. It was understood that they discussed the Middle East situation.

The Plenary Session of the Central Committee of the Communist Party of Syria and Lebanon ended after discussing the situation in the two countries and unanimously adopting resolutions on the establishment of a Syrian-Egyptian federation, strengthening of the Syrian United National Front, and the situation in Lebanon.

President Sukarno of Indonesia had a long talk with President Nasser.

January 14

The Spanish Government converted the area known as Spanish West Africa into the two provinces of Ifni and Spanish Sahara and placed them under military rule.

A Moroccan reply to Soviet Premier Bulganin's peace appeal letter stated that for the moment all its energies were directed to the consolidation of its independence.

The UN reported that the volume of exports from Middle Eastern countries was almost trebled between 1938 and 1956.

A trade agreement was signed between Morocco and Norway.

January, 1958

January 14

The Organization for European Economic Cooperation recommended steps to protect Western Europe from a second Suez Canal crisis.

January 15

The Turkish delegation to the Council of Europe's meeting at Strasbourg said that the Soviet Union's aim was to quietly take over the Middle East without any spectacular action.

Morocco and Spain signed an agreement for withdrawal of the peseta from circulation in Northern Morocco, implementing the agreement of July 7, 1957.

The Soviet press carried N. A. Bulganin's messages to Prime Minister Nehru and President Nasser.

France Presse reported resumption of fighting between Spanish regular troops and Moroccan Liberation Army units in Rio de Oro.

Jordan paid Britain 133,333 pounds sterling as the first installments, due for 1956 and 1957, of an interest free loan of 1 million pounds sterling for economic development. Britain had made the loan in 1950.

January 16

President Bourguiba of Tunisia refused to receive General Buchalet, who was sent from Paris as a special envoy to deliver a message from the French Prime Minister about a Franco-Tunisian quarrel which had resulted from fighting with Algerian insurgents near the Tunisian frontier on January 11, 1958.

France withdrew special envoy General Buchalet from Tunis and French Ambassador to Tunisia, George Gorse, complaining of President Bourguiba's deliberately unfriendly attitude.

Awni Khalidi of Iraq, Secretary General of the Baghdad Pact, said that the Pact was entering a new stage of development. He stressed the value of US support.

January, 1958

January 16

Syrian Foreign Minister Salah al-Bitar arrived in Cairo for talks on Syrian-Egyptian unity.

In a campaign against sabotage and terrorism, the Lebanese Government announced the formation of a new national guard for sentry duty at important installations.

The Yemeni Legation in Beirut issued a communique announcing that British troops in Aden had resumed hostilities against the Yemen and attacked the Beidha area with planes, tanks and artillery.

Arrangements were made for the US to deliver 2,700 tons of wheat, 378 tons of processed cheese and 30 tons of powdered milk to Tunisia for about 50,000 Algerian refugees.

January 17

King Saud's adviser Abd-al-Rahman Azzam met with US Secretary of State Dulles to ask US support for the Saudi view on the Gulf of Aqaba and to ask the US to try to settle the Buraimi dispute.

Meetings of Baghdad Pact Organization Committees opened in Ankara.

Francisco Urrutia, personal representative of UN Secretary General Hammarskjold, discussed the Mount Scopus issue with Israel Prime Minister David Ben-Gurion.

Jordan requested a meeting of the UN Security Council to discuss violations of the armistice agreement in the no man's land near Jerusalem. Israel maintained that its activity in that area consisted only of tree planting.

James H. Smith, Jr., director of the ICA (International Cooperation Administration), completed a two day tour of US aid projects in Lebanon.

The British Government was to take over and enlarge the Near East Arab broadcasting station in Zyghi, on the south coast of Cyprus, for

January, 1958

January 17

official propaganda to the Middle East. The station had been the "Voice of Britain" during the Suez crisis in 1956.

An official in Baghdad said that Iraq had given Jordan ID857,000 to help Jordan overcome its financial difficulties.

The US Information Agency asked Congress for increased funds, part of which would be used to complete a radio transmitter for the Middle East that was expected to be established in Turkey.

The foreign ministers of Denmark, Norway and Sweden arranged to meet on January 29 to decide whether or not new contingents should be sent to the UN Emergency Force when the service period expired April 4.

The South African External Affairs Minister, Mr. Eric Louw, said that the African-Asian conference in Cairo demonstrated the necessity for European governments with responsibilities in Africa to meet occasionally and discuss their common interests there.

January 18

Israel and Jordan reached agreement on the Mount Scopus dispute.

Abdallah Balkhair, Saudi Arabian Director of Information, announced that King Saud would donate nearly $1 million to the rebel cause in Algeria.

Tunisian President Bourguiba reaffirmed his country's allegiance to the "free world" and the need for friendly cooperation between France and Tunisia, but still refused to accept the special envoy, French Brigadier General Buchalet.

Urrutia, personal representative of UN Secretary General Hammarskjold, reported some progress in negotiations with Israel and Jordan over the demilitarized zone of Mount Scopus. He said that the two countries agreed that the 1948 agreement providing for the demilitarization of Mount Scopus should be followed.

January, 1958

January 18

The British Ambassador to Amman informed the Jordanian Government that Great Britain would give Jordan JD1,100,000, the balance of the loan promised for development projects in the agreement signed December 20, 1956.

The Upper House of the French Council of the Republic approved with moderate amendment a bill offering increased self government to Algeria.

Premier Chou En-lai of Communist China had accepted an invitation to visit Egypt in the spring.

January 19

A 150 ton shipment of arms was seized aboard the Yugoslav ship Slovenija that was stopped off Oran, Algeria, by two French vessels. French sources said that the arms were to have gone to Casablanca where they were to be transferred to the NLF (National Liberation Front) through an intermediary. Some of the weapons were believed to have been used to destroy the electric fence in Algeria.

It was reported that the Tunisian Government would soon receive about $700,000 worth of food from the US for Algerian refugees.

The Turkish Prime Minister, Adnan Menderes, replying to a November 22 message from Russian Premier Bulganin, said there was no conflict between Turkey and Syria or any other Arab country. Turkey was anxious about foreign activities in Syria which might damage the security of Middle Eastern countries including Syria.

Israel officials said that the Mount Scopus agreement benefitted both Israel and Jordan.

An Israel military spokesman said that Syrians had repeatedly opened fire on Israel fishermen in the northeastern section of the Sea of Galilee.

January 19

All restrictions imposed on Jordanians who traveled outside the country during the crisis of April, 1956, were abolished.

President Sukarno of Indonesia arrived in Damascus.

It was reported that the US was counseling moderation to both France and Tunisia.

A government bill was being prepared for stricter control of the traffic in arms in West Germany. West Germany had been used as a center for arms shipments to the Middle East and North Africa.

The Cairo daily Al-Ahram reported that Communist China's loan to Yemen would be 70 million Swiss francs, mainly for the building of textile mills, fish packing plants and other industries.

The French Catholic Popular Republican Movement recommended that a Franco-Tunisian force be formed to patrol the Algerian frontier and prevent incidents.

January 20

Representatives of Turkey, Iran, Iraq and Pakistan signed an agreement providing for cooperation among their customs administrations and greater exchanges of information to thwart smuggling.

Yugoslavia protested to France against the seizure of the ship Slovenija, demanded the immediate release of the arms cargo and reserved the right to demand compensation for damage. The Yugoslav official news agency said that the arms had been intended for a Moroccan company in Yemen.

The Turkish Government signed an agreement with the US under which Turkey would receive about $47 million worth of surplus American food, to be paid for in liras.

January 21

The Economic Committee of the Baghdad Pact nations ended a five day conference and asked for financial assistance from the donor governments (Britain and the US) to improve transportation and communications, free movement of goods and persons and a possible free trade area.

The Majors Federation in the Algiers region urged France to defend its honor by settling its differences with Tunisia.

The French announced that it would seize any arms cargoes in Algerian waters that appeared to be headed for the rebels.

Jacques Soustelle, a former Governor General of Algeria, opening a three day debate on foreign policy in the National Assembly, said that Tunisia's belligerence in helping the Algerian insurgents was delaying peace in Algeria. He also complained that the US policy towards the Arab world was helping Communism.

Britain and Egypt decided to resume their financial talks in Rome on January 30.

The East German press accused West Germany of imperialism in the Middle East, on the basis of an assumed arms deal with Israel.

The Soviet Foreign Ministry urged that the Middle East be kept free of nuclear and missile weapons and accused the US of using the Baghdad Pact meeting to force member states to accept such weapon bases.

Anglo-Libyan talks were begun in Banghazi, Libya, for an extension of the financial agreement due for review in March.

British troops, supported by planes and artillery, fought Yemenis on the Aden frontier.

A French parliamentary delegation which was arranging to visit Israel on January 26 said that talks with military leaders would be held there.

January 22

The UN Security Council unanimously adopted an Anglo-American resolution requesting that Israel suspend tree planting in the demilitarized zone of Zebel el-Mukabber, Jerusalem. Also Jordan and Israel were requested to remove or destroy all their military installations in the zone and to prevent their forces from crossing demarcation lines.

The Israel Foreign Minister, Golda Meir, criticized the UN Secretariat for not denouncing Egypt's seizure of the Israel fishing boat Doran near Al-Arish in September.

The US State Department branded Soviet accusations of January 21 as totally false; it declared that the purpose of Secretary of State Dulles' trip to Ankara for the Baghdad Pact Ministerial Council conference was to show US sympathy and support for the security and independence of Russia's southern neighbors who were menaced by the imperialistic aggressive designs of the Soviet Union.

US Secretary of State Dulles left Washington to attend the Baghdad Pact meeting as head of the US Observer Delegation and expressed his concern for the security and economic development of the member states.

The Security Council unanimously called for tighter UN control over the no man's land between Israel and Jordan.

Turkey rejected a Syrian protest that Turkish Prime Minister Menderes in December, 1957, told the NATO summit conference that Russia had taken over Syria. Turkey said Syria had misunderstood the statement. Communist expansionist activities were not limited to any particular area but were going on everywhere. This danger had led to developments in the Middle East that were harmful to the security of the Arab countries.

A group of Iraqi Parliament deputies demanded the restoration of freedom of action for political parties and trade unions.

January 22

The French National Assembly in Algeria approved French Premier Felix Gaillard's North African policy by a vote of 334-226.

January 23

In a reply to a letter from Soviet Premier Bulganin, Israel said that it agreed with the Soviet desire for peaceful coexistence in the Middle East and said it would be aided if Moscow would urge the Arabs to conclude a peace treaty.

The Minister of State of the British Foreign Office, Ormsby-Gore, said that it was an important part of the British Government's Middle Eastern policy that the UNEF should not leave the area until its missions had been completely fulfilled.

US Secretary of State Dulles visited with Foreign Minister Ahmad Balafrej of Morocco.

The Iraqi Prime Minister, Abd-al-Wahhab Marjan, suggested that his country should send a parliamentary mission to all the Arab countries to recommend that they federate.

General Maxwell D. Taylor, US Army Chief of Staff, said that US military cooperation in the Baghdad Pact had demanded no obligations in return and that the Military Committee of the Pact would discuss the area as a whole, not specifically in relation to US aid.

Dr. John Badeau, President of the Near East Foundation, warned that a new US policy in the Middle East was necessary to prevent that area's dependence on the Soviet Union.

Dr. Fadel al-Jamali, former Premier of Iraq, said that the Baghdad Pact meeting was the acid test of US policy in the Middle East and that the US must counter Soviet policy in the area quickly and effectively.

Israel officials expressed sorrow and anger over the resolution of January 22. They said that the UN had reopened the question of ownership of land in the no man's land and that this could lead only to further disputes.

January, 1958

January 23

Yemen complained to the UN of an attack by British forces from Aden December 30.

Lebanese Prime Minister al-Solh urged the Ministry of Justice to expedite the trial of persons accused of bomb throwing and subversive activity.

The Egyptian Middle East News Agency reported from Damascus that the establishment of an Egyptian-Syrian Federation would be announced soon.

The International Bank of Reconstruction and Development, participating in the talks between Egypt and the Universal Suez Canal Company as a good officer, said that these talks would be resumed in Rome the third week of February.

The UN Security Council unanimously approved certain recommendations regarding activities in the area of Government House in Jerusalem.

January 24

Yugoslavia demanded that France restore the arms cargo seized from the Slovenija January 19 after its interception off Algeria and compensate for the damage.

The Russian trade union paper Thrud said that Iraq's alliance with the West had greatly damaged its economy and interrupted traditional ties between Iraq and the other Arab countries.

Premier Adnan Menderes of Turkey went to Baghdad. Some suggested the purpose was to convince Iraqi Premier Abd-al-Wahhab Marjan to attend the Baghdad Pact meeting.

The Syrian Council of Ministers announced that it had approved the executive steps for federal union between the republics of Egypt and Syria.

January, 1958

January 24

William Allis, a leading scientist, said at Cambridge, Massachusetts, that success in the efforts to harness nuclear power through fusion of atoms would mean that Middle Eastern oil would no longer be a possible cause of armed conflict between the Communist and Western powers.

An official spokesman said that the Iraqi Government was still opposed to the scheme for a new pipeline crossing non-Arab territory after leaving Iraq.

The Tunisian Government charged that French heavy artillery had shelled a Tunisian army post from border positions in Algeria.

It was reported that 35 persons were arrested in an attempt to assassinate the Imam Ahmad of Yemen.

It was officially stated in Paris that France would do all it could to stop any ship known to be carrying arms for the Algerian insurgents, even if the ship were in the Atlantic Ocean.

US Secretary of State Dulles visited Tehran on route to Ankara for the Baghdad Pact Council Meeting.

January 25

Syrian President Kuwatli and Egyptian President Nasser met in Cairo to arrange the date for the announcement on the union of Egypt and Syria under Nasser.

Premier Menderes of Turkey returned from Baghdad. He said that both countries reached complete agreement.

The talks with Egypt on compensation for the shareholders of the Suez Canal Company would open in Rome February 17, it was stated in Cairo.

The Yemeni Crown Prince arrived in Saudi Arabia for a two day visit.

January, 1958

January 25

The Iraqi Minister of Economy, Said al-Hardan, told the Chamber of Deputies that the laying of oil pipelines from Iraq across Turkey in order to avoid Syria was out of the question. He also said that in Iraq's interests, his Ministry was considering how to obtain greater control of the policies of the companies.

January 26

On their way to Ankara the Pakistan and Iranian Prime Ministers had talks in Baghdad with the Iraqi Prime Minister, Abd-al-Wahhab Marjan, whom Turkish Prime Minister Menderes had visited unexpectedly the previous week.

It was announced that uranium deposits were found near the southwest border of Sudan.

Israel Major General Moshe Dayan resigned as Army Chief of Staff. He was succeeded by Major General Chaim Laskov.

US Secretary of State Dulles declared on his arrival in Ankara that the US looked forward to continued association with the Baghdad Pact.

Committee meetings of the Baghdad Pact meeting ended.

The President of the Zionist Organization of America, Dr. Neumann, called the Baghdad Pact a modern version of the Maginot Line mentality.

The US informed Syria that there was no truth in reports that it intended to try to force the Baghdad Pact countries to provide missile bases.

Turkish Foreign Minister, Fatin Rustu Zorlu, said that the Baghdad Pact members were gradually moving toward the formation of a joint military command.

January, 1958

January 27

Nominations for the Sudanese House of Representatives and the Senate were completed. There were 637 nominations for the 173 seats in the House and 135 for the Senate.

Syrian Foreign Minister Salah al-Bitar completed talks in Cairo with President Nasser on an agreement to merge Syria and Egypt into a united Arab state.

The Baghdad Pact Council began a four day meeting at Ankara.

Bulgaria signed a five year cultural agreement with Syria, automatically renewable for further terms of five years.

At the fourth ministerial session in Ankara, US Secretary of State Dulles told the Baghdad Pact nations that the US would supply mobile power of great force in the event of Communist attack.

The British Minister of State for Foreign Affairs, Allan Noble, said that the Anglo-Egyptian financial talks were a first step toward a renewal of diplomatic relations.

British Minister of State for Foreign Affairs, Allan Noble, told the House of Commons that British policy in the Arab-Israel dispute was still governed by the principles of the 1950 agreement with the US and France. He also said that Britain would welcome any proposals for disarmament in the Middle East.

Malik Firoz Khan Noon, the Prime Minister of Pakistan, said that if shortage of funds forced the UN Relief and Works Agency for Palestine refugees to reduce its aid, there would be political complications in Gaza and Jordan. He added that it was essential for the UNEF to remain in Gaza until permanent peace had been established.

President Tito of Yugoslavia described the French seizure of an arms cargo from the Yugoslav freighter Slovenija off Algeria as an act of piracy. He said that the arms were meant for Yemen and not for the Algerian insurgents.

January, 1958

January 27

The Moslem nations in the Baghdad Pact meeting stressed the need for more economic aid from the donor members.

The first conference of the Arab members of UNESCO opened in Fez, Morocco, with Egypt, Iraq, Jordan, Lebanon, Libya, Morocco, Saudi Arabia, Sudan, Syria and Tunisia participating.

Under the auspices of the UNEF Egypt returned to Israel the six man crew of the fishing trawler Doran which was seized in September, 1957, and Israel turned over to Egypt six Arabs taken from a fishing vessel December 13.

Discussing the financing of the Baghdad Pact, British Foreign Secretary Selwyn Lloyd of Britain said that he could not undertake any new commitments on behalf of his Government, but that Britain would be willing to re-examine the position later.

Manoucher Eghbah, Iran, suggested that Baghdad Pact members ask the US Import-Export Bank for credits needed for economic projects. Iran was ready to put 10 million rials at the Pact's disposal for technical aid.

Moscow radio said that the US was forcing the Baghdad Pact countries on the disastrous road of atomic war preparations.

January 28

The Combined Military Planning Organization of the Baghdad Pact was changed to Combined Military Planning Staff, headed by General Ekrem Akalin of Turkey. Major General Campbell, USAF, was named his deputy. The creation of this staff was a step toward a unified pact command.

Moroccan Crown Prince Moulay Hassan left Rabat for a ten day visit with King Saud in Saudi Arabia.

The Baghdad Pact's Council of Ministers approved a military committee recommendation for a long term defense building project. It called for

January, 1958

January 28

Brigadier Mordecai Makleff, General Manager of the Israel potash works at Sodom, left for the US to discuss with the works advisers, the Ebasco Corporation, plans for a pipeline from the Dead Sea to the Mediterranean or to the Gulf of Aqaba.

Nuri-Said, Premier of Iraq, urged a speedy settlement of the Palestine problem in private discussions with the leaders of the Baghdad Pact delegations in Ankara. Pact sources said that he asked the American Secretary of State to use his influence with Israel to secure a settlement.

January 29

Egypt and the Soviet Union signed a 12 year loan accord granting money, technical assistance, materials and machinery to Egypt at two and one-half percent interest. Egypt would repay by the export of goods and by hard currency.

At the Baghdad Pact meeting US Secretary of State Dulles announced a US gift of ten million dollars toward the improvement of the joint communications project of Pakistan, Iran, Iraq and Turkey. This was in addition to $12.5 million already given by the US.

Jordanian Foreign Minister Samir al-Rifai arrived in Saudi Arabia with a special message for King Saud from King Hussein.

US Secretary of State Dulles, British Foreign Secretary Selwyn Lloyd and Iraqi Prime Minister Nuri-Said conferred at the Iraqi Embassy in Ankara. There was no comment on what was discussed.

A delegate of the International Red Cross Committee had come to handle the distribution of Egyptian aid to Algerian refugees in Morocco. One hundred tons of clothing, blankets and foodstuffs were unloaded.

It was reported in Paris that a new oil strike was made by French drillers 40 miles northwest of the proven field at Edjeleh, Algeria, in the Eastern Sahara. The daily yield was some 400 tons of crude oil.

January, 1958

January 28

communications channels from Western Turkey to Pakistan, harbor and storage facilities on the Mediterranean, Persian Gulf and Arabian Sea, and civil airports that could be converted for military purposes.

The Military Committee of the Baghdad Pact recommended that any major assault from the North be met in the mountain passes between Russia and Turkey, Iran and Iraq.

The Syrian Cabinet gave final approval to union with Egypt.

The Syrians said that an Israel unit of 25, supported by an armored car, had crossed the demilitarized zone and fired on Syrian farmers near Baniyas. The Israelis had retreated under cover of heavy fire from Dan.

The Egyptian Government announced that the oil refinery at Alexandria would be expanded and its capacity considerably increased.

Said Barka, the President of the Moroccan Consultative Assembly, said after talks with Tunisian President Bourguiba and leaders of the Algerian National Liberation Front in Tunis that France should stop being intransigent and accept the Moroccan-Tunisian offer to mediate over Algeria.

Khaled Bakdash, Secretary of the Communist Party in Syria and Lebanon, opposed dissolution of the Party during discussions of the present Syrian moves for a national union.

Sixty Turkish soldiers reportedly attacked the Syrian border village of Huban and were forced to retreat to their territory after a three hour engagement with the Syrian militia.

January, 1958

January 29

Israel had spent IL2,000 million on direct security since its founding in 1948, Finance Minister Levi Eshkol said in presenting the budget.

The Egyptian Government decided to free the sequestrated Australian property whose value was estimated at about LE200,000.

It was reported in Cairo that the Imam Ahmad of Yemen had rejected an American offer of $1 million in economic assistance because the aid mission requested permission to install four radar stations in the Yemeni mountains.

Israel submitted a strong protest to the Truce Supervision Organization against the Syrian attack of the previous day.

Syrian President Kuwatli accepted an Ilyushin 14 airliner as a gift from Soviet President Kliment Y. Voroshilov.

Conference sources in Ankara said that Iraqi Prime Minister Nuri-Said raised the question of Palestine with US Secretary of State Dulles at a private meeting. There was a heated exchange of views. Dulles had reportedly replied sharply that the question should be settled at the UN and not by the Baghdad Pact Organization.

French Foreign Minister Christian Pineau said that France could not agree to return the arms seized from the Yugoslav ship Slovenija off Algeria. He also said that it was impossible to resume negotiations with Tunisia on outstanding problems so long as arms traffic across the frontier and Tunisian complicity with the Algerian insurgents continued.

The Egyptian Foreign Ministry informed US Ambassador to Egypt Raymond Hare that Egypt opposed construction of atom and rocket bases in the Mideast.

Lebanese Premier Sami al-Solh declared that his country would not join the Baghdad Pact or any of its committees.

January 29

The British Foreign Under Secretary, Lord Gosford, replying to members of the House of Lords who urged the Government to do more for the Palestine refugees, said that the problem was one for the UN. Experience had shown that there was little possibility of persuading either side to take the problem out of politics. Britain could help only by continuing its generous contribution to relief and by urging other countries to bear their share.

Egypt presented a memorandum to the Sudan protesting the holding of elections in what Cairo considered to be Egyptian territory.

January 30

A communique issued at the close of the Baghdad Pact Conference pledged the Pact members to closer cooperation in the political, economic and military fields and in countering the threat of Soviet penetration into the Middle East.

US Secretary of State Dulles told the Baghdad Pact nations that the Eisenhower Doctrine committed the US as effectively to the Middle East as membership in the Baghdad Pact Organization.

In a letter to the President of the UN Security Council, Israel protested against a new wave of Syrian aggressions since December which were of "a planned and premeditated character."

Syrian Minister of Economy Khalil Kallas said that the proposed union of Egypt and Syria would leave Syria's economy strong and its currency stable.

The Algerian Council of the Republic adopted a reform bill that differed from that of the Assembly. A third reading of the bill in the Assembly would therefore be necessary.

Anglo-Egyptian talks were resumed in Rome after an adjournment of more than six weeks.

A report from Bonn said that the German Federal Republic would supply the Israel armed forces with war material in accordance with Israel's compact with Adenaur and the so-called reparations agreement.

January 30

The Egyptian Embassy in Bonn informed the West German press that Egypt had rejected East German advances seeking diplomatic recognition.

Yemen had requested Britain to withdraw its Charge d'Affaires, it was officially stated in London.

French Minister for Algeria Robert Lacoste was reported to have informed the French Cabinet that 6,000 Algerian insurgents were in Tunisia near the frontier, forming a permenent threat. The insurgents reportedly had been abundantly armed by Communist countries.

Iraqi Prime Minister Nuri-Said told reporters after he left the Baghdad Pact meeting that he had been able to discuss Arab problems with the other heads of delegations and that they were in complete agreement on almost every issue.

January 31

The Algerian reform bill of the "framework law" passed the National Assembly on the third reading by a vote of 296-244. It established regional autonomy, voting equality between Moslems and non-Moslems and maintained full French sovereignty. It would be implemented by about fifty decrees. The French Minister for Algeria, Robert Lacoste, said that he expected to divide Algeria into five regions each with its own freely elected assembly and local government.

Ali Amini, Iranian Ambassador to the US, urged the pooling of oil income in the Middle East to combat poverty.

President Kuwatli of Syria arrived in Cairo to confer with President Nasser.

Sweden would send an additional 500 men to the UNEF in the Gaza Strip when the service period of the contingent expired in April, it was announced in Stockholm. According to the Swedish press, Colonel Carlson Von Horn, head of the Malmo defense area, was being nominated to succeed Major General E. L. M. Burns, Commander

January 31

of UNEF, as Chief of Staff of the UN Truce Supervisory Organization in Palestine. Colonel Leary, Acting Chief of Staff, was due to retire soon.

Yugoslavia said that it would take further measures if France refused to return the arms cargo seized from the Slovenija off Algeria.

Japanese delegates completing 15 days of talks with Egyptian officials said that President Nasser had asked Japan to help Egypt to carry out 50 to 60 industrial projects.

February 1

Egypt and Syria announced the merger of the two countries into the United Arab Republic. The new state was to be subject to a plebiscite to be held within 30 days.

Presidents Nasser and Kuwatli said that the union of Egypt and Syria was the first step toward the federation of all Arab states.

Egypt sent a note to Sudan disputing its right to include in its election constituencies frontier areas bordering the Red Sea in Kassala Province and a small enclave along the Nile north of Wadi Halfa.

King Hussein of Jordan was said to have proposed to King Faisal of Iraq and King Saud of Saudi Arabia a discussion of ways and means to achieve Arab unity among the three countries.

France and Morocco agreed on the creation of a special compensation fund to keep down prices on essential imports. They agreed on the transfer of the Moroccan Bureau of Currency Exchange from Paris to Rabat. Morocco was also to remain in the franc zone while pursuing an independent financial policy.

A Spanish communique said that Spanish troops attacked Moroccan irregulars in the eastern zone of Ifni.

Italian Foreign Ministry sources disclosed that their Ambassador to Turkey had talked with the US delegation there about pooling Western aid to the Middle East.

US Secretary of State Dulles, on his return from Ankara, said that excessive military efforts from the five Baghdad Pact members and the US could create economic and social conditions that would facilitate Communist subversion in the Baghdad Pact countries. He stressed the emphasis on economic and social development and the Pact's solidarity.

Mayor Jacques Chevallier of Algiers urged speedy implementation of the reform bill and the section of Moslem leaders to assume positions of leadership in the interim.

February, 1958

February 2

It was announced that the Imam Ahmad of Yemen had sent a message to President Nasser and Kuwatli requesting to join the new United Arab Republic.

Thirty-seven went on trial in Nablus, Jordan, on charges of attempting to overthrow the Government.

The Israel Cabinet discussed the merger of Syria and Egypt and reportedly thought it brought no immediate danger.

Dr. Fadel al-Jamali, former Premier of Iraq, said that the Syrian-Egyptian union was unnatural because the two countries lacked geographical contact, complimentary economic interests and the possibility of mutual support for defense.

More than 100,000 Syrians paraded in Damascus to hail the merger of Syria and Egypt.

Menahem Morgalioth, a senior official of the Israel Government, said that his Government was slightly worried that the aim of the UAR was continued warmongering and renewal of aggressive action.

Jean Raymond-Laurent, Deputy Chairman of the French Council of the Republic, who was a member of a parliamentary mission visiting Israel, urged Israel's admission to NATO and the European Community.

The Yemeni Government reportedly uncovered an "imperialist plot" against King Ahmad and Crown Prince al-Badr.

February 3

President Nasser made known the decision to dissolve all Syrian political parties and to set up a National Union in Syria to realize the same objectives as those of the National Union of Egypt.

Tatsunorsuke Twkasaki, leader of the Japanese industrial mission to Egypt, said that the Egyptian Government was willing to authorize

February, 1958

February 3

Japanese cooperation in developing oil resources in the Sinai. The mission also offered to build a shipyard in Egypt for vessels under 5,000 tons.

The Algerian National Movement and the NLF (National Liberation Front) rejected the French reform plan.

Jamil Makkawi, Finance Minister of Lebanon, resigned after the budget was decreed. Farid Quzma, Minister of Education and Information, was appointed to the post.

Syria denied charges by Israel that Syrian attacks were made along the border on January 28.

Hassan Abbas Zaki returned to Cairo from the Anglo-Egyptian talks in Rome with a British draft agreement which included the problem of the machinery to be set up for the valuing of compensation claims for sequestrated and nationalized British property in Egypt.

Sudanese Foreign Minister Muhammad Ahmad Mahgoub declared that the Sudan would not permit any foreign country to set up rocket or other bases on its territory.

Egyptians at the UN said that they believed that the constitution of the United Arab Republic would enable Egypt and Syria to continue their separate membership in the UN.

February 4

Diplomatic missions in Damascus were officially informed of the union of Egypt and Syria (UAR).

A Jordanian military court sentenced 41 Communists to life imprisonment for plotting to overthrow the regime and spying for Syria.

Syria complained to the UN Security Council that Israel troops and armored cars supported by jet aircraft had penetrated the demilitarized zone between Israel and Syria.

February, 1958

February 5

Syrian President Shukri Kuwatli formally announced Syria's union with Egypt. He nominated President Nasser to head the United Arab Republic. The Egyptian National Assembly also nominated Nasser, who was the only candidate for President of the UAR.

In simultaneous actions the Parliaments of Syria and Egypt unanimously approved the 17 point provisional constitution for the UAR as outlined by Nasser.

US Senator Mike Mansfield (Democrat) recommended US intervention in the Algerian conflict and proposed a North African confederation.

Robert Lacoste, French Minister for Algeria, outlined initial plans for political reforms in a closed door session with the Inspectors General of Algiers, Oran and Constantine and nine territorial Prefects.

King Muhammad V of Morocco said that an early peaceful solution of the Algerian revolt would reinforce Moroccan-French relations and strengthen the French position in Africa.

The Algerian rebels accused the French of imposing the death sentence on captured Algerians in violation of the Geneva Convention on guerrilla warfare.

Yemeni Crown Prince Muhammad al-Badr arrived in Cairo to discuss Yemen's joining the United Arab Republic. He said that Yemen wanted complete unification in defense, economy, foreign affairs and education.

Khaled Bakdash, leader of the Syria Communist Party, left for Moscow after making a statement on the party's future which conflicted with Nasser's statement of February 3.

President Celal Bayar of Turkey arrived in Tripoli, Libya, for a five day state visit.

The Iraqi Minister of Economy told Parliament that uranium and phosphate were discovered in the western desert of Iraq.

February, 1958

February 5

The Arabia Oil Company was formed by the Japan Petroleum Trading Company to explore offshore oil fields in the Neutral Zone.

Britain made strong protests to Yemen and took counter-action against new border attacks, it was stated in the House of Commons.

The Iraqi Minister of Economy, Sayyed al-Hardan, said that repairs to the IPC (Iraqi Petroleum Company) pumping stations which the Syrian Army sabotaged were being delayed by obstacles created by Syria.

February 6

Students in Rabat, Morocco, demonstrated in front of the French Embassy in protest against the dissolution of the General Union of Algerian Moslem Students.

Ethiopia announced that it would call a conference of all the countries of the Nile valley.

Tunisian President Bourguiba declared in a broadcast to the US and France that if the Algerian war continued and if the Algerian people despaired of the West and let themselves slide downhill by depending on Russia for arms and economic support, there would be a strong chance that all North African countries would follow.

Premier Abd-al-Wahhab Marjan of Iraq told his Parliament that he wished the Egyptian-Syrian merger success, although it had been expected that Iraq's opinion and that of other sister Arab states would have been sought on the union.

February 7

King Saud of Saudi Arabia and Moroccan Crown Prince Moulay Hassan issued a joint communique regarding the signing of a treaty of friendship, alliance and large scale cooperation.

February, 1958

February 7

The Saudi Arabian Ministry of Commerce announced a Royal Order prohibiting the importation of merchandise carried by airlines or shipping companies dealing with Israel.

It was announced that the Algerian rebel leaders were to meet in Cairo rather than Tunis. President Bourguiba of Tunisia regarded this change as a tendency to draw away from the Western World.

A plan to eliminate reciprocal passports for Tunisia and Morocco was under consideration.

Yugoslavia's President Tito sent his congratulations on the formation of the UAR.

About 20 British Army officers were to be seconded for service with the forces of the Sultan of Muscat and Oman.

February 8

The Tunisian Government ordered the French forces to remain in their camps and said an appeal would be made to the UN. The Government also demanded the withdrawal of all French troops from Tunisia.

French aircraft from Algeria bombed the Tunisian village of Sakiet Sidi Youssef near the Algerian border, charging that it was an Algerian rebel base.

Crown Prince Hassan of Morocco said in Paris that Morocco would not join the UAR.

The Yemeni Legation in Cairo made public a telegram reporting British air and land attacks on the towns of Horib and Abu Deif, Yemen.

Syria accused Israel of opening fire on villagers in Kifrhareb, in the southern demilitarized zone.

February, 1958

February 9

US relief to 2,000 flood victims in eastern Algeria began arriving in Constantine, Algeria.

It was reported from Cairo that Saudi Arabia was negotiating with the UAR for possible federation.

King Faisal of Iraq postponed his meeting with King Hussein of Jordan on the latter's proposal for a union of Arab monarchies.

Major General Dayan, formerly Israel Chief of Staff, said that European countries which hitherto refused to sell arms to Israel were now ready to do so as they realized that it was better to have a strong Israel than a war in the Middle East.

February 10

At the end of Turkish President Celal Bayar's visit, it was announced that Libya and Turkey agreed to work together to promote peace in the Middle East. A cultural agreement was also signed.

The Tunisian Constituent Assembly recessed so that its members could return to their constituencies.

Diplomatic representatives of 15 countries visited the site of the bombing in Tunisia to ascertain for their governments the extent of the damage.

The assistant chief of ICA (International Cooperation Administration) in Tunisia offered all the aid necessary in food, clothing and supplies to the survivors of the Sakiet Sidi Youssef bombing.

Official sources in Amman, Jordan, predicted a union of Iraq and Jordan.

Vice President Kuwatli of the UAR advised the heads of all Arab states to join the UAR.

February, 1958

February 8

Egyptian President Nasser and Yemeni Crown Prince al-Badr discussed Yemen's possible entry into the UAR. Reports declared that Yemen was interested in Egyptian military aid.

The Egyptian Education Minister, Major Kamal-ad-Din Hussein, advised all Arabs along the Mediterranean from Morocco to Syria to unite under one Government.

Iraqi King Faisal was to meet King Hussein in Jordan February 9 to discuss the possibility of their countries uniting.

February 9

Tunisia protested to the UN against the bombing of Sakiet Sidi Youssef and denied that the attack followed the destruction of a reconnaissance plane.

Lieutenant General Raoul Salan, French Commander in Algeria, said that 80 percent of Sakiet Sidi Youssef was intact. He claimed that only military objectives were hit.

Libya and Turkey signed an agreement on cultural cooperation and rights of domicile.

French military bases in Tunisia were blockaded by Tunisian military forces.

US Secretary of State Dulles called the Tunisian Ambassador for talks on the French bombing of Sakiet Sidi Youssef. The US State Department was reportedly disturbed and embarrassed over the incident because the French used US planes in the attack.

President Kuwatli of Syria invited Lebanon to join the UAR with the right to maintain its own integrity and special position.

A $23 million contract for the reconstruction of port facilities in Kuwait was awarded to two US companies.

February, 1958

February 10

President Chamoun of Lebanon said that he did not want leaders of the other Arab countries to meddle in the internal affairs of Lebanon.

Saeb Salam, former Lebanese Premier and leader of the Opposition, was reported to have been told by Nasser that he would not interfere in Lebanese affairs, but that Lebanon should join the UAR to protect its independence.

President Eisenhower pledged continued collaboration with Lebanon in promiting the principles of independence and human dignity.

The Moroccan Government recalled Crown Prince Hassan and Foreign Minister Ahmad Balafrej from a private visit to Paris because of the French bombing of the Tunisian village Sakeit Sidi Youssef.

French forces in northern Mauritania were in a state of alert following two clashes with Moroccan irregulars in the past two weeks.

The Egyptian National Assembly approved the agreement with the Soviet Union to provide $175 million in credits.

The Tunisian Ambassador to France, Muhammad Masmoudi, said before leaving Paris for Tunis that he would strive to renew Franco-Tunisian friendship.

The Tunisian Ambassador to Washington and the UN, Mongi Slim, appealed to the US to take action in the French air attack.

The Tunisian Government demanded that all French forces leave Tunisia. To be sure of receiving compensation for the attack on Sakiet Sidi Youssef, the Government seized the farms of 15 French families, and recalled its Ambassador from Paris.

February 11

It was officially announced in Cairo that an agreement on Yemen's federation with Egypt and Syria would be signed after the February 21 plebiscite on the UAR.

February, 1958

February 11

US Secretary of State Dulles said that the US role in Tunisia would be that of a benevolent but neutral peacemaker.

Italy urged France to settle the Tunisian dispute by private talks before the UN took it up.

Official sources in Amman, Jordan, said that King Saud of Saudi Arabia would not join any federation of Arab states.

Kings Faisal and Hussein began talks in Amman on a union of Iraq and Jordan.

The Sudanese Premier asked for an explanation from the Egyptian Ambassador of the memorandum from Cairo concerning the territories north of the 22nd parallel.

Syria charged that a force of 50 Israel soldiers and two armored vehicles penetrated the demilitarized zone. Israel denied the charges.

US Secretary of State Dulles said that there were suggestions for stationing joint Franco-Tunisian patrols and UN observers on the Tunisian-Algerian frontier.

The Shah of Iran said that if his country had not joined the Baghdad Pact its defense expenditure would have increased sevenfold.

The Tunisian Government banned French warships from entering the base at Bizerta and said that if the ships tried to force their way in they would be fired at. The Government requested France to close four of its seven Consultates General in Tunisia.

Norway announced that it proposed to ask NATO to consider tne Franco-Tunisian situation because of concern about the effect of the Sakiet raid on relations between the western powers and the uncommitted countries.

The French Ambassador to the US, Herve Alphand, said that France was considering whether or not to pay compensation for civilian losses in the Sakiet raid.

February, 1958

February 12

The British Government said that it had recalled its Charge d'Affaires in Yemen at the request of the Yemeni Government.

Among others, former Syrian President Adib Shishakli and Colonel Husseini, former Military Attache in Rome, received life sentences for plotting against the Syrian Government.

It was reported that the US State Department was debating the possibility that the Baghdad Pact would be dissolved as a consequence of the Arab Federation.

Tunisia announced plans to build a new village of Sakiet Sidi Youssef near the ruins of the old as a symbol of the Algerian war and colonialist atrocities. The major of Tunis said that very few of the raid victims were Algerians; they were not rebels but refugee women, children, and old men.

Three Algerian NLF leaders, Dagin, Yahya and Abbas, met in Cairo.

British Minister of State for Foreign Affairs, Commander Allan Noble, said that Britain had been consulting with the US and France to determine the status of the 1950 Tripartite Agreement in regard to the UAR.

King Muhammad V and members of the Moroccan Government visited the frontier zone bordering Algeria to preside over the distribution of 187 lots of land to needy persons.

A basic law unanimously adopted by the Israel Knesset defined the status of the Knesset, its term of office, the procedure by which its members were to be elected, the right to vote and be elected, the procedure of its opening and dissolution, and immunity of its members and buildings.

February, 1958

February 12

The US said that it was prepared to assist in any way possible to reach a solution of the Franco-Tunisian dispute.

In a report to the NATO Council, France said that the Sakiet raid was an initiative of local commanders under a general authorization to strike back in self defense at rebels using Tunisia as a sanctuary.

The French National Assembly by a vote of 335-179 endorsed the Government statement that the raid on the Tunisian village was a legitimate action of self defense.

Tunisian Ambassador to the US Mongi Slim conferred with UN diplomats and said that Tunisia would submit the question of the village of Sakiet to the Security Council.

Tunisian President Bourguiba formally demanded the withdrawal of French troops from Tunisia as a condition of restoring friendship with France.

February 13

Crown Prince Abd al-Ilah of Iraq arrived in Amman, Jordan, to join the federation discussions. A draft document on federation was completed between Iraq and Jordan.

The Japanese Ministry of Trade confirmed that Saudi Arabia had requested arms and military equipment. It was reported that Japan had agreed in principle to supply $50 million worth of arms to Saudi Arabia.

The Aden Legislative Council approved a 4,283,165 pound sterling budget.

Tunisia submitted a formal request for a meeting of the UN Security Council, to consider the French act of aggression on Sakiet Sidi Youssef. It would regard itself in a state of legitimate self defense if France violated new restrictions on the movement of forces into Tunisia.

February, 1958

February 13

President Bourguiba of Tunisia said that if France would accept mediation by the US, so would his country. In this event Tunisia would withdraw its request from the Security Council.

French Foreign Minister Christian Pineau, in a report to the National Assembly, said that France could not attempt to restore normal relations with Tunisia as long as French troops were restricted to their camps and civilians were being harassed.

A Syrian Army spokesman said that a Western backed plot to prevent the merger of Egypt and Syria had been uncovered and arrests made.

The US provided $75,000 worth of help for the Sakiet victims in Tunisia.

The Moroccan Foreign Ministry protested against Spanish planes flying over southern Moroccan territory.

Morocco protested to the US that US equipment might have been used by Spanish troops defending the Ifni enclave against Moroccan irregulars.

The World Federation of Trade Unions decided to send Tunisian trade unions 1,000 pounds sterling from its solidarity fund for distribution among the working people of Sakiet Sidi Youssef and their families, who lost their homes and jobs as a result of the French air raid.

The Tunisian Government ordered the French Consulates General at Medjez al-Bab, Le Kef and Gafsa to close down after the Charge d'Affaires had insisted on their remaining open because he regarded the order to close as a violation of the Franco-Tunisian Consular Agreement.

February 14

King Faisal of Iraq and King Hussein of Jordan announced the formation of the Arab Federation, a union of the two countries with Faisal

February 14

as Head of the federal union, King Hussein as his Deputy, and a Cabinet to be composed equally of Iraqis and Jordanians. Each monarch retained sovereignty in his own country. The question of Iraq's membership in the Baghdad Pact was settled by an agreement that treaties signed before the union were binding only on the signatory party.

King Hussein of Jordan pledged to restore Arab rights taken by Israel in the Palestine war.

President Nasser sent a message of congratulations to Iraq's King Faisal on the merger of Iraq and Jordan.

The US endorsed the Iraq-Jordan union.

Both Great Britain and France said that the new merger of Iraq and Jordan would add stability to the Middle East.

Radio Moscow said that Jordan had come under the control of Iraq and therefore under the Baghdad Pact.

It was announced that plans were to be drawn up for a university in Baghdad.

Fears were expressed in Tel Aviv that Israel might be faced with Iraqi troops on its border with Jordan instead of with only the weaker Jordanian forces.

Israel informed the UN Security Council that mine clearing operations in the demilitarized zone between Israel and Syria were completed February 10.

Lebanese Premier al-Solh denied Syrian charges that armed agitators had moved into Syria from Lebanon in a plot against the UAR.

It was confirmed that all nine members of the Algerian National Liberation Front's Coordination and Executive Committee were in Cairo to attend a council of war meeting.

The Tunisian National Assembly passed a law abrogating the extraterritorial status of the harbor of Bizerta.

February 14

France filed a counter complaint with the Security Council charging that Tunisia had permitted Algerian rebels to operate from Tunisian territory.

The US said that neither France nor Tunisia had requested that the US mediate their dispute.

Reporting to the Foreign Affairs Committee of the French National Assembly, Foreign Minister Pineau said that neither he nor Premier Gaillard nor Minister for Algeria Lacoste had been informed in advance of the Sakiet bombing.

French sources in Tunis reported that Tunisia sent a note rejecting French proposals for talks on outstanding problems.

February 15

A French Government spokesman said that France would accept the good offices of the US, but not arbitration, to settle the Tunisian dispute.

Tunisian President Bourguiba said that the French should withdraw their troops and immediately begin to concentrate all forces at Bizerta and Sfax. After this was accomplished, Tunisia would be prepared to negotiate an arrangement by which Bizerta would be converted into a NATO base.

Moshe Sharett, former Israel Prime Minister, said that Israel must be strong enough to defeat any possible pincer attack by the UAR.

Morocco protested to France against frequent and massive movements of French troops in the Agadir area of southern Morocco.

The Sudanese Prime Minister, Abdallah Khalil, said that the existence of two opposing Arab unions was liable to weaken the efforts of the Arab League.

Tunisian President Bourguiba instructed Ambassador to the US, Mongi Slim, to lodge a complaint with the UN Security Council that the Algerian war was a threat to North African peace.

February 15

The US State Department drafted a good offices offer. It was learned that Great Britain had already submitted such a proposal, hoping to avert a UN Security Council debate on the Sakiet Sidi Youssef bombing.

The Soviet Ambassador in Paris called on the French Foreign Minister and informed him that Moscow was seriously disturbed by the French air raid on Tunisia, an independent state and a UN member.

February 16

At the United Nations' request the Tunisian Government authorized local supplies of food to be given to French forces blockaded in their camps in Tunisia.

The Crown Prince of Yemen, Muhammad al-Badr, returned from Cairo to Taizz for the Imam's signature to Yemen's federation with Egypt and Syria in the UAR. He said that the Imam was eager for complete Arab unity.

The territorial waters of Saudi Arabia were extended to 12 nautical miles from the inland waters.

Syrian Foreign Minister Salah al-Bitar indicated that the UAR would not attempt to retain two seats in the UN General Assembly.

February 17

The Parliament of Iraq unanimously ratified the Arab Federation agreement between King Faisal and King Hussein of Jordan uniting their two countries.

Sudanese Foreign Minister Muhammad Ahmad Mahgoub declared that the UAR had laid claim to Sudanese territory north of the 22nd parallel before February 21 in return for which it had offered the Sudan a small piece of land south of the 22nd parallel. He said that the UAR troops were moving into the area. The UAR denied the troop movement into the Sudan.

February 17

Algerian authorities said that it was difficult to find responsible Moslems to fill political positions in the interim before elections.

King Muhammad V of Morocco proclaimed the economic and monetary unity of Morocco.

Westinghouse Electric International Company announced plans to build the world's largest seawater evaporator in Kuwait.

Syrian Prime Minister Kuwatli said that he had no doubts that the federation of Iraq and Jordan was against the true wishes of the Arabs for a free union and was therefore "doomed to failure."

US Ambassador to the UAR Raymond Hare conferred with President Nasser.

Turkish Prime Minister Menderes said, after a meeting with the Iraqi Ambassador, that Iraq would not withdraw from the Baghdad Pact.

France and Tunisia accepted the good offices offers of the US and Britain to resolve the Tunisian-French dispute.

Tunisia asked the UN Security Council to consider the Algerian war and the overflow of the Algerian war into its territory.

French troops killed 1,040 insurgents and captured 156 and large amounts of war material in the fighting in Algeria the week of February 8-15.

The m/v Frolovo arrived in Tunis with a cargo of food, clothes, and medicines donated by the Soviet Red Cross to Algerian refugees.

February 18

The UAR sent an ultimatum to the Sudan demanding the immediate withdrawal of troops from the village of Halaib, a village claimed by both Egypt and Syria. The Sudanese Foreign Minister, Mahgoub, left

February, 1958

February 18

Khartoum for Cairo to discuss this matter with Nasser. Sudan refused to withdraw troops from Halaib and asked the UAR to accept negotiation.

The UN Security Council postponed debate on the French-Tunisian issue pending US-British action to mediate the dispute.

France proposed the formation of a French-Tunisian commission under neutral chairmanship to control the frontier. Other subjects proposed were action to relieve pressure on French military personnel in Tunisia, the formation of a no man's land on the Algerian side of the border and the re-establishment of the bilateral negotiations that had been broken off in January.

President Bourguiba of Tunisia said that the settlement of the Algerian war must await pressure by the US and other Western nations to change the French position.

The Jordanian Parliament unanimously approved the federation agreement with Iraq.

The Lebanese Foreign Ministry said that Lebanon intended to cooperate with both unions without joining either.

It was reported in Amman, Jordan, that a military court in Ramallah sentenced 14 persons to 16 year prison terms for membership in the outlawed Communist Party.

Tunisian President Bourguiba wrote to King Muhammad V of Morocco to ask him to take measures to support Tunisia's national aims within the framework of the friendship treaty between the two countries.

The French Government instructed five Consulates, which the Tunisian Government had ordered to close, to remain open, although the Tunisian Government had withdrawn its recognition of them.

Pierre Gilbert, French Ambassador to Israel, promised French support for Israel in the face of recent Arab unity moves.

February, 1958

February 19

French Conservative Party leaders threatened to withdraw their three ministers from the Tunisian Government if the Prime Minister failed to say unequivocally that the Bizerta naval base would remain French.

Yugoslavia said that France's lack of good will over the seizure of arms from the merchant ship Slovenija off Algeria on January 18 was forcing Yugoslavia to consider measures to protect its interests.

Hugh Gaitskell, leader of the Opposition, said in the British House of Commons that the proposed summit conference with Russia should discuss not only renunciation of force in the Middle East for peace and security, but a guarantee of the existing frontiers between Israel and the Arab countries, an arms embargo and an economic development plan for the Middle East. He would also like a contribution from the oil revenues of Arab Governments and of the oil companies to a fund for the whole Middle East.

Tunisia's demand for the withdrawal of the French troops reportedly raised important problems of NATO strategy.

The US State Department appointed Deputy Under Secretary Robert Murphy to negotiate with France and Tunisia on their border dispute.

France decided to set up a no man's land about 200 miles long and 15 miles wide on the Algerian-Tunisian border. Seventy thousand people were to be forcibly moved from the area.

It was reported in Rabat that Spanish planes bombed Tabelkorekt, the northern part of the Ifni enclave and then dropped about 500 paratroopers.

UN Secretary General Hammarskjold said that the good offices of the US and Britain might lead to at least a partial solution of the issues between France and Tunisia.

February 20

Tunisia warned the US and Britain that its crisis with France was worsening.

February, 1958

February 18

Egyptian propaganda outlets were said to be launching an offensive against the Baghdad Pact on the basis of the federation of Iraq and Jordan. They claimed that the Arab Federation could not work unless Iraq withdrew from the Pact.

Syria gave foreign embassies and legations two months to terminate their functions after the merger of the UAR was ratified.

Indian Prime Minister Nehru said that he welcomed the UAR because it was obviously what the people of Syria and Egypt wanted.

February 19

Negotiations between the shareholders in the Universal Suez Canal Company and the UAR began in Rome. Abd-al-Galil al-Imari headed the UAR delegation.

Negotiations between the UAR and Sudan over control of the disputed border area were suspended after UAR President Nasser conferred with Sudanese Foreign Minister Mahgoub.

It was reported that Israel had opened an all-Arabic radio station reaching all parts of the Arab World.

Moroccan Foreign Minister Ahmad Balafrej accused France and Spain of waging concerted combat against the Moroccans in Ifni and the Moroccan Sahara.

King Muhammad V emphasized that Spain had not yet restored its Saharan protectorate to Moroccan control as had been agreed in 1956.

The Moroccan Liberation Army accused France and Spain of organizing a bilateral plot in the Sahara to consolidate their colonial possessions.

The Spanish Foreign Ministry was said to have ordered a blackout of all news of military operations during talks with Morocco about Ifni.

February, 1958

French Foreign Minister Christian Pineau told the Council of the Republic that the good offices of the US and Britain were concerned with the normal movement of their troops in Tunisia, the security of the Algerian-Tunisian border and eventual resumption of Franco-Tunisian talks to the exclusion of third parties instead of mediation.

The Tunisian Government closed the French consultates at Medjez al-Bab, Souk al-Arba, Gabes, Gafsa and Le Kef.

The federal union of Jordan and Iraq did not mean the end of US economic aid to Jordan, Sayyed Hazza al-Majali, Deputy Chairman of the Development Board, said.

The Sudanese Government, in a note to UN Secretary General Hammarskjold, asked for a meeting of the Security Council to stop Egyptian aggression in the Sudan.

The efforts of Abd-al-Khaleq Hassouna, Secretary General of the Arab League, as arbitrator in the Sudanese-Egyptiam dispute, failed.

Talks in Cairo between Egypt and the Sudan were suspended.

Iraqi Finance Minister Nadim al-Pachachi resigned after making a speech on oil policy in the House of Notables.

British planes reportedly again raided the Yemeni towns of Shuqueir and Harib.

Israel was the first country in the Middle East to produce liquid hydrogen and liquid helium.

The Italian press was split in its reactions to the announcement of President Nasser's visit. The Foreign Ministry said that the visit would be helpful not only to Italy, but to all Western countries.

Egypt rejected a Sudanese proposal that its plebiscite officers should be withdrawn from the disputed area north of the 22nd parallel and that Sudanese elections should be held there without prejudice to its claims.

The French Government decided to set up a 50 kilometer wide restricted zone along the Tunisian border in Algeria. This zone would cause forcible removal of 70,000 people from the area.

February, 1958

February 21

A plebiscite took place in Syria and Egypt to approve the merger and the election of Nasser as President of the UAR. Approval was voted by 99.99 percent in Egypt and 99.98 percent in Syria.

The Sudan formally asked for a meeting of the Arab League to consider its border dispute with Egypt.

It was officially announced in Beirut that armed persons had crossed the Syrian border and attacked Lebanese security forces in North Lebanon.

US Deputy Under Secretary of State Robert Murphy in Tunisia left for London for talks with his British opposite number, Beeley, Prime Minister Macmillan and Foreign Secretary Selwyn Lloyd. He would then proceed to Paris.

The French Embassy in Tunis delivered a note to the Tunisian Government protesting against the closing of the consulates.

The Tunisian Ambassador to the US, Mongi Slim, said that the US should take the same stand against France in the Tunisian dispute as it had maintained in the Suez crisis.

Harold Beeley, Foreign Office Assistant Under Secretary, was given charge of the British good offices in the dispute between Tunisia and France.

French Minister for Algeria Lacoste said that African-Asian countries had greatly increased their aid to the insurgents since the Cairo conference.

British exports to the Middle East were worth 190 million pounds sterling in 1957, compared with 176 million pounds sterling in 1956 and 162 million pounds sterling in 1955.

Negotiations for the settlement of claims from the nationalization of the Suez Canal were suspended. They would be resumed in Cairo.

February, 1958

February 21

The Moroccan Government expelled the Spanish Vice Consul at Agadir. It was said that he was linked with Spanish intelligence agents in Ifni.

The UN Security Council shelved the Sudan-Egypt issue without either introducing a resolution or taking a formal vote. Settlements would begin after a new Sudanese government took office.

Omar Loutfi, the Egyptian Delegate to the UN, said that Egypt would postpone the frontier question until after the Sudanese elections.

Egypt did not attempt to carry out the plebiscite in the disputed Egyptian-Sudanese territory.

The Sudanese Prime Minister protested to Egypt that it had told its people about the postponement of discussions on the frontier question but had ignored the Government of Sudan.

February 22

Saudi Arabia and Bahrain signed an agreement on offshore boundaries.

The United Arab Republic was formed as a union of Syria and Egypt.

President Nasser named Lieutenant General Amer Commander in Chief of the UAR Army, with the rank of Field Marshal.

King Muhammad V of Morocco sent his congratulations to President Nasser on the merger of Egypt and Syria in the UAR. He also congratulated King Faisal on the merger of Iraq and Jordan.

Saudi Arabia and Egypt signed a trade agreement regarding the reduction of duties and the Egyptian import of Saudi oil.

The talks between Egypt and the Suez Canal Company in Rome were postponed until March 31, apparently to give each side time to consider the other's views.

February, 1958

February 22

Emperor Haile Selassie of Ethiopia revealed that he had personally intervened in an effort to settle the Egyptian-Sudanese dispute. He urged the two Governments not to take any action until after the Sudanese elections.

France protested to the UN against the closing of its consular offices in Tunisia.

The French Government reiterated its insistence that British-US good offices could not be extended to the Algerian issue.

The Soviet Union recognized the UAR.

Tunisian President Bourguiba said that he would not consider France's proposal that French and Tunisian troops with troops of a third country control the Algerian-Tunisian frontier.

A Jordanian Army spokesman said that Israel and Jordanian troops exchanged fire in the area of Latrun after Israel troops penetrated into no man's land and opened fire on the Jordanians.

February 23

The Soviet Union sent congratulations on the formation of the UAR. Several other countries sent their Ambassadors to present their credentials to the UAR.

King Saud of Saudi Arabia sent identical congratulatory messages to the UAR and the Arab Federation.

King Saud of Saudi Arabia offered to assist in the peaceful solution of the Egyptian-Sudanese dispute.

It was reported that Algerian rebels were moving into Tunisia in sizable numbers.

US Deputy Under Secretary of State Robert Murphy conferred with British Prime Minister Macmillan and Tunisian Ambassador to London Tayeb Slim.

February, 1958

February 23

About 250 French liberals and non-Communist leftists met in Orleans to ask the Government to negotiate with the Algerians for independence.

The Iranian Prime Minister, Dr. Manushar Eghbal, told the Majlis that there was no official confirmation of press reports that Saudi Arabia, Kuwait and Bahrain were to form a federation of their own.

The Sudanese Prime Minister, Abdallah Khalil, said that a company of Egyptian troops had been seen in a distant part of the frontier area claimed by both Egypt and the Sudan.

February 24

An Israel official said that the merger of the Arab states was not considered an immediate danger to Israel.

Israel Foreign Minister Golda Meir said that she regretted that the new Arab states still maintained hostility toward Israel.

US Deputy Under Secretary of State Robert Murphy conferred with French Premier Gaillard and Foreign Minister Pineau.

Cairo reported recognition of the UAR by Afghanistan, Albania, Belgium, Bulgaria, Ceylon, Communist China, Czechoslovakia, Denmark, Greece, Hungary, Indonesia, Italy, Japan, Norway, Poland, Rumania, Spain, Sweden, Switzerland, Tunisia, the USSR, the Vatican, West Germany and Yugoslavia.

Military sources said that French and Spanish troops had rounded up all Moroccan irregulars in the Spanish Sahara in two large pockets.

Prime Minister Khalil of the Sudan accused Egypt of interference in the forthcoming Sudanese elections in cooperation with the Communists. It was reported that the Sudan had asked the UN Security Council to reconvene to discuss the border question between Egypt and the Sudan.

February 24

Forty members of the Iraqi Parliament arrived in Amman, Jordan.

Egypt officially informed the Sudan that it would not now press its claim to territory north of the 22nd parallel.

February 25

President Nasser, in a speech in Damascus, accused imperialists of trying to undermine Arab unity by spreading false reports about the Egyptian-Sudanese dispute. He said that the UAR would maintain solidarity with the Sudan against imperialism, asserting that the UAR would never "carry arms" against an Arab State.

French Foreign Minister Pineau told the Council of the Republic that he had warned the US of errors in its Middle East policy in 1956, concerning dangers of the Baghdad Pact, when the US stopped the Suez invasion and when the Eisenhower Doctrine was declared.

King Muhammad V proclaimed Morocco's determination to recover the Sahara.

French authorities seized a case of arms destined for Morocco aboard the Italian vessel Maria Luisa in the harbor of Bone, Algeria.

Tunisian President Bourguiba told US Deputy Under Secretary of State Robert Murphy that one of the fundamental issues to be discussed by the US and Britain would be the Algerian war.

Krim Belkacem and Mahmoud Sharif of the NLF arrived in Tunis as guests of President Bourguiba.

The US extended recognition to the UAR.

The UAR had reportedly asked Japan for a loan of nearly 18 million pounds sterling toward the $180 million worth of foreign aid needed for the industrialization plan in Egypt.

The Jordanian and Iraqi Ministers of Foreign Affairs arrived in Riyadh, Saudi Arabia, for talks.

February 25

French right wing Deputy Jean Dides said that the French police were not being helped by the Government in the new wave of Algerian terrorism in Paris. Communist Deputies accused the police of harassing the Algerians.

King Saud of Saudi Arabia offered to help settle the Egyptian-Sudanese dispute.

Egyptian troops left Ramada, Sudan, and took their flag with them.

Corsair fighter aircraft obtained under US aid were used in the French attack on Sakiet Sidi Youssef, Tunisia, February 8, the US State Department said.

Anglo-Egyptian financial talks were resumed in Rome. Egypt replied to a British draft agreement which offered to release 24 million of Egypt's sterling balances if Egypt would accept independent assessment of British commercial losses in Egypt.

The Ghananian Government said that it would protest to Jordan if it should be confirmed that the Jordanian Government had blacklisted ships of the Ghana Black Star Line for dealing with Israel.

February 26

An Iraqi-Jordanian mission went to Riyadh, apparently to invite Saudi Arabia to join the Arab Federation.

President Nasser of the UAR stated that the union of Iraq and Jordan was doomed to failure.

US Secretary of State Dulles said that there was some reason to hope that now Egypt and Syria had combined they would be more determined to avoid falling under the control of international Communism.

Israel Prime Minister David Ben-Gurion said that Israel would be free to act if Iraqi troops appreached the Jordan River. He said that Israel

February 26

would be glad to cooperate with the United Arab States politically, economically and culturally if they were free, peace loving and democratic.

It was reported that on February 15, Soviet Ambassador to Paris, Sergei A. Vinogradov, told French Foreign Minister Pineau that any step to make the Bizerta base in Tunisia a NATO base would be regarded as an unfriendly act.

The general elections began in the Sudan.

French Prime Minister Gaillard reaffirmed that France intended to stay in Bizerta, Tunisia.

It was reported from Rome that Egypt had rejected the British view that claims for compensation for the attack on Port Said should be written off against the Egyptian seizure of the Suez Canal base.

February 27

President Bourguiba of Tunisia voiced a strong protest to the UN Security Council against the French plan to establish a no man's land along the Algerian border and to evict 250,000 inhabitants who sought refuge in Tunisia, and violation of Tunisian air space.

Jacques Chaban-Delmas, French Minister of National Defense, said that Algeria must be isolated from Tunisia and Morocco and that the announced no man's land would cover 976 miles.

The French reported 3,371 rebels killed in Algeria since February 1.

The Syrian Government imposed a SL50 tax on all Jordanian military and civilian planes using Syrian air space.

President Nasser attacked the Arab Federation and pledged to fight against imperialist influences in their countries.

February 27

Crown Prince al-Badr, Yemeni Deputy Premier and Foreign Minister, arrived in Cairo for talks on Yemen's adherence to the UAR on the basis of a federal union.

Israel Ambassador to the US Abba Eban called on Secretary of State Dulles to discuss the significance of the Arab mergers.

Sudanese voters went to the polls to elect a parliament in the first free elections since the Sudan had gained its independence. The vote resulted in victory for the Umma Party.

February 28

Crown Prince Muhammad Al-Badr of Yemen returned to Cairo from Yemen with authorization to sign a pact of confederation with the UAR.

US Under Secretary of State Robert Murphy conferred again with President Bourguiba of Tunisia and discussed the problem of Algerian refugees arriving in Tunisia and the evacuation of French troops.

King Hussein of Jordan praised the Arab Federation and said that his country had found an ally to protect and support it.

The Jordanian Government announced that work was to begin immediately on a project to divert the Yarmuk River to irrigate 60,000 acres.

The Independent wing of the Algerian Government coalition asked French Prime Minister Gaillard to send 50,000 to 80.000 more troops to Algeria.

Sheikh Muhammad Sulman al-Khalifah, Chief Adviser to the Ruler of Bahrain, said that the Ruler was in Saudi Arabia to discuss a union of Saudi Arabia, Bahrain and Kuwait.

The Franco-Egyptian talks were resumed in Geneva.

Charles Yost, former US Ambassador to Syria, discussed the downgrading of the Damascus Embassy to a consulate general with US Ambassador Raymond Hare of the UAR.

President Nasser said the Iraqi and Jordanian Foreign Ministers were traitors and imperialists.

March 1

In a statement directed at the UAR and the Arab Federation, King Saud of Saudi Arabia confirmed his stand to cooperate with all Arab states within the commitments he had already undertaken.

Crown Prince Muhammad al-Badr of Yemen flew to Damascus to confer with President Nasser, supposedly to deliver a message from King Saud of Saudi Arabia.

The Bahrain Government announced that Chief Advisor to the Ruler Sheikh Muhammad Sulman al-Khalifah and King Saud of Saudi Arabia agreed to a 50-50 split of ore profits from the disputed underwater territory between their countries.

The Bahrain Government officially denied reports that Sheikh Muhammad Sulman al-Khalifah, Chief Advisor to the Ruler, was in Saudi Arabia to discuss possible federation.

President Bourguiba of Tunisia sent messages expressing his anxiety over the French establishment of a no man's land in Algeria to President Eisenhower, Queen Elizabeth II of England, the Kings of Norway, Denmark and Sweden, President Heuss of West Germany and the Pope.

Morocco accused the Spanish press of carrying out an organized campaign denigrating North African countries, particularly Morocco.

The UAR notified the UN Secretary General that it would be represented in the UN as a single member.

The Spanish Army Ministry said that the rebel bands in the Spanish Sahara had been completely broken up with the cooperation of French forces in French Mauritania.

March 2

Crown Prince Muhammad al-Badr of Yemen and President Nasser announced that Yemen would federate with the UAR.

March 2

The newspaper Al-Shaab said that President Nasser and the Imam Ahmad of Yemen would form a Supreme Council with veto power over any decisions relating to the new federation. A broader Federal Council was to be formed of an equal number of members from both countries. This council would act on foreign policy and economic, cultural and defense affairs; all of its decisions would be submitted to the Supreme Council.

President Nasser said in Damascus that he pitied Iraqi Prime Minister Said Abd-al-Wahhab Marjan for having described Syria as weak. He said that the Iraqi people were in chains, but in spite of that they were the only force in Iraq today. He also said that the Hashemite union was imperialist inspired and did not represent the desire of the people.

The Iraqi Government of Abd-al-Wahhab Marjan resigned.

Thomas K. Finletter, former US Secretary of the Air Force, said that the US should take steps immediately to prevent a Middle East war and should increase support of Greece, Iran, Morocco, Tunisia, Turkey and Israel.

US Deputy Under Secretary of State Robert Murphy, exercising good offices on behalf of the US in the Franco-Tunisian dispute, said after meeting President Bourguiba of Tunisia that he did not think there was any problem in the present situation "which able and farsighted statesmanship should be unable to solve," and that he was optimistic about settlement of the dispute.

March 3

Ahmad Shukairi, Minister of State in Saudi Arabia, told a Geneva conference on the law of the sea that the Gulf of Aqaba enclosed Arab water and was under exclusive Arab jurisdiction. Saudi Arabia's attendance at the conference was not to be construed as recognition of Israel, which was also present.

March 3

French Minister for Algeria Robert Lacoste said that the creation of a no man's land on the Algerian side of the Tunisian frontier would displace about 500 familes. French officials had estimated that 35,000 to 40,000 persons would be displaced and Tunisia complained to the UN that the number was about 250,000. Lacoste also said that the no man's land had been necessitated by Tunisian aid to the Algerian insurgents, who had received more than 18,000 weapons from that country so far this year.

The Algerian National Liberation Front warned the French Government that it would react if insurgent prisoners continued to be executed.

Morocco proposed a union of Tunisia, Algeria and Morocco to settle the North African controversy. The Executive Committee of the Istiqlal in Morocco drew up a program of action calling for immediate steps to strengthen ties uniting the North African countries.

The Council of Ministers in Lebanon adopted a new press law providing that journalists accused of press offenses would not be put under arrest unless they had published something derogatory to the head of state or affecting the security, integrity, sovereignty or frontiers of the state. This amended a law passed February 24 which allowed for provisional arrest.

Negotiations between the Syrian Government and Tapline for increased transit royalties were resumed from January.

US Deputy Under Secretary of State Robert Murphy arrived in Paris to confer with French Premier Gaillard.

Badr ad-Din Hamdi, Deputy Director of the Egyptian Finance Ministry, was appointed head of the financial division of the International Atomic Energy Agency.

Cotton exporters in Egypt were enabled to offer a discount of 23 percent on all sales in hard currencies, including sterling.

March 3

UN Secretary General Dag Hammarskjold appointed Major General Carl Carlsson Von Horn Chief of Staff of the UN Truce Supervision Organization, to succeed Lieutenant General E. L. M. Burns.

Ex-President of the US Harry Truman, in a New York Times article, said that the Soviet Union's preoccupation with the summit meeting and missiles could be a blind for penetration of the Middle East. He called for a US plan of economic aid to the region as a whole to discourage rivalries.

Iraqi Prime Minister Nuri-Said formed a new government, in which Fadel al-Jamali, the most persistent critic in Iraq of the UAR, would be Foreign Minister.

Syrian Lieutenant General Afif Bizri, Chief of Staff of the Syrian Army, resigned. This action was taken as evidence that Nasser had gained total control of the Syrian Army.

March 4

French Prime Minister Felix Gaillard agreed with other Ministers that reinforcements must be sent to Algeria, where about 400,000 French troops were already pitted against the insurgents.

A new Municipal Council in Oran, Algeria, composed of 35 Europeans and 35 Algerians, was sworn in under the "framework law" passed by France in January. All parties except the Communist were represented.

The first tanker load of oil from the Sahara left Philippeville.

The French Cabinet gave the Algerian war priority in the military budget.

Washington agreed to the use of half of a $10 million aid grant to cover the budget deficit of Jordan. The Director of the US aid program reported that since 1956 the US had given Jordan assistance totaling $43,750,000.

March, 1958

March 4

Dr. Hassan Abbas Zaki, Head of the Egyptian Delegation to the Rome financial talks with Britain, said in Cairo that agreement had been reached on most questions previously unresolved.

It was reported that the holders of founders shares in the Universal Suez Canal Company had approved a reorganization of the company's capital structure.

Sheikh Salam al-Sabah, Chief of Police of Kuwait, said that the UAR answered Kuwait's national aspirations.

A 15 member parliamentary delegation from Lebanon went to Jedda at the invitation of the Saudi Arabian Government.

March 5

President Eisenhower said that the US doctrine in the Middle East had played a decisive part in the past year in strengthening countries there to resist the insidious and ever present threat of international Communism.

The French Council of Ministers approved a series of decrees to divide Algeria into five autonomous areas — Oran, Chelif, Algiers, the Kabylia highlands and Constantine. Each area would have a local assembly, and a Government responsible to it elected by universal suffrage.

Syrian Army headquarters charged that a Jordanian mobile patrol had shelled Syrian border guards.

Lieutenant Colonel Abd-al-Hamid Sarraj of Syria accused King Saud of Saudi Arabia of plotting to assassinate President Nasser and of attempting to bribe him to thwart the Syro-Egyptian union.

March, 1958

March 5

Tunisia protested to Cairo concerning the plot against President Bourguiba.

US Deputy Under Secretary of State Robert Murphy conferred with British and French officials in Paris on the question of French troops in Tunisia and Tunisian treatment of French civilians and consular officials.

The Egyptian Government announced that it would give tourists a 23 percent discount on the exchange for Egyptian pounds.

King Hussein of Jordan described as "mean lies" UAR allegations of a Saudi Arabian plot.

President Nasser proclaimed the UAR's temporary constitution at a mass meeting in Damascus.

March 6

Iraqi Foreign Minister Fadel al-Jamali said that Iraq would not recognize the UAR because it was "a forgery and a farce."

President Nasser named four vice presidents of the UAR. He also named the heads of the joint Egyptian-Syrian ministries. Egyptians held the key posts of defense and foreign affairs.

President Bourguiba of Tunisia threatened to break off diplomatic relations with the UAR unless they provided convincing explanations of why a plot was hatched in Cairo to overthrow the Tunisian Government.

The membership of the UN was reduced to 81 as the credentials of the permanent representative of the UAR, comprising Egypt and Syria, were presented to the Secretary General.

It was reported that US and British negotiators suggested that France begin evacuation of its forces while Tunisia lifted the blockade of the bases.

March, 1958

March 6

Sayyed Tayeb Slim, Tunisian Ambassador to Britain, said that although Tunisia sympathized with the UAR it did not envision that it would have any connection with a North African union. The UAR was not moved by the same spirit of friendship or pro-Western ties as the union visualized for North Africa.

King Muhammad V of Morocco proposed the establishment of a North African federation linking Morocco, Tunisia and Algeria.

Full political rights for women in Iraq were announced.

King Idris of Libya sent messages to President Eisenhower and Queen Elizabeth asking them to intervene to end the war in Algeria.

The Saudi Arabian Government said that it knew nothing of plot allegations made by President Nasser and was astonished at them. The allegations contradicted Saudi Arabia's neutral attitude toward the United Arab States and were inconsistent with King Saud s principles.

The State Department emphatically denied that the US was involved in any plot against the United Arab States.

March 7

Britain said in a letter to the UN that its forces had never committed aggressive actions against any place within Yemeni territory. There had been 71 Yemeni attacks in the Aden Frontier area between January 21 and February 27.

French Premier Felix Gaillard received a 286-147 vote of confidence on his Algerian policy.

All Roman Catholic Cardinals and Archbishops in France called on French leaders to avoid excesses in the Algerian war.

Pierre Maisonneuve, Economic Planner of the Ministry for Algeria, said that the Government was drawing up a ten year economic program for Algeria at the cost of $9.5 billion.

March, 1958

March 7

Saudi Arabia formally denied Nasser s charges that King Saud had plotted against the UAR.

The Moroccan Government banned the railway transport of all foreign troops and materiel without prior Moroccan authorization.

Foreign Minister Samir al-Rifai of Jordan left for Baghdad to begin consultations on a constitution for the Arab Federation.

The UN accepted credentials from Omar Loutfi as permanent representative of the UAR.

Aziz Abbad, a Syrian Deputy, said that he went to Riyadh February 12 and was told by King Saud that he wanted Syria to remain independent. The Syrian Deputy made two more trips to Riyadh to collect money to pay Sarraj, the leader of the Arab Socialist Resurrectionist Party, to organize a coup.

March 8

King Saud of Saudi Arabia, replying to a message from King Hussein of Jordan denouncing Egyptian and Syrian accusations against him, expressed regret over dissension in the Arab ranks when the Arab world needed solidarity and unity. King Saud warned that the Arab countries were faced by enemies who were ready to seize any opportunity.

It was announced in Cairo that President Nasser withdrew the Egyptian military mission that had been training Saudi Arabian forces.

A federation between Yemen and the UAR was established by the signing in Damascus of a "Charter for the Establishment of the United Arab States." Article I provided for the new "Union" including the UAR, the Kingdom of Yemen and those Arab States which had agreed to join the Union.

March, 1958

March 9

President Nasser said that the UAR would maintain a neutral policy between the East and West. He warned that imperialist powers and Israel wanted to take Jordan, Lebanon and parts of Syria and Iraq.

A Damascus note from about 5,000 Palestinian refugees proclaimed President Nasser their President in the name of the Arab people of Palestine. They said that they considered Palestine part of the UAR.

President Nasser said that the 1952 revolution was not only Egyptian but Arab. It had succeeded because it depended on the people, whereas the first revolution against the Turks during the first World War had failed because it had depended on imperialism.

Iraqi Foreign Minister Fadel al-Jamali denied reports that Iraq intended to leave the Baghdad Pact.

Iraqi and Jordanian ministers began detailed talks in Baghdad on the Arab Federal State constitution, which had to be enacted by May 14.

Lebanese Foreign Minister Charles Malik said that Lebanon would not accept any limitation or weakening of its independence.

Eighty-four ships passed through the Suez Canal, establishing a record.

March 10

It was reported in Baghdad that the Arab Federation's Federal Council would have 15 Iraqi and 15 Jordanian members who would not be allowed to hold office in their respective governments simultaneously.

Hodeida, a Yemen seaport, was to be the headquarters of the United Arab States' Federal Legislature, it was reported in Damascus.

The first Russian technicians to help carry out the provisions of the technical and financial aid agreement between Syria and the Soviet Union were expected to arrive in Damascus March 24.

March, 1958

March 10

Al-Alam said that Morocco could not consider joining a Mediterranean pact before agreement had been reached on the evacuation of foreign troops.

It was reported that US Deputy Under Secretary of State Murphy and his British counterpart Beeley would offer Tunisia a plan consisting of the regrouping of forces in Bizerta and progressive withdrawal of troops not needed to maintain the base in exchange for a promise of no further expulsion of Frenchmen and approval in principle of a neutral frontier surveillance.

Iranian Foreign Minister Ali Gholi Ardalan denounced the Saudi-Bahrain oil agreement.

Trade union leaders from Morocco, Tunisia, Libya and Algeria unanimously agreed in Geneva on a resolution calling for peace in Algeria.

Esso Standard Oil found deposits of natural gas with a daily capacity of about one million cubic feet near Atshan, West Fezzan, Libya.

March 11

The Algerian National Movement offered to open talks with France for a ceasefire and free elections for a "sovereign" Algerian constituent assembly. It was indicated that they were also seeking Vatican support for the talks.

French authorities said that many of the "Algerian refugees" displayed to foreigners in Tunisia were not Algerians but Tunisians.

Baha-ad-Din Touqan, new Jordanian representative to the UN, presented his credentials to UN Secretary General Dag Hammarskjold.

In the Sudan's first general election the Umma Party won 68 seats in the House, the National Unionists won 47 seats, and the People's Democratic Party, 26. Thirty-two went to other parties.

March, 1958

March 11

President Nasser said at an army camp near Damascus that during the 1948 Palestine war traitors and supporters of imperialism had ordered Iraqi troops not to fight even though they had wanted to do so.

The US considered whether or not to give economic help to Tunisia and Morocco if France should stop doing so, State Department officials said.

US Deputy Under Secretary of State Murphy and British Foreign Office Assistant Under Secretary Beeley conferred with Tunisian President Bourguiba. It was reported that the latter showed stiff resistance to their proposals.

It was announced that the Gaza Strip Palestinians would be given more voice in their Government. The Israel Government did not see any immediate danger in this development.

March 12

Tunisian President Bourguiba requested Britain and the US to choose between Tunisia and France, or "between freedom and colonialism," before March 20, the second anniversary of Tunisia's independence.

It was reported that Tunisian President Bourguiba demanded total evacuation of French troops from Bizerta.

Israel said at the Geneva Conference on the law of the sea that Arab claims that the Gulf of Aqaba was an internal Arab water under the exclusive jurisdiction of the Arab states were not based on law or on fact but on wishful thinking.

Michael Comay, the Israel delegate to the Geneva Conference, said that Israel was forced to increase its territorial limit from three to six miles, and that since its coasts were its only link with the outside world, freedom of the seas was essential.

The Afro-Asian bloc at the UN expressed deep concern to Secretary General Hammarskjold at the French plan for a no man's land on the Algerian frontier with Tunisia.

March, 1958

March 12

The Press Committee of the National Assembly of France protested the seizure of newspapers critical of the Algerian war.

In Lebanon the Cabinet of Sami al-Solh resigned. It was reported that the new Cabinet would modify foreign policy to suit developments in other Arab states. Charles Malik remained as Foreign Minister.

In Kuwait two new refining units designed to handle 160,000 barrels of crude oil a day were inaugurated. This brought Kuwait's total refining capacity to 190,000 barrels daily, or about 11 percent of its normal crude production.

The UAR denied rumors that oil pipelines passing through Syria would be destroyed or molested.

President Nasser ordered the immediate dissolution of all political parties and associations in the Syrian Region of the UAR.

President Nasser appointed Lieutenant General Afif Bizri Commander of the UAR First Army.

March 13

Saudi Arabia announced to the Geneva Maritime Conference that it had extended its territorial waters in the Gulf of Aqaba to 12 miles.

The Istiqlal Party in Morocco accused Egypt of showing a lack of comprehension and good will in its policy toward Morocco.

Thousands of Parisian policement demonstrated for higher pay and bonuses because of Algerian terrorism. They were met at the gates of the National Assembly by government security troops.

Yugoslavia rejected as groundless, explanations from the French Government for the seizure of an arms cargo from the Yugoslav ship Slovenija off Algeria January 18. It expressed the hope that France would yet agree to pay compensation.

March 13

It was announced that demonstrators had tried to attack the Egyptian Embassy in Saudi Arabia.

March 14

Responding to the call of Lebanese President Camille Chamoun, Sami al-Solh formed a new 14 man cabinet. He retained the Interior Ministry portfolio as well as the Premiership.

Nikita Khrushchev, Russian Communist Party leader, said that the French must understand that if they did not change their policy in Algeria they would suffer the same failure as in Indo-China.

It was reported in Jordan that a drought was expected to ruin many of the crops to be harvested. The press urged the establishment of price controls on basic necessities.

Yugoslavia sent a new protest to France demanding compensation for the arms cargo seized January 18 from the freighter *Slovenija*.

French Defense Minister Jacques Chaban-Delmas said that the creation of a no man's land between Algeria and Tunisia would be expedited as it was essential to isolate the Algerian insurgents from their bases in Tunisia.

March 15

A Council composed of ten Egyptians and 20 Palestinians was established in Gaza to advise the Egyptian Governor on administration of the strip.

It was reported from Baghdad that the draft constitution of the Arab Federation was completed.

President Eisenhower replied to the March 1 note from Tunisian President Bourguiba concerning the French establishment of a no man's land. The note focused on the situation in the dislocation of civilians in the Algerian-Tunisian border area.

March 15

The Egyptian press said that King Saud of Saudi Arabia had arrested four Saudi officers and executed one of them on charges of having formed a pro-Nasser underground and plotting to overthrow the monarchy several months before.

A New Delhi announcement said the Indian and Tunisian Governments had agreed on exchange of ambassadors with a view to promoting friendship between the two countries.

Lebanese press favoring the UAR gave divergent views of the new Lebanese Cabinet. *Al-Jorida* said that the Government had taken the initiative for reconciliation with the Opposition. *Al-Masa* condemned the new Government.

The Lebanese Government issued orders prohibiting political demonstrations and political pictures.

March 16

Premier Nuri-Said would resign as head of the Iraqi Government after the formation of the Arab Federation, the Iraqi Parliament was told.

A Soviet Embassy spokesman said that the Soviet Union would help Libya build and equip two hospitals under a $2.8 million aid program which included the training of Libyan health workers at Soviet universities.

The American Council for Judaism said that expansionist Zionism and Arab refusal to recognize the political fact of the State of Israel were obstacles to peace in the Middle East.

It was announced that Israel had received more than 71,000 immigrants in 1957 including 30,600 from Poland, 13,000 from Egypt and 12,000 from North Africa.

French Minister for Algeria Robert Lacoste said it was to be feared that more than 50,000 weapons were stocked in Tunisia and destined for the Algerian insurgents. Talks of extending the American good

March 16

offices to Algeria had encouraged some countries to send there as many arms as possible.

President Tito of Yugoslavia said that France, in proposing a Mediterranean pact, aimed to divide the African and Arab worlds. He said that the pact would be a disaster.

The Sudanese Government formally recognized the UAR.

President Nasser pledged all-out support to all Arabs fighting for the liberation of their countries from "imperialism, foreign intervention or domination."

The French Independent Party warned the French Government that if concessions were made to Tunisia it might withdraw its Ministers from the Government.

Al-Ahram of Cairo reported that an Egyptian military mission to Saudi Arabia had returned as ordered after allegations of bribery by King Saud. The newspaper did not say whether Saudi Arabia or Egypt gave the order.

International bankers in London estimated the overseas value of the Egyptian pound — when negotiable at all — at less than three-fifths of the official rate in Cairo.

March 17

British and US intermediaries flew to Paris with reportedly moderate Tunisian demands. The Tunisians demanded that France recognize Tunisian sovereignty over the port and naval base of Bizerta and asked for other concessions.

After conferring with Tunisian President Bourguiba on the Franco-Tunisian dispute resulting from the Sakiet Sidi Youssef bombing February 8, Special US Ambassador Robert D. Murphy declared that the "tendency in Tunis was conciliatory."

March 17

The British engineering firm of Sir Alexander Gibb and Partners said that it was arranging discussions in London the next month with representatives of the Aswan Dam Authority.

President Nasser returned to Cairo after a 21 day visit to Syria.

It was reported from Port Said that the Egyptian Canal Authority had dismissed two American pilots for allegedly engaging in "union organization" activities.

France gave asylum to Sayyed Loutfi, Egyptian Press Attache in Berne, because he had disagreed with the Nasser Government. *Le Monde* quoted him as saying that he was a member of an Egyptian opposition group of politicians, journalists and army officers.

Haji Amin Husseini, former Mufti of Jerusalem, told the Associated Press that the Palestine Arab Government formed in 1948, but since moribund, had asked for admission to the United Arab States.

British Minister of State for Foreign Affairs Commander Allan Noble told questioners in the House of Commons that no action had yet arisen calling for a formal British decision to give *de jure* recognition to the United Arab State.

Nahum Goldmann, President of the World Zionist Organization, said that a Middle Eastern political armistice between the two world blocs was Israel's only hope in the present dangerous situation in that area. The danger had been intensified by increasing Russian hostility toward Israel.

It was reported that Britain would strengthen its ground forces in the Aden Protectorate.

The Spanish Government prepared to help 30,000 Spanish colonists emigrate to the Spanish Sahara.

The Moroccan Economic Attache in Washington formally expressed his country's "strict reservations: about a French request for an IBRD (International Bank for Reconstruction and Development) loan for mining in Mauritania.

March, 1958

March 17

Sweden was to increase its strength in the UN Emergency Force from 365 to 510 men. India had increased its strength in the Force and Brazil intended to do so since the Indonesian and Finnish contingents had withdrawn.

March 18

The Council of Ministers of Iraq approved the Constitution of the Arab Federation.

Saudi Arabia complained to Lebanon about recent attacks on King Saud in the Lebanese Opposition press.

The first sitting of the Sudanese Parliament was postponed until March 20.

French Delegate to the UN, Herve Alphand praised Israel's "courageous struggle and miraculous achievement" and declared France's continued support of Israel.

Morocco complained to UN Secretary General Dag Hammarskjold that it was being taxed by refugees fleeing from surrounding Spanish and French territories.

March 19

The Constitution of the Arab Federation was proclaimed simultaneously in Baghdad and Amman.

Iraq would provide four-fifths of the budget, and Jordan the rest, in the first year of the Arab Federal State according to the Constitution now published.

Eigteen prominent French university professors asked the Government to negotiate with the Algerians and realize that independence for Algeria was the only way to stop the war.

March, 1958

March 20

President Nasser said that the Arab Federation was "London inspired" and had been conceived as an opposition grouping to the UAR.

March 21

The French Government made Tunisian "nonbelligerence" in the Algerian war an essential condition for settlement of the Franco-Tunisian dispute.

A foreign affairs official said that Morocco had almost reached the "end of its patience" with Spain. He emphasized the "pressing need" for Spain to fulfill its agreement to relinquish the Moroccan Southern Zone.

Israel and Jordanian army units supervised their respective Bedouin tribes in the Negev border area to prevent fighting over the few grassy spots. The Bedouin tribes had lost 95 percent of their winter wheat crop on account of drought.

March 22

The Sudanese Senate elected Amin al-Sayyed as Speaker of the Senate.

The Saudi Arabian royal court said in a telegram to the Arab News Agency that there were no difficulties between King Saud and the Amirs which would require the King to contemplate abdication. Any reports to the contrary were lies, it was stated.

March 23

King Saud of Saudi Arabia agreed that his brother, Crown Prince Faisal, who was Prime Minister and Foreign Minister, would now also supervise internal and financial policies. In Cairo this was interpreted as the King's "abdication" and in Damascus as partial atonement for his alleged conspiracy against the UAR. Elsewhere in the Middle East supporters of King Saud said that the agreement disproved Egyptian and Syrian reports that he and Crown Prince Faisal were quarreling.

March, 1958

March 19

The UAR declared its opposition to the three mile territorial sea limit and to the right of innocent passage for foreign warships in coastal waters without prior notification and authorization.

March 20

French President Gaillard said that his Government was ready to resign if part of its majority indicated lack of confidence.

Tunisian President Bourguiba expressed his willingness to cooperate with France and thanked the US and Britain for their good offices.

Tunisian President Bourguiba said that he had hoped to announce soon a just solution to the Franco-Tunisian dispute. If the Western world continued to help France in the war in Algeria it would lose the friendship and cooperation of Arab North Africa.

Abdallah Khalil continued as Premier of the Sudan as the newly elected House gave him a strong majority.

Diplomatic circles in Madrid said that Spain had offered to return the Southern zone to Morocco if Morocco accepted Latitude 27.40° N and Longitude 11° W as the northern and eastern borders of the Spanish Sahara.

Correspondents in Algiers were told that all dispatches on military operations must be submitted for official clearance.

The British Colonial Secretary, Alan Lennox-Boyd, said that measures would continue to be taken to protect the Aden frontier states against aggression by Yemen. He also said that Aden trade unions were reportedly contemplating a general strike in protest against what they considered a too lenient immigration policy.

President Nasser said in Cairo that the United Arab State was the front line in the defense of Arab Nationalism.

March, 1958

March 23

Tunisian political quarters and the press indicated that there would be no further concession to French demands.

Sharp rivalry had arisen between Czechoslovakia and Hungary over tendering for the new Damascus broadcasting station, it was reported in Vienna.

Cairo reported that President Nasser had issued a decree accepting the resignation of Lieutenant General Afif Bizri as Commander in Chief of the UAR forces in Syria.

The Tunisian Neo-Destour and Moroccan Istiqlal Parties arranged to meet the Algerian National Liberation Front in Tangier April 27 to discuss North African unity.

Israel Prime Minister David Ben-Gurion was reported by the Tel Aviv press to have advocated closer ties with all Western European countries except Britain, whose Middle Eastern policy he said was based on oil and a struggle for influence.

French Premier Gaillard asked France's allies to remember that "Algeria is as dear to our hearts as was Alsace-Lorraine."

March 24

Tunisian President Bourguiba agreed with the Anglo-American good offices mission that Tunisia should resume talks with France.

King Saud of Saudi Arabia turned over to his brother, Crown Prince Faisal, the "full power to lay down the state's internal, external and financial policies and to supervise implementation of these policies."

The first group of Soviet experts to visit Egypt under the new aid agreement arrived in Cairo.

The US Secretary of State, John Foster Dulles, said that some of the more radical pro-Communists in Syria seemed not to have as important a role in the UAR as they had had previously in Syria.

March, 1958

March 24

A UAR military spokesman said that an hour long fight had taken place at the border. The UAR made a formal complaint to the UN Mixed Armistice Commission about the Palestine border dispute.

March 25

Sayyed Awni Khalidi, Secretary of the Baghdad Pact Council, said that there was no question of a formal link between the Pact, NATO and SEATO, but that there might be a "harmless liaison" among them.

Crown Prince Faisal of Saudi Arabia was reported to have barred the King's five foreign advisors from all future Cabinet meetings.

US Secretary of State Dulles said that the power shift would not alter Saudi Arabia's position as an anchor of US policy in the Middle East. He said that there was no reason to believe that Crown Prince Faisal was anti-American.

Premier David Ben-Gurion said that peace between Israel and the Arabs was possible if the other powers guaranteed Israel's borders.

Foreign Minister Balafrej would reportedly head the Moroccan delegation to the pan-North African Conference in Tangier April 27.

The Government of Lebanon declared that it would not join either of the Arab unions or any other group that would limit its independence, sovereignty and freedom.

Russian leader Nikita Khrushchev told Le Figaro, a Parisian newspaper, that France would lose Algeria if it went on with the war there.

US Deputy Under Secretary of State Murphy and British Foreign Office Assistant Undersecretary Beeley met with French Premier Gaillard and Foreign Minister Pineau to discuss the Franco-Tunisian problem.

March, 1958

March 26

The Jordanian Parliament unanimously ratified the Constitution of the Arab Federation.

The Iraqi Parliament unanimously ratified a constitutional amendment giving King Faisal the right to form a union with one or more Arab countries.

In Iraq a constitutional amendment granting voting rights to women who had a primary school education was approved by Parliament.

In the Sudan Premier Abdallah Khalil announced the formation of his new Cabinet. He retained the post of Defense Minister.

The newspaper al-Ahram reported that President Nasser signed a decree defining the responsibilities of his four vice presidents.

Sporadic shooting continued around Lake Huleh as Israelis refused to stop work there as requested by Colonel Bertrand of the Mixed Armistice Commission.

March 27

The Iraqi Parliament was dissolved following its approval of a constitutional amendment to permit union with Jordan.

French Foreign Minister Christian Pineau said that there was no point in resuming negotiations with Tunisia unless Tunisia accepted in advance some kind of control over the frontier with Algeria.

The Lebanese Government received a vote of confidence 38-15 in the Chamber of Deputies.

A group of 82 Lebanese leaders warned President Chamoun in a manifesto against seeking re-election.

The World Zionist Organization urged Jewish organizations everywhere to take concerted action to fight the Arab boycott of Israel.

March, 1958

March 28

Iraqi Foreign Minister Fadel al-Jamali was reported to have told Arab envoys in Baghdad that Egypt had published a map which was a challenge to the sovereignty of independent Arab states. The map showed all the Arab states in one color as part of the UAR, omitting both the Arab Federation and the other independent states.

Major General Von Horn of the UN visited the Gaza Strip and inspected observation posts there.

Four Mauritanian leaders pledged loyalty to Morocco. France did not recognize Morocco's claim to suzerainty over Mauritania, a province in French West Africa.

The French Government defeated a motion to delineate the details of its position on US-British efforts to end the Tunisian dispute by a vote of 317-255.

Crown Prince Faisal of Saudi Arabia was reported to have dismissed the Minister of Finance.

March 29

The Minister of the Interior of Iraq announced that a general election would be held May 5.

It was officially announced in Amman that Great Britain had paid the last of its commitments to Jordan, 500,000 pounds sterling. The funds were to be used for public projects under the supervision of the Jordanian Development Board.

The Egyptian Consul in Jerusalem, Muhib al Samra, was expelled from Jordan without explanation.

The Saudi Arabian Defense Ministry, according to reports released to a Cairo newspaper, had been taken over by Crown Prince Faisal, who ousted Defense Minister Prince Fahd. Saudi troops were being withdrawn from Jordan.

March, 1958

March 30

Russia had offered "unconditional" financial aid to Libya, it was officially announced in Tripoli. The Libyan Government was understood to have asked the US to increase its financial aid. Libyan newspapers reported a deadlock in the talks on British financial aid for Libya. The British Foreign Office denied this.

The Soviet Union, Communist China and North Vietnam marked Algeria Day with unofficial expressions of support for the nationalists.

US Deputy Under Secretary of State Robert Murphy and British Foreign Office Assistant Undersecretary Harold Beeley met with the UN Secretary General Dag Hammarskjold in London to discuss the Franco-Tunisian dispute.

The Tunisian newspaper, L'Action, said that Tunisia would agree to UN supervision of the border if French troops left Tunisia.

A spokesman for the Arab League at the UN said that the League would favor UN observers in Tunisia.

A national conference for peace in Algeria, organized by 110 French public and political leaders, opened in Paris.

A Syrian spokesman said that Israel tanks had shelled two Arab villages and that Israel troops had fired on Syrian villagers. He accused Israel of aggression and of having violated a UN order to cease activities in the Lake Hula area.

March 31

Israel Prime Minister David Ben-Gurion said in an interview published by Look Magazine that he would meet with President Nasser in Cairo any time he was invited to do so. He was willing to consider an invitation to Israel to join the UAR, as offered in a Cairo broadcast in Hebrew recently.

Israel Foreign Minister Golda Meir told the UN Truce Supervisory Organization that Israel was determined to proceed with the drainage

March 31

work near Lake Huleh, which was being done entirely within its boundary and rights. Replying to critics in the Israel Parliament, she said that the Government had left nothing undone in its effort to improve relations with Russia, but it had all been without success.

The UAR complained in a letter to UN Secretary General Hammarskjold against "Israel aggression on the borders of Syria" between March 24 and 27.

Robert Schuman, head of the European Economic Assembly, said that the North Atlantic, Baghdad and Southeast Asia alliances should help in preventing the loss of Algeria to outsiders hostile to Western interests.

An agreement was signed between the Sudan and the US for the establishment of an International Cooperation Administration operations office in Khartoum to provide technical assistance in agriculture, vocational education, road development and communications.

April 1

Israel agreed to suspend work on the Lake Huleh drainage project pending a survey by UN investigators to determine whether the work touched on Syrian territory.

The Arab League Council telegraphed asking the UN to carry out its obligations resulting from the fighting near Lake Huleh.

The United Arab Republic's mission at the UN said that it would ask immediately for a meeting of the Security Council to consider Israel s aggression.

American Secretary of State, John Foster Dulles said that the present dispute between Syria and Israel centered on whether the latter's irrigation project in the Lake Huleh area impinged on a demilitarized zone, the precise limits of which were not altogether clear.

Spanish Government sources said that Morocco would control the Southern Protectorate. Transfer of control was slated for April 10.

Ahmad Zaki Saad, member of the Board of Directors of the International Monetary Fund, was asked by Crown Prince Faisal to come to Saudi Arabia to take charge of preparing the budget and reforming the Ministry of Finance and National Economy.

The Egyptian Treasury Ministry said that an offer by France to pay eight million pounds sterling in compensation for harm done during the 1956 invasion had been rejected. Egypt was demanding 72 million pounds sterling from France and Britain jointly.

In Lebanon, Kazem al-Khalil, Minister of Economy, threatened to resign in protest against the sentencing of three pro-Egyptian youths in Tyre.

April 2

The UAR Foreign Minister, Mahmoud Fawzi, flew to Switzerland to see Mr. Dag Hammarskjold, Secretary General of the UN, with whom

April 2

he said he would discuss the new position of the UAR in the UN and its representation in international agencies. Reports from Cairo said Dr. Fawzi would also seek to discuss the Lake Huleh fighting.

The UAR changed its mind about asking for an urgent meeting of the UN Security Council, but said that it would make the request if hostilities were resumed by Israel.

Israel informed the UN that the drainage work was an integral part of the Lake Huleh reclamation project designed to hasten its completion, and that it was being done with the full knowledge of the UN Truce Supervisory Organization and in the presence of UN observers.

The US-British good offices team arrived in Paris to try anew to settle French-Tunisian differences.

UN Secretary General Hammarskjold conferred with Britain's Prime Minister Macmillan concerning France and Tunisia. No details of the talks were released.

Sir Leslie Munro, President of the UN General Assembly, said that the failure to solve the Palestine problem had encouraged political extremism and multiplied Communist opportunities in the Middle East. A transition from an uneasy truce to a permanent settlement was still the urgent need. The UN could not be expected to play the decisive role in this. That role remained to be assumed by the Arabs and Israelis.

Two Syrian newspapers reported that Iraqi troops were massing on the Syrian-Iraqi border. Iraq denied the reports.

Theodore Green, Chairman of the US Senate Foreign Relations Committee, suggested that the US might provide aid for the UAR to replace that from Russia. President Nasser reportedly might respond to the US overtures, but it should be made clear to him that the US did not like his brand of imperialism any better than any other brand.

April 3

Foreign Minister Mahmoud Fawzi of the UAR met in Geneva with UN Secretary General Dag Hammarskjold to discuss matters involving relations of the UN to the new UAR.

The Moroccan Cabinet announced that a committee had been formed to judge persons who had engaged in anti-national activities during Morocco's struggle for independence.

The Lebanese Council of Ministers considered clashes and strikes during the week at Tyre and elsewhere. It announced that it would suppress any act which might disturb peace.

The newly formed Gaza Legislative Council approved a resolution stated that the inhabitants of the Gaza Sector had expressed their wish to join the UAR. The council decided that this resolution should be put into effect at the appropriate moment.

The Anglo-American good offices envoys, Harold Beeley of Britain and Robert Murphy of the US, arrived in Tunis from Paris for a new attempt at a Franco-Tunisian reconciliation. They had discussed their mission in London with Dag Hammarskjold, UN Secretary General.

The Jordanian Government took over control of all petroleum supplies, as well as fuel imports and distribution.

Suez Canal tolls were ordered to be paid in the currency of the country under whose flag the ship was sailing. This was interpreted as a move to obtain more dollars, as many ships flew flags of convenience of countries within the dollar area.

The UAR Government disclosed the purchase from the Soviet Union of an unspecified number of new TU-104 jet transport planes for passenger service.

President Nasser announced that three new submarines, purchased from Poland, had arrived to make his submarine fleet the strongest in the Middle East.

April 3

The Syrian daily newspaper, al-Sham, said that Syrian newspapers were suffering as a result of that country's merger with Egypt. Cairo newspapers were being favored and many Syrian newspapers lost the support of political parties that had financed them.

The State Department confirmed that the US had intervened to aid the UN s truce efforts in the Syro-Israel clashes.

Tunisian President Bourguiba rejected a French demand for international control of the Algerian-Tunisian frontier on the ground that it implied Tunisia s recognition of French sovereignty in Algeria. He said that the NLF had threatened to establish a Government in exile in Cairo within a month if he yielded to this demand.

April 4

Dag Hammarskjold, UN Secretary General, and UAR Foreign Minister Mahmoud Fawzi completed talks in Geneva mainly on questions which concerned the relationship of the UAR to the UN. According to Akhbar al-Yom, of Cairo, Dr. Fawzi told Hammarskjold that the UAR would meet with force any new attack by Israel against Syria.

UN observers completed their investigation of this week's clashes between Syrian and Israel forces near Lake Huleh and reported to the Mixed Armistice Commission.

It was reported from Paris that the Socialist International Mission to Algeria had reported that talks between France and the insurgents were impossible at present.

April 5

US Deputy Under Secretary of State Robert Murphy delivered a note to Tunisian President Habib Bourguiba from US Secretary of State Dulles, asking the Tunisian President to take a broad view of the present situation.

April 5

Egypt announced that it would start exporting oil for the first time on May 1 from fields in the Sinai Peninsula.

The Arabia Oil Company, which had been incorporated in February by Japanese businessmen seeking Middle Eastern oil concessions, said that it was urging the Japanese Government to authorize payment of rent for this year to Saudi Arabia.

April 6

Tunisia refused to consider French demands for international control of the Tunisian-Algerian border.

Jordanian Foreign Minister Samir al-Rifai said that Saudi Arabia had not cut off its subsidy to Jordan. He added that the Government might dispense with it since Jordan was federated with Iraq.

Israel announced that work would be resumed at Lake Huleh.

April 7

The World Bank announced that it would help Egypt draft plans to increase the capacity of the Suez Canal.

Egypt and the Soviet Union agreed to a $9.8 million barter pact involving Soviet wheat and Egyptian cotton.

India and Saudi Arabia signed a joint trade communique.

President Nasser said that nine secret broadcasting stations administered by the West were making propaganda attacks on him.

The UN survey results showed that one of the Lake Huleh canals would go through the demilitarized zone. Israel said that the direction of the canal would be changed if this were true.

The US and British conciliators, Robert Murphy and Harold Beeley, returned to Paris with the Tunisian demand that the border question be

April 7

postponed until after the issue of the evacuation of French troops had been settled.

April 8

King Muhammad V of Morocco declared that any new military agreement with a foreign country must be preceded by recognition of the principle of withdrawal of foreign troops.

The French stopped a diplomatic shipment to Tunisia containing radio equipment that the French said was bound for Algeria.

Saudi Arabia was to give a check of LE80,000 to the Arab League as its share of the budget.

A French military communique reported 243 Algerian rebels killed that day in fighting near the Algerian border.

April 9

It was reported that technicians from the Soviet bloc were helping to build harbor installations at Ras al-Khitab, Yemen.

The Jordanian Government announced approval of twelve constitutional amendments that delegated the powers of King Hussein to King Faisal of Iraq. This limited King Hussein's power to ratify treaties and declare war.

The Iraqi and Jordanian Army Chiefs of Staff, Lieutenant Generals Rafiq Aref and Habes al-Majali, reported to King Hussein of Jordan on their talks about uniting the two armies under the Arab Federation.

Fifty-five Iraqi opposition leaders, including former premiers, party chairmen and ex-MP's, urged the people to boycott the May 5 parliamentary elections.

The Jordanian Government broadcast the text of a Cairo Radio report inviting Israel, February 10, to join the UAR.

April 9

J. K. Vaughan Morgan and W. H. McFadzean of the British Advisory Council on Middle Eastern trade announced that they would visit Iraq, Iran, Lebanon and the Persian Gulf states during May and June to discuss trade opportunities.

Premier Felix Gaillard of France conferred with the US-British good offices team, Robert Murphy and Harold Beeley. He called the vacationing Cabinet into session.

April 10

The State Department announced that the US agreed to make available 20,000 metric tons of surplus wheat for an emergency relief program in Tunisia.

An accord between the UAR and the Soviet Union concerning cooperation in science, culture and education was signed in Cairo.

President Chamoun of Lebanon called an emergency meeting to discuss a battle the previous night between security forces and Druses in the Shuf.

Israel completed work, suspended for more than a week, on the last Lake Huleh drainage canal.

A Baghdad Pact Committee met in Baghdad to consider development plans for the Tigris and Euphrates River basins.

April 11

The US and Britain warned French Premier Gaillard against taking his conflict with Tunisia before the UN Security Council. They also appealed to France to continue conciliation.

Ahmad Balafrej, the Moroccan Foreign Minister, said that the major problem in Morocco was the evacuation of all foreign troops.

April 11

The Lebanese Government moved reinforcements into the mountain passes along the Damascus road to combat smugglers.

The American Embassy in Amman announced that the US was sending two million pounds of wheat and flour as a gift to needy families in Jordan.

April 12

The French Government accepted the suggestions made by the Anglo-American good offices team, Robert Murphy and Harold Beeley, that direct talks be resumed with Tunisia on issues arising from the bombing of Sakiet.

Spain cut off the Cape Juby zone of the Moroccan Southern Protectorate. Spanish authorities there refused to transfer the zone to the Moroccans.

The Egyptian Government and British engineers met to discuss plans for the Aswan High Dam.

It was reported that propaganda attacks by Cairo Radio against the US had stopped.

April 13

Syria reported an exchange of gunfire between an army patrol and Turkish soldiers within Syrian territory.

The French right wing expressed hostility to the Government's decision to renew negotiations with Tunisia.

Spain denied that it was being difficult about transferring the Southern Protectorate to Morocco.

April 14

Tunisia became a member of the International Monetary Fund and the International Bank for Reconstruction and Development.

April 14

The UNRWA for Palestinian refugees asked for an extra $7,000 to carry on its work.

New press and radio attacks from Cairo were reported to be directed against King Hussein of Jordan.

Levi Eshkol, the Minister of Finance in Israel, urged widespread support of the Israel bond campaign in the US.

Muhammad Yazid, NLF representative in New York, and two others, arrived in Accra to focus the attention of the African Conference on the issue of Algerian independence.

April 15

In Morocco opponents to the Istiqlal formed a coalition and presented Premier Barek Bekkai with a motion addressed to King Muhammad.

A conference of independent African states, including Ethiopia, Libya, Morocco, Sudan, Tunisia and the UAR, began in Accra.

The Council of Ministers of the Sudan held an informal meeting to discuss the development program for the next five years.

Britain accused Yemen of aggression against Aden on April 13.

French Premier Gaillard submitted his resignation after the National Assembly refused, 321-255, to support his policy of resuming direct talks with Tunisia.

April 16

King Muhammad V of Morocco dissolved the Government of Premier Bekkai following the resignation of ministers of the Istiqlal Party. The

April 16

ministers charged the Premier with supporting a resolution by Opposition leaders criticizing the Government's policy and the lack of fundamental democratic liberties in Morocco.

The Algerian NLF representatives at Accra were accorded nonvoting status at the African Conference.

It was announced that a conclusion in principle was reached for Egyptian-British and Egyptian-French barter agreements.

President Nasser was reported to have made an important compromise offer toward a settlement of the issue of compensation to shareholders in the Universal Suez Canal Company.

The International Chamber of Shipping decided to pay a three percent surcharge to be applied to Canal tolls by the UN in order to defray the costs of $8 million for repairing the canal after the Anglo-French invasion in 1956.

The Anglo-American good offices mission to settle the Franco-Tunisian dispute was suspended in Paris.

The third consignment of US armaments promised in 1957 arrived at Aqaba, Jordan.

Felix Gaillard resigned as French Premier on the defeat of his Tunisian policy.

An Iraqi committee of judges and senators ruled that civil courts could not revise military tribunal decisions when interpreting Article 73 of the constitution. In interpreting Article 66, the committee said that the Council of Ministers was the only authority in charge of state affairs.

The UAR invited the prospective economic commission of the UN for Africa to make its headquarters in Cairo.

Burhan ad-Din Bashayan was appointed acting Minister of Information and Guidance, a new Ministry in Iraq.

April 17

Khulusi al-Khairi, Minister of Economy in Jordan, left for West Germany to discuss the possibility of German capital investment in Jordan.

The Algerian representatives in Accra asked the African Conference for material aid against the French.

It was reported that the US was convinced of the need for a nonmilitary settlement of the Algerian rebellion.

Tunisian President Bourguiba declared that he would take the French-Tunisian conflict before the UN but that he would defer such action until a new Cabinet had been formed.

April 18

The Saudi Arabian Premier, Crown Prince Faisal, announced in a major policy statement that his Government would not join either the UAR or the Arab Federation but would pursue a policy of positive neutrality and avoid membership in any foreign pacts which would contradict Arab interests. He agreed to cooperate with both groups.

It was reported in Morocco that preliminary discussions among the Istiqlal, Neo-Destour and NLF (National Liberation Front) Parties would begin, April 23, prior to a conference in Tangier.

US Under Secretary of State Christian Herter assured French Ambassador Herve Alphand that the US policy toward Algeria had not changed.

April 19

A Soviet-Moroccan trade and payments agreement was signed in Moscow.

April 20

The Accra Conference members recognized the Algerian National Liberation Front as the sole legitimate authority in Algeria and asked

April 20

France to negotiate an end to the war. The Conference members decided to meet at least every two years and to set up a permanent staff.

Two mediators for the IBRD left Cairo and said that the UAR and the shareholders in the Suez Canal Company were near to settlement of their dispute.

The Istiqlal Political Commission of Morocco called for a one party Government and a representative assembly with constitutional powers.

Spain was requested to remove all of its troops from Morocco. This action was precipitated by Spanish refusal to withdraw from Villa Bens in the Southern Protectorate under Moroccan control.

US Deputy Under Secretary of State Murphy stated on his return to the US that his mediation efforts between France and Tunisia were in suspension.

Jordan filed a complaint with the UN Truce Supervisory Organization that the gathering of Israel military forces in Jerusalem in connection with the forthcoming Independence Day parade was in violation of the 1949 Armistice Agreement. The complaint said that the Jordanian Army had been directed to send reinforcements to the Jordanian Sector of the city for the parade.

April 21

The Accra Conference states adopted a common foreign policy of non-entanglement.

The Mixed Armistice Commission met to discuss Jordan's objections to the Israel Independence Day parade.

Jordan walked out of the Mixed Armistice Commission meeting, charging that Colonel Flint of the UN had come under Israel's influence.

The Arab League complained to the UN concerning the Israel parade.

April 22

Crown Prince Muhammad al-Badr said that Yemen would accept arms at any price from any place they could get them.

President Nasser said that his country would remain neutral between East and West.

Official sources said that the UAR would probably pay about $40 million in compensation for the nationalization of the Suez Canal.

The UAR Ministry of Finance announced that agreement had been reached with representatives of the Universal Suez Canal Company concerning compensation for shareholders because of the nationalization of the Canal.

Representatives of the NLF arrived in Rabat, Morocco, for talks with Moroccan leaders prior to the Tangier Conference.

The Accra Conference ended with a plea to the great powers to stop the production and testing of nuclear weapons.

April 23

The first US trade mission to Morocco opened talks with government officials.

A delegation from Libya was to attend the Tangier meeting of North African parties, it was announced.

Britain and Saudi Arabia had been in communication in order to resume diplomatic relations, it was reported.

Jordan and Israel agreed to permit UN observers in both the Israel and Jordanian sectors of Jerusalem.

Algerian-French Defense Minister Jacques Chaban-Delmas announced that in the three and one-half years of the rebellion 62,000 rebels and 6,000 French military personnel had been killed.

April 23

Lieutenant Colonel Flint, Chairman of the Israel-Jordan Mixed Armistice Commission, refused to vote on Jordan's complaint on the ground that the MAC had no authority to rule on it. He noted, however, that any Jordanian reinforcements brought to Jerusalem would also be a formal breach of the 1949 Armistice.

April 24

The Israel Independence Day parade in Jerusalem proceeded without incident.

President Bourguiba of Tunisia said that he had discarded a plan to renew charges against France in the UN.

The US State Department released Egypt's frozen assets in the US.

April 25

Moroccan King Muhammad V opened the Fourteenth International Casablanca Trade Fair.

Morocco joined the International Monetary Fund and World Bank.

Discussion began in Rabat, Morocco, to fix the agenda for the Tangier North African Party Conference.

Three Algerian revolutionaries, Abd-al-Rahman Taleb, Gharbi Said and Saab Ben-Belkacem, were guillotined in Algeria by the French for taking part in the national liberation movement.

There was a general strike in Aden against the British "imperialist domination."

About 5,000 Israel troops, equipped with tanks and artillery, completed their withdrawal from Jerusalem without incident following the Independence Day parade.

April 26

The Jordanian House of Notables unanimously approved amendments to the Constitution to bring it into line with the Constitution of the Arab Federal State.

Tunisia gave the Conorada Petroleum Company of America prospecting rights in southern Tunisia.

King Paul and Queen Frederika of Greece arrived in Lebanon for a four day state visit.

The conference agenda for Tangier was set; it included discussions about independence for Algeria, the liquidation of remnants of colonial domination in the Maghreb and North African unity.

April 27

The UN conference on maritime law adopted an article permitting innocent passage of foreign ships through straits connecting high seas or national and international waters, thus upholding Israel shipping rights in the Gulf of Aqaba. The Arab states abstained from voting.

Libyan Premier Abd-al-Majid Kobar arrived in London to discuss the British-Libyan Treaty of 1953.

Premier Kobar of Libya made some changes in his Cabinet.

Iraq informed the Arab League that it would not pay its share of the League budget for the coming year nor settle its debt of LE256,000 because of its economic condition.

Iraqi Foreign Minister Fadel al-Jamali began a tour of neighboring countries.

The Syrian people were told that luxury goods valued at more than $300 would not be imported without an irrevocable letter of credit.

April, 1958

April 27

The Arab League Council denounced the latest British attacks on Yemen.

At a conference in Morocco, delegates from the Moroccan Istiqlal Party, the Tunisian Neo-Destour Party, and the rebel Algerian National Liberation Front issued a communique outlining agreement on a practical program to achieve Algerian independence.

April 29

President Nasser arrived in Moscow for an 18 day state visit and expressed his gratitude for Soviet support in the 1956 Suez Crisis and for arms supplied by Russia to Egypt and Syria.

The UN Conference on the Law of the Sea (Geneva) adopted a covenant recognizing rights of states to exploit natural resources on their continental shelves. The Covenant did not set a territorial water limit.

An agreement on compensation to stockholders of the nationalized Universal Suez Canal Company was signed in Rome between the UAR and Company representatives. LE28.3 million would be paid to stockholders over a five year period.

April 30

The Tangier Conference final communique urged the establishment of an Algerian government in exile, the formation of a Maghreb federal union and the evacuation of foreign troops from the Maghreb states. The communique also recommended that North African governments not commit themselves separately in foreign relations or defense plans until after their federation.

The US Treasury Department announced that on the advice of the State Department it was releasing $26 million of Egyptian Government funds and $44 million of Universal Suez Canal Company assets that had been frozen when Egypt nationalized the Suez Canal.

May, 1958

May 1

Iraqi Prime Minister Nuri-Said said that 114 of his supporters were unopposed in the general elections for the Chamber of Deputies.

Henry R. Labouisse announced his resignation as Director of the UN Relief and Works Agency for Palestine Refugees in the Near East.

King Muhammad V of Morocco endorsed plans for the creation of a North African Federation composed of Algeria, Morocco and Tunisia.

King Hussein ratified the amendments to the Jordanian Constitution.

US Secretary of State Dulles asserted that the Soviet Union was not a market for Middle East oil.

May 2

It was reported that the Soviet Union had offered the Sudan technical and economic aid.

A state of emergency was declared in the Protectorate of Aden following two bombing incidents.

May 3

President Nasser started a tour of the Soviet Union. It was reported from Cairo that an accord had been reached with Russia on economic issues.

Tunisian President Bourguiba announced three changes in his Cabinet: 1. Health Minister Ahmad Ben Salah took over the Ministry of Social Affairs, formerly headed by Muhammad Chakroun; 2. Education Minister Lamine Chabbi took over the Ministry of Sports and Youth, succeeding Muhammad Messadie; and 3. Bashir Mahdebi was made Chief of the Cabinet, his former position of Radio Chief being filled by Shadli Klibi.

An official statement said that the presence of large stocks of arms on the borders of Aden constituted a grave threat to the security of Aden colony which in the present state of emergency could not be tolerated.

May, 1958

May 4

A military good will mission from the UAR ended its five week stay in Communist China.

President Nasser visited Tashkent, capital of Uzbekistan, a republic of the USSR.

Sheikh Abdallah al-Salem al-Sabah, Ruler of Kuwait, accepted an invitation from King Faisal to visit Iraq.

Abd-al-Hamid Mehri and Ahmad Francis, NLF leaders, said that US support of France was alienating the Algerians.

Yemen sent a letter to the UN Security Council proposing a neutral investigation of alleged British attacks. The British Foreign Office termed the letter inaccurate and misleading.

May 5

Iraq elected a new Parliament; only 27 of the 145 seats in the Chamber of Deputies were being contested. The general election ended in victory for General Nuri-Said.

Britain agreed to strengthen the Libyan Army and provide technical assistance to that country for the next five years.

President Nasser was reported to have told the Soviets that the Suez Canal would remain open to all in case of war.

It was announced after a Cabinet meeting that Lebanon would ask the US for a loan of about $230 million.

May 6

The West German Government announced it would give the UAR industrial credits amounting to about 400 million marks.

The UAR was to return part of the German assets seized in Egypt and Syria during World War II.

May, 1958

May 6

The US State Department said that discussions with Lebanon indicated that country would seek about $10 million in US aid.

Jordanian Finance Minister Anastas Hananiah said that the $36.5 million deficit in the 1958 budget resulting from the failure of Egypt, Syria and Saudi Arabia to honor their pledges would become the responsibility of the Arab Federation Government.

It was reported in Baghdad that Great Britain had informed the Iraqi Government of its willingness to give up its special treaty arrangements with Kuwait if that sheikhdom joined the Arab Federation.

May 7

In a bilateral agreement signed in Bonn, West Germany granted the UAR 400 million German marks credit for the purchase of industrial goods and provided the framework for West German technical assistance to the Arab Republic.

Yusuf al-Sibai, Secretary General of the Afro-Asian Conference, said that Communist China gave the Algerian nationalists $172,000 to be used for their rebellion.

Jordan halted Israel's bi-monthly supply convoy to Mount Scopus allegedly because two of the men accompanying it were intelligence agents. Israel refused to proceed without them and accused Jordan of a contradiction of the agreement negotiated by UN representative Dr. Francisco Urrutia.

May 8

Moroccan King Muhammad V promulgated a Royal Charter providing for a Deliberative Assembly that would share legislative power with the ruler, and enunciating the principle of collective responsibility of Cabinet members to the throne. The King called on Ahmad Balafrej, Secretary General of the Istiqlal Party and former Foreign Minister, to form a new Government.

May, 1958

May 8

A new Government was formed in Libya.

Tunisian President Bourguiba warned that there would be danger of war in North Africa unless Algeria was independent.

President Habib Bourguiba of Tunisia said he had no doubt that the projected Algerian government in exile would be recognized by the Communist countries and most of the Afro-Asian states. He said that the formation awaited agreement between the Tunisian and Moroccan Governments.

Britain protested to Yemen against attacks by Yemeni guns on planes flying over Aden territory.

The Iraqi Foreign Minister said that the Iraq Government had sent a strong note of protest to Egypt against the Voice of the Arabs broadcasts inciting Iraqis to revolt.

Nasib al-Mitni, owner of the anti-Government pro-Nasser newspaper Telegraphe, was assassinated in Beirut, Lebanon.

May 9

The Israel supply convoy halted by Jordan May 7 was allowed to proceed to Mount Scopus.

The US Information Service Library in Tripoli was sacked and burned by armed rioters demonstrating against the Lebanese Government.

Lahej Sultan Sir Ali Abd-al-Karim al-Abdali protested against the presence of British troops in Lahej and proposed that Britain empower him to approach Yemen in order to solve their border problems.

Twenty-one persons were reported killed and at least 128 seriously injured in Tripoli, predominantly Moslem seaport in northern Lebanon, when armed mobs rioted against the Lebanese Government and looted and burned the US Information Service Library.

May, 1958

May 11

Ralph J. Bunche, special UN Representative on Mount Scopus affairs, said that he had concluded a series of satisfactory talks with Samir al-Rifai, Jordan's Foreign Minister and Deputy Premier, Israel Prime Minister David Ben-Gurion, and other Israel and Jordanian leaders.

May 12

The Arab Federation of Iraq and Jordan became effective with the approval of the federal constitution.

Israel Premier Ben-Gurion met with Ralph Bunche to discuss the Palestine problem.

Anti-government fighting, directed against Lebanese President Camille Chamoun, occurred in Beirut.

The Lebanese Government decreed a state of alert and imposed a curfew from 8 pm to 5 am in Beirut.

Major oil pipelines in Lebanon belonging to Iraq Petroleum Company were cut by rebels.

A new Moroccan Cabinet with Ahmad Balafrej as Premier was invested. The Cabinet was composed entirely of members of the Istiqlal Party with the exception of the non-political Minister of Health.

May 13

Nuri-Said submitted his resignation as Premier of Iraq in order to form the cabinet for the Arab Federation.

It was reported that the German Cabinet was considering the use of former Marshall Plan funds to finance long term credits for development in the Middle East.

King Hussein of Jordan arrived in Baghdad for discussions on the administrative structure of the Arab Federation.

May, 1958

May 10

The Iraqi Chamber of Deputies ratified a constitutional amendment legalizing entry into the Arab Federation.

The Sheikh of Kuwait, Abdallah al-Salem al-Sabah, arrived in Baghdad for a state visit.

President Nasser visited Leningrad.

The Lebanese Journalists' Union and Newspaper Publishers' Association called a strike in protest against the assassination of Nassib al-Mitni, publisher and chief editor of the Telegraphe.

Spain was reported to have agreed to withdraw its troops from the Southern Protectorate of Morocco.

Morocco and Austria signed a trade agreement.

Serious disturbances broke out in Lebanon with increasing moral and material support from within the UAR.

May 11

Iraq s Senate ratified a constitutional amendment to permit the merger of Iraq and Jordan.

An official source in Cairo said that the US had authorized the purchase of $2 million worth of Egyptian cotton. This was the first trade agreement between Egypt and the US since the nationalization of the Suez Canal.

The Kuwait Government announced that it had granted the Japan Petroleum Trading Company offshore oil rights in the neutral zone between Kuwait and Saudi Arabia, in return for 57 percent of the profits.

The Saudi Arabian organization of the Council of Ministers was provided for by a Royal Decree.

Fighting was reported between rival political groups in Tripoli, Lebanon. This was the third day of rioting.

May, 1958

May 13

The Jordanian Chamber of Deputies approved the budget for 1958.

Lebanese Foreign Minister Charles Malik accused the UAR of having instigated and aided the rebellion in Lebanon.

Lebanese President Chamoun called in the US, British and French Ambassadors to report that his nation was under attack from abroad.

Rebel leader Saeb Salam of Lebanon made a statement criticizing US Secretary of State Dulles for blaming Communists for the trouble in Lebanon. The US Embassy replied that the allegation was false.

French generals and European rioters in Algiers staged demonstrations in Algiers, overwhelmed police and occupied French Government headquarters. They demanded the return of General Charles De Gaulle as premier of France. Jacques Massu, the French parachute troops commander, announced the formation of a Committee for Public Safety.

Israel Premier Ben-Gurion said that his state was ready to establish relations with the Arab states and that the Arabs should open their countries to the Palestinian refugees.

President Nasser visited the Joint Nuclear Research Institute in Dubna near Moscow.

A Soviet-Arab friendship rally was held at the Central Lecture Hall in Moscow.

New citizenship was established for the people of Syria and Egypt who were designated Arabs.

May 14

The US doubled the size of its Sixth Fleet in the eastern Mediterranean.

Kings Faisal of Iraq and Hussein of Jordan completed talks on the governing of the Arab Federation.

May, 1958

May 14

The oil flow through the Kirkuk-Tripoli pipeline was resumed in Lebanon.

Britain endorsed Lebanon's charge that the UAR had instigated the Lebanese uprisings.

The UAR refused to accept the Lebanese note complaining of interference in Lebanese internal affairs, rejecting it as "mere unjustifiable allegations."

Opposition parties combined in a Lebanese National Union Front announced that its general strike would continue until President Chamoun resigned.

The US State Department announced that at the request of the Lebanese Government it was rushing shipments of police equipment provided for under a program inaugurated in 1956.

Pierre Pflimlin was elected Premier of France after 28 days without a government. Premier Pflimlin authorized General Salan to assume civil as well as military power in Algeria.

Mecca Radio reported that King Saud of Saudi Arabia had ordered two Syrian and two Palestinian ministers dropped from the cabinet under a decree requested by Saudi Arabian Crown Prince Faisal, making it mandatory for all ministers to be Saudi Arabians.

The Tunisian government expressed anxiety to the US over the French army takeover in Algeria.

Incidents began in Tunisia involving French troops stationed there and French planes from Algeria.

The Moroccan-Algerian border was completely closed because of recent Algerian developments.

May, 1958

May 15

President Nasser and Soviet Premier Khrushchev signed a joint communique which committed the UAR to support the major Soviet foreign policy planks. The Soviet Union agreed to support liberation for the peoples of Asia and Africa.

Lebanese Foreign Minister Charles Malik said that hundreds of armed men had infiltrated his country from Syria. The Lebanese Army began action against the rebels.

The UAR protested against the deportation of Syrians from Lebanon.

Lebanese rebel leader Saeb Salam, in a note to the US Ambassador, said that the Opposition did not seek outside aid nor did it want Lebanon to join the UAR.

The Arab States Observed five minutes of mourning to commemorate the loss of Palestine to the Israelis.

General Charles De Gaulle announced, "I hold myself ready to take over the powers of the Republic."

The British Colonial Secretary told the House of Commons that he was not considering any proposal to revise the treaty relations with the rulers in the Protectorate of Aden.

Sheikh al-Salem Abdallah of Kuwait left Baghdad after his state visit. He cancelled plans to go to Cairo.

The Egyptian Minister of Economy and Trade, Abd-al-Moniem al-Kaissouni, said that Egypt expected the IBRD to help finance the Aswan High Dam.

Sheikh Yusuf Yasin, Rashid Firawn, Dr. Ahmad Shukairi and Jamal Husseini were reported to have been dismissed from the Council of Ministers of Saudi Arabia.

The UAR rejected Baghdad's protest against propaganda attacks broadcast by Cairo and Damascus Radios.

May, 1958

May 16

The US State Department said that it would send tanks to Lebanon in the near future, under the military assistance program.

UN officials were concerned about their inability to deliver food from Lebanon to the refugees in Syria due to the Lebanese crisis.

On his return from Moscow, Nasser told Egyptians that charges of his fostering the Lebanese rebellion were lies and fabrications.

The Government of French Premier Pflimlin was granted emergency powers to cope with the army insurrection in Algeria.

Clashes between the army and rebels were reported in many parts of Lebanon.

At the direction of Algerian General Salan, Andre Regard was named the new Secretary General of the Ministry for Algeria, and Colonel Godard was appointed Director of National Security.

The Ambassadors of Tunisia and Morocco in the US expressed their concern about the Algerian junta to US Secretary of State Dulles.

A trade agreement was signed between Morocco and Japan.

May 17

The UAR got a 20 to 30 percent reduction on the price of arms from the Soviet Union. Industrial equipment prices were cut by 15 percent.

Premier Khrushchev gave President Nasser an Iluyshin-14 plane and presented the UAR Government with a cotton research laboratory.

Jacques Soustelle, former Governor General of Algeria, arrived in Algeria.

An official stated that most of the Saudi Arabian troops stationed in Jordan would be withdrawn in the next few days.

May, 1958

May 17

The US State Department confirmed reports that consideration was being given to the dispatch of troops to Lebanon if Lebanese President Chamoun requested them.

A truce was reported to have been reached between followers of Amir Majid Arslan and Kamal Jumblat in the Lebanese Shuf.

Emile Bustani, Jamil Makkawi, John Aziz, Salim Lahoud and Nicola Salim, members of the Lebanese Chamber of Deputies, suggested the formation of a national coalition Government with a general principle of non-alignment.

May 18

A new Government was formed in Iraq with Ahmad Mukhtar Baban as Prime Minister.

Jordanian King Hussein accepted the resignation of the Hashem cabinet. Samir al-Rifai became the head of the new Government and formed a new Cabinet.

The French Government dismissed Serge Maret, Chief Prefect of Algiers.

May 19

The Arab Federation's first Cabinet was sworn in by King Faisal of Iraq with Nuri-Said as Premier and Ibrahim Hashem as Deputy Premier. Premier Nuri-Said declared that the Federation would cooperate with all Arab countries without interfering with their domestic problems and would seek a solution to the Algerian problem.

Soviet newspapers published a Tass statement on foreign interference in the domestic affairs of Lebanon.

Libyan Premier Kobar announced to Parliament that Britain would give Libya 3,250,000 pounds sterling a year for the next five years. The US would contribute $5.5 million a year to the Libyan Development Agency.

May, 1958

May 19

A Public Safety Committee for all Algeria was formed. They stated that this was not a government since all power remained in the hands of the army.

General Raoul Salan, Commander of French forces in Algeria, offered a pardon to all Algerian rebels who turned their arms over to the French Army.

Fighting was reported in the south of Lebanon for the first time since the outbreak of the rebellion.

General De Gaulle praised the achievements of the army of Algeria.

The US and Great Britain decided to act jointly in the Lebanese crisis, should action be necessary.

Lebanese Druze Chieftain Kamal Jumblat, in a letter to US Ambassador to Lebanon Robert McClintock, protested against US support of the Lebanese Government.

May 20

Jacques Soustelle, former Governor General of Algeria, called for the complete integration of Moslems and Europeans in Algeria.

Muhammad Sid Gara, Secretary of State in the former Algerian Ministry of Robert Lacoste, accepted the Presidency of the Pan-Algerian Committee of Public Safety.

The French Information Ministry said that French forces had killed 95 insurgents and captured 230 in the past 24 hours; French losses were listed as seven killed, 16 wounded and two missing.

The French National Assembly voted 475-100 to renew the Government's special powers to combat the Algerian rebellion.

Lebanon was reported to be consulting the US and Britain about a complaint to be filed against the UAR with the UN Security Council.

May, 1958

May 20

Rashid Karami, Raymond Edde, Saeb Salam and Abdallah al-Yafi were reported to be in consultation in Beirut, Lebanon. They reiterated their demand for President Chamoun's resignation.

Israel and Jordan signed an agreement to control malaria-breeding mosquitoes along their common border.

Lebanon deported 1,000 Syrians.

The Jordanian Government refused an Israel offer to supply Salk vaccine to combat the rising polio rate in western Jordan.

May 21

Lebanese President Chamoun announced his determination to serve out his term.

The Lebanese Government asked the Arab League Council for an immediate meeting to hear its complaint against the UAR.

In Lebanon, mediation efforts were made on the basis that General Chehab should lead a new Government and President Chamoun continue in office. Rebel leader Saeb Salam said that no proposal would be acceptable unless it included the immediate resignation of President Chamoun.

The Sudanese Government received a vote of confidence in the House of Representatives after a debate concerning US aid acceptance.

The Tunisian Government accused France of aggressive incursions, charging that four French jets had landed at the Gafsa Airport.

The French Government abolished censorship on news dispatches entering and leaving France, but continued restrictions on news published in the country.

May, 1958

May 22

British Government sources announced that Great Britain would give Libya 3,250,000 pounds sterling annually in financial aid for the next five years under a 1953 treaty.

President Bourguiba alerted Tunisia to the possibility of French aggression.

Fadel al-Jamali, former Iraqi Foreign Minister, urged a joint defense agreement between Iraq and Lebanon.

The evacuation of Spanish troops from the Southern Protectorate of Morocco was completed.

The Moroccan Government decided to authorize the establishment of a Soviet economic mission in Morocco.

The Lebanese Defense Minister, Rashid Baidun, resigned.

Lebanon lodged a complaint with the UN Security Council charging that the UAR had imperiled Middle Eastern peace by sending Syrian infiltrators into Lebanon and interfering in the internal affairs of Lebanon.

Ferhat Abbas, NLF leader, said that General De Gaulle might be able to solve the Algerian problem and stressed that the NLF would negotiate only with a legally constituted French Government.

May 23

Algerian General Salan issued a decree officially establishing the All Algerian Committee of Public Safety. It was jointly headed by Brigadier General Jacques Massu and Dr. Muhammad Sid Cara, Secretary of State in the former Algerian Ministry of Robert Lacoste.

French Premier Pflimlin, in a nationwide radio and TV address, rejected renewed demands of dissidents in Algeria that General De Gaulle be called to power.

May, 1958

May 23

It was reported that major projects to enlarge the Suez Canal would not begin for five years.

The Moroccan Federation of Labor, with government backing, prevented 900 French soldiers from disembarking at Casablanca.

It was announced in Rabat that the US had agreed to provide Morocco with $10 million in emergency assistance, in addition to the $20 million US aid program.

The UAR, according to Lebanese Foreign Minister Charles Malik, had agreed to a meeting of the Arab League Council to consider Lebanese charges of interference.

Premier al-Solh of Lebanon said that his government would not ask for a constitutional amendment to allow President Chamoun to run again.

Lebanese President Camille Chamoun accepted the resignation of Defense Minister Rashid Baidun and Minister of Communications Bashir Uthman; their posts were filled by Premier Sami al-Solh and Minister of National Economy Kazem al-Khalil.

May 24

Soviet and Sudanese sources in Khartoum officially confirmed that the Soviet Union offered technical and economic aid without obligations attached, to the Sudan.

Crown Prince Moulay Hassan of Morocco flew to the Southern Protectorate to receive official control of the military installations evacuated by the Spanish.

It was announced that President Nasser would visit Yugoslavia's President Tito in July.

The Committee of Public Safety, proclaimed in Algeria, seized control of Corsica.

May, 1958

May 24

King Faisal, head of the Arab Federation, arrived in Amman to open the first Parliament.

In Saudi Arabia, Crown Prince Faisal and members of the Council of Ministers took an oath of allegiance to King Saud in Dhahran.

Lebanese President Chamoun conferred with the American, French and British Ambassadors.

The Syrian Government reported 10,000 Syrians deported from Lebanon.

The Algerian Committee of Public Safety urged the establishment of a triumvirate to coordinate civil and political affairs, to be composed of General Massu and Messrs. Soustelle and Sid Cara.

The French Cabinet met in emergency session to consider the fighting at Remada between Tunisian and French troops. The US and Britain cautioned Tunisia and France against further clashes.

May 25

The twelfth anniversary of Jordan's independence was celebrated throughout the country.

King Faisal of Iraq said that the Arab Federation would protect the Arab countries from foreign influence and subversion.

Admiral Philippe-Marie Auboyneau, of the NATO Command in the Mediterranean, joined the Algerian insurrectionists.

Total mobilization of all Tunisian forces was ordered. President Bourguiba decreed a state of national emergency.

A British RAF transport plane from Cyprus reportedly delivered arms to the Lebanese Government.

Lebanese insurgents occupied Hasiya. Fighting in the country continued.

May, 1958

May 26

Saudi Arabia banned the entry of pilgrims by plane from Pakistan and India; others were allowed to enter the country if they were vaccinated.

Lieutenant Colonel George A. Flint, Chairman of the UN Mixed Armistice Commission, was killed during an exchange of fire by Jordanian soldiers and Israel police on Mount Scopus.

UN Secretary General Hammarskjold said that a radical change of attitudes was needed to restore peace in the Middle East.

President Bourguiba told Tunisians that he had asked for British-US intervention in easing tension with France.

Members of the Arab League met in Cairo to try and resolve the dispute between Lebanon and the UAR before it was brought before the Council.

Nassim Majdalani, Deputy Leader of the Social Progressive Party in Lebanon, said that the opposition movement was against the Government, not the state, and was a result of President Chamoun's attempts at being re-elected.

The UAR described as "baseless" Lebanese charges that it was behind the internal crisis in Lebanon.

The Lebanese Government formed a Militia of National Volunteers and distributed arms to them.

May 27

Despite a 408-165 vote of confidence from the Algerian National Assembly, French Premier Pflimlin submitted his resignation, under Gaullist pressure. He agreed to continue in office until a successor was found.

Iraqi King Faisal was sworn in as Head of the Arab Federation in Amman. Federal Parliament members were sworn in.

May, 1958

May 27

Lebanese Premier al-Solh, in a broadcast, said that his Cabinet did not intend to seek the re-election of President Chamoun.

The UN Security Council, at the request of Lebanon, postponed debate on the Lebanese complaint against the UAR to give the Arab League time to settle it.

US Ambassador to Lebanon Robert McClintock, having heard that American arms were being diverted to unofficial partisan forces in Lebanon, threatened to stop shipment unless the arms were given only to security forces.

Tunisians demonstrated, calling for the evacuation of French forces from their country and for arms from the US and Britain.

Tunisian Ambassador to the US and UN Mongi Slim discussed the Tunisian-French crisis with UN Secretary General Hammarskjold.

It was reported from London that Baghdad Pact preliminary meetings would begin July 16 and a ministerial session was set for July 28-31.

King Faisal of Iraq, Head of the Arab Federation, opened the first Parliament of the Arab Federation.

Syria accused Israel of an armed attack across the Syrian border.

May 28

Five men were convicted of having taken part in a plot against President Nasser in Cairo.

Indonesian pilots were to be trained in Egypt in Czech and Polish fighter planes.

A communique from the Tangier meeting said that the Maghreb delegates had agreed on political and practical means of action to free Algeria.

May, 1958

May 28

Emile Bustani, a member of the Lebanese Chamber of Deputies, in a press conference, called for the re-establishment of the national covenant between Christians and Moslems.

In Lebanon the National Union Front said that the security forces were giving US arms to unofficial partisan forces. Other arms had fallen into the hands of the rebels.

May 29

Kamal-ad-Din Hussein, Education Minister of the UAR, said that Russian would be taught in all schools in the UAR.

A joint letter by the Mufti of Lebanon, Sheikh Muhammad Abu-Shakra of the Druzes and Sheikh Muhammad al-Taqi al-Sadiq of the Shiites, protested to General Chehab against the formation of a militia.

The Sudanese Minister of Finance presented the budget to Parliament.

Israel presented a note to the Security Council charging Jordan with responsibility for the death of Colonel Flint.

French President Rene Coty asked the French National Assembly to vote Premiership to General De Gaulle or risk civil war. He said he would resign if the Assembly did not comply.

The US Federal Grand Jury in Alexandria, Virginia, returned an indictment charging 29 US oil companies with price fixing of crude oil and gasoline after the 1956 Suez Canal crisis.

The Tunisian Government asked the UN Security Council to meet to consider armed aggression by France in Tunisian territory. In a counter-complaint, France asked the Council to consider the situation in Algeria resulting from aid furnished by Tunisia to the rebels.

May 30

Renewed fighting was reported at Remada, Tunisia.

May 30

The UN Security Council was summoned to meet to consider both the Tunisian complaint and the French counter-complaint of the previous day.

Prominent Lebanese leaders issued a statement drawing public attention to the danger of foreign intervention in their country.

Maronite Patriarch Paul Moushi recommended in a press conference that Lebanese President Chamoun be replaced by General Chehab to exercise government powers. He said that Chehab was the only one capable of preventing war.

May 31

A decree issued by General Salan, the French Commander in Chief of the Armed Forces in Algeria, put all departments and regions under direct control of local commanding generals.

The US and Jordanian Governments signed an agreement under which the US would provide $2.5 million for work on the Jordan Valley irrigation project.

Colonel S. G. H. Norstrum of Sweden was appointed Chairman of the Israel-Jordan Mixed Armistice Commission, succeeding Lieutenant Colonel George Flint.

Czechoslovakia announced the beginning of economic projects in India and Yemen.

Adel Usaran, Speaker of the Chamber of Deputies in Lebanon, said that the proposal to recruit volunteers to form a militia could not be carried out due to lack of financial appropriation.

The Lebanese Cabinet decided not to dismiss General Chehab, although he had failed to take strong measures to quell the revolt.

The Arab League met in Benghazi, Libya, to consider the complaint by Lebanon of UAR intervention in its internal affairs.

June 1

General Charles De Gaulle was elected Premier of France by a National Assembly vote of 329-224 and granted power to rule France by decree for six months.

Jacques Chevallier, Mayor of Algiers, endorsed a federal solution to end the Algerian war.

Leon Delbecque, Vice President of the All Algeria Committee of Public Safety, said that the Cabinet submitted by General De Gaulle was not yet the Government of Public Safety the Committee had hoped for.

Bashir al-Ahwar, Lebanese Minister of Justice, charged before the Arab League meeting in Benghazi that the UAR was interfering in Lebanon's affairs and fomenting anti-Government riots.

The US was charged with being behind the plot to sabotage the merger of Egypt and Syria into the UAR.

Ahmad Ibn-al-Thani, eldest son of the Sheikh of Qatar, arrived in Teheran for an official visit.

June 2

French Premier De Gaulle sent a message to King Muhammad V of Morocco expressing his intention to maintain and develop with the Moroccan Government relations corresponding to the friendship already existing between their two countries.

Tunisia asked the UN Security Council to take all necessary measures to assist it in the evacuation of French troops from Tunisia.

Lieutenant General Muhammad Rafiq Aref of Iraq was appointed Chief of the General Staff of the Arab Union Army.

French Premier De Gaulle asked for the authority to submit to a referendum reforms of the French Union.

The Lebanese Government again requested postponement of the UN Security Council meeting on its complaint against the UAR until June 5.

June 2

The US Ambassador to Lebanon said in Beirut that US arms were and would be going to legitimate security forces in Lebanon.

Work began on a potash factory in Jordan to be built by a West German firm on the north shore of the Dead Sea.

French Premier De Gaulle appealed to Tunisian President Bourguiba to help settle the difficulties between their countries themselves.

The UN Security Council began discussion of the French-Tunisian dispute. Debate was to be renewed June 4.

June 3

King Muhammad V of Morocco, in a note to French Premier De Gaulle, expressed hope that De Gaulle would be able to establish free cooperation between France and the countries of North Africa.

Jacques Chevallier, Mayor of Algiers, tendered his resignation.

Tunisian President Bourguiba told French Premier De Gaulle that he, too, wished to settle the differences between Tunisia and France.

Tunis expressed disappointment in French Premier De Gaulle's speech to the Algerians promising elections in three months. Tunisian sources said that the Algerians wanted Algerian, not French, citizenship.

The last of five USIS libraries was closed in Lebanon.

June 4

Premier De Gaulle arrived in Algiers and pledged equality of voting for the French and Moslems of Algeria. He invited the Algerian nationalists to participate in the elections. A spokesman for the NLF spurned De Gaulle's offer and said that the rebellion would continue.

June 4

The UN Security Council unanimously accepted a French suggestion to postpone for two weeks its discussion of the Franco-Tunisian dispute in order to permit direct negotiations between the two countries.

A communique from Riyahd announced that all imports would be subject to licenses issued by the Council of Ministers in Saudi Arabia, and that imports of motor cars and luxury items would be banned.

An Israel Foreign Ministry spokesman denied reports that Israel was supplying arms to the Lebanese Government.

June 5

The Lebanese Parliament was called to meet July 24 to elect a new President to succeed Chamoun, whose six year term was to end September 23.

Clovis al-Khazin, Lebanese Minister of Information, said that the government had decided to forbid publication of statements by leaders of the Opposition.

Lebanon again requested postponement of the UN Security Council discussion of its complaint against the UAR until June 6.

The Council of Ministers instructed the Lebanese delegation at Benghazi to reject a proposed resolution calling for a stoppage of radio propaganda.

Moroccan Premier Balafrej received the French Ambassador. It was presumed that Balafrej had asked for a clarification of the intentions of Premier De Gaulle concerning North Africa.

Sultan Saleh Ibn-Hussein of Audhali, Aden, declared that his people should stand on their feet and resist the propaganda and subversion from Yemen and the UAR if they were adequately backed by the British Government.

UAR delegates arrived in Paris to draft a final agreement on compensation for shareholders of the Suez Canal Company.

June 5

De Gaulle told Algerians that all distinctions between the nine million Moslems and the one million Europeans would disappear. This meant that the ten million Frenchmen of Algeria must have the same laws and the same duties.

President Nasser clamped down on pro-Communist writers in the press and allowed criticisms of the Soviet Union to appear in magazines and newspapers in Egypt as he revised his relationship with the Communist bloc. Censors also ordered Soviet propaganda pamphlets and books out of bookshop windows.

June 6

De Gaulle told the Committee of Public Safety for Algeria that he was leaving control of Algeria in the hands of General Raoul Salan, who must take his instructions from Paris. He cracked down on the Committees of Public Safety whose limited activity was put under Salan's direction.

Foreign Minister Charles Malik of Lebanon asked the UN Security Council to halt UAR interference in Lebanon's internal affairs.

Lebanon's Army met rebel forces near Tripoli and Halba in the most intense battle since the start of hostilities May 10.

The Arab League Council ended its consideration of Lebanon's complaint after the Lebanese delegation rejected the paragraph in a four-part draft resolution which requested the Lebanese Government to withdraw its complaint from the UN Security Council.

The Arab League Council meeting ended. No resolution had been passed.

The UN held its first debate on the Lebanese situation. Lebanese Foreign Minister Charles Malik presented to the UN Security Council the Lebanese accusations of gun running, training terrorists and press and radio propaganda against the UAR. He presented no resolution and asked for no specific measures but left action to the discretion of the Council. The charges were denied by UAR delegate Omar Loutfi. The Council then adjourned until June 10.

June 6

Fifteen Moslem judges issued statements condemning Premier al-Solh of Lebanon for his support of the Government.

June 7

It was reported that Saif al-Islam Abdallah returned to Yemen.

The UAR was to send 300 students to study in the Soviet Union, and in return the Soviet Union agreed to send technical and scientific equipment, cultural experts and professors to the UAR.

It was announced that municipal elections would be held in Algeria in about a month.

The Algerian Cabinet confirmed Premier De Gaulle's decision to assume the powers of Minister for Algeria.

An NLF spokesman in New York said that his organization was preparing for debate on the Algerian war in the UN General Assembly.

The Committee of Public Safety for Algeria placed itself "without condition or reservation" under General Salan's authority.

Three French policemen in Bone were killed in a surprise rebel attack.

June 8

Syria imposed an exit head tax of LS10 on all UAR citizens leaving for countries outside the UAR.

The UAR denied an Israel report that on June 6 smugglers from Syria had tried to make their way through Israel to Lebanon with guns.

June 9

The leaders of Ghana and Libya discussed the establishment of a communications network between the two countries. Premier Kobar of Libya also accepted an invitation to visit Ghana.

June 9

The Higher Planning Council of Morocco met to study the draft of the 1958-1959 Two Year Plan.

General Salan, French Commander in Chief of the Armed Forces in Algeria, accepted the resignation of the Mayor of Algiers, Jacques Chevallier.

Prime Minister Kwame Nkrumah of Ghana arrived in Tunis for a state visit.

Algerian NLF leaders meeting in Cairo called for an all out attack against the French forces.

The US allotted ten million dollars in aid to Morocco, bringing the total for the year to $30.5 million.

It was reported that Syria had decided to raise import tariffs on a number of consumer goods without approval from Cairo. President Nasser was reported to have summoned the two Vice Presidents of the Syrian Region to Cairo to discuss the tax increase on imports.

President Chamoun of Lebanon decreed that harsh action would be taken against government employees who were found to act against the interest of the state, or who joined a political party or participated in strikes.

Lebanese Premier al-Solh, in a nationwide broadcast, denied foreign reports that Lebanon had accepted foreign mediation offers.

June 10

The All Algeria Committee of Public Safety sent a message to French Premier De Gaulle calling for the abolition of political parties, the formation of a real Government of public safety and the postponement of Algerian elections.

The UN Security Council resumed debate on the Lebanese situation. Lebanon was supported by the US, Great Britain, France and Iraq. The Soviet Union accused the US and Britain of intervention in Lebanon because of their oil interests there.

June 10

Sweden proposed in the UN Security Council that observers be sent to Lebanon to investigate its charges against the UAR.

US Secretary of State Dulles said that there was irrefutable evidence of UAR interference in Lebanon.

In Lebanon, Munir Taj-ad-Din, Director General of the Ministry of Defense, and Abd-al-Aziz Chehab, Director General of the Ministry of Interior, resigned.

UN Secretary General Hammarskjold named his executive assistant, Andrew W. Cordier, as his special representative to Mount Scopus.

The US and Britain completed arrangements to reinforce Iraq, Jordan and Lebanon with about 50 jet fighters.

June 11

The International Bank announced that a final agreement had been reached to compensate Suez Canal Company shareholders. This agreement, based on the Rome Treaty of April 29, was to be signed in July.

The UN Security Council adopted a resolution by a vote of 10-0-1 (Soviet Union) creating Observation Group in Lebanon (UNOGIL), to ensure that there would be no illegal infiltration of personnel or supply of arms or other material across the Lebanese border.

Ghana pledged complete support of Tunisian demands of French troop withdrawals.

France charged that Jordan had occupied part of the French Embassy in Amman June 8.

French Premier De Gaulle reprimanded the Algerian Committee of Public Safety for its demand of June 10.

June, 1958

June 12

UN Secretary General Dag Hammarskhold said that the UNEF would need $20 million to maintain itself in 1958.

In outlining his plans for UNOGIL, UN Secretary General Hammarskjold set up a three man committee to head the UN observation team in Lebanon.

Jordanian King Hussein arrested 60 army officers whom he accused of having plotted to assassinate him with the help of the UAR.

It was reported that the Council of Ministers in Lebanon had decided to raise 1.5 million pounds sterling for an emergency militia, under military discipline, to serve for six months.

Asaad al-Asaad, Director General of Information in Lebanon, resigned.

Five officers of the Palestine Truce Supervision Organization, on temporary duty with UNOGIL, arrived in Lebanon as part of the UN observation group.

Prime Minister Kwame Nkrumah of Ghana arrived in Rabat, Morocco.

It was reported from Paris that the De Gaulle Government was seeking settlement of the French-Tunisian dispute on the basis of the plan submitted by the US-British good offices mission.

Tunisian President Bourguiba said that his country was always ready to cooperate with France.

Muhammad Jabari, Minister of Justice in Jordan, was appointed Minister of Education to replace Ahmad Tarawnah.

June 13

Syria opened all its main cities for international transit trade.

Lebanese insurgent units under the leadership of Druze Chieftain Kamal Jumblat launched a large scale offensive against Beirut.

June, 1958

June 13

Foreign Minister Malik of Lebanon discussed the possibility of increased aid to his country with US Secretary of State Dulles.

The Lebanese Ministry of the Interior cancelled all curfew passes in Lebanon beginning June 15.

French Premier De Gaulle stated French policy as: "To pacify Algeria . . . in such a way that it should always be body and soul with France."

French and Tunisian officials consulted on the withdrawal of French troops from Tunisia.

French Ambassador to Morocco Alexandre Parodi, after a week of consultation in Paris, returned to Rabat to resume negotiations on problems between France and Morocco.

June 14

UN Secretary General Hammarskjold announced the appointment of Major General Odd Bull of Norway, Galo Plaza of Ecuador and Rajeswar Dayal of India to head the UN Observation Group in Lebanon.

Heavy street fighting was reported in Beirut as rebel forces carried out numerous attacks.

The French Ambassador informed Premier Balafrej of Morocco that six French military posts in Eastern Morocco would be evacuated within two weeks. Five others in the South would be evacuated by July 15.

June 15

A joint communique issued by Morocco and Ghana said that the two Governments agreed on the necessity of strengthening the ties of solidarity binding independent African nations, of raising the standard of living and of working toward the liberation of still dependent African countries.

June, 1958

June 15

A six man delegation, headed by Ahmad Balafrej and Abderrahim Bouabidl, left Morocco for Tunis to lay the foundations for a Maghrebi Federation.

Ghana's Prime Minister, Kwame Nkrumah, arrived in Cairo for a state visit.

It was reported in Khartoum that the Sudanese Government had informed the Soviet Union of its readiness to enter into negotiations for an economic assistance and trade barter agreement.

It was reported that key units of the French Army in Algeria had gone on the alert to stage an offensive designed to wipe out the rebellion.

General Salan, French Commander in Chief of the Armed Forces in Algeria, named General Edmond Jouhad as his Deputy Commander in Chief.

Heavy street fighting occurred in Beirut. The Lebanese Government used tanks against rebel forces in the capital.

US Ambassador to Lebanon McClintock said that all US personnel who requested would be evacuated from Lebanon.

June 16

General Salan of Algeria was officially installed as Premier De Gaulle's Delegate General in Algeria. Brigadier General Jacques Massu was named Governor of the Algiers Department.

The Arab Federation budget of $91,296,800 was presented to Parliament. Iraq was to pay 80 percent.

June, 1958

June 16

In Lebanon, rebel leader Saeb Salam warned that President Chamoun risked a full scale war if he refused to resign.

UN Secretary General Hammarskjold reported that the work of UNOGIL was "greatly complicated by the fact . . . that only a small part of the total frontier appears to be controlled by [Lebanese] government forces."

Andrew Cordier, Executive Assistant to the UN Security General, conferred with Premier David Ben-Gurion and other Israel leaders on the dispute over Mount Scopus.

Tunisia imposed full censorship on all outgoing news dispatches.

June 17

The Japanese Arabian Oil Company signed an agreement with Great Britain implementing the grant of exploitation rights by Kuwait.

The North African Conference began in Tunis.

It was announced that 57 Middle Eastern banking and business establishments had bought voting shares in the Middle East Industrial Development Corporation.

Andrew Cordier of the UN conferred in Amman, Jordan, with Premier Samir al-Rifai.

The Lebanese Cabinet granted President Chamoun power to ask for international assistance to help bring peace to the country.

Lebanese Foreign Minister Charles Malik said that captured Syrian army officers had admitted that the UAR had interfered in Lebanon's affairs.

Bashir al-Ahwar, Minister of Justice and head of the Lebanese delegation to the Arab League Council meeting in Benghazi, resigned.

June, 1958

June 17

US Secretary of State Dulles renewed pledges that the US was ready to use troops, if necessary, to maintain Lebanese independence.

UN Secretary General Hammarskjold went to Beirut to attend the first meetings of UNOGIL.

Tunisia made an agreement with France that provided for provisional maintenance of French forces in Bizerta and for the evacuation of all other French military posts within four months.

The Iraqi Government accused Mustafa Abbas, Press Attache of the UAR in Baghdad, of carrying on activities against the interests of the Arab Union, and asked him to leave the country.

In a message to French Premier De Gaulle, Moroccan King Muhammad V expressed his hope that friendly relations between Morocco and France would be expanded to include all of North Africa.

June 18

Iraqi Premier Nuri-Said said that friendly relations between the two Arab unions could be brought about only on the basis of noninterference in the private affairs of the other Arab states.

Diplomatic sources reported that the US had asked President Nasser to cease all aid to rebel forces in Lebanon. President Nasser denied aiding the rebels.

Lebanese Premier al-Solh said that he had hoped that UN observers would ask the UN Security Council to take measures to stop infiltration of his country.

Lebanese Foreign Minister Charles Malik said that the UN observers had been asked to interrogate Syrian army officers who had crossed the Lebanese border.

US President Eisenhower said that any US military action in Lebanon was dependent upon the judgment of the UN observer team.

June, 1958

June 18

An agreement for evacuation of French troops from Tunisia was reported to the UN Security Council.

The Conciliation Commission for Palestine reported that as of April 30, 1958, Israel had released $7,444,335 of Arab blocked accounts. It also announced completion of its program of identification of individual Arab property holdings in Israel. It recommended valuation of holdings to facilitate the possible compensation to Arabs by Israel. The Commission stated that the situation in Palestine remained the same as reported in 1951 "in view of the unchanged attitudes of the parties and their failure to avail themselves of the commission's services."

A four day conference of Moroccan, Tunisian and Algerian nationalist leaders in Tunis deferred the establishment of an Algerian Government in Exile, but decided to set up a North African Assembly.

June 19

Iraqi and Jordanian diplomats stated that the merger of their two countries was to be officially called Arab Union rather than Arab Federation.

UN Secretary General Hammarskjold conferred with Lebanese leaders and UN observers in Beirut, Lebanon.

June 20

A communique issued at the close of a four day conference in Tunis of Moroccan, Tunisian and Algerian nationalist leaders said that the participants would act together on the diplomatic plane to achieve a peaceful solution of the Algerian problem. The communique also announced the establishment of two permanent mixed commissions to study economic cooperation and cultural and technical cooperation.

The Governments of Tunisia and Morocco joined the NLF in condemning the policy of integration with France for Algeria, as advocated by the Public Safety Movement there.

June, 1958

June 20

France announced that it would withdraw all ground forces, leaving only air and naval units in Tunisia.

Israel said that it would open the road between the Jordanian village of Issawiya and Jerusalem at their Mount Scopus enclave for a few hours each day. It had closed the road May 26.

The All Algerian Committee of Public Safety, in a two hour debate, expressed disapproval of Premier De Gaulle's policies and was unable to give him a vote of confidence.

June 21

UN Secretary General Hammarskjold conferred with Israel Premier Ben-Gurion in Jerusalem following talks in Amman with King Hussein and Jordanian Premier al-Rifai.

UAR Ambassador to Bonn, Farid Zain-ad-Din, said that foreign pilots were flying government planes for the Lebanese. There were no rumors to this effect in Beirut since there were more Lebanese pilots than planes.

Henry Labouisse of the UN said that former Palestinians had played an active role in the Lebanese disturbances although there had been no trouble in the UNRWA camps.

It was officially reported that many of the restrictions imposed on French troops in Tunisia after the bombing of Sakiet Sidi Youssef in February had been lifted as a result of the troop withdrawal agreement with Tunisia.

The UAR and Spain were reported to have signed a commercial barter agreement for exchange of Spanish flour and wheat for Egyptian cotton.

June 22

It was reported that the North African Conference held in Tunis the previous week decided to form a Maghrebian Permanent Secretariat and a Maghrebian Consultative Assembly.

June, 1958

June 22

Muhammad Ali al-Jifri, President of the Lahaj Legislative Council, and Muhammad Salim Bawazir, Acting General Secretary of the South Arabian League, protested that Britain had forced federation on territories that rightfully belonged to Yemen.

UN Secretary General Hammarskjold arrived in Cairo to consult with President Nasser and Foreign Minister Mahmoud Fawzi about the Lebanese situation.

Syria said that 25,000 Syrians had been expelled from Lebanon. President Nasser requested that 50,000 pounds sterling be distributed among them, and that accommodations and jobs be found for them. The UAR also threatened to send volunteers to Lebanon.

June 23

UAR President Nasser was reported to have expressed conditional willingness to use his good offices with Lebanese rebels to bring about a ceasefire.

Two members of the Algerian NLF had a two hour meeting with Libya's Premier Kobar in Benghazi.

Premier Nuri-Said of the Arab Union arrived in London for talks with British officials.

Moroccan Premier Balafrej conferred with US Ambassador Cannon concerning US air and naval bases in Morocco.

Moroccan King Muhammad V held an extraordinary Cabinet meeting to discuss the evacuation of foreign troops.

June 24

UN Secretary General Hammarskjold returned to Beirut and conferred with President Chamoun of Lebanon.

Fawzi al-Hass, a Beirut member of the Chamber of Deputies, switched allegiance from the Lebanese Government to the rebels.

June, 1958

June 24

The Soviet Union charged the US and other Western powers with armed intervention in the affairs of Lebanon. It said it would not stand by in case of such intervention.

French government spokesman Andre Malraux said that France would try to reconcile the French and Moslems in Algeria. He said also that a "model" department would be set up in Algeria.

A trade agreement was signed between Morocco and Italy.

Moroccan Premier Balafrej informed the French Ambassador of the extreme urgency of the evacuation of French troops.

June 25

The French Cabinet approved drafts of three decrees that would limit the power of the French Army in Algeria. Formal approval was pending.

The Afro-Asian bloc in the UN decided to ask the General Assembly to take up the Algerian question.

Lebanon asked the UN to seal its land and sea frontiers with armed forces.

President Chamoun of Lebanon said that he might ask for outside aid under Article 51 of the UN Charter.

Bashir al-Ahwar, who was reported to have resigned as Minister of Justice in Lebanon June 17, resumed his post.

The Soviet news agency, Tass, published a statement on the Western powers' projected armed intervention in Lebanon.

June 26

One-third of the regular Army of the state of Lahej deserted to Yemen, reportedly taking a substantial amount of state treasury funds with them.

June, 1958

June 26

UN Secretary General Dag Hammarskjold returned to New York from Lebanon. He said that UNOGIL was "an observation operation, and the word 'observation' is decisive."

June 27

The Iraq Petroleum Company reported that Iraq's export of crude oil to the Mediterranean, disrupted by sabotaged pipelines during the Suez crisis in November, 1956, was operating normally.

Lebanese Premier Sami al-Solh issued a statement that he had never made a formal request for UN troops to be sent to Lebanon.

The Lebanese UN delegation stated that "illegal infiltration of men and smuggling of arms into Lebanon" was increasing. UN Secretary General Hammarskjold asked Lebanon to provide this evidence to UNOGIL.

The US announced that it was shipping 65,000 tons of wheat to Lebanon.

June 28

Seven main UN observer outposts were established in Lebanon.

June 29

UAR President Nasser said that the Lebanese crisis was due to the Lebanese government's attachment to foreign alliances. He denied any UAR intervention.

Moroccan Premier Balafrej protested against the change in the status of the US base at Nouaseur, without prior notification given the Moroccan Government, from a supply base to an operational SAC (Strategic Air Command) base.

June, 1958

June 30

Lebanese President Chamoun said that he would not run for re-election.

The Foreign Ministry of Lebanon stated that if the UN Security Council were asked for and agreed to send a police force, but Russia vetoed the resolution, Lebanon would request a meeting of the UN General Assembly.

A French-Tunisian accord was signed for the construction of a pipeline from the new Algerian oil field of Edjele through southern Tunisia to port al-Skirra near Gabes. The Tunisian signing of the agreement was assailed by the NLF as "playing into hands of French Colonialists."

July, 1958

July 1

The Sudan began diverting the waters of the Nile River into the new Managil irrigation project without waiting for the concent of the UAR.

The Ohio Oil Company announced the finding of oil on their concession area in Libya.

Kamal Jumblat, Druze Chieftain in Lebanon, said that if there was any Western military intervention in Lebanon the insurgents would accept foreign volunteers.

Lebanese President Chamoun said that the rebel drive toward the Beirut Airport was part of an all out attempt to overthrow his Government. He predicted a government offensive in the next week that would be coordinated with an attack on Tripoli.

Lebanese President Chamoun conferred separately with the American and British Ambassadors.

US Secretary of State Dulles said that the UN observers in Lebanon might be slowing down or even stopping infiltration from Syria.

Chairman of the US Joint Chiefs of Staff General Nathan Twining said that the US was ready to send troops to Lebanon if the situation called for it.

July 2

Premier De Gaulle toured isolated army posts in Algeria, where he promised Moslems equal rights with Europeans.

Yemen Crown Prince Muhammad al-Badr announced that Yemen had received and was still receiving arms from the Soviet Union.

The Moroccan Government accepted the nomination of Charles Woodruff Yost as US Ambassador to Rabat.

General Cheneliere succeeded General Cogny as the Commander of the French forces in Morocco.

July, 1958

July 2

Amir Talal Ibn Abd-al-Aziz returned to Jedda, Saudi Arabia, from Cairo.

The Iraqi Minister of Finance proposed that the allocation for foreign affairs and defense in the national budget be transferred to the federal budget.

UAR President Nasser met with Yugoslavian President Tito at Belgrade.

The Lebanese Foreign Ministry handed copies of a note to diplomatic envoys in Beirut accusing the UAR of using the Lebanese rebels as a means to obtain its ends.

The American Friends Service Committee approved a $3,000 grant to meet emergency needs among Christian and Moslem groups in Lebanon.

July 3

Ending his three day fact finding tour in Algeria, Premier De Gaulle proclaimed a plan to give Algeria its rightful share in the progress of France. The plan provided for economic expansion, social improvement and political reform. For this plan, $36 million would be added to the French budget.

The withdrawal of the first contingent of French troops stationed in southern Tunisia began.

Hassan Jabbara, the Syrian Minister of Planning, said that SL80 million would be allocated in the general budget for the Economic Development Council in Syria.

Jordan suspended a 1956 criminal exchange agreement with Syria.

The Moroccan Executive Committee of the Istiqlal Party condemned the French plan for atomic tests in the Sahara.

The US State Department announced an agreement to lend Tunisia the equivalent of $100 million to finance economic development projects.

July, 1958

July 3

UN Secretary General Hammarskjold said that observation teams in Lebanon had found no evidence of mass infiltration of men and arms from Syria. A Lebanese government spokesman disputed UN Secretary General Dag Hammarskjold's statement and said that the rebels were supported by 3,000 Egyptians, Syrians and Palestinians from Gaza armed with 36,000 fire arms, machine guns and heavy mortar.

Israel charged Syria with opening fire with heavy automatic weapons in the Lake Huleh area.

July 4

The De Gaulle Government published decrees in Algeria establishing a single electoral college for Europeans and Moslems and enfranchising Moslem women.

Stockholders of the Universal Suez Canal Company approved the final compensation agreement with the UAR.

The UN observer group, reporting to the UN Security Council, said that there was no evidence of Syrian infiltration into Lebanon, as charged by Lebanon.

The Lebanese Government declared six UAR diplomats personae non gratae and gave them 48 hours to leave the country for allegedly inciting the Lebanese to revolt and for giving financial aid to the revolution.

July 5

Galo Plaza, Head of the UN observer team, termed the Lebanese conflict a civil war.

Emile Bustani, Member of the Lebanese Chamber of Deputies, called for the immediate resignation of the Lebanese Government and the appointment of a new President to settle the dispute. The new Government, he said, should depend on the Lebanese economy, dispensing with outside aid, and should join with no Arab or international group.

July, 1958

July 5

Negotiations between the Iraq Petroleum Company and the Iraqi Government opened to discuss the outstanding issues between the two.

President Nasser and Tito began conferences at Brioni, Yugoslavia.

The NLF called for a general strike in Algeria that was not to affect the major cities.

Kuwait and the Japanese Arabian Oil Company signed an agreement for offshore oil prospecting rights in the Kuwait half of the neutral zone shared with Saudi Arabia.

Giuseppe Saragat, Italian Social Democratic leader, stated that Italy's new Government would not allow its Atlantic alliance to prevent it from supporting the emancipation of the Arab peoples still deprived of the benefits of autonomy.

July 6

Tunisian President Bourguiba said that the Government was planning to recognize the Soviet Union and Communist China before the end of the year.

General Raoul Salan, Commander in Chief of the Armed Forces in Algeria, in a speech in Algiers, pledged his loyalty to Premier De Gaulle and praised his program for Algeria.

Pro-Government spokesmen rejected all idea of compromise with the Opposition to end the revolt in Lebanon.

July 7

Jacques Soustelle, former Governor General of Algeria, was appointed Minister of Information in the French Cabinet.

The Iraqi Basra Petroleum Company announced that it would build a deep water terminal at the head of the Persian Gulf.

July, 1958

July 7

The Sudanese House of Representatives ratified the US aid agreement by a vote of 101-49.

The Jordanian Federal Council ratified a bill regulating conditions in the civil service.

The Federal Foreign Ministry informed all Governments which had diplomatic relations with Jordan and Iraq that such representation would now be to the Federal Government.

The Moslem countries of the Baghdad Pact were reported to have pledged their support to President Chamoun of Lebanon.

Saeb Salam, leader of the opposition in Lebanon, accused the US of "gunboat diplomacy" in its support of the Lebanese Government.

The International Red Cross announced that it had supplied medical equipment and blood plasma to the Lebanese Red Cross and the rebels.

July 8

Former French Premier Georges Bidault said that the heart of the Christian Democracy of France Movement was the belief that Algeria must remain French.

UAR Foreign Minister Mahmoud Fawzi conferred with Greek Foreign Minister Evangelos Averoff-Tositsas and Yugoslav Foreign Minister Koca Popovic.

Abd-al-Majid Abbas of Iraq presented his credentials to UN Secretary General Dag Hammarskjold as the new Iraqi representative to the UN.

A Syrian delegation of cotton exporters went to Cairo to consult the Minister of Agriculture on the need for new markets for Syrian cotton.

Three British planes were downed during a Royal Air Force attack on Harib, Yemen.

July, 1958

July 8

A Soviet military delegation headed by Air Minister Sergei Rudenko arrived in Cairo on the invitation of Field Marshal Abd-al-Hakim Amer, UAR War Minister and Commander in Chief.

The Turkish Ministry of the Interior said that Turkey had closed its border and banned Syrians from entering Turkish territory.

A law prohibiting polygamy went into effect in Tunisia.

July 9

A joint communique issued at the end of the meeting between the foreign ministers of the UAR, Greece and Yugoslavia stated that the ministers had exchanged views on the international situation. It also commented on the friendly ties among the countries.

The Saudi Arabian Ministry of Defense and Aviation began soliciting applicants to study at the War, Naval and Air Colleges in Egypt.

Atlantic Gulf Pacific Company, Standard Dredging Corporation and Hawaiian Dredging and Construction Company signed contracts with the UAR Government for a two year widening and deepening program for the Suez Canal.

Visa restrictions between Tunisia and France were relaxed.

The Belgian Consul General for Damascus, Louis de San, arrested on May 10 for smuggling arms, was brought to trial. He claimed diplomatic immunity and the court was adjourned pending a defense appeal to a higher court on the question.

Lebanese President Chamoun said that he would definitely leave office at the end of his term.

July 10

The joint communique issued by UAR President Nasser and President Tito of Yugoslavia called for the termination of the cold war, the abolition of nuclear tests, a summit conference and support of the UN.

July, 1958

July 11

The Sultan of Lahej said in Rome that he would ask President Nasser and other Arab leaders to support him against the British.

The British Foreign Office said that Horace Phillips, Protectorate Secretary to the Aden Government, had flown to Diredawa, Ethiopia, to negotiate with a Yemeni representative to halt border fighting.

US Ambassador McClintock reaffirmed the US pledge to support the Lebanese Government.

July 12

The final accord between the UAR Government and the Suez Canal Company, scheduled to be signed, was indefinitely postponed due to a difference in the interpretation of a clause intended to fix the level of indemnification.

It was reported that the US had informed Lebanon that it was ready to consider favorably requests for financial help to rebuild the economy.

UN observers gained access to the border controlled by Sabri Hamadi, Opposition Deputy in Lebanon, which meant all the borders were open to the UN.

Saeb Salam of Lebanon accused US Ambassador McClintock of meddling in the internal affairs of Lebanon.

The Soviet Union accused the US and other Western powers of planting Russian guns in the hands of the Lebanese rebels.

It was reported that the French Government had offered to evacuate all ground forces from Morocco in return for the maintenance of air bases at Meknes and Marrakech and naval air bases at Port Lyautey (Qunaytra) and Agadir.

July 13

Final agreement in Geneva between the UAR and the Universal Suez Canal Company called for compensation payments to stockholders of 23 million pounds sterling on a five year installment plan.

July, 1958

July 10

Soviet Air Force Commander, Marshal Sergei I. Rudenko, was reported to have offered the UAR TU-114 commercial airliners.

The French Army announced that it was conducting an offensive to contain the rebels in their strongholds so that they could not interfere with the referendum to be held on September 28.

The Afro-Asian bloc in the UN signed a request that the Algerian problem be brought before the fall session of the General Assembly.

The Moroccan Government signed an agreement with the US to provide Morocco with $30 million for development projects.

The UAR accused the Sudan of violating the 1929 Nile Waters Agreement by diverting water into the main canal of the Managil extension without the UAR s consent.

Saeb Salam, leader of the Opposition Party in Lebanon, said that the Opposition would call off the revolt as soon as President Chamoun resigned.

About 17 members of the Lebanese Chamber of Deputies met to discuss the election to be held July 24.

Lebanese Finance Minister Pierre Edde said that the Government's financial position was sound and that the treasury would continue to face its commitments without inflation.

The manager of the Jordanian Phosphate Company said that Yugo Metal of Belgrade had agreed to take shipments of phosphate via Aqaba rather than Beirut.

British Colonial Secretary Lennox-Boyd told the House of Commons that the British Government had withdrawn recognition from Sultan Amir Fadel Ibn-Ali of Lahej and had forbidden him to return to Aden.

July, 1958

July 13

In a speech, Premier De Gaulle called for Federal Union between France and Algeria, with Algeria in a "choice place."

The Minister of Education in Jordan announced that the services of all the 50 Egyptian school teachers in Jordan would be terminated during the month of July.

Sir William Luce, Governor of Aden, left London for Lahej to study the situation there.

A trade agreement was signed between Morocco and the UAR.

Some units of the Twentieth Brigade of Iraq under the command of Abd-al-Karim Kassem were ordered to proceed to Jordan to reinforce the Iraqi troops there.

Saeb Salam, leader of the Opposition Party in Lebanon, said that any meeting of the Chamber of Deputies in the present circumstances would have no effect on the revolt.

July 14

Iraqi revolutionists seized Baghdad, proclaimed a republic, killed King Faisal, Crown Prince Abd-al-Ilah and Premier Nuri-Said. The British Embassy was sacked and burned. Brigadier General Abd-al-Karim Kassem was proclaimed Premier.

King Hussein of Jordan announced that he had assumed power as Head of the Arab Federation of Iraq and Jordan following the death of Iraqi King Faisal.

It was announced that King Hussein of Jordan had asked the US and Turkey for aid to meet the situation in Iraq.

General Kassem was reportedly in control of the Premier's office in Iraq.

The US halted all military aid to Iraq.

British Prime Minister Harold Macmillan ordered 6,000 British troops to prepare for speedy movement to the Middle East.

July, 1958

July 14

A Cabinet was formed under a Council of Sovereignty in Iraq. The Council members were General Nagib al-Rubai, Muhammad Mahdi Kubbah and Khaled al-Naqshabandi.

The British Cabinet met in emergency session after confirming that the British Embassy in Baghdad had been ransacked and set on fire.

British and American officials urged all dependents to leave Lebanon at once.

President Nasser extended recognition to the newly proclaimed Iraq Republic, and the Iraqi Republic recognized the UAR.

Iraqi troops in Jordan were ordered home.

US President Eisenhower called an emergency meeting of the UN Security Council to consider the Middle East situation.

The proposed meeting of the four Moslem members of the Baghdad Pact was transferred from Istanbul to Ankara. Iraq did not participate.

The new Iraqi Government announced that it intended to withdraw from the Baghdad Pact alliance.

UAR President Nasser left Yugoslavia for Cairo.

President Camille Chamoun of Lebanon appealed to President Eisenhower for military assistance because Iraq had been taken over by rebel forces. He also asked Britain and France to send troops.

July 15

Three thousand five hundred US Marines landed in Lebanon. US naval, air and army units were ordered into improved readiness positions in support of the Marines who had landed.

US President Eisenhower said that he had sent Marines to defend the sovereignty and independence of Lebanon following an appeal by President Chamoun.

July, 1958

July 15

Iraq asked the UN Security Council to postpone its meeting pending the arrival of Hashem Jawad to replace Abd-al-Majid Abbas as the government spokesman. The request was denied.

Gharbi Hajj Ahmad was appointed Director General of Guidance and Broadcasting in Iraq.

The IPC said that there had been no interruption in the flow of oil from Iraq.

The Amman Radio said that a large force of Iraqi soldiers loyal to King Faisal was marching on Baghdad.

Martial law was declared throughout Iraq and assemblies of more than five persons were prohibited.

US Delegate to the UN Henry Cabot Lodge announced that Fadel al-Jamali, Foreign Minister of Iraq, had been killed.

The Council of Ministers announced Iraq's withdrawal from the Arab Union.

Communist China hailed the coup as victory for national independence in Iraq.

The Iraqi Government was recognized by Yemen.

Iraqi Premier Kassem received the British and US Ambassadors.

The US Senate Foreign Relations Committee called for an inquiry into US foreign policy, especially that in the Middle East.

The UN Security Council met and heard two proposed resolutions. The US asked the Council to establish an international military force to protect the integrity of Lebanon. A Soviet resolution called on the US to cease its intervention in the affairs of the Arab states.

The Mixed Armistice Commission censured Israel for holding exercises with live ammunition near the Jordanian border July 8.

July, 1958

President Chamoun, in a broadcast to his nation, said that he had exhausted all other resources before asking for direct armed support. He said that requests to the UN and Arab League had not been effective.

The Soviet news agency Tass called the US Marine landing an "open act of aggression."

Yugoslavia warned that the landing of US Marines in Lebanon threatened a world war.

France said that it would come to the support of the US only if the US action in Lebanon was insufficient to safeguard Western interests and preserve the independence of Lebanon.

Ambassador Randolph W. Burgess, US representative to NATO, reported on the US Marine landings in Lebanon to the emergency session of the Permanent Representatives or that of the Foreign Ministers.

British Foreign Secretary Selwyn Lloyd said that his Government fully supported as necessary the American troop landing in Lebanon.

Officials of the UAR called the US landing of troops in Lebanon another Suez.

The People's Resistance was mobilized throughout Syria.

British reinforcements were sent to Aden.

Five Arab rulers in the Aden Protectorate who were in London discussing federation said that they would attain federation before the end of 1958

Jordan's Samir al-Rifai was given the portfolios of the Foreign and Defense Ministries after the Iraqi Republic named Ministers of Foreign Affairs and Defense.

The National Consultative Assembly of Morocco convened to debate a two year development plan submitted by the Higher Planning Council.

At an emergency meeting of the UN Security Council, called at the request of the US, US Delegate Henry Cabot Lodge informed the Council of the dispatch of US troops to Lebanon. He also said that American forces were instructed to cooperate with UNOGIL.

July, 1958

July 15

The heads of state of Turkey, Iran and Pakistan conferred in Ankara and approved the dispatch of US forces to Lebanon.

July 16

It was reported that the Heads of State of Pakistan, Iran and Turkey had urged King Hussein of Jordan to ask for American military aid.

Jordan's King Hussein, in a broadcast to the Iraqi people, called on them to quell the revolution.

Fawzi al-Mulki was appointed Royal Court Minister of Jordan.

The Middle East News Agency reported that Jordanian Cabinet members Ibrahim Hashem, Sulaiman Touqan and Khulusi al-Khairi and General Sadeq al-Shari, Deputy Commander of the Jordanian Army, were arrested in Baghdad.

The UN Observation Group in Lebanon (UNOGIL) reported full freedom of access to the borders of Lebanon.

The Jordanian Government asked the US for gasoline, kerosene and other oil products to replace supplies cut off after the coup in Iraq, Jordan's normal source of supply.

Sudanese Prime Minister Abdallah Khalil said that American troop landings in Lebanon were the turning point toward stability.

The three Moslem heads of state of the Baghdad Pact — the leaders of Turkey, Iran and Pakistan — ended a two day conference with praise for US military intervention in Lebanon.

Admiral Holloway, Commander of the US forces in Lebanon, met with General Faud Chehab of Lebanon. He said that the US Marine mission was to insure the safety of the port area and of the airport and to guarantee communications between the two.

US President Eisenhower sent Under Secretary of State Robert Murphy to Lebanon as his special political representative.

July 16

The UN observers group issued a statement saying that they would not establish any contact or working relationship with the US or other non-Lebanese forces in Lebanon.

More US forces were moved into Lebanon. Airlifts were working from the US to West Germany to Adana, Turkey.

The Permanent Council of NATO indicated approval of the US dispatch of troops.

Representative at the UN of 24 Afro-Asian nations requested that "the Question of Algeria" be included in the agenda of the General Assembly.

Red China, the Soviet Union, Ghana, Japan and India disapproved of the US troop landings in Lebanon.

Emile Bustani issued a statement which he said was signed by four other deputies in Lebanon — Jamil Makkawi, Nicola Salim, Salim Lahoud and Jean Aziz — stated that foreign troops on Lebanese soil should be removed, no matter what their purpose or nationality.

The Lebanese Prime Minister called on men who had received arms from Syrian army intelligence to surrender them and they would be treated justly.

The Soviet Union called for the immediate withdrawal of US troops from Lebanon. It asked the UN to take steps to stop American aggression, and reserve the right to take necessary measures dictated by the interests of peace and security.

UAR President Nasser declared that the occupation of Lebanon by American armed forces endangered world peace and was a direct threat to the Arab countries.

The US Government sent documentary evidence to the UN, listing more than 125 instances of infiltration and indirect aggression against Lebanon by Egypt and Syria between May 11 and June 21.

July 16

The Japanese Government expressed misgivings over the US military action in Lebanon, saying that the move could make a permanent settlement more difficult.

Sweden told the UN Security Council that the landing of US marines in Lebanon was not justified because no intervention from Syria had been detected by the UN Observation Group in Lebanon.

Talks between Aden and Yemen, to settle their border dispute, opened in Diredawa, Ethiopia.

The Finance Minister of Iraq authorized banks to pay out sums of up to ID100 and not exceeding ID300 per month for individual accounts. Merchants were allowed to draw enough to cover bank loans and companies to pay wages. The Minister said that this was a temporary measure.

The new Iraqi Cabinet assumed office and General Nagib al-Rubai, President of the new Republic, arrived from Jedda, where he had been Ambassador to Saudi Arabia.

Iraqi Premier Kassem received the American and Turkish Ambassadors.

The Soviet Union and Cummunist China officially recognized the Republic of Iraq.

President Nasser said that any aggression against the Iraqi Government would be considered aggression against the UAR under the terms of the Arab Collective Security Pact. He also condemned the US troop landings in Lebanon as a threat to peace in the Middle East.

British Foreign Secretary Selwyn Lloyd flew to Washington to discuss with US Secretary of State Dulles the critical position of the Western powers in the Middle East.

Israel Premier Ben-Gurion called his Cabinet into an emergency session to plan stretegy for the current Middle East situation.

July 16

The Sudanese Council of Ministers, after reviewing the tense situation in the Middle East, declared that the foreign policy of their country was based on neutrality between the West and East and among the Arab states.

July 17

The pro-Western Speaker of the Lebanese Chamber of Deputies protested against the landing of US Marines in his country and contended that a majority in Parliament supported his protests.

US Deputy Under Secretary of State Robert Murphy arrived in Beirut to "do everything possible to restore peace and tranquility in Lebanon" and to assist the Government of President Chamoun in so doing.

The Government of Israel granted permission for flights over Israel by planes carrying British troops to Jordan.

Russians marched on the US Embassy in Moscow and great crowds in Peking condemned the US troop landings in Lebanon.

The British Cabinet met in emergency session to consider an appeal from King Hussein of Jordan for military aid.

Abd-al-Moniem Rifai, Jordanian Ambassador to London, said that military aid had also been requested by Jordan from the US.

The US announced that it was beginning the airlift of petroleum products to Jordan. It stated that the US had no plans for sending troops to Jordan at that time.

Jordan complained to the UN Security Council about interference in its internal affairs by the UAR.

Sweden submitted a resolution to the UN asking for the suspension of the Observation Group in Lebanon.

July 17

The Soviet Union said that if the UN Security Council did not request the immediate withdrawal of US troops from Lebanon and Jordan it would call the General Assembly into special session.

US Ambassador to the UAR Raymond Hare delivered a note to the UAR Foreign Ministry stating that any attack on American troops in Lebanon by units of the UAR Army or by forces under UAR control would result in grave consequences.

Saeb Salam, former Lebanese Premier and leader of the rebel forces in Beirut, warned US forces to leave the country immediately under the threat that he would "seek support against them wherever he could find it."

The US and British Governments decided that intervention in the Middle East would not be extended to Iraq as long as the revolutionary government in Iraq respected Western oil interests.

Sir Pierson Dixon of Great Britain informed the UN Security Council of British troop movement to Jordan. The Soviet delegate labeled the British action aggression aimed at permitting Jordanian King Hussein, with British and American help, "to march on Baghdad" to crush the Iraqi revolution.

The UN Observation Group asked for additional men and planes to keep a direct and constant patrol along the 179 mile border between Lebanon and Syria.

French Foreign Minister Maurice Couve de Murville said that the discord and disorder in regard to Middle East nationalism was due to the lack of agreement among the Western powers in dealing with that area.

Turkey, Iran and Pakistan, after the heads of states meeting, welcomed US intervention in Lebanon and looked forward to the extension of such initiative in other countries similarly threatened.

President Eisenhower and British Foreign Secretary Selwyn Lloyd met in Washington to discuss their joint efforts in Lebanon and Jordan.

July, 1958

July 17

The Iraqi Government decided to recognize Red China and establish diplomatic relations with the Soviet Union.

North Korea recognized the new Government of Iraq.

Amir Fahd Ibn-Saud, Minister of Defense and Avaiation, returned to Riyahd, Saudi Arabia, from Cairo.

Two thousand British troops, backed by US jets, landed in Amman, Jordan. British Prime Minister Harold Macmillan explained to the House of Commons that the action had been taken at the urgent request of King Hussein and with the full support and approval of the US. The action was upheld by a 314-251 vote.

The French Ambassador to Tunis lodged a protest with the Government of Tunisia concerning a clash of French and Algerian troops near the Tunisian border. He accused the Tunisians of furnishing artillery support to the rebels.

July 18

In a UN Security Council session, the Soviet Union vetoed the US proposal to send UN forces to Lebanon. At the same session, the Security Council voted down a Soviet resolution demanding that the US and Britain withdraw their troops from the Middle East and a Swedish resolution to suspend operations of the UN Observation Group while US forces were in Lebanon.

US Deputy Under Secretary of State Robert Murphy met with General Chehab, Lebanese Prime Minister al-Solh and the Speaker of the Chamber of Deputies.

The US Sixth Fleet was reported to be in the Eastern Mediterranean in full force. Forty-nine ships were in the Beirut area.

Additions to the US Marines raised the total force in Lebanon to about 6,200.

July, 1958

July 18

Yemen sent a letter of protest to the UN Security Council accusing Britain of unprovoked air attacks on Harib on July 8.

President Nasser flew to Moscow, reportedly to ask Premier Khrushchev what help he could expect from the Soviet Union in the event the Western powers attacked Syria or Iraq.

India called for the withdrawal of US forces from Lebanon.

US Secretary of State Dulles said that he doubted that the Soviet Union would intervene in the Middle East militarily.

The US and the Soviet Union introduced resolutions in the UN calling for a General Assembly meeting.

July 19

Baghdad Radio announced that the Jordanian Charge d'Affaires in Baghdad, Badri al-Mulki, had been granted political asylum.

The US arranged to evacuate any Americans who wished to leave Iraq.

Soviet Premier Khrushchev proposed the immediate convening of a summit conference on the Middle East crisis between the heads of Government of the Soviet Union, US, Great Britain, France and India, with the participation of the Secretary General of the UN.

Iraq and the UAR concluded an agreement to stand as one bloc in the defense against any attack on one or both countries. They also agreed to take immediate steps to promote economic and cultural cooperation. The UAR undertook to supply all the arms Iraq would require.

Iraqi Deputy Premier Colonel Abd-al-Salam Muhammad Aref said that a military tribunal had been formed to try persons arrested after the revolt in Iraq.

President Nasser conferred with Sheikh Abdallah al-Salem al-Sabah of Kuwait in Damascus.

July, 1958

July 18

US Secretary of State Dulles charged the Soviet Union with playing a major role in the concerted movement that had liquidated the lawful Iraqi Government and turned internal differences into a cover for violent indirect aggression in Lebanon.

The Kuwait-Iraq border was closed.

Hashem Jawad, the Iraqi Representative to the UN, said that Iraq would remain in the Baghdad Pact, and that it would uphold the commitments of the last regime and change them only by peaceful and diplomatic means.

Fayeq al-Samarrai, President of the Iraqi Bar Association, said that if the situation in the Middle East could be stabilized, the Iraqi revolutionary Government would present a constitution to the people for ratification and general elections would be held.

Iraqi Premier Kassem said that his Government wanted to continue the production and export of oil to world markets and would uphold its obligations to all concerned.

James Hagerty, US Presidential Press Secretary, denied that the US-British agreement not to intervene in Iraq was based on the condition that Iraq not violate its oil agreements.

The US Government announced that it would start an airlift of petroleum products to Jordan, since the closing of the Lebanese and Iraqi frontiers had halted all oil shipments.

The Moroccan National Consultative Assembly condemned the US and British troop landings as colonialist aggression and a threat to Middle Eastern peace.

A general mobilization was declared in Israel.

A communique from the Presidency of the Council of Ministers denied that Saudi Arabia had given permission for US planes to fly over its territory when carrying oil from Bahrain to Jordan.

July, 1958

July 19

In a radio broadcast, President Eisenhower said that the US troops would be withdrawn as soon as the independence and integrity of Lebanon were secure.

The Jordanian Government ordered a UAR diplomat, accused of making contact with certain destructive elements, to leave Jordan within 24 hours.

Marshal Rudenko, Chief of Staff of the Soviet Air Force, returned to Moscow after a ten day official visit to Cairo at the invitation of Field Marshal Amer, Vice President and War Minister of the UAR.

Imam Ahmad of Yemen summoned a meeting of his advisers to consider general mobilization and the declaration of a state of emergency.

King Hussein of Jordan said that he had asked for American troops and expected them to arrive.

British commandos landed at Tobruk, Libya, to help the Government of King Idris I, in accordance with the 1953 Treaty of Friendship and Alliance, against rumored Egyptian plans to overthrow the regime.

The Chinese Government protested to Great Britain against the landing of British forces in Jordan and the threat it created for the Republic of Iraq.

The Soviet Union decided to exchange ambassadors with Iraq.

Italian Premier Fanfani said that he would visit the US soon to confer on Middle Eastern policy with Secretary of State Dulles.

The US Secretary of the Interior summoned representatives of 16 oil companies to meet July 23 to prepare plans for an oil life to Western Europe in case Middle East oil supplied were cut off.

July 20

The Arab League recognized the new Government of Iraq.

July 20

Fayeq al-Samarrai of Iraq was appointed Ambassador to the UAR.

The military Governor General of Iraq closed unauthorized recruiting centers for the People's Resistance. He said that the Government would organize civilian defense but did not need the help of those not authorized to do so.

The Director of the Arab League's oil department said that Iraq would join the League's oil conference in November.

Great Britain built up army, air and naval forces in Kuwait and Bahrain. The US bolstered forces at the Dhahran air base in Saudi Arabia.

Iraqi Embassies and the Iraqi UN Delegation declared their allegiance to the Iraqi Government regime.

Japan introduced a draft resolution to the UN Security Council which would allow the UN Secretary General to decide what additional measures the UN would take "to make possible the withdrawal of US forces from Lebanon."

Talks between Aden and Yemen were suspended.

Jordan received $12.5 million in economic grants from the US.

Sheikh Abdallah al-Salem al-Sabah, Ruler of Kuwait, met with UAR President Nasser in Damascus.

Lebanese rebel leader Saeb Salam was reported to have said that he would call for volunteers from the Soviet Union and the UAR if US forces tried to enter rebel territory in Lebanon.

In Lebanon, US Deputy Under Secretary of State Robert Murphy conferred with US Ambassador to Lebanon Robert M. McClintock and Monsignor Paul Maoushi, Maronite Patriarch in Lebanon.

Syrian troops were reported to be strengthening their positions close to the Lebanese border.

July 20

Indian Prime Minister Nehru told Premier Khrushchev that India would gladly attend a summit conference on the Middle East.

US Secretary of State Dulles and British Foreign Secretary Selwyn Lloyd, after conferring three and a half days, agreed on joint action, if necessary, to maintain western oil supplies from the Middle East.

It was reported that Russian Premier Khrushchev had promised UAR President Nasser volunteers, if requested.

Jordan broke off relations with the UAR because of that country's recognition of the new Government of Iraq.

July 21

Japan submitted a resolution to the UN Security Council calling for the Secretary General to take any necessary measures to enable the US to withdraw its troops from Lebanon.

David Ormsby-Gore, the British Minister of State at the Foreign Office, said that the British Government had no intention of interfering in the internal affairs of Iraq.

The Israel Knesset agreed to postpone immediate debate of the current Arab crisis. Premier Ben-Gurion said that events in the Arab world had increased the threat of encirclement by UAR President Nasser.

It was reported in Baghdad that former Premier and Foreign Minister Fadel al-Jamali was being held in prison on charges of stealing from the Government.

Libyan King Idris proclaimed two weeks of official mourning for King Faisal of Iraq.

US Deputy Under Secretary of State Robert Murphy met with Hussein al-Uwaini, Abdallah al-Yafi, and Henri Firawn in Lebanon. He later conferred with Monsignor Antoine al-Abdal, the Bishop of Tripoli.

July 21

Henri Firawn conferred with Adil Usayran and Saeb Salam in Lebanon.

Lebanese President Chamoun met with the US and Turkish Ambassadors.

The UN Observation Group in Lebanon said that the work of its mission had been abruptly curtailed by the US Marine landings but was now back to normal.

Prime Minister of Ghana, Kwame Nkrumah, said that a UN force should replace US troops in Lebanon. Then a general election should be held under UN supervision and Lebanon should have a neutral status under international guarantee.

Muhammad Sulaiman al-Unaibi, Chairman of the Advisory Council for the Ruler of Kuwait, said that Kuwait did not want British troops on its soil.

The Economic Committee of the Baghdad Pact met in London without an Iraqi representative.

The African-Asian Secretariat in Cairo telegraphed US President Eisenhower and British Prime Minister Macmillan demanding the withdrawal of US and British troops from Lebanon and Jordan.

The IBRD announced it would lend $39 million to the Sudan to develop transportation facilities. The loan was to be of 20 year duration with five and three-quarter percent interest.

The Council of Ministers of the Sudan met to discuss the change of regime in Iraq. They then recognized that Government.

The Jordanian Embassy in Tehran claimed that it represented the Arab Federal State.

July 22

Full communication between Iraq and Syria was resumed.

July 22

Abd-al-Majid Abbas of Iraq attended the UN Security Council session under guard.

US President Eisenhower, in a note to Soviet Premier Khrushchev, advised that a summit meeting on the Middle East should be held within the framework of the UN Security Council.

British Prime Minister Harold Macmillan rejected Soviet Premier Khrushchev's proposal for immediate summit talks on the Middle East and suggested a special meeting of the UN Security Council.

In a reply to Soviet leader Khrushchev, Premier De Gaulle also stated that a top level conference should be arranged under UN auspices.

President Nasser, in his Independence Day speech to a crowd of 250,000 in Cairo, predicted the triumph of Arab nationalism under his flag in Jordan, Lebanon and Algeria, and condemned the US and British troop landings in Lebanon and Jordan.

The Secretary General of the UN, Dag Hammarskjold, said that he was going ahead with plans to strengthen the Observation Group.

Iraqi Premier Kassem said that it was his Government's aim to increase cooperation with the West, especially in oil production.

Colonel al-Aref, Deputy Premier of Iraq, said that the revolution in his country had been precipitated by the corruption of the ruling class that had encroached upon the rights of the people.

The Soviet Union vetoed a Japanese resolution to strengthen the UN Observation Group in Lebanon. The Security Council suspended its debate on the Middle East to await the outcome of East-West negotiations on a summit conference.

British Foreign Secretary Selwyn Lloyd told the House of Commons that the first priority of the British intervention in Jordan was achieved, that of foiling a coup organized outside the country.

July 22

In the UN Security Council, the Soviet Union veered from traditional opposition to UN military units by asking for strengthening of UNOGIL. The proposal was contained in one of three amendments to the Japanese resolution, proposed by the Soviet Union. The amendments were rejected by a vote of 1-8-2.

Demonstrations were reportedly held throughout Jordan against the landing of British forces there.

Tunisia recognized the Republic of Iraq.

The Jordanian Government reported the murder of Ibrahim Hashem, Deputy Premier of the Arab Union, and Sulaiman Touqan, Defense Minister of the Union, in Baghdad.

A Jordanian Royal Decree was issued making any attempt on the King's life or any attempt to overthrow his Government punishable by death.

US Deputy Under Secretary of State Robert Murphy met with the Greek Orthodox Primate and the Greek Catholic Bishop of Beirut.

July 23

Russian Premier Khrushchev said that he would attend a summit meeting in the UN Security Council if the Indian Prime Minister and representatives of the Arab States were also invited. He also insisted that discussions take place only among the powers designated.

The American Charge d'Affaires delivered a note to Moroccan King Muhammad V concerning the US position in the current Middle East situation.

In Lebanon, Adel Usairan, the current President of the Chamber of Deputies, notified the Chamber that it would meet July 31 to elect a new President.

US representative Robert Murphy conferred with Phalange leader Pierre Jumayil in Lebanon.

July 23

The UAR Ambassador to Lebanon was notified that he had three days in which to leave the country.

The British landed troops in Benghazi, Libya.

The death of Khulusi al-Khairi, Minister of State for Foreign Affairs in the Arab Federation Government, was announced.

President Nasser was reported to be willing to attend a summit conference meeting in the UN Security Council as an observer.

Mustafa Kamel, new UAR Ambassador to the US, arrived in New York.

The US Secretary of the Interior presented a plan to representatives of 16 oil companies to provide for action to meet the cut off of Middle East oil production and transportation.

Iraqi Foreign Minister Abd-al-Jabbar Jumaa said that no unilateral action concerning treaties would be taken and that Iraq would uphold all international obligations, both political and commercial. No changes were contemplated in the economy.

Seven senior Iraqi government officials were suspended for five years. Among them were: Yusuf al-Kailani, Ihsan Rifat and Amin al-Mumayiz of the Foreign Ministry.

The new regime in Iraq was recognized by the Soviet Union, Communist China, Poland, Czechoslovakia, Hungary, the UAR, Tunisia, the Sudan, India, Indonesia, East Germany and Yemen.

July 24

Iraqi Finance Minister Muhammad Hadid said that the general economic policy of the Government would resemble that of a welfare state. Income taxes would be graded equitably, a direct tax would be put on agriculture, and indirect taxation would be reduced. Industries would be protected and imports limited.

July 24

The Iraqi Council of Ministers announced that it would place 64 politicians of the former regime under official control.

Premier Kassem stated that Iraq was unable to say if it would attend the London meetings of the Baghdad Pact since other members of the Pact had not recognized the new Government.

It was announced in Cairo that Iraq and the UAR had set up joint committees to deal with military, political, economic and educational matters.

Saudi Arabia recognized the new Iraqi Government.

Jordan announced that it would not allow Egyptian passenger planes to fly over its territory.

Lebanese Foreign Minister Charles Malik said that the infiltration of men and arms from the UAR into his country was continuing.

Afghanistan recognized the Republic of Iraq.

The US Embassy in Beirut reported that the current crisis had resulted in a general economic paralysis in Lebanon.

Lebanese President Chamoun conferred with US Deputy Under Secretary of State Robert Murphy and US Ambassador McClintock.

The scheduled presidential election for Lebanon was postponed because government and opposition leaders failed to agree on a compromise candidate.

July 25

The Moroccan Council of Ministers decided to recognize the Republic of Iraq.

Jordanian King Hussein said he thought the new Iraqi Government had every intention of stopping the flow of oil to Europe.

July 25

Rebel leader Saeb Salam of Lebanon said that the Opposition would not permit presidential elections to be held so long as President Chamoun was in power and foreign troops occupied the country.

US Deputy Under Secretary of State Robert Murphy visited President Chamoun, Secretary General of the Foreign Ministry Victor Khouri and Kamal Jumblat in Lebanon.

The Industrialist and Merchants Association of Lebanon announced that their businesses would close for three days beginning August 1 if a President was not elected July 31.

US Marine and Army landings in Lebanon were resumed; reserves were put ashore. This was announced to be the completion of the build up of forces in that country to 10,000.

Sidney Smith, Canadian Secretary of State for External Affairs, proposed that Lebanon be neutralized. He said that British and US reactions to the plan were favorable.

President Eisenhower notified Premier Khrushchev that the US would not be limited at any UN summit conference to discussion of US-British intervention in Lebanon and Jordan. He also said that any such meeting would be guided by rules determined by the UN Security Council rather than by any of its permanent members.

Tunisian President Bourguiba said that the US had to change its policy toward the Arab countries before these countries were turned too far toward Russia.

July 26

The provisional constitution of Iraq was announced. The Iraqi Premier promised a plebiscite on the constitution, but said that general elections would not be held until basic reforms were made.

General De Gaulle, in reply to Khrushchev's letter of July 23, insisted that other Middle East countries be represented at a summit conference, and urged that notwithstanding special Security Council

July 26

meetings, preparations be made for a five power summit conference first proposed, preferably in Europe.

Britain promised the Sultan of Muscat and Oman military aid to defeat the Imam of Oman.

The Italian State Petroleum Corporation was granted oil exploration rights in the province of Tarfaya, Morocco.

US Deputy Under Secretary of State Robert Murphy again met with President Chamoun of Lebanon.

It was officially announced that additional US forces were en route to Lebanon. It was not decided whether they would be put ashore.

The press in Cairo came out against the idea of a summit conference in the UN.

US Secretary of State Dulles met with West Germany's Chancellor Adenauer to discuss the Middle East. They agreed on what procedures would offer the best opportunities for a solution of the Middle East crisis.

July 27

UAR President Nasser conferred with the Soviet Charge d'Affaires and with Colonel Abd-al-Hamid Sarraj, a Syrian Army Intelligence officer.

Iraqi funds totalling 80 million pounds sterling that had been frozen in the Bank of England on July 20 were released.

A public safety committee was formed in the Algiers region of Algeria.

It was reported that President Chamoun of Lebanon had sent a letter to President Eisenhower on July 21 expressing his thanks for US assistance.

July 27

The Jordanian Government announced that the British troops would leave Jordan as soon as the UN took steps to stabilize the Middle East.

A Royal Decree imposing a tax of 10 percent on real estate sold by foreigners was signed in Saudi Arabia.

Fakher al-Kayali, Minister of the Treasury in Syria, went to Cairo to submit the proposed Syrian budget to President Nasser.

The West German Government said that if the Arab States were invited to a summit conference, Israel should also be included.

US Secretary of State Dulles and British Prime Minister Macmillan met to discuss the problems of the Baghdad Pact and the general Middle East situation.

President Nasser opened a West German built steel mill at Helwan in the UAR.

The Iraqi Republican Government issued a provisional constitution declaring Iraq to be part of the Arab nation and vesting supreme power in the Council of Ministers pending general elections.

Spain's Generalissimo Franco said that the Western policy in the Middle East was a failure because it sent against the natural course of events in that area.

July 28

US Secretary of State Dulles committed the US to partnership in the Baghdad Pact. He told Britain, Turkey, Iran and Pakistan that the US would not fail to act in defense of their independence and integrity.

Russian Premier Khrushchev said that the Baghdad Pact conference looked like a plot against the Arab States.

July 28

Soviet Premier Khrushchev sent letters to the US, Britain, and France insisting that a date be named for a summit meeting on the Middle East. He was still prepared to meet within the framework of the UN Security Council, but reasserted preference for a five power meeting as suggested by General De Gaulle.

Premier Khrushchev rejected proposals that the UN Security Council be given responsibility for arranging a summit conference. The US quickly rejected the Soviet demand for a summit conference untrammeled by Security Council rules.

Crown Prince Faisal assumed the duties of Minister of Finance and National Economy in Saudi Arabia.

The US Government announced that a shipment of 2,000 tons of surplus flour was being sent to Jordan for free distribution.

The US agreed to furnish the British troops in Jordan with supplies.

General Fuad Chehab agreed to be a candidate for the Presidency in Lebanon.

Baghdad Radio announced the retirement of Ibrahim al-Khudayri, Iraqi Ambassador to Cairo, and the dismissal of Abd-al-Majid Abbas, Iraqi representative to the UN.

Iraqi Minister of Economics Ibrahim Kubbah said that oil negotiations had been resumed with the IPC (Iraqi Petroleum Company).

It was announced that tribal courts had been dissolved in Iraq.

Jordan formally accused Syria of plotting to overthrow King Hussein's regime.

July 29

The final communique issued by the Baghdad Pact meeting in London took note of the danger of indirect aggression and supported the

July 29

American and British prompt action in Lebanon and Jordan to combat aggression by indirect means.

Italian Premier Fanfani told the US Congress that his country would join endeavors to increase freedom and prosperity in the Middle East.

The ambassadors of Ethiopia, Libya, Tunisia, Morocco, Italy and West Germany were called to the UAR Foreign Ministry to ascertain their positions should the US and Britain launch an attack on the UAR from bases in their countries.

Kamal Jumblat, Druze Chieftain in Lebanon, warned that agreement by the Chamber of Deputies on a new president in Lebanon would not bring peace unless it was coupled with the immediate withdrawal of US troops.

Burma officially recognized the Republic of Iraq.

The Lebanese Chamber of Deputies issued a ruling granting immunity to deputies for 48 hours before and after the election.

Premier al-Solh of Lebanon told a cabinet meeting that he would not attend the election meeting if it was to be held in an atmosphere of terrorism.

July 30

Two members of the Baghdad Pact, Pakistan and Iran, announced recognition of the Iraqi Republic.

The Soviet Government accused the Western Powers of planning to attack Iraq.

The new Government of Iraq was recognized by West Germany and Greece.

A US press service reported that censorship was tight and capricious in Jordan.

July, 1958

July 30

US Deputy Under Secretary of State Robert Murphy left Beirut, where he had conferred with General Chehab, for Amman to talk with King Hussein and Premier Samir al-Rifai.

Lebanese Opposition sources were reported to support General Chehab and said that they would attend the election meeting of the Chamber of Deputies.

It was officially announced in Jedda, Saudi Arabia, that Crown Prince Faisal had assumed the post of Finance Minister, replacing Muhammad Sorar Sabban, who was dismissed March 28. Prince Faisal was also Premier and Foreign Minister.

July 31

General Fuad Chehab, a compromise choice approved by the Opposition National Front, was elected President of Lebanon by Parliament over the strong objections of Premier Sami al-Solh.

In its second report to the UN Security Council, the UN Observation Group declared that arms infiltration from the UAR into Lebanon could not be on anything more than a limited scale, and was largely confined to small arms and ammunition. In no case had the observers been able to detect the presence of persons who had indubitably crossed the border for the purpose of fighting.

In Lebanon, Opposition deputies and leaders met with rebel leader Saeb Salam. Among them were Sabri Hamadi, Shafiq Murtadad, Abd-al-Karim Kaddur and Rashid Karami.

General De Gaulle, in reply to Khrushchev's letter of July 28, proposed a five power summit meeting at Geneva August 18.

US Secretary of State Dulles said that US troops would be withdrawn as soon as the Lebanese Government requested their evacuation.

King Hussein of Jordan told loyal tribal leaders from the north that he was ready to sacrifice his life for his country.

August, 1958

August 1

President Eisenhower told Soviet Premier Khrushchev that he would attend and participate in a UN summit meeting on August 12 and urged Khrushchev to do likewise.

The Soviet Union and Great Britain submitted a formal request to the UN Security Council to hold a special meeting August 12 to discuss the Middle East. The British and Canadian Prime Ministers said that they would attend.

UN Secretary General Hammarskjold announced that as of September 15 all ships using the Suez Canal would be asked to pay a three percent surcharge to cover the cost of clearing the waterway after the 1956 attack by Israel, France and Britain.

Italian Premier Fanfani met with British Prime Minister Macmillan in London to discuss the Middle East.

Pierre Edde, the Finance Minister of Lebanon, resigned. The Minister of General Planning, Joseph Shader, was appointed in his place.

Abd-al-Jabbar Jumaa, the Foreign Minister of Iraq, said that Iraq would accept technical aid from Russia but would not buy arms there. He said that his Government had not renounced the Baghdad Pact but had made it ineffectual.

Great Britain recognized the new Iraqi Government.

Crown Prince Faisal of Saudi Arabia arrived in Cairo and conferred with UAR President Nasser.

A trade agreement was signed between Tunisia and the Benelux countries.

Lebanon recognized the Republic of Iraq.

The Soviet press published a joint statement by representatives of the Arab Peace Movement, the USSR Peace Committee, and the USSR Committee of Afro-Asian Solidarity regarding the situation in the Middle East.

July, 1958

July 31

Morocco signed a three billion franc trade agreement with the UAR under which Morocco would deliver ores, canned sardines and cardboard in exchange for sugar, cotton goods and books.

Special US Envoy Robert Murphy arrived in Israel to confer with Prime Minister David Ben-Gurion and other Government officials.

Turkey became a third member of the Baghdad Pact to extend recognition to the Iraqi Government.

Iraqi Foreign Minister Jumaa said that Iraqi foreign policy was the same as that adopted by the UAR.

British Prime Minister Macmillan told Premier Khrushchev that Britain favored an August 12 summit meeting of the UN Security Council, with permanent members of the Council deciding the details.

Austria, Belgium, Malaya, Japan, and Italy recognized the Republic of Iraq.

August, 1958

August 1

The Soviet Government protested to Italy and Israel against the permission given the US to use Italian territory and Israel air space for air attacks against Arab nations.

Selwyn Lloyd announced that his Government had agreed "in principle" to reimburse British shipowners and charterers for the Suez surcharge paid if other countries would do the same.

It was reported that the British Army had been moving armored equipment into Aqaba, on its way to Amman, Jordan.

August 2

King Hussein of Jordan decreed the formal dissolution of the Arab Union of his country and Iraq.

Fawzi al-Mulki was replaced by Hazza al-Majali as Court Minister in Jordan.

It was announced that West Germany had agreed to grant aid to Jordan for development.

The US extended recognition to the Iraqi Regime when US Envoy Robert Murphy flew to Baghdad and conferred with Premier Kassem and other Iraqi leaders.

The Middle East News Agency said that an imperialist plot that aimed to use the Sudan to overthrow President Nasser had been discovered in Khartoum.

Sheikh Abdallah al-Salem al-Sabah, the Ruler of Kuwait, arrived in Tehran for a state visit.

A bill was promulgated forming a People's Resistance organization to cooperate with the Army in Iraq.

The Lebanese Cabinet met with President Chamoun presiding. It was reported that the members decided not to resign.

August, 1958

August 2

Rebel leader Saeb Salam met with General Chehab in Lebanon and declared that he was well satisfied with their talk.

Iraqi Premier Kassem's representatives took the seat of Iraq in the UN Security Council.

Adel Usairan of Lebanon said that there was the possibility that a caretaker Cabinet would be formed for the duration of President Chamoun's term.

It was reported that when all the US forces were ashore in Lebanon the total US force would be around 13,000.

August 3

Hasan Jabarra, the Minister of Planning in Syria, announced that shipments of technical equipment for development plans had arrived from the Soviet Union.

The Sultan of Lahej in Aden conferred with the Arab League's Secretary General, Muhammad Abd-al-Khaleq Hassouna, in Cairo.

General Habes al-Majali was appointed Chief of Staff in Jordan.

Israel withdrew permission for British and US military planes to fly over its territory to Jordan. Syria closed the Jordanian frontier to all travel. Israel's action left Jordan with only the port of Aqaba as a means of supplying British troops.

Twenty-seven Jordanians went on trial before a military court in Amman on charges of entering from Syria with arms and explosives to help overthrow King Hussein's Government.

Hashem Jawad, the newly appointed Iraqi Delegate to the UN, affirmed that Iraq considered itself still bound by all provisions of the Baghdad Pact.

August, 1958

August 4

Three-fourths of the populations of the Departments of Algiers, Constantine and Oran registered to vote in the referendum of Algeria.

Russian Premier Khrushchev said that he was opposed to the sending of either regular military forces or volunteers from other countries into the Middle East.

August 5

Foreign Minister Golda Meir of Israel met in Paris with Premier Charles De Gaulle to discuss the Middle East situation.

A 60 percent increase in the tax on livestock and dairy exports went into effect in Syria.

Italian Premier Fanfani met with opposition in the UAR Parliament against dealing with President Nasser and Nasser's planned trip to Rome.

The US Defense Department said that the American troop landing operation was virtually completed; there were about 14,300 American service personnel in Lebanon.

Abd-al-Majid Abbas, UN representative of the pre-revolutionary Iraq Government, informed the UN that the termination of the Arab Union had "terminated my mission."

General Chehab of Lebanon sent a message to President Eisenhower assuring him that he would do everything possible to maintain the traditional friendship between the US and Lebanon.

US Deputy Under Secretary of State Robert Murphy said that he had discussed the issue of US troop withdrawals from Lebanon with General Chehab but said that it was impossible to tell when the withdrawal would begin.

It was reported that the Lebanese Government had placed its resignation at the disposal of President Chamoun.

August, 1958

August 3

Premier Kassem said that Iraq would make no decisions on the Baghdad Pact without consulting other members.

It was announced that Premier Khrushchev of the Soviet Union had spent four days in Peking consulting with Mao Tse-Tung. A joint communique called for the convening of a Big Powers meeting to discuss the Middle East and demanded the immediate withdrawal of Western troops from that area.

August 4

President-elect Chehab said that his first aim was to rid Lebanon of foreign troops. He stressed the importance of restoring unity in Lebanon.

US Deputy Under Secretary of State Robert Murphy talked with General Chehab, President Chamoun and rebel leader Saeb Salam in Lebanon.

The Lebanese Foreign Ministry announced that both President Chamoun and General Chehab supported the candidacy of Dr. Charles Malik for President of the UN General Assembly.

Secretary General of the French Ministry of Foreign Affairs Louis Joxe conferred with Moroccan Muhammad V and later with Premier Balafrej.

The Soviet Ambassador to Iraq, Grigory T. Zaitsev, arrived in Baghdad to resume diplomatic relations that had been broken in 1955.

Telephone and telegraph communications between Jordan and Syria were suspended.

Two American railroad experts arrived in Amman, Jordan, to help reorganize the national railway administration.

Jordanian Government officials said that Jordan had sealed off its side of the Syrian border in retaliation for the sealing off of the Syrian side by the UAR.

August, 1958

August 5

Soviet Premier Khrushchev refused the proposal that the Middle East be discussed in the UN Security Council and requested that the General Assembly be brought into special session.

US President Eisenhower accepted Soviet Premier Khrushchev's proposal for a special session of the General Assembly to discuss the Middle East situation.

Robert Murphy, President Eisenhower's Special Envoy, suggested that US troops not leave Lebanon before the end of President Chamoun's term, September 23.

The Governor of the Ahmadi area of Kuwait pledged that Western oil interests would be defended as long as Kuwait received its full rights.

August 6

The Israel Government agreed to a US request for resumption of flights over its territory for a few more days to build up necessary supplies. The ban on British planes continued.

Macmillan accepted a proposal for a special session of the UN General Assembly on the Middle East.

UAR President Nasser, Foreign Minister Fawzi and Minister of State for Presidential Affairs Sabri met with US Ambassador to the UAR Raymond Hare and Deputy Under Secretary of State Robert Murphy.

Lebanese President Chamoun conferred with General Chehab and President of the Chamber of Deputies Adel Usairan. It was reported that they discussed the possibility of a caretaker government.

Eliahu Elath, the Israel Ambassador to London, conferred with Prime Minister Macmillan. It was reported that the Israel Ambassador had asked for arms and a guarantee of Israel's borders against direct or indirect aggression.

King Saud and Crown Prince Faisal of Saudi Arabia conferred with Field Marshal Amer, UAR Vice President and War Minister.

August, 1958

August 6

An amended electoral law, allowing for a parliament of 50 members, was ratified in Jordan.

The US Government agreed to pay the surcharge for all US owned ships, including those under flags of convenience, when passing through the Suez Canal.

Bertram Dickson, an Australian expert on arid zone problems, accepted an invitation to advise the UAR Government on the establishment of a desert institute near Cairo.

A trade agreement was signed between Morocco and the Benelux countries.

It was reported that Tunisia planned to triple its Army within the next few months.

August 7

The UN Security Council unanimously adopted a US resolution calling for an emergency session of the General Assembly August 8 concerning the Middle East situation.

The resumption of international airline flights to Baghdad was sanctioned by the Iraqi Government.

Hashem Jawad, the Iraqi delegate to the UN, was seated in the UN Security Council without debate.

The Government of Iraq lowered rents 10-20 percent on dwellings and some shops. The decree followed Government imposed cuts in the prices of bread and other consumer items, and a limitation on the landlord's share of crops harvested by tenant farmers.

The Jordanian Government started the East Ghor Canal Development Program.

August, 1958

August 7

The Syrian Ministry of Labor and Social Affairs decided to send 15 mechanical and chemical workers to East German factories for training.

The Secretary General of the Ministry of Trade and Economy and the American Consul General in Damascus met to discuss the promotion of trade exchanges between Syria and the US.

UAR Vice President Abd-al-Hakim Amer returned to Damascus from Saudi Arabia, where he had discussed ways and means of improving relations between the two countries.

British Prime Minister Macmillan wrote to Soviet Premier Nikita Khrushchev on the settlement of the Middle East conflict.

August 8

At the opening meeting of the third Emergency Special Session of the General Assembly, Secretary General Hammarskjold proposed that the UN step up its political and economic activities in the Middle East to stabilize the area.

The UN General Assembly adjourned until August 13 to give the foreign ministers time to get to the UN.

The UN Security Council received a complaint from the Jordanian representative that increasing numbers of heavily armed infiltrators had been crossing into Jordan from the UAR.

Paul Rykens, Chairman of the Middle East Industrial Development Corporation, said that the company had five plant developments under consideration and a tentative $25 million in local capital in various Middle Eastern countries.

Prime Minister Jawaharlal Nehru of India declared that a peaceful settlement between the Arab nations and Israel obviously involved the continuation of Israel and its acceptance by the Arab countries and other countries in the area.

August, 1958

August 8

Italian Premier Fanfani, after conferring with French leaders, said that Italy would work closely with its allies to insure peace in the Middle East.

A new Iraqi law was promulgated providing the maximum penalty of life imprisonment for those convicted by a military court for conspiring against national security.

August 9

The Jordanians announced the start of the long awaited East Ghor Canal Development Program. The program, financed largely by US Point Four plans, would eventually irrigate more than 25,000 acres of land.

Jordanian authorities reported that the Syrian-Jordan border had been re-opened by both sides.

The American Embassy in Amman announced a US grant to Jordan of $3,830,000 in economic aid. This was to free Jordanian funds so that the country s armed forces could be paid.

The US Government advised dependents of Americans in Jordan to leave the country.

King Hussein of Jordan gave Jordanian citizenship to General Baha-ad-Din Nuri, former Iraqi Ambassador in Amman.

The Minister of Economy of Jordan conferred with representatives of fuel dealers about the possibility of buying a floating oil tank to store fuel brought in at Aqaba.

UN Secretary General Hammarskjold met with the representatives of Iraq and Jordan and with the President of the Security Council to discuss his plan for peace in the Middle East.

The Minister of Economy in Iraq said that the Government had no intention of nationalizing the oil industry.

August, 1958

August 9

Jordan submitted three complaints to the Mixed Armistice Commission, accusing Israel of opening fire on an army outpost in the Arbona village and of flying 12 airplanes over the Hebron district and one plane over Saffin village.

An official communique said that talks in Rome between Israel Foreign Minister Golda Meir and Italian Premier Fanfani resulted in a useful exchange of the views of the two Governments on the Middle East situation and on the special assembly of the UN.

The Moroccan Government sent a note to the IBRD about a projected loan to the Miferma Company which was engaged in the exploration of iron deposits in Mauritania. The note expressed the Government's reservations about the request for the loan due to the status of Mauritania.

The Iraqi Government announced the establishment of military courts to try some 100 persons arrested since July 14.

The first shipment of US wheat arrived in Lebanon. It was part of the 65,000 tons sold to Lebanon against local currency.

The Soviet Ambassador presented his credentials to Nagib al-Rubai, President of the Supreme State Council of the Republic of Iraq.

General Odd Bull, Chief of Staff of the UN observers in Lebanon, appointed Colonel Justin MacCarthy of Ireland his Deputy Chief of Staff.

Lebanese Minister of Justice Bashir al-Ahwar tendered his resignation.

August 10

Jordanian King Hussein called President Nasser the main agent of Communism in the Middle East.

The Jordanian Government blamed members of the Lebanese Opposition and the Syrian Army Intelligence for terrorist activities in Jordan.

August, 1958

August 10

It was reported in Amman, Jordan, that authorities had uncovered a widespread pro-Nasser espionage and sabotage ring which was allegedly using UN facilities to bring explosives into the country.

The US airlift of supplies to British troops in Jordan ended.

Iraq banned the export of cattle and put price restrictions on meat.

Soviet Premier Khrushchev replied to British Prime Minister Macmillan's note on the settlement of the Middle East conflict.

August 11

President Nasser approved a $130 million budget for Syria some $14 million was allocated for defense spending.

It was reported in Rabat that the Moroccan Government had blocked the unloading of a ship bringing munitions to US forces in Morocco.

Foreign Minister Golda Meir of Israel and British Foreign Secretary Selwyn Lloyd held a series of "useful" talks in London.

The Muscat, Oman and British agreement was published, providing for British military and economic assistance to the territory.

A Jordanian delegation headed by Abd-al-Moneim al-Rifai left for the UN emergency session.

Mustafa Kamel, new UAR Ambassador to the US, presented his credentials to President Eisenhower.

August 12

The Iraq Development Board was abolished. It was replaced by a Development Guidance Committee composed of the following Cabinet members: the Deputy Premier and the Ministers of Development, Finance, Economy, Agriculture, Social Affairs and Communications, under the chairmanship of the Premier.

August, 1958

August 13

Foreign Minister Gromyko of the Soviet Union demanded the withdrawal of US and British troops from Lebanon and Jordan in an address before the UN General Assembly.

The Arab League announced that its Political Committee would meet in Cairo September 6.

Sudanese Foreign Minister Muhammad Mahgoub denied reports that the Premier of the Sudan, Abdallah Khalil, approved of US intervention in Lebanon.

Tawfiq al-Suwaidi, former Deputy Premier of the Arab Union, and Burhan-ad-Din Bashayan, who had been the Iraqi Foreign Minister in 1955, were interrogated by a five man investigating committee prior to trial for plotting to overthrow the Syrian Government.

Jordanian Premier Samir al-Rifai said that Jordan would reject any UN proposal his Government considered impractical. He indicated that he and King Hussein did not consider it practical to replace the 4,000 British paratroopers with a UN force.

The UN Children's Fund director recommended an allocation of $270,000 for emergency aid to destitute mothers and children in Jordanian border villages.

The Jordanian Government lifted censorship on outgoing reports, which had been in effect since May.

The Lebanese Industrialists' Association requested the Government to refrain from paying any compensation to the victims of the revolution before indemnifying industralists.

US President Dwight Eisenhower proposed at the UN a Middle East regional development institution financed partly by oil countries.

It was reported that Foreign Minister Charles Malik of Lebanon did not leave for the UN session on schedule because the Opposition refused to name delegates to accompany him.

August, 1958

August 12

The Lebanese Council of Ministers decided that Dr. Charles Malik, the Foreign Minister, should represent Lebanon at the special meeting of the UN General Assembly.

Iraq's Deputy Premier al-Aref said that rumors of a disagreement between himself and Premier Kassem were "imperialist propaganda."

On his return to the US from Lebanon, US Deputy Under Secretary of State Robert Murphy described the results of his mission, which began July 16, as very satisfactory, and said that prospects for peace looked brighter.

Abd-al-Moneim al-Kaissouni, the Minister of Trade and Economy in Egypt, announced that the US had resumed deliveries of road building equipment, which had been suspended for two years.

The head of Jordan's permanent delegation to the UN, Baha al-Din Touqan, was recalled because of a policy disagreement.

Tunisian President Bourguiba conferred with Louis Joxe, Secretary General of the French Ministry of Foreign Affairs. No communique was issued.

Soviet Foreign Minister Andrei Gromyko submitted to the special session of the UN General Assembly the Soviet draft resolution demanding the immediate withdrawal of US and British armed forces from Lebanon and Jordan.

The Ruler of Kuwait ended his visit to Iran after agreeing in principle to set up consular, commercial and cultural relations with Iran.

President Nasser awarded a medal to Russian Air Marshal Rudenko to mark his visit to the UAR.

August 13

President Eisenhower presented the framework of a plan for peace in the Middle East to the UN General Assembly

August, 1958

August 13

The first major withdrawal of American forces from Lebanon began with the evacuation of some 1,700 Marines.

The French Foreign Ministry said that France approved the US and British decision to ship arms to Tunisia.

Under an agreement signed in Geneva, France agreed to pay the UAR the equivalent of $57.4 million in compensation for damage inflicted in the 1956 Suez landings. The agreement also provided for the release of properties seized in Egypt and in France.

Amir Abdallah al-Mubarak al-Sabah, the Deputy Ruler of Kuwait, arrived in Cairo for talks with President Nasser.

August 14

Decrees adopted by the French Committee of Ministers, concerned with Algerian problems, to insure free voting on the referendum in Algeria, were announced.

The US and British Governments confirmed reports that they would supply arms to Tunisia.

The Jordanian UN representative said that his Government would not permit UN forces or observers to be stationed on Jordanian territory.

Jordan accused the UAR of indirect aggression by means of radio propaganda and infiltration of arms.

Lebanese Foreign Minister Charles Malik left for the UN emergency session.

Exit permits were refused Lebanese Opposition leaders wishing to go to the UN General Assembly meeting on the Middle East as a separate delegation.

Iraq announced that it would establish diplomatic relations with Communist China, Yugoslavia, Rumania, Czechoslovakia, Hungary, Poland, Bulgaria and Albania.

August 14

Iraq informed the diplomatic missions in Baghdad that it would aid Jordan if the latter were attacked by Israel.

In the UN General Assembly, British Foreign Secretary Selwyn Lloyd said that indirect aggression by means of radio propaganda beamed from Cairo should be stopped. He also called for the formation of a UN force that could act in an emergency.

Foreign Minister of Israel, Golda Meir, said that an arms embargo in the Middle East at the present time would be of benefit to the Arabs.

August 15

Iraq assured the West German Government that it would not open diplomatic relations with East Germany.

The Second Battalion, First Regiment of US Marines completed their evacuation of Lebanon.

The UN Observers' third report said that there might have been a few arms brought into Lebanon illegally but the smuggling had declined after the election of General Chehab for the presidency July 31.

Crown Prince Faisal, Premier of Saudi Arabia, arrived in Cairo and conferred with President Nasser.

A delegation of 14 industrial experts from the UAR left for the Soviet Union to study Soviet techniques. They also planned to visit East Germany and Czechoslovakia.

Ahmad Shukairy, Saudi Arabian UN representative, declared to the UN Third Emergency Special Session, "Arab oil is our own. . . . it falls entirely within our jurisdiction. It does not admit any discussion before any international forum. . . . Oil, our oil, is not a political commodity."

The British Treasury said that unofficial Anglo-UAR contacts had recently taken place in Geneva.

August 15

French military sources said that 20,757 rebels had been killed in Algeria during the first seven months of the year.

UN Secretary General Hammarskjold met with US Secretary of State Dulles, British Foreign Secretary Selwyn Lloyd and Deputy Foreign Minister Hans Engen of Norway.

The Japanese Foreign Minister consulted with the Foreign Ministers of the Soviet Union and the UAR.

The representatives of Saudi Arabia and Turkey both stressed that Arab problems should be settled with the Arab League.

August 16

The UAR Ministry of Education announced that it would send a four man delegation to Baghdad August 17 to negotiate an educational and cultural agreement with Iraq.

Crown Prince Faisal of Saudi Arabia and President Nasser conferred for a second time. Prince Faisal said that the talks had covered every topic of interest to Arabs, particularly to the UAR and his country.

General Sir Roger Bowler, Commander in Chief of British Middle East Land Forces, arrived in Amman from Cyprus.

US Ambassador to the UN, British Delegate Sir Pierson Dixon and Norwegian Delegate Hans Engen met with UN Secretary General Hammarskjold to discuss a prospective Western sponsored resolution.

The UN Secretariat published a report by the UN Observer Team in Lebanon, confirming the conclusions given in its first two reports, refuting allegations of UAR intervention.

The trial of the leaders of the former Iraqi regime opened before a five man military court in the Chamber of Deputies.

August 16

In Iraq, General Rafiq Aref, former Army Chief of Staff, testifying against General Ghazi Daghistani, former Deputy Chief of Staff, said that the US had wanted Iraq to attack Syria in 1956.

The US Government denied the claim of Iraqi General Aref that it had pressed Iraq to attack Syria in 1956.

Former Iraqi Deputy Premier Ahmad Mukhtar Baban, testifying in the trial of General Daghistani, said that Crown Prince Abd-al-Ilah had been the instigator of the plan to attack Syria. He said that General Daghistani and General Rafiq Aref did not approve of the plan.

The Iraqi Government opened negotiations with Communist countries for the export of dates.

In Iraq a new law was promulgated which obliged all civil servants and government officials to make an accounting of all their assets and debts from 1939.

August 17

In Lebanon, Leader of the Opposition Party Saeb Salam called for the immediate withdrawal of the UN Observation Team since, he said, their third report showed that there was no massive infiltration.

The West German Government turned down a Soviet protest of July 26 that the Bonn Government had approved of US aggression against the Arab Countries.

August 18

The Jordanian Parliament passed resolutions restoring the constitution and returning to King Hussein powers that he had relinquished under the Arab Union. It also voted to enlarge the House of Deputies from 40 to 50 to accommodate the Jordanian members of the former Arab Union Council.

It was announced that the Jordanian Government had refused permission to the Eagle Aviation Company to fly between Cyprus and Amman via Lydda, Israel.

August 18

The British Foreign Office denied reports that Britain and the US were contemplating the abdication of King Hussein of Jordan.

Following a series of meetings in Cairo, President Nasser of the UAR and Premier Faisal of Saudi Arabia signed a communique condemning the presence of foreign troops on Arab soil. Crown Prince Faisal announced that previous differences between his country and the UAR had been resolved.

The US and Britain pledged to withdraw troops from the Middle East as soon as the General Assembly voted that UN action was sufficient to maintain peace.

A spokesman for the International Cooperation Administration said that a request for LL150 million had been received from the Lebanese Government to repair damage sustained since the outbreak of violence May 10.

President Chamoun of Lebanon said that he did not expect American troops to be withdrawn from the country before his term of office expired (September 23).

Lebanon withdrew its complaint to the UN Security Council of May 22 concerning a threat to its territorial integrity.

The UN General Assembly reconvened and a resolution sponsored by Norway, Canada, Colombia, Denmark, Liberia, Panama and Paraguay was introduced. The resolution called upon the Secretary General to take such action as he deemed adequate to uphold the principles of the UN Charter; it made no specific reference to the withdrawal of US and British troops from the Middle East.

August 19

The Indian delegate to the UN met with the Afro-Asian delegates to get approval of a draft resolution to be sponsored by India, Indonesia and Ceylon calling for the withdrawal of US and British troops from the Middle East at an early date.

August, 1958

August 19

The British-UAR talks in Geneva were suspended due to the wide divergence of views over compensation.

Crown Prince Faisal of Saudi Arabia termed the US and British intervention in Lebanon and Jordan "aggression."

The Iraqi Government set up a special administration to deal with confiscated property.

The World Health Organization appropriated $108,042 for health projects in Jordan, the Minister of Health announced.

The Sultan of Lahej in Aden said that President Nasser completely supported his case against Britain.

The Lebanese Ministry of Finance announced that the country was financially sound and that the rate of gold cover for its currency was over 71 percent.

August 20

The first shipment of American military aid since July 14 arrived in Basra, Iraq. A US State Department spokesman said that this was merely a fulfillment of previous obligations.

The first official contact between the IPC (Iraq Petroleum Company) and the Iraqi Government was made when the Managing Director of the IPC called on the Minister of Economics.

Premier Kassem of Iraq said, in a press conference, that the status of the British Airbase at Habbaniya would be settled in a friendly manner with understanding for mutual interest, once British and US troops had left Jordan and Lebanon. He also said that the USIS offices would be allowed to reopen as soon as tensions were eased.

The Arab Countries drafted a compromise resolution calling on the UN Secretary General to make practical arrangements for an early withdrawal of US and British troops. The resolution also reaffirmed the countries' Arab League ties.

August, 1958

August 21

By unanimous vote of all 80 UN member nations present, the UN General Assembly adopted a resolution sponsored by the ten Arab States, including both Jordan and Lebanon. It requested the Secretary General, Dag Hammarskjold, to make arrangements for the early withdrawal of British and US troops from Jordan and Lebanon.

Twenty pro-government deputies told General Chehab of Lebanon that they would support any measures he might take to restore stability to the country.

Lebanese Leader of the Opposition Party Saeb Salam issued a statement approving the UN Arab resolution.

A US State Department spokesman said that no indication had been received that Saudi Arabia would oust the US from the Dhahran Airbase.

The British Foreign Office disclosed that the Sudanese Government had imposed a ban on flights over its territory by British aircraft carrying troops or military equipment.

King Hussein said that the Jordanian Army was capable of defending the country if given sufficient military and financial aid.

August 22

A France-UAR agreement signed in Zurich allowed French nationals to return to the UAR and regain a large part of their property seized as a result of the 1956 invasion. The French Institute of Archaeology in Cairo, the French Law Institute and lycees in Cairo and Alexandria were to be reopened.

August, 1958

August 20

Izzat Tannous, Director of the Palestine Refugee Office in New York, urged the UN General Assembly Emergency Session to consider the question of the refugees.

The Sudanese Government banned flights over Sudanese territory by British planes carrying troops or military equipment.

It was reported that Saudi Arabia was planning not to renew the US lease on the Dhahran Airbase.

Aziz Sidqi, UAR Minister of Industry, said that the plant equipment promised by the Soviet Union under the loan agreement negotiated in January was scheduled to start arriving within the next few months.

Monsignor Paul Maoushi of Lebanon said that he was against the neutralization of Lebanon.

The fifth anniversary of King Muhammad V's exile was commemorated in Morocco. In his speech, the King said that he was determined to realize the national objectives: the complete integration into Morocco of all parts under colonial rule, the evacuation of foreign troops and a Maghreb union, including Algeria.

French General De Gaulle's Government issued a decree reactivating the Commission to Safeguard Individual Rights and Liberties. In its new form the Commission was empowered to demand information or documents from the civil, military, or judicial authorities, and was granted the right of access to any place at any time, whereas its field of activity was extended to cover France as well as Algeria.

The Jordanian House of Notables approved the amended constitution and electoral law that had been approved by the Lower House August 18.

The Suez Canal Authority placed an order with a Dutch firm for two of the world's most powerful tugboats, each with a capacity of about 6,400 horsepower.

August, 1958

August 22

UN Secretary General Hammarskjold announced that he would leave for the Middle East August 25 to make arrangements for the withdrawal of British and US troops. He said that a radio truce should be declared in the area.

British Foreign Secretary Lloyd had a confidential conference with Foreign Minister Fawzi of the UAR, arranged and attended by UN Secretary General Hammarskjold.

Crown Prince Muhammad al-Badr, Foreign Minister of Yemen, arrived from Cairo on a state visit to Iraq.

French Premier De Gaulle at Tananarive, Madagascar, offered African territories either complete separation from France or a part in a "federal community" under French leadership.

Radio Mecca reported that a responsible source had refuted reports that President Nasser told Crown Prince Faisal of Saudi Arabia that no country could join the UAR while it had foreign bases on its soil. It went on to say that Saudi Arabia was not bound by any agreement with a foreign country that made it subservient and that it had no secret agreement with the US.

August 23

Ali Abu Nuwar, former Jordanian Chief of Staff, testifying in the trial of General Daghistani, said that there was a British backed plot to assassinate President Nasser. He said that it was part of a bigger plan sponsored by the US, Great Britain, Saudi Arabia, Israel, Turkey and Iraq.

Jordanian Premier al-Rifai said that he welcomed the UN Arab resolution and that he was prepared to meet President Nasser for personal negotiations.

The Lebanese Minister of Finance announced that his Government had requested a cash assistance of LL90 million from the US Government.

August 23

The Lebanese frontier with Syria was reopened for the first time since May 10.

August 24

The Syrian Ministry of Economy and Commerce announced that rationing of rice had been lifted.

A UAR Government delegation arrived in Berlin to discuss expansion of economic relations with the East German Government.

August 25

UN Secretary General Hammarskjold left for the Middle East for talks to facilitate the withdrawal of US and British troops from Lebanon and Jordan.

US tanks approached Beirut and took up battle positions opposite the city districts controlled by the insurgents.

In a note to Cairo, the Sudan rejected a UAR protest, made in July, that Sudan's diversion of Nile waters for an irrigation project was in violation of the 1929 pact.

Members of the Lebanese Cabinet met with President Chamoun while 32 members of the Opposition met with their leader, Saeb Salam, to discuss political tactics.

Opposition leaders in Lebanon issued a statement accusing subversive and foreign elements of conspiring to keep General Chehab from performing his duties.

Gaston Lesneau, Assistant Financial Attache of the French Embassy in Beirut, arrived in Damascus to discuss the desequestration of French properties in Syria.

August 26

Crown Prince Muhammad al-Badr of Yemen and Iraqi Premier Kassem issued a joint communique expressing determination to align their foreign policies. The Crown Prince then flew to Cairo.

The UAR charged Israel with crossing the demarcation line between Israel and Sinai.

UN Secretary General Hammarskjold arrived in Beirut, Lebanon.

The UN Observation Group in Lebanon (UNOGIL) reported 190 military observers from fifteen countries in Lebanon.

In Lebanon censorship was reimposed on outgoing telegrams by newsmen.

The Soviet Government drew the attention of the Italian Government to the serious responsibility it had taken upon itself in supporting the British and US actions in Lebanon and Jordan.

In Lebanon, 33 Opposition leaders pledged that when General Chehab became President September 24, they would not cooperate with anyone who had worked with the present administration.

August 27

Talks opened in Baghdad with the UAR for trade extension. Iraq approved a payments agreement between the two countries.

Premier De Gaulle arrived in Algiers and conferred with civil and military leaders.

The Moroccan Foreign Ministry said that the Government had agreed to establish diplomatic relations with the USSR.

Gaston Lesneau, Assistant Financial Attache of the French Embassy in Beirut, offered on behalf of the French Government to buy 15,000 tons of the Syrian cotton crop.

August 27

UN Secretary General Hammarskjold met with members of the UN Observation Group in Lebanon before going to Amman.

UN Secretary General Hammarskjold arrived in Amman, Jordan, and conferred with King Hussein and Premier al-Rifai.

It was announced in Jordan that state land would be distributed to landless farmers.

The Lebanese Minister of National Economy announced that the US would pay Lebanon $2.5 million. The remainder of the LL90 million requested was promised for a later date.

The United Parliamentary Bloc of Lebanon, composed of 25 pro-government deputies, asked that an ultimatum be given to all armed groups to surrender their arms. They also stated their refusal to cooperate with any Government that included Opposition leaders.

August 28

Premier De Gaulle, in a speech in Algiers, said that if the Algerians voted in favor of the September 28 referendum it would prove that they wanted Algeria to evolve in a French framework.

French units launched an air supported operation against the Algerian National Liberation Army in the Seddouk area.

An agricultural delegation of the UAR, headed by Sayed Marei, Minister of Agriculture of the Egyptian sector, and Ahmad Al-Hag Younes, Agricultural Minister of the Syrian sector, arrived in Moscow at the invitation of the Soviet Ministry of Agriculture.

President Camille Chamoun of Lebanon approved the establishment of the National Rally Party.

Philip de Saynes, UN Under Secretary for Economic and Social Affairs, met with Prime Minister Abd-al-Majid Kobar and other officials of

August 28

Libya. Seynes said that Libya would benefit greatly from the technical aid it was to receive from the UN Economic Commission for Africa

Yusuf Salim, President of the Traders Association in Beirut, conferred with Saeb Salam over the question of gradually calling off the strike that had been in effect since May so that economic life would be normal when General Chehab assumed the presidency.

August 29

After three days of discussions, a joint communique was issued by the Jordanian Government and the UN Secretary General.

Agreements on economic, technical and scientific cooperation were concluded between the UAR and East Germany. A credit of LE million in the form of industrial plants and equipment was extended to the UAR.

The Arab States in the UN protested against the extension of the French referendum to Algeria.

The US Embassy in Lebanon said that the amount of US aid to be given to that country was still under discussion, and denied that any agreement had been reached.

It was reported that Monsignor Paul Maoushi was renewing his efforts to convince the Opposition in Lebanon to change its attitude.

It was reported that Syria had been supplying Iraq with small arms and ammunition for the People's Resistance in exchange for petroleum products.

Premier Kassem of Iraq said that any union with the UAR would be gradual.

August, 1958

August 30

A delegation headed by Ibrahim Kubbah, Iraqi Minister of Economics, went to Damascus to discuss commercial and economic relations with Syrian officials.

US Ambassador McClintock and Admiral Holloway, Commander of US troops in Lebanon, met with Opposition leader Saeb Salam in Lebanon.

President Chamoun of Lebanon and General Chehab were reported to be conferring over measures to restore law and order in that country.

UN Secretary General Hammarskjold left Beirut after a one day stay. He did not confer with any government officials.

Premier De Gaulle presided over a Cabinet meeting which decided to give the necessary supplementary means to the Ministry of the Interior to stop terrorism and sabotage in Algeria.

It was announced that President Nasser had invited Italian Premier Fanfani to Cairo.

August 31

A new Amman-Jerusalem road was opened to traffic on the completion of a bridge over the Jordan River.

September, 1958

September 1

Members of the NLF ended a two day conference with Tunisian and Moroccan leaders. A communique said that the participants agreed on diplomatic steps for UN action on the Algerian question.

The US land forces began a three week training period in tank tactics for Lebanese army personnel.

Jordanian King Hussein approved the Cabinet's decision to replace Baha-ad-Din Touqan as permanent delegate to the UN.

Syrian Vice President Akran Hourani formally opened the Fifth Damascus International Fair.

Crown Prince Muhammad al-Badr of Yemen said that he had uncovered evidence that the former Iraqi Government had plotted to make the late Crown Prince Abd-al-Ilah King of the Aden protectorates.

The Communist Chinese Embassy in Cairo said that UAR labor union leaders had volunteered to fight Formosa.

September 2

A UAR Government Delegation arrived in Moscow to open talks on direct air service between the UAR and Russia.

Khalil Kallas, Minister of Economy for the Syrian Region, said that the UAR and Iraq would soon conclude a trade and payments agreement that would be the first step toward total economic unity.

East German and Yugoslav delegations arrived in Baghdad to discuss trade relations with Iraq.

A 16 member control commission was set up to supervise preparations for the referendum in Algeria.

Syria reported that Turkish soldiers had opened fire on Syrian outposts.

September, 1958

September 3

Victor Khouri, Secretary General of the Lebanese Foreign Ministry, was to be appointed leader of the Lebanese UN delegation of Dr. Malik who became President of the General Assembly.

Adib Firzli, Deputy Speaker of the Chamber of Deputies of Lebanon, flew to Cairo to meet President Nasser in an attempt to relax tensions between their countries.

British and UAR representatives met in Rome to discuss financial claims.

The US State Department announced that relatively small quantities of arms of a defensive character were being purchased by Israel from the US.

Israel did not send a representative to the emergency meeting of the UAR-Israel Mixed Armistice Commission to review the incident of August 26.

Allal al-Fassi, leader of the Istiqlal Party in Morocco, indicated that Morocco would join the Arab League.

UN Secretary General Hammarskjold arrived in Cairo and conferred with UAR Foreign Minister Fawzi.

President Nasser, in his speech opening the Executive Council of the United Arab States, accused the US and Britain of seeking to destroy Arab nationalism by arming Israel.

A conference of 150 delegates from Mauritania and the Moroccan Sahara met in Rabat, Morocco. Babana, a leader of the Mauritanian nationalist movement, said that Mauritania and the Sahara were integral parts of Morocco. He noted that independence would be won by negotiation with the powers concerned.

September, 1958

September 4

A Foreign Ministry spokesman announced that the Soviet Union had offered financial and technical aid for economic development in Libya. The Libyan Government was considering the offer.

The British Government agreed that an annual payment of 500,000 pounds sterling from Jordan for British stores and installations would be deferred for six years.

Sudanese Foreign Minister Mahgoub arrived in Khartoum, Sudan, after spending several days in London on his trip from the UN. While in London he conferred with British Prime Minister Macmillan.

President Nasser approved a ten year economic development program for the Syrian Region.

UAR President Nasser conferred with UN Secretary General Hammarskjold.

The Iraqi Government approved a cultural agreement with the UAR which reportedly included the unification of school curricula.

Ways of expanding Iraqi-Soviet trade were discussed by the Chairman of the Baghdad Chamber of Commerce and the Soviet Commercial Attache.

The UAR proposed that a conference be held with the Sudan to settle water and other disputes that were left pending when the Sudan became independent.

The US State Department announced the release of 73 million pounds of surplus food, valued at $8 million, to help feed UAR school children.

September 5

Morocco formally applied for admittance to the Arab League, which was composed of the UAR, Iraq, Jordan, Saudi Arabia, Libya, Lebanon, the Sudan and Yemen.

September, 1958

September 5

The Moroccan Government passed a new law to attract foreign capital.

The Mauritania-Sahara conference in Morocco rejected French Premier De Gaulle's constitutional referendum.

The UN Secretary General completed three days of talks in Cairo with President Nasser, Foreign Minister Mahmoud Fawzi, and Abd-al-Khaleq Hassouna, Secretary General of the Arab League. No communique was issued at the conclusion of their discussions.

September 6

The Political Committee of the Arab League opened its meeting in Cairo. They decided not to bring up the Palestine political issue before the next UN General Assembly.

Britain announced cession by Muscat and Oman to Pakistan of the small enclave of Gwadar on the coast of Baluchistan, effective September 8.

Hassan Jabarra, the Minister of Planning in Syria, said that oil in commercial quantities had been discovered in the northeast, near the Iraq border, by an American owned drilling concern.

September 7

UN Secretary General Hammarskjold conferred with Iraqi Premier Kassem and other government leaders.

In Baghdad, talks between a Yugoslav mission led by the Minister of Industry and the Iraqi Government began. A trade agreement was to be signed.

Iraqi Foreign Minister Abd-al-Jabbar Jumaa conferred with President Nasser in Cairo.

The Jordanian Council of Ministers decided to grant loans to farmers for drought damage.

September, 1958

September 9

It was reported in Amman that the Jordanian Government had asked the US for an additional $40 million worth of military aid.

Abd-al-Moneim al-Rifai was appointed head of the Jordanian UN delegation.

President Nasser of the UAR accepted an invitation to visit Czechoslovakia.

The British-UAR financial talks in Rome were indefinitely suspended so that the representatives could have time to report back to their Governments.

It was announced that farmers in Syria whose crops were damaged by drought would receive wheat loans from the Syrian Board of Cereals.

The Lebanese delegation to the UN announced that their country would uphold the candidacy of their Foreign Minister Malik for President of the UN General Assembly.

September 10

UN Secretary General Dag Hammarskjold met with Lebanese President Chamoun, Acting Minister of Foreign Affairs Mukhaybir and General Chehab regarding implementation of the special General Assembly resolution on the early withdrawal of US troops from Lebanon.

Lebanese Premier al-Solh announced that he would leave Lebanon after his resignation September 24.

The Lebanese Ministry of the Interior accepted an application from eight pro-government deputies to form a new party, the "Free Patriots." The founders, it was reported, would proclaim President Chamoun the party leader.

It was announced that Foreign Minister Mahgoub of the Sudan would run for the Presidency of the UN General Assembly.

September, 1958

September 7

US Charge d'Affaires in Jordan, Thomas Wright, conferred with Jordanian Premier al-Rifai on the subject of American financial aid to Jordan.

The Arab League decided to contact League member UN delegations to bring up the Oman question before the General Assembly. They also condemned the French draft constitution for Algeria.

Soviet newspapers published the Soviet Government's note to Israel regarding its direct complicity in the British and US actions in the Middle East.

September 8

The Moroccan Government formally announced that it would exchange diplomatic missions with the Soviet Union on the ambassadorial level.

Israel Prime Minister Ben-Gurion said that the objectives of Israel foreign policy were: to maintain the status quo in the Middle East, to increase military preparedness, to win friends and make peace with all peaceful nations.

The Council of Heads of Departments decided that Tunisia would join the Arab League.

A meeting of the Council of the League of Arab States voted opposition to a French plebiscite in Algeria and said that such an action was illegal and void and could have no binding effect upon the Algerian people.

UN Secretary General Dag Hammarskjold returned to Amman, Jordan, and conferred for a second time with Jordanian leaders on ways to implement the UN resolution.

The Sudanese Ambassador to Baghdad held talks with the Iraqi Minister of Education, Jabr Omar, concerning the improvement of cultural cooperation between their countries.

September, 1958

September 10

The Norwegian Government agreed to pay the surcharge on Suez Canal passage for all Norwegian ships.

It was announced after a French Cabinet meeting that France would not participate in any UN debate of the Algerian question.

The US replied to a Moroccan demand for evacuation of airbases in a note handed to the Prime Minister by the US Ambassador.

The Iraqi Military Court accused a former Baghdad Radio announcer of helping to organize the "Voice of Free Egypt," a radio program designed to subvert the Nasser regime in the UAR.

September 11

It was reported in Iraq that Baghdad Radio had taken an anti-US and pro-Soviet view of world issues.

Brigadier Shaker Mahmound Shukri was appointed Deputy Chief of Staff of the Iraqi Army.

Iraq, it was announced, was discussing a cultural agreement with Morocco.

Lebanese General Chehab supported Charles Makik for President of the UN General Assembly.

UN Secretary General Dag Hammarskjold met with senior members of the UN Observation Group and later conferred with General Chehab in Lebanon.

September 12

Moscow Radio announced that the Soviet Union and the UAR had agreed to establish regular air service between the two countries.

September, 1958

September 12

Colonel Abd-al-Salam Aref was relieved of his post as Assistant Commander in Chief of the Armed Forces in Iraq.

A British mission in Libya to discuss the formation of the nucleus of a navy met with the Libyan Prime Minister and later with the Minister of Defense.

Muhammad Masmoudi, Tunisian Ambassador to France, was expelled from the Political Bureau for "grave indiscipline." Masmoudi had refused to sign a condemnation of L'Action.

The Algerian Minister of the Interior announced the start of a 25 billion French franc five year plant to provide adequate housing for Algerian workers in Metropolitan France.

Gaston Defferre, a leading member of the Socialist Party in Algeria, asked for a policy of negotiation to end the Algerian war.

September 13

Secretary General of the UN Dag Hammarskjold returned to New York from a Middle East trip, terming his talks with Arab leaders highly useful.

Sudanese Foreign Minister Muhammad Mahgoub arrived in New York for the UN General Assembly meeting. He said that he would "fight the battle to the end" for election as President of the General Assembly.

Representatives of fuel companies completed a draft agreement to form a consortium to organize the import and distribution of fuel in Jordan.

September 14

The US began withdrawal of two battalions of Marines from Lebanon.

Discussions between Iraqi Premier Kassem and the Bulgarian Ambassador were held to strengthen trade relations.

September, 1958

September 14

The British Foreign Office announced that it would grant Jordan one million pounds sterling to help balance the budget.

Moroccan officials disclosed that the US had agreed to gradual evacuation of its bases in Morocco.

The Jordanian Government announced its candidature for membership in the UN Trusteeship Council.

September 15

Under an agreement signed in Tokyo, Japan was to lend the UAR $30 million for industrial development. Japan was also to send equipment for 19 different industries.

President Bourguiba of Tunisia disclosed that he had rejected a French offer to sell arms to Tunisia.

The Suez Canal surcharge went into effect. Communist bloc ships were not paying the charge.

A joint Yugoslav-Iraqi committee was formed to investigate the expansion of trade relations.

September 16

Charles Malik, the Foreign Minister of Lebanon, was elected President of the UN General Assembly over Muhammad Ahmad Mahgoub of the Sudan. The vote was 45-31-4. The Israel delegation was absent.

The former Iraqi Ambassador to Jordan, Baha-ad-Din Nuri, was named to an Ambassador's post in the Jordanian Foreign Ministry by Royal Decree.

The US Embassy in Amman announced that the US granted Jordan $5 million, bringing total US support for the 1959 fiscal year to $24 million.

September, 1958

September 16

The Iraqi Military Attache in Cairo announced that Colonel Abd-al-Salam Muhammad Aref had resigned as Deputy Commander of the Army at his own request in order to be better able to attend to his other government posts.

US Ambassador to Lebanon Robert M. McClintock and Major General Paul D. Adams, Commander of US forces in Lebanon, conferred with General Chehab, President elect of Lebanon.

A trade agreement was signed between Tunisia and Finland.

It was reported that the US had asked the Moroccan Government to sign a contract for continued use of five military bases in Morocco for seven more years. It was also reported that the US had agreed to eventual evacuation.

President Habib Bourguiba of Tunisia, in a press interview, recognized a trend toward growing authoritarianism in his country.

September 17

It was reported in Washington that Jordan, Lebanon and the UAR had approved the Hammarskjold plan for a UN Committee with its main office in Amman, Jordan, and branch offices in Damascus and Beirut.

It was reported that the US would soon release about $5 million in foreign aid to the UAR. These funds had been frozen when Egypt nationalized the Suez Canal in 1956.

It was announced that President Tito of Yugoslavia would visit the UAR as part of a projected tour of Asian countries.

Nuritdin A. Mukhitdinov, a member of the Soviet Communist Party's Presidium, arrived in Cairo on a cultural visit.

The Saudi Arabian Monetary Agency announced a reduction of two gurushs (piastres) in the free market rate of the Saudi riyal, in relation to the US dollar.

September, 1958

September 17

French Foreign Minister Maurice Couve de Murville stated at the UN that he opposed all UN action on Algeria, that the UN General Assembly was not empowered to deal with the Algerian question and that the French Delegation would in no way participate in the debate on Algeria.

Police and military guards were strengthened throughout France, as Premier De Gaulle conferred with government officials on further measures to halt Algerian terrorist attacks.

September 18

A three year Maritime Agreement was signed between the UAR and the Soviet Union, providing for the establishment of permanent sea routes between the two countries.

Libya became the 68th member of the International Monetary Fund and the International Bank for Reconstruction and Development.

The Egyptian Government freed French assets frozen in 1956 when Britain and France attacked Egypt.

Many dwellings and palm plantations reportedly were destroyed in a British air raid in Oman.

The UN announced that steps had been taken to bolster its team of military observers in Lebanon.

September 19

The Coordination and Executive Committee of the Algerian National Liberation Front announced in Cairo the formation of a Provisional Government for a Republic of Algeria. Ferhat Abbas was designated Premier. The UAR, Iraq, Libya, Yemen, Tunisia and Morocco immediately announced recognition of the regime.

The French Government declared that recognition of the Algerian government in exile by foreign states would be considered an unfriendly act.

September, 1958

September 19

UN Secretary General Hammarskjold appointed a three man team to go to Jordan to work out organizational details of the practical arrangements on which agreements had been reached by the Secretary General in relation to Jordan.

It was reported that members of the Lebanese Parliament were opposed to rebel demands that Rashid Karami, the rebel leader in Tripoli, become the first Premier of Lebanon under General Chehab.

The French Defense Ministry denied Tunisian charges that French forces had violated Tunisian territory.

September 20

The outgoing Premier of Lebanon, Sami al-Solh, left secretly for Turkey four days before his term of office ended.

The UN Observation Group in Lebanon (UNOGIL) reported 214 military observers from 21 countries in Lebanon.

The Saudi Arabian Government recognized the Provisional Government of Algeria.

Nuritdin A. Mukhitdinov of the Soviet Union arrived in Damascus from Cairo to visit the Syrian Province.

The Provisional Government of Algeria announced that it would establish its headquarters in Cairo.

The Provisional Government of Algeria protested to the UN against the extension to Algeria of the French constitutional referendum, alleging that Algerians had been forced to the polls by French soldiers and police during the first stage of the referendum in Algeria.

September 21

It was reported from Cairo that President Nasser planned to centralize the administration of the UAR by replacing the dual ministerial arrangement with a stronger central government. The reports also

September, 1958

September 21

indicated that the Egyptian-Syrian union had not been functioning as smoothly as hoped.

Algerian rebel forces opened a general offensive against the French, occupying territory west of the Tunisian border.

Baghdad Radio announced that no publication could in the future be printed in Iraq without the permission of a special military committee.

September 22

Lebanese Premier Sami al-Solh and his pro-Western Cabinet formally resigned.

Jordan and the Sudan recognized the Provisional Government of Algeria.

Communist China recognized the Algerian Provisional Government.

The French Government protested to Morocco, Libya and Tunisia against their recognition of the Provisional Government in Algeria.

September 23

Fuad Chehab was sworn in as President of Lebanon. General Chehab said that he would work for the early withdrawal of US troops. Outgoing President Chamoun left for a vacation in the mountains, but said that he would return to serve Lebanon as a simple citizen.

September 24

Lebanese President Chehab appointed a Cabinet headed by former rebel leader Rashid Karami.

King Saud of Saudi Arabia formally sent congratulations to the new President of Lebanon.

It was reported that the Saudi Arabian Minister of Agriculture promised Saudi businessmen assistance from the Ministry if they would invest in agricultural projects.

September, 1958

September 25

The US State Department announced that the US would not recognize the Algerian Provisional Government.

A trade agreement was signed between Tunisia and Communist China.

The UAR and India signed a ten year cultural agreement.

It was reported that US officials expected their forces in Lebanon to withdraw by the end of October, depending on UN arrangements and Lebanese Premier Karami's ability to maintain order.

Premier Karami of Lebanon said that he would ask for the immediate withdrawal of US troops. He added that in foreign affairs, his government would work for the continued independence of Lebanon, brotherhood with all Arab countries and for neutrality between East and West in world politics.

It was reported in Jerusalem that the Israel Government had allocated more than IL20 million for a program designed to rehabilitate former Arab refugees and displaced persons who had returned to Israel legally since 1948.

Lebanese Premier Karami said that his Government did not adhere to the Eisenhower Doctrine, but that it would continue to accept American aid if given unconditionally.

September 26

Prime Minister Ferhat Abbas of the Algerian Provisional Government announced the Government's program at a press conference in Cairo. He offered to stop the killing in Algeria and to negotiate a peaceful settlement with France. The declaration also said that Algeria was not France and that Algerians would never submit to integration.

The referendum on the French Constitution began in Algeria.

Pierre Jumayil, leader of the Phalange in Lebanon, presented his demand for at least one seat in the Cabinet, to Lebanese President

September, 1958

September 26

Chehab. The Phalange charged that the Cabinet was composed only of rebels and neutrals.

It was announced in Riyadh, Saudi Arabia, that Fahd Ibn-Saud, eldest son of the King, had been reinstated as Minister of Defense.

September 27

UAR President Nasser introduced, by decree, a land reform law for the Syrian Region effective January 1959.

The US assured the Karami Government of Lebanon its full support.

Morocco established an agency to set up an Arab cultural center under UNESCO.

The official Communist Party newspaper Pravda reported that the Soviet Government had established high level contact with the rebel Algerian Government.

September 28

A Presidential Decree created a General Petroleum Authority to plan petroleum policy and to supervise the administration and exploitation of oil in the UAR.

President Nasser issued a Decree repealing tribal laws in the Syrian region; the tribes would be subject to the same laws and decrees as town dwellers.

The French Constitution of the Fifth Republic, which was submitted to national referendum throughout France, Algeria, and France Overseas, was approved everywhere except Guinea. It gave the president greater powers and strengthened the position of the Government in the Assembly.

It was reported that Iraq had opened economic and trade negotiations with the UAR.

September, 1958

September 28

Ali Ibn-Abd-al-Karim Abdali, the deposed Sultan of Lahej, asked his people to boycott any referendum on the proposed Consultative Assembly.

September 29

It was revealed in Washington that the US would grant the Sudan $19.5 million in foreign aid; $15 million was for aid in the balance of payments difficulties and the rest for technical assistance.

UN Secretary General Hammarskjold reported to the General Assembly that the US and Britain had given him renewed assurances regarding their early troop withdrawal from the Middle East as soon as the area had been stabilized. Furthermore, he asserted that both the UAR and Iraq had assured him that they would end their economic blockade of Jordan after US troops had withdrawn from Lebanon and the British had evacuated Jordan.

The vote in Algeria was 96 percent in favor of Premier De Gaulle's new constitution. The unusually favorable vote was believed to be due to the fact that Moslems, who risked the reprisals of Algerian rebels by going to the polls, voted affirmatively to avoid the anger of the French Army.

Arab League Secretary General Hassouna indicated that Kuwait wanted to join the League.

The USSR Society for Friendship and Cultural Relations with the Arab East held a meeting in Moscow to honor the Algerian people in their intrepid fight for freedom and independence.

The last contingent of US Marines left Lebanon; it was believed that US army forces were also preparing to leave.

September 30

The Iraqi Government proclaimed an agrarian reform law limiting individual land holdings.

October, 1958

October 1

Tunisia and Morocco, on their own application, were elected the ninth and tenth members of the Arab League.

King Hussein of Jordan announced to Parliament that British troops would begin withdrawing from Jordan October 20. He also said that some security restrictions would be relaxed.

Details of the meeting of Lebanese leaders arranged by Ambassador McClintock were announced by the Ambassador to the press. He reported that he had made three proposals to the two factions.

The UN Observer Group in Lebanon reported that armed infiltration across the border from Syria had virtually ceased.

The Minister of State in Saudi Arabia, Ahmad Shukairi, suggested that France negotiate directly with the Provisional Algerian Government in Cairo and that UN Secretary General Hammarskjold act as mediator.

The French Cabinet, in a special meeting, approved emergency measures to stem Algerian terrorist attacks in metropolitan France.

October 2

An Iraqi-Yugoslav trade agreement, providing for an exchange of Iraqi agricultural products and Yugoslav industrial goods, was signed in Baghdad.

Former President of Lebanon Chamoun reportedly did not consider the proposals of US Ambassador McClintock a suitable basis for a settlement.

US Ambassador to Lebanon Robert McClintock came under fire from several segments of the population of Lebanon for what was charged as interference in the affairs of Lebanon.

A ten man trade delegation from Communist China arrived in Rabat, Morocco.

September, 1958

September 30

Baghdad Radio announced that Abd-al-Salam Muhammad Aref, Deputy Premier and Iraqi Minister of Interior, had been appointed Ambassador to West Germany. Jaber Omar, Minister of Education, and Faud al-Rikabi, Minister of Development, were removed from their posts.

UN Secretary General Hammarskjold acknowledged that the UAR and Iraq had refused to permit him to establish a UN presence in Cairo and Baghdad, but he said that the UN special representative in Amman would have liaison representatives in Damascus and Beirut. He also reported that he had encouraging contacts about the supply of oil to Jordan through the Syrian region and the supply of oil from Iraq on a commercial basis.

US Ambassador to Lebanon Robert McClintock brought top leaders of the new Lebanese Government and the Phalange together for talks. The only Cabinet member present was Philippe Taqla, the Foreign Minister. Pierre Jumayil also attended.

A UN General Assembly discussion of the Middle East began.

October, 1958

October 2

The Soviet Union requested the UN General Assembly to open debate on the failure of the US and Britain to withdraw troops from the Middle East. US Delegate Henry Cabot Lodge assailed the request as a "typical statement from the Moscow propaganda factory."

Premier De Gaulle arrived in Algeria. In a speech he reaffirmed France's determination to remain in Algeria, although he hinted that his policy might favor a special status for Algeria rather than total integration.

An investigation commenced in Cairo to weigh charges that the UAR's Syrian Vice President Sabri al-Assali had conspired to link Syria with Iraq.

October 3

In a speech at Constantine, Premier De Gaulle outlined a five year program for the agricultural and industrial development of Algeria.

The Constantine Plan for Algeria envisioned increased education and employment, new housing, and land reform.

Morocco broke off trade talks with West Germany.

Tunisian President Bourguiba took steps to decentralize the political control of the Neo-Destour Party. He announced that Political Commissioners in each of the 14 provinces would replace party federations.

Lebanese women blockaded roads into Beirut, demanding that pro-Chamoun elements of the population be represented in the new Cabinet under Premier Karami.

The UAR and the Provisional Government of Algeria recognized the independence of the Republic of Guinea.

October, 1958

October 3

The founding of an Israel Arab Labor Party was proclaimed in Haifa by 732 delegates from 60 Arab settlements.

Abd-al-Moniem Rifai, the Jordanian Delegate to the UN, warned the Soviet Union not to interfere with Middle Eastern affairs.

October 5

The Arab League Council postponed consideration of adopting a budget for the Algerian nationalists on account of Tunisia's failure to send a delegate to the Council meeting.

The exploration concession of the American Menhall oil interests was cancelled by the Syrian Government for alleged violation of their exploration license.

October 6

Sabri al-Assali, the Syrian Vice President, resigned amidst an investigation into charges the before the Syrian-Egyptian merger he had been involved in a plot to establish a pro-Western Government with Iraq.

A Finance Ministry spokesman announced that Great Britain had given Jordan 575,000 pounds sterling as the first installment of a recently announced million pound loan.

Sudanese Foreign Minister Mahgoub called on the US and Britain to hasten their troop withdrawals from Lebanon and Jordan.

Premier Ferhat Abbas of Algeria left Cairo for Tunis to talk with Tunisian leaders.

October 7

President Nasser announced the formation of a Central Cabinet of 21 members and a 15 member Executive Council for Egypt and Syria. He also announced the resignation of al-Assali of Syria as Vice President.

October, 1958

October 9

It was reported that the first British army truck convoy left Amman for the port of Aqaba. This marked the beginning of the British troop withdrawal from Jordan.

October 10

Algerian Premier Farhat Abbas announced that his Provisional Government was ready to negotiate with France to determine the political and military conditions for a ceasefire.

A record cotton crop in the UAR for the year of 1958 was announced by the Government.

Moroccan officials reported that the French Government had officially protested to Morocco against proposals for oil prospecting in the Moroccan-Algerian border region.

In Lebanon, President Chehab's attempts to set up a coalition cabinet failed.

Premier De Gaulle's Government announced its decision to allot 66 seats to Algeria in the next French National Assembly; 45 seats would be given to Moslems.

October 11

The new Iraqi regime signed an economic and trade agreement with the Soviet Union. A protocol signed established a Soviet trade mission in Iraq.

Lebanese Premier Karami agreed to enlarge his Cabinet to include supporters of former President Chamoun.

The UAR delegation walked out of an Arab League Council meeting in protest against a Tunisian charge that the League was dominated by some big countries. The Tunisian delegate, al-Shatti, announced that he would not return to the meeting because of the actions of the UAR representatives.

October, 1958

October 7

Radio Cairo unleashed an attack against the US for failing to withdraw troops from Lebanon. Broadcasts also attacked President Eisenhower.

King Muhammad V of Morocco accepted the appointment of Dmitri P. Poxihdayev as the first Soviet Ambassador to Morocco.

A new wave of violence started in Lebanon.

It was reported in Baghdad, Iraq, that Premier Kassem had put down a revolt by soldiers supporting his chief rival, Colonel Aref.

October 8

A group of Lebanese Deputies in Parliament demanded that the Cabinet appear before that body within 48 hours or resign. It was reported that Premier Karami had been unable to muster a vote of confidence from Parliament.

Tunisia, Argentina and Italy were elected to non-permanent seats on the UN Security Council.

The US State Department announced that by agreement with Lebanon, American forces would be withdrawn from that country by the end of October, barring unforeseen developments.

October 9

Habib Bourguiba, Jr., son of the Tunisian President, was appointed Tunisian Ambassador to France.

Prime Minister Macmillan of Britain and West German Chancellor Adenauer concluded their talks on NATO, the German problem, and the Middle and Far East.

It was reported that Lebanese Premier Karami and his Cabinet had offered to resign. There were no indications that President Chehab had accepted the resignations. It was rumored that he was forming an emergency cabinet to meet the mounting crisis in Lebanon.

October, 1958

October 11

The US State Department announced that a nine man army mission was on its way to Jordan to study possible reorganization and re-equipment of the Arab army. The mission was sent at the request of King Hussein.

Paris newspapers reported the withdrawal of French troops from all parts of Tunisia except Bizerta.

The Saudi Arabian Government confirmed a Royal Decree appointing Anwar Ali Governor of the Monetary Agency as of April 1, 1958.

October 12

Colonel Abd-al-Salam Aref left Baghdad for Bonn to assume his duties as the new Iraqi Ambassador to West Germany. Premier Kassem bade him farewell at the airport.

It was reported that other delegations to the Arab League were attempting to mediate a dispute between the UAR and Tunisia.

A US military spokesman in Beirut said that US forces were in the final stage of withdrawal from Lebanon.

October 13

According to an American Embassy spokesman, the US signed an agreement granting Jordan $7.5 million in economic aid.

Premier De Gaulle told the French Army to stay out of Algerian politics and to permit free legislative elections. He also decreed that Moslems representing all shades of opinion, including those espousing Algerian independence, would be permitted to campaign freely for election to the French Parliament.

Premier Abd-al-Majid Kobar took over the Libyan Ministry of Foreign Affairs by Royal Decree. The former Foreign Minister, Wahbi al-Buri, became Minister of State, succeeding Khalil Kallal, who had resigned.

October, 1958

October 13

Tension mounted in Lebanon over the issue of whether Premier Karami would resign or agree to form a coalition cabinet which would include supporters of the former Chamoun Government.

A Permanent Bureau of Asian and African Writers composed of representatives of the Cameroons, Ceylon, China, Ghana, Indonesia, Japan, the Soviet Union, the Sudan and the UAR was established.

The Council of the League of Arab States formally and unanimously dissociated itself from Tunisia's charges that the League was dominated by the UAR.

October 14

Final agreement was reached on the formation of a compromise cabinet for Lebanon following a conference at the residence of President Chehab. A four man Cabinet, headed by Premier Rashid Karami and including Phalangist Party leader Pierre Jumayil, National Block leader Raymond Edde, and leader of the Islamic Council Hussein Uwaini, was formed.

Tunisian Foreign Minister Sadok Moqaddem said that his Government was studying the possibility of breaking diplomatic relations with the UAR.

The US military mission to Jordan arrived in Amman.

The UAR delegation to the Arab League returned to the Council meeting in response to pleas of other members. The Tunisian representative left for Tunis.

It was reported that Saudi Arabia had presented a proposal for an oil concession to the Standard Oil Company of Indiana.

Algerian Major General Jacques Massu, leader of the All Algeria Committee of Public Safety, and 11 other officers left that organization in obedience to orders from Premier De Gaulle.

October, 1958

October 15

Tunisia broke diplomatic relations with the UAR. President Bourguiba said that President Nasser was meddling in Tunisia's internal affairs and harboring enemies of Habib Bourguiba himself.

The new Lebanese Cabinet met under the chairmanship of President Chehab to study the necessary steps toward restoring law and order and disarming civilians.

October 16

It was reported that the UAR Government had rejected a Soviet bid to build schools, hospitals and orphanages in the UAR.

In Lebanon, the highways leading out of Beirut that had been blocked by supporters of former President Chamoun were reopened. Curfew regulations were eased.

It was reported that Saudi Arabia's offer of a new oil concession to the Standard Oil Company of Indiana was rejected.

October 17

The French Cabinet set November 30 as the date for Legislative elections in Algeria.

It was announced that UAR Field Marshal Amer would visit the Soviet Union at the invitation of the Soviet Government.

It was reported at the UN that Tunisia was willing to re-establish diplomatic relations with the UAR if Salah Ben-Youssef, the dissident Tunisian leader, was expelled from Cairo.

The Lebanese Parliament gave a unanimous vote of confidence to a four man cabinet headed by Premier Rashid Karami.

The Baghdad Pact Headquarters was moved temporarily from Baghdad to Ankara, in view of existing conditions.

October, 1958

October 18

The Arab League Council agreed to assess its ten members LE12 million for support of the Algerian rebellion. A communique requested all members whose pledges from the previous year remained unfulfilled to pay immediately.

The UN announced that Secretary General, Dag Hammarkjold, had requested Major General Odd Bull, executive member of the UN Observation Group in Lebanon, to begin arrangements for UN participation in the British troop withdrawal from Jordan.

The British Foreign Office announced that it would give the Sudan an undisclosed quantity of arms and equipment without charge, and that it would provide free training for Sudanese pilots.

Al-Kaissouni, the UAR Minister of Economics, said that a new currency, the Arab dinar, would replace the Egyptian pound and the Syrian lira by July, 1959.

It was reported that final preparations were being made to airlift all US troops out of Lebanon. London announced that all British troops in Jordan would be withdrawn by November 11.

The new Government of Lebanon issued an order rescinding a previous order which expelled the UAR Ambassador from Lebanon.

Field Marshal Abd-al-Hakim Amer, Vice President and War Minister of the UAR, arrived in Moscow.

October 19

The airlifting of the last US military personnel from Lebanon to Germany began.

October 20

The Sahara Petroleum Company, an operating subsidiary of the Continental Oil Company, announced that it would abandon prospecting operations in the Western Desert of Egypt. The announcement also stated that about $30 million had been spent on the operation in four and one half years.

October, 1958

October 20

British troops began their withdrawal from Jordan.

October 21

The US confirmed that it was sending approximately $1 million worth of surplus commodities for the relief of Algerian refugees in Tunisia. The Algerians conceded that a large part of the aid found its way back to Algeria and the rebel army.

The All Algeria Committee of Public Safety dissolved itself and regrouped to form a new body known as the Organization of Public Safety Committees.

Lebanese Foreign Minister Uwaini said that adoption of the Arab resolution by the UN General Assembly had made obsolete charges which the former Chamoun Government had presented to the UN against the UAR May 22. Lebanon then accused the UAR of interfering in its internal affairs.

October 22

It was reported that the UAR had asked the Soviet Union to warn the US, Britain, and France against aiding Israel should war again occur between Israel and the Arabs.

It was reported that the Arab States were considering formation of a Middle East Common Market.

Leslie J. Carver, acting head of the UN aid program for Arab refugees, reported to the UN that Arab Governments were interfering in the relief operation. He requested a UN budget of $37.5 million for UNRWA for 1959.

Jordanian Premier Samir al-Rifai stated that Jordan's security rested on three formidable pillars: the popularity of King Hussein, the loyalty of the army, and the recent growth of an enlightened public opinion that would answer a call to reason.

October, 1958

October 23

Crown Prince Faisal of Saudi Arabia said, in a press conference, that his country had achieved an independent foreign policy based on neutralism and Arab nationalism.

Alternate members of the Baghdad Pact Council met in Ankara and decided to make that city the Baghdad Pact's temporary headquarters.

Premier De Gaulle extended an invitation to the Algerian revels to come to Paris to negotiate a ceasefire. He promised them safe conduct in France and also made it clear that he would not discuss Algeria's political future with them, but would reserve such discussions for democratically elected representatives of the Algerian people. He also offered an amnesty to all rebels who surrendered.

Soviet Premier Khrushchev announced in his speech at a reception given in honor of Vice President Abd-al-Hakim Amer of the UAR that the Soviet Government had consented to participate in the construction of the first section of the Aswan Dam, and would loan the UAR 400 million rubles for the first stage of the construction.

October 24

The evacuation of US forces from Lebanon was completed.

Saudi Arabia warned Israel that an attack on Jordan would call for collective military action by all the Arab States.

It was reported that the Soviet offer to the UAR, of aid in the building of the Aswan Dam, was enthusiastically received throughout the Middle East.

October 25

The Algerian Provisional Government in Cairo rejected Premier De Gaulle's offer to confer in Paris to negotiate a ceasefire. The Government said that it was ready to appoint representatives to meet with those of the French Government to negotiate a real solution to the whole of the Algerian problem. This meeting could take place only in a neutral country.

October, 1958

October 25

The Ruler of Kuwait, Sheikh Abdallah al-Salem al-Sabah, arrived on an official visit in Baghdad. It was reported that he would discuss with Premier Kassem the improvement of economic and cultural relations between the two states.

Premier and Crown Prince Faisal of Saudi Arabia, in a radio broadcast, affirmed Saudi neutrality.

Abba Eban, Israel Ambassador to the US, said that the key to peace in the Middle East lay in the rapid strengthening of Israel.

Cairo declared that it was still open to Western offers of aid for the Aswan High Dam construction.

October 26

An economic agreement between Iraq and East Germany was signed in Baghdad.

October 27

Reports from Cairo indicated that the UAR and the Sudan would resume negotiations over a long standing dispute on division of the Nile waters.

The British Foreign Office denied knowledge of any intention by Qatar to join the Arab League.

The US called on the Arab States and Israel before the UN for renewed efforts to resolve the problem of the Arab refugees.

The UAR and Yugoslavia signed an agreement for exchange of technical information, educational experts and technicians.

Morocco and Communist China signed a $20 million trade agreement.

Thirty-two governments, members of the UN, pledged $27.5 million for the UN Relief and Works Agency for Palestine Refugees in the Near East (UNRWA).

October, 1958

October 27

The British Petroleum Company Ltd. and the Sinclair Oil Corporation announced plans for joint operations in the production and marketing of crude oil produced in Latin America and the Middle East. This joint action was designed to provide each company with greater strength and wider flexibility of crude oil supply and markets in both hemispheres.

October 28

Dr. Charles Malik, President of the UN General Assembly, conferred with Muhammad Yazid, Minister of Information in the Algerian Provisional Government.

A general mobilization took place in Israel. Troops were moved toward the Jordan border.

Secretary General Hammarskjold told the UN that the UNEF should be maintained along the borders of Egypt and Israel.

October 29

Premier Karami of Lebanon said that the US had offered Lebanon economic aid to help make up for losses incurred during five months of civil strife. The Premier's statement was confirmed by the US State Department.

It was announced in Tokyo that Japan still hoped to participate in the Aswan Dam project in Egypt.

Pier Spinelli announced that a plan for the establishment of a permanent UN mission in Jordan had been completed. The plan called for a mission of three men in Amman under the leadership of a special representative for Jordan.

Premier Ben-Gurion of Israel said that if there was a change in the status of Jordan, Israel should insist on demilitarization of Jordanian territory west of the Jordan River.

October, 1958

October 30

Dr. Galo Plaza, head of the UN Observation Group in Lebanon, said that he considered the work of his mission complete and hoped to arrange for the Group's withdrawal as soon as possible.

Charles Malik, President of the UN General Assembly, conferred with the Head of the French delegation on the Algerian problem. He later announced that he was not engaged in mediating the French-Algerian dispute.

A delegation of Iraqi public and cultural leaders, headed by the lawyer Nadji Youssef and Sheikh Latif, arrived in Moscow.

Aden Protectorate trade unions and public organizations called a general strike in protest against British persecution and mass terror.

President Bourguiba of Tunisia announced that a new currency, the dinar, valued at 1,000 French francs, would be issued the next week.

October 31

The British Foreign Office announced that Britain would send urgent shipments of arms, ammunition and equipment to the Sudan.

It was reported that some countries using the Suez Canal had refused to pay the three percent surcharge.

Moscow Radio reported that a delegation of Iraqi peace partisans had arrived in Moscow to strengthen relations between Iraq and the Soviet Union.

The Algerian Provisional Government's Minister of Information, as the Algerian revolt entered its fifth year, called upon the French to negotiate a peaceful settlement or to face a more intensive war effort.

November, 1958

November 1

Air, road and telephone communications between Jordan and the UAR were restored after an interruption of more than three months.

Informed sources in London reported that Great Britain had rushed troops to Muscat and Oman to repel increased rebel activity against Sultan Said Ibn-Taimur.

Morocco and Communist China announced the establishment of diplomatic relations at the ambassadorial level.

The US Embassy in Beirut announced that the US was to begin delivery of six jet fighters for the Lebanese Air Force.

Anti-British demonstrations continued in Aden.

November 2

British troops sent to Jordan at the request of King Hussein after the overthrow of the Iraq monarchy July 14 completed their withdrawal from Jordan.

November 3

The Central Bank of Tunisia was officially opened.

It was reported that an official UAR source disclosed that Britain had supplied Israel with a number of jet bombers.

The US State Department said that it had uncovered no evidence that Israel was preparing an invasion of Jordan.

Voting 49-9 in the UN General Assembly's Special Political Committee, members approved the continuing of the UNEF patrolling the Israel-UAR border.

Former Lebanese Premier Sami al-Solh said in Paris that the UAR had not ceased to meddle in Lebanese domestic affairs.

November, 1958

November 3

Baghdad Pact countries started their 18 day "Midlink" manoeuvers in the Arabian Sea, with Britain, the US, Pakistan and Turkey participating.

November 4

The Lebanese Government sent a bill to Parliament requesting power to rule by decree for six months. It was announced that such power was essential to effect urgent reforms, disarm civilians and restore peace and order.

Baghdad Radio announced that Colonel Aref was arrested for having returned to Baghdad from Europe without permission. The broadcast said that on account of the colonel's repeated attempts to disturb general security, he had been arrested and would be tried on a charge of plotting against Iraqi interests.

November 5

The heads of the Tunisian and Moroccan delegations to the UN formally presented to Secretary General Hammarskjold an Algerian rebel request that French authorities release five members of the Provisional Government, including Ahmad Ben-Bella, from prison.

Events in Baghdad last week — the rioting and the arrest of Colonel Aref — were reported to be part of a pro-Nasser coup which was foiled by Premier Kassem.

Tunisia accused France of sending two regiments of French troops across the Tunisian border in the vicinity of Kalaat-as-Senam.

November 6

General Abd-al-Hamid Ghaleb, Ambassador of the UAR from Lebanon who was declared persona non grata during the presidency of Chamoun, returned to Beirut.

The French Command in Algiers formally denied Tunisian charges that French forces had penetrated Tunisian territory.

November, 1958

November 7

Demonstrations in support of the regime of Iraqi Premier Kassem continued in Baghdad.

King Hussein of Jordan presided over a special meeting of the Council of Ministers. It was reported that he issued directions concerning Jordanian affairs prior to his departure for a vacation in Europe.

It was reported that the UAR and the Sudan might invite the World Bank to use its good offices in the Nile River waters dispute.

The Algerian rebel government announced that any Moslem who presented himself as a candidate in the forthcoming elections for the French National Assembly would be considered a traitor.

November 8

The Tunisian Foreign Ministry announced that Tunisia would not agree to any restrictive conditions attached to arms supplies it was seeking from the US and Britain. The announcement also said that Tunisia would renounce the arms rather than have its right to buy them submitted to the agreement of a third party.

It was reported that Saudi Arabia had granted an oil exploration and mining concession to the Italian Sani Company covering 13,000 square miles in the Qizan area, including the Farasan Islands.

A three man council was appointed to act in behalf of King Hussein during his absence from Jordan.

In an address at the opening of the National Consultative Assembly in Morocco, King Muhammad V reaffirmed his determination to transform that country into a democratic constitutional monarchy.

November 9

The deadline for candidates to file for election to the French National Assembly in Algeria ended. It was announced that Moslems who held nationalist views had failed to file. The only candidates running expressed the views of the French Army and the Committee of Public Safety.

November, 1958

November 9

Charles Malik, President of the UN General Assembly, said that the US should make a gift to the UAR to help in the construction of the Aswan Dam.

Jordanian King Hussein announced that the crisis in Jordan had ended, and promised to return soon to continue working and sacrificing himself for his people.

November 10

King Hussein of Jordan charged that his plane had been attacked by Syrian jets while flying over Syrian territory en route to Beirut.

It was reported in Washington that the US was negotiating defense agreements with Iran, Turkey and Pakistan as a means of bolstering the Baghdad Pact.

The UAR, in an official statement, denied that Syrian jets had attacked King Hussein's plane.

Former Iraqi Premier Fadel al-Jamali, former Chief of Staff General Muhammad Aref, and former Deputy Chief of Staff General Ghazi Daghistani were sentenced to death for treason.

The US told the UN that it did not favor continuance of relief to the Arab refugees after 1960. It suggested that the UN help them to become self-sufficient in the areas where they were then located.

Bouabid, Moroccan Deputy Premier and Minister of National Economy and Agriculture, submitted his resignation.

It was reported in Cairo that two groups of Sudanese, representing a government party and the chief opposition party, had been meeting in Cairo for several days with UAR officials.

November 11

Ferhat Abbas, Premier of the Algerian Provisional Government, stated that he was ready to accept a temporary ceasefire in Algeria, provided that the UN supervised negotiations between France and the free Algerian government.

The Israel Foreign Ministry announced that it favored the suggestion of the US on the Arab refugee problem.

Saudi Arabia expressed opposition before the UN to the US suggestion that the UNRWA relief program be discontinued after 1960.

After Jordanian King Hussein announced that his plane had been attacked in flight over Syria, Jordan asked the UN Security Council to consider the unfriendly act.

November 12

The Lebanese Parliament voted emergency powers to Premier Rashid Karami to rule by decree for six months in all matters relating to finance, economy, public security, civil service and judiciary. The vote was 39-1-1.

The US State Department announced that Tunisia had been assured that its arms agreement with the US was not subject to any kind of veto by France.

Sudanese Premier Abdallah Khalil decided to accept a US aid grant for development of Sudan's textile industry. The program had been rejected earlier by Ali Abd-al-Rahman, Minister of Commerce, who was in Cairo conferring with UAR officials.

November 13

Tunisian President Bourguiba said that Tunisia was trying to buy arms from two Communist states, Czechoslovakia and Yugoslavia. He also asserted that his traditional Western friends had offered to supply arms only under unacceptable circumstances.

November 13

The British Foreign Office issued a statement that it still considered it possible to sell arms to Tunisia.

The US State Department denied that it was seeking French approval before selling arms to Tunisia.

It was announced in Cairo that Premier Khalil of the Sudan would confer with President Nasser in Cairo on outstanding problems between the two countries.

It was reported that the Arab League members at the UN had agreed to raise the question of British aggression against the Imam of Oman at the UN General Assembly in 1959.

Former Foreign Minister Burhan-ad-Din Bashayan of Iraq was sentenced by the Supreme Military Court to be hanged for treason.

The Jordanian Government announced that on account of an administrative error, King Hussein had not received proper clearance to cross Syrian territory.

Anti-Nasser demonstrations continued in Amman, Jordan.

November 14

President Nasser pledged continued support of the UAR for the Algerian nationalist cause. He also declared that the UAR would support Aden.

A group of Soviet experts arrived in Cairo to work out details of Russian aid in the building of the Aswan High Dam.

It was reported in Damascus that Crown Prince Saif-al-Islam Muhammad al-Badr of Yemen had announced the establishment of a military air college which could accommodate about 100 students. The Crown Prince said that the UAR and other friendly powers would provide instructors and planes.

November 14

The UN General Assembly adopted a resolution by a vote of 51-9-17, including the Soviet bloc, to continue the UNEF in the Gaza Strip.

Archbishop Theodoseos Abu Rjaileh of Lebanon was elected Patriarch of Antioch and the Entire East by the Sacred College of Orthodox Archbishops. The oldest throne in Christianity commanded fealty from Orthodox groups in Syria, Lebanon, Iraq, part of Turkey, the US and Latin America.

November 15

Trade, economic and technical assistance agreements between Iraq and the UAR were signed in Baghdad.

Secretary General Hassouna of the Arab League conferred in New York with UN Secretary General Dag Hammarskjold.

Official sources in London reported that senior British officers had resumed the training of Jordanian army personnel for the first time since March, 1956, when King Hussein dismissed General Glubb.

November 16

The Sudanese Commerce Minister, Ali Abd-al-Rahman, said in Cairo that a basis had been laid in cordial discussions with President Nasser for UAR-Sudan discussions of outstanding problems. He also announced that a new trade payments agreement between the two states had been drawn up.

The Lebanese Government withdrew its complaint at the UN against interference in its internal affairs by the UAR.

It was reported that Jordan had protested to the US and the UN that the UAR was blocking US military assistance by refusing to grant permission for the flight of ten US jets over UAR territory.

An Israel government sponsored Afro-Asian seminar on cooperation opened in Tel Aviv. Delegations from twelve non-Moslem Far Eastern and African states attended.

November 17

The Iraqi Government was reported to have delivered notes to the British, American and Turkish Embassies requesting early closure of their consular offices in Kirkuk and Mosul.

The Sudanese Army, under the leadership of its Commander in Chief, General Abboud, seized control of the Sudanese Government. Abboud issued three decrees, proclaiming a state of emergency, suspending the constitution and dismissing Parliament, and suspending all newspapers. The Khalil Government resigned.

Premier Samir al-Rifai announced that Jordan would not press the issue of the incident involving a Syrian attack on King Hussein's plane before the UN.

Israel Ambassador Abba Eban told the UN General Assembly Political Committee that Israel was willing to give compensation to the Palestine Arab refugees without insisting, as it had in the past, that such payment await a general Arab-Israel peace settlement. Israel also asked that international financial help be made available to Israel to help settle the refugee claims.

November 18

General Ibrahim Abboud declared that the Sudan would remain a democratic republic, and he appointed a Supreme Council and a Cabinet to govern the country.

The UAR recognized the new Sudanese regime.

Ahmad Shukairi of Saudi Arabia rejected Israel's offer concerning refugees.

President Eisenhower extended his warmest wishes for success and prosperity to King Hussein through the new Jordanian Ambassador to the US, Midhat Juma.

Iraq's territorial waters were fixed at 12 nautical miles.

November, 1958

November 18

The Israel Government announced that protocols of trade agreements for an exchange of goods totaling $13 million had been signed with Bulgaria and Rumania.

President Nasser issued a decree delegating the power of Syrian Vice President Hourani to Nur-ad-Din Kuhala, President of the Executive Council of the Syrian Region. Hourani retained his post as UAR Vice President and Minister of Justice.

A new Sudanese Cabinet was formed. Ibrahim Abboud was Prime Minister and Minister of Defense, General Ahmad Abd-al-Wahhab was Minister of Interior and Local Self Government, and Ahmad Khair was Foreign Minister.

In his annual message to Parliament, King Muhammad V of Morocco announced that his country's determination to obtain total and unconditional evacuation of US bases as well as of French and Spanish troops. He asserted that their presence constituted a constant threat to Morocco.

November 19

General Abboud was sworn in as Premier, Defense Minister and President of the Armed Forces Supreme Council of the Sudan.

Sudanese Premier Abboud announced that the Sudan would honor its obligations to the UN and the Arab League, and would honor accords concluded since the nation became independent in 1956.

Britain and Ethiopia recognized the new regime of the Sudan.

The British Foreign Office confirmed that rebel leaders from Muscat and Oman had made unofficial contacts with an intermediary of the Sultan to negotiate terms of surrender.

UN Secretary General Hammarskjold announced that the UN Observation Group in Lebanon would be abolished now that the Lebanese Government had withdrawn its charges against the UAR.

November, 1958

November 19

The Lebanese Government announced that all work permits for foreigners would be suspended and that the number of new permits granted would be cut by 80 percent. The reason given for this action was to reduce unemployment among the Lebanese.

President Bourguiba of Tunisia said that he still intended to make limited purchases of arms from Czechoslovakia and Yugoslavia. He also expressed hope that arms shipments from the US would also begin soon.

November 20

The Saudi Arabian Government recognized the new Government of the Sudan.

Muhammad Zainal resigned as Minister of Commerce in Saudi Arabia.

Waldemar Gallman resigned as US Ambassador to Iraq.

November 21

It was announced that the new regime of the Sudan had been recognized by Great Britain, France, West Germany, the UAR, Jordan, Greece, Turkey, Italy, Iraq, Tunisia and Ethiopia.

The US Embassy announced that the US had ordered $484,000 worth of railway equipment from Japan to renovate Jordan's 200 mile railroad.

The rebel Provisional Government in Algeria asked UN Secretary General Hammarskjold to use his good offices in an attempt to effect negotiations with France.

The Iraqi Government annulled the concession agreement with the British Khanaqin Oil Company.

Sudanese Interior Minister Abd-al-Wahhab declared that the Sudan would reconsider all of its agreements with foreign states and reject those unfavorable to it. He added that the Sudanese Government would carefully consider any offer of help from the Soviet Union.

November, 1958

November 21

The Lebanese Government lifted the curfew in Beirut which had been in effect for six months.

November 22

King Muhammad V of Morocco accepted the resignation of Deputy Premier Bouabid who was also Minister of National Economy and Agriculture.

The Shah of Iran, at a monthly press conference, said he considered Bahrain an integral part of Iran and would gladly accept the allegiance of the present ruler in the capacity of governor of the island.

It was reported that the UAR had agreed to allow Britain to fly jets over Syrian territory into Jordan.

Sudanese General Ibrahim Abboud promised that as soon as the country's ills had been corrected, he would hand control back to civilian authorities.

The US extended recognition to the new Sudanese Government.

The UAR loaned 84 school principals, men and women, to Iraq, Gaza, Kuwait, Libya, Qatar, Morocco and Yemen.

November 23

India recognized the new regime of the Sudan.

Abd-al-Wahhab, Minister of the Interior of the Sudan, was quoted as saying that the Sudan's policy was now neutralist rather than pro-Western.

Major General Von Horn, Chairman of the UN Truce Supervision Organization for Palestine, met with UAR President Nasser to discuss the reactivation of the Israel-UAR Mixed Armistice Commission, boycotted by the Israelis since 1956.

November, 1958

November 23

Tunisian President Bourguiba said that several officers of the UAR and supporters of the exiled Salah Ben-Youssef had been arrested in Tunisia on charges of plotting to assassinate him and overthrow his regime.

November 24

The Soviet Union granted recognition to the Sudanese Government.

It was reported that Venezuela would send a delegation to the First Arab Petroleum Conference to be held in Cairo, April 16, 1959.

King Muhammad V of Morocco signed a decree establishing martial law in the Rif mountain area.

The UAR filed a complaint with the MAC (Mixed Armistice Commission) against alleged mine laying by Israelis in the northern demilitarized sone.

November 25

The US State Department said that the United States would soon sign an agreement with Tunisia to sell that country enough arms for one Tunisian battalion. This was to be done in conjunction with the British.

At Lebanese request, the UN Security Council took off its agenda the complaint lodged in May by the Chamoun Government against the UAR's hostile actions and decided to withdraw the UN Observer Group, sent to Lebanon during the Lebanese crisis.

It was reported that Moroccan King Muhammad V consulted Allal al-Fassi, leader of the Istiqlal Party, about a Cabinet reorganization. It was also reported that Premier Balafrej would resign soon.

Ten jet fighter planes, a gift from the US to Jordan, arrived in Amman.

November, 1958

November 26

Former Premier Khalil of the Sudan said that he knew in advance of the coup in his country and had approved of it. He also said that the coup had saved his country from a foreign sponsored move to end Sudanese independence.

Agreement was reached between the Iraq Petroleum Company and Syria on a pipeline revenue increase.

The Sudanese Government ordered the removal from Khartoum of the monuments to Lord Kitchener and General Gordon, the colonizers of Sudan.

The Soviet Union announced that it would commence an Arabic class by radio on December 1. It would consist of lectures on Soviet history, economy and politics.

November 27

It was reported in Baghdad that one of the largest British contractors in Iraq had withdrawn from its 5 million pounds sterling road building contract with the Development Board on account of extra difficulties encountered since the July 14 revolution.

Sudanese Premier Abboud said that he favored in general the $31 million US economic aid program for the Sudan.

The UAR Foreign Ministry announced that it had refused to grant permission to the US to land MAT (Military Air Transport) service planes at Cairo.

The Provisional Government of Algeria announced that it would send a three man delegation to Communist China on a visit in the near future. Arms and Supply Minister Mahmoud Sherif would be a member of the delegation.

November, 1958

November 28

Both Europeans and Moslems in Algeria went to the polls as a three day voting period opened for elections to the French National Assembly.

A joint statement by a delegation of Iraqi public leaders, the USSR Peace Committee and the USSR Society for Friendship and Cultural Relations with the Arab East was made public at a press conference held for Soviet and foreign journalists at the Peace Committee in Moscow.

Israel Premier Ben-Gurion said that he expected to confer with UN Secretary General Dag Hammarskjold on the implementation of Article Eight of the Jordanian-Israel Armistice Agreement, which would permit Israel to have access to the Jewish holy places within the Old City of Jerusalem, now Jordanian territory.

Saudi Arabia charged Britain with armed aggression before the UN. The Saudi delegate said that Britain occupied the area of Khor al-Udayd, south of the Persian Gulf, in violation of a bilateral agreement to maintain the status quo in disputed territory on the fringes of the Arabian Peninsula.

It was reported that Fassi, leader of the Istiqlal Party, had failed in his attempt to form a new Cabinet in Morocco.

A Japanese company announced plans to ship $18.5 million worth of diesel cars to the UAR National Railways.

November 29

The Sudan recognized Communist China.

It was reported that Tunisian President Bourguiba planned to buy all agricultural lands held by foreigners in his country.

A large delegation of educators and publicists represented the UAR at the All Africa Peoples' Conference at Accra, Ghana, it was announced.

November, 1958

November 29

Ferhat Abbas, the head of the rebel government in Algeria, declared that the government would hold invalid the results of the French legislative elections.

November 30

Libyan Premier Kobar opened Parliament. He told the body that his Government would review the four year old pact with the US providing for US Air Force bases in Libya.

Former Deputy Premier Bouabid, generally considered the leader of the left wing of the Istiqlal Party, said that Moroccan leftists were ready to form a cabinet if called upon by the King, Muhammad V.

Muhammad Yazid, Minister of Information in the Algerian Provisional Government, said that Algerian nationalists might eventually be supported with military supplies from Communist China. He also said that an Algerian delegation was traveling to Peiping for negotiations.

The three day voting period in Algeria ended. It was reported that about 70 percent of the registered voters had gone to the polls. Candidates of the Committee of Public Safety were leading.

December, 1958

December 1

Martial law ended in Jordan after 19 months.

The Sudanese Government decided that a $30 million US aid agreement should stand, since there was nothing in the offer which limited Sudanese sovereignty.

December 2

The US State Department announced in Washington that Assistant Secretary of State Rountree would tour the Middle East beginning December 6.

It was reported that Iraq had agreed to a UAR request to investigate accusations by Tunisian President Bourguiba that the UAR was involved in a plot to assassinate him.

Tunisian President Habib Bourguiba, in a speech the previous weekend, expressed the desire to buy up all foreign landholdings in his country. French farmers held seven to eight percent of Tunisia's arable land.

The Iraqi Ambassador in Cairo reportedly said that Iraq was deeply concerned about an alleged military pact between the US and Iran. He also said that if the agreement was implemented, it would threaten the peace of the Middle East and the world.

A British Foreign Office spokesman said that Britain had information to confirm a report that the Soviet Union was supplying Iraq with jet fighters, tanks and other arms.

A joint Iraqi-Indian statement announced that the two states had agreed to treat each other as most favored nations for purposes of increasing mutual trade.

It was reported in Khartoum that the Sudanese Defense Ministry had agreed to buy an ammunition factory from West Germany and would send specialists to that country for training in operating the plant.

December, 1958

December 3

Lebanese Premier Karami announced that his country had accepted a $10 million grant from the US in economic aid.

The US reported that the Soviet Union had delivered a cargo of light and heavy arms to Iraq.

It was announced that King Muhammad V of Morocco had accepted the resignation of Premier Ahmad Balafrej, but had requested all ministers to remain in office until a new Government could be formed.

Eight French soldiers were released by the Algerian National Liberation Army.

UAR President Nasser accused Tunisian President Bourguiba of manufacturing an assassination plot against himself to distract attention from his subservience to the French.

The UN Economic and Financial Committee approved a resolution that would invite member governments to extend to Libya financial aid for economic development through the UN.

December 4

The US Embassy in Amman announced that the US had ended emergency deliveries of gasoline to Jordan.

Israel requested an urgent meeting of the UN Security Council to discuss armed aggression on border villages in the Huleh sector.

It was reported in Khartoum that the Council of Ministers had suspended trade unions for the duration of the state of emergency.

December 5

UAR President Nasser met with President Tito of Yugoslavia on board Tito's yacht at Suez.

A Soviet TU-104 jet plane arrived in Cairo, inaugurating a twice weekly air service between Cairo and Moscow.

December, 1958

December 5

Premier De Gaulle visited the Hassi-Messaoud and Edjele oil fields in Algeria. He said that France may have found a "new destiny" in the Sahara.

December 6

Delegates from the Arab States began discussions in Cairo on the feasibility of establishing an Arab common market at a conference sponsored by the Federation of Egyptian Chambers of Commerce.

Assistant US Secretary of State William Rountree left for a fact finding tour of the Middle East.

The Lebanese Foreign Ministry announced that Lebanese and Syrian troops along Israel's frontier had been alerted following reports of unusually heavy Israel troop concentrations near the borders. Israel denied any such troop movement.

December 7

The Iraqi Development Board said that it had canceled projects with British, Italian and Lebanese concerns because they had failed to fulfill agreements signed under the monarchy. The Board also declared that it had canceled all special privileges granted to foreign companies by the former regime.

Ending his five day visit to Algeria and the Sahara, Premier De Gaulle stated that Algeria was not yet ready for a political solution in a rebuff to Algerian Europeans. De Gaulle's staff revealed that the Premier intended to emphasize economic reforms.

December 8

An Afro-Asian economic conference opened in Cairo where Muhammad Rushdi, President of the Federation of Egyptian Industries, was named chairman. A protest against the presence of the Soviet Union as a country which was neither Asian nor African was overruled.

December, 1958

December 8

Iraqi Premier Abd-al-Karim Kassem announced that a serious plot against the Government, the work of some corrupt elements with the help of foreigners outside Iraq, had been foiled, and that the plotters would be tried for treason by a people's court.

Tunisia proposed to the UN that negotiations be conducted between France and the Algerian Provisional Government to bring about a settlement in harmony with the natural rights of the peoples to freedom and independence.

France walked out of the UN General Assembly Political Committee in protest against its debate of the Algerian question.

A delegation from the Algerian National Liberation Front was seated at the All-African People's Conference which opened in Accra, Ghana.

The 60 newly elected Deputies to the French National Assembly formed a united bloc and adopted a program calling for integration of Algeria with France.

US Assistant Secretary of State William Rountree arrived in Beirut for talks with Lebanese officials.

It was announced that Amir Fadel Ibn-Ali, cousin of the exiled former Sultan, Ali Ibn-Abd-al-Karim Abdali, was elected new Sultan of Lahej in Aden.

At the meeting of the UN Security Council to discuss Syrian border aggression against Israel, the Council heard both parties and received the report prepared by UN Truce Chief Major General Carl C. Von Horn of Sweden.

The UAR charged that Israel had committed daily violations of the 1949 Palestine Armistice Agreement.

December 9

The UN Observation Group in Lebanon (UNOGIL) ceased operation.

December, 1958

December 10

Lebanese Premier Karami decalred that his Government was not bound to observe President Eisenhower's Middle East doctrine.

The Jordanian Government reported the discovery of a plot to smuggle UAR arms into Jordan.

The closing session of the Afro-Asian countries' Economic Conference took place.

The Tunisian Government informed the UAR through the Iraq Embassy that it banned Egyptian airline flights between Tunis and Cairo.

December 11

A $6 million trade and payments agreement was signed between Yugoslavia and Israel.

US Assistant Secretary of State Rountree conferred in Amman with Premier Samir al-Rifai and other Jordanian government officials.

The Afro-Asian People's Conference ended with a unanimous agreement in principle to set up a permanent organization for economic cooperation in the Middle East.

December 12

Replacing General Raoul Salan in Algeria, Paul Delouvrier was given the top civil administrative post of French Delegate General, answerable only to the Premier, and Air Force General Maurice Challe filled Salan's former position of Commander in Chief of the Armed Forces in Algeria. Salan himself was appointed to the newly created post of Inspector General of National Defense.

A resolution was passed by the UN General Assembly Political Committee which had been sponsored by 17 Afro-Asian states. The resolution recognized the right of the Algerian people to independence and urged negotiations between the Provisional Government of Algeria and the French Government with a view to reaching a solution in conformity with the Charter of the UN.

December, 1958

December 12

The UN General Assembly adopted a resolution asking for continued aid to Palestine Arab refugees.

December 13

The Afro-Asian resolution on Algeria failed to be adopted by the UN General Assembly by a vote of 35-18-28 with France absent from the debate.

December 14

A trade agreement between Iraq and Czechoslovakia, containing a protocol on scientific and technical exchanges, was signed in Baghdad.

UAR President Nasser met for three hours with US Assistant Secretary of State William M. Rountree, who was on a fact finding tour of the area.

The UN General Assembly failed to reach a decision on Algeria. A resolution calling for negotiations between France and Algeria failed to receive the necessary two-thirds majority vote.

December 15

UAR officials described US Assistant Secretary of State Rountree's two day talks with President Nasser as very useful and held in a friendly atmosphere.

UN Secretary General Hammarskjold announced that he would leave December 18 for the Middle East to try to settle the most recent border troubles between Israel and the UAR.

US Assistant Secretary of State William Rountree arrived in Baghdad on an official visit. He was greeted by an anti-US demonstration.

The US officially demanded that the Iraqi Government take measures to guarantee the protection of William Rountree, US Assistant Secretary of State.

December, 1958

December 16

A trade and payments agreement was signed between the UAR and Communist China. It increased the volume of trade to LE15 million for each country.

Moroccan King Muhammad V asked Abdallah Ibrahim, leader of the left wing of the Istiqlal Party, to form a new Government on a non-party basis which would include individuals who had no party affiliation. It was also reported that the left wing favored stronger ties with the UAR.

A UAR Army spokesman charged that Israel was massing troops on the Israel-Syrian border. He denied that Syria had committed aggressions against Israel the previous day.

US Assistant Secretary of State William Rountree met with Iraqi Premier Abd-al-Karim Kassem.

December 17

US Assistant Secretary of State Rountree arrived in Beirut on his fact finding tour.

It was announced that the UAR had protested to the UN Mixed Armistice Commission.

December 18

A UAR Ministry of Economy spokesman said that a new oil exploration concession had been granted to Anglo-Egyptian Oilfields Ltd., a Shell Oil Company subsidiary that had been sequestered in 1956. The agreement, effective until 1961, followed the initialing of an agreement settling all outstanding questions between the UAR and the Shell Anglo-Egyptian group.

The Soviet Union signed an agreement with the UAR for Soviet aid in the construction of five airports and a number of industrial installations in Egypt.

December, 1958

December 18

The Bonn Government reported that a West German industrial group and firms from other Western countries had offered to contribute 200 million West German marks to the UAR to build the Aswan High Dam.

Brigadier Muhammad Ahmad Irwa was appointed Minister of Commerce of the Sudan, succeeding Abd-al-Majid Ahmad, who was also Minister of Finance.

UN Secretary General Hammarskjold announced his intention to visit Saudi Arabia January 5.

Jordan and Nationalist China opened talks on the possibility of improving trade relations.

Trade talks opened between Iraq and Communist China in Baghdad. The Iraqi Minister of the Economy Ibrahim Kubbah told the visiting Chinese delegation that Iraq would accept unconditional economic and technical assistance from all quarters.

General Raoul Salan told the European colony in Algiers that he would continue to work for a French Algeria in his new post of Inspector General of the Armed Forces.

December 19

The French Cabinet in Paris announced that 100 billion francs a year would be set aside in the French budget for the next five years for Algerian development.

December 20

A treaty of amity, economic relations and consular rights was signed between the Sultan of Muscat and Oman and the US.

It was reported that 50,000 Iraqis attending a peace rally at Najaf approved of cables sent to the Embassies of Iran and Turkey condemning the establishment of US military bases in those countries.

December, 1958

December 20

A joint communique issued in Peking stated that Red China and the visiting Algerian Provisional Government delegation had reached a unanimity of views on a wide range of international problems, and planned to strengthen mutual cooperation.

King Saud of Saudi Arabia appointed Ahmad Jamjum a Minister of State and member of the Council of Ministers.

The UAR and Israel had an air battle over Negev.

December 21

Charles De Gaulle was elected President of the French Republic.

William M. Rountree, Assistant Secretary of State for Near Eastern and South Asian Affairs, returned to Washington after his trip to the Middle East. He noted that the Iraqi Government conducted "useful and friendly discussions" with him.

December 22

France signed a LE2,000,000 trade agreement with the UAR.

The Iraqi Ministry of Economy announced over Radio Baghdad that as a result of negotiations with oil concerns in Iraq, the Basra Oil Company had agreed to forego its concession rights in Iraq territorial waters.

It was reported that a West German industrial group had offered the UAR $48 million for the Aswan Dam project.

The UAR and the Soviet Union signed an agreement providing for Soviet cooperation in building five airfields, several factories in Egypt, a thermal power station at Suez, and the creation of industrial projects in accordance with the agreement of January 29.

December 23

It was announced in Rabat, Morocco, that a new Government had been formed.

The Sudanese Government announced in Khartoum that it had accepted a West German offer to build a $2 million sugar refinery in the Sudan.

Victory Day, commemorating the failure of the British, French and Israel aggression in 1956, was celebrated in the UAR.

President Nasser accused the Syrian Government of being enemies of Arab nationalism and of attempting to break up the Egyptian-Syrian union. He announced the appointment of a three man reform committee to cope with the Communist problem in Syria.

Lebanese Foreign Minister Uwaini left Beirut on a visit to Saudi Arabia.

December 24

The US signed an agreement to sell $24.9 million worth of surplus wheat and flour to the UAR. The shipments had been suspended during the Suez crisis.

Moulay Abdallah Ibrahim formed a new Moroccan Government, the fourth since the procalamation of the country's independence.

The World Federation of Trade Unions protested against the violation of union rights and democratic freedoms in the Sudan and demanded the restoration of union freedoms and release of union militants.

It was disclosed that the UAR State Department was supporting possible West German participation in the construction of the Aswan High Dam.

December 25

A trade agreement was signed between Iraq and Rumania. The Iraqi Minister of the Economy, Ibrahim Kubbah, said that Iraq would

December 25

cleanse its national economy of imperailist control, safeguard private enterprise and consolidate national capital.

Syrian Communist leader Khaled Bakhdash and many of his supporters were reportedly arrested.

The Sudanese Government decided to recognize and exchange ambassadors with the Peoples' Republic of China.

December 26

The Syrian Executive Council closed down the Communist daily, al-Nour.

The Sudan signed a $2.8 million barter agreement with Poland providing for the exchange of Sudanese cotton and Polish manufactured goods.

UN Secretary General Hammarskjold ended a three day visit to UNEF bases and UNRWA camps in the Gaza Strip.

An Afro-Asian Peoples' Solidarity Conference met in Cairo and decided to set up an Afro-Asian Permanent Solidarity Council.

December 27

The Soviet Union and the UAR signed an agreement in Cairo for $100 million worth of Soviet assistance for the construction of a high dam at Aswan, using only Soviet technicians and Soviet equipment.

December 28

Jordan and the US signed an agreement under which the US would grant $50,000 in technical aid to teachers' training centers in Jordan.

December 29

It was reported that tribal leaders in the Rif Mountains had demanded that Morocco bring about the immediate withdrawal of all French

December 29

forces from the country and threatened to attack French garrisons if the Government were unable or unwilling to achieve this.

A spokesman for the Algerian Provisional Government reported that some 354 French soldiers were killed the previous week.

The Moroccan Government announced that it would not evaluate its currency to conform to the devalued French franc.

It was reported that every Communist Party member in Syria was either under arrest or being sought. The report indicated that hundreds had been arrested.

The UAR granted an Italian-Egyptian oil company new concessions for oil prospecting during the next 13 years in the Sinai Desert.

It was reported from Bonn that West Germany was reconsidering possible participation in the Aswan Dam project.

The Israel-UAR Mixed Armistice Commission meeting with Israel absent condemned Israel for violating UAR air space December 20.

December 30

President Bourguiba of Tunisia reorganized his Cabinet.

Tunisia officially announced the unpegging of the Tunisian dinar to the French franc.

It was announced that Italian Premier Fanfani would go to Cairo in a few days for talks with President Nasser.

Eugene Black, President of the World Bank, conferred with British officials in London in preparation for a mediation mission to Cairo on the UAR-British financial disputes that resulted from the Suez crisis in 1956.

December 30

Iraq and India signed a trade agreement providing for an expansion of trade between the two states. Indian tea was to be exchanged for Iraqi dates.

It was reported that Israel Premier David Ben-Gurion promised to recommend the easing of restrictions on Arab citizens in Israel. The promise was made to five Arab members of the Knesset who had been pressing for the abolition of a military Government in the Arab areas.

December 31

New taxes on gasoline, alcohol, wine and tobacco were announced by the French in the Algerian budget. It was reported that the new taxes would net about $41 million.

The UAR Government ordered the arrest of some 100 Communists in widespread action against persons suspected of anti-government activities in the Egyptian and Syrian regions of the UAR.

The Iraqi National Front accused Western imperialists of conspiring against Iraq, the UAR and the free Arab movement, and described the recent visit by US Assistant Secretary of State William Rountree to the Middle East as an attempt to create a schism between Iraq and the UAR.

UN Secretary General Dag Hammarskjold arrived in Jerusalem under instructions from the Security Council to try to stop the intermittent clashes along the Israel-Syrian border.

Amnesty was proclaimed in Lebanon.

January, 1959

January 1

A trade and payments agreement and a technical and scientific exchange agreement were signed between Iraq and Poland.

The third anniversary of the Sudan's independence was celebrated.

Evidence of great unrest and disorder in Iraq was reported. Communists and pro-Egyptian nationalists were believed to be battling.

UN Secretary General Dag Hammarskjold and Israel Prime Minister David Ben-Gurion exchanged views at Sde Boker, Israel.

Eugene R. Black, President of the International Bank for Reconstruction and Development, opened negotiations in Cairo with UAR officials to discuss the question of a possible financial settlement with the UK over the Suez Canal.

An explosion rocked central Beirut, Lebanon. No casualties were reported.

Reliable sources in Cairo reported that over 200 suspected Communists had been arrested in a large scale drive against "separatist" elements in Egypt and Syria, and that three Communist oriented publishing houses were shut down.

January 2

A French Army spokesman reported that French forces in Algeria had killed 136 rebels and captured stores of explosives and supplies in a two day battle that ended January 1.

The Lebanese Council of Ministers decided to refer the question of granting recognition to the Algerian Provisional Government to the Foreign Affairs Committee of Parliament.

UN Secretary General Dag Hammarskjold ended his talks with Israel Premier David Ben-Gurion on ways to prevent further incidents along the Israel-Syrian border.

January 3

Morocco rushed troops into the Fez region for a showdown with supporters of rebel Chief Lyoussi.

Lebanese Premier Rashid Karami left Beirut for Cairo to visit the UAR after a long period of strained Lebanese-UAR relations.

A three man mission, composed of UAR Vice Presidents Abd-al-Latif al-Baghdadi and Akram Hourani and Minister of the Interior Zakariya Mohi-ad-Din, arrived in Damascus from Cairo for an indefinite stay on orders from President Nasser to speed development projects in the Syrian Region.

UN Secretary General Dag Hammarskjold conferred in Amman with King Hussein and Premier Samir al-Rifai of Jordan on a wide range of Arab-Israel problems, including the Palestine refugees and free access for Israelis to Mount Scopus.

January 4

East German Premier Otto Grotewohl arrived in Cairo on an unofficial visit and conferred with UAR President Nasser.

Twelve political moderates were elected to the Legislative Council in Aden by 30 percent of the electorate. A boycott of the elections had been urged by the Aden Trades Union Congress.

It was announced in Djakarta, Indonesia, that President Nasser of the UAR would visit Indonesia in 1959.

UN Secretary General Dag Hammarskjold arrived in Riyadh, Saudi Arabia.

The Algerian Provisional Government announced that 433 French soldiers had been killed and 189 wounded in rebel operations between December 28, 1958 and January 1, 1959.

A trade and payments agreement was signed in Baghdad between Iraq and China.

January 4

The Israel Oil Company, Pazit, announced its purchase from the UK owned Iraq Petroleum Company of the part of the Iraq-Haifa pipeline that lay in Israel territory.

January 5

The fifth session of the Arab League Economic Council opened in Cairo. Premier Rashid Karami of Lebanon presided.

UN Secretary General Dag Hammarskjold met in Riyadh, Saudi Arabia, with King Saud.

The USSR news agency Tass said that a five member delegation of Russian education officials arrived in Baghdad for a visit, at the invitation of the Ministry of Education of Iraq.

The UK agreed to grant Sudan up to five million pounds ($14 million) in export credits.

King Muhammad V of Morocco issued a 48 hour ultimatum to rebellious tribesmen in the Rif mountain area to lay down their arms or face cruel punishment.

Two Arabs were sentenced to life imprisonment by the Israel Government for slaying an Israel border patrolman in 1956.

Libya announced that it was prepared to join the UAR, Jordan and Saudi Arabia in the formation of an Arab Development Bank.

Saudi Arabian King Saud, in discussions with UN Secretary General Hammarskjold, outlined Saudi Arabia's foreign policy with respect to Algeria, Palestine, Oman and the Buraimi dispute. The King reportedly said the latter dispute would be reported to the UN.

It was reported from Algiers that the administration of French Delegate General Paul Delouvrier was settling down to civilian rule in Algeria after nearly eight months of military control.

January 5

Equipment for a machine and tractor station, the USSR Government's gift to the UAR, was presented at a ceremony at the Saha State Farm near Kafr ab-Sheyh, UAR.

January 6

It was reported from Baghdad, Iraq, that Communists were in control of the People's Militia, and also held key positions in the police force and army.

Iraq and Hungary signed a trade agreement in Baghdad.

Colonel Ismail al-Aref, Iraqi military attache in Washington D.C., told the press that reports of Communist strength in his country were absolutely false. He added that there were no Communists in the Cabinet or top levels of the Government of Premier Abd-al-Karim Kassem.

Iraqi Premier al-Kassem was promoted to the rank of Major General in the Iraqi Army.

The US State Department announced that Sheldon T. Mills would be designated as US Ambassador to Jordan.

Jordan refused permission for 35 nuns and monks holding USSR passports to cross from Israel into Jordan to celebrate Orthodox holy days in Bethlehem.

Italian Premier Amintore Fanfani arrived in Cairo on a four day official visit. He planned to attempt to explain Western attitudes and aspirations to UAR President Nasser.

UN Secretary General Dag Hammarskjold consulted in Cairo with UAR officials on the problem of Israel and the Arab refugees.

It was reported in Beirut that the Syrian Minister of Agrarian Reform, Mustafa Hamdoun, issued a decree confiscating about 35,000 acres of land from 39 Syrian landowners.

January, 1959

January 6

A subcommittee of the Arab League's Economic Council recommended that oil pipelines should be owned by an Arab company, and that Trans-Arabian Pipeline should not receive a renewal of its concession.

It was reported from Amman that King Saud of Saudi Arabia had told UN Secretary General Hammarskjold that either Palestine refugees could be returned home or the Arab states could declare a holy war to regain their usurped land.

An East German delegation, headed by Premier Otto Grotewohl and including Deputy Premier and Foreign Minister Lothar Bolz and other government leaders, arrived in Baghdad at the invitation of the Iraqi Government.

January 7

The French Army announced that at least 220 Algerian rebels had been killed in one of the biggest battles in Algeria since last spring, in the region of Kabylia, and that French planes and artillery had pounded rebel strongholds in the region.

French military authorities announced the slaying of 21 Algerian insurgents in a battle south of Oran.

French Army headquarters in Algiers reported the capture, near Colomb Bechar, of a rebel camel caravan heading toward the Sahara missile testing grounds with a load of mines and ammunition.

East German Premier Grotewohl announced in Cairo that his Government and the UAR would establish consular relations. He conferred with UAR President Nasser.

A communique issued in Cairo at the conclusion of UN Secretary General Dag Hammarskjold's visit said that Mr. Hammarskjold had met with authorities of the UAR and they had consulted on the latest aspects of matters of common interest.

January, 1959

January 7

It was reported in Rabat that 5,000 Moroccan tribesmen in the Rif and in the northern provinces surrendered their arms in response to King Muhammad V's ultimatum.

The Japanese Government announced plans to establish a diplomatic office in Riyadh, Saudi Arabia.

January 8

General Charles De Gaulle, in his inaugural address on becoming President of France, declared that in the French Community, place was reserved for the Algeria of tomorrow, pacified and transformed, developing itself, its personality, and closely associated with France.

A French Army communique said that 265 Algerian rebels were killed and 24 captured in a three day battle in the Kabylia mountain region about 60 miles east of Algiers.

Israel and UAR jet fighters clashed over the desert along the Egyptian-Israel border. Each side contended that the other violated its airspace.

The West German Government asked UAR President Nasser for clarification of East German Premier Grotewohl's announcement that East Germany and the UAR would establish consular relations.

The UAR and Italy signed agreements designed to increase economic and cultural cooperation between them. The joint statement settled outstanding problems from the Second World War, the Suez crisis and trade.

A UAR Government statement said that President Nasser and East German Premier Grotewohl discussed economic and trade relations and ways and means of strengthening them.

East German Premier Otto Grotewohl arrived in Baghdad for a three day visit and conferred with Iraqi Premier Kassem.

January, 1959

January 8

Moscow Radio reported that a Soviet trade delegation in Baghdad had discussed the possibility of Russian economic and technical aid with Iraqi officials.

January 9

As a result of the UAR's reception of East German Premier Grotewohl, West Germany recalled its ambassador from Cairo for consultations.

Premier Kwame Nkrumah of Ghana arrived in Cairo for a two day official visit to the UAR.

It was announced in Cairo that Britain and the UAR would resume talks on financial problems that had arisen from the Suez crisis.

Eugene Black, President of the World Bank, announced after consultations with Abd-al-Moneim Kaissouni, that they had worked out a basic understanding, acceptable to both sides, to resume negotiations between Great Britain and the UAR.

According to military sources, some 20,000 men, or four-fifths of the Royal Moroccan Army, were operating in the Rif Mountains against tribal insurgents, under the command of Moroccan Crown Prince Moulay Hassan.

January 10

West German Ambassador to the UAR, Walther Backer conferred for three hours with UAR President Nasser.

Iraqi Communists reportedly attempted to disrupt prayer services in the mosques in Baghdad on January 9. Pamphlets advocating atheism were circulated.

French President De Gaulle was reportedly considering amnesty for four members of the Algerian Provisional Government imprisoned in France. The prisoners were Ahmad Ben-Bella, Muhammad Khider, Hocine Ait-Ahmad and Muhammad Boudiaf.

January, 1959

January 10

The President of the Iraqi People's Court announced that former Premier Fadel al-Jamali and four other leaders of the former regime would be hanged soon.

The Saudi Arabian Ministry of Finance ordered all commerical banks to deposit at least 15 percent of their capital with the Monetary Agency.

Israel Army headquarters reported that an Egyptian infiltrator was killed the previous day near the Sinai border by an Israel patrol.

January 11

The Council of the Arab League decided to set up a financial organization for Arab development.

Concluding a three day meeting with East German Premier Otto Grotewohl, Premier Abd-al-Karim Kassem refused to grant diplomatic recognition by Iraq to East Germany.

A joint announcement at the conclusion of the talks stressed complete agreement on increasing economic and cultural relations between East Germany and Iraq.

Israel naval authorities captured off Israel territorial waters a Lebanese fishing boat and its five man crew which was illegally using dynamite to blast fish to the surface.

The Tunisian Government suspended all transfers of capital from Tunisia to France.

Tunisian President Bourguiba, in his weekly radio address to the nation, attacked France for having devaluated the franc. He said that the French-Tunisian customs union had practically ceased to exist.

The French Army announced that French Legionnaires wiped out a rebel command post near Sidi Bel Abbes in Algeria; four rebels were killed and five captured. Four insurgents were slain, five wounded, and one taken prisoner in a similar operation near Constantine.

January 12

The Lebanese Government and the USSR agreed to raise their annual trade from LL10 million to LL15 million.

British and Egyptian delegations formally began negotiations in Cairo on a settlement of Suez compensation claims.

A Syrian State Security Court in Aleppo sentenced 15 members of the outlawed Syrian Social Nationalist Party to prison terms.

The Arab Financial Institution for Economic Development came into being when Libya subscribed to its charter and raised the level of stock subscriptions to more than 75 percent of the projected total.

The Moroccan Government imposed a 10 percent tax on all monetary transfers from Morocco to other countries in the franc zone.

The Moroccan Army succeeded in clearing rebel roadblocks in the Rif mountains and relieving the port city of Alhucemas, which had been cut off from the interior by rebel tribes for five days.

US Ambassador John T. Jernegan presented his credentials to the Iraqi Sovereignty Council in Baghdad.

Christopher Soames, British Secretary for War, completed a four day inspection visit to British Army units stationed in Cyrenaica and Tripolitania in Libya.

The West German Foreign Ministry announced that West Germany was ready to negotiate a loan to Sudan for industrial development.

January 13

President De Gaulle of France decreed wide measures of clemency for Algerian rebels. The measures included transfer of Ahmad Ben-Bella and three other rebel leaders from Sante Prison in Paris to an undisclosed fortress; permission for Hajj Messali, leader of the Algerian National Movement to live anywhere in continental France; commutation of the death sentences of about 140 rebels to life imprisonment;

January 13

reduction of the prison sentences of all rebels by one-tenth or more, and release of nearly 7,000 persons interned in Algeria by administrative decision.

Ghana and the UAR signed a trade agreement.

The Algerian Army Command reported more than 900 nationalists killed, wounded or captured during the past week; it listed French casualties at 46.

The Egyptian-Israel Mixed Armistice Commission condemned Israel for a January 8 air clash over Egyptian territory. Israel was absent.

Saeb Salam, a leader of the revolt in Lebanon, returned to Beirut after a month's stay in the UAR.

A Jordanian Finance Ministry spokesman announced that Jordan had received a grant of $5 million from the US to support its budget.

It was announced in Damascus that a new harbor and oil pipeline terminal for Syrian oil would be built at Tartus.

The Tunisian Ministry of Information announced the arrival in Bizerta of a cargo of US arms.

A Syrian spokesman said two Israel infiltrators entered the demilitarized zone and were arrested when they tried to seize a herd of cattle.

The Israel Foreign Ministry announced that two Americans studying agriculture in Israel were seized by Syrians near the Syrian border. They were questioned and then turned over to the UN observers.

A Royal Decree approved a new law under which Jordanians could be deprived of Jordanian nationality if they were declared dangerous to public and state security or if they had committed crimes against state security.

January 14

Britain and the UAR came to an agreement on the financial problems arising from the Suez crisis.

The Algerian Provisional Government said in Cairo that France's decision to release thousands of Algerians could be positive only if backed by France's willingness to negotiate directly with the rebel Government.

The Saudi Arabian budget for 1959 was promulgated by Royal Decree. Revenue was estimated at 1,410 million riyals and expenditures at 1,250 million rials. The difference was to be devoted to debt retirement.

A spokesman for the West German Government said that UAR President Nasser had assured West Germany that the UAR's establishment of trade missions with East Germany did not imply recognition.

Fernando Castiella, Spanish Foreign Minister, left Madrid for Cairo on an eight day visit to the UAR.

Iraqi Premier Kassem ordered the People's Militia to refrain from any police activity except under direct orders from the Army or the military Governor General. The order also applied to the activities of the Iraqi Students Union.

The US Embassy in Beirut announced that the US would lend Lebanon a helicopter and crew to help fight an invasion of locusts.

The Israel Government instructed its Ambassador to the US, Abba Eban, to take up two violations of the Arab-Israel Armistice Agreement with UN Secretary General Dag Hammarskjold.

The US State Department said it was trying to secure the release of an American, Gary Schwartz, who was jailed in Jordan after having crossed the border from Israel nine days ago.

The Jordanian Council of Ministers approved a bill establishing a Central Bank for Jordan.

January 15

French Premier Michel Debre affirmed French sovereignty over Algeria before the French National Assembly and renewed France's offer to provide safe conduct for rebel leaders to come to France to discuss a ceasefire in Algeria. President De Gaulle sent a message to the French National Assembly in which he declared that a political solution for Algeria could arise only from universal suffrage, and added that France would make no political settlement with the Algerian Provisional Government.

An Israel Army spokesman said that Syrians had opened machine gun fire on an Israel fishing boat and that an Israel police boat replied with several bursts.

Amin Mahmoud, an Egyptian school headmaster, was hanged in Cairo for spying for Britain in 1957.

"Reliable sources" said at the UN that Israel and the UAR had agreed to allow stone and concrete markers to be set up along the Israel-Syria frontier.

A UAR Army spokesman charged that an Israel armored boat on the Sea of Galilee had opened fire on Arab villages.

Iraqi Premier Kassem reportedly put restraints on two Communist infiltrated groups: The People's Militia and the Iraqi Students Union.

January 16

UN Secretary General Dag Hammarskjold reported after a two week tour of the Middle East that in spite of certain signs to the contrary, relations among the Arab states were much more favorable than they were a few months before.

Disregarding the recommendation of its parliamentary Foreign Affairs Committee, the Lebanese Government decided to recognize the Algerian Provisional Government based in Cairo.

January, 1959

January 16

President Eugene R. Black of the International Bank for Reconstruction and Development pledged the full cooperation of the bank, in the form of technical advice and services, to the new Arab Financial Institution for Economic Development, set up by the Arab League's Economic Council.

The French National Assembly approved, 453-56, Premier Michel Debre's Algerian policy: Algeria to continue to be under French sovereignty; Algerian economic, social and human advancement to be the work of France; ceasefire offers but no political negotiations.

The first of the clemency measures for Algeria announced by President De Gaulle on January 13 went into effect; some 100 Moslems were released from internment camps in various parts of Algeria.

The Jordanian Government temporarily suspended an expulsion order against seven Armenian Orthodox churchmen, including three Americans, in the Jordanian sector of Jerusalem.

January 17

It was reported that Moslem religious leaders were exerting pressure on Premier Kassem of Iraq to curb the growing influence of the Communists in his country.

Representatives of the UAR and Great Britain initialed a financial agreement on the claims and counterclaims resulting from the 1956 Suez affair; the exact terms were to be made public when the agreement was formally signed.

A cultural agreement was signed in Cairo between the UAR and a Czechoslovak delegation headed by the Minister of Education and Culture.

The USSR Central Council of Trade Unions cabled to UN Secretary General Dag Hammarskjold, asking him to demand that the Sudanese Government release Shafle Ahmad al-Sheikh, the Secretary General of the Sudan Federation of Trade Unions, and 13 trade militants.

January, 1959

January 18

Abd-al-Ilah Ibn-Hassan al-Sheikh, Chief Qadi of the Hejaz, died in Mecca, Saudi Arabia.

The UAR and the Soviet Union signed an undertaking for building a shipyard in Alexandria. The agreement was an annex to the overall economic pact of January 29, 1958.

Several Arab states reportedly were planning to form a united front to demand an increased share of the proceeds from Middle East oil.

US Ambassador to Iraq John T. Jernegan conferred with Premier Kassem of Iraq.

January 19

The Ministry of Education of Iraq announced that an agreement was signed in Baghdad on January 5 between Iraq and West Germany, under which the latter would participate in the establishment of an industrial college in Baghdad.

President Fuad Chehab of Lebanon ended a strike of law students at St. Joseph University in Beirut by naming a parliamentary Education Committee to decide whether classes should be conducted in Arabic, as demanded by students backed by Premier Rashid Karami, or in French, as advocated by Pierre Jumayil, Minister of Education.

The Yemeni State Department announced that the US would send Yemen 15,000 tons of wheat, flour, and animal foodstuffs to relieve a severe drought in Yemen.

The Jordanian Government announced that an informal agreement had been reached with the UAR on shipments to and from Mediterranean ports across Syrian territory.

January 20

It was reported from Cairo that three Canadian soldiers belonging to the UN Emergency Force had been arrested by the UAR in Gaza. Three Israel girls accompanying them were also arrested.

January, 1959

January 20

The World Jewish Congress reported that the Provincial Government of Tripolitania, Libya, had by decree taken over all operations of the Jewish community. It also reported that there were about 3,000 Jews in Libya.

January 21

Informal trade talks were held between Libyan officials and a West German parliamentary delegation visiting Libya as guests of the Government.

A World Bank mission arrived in Libya to survey the Libyan economy and to help draw up a development program.

A British Foreign Office spokesman disclosed that negotiations were under way with the UAR for the establishment in Cairo of a British mission with diplomatic immunity. The Cairo newspaper al-Ahram declared that Great Britain officially asked for renewal of full diplomatic relations.

President Nasser of the UAR said in an interview that despite his crackdown on Communists in Egypt and Syria, the UAR would continue to seek trade with the Soviet Bloc.

The Israel Government demanded the return of three Israel girls who crossed the border into Gaza with three UN Emergency Force Canadian soldiers. The report said that the three girls had records as prostitutes.

The Egyptian police turned over to the UN Emergency Force a Canadian sergeant arrested for illegally crossing the border from Israel.

French authorities in Algeria reportedly were releasing Algerian prisoners in accordance with President De Gaulle's order. Between 18,000 and 19,000 rebels would reportedly be kept in custody after release of the 7,000 ordered by the French President.

A group of eight African UN delegations said that the new French proposal for ending the Algerian war was not acceptable to the African governments.

January, 1959

January 21

The US gave Jordan 10,000 tons of wheat and 20,000 tons of livestock feed to help meet shortages resulting from a severe drought.

The Lebanese Government decided to establish a college of law consisting of two sections, one with classes conducted in Arabic, the other in French.

January 22

As the sixth session of the Economic Committee of the Baghdad Pact opened in Karachi, Pakistan, US delegate Donald D. Kennedy asked Pact nations to share more fully in meeting the costs of economic development projects.

An American student, Gary Schwartz, from the Hebrew University, who crossed into the Jordanian section of Jerusalem, was returned to Israel after being held since January 5 by Jordanian authorities.

The formal signing of the UAR-British agreement was reported to have been held up by UAR objections to the diplomatic rights demanded by Britain for personnel who were to supervise implementation of the agreement.

France signed a 50-50 profit sharing agreement for Saharan oil prospecting with the Standard Oil Company of New Jersey.

January 23

The French Army announced that Algerian rebels had destroyed a train carrying oil from Touggourt in the Sahara to the Mediterranean coast. No victims were reported.

The Economic Committee of the Baghdad Pact decided to create a Multilateral Technical cooperation Fund with a capital of $150,000.

The Military Committee of the Baghdad Pact met in closed session to discuss mutual defense along the Soviet frontier from Pakistan to Turkey.

January 23

Nine persons, including two Americans, were killed when a passenger plane crashed near Amman, Jordan. King Hussein, who was flying in a helicopter at the time of the crash, was the first person to arrive on the scene. He directed rescue operations.

The Moroccan Army, successful in its efforts to put down tribal insurgents in the Rif Mountains, had reportedly shifted its operations to the Atlas Mountains.

January 24

An Iraqi Government prosecutor announced that Colonel Abd-al-Salam Muhammad Aref, former Army Commander in Chief, Deputy Premier and Interior Minister in the government under al-Kassem, and former Premier Rashid Ali al-Gailani, who led a pro-Axis revolt in 1941, were tried in secret by a people's court and convicted of treason.

Hajj Messali, leader of the Algerian National Movement, who was released from forced residence in a general amnesty, declared that France should organize a round table conference with Algerian representatives. He also declared that independence was still the goal of the movement he leads.

January 25

King Hussein of Jordan said in an interview that the next move in an improvement of Arab relations with Jordan was up to those Arab states that he felt had inflicted a lot of injustice and bad treatment upon Jordan. He hinted that he would be willing to end his feud with the UAR.

A new law was promulgated imposing the death penalty on any Iraqi citizen who takes up arms against Iraq or any other Arab country.

It was announced in Baghdad that three top Iraqi Communists hanged in 1949 had been granted a posthumous amnesty to mark the country's appreciation of their services.

January 25

Colonel Richard Rickert, acting UN Truce Chief, was summoned to the Israel Foreign Ministry and told of the grave view taken by the Israel Government of the continuing incidents in which Syrians were involved.

It was reported from Tunis that the Algerian Provisional Government would directly appeal to US and European business concerns to keep their companies and investments out of Algeria.

The sixth session of the Ministerial Council of the Baghdad Pact opened in Karachi, Pakistan.

Three new Soviet submarines reportedly arrived in Alexandria, Egypt.

The UAR reportedly had conceded in part to the British request that diplomatic status be given its mission to Cairo to sign the Suez financial accord.

An Israel Foreign Ministry official was reported to have said that the US and Britain had assured Israel that their recent moves toward a rapprochment with the UAR would not be at Israel's expense.

In mass meetings throughout Morocco, left wing political leaders of the Istiqlal [Independence] Party accused the Party leadership of three years of weakness, negligence, and grave errors, and set up autonomous organizations with regional administrative committees. The leftist leaders declared their support of Premier Abdallah Ibrahim. The expulsion of Mahdi Ben-Barka, President of the National Consultative Assembly, from the Istiqlal Executive Committee January 24 was reported as the immediate cause of the mass mutiny.

January 26

Israel requested a meeting of the UN Security Council to consider the renewal of aggression by the UAR armed forces on the Israel-Syrian border.

The UAR Ministry of Education closed three Jesuit primary and secondary schools, known jointly as the College de la Sainte Famille, because their curriculum allegedly encouraged religious differences and did not truly reflect Arab history.

January 26

The French Government denied that it was turning control of Sahara oil over to foreign concerns. The denial followed criticism in the French press of an agreement between the Standard Oil Company (New Jersey) with two French concerns to exploit a new oil area in Algeria.

Allal al-Fassi, leader of the Istiqlal (Independence) Party of Morocco, announced the expulsion of several of the Party's members including Tihami Amar, Minister of Agriculture, and Ben-Barka, President of the Consultative Assembly.

The Jordanian citizenship of General Ali Abu-Nuwar, former Army Chief of Staff, his successor, Major General Ali Hayari, and 46 others accused of plotting against King Hussein was revoked. All 48 fled to Syria after an abortive revolt.

January 27

Mahdi Ben-Barka, President of the Consultative Assembly expelled from the Istiqlal (Independence) Party, announced the formation of a new party of the masses called the Democratic Istiqlal Party.

Baghdad Pact's Ministerial Council ended a meeting in Karachi, Pakistan, with a warning that threat of aggression against the Middle East was not diminishing.

Allal al-Fassi, leader of the Istiqlal Party of Morocco, appealed to the people to defend the principles of fidelity to God, country and King.

The Algerian Provisional Government Information Minister, Muhammad Yazid, declared that his Government saw no prospect for peace in Algeria at the present time. He also warned that contracts such as the one signed by the Standard Oil Company, New Jersey, for the exploitation of Saharan oil, would not be binding on the nationalist regime once independence was achieved.

Soviet Premier Nikita S. Khrushchev, at the Soviet Communist Party Congress, warned unidentified officials of the UAR not to persecute Communists. He was reported to have said that Communists were the most steadfast supporters of the Arabs against imperialism.

January 27

The Jordanian Government announced the following Cabinet shifts: Ahmad Tarawnah—Minister of Defense, Samaan Daoud—Minister of Finance and Economy, Muhammad Jabari—Minister of Justice.

A Syrian official announced that a Bulgarian concern, Tecno Impex, would build the 2,154 million cubic foot Mharda Dam.

Dr. John H. Davis was appointed Director of the UN Relief and Works Agency for Palestine Refugees in the Near East.

An Arab League Official, Abu-Bakr Bayar, was arrested in Cairo and charged with communicating reports and information to a foreign country in time of war.

The UAR Ministry of Education said that the three Jesuit schools closed by the Ministry on January 26 would be reopened as soon as offending textbooks could be replaced and faculties questioned.

January 28

A communique issued at the close of the session of the Baghdad Pact's Ministerial Council said that the Council decided to strengthen the Pact's central military organization and to set up a nuclear center in Teheran, Iran.

It was revealed in London that the British Government was pressing Jordan to account for British subsidies from 1955 through 1957.

The US concluded an agreement in Washington D.C. with Yemen to ship immediately on a grant basis, 15,000 tons of food grains to aid famine victims.

Minister of State for UN affairs of Saudi Arabia, Ahmad al-Shukairy, said in Cairo that Saudi Arabia was grateful for the UAR's stand during the Anglo-Egyptian financial negotiations. He also reportedly said that Saudi Arabia would refuse to establish diplomatic relations with the British until the Buraimi dispute was settled.

January, 1959

January 28

It was announced in Paris that President De Gaulle had appointed General Jacques Massu interim Commander of the French Army in Algeria.

A spokesman for the Istiqlal (Independence) Party of Morocco charged that the Government had violated its nonpartisan role by supporting the leftists in their battle with Party leadership, and alleged that the Government had begun to close Party offices and to arrest right wing sympathizers.

Two Turkish jet planes reportedly violated the air space of the Syrian Sector of the UAR near the town of Qamishliye.

January 29

President Habib Bourguiba of Tunisia endorsed the January 27 statement of the Algerian Provisional Government. He asserted that French policies alone were to blame for the war in Algeria. He appealed to the Western powers to show at least a modicum of understanding for the Algerian cause and to realize that the West, in blind solidarity with France, was driving the Algerians into the arms of anti-Western powers.

The three Roman Catholic Jesuit schools closed January 26 by UAR officials were reopened under Egyptian supervision.

Muhammad Hassanein Haikal, editor of the Cairo newspaper, al-Ahram, said in an article that Soviet Premier Nikita S. Khrushchev's criticism on January 27 did not meet the criteria of the peaceful coexistence that he preached, nor was it in line with his previous statements on meddling with the affairs of other countries.

Abd-al-Rahim, Deputy Premier of Morocco, said that he sympathized with the left wing movement to take over the leadership of the Istiqlal (Independence) Party of Morocco. He announced that he would resign from the Executive Committee of the Party.

Thirteen Iraqi industrial graduates and skilled workers left for East Germany for industrial and technical training, under a technical assistance program.

January, 1959

January 31

The Moroccan High Court sentenced to death former Governor Add-Bihi and three other leaders of a 1957 revolt plot.

Authoritative Moroccan sources disclosed that the US had offered Morocco $40 million in economic aid for the 1959-60 fiscal year.

Thirty-two persons arrested after an attempt to overthrow the Jordanian Government in 1957 were released.

It was reported from Tunis that high Tunisian officials feared that the Algerian revolt would spread into other countries if there was no political negotiation between France and the rebels. They also feared that Tunisia and Morocco might be drawn into conflict.

West Germany and Sudan announced arrangements for Federal Government guarantee of credits for Sudanese economic development and purchase of capital goods from West Germany.

The Cairo newspaper, al-Ahram, charged that Premier al-Kassem of Iraq first accepted and then rejected an invitation from President Nasser of the UAR for a meeting.

The UAR Government ratified the agreement on USSR participation in the construction of the Aswan Dam.

January, 1959

January 30

The UN Security Council met to consider Israel's complaint against Syria. It urged full use of the UN pacification machinery. No formal action was taken and no date was set for another meeting.

President De Gaulle renewed his October 23, 1958, offer of "honorable conditions" to the Algerian rebel leaders to come to Paris under safe conduct to discuss a ceasefire.

It was announced that the US had given $100, 000 to the UN to assist Algerian refugees in Tunisia.

Israel complained to the UN Security Council that constant attacks were being made on its territory from Syria. Israel's Ambassador to the UN Abba Eban urged that an injunction rigorously binding on Syrian forces be issued by the UN.

Five Soviet specialists in the field of rocket and space research arrived in Cairo for a months visit. They were to take part in lectures on UAR scientific planning and problems.

British-UAR negotiations on financial problems had reportedly developed a new dispute over which British assets were seized permanently and which were seized temporarily by Egypt in the Suez crisis.

The UAR Minister of Economy arrived in Beirut for talks with Lebanese officials on relations between the two countries.

Egyptian pilots training Iraqis to fly Soviet jets had reportedly returned to Cairo.

Premier Abd-al-Majid Kobar of Libya told the press that the US was willing to negotiate for a revision of the Libyan-US base agreement.

L'Humanite reported about 300 French soldiers and Algerian insurgents were killed in two days. The French command admitted heavier fighting.

February, 1959

February 1

An agreement which the UK announced on January 5, 1959, to make available to Sudan export credits up to 5 million pounds sterling was signed.

The British announced that the forces of the Sultan of Muscat and Oman had attacked the Jabal Akhdar stronghold of rebel tribesmen and captured three villages.

The first anniversary of the Syrian-Egyptian union was celebrated throughout Syria.

February 2

The first Afro-Asian Youth Solidarity Conference in Cairo opened with 500 delegates representing 34 countries.

Khaled Bakdash, leader of the Syrian Communist Party, declared at the Twenty-First Communist Party Congress in Moscow that Syrians had known Communists for more than 30 years and that it was difficult to convince them that Communists were enemies of national unity.

An Israel company took formal possession of the properties of the Iraq Petroleum Company, including a section of pipeline, storage tanks and loading facilities.

A shipment of arms from Yugoslavia arrived in Tunisia.

February 3

The Colonial Office in London announced that six Western Aden Protectorate states had agreed on a proposed federation and a constitution.

Lebanon and the UAR agreed to promote trade relations. A joint communique said that the UAR would import Lebanese apples and tobacco, and would export to Lebanon wheat and cigarettes.

February, 1959

February 3

The first meeting of the French Overseas Community Executive Council which included the premiers of the 12 African States, met in Paris.

February 4

Iraq's Military Supreme Court sentenced Said Qazzaz, a former Interior Minister, Abd-al-Jabbar Fahmi, former Governor of Baghdad, and Bahjat Attiyah, former Chief of Security, to be hanged.

The UN Emergency Force headquarters stationed along the Gaza Strip and the Sinai Desert stated in a communique that one of its patrols found four armed Israelis on Egyptian territory south of Rafah and that it subsequently learned that the Israelis had attacked a Bedouin camp in Egypt with the result that one woman and one child were killed by small arms fire and one woman wounded.

Israel Army Headquarters acknowledged that an Israel patrol had entered UAR territory, but explained that the entrance was inadvertant. The report stated that the Israel patrol was engaged in a running fight with Arab infiltrators.

Cardinal Spellman, Roman Catholic Archbishop of New York, received the highest decoration of the Jordan Government in recognition of his work for Palestine refugees in Jordan.

A Jordanian Royal Decree placed the responsibility for the control and administration of Jordan's armed forces on the Minister of Defense. The Commander of the Army had previously carried this responsibility.

Official Tunisian sources said that eight French civil servants were arrested on charges of espionage.

February 5

Finance Minister Muhammad Hadid of Iraq said that he favored government to government deals for capital to finance industry. He described Baghdad's economic policy as progressive toward a welfare state.

February, 1959

February 5

UN Secretary General Dag Hammarskjold said that a full report by UN truce officials confirmed earlier findings that no evidence was found of infiltration or hot pursuit to justify the actions of the Israel patrol in entering Egypt on February 3.

In a letter to the UN Security Council, the UAR complained of Israel aggression in the Syrian region. (Documentation: S/4151)

USSR-Iraqi economic talks ended in Baghdad.

February 6

A US Embassy official in Rabat, Morocco, announced that Morocco accepted $40 million in economic aid for the 1959-60 fiscal year from the US.

February 7

A 40 ton US shipment of small arms and ammunition for the Tunisian Army was unloaded near Tunis.

A trade, payments and navigation agreement between the UAR and Czechoslovakia was signed in Cairo. It provided for a LE30 million exchange between the two countries.

Colonel Abd-al-Salam Muhammad Aref of Iraq was sentenced to death by the highest military tribunal. He was former Army Commander in Chief, Deputy Premier and Interior Minister in the Government under Kassem.

Iraq Premier Abd-al-Karim al-Kassem accepted the resignations of six Cabinet ministers and appointed eight new ministers in the first major government reshuffle since the July revolution.

Two Algerian rebels were sentenced to death by a military court in Paris for attempting to assassinate Jacque Soustelle on September 15, 1958, the former Minister of Information in the De Gaulle Government.

February, 1959

February 7

The Egyptian-Israel Mixed Armistice Commission (Israel absent) found Israel guilty of an unprovoked attack on an unarmed Bedouin family in Egyptian territory. The attack occurred on February 3.

USSR participation on a vast scale in Iraq's economic development was pledged in a joint communique from Baghdad.

February 8

Sheikh Abdallah Salim Sabah, Ruler of Kuwait, issued a decree transferring a number of department heads and appointing new heads. A treasury chief was appointed for the first time.

A number of political detainees held since 1957 for attempting to overthrow the regime of King Hussein of Jordan were released.

The Jordanian Government announced that no person who had been a former member of a foreign political party would be allowed to enter Jordan.

Premier Michel Debre of France, in a speech on his arrival in Algiers, declared that the French Government would forthwith bring a new determination to bear on the French sovereignty which covered the Algerian side of the Mediterranean as it did the other.

Israel Army headquarters in Tel Aviv announced that an Israel officer would be court martialed on charges of having led a patrol into Egypt in pursuit of Arab attackers on February 3.

The Iraqi Government was reshuffled, with Hashem Jawad appointed Foreign Minister in place of Abd-al-Jabbar Jumard and Dr. Talaat al-Shaibani becoming Minister of Construction.

February 9

Thousands of French Algerians demonstrated against French Premier Debre of France and the De Gaulle regime's Algerian policy.

February, 1959

February 9

French Premier Debre said that the French Government would not negotiate abroad with leaders of the Algerian Provisional Government.

The UAR and Yugoslavia signed a protocol providing for extensive cultural exchanges.

US negotiations with Libya on the status of the base agreement were opened.

The Communist Iraq newspaper, Ittihad al-Shaab, was suspended for two weeks by the Iraq Government for having criticized recent cabinet shifts.

US Senator John Marshall Butler accused Iraq of having disclosed to the Soviet Union secret American bids on projects in Iraq. He added that the disclosure had enabled the Russians to win 20 choice contracts.

It was reported from Damascus that the Iraqi Government had arrested 200 Arab nationalists since the announcement of Cabinet changes.

Dr. Amin al-Sayyed, former Minister of Health and later Speaker of the Senate of Sudan, died.

The London Times published a letter from a group of Labour Members of Parliament concerning Prime Minister Macmillan's forthcoming visit to the USSR. The letter urged the UK Government to modify its rigid position on all the major questions at issue in Europe, the Middle East and the Far East, and on disarmament.

February 10

Sheikh Abdallah Mubarak, Deputy Ruler and head of the Army Security Department, banned pro-Nasser and pro-Kassem demonstrations in Kuwait.

Sheikh Abdallah Salim Sabah, Ruler of Kuwait, had reportedly restored order following pro-Nasser rioting.

February, 1959

February 10

French Foreign Minister Maurice Couve de Murville protested against the suicide of a French communications worker arrested in Tunisia for alleged espionage activities on behalf of France.

Minister of Information Muhammad Masmoudi of Tunisia charged that on February 9 a French Army post in Algeria shelled a Tunisian frontier village in the Kasserine Pass region, killing one person, wounding several others and causing considerable damage.

Iraq had reportedly received from 100 to 150 Soviet tanks since the revolution in July, 1958.

Several incidents of violence were reported to have marred French Premier Debre's visit to Algiers.

French Premier Debre presided over the first meeting of a 46 member commission established to work out the details of an economic development plan for Algeria announced in the fall of 1958 by French President De Gaulle. The commission appealed for French and foreign investments in Algeria.

French President De Gaulle signed a decree which abolished the Moslem custom for obtaining a divorce in Algeria.

February 11

The Tunisian Government dismissed all the French employees in its Postal Telephone Telegraph (PTT) Service and announced that the "Tunisification" of the PTT would be effective as of the morning of February 12.

Before leaving Algeria, French Premier Debre made a statement in which he declared that the future of the French position in Algeria was linked to the opportunities they would be able to give to young Moslems.

The French ordinance which changed Moslem marriage rules, decreed February 10 by French President De Gaulle, was published.

February, 1959

February 12

President Tito of Yugoslavia arrived in Khartoum, Sudan, for a seven day visit as the guest of the Sudanese Government.

The French Government said that Tunisian support of the Algerian rebels violated international law, and warned that Tunisia's actions might cause more and more painful incidents between Tunisia and France.

President Bourguiba of Tunisia charged that French consular officials had used their diplomatic immunity to shelter a spy ring in Tunisia.

Premier al-Kassem of Iraq stated that Iraq was out of all foreign alliances, and that the Baghdad Pact had been reduced to less than a shadow.

Husseim Jamil, new Minister of National Guidance of Iraq reportedly resigned after violent friction with Premier al-Kassem.

Premier al-Kassem of Iraq had disclosed that Iraq was supplying arms to the Algerian rebels.

French President De Gaulle instructed government ministers to visit Algeria frequently for the purpose of defining government policy there and seeing that it was implemented.

BP Trading, Limited, an affiliate of the British Petroleum Company, Limited, announced a reduction on Middle East crude oils of 18 cents a barrel, or about 10 percent of its listed prices.

A spokesman for the Ministry of Development of Israel announced that IL2.5 Million would be invested that year in development works in Arab and Druze villages; these would include construction of school buildings, water plants, electricity installations and roads.

February 13

President Bourguiba of Tunisia appealed for French-Tunisian cooperation and proposed a personal meeting with French President De Gaulle.

February, 1959

February 11

The rulers of six British protected sultanates, emirates and sheikhdoms in West Aden signed a constitution establishing the Federation of the Arab Emirates of the South. In a treaty signed with the new Federation, the UK promised eventual independence. British Colonial Secretary Alan Lennox-Boyd pledged continued British support and military and financial aid.

Histadrut, an Israel trade union federation, announced that it would admit Israel Arab workers to full membership.

A Lebanese decree extending for five years the exemption of certain companies from income tax in accordance with the law of February 4, 1954, came into force.

Prime Minister Karami of Lebanon announced that talks to revise the 1948 financial agreement between Lebanon and France would begin in one week.

Delegates from 40 countries took part in the Afro-Asian Peoples' Solidarity Council's second session in Cairo.

An Algerian National Liberation Army communique published in Cairo reported 237 encounters with French troops between January 31 and February 6, in which 575 French officers and soldiers were killed, 275 wounded and eight French planes shot down.

A state of emergency was proclaimed in Kuwait. The country was reportedly swept by demonstrations protesting against the reactionary elements' attempts to turn Kuwait into a center of intrigue against Iraq.

February 12

Sudan signed an agreement with an Anglo-German consortium for construction and related work on a hydro-electric power station at the Sennar Dam on the Blue Nile.

The US Development Loan Fund announced a $1.2 million loan to a Jordanian electricity company to expand its power system in the Amman area.

February, 1959

February 13

The French Foreign Minister Couve de Murville reported to the National Assembly's Foreign Affairs Committee on the progressive deterioration of relations with Tunisia.

France vs. Lebanon cases involving taxes on French companies in Lebanon were referred to the International Court of Justice.

The Afro-Asian Peoples' Solidarity Council adopted a resolution establishing a special section of the secretariat to help freedom movements in still dependent countries of Africa, in particular, Portuguese colonies. They also established "The Permanent Organization for the Solidarity of the Afro-Asian Peoples'."

The Syrian press reported that 132 persons had been killed in clashes betwen Communists and Pan-Arab nationalists in Mosul and Basra, Iraq.

The USSR Supreme Soviet Presidium ratified the Cairo agreement of December 27, 1958, on economic and technical assistance to the UAR in the construction of the first section of the Aswan Dam.

February 14

The French Government protested the Tunisian refusal to permit the French Consul General to see two Algerians held in Tunis on a charge of espionage.

Three Israel girls were convicted of illegally entering UAR territory (with three Canadian UN Emergency Force soldiers) by a military court, and were sentenced to five years in prison.

February 15

The first shipment of a Soviet gift of wheat to Yemen reportedly left Russia for Yemen.

February, 1959

February 15

Arab League Secretary General Abd-al-Khaleq Hassouna said that the migration of Jews to Israel was the greatest peril faced by Arabs since the creation of the State of Israel.

The Aden Sultanate of Lower Aulaqi formally applied to join the Aden Federation.

The Jordanian Government announced the release of 53 persons arrested in 1957 on charges of Communist activity. The former prisoners were reported to have denounced Communism.

February 16

Ten alleged Communists were released from a Jordanian prison under a Royal Decree freeing detainees not considered risks to public security.

The American Topps Chewing Gum Company was blacklisted by the Jordanian Government for allegedly trading with Israel.

Premier David Ben-Gurion of Israel reportedly rejected a UN proposal for a survey of Israel's border troubles with the UAR. There was no official confirmation of this report.

UN Secretary General Dag Hammarskjold conferred with the Israel Ambassador to the UN Abba Eban.

The Tunisian Government officially mourned the deaths of four persons allegedly killed by a French attack on a border village.

Tunisia's permanent representative in the UN informed the President of the Security Council of continued French air raids on Tunisian territory.

February 17

A joint communique issued following talks between President Tito of Yugoslavia and Ibrahim Abboud, President and Premier of Sudan, said that Yugoslavia agreed in principle to give Sudan credit for financing industrial projects and buying machinery and cargo vessels.

February, 1959

February 17

UAR Foreign Minister Mahmoud Fawzi declared that the UAR would oppose mass migration of East European Jews to Israel.

A Lebanese Foreign Ministry source said that Lebanon would approach other Arab countries with a view to adopting a common plan to counter Jewish migration from Eastern Europe to Israel.

The Association for the Safeguard of Judicial Institutions and Individual Liberties, a nonpolitical group formed in France in 1957, renewed its charges that inhumane methods were being employed in continental France and in Algeria to put down the Algerian rebellion.

President Bourguiba of Tunisia declared that his country might demand the liquidation of the remaining French military base in Tunisia if peace in Algeria was not in sight within four months. He indicated that Tunisia would allow the French to retain the naval base at Bizerta in exchange for French recognition of nationalist aspirations in Algeria.

February 18

The US State Department said that Libya wanted more US economic assistance in exchange for continued US operation of Wheelus Air Base at Tripoli in Libya.

Tunisia formally protested to the UN Security Council against an attack by three French fighter planes on February 14 in which four Tunisians were reported killed and nine wounded.

Nine swarms of locusts entered Jordan from neighboring countries.

The Royal Cabinet of Morocco decided to establish an Industrial Development Bank, a Trust and Administration Fund to collect and manage the various Government funds and a National Savings Bank.

February 19

The British Foreign Office announced that Britain had delivered arms to Iraq mainly for logistic support of British arms already possessed by the Iraq Army.

February, 1959

February 19

A Cairo court sentenced the first three of hundreds of Communists arrested in both regions of the UAR to three to five year prison terms.

King Muhammad V of Morocco arrived in Corsica for a visit. In a gesture of friendship he turned over to the French authorities a French sergeant held captive for two years by Moroccan irregular forces.

Mid-East Crude Oil Sales Company, an affiliate of California-Texas Oil Corporation, announced reductions of 15 to 18 cents a barrel on Saudi Arabian crude oil prices.

The Shell Oil Company reduced the price of Abadan refinery products by about 15 cents a barrel.

George Hakim, Lebanon's new representative to the UN, presented his credentials to UN Secretary General Hammarskjold.

The Algerian rebels released six French soldiers captured in 1958 and detained in Morocco.

Israel Premier David Ben-Gurion said that Israel could absorb a great many more refugees.

President Marshall Tito of Yugoslavia was greeted by UAR President Nasser as he began a ten day visit in Cairo.

The agreement on USSR assistance to the UAR in the construction of the Aswan Dam came into force.

February 20

UN Security Forces in southern Lebanon occupied the town of Jwaya, scene of an armed clash between the private forces of two political opponents.

Israel Premier David Ben-Gurion said that peace between his state and the Arab countries was possible at any time, but that it depended on when Israel's Arab neighbors became democratic and spent money not on buying armaments but on raising the health and education standards of their people, when they realized that Israel could not be destroyed and when world tension lessened.

February, 1959

February 21

King Muhammad V of Morocco returned from Corsica to celebrate Morocco's third anniversary of Independence from France.

The Soviet Government said that it would not alienate its Arab friends by permitting the emigration of Soviet Jews to Israel.

The Egypt-Israel Mixed Armistice Commission (Israel absent) condemned Israel for the slaying of two Egyptian auxiliary police officers by an Israel armed patrol which crossed into the Gaza Strip.

US President Eisenhower sent a message of felicitations and best wishes to President Nasser on the first anniversary of the UAR.

Addressing a mass rally on the eve of the first anniversary of the UAR, President Nasser of the UAR revealed that he and Soviet Premier Nikita S. Khrushchev exchanged letters renewing their pledge of friendship and cooperation. Nasser also assailed those who accused him of designs to annex Iraq to the UAR. He said that cooperation was what was important, and not union. Nasser quoted Khrushchev as saying that the Soviet Union would continue to support the UAR, that these relations would never change and that the attitude of the UAR toward Communism was a matter of internal policy which concerned the UAR alone. President Nasser declared that the UAR would not let the friendship between them and the Soviet Union be broken.

The Iran Senate ratified the cultural agreement concluded between Iran and the UAR.

Fighting broke out at the American University of Beirut, when 150 students staged a pro-Nasser demonstration to mark the UAR's National Day.

February 22

President Nasser of the UAR arrived in Damascus to celebrate the first anniversary of the UAR. He was accompanied by President Tito of Yugoslavia and Crown Prince Saif-al-Islam Muhammad al-Badr, Yemen's Deputy Premier.

February, 1959

February 22

Eugene Black, President of the World Bank, arrived in Cairo to make a new attempt to iron out differences between Britain and the UAR in current financial negotiations.

The Lebanese Government publicly congratulated the UAR on its first anniversary.

Pro-Nasser crowds in Beirut wrecked five street cars in rioting during the celebration of the first anniversary of the UAR. The Lebanese Army sent troops to quell the riots.

A mob of Frenchmen in Algiers clamored for the death of Algerian rebel leaders and of President Bourguiba of Tunisia. Police squads broke up the demonstration.

Hajj Messali, Algerian nationalist leader, appealed for unity among his countrymen in a statement issued in Paris.

President Nasser of the UAR formally launched Syria's land reform program by giving deeds for new small holdings to 60 farmers.

February 23

Muhammad Salah M'zali, former Tunisian Premier under the French Protectorate, was to go on trial for treason, it was announced in Tunis.

The Algerian Provisional Government announced that Premier Ferhat Abbas would visit King Saud of Sauid Arabia within the next week. The announcement said that he would then visit Kuwait, Beirut, Baghdad and Damascus. The purpose of the trip was reportedly to speed up Arab League financial support for the Algerian rebels.

February 24

President Nasser of the UAR reportedly would meet with Premier Kassem of Iraq to settle their differences.

February, 1959

February 24

President Bourguiba of Tunisia had reportedly threatened to end instruction in French in Tunisian schools.

In a letter to all newsmen and publications accredited to France's Ministry of the Armed Forces, the Ministry warned the French and foreign press against premature or erroneous stories on military problems, and in particular, the operations in Algeria.

The UAR made representations to the Rumanian Government on the emigration of Rumanian Jews to Israel.

The Rumanian Government issued a statement accusing Israel and "imperialistic circles" of using the migration of Rumanian Jews to Israel to harm relations between the Eastern Bloc and the UAR.

February 25

French military authorities announced that their forces killed 105 rebels and captured 18 in a battle with a detachment of the Algerian National Liberation Front in the Guillaumet region 12 miles from Orleansville.

Moscow Radio reported that an Iraqi delegation had arrived in Moscow to complete negotiations for an agreement on economic and technical collaboration between the two countries.

Sources disclosed that UAR President Nasser had offered to meet with Premier al-Kassem of Iraq to improve understanding between them.

February 26

The Egyptian Ministry of Education returned to the Jesuits control of three Roman Catholic schools in Cairo after their textbooks and curricula were revised in accordance with Egyptian regulations.

French Delegate General Paul Delouvrier announced an electoral decree under which Algerians would elect municipal councils throughout Algeria between April 19 and 26. Elections would take place in all but the most

February, 1959

February 26

troublesome fighting zones. The decree assured Moslems of a majority on the municipal councils in those areas where Moslems outnumbered the French.

UAR authorities detained at Port Said the Liberian ship Capetan Manolis carrying a cargo of Israel cement and potash.

February 27

Five persons were reported injured in clashes in downtown Beirut between friends and foes of President Nasser of the UAR. These clashes were considered to be a continuation of disorders that broke out on February 22 when Nasser partisans celebrated the first anniversary of the Egyptian-Syrian merger (the formation of the UAR).

It was reported from Cairo that the Algerian Provisional Government signed a financial and military agreement with Communist China.

The High Court of Tunisia sentenced former Premier Muhammad Salah M'Zali to ten years imprisonment for collaborating with French authorities while Tunisia was a French protectorate.

British Colonial Secretary Alan Lennox-Boyd said in a press interview that the new Aden Federation was in the best interests of the people and their rulers. He also affirmed Britain's pledge to support the Federation against aggression from without and subversion from within.

February 28

The UK and Egypt formally signed the financial agreement on claims arising from nationalization or sequestration of British property after the 1956 Suez crisis.

The Lebanese Government banned the newsreel pictures of President Nasser of the UAR that sparked the bloodiest fighting in Beirut between rival factions since the revolt of the summer of 1958.

Lebanese Minister of the Interior, Raymond Edde charged that the clashes in Beirut on February 27 were instigated by some politicians who did not want to see relations among the Lebanese returned to normal.

March, 1959

March 1

King Hussein of Jordan opened a new broadcasting station in Amman. He said that the new station would be used as a medium for unity and brotherhood among Arabs.

Through the mediation of the IBRD a financial agreement was signed between Britain and the UAR which determined the amount of compensation to be paid by Egypt in connection with the British properties that it had taken over at the time of the Suez crisis of 1956.

March 2

Premier Abd-al-Karim al-Kassem of Iraq called for a Pan-Arab political and economic boycott of France until Arab Algeria was liberated.

At the opening of a congress of the Neo-Destour Party, President Bourguiba of Tunisia urged the western powers to relinquish colonialism.

Minister of Economy of Egypt Abd-al-Moneim al-Kaissouni, revealed that under a settlement with the Shell Oil Company on December 18, 1958, Shell agreed to waive LE11 million in claims, and to pay Cairo LE3 million for new concessions.

The UK made public the details of the financial settlement with the UAR. Both sides agreed to waive all claims for war damages; the UAR Government asked to release sequestered British properties; the UAR agreed to pay the UK a lump sum of 27.5 million pounds sterling for British private property that was Egyptianized. The UK agreed to release blocked Egyptian accounts.

Israel fined an American, Gary Schwartz, a student at Hebrew University, IL30 for having left the country without authorization.

The UN reported that an Israel patrol fired on a UN Emergency Force unit in the Gaza Strip on February 27, and that the Israelis had opened fire by mistake and had expressed regret.

Tass, the USSR News Agency, denied reports appearing in US and certain Beirut and Cairo papers on the USSR's alleged intention to carry out mass emigration of Jews to Israel.

March, 1959

March 3

A trade agreement was signed between Morocco and West Germany.

It was reported from Cairo that a battle over the direction of the Algerian movement had broken out in the ranks of the Algerian Provisional Government.

Abd-al-Kader Chanderli, the Algerian Provisional Government's representative at the UN, declared that reports of discord in his Government were pure press speculation.

March 4

Israel began constructing an aqueduct that would transport water from the Jordan River to the Negev Desert.

Premier Ibrahim Abboud of Sudan dismissed all 12 members of the Supreme Council of the Armed Forces which had ruled Sudan since the November, 1958, coup. The Premier assumed full powers.

March 5

Premier Abboud of Sudan appointed a new ten member Supreme Military Council.

The US signed, in Ankara, identical but separate defense agreements with Turkey, Pakistan and Iran, pursuant to the declaration signed on July 28, 1958, by the governments participating in the Baghdad Pact Ministerial Council session.

The British Foreign Office welcomed the conclusion of the agreements of defense which reaffirmed the close association of the United States with the three allies in the Baghdad Pact.

President Bourguiba of Tunisia was re-elected President of the Neo-Destour Party. He reportedly declined the Presidency for life.

March 6

The UAR was reported to be planning a vast oasis project for the Western desert.

March, 1959

March 8

A revolt by several brigades of the Iraqi Army was reported to have occurred in northern Iraq under the leadership of Colonel Abd-al-Wahhab al-Shawwaf. Mosul (Iraq) Radio announced that the revolutionary group was opposed to the Government of Premier al-Kassem, and had established headquarters in Mosul. Colonel al-Shawwaf favored a policy of positive neutrality and good relations with all states, especially with the UAR, according to the broadcast.

The US State Department officials termed the uprising in Iraq a "family affair."

The government in Baghdad, Iraq, appealed to the entire nation to join in a hunt for the Army Commander, Colonel Abd-al-Wahhab al-Shawwaf, charged with plotting against the state.

March 9

The Kassem Government of Iraq asserted that the pro-Nasser revolt was over, and that the Iraqi Air Force bombed and destroyed the rebel headquarters in Mosul. Colonel al-Shawwaf, who led the revolt, was killed by his own men, according to the Kassem Government report, and the units supporting Premier Kassem were in full control in Mosul.

Radio Mosul reported that the Iraq insurgents were still battling the Baghdad regime in northern Iraq and were still determined to overthrow General al-Kassem.

Moscow Radio charged that the US might have deliberately stirred up the Iraqi revolt.

Both US officials and Turkish officials were reported to have expressed fear that the pro-Nasser uprising in northern Iraq might pave the way for far reaching Soviet penetration of Iraq.

Demonstrations broke out in Baghdad when the Iraqi Government announced that the pro-Nasser revolt, led by Colonel al-Shawwaf in northern Iraq, had been suppressed.

March, 1959

March 6

Syrian officials said that the UAR lodged a strong protest with the Turkish-Syrian Mixed Border Commission against the destruction by Turks of a Syrian dam on the Jula River.

March 7

An Israel Army spokesman said that an Egyptian was killed when an Israel military patrol intercepted a group of infiltrators five miles inside Israel territory. Israel lodged a complaint with the Israel-Jordan Mixed Armistice Commission.

Following intervention by the Greek Embassy, a Greek ship carrying cargo from Israel was allowed to go through the Suez Canal after two days under detention.

A French Command communique announced heavy fighting in the past few days in Algeria.

March 8

UAR President Nasser was reported to have accused international Zionism of planning to establish an Israel motherland stretching from the Nile to the Euphrates.

Baghdad Radio confirmed a reported army revolt at Mosul, Iraq, which had gone on for more than a week.

Jordanian King Hussein left Jordan on a six week trip to the Far East, the US and the UK. In a farewell message, he said that he would discuss outstanding Arab problems.

Premier Muhammad Daoud of Afghanistan attacked US military pacts with Middle Eastern countries; he declared such agreements aggravated international tensions.

The Iraq Government dismissed Colonel Abd-al-Wahhab al-Shawwaf for cooperating with a foreigner against the nation's interest and plotting against the republic, and ordered his arrest.

March, 1959

March 9

Unidentified oil executives told the press that there had been no interruption of the flow of oil from northern Iraq to the Mediterranean coast.

King Hussein of Jordan arrived in Formosa (The Republic of China).

Major General Ahmad Abd-al-Wahhab of Sudan was relieved of his duties as a member of the newly reshuffled Supreme Military Council and as Minister of the Interior and Local Government.

The Supreme Military Council of Sudan was sworn in.

The Council of the Arab League adopted a resolution warning Hungary, Poland and Rumania that their relations with the Arab countries would be endangered if they permitted Jewish emigration to Israel.

Israel Foreign Minister Golda Meir said in New York that Israel had no intention of evicting Arab citizens to make room for Jews emigrating to Israel from Eastern Europe.

The UAR acceded to the Convention on the Recognition and Enforcement of Foreign Arbitral Awards adopted by a UN conference on June 10, 1958.

All but three members of the UAR mission in Baghdad, Iraq, were ordered to leave the country within 24 hours.

Israel resumed participation in the Israel-Jordan Mixed Armistice Commission (MAC).

March 10

It appeared that Colonel al-Shawwaf's pro-Nasser revolt in northern Iraq had been successfully crushed.

Baghdad Radio warned a country, interpreted to be the US, to stop meddling in Iraqi affairs.

Lebanese Ambassador to the US, Nadim Dimashqiyyah told US Senator J. W. Fulbright that he doubted the usefulness of a study being conducted for the US Senate Foreign Relations Committee by the Institute

March 10

of Mediterranean Affairs on the effect of US policies in the Middle East. The Ambassador alleged that "several Israeli Zionists" were among the consultants to the Institute.

An official UAR report stated that two Iraqi fighter planes strafed the Syrian village of Hamoudiya, about three miles from the Iraqi border.

March 11

President Nasser of the UAR accused Premier Abd-al-Karim al-Kassem of Iraq and Communist "agents of a foreign power" of trying to split the Arab world and of engineering demonstrations in Baghdad against the UAR.

According to Baghdad newspaper reports, the pro-Nasser army revolt in northern Iraq was broken mainly by Kurdish tribesmen who swarmed into rebel held Mosul from the surrounding countryside.

Iraqi demonstrators hanged President Nasser of the UAR in effigy in Baghdad, Iraq.

The offices of three right wing newspapers in Baghdad were wrecked. A fourth paper was suspended.

A Turkish Ministry of Foreign Affairs communique said that the Turkish Government's policy toward the Government of Iraq had always been inspired by the fraternal sentiments between the two nations.

March 12

Baghdad Radio made its first open and official charge that the UAR engaged in conspiracies against the Kassem Government.

The French Government seized an edition of the Paris newspaper, Express, which contained an interview with an Algerian rebel. The Government stated that the article constituted an indecent eulogy of the rebel forces against which the nation and the army were fighting.

March 12

President Nasser of the UAR denied that a foreign power or the UAR inspired the army revolt in Mosul, Iraq. He accused the Iraqi Premier Kassem of trying to subject the Arab peoples to a Communist reign of terror.

A UAR Foreign Ministry spokesman reported that a strong protest was sent to Iraq on the Hamoudiya air raid in Syria and the anti-Nasser demonstrations in Baghdad.

Jews emigrating from Rumania to Israel were reported to have arrived in Vienna.

March 13

In a speech given in Damascus, UAR President Nasser's third speech in as many days attacking Iraqi Premier Kassem, Nasser revealed that he had offered four times to meet General Kassem to settle their differences, but that the Iraqi Premier refused the invitation. Nasser asserted that the banners of Arab nationalism would some day fly over Baghdad. He charged that the Communists in Iraq were trying to tear Syria away from the UAR and annex it to Iraq in a "Communist Fertile Crescent."

Paul Delouvrier, French Delegate General in Algeria, informed army officers that the political and administrative decisions of their civilian advisers were final.

Large scale political demonstrations were held in all major Syrian cities in conjunction with the funeral for Muhammad Said Chehab, an Iraqi Army officer who had fought on the rebel side at Mosul, Iraq, and escaped to Syria, where he had died of his wounds.

Iraqi Director General of Broadcasting and Guidance said that the burial with honors in Damascus, Syria, of the Iraqi officer, Mohammad Said Chehab, was a provocative act of the UAR against Baghdad (the seat of the Kassem Government of Iraq).

The Israel Army announced that Syrian soldiers, firing across the border, wounded an Israel farmer.

March 13

Two Algerians were reported killed and two wounded when gunmen fired into a bar in northeast Paris, France.

March 14

President Nasser of the UAR said in Syria that when there was a Communist party, it operated under the word "democracy," and when this succeeded, it worked for the "red dictatorship."

A UAR Army communique stated that three Iraq planes staged a rocket attack inside Syrian territory and strafed two villages with machine guns. The communique blamed the ruler of Iraq for the incident.

Iraqis charged that the recent uprising in Mosul, Iraq, was carried out with supplies received from Syria.

It was reported from Baghdad, Iraq, that 2,000 persons were killed and hundreds wounded in the Mosul uprising against the Kassem Government.

King Hussein of Jordan watched a Chinese Nationalist airborne exercise and an amphibious landing in southern Formosa.

March 15

Iraqi Foreign Minister Hashem Jawad said that a preliminary investigation showed a 100 percent connection between the Mosul, Iraq, revolt and the UAR.

The Iraqi Foreign Ministry called on the UAR to stop the infiltration of Syrian tribesmen into Northern Iraq for the purpose of creating disorder in Iraq.

A spokesman for the UAR First (Syrian) Army charged that 30 Iraqis crossed the frontier and attacked two Syrian guards near the village of Talhamar.

An official spokesman for the Foreign Ministry of Iraq denied the UAR's allegation that two Iraqi planes strafed a Syrian village.

March 15

The National Union, the only legal political organization in the UAR, urged the Arab world to assist the free Iraqi people in the struggle against evil and Communism.

The Sudanese Cabinet endorsed a SP2.23 million trade exchange agreement with Russia whereby Russia would buy Sudanese cotton in exchange for machinery, trucks and cars.

The building containing the Soviet motion picture center in Beirut was heavily damaged by an explosion. At about the same time a bomb was thrown at the home of Mustafa al-Aris, a Lebanese Communist leader.

March 16

Abd-al-Isam Rashid Huwaish, a nephew of Colonel Abd-al-Salam Aref of Iraq, reportedly made an armed attack on the town of Ramadi, 60 miles west of Baghdad.

A memorial service was held in Cairo for the dead of the Mosul revolt against the Government of Iraq Premier al-Kassem.

UAR Vice President Abd-al-Hakim Amer declared in Cairo that the Iraq Communists had deliberately provoked the Mosul uprisings as an excuse to crush Iraqi nationalism.

An economic and technical cooperation agreement between Iraq and the Soviet Union, signed in Moscow, called for a loan to Iraq of 550 million rubles ($37.5 million at the official exchange rate) repayable at two and one-half percent interest.

Soviet Premier Nikita S. Khrushchev said at a Kremlin reception for an Iraqi Government delegation, that President Nasser of the UAR should abandon insistence on uniting Iraq with the UAR and that the present regime in Iraq had reliable and selfless friends who were ready to come to its aid whenever it was in trouble. He said that anti-Communist policy was doomed to failure.

March 16

President Nasser of the UAR said that Soviet Premier Khrushchev's charges about the UAR designs on Iraq involved distortion of fact because they had always announced that the UAR path was Arab solidarity. He declared that the UAR appreciated Soviet friendship as long as it was established on the basis of non-interference in internal affairs and did not involve the backing of a Communist minority in the country against the unanimity of the Arab people.

Khaled Bakdash, Syria's outlawed Communist leader, said at the Congress of the Polish Communist party in Warsaw that Nasser's Government was the chief obstacle in the way of Arab unity. He applauded Iraq as the unconquered bastion of the Arab nationalist movement.

The Foreign Ministry of the UAR formally protested to Iraq against the strafing of two villages and an automobile in Syria on March 14, by the Iraqi Air Force.

March 17

A trade agreement between Sudan and the Soviet Union, endorsed by the Sudanese Cabinet on March 15, was signed in Khartoum. The one year, automatically renewable agreement provided for SP2.23 million worth of trade in each direction.

In a joint communique issued at the end of King Hussein's eight day visit to Taiwan, the Jordanian ruler and President Chiang Kai-shek agreed that their countries should act in cooperation against aggression. King Hussein left for an official visit to the US.

King Saud of Saudi Arabia received Amir Saleh Ibn-Isa al-Harithi, the Representative of the Imamate of Oman in Riyadh.

The Iraqi Minister of Economy Ibrahim Kubbah expressed confidence that the agreement between Iraq and the Soviet Union signed March 16 would constitute the solid foundation for the strengthening of the friendly relations between the Soviet Union and Iraq and all the countries of the Middle East.

March 17

The UAR's semi-official news agency said that Soviet Premier Khrushchev had opened a showdown between Arab nationalism and the new Communist imperialism in the Middle East.

Gharbi Ahmad, Director General of National Guidance in Iraq, was replaced by Dhummun Aib.

USSR newspapers published an Iraqi-USSR communique on the visit to the USSR (February 25-March 17) of an Iraqi Government delegation.

March 18

A crowd of Libyan students marched through Tripoli to the Soviet Embassy shouting pro-Nasser and anti-Communist slogans. Police dispersed the crowd.

A LE25 million UAR Government development loan, issued on March 16, was fully subscribed.

It was reported from Damascus that Iraqi authorities arrested Muhammad Mahdi al-Kubbah, a member of the Sovereignty Council and head of the Istiqlal (Independence) Party in Iraq.

Israel protested to the UN Security Council against the UAR for flagrant violations of Security Council resolutions and the Suez Canal Convention in seizing Israel cargoes from two non-Israel freighters passing through the Suez Canal.

Israel Prime Minister David Ben-Gurion warned that Israel might be forced once again to fight for freedom of shipping in the Red Sea if the UAR continued to put obstacles in the path of Israel's navigation.

It was reported from Damascus that President Nasser of the UAR and President Chehab of Lebanon had agreed to meet. Time and place were not disclosed.

About 250,000 people reportedly jammed Alexandria's Liberation Square to honor the Iraqi "martyrs" of the Mosul, Iraq revolution.

March 19

Soviet Premier Khrushchev said in a press interview in Moscow that President Nasser of the UAR was a hot headed young man who took upon himself "more than his stature permitted" when he assailed Communists in the Middle East and in the Iraqi regime.

The UAR Finance Ministry announced that Cairo was considering an offer from the International Bank for Reconstruction and Development (IBRD) to finance some development projects in the UAR.

In a press conference in Baghdad, Dr. Ibrahim Kubbah, the Economy Minister of Iraq, announced the projects which would be carried out with the new Soviet loan. He listed 23 industrial and research projects already decided on under the Soviet aid agreement. He stated that 80 Russian technicians were to come to Iraq to supervise the projects.

In an effort to disarm the Lebanese political factions and mountain tribes, the Lebanese Government cancelled all firearms licenses, effective April 1.

The official newspaper of the Neo-Destour Party in Sudan, al-Amal, protested recent French rocket tests made near Colomb-Bechar in the Sahara.

Several shipments of US wheat left for Yemen as emergency aid to the famine ravaged country.

The Iraqi Government allocated ID50,000 in relief for the victims of the reactionary Mosul revolt.

The Iraqi Government decreed the establishment of a general committee for oil.

Israel was reported to have appealed to neutral maritime nations to support its demand for release of cargoes allegedly seized by the UAR in the Suez Canal.

March 20

Paul Delouvrier, French Delegate General for Algeria, announced two important decisions to advance the industrialization for Algeria: the construction of a large steel plant in the port city of Bone and the establishment of low prices for natural gas used in homes and factories in the Algiers and Oran areas.

The French Army announced that 6,000 persons were killed during the first two years of the Algerian war. In the same period, 2,000 persons, most of them Moslems, disappeared, 400 schools were burned or raided, 50,000 telegraph poles were felled, and 6,000 farms attacked.

UAR President Nasser in a speech in Damascus denounced Soviet Premier Khrushchev for interference in Middle Eastern affairs, and said the Communists in the UAR must be crushed as agents of foreign powers. He said that the UAR would not accept Communism and satellite status.

The Israel Army reported that an Egyptian infiltrator was killed by an Israel patrol near Sikim, in the Negev Desert.

It was reported from Cairo that informed sources told the press the UAR would continue to seize Israel cargoes shipped through the Suez Canal.

A St. Helena court reportedly dismissed an application for a writ of habeas corpus to release Abd-al-Rahman al-Bakr, a Bahraini nationalist leader imprisoned there since 1956.

The Lebanese Council of Ministers announced creation of a special department in the Ministry of Interior to handle Palestinian refugees in Lebanon.

Police used tear gas to break up a second anti-Communist demonstration in Tripoli, Libya.

The Libyan Embassy in Washington said that the Libyan Government was drafting new laws for the Jewish Community Organization in Libya and had taken charge of that Organization at its request to investigate charges that the Organization's funds had been mishandled. It said that only the Jews in the Community Organization were affected.

March, 1959

March 21

There were reportedly large scale arrests of pro-Nasser army officers in Jordan. The officers were accused of participating in a conspiracy against the King.

A demonstration was held in Baghdad in support of Iraq Premier Kassem.

The French Army command announced that 156 Algerian rebel soldiers in the National Liberation Army and their commander gave themselves up at a French Army post near the Tunisian border, in the first mass surrender of the four year rebellion.

French Premier Debre announced in Paris that he would renew the French offer to negotiate with the Algerian rebel forces for a cease-fire in Algeria.

Ferhat Abbas, Premier of the Algerian Provisional Government, arrived in Tunis to confer with Tunisian President Habib Bourguiba.

March 22

President Nasser of the UAR said in a speech broadcast from Damascus that late in 1958 the UAR decided to enter a decisive battle against Israel after a number of incidents along the Syrian-Israel border, but that Premier Abd-al-Karim al-Kassem of Iraq had refused to stand with them against Israel and to send Iraqi Army units. He declared that the Soviet Union gave Egypt no help during the actual fighting over Suez in 1956.

UAR President Nasser, visiting in Damascus, received representatives of various Lebanese organizations. They denounced the agents of Communism in the Arab homeland and pledged their allegiance to Nasser in the form of a proclamation written and signed in blood by 5,000 Lebanese who promised to carry arms in defense of Arab nationalism.

Israel reportedly arrested 16 Lebanese women who had crossed into Israel to cut grass.

March, 1959

March 23

Adnan Pachachi was appointed as Acting Permanent Representative of Iraq at the UN.

The Iraq Health Ministry announced an agreement with the USSR to send an unspecified number of Iraqis to Moscow for medical treatment.

Iraq and Yugoslavia signed a cultural, scientific and educational cooperation agreement in Belgrade.

Sheikh Shaltout, the Rector of al-Azhar University in Cairo, called on all Moslem people to "rise as one man" to defend their religion against atheistic Communism.

French Premier Debre said that France must remain in Algeria to maintain the security of the nation, to assure development of the oil and mineral wealth of the Sahara and to retain physical links with members of the French Community farther south.

French military units, stationed at the four US Air Force bases in Morocco under an agreement with France when Morocco was a French Protectorate, reportedly would be withdrawn on March 31.

Hungary and Yemen reportedly would establish diplomatic relations.

It was reported from Cairo that President Nasser of the UAR and Chehab of Lebanon planned to meet later in the week to discuss joining the two countries in a loose federation similar to that of the UAR and Yemen.

A Jordanian Government spokesman told the press that there was no truth to a Damascus report that a plot to overthrow the Government of King Hussein had been uncovered in Jordan.

Jordanian King Hussein arrived in Washington for informal discussion with President Eisenhower, acting Secretary of State Christian A. Herter and other government officials.

March, 1959

March 22

It was reported from Damascus that an Iraqi plane attacked a convoy of Iraqi refugees en route to the Syrian border and wounded six.

Clashes between Communist sympathizers and pro-Nasser Arabs were reported to have occurred in several Arab villages in Israel.

The offices of the Communist newspaper in Lebanon, al-Akhbar, were damaged by two bomb explosions.

President of the Zionist Organization of America, Abraham A. Redelheim, criticized what he termed falsehoods spread by the Arab propaganda machine to try to stop Jewish emigration from Eastern Europe to Israel.

The Omani leaders were feted in Riyadh as guests of King Saud of Saudi Arabia.

French Premier Michel Debre, on an inspection tour of Algeria, gave his solemn affirmation that there would never be a separation of France and Algeria.

The Algerian Provisional Government announced that a rebel delegation would visit Communist China at the request of Peking. The delegation would be a military mission.

King Hussein of Jordan arrived in San Francisco.

Prime Minister Macmillan of the UK told President Eisenhower in Washington that Britain was willing to supply arms to the regime of Premier al-Kassem of Iraq.

Baghdad residents reportedly demonstrated against the plots and intrigues of the imperialists and their agents.

March 23

The Iraqi Government announced the closing of the town of Khanaqin and of villages surrounding it.

March, 1959

March 24

Premier Abd-al-Karim al-Kassem of Iraq announced in Baghdad, Iraq's formal withdrawal from the Baghdad Pact. He also urged the press to ignore President Nasser of the UAR.

A British Foreign Office spokesman said that Iraq's withdrawal from the Pact formalized what had been a fact since the overthrow of the Iraqi monarchy in the summer of 1958.

Unidentified US officials told the press that Iraq's action in withdrawing from the Baghdad Pact might be interpreted as a gesture to deprive Nasser of a political stick and to appease Iraq's Communists.

Leaders of the abortive revolt in northern Iraq went on trial for treason in Baghdad.

Following a conference with King Hussein of Jordan, President Eisenhower told the press that the King was a man who had withstood the temptations to weaken his defense of his principles and rights.

Sayyed Abd-al-Rahman al-Mahdi died in Khartoum, Sudan. Although a patron of the Umma Party, his leadership in the country remained religious and nonpolitical. It was felt in Cairo that al-Mahdi's death would weaken the Umma faction and those forces within the army wishing to pursue the rigorously independent policy laid down by former Sudanese Premier Khalil.

A communique from the Algerian Provisional Government asserted that only about 30 rebel soldiers surrendered to the French on March 21, not 156 as announced by the French Army.

March 25

The Iraqi Cabinet designated March 24, the day Iraq withdrew from the Baghdad Pact, as a national holiday, "The Freedom Day."

Demonstrators paraded before the US Embassy in Baghdad shouting their approval of Iraq's withdrawal from the Baghdad Pact.

March 25

A British Foreign Office spokesman said that the British Government had received an assurance from the Iraq Government that the withdrawal from the Baghdad Pact would not disturb Britain's rights at Habbaniya Airfield for the time being. Britain hoped to maintain good relations with Iraq.

Iraq's Foreign Minister Hashem Jawad told the Turkish Ambassador to Baghdad that with his country's withdrawal from the Baghdad Pact, efforts would be exerted to improve Iraq's friendship with Turkey.

It was reported from Baghdad that Premier al-Kassem of Iraq had dismissed Salim Fakhri, reputed to be a pro-Communist, from his position as Director General of Broadcasting, and had replaced him with Shunun Ayyoub.

French President Charles De Gaulle said that the destiny of Algeria depended upon an immense task of long duration. Algeria must reveal itself to itself and the outside world, and that this was inconceivable without the action and presence of France.

The Soviet Union declared in a formal statement that it would take steps to protect its southern frontiers in the face of new US bilateral military agreements with Turkey, Iran and Pakistan.

It was reported that four Arabs were killed when three mines exploded on the Syrian-Turkish frontier.

A joint communique issued after a meeting with President Fuad Chehab of Lebanon and President Nasser of the UAR at the Syrian-Lebanese border said that the two leaders agreed to foster brotherly relations and fruitful cooperation within the framework of the Arab League and the United Nations. Nasser promised to respect Lebanon's independence; Chehab reaffirmed Lebanon's solidarity with the Arab cause.

Siddiq, the eldest son of al-Mahdi who died in Khartoum on March 24, was named head of the Ansar, a reformist sect in Sudan. He was the former head of the Dairat, the commercial part of the movement.

March 26

After detaining the ship for two days, Egyptian authorities allowed the Greek freighter Nicolas Kairis, carrying an Israel cargo, to pass through the Suez Canal.

The halting of foreign owned freighters attempting to carry Israel cargoes through the Suez Canal was reported to be threatening the budding trade between Israel and Africa and the Far East.

Three US press correspondents were expelled from Iraq. No reason was given other than that they had "been here long enough."

A new three year trade agreement between Hungary and the UAR provided for an exchange of goods valued at LE10 to 14 million annually.

Switzerland and the UAR signed an agreement for the loan of 25 million Swiss francs to the UAR to buy Swiss textile machinery.

Ali Khodja, a prominent Algerian Moslem and businessman, urged rebel leaders to negotiate with the French for a ceasefire.

An Algerian rebel military mission left Cairo for Peking to discuss the purchase of Communist arms supplies.

King Hussein of Jordan criticized President Nasser of the UAR for having opened the way for Soviet penetration of the Middle East and then shifting to a policy of anti-Communism for which the Jordanian ruler previously had been attacked.

March 27

An Israel Foreign Ministry spokesman announced that Israel would continue to attempt to obtain a commitment from the UAR that foreign owned vessels carrying Israel cargoes would be assured passage through the Suez Canal.

The Arab foreign ministers' meeting, scheduled for Beirut, to discuss the Iraqi-UAR dispute was postponed until April 2 at Morocco's request.

March 27

It was reported from Beirut that a widespread purge took place in Iraq and that 5,000 to 6,000 civil servants, army officers and political leaders were arrested.

Winston Burdett, ousted CBS correspondent (from Iraq on March 26) said in Beirut that Baghdad prisons were filled until there was no more room in them for all the political prisoners.

Iraq's Ambassador to the UAR, Fayeq al-Samarrai, resigned in protest against the policy of the al-Kassem regime.

The Communists in Iraq were reported to have presented Iraqi Premier al-Kassem with several demands, among which were the demands that the just verdicts of the People's Court against members of the former regime be carried out, and that the people be armed in order to defend effectively the safety of the republic side by side with the army. The report was not confirmed.

French forces reported that they killed 135 rebels and took 62 prisoners near Bou Saada, Algeria, about 200 miles southeast of Algiers. French losses were put at six dead.

The US gave Jordan $4.4 million; this was the final grant of budgetary assistance for the fiscal year 1958-1959 and brought the year's total to $43.2 million.

Jordanian King Hussein and Premier Samir al-Rifai ended their conversations with US President Eisenhower and Acting Secretary of State Herter.

March 28

An Iraqi People's Court sentenced to death four Air Force officers convicted of bombing a Baghdad Radio station during the Mosul revolt.

King Hussein and his entourage from Jordan began a tour of the US.

March 29

Fayeq al-Samarrai who was expelled as Iraqi Ambassador to the UAR three days ago accused the Baghdad Government of having killed former Foreign Minister Abd-al-Jabbar Jumard.

King Hussein of Jordan, in an interview over CBS radio in the US said that there was danger that Communists would come to power in Iraq. He added that the Soviet Union had a plan to take over the entire Middle East.

Ferhat Abbas, Premier of the Algerian Provisional Government, said that membership in the French Community was incompatible with Algerian independence, but that a free and unified North Africa would not be opposed to association with France under certain circumstances.

The French Army announced that Colonel Amirouche, commander of about 5,000 rebel troops in northeast Algeria, was killed in battle with French forces.

Ferhat Abbas, Premier of the Algerian Provisional Government, said in Tunis that the French community taking shape in Algeria resembled a prefabricated cage.

March 30

The Iraqi Government announced that the four Air Force officers convicted on the 28th of March were executed by a firing squad.

The British Foreign Office announced that Great Britain and Iraq agreed that the British regiment and its stores should leave the Habbaniya Air Force Base at an early date.

It was reported from Baghdad that nine members of the Iraqi Foreign Service, including the Iraqi Consul in New York and the Counselor of the Iraqi Embassy in Washington, had either been retired or suspended.

March, 1959

March 30

Morocco and Tunisia signed six conventions for cultural, economic and technical cooperation.

President Nasser of the UAR disclosed in a speech at Cairo that during his visit to Moscow last year, Premier Khrushchev asked him to allow Communists to operate in the UAR, but that he refused because he considered it an interference in internal affairs. He also revealed that he complained to Khrushchev that Soviet diplomatic envoys in the Arab world had opposed the Egyptian-Syrian union. Nasser said that an elected Parliament in the Soviet Union was dismissed in 1917, and now they were governed by the Communist Party, where no one had the chance to speak except the Communists.

Israel Foreign Minister Golda Meir said that there was no ground for Western circles to hope that by strengthening President Nasser of the UAR in his current dispute with Baghdad, he could be attracted to the West.

An Algeria Week opened in the USSR in accordance with the resolution of the Afro-Asian Peoples' Solidarity Council.

March 31

In Columbus, Georgia, King Hussein of Jordan cautioned Americans not to confuse Arab nationalism with Nasserism.

French military units used to maintain safety and security were withdrawn from the four US Air Force bases in Morocco, under an agreement between France and the US.

Ferhat Abbas, Premier of the Algerian Provisional Government, returned to Cairo after a ten day visit in Tunis.

Abu-al-Kassem Karim, Minister of War in Algerian Provisional Government, issued a statement mourning the death of Colonel Amirouche, and said that the revolution would continue; it was producing scores of leaders just like him.

April, 1959

April 1

US Senator Hubert Humphrey, Democrat from Minnesota, urged that the US place greater emphasis on the Middle East and fashion adequate policies for the area.

The Egyptian press reported that Communists from Iraq had attempted to overthrow the Government of Kuwait, but had been foiled by Kuwait authorities.

Premier Samir al-Rifai of Jordan warned the West against hasty conclusions about the political developments in Iraq.

Eastern Germany and Iraq signed an agreement on cultural and scientific cooperation.

The Secretary General of the Arab League Hassouna announced that Iraq had given no positive response as to whether it would send a representative to the political meeting of the League scheduled for April 2.

Israel broadcast an order over the radio for the partial mobilization of the Israel Army. Syria reportedly mobilized its troops along the borders of Israel soon after.

Thirteen Jews were arrested for trying to leave Morocco illegally for Algeria.

April 2

Iraq terminated its contract with Mackenzie & Company, British engineering consultants, for construction of a steel plant in Baghdad. The work would be carried on by the Soviet Union under the economic cooperation agreement with Iraq. Contracts of two French concerns engaged in yarn spinning projects and natural gas production were also ended.

Crown Prince Faisal of Saudi Arabia attended the meeting of the Arab League Political Committee to mediate the dispute between Iraq and the UAR.

Poland and Iraq signed an agreement on cultural and scientific cooperation.

April, 1959

April 2

The Arab League's Political Committee convened in Beirut, at the request of Sudan, to consider the Iraq-UAR dispute. Iraq, Tunisia and Jordan declined to attend because of strained relations with the UAR. Libya, which accepted the invitation, did not send a delegation.

UN Secretary General Dag Hammarskjold said he was in touch with Cairo about the seizures by the UAR of Israel cargoes on foreign flag vessels going through the Suez Canal.

An agreement for prospecting in 13 areas in the eastern part of the UAR and on the continental shelf of the Gulf of Suez was signed in Cairo between the Eastern Oil Company and the UAR Ministry of Industry.

The Jordanian security police raided Communist cells in Nablus, Jordan, and arrested several Jordanian Communists.

April 3

The Israel Military High Court of Appeals closed the Kafr Kassem case; it upheld the guilt of the eight policemen convicted for the killing of 43 Arabs on the eve of Israel's action in Sinai in 1956. The Court reduced penalties, however, since the men were acting under orders.

The UAR urged the Arab League to take collective measures against Communism in Iraq.

King Hussein of Jordan piloted a Lockheed jet at 1,520 miles an hour at Los Angeles, California, USA.

Lebanese Minister of the Interior Raymond Edde said that a general election in Lebanon could not be held as long as civilians continued to be armed.

April 4

Iraq signed a cultural pact with Communist China.

April, 1959

April 4

At a meeting of the Arab League called by Sudan to discuss the rift in Iraqi-UAR relations, the six nations present agreed that Iraq's pro-Communist Government might be a threat. The six nations represented were the Sudan, the UAR, Saudi Arabia, Morocco, Lebanon and Yemen.

French military headquarters stated that 1,138 Algerian rebels were killed or captured between March 23 and 29. French casualties were given as 58 soldiers and 60 civilians killed. According to a rebel spokesman, the French suffered 44 fatalities on March 29 alone.

It was reported from London that the restoration of diplomatic relations between Britain and the UAR might be forthcoming.

US Secretary of Defense Neil McElroy gave an encouraging picture of the Western political position in the Middle East before the House Foreign Affairs Committee.

April 5

The meeting of the Arab League Political Committee to mediate the quarrel between President Nasser of the UAR and Premier al-Kassem of Iraq was expected to adopt a noncommittal position on the dispute between the UAR and Iraq.

Premier al-Kassem of Iraq said at a press conference that he would carry out a revolution in the organization of his Government this month.

It was reported from Cairo that the UAR was arranging for the immediate recall of some 700 experts and employees lent to the Iraq Government.

President Nasser of the UAR appointed Abd-al-Hamid Sarraj as Minister of Waqfs for the Syrian region. This post was in addition to his Interior Ministry portfolio.

It was reported from Tunis that Saleh-ad-Din Baccouche, a former Premier of Tunisia who was sentenced last November to a 10 year prison term for collaborating with French protectorate authorities was freed.

Four Israel planes reportedly violated the airspace of the UAR in the Gaza area.

April 6

Premier al-Kassem of Iraq conferred for two hours with R. G. Seawright, chief British representative in Baghdad of the Iraq Petroleum Company, and other oil officials. It was announced that the meeting concerned certain important questions about oil and production in Iraq.

It was reported in Baghdad that Iraq had protested UAR violation of Iraqi airspace.

The first group of British servicemen and their families being withdrawn from the Habbaniya Base in Iraq left the country.

The Political Committee of the Arab League began bargaining about a proposed resolution by Lebanon concerning the dispute between Iraq and the UAR.

Egyptian port officials said that the Soviet passenger ship Gruziya, with 855 armed Kurds of Soviet origin aboard, passed through the Suez Canal on its way from Odessa to Basra.

The Liberian Government declared that it protested to the UAR against the seizure of cargoes from ships flying the Liberian flag which were passing through the Suez Canal.

General E. L. M. Burns, Commander of the UN Emergency Force, said that the Force was still needed to help keep the peace because of the tensions existing on either side.

The Tunisian Government charged that two French Army tanks penetrated about a mile into Tunisian territory last week. The charge said that the tanks captured an Algerian refugee before withdrawing.

French authorities in Algeria denied Tunisian charges that French tanks had penetrated Tunisian territory.

The Czechoslovakian freighter, Lidice, with 581 tons of arms and ammunition for the Moroccan Army was overdue at Casablanca. The ship reportedly might have been seized by the French.

The US handed over $5 million worth of railroad equipment to Jordan, it was announced; this was part of the aid allocated during 1958 for Jordan.

April 7

A resolution adopted at the conclusion of the meeting of the Arab League Political Committee appealed to the Iraqi Government to follow the example of the other Arab states by adhering to the policy of neutrality, nonalignment and Arab unity and solidarity.

The Arab League Political Committee declined to commit itself on the questions of Communism in the Arab world and the dispute between Iraq and the UAR.

The Cairo Radio reported that a revolt against the Kassem pro-Communist regime had started in northern Iraq and that the Kurds on their way from the Soviet Union were coming to help quell the revolt.

Iraqi Premier Kassem promised a pardon to Shammar tribesmen who fled to Syria if they returned to their family villages. The tribe participated actively in the Mosul rebellion.

The Iraq Petroleum Company announced in London that it was discussing plans with the Iraqi Government to give up parts of its concessions in Iraq.

Dr. Ibrahim Kubbah, Iraq Minister of Economy, said in Baghdad that it was absolutely untrue that the Iraqi Government was making any demands for nationalization of the oil industry.

The Israel Army said that two Egyptian infiltrators were killed by an Israel patrol which found them stealing irrigation pipe in Israel territory.

Three Lebanese fishermen were sentenced to two year prison terms for using explosives while fishing in Israel territorial waters.

Algerian terrorists attacked two Paris suburban police stations following police raids on Moslem neighborhoods in Paris.

April 8

A cultural agreement between Iraq and Bulgaria was signed in Baghdad.

April 8

The Cairo press reported that Kurds from the Soviet Union had begun arriving in Baghdad to help quell a reported revolt against the Kassem regime beginning in the north of Iraq.

The Baghdad Radio described the Gruziya passengers as Kurds who had fled to the Soviet Union in 1947 to escape persecution by the Iraqi monarchy. They were said to be followers of Sheikh Mustafa Barazani.

The Iraqi Army Chief of Staff, Brigadier Ahmad al-Abdi, said that the Popular Resistance Forces (the Civilian Militia) had been supplied with adequate arms to enable them to carry out their duties.

It was reported from Cairo that members of the Shammar tribe near Mosul, Iraq, were waiting for a signal from their leader, Ahmad Ojale, before clashing with Iraq Premier al-Kassem's supporters.

Britain had reportedly received no confirmation of disturbances in northern Iraq.

Major Salah Salem, former Minister of National Guidance of Egypt who resigned in 1956 after differences with President Nasser, was named Chairman of the Tahrir Publishing House owned by the Egyptian Government.

Morocco protested to Paris against the seizure by French authorities in Algeria of the Czech freighter Lidice, which was on its way to Casablanca with arms for the Moroccan armed forces. The French said they suspected that the arms were for the Algerian rebels.

April 9

At a press interview Saudi Arabian Crown Prince Faisal stated that Saudi Arabia did not object to a restoration of diplomatic relations with Great Britain provided that Britain was willing to work for a solution of the outstanding disputes between the two countries.

The American delegate to the Intergovernmental Committee for European Migration announced a US contribution of $150,000 for the relief of Algerian refugees in Tunisia and Morocco.

April 9

A British Government spokesman announced that organized rebel resistance in the Jebel Akhdar area of Oman had ceased and that British units had withdrawn.

The Iraqi Minister of Economy Dr. Ibrahim Kubbah, in a more complete statement than that of April 7, declared that Iraq did not intend to nationalize the oil industry, that the Government policy was based on keeping the oil agreement with the companies working in Iraq, provided that these agreements would not be amended without the acceptance of the aforementioned companies.

Iraq reported that it would not be represented at an Arab League oil conference in Cairo April 16 because of the "hostile attitude" of the UAR.

Jordanian security forces reported the arrest of Isa Sulaiman Naber, a "dangerous" Communist who had been sentenced in absentia to 15 years imprisonment for taking part in the riots in April, 1956.

Akram Hourani, a Vice President of the UAR, said that Soviet interference in internal Arab affairs had convinced Afro-Asian countries that cooperation with the Soviet Union was now illusory.

The Iraqi-Chinese Friendship Society was inaugurated in Baghdad.

April 10

It was reported from Paris that French Premier Debre would meet with UK Prime Minister Macmillan in London to discuss, among other problems, the status of Western oil concessions in Iraq.

It was reported that French police arrested 465 Algerians in raids throughout continental France. The police reportedly described them as "nationalist agitators."

April, 1959

April 11

It was announced that the flag of the Algerian Provisional Government would be displayed with those of nine independent African states at Carnegie Hall in New York during the celebration of African Freedom Day.

The official Soviet News Agency Tass said that reports from Cairo that 855 "young Soviet armed Kurds well trained" in guerrilla warfare were on their way to Iraq aboard the Soviet vessel Gruziya were false from beginning to end. The statement from Tass said that the Kurds were Iraqi repatriates.

The Middle East News Agency reported that a second Soviet ship, the Argun, arrived at Port Said with several hundred armed Kurds bound for Iraq.

A Cairo newspaper reported that MIG fighter jets flown by Soviet pilots had arrived in Iraq to strengthen the Iraqi Air Force.

April 12

The French seized 581 tons of arms and ammunition from a Czechoslovakian ship in Algiers.

A crowd of about 2,000 Europeans in Algiers, organized by a group called the "Popular Movement Thirteen," staged an anti-De Gaulle demonstration and applauded a call for a formula of replacement of his government.

Thirty-five Roman Catholic priests, serving with the French Army in Algeria, charged that the Army was torturing Moslem rebels and summarily executing wounded insurgents.

A Soviet Committee for African-Asia solidarity arrived in Baghdad to attend a Congress of Iraqi Peace Partisans.

The American Committee for Liberation, which monitored Soviet broadcasts, quoted Radio Moscow as saying that Israel military preparations showed the shortsightedness of those Arab statesmen who claimed that imperialism had left the Arab world.

April, 1959

April 12

An Israel Foreign Ministry spokesman said that Radio Moscow and Tass reports alleging Israel plans to attack Arab states were "fantasy" and "pure fiction."

April 13

Kamal Rifaat, UAR Minister of State, declared that the Government would take drastic action if the situation in Iraq constituted a threat to the UAR at any time. He compared Communist intervention in Iraq to US and UK interventions in Lebanon and Jordan in July, 1958.

The US announced authorization by the Development Loan Fund of a $2.5 million loan to the Jordan Phosphate Company, a private concern, for expansion of its mines at Ruseifa, Jordan.

The Reverend Harold Davenport, last of four American Protestant missionaries expelled by the Iraqi Government, left Iraq for Beirut.

Ferhat Abbas, Premier of the Algerian Provisional Government, arrived in Karachi, Pakistan, for talks with Pakistani President Ayyoub Khan.

It was reported from Amman that Khalil Qunsul, Secretary of the Jordanian Communist Party, had been arrested by Jordanian security police.

Jordanian King Hussein arrived in New York City after a visit to the US Military Academy at West Point, New York.

April 14

A Congress of Iraqi Peace Partisans opened in Baghdad with an address by Premier al-Kassem of Iraq who said that his country was a country of peace partisans.

French police were reported to have arrested for questioning about 800 people suspected of terrorist activity in Algeria. All but 30 were later released, the report said.

April, 1959

April 14

Abba Eban, Israel's Ambassador to the US, forecast failure for Nasser's attempt to establish centralized domination of the Middle East.

The Moroccan Government announced that a Spanish-Moroccan Mixed Commission would be established to examine relations between the two countries. The Commission would sit alternately in Madrid and Rabat.

It was announced in Rabat that the Moroccan Crown Prince Hassan would visit the UAR at the invitation of Field Marshal Abd-al-Hakim Amer.

King Hussein of Jordan said in New York that he would aid his people "in the pursuit of happiness" if the US continued to help Jordan not as charity, but as investment in the future of a free and determined people.

The High Council on Agrarian Reform in Iraq decided to expropriate the lands of persons whose holdings exceeded the maximum permitted under the Agrarian reform law.

The Baghdad Radio stated that the Soviet ship Argun, which the Cairo press alleged was bound for Basra carrying hundreds of Kurds and Soviet arms, was loaded with sugar for the UAR.

An Israel Army spokesman announced that an Israel watchman was killed by Jordanian infiltrators near Ramat Rahel, south of Jerusalem. Israel lodged a complaint with the Israel-Jordan Mixed Armistice Commission.

An Israel military court sentenced to ten years imprisonment an Egyptian infiltrator captured inside Israel territory carrying a submachine gun and notes on Israel troop movements.

The Middle East News Agency reported that a Jordanian patrol and Syrian villagers exchanged fire in southwest Syria.

April 15

Syrian and Israel surveyors met under UN auspices to arrange for demarcation of the border between Israel and Syria.

April, 1959

April 15

Jordanian and Israel investigators cooperated in tracking down the murderer of an Israel night watchman in Jerusalem.

Prime Minister Nehru of India said that India's entire sympathy was with the Algerians in their war for independence from France.

Ferhat Abbas, Premier of the Algerian Provisional Government, told reporters in Karachi, Pakistan, that Pakistani President Ayyoub Khan assured him of Pakistani support for Algerian independence.

The National Liberation Front in Tunis criticized the leaders of African states in the French Community for failing to support the nationalist cause in Algeria.

Czechoslovakia demanded that the arms taken from the Czechoslovakian ship Lidice be sent on to Casablanca; it claimed that the material was for the Moroccan Army and not for Algerian rebels.

An agreement signed in Tunis provided for the continuation of French technical assistance to Tunisia, for 18 months. France agreed to increase its share of the salaries of 1,100 French teachers and 600 technicians and administrators from 15 to 45 percent.

Sir Humphrey Trevelyan, British Ambassador to Iraq, arrived in London for talks with the British Foreign Office.

Great Britain announced a grant in aid to Jordan of two million pounds sterling ($5.6 million) and an interest free loan of 500,000 pounds sterling ($1.4 million).

The Director General of the Petroleum Affairs Office in Saudi Arabia expressed the hope that the Arab oil conference would pave the way for a unified oil policy linking Middle Eastern and Caribbean oil producing countries.

Premier and Foreign Minister Crown Prince Faisal of Saudi Arabia took charge of the Defense Ministry when the Defense Minister resigned.

UN Under Secretary for Special Political Affairs Ralph Bunche left for the UAR and other nations in the area to talk about regional differences.

April, 1959

April 15

The first congress of Iraqi peasant associations opened with about 1,800 Arab and Kurd delegates from all over the country taking part. The ceremony was attended by Iraqi Prime Minister Kassem.

April 16

The first Arab Petroleum Conference and the petroleum exhibition opened in Cairo with the UAR, Lebanon, Saudi Arabia, Kuwait, Qaṭar, Yemen, Libya, Sudan, Morocco and Algeria attending. Venezuela and Iran sent observers; Iraq, Bahrain, Jordan and Tunisia refused the invitation.

President Nasser of the UAR said that Egyptian intelligence uncovered a "Communist master plot" planned by Arab Communists at the Twenty-First Congress of the Soviet Party in Moscow in January, for a "Red Fertile Crescent" federating Iraq, Syria, Jordan, Lebanon and Kuwait, aimed at giving the USSR access to the Persian Gulf, the Gulf of Aqaba and the Indian Ocean.

The UAR Government sponsored Middle East News Agency reported that the UAR had accepted a Libyan request to provide that country with arms, including tanks, anti-aircraft guns and two training planes.

A UAR Army spokesman said that five Iraqi Yazidi tribesmen were killed when they attacked the Khazaa post in northeastern Syria.

It was reported that Awni Khaledi, former Secretary General of the Baghdad Pact, resigned from the Iraqi Foreign Ministry.

Richard P. Hunt, a correspondent for The New York Times, was refused admission into Iraq.

It was reported from Moscow that the Iraq-Soviet Economic and Technical Aid Agreement was officially approved by the two governments, and that the USSR initiated its aid to Iraq with a loan of $55 million.

UN Secretary General Dag Hammarskjold said that he considered it essential that the UN aid program for Arab refugees be continued, and that he was preparing a special report on the issue to be presented to the General Assembly.

April, 1959

April 17

A procession of Iraqi Peace Partisans, in which Kurds were strongly represented, marched through Baghdad. Iraqis carried banners urging peace and friendship with the Soviet Union.

It was reported from Moscow that the Communist Party of Iraq was to be permitted to carry on its activities without hindrance from the Iraq Government, even though political parties were still not legalized.

The British Foreign Office announced that a British airliner, carrying servicemen from London to Hong Kong, was forced to land in Baghdad. The flight had previously been cleared through formal channels.

It was reported from Cairo that the Iraqi Government had asked a Western oil company to construct an $800,000 oil pipeline from the Mosul fields in Iraq to the Persian Gulf.

An Israel fisherman was killed by a Syrian sniper in the Sea of Galilee.

The French Army reported that 1,600 Algerian rebels were killed and 460 captured in a three week offensive south of Oran. French casualties were said to have been about 10 percent of rebel losses.

Cardinal Spellman, Roman Catholic Archbishop of New York, presented King Hussein of Jordan a check for $5,000 to "alleviate the suffering of the poor and homeless in Jordan, regardless of race, color or creed."

Imam Ahmad of Yemen arrived in Rome for medical treatment for a form of arthritis.

April 18

Two explosions in Algiers on the eve of the countrywide municipal elections organized by the French authorities marked the renewal of terrorist activities in Algeria.

Three right wing organizations, the French National Front, the Friends of the Young Nation and the National Student Movement signed tracts in Algiers calling for massive abstentions in the municipal elections to be held on April 19.

April, 1959

April 16

Street crowds in Algiers lynched two Algerians after a grenade carried by one of them accidentally exploded.

The French Army was ordered to stop the mass resettlement of Algerian Moslems; more than a million persons had already been uprooted from their homes.

King Hussein of Jordan said in New York that Jordan would fight on the side of the free world in any world wide clash. The monarch said that Jordan would not hide behind any expressions such as "neutralism."

The Libyan newspaper, al-Libi, criticized the slow pace of the US-Libyan negotiations to amend the 1954 Base Agreement.

An official announcement issued by Premier Abdallah Ibrahim of Morocco on his return from five days of talks in Madrid said that Morocco and Spain agreed to establish a permanent Spanish-Moroccan Commission.

Foreign Minister Sadok Moqaddem of Tunisia lodged a protest with French Ambassador to Tunisia Georges Corse over the artillery shelling of the Tunisian village of Bour Jaber by French forces based in Algeria.

The US State Department announced that the US Government's investment guarantee program had been made applicable for new private American investments in Sudan and Tunisia through the formal exchange of notes between Washington and the respective governments.

Six Army officers and enlisted personnel sentenced up to 20 years in prison on a charge of attempting to overthrow the Sudanese Government in 1957, were released.

The Soviet Union and Sudan agreed to study the possibilities of producing asbestos, cement and fertilizers in Sudan.

The USSR ship Gruziya arrived in the Iraqi port of Basra with a large group of Kurds and their families, returning home after 11 years.

April, 1959

April 18

On leaving the US, King Hussein of Jordan said that he was most satisfied with his discussions with American officials on matters of mutual interest.

The legal adviser to the Saudi Arabian Department of Petroleum and Mineral Affairs, Frank Hendryx, said that a sovereign nation had virtually unlimited legal right to modify unilaterally or to eliminate provisions in existing oil agreements.

A statement issued at the conclusion of the Second Congress of the Iraqi Peace Partisans denounced the UAR for plotting against Iraq and accused the UAR of concentrating troops on Iraq's borders with aggressive intentions.

A communique was signed in Khartoum at the conclusion of the USSR-Sudanese talks on economic and technical cooperation.

April 19

Algerian rebel terrorists killed eight persons, wounded about 80, and kidnapped two during the first day of the municipal elections in Algeria. Almost all were Moslems and many were candidates for local offices.

During the first day of the muncipal elections in Algeria about 95 percent of the registered voters in rural areas went to the polls, but participation in the cities ranged from 33 to 65 percent.

King Hussein of Jordan said in London, where he came for informal talks with Prime Minister Harold Macmillan and Foreign Secretary Selwyn Lloyd, that the Communist danger in the Middle East was not confined to Iraq. The Communists were, according to Hussein, very interested in the Middle East because of its oil, and as "a bridge to further their interests in Africa."

Spain agreed to purchase 12,000 tons of Syrian cotton for $7 million.

A large number of Communists and Kurds were reportedly dismissed from the Syrian military forces.

April, 1959

April 19

Representatives of Arab governments and oil companies attacked the argument of Frank Hendryx, legal adviser to the Saudi Arabian Department of Petroleum and Mineral Affairs, that sovereign nations had virtually unlimited legal rights to unilaterally modify existing oil agreements or to eliminate provisions in them.

It was reported from Jerusalem that the UAR War Prize Court ordered confiscation of the Israel cargoes carried by a West German ship and a Liberian freighter which were detained as they went through the Suez Canal en route from Haifa to the Orient.

Kyrillos VI was enthroned as Patriarch at St. Mark's Cathedral in Cairo, the Mother Church of Coptic Christianity.

April 20

Fayeq al-Samarrai, former Iraqi Ambassador to Cairo, appealed to the UN to aid 40, 000 political prisoners who he said were detained in Iraq.

It was reported from Baghdad that the Iraq Ministry of Foreign Affairs sent a memorandum to the UAR asking it to put an end to the anti-brotherhood behavior of Syrian officials toward Iraqi drivers on the commercial transport transit service between Beirut and Baghdad.

The Iraqi military prosecution demanded the death penalty for 17 officers charged with supporting the Mosul uprising against Premier Kassem's Government.

King Hussein of Jordan in London called upon the US and Britain for a more positive policy toward the Middle East and the countries who were fighting there to preserve their independence.

It was reported from Cairo that Soviet Ambassador to the UAR Yevgeny D. Kiselev handed President Nasser of the UAR a message from Premier Nikita S. Khrushchev at the first meeting between the Ambassador and the President of the UAR since relations between the two countries deteriorated. The nature of the message was not disclosed.

April, 1959

April 20

Derek Martin Riches, new British Ambassador to Libya, presented his credentials to King Idris of Libya.

Libyan Crown Prince Hassan al-Rida al-Sanusi was married in Tobruk, Libya.

The Parliamentary Internal Security Committee of Lebanon recommended that LL100 be deducted from the salary of any Deputy who absented himself from a meeting of the Chamber without excuse.

It was reported from Baghdad that labor unrest and other disturbances had broken out in Iraq.

The right wing Algerian extremists reportedly lost some support in the Algerian municipal elections to liberal candidates, who sought a compromise solution to the Algerian problem.

Crown Prince Moulay Hassan of Morocco arrived in Cairo for a ten day visit at the invitation of Field Marshal Abd-al-Hakim Amer, UAR Vice President and Minister of War.

A five member mission of the International Bank for Reconstruction and Development arrived in Cairo for a months study of the UAR economy.

After several delays, Israel and Syrian surveyors began to measure checkpoints on the Israel-Syrian frontier as the first step in a UN plan to place whitewashed marker barrels along nearly eight miles cf the boundary.

Farm experts from 14 Middle Eastern and South Asian countries attended the opening of a conference in Beirut sponsored by the International Cooperation Administration, to discuss farm projects and training programs in the area.

April 21

French Delegate General to Algeria Paul Delouvrier arrived in Paris. He told a press conference that the municipal elections in Algeria showed a more moderate trend.

April, 1959

April 21

An agreement to release from sequestration four Royal Dutch Shell Oil Company affiliates was signed by the UAR and Britain in Cairo.

Israel's Ambassador to the UN, Abba Eban, conferred with UN Secretary General Dag Hammarskjold at UN headquarters. It was reported that they discussed UAR seizures of cargoes passing through the Suez Canal.

Iraqi Premier al-Kassem welcomed a delegation headed by Premier Ferhat Abbas of the Algerian Provisional Government on its arrival in Baghdad for an official visit.

Two Israel Arabs, found guilty of collecting information on behalf of the Jordanian intelligence, were sentenced in Israel to four and one-half years imprisonment.

The trial of the Mosul anti-Government plotters opened at the Baghdad Supreme Military Tribunal.

April 22

The Peoples Resistance Organization in Lebanon issued a warning to former Lebanese Premier Sami al-Solh not to return to Lebanon from Paris as some reports suggested that he might.

Baghdad newspapers reported a "wave of arrests" of Iraqi army officers on charges of plotting against the Government of Iraq. Among them was Brigadier Shaker Mahmoud Sukr, Deputy Chief of Staff for Operations.

It was reported from Baghdad that the Communist Press was waging a determined attack on the Iraqi Foreign Ministry.

According to the Secretary General of the Baghdad Pact, the possibility of Communist domination in Iraq had put new life into the Pact Secretariat now located in Ankara.

In the text of the Soviet note to the US on West Germany, Russia warned that the atomic arming of Turkey would result in a bigger war menace in the Middle East.

April, 1959

April 22

King Hussein of Jordan conferred with Prime Minister Macmillan in London.

At the close of the first Arab Petroleum Conference, the delegates agreed that the Arabs should have a share of the profits of oil transportation, refining and marketing as well as production. They recommended that special machinery be set up to coordinate at the national level the conservation, production and exploration of petroleum to help maintain stable price levels.

April 23

Viscount Monckton, chairman of the Iraq Petroleum Company, said on his return to London from a 17 day tour of the company's installations that neither the threat of nationalization nor a demand for a change in the profit sharing agreement arose during his discussions with Iraqi leaders.

Ibrahim Kubbah, Iraqi Minister of Economy, said that the Government had agreed with the Khanaqin Oil Company that Iraq would take over the internal distribution of oil.

A committee of three Sudanese Army colonels was formed by Sudan's Supreme Military Council to carry out a complete purge of the civil service.

Two French Army jeeps were blown up by Algerian rebel land mines on a military airfield near Azazga in Kabylia; one officer was killed and an officer and four enlisted men were wounded.

The French Government proclaimed as an official Algerian holiday the anniversary of the uprising of May 13, 1958. It warned against all demonstrations of disunity.

A Jordanian official communique said that a large Syrian force penetrated Jordanian territory near Mafraq and slightly wounded two Jordanian soldiers on patrol duty. The Syrians were said to have left behind two wounded.

April 23

A UAR Army spokesman charged that 18 Jordanian armored cars penetrated two miles into the village of Gharoyah in Syria, killing a policeman and wounding four home guardsmen. He called the clash flagrant, unprovoked aggression.

It was believed by some US observers that the main effort of Soviet strategy was concentrated in the Middle East and that Russia was using the Berlin crisis as a diversion.

The Government of Aden announced that the newspaper al-Nidhal, an organ of the South Arabian League which advocated a union of the Aden Protectorate with the United Arab States, would be banned in Aden.

Dr. Ralph Bunche, Under Secretary for Special Political Affairs of the UN, toured the Israel-Egyptian border and conferred with Lieutenant General E. L. M. Burns, Commander of the UN Emergency Force.

Tunisian President Bourguiba announced that a new Constitution for Tunisia would be promulgated on June 1. He also announced that the price of tobacco had been raised to secure revenue to furnish the Tunisian Army with equipment from Britain, the US and Yugoslavia.

April 24

French President De Gaulle commuted the death sentences of 30 convicted Algerian nationalists.

The Second Conference of the International Federation of Arab Labor Unions opened in Cairo.

Father Badre, Director of Roman Catholic chaplains in the French Army, condemned the torture and summary executions of Moslem rebels in Algeria as gravely tarnishing the honor of the Army and the nation.

French Premier Debre arrived in Oran for a round of conferences with Algerian leaders. He reaffirmed France's determination to crush the Algerian revolt.

April 24

Former French Premier Guy Mollet, leader of the French Socialist Party, denounced plans for a celebration of the first anniversary of the May 13, 1958, uprising in Algeria. He said the movement, which brought President De Gaulle to power, had threatened French unity.

Abd-al-Aziz Ben-Driss, a member of the Moroccan Consultative Assembly, was killed at a political meeting in Rabat.

April 25

The Saudi Arabian Council of Ministers nominated Hafez Wahbah and Abdallah al-Tariqi to serve as members of Aramco's (Arabian American Oil Company) Board of Directors.

Premier Ibrahim of Morocco was expelled from the ruling Istiqlal (Independence) Party following the slaying of Abd-al-Aziz Ben-Driss, a member of the Party's Executive and the National Consultative Assembly. Allal al-Fassi, president of the Istiqlal Party, announced the action in a statement attacking the Premier and the Government for failing to control banditry and disorder.

French military headquarters said that a French patrol killed 32 Algerian rebels in a battle near the Tunisian border. French losses were put at five dead and four wounded.

The delegations of the UAR, Algeria, Lebanon and Morocco to the Yugoslav Trade Union Congress decided to boycott the sessions in protest against the presence of Israel delegates.

President Nasser of the UAR said that the UAR was the only stumbling block in the Middle East for Eastern Communism and Western imperialism.

April 26

A joint communique issued at the conclusion of Algerian Premier Abbas' visit to Iraq said that Iraq gave ID75,000 ($210,000) to the Algerian Provisional Government, and that the remaining installments

April 26

of ID2 million ($5.6 million) allocated in the budget for aid to the Algerian rebels would be paid by October, 1959.

Of the 13,995 municipal councillors elected in the Algerian municipal elections the past seven days, 11,558 were Moslems.

Jordanian Security Forces reportedly clashed in a battle with smugglers allegedly taking food and other goods into Israel.

The Saudi Arabian Government withdrew the citizenship of Omar Haleq, its former alternate delegate to the UN, because of improper conduct.

The Jordanian Government banned the book Strange Lands and Friendly People by US Supreme Court Justice William O. Douglas, for allegedly criticizing the Arab peoples.

Iraqi Minister of Economy Ibrahim Kubbah said that Iraq and the Iraq Petroleum Company (IPC) had agreed to increase the production and exportation of Iraqi oil, leading to a doubling of the amount of production within a period of not more than three years. The Iraq Government had laid down plans for Iraqization of oil companies.

April 27

The Sudanese Government rescinded its suspension of al-Ayyam, Khartoum's leading Arab daily newspaper, which had been shut down in January after it published an article demanding that the proceedings of a secret military trial of some civilians be made public.

Two Arab infiltrators were killed in a clash with an Israel patrol near the Jordanian border south of Beersheba.

The UAR agreed to let a British mission come to Egypt to help implement a financial agreement signed between the two countries on February 28.

The French Cabinet issued a communique outlining progress in pacifying Algeria and demanding that all persons with common sense get behind the De Gaulle policy for Algeria. It declared May 13 as a day of "fraternization and renovation."

April 27

A British Government spokesman reasserted in the House of Commons his Government's opposition to continuing Arab attempts to boycott British firms for dealing with Israel, and said that further representations would be made whenever it seemed that these would be fruitful.

April 28

Two Baghdad newspapers said in editorial comments that Communists should be represented in Iraq Premier al-Kassem's Cabinet.

Part of the funds granted to the UAR by the World Bank would be used to widen and deepen the Suez Canal.

Ferhat Abbas, leader of the Provisional Algerian Government, arrived in Beirut for discussions with Lebanese leaders.

A Sudanese livestock delegation arrived in Beirut for conferences with the Lebanese Ministry of Agriculture.

An Israel Army spokesman announced that Israel jet fighers intercepted four UAR MIG-17's over Israel territory and chased them back over the border.

Libyan King Idris promulgated a law providing for the importation and exportation of goods without duties and restrictions in a number of Libyan ports.

The Algerian rebels warned Tunisia that the French planned to extend their operations against the Algerians to Tunisia next year.

Allen W. Dulles, Director of the US Central Intelligence Agency, was quoted as telling the US Senate Foreign Relations Committee that the situation in Iraq was "the most dangerous in the world today." Mr. Dulles reportedly said that the Communists were close to a "complete takeover," although Premier al-Kassem was not considered a Communist.

April, 1959

April 28

Abd-al-Kader Chanderli, representative in the US of the Algerian Provisional Government, submitted a memorandum to UN Secretary General Dag Hammarskjold appealing for UN intervention to "save one million Algerians" from imminent danger of death, famine or disease.

K. Chadarchi, prominent Iraqi public figure and leader of the National Democratic Party, arrived in Moscow.

April 29

Moulay Merbah, Secretary General of the Algerian National Movement, was arrested in Bonn.

US President Eisenhower indicated that the US policy in the Middle East was to maintain friendly relations with all of the countries in the area.

A manifesto signed by the Central Bureau of the Iraq Communist Party demanded full membership in Iraqi Premier Kassem's Government and called for establishment of a popular front with representatives of other "loyal democratic parties and forces."

The Greek vessel Aegeos, chartered by the Israel Company Netivei Yam, arrived in Elath after going through the Suez Canal.

An economic agreement signed between the Egyptian region and Italy provided for direct purchases by Italy of Egyptian cotton, for technical assistance to Egypt and for measures to be taken by Italy to encourage Italian investments in Egyptian projects.

April 30

Pope John XXIII received King Hussein of Jordan in a 20 minute audience in the Vatican.

Twenty opponents of the Ruler of Upper Aulaqi in Aden had fled into the hills near the border of Yemen.

May, 1959

May 1

Premier al-Kassem of Iraq declared in a May Day speech that he was opposed to political party activity in Iraq at the present time.

It was reported from Washington that US Government officials said that Point Four Programs in Iraq had been slowed down almost to a halt and that American contractors and technicians had been increasingly harassed and threatened during recent months.

Golda Meir, Israel's Foreign Minister, said that Israel still held out its hand in peace to the Arab countries, and that if peace came it would be ready to extend its experiences and know-how to the Arab countries in helping them reclaim their vast uncultivated land areas.

Speaking for the Algerian Provisional Government, Abd-al-Kader Chanderli charged that by favoring the integration of Algeria with France, President De Gaulle had adopted a policy of war. He said there would be no peace until French authorities agreed to negotiate directly with the Algerians.

The distribution of US flour, corn meal and powdered milk to 700,000 needy Egyptians began.

The Omani office in Cairo reported that the British in Muscat and Oman had instituted widespread troop movements to combat the activities of Omani nationalists.

May 2

President Bourguiba of Tunisia announced that all land neglected by its owners would be seized and exploited by the Government as part of a plan to increase agricultural productions.

King Hussein of Jordan returned to Jordan after an eight week world tour.

The Afro-Asian Organization for Economic Cooperation in Cairo stated that the Soviet Union had been excluded from that organization following the decision of the 11 member consultative committee set up in December, 1958.

April, 1959

April 30

President Charles De Gaulle said in an interview, published in a leading newspaper in Oran, that his policy in Algeria was one of integration with France, but that he had not used the term publicly because there had been attempts to impose it on him.

A new power station, operating on gas supplied by the Bahrain Petroleum Company, was opened in Jufair, Bahrain.

It was reported that Dr. Ralph Bunche, Under Secretary for Special Political Affairs of the UN, presented informal proposals by the UAR regarding passage of Israel cargoes through the Suez Canal to Israel Foreign Minister Golda Meir in Jerusalem.

An Iraqi People's Court sentenced to death seven Iraqi officers for participating in the Mosul revolt against the al-Kassem Government.

May, 1959

May 2

French President Charles De Gaulle removed the Deputy Secretary of the Algerian Administration Andre Regard.

According to a report from Ankara 555 Kurdish tribesmen attempting to flee to Turkey were stopped by Iraqi troops.

May 3

The French announced that 46 rebels were killed in the eastern Constantine area; French losses were listed as 14 dead.

The Moroccan Government charged seven persons with the murder of Abd-al-Aziz Ben-Driss, a member of the consultative Assembly.

The Arab News Agency, a British concern sequestrated by the Egyptian Government in 1956, was returned to its owners.

The Israel-Lebanon Mixed Armistice Commission found that infiltrators who attacked a bus in Upper Galilee on April 30 had crossed Lebanese territory from Syria.

May 4

The French Army reported that 2,000 Algerian nationalist soldiers were executed by their commander during a three month period last fall, and that a new purge of those favoring peace was under way in the rebel army.

Muhammad Yazid, Information Minister of the Algerian Provisional Government, warned the West that if they did not persuade France to work out a peace settlement for the Algerian war, the Provisional Government would seek help from the Communists.

Crown Prince Hassan of Morocco said on his return from a visit in Cairo that the West still had great chances in the Arab world, but that it must know how to seize them. He noted a "veritable crusade" against Communism in the UAR.

May, 1959

May 5

A scientific and cultural agreement was signed in Baghdad between Iraq and the Soviet Union.

Colonel Taha Bamirni, commander of the Iraqi civil militia, said that about 300 Kurdish tribesmen, followers of Sheikh Rashid, were opposing Government forces in the mountain area in northeastern Iraq bordering Turkey and Iran. He also charged that they were getting money from the Turks and Iranians.

US Ambassador to Iraq John T. Jernegan arrived in Washington for consultations with the US State Department.

Tawfik al-Medani, Minister of Culture in the Algerian Provisional Government, reported from Cairo that the Algerians were losing some 500 men daily in the struggle against France and that the total dead since the rebellion began in 1954 numbered 750, 000. He noted, however, that the Liberation Army had grown from 20, 000 to 120, 000.

Disturbances raged in Constantine in Algeria. French youths staged an anti-De Gaulle demonstration. Arabs protesting against an attack on their people by 1, 000 French settlers the night before were turned back by police.

Premier Samir al-Rifai of Jordan submitted his resignation, pleading ill health. The King asked Hazza Majali, Minister of Court, to form a new government; he was instructed to maintain the present anti-Communist policy and to seek friendly relations with other Arab states.

US President Eisenhower said that the US was trying to get all the Middle Eastern nations to recognize that they would realize their aspirations more surely in freedom and independence than in an association with the Soviets.

Former King Farouk of Egypt became a citizen of Monaco.

Several incidents between Italian photographers and Yemeni guards protecting the Yemeni Imam's harem were reported when the photographers attempted to obtain pictures of the Imam's three wives and several concubines.

May, 1959

May 6

Three Iraqi ministries—Economics, Development and Communications and Works—were to be eliminated and eight new ministries created.

The Iraqi Ministry of Education announced that it accepted 70 American college scholarships offered by the American Point Four Program, and that under a cultural agreement with the USSR ten Iraqi students would study in Soviet institutions.

A Jordanian Royal Decree listed the members of Premier Hazza Majali's new Cabinet.

The Cairo press of the UAR attacked Jordanian Premier Majali as an agent of British policy.

Abd-al-Kader Chanderli, Algerian rebel spokesman, speaking at a meeting of the Afro-Asian Bloc in the UN, asked that the Algerian issue be laid before the UN General Assembly this year because France had failed to take account of previous Assembly resolutions recommending that the matter be settled by negotiations.

General Maurice Challe, French Military Commander in Algeria, warned the Algerian population against being provoked into blind vengeance by rebel acts of terror. He declared he would not tolerate reprisals from either side.

French authorities released two Italian ships that had been escorted into the port of Bone for cargo checks.

King Muhammad V of Morocco released 40 Spaniards captured during the Ifni fighting in 1957. He said he was freeing them in the hope that a commission now studying Spanish-Moroccan differences could work in the climate of complete serenity and achieve positive results.

A delegation of the UAR Aswan Dam Committee, headed by Minister of Public Works Mousa Arafa, arrived in Moscow.

The first session of the ad hoc Committee on the Peaceful Uses of Outer Space took place. The USSR, Czechoslovakia and Poland officially announced their refusal to take part in its deliberations. India and the UAR did likewise.

May, 1959

May 7

Under a cultural agreement signed in Baghdad between Czechoslovakia and Iraq, Czech teachers would help replace the approximately 400 UAR teachers who resigned their posts in Iraqi schools.

The Iraqi Health Ministry announced that the Government took steps to requisition the Dar al-Salam Hospital and mission of the American Seventh Day Adventists.

The number of Iraqi Ministries was increased by a special law, from 15 to 18.

Iraqi authorities released an Italian airliner after detaining it for 27 hours for flying across Iraq without specific authorization.

French President De Gaulle said in Paris that the Algerian problem would not be resolved by war or by words, but only by an immense effort of human transformation whereby Algerians by their own accord would want to remain forever linked to France. He declared that the pacification of Algeria was in sight.

President Bourguiba of Tunisia said that he intervened several times with French and Algerian rebel officials for cessation of clashes along the Algerian-Tunisian frontier. He warned both sides that Tunisia would oppose any extension of the Algerian conflict to Tunisian soil.

A military mission of Sudan, headed by Brigadier Awwad Abd-al-Rahman, left for Belgrade for an official tour of Yugoslav military installations.

Peace champions from all over Iraq held a mass meeting in Basra.

May 8

Authoritative sources in London told the press that Iraq had requested from Britain enough arms to re-equip its entire army.

The Spanish Embassy in Rabat, Morocco, announced the release of Moroccan prisoners captured during clashes in November, 1957, near Rio de Oro, the Spanish enclave in Morocco.

May, 1959

May 8

King Muhammad V of Morocco reportedly would probably not meet with French President De Gaulle on the Algerian problem.

The Shah of Iran reiterated his country's adherence to the Baghdad Pact, but said that Iran would never grant military bases to any country.

The Ninth Middle Eastern Medical Conference opened in Beirut. The group was addressed by Pierre Jumayil, Lebanese Minister of Health.

Dr. Charles Malik of Lebanon, President of the UN General Assembly, visited a Trade Fair in New York. The Fair included an Israel exhibition.

May 9

The Lebanese Council of Ministers approved a plan to reorganize the Lebanese Foreign Ministry. In part, the plan would restrict diplomatic appointments to highly qualified candidates who must sit for a special examination.

May 10

In a policy statement, Premier Hazza Majali of Jordan said that Jordan had not and did not intend to tie itself to any foreign political or military pact, except for commitments under the Arab League.

Kyrollos VI was crowned as Pope of Alexandria, Egypt, and Patriarch of the Coptic Orthodox Church of 3 million members. Because of a dispute over the manner of election of the new Patriarch, the Church in Ethiopia might refuse to recognize his authority.

May 11

In the first declaration of support for Communist participation in the Government of Iraq, Economy Minister Ibrahim Kubbah said that such participation was dictated by the nature of the July, 1958, revolution and would be a decisive factor in cementing the structure of the Republic.

May, 1959

May 11

Iraqi Premier Kassem said that Iraq's withdrawal from the Baghdad Pact strengthened its relations with Iran and Turkey.

The British Government announced its approval of a substantial sale of arms to Iraq, including tanks and jet planes, to allow Iraq Premier Kassem to maintain an independent line of action which he said was what he wished to do.

UAR President Nasser named Lieutenant General Muhammad Ibrahim Minister of War. Lieutenant General Ali Amer succeeded to the new minister's former post, UAR Army Chief of Staff.

President of the World Bank Eugene R. Black ended talks in Cairo with UAR officials. One of the topics under discussion was a loan for widening the Suez Canal.

Ten member Arab countries of the UN protested to the UN Secretary General that continued Jewish immigration into Israel was detrimental to the rights, property and interests of the Palestine Arabs and directly threatening to the peace and security of the Middle East.

U Thant, Burmese delegate to the UN, said at a farewell dinner for Abba Eban, Israel Delegate to the UN, that only peaceful coexistence between Arabs and Jews could offer any hope of reconciling these two great peoples of the Middle East.

An anti-De Gaulle demonstration broke out in Algiers. Police dispersed a mob of about 500 extreme right wing colons.

Twenty-five graduates of the Lebanese University Teachers' College began a hunger strike in protest against not being given government posts.

May 12

Iraqi Minister of Health, Dr. Muhammad al-Shawwaf, urged Iraqi Premier al-Kassem to include Communists in his Cabinet.

May, 1959

May 13

Algerian Moslems celebrated the first anniversary of the May 13 uprising by massing together on the Forum in Algiers. The large majority of Algerian Europeans boycotted the celebration in accordance with a right wing directive to observe a day of mourning.

It was announced in Khartoum that the Sudanese Government and the Italian state owned Azienda Generale Italiana Petrole (AGIP) would sign a 30 year agreement under which AGIP would acquire oil prospecting rights along the Red Sea. Profits would be equally divided between Sudan and the Company.

Sudan announced that it would protest to the UN against France's proposed nuclear tests in the Sahara.

Jordan accepted an Arab League proposal for an Arab summit conference on the Palestine problem.

Premier Karami of Lebanon said at a press conference that the Government did not intend to seek from the Chamber of Deputies an extension of its special authority to issue legislative decrees. This authority was to expire on June 15, 1959.

The World Peace Council session ended in Stockholm after adopting resolutions on, among other things, the Mideast and the Algerian problem.

May 14

Premier al-Kassem of Iraq told the Iraqi Federation of Industry that he was gradually bringing Iraq toward a democratic regime, that he did not at present encourage the formation of political parties, and that he did not want a certain group to control the country.

Abu-al-Kassem Karim, a Vice Premier and the Minister of War of the Algerian Provisional Government, charged in Tunis that the French Army in Algeria was replacing its equipment with many items from the US. He said that transfer of equipment was contrary to assurances given by the US State Department.

May, 1959

May 12

Iranian Government authorities reported that a group of Kurds had crossed the frontier into Iran and sought asylum after fighting in Iraq.

The UAR and Yugoslav Foreign Ministers reportedly met secretly at Maribor, near the Austrian border, to discuss relations between their two countries.

Six Syrian Communists were jailed on charges of belonging to a secret organization and spreading rumors that caused confusion.

French Premier Debre, in a speech to the French nation, acclaimed the first anniversary of the May 13 uprising in Algeria. The Premier said it represented a break with the past and the beginning of the fraternization of the Algerian European and Moslem populations.

Monsignor Paul Maushi, the Maronite Patriarch, left Beirut for Rome on an official visit to the Vatican.

A spokesman for the Israel delegation to the UN said that immigration into Israel was the concern of Israel alone, just as Israel claimed no rights to influence the immigration laws and policies of the countries of the Arab League.

The American Council for Judaism Philanthropic Fund gave $25, 000 to help Jewish refugees from Rumania and Egypt to settle in Europe instead of Israel. The Council also announced financial assistance to Arab refugees in Jordan.

Jordan complained to the Jordanian-Israel Mixed Armistice Commission that the Israelis displayed a Star of David over buildings on Mount Scopus, a demilitarized zone on the outskirts of Jerusalem.

The US Operations Mission announced that it had offered Morocco $40 million to help finance about half of Morocco's Development Program for 1959.

Israel Premier David Ben-Gurion in an Independence Day address promised that Israel would strive for agreement with its Arab neighbors.

May, 1959

May 14

The US State Department said that there were no restrictions on US military equipment once it was turned over to France. The Department added, however, that US military aid to France in recent years consisted mainly of advanced weapons useful for the defense of NATO, but not for operations in Algeria.

President Nasser of the UAR sent a reply to USSR Premier Khrushchev's letter delivered by the Soviet representative in Cairo on April 20. The contents of Khrushchev's note and Nasser's reply were not disclosed.

It was announced that Jordan would establish a consulate in New York.

May 15

A communique issued by the Algerian Provisional Government in Cairo said that from May 5 to 11 the rebels killed 140 French soldiers, wounded 63, shot down four planes and destroyed a number of combat vehicles.

A World Bank mission arrived in Khartoum to continue discussions with Sudanese officials on an extension of the Roseires Dam project.

A UAR presidential decree provided for the reorganization of the National Union, the only representative body designated in the constitution for both regions of the Republic.

May 16

Basra, Iraq, reportedly had been placed under curfew to curb anti-Soviet agitation.

May 17

President Nasser of the UAR said that Soviet Premier Khrushchev gave him renewed assurances of non-intervention in Arab affairs.

May, 1959

May 17

West Germany and Saudi Arabia reportedly had agreed to raise the status of their diplomatic representation in Bonn and Riyadh to that of embassies.

President Nasser of the UAR proposed to India, Yugoslavia and Indonesia that the three nations meet soon with the UAR to discuss any position taken at the Geneva meeting of the US, Britain, France and the Soviet Union.

The Iraqi-USSR Friendship Society was inaugurated in Baghdad.

May 18

Fifteen persons were arrested following two bomb explosions in a soccer stadium in Beirut.

A three man delegation of Algerian rebels headed by Vice Premier Abu-al-Kassem Karim met with King Muhammad V of Morocco.

In reply to a charge by the American Jewish Congress that William Rountree, Assistant Secretary for Near East and South Asian Affairs in the US Department of State, had condoned Saudi Arabian discrimination against Jews by denying them entry and transit visas, refusing to permit their employment, and by boycotting American Jewish businesses, the State Department said that it would seek improvement in the Arab attitude towards Jews whenever possible, but it saw little hope as long as the Arab-Israel conflict persisted.

An Israel military spokesman said that a Lebanese plane carrying UN Emergency Force soldiers from Egypt to Lebanon on leave was intercepted by Israel fighter planes over the Mediterranean but well within the Lydda airport control area. It was released four hours later.

A Yemen delegation arrived in Aden to discuss mutual problems with the Aden Governor and the Federation of Arab Emirates of the South.

May, 1959

May 20

Abd-al-Kader Chanderli, spokesman for the Algerian Provisional Government, said that Communist China agreed to supply military aid to the Algerian rebels.

A Soviet freighter arrived in Casablanca with a cargo of 1,000 tons of wheat, 100 tons of sugar and 50,000 cans of milk given by the Soviet Red Cross for Algerian refugees in Morocco.

The French Foreign Ministry described as complete nonsense a report broadcast by Radio Tunis earlier in the day that France accepted a UAR proposal that it stop supplying arms to Israel in return for Egypt's cutting off aid to the Algerian rebels.

The Lebanese Parliament requested former Foreign Minister Charles Malik, now President of the General Assembly, to submit a report as to why he visited an Israel exhibit at New York's World Trade Fair on May 8.

It was reported from India that Soviet Premier Khrushchev stated recently that the people of the UAR had no friend more sincere and true than the Soviet Union.

May 21

The Iraqi Government announced that 12 Soviet engineers were employed at the Government owned oil refinery and that 12 more would be hired. It was also announced that the Development Board terminated its contract with the Site Investigation Company, a British firm, on the grounds that its work was provided for in the Soviet-Iraq economic and technical aid agreement.

UN Secretary General Dag Hammarskjold said that there had been many more recent Israel overflights over Arab airspace than of Arab flights over Israel areas. An Israel spokesman declared that the statistical picture was quite incomplete, since Israel did not submit complaints to the Israel-Egypt Mixed Armistice Commission, whereas Egypt did.

A 600 mile telephone link between Tripoli and Benghazi, Libya, was opened.

May, 1959

May 19

A strike in Aden of about 4,000 local employees of the British forces was settled after a pay increase and improved conditions of service were granted to the strikers.

Abd-al-Hafid Boussouf, Minister of Liaison and Communications in the Algerian Provisional Government, charged that the US blocked shipments of arms to Algerian guerrilla forces that certain countries were prepared to give them. The US State Department said they had no idea what the Algerian Minister meant by his charge. The Department stated that American policy was not to ship arms to rebels against a recognized or friendly government, and that US arms supplied to one country could not be shipped to a third country without express approval from Washington.

Algerian rebels were reported to have killed 24 French soldiers in heavy fighting in southeast Algeria.

The French Command said that from May 11 to 17, 861 rebels were put out of action and 59 rallied to the French; French forces suffered 37 dead. An Algerian spokesman in Cairo said that Algerian insurgents killed 439 French troops and wounded 103 (May 12-16).

It was reported from Algiers that eight Algerians under sentence of death for terrorist activities were reprieved by French President De Gaulle, and that the Algerian rebels freed 15 French prisoners.

It was announced in Cairo that a group of alleged Communists would be tried by a military court on a charge of trying to overthrow the UAR Government.

A large Norwegian oil tanker caught fire off the coast of Muscat. The crew was saved.

May 20

The non-Communist National Democratic Party of Iraq declared that it would cease all political activity in response to Premier Kassem's call for an end to such activity.

May, 1959

May 22

It was reported from Cairo that the Danish freighter Inge Toft was being detained at Port Said while a war prize council in Alexandria decided whether to confiscate its cargo of Israel potash, cement, scrap iron and marble.

Seventeen members of an extreme right wing organization in Algeria called Jeune Nation were warned by the Commander of the Military District of Algeria to behave or risk being expelled from Algeria or drafted into the Army.

The US Development Loan Fund announced the signing of an agreement with the Sudanese-American textile firm, John Theodoracopulos Company, Limited, for a $1 million loan to help finance construction and equipment of a textile plant in Khartoum.

The Arabian American Oil Company announced that Sheikh Hafez Wahba, Saudi Arabia's Ambassador at Large to the Arab world, and Sheikh Abdallah Tariqi, Director General of Petroleum and Mineral Affairs, were appointed to the Board of Directors.

An Australian charged that Syrian fighters forced his plane down in Damascus. He was flying from Australia to Paris.

May 23

Premier Manouchechr Eghbal of Iran met with 100 representatives of the Kurds of Iraq and promised that the Iranian Government would help them. The Kurds pledged their loyalty to the Shah of Iran.

An official announcement by the Political Bureau of the Communist Party in Iraq said that in the interests of national unity it would drop its campaign to get its members in Iraq Premier Kassem's Cabinet.

The Premier of Iraq al-Kassem openly rebuked Iraq's Communist Party in a news conference for refusing to end party activity. He declared that he did not encourage political party activity during the present transitional period, and that any group so engaged would be considered as having committed an act of conspiracy against the Government.

May, 1959

May 23

The special Supreme Military Court of Iraq sentenced to death six more officers for participating in the Mosul rebellion. Five other army officers were sentenced to life imprisonment at hard labor.

Representatives of IPC (Iraq Petroleum Company), negotiating with Lebanese officials over oil transit royalties in Beirut, left for London to present Lebanon's latest proposals to high company officials.

The Lebanese Council of Ministers approved a new law dealing with pension, age, discharge and indemnity for government employees.

It was reported from Beirut that Lebanon had begun to deport Arab Communists who allegedly had been operating an international party center in Lebanon. Minister of Interior Raymond Edde told the press that his intention was to stop all infiltration and all activities of Communism.

Cairo press reports said that Egyptian authorities informed Dr. Ralph Bunche, UN Under Secretary for Special Political Affairs, during his recent visit that the UAR would not allow the passage of Israel goods through the canal whatever the flag hoisted on the ships hired by Israel. There was no alternative but to confiscate the ships' cargoes.

An Israel Foreign Ministry spokesman called Egypt's seizure of the cargo of the Danish ship Inge Toft an act of international piracy.

It was reported from Aden that Yemeni troops mutinied and burned a number of houses in the capital city of Sanaa and that 180 soldiers were arrested after Yemeni Crown Prince Saif-al-Islam Muhammad al-Badr quelled the rebellion.

A Jordanian Government spokesman announced that Major General Sadeq Sharaa, Deputy Commander of the Armed Forces, was arrested on suspicion of having been involved in a plot against the safety of the state.

May, 1959

May 24

Several Algerian Moslem and European candidates opened their campaigns for election to the Senate of the French Republic. The candidates lined up into conservative and liberal groupings.

It was reported from Beirut that Baghdad Radio broadcast a warning to Iraqi Communists not to obstruct the course of the Iraq revolution.

An Israel Army spokesman reported that Israel coastal police seized a 75 ton UAR boat off Naharia, within the six mile limit Israel set for its territorial waters. The vessel was en route from Port Said to Lebanon with a cargo of onions and garlic.

May 25

Refugee Kurds from Iraq told the press in Turkey that 6,000 of their tribe were opposing the forces of Premier al-Kassem of Iraq and their own leftist tribesmen in Iraq.

King Muhammad V of Morocco declared that foreign aid was acceptable to Morocco only if it were tendered with respect for Moroccan independence, its liberty of action, and the superior interest of the nation. He said that Morocco would continue its efforts to obtain evacuation of foreign troops and recover the rest of its territory.

US and Libya reached a new agreement on financial assistance. The Libyan Government was to receive funds directly from the US Government instead of through US aid organizations.

The acting Ruler of Kuwait, Sheikh Abdallah Mubarak al-Sabah, arrived in Bahrain to visit the Ruler of the island.

A USSR plan of construction work on the first section of the Aswan Dam and a variant of the dam with an open canal were submitted to the UAR Government in Cairo.

Ahmad Saleh al-Abdi, Military Governor of Iraq, lifted the curfew decreed throughout the country after the July 14, 1958 revolution.

May, 1959

May 26

The Iraqi Foreign Minister Hashem Jawad in what was described as a restatement of foreign policy over Baghdad Radio, said that Iraq aimed at keeping clear of participating in the cold war through nonalignment with any of the existing blocs in the international level.

Israel Foreign Minister Golda Meir said in Buenos Aires that her nation was astounded that the UN was not enforcing free navigation through the Suez Canal, and warned that if the UAR continued to violate international law, Israel would be compelled to change its policy of releasing UAR ships which entered Israel's territorial waters.

The UAR protested to the Mixed Armistice Commission against Israel's piracy in retaining an Egyptian vessel on May 23, and asked for an urgent meeting to investigate the incident.

According to a Cairo governmental source, the World Bank had offered to advance part of a $40 million loan for improving the Suez Canal.

French military headquarters in Algeria said that the rebel chieftain of the Tlemcan region near the Moroccan border surrendered, and that the information he supplied led to the arrest of 40 persons.

Nine African states announced at the UN that they would hold a ministers conference in Monrovia in August to consider the conflict in Algeria.

Authorities arrested 24 leading members of the outlawed Communist Party in Sudan who were accused of working to undermine the security and peace of the country.

A Yemeni diplomat in Cairo, Hassan Ibn-Ibrahim, said that the Yemeni Crown Prince, who held the titles of Foreign and Defense Minister, carried out a major purge of elements trying to sow dissension in the kingdom, and that he announced the formation of a representative council to supervise administrative affairs.

Former Lebanese Foreign Minister Dr. Charles Malik, in a cablegram to the Lebanese Parliament, said that he had attended the World Trade Fair with Mayor Wagner of New York City in his capacity as President

May, 1959

May 26

of the UN General Assembly. On May 20 the Lebanese Government had requested that Dr. Malik explain his attendance at the Fair.

A clash between Moroccan irregulars and the Moroccan Army was reported. The clash, in which several were killed and wounded, reportedly occurred when King Muhammad V arrived in Agadir.

May 27

An Israel Army spokesman announced that a Lebanese military aircraft was intercepted as it was photographing Israel border positions and forced to land at Haifa Airport. Israel protested to the Israel-Lebanon Mixed Armistice Commission.

Two Lebanese, one Jordanian and two Iraqis, charged with establishing an anti-Communist people's front to overthrow the Iraqi regime, were sentenced by a Baghdad military court to prison terms ranging from six months to five years.

Premier Karami of Lebanon said at a press conference that he would like to visit Cairo soon to meet UAR President Nasser.

The French Cabinet approved three bills designed to further Algeria's integration with France. The Assembly would debate the bills in early June.

King Muhammad V of Morocco reportedly would probably meet with French President De Gaulle at the end of July in Paris to discuss the Algerian problem.

A Moroccan Royal Decree forbade all radio transmissions in Morocco, starting January 1, 1960, except that of the state radio.

The US signed an agreement with Tunisia under which the US would lend the Tunisian National Railways $12,400,000 to help purchase diesel powered and trailer passenger coaches.

May, 1959

May 27

The French Army in Algeria announced that its forces crossed into Tunisia after having been attacked by Algerian rebels across the border. The announcement explained that a French patrol in Algeria was fired upon from Tunisia in the area of Djebel Harraba.

May 28

The Afro-Asian Bloc in the UN decided to bring the Algerian conflict before the next General Assembly. A statement made by Muhammad al-Farra of Jordan, current Chairman of the Bloc, reaffirmed the Bandung and Accra Conference declarations supporting Algerian independence and said that a just solution of the problem could only be found through direct negotiations between the French Government and representatives of the Algerian people.

Tunisia declared that French troop movement on May 27 did not impair Franco-Tunisian unity.

Premier al-Majali of Jordan received 30 visiting Americans traveling throughout the Middle East under the auspices of the American Friends of the Middle East.

May 29

The Governing Council of the UN Special Fund approved the first 13 technical aid projects to be undertaken by that body, including the establishment of a pilot plant in Israel to test and demonstrate techniques for utilizing water from ephemeral streams that ran off into the sea, an aerial survey of areas in the UAR scheduled to be developed as new irrigation facilities became available and expansion of the facilities of the Middle East Technical University in Ankara.

Reports from Amman indicated that the Deputy Commander of the Jordanian Armed Forces was at the center of a conspiracy against the Government.

May, 1959

May 29

A roundup of Communists by the Sudanese Government had reportedly been extended, and about 40 alleged Communists were detained.

The Algerian rebels announced in Tunis that the only negotiations with France acceptable to them would be negotiations held on neutral territory.

May 30

Iraqi Premier Kassem said in a three hour interview with five Western correspondents that he did not now consider the Communists a menace. He declared they were working with others for the good of the country, and he felt ready and able to check the Communist Party if ever he deemed it a threat to the rights of the people. He stated that he had no grudge against President Nasser of the UAR, that he hoped for improved friendship with Western countries and wanted most of all to concentrate on the development of his own country.

The Lebanese Government announced that it would not accept the crew of the Lebanese bomber forced down by Israel planes on May 27 unless the plane were also released. The crew was turned over to the Lebanese-Israel Mixed Armistice Commission at Ras Tanura.

The Arab League "Boycott of Israel" office in Alexandria announced that the cargo of the Danish freighter Inge Toft, consisting of potash, cement, scrap brass and marble, was seized as a war prize because it was related to the war effort.

The UAR Government announced that it had decided to stop all barter deals in cotton.

A clash broke out between Brazilian members of the UN Emergency Force and some Arab inhabitants of Port Said. The Brazilians were there to sail for Brazil.

The Iraqi Government denounced the US imposed military aid treaty of 1954, the 1955 agreement on the use by Iraq of US arms and equipment and the economic aid agreement based on the Eisenhower Doctrine.

May, 1959

May 30

The USSR Red Crescent sent another 1,000 tons of wheat, 50 tons of sugar and 50,000 tins of condensed milk as a gift to the Algerian refugees in Morocco.

May 31

The British evacuation of the Royal Air Force base at Habbaniya, Iraq, was completed when 90 British airmen left Iraq.

Twenty Moslems and 12 Europeans were elected to the French Senate by 6,134 grand electors designated by the municipal council in each community throughout Algeria.

The Soviet Ambassador to Iraq conferred with Iraq Premier al-Kassem for two hours in Baghdad.

The Protestant Church of France offered French President De Gaulle its support if the President would make a just and fraternal peace in Algeria.

Sudanese Interior Minister Ahmad Maghoub al-Bahari announced that 15 army officers were arrested after a bogus telegram brought platoons of the Eastern Command to the outskirts of Khartoum.

Crown Prince Moulay Hassan of Morocco flew to Paris to make preliminary arrangements for the July meeting between King Muhammad V of Morocco and French Premier De Gaulle.

The UAR handed over the firms of British Petroleum (Egypt) and Shell Chemicals (Egypt), to the Shell Oil Company.

A Yemeni delegation left Aden after attempts to begin talks on Aden-Yemeni frontier problems failed. The Yemenis refused to sit with Protectorate chiefs who were ministers in the Federal Government because, they stated, such action would be tantamount to Yemen's recognizing the Federation.

June, 1959

June 1

The US Embassy in Baghdad announced that it received a note from the Iraqi Foreign Ministry terminating the military assistance agreement of April 21, 1954, the 1955 supplement and a 1957 economic aid agreement under the Eisenhower Doctrine on the grounds that they conflicted with Iraq's policy of positive neutrality. The note emphasized that this action was not meant as an unfriendly act toward the US.

Baghdad Radio announced that Field Marshal Afif Bizri, former Syrian Army Chief of Staff, was granted political asylum in Iraq.

A French Army spokesman said that during the past week 1,057 Algerian nationalists were killed, wounded or taken prisoner, and that Algerian rebel fighters were surrendering in greater numbers than at any time since the beginning of the rebellion.

Ferhat Abbas, Premier of the Algerian Provisional Government, arrived in Amman where he was greeted by King Hussein of Jordan.

The French Socialist Party condemned the integration of Algeria into France.

A new trade agreement was signed between Morocco and Finland, in Paris. The agreement is valid for one year from June 1, 1959 to May 31, 1961.

Tunisia's new Constitution, patterned on the US model, went into effect.

In a speech to the nation, President Bourguiba of Tunisia said that Tunisia's new Constitution was aimed at preserving the State from excess of power and declared it was in harmony with the realities of the country.

Six persons were hurt and 35 arrested in a suburban clash in Beirut. The clash occurred when Communists, distributing literature, were attacked by members of the Baath Party.

Two members of the ruling Supreme Council of Sudan, Brigadier Abd-al-Rahim Shinana and Brigadier Ahmad Abdallah were arrested as accomplices in a conspiracy.

June, 1959

June 1

A proclamation was issued with the new Tunisian Constitution declaring Tunisia's fidelity to the unity of the Grand Maghreb (Arab North Africa) and cooperation with the African people with a view to building a better future.

June 2

Raymond Edde, the Lebanese Minister of Interior, announced to the press that he would resign from the Lebanese Cabinet about June 22. He stated that he considered his task at an end now that the domestic situation was calm.

Hussein al-Uwaini, Minister of Foreign Affairs, Justice and General Planning in Lebanon, announced that he would leave the Cabinet.

It was reported from Cairo that the captain of the Danish ship *Inge Toft* refused to unload his cargo of Israel cement, potash, marble and scrap brass, as ordered by a UAR war prize court.

June 3

The Lebanese Government and the Iraq Petroleum Company announced that the Company agreed to increase royalty payments from LL360, 000 to LL235, 000 annually on oil passing through pipelines in Lebanon. The Company also agreed to pay an additional lump sum of LL5, 818, 000 in settlement of all past claims.

Premier David Ben-Gurion of Israel said that Egypt's refusal to permit the Danish freighter *Inge Toft* to pass through the Suez Canal was a blow not only to the interests of Israel, but also to the Charter of the UN, the Treaty of Constantinople and the decisions of the UN Security Council.

A shakeup of the UAR diplomatic corps, affecting 21 ambassadors and 159 other officials, was reported. Details were not disclosed.

June, 1959

June 3

The UAR proposed at a meeting of the International Labor Conference in Geneva that a study be made of undesirable mass migratory movements.

French President Charles De Gaulle said that whether it was wanted or not, democracy now existed in Algeria. He declared that present difficulties did not prevent free elections, and that the elections were proof of the Moslem accession to political equality, equality of rights and finally to establishment of democracy in Algeria.

Sudanese authorities said that Muhammad Ahmad al-Maradi, Minister of Local Government in the first Cabinet of former Premier Ismail al-Azhari, was put under house arrest.

Syria reportedly planned to construct a huge dam on the Euphrates River in northern Syria. Costs were estimated at $140 to $170 million, according to the report.

French employees of the State Bank of Morocco went on strike to enforce their demand for guarantees of their future status after the Moroccanization of the Bank on July 1.

June 4

Premier al-Kassem of Iraq announced that Iraq would withdraw from the sterling currency area in the near future.

French Premier Michel Debre, in a speech before the French National Assembly, warned that unless France received the complete understanding of its allies on the Algerian problem, it might be forced to reconsider its participation in NATO and other Western alliances.

The French Government granted an oil exploration permit covering 8, 000 square miles of the Sahara Desert in eastern Algeria to Esso Saharienne, owned 50 percent by Standard Oil of New Jersey and 50 percent by French interests.

The Sudanese Government banned the Cairo newspaper, *al-Akhbar*, for allegedly misquoting the Sudanese Minister of Information as saying that there was a Communist plot to overthrow the Sudanese regime.

June, 1959

June 4

UN Secretary General Dag Hammarskjold said he hoped the dispute over seizure by the UAR of Israel cargoes in the Suez Canal could be settled as a legal and not a political issue.

Israel Premier David Ben-Gurion reportedly conferred with the Soviet Ambassador to Israel on the right of unrestricted navigation through the Suez Canal and requested Soviet support for Israel's position.

One Israel soldier was killed and five were wounded when their vehicle was blown up by a mine at Nitzana, near the Egyptian border.

Premier Karami of Lebanon signed a new transit agreement with the Iraq Petroleum Company, which would pay Lebanon about three and a half times as much in royalties annually as it did in the past.

Greek Catholic Archbishop George Hakim, spiritual head of 20, 000 Christian Arabs in Israel, said that many thousands of Arab refugees in Lebanon and Jordan, as well as in Europe, were ready to give up immediately any claims to abandoned property in Israel if they were compensated in accordance with the 1948 value of the property.

June 5

An Israel Foreign Ministry spokesman was reported to have told the press that Israel would not agree to a court test of its right to navigation through the Suez Canal, a right, according to the report, which had already been established by the UN.

June 6

Jordan notified the UN of the tense situation on its borders after Syria cut all road and rail transport between the two countries.

Hussein Ibn-Ahmad al-Habili, Minister of Interior in the Aden Federation, said in a broadcast that the Federation did not need Yemeni recognition.

June, 1959

June 6

Premier Karami of Lebanon left Beirut for Cairo to sign an economic agreement between Lebanon and the UAR.

The Moroccan Government reportedly had decided to speed up the Moroccanization of the state radio.

Egypt handed over to the Shell Company the Shell Company of Egypt (Marketing).

An official Israel report said that Israel jet planes drove off four UAR MIG-17s in an encounter over the Negev Desert.

June 7

Prime Minister David Ben-Gurion of Israel said that Israel would agree to an arms embargo in the Middle East, provided equality and security were assured.

The Egyptian Air Force said that two Israel planes violated UAR airspace over Sinai and were engaged by an Egyptian aerial patrol.

An agreement clarifying the economic relations between Lebanon and the UAR, particularly the Syrian region, was signed in Cairo.

The Lower House of the Jordanian Parliament voted 49-0-1 confidence in Premier Hazza al-Majali's new Government

It was reported from Damascus that the UAR protested alleged Turkish violations of Syrian airspace.

June 8

A Yemeni spokesman in Cairo announced that Yemen's Director of Public Security, Qadi Yahya al-Amari, was arrested and charged with being behind the army disturbance last month.

June, 1959

June 8

UAR Ambassador to Sudan Saif-al-Yazal Khalifah delivered a note to the Sudanese Government expressing Cairo's readiness to resume talks with Sudan over the distribution of Nile waters.

Syrian authorities reported from Damascus that ten Turks were arrested by UAR security forces in the Kamishli District in northeastern Syria.

The Israel-Egypt Mixed Armistice Commission opened an inquiry into the Israel-Egypt air clash of June 6.

Polling to choose local committees of the Egyptian National Union Party in preparation for the election of an Egyptian Parliament began.

Jordanian Air Force planes rescued a Saudi Arabian airliner that made a forced landing 50 miles east of Amman with 36 passengers aboard.

June 9

An Israel Government spokesman announced that a Lebanese reconnaissance plane, forced to land at Haifa while allegedly photographing Israel sites, was returned to Lebanon as a gesture of Israel recognition of Lebanon's positive behavior in the past.

Algerian rebels released three French civilian prisoners, two of them women.

June 10

Baghdad Radio announced that a special military court sentenced four army officers to death and five others to life imprisonment for participating in the Mosul revolt in March.

A 23 year old Moslem was shot to death in Setif about the time his sister-in-law, Madame Rebiha Khebtani, one of the first Moslem women Deputies from Algeria, was speaking in the French National Assembly in support of French President De Gaulle's program for Algeria.

June, 1959

June 10

The French Army announced that two camel caravans of arms of the Algerian rebels were captured by French air commandos in the Sahara.

The 21 member Afro-Asian Bloc in the UN, in a letter to the Security Council President, criticized French excesses in Algeria, and the entire Algerian situation as a threat to international peace.

UAR Minister of State Ali Sabri declared that Israel cargoes would not be permitted transit through the Suez Canal regardless of any action taken by the UN, the World Court or the Big Powers.

Premier Karami of Lebanon told a press conference that the question of enlarging the present Government had not been considered because all its time was taken up with the preparation of legislative decrees under its extraordinary powers.

June 11

The French National Assembly, by a vote of 466-57, approved the first measures to integrate Algeria with France. It decided that the Algerian budget, formerly adopted by the Algerian Assembly, should be voted by the French Parliament and that French and Algerian money should be legal tender in both areas. Opposition to the measures came from the Socialists and Communists in the Assembly.

The French Army announced that the two large camel caravans it intercepted on June 10 were carrying munitions from southeastern Morocco for the Algerian rebels.

King Muhammad V of Morocco visited the troubled areas of the Rif Mountains. He was cheered in the port of Alhucemas.

President Bourguiba of Tunisia praised the US for its economic assistance to Tunisia, saying that it was given with no conditions imposed.

The UAR announced that it would participate in the activities of the World Refugee Year.

June, 1959

June 12

Speaking at a news conference on the final day of a week long visit to Yugoslavia, Premier Ferhat Abbas of the Algerian Provisional Government called for direct peace talks with France in Switzerland, Yugoslavia or another neutral country.

The French Government declared that it appropriated funds necessary to care for Algerians who have taken refuge in Tunisia and Morocco in consequence of the happenings in Algeria, and that it needed no outside aid to care for French nationals.

It was announced that the US labor organization AFL-CIO had donated $2, 500 for aid to the Algerian refugees.

Esso Standard Oil Company of Libya announced that it had brought in a wildcat oil well producing 17, 000 barrels a day. The well was 100 miles from the Mediterranean and 200 miles south of Benghazi.

Monsignor Paul Maushi, the Maronite Patriarch of Lebanon, was awarded the Pallium by Pope John XXIII at a ceremony in the Vatican.

June 13

An Iraqi Education Ministry Spokesman said that the US Government was making a gift to the ministry of books and equipment from the US Information Agency office in Baghdad which had been closed since the revolution in July, 1958.

The Lebanese Council of Ministers completed the legislative decree for reorganizing the governmental administration and referred them to the Chamber of Deputies.

The Tunisian Government announced an influx of 1, 200 new refugees from Algeria. Muhammad Masmoudi, Tunisia's Secretary of State for Information, declared that he found the French statement of June 12 on the Algerian refugees astonishing because it suggested no hope for peace in Algeria.

June, 1959

June 14

Iraq ordered a French bank, Banque Nationale pour le Commerce et l'Industrie (Afrique), to cease activity.

The UAR Government ordered 15 to 30 percent reductions in the retail prices of 450 items, including shoes, wearing apparel, kerosene and bottled gas for cooking stoves.

President Nasser of the UAR announced that persons seeking political office would no longer be screened.

June 15

A clash reportedly took place between farmers and townsmen outside the Iraqi Defense Ministry in Baghdad.

Premier Abdallah Ibrahim of Morocco arrived in Cairo for an official visit at the invitation of the UAR Government.

Dr. Subandrio, Indonesian Foreign Minister, met President Nasser of the UAR and Dr. Fawzi, UAR Foreign Minister, after his arrival in Cairo for a one day visit. He came to discuss world problems that affected the governments of uncommitted nations.

Cuban Premier Fidel Castro's envoy, Ernesto (Che) Guevara, arrived in Cairo together with three others to talk with President Nasser on strengthening the two countries' relations and to study Egyptian land reform.

In a report submitted to the UN General Assembly, UN Secretary General Dag Hammarskjold recommended the continuation of the UN Relief and Works Agency pending, as expressed by the General Assembly, the reintegration of the refugees into the economic life of the Near East, either by repatriation or resettlement.

June 15

Preliminary talks began between the Jordanian Government and John Noble, of the American Trans-Arabian Pipeline Company (Tapline), on amending the company's agreement with Jordan with a view to increasing transit royalties.

The President of the Syrian Executive Council announced that the state owned refinery near Homs, built by the Czechoslovakian Techno-Export Company, had been completed 15 days ahead of schedule.

June 16

French Premier Michel Debre told the Senate that the French Government would publish a list of private concerns helping the Algerian rebels.

The 27th annual Arab Medical Conference opened in Damascus with about 1,500 physicians in attendance.

A spokesman for the Imam of Yemen dismissed reports that the Yemen Army had seized control of the Yemeni capital of Taizz and the port of Hodeida.

The Resolutions Committee of the International Labor Organization's Annual Assembly, meeting in Geneva, rejected 170-62 a UAR resolution aimed at stopping the flow of Jewish emigrants from Eastern Europe to Israel.

Sheikh Fahd al-Salem al-Sabah, brother of the Ruler of Kuwait, died of a heart attack in Saudi Arabia after having made courtesy visits to that state and the Trucial Sheikhdoms.

June 17

The Ruler of Bahrain, Sheikh Salman Ibn-Hamad al-Khalifah, collapsed in his palace from a heart attack.

The Beretta arms manufacturing company of Italy denied a French charge that it had supplied weapons to Algerian insurgents.

June 17

The Swiss Bank Corporation expressed astonishment at being accused of having received funds collected in France for the Algerian rebels.

The Government of the UAR detained the 4,500 ton Liberian register freighter Nord at the entrance to the Suez Canal on the suspicion that it carried a cargo originating in Israel.

The UN Food and Agriculture Organization announced that it would undertake a pilot project in drainage practices in the UAR at a cost of $300,000 and an aerial soil survey which was estimated at $265,000.

Lebanon signed an economic agreement with the UAR, revising customs and export charges, and Syrian import facilities.

June 18

President Habib Bourguiba of Tunisia said that the status of the French naval base at Bizerta must be defined in terms consonant with Tunisian sovereignty. He declared that the presence of French troops at Bizerta was against the will of the Tunisian Government.

King Hussein of Jordan left the military hospital in Amman after a medical check for a complaint of sinusitis. The results showed a satisfactory improvement.

The UAR celebrated the third anniversary of the evacuation of British troops from Egypt.

The Director General of Pilgrimage announced in Saudi Arabia a total of 557,801 made the pilgrimage to Mecca this year.

UN Secretary General Dag Hammarskjold was undecided as to whether to make his scheduled trip to Cairo to try to settle disputes over the UAR seizure of Israel cargoes.

The Liberian registered freighter Nord, detained for 24 hours on suspicion of carrying Israel cargo, was permitted to pass through the Suez Canal.

June 18

The Bureau of the Imamate of Oman announced that Imam Ghaleb Ibn-Ali would arrive in Cairo, by invitation of UAR President Nasser, to discuss with him the Oman issue and continued British aggression in Oman.

June 19

The French Army announced the surrender of Youssef Smail, regional rebel leader in the Macarasaida area of eastern Algeria. The statement declared that Smail sent a letter to his troops recalling French President De Gaulle's offer of a peace of the brave.

The French Ministry of Interior ordered the seizure of a book accusing police officials of torturing Algerian rebel suspects arrested in Paris.

Four hundred persons escaped to safety after a violent explosion set fire to a six floor block of apartments and stores in an Algiers suburb.

In Rome, the UN Food and Agricultural Organization Council deferred official action on a draft agreement between the Arab League and the FAO.

June 20

The US offered to aid the Kingdom of Yemen in the building of an internal road linking Taizz with Sanaa.

June 21

A young Algerian threw a grenade into a crowded cafe in Algeria; 16 persons were injured, three seriously.

Dr. Ibrahim Kubbah, Minister of Economy in Iraq, announced that Poland had offered to buy crude oil from Iraq and that a Polish delegation was expected in Baghdad to discuss the deal.

Amir Muhammad Ibn-Saud, son of King Saud of Saudi Arabia, was appointed by Royal Decree as the Chief of the Royal Cabinet.

June 21

A Phalange candidate, Dr. Basile Abboud, won the first by-election since the civil strife in Lebanon in 1958, defeating ex-President Chamoun's candidate.

Nine Turks were arrested while crossing into Syrian territory.

June 22

A joint communique issued by the British and Iraq Governments announced the Iraqi Republic's decision to terminate its membership in the sterling area and to vary the backing of the Iraqi currency and the Iraqi foreign balances. The withdrawal was to take effect as of June 23, 1959.

An Iraqi Government spokesman denied an Egyptian newspaper report that Iraqi Premier al-Kassem had foiled a Communist plot.

The Jordanian Government approved a law providing for the establishment of a court to try persons accused of plotting against or disturbing the security of the State.

The International Confederation of Free Trade Unions protested against the continued detention by the French of an Algerian Trade Union leader.

An attempt by French leftists to arouse public opinion against the fighting in Algeria drew a warning from the French Government that it would not tolerate any defense of rebellion or attack on the French Army.

President Nasser of the UAR decreed the formation of a Supreme Planning Committee for Palestine, to be headed by Field Marshal Abd-al-Hakim Amer, the UAR's Vice President and War Minister, and to draft UAR policy regarding the Palestine problem.

After reaching agreement at a meeting of the Israel-Jordan Mixed Armistice Commission, Israel and Jordan started a joint campaign to fight a locust invasion.

June, 1959

June 22

It was officially announced in Cairo that 40 Arab experts would leave for Yemen to direct various development plans, including supervision of the issue of currency and the organization of customs, trade and social welfare affairs.

Peace in Algeria Fortnight started in France. In the course of these two weeks there would be meetings, rallies and forums to demand peace negotiations with the Algerian Provisional Government.

June 23

Consequential to Iraq's withdrawal from the sterling area, the Bank of England issued an exchange control notice to give administrative affect to the removal of Iraq from the list of schedule territories.

A French Army communique stated that 534 Algerian rebels were killed and 269 captured during the past week. French losses were put at 39 dead.

Seven Algerians, apparently members of the rebel National Liberation Front, were massacred in a shantytown on the outskirts of Lyons, France, by members of the rival Algerian National Movement.

UN Secretary General Dag Hammarskjold was to arrive in Cairo on July 1 in an attempt to settle the Israel cargo dispute. The UAR had indicated that there was no possibility of the release of the cargo aboard the Danish freighter, Inge Toft, which was stopped May 21.

The leader of the conservative Independence (Istiqlal) Party in Morocco announced that the problem of American, French and Spanish troops still occupying the Moroccan soil should be brought up before the UN if negotiations on their evacuation brought no results.

A cultural agreement between Lebanon and Turkey was signed.

A cultural agreement which provided for an exchange of cultural missions, teachers, students, books and films was signed in Cairo by UAR Foreign Minister Fawzi and Prime Minister Ibrahim of Morocco.

June, 1959

June 23

It was revealed in Cairo that six members of the Arab League—Jordan, Lebanon, Saudi Arabia, Sudan, the UAR and Yemen—had arranged an extraordinary meeting of their foreign ministers to consider the problem of Israel and the Suez, Jewish immigration and other questions.

June 24

The Iraqi Communist Party newspaper said that official telegrams had been sent from Baghdad allegedly ordering the arrest of Communists and the leaders of democratic organizations throughout Iraq.

The UAR accepted the USSR plan for the Aswan High Dam which would provide for an open channel instead of seven tunnels to lead water from the dam.

Emperor Haile Selassie of Ethiopia arrived in Cairo for an official visit.

During the fighting which took place five miles from Bone, the French forces killed 31 Algerian rebels and took 16 prisoners. Six Frenchmen were killed.

The Moroccan Minister of Economy announced that the US had agreed to grant to Morocco $40 million in the form of a long term, low interest loan to be spent on irrigation, road building and modernization of agriculture.

A law providing for censorship of all nonstate radio broadcasts in Morocco was scheduled to go into effect June 25, 1959.

Irrigation Minister of Sudan Brigadier Ahmad Abdallah Hamad was arrested because of evidence brought out at the court martial trying former cabinet Ministers Brigadier Abd-al-Rahim Shennan and Brigadier Mohi-ad-Din Ahmad Abdallah.

Led by the Jordanian Royal Cabinet Chief Bahjat al-Talhouni, a three man Jordanian delegation visited Saudi Arabia on a goodwill mission.

A Jordanian delegation consisting of three ministers left Amman for Saudi Arabia, Kuwait and Sudan with messages from Jordanian King

June, 1959

June 24

Hussein to Saudi Arabian King Saud, Sheikh Abdallah al-Salim al-Sabah, Ruler of Kuwait and Lieutenant General Ibrahim Abboud of Sudan, in an attempt to forget feuds, clear the Arab atmosphere, give priority to Arab issues requiring urgent attention, unite the Arabs, study UN Secretary General Hammarskjold's report and prepare Arab countries for the next meeting of the UN General Assembly by holding contacts with friendly supporters of the Arab cause.

June 25

The Jordanian delegation of three ministers left Riyadh, Saudi Arabia, for Kuwait, after having had an audience with King Saud and Premier Faisal of Saudi Arabia.

Colonel Fadel Abbas Mahdawi, President of the Iraqi People's Court, said during the trial of 21 Iraqi Army officers and civilians on charges of complicity in the Mosul uprising, that the re-equipment of the Army with the most modern arms, including nuclear weapons, was completed.

Premier Abd-al-Karim al-Kassem of Iraq granted an amnesty to all those who indulged in conflict which endangered the security and order of the country, if they returned to their homes before July 31.

A Mexican mission arrived in Beirut on its tour of oil producing and oil transit countries in the Middle East.

A new financial agreement between Lebanon and France, replacing the 1948 agreement, was signed in Beirut. It guaranteed the exchange rate of Lebanon's franc assets until they were liquidated and provided for tax exemption of French concessionary companies.

The Phillips Petroleum Company and its French partners were awarded a second exploration permit in Algeria.

The Moroccan Government censorship of commercial radio news broadcasting went into effect, in accordance with the law of June 24 providing for supervision of all nonstate radio transmissions.

June, 1959

June 25

The Premier of the Nationalist Provisional Government of the Algerian Republic flew to Cairo for a major policy meeting of the Algerian Ministers in exile to determine the Nationalist position on the prospective meeting of French President Charles De Gaulle and King Muhammad V of Morocco in August.

Walter N. Walmsley, Jr., was appointed to succeed G. Lewis Jones as US Ambassador to Tunisia.

The Egyptian War Prize Commission upheld the seizure by the UAR of an Israel cargo of phosphates and cements from the Liberian ship Capetan Manolis at Port Said in March. The Court declared the cargo was stolen property because a state of war with Israel still existed.

June 26

It was reported from Baghdad that Iraqi Premier Kassem curbed the Popular Resistance forces on the grounds that the nation was secure and had no immediate need of such forces. The Resistance forces were a pro-Communist militia.

The editor of the weekly French newspaper L'Express, a persistent critic of French policy in Algeria, was attacked by members of a right wing extremist veterans group at Lyons.

Four left of center French Senators criticized French Government bills adopted by the Assembly to start the process of integration of Algeria and France.

June 27

A commercial attache of the Japanese Embassy in Cairo ended a two week visit to Yemen where he discussed methods of strengthening commercial relations between Yemen and Japan.

June, 1959

June 27

The Industrial Health Training Course, under the joint auspices of the UAR and World Health Organization (WHO), opened at Alexandria with 27 physicians, engineers and chemists from seven countries of the Eastern Mediterranean participating.

The Maronite Patriarch, Monsignor Paul Maushi, expressed sympathy for the Algerian cause when he received Sayyed Maluloud Boukarmouh, the Representative of the Algerian Provisional Government in Lebanon, and Sayyed Muhammad al-Ghasiri, its Representative in Damascus.

After a three month boycott, Iraq's Charge d'Affaires in Cairo indicated that Iraq would send a representative to the coming foreign ministers meeting of the Arab League.

June 28

The UAR President Nasser signed a decree approving final plans for the Soviet backed Aswan High Dam project.

The Jordanian Government announced that 14 Communists were arrested in a police raid in Ramallah.

Jordan's Grand Mufti Sheikh Abdallah Kalaili had issued an appeal to all Moslems to assist the Algerian insurgents by supplying them with men and money for their fight against France.

An armed clash between two Lebanese tribes on the Syrian border resulted in two persons being killed and 12 others wounded.

Counterfeit notes and checks in the amount of $100,000 were confiscated from two Lebanese who were trying to smuggle them to Khartoum.

June 29

It was reported from Baghdad that the Communist, National Democratic and Kurdish Democratic Parties had formed a United National Front. A charter signed by 163 persons, including trade union officials and the editors and proprietors of 13 newspapers and magazines was sent to Iraqi Premier al-Kassem to force him to permit continued political party activity in Iraq.

June, 1959

June 30

About 700 Algerians who had demanded treatment as political detainees rather than as criminals ended a two week hunger strike.

The Italian and Saudi Arabian Foreign Ministries were to raise their respective diplomatic missions from the rank of legations to that of embassies.

An official Cairo announcement said President Nasser of the UAR had approved the USSR project for the first section of the Aswan Dam earlier endorsed by UAR experts.

June, 1959

June 29

George V. Allen, Director of the US Information Agency, assured France that President De Gaulle had the wholehearted support of the US in his efforts to find an equitable and liberal solution to Algeria.

It was reported from Amman that Jordanian security forces arrested nine Communists, including Khaled Ali al-Said of Jenin, who had been sentenced to life imprisonment *in absentia* for organizing armed bands.

A Saudi Arabian delegation attended the meeting of the Desert Locust Control Committee of the UN Food and Agriculture Organization in Rome.

A joint communique issued at the end of Ethiopian Emperor Haile Selassie's visit to Cairo said that special attention was paid to economic and cultural relations between Ethiopia and the UAR during this visit and that another meeting was set for August to discuss a trade and payments agreement.

Yugoslavia and Sudan signed a cultural cooperation agreement.

The US Development Loan Fund signed an agreement with the Government of Libya for a $5 million loan for electric power generating and transmission facilities to serve Tripoli and the surrounding area.

June 30

The Ministry of Economics of Iraq announced that the concession granted to the Khanaqin Oil Company for the distribution of oil on behalf of the Iraqi Government had ended.

UAR President Nasser accused Israel of aggressive actions in trying to send ships through the Suez Canal. He said that the UAR could not allow vessels under Israel charter or flying the Israel flag to use the Canal while a state of war existed between the two countries.

UN Secretary General Hammarskjold arrived in Cairo on a two day visit.

French authorities ended the military deferment of a young European right wing agitator in Algiers who had been critical of French President De Gaulle.

July, 1959

July 1

UN Secretary General Dag Hammarskjold conferred in Cairo with President Nasser about the UAR's refusal to permit Israel commerce to go through the Suez Canal.

UN Secretary General Dag Hammarskjold reportedly proposed to Nasser that the International Court of Justice decide whether the Danish freighter *Inge Toft* should be allowed to pass through the Suez Canal.

King Muhammad V of Morocco officially opened the Bank of Morocco which would issue currency, provide credit for other banks, and handle foreign exchange and monetary transfer. The opening of the bank was hailed as the first step in freeing the country's economy from French and other foreign banking interests.

Under a recent agreement with France, Moroccan troops replaced French soldiers guarding US bases in Morocco.

A Moroccan organization replaced the French body charged with recruiting local labor for the US bases in Morocco; this replacement was considered a step toward solving the base problem between the US and Morocco.

The US Embassy in Cairo disclosed that the US and the UAR signed an agreement on technical assistance unofficially estimated at $8 million. This was the first such agreement to be concluded since US aid to Egypt was broken off during the Suez Crisis in 1956.

Radio Cairo stated that President Nasser would distribute two million *feddans* of new agricultural land to farmers during the next ten years. The land would be made available after the erection of the Aswan High Dam.

The duty on practically all important items in Sudan was increased, on the average, between 25 and 40 percent *ad valorem*.

The twenty-nine Afro-Asian states agreed unanimously on the tentative text of a letter requesting UN Secretary General Hammarskjold to place the question of Algeria on the agenda of the next UN General Assembly session.

July, 1959

July 1

Two Algerian rebel chiefs died before a French firing squad in Oran.

The Lebanese Cabinet rejected the report of Dag Hammarskjold, Secretary General of the UN, on the future of the Palestinian refugees. The Cabinet endorsed the idea of a meeting of foreign ministers of Arab States to discuss the report.

The National United Front, comprising the Communist National Democratic and United Kurd Democratic Parties, as well as a number of mass public organizations, was established in Iraq.

The Iraqi Minister of Economics announced the closure on June 30 of the marketing service of the UK Khanaqin Oil Company. Iraqi oil products were now to be marketed in the country by the General Oil Board.

July 2

The Iraqi Ministry of Economy announced that Iraq and Czechoslovakia agreed to exchange 5,500 tons of Iraqi dates for about 150 Czech cars.

In an interview with the Cairo newspaper al-Ahram, President Nasser of the UAR announced that a period of radical change in social and economic life was about to begin in the UAR.

The UAR Minister of Education arrived in Belgrade, Yugoslavia, for talks on cultural cooperation.

The US State Department announced the signing of a $40 million loan agreement to finance Morocco's economic development program.

Premier Hazza Majali of Jordan officially announced cancellation of all old identity cards and ordered all government departments to accept only the new cards.

UN Secretary General Dag Hammarskjold ended his talks with UAR officials with no evidence of progress in resolving the dispute over Israel shipping in the Suez Canal.

July, 1959

July 2

The US agreed to resume technical cooperation with Egypt and signed two agreements on aid for the UAR totaling $291,300 for civil aviation and road development.

July 3

The International Atomic Energy Agency decided to grant technical assistance of $8.4 million to the UAR.

A Tunisian delegation arrived in Rome for a two week tour of Italian industry and for trade talks.

Israel officials considered more forceful steps to obtain the free passage of Israel cargoes through the Suez Canal should the UN Secretary General's intervention in the Israel-UAR dispute fail to produce a solution.

July 4

Twenty-five soldiers in a column of Moslem and French troops were killed in a rebel ambush 50 miles southwest of Algiers.

A military spokesman for the General Secretariat of Algerian Affairs said that the armed rebellion in Algeria was back to its beginnings in 1954.

An official UAR decree made the Arabic language obligatory for all official and commercial correspondence in the UAR. This applied to foreign as well as to domestic firms.

In answer to the recent French decision to block Morocco's access to the Franc Zone foreign currency pool, the Moroccan Government established control over all capital transfers with other countries in the Franc Zone. The new measures would not apply to Tangier.

July, 1959

July 5

Premier Kassem of Iraq told the Communists to stop their attempts to form a popular front with other left wing groups. At the same time he placed the Popular Resistance Forces, a Communist dominated militia organization, under direct army control.

Yemen charged that British planes bombed the Baida area of Yemen and that British land forces launched a two and one-half hour battle on al-Daleh on July 3.

Neither British Air Ministry nor the British War Office had information on the reported attacks on the Baida area in Yemen, on July 3.

French forces searched the hills southwest of Algiers where a French military convoy was ambushed on July 3.

It was reported that Georges Aigrot, Mayor of the Algerian village Paul-Robert was killed by nationalist insurgents at his home.

King Muhammad V of Morocco left on a six to eight week rest tour of Europe.

Raymond Edde, the Minister of Interior in Lebanon, promised protection for former Premier Sami al-Solh who returned from exile in France.

July 6

Lebanon's first television company went into operation on two channels—one in Arabic and the other in English and French.

Iraqi Premier Kassem decreed a 15 percent decrease in all prison sentences, effective July 14, as part of the celebration of the first anniversary of the 1958 revolution. He also decreed half a month's pay, together with cost of living allowances, to all government officials, to be paid in the new currency that would be issued on July 14.

July 7

According to figures compiled from official French sources, the number killed in the Algerian revolt reached 114,500.

July, 1959

July 7

A Jordanian Royal Decree dismissed 18 high army officers, including Major General Sadeq al-Shar. They were brought before a special tribunal and charged with plotting against the State.

July 8

A trade and payments agreement between Iraq and the Democratic Republic of Vietnam was signed in Baghdad.

Elections were held throughout the UAR to choose about 40,000 delegates to the local councils of the government sponsored National Union, the only political party in the country. Scattered violence was reported. One man was killed. By holding these local elections, President Nasser launched a school for democracy experiment.

Morocco inaugurated the opening of the annual three day Youth Festival in Casablanca.

Lieutenant General E. L. M. Burns, Commander of the UN Emergency Force, presented the UNEF Medal to members of the Indian contingent serving with the Force in the Gaza Strip.

July 9

The Government of Ghana decided to give de facto recognition to the rebel Provisional Algerian Government.

Ninety Arab students from Turkish universities arrived in the UAR for a visit.

The Jordanian Education Ministry banned Indian Prime Minister Nehru's book, Glimpses into World History.

At a meeting of the Executive Council of the French Community, France announced its intention of conducting atomic tests in the Sahara.

July 10

Ibrahim Sabri, new UAR Ambassador to West Germany, arrived in Bonn.

July, 1959

July 10

Nuclear aid for the UAR, Thailand and Indonesia worth nearly $250,000 was approved by the Board of Governors of the International Atomic Energy Agency (IAEA) in Vienna.

In a letter to the UN Security Council, 21 Asian and African countries stated that the Algerian conflict had become a threat to international peace.

July 11

The UAR Government returned the Anglo-Egyptian Oilfields, Limited, confiscated in 1956, to its British parent company, Shell.

The Soviet Union and Yemen signed an economic cooperation agreement.

The UAR Customs Department auctioned the Israel cargo of potash, cement and fruit juices taken from the Liberian vessel Capitan Manolis when it attempted to pass through the Suez Canal.

A Sudanese official mission arrived in Yugoslavia for talks on long term credit to finance imports of industrial equipment.

July 12

The Iraqi Government announced that in celebration of the first anniversary of the 1958 revolution, government offices and departments would be closed from July 14-17.

The Socialist Party which continued to support President De Gaulle's efforts for peace in Algeria, told the President to hurry lest the political consequences of the Algerian war be disastrous for the Fifth Republic.

An Algerian communique said that 103 nationalists had been killed and 70 captured in a battle in the Hodna Mountains which served as the major arsenal and training ground for the rebel army.

July, 1959

July 14

Clashes between army units and Communist led factions were reported taking place at Kirkuk, a north Iraqi oil center.

The new Iraqi flag was flown for the first time in the UN. The flag was black, white and green with an eight pointed red star in the center of a vertical white strip; and within this star was a yellow circle bordered in white.

Imam Ahmad of Yemen left Rome by airplane after twelve weeks of medical treatment in Italy but returned to the city an hour later after complaining of not feeling well.

Asian and African states asked UN Secretary General Dag Hammarskjold to put the Algerian question on the agenda of the forthcoming General Assembly session. The French, in a letter to the Security Council, stated that the UN was not competent to take up a matter which under the UN Charter fell within France's national sovereignty.

As part of the Bastille Day celebrations in Algeria, about 5,000 Moslems were released from camps in Algeria where they had been interned by administrative decision on charges that they were helping the rebellion against France.

At the opening session of the Congress of the Socialist International at Hamburg, West Germany, the French Socialist Party was criticized on its position on Algeria.

Four ministers of the Algerian Provisional Government returned to Tunis from Cairo where they had been conferring since June 25.

Fifteen French soldiers were killed and ten were wounded in a rebel ambush near the Moroccan frontier.

Patriarch Theodosius of Antioch and All the East arrived in Moscow at the invitation of Alexus, Patriarch of Moscow and All Russia, to acquaint himself with the life of the Russian Orthodox Church.

July, 1959

July 12

Final results in the elections of delegates to the UAR National Union, the organization from which a Parliament would be selected, showed big majorities for all Cabinet Ministers for the Egyptian and Syrian Regions.

King Muhammad V of Morocco arrived at Montreux, Switzerland, to vacation until his scheduled meeting with French President De Gaulle near Paris in August.

American Overseas Petroleum, Limited, announced that a drill seismic test at its Baida well in Libya recovered oil at a rate of 875 barrels a day from 4,000 feet. This was the second biggest oil strike after the one at Zeltan, south of Agheila, Libya.

July 13

Premier Kassem of Iraq reorganized and expanded his Cabinet.

A trade agreement which provided for exchanges of up to 1,880 million Moroccan francs, a 56 percent increase in trade, during an initial period of one year was signed in Rabat by representatives of Morocco and the UAR.

UAR Minister of Finance, Abd-al-Moneim Kaissouni said that the trade deficit in 1958 was about $300 million. This compared with a deficit of $31 million in Egypt in the previous year, and the trade surplus in Syria.

The Sudanese Military Court trying the former Minister of Communications and Minister of Local Government on charges of mutiny completed its hearings.

The Iraqi-USSR Friendship Society was inaugurated in Baghdad.

July 14

Iraq began five days of celebrations for the first anniversary of the 1958 revolution. Premier Kassem promised to restore political life and to hold elections within a year.

July, 1959

July 15

The UAR and Yemen signed an agreement for the establishment of the Arab Company for Foreign Trade to carry out domestic and foreign trade operations in the two countries and abroad.

Russians who had been visiting Egypt to work on the projected Aswan High Dam left for Moscow.

Two armed Egyptians were killed and one was captured in a clash with an Israel patrol three miles from the Gaza Strip.

Moroccan Premier Abdallah Ibrahim said that Morocco still favored a meeting between King Muhammad V and President Charles De Gaulle of France in spite of increased tension between the two countries.

More than 500,000 persons gave Premier Kassem of Iraq an ovation as he reviewed a colorful five hour procession devoted mainly to proclaiming loyalty to him.

July 16

King Saud of Saudi Arabia was greeted by dignitaries of the UAR and the Arab League as his ship passed through the Suez Canal on its way to Europe.

The Ghana Government received a message of appreciation from the Provisional Algerian Government for extending recognition to it.

The US Development Loan Fund announced approval of a $500,000 loan to the Societe d'Electricite d'al-Bared to help reconstruct a power plant on the al-Bared River in Lebanon.

July 17

The first agrarian land reform move in Iraq was made: 1,200 peasants received a total of 10,000 acres taken from a large estate.

The UAR decided to increase sharply its participation in the International Monetary Fund and the International Bank for Reconstruction and Development.

July 17

Premier Kassem of Iraq opened a model village at Latifiva with homes for 100 families, a school and a dispensary.

Customs officials reported that three Syrians were arrested when trying to smuggle 11 kilograms of hashish by air from Damascus to Cairo.

July 18

Premier Kassem of Iraq received the Saudi Arabian Ambassador and other members of the delegation sent from Saudi Arabia to attend the July 14 celebrations.

Yugoslavia and Sudan signed an agreement on economic, scientific and technical cooperation.

July 19

US Middle East experts saw no likelihood that the Communists would take control of Iraq at this time.

A pro-Communist revolt and armed mutiny were reported to have broken out at Kirkuk, oil center in northeastern Iraq, with casualties in the hundreds. The revolt brought a declaration from Premier Kassem that he would settle accounts with the Communists and mutineers.

British Foreign Office reports from the Middle East indicated that British oil installations and personnel in Kirkuk were not affected by the last week's rioting.

THE UAR Government made public the national budget of approximately LE700 million (about $1.8 billion). The outstanding aspect of the new budget was that about 25 percent was devoted to production and economic development projects. Included was a $331 million national defense budget for the coming year.

UAR President Nasser's decision to give LE2 million to the Algerian Provisional Government was announced.

July 19

At Saniquellie, Liberia, chiefs of state of Liberia, Guinea and Ghana, supported requests that the Algerian question be included on the Agenda of the UN General Assembly. They also stated their opposition to French nuclear tests in the Sahara.

In Lyons, France, the police arrested about 15 men identified as leaders of the local Algerian nationalist rebel movement.

The Provisional Government of Algeria accused the French Army of plotting to have French soldiers disguised as insurgents carry out massacres in Algerian villages.

An appeal was made by the Afro-Asian People's Solidarity Secretariat in Cairo for all peace loving nations to join in a campaign to stop the proposed French Atom bomb tests in the Sahara.

King Saud of Saudi Arabia conferred with King Paul of Greece on the island of Corfu.

After talks with Italian leaders, President Bourguiba of Tunisia, in an audience with the Pope, was believed to have emphasized that the Roman Catholic Church would enhance its prestige in the Arab world if it convinced France of the futility of continuing to seek a military solution of the Algerian problems.

July 20

The UAR Minister of Industry held talks with representatives of the West German firm Concordia concerning the company's offer to participate in the execution of some of the petroleum projects included in the UAR Five Year Industrialization Program.

The Japanese Arabian Oil Company announced that it started test drilling on the sea bed in the neutral offshore zone between Saudi Arabia and Kuwait.

The first motor car produced in Egypt, the Rameses, made its appearance in Cairo.

The Baghdad Radio announced that the Iraqi Government cancelled a number of the national holiday celebrations because of continued fight-

July 20

ing in the north. It also announced that the mutiny in Kirkuk was quelled and that the Government was in full control of the situation.

Iraqi government bonds valued at ID5 million were issued for subscription.

The British Foreign Office estimated that 50 persons were killed last week in the Kirkuk riots in Iraq.

July 21

Premier Khrushchev of the Soviet Union invited Premier Kassem of Iraq to pay a state visit to the Soviet Union.

Premier Khrushchev's invitation to Iraqi Premier Kassem to visit the USSR was interpreted in Washington as a reflection of Soviet concern over anti-Communist developments in Iraq.

UAR Minister of Industry Aziz Sidqi reported that an oil well with an annual capacity of 60, 000 tons was discovered in the Sinai desert.

Muhammad Abd-al-Khaleq Hassouna, Secretary General of the Arab League, said in Amman, Syria, that Syria would reopen its border to traffic from Jordan and that diplomatic relations between Jordan and the UAR would be re-established.

One million pounds was paid to Jordan by the British Treasury; this was the first installment of two million pounds aid to cover Jordan's budget deficit. The second installment was to be paid six months later.

A Moslem Deputy from Algeria proposed to the French National Assembly the formation of a commission of appeasement and reconciliation to end the nearly five years of violence in Algeria.

The new Sennar Dam in Sudan, completed by two West German concerns, was put into operation and the Manaqil Canal, which would bring 600, 000 acres of desert under cultivation, began to fill.

The exchange rate of the Saudi Arabian riyal on the free market improved to 4.75 riyals to the US dollar.

July 21

The US Government's Development Loan Fund authorized a loan of $5 million to enable Lebanon to make credits to industrial enterprises.

A Syrian shepherd was killed when a Turkish land mine exploded at ain-al-Arab on the frontier. Four Turkish soldiers who had infiltrated to the Syrian Khirb Nass post were arrested.

The exiled Imam of Oman, Ghaleb Ibn-Ali, arrived in Damascus from Jedda.

July 22

The court martial of Brigadier Hamad, the suspended Minister of Agriculture and Irrigation of Sudan, was opened.

His Royal Highness Amir Faisal of Saudi Arabia stated that the current budget surplus would be devoted to debt retirement.

Seven union leaders from Tunisia arrived in the US to study vocational education methods.

The Iraqi Government announced that the domestic situation had returned to normal in Kirkuk, scene of a pro-Communist rebellion.

Speaking in Cairo on the eve of the seventh anniversary of the Egyptian revolution, President Nasser said that his recent friendly overtures to Premier Kassem of Iraq were met with silence.

July 23

Rashid Ali al-Gailani was sentenced to be hanged for attempting to overthrow the Kassem regime in Iraq.

Iraq and Communist North Korea signed a cultural agreement and a trade and payments agreement in Baghdad.

July, 1959

July 23

Spearheaded by nearly 1,000 paratroopers, French land, sea and air forces began what was described as the biggest offensive of the Algerian war in the Kabylia mountain region.

In a three hour parade marking the seventh anniversary of the overthrow of the Egyptian monarchy, the UAR displayed its military striking power.

Talks between King Muhammad V of Morocco and President De Gaulle of France were reported delayed until after August 10 because some members of the Algerian Provisional Government were opposed to any action which appeared to be a concession by them to France and because the Algerian nationals wished to keep the Monrovia Conference of independent African states free from competition for world attention.

July 24

Twenty-six Soviet physicians arrived in Baghdad to train Iraqi doctors.

Oil operations in Iraq were proceeding at a record pace despite the recent rebellion and the other disquieting incidents.

A trade agreement between Iraq and the People's Republic of Korea was signed in Baghdad, Iraq.

UN Secretary General Hammarskjold was to fly to Paris in the coming week to visit President De Gaulle of France.

In Paris, the forthcoming visit of UN Secretary General Hammarskjold focused attention on the pessimistic outlook for France in this year's debate on Algeria in the UN General Assembly.

Seventeen Algerian nationalist students were in the US on public grants and scholarships. Seven of them had State Department grants even though the US did not recognize Algerian nationality.

According to the French High Command, the offensive by 20,000 French troops against the Algerian rebel stronghold in Kabylia was proceeding according to plan.

July, 1959

July 26

Speaking on the third anniversary of Egypt's nationalization of the Suez Canal, President Nasser said that the UAR would not shy away from a decisive battle with Israel.

Crown Prince Moulay Hassan and Vice Premier Abd-al-Rahim Abu-Abid flew to Switzerland to submit the Moroccan Cabinet decisions on the devaluation issue to Muhammad V, the King of Morocco.

An agreement was signed between Sudan and Yugoslavia for the delivery of two 4,700 ton ships.

A military tribunal in Damascus sentenced former Premier Husni Barazi to life imprisonment <u>in absentia</u> on charges of provoking foreign powers to commit aggression against Syria.

July 27

France was expected to demand US support of its policy in Algeria in the UN General Assembly debate this fall.

According to a report on the first six days of the operation to rout rebels from the Kabylia Mountains in Algeria, French forces had not yet encountered the main body of rebels.

A hunger strike of Algerians in Rouen and Fresnes prisons in France spread today to jails in Versailles, Lille, Douai, Charleville and Chalon-sur-Marne.

A two week conference of the Arab League to discuss and decide on plans for intensifying the Arab boycott against Israel opened in Beirut.

Naim Mughabghab, a former Cabinet Minister and member of the Lebanese Parliament, was assassinated on his way to President Chehab's summer place.

July 28

The Senate of Tunisia confirmed the nomination of Walter N. Walmsley, Jr. as US Ambassador to Tunisia.

July, 1959

July 24

Ethiopia joined the signatories of the letter of July 10 sent by 21 Asian and African states to the President of the Security Council on the subject of Algeria.

July 25

Iraq decided to conclude an agreement with Britain for scholarships, cultural exchanges and technical fairs.

Three agreements between Sudan and Yugoslavia involving the building of factories, the delivery of two cargo ships, and the formation of a Sudanese-Yugoslavian navigation company were signed after extensive negotiation.

The Moroccan Cabinet met for seven hours reportedly to discuss the question of the devaluation of the Moroccan franc which was presently worth 420 to the US dollar.

The Moroccan Government censorship of all commercial radio news broadcasts, except the Voice of America, went into effect in accordance with a law providing for supervision of all nonstate radio transmissions.

French troops in Algeria continued to move into the Kabylia Mountain region swelling the number of soldiers to 30,000.

The radio telephone circuit between Lebanon and Bahrain was expanded to include Dawhat al-Qatar.

Representatives of nine Arab countries began to prepare for a two week conference on ways to apply more economic pressure against Israel.

Asian-African states requested UN Secretary General Hammarskjold to bring the question of Algeria before the 1959 UN General Assembly session.

July, 1959

July 28

The denunciation by political groups on all sides of the assassination of Mr. Mughabghab dampened fears that the attack would lead to a civil war similar to the one which caused the US marines to enter Lebanon last year.

In a speech at the ceremonies near Alexandria to distribute land to 1,200 families under an agrarian reform program, President Nasser told the Egyptians that he would welcome them to battle if the Israelis tried to invade the UAR.

July 29

The Military Governor of Iraq cancelled all licenses to carry firearms and ordered that all firearms be turned in. He also banned the wearing of the Popular Resistance uniform.

Premier Kassem of Iraq accused the Communists of plotting simultaneous uprisings in all major cities of Iraq on July 14.

The acting Minister for Local Government and member of the Supreme Council for the Armed Forces in Sudan received the US Ambassador at his office.

Imam Ghaleb Ibn-Ali of Oman declared that the Omani people would not consider themselves bound by any contract made by the Sultan of Muscat and companies prospecting for oil in Oman.

July 30

President Bourguiba of Tunisia announced that Tunisians would vote November 8 to elect their first legislative assembly of 90 members to replace a constituent assembly elected in March 1955.

President Bourguiba of Tunisia stressed that in spite of the border incidents Tunisia would go on with the housing plans and with projects towards progress.

July 30, 1959

July 30

UN Secretary General Hammarskjold left for Paris for his first meeting with President De Gaulle.

The death of Ayssat Idir, an Algerian labor leader, of accidental burns while in French custody in Algiers provoked a demand by the International Confederation of Free Trade Unions for an independent investigation.

Omar Abd-al-Hamid Adil, new Permanent Representative of Sudan to the UN presented his credentials to UN Secretary General Dag Hammarskjold.

The Moroccan representative at the UN called on the UN Secretary General Hammarskjold to draw to his attention the grave situation on the border of southern Morocco and the French Sahara. Morocco had protested to France against the projected atomic bomb experiments in the French Sahara but France had rejected the protest.

The US signed an agreement with Egypt to supply 29.5 million bushels of surplus wheat and flour at a cost of $57.7 million.

Iraq and Tunisia refused to attend the Arab League Council session scheduled to meet in Casablanca.

As a result of talks between the UAR and Jordan, the border between Syria and Jordan, which was closed by Syria on June 5, was opened to normal traffic.

Lebanon acceded to the Universal Copyright Convention that gave foreign works the same protection as that given to national works.

Premier Abdallah Ibrahim of Morocco charged that Ayssat Idir, an imprisoned Algerian labor union leader, had been assassinated by the French Army.

August, 1959

August 1

UN Secretary General Hammarskjold left for New York after conferring with French President De Gaulle and Premier Debre for two days.

Five Tunisians accused of having given political and military information to French local affairs officers were sent to prison by a military tribunal.

The Moroccan Government banned all public demonstrations to avoid disturbances and possible anti-French disorders while it was engaged in delicate monetary negotiations with France.

August 2

The US negotiated an agreement with Morocco whereby the Government of Morocco became the employer and paymaster of all local civilian labor on US bases in Morocco.

King Hussein of Jordan announced that Jordan would re-establish diplomatic relations with the UAR in the near future and hinted his willingness to re-establish relations with Iraq.

A Decree approved by Jordanian Cabinet decision discharged Jordan's Ambassador to London and its Ambassador to Nationalist China.

Jordan's Development Board appropriated $105,000 for improvements at the Amman and Jerusalem airports.

A French vice consul and a Moroccan administrative official were released after being held prisoner for more than 48 hours by Algerians.

Three delegates of the Algerian nationalist regime left for Monrovia, Liberia, to attend the conference of members of North and West African governments.

Si Boucif, organizer of the rebels in the Oran region of Algeria was killed in a battle with French security forces.

Lebanese aircraft attacked the village of Erawbah in northern Lebanon to quell clashes between villagers and tribesmen.

August, 1959

August 2

The Imam of Oman said that he considered himself president of an independent republic, and that he remained in control of active guerrilla warfare against the British.

A British Foreign Office spokesman described the Imam of Oman's statement that he considered himself the president of an independent state as ludicrous and said that the religious leader was not a rebel against the British but a rebel against the Sultan of Muscat.

The Iraqi nationalist newspaper, al-Hurriyah, whose press was attacked and damaged allegedly by anarchists about three months ago, resumed publication.

August 3

Premier Kassem of Iraq announced that 79 persons were killed—40 of them buried alive—in recent disturbances in Kirkuk. He said that reports indicated that many more persons were unaccounted for and were probably dead.

The 63 year old ruler of Yemen left for Yemen after a three month stay in Italy for the treatment of arthritis.

The Iraqi Communist Party publicly condemned itself for criminal acts, emotionalism and miscalculations.

The Imam of Oman spent a few days on tour of the UAR.

Syrian authorities charged Turkey with planting mines inside Syrian territory.

Accusations of allegiance to Israel instead of to Lebanon were levelled against the Lebanese Jewish community in a Parliamentary debate over a bill dealing with the right of Jews to buy Lebanese land.

Dr. Said Karem, a town planning specialist of the UN, arrived at Amman at the request of the Jordanian Government to plan Aqaba as an industrial, commercial and residential town.

August, 1959

August 4

Tunisia, Iraq and Jordan were absent from a meeting of the Arab League Council in Cairo when Lieutenant General Ali Amer, Chief of Staff of the UAR Army, took the oath of office as the Arab League's Assistant Secretary General for Military Affairs.

The Conference of Representatives of nine independent African States—Ethiopia, Ghana, Guinea, Liberia, Libya, Morocco, Sudan, Tunisia and UAR—met at Monrovia, Liberia, from August 4-8. President William Tubman of Liberia made an appeal at the opening of the conference for both the Algerian nationalists and the French to ease their extreme positions and agree to a negotiated settlement. A delegation of the Provisional Algerian Government also attended.

A cultural cooperation agreement with Bulgaria was signed by the Iraqi Government in Baghdad.

King Muhammad V of Morocco cut short his vacation in Europe and returned home reportedly because of the political and monetary problems of his kingdom.

News of the Eisenhower-Khrushchev visits was enthusiastically welcomed in the UAR.

August 5

French Premier Debre flew to Algiers for a 36 hour visit to discuss military, administrative and economic problems with Moslem and French officials.

Jordan decided to send an envoy to Cairo to negotiate for resumed diplomatic relations with the UAR.

An Algerian Nationalist flag was raised on the Liberian capitol in Monrovia.

Premier Kassem of Iraq accepted an invitation by Premier Khrushchev to visit the Soviet Union. No date had been set.

August, 1959

August 6

It was announced from Monrovia, Liberia, that Guinea would exchange diplomatic missions with the Provisional Government of Algeria.

The French offensive against the Algerian rebel groups in the Kabylia region entered its third week.

Iraq and Britain began talks toward a cultural agreement.

The Foreign Ministry of Morocco issued a communique declaring that the recent arrangements between the US and Morocco regarding US air bases did not constitute an agreement between the two countries and that the Moroccan Government had not deviated from its policy of non-dependence in dealing with the US.

The Jordanian Government announced in Amman last week that $90, 000 in the budget was earmarked to aid the Algerian Provisional Government.

President Nasser greeted Imam Ahmad of Yemen at Port Said, UAR, in their first meeting since the UAR and Yemen formed a federation in 1958.

US Senator Javits, a Republican from New York State, proposed in the US Senate that the US ban all aid to the UAR unless it guaranteed freedom of passage through the Suez Canal for Israel cargoes.

August 7

French President De Gaulle decided to receive President Eisenhower of the US after the latter's trip to London in order to enable the French President to make a scheduled trip to Algeria beginning August 27.

The UN Technical Assistance Board appointed Jens Henrik Malling of Sweden as resident representative in Iraq.

The Russian Ambassador to the UAR, Evgeni Kisselev, was transferred back to Moscow.

Informed sources in Amman said that Jordan and the UAR would re-establish relations broken off after the Iraqi revolt last year.

August, 1959

August 8

Premier Abdallah Ibrahim of Morocco returned from the Conference of Independent African States in Liberia.

Three persons were killed and 28 injured by a bomb thrown into the crowded market place at Redeyef, Tunisia.

August 9

Twenty-two rebels were killed and two captured in a skirmish 25 miles east of Algiers. Several French soldiers were wounded, two seriously.

The French Government had not yet commented on an appeal by sixteen US Congressmen to negotiate for peace in Algeria.

In Amman, a Royal Decree approved the discharge from the Jordanian Armed Forces of 22 officers, ranking from Lieutenant Colonel down to Second Lieutenant. No reason was given.

A five member UN mission was to conduct a six week narcotics survey in the Middle East this fall.

Premier Kassem of Iraq distributed title deeds for 25, 000 acres of agrarian reform land to peasants in the Lafifiyah area.

August 10

The French Minister Delegate concerned with atomic energy denied the rumor that France planned to explode an atomic bomb in the Sahara in the near future.

August 11

The Iraqi Government signed an agreement with the Soviet Union for the construction of a shipbuilding yard in Basra.

August, 1959

August 7

The new Cairo-Alexandria Delta Expressway opened in the UAR. The highway is 72 feet wide and 137 miles long.

King Muhammad V of Morocco underwent a tonsillectomy in a private clinic in his palace.

Iraq sent an emissary to Russia to secure an agreement for Iraq to receive technical and material help in the peaceful uses of atomic energy.

August 8

Muhammad Yazid, Algerian nationalist Information Minister, declared that his Government was preparing for many years of war.

In response to Iraq's request, the UN Children's Fund (UNICEF) planned to help Iraq carry out an extensive child aid program.

Delegates from nine independent African States ended their conference in Monrovia, Liberia, with an appeal to peoples and governments of the world to support and recognize the Provisional Government of the Algerian Republic.

The Conference of Independent African States designated November 1 as Algerian Day, to be observed throughout Africa.

Premier Michel Debre of France completed his brief visit in Algeria.

A spokesman for the Algerian Provisional Government said that 226 French soldiers had been killed by rebel forces in Algeria during the past three days.

President Nasser of the UAR said in Cairo that Israel would not be allowed to use the Suez Canal. He reportedly scoffed at reports that Israel planned to raise the Suez Canal issue before the UN.

The Israel Army reported that an Israel patrol fired at a marauding party from the Gaza Strip and killed one member. An Army spokesman said the infiltrators had been caught dismantling irrigation pipes near the Israel village of Nir Am.

August, 1959

August 12

Iraqi Brigadier Nadim Tabaqchali, former Commander of the Second Division Army in Kirkuk, Iraq, eight other officers and one civilian went on trial before a special military court on charges of complicity in a mutiny against the Iraq regime in March.

A special security court opened hearings in Amman of 17 army officers and one civilian accused of plotting to seize power and establish a republic in Jordan while King Hussein was out of the country. Among the accused was the former Army Chief of Staff.

The Homs Refinery in Syria was officially opened.

Sudan gave France a protest against the projected atomic explosion in the Sahara.

The US Senate asked to go on record in opposition to foreign aid for Saudi Arabia and other nations that discriminate against American Jews.

The Moroccan Ministries of Public Health and Interior promoted the eating of fish to improve the Moroccan diet and to give stimulus to the fishing industry.

An International Monetary Fund press release disclosed that an initial par value for the Libyan pound, at LP0. 357143 per US dollar was established by an agreement between Libya and the IMF.

August 13

Colonel al-Mahdawi, president of the Baghdad People's court admitted that witnesses had been tortured.

The Moroccan Government decided to join the Arab Postal Union.

Morocco was expected to nominate itself to the position of vice president of the Fourteenth Session of the UN General Assembly.

Lieutenant General E. L. M. Burns, Commander of the UN Emergency Force, presented UNEF medals to 350 men of the Swedish contingent serving with the Force in the Gaza Strip.

August, 1959

August 13

The Israel Military Governors of Upper Galilee and the North Central area ordered relaxation of the restrictions on the movement of Arabs living in those two areas.

A trade agreement was signed between Morocco and Bulgaria.

Israel Foreign Minister Golda Meir said in Jerusalem that Israel still insisted that Egypt must obey the rulings of the UN Security Council on free passage through the Suez Canal, and that Israel would not accept any conditions that would qualify the right to send Israel cargoes through the canal in foreign owned vessels.

An Arab armed marauder was shot by an Israel patrol in the Lachish district.

The Arab League ended a conference in Bhamdun, near Beirut, with a recommendation that the economic blockade of Israel should be tightened.

The Moroccan Government decided to take its protest against the projected French atomic explosion in the Sahara to the UN.

August 14

An Iraqi Commerce Ministry committee accepted 17 of 56 factories for small industries offered by East Germany to the Iraqi Government.

Iraq began work on an $18 million broad-gauged railway between Baghdad and Basra.

An Egyptian authority implied that the thefts or loss of Egyptian antiquities was a result of the Suez invasion of 1956.

A mission from the International Bank for Reconstruction and Development was in Cairo looking into the financial aspects of a loan to Egypt to enable the widening and deepening of the Suez Canal.

The leader of a delegation of visiting Americans of Arab descent said that the US must give the UAR the economic help it needed or risk driving the UAR into the arms of the Soviet Union.

August, 1959

August 15

Baghdad reported that the Iraqi Trade Ministry decided to accept 17 of the 56 factories offered by East Germany.

The Tunisian Government charged that a French plane based in Algeria had twice attacked the Tunisian town of Bharet Zitouna. A demand for a ceasing of the operations was presented.

The French Army in Algiers denied that French planes had bombed a Tunisian town. An Army communique declared that the plane, pursuing rebels fleeing to Tunisia, strafed but did not bomb the town.

August 16

Jordan and the UAR resumed diplomatic relations which had been severed on July 20, 1958.

It was reported that Arab pressure was delaying the transfer of two Israel frigates purchased by Ceylon.

The UAR Railway Authority was expected to buy 16 electric diesel locomotives from the General Electric Company for use on principal railway lines.

The ruins of a fourth century city, covering nearly 25 acres and including the remains of big churches and a burial ground, have been discovered near Skhira, Tunisia, south of Tunis.

It was announced that the new Jordanian Ambassador in Cairo would be Muhammad Sharaiki (a former Jordanian Foreign Minister) and the new UAR Ambassador in Amman Mr. Fathi Radwan, director of the Arab Affairs Department in the UAR Foreign Ministry, following the August 15 resumption of diplomatic relations.

August 17

The Imam of Yemen dealt strongly with rebel elements who tried to overthrow the regime during his stay in Italy for medical treatment. According to informed sources, more than six persons were executed without trial.

August, 1959

August 14

Saif-al-Islam Muhammad al-Badr presented his credentials to King Paul of Greece as the Ambassador of the Republic of Sudan to that country.

An offshore oil well fire in the Arabian Oil Company of Tokyo's prospecting concession zone was extinguished by dynamite after blazing for eleven days.

Morocco asked the UN General Assembly to place the question of French nuclear tests in the Sahara on its agenda.

President Nasser of the UAR dismissed Riyad al-Malki, Minister of Guidance in the Syrian Region.

Jacques Verges, a left wing lawyer from Paris, was expelled from Algeria by the police.

August 15

Muhammad al-Fasi, the Rector of Moroccan Universities, arrived in the US for a tour of the schools and universities of that nation.

It was reported from Rabat that nine persons were killed and 35 injured when a bus plunged off a twisting mountain road.

Premier Hazza al-Majali of Jordan lifted all restrictions imposed on foreign correspondents by former Premier Samir al-Rifai.

A trial of persons charged with trying to overthrow President Nasser opened in Alexandria.

The UAR Minister of Industry announced that the biggest oil field in the UAR had been discovered in the Sinai Peninsula.

The Sudanese Minister for Presidential Affairs discussed with the Ambassador of Yugoslavia the question of training Sudanese officers in Yugoslavia.

August, 1959

August 17

Aziz Sidqi, the UAR Minister of Industry, declared in Cairo that the UAR had reached a stage of self sufficiency in oil, producing at a rate of 4 million tons annually.

U Thi Han, Burmese Minister of Trade and Development, concluded talks with UAR Ministers.

The emergency curator of the Egyptian Museum accused former King Farouq of pilfering antiquities and selling them to collectors through a New York City store.

Ferhat Abbas, Premier of the Algerian Provisional Government, refused to meet President De Gaulle of France anywhere except on neutral territory.

The French Army announced that its offensive in Kabylia, Algeria, had put 1, 015 nationalist guerrilla fighters out of action.

An International Cooperation Administration staff arrived in Yemen from the US to carry out a wheat distribution program.

The Soviet Union and Iraq signed an agreement on cooperation in peaceful uses of atomic energy.

August 18

It was reported in Iran that the name of the Baghdad Pact was now the Central Treaty Organization, or CENTO because Iraq had left the Pact. Members of the pact still remaining were Britain, Iran, Pakistan and Turkey.

Spokesmen of nine Arab states declared at the end of a ten day conference in Beirut that their countries would support the demand that the Palestine refugees be returned to their former homes in Israel. They unanimously rejected the UN Secretary General's plan for economic aid to Palestinian refugees.

The British Ballet Rambert made its first appearance at the Baalbak International Festival in Lebanon.

August, 1959

August 19

The trial of Brigadier Tabaqchali on charges of complicity in a mutiny against the Iraqi regime last March was continued.

The special military court sentenced five Iraqi army officers and one civilian to death for participating in the Mosul uprising last March against the Iraqi regime.

The Moroccan Government party newspaper, al-Alam, said the agenda of the Arab League Council meeting, which would open in Casablanca September 4, included an appeal for the formation of a Palestine Government and an army able to take the offensive against Israel.

About $40, 000 was collected for Algerian nationalists at a dinner given in honor of a group of Algerian women visiting the UAR.

August 20

An exploration agreement was signed between the Sudanese Government and the Italian state owned oil corporation, ENI.

At a press conference in Khartoum, the Sudanese Minister of Information presented the proposed development program for 1959-60, which was estimated at SP8, 567, 334 excluding American aid.

King Saud of Saudi Arabia accepted an invitation to visit President Nasser on August 31.

The Sultan of Muscat and Oman conferred with British Minister of State for increased assistance to his army and for British officers to train his soldiers.

The leader of Morocco's conservative Istiqlal (Independence) Party accused France and Spain of plots against Morocco's Saharan territories.

Ibrahim Kubbah, Agrarian Reform Minister, said that Iraq had signed an agreement with the Soviet Government agency, Techno-Export, for the provision of 34 Soviet experts and ten translators to help Iraq implement its agrarian reforms.

August, 1959

August 20

The former Army Chief of Staff, Sadeq al-Sharaa, confessed in a security court that he took part in a plot to overthrow the Jordanian regime.

President Bourguiba of Tunisia announced that Tunisia had left the French customs union. A new French-Tunisian agreement would be sought and no new Tunisian tariffs would be applied to French goods until October. Tunisians would now be allowed to make purchases in the dollar market.

The Jordanian Cabinet decided that the Jordanian sector of Jerusalem would be considered Jordan's second capital, that a royal palace would be built there, and that the Cabinet meetings would be held there frequently.

August 21

The Lebanese prosecution requested the death sentence for three men not in custody who were accused of murdering Mr. Moghabghab. The accused, including those charged with aiding and abetting the murder, were to be tried in absentia by the state council if they could not be arrested.

More than a thousand French army troops engaged in a battle against 100 Algerian nationalists near Aumale killed 63 rebels.

The US granted the UAR a loan of $12 million, repayable in five years.

August 22

A statement by Joseph Satterthwaite, US Assistant Secretary of State for African Affairs, that the US would like to see Algeria develop with France as a friend and partner has caused concern in diplomatic circles in France.

The Soviet newspaper Pravda expressed disapproval of the proposed French atomic tests in the Sahara.

August, 1959

August 22

According to a communique published by Tass, the Soviet press agency, the Soviet Union planned to help Iraq launch a program of atomic research for peaceful purposes.

Dr. Rifaat Awdah, described by the prosecutor as the mainspring of an army plot against King Hussein's regime in Jordan repudiated his confession and denied all knowledge of the plot before the State Security Court.

The UAR stepped up its radio services to make Cairo broadcasts audible in most parts of the world.

King Saud of Saudi Arabia was scheduled to arrive in Cairo on August 31, and the city was planning a full reception for him in the name of Arab unity.

August 23

Qadi Ahmad Ibn-Ahmad Assayaghi, Secretary to the Imam of Yemen, fled to the tribal area of Beihan with a number of his followers after a threat of vengeance by the Imam.

The new UAR-Sudanese Solidarity Hospital was opened in Port Said, and was named in honor of Sudan, which contributed $300, 000 to construction.

After a five day stay in Tunis, the Secretary General of the Arab League said that he hoped that diplomatic relations between the UAR and Tunisia would be resumed shortly, and that Tunisia would participate in the forthcoming League Council session in Casablanca to open on September 1.

August 24

Reports from Aden said that the Imam of Yemen had had several Christian agitators beheaded and others mutilated in a move against liberal reforms instituted by his son, Crown Prince Amir Saif-al-Islam Muhammad al-Badr, during his absence.

UAR customs officials at Port Said confiscated eight bags of mail addressed to Israel, from the Norwegian ship Tarn.

August, 1959

August 25

Ambassadors to Washington D.C. from ten Arab countries told US Secretary of State Christian A. Herter that a solution to the Algerian war must come through political negotiation. They urged the US to support their stand at the forthcoming session of the UN General Assembly.

French forces reported that they killed or captured 739 rebels during the week ending August 23, and that French losses were 36 killed.

The Sahara oil pipeline joining the Hassi-Messoud oil fields with Bougie on the Mediterranean coast was completed; it extended for 420 miles and cost more than $93 million.

A high French official called upon President De Gaulle to assume dictatorial powers to consolidate the French Community and settle the Algerian problem.

The Arab League Boycott Committee announced a ban against 15 American and European companies, prohibiting them from operating in or sending products into the Arab world because they were doing business with Israel.

Turkey defied the Arab League's threat to boycott Turkish cigarettes if trade with Israel continued.

Israel asked the Universal Postal Union in Switzerland to recover mail impounded by the UAR in the Suez Canal.

Five Iraqi Army officers and a civilian were executed for complicity in the March revolt in Mosul in which the prosecution said there was a plot to annex Iraq to the UAR.

The first agreement for oil prospecting in Sudan was signed in Khartoum by the Minister of Works and Finance and representatives of the Italian company AGIP (Azienda Generale Italiana Petroli).

August 26

Premier Majali of Jordan said that all Palestine Arab refugees desiring to live in Jordan as citizens would be accepted.

August, 1959

August 26

French President De Gaulle polled the views of his ministers in an effort to find a solution for the Algerian conflict.

August 27

French President De Gaulle flew to Algeria to begin four days of visits to the French Army units before meeting with US President Eisenhower.

The Agenda of the Arab League meeting to be held September 1 at Casablanca was expected to include proposals that Palestine Arab refugees be restored to their former homes, that an army be raised from the ranks of the refugees, and that a charter of a Palestinian Arab nation be drafted.

King Saud of Saudi Arabia motored to Geneva, Switzerland, for a short visit with the Sheikh of Qatar.

August 28

French President De Gaulle's intentions concerning the Algerian problem remained unclear as he encouraged both conservatives and liberals.

US Secretary of State Christian Herter and British Foreign Secretary Selwyn Lloyd were believed to have agreed to support efforts by French President De Gaulle to reach a liberal solution in Algeria.

A meeting was held in Alexandria between the Director General of the Ports Administration and representatives of the UAR General Petroleum Authority to consider bids for the supply of five new oil tankers to the UAR.

In two circular letters from the UAR Foreign Ministry to all embassies in Cairo, the Government of the UAR made known that it expects all foreign representatives to keep propaganda activities friendly and within bounds.

Algerian Moslem Senator Sherif Ben-Habyles, who was opposed to Algerian integration with France, was assassinated in the streets of Vichy, France.

August, 1959

August 31

In a letter to UN Secretary General Dag Hammarskjold, Israel complained about the UAR's stoppage in the Suez Canal of neutral ships carrying Israel cargoes.

King Saud of Saudi Arabia arrived in Cairo for a four day state visit. He was scheduled to discuss Arab affairs with President Nasser of the UAR.

August, 1959

August 29

French President De Gaulle promised a crowd of Moslems in Tebessa, Algeria, that the Algerians would make their destiny themselves. This was to be done after peace had been restored.

The Syrian Minister of Economy approved the articles of association of the National Oil and Asphalt Company of Latakia, Limited.

A trade agreement containing the most favored nation clause was signed in Cairo for one year between the UAR and Cuba.

August 30

Premier Kassem of Iraq ordered all students and teachers detained in prison for taking part in various incidents be released.

The French Army in Algeria accepted the idea of self determination as the ultimate goal for Algeria and abandoned the previous goal of integration of Algeria as part of France.

French President De Gaulle returned to Paris after completing a tour of Algeria in preparation for an announcement of a new policy for that country.

US Senator Fulbright said that the US should formulate a long range policy for the Middle East.

August 31

Cairo welcomed US Senator Fulbright's call for a new US policy on the Middle East as a show of confidence in the ability of the Arab countries to handle their own affairs.

A UAR diplomat arrested recently on allegations of trying to sell out of date Egyptian banknotes hanged himself in his cell in Basel, Switzerland.

Jordan complained to the UN chief truce supervisor that Israel had violated the special agreement for the demilitarized zone on Mount Scopus, Jerusalem, when an Israel patrol crossed the zone into Jordanian territory.

September, 1959

September 1

King Saud of Saudi Arabia said in Cairo, after private talks with President Nasser of the UAR, that his country renewed full cooperation with the UAR against the enemies of the Arab nation.

The thirty-second session of the Council of the Arab League opened in Casablanca. Of the 23 items on the agenda, the most important were those dealing with the Palestine problem. Iraq and Tunisia boycotted the session. The Algerian people's struggle received full support by all members of the Arab League Council.

The UAR delegation to the Arab League Council meeting in Casablanca submitted a resolution stating that there was no longer any reason for Tunisia to be absent from the Arab League meetings. The resolution was adopted and a telegram was sent to President Habib Bourguiba inviting him to send a delegation. The council also sent a telegram to Premier Kassem of Iraq inviting him to send a delegation.

The Ministry of Economy of the UAR banned all direct barter export transactions and also removed the export tax on long staple cotton. The Ministry said that it would take all possible steps to prevent the re-export of Egyptian goods, and would prohibit trading in currency.

The Italian-Iranian SIRIP Company began offshore drilling operations in the Persian Gulf area from a permanent type drilling platform set in the water.

The Economic Committee of the CENTO (Central Treaty Organization) opened a three day meeting in Ankara, Turkey, to review progress in improving road, rail and radio links of member countries.

Britain told the UAR, Ethiopia, Sudan and Belgium that three of its East African territories would need a larger share of the Nile waters.

September 2

President Nasser was expected to visit Saudi Arabia at the invitation of King Saud, who just completed a visit to Cairo.

September, 1959

September 2

The Iraqi Government blacklisted 24 British, 11 American, 7 Swiss, 7 Dutch, 5 West German, 4 Italian, and 4 Norwegian, 2 Greek, 1 Danish and 1 Rumanian ships for engaging in business with Israel.

Morocco announced that a Protocol was signed in Rabat between Morocco and Guinea fixing bilateral trade between the two countries at one millard francs in each direction.

The Arab League's Political, Financial and Economic Committees met in Casablanca. Dr. Zain-ad-Din told the Political Committee that the UAR had carried out the League's decision to form military units among the Palestinians and recognize the separate existence of these people.

September 3

The Arab League Council voted to support the UAR's closure of the Suez Canal to Israel ships and cargoes. It accepted the recommendation of the Arab experts who met in Beirut last month and rejected the resettlement plan for Arab refugees proposed by UN Secretary General Dag Hammarskjold.

The Tunisian Government refused to attend the Arab League Council meeting in Casablanca unless the UAR would release Said Salah Ben-Youssef.

General De Gaulle offered a plan for ending the Algerian war by creating an Algerian elected assembly and an Algerian executive.

Colonel S. W. Griffith, Commander of the US Air Force Wheelus Base in Libya, said that expenditure there had benefited the Tripoli area's economy by about LP2,719,346 in the fiscal year from July 1, 1958 to June 30 last.

September 4

It was reported at the end of King Saud of Saudi Arabia's four day state visit to Egypt that he and President Nasser agreed to resume diplomatic relations with Great Britain and to apply pressure on Iraq to thwart Communist inroads in that country.

September, 1959

September 4

The Arab League's Economic Committee approved a recommendation banning any film where actors were of Zionist origin or were known to be supporters of Israel.

Acting Permanent Representative of Israel to the UN, Yosef Tekoah, brought to the attention of the Security Council once again the unlawful practices pursued by the UAR in violation of the UN Charter, Security Council decisions, and general principles of International Law, by obstructing freedom of passage through the Suez Canal.

Authoritative Algerians in Morocco indicated that there will be no ceasefire in Algeria without negotiations between the nationalist rebels and the French Government because a statute handed to Algeria by French President De Gaulle could not help solve the Algerian problem.

September 5

France and Tunisia signed a new monetary and commercial agreement that maintained close relations between the two countries in an effort to maintain French-Tunisian trade at the present level of about $90 million a year each way. It permitted Tunisia to stay in the Franc Zone and gave preferential customs treatment to many French products entering Tunisia.

The Arab League Council decided at Casablanca to support the UAR as successor in the UN Security Council. It also confirmed a plan for a pro rata contribution by its members of LE2 million to help Oman achieve independence.

An Arab League spokesman said that the UAR suggested amending the reply to the Hammarskjold report to the UN Relief and Works Agency in which he recommended eventual resettlement and integration of Palestinian refugees into the economy of the Arab countries. The amendment called for an international organization to look after and invest the revenue from Arab property in Israel and was approved by the political committee.

September, 1959

September 5

Dr. Kaissouni, UAR Minister of Economy and chief economic adviser to President Nasser, began an extended tour to sell Egyptian cotton and other UAR products to the West for hard currency.

After completing one-half of his term, Mr. James Swinburn, the British businessman serving a five year sentence in Egypt for espionage, was to be released.

A military court in Damascus sentenced to death six Syrians and two Lebanese found guilty of having spied for Israel. Three other Syrians received life terms.

September 6

Morocco left wing leaders who split with the Istiqlal Party in January, 1959, Mahdi Ben-Barka, formed a new political front under the name of the National Union of Popular Forces to oppose Crown Prince Moulay Hassan.

National Economy Minister Khalil Kallas of Syria announced a new law issued by President Nasser of the UAR which stipulated that at least 70 percent of any bank capital stocks should be owned by UAR citizens, who should in turn be represented on bank boards of directors in the same proportion. The operation of insurance companies in the Syrian Region should be under direct state supervision and only Arab owned insurance agencies can be established in the future.

The Arab League, meeting in Casablanca, issued a statement declaring that the Algerian war threatened to spread and that a peaceful settlement could be achieved only through negotiations with the rebel Algerian Provisional Government.

King Hussein of Jordan said in a Sunday Times interview that in spite of diplomatic relations with the UAR he would not accept any revival of the military convention of 1956 between Egypt, Saudi Arabia and Jordan.

A new wave of nationalist attacks was reported in several parts of Algeria.

September, 1959

September 6

Maqboul al-Amin al-Hajj, acting Minister of Agriculture and Irrigation in Sudan, stated that the Nile water talks between the Sudan and the UAR would begin immediately after the current military courts finish their work.

September 7

The Arab League Council meeting at Casablanca adopted four resolutions aimed against Israel and Zionism. Other issues of the Palestine problem were postponed for a meeting to be convened in January, 1960.

Israel transported a torpedo boat 249 miles overland to avoid the Suez Canal ban imposed by the UAR.

The National Union of Popular Forces in Morocco published its charter advocating nationalization of vital sectors of the economy.

The French Army reported that it killed or captured 2,058 Algerian rebels in the Kabylia region since the massive offensive began on July 22.

September 8

The Arab League Council session concluded its 8 day meeting in Casablanca with a decision to modernize the League's charter, as suggested by King Muhammad V of Morocco.

Archbishop Makarios announced that a Lebanese official delegation would discuss with him in the coming week the position in the new constitution of Cyprus of the 6,000 Maronite Christians in Cyprus who claim Lebanese descent.

Premier Karami of Lebanon was expected to head the Lebanese delegation to the UN General Assembly and hand the gavel to the incoming president in place of Dr. Charles Malik who would not be a member of the delegation.

September, 1959

September 8

French Premier Debre confirmed reports that US President Eisenhower had given no commitment for US support for France on the Algerian question.

The Soviet Union signed a general contract for technical assistance and equipment for the first stage of the Aswan High Dam.

About 1,000 Algerian prisoners had reportedly been on a hunger strike since August 27 in a camp at Mourmelon-le-Grand in northeastern France.

September 9

Three Norwegian unions representing seamen, engineers and transport workers protested to the Norwegian Foreign Ministry against UAR action against ships carrying cargo from Israel.

The Military Committee of the CENTO opened a two day meeting in London to discuss Middle Eastern defense problems.

It was officially announced that complete agreement had been reached between Quaiti and Kathiri states in Aden on sharing profits from oil concessions and negotiations for the next stage in the oil search were expected to be held with Petroleum Concessions, Limited.

September 10

UN Secretary General Dag Hammarskjold said his report on the Palestine Arab refugee problem had been widely misread. He had written that he did not see any possibility of solving the problem without economic development of the Middle East, but he never said that economic development was the means by which the refugee problem could be solved.

A World Bank spokesman said it had not so far decided on a loan to the UAR for widening the Suez Canal, as Cairo officials had claimed.

September, 1959

September 10

French President De Gaulle was expected to address the French nation on September 16 on Algeria's future.

An Executive Council of the French Community met to hear President De Gaulle's new proposals for settling the Algerian rebellion.

UAR Minister of Economy Abd-al-Moneim al-Kaissouni arrived in Britain on an unofficial visit, reportedly to urge increased trade.

Secretary General Hammarskjold submitted his third report on the organization and financing of the UN Emergency Force.

In a speech before the annual convention of the Zionist Organization of America, Senator Keating (Republican from New York) said that short sighted leaders in the Middle East were condemning their own people to needless sacrifice because of their obsession with Israel.

September 11

It was announced that the Ninth Session of the World Health Organization Regional Committee for the Eastern Mediterranean, would open on Monday, September 14, at Alexandria.

The Premiers of the twelve autonomous African republics in the French Community have given their support to President De Gaulle's new attempt to settle the Algerian question.

The Moroccan Interior Minister said in a news conference on the new electoral law that all Moroccan men and women of 21 years would have the right to participate in free and secret municipal elections to be held early in 1960.

An Iraqi cultural delegation returned from Ankara, Turkey, where talks were held between Iraq and Turkey.

The UAR Ambassador to Libya presented a gift of arms to the Libyan Defense Minister.

September, 1959

September 12

Spain began cutting back its Spanish Foreign Legionnaires stationed in Morocco from 60,000 to 5,000 men in an effort to improve relations with Morocco and to save money. The US has decided to evacuate 8,000 airmen and dependents from Morocco over a period of five and one-half years.

Algiers remained calm despite efforts of extremists to arouse feelings in anticipation of the forthcoming announcement of French President De Gaulle's policy regarding Algeria.

US Senator Hugh Scott of Pennsylvania denounced the UAR policy towards Israel and suggested that the Arab states contribute towards world peace by agreeing to a settlement of the Arab refugees, allowing unrestricted use of the Suez Canal, and ending their discrimination against Americans because of religion.

September 13

It was reported from Tangier that the Moroccan franc fell to a new low of 500 francs to one US dollar on the free money market.

Cairo reported that four Israel fighter planes fired warning shots at a UAR plane over the Gulf of Aqaba. The Israel Army denied the report.

Sir Anthony Eden of Great Britain completed a book explaining his role in the Suez Canal Crisis of 1956.

September 14

The Moroccan Communist Party was suspended by the Government of Morocco under a law which provided for such action against any association which infringes upon the national entity and monarchical structure of the state.

President Bourguiba of Tunisia was quoted in an interview published in Tunis as having said that he had offered France the naval base at Bizerta in return for the granting of independence to Algeria.

September, 1959

September 15

The US paid Jordan a grant in aid installment of $10 million to cover budgetary expenses.

The USSR Afro-Asian Solidarity Committee cabled to the UN Fourteenth General Assembly, which was to discuss the Algerian question, demanding on behalf of millions of USSR people that effective measures be taken to put an early end to bloodshed in Algeria.

September 16

In a television and radio address to France and Algeria, French President De Gaulle outlined his plan for solving the Algerian problem. He offered three possible alternatives to be chosen by referendum by the people of Algeria: independence; integration with the French Republic; or a federal autonomy retaining close ties with France. The choice would have to be preceded by a peaceful period of not more than four years.

The Steering Committee of the UN General Assembly approved for debate the item: "The Question of Algeria."

US officials expressed the hope that Arab leaders would not reject out of hand French President De Gaulle's plan for ending the Algerian war.

France would inform the UN General Assembly of President De Gaulle's plan for Algeria, but would not take part in the Assembly debate on Algeria.

The People's Court of Iraq sentenced Nadim al-Tabaqchali, formerly Commander of the Second Division in Kirkuk, Colonel Rifaat al-Hajj Sirri, formerly head of army intelligence in Baghdad, Lieutenant Colonel Aziz Ahmad Shihab and Captain Daud Khaled to death before a firing squad for complicity in the Mosul revolt last March.

General Abdi of Iraq said that the Iraqi airports would now remain open at all times.

September, 1959

September 16

The Minister of Agrarian Reform in Syria, Mustafa Hamdoun, issued a decision providing for the expropriation of excessive land belonging to 2,697 landlords in the provinces of Damascus, Dara, Hama, Aleppo, Latakia, al Hasakuh and Dar al-Zor.

September 17

In Paris, an attempt was made on the life of Hajj Messali, leader of the Algerian National Movement, rival of the Algerian National Liberation Front.

US President Eisenhower endorsed the De Gaulle plan for Algerian self determination as completely in accord with his hopes to see proclaimed a just and liberal program for Algeria.

Christian A. Herter, US Secretary of State, said at the UN General Assembly, that the US continued to support the principle of freedom of passage through the Suez Canal.

Britain went on record at the UN in support of free passage for all through the Suez Canal.

The Spanish Government passed up a chance to cooperate with French, British, West German and Italian interests in the exploitation of rich iron ore fields in northwestern Africa.

Khulusi al-Khairi, the Jordanian Minister of National Economy, announced in Amman that the Council of Ministers had approved the request of the Phillips Petroleum Company for an extension of its oil exploration concession in Jordan.

A Republic Decree was issued placing the Egyptian Petroleum Cooperative Society under the supervision of the UAR General Petroleum Authority.

Cairo Radio reported that Raymond A. Hare, US Ambassador to the UAR, was received by President Nasser.

September, 1959

September 18

The Soviet news agency Tass charged that some persons in the UAR were trying to poison Soviet-Arab friendship, even criticizing Premier Nikita S. Khrushchev's mission to the US.

September 19

President Nasser of Egypt declared at Rosetta, near Alexandria, that Israel shipping would not pass through the Suez Canal.

Three Bedouins were killed in an exchange of fire in the Negev Desert in southern Israel after they attacked an armed Israel Patrol searching for outlaws.

The Political Bureau of the French Communist Party's Central Committee urged peaceful settlement of the Algerian problem.

The Jordanian prosecution demanded the death penalty for 14 army officers accused of attempting to overthrow the regime last March while King Hussein was on a world tour.

A trade agreement between Tunisia and Russia was signed in Tunis by Said Ahmad Mistiri, Secretary of State for Finance and Commerce, and Mr. Pankratov, Russian Deputy External Trade Minister.

The Cairo weekly, Akhbar al-Yawm reported that Premier Kassem of Iraq's request for an Iraq Petroleum Company loan of ID50 million was refused and that he subsequently threatened to nationalize the company.

September 20

Thirteen army officers sentenced to death for participating in the Mosul uprising last March against the regime of Premier Kassem were executed.

September, 1959

September 17

French soldiers early in the morning and again in the evening covered the walls of nearly every building downtown in Algiers with posters advocating Algerian integration with France.

September 18

The Algiers Public Safety Committee attacked President De Gaulle's offer to Algeria of independence, semi-autonomy, or union with France as "this new demoniacal wager."

Algerian National Liberation Front ministers discussed De Gaulle's three way proposal for an Algerian settlement with the Provisional Government's President, Ferhat Abbas.

It was learned today that French troops killed 41 Algerian insurgents and captured five in the past 24 hours.

Three years after Egyptian martial law put them out of business, the British and French were able to return to their businesses and property in Cairo.

A series of paralysis attacks caused consternation in the Maknes region in central Morocco. The causes were believed to be from food poisoning.

The Committee of the Iraq Petroleum Company's Dismissed Workers completed a detailed report of their case which the Lebanese Ministry of Social Affairs requested.

The Tunisian newspaper al-Amal published an editorial which was clearly favorable in its reaction to President De Gaulle's declaration with regard to Algeria.

It was reported in the Jerusalem daily, Falastin, that assistance in the form of heavy equipment and technicians to assist Jordanian government engineers in the laying of water pipelines to Amman, had been supplied by Tapline to the Jordan Water Project.

September, 1959

September 20

The President of the Special Supreme Military Court of Iraq, Colonel Fadel Abbas Mahdawi, accompanied by the Prosecutor General, Colonel Majid Muhammad Amin, left by plane for a six weeks visit to Communist China.

Signor Pier Spinelli, UN Ambassador in the Middle East, returned to Amman from Geneva.

A ministerial reshuffle announced by Premier Majali of Jordan disclosed the following changes: former Finance Minister, Musa Naser, as Foreign Minister; Minister of Justice, Anastas Hananiya, replaced by Anwar Nashashibi, Minister of National Defense, for an ambassadorial appointment; and in addition to his portfolio, Khulusi al-Khairi received the Portfolio of Development and Reconstruction.

The Syrian Ministry of Industry announced that the oil storage facilities to be constructed at the Homs refinery would have sufficient capacity to meet Syrian fuel requirements over a period of 80 days.

The UAR agreed to the loan of 12 Egyptian specialists in eye diseases and radiology to work in the Saudi Arabian Ministry of Health for two years.

Arabs and Israelis began a joint campaign against malaria in Wadi al-Sanabra, Hebron district, near the truce line, under UN supervision.

September 21

General Maurice Challe, French Commander in Chief in Algeria, told his troops that the struggle against the Algerian rebellion would be intensified until total pacification was reached.

It was reported in Paris that Hajj Messali, the father of Algerian nationalism, approved French President De Gaulle's proposals of self determination to bring peace to Algeria.

September, 1959

September 21

Mr. James Swinburn, convicted in 1957 by an Egyptian court of spying for Great Britain and sentenced to five years imprisonment at hard labor was released in the general amnesty granted by President Nasser of the UAR on September 13 for the seventh anniversary celebration of the establishment of the Egyptian republic.

Dr. Abd-al-Moneim al-Kaissouni, UAR Minister of Economy, conferred with Mr. Eugene Black, President of the International Bank for Reconstruction and Development, about a possible loan for the development of the Suez Canal.

Lieutenant General Ali Amer was appointed Chief of General Staff of the Armed Forces of the UAR.

Baghdad reported that Kamel al-Chadirchi, leader of the National Democratic Party of Iraq, returned to Baghdad after spending about four months at Soviet resorts.

Jordan Radio called the hanging of the four Iraqi civilians on September 20 a disgusting crime committed by Communist agents of Moscow and Peking and Communist imperialism.

Premier Rashid Karami of Lebanon conferred with US President Dwight D. Eisenhower in Washington, D.C. They discussed the relations between the Arab World and the US.

September 22

A US State Department official denied that the US had strongly urged the Algerian rebels to accept the De Gaulle peace proposals.

US Secretary of State Christian A. Herter, addressing a luncheon of UN correspondents, expressed the hope that the UN would not take any action to imperil the Algerian settlement set forth by French President De Gaulle for Algerian self determination. France has feared a UN resolution calling for Algerian independence.

September, 1959

September 22

Sentences were pronounced by President Ibrahim Abboud of Sudan on 12 army officers courtmartialed for plotting last May to overthrow the Government.

The seventeenth progress report of the UN Conciliation Commission for Palestine, covering the period from June 1, 1958, to August 31, 1959, was issued.

Representatives of the Iraq Petroleum Company's Dismissed Employees Committee met with the Director General of the Ministry of Social Affairs of Lebanon and discussed their report of their case with him. The committee also announced that a meeting of all the dismissed employees would be held in Tripoli on September 27.

Sayyed Salah Ben-Youssef, a Tunisian political leader in exile in Cairo, accused President Habib Bourguiba of odious blackmail against the Algerian Provisional Government in order to induce it to accept the enslaving De Gaulle Plan.

Foreign Minister Musa Naser of Jordan said that Jordan and other Arab delegations to the current session of the UN General Assembly would concentrate on Palestine, including Mr. Hammarskjold's report on the future of the refugees and Algeria.

Turkish soldiers were officially stated to have crossed into Syria in the Ifrin area, Aleppo province, and tried to kidnap shepherds and steal their flocks.

The decision of Morocco to adhere to the Arab Postal Convention and cut all postal links with Israel was implemented.

King Saud of Saudi Arabia telegraphed President Nasser of the UAR supporting the barring of Israel ships and cargoes from the Suez Canal.

September 23

A report from Baghdad stated that Iraq had decided to form a board of directors for the General Petroleum Authority in Iraq, the members of which would be appointed by the Iraqi Council of Ministers and their term of office would be three years.

September, 1959

September 23

The Egyptian press reportedly launched a violent attack on US Secretary of State Christian A. Herter for his appeal at the UN for freedom of transit through the Suez Canal.

Jordan's chief delegate to the UN, Abd-al-Moneim Rifai, told the General Assembly that the Arab states were united in opposing Israel's claim to the right to use the Suez Canal. In regard to the Arab refugees, he stated that the Arabs would continue to insist that they must go back to their former homes. He warned that Arabs would not accept an economic approach to the problem.

Some 5,000 students and workers rallied in protest against the Iraqi execution of 13 revolutionary leaders on September 20. The protest took place in Cairo.

King Muhammad V of Morocco was faced with a grave domestic dilemma whether to support the present Government in its new plan of economic liberation from the French monetary zone or to call on the opposition to present a counter program and the names of a governing team to apply it.

Two leading Jordanian newspapers, al-Difa and al-Jihad, attacked the Iraqi Government execution on September 20 of army officers and civilians purported to be enemies of General Kassem.

September 24

Israel's Foreign Minister, Mrs. Golda Meir, speaking in the UN General Assembly, accused the UAR of violating international commitments and Security Council resolutions by closing the Suez Canal to Israel ships and Israel commerce.

Farid Zain-ad-Din, acting head of the UAR delegation to the UN, stated that his country was adhering strictly to the 1888 Convention of Constantinople, which made the Suez Canal an international waterway open to all countries.

September, 1959

September 24

The Egypt-Israel Mixed Armistice Commission (Israel absent) blamed Israel for an attack by four Israel fighter planes on an Egyptian airliner over the Gulf of Aqaba on September 13. It called the incident a flagrant breach of the armistice agreement.

The Palestine Conciliation Commission reported that Israel released $7,800,000 of blocked Arab refugee bank accounts.

It was disclosed in London that the Burden-Turiff construction company would build 314 miles of oil pipeline for Iraq for the Iraq Petroleum Company.

It was disclosed in Baghdad that the Iraqi Cabinet approved a draft law creating Iraq's first news agency.

A Chief of Staff for the Saudi Arabian Army was instituted by Royal Decree. General Ibrahim al-Tasan was appointed to the post.

King Hussein of Jordan received seven West German parliamentary delegates in Amman. On the same day four members of the US House of Representatives, led by Mr. Otto Passman, Chairman of the Foreign Aid Subcommittee, called on King Hussein.

September 25

France's delegation walked out of the General Assembly in protest against an Arab statement picturing the French Army in Algeria as torturers with a thirst for blood.

Terrorists killed nine French civilians and wounded 20 as Algeria awaited the nationalist rebels' reply to the French offer of self determination outlined by French President Charles De Gaulle.

Anti-Kassem demonstrators surged toward the Iraqi Embassy in Beirut in protest against the September 20 execution of the 13 men accused of plotting against the Kassem regime.

The chairman of the Saudi Arabian educational mission visiting Jordan announced the 140 Jordanian teachers had been hired to work in Saudi Arabia.

September, 1959

September 25

President Ibrahim Abboud of Sudan announced the permanent appointment of Major General Maqboul al-Hajj as Minister of Communications, Irrigation and Agriculture.

September 26

The appointment of Mr. Walter Eytan, Director General of the Israel Foreign Ministry, as Ambassador to France, was officially confirmed.

In an interview with the newspaper Ethnos in Athens, the Israel Foreign Minister, Mrs. Golda Meir, declared that Israel stood ready to negotiate a total or partial settlement of all outstanding questions as soon as its Arab neighbors, singly or collectively, were willing to do so.

The Algerian Nationalists informed King Muhammad V of Morocco of the broad lines of their answer to French President Chares De Gaulle's offer of self determination.

Algerian rebels ambushed an eight vehicle French convoy near Aflou, 190 miles south of Algiers, destroyed the military escort, and killed 26 people, among them a local Moslem leader.

The Tunisian Government reported two incidents on the Algerian border in which one civilian was killed and a soldier wounded when a French artillery fired barrages across the border.

September 27

A by election was held in al-Mukhtara, Lebanon, to fill a seat in Parliament left vacant by the murder of Deputy Naim Moghabghab two months ago. Candidate Kamal Jumblat won by almost 3,000 votes over the candidate backed by Mr. Camille Chamoun and the Socialist Party.

A special ministerial committee of Jordan met with representatives of the Phillips Petroleum Company and the Director of the Bureau of Mines

September, 1959

September 27

in the Jordanian Ministry of National Economy to draw up the final draft of an amendment, to be introduced into the concession agreement of the Phillips Company, which would provide for the addition of part of the Ghor district to the company's concession area against payment by the company of additional rent.

Award of the contract for completing the Ghor canal had been postponed for a month, Sayyed Muhammad Ismail, Director of the Canal Authority, disclosed in Amman.

The Syrian Communist leader in exile, Sayyed Khaled Bakdash, made a speech about the UAR during the 10th anniversary of the Communist regime in Peking which gave rise to a protest by the UAR Charge d'Affaires there.

Algiers waited tensely today for nationalist rebel leaders to reply to French President De Gaulle's offer of self determination for Algeria.

Algiers experienced its fifth bomb incident in three days.

September 28

A communique issued in Tunis by the Provisional Algerian Government said that it was ready to enter into conversations with the French Government to discuss the political and military conditions of a ceasefire, and the conditions and guarantees of the application of self determination.

A French Information Ministry spokesman disclosed in Paris that the French Government would officially ignore the declaration in Tunis by the Algerian Provisional Government.

Premier Ferhat Abbas of Algeria accepted the principle of self determination and said his regime was ready to discuss the political and military conditions of a ceasefire and the application of self determination.

Conservative Europeans in Algeria for the most part breathed a sigh of relief in the hope that a negotiated settlement would result in view of the reply of the Algerian Provisional Government to the De Gaulle offer.

September, 1959

September 28

Moroccan royal palace and political leaders welcomed the Algerian nationalist declaration to accept the principle of self determination as a positive factor toward a solution of the Algerian problem.

A storm of indignation arose in Cairo upon the execution of 13 Arab nationalist officers on September 20 for their participation in the Mosul revolt.

The Communist daily newspaper in Cairo, Ittihad-al-Shaab, defended the execution of 13 Arab nationalist officers implicated in the Mosul revolt as prudent and necessary.

The execution September 20 of 13 Iraqi army officers produced public demonstrations in the streets of Baghdad. Compared with other demonstrations in Iraq, these were mild, with no violence and no casualties reported.

The Sultan of Lahej in Aden, Fahd Ibn-Ali, laid the foundation stone at Ittahad city, a new Aden Federation capital, at Bir Ahmad.

Premier Karami of Lebanon said that his Government firmly supported the exclusion of Israel ships and cargoes from the Suez Canal.

The Cairo weekly Ruz-al-Yusuf reported that it had gained possession of a secret document giving details of an Iraqi plan to annex by force of arms if necessary the oil rich Sheikhdom of Kuwait, and other oil producing states of the Persian Gulf. Iraq's present financial crisis had compelled Iraq to do this, the weekly reported.

Prime Minister Sayyed Hazza al-Majali of Jordan said that an agreement to organize relations between the Ministry of Education and Christian missionary and private schools was contemplated, and denied the accusation that the ministry had requested the Christian community schools to teach the Moslem religion.

The US and the UAR signed an agreement in Cairo establishing a new Fulbright educational exchange program. This was actually a renewal of the old Fulbright program that was suspended during the Suez Crisis in 1956.

September, 1959

September 29, 1959

The Jordanian State Security Court heard the final evidence in the trial of seventeen discharged officers and civilians accused of plotting to overthrow the monarchy while King Hussein was on a world tour. The verdict was to be announced later.

King Hussein of Jordan approved a provisional military pension law submitted by the Council of Ministers which would entitle officers to pension on resigning after 20 instead of 25 years' service and on discharge after 12 instead of 15 years.

A courtmartial in Baghdad sentenced ten persons to prison terms, ranging from six months to four years at hard labor, for attacking the house of the President of the Special Supreme Military Court.

Iraq called on France to accept the offer of the Algerian Provisional Government to negotiate a ceasefire and conditions for self determination in Algeria.

September 30

On the first anniversary of the promulgation of the agrarian reform law, Premier Kassem of Iraq reported that the law had successfully laid down the outlines of its plan and marked about 5 million dunums of land for seizure.

It was reported in Cairo that Premier Kassem of Iraq had ordered the suspension of three newspapers for their attacks on the growing Communist influence in Iraq.

The French Foreign Minister, Maurice Couve de Murville, declared in the UN that only the French Government would carry out the arrangements for Algerian self determination offered by President De Gaulle of France.

President Charles De Gaulle of France was accused of treason in Algiers in a public statement by Pierre Lagaillarde, Deputy from Algiers in the French National Assembly saying that De Gaulle started a process of deliberate sell out of Algeria immediately after coming to power.

September, 1959

September 30

Mohan Ait-Ahmad, head of the Algerian rebel organization in the Paris suburbs, was arrested in Paris by French police.

Walter N. Walmsley, Jr., new US Ambassador to Tunisia, arrived in Tunis.

The Foreign Ministers of France, Sweden and Australia advocated free passage for all ships through the Suez Canal, including those of Israel.

It was reported from Tel Aviv that two sacks of mail sent from Israel to Morocco the previous week were returned by the Moroccan post office with the explanation that postal communications between the two countries had been severed.

The UAR Government expressed grave concern at the inclusion of Khaled Bakdash, leading Syrian Communist and an avowed opponent of the UAR regime, among the speakers at the celebration of the tenth anniversary of the establishment of Communist China on September 27, and announced that its Charge d'Affaires in Peking withdrew from the ceremonies.

The UAR Deputy Foreign Minister handed a protest note to the Chinese Ambassador in Cairo which demanded an explanation of the violation of the principle of peaceful coexistence by allowing a renegade, Khaled Bakdash, to make a flagrant attack that would do damage to relations between the two countries.

President Bourguiba of Tunisia urged each side in the Algerian rebellion to display an understanding of the other's basic political difficulties and not to set up minor obstacles to the achievement of peace.

French Foreign Minister Couve de Murville, at the UN General Assembly, assured the African countries, who had expressed fear of radioactive fallout from proposed Saharan atomic tests, that the precautions of the French Government "will absolutely eliminate all risks."

October, 1959

October 1

Rahdain Bank funds in Amman were released. A defense order freezing the funds and sequestrating the bank in July last year, after the federation of Iraq and Jordan was cancelled, was withdrawn.

Aden colony's 16 month old state of emergency was ended today.

A large part of the middle class in Iraq including businessmen, some religious leaders and professional men expressed their discontent over General Kassem's indifferent stand against Communists.

October 2

France boycotted a UN General Assembly speech by Guinea criticizing French excesses in Algeria.

The Moroccan Government explained that the ban on mail to or from Israel was a result of Morocco's ratification of the Arab postal convention, which barred its members from postal communication with Israel.

October 3

The UAR Foreign Ministry charged that the Chinese Communist Government deliberately held up diplomatic cables sent by the UAR Embassy in Peking.

It was reported in Ismailia, UAR, that the Suez Canal was exceeding pre-1956 records and that the new regime was able to handle the heavy traffic efficiently.

The High Court of Justice in Tunisia sentenced 15 men to death, seven in absentia, and 108 to varying terms of imprisonment, for plotting to assassinate Tunisian President Habib Bourguiba.

Following the decisions of the Arab League Higher Economic Council, the first meeting of the provisional Arab Economic Council began in Beirut, with the stated purpose of coordinating the economic and social policies of the Arab states.

October, 1959

October 1

The Sudanese and Libyan delegates in the UN appealed to France to accept the Algerian rebel government's offer to begin discussions on the application of Algerian self determination as offered by French President De Gaulle.

Electric light and power over a wide area in the Blida region in Algeria were cut off during the night when insurgents blew up a transformer and cut two main power lines.

French army headquarters said that Tunisian troops had been battling since September 28 against Algerian insurgent units north of Haidra and several Tunisians had been wounded.

Tunisia began its new policy of non-adherence to the French Customs Union by which it would continue to trade with France and other members of the Customs Union of the French bloc but at the same time carry out trade negotiations with markets competing with the Zone.

The UAR Foreign Ministry sent notes to the 25 nations that participated in the Bandung Conference, suggesting that they recall their ambassadors to Peking in protest against Communist China's recent aggression against Tibet, India and Laos.

UAR President Nasser ordered all government officials not to attend a large dinner party to be given at the Chinese Embassy in Cairo in honor of Communist China's tenth anniversary.

The UAR Minister of Culture and National Guidance announced the Egyptian decision to offer surplus antiquities in exchange for international help in excavating, recording and preserving the archeological sites in Nubia, which would be flooded with waters behind the proposed Aswan High Dam.

It was announced in Rabat that Morocco signed a commercial agreement with Communist China totaling $11.6 million.

Dr. John H. Davis, Director of the UN Relief and Works Agency, stated in a report to the UN General Assembly that the agency's life should be extended to allow time to arrive at a more permanent solution to the Arab refugee problem.

October, 1959

October 3

Lebanese President Fuad Chehab refused to accept the resignation of Sayyed Raymond Edde from the Lebanese Cabinet.

All the speakers at an Algiers meeting of 250 mayors and members of the French National Assembly pledged themselves to the integration of Algeria with France and repudiated any possibility of another solution.

October 4

The Istiqlal Party of Morocco announced the suspension of its five news organs in protest against the press decree of September 18 in which penalties were provided for criticizing a government official or a member of the army or police. The Party accused the Government of infringing on the freedom of the press.

Dr. Amin Ismail Sidqi, epidemics specialist at the World Health Organization's office in Alexandria, arrived in Amman for talks with the Health Ministry about aid for Jordan project to produce dry anti-smallpox vaccine to be used for Bedouin tribes which move between Jordan and other Arab countries.

M. Jean Querton, Belgian Ambassador to Jordan and Lebanon, presented his credentials to Jordanian King Hussein today following the raising to embassy level of diplomatic representations between Jordan and Belgium the previous week.

A herdsman in the Israel Village of Yad Hanna, near the Jordanian border, was shot to death.

October 5

UAR Foreign Minister Mahmoud Fawzi, speaking in the UN, attacked Israel Foreign Minister Golda Meir and the British Foreign Secretary Selwyn Lloyd for complaining to the General Assembly about Cairo's action in closing the Suez Canal to Israel shipping and cargoes. He

October 5

charged that Israel was creating a crisis by insisting on using the Suez Canal. The UAR would lift the anti-Israel blockade when the Palestinian refugee question was settled, he said.

Israel's chief delegate to the UN, Arthur Lourie, replied to UAR Foreign Minister Mahmoud Fawzi's attack on Israel, that the Egyptians having failed on the field of battle now asserted that they were entitled to maintain against them a one sided state of war. Lourie observed that the UN Charter emphatically rejected any such alleged right. He then challenged the UAR, saying that Israel would be prepared to enter into immediate negotiations for a full and final settlement of all outstanding Israel-Arab problems, at any time and place the Arab leaders may wish, and without any pre-conditions.

Syrian security and customs men fought with a 60 man band of smugglers said to have been guarded by six Turkish soldiers on the Turkish-Syrian border.

The newspaper *al-Nasr* reported that exiled Syrian Communist leader Khaled Bakdash would be tried *in absentia* on charges of high treason and intriguing against the UAR and Syrian-Egyptian unity.

Anti-Communists in Iraq were gaining influence over professional bodies. They recently gained control of the small but influential lawyers association and were continuing their efforts to counteract the Communists' move to gain power in these organizations.

The French Army produced today a document purporting to show that 483 Algerian rebel fighters had been executed by their commander for advocating ceasefire talks with France.

Lahej joined the Federation of Arab Emirates of the South.

October 6

The Egyptian-Israel Mixed Armistice Commission (Israel absent) condemned Israel for expelling several hundred Bedouins of the Azamah tribe from the Negev.

October 6

Israel declared at the UN that its offer to negotiate a Palestine peace settlement with the Arab states had been rejected.

Sayyed Muhammad Kamel Abd-al-Rahim of Yemen urged the UN General Assembly to send a mission to Yemen to investigate what he described as Britain's secret war against the people of Oman.

The Jordanian House of Representatives approved an amendment to the State Security Court act empowering the Prime Minister to form more of such courts to try Communists and others, the main aim of which was to speed up trials.

October 7

In a memorandum to UN Secretary General Dag Hammarskjold, the Arab League rejected his proposals concerning the continuation of UN assistance to the Palestine refugees and insisted on the return of all the refugees to Israel.

At a meeting of the Jordan-Israel Mixed Armistice Commission, Israel and Jordan promised each other to make efforts to maintain tranquility on their common border and avoid incidents.

It was announced in Jerusalem that Israel maintained its boycott of the Egyptian-Israel Mixed Armistice Commission.

President Nasser of the UAR said that he was ready to accept a UN commission that would implement all UN resolutions relating to Israel and the Arabs, including the 1951 Security Council resolution calling for freedom of shipping in the Suez Canal.

Premier Kassem of Iraq was wounded in the shoulder in an assassination attempt while driving in his car in al-Rashid Street in Baghdad.

The Iraqi Military Governor imposed a 9 pm to 5 am curfew in Baghdad and its suburbs. He banned all demonstrations and gatherings throughout the country. A gathering of five or more persons for any purpose was considered to be a violation of the ban.

October 7

The Jordanian House of Notables approved the amendment to the State Security Court Act.

Dr. Chun Jien-pae, the new Nationalist Chinese Ambassador to Jordan, submitted his credentials in Amman, taking the place of Mr. Chun Chehping, who was transferred to Libya.

The Jordanian State Security Court sentenced former Army Chief of Staff, Sadeq al-Sharaa, his brother and a civilian to death for attempting to overthrow the regime.

Arab delegates at New York said that someone had threatened Saudi Arabian delegate to the UN, Ahmad Shukairy, that he would be shot if he did not abandon his attacks on Israel.

W. R. Cooper, Arabian-American Oil Company's General Manager for Engineering and Construction, was elected a Vice President of ARAMCO.

CENTO's Council of Ministers met in Washington D. C. from October 7-9.

A Sudanese ministerial mission with numerous advisers arrived in Cairo to resume negotiations for an equitable share of Nile waters now that the UAR was going ahead with the Aswan High Dam projects.

The National Mining and Geological Department of Morocco awarded to the Fairchild Aerial Surveys Incorporated, of Los Angeles, California, a contract for an extensive geophysical air survey of the eastern part of Morocco to determine mineral resources.

The Arab League's Provisional Council for Economic Union ended its two week meeting in Beirut.

October 8

Premier Karami of Lebanon enlarged his cabinet from four to eight men. One minister was dropped and five new ones were added. Karami was now Premier, and Minister of Finance and Defense. Hussein Uwaini was the new Minister of Foreign Affairs.

October 8

It was announced officially that the Iraqi Cabinet decided to form a medical committee to treat and restore the health of the sole leader, Abd-al-Karim Kassem. It would also issue bulletins on his condition, which was reported then as good.

US President Eisenhower sent a message of sympathy to Premier Kassem.

The Iraq Military Governor extended the curfew in Baghdad from 9 pm to 6 am. Armored cars took up stations throughout Baghdad.

The Arab delegations at the UN informed Secretary General Hammarskjold that they would oppose any effort to reintegrate Palestine refugees in the Arab host countries. They said that Dag Hammarskjold's recent recommendation had anticipated a situation in which the refugees would be forced to give up their rights.

Royal approval of the appointment of Sayyed Anatas Hananiya of Jordan as Ambassador in London was given today.

October 9

France and Tunisia agreed to release political prisoners of Tunisian and French nationality.

Communist China accused President Nasser of the UAR of waging a systematic campaign of vilification against it, while Peking held out the hand of friendship.

October 10

President Habib Bourguiba of Tunisia inaugurated the National Agricultural Bank of Tunisia which could lend to peasants at 2 percent interest. He thanked the US for financial contribution to its initial capital.

October, 1959

October 10

The Russian consulate in Cairo cancelled its lease of a Port Said cinema where it had been presenting Russian films because the public had been boycotting the shows. Moscow Radio complained that prospective patrons were intimidated by the authorities.

An agreement on the avoidance of double taxation was signed by UAR and US representatives in Washington for the purpose of encouraging private American investments.

Yemen was reported to be signing an oil agreement with ENI (Entente Nationale Italienne).

Sudan and the UAR opened talks on the long standing issue of sharing the waters of the Nile.

A special committee of high ranking officers and judges was appointed in Iraq to investigate the attempt on Premier Kassem's life.

A Royal Decree issued in Amman authorized Premier Majali to establish new State Security Courts to try Communists and other "dangerous" Jordanians.

The Premier of Morocco, Abdallah Ibrahim, expressed hope that his visit to the US would result in a solution to the question of five US military bases in Morocco.

October 11

About 250 doctors met in Beirut and decided to ask the Government for legislation prohibiting precautionary detention of doctors and for changes in the rules of medical practice in Lebanon.

It was reported in Algiers that Moslem rebels stepped up their activities in Algeria this weekend resulting in the death of eight persons.

A group of French paratroopers on leave clashed with Moslem civilians after six paratroopers had been wounded in a terrorist attack in Algeria.

October, 1959

October 11

French Foreign Minister Couve de Murville made public an offer to negotiate a ceasefire with the Algerian National Liberation Front.

French military sources reported that 26 Algerian rebels were killed and five wounded and taken prisoner in a clash near Diderot in western Algeria.

Popular sympathy over the attempted assassination of Kassem had, in the opinion of the diplomats, helped to stabilize Kassem's regime in Iraq while US analysts expressed the gloomy view that his regime was being maneuvered into a position from which Communists could at some future time take over.

October 12

M. Noel Fieschi, mayor of Behagle, eastern Algeria, and his wife were shot to death by insurgents.

Al-Ahram accused Moscow Radio of lying when it alleged that the UAR was angling for western military aid. The paper said that the West refused to sell arms to the UAR and not because the latter was unwilling to buy them.

The Jordanian financial undersecretary disclosed that the US promised to pay a second installment of aid to Jordan early next month.

An-Nahar reported that the appropriate departments in the Lebanese Ministries of Finance and Planning were preparing to resume oil transit royalty negotiations with Tapline.

The curfew hours in Iraq were changed again, from 6 pm to 5 am, and were extended to cover the entire country.

October 13

The French Government again offered safe conduct to leaders of the Algerian Provisional Government to come to France to discuss a ceasefire.

October, 1959

October 13

French Premier Michel Debre opened a National Assembly debate on France's three way proposal of self determination for Algeria.

The President of the Special Supreme Military Court of Iraq, Colonel Mahdawi, and the Prosecutor General, Colonel Amin, cut short their visit to Communist China and returned to Baghdad after the attempt on Premier Kassem's life.

According to the Iraq Times, the Iraq Government's income from oil royalties amounted to ID63, 784, 886 so far in 1959, or about ID6 million more than in the same period last year.

The Ministry of Health of Jordan reported that it intended to give three million doses of vaccine produced in its laboratories to the World Health Organization each year as a contribution to the campaign to eradicate smallpox in the Middle East.

October 14

It was learned at the UN that Premier Abdallah Ibrahim of Morocco was trying to lay the groundwork for UN action to pave the way for talks between France and the Algerian nationalists.

Eight of the prisoners sentenced to death by the Tunisian High Court of Justice for attempting to assassinate President Bourguiba and for charges of subversion were hanged.

The Renault automobile company of France decided to end operations in Israel, apparently because of Arab boycott threats.

Eight members of the Gaullist group in the French National Assembly broke away from the group because they were not being allowed to defend Algeria's integration with France.

It was announced that Shah Muhammad Riza Pahlevi would make an official visit from Iran to Jordan on October 28 at the invitation of King Hussein of Jordan.

A trade agreement was signed between Tunisia and Czechoslovakia.

October, 1959

October 14

The leader of the Sudanese delegation in Cairo announced that representatives of the first subcommittee had drawn up a trade and payments agreement which would be put in its final form before the weekend.

Top level talks between Algeria and Morocco began in Rabat. Premier Abbas of the Algerian Provisional Government was reported to be desirous to clarify the French and Algerian positions with regard to the new regime in Algeria.

October 15

Premier Abdallah Ibrahim of Morocco conferred with US President Eisenhower in Washington. They discussed the future of the American military bases in Morocco.

Another attempt on General Kassem's life was reported by the Military Governor General.

The Lebanese Minister of Social Affairs, Maurice Zywain, submitted a draft decision to the Council of Ministers providing for the formation of a ministerial committee to follow up the case of the dismissed Iraq Petroleum Company employees.

The UK rejected as unfounded Yemen's allegations of infringement of the frontier between Yemen and the Aden Protectorate, and said that it was perturbed by Yemen's unsubstantial allegations.

French Premier Debre said military pacification of Algeria would continue with the French Army kept at full strength and declared that conversations with the rebels would concern only military and not political questions.

October 16

It was announced in Baghdad that the Iraqi Ministry of Agrarian Reform ordered all its directorates in the provinces to guard against the migration of peasants and to take legal measures against anyone who violated the Military Governor General's ban on such movements for any reason whatsoever.

October, 1959

October 16

Syrian troop movements on the Iraqi border were rumored following an Iraqi charge to this effect.

A UAR spokesman said in Cairo that the UAR rejected a charge that they were massing troops along the Syrian-Iraqi border.

The French National Assembly voted confidence, 441-23, in President Charles De Gaulle's plan for Algerian self determination of the solution to the Algerian problem.

A promoter of a liberal Algerian policy, French Senator Francois Mitterrand, survived an attack on his life.

The Moroccan Government announced a change of name for the Moroccan currency from the Moroccan franc to the Dirham (equivalent to 100 Moroccan francs). The measure was considered a prelude to new economic measures that may involve a break with the franc zone.

The Lebanese Minister of Social Affairs received Hussein al-Hussein, President of the Association of Lebanese Labor Unions.

The Presidium of the USSR Supreme Soviet ratified the USSR-Iraqi cultural cooperation agreement, signed in Baghdad on May 5, 1959.

October 17

The International Monetary Fund in Washington announced that it agreed to a one year $25 million standby credit arrangement with Morocco.

The Moroccan Government announced a 20.44 percent devaluation of the Moroccan franc as one in a series of measures to strengthen the country's economy. To counter the effect of devaluation on prices, the Government has established strict control of the prices of consumer goods and luxury items would be highly taxed.

A UAR decree abolished the separate posts of Chief of Staff in the army, navy and air force, and assigned to them the title of Commander in Chief.

October, 1959

October 17

A French Army spokesman said that French forces killed 61 insurgents and wounded twelve in the preceding 48 hours.

October 18

The Council of the Arab League decided to make a grant of LE12 million in response to the Algerian Government's request.

Dr. Moshe Prywes, Associate Dean of Hebrew University Haddasah Medical School of Jerusalem deplored the fact that Israel's health and medical programs could not be applied at the present to neighboring Arab countries because of the lack of contact between these countries and Israel.

The Soviet Ambassador in Lebanon, Sergei P. Kiktev, paid a private visit to Jordan, the first Soviet diplomat to visit the country.

The Egyptian Minister of Rural and Municipal Affairs told the press that a preliminary agreement had been reached for Czechoslovakian equipment and materials worth LE50 million to be supplied to Egypt on a long term credit basis.

The Ministry of Finance in Morocco announced that all Moroccan citizens must return to Morocco the liquid capital and deposits from their investments abroad.

October 19

The US made a voluntary contribution of $3.5 million to meet the cost of the UN Emergency Force in the Middle East.

Premier Hazza Majali of Jordan accused Israel of expelling 300 Bedouins of the Azazmah tribe from their homes and driving them into Jordan.

October, 1959

October 19

An Israel Army spokesman denied that any group of Arabs was driven from Israel into Jordan.

An Israel military patrol killed an Arab infiltrator near the Gaza Strip.

Rabat reported that the US agreed in principle to a loan of about $40 million to Morocco for the year 1960.

French troops killed or captured the total of 538 Algerian rebels in 233 operations in Algeria the previous week. The Army said that 56 French soldiers died.

A delegation of the dismissed employees of the Iraq Petroleum Company visited the Minister of Social Affairs in Lebanon and threatened to go on another hunger strike if their case was not settled by October 26.

In an interview with the Cairo daily al-Ahram, His Royal Highness Amir Faisal denied that any contacts were taking place between Saudi Arabia and Great Britain over the renewal of diplomatic relations.

A Gaullist leader confirmed reports that right wing forces in Algiers and Paris had plotted to overthrow the Government of Premier Michel Debre.

Australia and the UAR agreed to resume diplomatic relations.

October 20

Kaiser-Fraser of Israel said today that it would sue Renault Company of France for $2 million for breach of contract arising from the Arab League's removal of Renault from its blacklist and the halting of shipments to Israel.

The French-Israel Alliance Committee in Paris decided to campaign for reversal of the Renault Company's withdrawal from Israel.

The US granted the American University in Cairo $500,000 for a new science building, a student service center, and a scholarship program.

October, 1959

October 20

Dollars were in heavy demand on the Tangier free market, but on instructions from Rabat, banks were unable to sell them.

The Conference of Arab Oil Experts began in Jedda, Saudi Arabia.

Sayyed Sabri Hamadi was elected speaker of the Lebanese Chamber of Deputies by a 33-29 vote.

The Jordanian House of Representatives unanimously agreed to meet occasionally in Jerusalem in compliance with a resolution adopted by the Council of Ministers nominating Jerusalem as a second capital.

Employees at the Crescent Hotel in Aden went on strike for more money and shorter hours. The management claimed that one-third of them remained at work.

Local employees of the British Navy, Army and Air Force Institutes who had been on strike for a week returned to work.

The Soviet vessel Tenchin arrived in Alexandria, Egypt, with the first cargo of equipment for the building of the Aswan High Dam.

October 21

UAR President Nasser placed Field Marshal Abd-al-Hakim Amer, Vice President and Commander in Chief of the Armed Forces, in authority over the Syrian cabinet, responsible to Nasser himself. Amer was also entrusted with the organization of the National Union in Syria.

UAR President Nasser placed the Department of News and Propaganda under Colonel Abd-al-Hamid Sarraj, Minister of the Interior of the Syrian Region.

Israel offered to repatriate any Bedouins of Israel nationality who fled into Egypt during a search for the murderer of an Israel officer.

The Japanese owned Arabian Oil Company announced in Tokyo that it would resume its test drilling offshore from the Saudi Arabian-Kuwait Neutral Zone toward the end of November.

October, 1959

October 21

King Saud of Saudi Arabia announced that schools for girls would be established in Saudi Arabia under the supervision of a special committee of religious leaders.

Premier Ferhat Abbas, in an interview with the Arabic daily al-Tahrir, disclosed that foreign investments in the Sahara would be respected in independent Algeria on the condition that these investments did not interfere with the right of ownership.

October 22

A spokesman was reported to have said that $14, 399, 000 had been allotted for UN Relief and Works Agency's work in Jordan during the coming year.

King Hussein of Jordan nominated the 25 members of the new House of Notables, ten of whom were new.

Major General Moshe Dayan of Israel, one of the leading personalities of the Mapai Party, visited the Katamon quarter using the American political technique of personal call to tackle the only issue that had developed thus far in the Israel election campaign—the discontent of the so-called oriental immigrants from the Middle East and North Africa.

The UN Syrian-Israel Mixed Armistice Commission received a complaint from Israel that an Israel patrol was fired on in the Huleh valley near the Syrian line. The exchange of fire lasted 80 minutes.

October 23

French military sources reported that 30 nationalist insurgents were killed in a 48 hour battle near Oran, Algeria.

According to Iraqi trade reports, goods worth ID325, 000 were ordered by Iraqi merchants during the first week of the Czechoslovakian trade exhibition in Baghdad.

October, 1959

October 25

At a meeting of 200 representatives of the Gaullist Union for the New Republic in Algeria, French President Charles De Gaulle's proposal for secession, integration or autonomy for Algeria was accepted. It was also reported that some 300 mayors and other local officials resolved to accept the De Gaulle proposal.

The French Army intensified a psychological warfare campaign against the insurgents in Algeria.

An Iraqi courtmartial sentenced a lieutenant colonel and 12 privates to death for killing Colonel Jalal Ahmad Ismail, of the Basra garrison.

The US Development Loan Fund granted $1. 5 million to the Jordan Phosphate Mines Company, Limited, to help finance expansion of its operations from 320, 000 tons annually to 600, 000 tons.

In an interview with the Amman correspondent of the London News Chronicle, King Hussein said that Jordan would do all in its power to rescue Iraq from Communist control and that Jordan could not stand idly by if either Communists or a pro-Nasser group took over Iraq.

Field Marshal Amer began reorganizing Syrian administrative government machinery.

October 26

Leaflets criticizing President Nasser were confiscated by security officers as they were being distributed in the streets in Beirut. They originated from the Moslem Liberation Party and attacked the recent decision of giving Field Marshal Amer powers to supervise Syrian affairs.

The Arab League Petroleum Experts Committee held its seventh session in Jedda, Saudi Arabia. Sheikh Abdallah Tariki was elected chairman.

Two more protectorates would soon join the West Aden federation.

October, 1959

October 24

UAR President Nasser named Ahmad Abdallah Tuaima as Minister of Waqfs.

More than two-thirds of the Senators representing Algeria and the Sahara in the French upper house appealed tonight for a ceasefire between French troops and Moslem insurgents in Algeria.

Revised editions of two French newspapers, L'Express and France Observateur, were seized today by French authorities because they contained reprints about an alleged plot to overthrow the French Government.

The UN Egyptian-Israel Mixed Armistice Commission (Israel absent) condemned and strongly blamed Israel for an attack by four Israel fighters on an Egyptian airliner over the Gulf of Aqaba, September 13.

New governors were appointed for the five Lebanese provinces.

An intensive search went under way for two Americans, two Frenchmen, and their guide who have been reported lost in the Nubian Desert in Egypt.

Field Marshal Amer took over control of the Syrian Region.

October 25

Australia and Egypt resumed diplomatic relations severed November 6, 1956. The UAR agreed to transfer to Australia the ANZAC memorial at Port Said.

The UAR Government accepted an apology from Communist China for the speech made by Khaled Bakdash at a reception in Peking in celebration of the tenth anniversary of the establishment of the Chinese Communist regime.

It was learned that Sayyed Kilani would fly back to Peking as the UAR's dispute with Communist China was resolved and the Cairo press dropped its attacks.

October, 1959

October 26

Fifteen Britons received exit permits from Iraq, the first since the attempt to kill the Prime Minister.

An Egyptian frontier patrol reported that it had found the bodies of one American and two Frenchmen missing in the Nubian Desert.

October 27

The Petroleum Conference of the Arab League in Jedda approved a proposal to build a 1, 250 mile Arab owned pipeline linking the oil fields of Iraq, Kuwait and Saudi Arabia with Mediterranean ports in Syria and Lebanon.

The Iraqi Government confiscated the properties of 38 persons implicated in the assassination attempt on Premier Abd-al-Karim Kassem.

A UN Emergency Force communique said that fire had swept through the force's hospital burning it to the ground within an hour.

October 28

It was reported in Paris that French President De Gaulle called on the French Army and the civil administration in Algeria for devotion and discipline in seeking an end to the rebellion.

Paul Delouvrier, France's chief executive in Algeria, called in about 300 departmental heads of the civil administration and lectured them on the meaning of General De Gaulle's policies.

Talks between Crown Prince Moulay Hassan of Morocco and French President De Gaulle on the Algerian problem proved to be positive, fruitful and useful.

Reacting to a report that King Husein of Jordan was preparing to take over Iraq, Premier Kassem stated that Iraq was powerful enough to crush any aggression from abroad.

October, 1959

October 29

A UN Jordan-Israel Mixed Armistice Commission met to discuss a Jordanian complaint about the expulsion from Israel of 300 Bedouins of the Azazmah tribe.

French Army commanding officers expressed confidence and optimism that a ceasefire would not shake the army's control of Algerian territory.

The Iraqi Military Governor reduced the curfew. The new hours were from 9:30 pm to 5 am.

The US reiterated its intention of withdrawing from Morocco its naval and air bases.

The Casablanca civil court turned down the Moroccan Government's demand for the dissolution of the Communist Party of Morocco.

October 30

Ahmad Shukairy of Saudi Arabia denounced a suggestion by Israel that a regional arms limitation plan for the Middle East be considered while negotiations over world disarmament were proceeding.

In a speech at Algiers, French delegate general Paul Delouvrier vowed that France and its army would stay in Algeria. He declared that either through a negotiated ceasefire or a military campaign, France would still be the victor in Algeria.

The Petroleum Conference of the Arab League, meeting in Jedda, Saudi Arabia, recommended that no concession be granted to any company which had non-Arab government capital, that Arab Governments should demand that oil companies give up their concessions in territories which have not been exploited and for which no rent is paid, and that every Arab country should be supplied with the oil it needs if its own resources should fail, either in wartime or peace.

Socony Mobil Oil Company announced in New York that its Libyan affiliate had struck oil with a wildcat well 190 miles southeast of Benghazi.

October, 1959

October 30

The newspaper al-Thawra reported that a pro-Kassem political party in Iraq was being initiated in Baghdad in an effort to attract independent forces among the people to party life, curb the anarchists (Communists) and promote the economic life of the country as well as uphold the supremacy of the law.

UAR President Nasser accepted the resignation of Sayyed Hassan Ibrahim as Chairman of the Board of Economic Organization. His position was taken over by Dr. Kaissouni who was also Minister of Economy.

No agreement was reached on the Nile water talks between Sudan and the UAR, it was reported in Cairo, but Sudanese delegates expressed hopes that agreement would soon be reached.

The British Embassy in Tunis reported that a new trade agreement between Tunisia and Italy was signed in Tunis on October 31, 1959. The new agreement would be valid for one year with effect from November 1, 1959.

October 31

Parcels of state lands were distributed to 293 needy peasant families in Sidi Kassem by King Muhammad V in the advent of the Moroccan Government's new program of land distribution.

It was reported in Casablanca that 15 dock workers were injured in a clash between rival unionists.

The heavy cost, human and financial, of the Algerian war was examined by Le Monde on the eve of the conflict's fifth anniversary.

November, 1959

November 1

At a Cairo reception to commemorate the anniversary of the Algerian war, the Minister of Culture in the Algerian Provisional Government, Sayyed Tawfiq al-Madani, declared that the Algerians would go on fighting until final liberation. A solution of the war would only come if the French agreed to negotiate with the Provisional Government on conditions for a ceasefire and guarantees for a referendum on the future of the Algerian people.

In an interview, Premier Kassem of Iraq declared that Iraq was a friend of all countries, but he warned that Iraq would not tolerate interference from outside forces.

A wave of armed attacks swept through Algeria on the fifth anniversary of the outbreak of the nationalist rebellion.

The Sudanese Government announced that an overall agreement was reached with the UAR on all outstanding issues including the division of the Nile waters.

The Sudanese Minister of Communications said at Khartoum that Port Sudan was to be expanded and developed into an international harbor that would accommodate the largest ships in the world.

According to the Egyptian engineer in charge of the Aswan project, the Soviet Union fully expected to build all three stages of the Aswan High Dam. The Soviet loan of $92 million was intended for the first stage only.

The nine African state members of the UN declared that there was now hope for a just, peaceful and democratic solution in Algeria, now that it had accepted the principle of self determination.

It was learned in Rabat that after Premier Abdallah Ibrahim's talks in Washington, the US publicly recognized Moroccan sovereignty over the five bases and declared its determination to reach an agreement on withdrawing its forces from them.

November, 1959

November 1

Security forces were deporting all foreigners who were politically active in Lebanon, an authoritative source in Beirut said.

Jordanian security forces arrested an Israeli who allegedly tried to cross the armistice line into Jordan from Israel in the Jenin Mablus area. UN truce observers began an investigation upon notification.

Sixty-two tons of American munitions for Tunisia's military forces arrived in Tunis aboard a US navy cargo ship.

November 2

Muhammad Riza Shah Pahlevi of Iran arrived in Amman for a state visit.

President Nasser of the UAR issued a decree placing state land with the exception of the areas used by various ministries under supervision of the agrarian reform organization.

Spain sent notes to all Arab League member countries assuring them that Spain was anxious to preserve good relations with the Arab countries.

Israel notified the Jordan-Israel Mixed Armistice Commission that it was prepared to admit about 200 Bedouins from Jordan as a gesture of good will if Jordan dropped the charge that Israel forced the tribesmen to cross the border.

The Iraqi Foreign Ministry notified the UAR Embassy in Baghdad that Tawfiq Sulaiman Abazah its Second Secretary, was engaged in activities detrimental to the state and that he was therefore to leave Iraq as a persona non grata within 24 hours.

November 3

Premier David Ben-Gurion of Israel warned President Gamal Abdel Nasser of the UAR that any attempt to stage an uprising in Iraq would compel Israel to reserve freedom of action.

November 3

Al-Ahram reported the terms of the agreement between Sudan and the UAR. Sudan would receive LE15 million from the UAR for land in the Wadi Halfa that would be flooded for the Aswan High Dam. Allocation of the water after the Dam was built would be 18.5 billion cubic meters for Sudan and 55.5 billion cubic meters for Egypt. The Sudanese were to lend Egypt 1.5 billion cubic meters annually until they built irrigation canals to utilize additional water.

The trade agreement between the Sudan and the UAR provided for an annual exchange of products to the value of LE11 million: LE6 million in UAR exports to Sudan, and LE5 million in Sudanese exports to the UAR.

The Central Committee of the French Communist Party conceded, after Moscow lauded the De Gaulle plan for Algerian self determination that they had erred in attacking it.

Sayyed Jamal Mikkawa was elected chairman of the Lebanese Chamber of Deputies' Foreign Affairs Committee to replace Sayyed Philippe Taqla, now Minister of Justice and Economy.

Britain was expected to lend Jordan 500,000 pounds sterling interest free during the present financial year to finance the development of the desert road between Amman and Maan.

Premier Ibrahim of Morocco returned from a month long visit to the US.

Dr. Faisal al-Samar, Iraqi Minister of National Guidance, left for Moscow reportedly with a message from Premier Kassem to Premier Khrushchev.

Israel's fourth election since independence gave a plurality to the Mapai Party of Ben-Gurion.

November 4

Israel told UN supervisors in Jerusalem that four UAR MIG-17 fighter planes had invaded its territory that morning and had been driven off by Israel Air Force jet fighters while the UAR Command in Cairo reported the contrary, namely, that its planes had repulsed two intrusions. Egypt reported that six Israel Mystere planes were intercepted by Egyptian planes; one Israel plane was reportedly hit and all Egyptian planes were reported to have returned safely.

Jordan withdrew its complaint to the Mixed Armistice Commission that Israel drove a group of 200 Bedouins across the border into Jordan.

In Algiers, French Delegate General Paul Delouvrier announced that the French Government intended to spend the equivalent of $506,600,000 in 1960 for the economic and social development of Algeria, an increase of 38 percent over 1959.

The Moroccan Government announced that it had been authorized to borrow up to $312 million from the US Development Loan Fund for improving the electrification and water supply in Rabat and Casablanca.

The Moroccan Government proclaimed the death penalty for the manufacture or sale of dangerous food products after an outbreak of mass poisoning caused by table oil adulterated with fuel oils from US surplus stocks.

The Jordanian Council of Ministers decided to increase Jordan's yearly contribution to the International Monetary Fund from $3 million to $4.5 million to enable Jordan to draw from the Fund.

The Jordanian Minister of Economy said that it had informed the Foreign Ministry that it supported the economic boycott of France decided by the Arab League Economic Council. In conjunction with this, the Government banned all dealings with the Paris firm La Societe Bancaire et Financiere d'Orient and all its branches for violating the Arab boycott of Israel.

A medical report said that the death of an inexperienced guide who led two Americans and a Frenchman on a fatal trek across the Nubian Desert was caused by violence.

November 4

US President Eisenhower announced that in December he would visit nine countries in Europe, the Middle East and Asia. The Middle Eastern countries would be Turkey, Afganistan, Iran and Morocco.

The Ford Foundation announced in New York a grant of $745,000 for five projects in Jordan and the UAR.

November 5

Uproar broke out in the Lebanese chamber when the President, Sayyed Sabri Hamadi, stopped Sayyed Pierre Edde and his supporters from discussing the latter's proposal to amend a Government Decree integrating the municipal and ordinary police forces.

A French Army spokesman announced that French military planes dispersed a nationalist rebel caravan of 120 men near Bir Djedid.

An official Moroccan delegation left Rabat for Beirut, to ask for the hand of Miss Lamina al-Solh for Prince Moulay Abdallah of Morocco.

November 6

Communist China gave the Algerian nationalist insurgents the equivalent of $10 million in credits for the purchase of war materials or to carry out propaganda and administration, usually reliable sources in Tunis said.

The French in Algiers announced the death of Major Mira (Oumira Abderrahmane), nationalist rebel commander in the Kabylia area of northern Algeria. They claimed that all six rebel zones were without field commanders.

A joint communique issued at Amman at the conclusion of the Shah of Iran's four day visit announced that the diplomatic representation between Iran and Jordan was to be raised to embassy level. They pledged to spare no effort to preserve peace and security in the Middle East.

November 6

The Iraqi Premier Kassem declared in Baghdad that Syria and Iraq were neighbors and should eventually be united. He added that reports of troops being massed near its borders did not frighten Iraq.

November 7

On the eve of Tunisia's first national elections as a republic, President Habib Bourguiba, lone presidential candidate, was assured of re-election.

It was officially announced in Amman that the US would make four monthly grants of $4,100,000 each, starting in December, to the Jordanian Treasury to help cover budgetary expenses.

The British Embassy in Tunis reported that a new trade agreement between Tunisia and Poland had been signed in Tunis. The agreement would be valid for one year, effective November 1, 1959.

Two Algerian rebel chiefs were killed by French forces at Oran Willaya district.

November 8

The Sudan and the UAR signed an agreement in Cairo on the division of the Nile waters, a trade and payments agreement and a customs agreement.

A marriage contract between the second son of King Muhammad V of Morocco and a 23 year old Lebanese girl was signed in Beirut. Neither Miss Lamina al-Solh nor Prince Moulay Abdallah was present.

Habib Bourguiba, unopposed presidential candidate in the first Tunisian national elections, was elected president by over 90 percent of the registered voters. His Neo-Destour Party won a resounding victory by capturing all the 90 seats in the National Assembly. Women voters were unveiled for the first time.

November, 1959

November 8

Fifteen Czechoslovakian and eight Yugoslavian professors were engaged to teach at Baghdad University.

November 9

The Iranian newspaper Kayhan, reported from Abadan that 15 Soviet ships and more than 100 transport planes had unloaded a large number of jet planes, jeeps, heavy arms and ammunition at Basra, Iraq.

The council of the Federation of the Arab Amirates of the South opened its first meeting in Aden.

About 500 oil workers in Aden went on a 48 hour strike in response to an appeal by the BP (British Petroleum) Aden Employees Union in demand for better conditions.

Sayyed Khulusi al-Khairi announced that West Germany offered to give Jordan technical aid including a fully equipped geological mission to prospect for minerals.

November 10

Dr. John H. Davis, Director of the UN Relief and Works Agency, told the Special Political Committee of the General Assembly that assistance to the Arab refugees would be needed for a decade or even longer. He also said that at least 600,000 of the refugees would have to cross a demarcation line or a national boundary for permanent settlement.

Soviet Premier Nikita S. Khrushchev told Salah Salem, editor of the semi-official Egyptian newspaper al-Gumhuriya, that President Nasser's attacks on local Communists would not stand in the way of Soviet friendship for Egypt. He also said that he supported Cairo's ban on Israel shipping in the Suez Canal and gave assurances of a continued arms supply to Egypt as well as loans for economic development.

November, 1959

November 11

The Arabian Oil Company of Japan announced that it was to increase its capital from 5,250 million yen to 10,000 million yen in order to raise the additional funds necessary for oilfield development in its offshore concession in the Persian Gulf.

The news of US President Eisenhower's proposed trip to the Middle East was greeted with much satisfaction in Tunisia.

Seven arrests were reported in the wake of the unsuccessful Sudanese revolt the previous day. No state of emergency had been proclaimed.

Lebanese Prime Minister Rashid Karami, Sheikh Abdallah al-Tariqi, the Saudi Director General of Petroleum and Mineral Affairs, discussed the problem of the increase of Lebanon's oil transit royalties from Tapline.

The Beirut daily al-Bina reported that over the past eight years and nine months, 188,582,000 tons of Iraqi and Saudi Arabian oil had been piped across Lebanese territory to Lebanese ports.

Nations of the Arab League proposed a joint Arab owned pipeline and improved financial terms for countries granting oil concessions, it was reported to the Lebanese Government.

The Adenese strikers continued their strike for another three days while European employees handled the bunkering operations.

November 12

President Habib Bourguiba of Tunisia, host and ally of the ministers of the Algerian Provisional Government, urged them publicly at a press conference to accept the De Gaulle offer to go to Paris.

Tunisia was invited to become a provisional member of the General Agreement on Tariffs and Trade, pending negotiations in September next year at a tariff conference in Geneva.

November, 1959

November 10

King Hussein of Jordan left Amman for a month's holiday in Europe.

The Yemen Government announced in Taizz the signing of a joint exploration agreement for oil, gas and minerals with the American Overseas Investment Company.

Sudanese troops smashed an attempted mutiny at the army infantry school at Omdurman and the plotters were arrested. It was reported from Cairo that regular army forces fought mutinous troops in the streets of Khartoum and that both sides suffered casualties.

French President De Gaulle issued a very strong appeal to the Algerian rebels to stop fighting and to join in determining the country's future. He stated that the choice of the Algerians would be entirely free, and that the conditions for ending the fighting would be honorable. General De Gaulle added that if the rebel political leaders wished to come to France to discuss the question, they had only to give the word.

November 11

Shouts of "De Gaulle to the gallows" echoed through downtown Algiers for nearly three hours, but extremist demonstration leaders found no response from the rest of the populace.

Right wing opponents of President De Gaulle's efforts to end the war with the Algerian rebels indicated that they were not giving up the fight.

Saudi Arabia celebrated the sixth anniversary of the accession of King Saud.

The Middle East director of the International Monetary Fund pronounced Saudi Arabia nearly restored to fiscal health after eighteen months of economic restrictions.

November, 1959

November 12

King Saud of Saudi Arabia said through a spokesman that the UN Emergency Force units should be withdrawn from the Gulf of Aqaba area so that the Arab ban on Israel shipping in the Gulf could be restored.

Three American correspondents interviewed Gamal Bey of Saudi Arabia who said that Saudi Arabia wished to restore normal relations with Britain provided that the disputes over the south and southeastern borders of the country were solved.

Israel and Arab delegates clashed in a tense debate on Palestinian refugees at the UN.

In an agreement between the Iraqi Ministry of Communications and the Russian Techno-Export, this organization would carry out a survey of two important railway projects in Iraq.

The Moroccan Government announced the confiscation of property of sixty-five Moroccans for collaborating with the French Protectorate regime prior to independence in 1956.

November 13

The Ministry of Health in Morocco reported that at least 9,467 cases of partial paralysis of arms and legs had been caused by a fraudulent dilution of cooking oil with a mineral oil used to rinse aviation engines.

Morocco and the Soviet Union signed a trade agreement in Rabat providing for three billion francs in bilateral trade, an increase of 500 million francs over last year.

The Egyptian-Israel Mixed Armistice Commission (Israel absent) condemned Israel for a violation by Israel fighters of UAR airspace over the Sinai Peninsula on November 4.

The Egyptian-Israel Mixed Armistice Commission announced that on November 4 at least four Israel jet fighters crossed the international frontier at Sinai and penetrated deep into UAR's air space.

November, 1959

November 13

The Federal Council of the Federation of Arab Amirates of the South ratified acceptance of Lahej, and appointed a new Minister of Defense and Foreign Affairs.

November 14

Attributing the attempted assassination on October 7 of Premier Kassem of Iraq to imperialists, Kassem declared in a nationwide broadcast in Baghdad that Iraq had freed itself from imperialism by crushing the Baghdad Pact and withdrawing from the Eisenhower Doctrine.

Seventy-seven more cases of paralysis were reported in Morocco and 27 merchants were arrested for making or selling adulterated cooking oil which caused the epidemic of paralysis.

The Ninth Conference of Arab Chambers of Commerce, Agriculture and Industry, held in Kuwait for a progress review of the various proposals for economic cooperation between Arab countries, was the subject of special interest because for the first time the host was a Persian Gulf Amirate, and the meeting was attended by a large delegation from Iraq.

UAR Finance Minister Abd-al-Moneim al-Kaissouni and US Ambassador Raymond A. Hare signed an agreement to supply Syria with 150,000 tons of American surplus grain, valued at $9.5 million. This was the first time Syria would receive US aid.

As oil workers continued their strike in Aden the oil company announced that it would be unable to bunker merchant ships at Aden until there was a general return to work.

The financing of a dam to catch the waters of the Oued Nabana near Kairouan in central Tunisia was being discussed by the Government with the US Development Loan Fund.

Trial began in Khartoum of two armed officers, six former officers and two civilians charged with conspiring to mutiny.

November, 1959

November 15

At the trial in Khartoum of those conspiring to mutiny, an army captain gave evidence that the leaders of the latest abortive coup demanded that the Abboud Government should relinquish power, that all military prisoners should be released and that a national conference should be held to discuss Sudan's future.

A surprise gift of $500,000 worth of US military equipment was to be made public at ceremonies opening the three day national holiday tomorrow in honor of King Muhammad V and Moroccan independence.

The political orientation of Tunisia appeared to be veering toward the left as President Bourguiba studied socialism for methods of reform.

Ratifications were exchanged on the scientific and cultural cooperation agreement signed between the Soviet Union and Iraq.

Two US Representatives on a world tour study mission of possibilities for US private capital investment visited Iraq.

November 16

In an interview in the Baghdad newspaper al-Thawra, Premier Kassem of Iraq was reported as favoring union with Syria and Jordan.

Arabs and Israelis again clashed in the UN General Assembly's Special Political Committee, each trying to blame the other for the plight of the Arabs from Palestine.

Algerian nationalist rebels killed three Europeans in Algiers.

Britain and Tunisia signed a trade agreement under which two export lists were established for Tunisia, one for the UK and Ireland, and the other for dependent British territories.

Six young Jordanians went on trial in Rammallah on charges of being members of a ring spying for Israel. A death penalty was asked by the prosecutor.

November, 1959

November 17

In the course of his speech marking the first anniversary of the new regime in Sudan, President Abboud referred to his Government's plans for new industries in the Sudan.

In the UN General Assembly Special Political Committee, Ceylon supported Saudi Arabia's suggestion that the Palestine Conciliation Commission should be received with wider representation and stronger powers to try to solve the refugee problem.

It was officially stated in Beirut that negotiations begun three years ago between Lebanon and Russia for a civil aviation agreement could be considered suspended.

A Lebanese Government bill compensating members of the army, security forces and civil service who were seriously injured in last year's revolution was approved by the Chamber of Deputies.

The League of Red Cross Societies announced in Geneva the receipt of an appeal from the Moroccan Government for immediate aid for 10,000 victims of the fraudulent dilution of cooking oil.

Tunisia was to be the first country in Africa to use atomic energy, Sayyed Muhammad Ali al-Annabi, Tunisian Atomic Energy Commissioner said. The International Atomic Energy Agency agreed to send two officials to Tunis for six to nine months and provide materials worth $10,000.

A Polish economic mission called on Sayyed Khulusi al-Khairi of Jordan and agreed to buy Jordanian phosphate in return for Polish goods.

West Germany agreed on economic cooperation with Yemen and agreed to give technical aid.

November 18

Three infiltrators were killed near the Gaza Strip in an exchange of fire with an Israel patrol.

November, 1959

November 18

The Food and Agriculture Organization in Rome decided to sign an agreement with the Arab League to strengthen and expand its cooperation with that body.

King Muhammad V of Morocco expressed great satisfaction with French President De Gaulle's offer of self determination for the Algerians.

It was reported in Hassi-Messaoud, Algeria, that nearly everything was ready for the December 5 dedication of the new pipeline which would run from that point to Bougie on the Mediterranean.

Imam Ahmad rebuffed UAR President Nasser's offer of technical assistance to Yemen. Civil, educational and military advisers sent to Yemen, which was a confederate of the UAR, were returned to Cairo.

Work began in Irbid, in northern Jordan, on the first factory to make diesel motor engines and parts with private capital but with the encouragement of the Ministry of Economy of the Jordan Government. Imports would be exempt from customs duty and tools would be imported from West Germany.

A spokesman said that the UN Relief and Works Agency recently paid JD125,000 to the Development and Reconstruction Bank in Amman.

Mr. Leslie Carver, Deputy Director of the UN Relief and Works Agency for Palestine Refugees, was killed in a collision between his car and a military armored car at a road crossing in Beirut.

Lebanese State Security Council asked Commanders of Security Forces in the north and the Governor there to approach the Syrian authorities with a view to ending border clashes.

Radio Baghdad quoted official sources as stating that the Iraqi Government was asking Jordan for payment for deliveries of Iraqi oil made before the 1958 Iraqi revolution.

A Yemeni Government delegation arrived in Moscow, headed by Prince Saif-al-Islam Abd-al-Rahman, the King's brother, Vice Minister of Foreign Affairs and General Director of the Ministry of Foreign Affairs.

November 19

A Lebanese airliner, intercepted by Israel planes and forced to land at Haifa Airport, was permitted to continue on to Beirut. The plane, enroute from Port Said, penetrated Israel airspace.

A mission of the International Monetary Fund arrived in Cairo to study currency regulations in the UAR and ways and means of control on expenditure.

The weekly newspaper al-Libi reported that Libya was drafting a reply to a US note on Libya's request for changes in the American-Libyan Agreement of 1954. The reply included a request for increase in the rent for the Wheelus Air Base, separation of this rent from American aid, and payment of both rent and aid directly to the Libyan Government.

Oil from Hassi-Messaoud reached its terminal, the Algerian port of Bougie, after flowing through 410 miles of a new 24 inch pipeline.

Contracts for 45,000 tons of Syrian cotton had been concluded since the beginning of the season last September, the Ministry of Economy of Syria said.

November 20

The Algerian rebel Provisional Government in Tunis issued a communique designating five rebel chiefs, who had been captives of the French since October 1956, as a delegation to discuss with France ceasefire terms and conditions for holding an election in Algeria on political self determination.

French President De Gaulle rejected the Algerian rebel proposal that truce talks be conducted by five rebel leaders who had been French prisoners since 1956.

An agreement with the Becker Company of Munich, to carry out technical surveys for the building of an international airport 15 kilometers south-east of Damascus, was signed.

November 20

Speaking at the Special Political Committee of the UN General Assembly, Virgil M. Hancher, US Representative, said about the Arab refugee problem that relief alone was not a satisfactory way to serve the long term interests of the Palestinian refugees.

Premier Abd-al-Karim Kassem of Iraq told army officers assembled in his hospital room that there were no borders between Iraq and Syria. They would not attack Syria, he continued, but they would hold their Syrian brothers. He said that Jordan was still linked to imperialism, but when it wished to be liberated, they were ready to help. He also said that since Iraq was now liberated from imperialism, the Fertile Crescent Plan for unifying Iraq, Syria and Jordan had become an Arab national project and that it was part of Iraq's policy.

UN General Assembly adopted a resolution sponsored by 22 Afro-Asian countries expressing grave concern at the French intention to conduct nuclear tests in the Sahara and calling on France to refrain from such tests.

November 21

French Premier Michel Debre called in the American Ambassador in Paris and protested the granting of visas to the Algerian rebels. He said that it was an unfriendly act, not in keeping with the Western allies' solidarity.

The granting of visas to the three man delegation of Algerian nationalists who would attend the UN debate put an end to criticism of the US that had been growing in Tunis among Algerians and Tunisians because of the long delay.

The Soviet Union and the UAR signed a program of cultural cooperation.

Two American Senators, Albert Gore of Tennessee and Gale W. McGee of Wyoming, touring the Middle East, charged that thousands of UN Relief and Works Agency ration cards were being fraudulently used, while thousands of babies were denied ration cards. They asserted that the operations of the refugee program were immoral, dishonest

November 21

and unfair. They maintained that unless fundamental corrections were made, continuation of the program would not be justified. The main stumbling block to more systematic and honest operation was the Government of Jordan, which did not permit validation of the cards.

November 22

The Tunisian Government announced the nationalization of the French run electricity, gas and water services in Tunis.

An organization of armed European settlers called on its members to form combat troops to be ready to fight to keep Algeria French. They number 600 members in Algiers and an undisclosed number in other areas of Algeria.

President Sihanouk of Cambodia informed President Nasser of the UAR at the conclusion of his state visit that he was unwilling to join a third power bloc and that he wanted to be neutral.

An Israel Army spokesman said that two Arab shepherds crossing into Israel territory were killed by a patrol of border policemen. Jordan charged that they were kidnapped by Israel Armed Forces.

Seventy-one Communists, including Syrians, Iraqis, Jordanians, Lebanese and Iranians, were arrested in Kuwait according to the Public Security Department. They were found to have been organizing a cell in Kuwait.

November 23

Three Algerian nationalist leaders arrived in New York for the UN General Assembly debate on Algeria.

Iraqi Premier Kassem approved a ID400 million construction program prepared by the Ministry of Planning. It would be implemented over a period of four years.

November 23

General Kassem of Iraq told army officers that he frustrated a plan to occupy Syria in connivance with Syrian officers when the Iraqi Army was in Jordan before the 1958 Iraqi revolution.

Five Jordanians accused of being members of a spy ring that smuggled military secrets to Israel were sentenced to death at Rammallah.

The US revealed plans to donate an additional contribution of $3 million to maintain the UN Emergency Force in Egypt.

Israel accepted 203 Bedouin tribesmen from Jordan for resettlement in the Negev.

November 24

A new five year plan which was to take effect early next year was outlined by the Moroccan Minister of the Economy, Abd-al-Rahim. It provided for widespread state intervention in and control of industry.

The 150 dismissed employees of the IPC (Iraq Petroleum Company) and workers in Lebanon began a hunger strike in protest against the failure of the Lebanese Government to arrange for their reinstatement in the company.

US Secretary of State Christian A. Herter explained to France that US law did not permit the withholding of visas from the three Algerian nationalist leaders who desired to go to the UN.

The first group of Soviet experts who were to work on the building of the Aswan High Dam arrived in Cairo.

Israel and Jordan clashed over an appraisal of the Jewish religion during the debate in the UN General Assembly's Special Political Committee, on the Palestine refugee problem.

President Abboud of Sudan said in an interview published in Cairo by the al-Akhbar that the Communist danger in Sudan had increased recently. He attributed the recent conspiracies to them.

November 24

Lieutenant Colonel Ali Hamid was convicted by a court martial for leading the recent revolt in Sudan.

The Libyan Government suspended the only three independent newspapers in Benghazi, the English-language Cyrenaica Weekly News, al-Zamar, and al-Amal, under a press law issued recently.

King Saud of Saudi Arabia and his retinue arrived in Duha, Qatar, for a four day state visit to Sheikh Ali Ibn-Abdallah al-Thani.

Britain said it would not vote for a proposal to ask the UN Secretary General to consult member governments on developing the petroleum industry in underdeveloped countries.

A trades union mission en route to Saudi Arabia, the UAR, Lebanon, Western Europe and England appealed to the International Confederation of Free Trade Unions in Brussels for money for Aden's starving strikers.

George A. Kasem, a US Congressman of Lebanese origin, defended Washington against charges of favoritism for Israel.

November 25

The Egyptian Ministry of Supply said that oil reservoirs to meet domestic needs for a year at a time were to be built in several parts of Egypt at a total cost of LE1, 750, 000.

The Iraqi Government planned to spend ID400 million in the next three to five years on defense and development projects, including new industries, schools, housing and other social schemes.

November 26

Addressing a visiting Lebanese football team, Premier Kassem of Iraq asserted that Syria had become a playground for plotters against Iraq and that the Syrians themselves would one day chase them out.

November 26

Al-Akhbar reported that the Russians had selected Dibis, in Kirkuk, for a site for a factory for producing sulphur from natural gas.

Syria had a central executive again after months of operating like a state without a governor. Field Marshal Abd-al-Hakim Amer who arrived on October 12 began to restore the faith of Syrians in the Arab League by expediting Syrian development projects and organizing a National Union.

The Syrian Minister of Economy disclosed that Rumania was ready to contribute towards a proposed development project in Syria.

Dr. Conor Cruise O'Brien of Ireland suggested that an experimental group of 100 Palestine refugees be permitted to return to their homes. He told the UN General Assembly's Special Political Committee that this could be a first step toward breaking the political deadlock.

President Nasser of the UAR delivered a violent direct attack on the Premier of Iraq. He said that Kassem suffered from all kinds of psychological diseases and that he became neurotic and bitter after his attempt to play off the Communists and Arab nationalists in Iraq against each other.

A trade agreement was signed between Morocco and Finland.

US Development Loan Fund financing for at least seven projects in Cairo and in Syria would be given expenditious consideration by both Governments.

The Tunisian Government nationalized the Tunis electricity, gas and water services, formerly controlled by a French company with a subsequent protest from French employees and a request by the French Government to justify the decision and compensate the shareholders.

November 27

$500, 000 worth of American weapons were handed over at Rabat to Crown Prince Moulay Hassan, of Morocco, Chief of Staff of the Moroccan Armed Forces, by the US Ambassador.

November 27

Crown Prince Moulay Hassan expressed gratitude and praised the extreme importance of the US arms package, presented to Morocco.

A US Embassy spokesman in Morocco disclosed that an analysis was being made to determine whether jet engine flushing oil sold by the USAF in Morocco contained poison. The oil, basically a mineral oil, had been used to adulterate cooking oil sold to Moroccan citizens, resulting in the paralysis of nearly 10, 000 people.

Algerian nationalists held strategy sessions with their Asian and African supporters, planning for a full scale debate in the UN General Assembly's Political Committee.

Israel Premier David Ben-Gurion sided with Premier Kassem of Iraq in the Iraq's conflict with President Nasser of the UAR in spite of Ben-Gurion's differences with Kassem, because he considered Nasser's threat of domination the biggest danger.

Lebanese Prime Minister Karami announced that he had requested Mr. Paul Ensor, Chief Representative of IPC (Iraq Petroleum Company) in Lebanon, to try to find a solution to the strike of the IPC workers and employees in Lebanon.

Sir William Luce, Governor of Aden, returned from his visit to the British Charge d'Affaires in Yemen.

November 28

Delegations to the UN decided to give priority to the Algerian debate.

Hajj Messali, 60 year old leader of the Algerian Nationalist Movement which was at odds with the dominant National Liberation Front, called in Paris for a roundtable discussion of Algeria's future by all interested parties.

A French Army source said that Algerian forces, bolstered with arms and reinforcements from Tunisia and Morocco, were repelled by French forces.

November 29

Guerrilla warfare in the Buraimi Oasis in Saudi Arabia continued as scouts led by British officers surrounded Hamassa village in search of guerrillas and men who laid mines.

In a speech at a miliary camp in al-Suwaida, Syria, Field Marshal Amer accused Iraqi Premier Kassem of aggression toward Syria.

The Arabian Oil Company of Japan resumed its test drilling operations. The company expected its drilling to reach an undersea depth of 2, 500 meters by the end of February.

Al-Jihad of Jerusalem said, on King Hussein's arrival in London, that he would have talks on British financial and military aid for Jordan.

A spokesman for the Lebanese strikers announced the determination of the dismissed workers to continue their strike till death if necessary.

November 30

Comay, Israel's representative in the Special Political Committee of the UN General Assembly, declared that his Government was ready to negotiate, directly or indirectly, with Arab Governments on the problem of Arab refugees. He reiterated his country's opposition to the mass return of the refugees who were living in the Arab countries bordering Israel.

The Political Committee of the UN General Assembly opened debate on the Algerian question. France was not present. The first speaker, the delegate from Tunisia, urged France to agree to negotiate with the Algerian rebels on a ceasefire and arrangements for a referendum that would decide the future of Algeria.

An agreement was signed between the UAR and the UN Special Fund covering relations between the two parties in the operation of projects assisted by the Fund.

The Libyan Government moved its seat to Tripoli for a two year term as capital.

November, 1959

November 30

The Jordanian Foreign Ministry said that arrangements were being made to recognize the Republic of Cyprus as soon as it was proclaimed and diplomatic relations would open.

World Bank's Director of Middle Eastern Operations, Mr. Rucinski left Cairo for Washington after a six day visit for final talks on the proposed loan for the Suez Canal improvement program. Press reports said that a loan of $56.5 million repayable in 18 years had been agreed upon.

Fifteen Lebanese strikers of the IPC (Iraq Petroleum Company) were hospitalized in serious condition.

December, 1959

December 1

The UAR and the UK re-established diplomatic relations at the level of Charge d'Affaires. This was simultaneously announced in Cairo and London.

The UAR decided to call a special meeting of the Arab League to consider Israel's intention to divert the course of the River Jordan.

A protocol for Soviet technical aid for the development of agriculture in Yemen was agreed in Moscow. According to Cairo sources, the USSR agreed to a loan of 80 million rubles for this purpose.

The Governor of Aden flew to Thamud on a special tour. A British oil team was exploring the area for oil.

It was reported that Libya, which already had two capitals, was building a third one in Baida.

A Soviet IL-18 turbo-prop jet brought President Sekou Toure of Guinea to Rabat from Prague for a four day visit of state.

The Jordanian Parliament ratified a bill sanctioning the Government's supplementary agreement with the Phillips Petroleum Company under the terms of which the company's concession area was increased.

Two infiltrators from the Gaza Strip were killed and two Israel soldiers wounded in a clash north of the strip.

December 2

Twenty-one Afro-Asian delegations introduced a resolution in the UN urging that France and Algeria enter into pourparlers to determine the conditions necessary for implementation, as early as possible, of the right of self determination of the Algerian people, including the conditions for a ceasefire.

The US and Great Britain urged the General Assembly to refrain from adopting any resolution on Algeria. They maintained that any Assembly action would only complicate the situation.

December, 1959

December 2

Five army men were executed in North Kober Central Prison in Khartoum for attempting a coup against the Sudanese military regime.

Premier Kassem of Iraq announced that he was fully recovered from his bullet wound and was leaving the hospital. He charged that a new student organization was plotting a series of assassinations throughout the country.

In a debate in the UN General Assembly's Legal Committee on a proposed study of the status of historic waters and historic bays, Israel and the Arab states clashed over shipping in the Gulf of Aqaba.

The Syrian Minister of Industry told a press conference that new factories providing employment for at least 25,000 workers would be established in Syria during the next three years.

In private talks, both the Arabs and Israel resisted the American proposal to revive the Palestine Conciliation Commission so that it could try to arrange repatriation or compensation for the Palestinian refugees. The Arabs were said to suspect the US wanted the commission to concentrate on compensation rather than on repatriation.

The first group of Russian staff members left Cairo for the construction site of the Aswan High Dam, being built by the USSR.

December 3

France opposed the Asian-African resolution to the UN General Assembly presented December 2 because of its call for informal discussions was tantamount to recognition of the Provisional Government as the actual administration in Algeria.

Iraqi Premier Kassem left the hospital and celebrations were held throughout the country.

Following his discharge from the hospital, General Kassem of Iraq gave a six hour press conference in the course of which he announced that the Iraqi Government was urging the Iraq Petroleum Company and its associated companies to relinquish 60 percent of its present area.

December, 1959

December 3

An agreement was signed between the Jordanian Government and the United Storage Company under the terms of which the company would pay a minimum of ID150,000 this financial year for the use of 12 storage tanks built by the Government at Aqaba.

Water conservation schemes were outlined by the Sudanese Ministry of Irrigation and Hydro-Electric Power now that the Sudan was assured of a larger share of the Nile waters after the construction of the Aswan High Dam. The most important was the Roseires Dam on the Blue Nile, proposed to be completed by 1966, and a smaller dam at Khashm al-Girba. The cost of this dam would be met by part of the LS15 million which Sudan would receive from Egypt as compensation for the flooding of the Wadi Halfa area.

The Governor of Tripoli, Lebanon, proposed a compromise solution which was accepted with reservations by the Lebanese dismissed employees of the Iraq Petroleum Company. The proposal was to give these employees temporary employment for six months and thereafter they were to be reinstated.

December 4

On the occasion of the Premier of Iraq's recovery, the Military Governor, Saleh al-Abdi, changed the curfew hours for the day from 9 pm - 5 am to 12:30 am - 5 am.

Half a million Iraqis paraded before Iraqi Premier Kassem in Baghdad shouting anti-Nasser slogans as a tribute to their leader upon his discharge from the hospital.

To celebrate Iraqi Premier Kassem's full recovery and his release from the hospital, the Cabinet decreed that henceforth December 3 would be a national holiday which would be known as the Day of Safety and Happiness.

UN Secretary General Dag Hammarskjold announced that Lieutenant General E. L. M. Burns of Canada had resigned as Commander of the UN Emergency Force in the Middle East and that he was asking the

December 4

General Assembly to approve the appointment of Major General Prem Singh Gyani of India as Burns' successor. Burns would represent Canada in disarmament talks in Geneva early in 1960.

A statement issued at the UN in the name of the Cabinet of the Algerian Provisional Government said that the Government would not discuss a ceasefire with France without first having guarantees of an impartial referendum in Algeria.

The UAR denied a report that its diplomats in Panama were encouraging an anti-US group advocating violent seizure of the Canal Zone.

The Labor supported daily al-Tahrir in Morocco was seized because it accused palace personnel of refusing to permit a group of former members of the nationalist resistance to have an audience with King Muhammad V. The paper was charged with slander.

Talks between Lebanon and Italy on the agreement organizing air services between them were broken off because of what Lebanese delegation sources said was obstinacy on the part of the Italians.

The Oasis Oil Company of Libya, a subsidiary of the Ohio Oil Company, announced the completion of a big exploratory well in Syrtica, Libya, yielding 2,800 barrels daily.

December 5

French Premier Michel Debre officially inaugurated a 400 mile pipeline carrying oil from Hassi Messaoud in the Sahara Desert to the Mediterranean port of Bougie and reaffirmed his Government's determination to stay in Algeria.

Armand Berard, French delegate to the UN, issued a statement that France would boycott the General Assembly debate if the Assembly decided to discuss a proposal for talks between France and the Algerian Provisional Government.

December 5

The General Assembly of the UN approved the appointment of Major General Gyani of India as Commander of the UN Emergency Force in the Middle East, replacing E. L. M. Burns of Canada who resigned earlier this week.

Upon the announcement of US President Eisenhower's planned trip to Morocco, political leaders in Rabat were reported to have stirred widespread hopes that the US was ready to treat African states as separate entities.

The hunger strike of the Lebanese workers of the Iraq Petroleum Company entered its 12th day as labor union delegations visited Maronite Patriarch Paul Maushi and Kamal Jumblat and asked them to intercede on their behalf.

Ahmad Sulaiman Izzat, Commander of the UAR Naval Forces, stated that his country possessed the strongest fleet of submarines in the eastern Mediterranean.

December 6

French military authorities reported that 147 rebels were put out of action in the past 48 hours and that 38 were captured.

It was announced in Algiers that five Algerians were killed in a hit and run attack on a regrouping center for persons loyal to the French Government.

December 7

A so-called compromise resolution on Arab refugees submitted to the UN by Pakistan and Indonesia gained the approval of the US. The compromise was not between Israel and the Arab states but rather between the resolution's sponsors and the US. The resolution called for a three year extension of UN Relief and Works Agency aid and for a

December 7

review of its mandate at the end of two years. It also asked the Palestine Conciliation Commission to make further efforts to secure compliance with the repatriation and compensation resolutions adopted by the General Assembly of the UN in 1948.

Israel disclaimed any part in the compromise agreement because it felt that the agreement stressed settling the problem by renewed efforts to return the refugees to their homes which were now within Israel's borders.

The Political Committee of the UN General Assembly passed a resolution by a vote of 38-26, calling for discussions between France and the Algerian National Liberation Front. France, which boycotted the debate on the grounds that the UN had no jurisdiction in the matter, was absent. Since there must be a two-thirds affirmative vote for a resolution to be finally adopted, the vote was considered a victory for France.

The Iraqi News Agency quoted the Ministry of Oil Affairs as having said that Iraq this year would earn L86 million in oil revenue.

Foreign Minister Sayyed Hashem Jawad of Iraq said he thought US President Eisenhower's trip would be helpful to the whole world. He denied accusations that General Kassem had shifted to the Left and declared that the leader wanted the middle way, that he wanted a liberal kind of democracy.

The Jordanian Foreign Ministry informed the Arab League Secretariat that Jordan agreed to a UAR proposal that the League's Economic Council should meet in Cairo early next month instead of in Beirut.

December 8

The UAR was to ask the Arab League to approve the erection of a dam in Syria to stop the River Jordan's water from reaching Israel if the Israelis tapped the river for an irrigation project.

Mr. B. West of the UN Food and Agriculture Organization arrived in Amman to discuss with officials the prospects of a long term agricultural program in Jordan.

December 8

Israel Ambassador Abraham Harman asserted at the annual dinner of the Weizmann Institute of Science at the Waldorf-Astoria in New York that Israel was ready for direct communication with its hostile Arab neighbors for peace talks.

Informed Israelis scoffed at the reported Cairo proposal to dam the Jordan River in Syrian territory to prevent the Israelis from tapping it.

The Special Political Committee of the UN adopted the Pakistan-Indonesia resolution for a three year extension of UN assistance to Palestinian refugees by a vote of 71-0.

December 9

The General Assembly approved the Arab refugee resolution, 80-0.

Britain formally resumed diplomatic relations with the UAR when Colin Crowe, UK Charge d'Affaires, presented his credentials to Deputy Foreign Minister Hussein Dhu-al-Fiqar Sabri.

An agreement on transit trade between Syria, Jordan, Saudi Arabia and Lebanon was signed in Damascus.

The Directorate of Propaganda and Information in Syria banned the entry into Syria of the New York revue Confidential for supporting Israel and Zionism.

Representatives of all labor unions in Lebanon met and resolved to call a general strike if the demands of the dismissed employees of the Iraq Petroleum Company were not granted by the evening of Monday, December 14.

The Iraq Petroleum Company issued a statement to the effect that the case of the dismissed workers in Lebanon had been settled as of November 1958, and that IPC had met all obligations pertaining to them.

Sayyed Awni Abd-al-Hadi said that the Arab League's Permanent Legal Committee decided at its recent meeting in Cairo to postpone

December, 1959

December 9

discussion of a proposed constitution for an Arab court of justice and a proposed inter-Arab residence agreement so that preliminary studies could be completed.

The BP (British Petroleum) Employees Union in Aden decided to return to work.

A Yugoslav military delegation left Khartoum after a ten day visit of northern and southern Sudan.

French sources in Algiers reported that French troops launched a new offensive in eastern Algeria to clear some of the strongest insurgent pockets. Twelve thousand parachutists, legionnaires and sharp shooters took part.

In a press interview, General Kassem of Iraq affirmed his neutral course.

In a move to encourage a wider representation of opinions prior to Morocco's first nationwide elections, King Muhammad V replaced a decree curbing the press.

The UN General Assembly extended United Nations Relief and Works Agency mandate to June 1963.

December 10

Norman Burns, Director of the UN Operations Mission in Jordan, said that the deficit in Jordan's trade balance this year was $80 million.

Crown Prince Muhammad of Jordan, acting for his brother King Hussein, inaugurated a new deepwater port at Aqaba. Premier Majali stressed the importance of the port in his speech at the ceremony.

The International Bank for Reconstruction and Development made a loan equivalent to US $50 million to assist in financing the construction and operation of the 412 mile pipeline to bring crude oil from Hassi-Messaoud to Bougie in Algeria.

December, 1959

December 10

Two men from the Majd al-Shams village in Syria were sentenced to death on charges of spying for Israel.

President Bourguiba of Tunisia said in Tunis that he would look elsewhere for loans if the US did not grant them.

US and Libyan negotiators were having little luck in reaching an agreement on how much the US should pay for keeping a jet training center at Wheelus Field near Tripoli.

An exchange of diplomatic missions between Morocco and Cuba, its first delegation to Latin America, was announced.

December 11

The Communist Party of Iraq was split three ways and General Kassem was encouraging a dissident nationalist faction while al-Thawra was trying to found a new middle of the road nationalist party.

In an effort to increase the possibilities for the UN General Assembly to pass a resolution on Algeria, Pakistan introduced a milder draft. It removed from the draft passed by the Political Committee on December 8 references to the two parties to which the French took exception and the recommendation that informal talks be undertaken to determine conditions necessary for the implementation of the right of self determination by the Algerian people. Instead, it recommends only that talks be held with a view to arriving at a peaceful solution and asks the Assembly to recognize the right of the Algerian people to self determination.

December 12

The resolution suggested by Pakistan failed passage in the UN General Assembly; the vote was 39-22 with 20 abstentions. The Algerian issue was shelved by the UN.

December, 1959

December 12

French authorities in Algiers reported that about 250 tons of high explosives destined for the Algerian nationalist insurgents were found aboard a Dutch ship.

A bomb attempt on the life of Sayyed Ahmad Ibn-Ibraham, Minister of the Interior of the Independent Sultanate of Muscat, was made while he was on his way from Muscat to Bombay for medical treatment, was officially revealed.

The government newspaper in Cairo said that the UAR would fight if Israel carried out its plan to divert the Jordan River.

Two explosions rocked the Basta quarter of Beirut. They were directed at Adnan Hakim, a leader of the extremist Moslem Najjada Party. The inside of the Najjada headquarters was wrecked, but there were no casualties.

December 13

Ten French soldiers were killed in an ambush set by Algerian rebels near Port Tigzirt.

Two prominent politicians were among 20 fugitives summoned to appear before the Iraqi People's Court. They were Fuad al-Rikabi, former Minister for Reconstruction, and Faisal Habib Khaizaran, a leader of the Baath Party.

The UK and Iraq signed a cultural convention providing for the setting up of a mixed commission as a forum for working out practical details of future cooperation in the arts and sciences. It was the first cultural agreement signed between these countries.

Israel asked the UN Truce Supervision Organization for high-level intervention in Damascus to halt Syrian sabotage of Israel fishing nets in the Sea of Galilee.

The UN decided not to intervene in the question of Algeria.

December, 1959

December 14

Legal action against al-Tahrir for an offense against the religious and political institutions of the kingdom would be taken according to an announcement by the Royal Palace, in Morocco.

Yugoslavia and Sudan signed an agreement providing for training of Sudanese military personnel in the Yugoslavian Marine Force.

Conservative Europeans in Algiers ever fearful of a sell out by France studied the impact that the planned transformation of the French Community might have on the future of Algeria.

December 15

Two resistance leaders of Morocco's former independence movement were arrested for publishing attacks against the monarchy in their positions as director and editor in chief of the daily al-Tahrir.

Iraqi Prime Minister, Major General Abd-al-Karim al-Kassem, called for the formation of a Palestine state to be governed by its own people, in a speech inaugurating the first annual Iraqi Medical Congress.

December 16

The new Israel Government, with Ben-Gurion again as Prime Minister, said its basic principles included proposals to be made to Arab states for nonaggression pacts to replace the present armistice agreements and for disarmament in the Middle East to end the Arab-Israel strife.

Mr. Joseph Grimond, British Liberal Leader, asked the House of Commons whether the British Government would offer its services in negotiating a settlement of Arab refugees in view of Israel's reported willingness to negotiate such a settlement through an intermediary. The British Minister of State for Foreign Affairs passed the responsibility back to the UN.

December, 1959

December 16

Jordanian Prime Minister Hazza al-Majali emphasized in the House of Representatives that the East Ghor canal scheme to irrigate 120,000 dunums in the Jordan Valley did not affect any refugee rights and had nothing to do with refugee resettlement.

Jordan agreed to a request by Saudi Arabia for the postponement of the Arab communications conference until next April instead of December 25.

King Hussein of Jordan declared at a press conference in London that his country was ready to do everything in its power to defeat Communist objectives in Iraq and in the Arab world.

Abd-al-Karim al-Khattabi said that the current meeting of insurgent Algerian leaders in Tripoli, Libya, might lead to a reshuffle of the Cabinet of the Provisional Government.

Tass, the official Soviet news agency, reported that Russia was to give the UAR technical aid in building two factories which would produce radio apparatus and abrasive materials.

Sources in Washington reported that G. Frederick Reinhardt was expected to be named by US President Eisenhower as the next Ambassador to the UAR.

Colonel Mahmoud Yunis from the UAR left for New York on his way to the International Bank for Reconstruction and Development meeting which was expected to draw up the final agreement providing for a loan of $56,500,000 for Suez Canal development.

Field Marshal Abd-al-Hakim Amer of the UAR issued a decree setting up a five man committee to supervise the execution of the Agrarian Reform Law.

It was reported from Tehran that Iranian frontier guards were reinforced along the Iraqi border near the disputed Shatt al-Arab area, following a shooting incident.

December, 1959

December 16

The Iraqi Military Governor General, Ahmad Saleh al-Abdi, suspended the activities of the Red Crescent Society until it amended its basic law to put it in harmony with the spirit of the revolution and the republican era.

Hussein al-Uwaini threatened to resign from the Lebanese Cabinet in a protest against a decision of the Council of Ministers on the long promised purge of government staff. It was reported by Lebanese Government sources that the council did not act on his desire that some officials of the Foreign Ministry, now in the administrative department, should be transferred to the diplomatic corps.

Middle East Airlines agreed to seek the technical advice of BOAC (British Overseas Airways Corporation) exports before finally choosing the aircraft type to re-equip its fleet.

December 17

ON US President Eisenhower's arrival in Tunisia, President Bourguiba said in greeting that his visit to Africa would encourage the peoples of Africa fighting against the last vestiges of stubborn colonialism and against privations and ignorance.

In a joint communique issued in Tunisia by US President Eisenhower and President Habib Bourguiba of Tunisia, it was stated that they examined the situation created by the difficulties in Algeria. They agreed that the fact that a solution had not yet been achieved was a cause of grave concern.

Al-Libi said that the present meeting of the Algerian leaders in Tripoli, Libya, would discuss developments of the Algerian problem after the UN discussions and steps to be taken in the military and political fields.

The UAR was reportedly to buy at least five 10,000 ton ships from East Germany.

December, 1959

December 17

An authoritative source said that India wished to buy Syrian cotton from this year's crop.

The Advisory Committee of the Afro-Asian Economic Conference decided to call for a Second Afro-Asian Conference in Cairo in mid-April.

Turkey and Greece informed Lebanon that they did not agree to Israel's becoming a member of the Organization for European Economic Cooperation.

Premier Rashid Karami of Lebanon presided over the opening of the Casino du Liban, said to be the biggest gambling casino in the eastern Mediterranean.

Moroccan security forces were alerted to prevent disorders as tension increased between King Muhammad V and the labor supported National Union of Popular Forces.

Imam Ahmad of Yemen sent a force of 2,000 soldiers, backed by Russian made tanks, against rebel Hashid troops, and of that, 800 deserted on reaching Hashid territory.

Khulusi al-Khairi of Jordan stated that a technical committee would shortly be set up to study possible construction of a TV station to be established with neighboring Arab states.

The Iranian Majlis accused Iraqi General Kassem of adopting an aggressive policy toward Iran after the shooting incident in the disputed border area.

December 18

Major General P. S. Gyani, an Indian soldier, arrived in Gaza to take over command of the UN Emergency Force, succeeding E. L. M. Burns of Canada, who resigned earlier this month.

December, 1959

December 18

UAR authorities held up at Port Said the Greek cargo ship Astypalea which was reported to be on its way to Djibouti with 400 tons of cement from Haifa, Israel. The master was requested to unload before the ship would be allowed to go through the Suez.

Urged by his friends and opponents to resign because of the arrest of his main supports, Premier Ibrahim of Morocco appeared to be determined to avoid a government crisis at least until after US President Eisenhower's visit.

Diplomatic sources at the UN reported that Saudi Arabia and Britain were near agreement on preliminary steps to be taken leading to a settlement of outstanding frontier issues and the resumption of diplomatic relations.

A long procession of peasants, estimated at more than a half a million, marched toward the Iraqi Defense Ministry to page homage to Premier Kassem on his recovery from an assassination attempt.

For the first time, an Arab labor union federation, the Iraqi General Federation of Labor Unions, became affiliated with the Communist sponsored World Federation of Trade Unions in Prague.

Lebanese Foreign Minister Hussein Uwaini submitted his resignation in a dispute over Government administrative reforms.

December 19

The UAR signed an agreement with the US for a $12 million loan to build the country's first TV station. It would be repaid in 30 years at four percent interest. The money would be obtained from the sale of US surplus agricultural products.

West Germany offered a loan of 200 million West German marks to the UAR to build the second stage of the Aswan High Dam.

The UAR accused Israel of using the Astypalea (a Greek ship carrying cement from Haifa) in another attempt to block a loan to Cairo by the International Bank for Reconstruction and Development to improve the Suez.

December, 1959

December 19

Another New York Congressman, Representative Victor L. Anfuso, a Democrat, protested the pending International Bank for Reconstruction and Development loan to the UAR for Suez Canal improvements because such action, he said, would condone President Nasser's aggressive action against Israel and approval of his policy of continued tension in the Middle East.

It was announced in Amman that the Commander in Chief of the Armed Forces signed an agreement with a German factory to supply the Jordanian Army with a complete factory that would produce woolen blankets and army cloth. It was to have a capacity of 100,000 blankets a year.

The Jordanian Government expressed concern to foreign diplomats in Amman over an Israel plan to divert water of the Jordan River to irrigate parts of the Negev desert.

Algerian political and military leaders, according to al-Masa, would discuss during their present meeting the possibility of moving the headquarters of the Algerian Provisional Government from Cairo to Tripoli, Libya.

In a press interview, Tunisian President Habib Bourguiba disclosed that he had told US President Eisenhower that the time was not yet ripe for peace talks between the Algerian nationalist rebels and the French Government because the talks had been blocked on the secondary issue of the composition of the nationalist delegation instead of self determination.

Lebanese President Chehab refused to accept Hussein Uwaini's resignation, submitted December 18, and agreed to the latter's request to take 10 to 15 days sick leave at Luxor, Egypt.

December 20

Prime Minister Hazza al-Majali of Jordan said the Council of Ministers had approved a transit agreement signed in Damascus earlier

December, 1959

December 20

this month between representatives of Jordan, Lebanon, the UAR and Saudi Arabia. It was referred to the Regency Commission for ratification.

The Shah of Iran declared that Iran would defend its interest and rights in the border dispute with Iraq.

UN Secretary General Dag Hammarskjold protested to the UAR against the seizure in the Suez Canal of the Greek freighter, Astypalea.

December 21

It was reported in Teheran that mechanized units of Iranian artillery, armored cars and tanks were sent to the Iraqi border.

Premier Abd-al-Karim al-Kassem of Iraq said that he would not resort to force to regain his country's rights unless all peaceful methods for solving international issues failed.

The Union Jack (British flag) flew in Cairo for the first time in more than three years, signalling the resumption of British-UAR diplomatic relations.

Ahmad al-Hajj Yunis, Syrian Minister of Agriculture, said that government loans to farmers had reached a total of 20 million lire, 18 million of which were seasonal and the rest long term.

The managing editor of the Gulf Times, Arthur Edward Lawrence, was sentenced to one year imprisonment at the British court at Manama, in the Persian Gulf, for firing a pistol with intent to alarm. For discharging a pistol and causing injury, Lawrence was sentenced to a concurrent term of three month's imprisonment.

In a message of gratitude for Tunisia's hospitality to him, US President Eisenhower was quoted as having promised that he would work without pause for peace, justice and equality for all.

December, 1959

December 21

The Arabian Oil Company announced in Tokyo the signature of a $5.8 million contract with the Seacoast Offshore Drilling Company for a second drilling platform to be used in its Saudi Arabian-Kuwait offshore Neutral Zone concession.

A Saudi Arabian Government circular on aviation affairs announced the separation of the Civil Aviation Department, which henceforth would operate the airports of the kingdom and Saudi Arabian airlines, which would be under the supervision of the Ministry of Defense and Aviation.

December 22

The International Bank for Reconstruction and Development made a loan of $56.5 million to the Suez Canal Authority to widen, deepen and generally improve the canal. It was made over the objections of the Israel Government and the appeal of 66 US representatives to delay the loan as long as Cairo did not permit Israel goods to pass freely through the canal.

The UAR Government Planning Affairs Committee was reorganized under the Chairmanship of Abd-al-Latif al-Baghdadi, Vice President and Central Minister of Planning.

US President Eisenhower arrived in Morocco and met with King Muhammad V. At his departure, a joint communique was issued announcing that the US military forces would be withdrawn from Morocco by the end of 1963.

It was reported in Cairo that a shake-up of the Algerian Provisional Government had put rebel military leaders in all top posts.

Observers in Paris were skeptical about the reported shake-up in the Algerian Provisional Government, saying that even if the reports were true, their meaning was open to contradictory conclusions.

December, 1959

December 22

France was attacked in the Jordanian House of Representatives when deputies demanded a ban on its exports in protest against its policy in Algeria.

Morocco and Czechoslovakia signed a new trade agreement in Rabat to be valid for one year effective January 1, 1960.

Israel's Foreign Minister, Golda Meir, said in the Knesset that the Greek freighter carrying a cargo of Israel cement, which was seized at the entrance to the Suez Canal, was dispatched with the blessing of the Secretary General of the UN. She said that Mr. Hammarskjold and officials of other nations recommended that Israel send goods through the Canal as the property of the buyers.

The enlarging of the Aleppo Airport in Syria at a cost of two million lire was to be begun early next year, the airport director said. Jet craft would be able to use the airport, which would be in service day and night.

The Shah of Iran conferred in Teheran with his War Minister and other officials on the border dispute with Iraq.

December 23

The Iranian Government put jet aircraft on a 24 hour emergency watch and alerted Persian Gulf naval units. The army reported the massing of Iraqi forces along the frontier opposite Abadan.

It was reported from Washington that the US State Department was using its influence in Baghdad and Teheran in an effort to persuade both sides to negotiate an amicable settlement of their border dispute in the Shatt-al-Arab.

Israel Foreign Minister Golda Meir declared in Jerusalem that the World Bank loan to the UAR for widening the Suez Canal while the waterway remained closed to Israel shipping meant giving a reward to the violator of international practice.

December, 1959

December 23

The Jordanian Prime Minister, Sayyed Hazza al-Majali, received a delegation of Palestinian refugees who declared that they supported Jordan's policy toward refugees. They also denounced Iraqi General Kassem's call for a Palestine state.

The Arab League Israel Boycott Central Office announced the black-listing of British vessel Inchstuard, registered at Hong Kong, and the Danish ship, Danholm, for violating Arab boycott regulations.

General Kassem of Iraq warned against building up Iran forces on the Iraqi frontier and requested that Iran come to its senses or be beaten by the Iraqis.

Baghdad Radio introduced a half-hour program called Voice of United Arabs directed against the UAR.

The Second Conference of Iraqi Engineers recommended that crude oil production should be increased; that refinery throughout capacity should be expanded with a view to exporting oil products; that petro-chemical industries should be established as rapidly as possible and natural gas should be used in these industries.

The American Overseas Company struck oil at Baida, Libya, well No. 2, in its Syrtica concession in Northwest Cyrenaica at the rate of 600 barrels per day.

It was reported in Paris that independent observers in close touch with the Algerian nationalist organizations in West Germany and Tunisia tended to corroborate accounts of an important shift of power within the Algerian Provisional Government.

The Syrian Minister of Interior announced that a second meeting of Syrian and Turkish Governors of frontier provinces would be held in Turkey at the beginning of April, 1960.

BAPCO (Bahrain Petroleum Company) announced a general wage and salary increase of 7.5 percent for all rupee payroll employees in the Persian Gulf effective the first of next year.

President Habib Bourguiba of Tunisia handed out title deeds to 548 Tunisian farmers.

December, 1959

December 24

UN Secretary General Dag Hammarskjold was reported to have pressed President Nasser of the UAR for the fourth time for a reply to his query regarding the failure of the formula for the passage of Israel goods through the Suez Canal.

The Iraq Times published a report from Caracas, Venezuela, that Sheikh Abdallah al-Tariqi was making arrangements for the holding next year of a conference of Middle East oil producing countries to consider joint action aimed at increasing these countries' share of oil profits to conform to Venezuela's oil profit sharing formula.

Two persons were killed and 41 wounded in Algiers when a bomb exploded in front of one of the city's leading department stores which was crowded with Christmas shoppers.

December 25

Ahmad al-Hajj Yunis of Syria announced a five year program for the afforestation of 6,000 hectares of barren hills and other areas in the interior and 5,000 in coastal areas to check the advance of sand on surrounding areas. The project would be started in Damascus, Hama and Latakia.

The Teheran, Iran, radio attacked Premier Kassem of Iraq as a "red servant of black imperialism."

The Soviet Union and Syria signed two contracts under agreement on economic and technical cooperation providing for designing of 3,000 kilowatt hydroelectric station, a technical design for building a dam and hydroelectric station and a power transmission line.

Leaders of the Algerian Provisional Government denied that rebel leadership had changed hands.

According to the Ettelaat, Soviet oil experts began building an off-shore drilling platform in the Persian Gulf following the Soviet-Iraqi oil agreement a week ago.

December, 1959

December 24

The Iraqi Foreign Ministry announced that it relieved UAR diplomatic missions of looking after Iraqi interests abroad.

Ian Colvin, the Daily Telegraph's special correspondent, reported from Iraq that General Kassem's four year 390 million pound development plan was causing concern among ministerial officials because of the high cost of the plan in relation to estimated revenues.

Premier Kassem of Iraq accused the Iranian Government of encroaching several times on Iraqi territory to a depth of four to seven miles. He warned those massing troops on Iraq's border to withdraw. He reportedly charged Iranian imperialists with stirring up aggression against Iraq.

An agreement covering a $12 million US Export Import Bank loan to the Egyptian Railways was signed in Washington. The money was for the purchase in the US of locomotives and other railway equipment.

A trade mission from the UAR was to arrive in Djakarta, Indonesia, next month, Antara news agency reported. It would discuss with the Indonesian Government ways for the smooth functioning of the trade agreement the two countries recently concluded.

Dr. Nur-ad-Din Kahhalah, President of the Syrian Executive Council, announced that President Nasser of the UAR had authorized him in his capacity as Syrian Minister of Public Works to enter into contracts for the building of Tartus port without being confined to the laws and regulations concerning general accounting and tenders.

Syria signed a contract with Technoexport for preparing a preliminary project for the establishment of a Euphrates Dam. Construction will start in 1962 and the completion of the project was expected to be in four years.

Syrian and Israel forces exchanged fire east of the Sea of Galilee; one Israeli was killed.

December, 1959

December 26

Fifty-seven people were brought before the Iraqi People's Military Court in Baghdad to face charges of complicity in an October 7 attempt to assassinate General Kassem. In his indictment, Majid Muhammad Amin, the Iraqi prosecutor general, accused the Shah of Iran, President Nasser of the UAR and King Hussein of Jordan, by saying that they were threatening the Government and people of Iraq.

One hundred Iraqis were reported to have clashed with Iraqi guards while trying to flee into Iran. Four of them were killed along with one guard.

Army headquarters in Tel Aviv, Israel, reported that three Arabs were killed in an encounter between infiltrators from the Gaza Strip on an Israel army patrol in the northern Negev desert.

December 27

Iraq and the Soviet Union signed a technical training agreement in Baghdad. The USSR would set up ten large centers in Iraq for training Iraqis to become skilled personnel for industry.

Two students testified in the Iraqi People's Military Court that the plot to assassinate Premier Kassem was to have been followed by a liberation army from the UAR, and that the banned Arab Socialist Baath Party had arranged for the weapons they used.

Iranian officials appeared to be soft pedaling the martial aspects of the Iraq-Iran border disputes in spite of civilian demonstrations and troop movements from Iranian border points. The Army Chief of Information, Colonel Gulbadi, declared that military activities in the area were a result of routine maneuvers.

The US and UK advised Iran to use moderation in dealing with Iraq over the disputed border territory.

Iranian Premier Eghbal said at a news conference in Lahore that he did not believe the Soviet Union was behind Iran's current border dispute with Iraq.

December, 1959

December 27

It was reported by Syrian authorities that they had smashed a group of Communist youth cells believed to be the last secret Communist organization in the region.

Field Marshal Amer of the UAR issued Decision No. 73 providing for the amendment of the customs tariff in Syria which exempted butter, cheese and certain kinds of fish and meat from customs duty.

It was reported that Egyptian cotton exports from the beginning of the current season until the end of November 1959, totaled 1,264,594 cantars valued at 18,297,000 pounds. Cotton yarn exports for the same period totaled 4,456 tons valued at 2.2 million pounds.

December 28

Lieutenant General E. L. M. Burns handed over command of the UN Emergency Force to Major General P. S. Gyani of India.

It was stated in London that Britain urged the Governments of both Iran and Iraq to use restraint in handling the Shatt-al-Arab border dispute.

Iraq appealed to the world to indict Iran for endangering peace in the Middle East by continuing to concentrate its troops in the Shatt-al-Arab. Iran stated it would invoke aid from its allies in event of aggression by Iraq.

General Kassem of Iraq denied reports of Iraqi troop concentrations at Basra.

King Hussein of Jordan was greeted on his arrival after a tour of Europe during which he had talks with British and West German officials on financial and military aid to strengthen Jordan's economy and army.

UAR President Nasser authorized the Syrian Ministry of Public Works to sign a contract with a Yugoslavian firm to build a port at Tartus.

December, 1959

December 30

Field Marshal Amer of the UAR issued a decree setting up a committee of four ministers to help him organize the National Union.

It was reported in London that Britain would like to see direct discussions between Iran and Iraq which would reach some practical agreement on their border dispute.

Iraq wanted a postponement of the proposed meeting in January of the Arab League's Economic Council until February, it was officially stated in Beirut.

Two French prisoners were freed by a representative of the Algerian National Liberation Front and were turned over to the French Embassy in Rabat.

It was announced that President Nasser had accepted the resignations of four Syrian Ministers, all leading members of the Baath (Arab Socialist) party which was dissolved at the time of the union of Egypt and Syria in 1958.

December 31

UAR President Nasser named Tumah al-Awdatallah, Minister of Municipal and Rural Affairs in Syria, as Minister of Agriculture, and Interior Minister Abd-al-Hamid Sarraj as Minister of Social Affairs, filling two of the four posts which the UAR ministers had vacated.

Informed sources believe UAR President Nasser's drive to set up a National Union as an approach to popular government in the UAR was a major factor in the resignation of the four ministers on December 30.

French General Maurice Challe declared that the Algerian nationalist rebels, having seen their best units broken up during 1959, had decided to concentrate on blind terrorism.

December, 1959

December 29

The French Delegate General in Algeria, Paul Delouvrier, declared that France would spend the equivalent of $140 million in public funds next year for industrialization and power development in Algeria.

French forces foiled three attempts by Algerian nationalists to send reinforcements from Tunisia into the interior of Algeria.

Premier Manouchehr Eghbal of Iran said that Iran would fight back with all its might and would seek assistance from its allies if Iran were attacked by Iraq over the Shatt-al-Arab dispute.

The Iranian Government, confident of its legal position, held open the door to negotiations of the disputed border.

Iraqi Foreign Minister Hashem Jawad said that Iran was continuing to concentrate troops in the Shatt-al-Arab. He appealed to the world to indict Iran for endangering peace in the Middle East.

Four political parties in Iraq were reported ready to apply for licenses after January 6. These were the People's Party, the National Democratic Party, the Communist and the United Kurdish Democratic Parties.

It was reported in Beirut that four Syrian cabinet ministers resigned in a dispute with Field Marshal Abd-al-Hakim Amer, Egyptian head of the Syrian Region.

Al-Ahram reported that the UAR was now, for the first time, exporting gasoline produced at the Suez refinery to Europe.

Demag, a West German concern, concluded negotiations with the UAR for the exploitation of mineral ores in three areas in Egypt.

Moroccan King Muhammad V and Cardinal Spellman of New York had a forty minute conversation in Rabat about peace, liberty, Algeria and Moroccan-American friendship.

December, 1959

December 31

The law on the interim four year economic plan which would provide for appropriations of ID391.3 million to cover the cost of Iraqi projects to be carried out included ID10 million from the Soviet loan of March, 1959, was published in the Official Gazette.

A Libyan Royal Decree accepted the resignation of Abu-Bakr Naamah as Minister of Education and appointed him Governor of Tripolitania in succession to Taher Bakir, who has been transferred to the Foreign Ministry.

A Saudi Arabian Royal Decree, based upon a decision of the Council of Ministers, stipulated the unit of Saudi Arabian currency to be the Riyal, divided into 20 qurush, each divided in 5 hallahs.

A Saudi Arabian Royal Decree provided that a currency devaluation profit of SR232.5 million be added to the budget revenues of 1379-1380 thus raising the total level of revenues and expenditures from SR1,405 million to SR1,637.5 million, amending the announcement on December 30.